The Encyclopedia of the
United States Congress

Editorial Advisory Board

The
Encyclopedia
of the
United States Congress

Edited by

DONALD C. BACON
ROGER H. DAVIDSON
MORTON KELLER

Volume 3

SIMON & SCHUSTER

A Paramount Communications Company

New York   London   Toronto   Sydney   Tokyo   Singapore

Simon & Schuster
Academic Reference Division
15 Columbus Circle
New York, New York 10023

Printed in the United States of America

printing number
1 2 3 4 5 6 7 8 9 10

Library of Congress Cataloging-in-Publication Data
The encyclopedia of the United States Congress / edited by
Donald C. Bacon, Roger H. Davidson, Morton Keller.
p. cm.
ISBN 0-13-276361-3 (set : alk. paper)
ISBN 0-13-306671-1 (v.3 : alk. paper)
1. United States. Congress—Encyclopedias. I. Bacon,
Donald C. II. Davidson, Roger H. III. Keller, Morton.
JK1067.E63 1995
328.73'003—dc20 94-21203 CIP

*Funding for this publication was received from
the Commission on the Bicentennial of the
United States Constitution. The University of Texas
at Austin and the Lyndon Baines Johnson Library recognize
with gratitude this and other assistance rendered by the
Commission in the development of this project.*

Acknowledgments of sources, copyrights, and
permissions to use previously printed materials
are made throughout the work.

This paper meets the requirements of ANSI/NISO Z39.48-1992
(Permanence of Paper).

About the Editors

DONALD C. BACON is a Washington-based journalist specializing in Congress and the presidency. He has served as staff writer of the *Wall Street Journal* and assistant managing editor for congressional and political coverage of *U.S. News & World Report*. A former Congressional Fellow, he holds major prizes in journalism and has written and contributed to numerous books, including *Rayburn: A Biography* (1987) and *Congress and You* (1969).

ROGER H. DAVIDSON is Professor of Government and Politics at the University of Maryland, College Park. He has taught at several universities and served as a Capitol Hill staff member with the Bolling Committee, with the Stevenson Committee, and as Senior Specialist with the Congressional Research Service, Library of Congress. He is author or coauthor of numerous articles and books dealing with Congress and national policy-making, including the standard textbook, *Congress and Its Members* (4th edition, 1994).

MORTON KELLER is Spector Professor of History at Brandeis University. He has been a visiting professor at Yale, Harvard, and Oxford universities. Dr. Keller's books include *Regulating a New Society: Public Policy and Social Change in America, 1900–1933* (1994); *Regulating a New Economy: Public Policy and Economic Change in America, 1900–1933* (1990); *Parties, Congress, and Public Policy* (1985); and *Affairs of State: Public Life in Late Nineteenth Century America* (1977).

Abbreviations and Acronyms Used in This Work

AFL-CIO American Federation of Labor and Congress of Industrial Organizations
amend. amendment
app. appendix
Ala. Alabama
A.M. *ante meridiem*, before noon
Ariz. Arizona
Ark. Arkansas
Art. Article
b. born
c. *circa*, about, approximately
Calif. California
cf. *confer*, compare
chap. chapter (pl., chaps.)
CIA Central Intelligence Agency
Cir. Ct. Circuit Court
cl. clause
Cong. Congress
Colo. Colorado
Cong. Rec. Congressional Record
Conn. Connecticut
CRS Congressional Research Service
d. died
D Democrat, Democratic
D.C. District of Columbia
D.D.C. District Court (federal) of the District of Columbia
Del. Delaware
diss. dissertation
doc. document
DR Democratic-Republican
ed. editor (pl., eds); edition
e.g. *exempli gratia*, for example
enl. enlarged
esp. especially
et al. *et alii*, and others
etc. *et cetera*, and so forth

exp. expanded
F Federalist
f. and following (pl., ff.)
F. Federal Reporter
F.2d Federal Reporter, 2d series
FBI Federal Bureau of Investigation
Fed. Reg. Federal Register
Fla. Florida
F. Supp. Federal Supplement
Ga. Georgia
GAO General Accounting Office
GPO Government Printing Office
GS General Schedule (federal civil service grade level)
H. Con. Res. House Concurrent Resolution
H. Doc. House Document
H. Hrg. House Hearing
H.J. Res. House Joint Resolution
H.R. House of Representatives; when followed by a number, identifies a bill that originated in the House
H. Rept. House Report
H. Res. House Resolution
How. Howard (court reporter)
I Independent (party)
ibid. *ibidem*, in the same place (as the one immediately preceding)
i.e. *id est*, that is
Ill. Illinois
I.L.M. International Legal Materials
Ind. Indiana
J Jeffersonian
Jr. Junior
Kans. Kansas

Ky. Kentucky
La. Louisiana
M.A. Master of Arts
Mass. Massachusetts
Mich. Michigan
Minn. Minnesota
Miss. Mississippi
Mo. Missouri
Mont. Montana
n. note
N.C. North Carolina
n.d. no date
N.Dak. North Dakota
Nebr. Nebraska
Nev. Nevada
N.H. New Hampshire
N.J. New Jersey
N.Mex. New Mexico
no. number (pl., nos.)
n.p. no place
n.s. new series
N.Y. New York
Okla. Oklahoma
Oreg. Oregon
p. page (pl., pp.)
Pa. Pennsylvania
P.L. Public Law
Prog. Progressive
pt. part (pl., pts.)
Pub. Res. Public Resolution
R Republican
Rep. Representative
repr. reprint
rept. report
rev. revised
R.I. Rhode Island
S. Senate; when followed by a number, identifies a bill that originated in the Senate
S.C. South Carolina
S. Con. Res. Senate Concurrent Resolution
S. Ct. Supreme Court Reporter
S.Dak. South Dakota

S. Doc. Senate Document
sec. section (pl., secs.)
Sen. Senator
ser. series
sess. session
S. Hrg. Senate Hearing
S.J. Res. Senate Joint Resolution
S. Prt. Senate Print
S. Rept. Senate Report
S. Res. Senate Resolution
Stat. Statutes at Large
S. Treaty Doc. Senate Treaty Document
supp. supplement
Tenn. Tennessee
Tex. Texas
T.I.A.S. Treaties and Other International Acts Series
U.N. United Nations
U.S. United States, United States Reports
USA United States Army
USAF United States Air Force
U.S.C. United States Code
U.S.C.A. United States Code Annotated
USN United States Navy
U.S.S.R. Union of Soviet Socialist Republics
U.S.T. United States Treaties
v. versus
Va. Virginia
VA Veterans Administration
vol. volume (pl., vols.)
Vt. Vermont
W Whig
Wash. Washington
Wheat. Wheaton (court reporter)
Wis. Wisconsin
W.Va. West Virginia
Wyo. Wyoming

Years of Each Congress

This table provides a simple guide to the dates of each Congress, citing the year in which the following Congress begins as the year in which the previous Congress ends. For the exact opening and closing dates of each session of each Congress from the First Congress to the present, see the table accompanying the entry "Sessions of Congress."

1st	1789–1791	26th	1839–1841	51st	1889–1891	76th	1939–1941
2d	1791–1793	27th	1841–1843	52d	1891–1893	77th	1941–1943
3d	1793–1795	28th	1843–1845	53d	1893–1895	78th	1943–1945
4th	1795–1797	29th	1845–1847	54th	1895–1897	79th	1945–1947
5th	1797–1799	30th	1847–1849	55th	1897–1899	80th	1947–1949
6th	1799–1801	31st	1849–1851	56th	1899–1901	81st	1949–1951
7th	1801–1803	32d	1851–1853	57th	1901–1903	82d	1951–1953
8th	1803–1805	33d	1853–1855	58th	1903–1905	83d	1953–1955
9th	1805–1807	34th	1855–1857	59th	1905–1907	84th	1955–1957
10th	1807–1809	35th	1857–1859	60th	1907–1909	85th	1957–1959
11th	1809–1811	36th	1859–1861	61st	1909–1911	86th	1959–1961
12th	1811–1813	37th	1861–1863	62d	1911–1913	87th	1961–1963
13th	1813–1815	38th	1863–1865	63d	1913–1915	88th	1963–1965
14th	1815–1817	39th	1865–1867	64th	1915–1917	89th	1965–1967
15th	1817–1819	40th	1867–1869	65th	1917–1919	90th	1967–1969
16th	1819–1821	41st	1869–1871	66th	1919–1921	91st	1969–1971
17th	1821–1823	42d	1871–1873	67th	1921–1923	92d	1971–1973
18th	1823–1825	43d	1873–1875	68th	1923–1925	93d	1973–1975
19th	1825–1827	44th	1875–1877	69th	1925–1927	94th	1975–1977
20th	1827–1829	45th	1877–1879	70th	1927–1929	95th	1977–1979
21st	1829–1831	46th	1879–1881	71st	1929–1931	96th	1979–1981
22d	1831–1833	47th	1881–1883	72d	1931–1933	97th	1981–1983
23d	1833–1835	48th	1883–1885	73d	1933–1935	98th	1983–1985
24th	1835–1837	49th	1885–1887	74th	1935–1937	99th	1985–1987
25th	1837–1839	50th	1887–1889	75th	1937–1939	100th	1987–1989
						101st	1989–1991
						102d	1991–1993
						103d	1993–1995

INSPECTOR GENERAL OF THE HOUSE.

The Office of Inspector General is one of two House offices created in the aftermath of the post office and house bank scandals of 1992, the other being the director of Non-Legislative and Financial Services. The inspector general's office was established by House Rule VI, clause 2 (103d Cong.), pursuant to the House Administrative Reform Resolution of 1992 (H. Res. 423, 102d Cong.), which provides that the inspector general be appointed by the Speaker, the majority leader, and the minority leader of the House, acting jointly.

The duties of the inspector general, subject to oversight by the Subcommittee on Administrative Oversight of the Committee on House Administration, include conducting periodic audits of the financial functions of the offices of Non-Legislative and Financial Services, Clerk, Sergeant at Arms, and Doorkeeper. Reports of such audits are submitted to the Speaker, majority leader, minority leader, and the chairman and ranking member of the Subcommittee on Administrative Oversight. The purposes of the audits are to ensure that financial functions are efficient, reliable, and in compliance with laws and regulations and to prevent and detect fraud and abuse. The first inspector general, John W. Lainhart IV, was appointed on 14 November 1993.

BIBLIOGRAPHY

U.S. House of Representatives. *Constitution, Jefferson's Manual, and Rules of the House of Representatives, 103d Congress.* Compiled by William Holmes Brown. 102d Cong., 2d sess., 1992. H. Doc. 102-405.

RAYMOND W. SMOCK

INSPECTORS GENERAL.

Offices of inspectors general consolidate authority over auditing and investigations within federal departments and agencies. The contemporary effort to create such units by public law as permanent, nonpartisan, independent offices has succeeded in more than sixty federal organizations. These include all cabinet departments and the largest agencies, where the inspectors general are nominated by the president and appointed by the head of the organization.

Significant legislative initiatives occurred in 1976, when the first inspector general's office was created; in 1978, when the Inspector General Act was passed; and in 1988, when major amendments to the act were approved. These congressional initiatives emerged because of significant financial scandals in the affected agencies and the failure of existing investigative units to combat waste, fraud, and abuse. They reflected substantial bipartisan support in both chambers of Congress—led by Representatives L. H. Fountain (D-N.C.), Jack Brooks (D-Tex.), and Frank Horton (R-N.Y.) and Senators Thomas F. Eagleton (D-Mo.), John Glenn (D-Ohio), and William V. Roth, Jr. (R-Del.). Congressional support usually ran in the face of opposition from the affected departments and agencies. Conflicts between the executive branch and the legislature have also arisen over whether inspectors general should report directly to Congress (in the 1978 compromise inspectors general would report directly to the agency heads, who would then transmit these reports without alteration or clearance to Congress within a specified time), as well as over the summary dismissal of fourteen inspectors general by President Ronald Reagan in 1981 and over the inspection and investigative powers of inspectors general.

Inspectors general have broad authority to detect and prevent waste, fraud, and abuse, including the power to conduct audits and investigations, issue subpoenas, and hire their own employees. The inspector general offices established by statute have also been given a substantial amount of independence from political pressures.

The inspectors general are also obligated to keep agency heads and Congress fully and currently informed about their findings and recommendations for corrective action through semiannual reports, special immediate reports on particularly serious or flagrant problems, and other means, such as testifying at congressional hearings.

[*See also* Inspector General of the House; Oversight.]

BIBLIOGRAPHY

Light, Paul C. *Monitoring Government: Inspectors General and the Search for Accountability.* 1993.
U.S. House of Representatives. Committee on Government Operations. *The Inspector General Act of 1978: A 10-Year Review.* 100th Cong., 2d sess., 1988. H. Doc. 100-1027.

FREDERICK M. KAISER

INSTRUCTION.

In colonial times and during the Articles of Confederation, the right of electors to instruct representatives how to vote on pending matters was widely accepted. *The Federalist* and debates of the state ratifying conventions show conflicting views on the subject. The House of Representatives in 1790 firmly refused to recognize the validity of instruction by rejecting by a vote of 41 to

10 a proposal to add to the Bill of Rights a provision recognizing the right of electors to instruct representatives.

The Senate—which, like the Continental Congress, was elected by state legislatures—was generally more accepting of instruction. In 1791, Virginia's senators, acting on instructions passed by that state's legislature, proposed that Senate sessions be opened to public view. In 1808, Sen. John Quincy Adams of Massachusetts became the first senator to resign when faced with instructions he opposed. In more than a dozen instances before the Civil War, senators resigned after receiving instructions with which they disagreed. However, in the decade before the Civil War, a number of senators began to ignore state legislature instructions successfully, thereby weakening them as a political tool. Although the practice fell into disuse after the Civil War (the Confederate Constitution formally endorsed the doctrine of instruction), instructions from state legislatures to senators continued up until the twentieth century and the popular election of senators (Seventeenth Amendment, ratified 1913).

Within Congress, *instruction* now has several meanings. First, a party caucus can by majority vote instruct party members how to vote in committee on particular matters on the grounds that a member owes his or her committee assignment to party caucus action. A member acting contrary to instructions (which are rarely voted anyway) may be disciplined by removal from that committee in future Congresses.

Second, the House and Senate rules permit motions to instruct members of a conference committee, generally urging them to accept or reject contentious matters in House or Senate versions of a bill. The instructions must be offered before the conferees are actually named (or after conferees have failed for twenty days to reach an agreement) and are not actually binding on conference committee members. However, the instructions do serve as signals to conferees of the sentiments of their parent chambers on highly salient issues.

Third, both the House and Senate permit a motion to commit or recommit a bill to committee with instructions. In the Senate, this practice is generally used to strip from the bill certain floor amendments previously agreed to by the Senate. In the House, the motion to recommit with instructions is used by the minority to force a vote (just before the vote on final passage) on its preferred version of the pending bill. In neither chamber does the bill actually leave the floor, and the committee is presumed to have reported the bill in the instructed form forthwith. Recommittal motions are generally successful in the Senate and generally unsuccessful in the House, where they, however, serve as an important symbolic power for the House minority party.

BIBLIOGRAPHY

Freed, Bruce F. "House Democrats: Dispute over Caucus Role," *Congressional Quarterly Weekly Report*, 3 May 1975, pp. 911–915.

Luce, Robert. *Legislative Principles.* 1930. Repr. 1971.

U.S. House of Representatives. *Constitution, Jefferson's Manual, and the Rules of the House of Representatives, 103d Congress.* 102d Cong., 2d sess., 1993. H. Doc. 102-105. Sec. 910.

PAUL S. RUNDQUIST

INTELLIGENCE COMMITTEE, HOUSE PERMANENT SELECT.

On 14 July 1977—more than a year after the Senate had acted to establish its new intelligence panel—the House created the Permanent Select Committee on Intelligence, ending dispersed and limited congressional oversight of intelligence in favor of consolidated jurisdiction, enhanced authority, and increased resources. Establishment of the panel was based in part on a recommendation from the earlier temporary House Select Committee on Intelligence (known as the Pike Committee), headed by Rep. Otis G. Pike (D-N.Y.). The Pike Committee's investigation, like that of the Senate Select Committee to Study Governmental Operations with Respect to Intelligence Activities (known as the Church Committee), disclosed widespread abuses, illegalities, and improper conduct by the intelligence agencies, particularly the Central Intelligence Agency (CIA) and Federal Bureau of Investigation (FBI).

By a vote of 227 to 171, the House established the new panel, which is similar but not identical to the Senate Select Intelligence Committee. The two committees were granted nearly identical jurisdiction and authority, including exclusive control over authorizations and legislation affecting the CIA and the Director of Central Intelligence and consolidated jurisdiction over the remainder of the intelligence community, which is shared by other standing committees with appropriate jurisdiction. The House panel, however, has jurisdiction over tactical military intelligence, which its Senate counterpart lacks.

The House committee also differs from the Senate version in size, partisan composition, leadership structure, the number of seats reserved for other committees, length of service, and authority to disclose classified information. The House panel's original thirteen seats (nineteen in 1993) represent a much smaller proportion of the chamber's membership than does the Senate panel's fifteen seats. The House committee also calls for only one seat for each of four committees with overlapping jurisdiction—Appropriations, Armed Services, Foreign Affairs, and Judiciary—while the Senate requires two from each, a majority and a minority party member. Tenure on the House committee is limited to six years of continuous service, compared to eight years on the Senate panel.

The creation of an independent oversight panel occasioned more conflict in the House than in the Senate. This was reflected in the delay in creating a House committee, the restrictions placed on it, the closed process governing the debate and vote, and the narrower margin of victory. Only 57 percent of the voting representatives agreed to the resolution—with an unusual combination of Republicans and liberal Democrats in opposition—compared to 75 percent of voting senators endorsing that body's new panel.

More than a year passed after the Senate launched its effort, allowing the acrimony surrounding the Pike Committee, because of the leak of its 1976 report, to subside. Partly to alleviate concerns raised by the Pike Committee's experience, however, the new House panel was given less authority and less autonomy than its Senate counterpart. The House Intelligence Committee, for instance, is prohibited from disclosing classified information on its own; this power was reserved for the full House and then only under elaborate procedures, including referral to the president and a vote of the chamber. The new committee was directed to prescribe regulations governing the availability and accessibility of information in its custody and was directed to keep a written record of what information was made available and to whom. Suspected leaks of classified information from either Intelligence Committee are to be investigated by the Ethics Committee of its respective chamber.

Another distinguishing characteristic of the House Intelligence Committee is its partisan composition—a 9 to 4 majority-minority party ratio at the committee's inception—compared to the more bipartisan Senate panel (8 to 7 majority-minority ratio). This brought intense criticism from the Republican minority at the time. But the initial 9 to 4

interparty ratio was the same for other House committees with the authority to report legislation to the floor in the 95th Congress (when House Democrats held an advantage of better than two to one in the number of seats).

The House's delay in establishing the new panel worked to its advantage. Divided-party government ended in 1977, when Democrat Jimmy Carter, a proponent of reform of the intelligence community, became president. The alliance between the Democratic president and Democratic House was made clear during the debate on the Intelligence Committee when Majority Leader James C. Wright, Jr. (D-Tex.), asserted bluntly that the committee "was requested by the president of the United States." Rules Committee chairman Richard W. Bolling (D-Mo.) added that "not only is the Democratic leadership in support of the resolution but it also has the approval of the president"; indeed, the intelligence panel was expected to be "a committee run, in effect, by the leadership." To help accomplish this goal, the Rules Committee reported House Resolution 658 under a closed rule, which limited debate and prohibited amendments from the floor. Further reflecting the leadership's role in running the committee, the Speaker appoints committee members and designates the chairman.

The House Intelligence Committee thus relied on strong Democratic leadership and partisan appeals. The size of the Democratic majority proved significant, because a number of liberal Democrats defected; they feared that the new panel would become isolated and coopted by the intelligence community and that critical overseers such as they would be closed out of the oversight process.

Most features of the House Intelligence Committee have been in place since its inception. In part, the committee's stability can be credited to its first chairman, Edward P. Boland (D-Mass.), who led it for nearly eight years. A senior member of the Appropriations Committee, Boland was a longtime friend of the Speaker and a trusted ally of the leadership.

The only significant changes in the House Intelligence Committee have been in its size and interparty ratio, from an original thirteen seats (9–4) to nineteen (12–7) in 1993. The number of members was increased on four separate occasions—thereby altering interparty ratios—reflecting the Intelligence Committee's heightened prestige and demands for increased minority-party representation.

In addition, a 1989 amendment to the House rules gave the Speaker direct access to any information held by the Intelligence Committee. This change came about in the aftermath of an alleged inadvertent disclosure of classified information from the committee by then-Speaker Jim Wright. The Speaker was not granted any special status under House Resolution 658 but had access to committee information by custom and practice.

Several public laws have benefited the House (and Senate) Intelligence Committee. Most important was the 1980 Intelligence Oversight Act, which reduced the number of committees that the president had to notify about covert operations from eight to two—the two Intelligence committees—and required advance notification in most cases. The provision was retained in the amended version enacted in 1991, in the aftermath of the Iran-contra affair. In addition, the committee receives reports from a statutory inspector general at the CIA, a post created by statute in 1989.

[*See also* Central Intelligence Agency; Intelligence Committee, Senate Select; Internal Security.]

BIBLIOGRAPHY

Jeffreys-Jones, Rhodri. *The CIA and American Democracy,* 1989.
Johnson, Loch K. *America's Secret Power: The CIA in a Democratic Society.* 1989.
Kaiser, Frederick M. "Congress and the Intelligence Community." In *The Postreform Congress.* Edited by Roger Davidson. 1992.
Smist, Frank J. *Congress Oversees the United States Intelligence Community, 1947–1989.* 1990.

FREDERICK M. KAISER

INTELLIGENCE COMMITTEE, SENATE SELECT.

On 19 May 1976, the Senate agreed to create the Select Committee on Intelligence by a 72 to 22 majority. (The House followed suit with a counterpart committee a year later.) The Senate's action—establishing a committee with consolidated jurisdiction over the entire intelligence community and with unprecedented authorizing powers over it—climaxed a long and involved process of committee deliberation and debate on the floor.

Major attempts to restructure congressional jurisdiction and oversight of intelligence occurred in 1956 and again in 1966 in the Senate. In 1956, Sen. Mike Mansfield (D-Mont.) and thirty-two cosponsors introduced a concurrent resolution to create a Joint Committee on Central Intelligence, modeled after the Joint Committee on Atomic Energy. The

proposal, which mirrored a similar idea from the second Hoover Commission in 1954, was defeated 27 to 59, because some original sponsors defected. In 1966, Sen. J. William Fulbright (D-Ark.), chairman of the Senate Foreign Relations Committee, sponsored a resolution to create a Senate Committee on Intelligence Operations, a proposal initially promoted by Sen. Eugene J. McCarthy (D-Minn.); the Foreign Relations Committee reported the proposal favorably, 14 to 5. This plan was defeated on a point of order, however, when the resolution was referred to the Armed Services Committee, which claimed jurisdiction for the change, at the request of its chairman Richard B. Russell (D-Ga.).

In 1975, both the House and Senate created temporary select committees on intelligence to investigate a series of alleged illegalities, improper behavior, and unethical conduct on the part of intelligence agencies, allegations of which appeared in the *New York Times* in December 1974. Headed by Sen. Frank Church (D-Idaho) and Rep. Otis G. Pike (D-N.Y.), the highly publicized and sometimes controversial investigations found numerous long-standing, widespread, and serious abuses, including assassination plots against foreign leaders, drug testing on unwitting subjects, mind-control experiments, infiltration of domestic dissident groups, and a program to "neutralize" African American civil rights leaders that included wiretapping Dr. Martin Luther King, Jr. A presidential commission, headed by Vice President Nelson Rockefeller, also looked into the CIA's domestic operations. The Rockefeller Commission's findings built on 1973 discoveries by the Senate Watergate Committee, which documented White House attempts to manipulate intelligence agencies for political purposes.

Congress faulted itself for an ineffective, insufficient, or sometimes nonexistent oversight system. Reporting in 1976, both the Church and Pike committees—which were formally named, respectively, the Senate Select Committee to Study Governmental Operations with Respect to Intelligence Activities and the temporary House Select Committee on Intelligence—urged the formation of a permanent intelligence committee in each chamber to expand, regularize, and improve congressional oversight.

Senate Resolution 400, the vehicle creating the Senate Intelligence Committee, and companion proposals generated hearings and meetings by five standing committees, reports or recommendations from four standing committees and one select committee, five distinct versions of the basic resolution, and floor debate spanning ten days. It also spawned thirteen proposed amendments, ten of which were ultimately adopted. The extensive Senate debate occurred for several reasons, including the many issues that needed to be resolved, the controversy surrounding the choices, the high stakes involved, and the uniqueness of the venture. Divided government also played a role, with Republican president Gerald Ford and a Democratic Senate (and House) at odds. Eventually, the disputes were resolved in a final compromise version arranged by Rules Committee chairman Howard W. Cannon (D-Nev.) and Majority Leader Mike Mansfield in consultation with a large number of senators and representatives of the Ford administration.

The compromise succeeded in lessening the concerns of the several rival camps. One raised the prospect that a new panel would not be strong enough to oversee and control intelligence activities adequately if it lacked independence and important bill-reporting power. Another raised the prospect that a committee granted too much power and independence would handicap intelligence activities and operations. Some administration supporters and opponents of the intelligence panel, particularly senior Republicans on the Armed Services Committee, argued that a new panel might jeopardize classified national security information and legitimate intelligence activities—an especially glaring charge in light of the highly visible clashes with the executive branch over such access and the allegations of leaks involving the Church and Pike committees.

Balancing the competing forces, the compromise version created an improved system for overseeing and controlling intelligence through far-reaching authority, including legislative power, authorizing power, and far-ranging jurisdictions. The executive was directed to keep the new panel "fully and currently informed, with respect to intelligence activities, including any significant anticipated activities," a reference to advance notice for covert operations. The compromise version, however, also imposed a number of checks on the new committee. Among other things, it circumscribed the Intelligence Committee's ability to disclose classified information through an elaborate set of procedures, which formally involved the president, and through required investigations of suspected leaks by the Ethics Committee.

The Senate Intelligence Committee's institutional integrity and stability were enhanced when, in early 1977, the Senate realigned its committee jurisdictions but left the Intelligence panel undis-

turbed. In 1976 the Senate Select Committee to Study the Senate Committee System (known as the Stevenson Committee) had questioned whether the intelligence Committee's workload would justify its retention as a permanent committee and whether there was a need for continued oversight of intelligence activities independent of other standing committees. The Intelligence Committee was, however, rescued from the skeptical Stevenson Committee by the Senate Rules Committee, headed by Cannon (who had played a key role in the creation of the intelligence panel).

As of 1993 the Senate Committee still consisted of fifteen members; each member is limited to eight years of continuous service. It features a bipartisan structure, with an 8 to 7 majority-minority party ratio and with the vice chairman, who replaces an absent chairman, being a member of the minority party. Other panels with overlapping jurisdictions—Appropriations, Armed Services, Foreign Relations, and Judiciary—are assigned two members (one majority and one minority) on the Intelligence Committee, for a total of eight. Seven other members are selected at large.

Since its establishment, the Senate Intelligence Committee has benefited from several statutory changes. The most important were contained in the 1980 Intelligence Oversight Act. These provisions, retained in the 1991 revision, directed the intelligence agencies to keep the House and Senate Intelligence committees "fully and currently informed of all intelligence activities" and to "furnish any information or material concerning intelligence . . . which is requested by either of the Intelligence Committees." The 1980 act also reduced the number of committees receiving notification of covert operations; instead of the eight committees that used to receive such notice, only the House and Senate Intelligence committees would now do so.

In the mid 1980s, the two Intelligence committees were deceived over the Iran-contra affair. Although the Senate committee mounted an investigation when the news about the scandal broke in late 1986, both the House and Senate set up special temporary committees to investigate in 1987. Their jurisdiction and authority remained intact afterward, although the minority on the combined Iran-contra committees recommended replacing the Intelligence committees with a Joint Committee on Intelligence.

[*See also* Central Intelligence Agency; Intelligence Committee, House Permanent Select; Internal Security.]

BIBLIOGRAPHY

Jeffreys-Jones, Rhodri. *The CIA and American Democracy.* 1989.

Johnson, Loch K. *America's Secret Power: The CIA in a Democratic Society.* 1989.

Kaiser, Frederick M. "Congress and the Intelligence Community," In *The Postreform Congress.* Edited by Roger Davidson. 1992.

Smist, Frank J. *Congress Oversees the United States Intelligence Community, 1947–1989.* 1990.

FREDERICK M. KAISER

INTELLIGENCE POLICY. Congress has long recognized that national security and diplomatic decisions require reliable knowledge of conditions outside the United States. It has allowed the government to gather, analyze, and use such data obtained by stealth and other means. It also has allowed special agencies to advance U.S. foreign objectives through various covert programs. The lawmakers, however, have never been comfortable with the conflicting imperatives of strict secrecy—the essence of intelligence activity—and the public's demand for accountable government. It has preferred, by and large, to provide the president with the broad statutory authority and money to carry out the unsavory business, while Congress itself remained relatively aloof from the process. Only since the mid 1970s, following public disclosure of failed and illegal covert activities involving U.S. agencies, has Congress insisted on a full voice with the president in the conduct and oversight of U.S. intelligence policy.

The expression *intelligence,* when applied to questions of a country's foreign affairs or national security, has two primary meanings. The first meaning is broad and encompasses a set of activities: the collection, analysis, and dissemination of information deemed valuable for decision makers in their deliberations (dubbed "collection-and-analysis"); the protection of this information ("counterintelligence"); and, based upon this information, the secret use of government agencies to influence other nations through the use of propaganda, political action, economic measures, and paramilitary operations ("covert action" or "special activities"). The second meaning of intelligence is narrow, referring specially to the information itself that is gathered for decision makers.

The Evolution of Intelligence Policy. The leaders of the American Revolution were well aware of the vital role intelligence policy would play in a successful war of independence. In 1776, the Continental Congress established the nation's first intelligence service, the Committee of Secret Correspondence; and Gen. George Washington made use of an effective network of spies led by Paul Revere. Beyond gathering and interpreting information about threats to the new nation (the collection-and-analysis function), the American revolutionaries were concerned as well about protecting their army's secret plans from hostile foreign spies (the counterintelligence function).

None of these intelligence activities were given formal standing in the Constitution. The prevailing view at the time of the document's drafting was that matters of espionage, vital in times of war, were best left unstated. Indeed, until 1947, U.S. intelligence policy lacked any formal statutory underpinnings and was based wholly on secret executive orders. The experiences at Pearl Harbor, which catapulted the United States into World War II, corrected this omission.

On 7 December 1941, the Japanese air force struck the United States with a surprise attack against the military base at Pearl Harbor, Hawaii, destroying much of the U.S. Pacific fleet. The attack represented the most disastrous intelligence failure in U.S. history. Soon after the war, U.S. government officials established a modern intelligence service in hopes of forever avoiding another military shock like Pearl Harbor. In 1946, President Harry S. Truman issued an executive order establishing a Central Intelligence Group patterned after the Office of Strategic Services (OSS), the U.S. intelligence arm during World War II. On 26 July 1947, with passage of the National Security Act, Congress gave statutory authority to this concept, replacing the Central Intelligence Group with a Central Intelligence Agency (CIA)—the centerpiece of the modern U.S. intelligence apparatus. This landmark law, coupled with key amendments passed in 1949, placed the CIA under control of a new White House structure that would henceforth coordinate U.S. foreign policy: the National Security Council (NSC).

By law, the NSC consists of four principal members: the president, vice president, secretary of State, and secretary of Defense, though other officials are invited from time to time to participate in its deliberations, including the top intelligence chief: the director of Central Intelligence (DCI). The DCI serves in two capacities: as DCIA (that is, director of the CIA) and as the official in charge of the full assemblage of other intelligence agencies in the federal government.

The 1947 National Security Act gave the DCI five specific authorities, of which the last (written in ambiguous language) made a gesture toward duties beyond the original purpose of the modern intelligence mission—that is, the improved collection and coordination of information. The statute charged the CIA with the duty to advise the NSC on intelligence activities related to national security; make recommendations to the NSC for the coordination of such activities; correlate, evaluate, and disseminate intelligence within the government; carry out services for existing agencies that the NSC decides might be best done centrally; and, in the vague catchall phrase of the act, "perform such other functions and duties related to intelligence affecting the national security as the National Security Council may from time to time direct." While the founding statute overwhelmingly emphasized the collection mission, it also permitted the CIA and the other secret agencies to be used for "other functions and duties"—an invitation quickly accepted by the NSC as an opportunity for launching aggressive covert action and counterintelligence operations around the world in the struggle against communism.

The concept of centralized coordination lay at the heart of the efforts in 1947 to create a new, more formal intelligence system. But strong forces resisted the endeavors to subsume all existing intelligence entities under the plenary control of a DCI. Through the skillful bureaucratic leadership of its early incumbents, most notably Gen. Walter Bedell Smith (1950–1953) and Allen Dulles (1953–1961), some consolidation of authority for intelligence policy took place within the office of the DCI; but undisputed dominance by this office over all the other secret agencies in the government—including such giants as the National Security Agency (NSA, with its worldwide network of communications and intercept facilities) and the Defense Intelligence Agency (DIA, the military's top organization for the analysis of military intelligence)—remained an elusive goal. For intelligence policy, the principle of federation would prevail for the dozen major (and several minor) agencies comprising the U.S. intelligence establishment.

This cluster of secret organizations, with a budget of some $30 billion a year and over 150,000 personnel, has become known as the "intelligence community." Euphemisms aside, however, the relationships among these agencies can be (and often have been) discordant. For instance, when the imperious J. Edgar Hoover was head of the Federal Bureau of Investigation (FBI), DCIs found it next to impossible to influence—let alone direct—his handling of domestic intelligence and counterintelligence operations.

A Changing Intelligence Mandate. Throughout the Cold War, the U.S. secret intelligence agencies made monitoring the U.S.S.R. their first priority. With the end of the Cold War, the new mission has become much broader: to understand the world. Eyeing the new world, intelligence professionals point to a fresh set of security threats: weapons proliferation, the drug trade, ethnic terrorism, international economic competition, lingering tensions in the former Soviet republics (four of which still have nuclear weapons), aggressive "renegade" nations like Iraq, territorial disputes around the globe, the spread of AIDS and other diseases (which are undermining the political stability of some countries), foreign nuclear safety problems, and migration, as well as the international technology race. At the same time, economic distress within the United States following the Cold War has forced a reduction in funding for intelligence policy.

Trim the budget and move forward cautiously in exploring the new mandates for the intelligence agencies—these became the watchwords of intelligence overseers and managers in the 1990s. Central, too, was a need to improve the often shaky partnership that had evolved since 1947 between overseers and the leaders of the intelligence agencies.

A Hidden Policy Domain. Following the creation of the contemporary intelligence community in 1947, the public and even most government officials were privy to little information about its workings. Neither the NSC nor the Congress monitored intelligence operations with close scrutiny. Congressional supervision of the secret agencies was, ostensibly, the duty of four subcommittees. Both the Senate and the House Armed Services committees had CIA Oversight subcommittees, as did the Senate and House Appropriations committees. The subcommittees seldom convened: typically, during the 1950s, they met once or twice a year for a two-hour meeting, with only slightly more activity (up to five meetings a year, each for a couple of hours) during the 1960s.

The lassitude that characterized congressional monitoring of the secret agencies resulted in part from a paralyzing awe engendered by the sheer size and complexity of the intelligence community. Moreover, legislators have been reluctant to be-

Landmark Intelligence Legislation

TITLE	YEAR ENACTED	REFERENCE NUMBER	DESCRIPTION
National Security Act	1947	61 Stat. 495–510	Established the Central Intelligence Agency.
Central Intelligence Agency Act	1949	50 U.S.C. 403	Clarified and strengthened the office of the director of Central Intelligence.
Hughes-Ryan Amendment (Section 662 of the Foreign Assistance Act of 1961)	1974	22 U.S.C. 2422	Required presidential approval of all important covert actions and reporting to Congress "in a timely fashion"—the first statutory restraint placed upon the CIA since its inception in 1947.
Senate Resolution 400	1976	—	Established the Senate Select Committee on Intelligence.
House Resolution 658	1977	—	Established the House Permanent Select Committee on Intelligence.
Foreign Intelligence Surveillance Act (Foreign Electronic Surveillance Act)	1978	P.L. 95-511	Created a special judicial court to review executive branch requests for authority to conduct electronic surveillance within the United States for intelligence purposes.
Title V of Intelligence Authorization Act for Fiscal Year 1981 (Accountability for Intelligence Activities Act, or Intelligence Oversight Act of 1980)	1980	P.L. 96-450	Required prior reporting to Congress from all intelligence agencies on all significant intelligence activities, except in times of extraordinary circumstances when advance reporting was required only to eight designated leaders of Congress.
Intelligence Authorization Act for Fiscal Year 1987 (Boland Amendment)	1987	P.L. 99-569	One of six laws sponsored by Rep. Boland during the 1980s and bearing his name, all designed to place curbs on the use of covert action in Nicaragua. Reagan administration violations of these laws led to the Iran-contra scandal in 1986 and 1987.
Title VI of Intelligence Authorization Act, Fiscal Year 1991 (Intelligence Oversight Act of 1991)	1991	P.L. 102-88	Clarified the definitions and missions of the U.S. intelligence agencies; retreated from the congressional reporting standard of prior notice in times of extraordinary circumstances, returning to the "in a timely fashion" requirement of the 1974 Hughes-Ryan Amendment.

come involved in the often heated disputes between the agencies within the community. Concern over the possibility of inadvertent breaches of security has played a role as well. Another reason that members of Congress avoided the task of intelligence review was its perceived lack of political payoff; the subject matter in this field is often classified, which prohibits legislators from discussing their work with constituents—not an attractive feature for politicians seeking reelection. A tradition had also grown up in Washington that the intelligence agencies were led by honorable individuals who could be relied upon to do the right thing without meddlesome interference by outsiders uninitiated in the esoteric arts of espionage.

This is not to say that the history of congressional review over intelligence policy was without some bursts of close scrutiny; occasional flaps, like the Bay of Pigs fiasco, sired limited investigations. And

a few members of Congress have attempted, off and on, to introduce more vigorous monitoring. From 1947 through 1974, legislators introduced over two hundred resolutions calling for improvements in congressional oversight of the CIA, but only a handful represented serious initiatives. Few of these proposals emerged from committee, and none was approved by Congress. In 1956 and again in 1966, a small band of senators led by Mike Mansfield (D-Mont.) tried to create an intelligence oversight committee that would go beyond the limited and largely inactive CIA oversight subcommittees already in existence in each chamber. In both instances, opponents easily defeated the measures. Then, in October 1974, a few senators led by James Abourezk (D-S.Dak.) introduced a bill to prohibit CIA involvement in covert action; henceforth, according to this proposal, the CIA would engage strictly in intelligence gathering, analysis, and counterintelligence. The bill was defeated by a lopsided margin.

Missing from the reformers' arsenal was the essential element for success: an aroused public. Occasionally, sharp questioning of intelligence activities came from the media, as in the case of the 1967 *Ramparts* magazine exposé of secret ties between the CIA and the National Students Association, or the revelation that former CIA officers had broken into the Watergate Hotel in a burglary of the Democratic National Party headquarters. Even these significant news stories caused only a ripple of public concern over intelligence policy. A truly major scandal was required to stir the public toward demands for reform, in turn stimulating Congress into action. Such an event occurred in December 1974.

Intelligence Joins the Government. Reporter Seymour M. Hersh of the *New York Times* captured the attention of the public in a series of articles, beginning on 22 December 1974, that accused the CIA of "massive" spying and illegal intelligence operations directed against anti–Vietnam War activists and other U.S. dissidents. According to Hersh's sources inside the CIA, files on over ten thousand U.S. citizens had been compiled by the agency, despite the language of the 1947 National Security Act that barred the CIA from any security or police function within the United States.

Coming on the heels of the Watergate scandal, these new revelations provided the next media sensation and brought quick reaction. Letters and telegrams poured into congressional offices calling for an investigation into the alleged spying against American citizens by the CIA and the other secret agencies. Several senators, including Majority Leader Mike Mansfield, joined the voices demanding an inquiry. In another indication of legislative determination to restrain the CIA, Congress passed the Hughes-Ryan amendment during the last days of 1974 (cosponsored by Sen. Harold E. Hughes [D-Iowa] and Rep. Leo J. Ryan [D-Calif.]). This statute, which required the president to approve and report to Congress ("in a timely fashion") all important covert actions, represented the first successful effort by legislators to place controls over the CIA since its creation.

On 4 January 1975, President Gerald R. Ford established the Commission on CIA Activities within the United States, chaired by Vice President Nelson A. Rockefeller (the Rockefeller Commission); and, on 27 January 1975, the Senate voted 82 to 4 to establish a special committee to conduct an investi-

gation of U.S. intelligence operations. The House soon created its own committee of inquiry. The congressional panels were chaired, respectively, by Sen. Frank Church (D-Idaho) and Rep. Otis G. Pike (D-N.Y.).

After several extensions, the congressional investigative committees finished their work in April 1976. The Church and Pike panels offered over one hundred reform recommendations. The Senate was persuaded by the work of its committee that something had to be done, and in June 1976, it endorsed the Church committee's most important recommendation: the establishment of a permanent oversight committee for intelligence policy, officially called the Senate Select Committee on Intelligence (SSCI). A year later, the House followed suit by creating a House Permanent Select Committee on Intelligence (HPSCI).

With the creation of the two intelligence committees, intelligence policy had moved from out of the shadows into the sunlight of more open government—though this is a relative matter, since much of what the secret agencies do is highly sensitive and still remains classified. Nevertheless, the intelligence agencies now face annual and detailed budget reviews; regular (though usually closed) hearings on proposed legislation and program review; confirmation hearings in the Senate for the DCI and his or her deputy; and day-to-day monitoring by legislators and their staffs. The two committees feature an unusual term limitation for members: no legislator can serve longer than eight years as an intelligence overseer—an effort to reduce the risk of members being co-opted by the secret agencies, a common phenomenon observed by students of congressional oversight.

Strengthened Intelligence Oversight. After establishing the two intelligence oversight committees, the Congress passed several laws affecting the intelligence agencies, including the Foreign Intelligence Surveillance Act of 1978, which tightened the approval procedures for electronic surveillance (a power sometimes abused by the executive branch in the past). The centerpiece legislation was the Accountability for Intelligence Activities Act, passed in 1980. With this law, known less formally as the 1980 Intelligence Oversight Act, the Congress increased the rigor of its monitoring demands on the intelligence agencies. Legislative overseers clarified that Congress wanted to be informed of all important covert actions, not just those sponsored by the CIA. This seemed to close a possible loophole for presidential recourse to other agencies, with the

White House resorting to the legal defense that the Hughes-Ryan amendment explicitly required the president to report only on CIA covert actions. Henceforth, if the president assigned a covert action to the military—or to any other government entity—it would have to be reported to the two intelligence committees. The law emphasized, too, that overseers expected reports on all significant intelligence activities, not only on covert actions.

With this strongly worded 1980 act, Congress moved away from the ex post facto quality of its "in a timely manner" reporting requirement to embrace a tougher standard of prior notification to both intelligence committees for all important covert operations. In emergency situations, the law permitted the president to limit the prior notice to eight leaders in Congress—the so-called Gang of Eight. The statute provides: "[If] the President determines it is essential to limit prior notice to meet extraordinary circumstances affecting the vital interests of the United States, such notice shall be limited to the chairmen and ranking minority members of the intelligence committees, the Speaker and minority leader of the House of Representatives, and the majority and minority leaders of the Senate."

Despite the clear intent of the law, the Reagan administration secretly sold weapons to Iran in the mid 1980s (a paramilitary covert action) without notifying Congress. The profits from these sales, plus money raised in other countries and from private U.S. citizens, was then used to fund additional covert actions in Nicaragua designed to topple its Marxist government. This second phase of what became known as the Iran-contra scandal (the Reagan administration supported the Contras, the opposition faction in Nicaragua) was never reported to Congress, either, again violating the 1980 Intelligence Oversight Act. The second phase violated the Boland amendments as well, a series of six laws sponsored by Rep. Edward P. Boland (D-Mass.) during the 1980s designed to curtail covert actions in Nicaragua. The administration claimed, without credibility, that the 1980 law and the Boland amendments failed to apply to the Iran-contra operations because these covert actions were guided by the National Security Council in the White House—not the CIA. Congressional investigators subsequently argued to the contrary: both laws referred to any government entity involved in covert actions.

The American Intelligence Experiment. In the aftermath of Iran-contra, DCIs have tried to heal relations between the Congress and the intelligence community that were badly torn by the 1987 scandal. Tensions continued in the 1990s, however, particularly over two thorny issues: when the DCI should report to the intelligence committees, and the lingering concern that intelligence officials may still be less than forthcoming with their legislative overseers.

With passage of the 1991 Intelligence Oversight Act, the Congress stiffened the formal presidential approval process for covert actions, but relaxed the demand for prior notification to Congress before an operation is implemented. The new language explicitly requires a written approval by the president (this document is called a "finding")—not simply an oral approval, as provided by President Ronald Reagan for the Iranian arms sale. The president is also still expected to report in advance when possible, but is now given greater leeway ("in a timely fashion" is the expectation) in times of emergency—a problematic return to the ex post facto standard of the Hughes-Ryan amendment, in the view of the law's critics.

As for the honesty question, legislative overseers remain sensitive to the memory of evasive testimony provided to them by intelligence officials during the Iran-contra inquiry conducted by House and Senate select committees. During that investigation, one senior CIA officer, for example, finally admitted to investigators that his earlier testimony regarding his agency's involvement in Nicaragua had been "technically correct, [but] specifically evasive."

These ongoing tensions point to the experimental nature of the relationship between Congress and America's secret agencies—a unique attempt to bring democracy to the hidden side of government. The experiment rests on the belief that if secret power is allowed to run free of supervision, it has the capacity to turn against the liberties of an open society. It reflects an understanding of the irony of intelligence, which has the potential to destroy as well as to guard democracy.

[*See also* Boland Amendments; Central Intelligence Agency; Intelligence Committee, House Permanent Select; Intelligence Committee, Senate Select; Internal Security; National Security Act.]

BIBLIOGRAPHY

Cohen, William S., and George J. Mitchell. *Men of Zeal: A Candid Inside Story of the Iran-Contra Hearings.* 1988.

Colby, William F., and Peter Forbath. *Honorable Men: My Life in the CIA.* 1978.

Jeffreys-Jones, Rhodri. *The CIA and American Democracy.* 1989.

Johnson, Loch K. *America's Secret Power: The CIA in a Democratic Society.* 1989.

Johnson, Loch K. *A Season of Inquiry: Congress and Intelligence.* 1985.

Ransom, Harry Howe. *The Intelligence Establishment.* 1970.

Smist, Frank J., Jr. *Congress Oversees the United States Intelligence Community.* 1990.

Treverton, Gregory F. *Covert Action: The Limits of Intervention in the Postwar World.* 1987.

Turner, Stansfield. *Secrecy and Democracy: The CIA in Transition.* 1985.

LOCH K. JOHNSON

INTEREST GROUPS.

The intimate connection between interest groups and Congress becomes immediately evident to an observer taking a simple walk around Capitol Hill. The hallways of the House and Senate office buildings, the sidewalks between the offices and the Capitol, the hearing rooms, the corridors outside the chambers of the two houses—all are filled with an admixture of members, staff, and lobbyists. Capitol Hill is as much the home and workplace of lobbyists as it is of lawmakers and their staffs.

Interest groups and lobbyists have been viewed alternately—sometimes simultaneously—as staples of the American legislative process, protected by the Constitution, and as pernicious indicators of the kind of corruption and influence-peddling that is always a danger, and frequently a reality, in the political system.

The legitimacy of lobbying is set in the First Amendment to the U.S. Constitution, which guarantees all citizens the right to free speech and the right to petition the government for redress of grievances. Taken together, these rights have for centuries legitimized the actions of individuals and groups as they have pursued their own interests within the political system, often at the expense of the interests of others. At the same time, James Madison, in *Federalist* 10, both warns of the "mischiefs of factions" (groups less than the whole citizenry) and yet acknowledges the necessity of their existence and their activity. Indeed, Madison says that the only way to limit the mischief is to allow the growth and activity of groups to check and balance one another.

Types of Interest Groups. In the nineteenth century, the range of groups represented in the corridors of Congress was quite limited, and their activity was highly directed. Lobbyists of the time represented commercial, business, and trust interests in areas from banking to railroads to armaments and agriculture—all in keeping with the limited number of areas, such as tariffs, government finance, and territorial expansion, in which Congress and the federal government were involved. As the twentieth century unfolded, however, the range in number and types of groups expanded dramatically.

Business Groups. Business groups with representatives in Washington range from small local firms seeking a federal subcontract, to a national business interest seeking a particular government benefit or tax break, to a large multinational corporation that maintains permanent representation in the capital. Business groups generally aim their lobbying activity as much toward regulatory agencies and the federal bureaucracy as toward Congress. Rather than set up a Washington office or use their own personnel, many businesses hire Washington law firms for their representation and lobbying. Many others do both, while also relying on one or more trade associations and umbrella groups for broader business issues.

Traditionally, the two largest and best-known umbrella groups representing business interests have been the U.S. Chamber of Commerce and the National Association of Manufacturers. In recent years, smaller, more narrowly focused groups such

STAGE ACTRESS FERN ANDRA. Describing the difficulties faced by American actors in Europe to House Immigration and Naturalization Committee member John H. Kerr (D-N.C.), *left,* and committee chairman Samuel Dickstein (D-N.Y.), *center,* 3 March 1937. The committee was conducting hearings on a bill to restrict the admission of foreign actors to the United States in order to protect native talent. LIBRARY OF CONGRESS

as the Business Roundtable (representing larger corporations), the American Business Conference (representing entrepreneurial, fast-growth businesses), and the National Federation of Independent Business (representing smaller businesses) have also come into their own.

In addition, Washington is filled with hundreds of industry-specific trade associations, including the American Petroleum Institute, the National Association of Broadcasters and the National Cable Television Association, and lobbying offices of individual firms, from General Motors and General Electric to General Dynamics and General Mills. Large companies like General Motors have on their lobbying staffs substantial numbers of engineers and scientists, who mainly interact with the Defense Department, the Highway Traffic Safety Administration, and the Environmental Protection Agency, along with people who track policy developments and legislation and others whose jobs involve lobbying members of Congress and staff on legislative proposals and bills.

Labor. Labor interests are also represented en masse in Washington, even if the role and influence of organized labor has diminished significantly over the years. Some unions have their main headquarters in Washington, while others have established legislative offices in the capital whose sole purpose is to represent the views of the union's members on Capitol Hill.

The American Federation of Labor and Congress of Industrial Organizations (AFL-CIO) is the largest and most powerful labor organization in the country. The AFL-CIO is an umbrella organization that represents nearly one hundred affiliated unions with a total of fourteen million dues-paying members. It has a variety of interrelated internal components, operates through a large and hierarchical organization, and is housed in an impressive headquarters only two blocks from the White House. The United Auto Workers, Teamsters, United Mine Workers, and other unions are also represented in Washington. Labor has been an active and visible player in Congress for many decades, although since the late 1980s it has had little success with its basic legislative agenda, from labor law reform to legislation banning replacement workers during strikes.

Public interest groups. Groups that seek policy goals (and often governmental reform) without regard for the material benefits of their members have been present in Washington in one form or another since the progressive, prohibitionist, and suffragist movements at the turn of the century. But the expansion in the numbers and activity of so-called public interest groups is really a phenomenon of the 1970s. The two groups that have come to epitomize the goals and strategies of interest groups in general are Common Cause and Ralph Nader's Public Citizen.

Common Cause, founded in 1970 by John Gardner, has approximately 275,000 members and an annual operating budget of more than $11 million. Common Cause has fought for such causes as ending the Vietnam War, reforming Congress and the campaign finance system, and tightening government ethics codes.

Public Citizen, a mass-membership organization modeled on Common Cause, is part of a conglomerate of public interest groups headed by Ralph Nader, which include groups directed toward consumer, environmental, health, science, regulatory reform, energy, and other orientations. These groups conduct research, lobby, publish books and reports, and generally attempt to influence the course of public policy. Norman Lear's People for the American Way has become another major player in the broad public interest field. Both Nader's and Lear's groups raise a substantial part of their funds through direct-mail solicitations.

The multitude of public interest groups that exist in the 1990s include groups representing the interests of women, children, and the elderly and groups concentrating on legal and health issues as well as on social welfare and urban problems. Initially, public interest groups seemed to have largely a liberal coloration. But in recent years a number of more conservative public interest groups have been formed or have expanded their focus and influence, partly in reaction to their liberal counterparts. These include organizations such as Accuracy in Media, Americans United for Life, Citizens against Government Waste, the National Taxpayers' Union, and the Washington Legal Foundation.

Environmental groups. The number and stature of environmental groups have grown since the 1980s as environmental issues have risen in importance on the legislative agenda. These groups include several older, established conservation organizations such as the Sierra Club, the National Audubon Society, and the National Wildlife Federation. Newer groups, organized in the late 1960s and early 1970s when *ecology* became a common term in the political lexicon, include Environmental Action, Friends of the Earth, and the Environmental Defense Fund.

Since the late 1980s, a community-based environmental movement has begun to take hold at the state and local levels. At the same time, with increasing multilateral action to deal with global environmental problems such as global warming and the deterioration of the ozone layer, environmental groups have had to broaden their focus beyond Congress and the states.

Civil rights groups. For most of the twentieth century, civil rights groups have been a factor in the policy-making process. The National Association for the Advancement of Colored People (NAACP) was established in 1910 to promote the interests of African Americans. Along with the National Urban League and other organizations, including some representing Hispanics, Asians, and women, these groups have lobbied on behalf of black Americans and other minority groups on issues such as educational opportunity, voting rights, equal employment, and fair housing. An umbrella organization, the Leadership Conference on Civil Rights, headed by Ralph Neas, played a particularly prominent role in the 1990–1991 struggle over a new civil rights act and in the controversial Senate confirmation hearings on the Supreme Court nominations of Robert Bork in 1987 and Clarence Thomas in 1991.

Foreign lobbying. Foreign lobbying has been controversial at least since the 1930s, when questions were raised about foreign agents lobbying Congress and the White House on behalf of Germany as American hostility toward Adolf Hitler's Nazi government grew. Here, American ambivalence about the legitimate political role of interests takes on yet another aspect: how far do Constitutional protections extend to foreign interests?

Lobbying on behalf of foreign interests or for U.S. interests whose concern is foreign policy is nonetheless an important and growing part of the political scene in Washington. In the 1990s, virtually every foreign nation of significant size has a lobbying agent or agents operating in Washington. Many foreign agents are prominent political figures; they lobby Congress and the State Department on a variety of issues. In recent years, lobbying by domestic groups on foreign policy has clearly increased, with the American-Israel Public Affairs Committee (AIPAC) and the newer Arab-American Institute being two examples. At the same time, business and labor groups lobby frequently for tariff protection, trade provisions, or other policies on behalf of foreign interests.

If foreign lobbying has always been a sensitive subject, it has grown even more controversial. A book by Pat Choate, *Agents of Influence* (1990), decries the growing influence of Japanese interests in the United States, focusing on the number of prominent Americans who receive compensation, in one form or another, from groups in Japan, suggesting that their views are being bought and that they are giving unwitting legitimacy to a point of view that is inimical to U.S. national interests. While many observers do not share this alarmist view, additional, tougher regulation of the representation of foreign interests is on the congressional policy agenda, and is likely to be passed in coming years.

This list is by no means complete. Literally thousands of groups are active in Washington, tracking congressional action and lobbying Congress. Some of the most consequential are not encompassed by the categories mentioned above. These include, for instance, the American Association of Retired Persons (AARP) and the National Committee to Preserve Medicare and Social Security, two groups that represent elderly Americans and have wide influence in the debate over entitlements; the National Rifle Association (NRA), which has had enormous influence over gun control policy; the American Legion, one of many organizations active in policy affecting veterans; and the U.S. Catholic Conference, one of many religious organizations with a base in Washington, which has been active in many areas of social policy but particularly in the antiabortion movement. For every large trade association like the American Petroleum Institute, there are dozens of small specialty associations representing, for example, independent gas stations, fig growers, natural gas pipeline producers, oil pipeline manufacturers, wine growers, or ball-bearing makers.

As power has become increasingly decentralized in Washington and the points of entry into the system have multiplied, the number of interest groups has mushroomed and groups have become more and more specialized—and the sources they use to lobby on their behalf have become more specialized and numerous as well.

Theories about Groups. Early research and literature on lobbying and interest groups focused on the origins and dynamics of groups themselves. Through the years many theories have been propounded about the impact and desirability of groups in the U.S. political system—some positive and some negative.

In general, the various theories about groups that have been offered have centered on three questions.

First and most broadly, are interest groups good or bad forces in American politics and society? Second, do groups, in the sum of their actions and interactions, provide some approximation of the public interest, or is the public interest ignored or shortchanged by group behavior in the political process? And, third, do interest groups reflect a basic bias in favor of monied, upper-class or business-oriented segments of the society, or are they a fair cross section of all interests in the society?

Most of the group theories that have emerged tend to reinforce the ambivalent attitude most Americans hold toward groups in politics and society; that is, while most Americans decry the insidious influence groups seem to have over politicians, they jump at the chance to influence the system as members of a group in pursuit of their own goals and interests.

James Madison was probably the earliest American "group theorist." John C. Calhoun, writing in the mid 1800s, turned Madison's notion of factional checks and balances on its head. Calhoun's theory of the "concurrent majority" posited that, because the existence of varying group views and positions is vital to the nation, each of the various interest groups in the society should be allowed a veto power over any major policy proposition that affected it. Conversely, a "concurrent majority" of all interest groups would have to support a policy proposal for it to be adopted.

The most important aspect of Calhoun's theory was that it focused attention on the notion of a broad community interest—a public interest—that exists and is independent of the views of particular factions. To Calhoun, the various factions were the community interests and should be treated as such by allowing them veto powers.

In the early twentieth century, the debate over the role of groups in U.S. politics took on a new coloration as political science entered the arena. The focus of academic political science shifted away from the legal-institutional framework and toward the interplay of groups, or nongovernmental forces, in the U.S. political system. From Arthur F. Bentley's *The Process of Government*, published in 1908, through David Truman's *The Governmental Process*, some forty years later, theorists used groups to explore the entire political process, examining their overlapping membership, access to decision makers, and role as catalyst in the democratic governmental process.

Truman's book fit in well with the emerging stream of political science research in the 1950s and early 1960s, which emphasized "objective" analysis of how things worked in the political arena rather than speculating on how they ought to work. In general, these political scientists viewed groups positively, seeing them mainly as the central vehicle through which individuals participated in the political system.

Still, some observers questioned the benignity of interest groups. E. E. Schattschneider identified what he saw as a pattern of undue influence whereby interest groups gained access to politicians through campaign contributions and inside connections. Echoing Schattschneider's warnings and criticisms, more recent critics, such as Theodore Lowi, take the argument one step further by suggesting that the existence and acceptance of interest groups in the political system have contributed to an erosion of government authority.

In recent years the focus of much of the literature on groups has shifted away from the study of groups per se to focus more closely on specific types of groups and their impact on the political system. Narrowly focused special interest groups, it is argued, can have a major influence on government and policy in a system of divided power, where political parties are of very little significance and constituent influences hold a great deal of sway over politicians.

Group Functions. Why do groups form, how do they persist, and how are they able to use their resources to influence the course of public policy? Groups can serve several functions for members, ranging from the symbolic to the instrumental. The function a group performs will have a direct effect on how that group impacts the political process, because it will determine the motivation of the group members and the nature of the political action the group will take.

Some groups provide symbolic benefits for their members, allowing individuals to express certain values or interests without pursuing them in a concrete manner. For example, membership or activity in a religious interest group may be undertaken to reinforce one's identification in that group rather than to promote a particular goal or policy.

Some groups are in business solely to promote economic interests. Groups that are economically based or motivated may function to advance the economic interests of a broad class of individuals or institutions, or they may act more narrowly, to protect an individual entity.

Still other groups may perform ideological functions for their members. These types of groups may adopt far-reaching political ideologies (e.g., liberal, conservative, socialist) covering all policy areas or more narrow ideologies that reflect deep feelings about a single issue such as abortion or gun control.

Another important group function is to provide valuable information or data to its members, to the public, or to members of Congress. In fact, most U.S. interest groups have as part of their function the collection, analysis, and dissemination of information.

In addition to these four primary functions, groups share instrumental goals. Instrumental functions involve concrete and immediate goals that often involve legislative or government decisions. Groups organized to support or condemn U.S. involvement in Central America in the 1980s fit into this category, as do groups that lobby for increased funding for the AIDS epidemic.

Role of Interest Groups. The American Association of Retired Persons, or AARP, exists and thrives primarily as a service organization for Americans over fifty—providing discounts on prescription drugs, hotels and airlines, and supplemental health insurance, as well as a glossy magazine and other benefits. But it also plays a major role in the political process, working on the range of issues affecting the elderly.

While some groups target all or most of their efforts toward the executive branch and others direct their energies at the judicial branch, most lobbying activity takes place within the halls of Congress. In general, groups attempt to monitor governmental activity that might affect them, to initiate governmental action to promote their interests, and to block action that would work to their detriment. Each of these areas of activity requires, above all else, access—access to information on what the government is doing or is about to do and access to key decision makers.

One important role of lobbyists and interest groups is to monitor political activity. A group must keep track of, digest, analyze, and disseminate all the information relevant to its particular interests. Often, in order to have a political effect, a group must go beyond monitoring to take action, such as testifying at congressional hearings, drafting amendments to legislation, or notifying members of Congress of its support or opposition to a bill or amendment.

Besides monitoring political activity, groups may seek avenues for promoting their interests through governmental action. This can involve initiating a new program, increasing congressional appropriations, or awarding a government contract, among other things. Conversely, groups may seek to op-

pose government action in an effort to protect their own interests. In fact, because of the slow and complex nature of the U.S. political system, groups often find they have a better chance of blocking government action than of spurring it.

Interest groups' primary weapons are the incentives they can offer politicians and the sanctions they can use against them. Finding successful ways of deploying these resources is the key to effective lobbying. Lobbying can be a mutually beneficial process in which both the interests of the group and those of the politician are served. Sometimes even the public stands to gain from these relationships.

Group Resources and Strategies. The strategies a group employs are dictated in part by the resources that the group can draw on. There are various types of group resources, and each group has its own mix, depending on its membership base and primary function. The combination of a group's goals, focus of activity, motivation, mix of resources, and skill at using them determines the political influence of the group.

Physical resources. Money is perhaps the most important resource for influencing public policy because it can be used to attract many other resources, including substantive expertise, political and leadership skill, and public relations talent. Another important resource is sheer membership size. Members are voters, and politicians pay attention to voters. If its membership is spread across the country, that means that a group has a presence in more congressional districts, which in itself can bring greater influence. Membership works best when it is intensely interested and motivated; if lawmakers think that a group or its lobbyist represents people who care deeply about an issue, are united, are paying attention, and are motivated to vote on that basis, they will pay much more attention to the group. The National Rifle Association, to take one example, has had extraordinary influence because of the intense motivation of its members on gun control issues.

Organizational resources. To be effective, any group must have the ability to mobilize its membership for political action. Members must be informed, often very quickly, of impending congressional action, must be told how to respond, and must have their responses channeled to the appropriate places. The U.S. Chamber of Commerce and the AFL-CIO, to choose two examples, have begun to use teleconferencing as a way of effectively communicating with and mobilizing members. Leadership skill and substantive expertise are important components of a strong organization. Common Cause cleverly developed a strong and sophisticated team to analyze campaign finance information from the Federal Election Commission; the group's information about campaign contributions and political activity has become the most widely used and credible information available, adding to Common Cause's leverage in the campaign reform debate.

Political resources. Knowledge of the political process is vital to a group's legislative success, which is why many groups hire former members of Congress or former congressional staffers. In addition, a group's political reputation is a crucial element in its political success. If lawmakers believe a group is effective, knowledgeable, and trustworthy, it will tend to win greater trust and hence be more effective.

Strategies. How do groups use their resources? One major outlay is campaign support. While corporations and labor unions are barred by law from contributing directly to campaigns for federal office, they do manage to channel a significant amount of money to the candidates of their choice through political action committees (PACs). PACs grew significantly in number and influence in the 1980s. From 1978 to 1991 the number of registered PACs increased by more than 150 percent, and the amount of money PACs contributed to congressional campaigns more than quadrupled—although this can mean only that more groups now counter each other in the policy process.

Aside from campaign support there is, of course, direct lobbying of members of Congress and their staffs. In general, lobbyists seek out like-minded legislators. While lobbying is, in a sense, a practice of persuasion, the relationships that develop are often friendly and mutually beneficial. Access is obviously a major factor here, for lobbyists must have access to members of Congress to get their message across.

In order to maximize access and enhance their "inside" contacts, interest groups frequently employ former members of Congress, former staff aides, or "old Washington hands." Washington-based representatives cultivate relationships with members and their staffs by taking them to lunch, stopping by offices to chat, and providing whatever help and useful information members might need.

In addition to direct lobbying techniques and strategies, lobbyists use a multitude of indirect methods to influence legislators and the policy-making process. Indirect strategies, often featuring mass media campaigns, are designed to drum up grassroots support for a particular measure or movement. Utilizing modern communications technologies, interest groups have been able to reach more and more people with computer-based direct-mail campaigns, satellite links, and teleconferencing, in addition to public service messages on local and cable television stations.

By mobilizing grassroots support, groups are able to gain public support for their interests. The public, in turn, applies pressure on members of Congress; for obvious reasons, members often respond (especially when the pressure is coming directly from their constituents).

The ability to influence public opinion and to mobilize grassroots support has been at a premium in recent years, leading to the growth of firms that specialize in these areas. Public relations firms such as Hill & Knowlton and Ogilvy & Mather have expanded their Washington operations sharply to provide interests with public relations support. PR firms have not only helped business and commercial clients: the Roman Catholic church, for example, hired Hill & Knowlton to improve its communications on the abortion issue when that issue began to move from the courts to the legislatures in the 1990s.

Often different interest groups come together and work collectively on major pieces of legislation. This increasingly common practice is called coalition lobbying. While these coalitions have the advantage of sheer numbers, they are often difficult to control and navigate because of conflicting views within the coalition. Many analysts believe that, because there are now so many diverse and specialized interests represented in Washington, the influence and clout of the larger, more encompassing groups has been undercut. In the 1990s most legislation involves a variety of interests, and as a result more often than not coalitions of interests (sometimes competing interests) are necessary to get measures passed.

The Changing World of Group Influence. If the basic relationships between interest groups, their representatives in Washington, and Congress have remained fundamentally the same since Madison wrote *Federalist* 10, almost everything else that affects their interactions has changed. The change has been particularly marked since the late 1960s and early 1970s.

In particular, the landmark series of congressional reforms during the 1970s revolutionized the legislative process and ushered in the modern era of interest group politics. Congress was sharply decentralized and democratized, spreading power downward and outward from committees to subcommittees and rank-and-file members. Staffs were expanded sharply for individual members and subcommittees, and the legislative process was opened up dramatically to public, press, and group scrutiny—in the recording of members' votes on amendments on the floor, in the opening of previously closed committee meetings and mark-up sessions, and through the advent of televised proceedings via C-SPAN.

The deep divisions in Congress over the Vietnam War provided the catalyst for many of these reforms. Groups such as Common Cause were formed at this time in response to the demand for governmental reform. The origins of other public interest groups, including environmental, consumer, and antidefense groups, also date to this period since, as Congress changed, more and more points of access to the legislative process opened up, providing entry to more and more groups.

The reforms unleashed a large number of activist entrepreneurial lawmakers and staff looking for ideas to promote, bills to sponsor, and amendments to offer. They found natural allies in group representatives who had ideas and political skills to complement the insiders' needs. For many such groups, substantial sums of money or vast memberships were not required; sometimes a small storefront office and a copying machine could suffice.

As these ideas generated new legislation and regulations, they bred counterlobbying by business groups and others affected by the policies that were being implemented. The result was a veritable explosion in the number of groups, trade associations, and Washington offices throughout the 1970s and early 1980s.

All these changes altered the art of lobbying in fundamental ways. The need for up-to-date intelligence on congressional activity increased sharply; the decentralized, more fluid legislative process was less predictable than the old process had been and required more constant vigilance. New technologies were necessary for lobbyists to reach a broader range of lawmakers, meaning that more sophisticated direct-mail and teleconferencing techniques, among others, were needed.

Specialized lobbying became more prominent, along with a growing number of outside professionals selling their services to an expanding range of clients. Lawyers, specialized lobbyists, public relations firms, legislative strategy groups, direct-mail specialists, media consultants, grassroots organizers, and advertising agencies all mushroomed in Washington during the 1970s and 1980s.

By the 1990s, their growth had slowed, although it had not stopped, and additional questions about the role and focus of groups in the American political process were being raised. For instance, just as questions had long been raised concerning how an elected legislator could represent his or her constituents—as a "trustee" or as a "delegate"—questions increasingly were raised about how an unelected group official or lobbyist could represent an affinity group.

The American Association of Retired Persons was actively involved in 1987 and 1988 in the congressional debate and negotiations that led to passage of catastrophic-illness health insurance for the elderly; AARP's leadership actively supported the bill when it passed. But strong subsequent opposition from a core of affluent elderly put the organization's leadership on the defensive and eventually caused the group to disavow much of its earlier action. At the same time, the National Committee to Preserve Social Security and Medicare, an organization with a small national staff and none of the support services provided by AARP, mobilized vigorous opposition to the catastrophic-illness plan through dire warnings in direct-mail appeals to the elderly, but survey evidence suggested that most elderly people polled viewed the issue in a very different way.

Just as much of the political debate in 1992 revolved around whether Washington elites in elective office were out of touch with the American public "outside the beltway," some debate began over whether interest group elites in Washington pursued agendas that were out of touch with their constituencies. Controversies remain over the role of interest groups and lobbies in Washington.

[*See also* Common Cause; Congress Watch; Labor; Lobbying; Political Action Committees (PACs).]

BIBLIOGRAPHY

Bentley, Arthur F. *The Process of Government*. 1949.

Calhoun, John C. "A Disquisition on Government." In *Source Book of American Political Theory*. Edited by Benjamin F. Wright. 1929.

Judis, John B. "The Pressure Elite." *The American Prospect* 9 (Spring 1992): 15–29.

Lowi, Theodore. *The End of Liberalism*. 1969.

Olson, Mancur. *The Logic of Collective Action: Public Good and the Theory of Groups*. 1965.

1138 INTERNAL IMPROVEMENTS

Ornstein, Norman J., and Shirley Elder. *Interest Groups: Lobbying and Policymaking.* 1978.

Ornstein, Norman J., and Mark Schmitt. "The New World of Interest Politics. *The American Enterprise* 1 (January–February 1990): 47–51.

Peterson, Paul. "The Rise and Fall of Special Interests." *Political Science Quarterly* 105 (1990–1991): 539–556.

Rauch, Jonathan. "The Parasite Economy." *National Journal,* 25 April 1992.

Salisbury, Robert H. "An Exchange Theory of Interest Groups." *Midwest Journal of Political Science* 13 (February 1969): 1–32.

Schattschneider, E. E. *The Semisovereign People.* 1960.

Truman, David. *The Governmental Process.* 1971.

NORMAN J. ORNSTEIN

INTERNAL IMPROVEMENTS. Following independence, Americans clamored for "internal improvements," by which they meant roads, canals, turnpikes, navigable rivers and harbors, and eventually railroads. Such facilities commonly served localities in more than one state, so promoters naturally turned to Congress for aid and authorization. In the 1790s, Congress received these petitions with ambivalence. Proposals for federal aid to navigation (lighthouses, beacons, and buoys) elicited no apparent concern, but could the federal government build roads and canals in the states? Federalists said yes, pointing to the post-road system and the Constitution's "general welfare" clause; Jeffersonians objected to such enlargements of federal power. Internal improvements posed a difficult dilemma: those who built them risked offending local interests not served by the chosen route, while others, who needed federal aid for particular improvements, feared the power that distribution of such aid would confer upon government.

With the triumph of his Republican party in 1801, Thomas Jefferson assumed that federal power no longer threatened the liberties of the people. Thus he approved, in 1802, Congress's plan to finance the National (or Cumberland) Road with proceeds from the sale of Ohio lands. In 1805, he urged lawmakers to "repartition" surplus moneys among the states to improve "rivers, canals, roads, arts, manufactures, education, and other great objects." Pleas for aid piled up in Congress, and in 1807, while debating the merits of particular projects, the House ordered the secretary of the Treasury, Albert Gallatin, to sketch out a system of roads and canals.

Gallatin's *Report on . . . Roads and Canals* (1808) urged national action on a blueprint of interregional roads and waterways. Gallatin admitted (as Jefferson had suggested) that a constitutional amendment might be needed to secure for Congress the uncontested power to build roads and canals in the states. Pending that technical reform, however, he urged support for selected projects, and Congress set to work. In 1810, New York representative Peter B. Porter introduced a bill that incorporated all of Gallatin's routes *except* the Potomac route to the West (which competed with New York's projected canal). Condemned as a "partial" measure, the Porter bill disappeared in the subsequent chaos of the War of 1812. Congress returned to the Gallatin plan after the war; in 1817, in the House of Representatives, John C. Calhoun called for a "perfect system of roads and canals" to "bind the Republic together." Everyone supported internal improvements in principle, but local rivalries and partisan fears of government activism rendered the program controversial. Finally, Congress narrowly passed the Bonus bill, designed to promote roads and canals with the proceeds from a new national bank. However, in a surprise reversal, President James Madison vetoed the Bonus bill as an unconstitutional enlargement of legislative power.

Leaders in Congress, especially House Speaker Henry Clay, could not imagine that the Constitution prohibited the government from giving a free people what they wanted—and they wanted internal improvements! Strict constructionists, however, condemned internal improvements as a trick to consolidate power in the Union. Congress debated the issue every year. In 1822, President James Monroe vetoed a new Cumberland Road appropriation, reversing a major Jeffersonian initiative. Congress successfully revived the issue in 1824, when lawmakers slipped the General Survey bill past a reluctant Monroe, establishing a Board of Internal Improvements to conduct surveys for roads and canals of "national importance." The first river and harbor bills and a stock subscription to the Chesapeake and Delaware Canal marked the dawn of a new era, and the administration of John Quincy Adams (1825–1829) openly supported national roads and canals. Adams's political enemies nevertheless denounced his activism.

Unwilling to risk seeking an amendment that might fail, Congress evaded constitutional objections by using military appropriations, land grants, and corporate stock subscriptions to aid public works. In his 1830 veto of the Maysville Road bill, President Andrew Jackson condemned such grants when they served "strictly local" purposes—a discretionary principle that allowed Jackson to favor

Landmark Legislation

Title	Year Enacted	Reference Number	Description
Ohio Enabling Act	1802	2 Stat. 173	Set aside proceeds from land sales for roads.
Cumberland Road Act	1806	2 Stat. 357–359	"An act to regulate the laying out and making of a road from Cumberland, in the State of Maryland, to the State of Ohio." Direct federal implementation; beginning of the National Road.
General Survey Act	1824	4 Stat. 22	Authorized federal engineering assistance for planning roads and canals.
Ohio and Mississippi River Improvements	1824	4 Stat. 32	Direct federal spending on river improvements.
Presque Isle Harbor Improvement	1824	4 Stat. 38	Direct federal spending on harbor improvements.
Chesapeake and Delaware	1825	4 Stat. 124	Authorized federal aid by subscription of stock in the Chesapeake and Delaware Canal Company.
Illinois and Michigan Canal	1827	4 Stat. 234	Federal aid by land grant to state of Illinois for the purpose of opening a canal to connect the Illinois River with Lake Michigan.
Wabash and Erie Canal	1827	4 Stat. 236	Federal aid by land grants to state of Indiana for the purpose of opening a canal to connect the Wabash River with Lake Erie.
Distribution of Surplus Revenues	1836	5 Stat. 55	"Loans" of federal funds to states.
Distribution and Preemption Act	1841	5 Stat. 453	Cash grants to states from land sale revenues (in addition to loans of 1836).
Illinois Central Railroad	1850	9 Stat. 466	Railroad land grants to states, regranted to a corporation.
Pacific Railroad Act	1862	12 Stat. 489–498	Land grants directly to a railroad corporation.

particular pork-barrel projects while denouncing federal power and integrated systems of internal improvements. Henry Clay's alternative scheme, to distribute the proceeds from public land sales to the states for internal improvements, satisfied these constitutional objections. However, it prevailed just as the land bubble burst (1837) and revenues collapsed. Although Jacksonian public works appropriations doubled the amount spent under Adams, Democrats steadfastly rejected the principle of national internal improvements.

The last great internal improvement debates concerned interstate railroad development. As early as 1844, New York merchant Asa Whitney proposed to build a trunk line to the Pacific if Congress would sell him (at bargain rates) a strip of land along the route. Enthusiasm for interregional railroads quickly mounted. Congress pioneered a new approach in 1850, granting 3.75 million acres to three states to subsidize the private, north–south Illinois Central Railroad. The east–west transcontinental plan proved more difficult: Congress could not select a route without inflaming sectional hos-

tilities. Only in 1862, following the departure of the southern states, did the northern majority grant millions of acres to the Union Pacific and Central Pacific companies. The Civil War destroyed much of the states' rights fever that long had frustrated friends of internal improvements. However, the states and the private sector continued to dominate land-transportation development for another century. All kinds of public works have received the patronage of Congress since the Civil War, but the comprehensive framework of the antebellum internal improvements debates disappeared forever.

[*See also* Public Works; Railroads; Transportation.]

BIBLIOGRAPHY

Goodrich, Carter. *Government Promotion of American Canals and Railroads, 1880–1890.* 1960.

Larson, John Lauritz. "'Bind the Republic Together': The National Union and the Struggle for a System of Internal Improvements." *Journal of American History* 74 (1987): 363–387.

JOHN LAURITZ LARSON

INTERNAL SECURITY.

INTERNAL SECURITY. Congressional concern for the internal security of the United States has surfaced periodically since the Constitution's adoption in 1788. Concerns have arisen during periods of tension and fear associated with war, threats of war, xenophobia, and political conflicts over policy-making.

The Alien and Sedition Acts. The Naturalization and Alien and Sedition Acts of 1798 constitute the first and best-known efforts by Congress to proscribe seditious internal activity. These laws were enacted as the United States became involved in an undeclared naval war with France. They were designed to squelch the Democratic-Republican opposition to the pro-British stance of the Federalists during the war between France and Great Britain.

The legislation was directed against aliens, potential naturalized citizens, and citizens in the nation who favored France. The individual laws were the Naturalization Act of 18 June 1798 (1 Stat. 556), which made it more difficult for an alien to become a citizen by extending the required residency from five to fourteen years; the Alien Act of 25 June 1798 (1 Stat. 570), which authorized the president to imprison for up to three years any aliens he judged to be "dangerous to the peace and safety of the United States"; and the Alien Enemies Act of 6 July 1798 (1 Stat. 577), which authorized the arrest and deportation of "all natives, citizens, or subjects of the hostile nation or government" with which the United States was at war.

The fourth and most controversial law was the Sedition Act of 14 July 1798 (1 Stat. 596). It was intended to punish anyone "with intent to oppose any measure or measures of the government of the United States" or anyone who would "write, print, utter, or publish, or shall cause or procure to be written, printed or uttered or published . . . any false, scandalous and malicious writing or writings against the government of the United States," Congress, or the president. Violators were subject to a $2,000 fine and two years in prison. The Federalist authors of this legislation were clearly concerned with self-preservation, however, because they declared that this measure would expire on 3 March 1801, the day before a potentially new president and a new Congress would take office.

These laws delayed and discouraged citizenship and caused fearful aliens to leave the country. The Sedition Act was also a source of harassment: twenty-five people were arrested because of it (ten were convicted), the majority of them Democratic-Republican editors who criticized the Federalist-dominated government under John Adams. All but the Sedition Act continued to be the law of the land until after World War II.

The Civil War. Congressional actions on internal security subsided from 1801 until the Civil War. This happened despite a nativist crusade against immigrants and Catholics that was mounted during the second quarter of the nineteenth century. The influx of Catholic immigrants, mostly Irish, alarmed Protestants. By 1855 the so-called Know-Nothing party had sizable majorities in several state legislatures and held the balance of power in Congress. The Know-Nothing movement scapegoated foreigners to foment fear of a conspiracy undermining American republicanism. Its fruitless purpose was to heal the breach between North and South over the slavery controversy.

During the Civil War, Congress enacted special legislation to avoid a strict application of the Treason Act of 1790, because it mandated the death penalty against millions of Southerners who supported "rebellion" or bore arms against the United States of America. It could be applied also to citizens of Northern and border states who were engaged in sedition activities, bordering on the treasonable. Three acts were designed to punish, short of the death penalty, Confederate military and illegal activities by the so-called Copperheads (Northerners with Southern sympathies). The first, the Seditious Conspiracy Act of 31 July 1861, made it unlawful for two or more persons "to conspire to overthrow, put down, or to destroy by force the Government of the United States." Violators were subject to six years in prison and a $5,000 fine. The Confiscation Act of 6 August 1861 outlawed enlisting, engaging, or recruiting persons to serve in a military capacity against the United States. Finally, the Second Confiscation Act of 17 July 1862 punished "rebellion" against the United States by imposing up to a five-year prison sentence and a $10,000 fine.

These laws were rarely enforced. A policy of leniency generally prevailed during and after the war. Grand juries brought many indictments against individuals, especially in the border states, but few were prosecuted. The government did not execute a single person for treason or completely carry out a sentence or fine for rebellion. The executive branch dealt with these issues through military arrests and suspension of the writ of habeas corpus.

During another upsurge of antiforeign sentiment as a consequence of the assassination of President William McKinley in 1901, Congress passed two laws designed to screen immigrants for their political beliefs. The Immigration acts of 3 March 1903 and 20 February 1907 prohibited entry into the United States of aliens who were anarchists or who advocated overthrow of the government by force or the assassination of public officials. Subversives who entered the country illegally were to be deported.

World War I and After. Congress again became highly concerned with internal security during and after World War I. Soon after the United States entered the war, Congress passed the Espionage Act of 15 June 1917. This act punished spies with fines, prison sentences, and even death. Furthermore, it penalized oral or written statements that were considered injurious to the war effort. The following year Congress expanded section 3 of the 1917 statute, making it likewise unlawful to "promote the success of" enemies of the United States, to obstruct the sale of war bonds, to criticize the government or the flag, or to advocate overthrow of the government.

These measures drummed up a feverish patriotism, leading to restrictions on freedom of speech during the war. After the war, the Supreme Court upheld their constitutionality, and concerns for internal security persisted. The Bolshevik revolution in Russia, postwar economic decline, and a resurfacing of nativism created a red scare and demands for further restrictions on immigration. A series of immigration statutes in 1917, 1918, and 1920 sought more clearly to define which aliens were admissible and which were deportable, mostly on grounds of their political beliefs. Finally, Congress passed the Immigration Act of 26 May 1924, consolidating past laws and establishing a quota system that favored northern and western European immigrants, presumably because others were deemed less likely to support the "American way of life."

During the 1930s, Congress became concerned about communist, Nazi, and fascist propaganda and activities in the United States. Investigations were carried out by the Fish Committee, named after Rep. Hamilton Fish, Jr. (R-N.Y.); the Special Committee on Un-American Activities, led by Rep. Samuel Dickstein (D-N.Y.) and Rep. John W. McCormack (D-Mass.); and the so-called Dies Committee, named after Rep. Martin Dies (D-Tex.). These investigations—in part politically motivated to discredit the New Dealers—led to passage of three major laws. The first was the Foreign Agents Act of 8 June 1938, amended twice before 1950, which required registration with the secretary of State by any foreign principals in the United States

whose purpose was to disseminate propaganda that might incite "racial, social, political, or religious disorder." Though designed to curb subversive activities, this law proved difficult to enforce.

The Hatch Act of 2 August 1939, aimed chiefly at "pernicious political activities," was a civil service reform to eliminate alleged exploitation of federal workers by national political organizations, especially New Deal Democrats. Section 9A specifically banned government-employee membership in any organization that advocated overthrow of the government. In 1943, an unsuccessful effort was made to prosecute American fascists under Section 9A. The Hatch Act was declared constitutional in 1947.

World War II and the Cold War. After the outbreak in Europe of World War II, Congress tightened the espionage laws and increased their penalties and, most significantly, passed the Alien Registration Act of 28 June 1940. Known as the Smith Act for its major sponsor, Rep. Howard W. Smith (D-Va.), this was the first peacetime sedition act since 1798 (the United States did not enter the war until late 1941). It penalized anyone, including citizens, who might "attempt to commit, or to conspire to commit" any act to impair the loyalty or morale of the military forces, or who "knowingly or willfully" advocated the destruction of the government. Other portions of the act dealt with registration of aliens and deportation of subversives.

These measures were used mostly after U.S. entry into the war and were directed against persons of German, Italian, and Japanese extraction. The most notorious use of the law came after Pearl Harbor, when, in February 1942, President Franklin D. Roosevelt authorized the secretary of War to relocate people of Japanese descent from military areas in the West. This program involved removing thousands of Japanese Americans from the West Coast and interning them in camps. Congress approved this program by statute on 21 March 1942. The dislocation, humiliation, and loss of property suffered by many Japanese Americans was not remedied until 1988, when Congress voted to present each of the sixty thousand surviving internees with a formal apology and $20,000 in reparations.

The Smith Act was much more effective during the Cold War years; in 1948 it was declared constitutional and was afterward used to indict hundreds of persons in communist organizations for conspiracy. Several of these indictments resulted in convictions when the Supreme Court ruled in 1951 that the federal government could act on these matters during an "internal security crisis," namely, the Korean War.

In the postwar United States the politics of anticommunism advanced dramatically during the Truman and Eisenhower administrations, whereby more than one hundred congressional investigations of communist activities were held between 1945 and 1955. Most notable were the House Committee on Un-American Activities' revelations on Hollywood and the Hiss-Chamber case; investigations by the Senate Judiciary Committee on immigration and espionage legislation; a Senate Foreign Relations Subcommittee query into Sen. Joseph R. McCarthy's (R-Wis.) charges that the State Department was riddled with communists; and a series of hearings by the Senate Operations Committee on communists in government service that culminated in the infamous Army-McCarthy hearings in 1954. News coverage of committee revelations kept the communist issue before the public eye, particularly affecting political partisanship in Washington, state and local legislative leaders, and organizations like the American Legion and the U.S. Chamber of Commerce. The effect was to intimidate government employees, academics, and media personalities for fear of being branded "communist."

Two important legislative efforts to curb communist and subversive activities came in 1950 and 1954. The Internal Security Act of 1950 amended many of the statutes previously mentioned and added two new wrinkles. Title I provided for the registration of "Communist-action" and "Communist-front" organizations with the attorney general; Title II provided for the detention of suspected subversives during a presidentially proclaimed "internal security emergency." The Communist Control Act of 1954 was aimed at outlawing the Communist Party of the United States.

Affected by the fear of communism roused by Sen. Joseph R. McCarthy, these laws caused harassment of many persons but proved ineffective constitutionally. After eighteen years of legal battles, the federal courts declared the registration provision of the Internal Security Act unconstitutional. In 1971, when it was feared that its detention provisions would be used by the government against protestors of the Vietnam War, Title II of the Internal Security Act was repealed. The Communist Control Act proved equally ineffective as a legal measure.

Since the early 1970s and after the Vietnam War and the Watergate fiasco, Congress has been less eager to legislate on internal security. The lessening of international tensions and the lessons of overzealous and illegal enforcement of such measures by the Federal Bureau of Investigation, the Central Intelligence Agency, and other government agencies have had a sobering effect on measures to pursue "subversives" in the interest of national or internal security. However, in the event of a new and extended crisis, war, or tense political situation, the groundwork for invoking internal security measures has been firmly established.

[*For general discussion of related issues, see* Civil Liberties; Communism and Anticommunism; Crime and Justice; Intelligence Policy. *See also* Alien and Sedition Acts; Alien Registration Act; Army-McCarthy Hearings; McCarran Internal Security Act of 1950; Un-American Activities Committee, House.]

BIBLIOGRAPHY

Davis, David Brian, ed. *The Fear of Conspiracy.* 1971.

Higham, John. *Strangers in the Land: Patterns of American Nativism, 1860–1925.* 1969.

Kelly, Alfred, W. A. Harbison, and H. Belz. *The American Constitution.* 6th ed. 1983.

Latham, Earl. *The Communist Controversy in Washington.* 1966.

Murray, Robert K. *Red Scare: A Study in National Hysteria.* 1955.

Smith, James M. *Freedom's Fetters.* 1956.

WILLIAM R. TANNER

INTERNAL SECURITY ACT OF 1950.
See McCarran Internal Security Act of 1950.

INTERN AND FELLOWSHIP PROGRAMS.
Each year thousands of people, from undergraduate students to midcareer professionals and senior citizens, serve internships on the staffs of members of Congress and with congressional committees and other staff agencies. Interns use the experience to develop an understanding of the legislative process and to explore career possibilities. For Congress, interns provide free staff help, possible professional expertise, new perspectives, and the potential for building political bridges with educational, private sector, and governmental entities. Internship programs were largely informal until the 1960s, when formal programs offering academic credit or professional credibility were developed by academic institutions and professional associations.

Undergraduate Internships. On the undergraduate level, a number of patterns have developed.

Many schools send individual students to Washington independently to serve internships, carry out study projects, and receive credit for experiential education. Over forty schools send small groups of students to Washington, often accompanied by a faculty member, to serve congressional internships and participate in academic seminars. Some of these programs accept a limited number of students from other schools. American University operates the cooperative Washington Semester Program, which provides internships and seminars with academic credit to students from member schools. Other cooperative programs include those of the State University of New York and the Lutheran College Consortium. For students whose school is not involved in any formal program, the privately operated Washington Center for Internships provides help with internship placement and housing and conducts seminars of its own.

Most internships are unpaid and quite competitive. Internship policies and procedures are determined by the individual offices and vary considerably. Some interns are responsible for significant legislative research, but all should expect some routine office work. House members receive funds to pay one student or teacher a modest stipend to work during the summer under the Lyndon Baines Johnson Congressional Internship Program. Some Senate offices designate funds for interns. Applications for internships are generally made directly to the member, committee, or congressional support agency and should precede the planned time of placement by several months.

Midcareer and Other Fellowships. A number of professional associations fund and place midcareer professionals in congressional offices and on committee staffs. The largest of these, the Congressional Fellowship Program coordinated by the American Political Science Association, places over forty academics, journalists, medical school faculty, foreign professionals, and federal agency executives on Capitol Hill. Since 1953, over fourteen hundred fellows have spent a year in congressional offices and attending seminars. Other groups such as the American Association for the Advancement of Science, the American Anthropological Association, the Congressional Black Caucus, the Congressional Senior Citizens Internship Program, and the Women's Research and Education Institute operate congressional fellowship programs. Such programs are designed not only to educate the interns, but also to assist Congress by having highly qualified professionals serve temporarily on congressional staffs.

BIBLIOGRAPHY

Frantzich, Stephen E. *Storming Washington: An Intern's Guide to National Government.* 1991.
Grabowski, Sue. *A Congressional Intern Handbook.* 1989.
Reifsnyder, Betsy. *Internships and Fellowships: Congressional, Federal, and Other Work Experience Opportunities.* 1990.

STEPHEN E. FRANTZICH

INTERNATIONAL ORGANIZATIONS. All international organizations are established by treaties among member states; therefore, the Senate, under the provisions of the U.S. Constitution, must give its consent by a two-thirds vote to each treaty as a necessary requirement for U.S. membership. Relatively few international organizations existed before World War II. Early examples of organizations joined by the United States are the International Telecommunication Union (ITU), established in 1865, and the International Union of American Republics, formed in 1890 as the forerunner of the Organization of American States (OAS). The only notable example of the ability of a Senate minority to block U.S. membership in an organization was the failure of the United States to join the League of Nations (1919–1946). By contrast, the Senate accepted the United Nations charter in 1945 by an overwhelming vote of 89 to 2 and has approved U.S. membership in more than seventy global and regional organizations since 1945. The Senate by similar margins endorsed the monetary and financial agencies of the Bretton Woods system—the World Bank (1945), the International Monetary Fund (1945) and later affiliates, the International Finance Corporation (1956), and the International Development Association (1960).

Through its budgetary process, Congress provides the U.S. share of the funds to support the international organizations to which the United States belongs. Some international programs rely on voluntary contributions, but in other cases the U.S. share is prescribed in the treaty establishing membership and thus becomes a part of international and U.S. law. In 1985, Congress ignored these treaty obligations and voted to withhold about half of its assessed dues to the United Nations in order to effect administrative reform and greater U.S. control of the U.N. budgetary process. After numerous U.N. reforms, Congress approved plans to pay arrearages over a five-year period, but by 1992 most of the $500 million deficit remained.

Bipartisanship has been the prevailing approach

to U.S. relationships with international organizations. Congress has generally followed White House and Department of State recommendations in such matters as budgetary policy and temporary withdrawals from membership in the International Labor Organization (ILO) and the United Nations Educational, Scientific, and Cultural Organization (UNESCO).

[See also Interparliamentary Organizations; United Nations.]

BIBLIOGRAPHY

Crabb, Cecil V., Jr., and Pat M. Holt. *Invitation to Struggle: Congress, the President, and Foreign Policy.* 4th ed. 1992.
U.S. Department of State. *United States Contributions to International Organizations.* Annual reports to Congress.

A. LeRoy Bennett

INTERPARLIAMENTARY ORGANIZATIONS.

Congress has participated in international organizations that address problems of common interest to lawmakers of various nations since the founding of the first such group in 1889. House and Senate delegations regularly attend conferences of four principal assemblies—the Interparliamentary Union (IPU), North Atlantic Assembly, Mexico–United States Interparliamentary Group, and Canada–United States Interparliamentary Group—which meet, usually once a year, at locations rotated among the member countries.

Critics argue that such organizations serve mainly as an excuse for members to travel abroad at public expense. Supporters, however, counter that the groups have a serious intent—the exchange of ideas for solving global problems, especially the peaceful settlement of political, economic, social, and cultural conflicts between nations—and a history of occasional substantive achievement.

The IPU is the oldest and largest of these groups, dating from 1889. Its membership by 1993 included the parliamentary assemblies of 188 sovereign nations.

The 1895 IPU Conference in Brussels drafted the first articles for what became the Permanent Court of Arbitration in The Hague. The group also arranged the first Hague Peace Conferences in 1899 and, at the urging of U.S. Rep. Richard Bartholdt (R-Mo.), founder of the IPU's American Group, initiated a second Hague Peace Conference in 1907. Since World War II the Geneva-based IPU has become a major forum for discussion and diplomacy on global topics such as human rights, the environment, disarmament, and drug trafficking.

Despite its long active role in the IPU, Congress did not provide statutory authority for its participation until 1935. The three other interparliamentary groups in which Congress is statutorily authorized to participate all were organized in the 1950s to deal with particular economic and military concerns of their member nations.

BIBLIOGRAPHY

Interparliamentary Union, Information Office. "Inter-Parliamentary Union 1993." Pamphlet prepared by the Information Officer, IPU, Geneva.
Lange, Christian L. *The Interparliamentary Union.* 1913.
Schmeckebier, Laurence F. *International Organizations in which the United States Participates.* 1935.

Donald C. Bacon

INTERSTATE COMMERCE ACT (1887; 24 Stat. 379–387).

Nineteenth-century railroads had effective monopolies except at those points where they intersected with competing lines or modes of transportation. To meet such competition railroads charged lower rates. And to attract large shippers they departed from their published rates, offering illegal rebates. Rate discrimination outraged shippers who could not obtain rebates and those in monopolized areas who often paid more to ship goods a short distance than those who shipped goods farther between competing points. At the behest of farmers and merchants, midwestern states passed laws regulating railroad rates. In 1886, however, when the Supreme Court in *Wabash v. Illinois* declared those laws unconstitutional, the pressure on Congress for federal regulation of railroads became irresistible.

Several disparate influences—merchants, farmers, industrialists, and railroads—shaped the Interstate Commerce Act. But its hard-core support in Congress came from the Midwest and the South. In the House, John H. Reagan (D-Tex.) sponsored a bill that prohibited rebates, the long haul–short haul abuse, and pooling; this bill relied on the courts for enforcement. Sen. Shelby M. Cullom (R-Ill.) proposed a less stringent bill that would be enforced by a commission. Both bills passed. In the conference committee Reagan accepted a commission but stiffened Cullom's long haul–short haul provision and insisted on the antipooling clause. Although the law did not specifically give the Interstate Commerce Commission (ICC) power to set rates, subsequent amendments (Hepburn Act, 1906; Transportation Act, 1920) did.

BIBLIOGRAPHY

Hoogenboom, Ari, and Olive Hoogenboom. *A History of the ICC: From Panacea to Palliative.* 1976.
Martin, Albro. "The Troubled Subject of Railroad Regulation in the Gilded Age—A Reappraisal." *Journal of American History* 61 (1974): 339–371.

ARI HOOGENBOOM and OLIVE HOOGENBOOM

INTERSTATE COMPACTS. The Framers of the Constitution gave Congress authority to approve compacts among the states in order to prevent the states from organizing to wrest power from the federal government. Article I, section 10 provides that "No State shall, without the Consent of Congress, . . . enter into any Agreement or Compact with another State."

Compacts are formal agreements among states somewhat akin to treaties among nations. Ordinarily, they are approved by the legislatures of the states concerned and then submitted to Congress for its approval. They are binding on all the citizens of the signatory states, protecting their rights as individuals as well as rights of the public as a whole. States cannot escape their financial obligations under these agreements since compacts are protected by the contract clause of the Constitution. The U.S. Supreme Court has original jurisdiction over their enforcement. Congress also can compel compliance.

Despite the constitutional requirement, some compacts are not submitted to Congress. A few, such as the Southern Regional Education Compact, operate without congressional approval. No precise line separates compacts requiring congressional consent and those that have taken effect without it; the U.S. Supreme Court has made the final determination in each instance. The Court held in *Virginia v. Tennessee* (1893) that express congressional consent was not required in every instance but could be implied. A 1978 case, *U.S. Steel v. Multistate Tax Corporation,* identified interstate agreements that increase the political power of the states or encroach on the supremacy of the United States as ones requiring specific approval.

Until the 1930s, Congress rather routinely consented to compacts. Since that time Congress has occasionally refused approval or given it for a limited time period. Congress has also stipulated that it could amend, alter, or repeal compacts or could require compact agencies to provide information about the agreements; the Supreme Court has yet to determine the enforceability of such limitations.

Only thirty-six compacts were ratified before 1920. Subsequently, with population growth and mobility and technological advancement, the pace of adoption accelerated. The Council of State Governments estimated that more than 150 compacts were in effect in 1992. All states have signed the Interstate Compact on the Supervision of Parolees and Probationers and the Interstate Compact on Juveniles. The typical state is a signatory to at least twenty agreements.

Early compacts were agreements between two states, but today they frequently include several states and occasionally Canadian provinces. The federal government has become a signatory to as well as the ratifier of a few compacts, including the Delaware River Basin Development Compact and the Susquehanna River Basin Compact, and engages actively in their administration.

States use compacts to solve intractable jurisdictional problems and to avoid service duplication. From oil regulation to water rights, these devices allay sibling rivalry among the states. They facilitate the settlement of disputes, although they sometimes elevate private controversies to the state level (as has happened in river basin development). Compacts help maintain state power in the federal system by blocking federal action, by disrupting direct federal-local relations, and by preventing the transfer of state functions to the national government.

Critics have attacked interstate compacts for the lack of attention they receive, both at adoption and during administration; for operating in improper spheres; for the possibility that compact commissions will be responsive to special interests and unresponsive to state control; and for their unrepresentativeness, since each signatory usually has only one member on a compact commission regardless of the state's size. Moreover, critics point out that Congress does not perform systematic reviews of interstate compacts.

BIBLIOGRAPHY

Barton, Weldon V. *Interstate Compacts in the Political Process.* 1967.
Glendening, Parris N., and Mavis M. Reeves. *Pragmatic Federalism.* 2d ed. 1984.
Ridgeway, Marian E. *Interstate Compacts: A Question of Federalism.* 1971.

MAVIS MANN REEVES

INTERSTATE HIGHWAY SYSTEM. It is arguable that, along with civil rights legislation, the congressional enactments that made possible the Interstate highway system have done more to shape the character of American life than any other contemporary laws.

Federal aid for road building in the age of the automobile began with the Road Act of 1916, which initiated a program of dollar matching by the states and the federal government. In order to qualify, the states had to create highway departments, and every commonwealth did so by 1917. Year after year the program continued, with federal expenditures substantially increased in 1921 and 1934. Initially, federal aid was directed at the system of rural post roads. It was extended in 1934 to urban roads and in 1944 to secondary roads linking farms to markets and in urban areas.

In January 1944, President Franklin D. Roosevelt proposed the construction of a 34,000-mile system of highways designed not only to satisfy the demands of road and truck traffic but "also as a means of utilizing productively during the postwar readjustment period a substantial share of the manpower and industrial capacity then available" (Congressional Quarterly, 1965, p. 527). Congress responded with the Federal Aid Highway Act of 1944, a scaled-down proposal allocating about $558 million a year for three years for various types of road building. It also committed the government in principle to a national system of interstate highways of up to forty thousand miles.

Despite the huge and speedy buildup of postwar auto and truck traffic, the traditional mix of federal, state, and local spending devoted primarily to state and local roads, inflation, and federal policy emphasis on housing and the Cold War all constrained the construction of the Interstate system. Like tariffs in the nineteenth century, highway acts extending expenditures came every few years: in 1948, in 1950, in 1952. But by the latter date only $1 billion had spent for the construction of 6,500 Interstate miles.

Strong and varied interests—truckers, car manufacturers, automobile clubs, state highway engineers, and farm groups—exerted pressure for an integrated national system. A 1954 law increased the federal share of Interstate costs to 60 percent of the total and dealt with the greater needs of urban areas by distributing money on the basis of state population.

Responding to the growing traffic strangulation in the country, President Dwight D. Eisenhower in 1954 asked Gen. Lucius D. Clay to come up with an integrated plan for the construction of the Interstate Highway System. Clay proposed a highly nationalized scheme in which the government would assume 90 percent of Interstate costs, a commissioner of Public Works would oversee construction, and a Federal Highway Corporation would handle financing through a $25-billion bond issue financed by a federal gasoline tax. But interests with a stake in the existing system of state-dominated, decentralized highways defeated the bill. The president gave some thought to convening a special session of Congress to reconsider the bill but decided that to do so "could be at the cost of the sanity of one man named Eisenhower."

Nevertheless, in 1956 Congress enacted the Interstate Highway Act, which led within two decades to what Eisenhower had predicted would be "the greatest works program in history." The law did little to threaten the interests of those most involved in road building, provided a relatively painless method of financing the Interstate system, and above all promised to meet the widely felt economic, social, and strategic need for a modern national highway system.

The key elements of the 1956 act—the primary shapers of which were House Democrats Hale Boggs of Louisiana and George H. Fallon of Maryland—were the creation of the Highway Trust Fund, based on a (relatively low) federal gasoline tax, and the provision that the federal contribution to Interstate construction would be 90 percent of the cost. The Interstate system (renamed the National System of Interstate and Defense Highways) was to total forty-one thousand miles; its cost was to be $31 billion in federal and state funds spent over thirteen years. The Senate passed the measure by a vote of 89 to 1, the House approved by a voice vote, and Eisenhower signed the bill on 19 June 1956.

Large annual expenditures assured the rapid construction of Interstate segments during the late 1950s, the 1960s, and the 1970s. Highway routing remained in the hands of county, state, and federal engineers. But from the mid 1960s on, criticism began to rise, focusing on two issues: the need to arrest the decay of mass transportation (especially in urban areas) and the harm to businesses and, often, poor and black urban residents wrought by large-scale land condemnation for the Interstates. Horror stories multiplied of the damage caused to individuals and communities, and congressional investigations of suspected profiteering in the sale of land acquired for rights-of-way in Indiana and Massachusetts added to public uneasiness.

In 1968 a fierce controversy erupted between supporters of uninhibited expansion of the Interstate system and those who wanted a slowdown while greater stress was placed on mass transportation. The District of Columbia itself was the battleground. Representatives John C. Kluczynski (D.-Ill.), who chaired the Public Works Subcommittee on Roads, and William H. Natcher (D.-Ky.), head of the District of Columbia Appropriations Subcommittee, insisted on legislation requiring that the Interstate projects in the District be completed before a rapid transit system could be funded. President Lyndon B. Johnson found this objectionable but finally signed the bill.

These concerns had political effects. Beautification provisions (beyond antibillboard clauses in effect since 1958) began to be added to the highway appropriations bills, and President Richard M. Nixon pushed for more support for urban mass transportation. The Federal Aid Highway Act of 1973 for the first time allowed some use of Highway Trust Fund moneys for bus and rail transit. Local governments were allowed to favor public transportation over Interstate construction if they so chose—but would have to get federal aid from sources other than the trust fund.

In 1991, $14.8 billion was expended by the federal Highway Trust Fund, most of it on an all-but-complete Interstate system totaling about forty-five thousand miles. It had lived up to many of the fondest hopes of its supporters—and to some of the darkest forebodings of its critics.

[See also Rural Post Roads Act.]

BIBLIOGRAPHY

Congressional Quarterly. "Postwar Highway Program." In *Congress and the Nation.* Vol. 1: *1945–1964.* 1965. Pp. 524–535.
Rose, Mark H. *Interstate: Express Highway Politics, 1939–1989.* 1990.

MORTON KELLER

INVESTIGATIONS. Congress conducted its first formal investigation in 1792. The subject was Maj. Gen. Arthur St. Clair's disastrous expedition against Native Americans in the Ohio Territory. Ever since, rarely has a session of Congress gone by without a formal inquiry by one or another of its committees or subcommittees.

The Objectives of a Congressional Investigation. The topics for investigation selected by members of Congress have been as plentiful as the problems faced by the nation. The wide range of subjects has included the migration of African Americans from the South to the North after the Civil War; the immigration of foreign contract labor during the 1800s; strikebreaking in the railroad industry; western land reclamation; grain speculation; the stock exchange (following the onset of the Great Depression); the munitions industry (on the eve of World War II); the unfairness of monopolies; the surprise attack on Pearl Harbor; communists in the federal government; mismanagement of the Atomic Energy Commission; the Internal Revenue Service; a suspected lag in U.S. nuclear missile production; the use of lie detectors by federal agencies; a criminal cover-up in the White House (the infamous Watergate scandal of the Nixon administration); illegal domestic operations carried out by the Central Intelligence Agency (CIA); and the covert sale of weapons to Iran with diversion of the profits to support a secret CIA war in Nicaragua (the Iran-contra scandal of the Reagan administration).

Congress has resorted to investigations for five primary purposes. First, investigations have proved useful in gathering information for the drafting of legislation. Second, investigations have been important instruments for the legislative supervision of agencies within the executive branch—the oversight or review function of Congress urged by James Madison in *Federalist* 51. Third, investigations have provided a highly visible means (especially since the advent of television) by which legislators can inform and educate the citizenry on the pressing issues of the day. Fourth, investigations have been used by legislators to police themselves through the congressional ethics committees or to improve their internal organization and procedures by way of ad hoc reform committees. And, fifth, an investigation can serve the subtle purpose of defusing potentially divisive issues in the nation, working them out in the hearing rooms of Congress rather than in the streets.

This last, the "safety-valve" function, was important in 1951, for example, when the controversy over President Harry S. Truman's firing of Gen. Douglas MacArthur threatened to stir a national donnybrook between the political parties. A congressional inquiry, led by Sen. Richard B. Russell (D-Ga.), managed to deflate the rising anger by allowing a thorough airing of the issue in public hearings. During this inquiry, many of America's other leading generals testified in support of the president's dismissal of MacArthur. The public became convinced that the general had overstepped the boundaries of civilian supremacy over the military, a well-established principle in the United States.

Although congressional investigations serve many purposes, at the heart of most inquiries is a search for information that can guide legislators in their lawmaking duties. A noted member of Congress, J. William Fulbright (D-Ark.), the longtime chairman of the Senate Foreign Relations Committee, looked upon the congressional investigation as "primarily a search for information which it is believed is needed in order to solve a governmental problem."

Investigations Good and Bad. The authority for legislative inquiries, although nowhere explicitly mentioned in the nation's founding document, has been generally upheld in the courts by virtue of the Constitution's "elastic clause." This clause affirms the right of Congress "to make all Laws which shall be necessary and proper for carrying into Execution the foregoing Powers" (Article I, section 8). If legislators were to be granted the right to make laws, by implication they would also have to have a way to ensure that the laws were faithfully executed. So long as Congress has remained loyal to this purpose of improved lawmaking, the courts have granted broad—but not unlimited—discretion to investigators (*McGrain v. Daugherty*, 273 U.S. 135 [1927]; *Watkins v. United States*, 354 U.S. 178 [1957]).

This is not to say that Congress's investigative powers have been free of controversy. They have long had articulate proponents and opponents. In their favor, Woodrow Wilson once opined that the "informing function of Congress should be preferred even to its legislative function" (*Congressional Government*, 1885). Other proponents have applauded legislators for defending freedom in the United States by asking pointed questions of executive bureaucrats, admirals and generals, cabinet members, and presidential advisers during formal investigative hearings. In contrast, opponents have looked with disdain upon the investigation as a dangerous weapon often misused by legislators in an attack on the civil liberties of the accused.

Most observers agree that throughout the history of this nation congressional investigative committees have ranged in quality and professionalism (as gauged by their adherence to the goal of improving legislation) from the egregious to the exemplary. By all accounts, the worst investigative committee ever assembled on Capitol Hill was the Joint Committee on the Conduct of the [Civil] War, which trampled extensively on the rights and reputations of its witnesses. A more recent example was the notorious McCarthy inquiry of 1954, an anticommunist witch-hunt into alleged communist influences in the U.S. Army, led by Joseph R. McCarthy, the junior Republican senator from Wisconsin, who chaired the Senate Government Operations Committee and the Permanent Subcommittee on Investigations. In the course of his "investigating," Senator McCarthy tossed out the window any semblance of preserving the rights of witnesses; instead, he engaged in smear tactics and innuendo against individual citizens inside and outside the government.

By consensus, one of the best congressional inquiries was the Senate's Special Committee to Investigate the National Defense Program (1941–1948). Its careful marshaling of evidence and fair treatment of witnesses drew extensive praise—and catapulted one of its chairmen, an obscure senator from Missouri by the name of Truman, into national prominence and soon thereafter the vice presidency.

Fairly or not, investigations have often been criticized as exercises in self-promotion by legislators, turning relatively unknown personalities into household names—Senators Truman, McCarthy, Richard M. Nixon (R-Calif.), Estes Kefauver (D-Tenn.), and Samuel J. Ervin, Jr. (D-N.C.), among others. And, as McCarthy found out, they can destroy as well as make a career. The line between a legislator's trying to publicize an inquiry in order to attract public support for legislative reform in one instance, and his or her self-promotion in another instance, can often be thin and hard to distinguish. The chairman of an investigative committee will find it difficult to muster public support for proposed remedial legislation without at the same time jumping into the limelight. Whether political ambition (and the phototropism it induces, bending legislators toward the television lights) or a sincere desire to inform the public of the need for new legislation is the more powerful consideration for the chairman is a matter that may fall beyond the competence of even a close observer to judge with assurance. In the best of cases, when a legislator is strongly driven by a sense of the public good, the two motivations are most likely intertwined in complicated ways—although self-interested grandstanding can become so transparent that it is easily seen through by observers (as McCarthy learned).

The Phases of a Congressional Investigation. A congressional investigation must normally go through six major phases: start-up, discovery, interrogation, presentment, reform, and follow-through. Once stimulated to establish an investigative committee (say, by indications of corruption in an executive agency; by a major societal problem outside the government, such as widespread failures in the banking industry; or by an international controversy, such as the CIA's covert-action disaster in 1961 at the Bay of Pigs in Cuba), Congress must sort out in its start-up phase a series of key decisions that will guide its probe.

Start-up. Congressional leaders must determine the precise mandate to give their investigative committee, ascertain the extent of resources (time, money, staff) that they are willing to make available for the inquiry, and select the committee members (who then select the staff).

Each decision is laden with implications for the course of the investigation. In the absence of a specific mandate, along with clear rules of conduct and a manifest legislative intent, investigators may flounder, because they lack a sense of direction. Inadequate time, money, or staff can similarly dim the prospects for a thorough inquiry. In particular, time is rarely on the side of congressional investigators. They are expected to show results quickly, often to the drumbeat of media hungry for dramatic revelations and bored by a methodical search for facts, however essential to a complete and fair inquiry.

The nature of the committee's membership is also vital. Have impartial individuals been appointed? Are they senior legislators, with extensive experience and wide respect in the chamber and the country? Do the members exhibit a wide disparity in ideological orientations, or are they a relatively cohesive group? Are would-be presidential aspirants—notoriously eager for publicity—among the members? Decisions on staffing are critical as well. Are the staff aides chiefly lawyers, social scientists, political aides (or, in some instances, political hacks)? Each brings a different, and sometimes clashing, set of cultural norms and investigative approaches to an inquiry.

Discovery. Once the committee is in place (which can take months), the next step is gathering evidence about the subject the committee is investigating. The most reliable evidence usually comes in the form of documents, broadly defined to include memoranda, minutes of meetings, letters, tapes, diaries, notes, appointment calendars, and other records. In the lexicon of law (and Capitol Hill), the gathering of documents is known as *discovery.* The staff of an investigative committee is expected first to lay out the chronology of the event under probe, then to substantiate this record with documentary sources.

Discovery can be a difficult undertaking. The required documents may be classified, posing special problems of access. Those individuals being investigated may do their best to stymie access through legal maneuvering. During the Watergate inquiry, President Nixon, citing executive privilege, tried to bar investigators from his papers—a move partially rebuffed by the Supreme Court in the celebrated case of *United States v. Nixon* (418 U.S. 283, [1974]). Or those under investigation may employ less overt actions. A key portion of taped White House conversations was mysteriously—suspiciously—erased by Nixon's secretary in the midst of the Watergate inquiry. During congressional investigations into the CIA and other intelligence agencies in 1975, one ploy used by an executive agency to slow and discourage discovery was to send literally truckloads of documents to investigators—almost all of which proved worthless. (The ruse was used fifty years earlier by the executive branch during the Teapot Dome investigation.) As Congress's Iran-contra investigation moved forward in 1986 and 1987, the White House shredding machines worked overtime, and some documents were surreptitiously removed from the premises.

As weapons against stalling ("stonewalling," in Washington argot), members of Congress sometimes resort to subpoenas and votes of contempt, which can carry stiff penalties, including imprisonment. Often, threats from Congress that these instruments of punishment will be used prove sufficient to gain compliance.

Interrogation. Once an investigative committee has collected enough documentation to understand the essential facts related to the subject of inquiry (again, a process that can take months), its members and staff augment the record by interviewing knowledgeable individuals, the interrogation phase. And frequently some early interviewing will take place as part of the discovery process—particularly attempts to learn about the existence and location of key documents.

Investigative staffs (and the few legislators who may wish to become involved in the proceedings at this early stage) use a range of approaches to interviews. At the less formal end of the continuum are friendly conversations with people who may know about the subject—for instance, individuals who have worked in the government for decades and have a deep understanding of the agency under in-

"SUGGESTION FOR A NEW DOME ON THE CAPITOL." Political cartoon commenting on the Teapot Dome affair, a Harding administration scandal involving the improper leasing of government oil reserves in Wyoming and California. The investigation into the affair, launched by the Senate Committee on Public Lands and headed by Sen. Thomas J. Walsh (D-Mont.), resulted in the conviction and imprisonment of Warren G. Harding's secretary of the Interior, former senator Albert B. Fall. Billy Borne, *Asheville Citizen*, 21 February 1924.

LIBRARY OF CONGRESS

vestigation. The approach in this instance is to be nonthreatening and cordial, in hopes of ferreting out information helpful to the probe. At the opposite end of the interview continuum is the full-blown—and sometimes hostile—interrogation, with the witness testifying under oath (at risk of perjury and usually accompanied by counsel) and a verbatim record kept of the proceedings.

The softer data obtained through interviews can be less reliable than documentary evidence. It was the still-extant White House tapes that established Nixon's involvement in the Watergate cover-up—the "smoking gun" of hard, culpable fact that investigators dream of in the discovery phase. Officials widely known for their intellectual acuity suddenly can be struck by profound bouts of amnesia regarding key points of evidence—especially if they are under investigation for wrongdoing. Nixon went so far as to explicitly advise his aides to resort to amnesia during the Watergate probe. And sometimes officials flatly mislead, even under oath and in executive (closed) session, as did former CIA director Richard Helms before investigators on the Senate

Foreign Relations Committee during the Vietnam War. Another senior CIA official conceded before an investigative committee that in earlier testimony before the House Permanent Select Committee on Intelligence, he had been "technically correct, [but] specifically evasive"—bureaucratic gobbledygook meaning he had intentionally sidestepped the House committee's attempts to probe the improper diversion of funds to the Contras in Nicaragua, in violation of the law. These problems are not limited to investigations of government agencies. Probes into private-sector misconduct have been plagued by evasiveness as well—as recently exemplified by inquiries into the operations of some savings and loan companies.

Yet, a committee cannot always expect to find a rich documentary trail (let alone a smoking gun), especially in the modern era, when shredding machines are ubiquitous and government officials are leery of writing down sensitive information. Interviews become an important means for filling in the inevitable gaps.

Presentment. The purpose of discovery and interrogation is to build a solid record of evidence for public presentation, on the road to legislative remedy. Presumably, public understanding and support will encourage legislators in the full Congress to support corrective measures. The centerpiece of the presentment phase is the hearing. Ideally, the hearing is held in public, to help build citizen support for the investigative findings and recommendations; sometimes, the hearing must be held in executive session, if the inquiry involves a topic that must be kept classified in order to protect sensitive national security information or the identity of endangered witnesses.

During this phase, members of the investigative panel may resort to political combat, attacking or protecting witnesses during the hearings, arguing among themselves (although usually with the veneer of Capitol Hill collegiality), emphasizing different sets of documents to make their point, and advancing their own brand of legislative remedies (or countering those proposed by adversaries)—all shaped by the partisan, philosophical, and constituency leanings of the individual committee members. Insiders already have seen these political stresses, for they immediately became apparent in member and staff selection during the committee's start-up phase, throughout the period of document requests and witness selection, and with all the other decisions an investigative panel must make in its early workings.

Investigative committees can also be quite cohesive. Often they are less divided by the forces of partisanship, ideology, or constituency—politics—than they are united by a desire to expose and correct wrongdoing; by a common sense of dismay over the mistakes, excesses, or crimes of government officials; and by institutional pride, especially when the executive branch is perceived as having affronted the constitutional prerogatives of Congress.

Of particular importance during the presentment phase is the development of public support for the investigative committee's work and recommendations. Without public interest (outrage directed against those being investigated is even better, from the committee's perspective), it becomes difficult to garner support among the plenary assembly of legislators for new laws or regulations designed to ameliorate the conditions that stimulated the investigation.

Reform. The success or failure of a congressional investigation is typically judged by whether it produces tangible reforms. This benchmark can be spurious, for sound and fury alone can lead to important changes, as bureaucrats (or other targets of investigation) correct their ways without further and more formal prodding from Congress, the institution upon which they depend for future funding. As government bureaucrats and private-sector officials anticipate the negative reactions that wrongdoing will bring on Capitol Hill, this latent check helps to keep potential miscreants in line. This so-

SENATE SUBCOMMITTEE ON LABOR INVESTIGATIONS, C. 1920.

called law of anticipated reactions is often subtle and difficult for the outside observer to detect, but it can be all important.

Explicit manifestations of reform provide, however, the most persuasive evidence of a committee's success—most visibly in the guise of new statutes (for example, the sweeping and widely supported National Security Act of 1947, which followed a legislative investigation into the Pearl Harbor attack and the nation's inadequate security and readiness). More frequent, the result of an inquiry is likely to be not so much new law as a fresh understanding between Congress and the executive agencies about expected behavior. Beyond a tacit sense of "anticipated reactions," the understanding may acquire official or semi-official status through an exchange of letters, by way of a legislative record (frequently a colloquy among members on the floor), by updated executive regulations insisted upon by key legislators (holders of the purse strings), or simply by informal verbal agreements.

While the informal arrangements often succeed, they lack the permanence of law. Like sand castles, they can wash away with the incoming tide of a new administration or even with the retirement of a key legislator, a change in staff, or secret executive codicils to public documents. Herein lies the attraction of formal statutes for those who seek more lasting protection against the abuse that initially triggered an investigation. A further hazard in the reform phase is that legislators will propose unneeded change. They may feel compelled to justify their long (and expensive) inquiry with new law, however unnecessary.

Follow-through. The best legislative reforms may be to little avail if they are never properly implemented. When the investigative committee has filed its report, passed its legislation, and (unless it is a permanent panel) disbanded its staff and dismantled its offices, who is left to see that the malfeasance that led to the inquiry will not occur again? Indeed, the mistake, crime, or scandal might well happen again. Government officials are like other human beings; they may err once more. They may even decide to ignore Congress in deference to a "higher law" spelled out by a president or some other lofty executive official (as one conspirator testified before Congress's Iran-contra investigators). So follow-through is necessary.

Part of the follow-through phase is to conduct periodic probes—especially oversight hearings, with or without immediate cause—into the same agencies and policies that have caused problems in the past. Legislators can also be more thorough in their confirmation hearings for high officials, guarding at the outset against the placement of dubious individuals in positions of authority. The avoidance of crime and scandal depends in part on the quality of government officials; the greater their integrity, the less likely it is that a formal investigation into their activities will prove necessary.

Others, including the media and the courts, as well as inspectors general and legal counsels within the agencies, have an important role in curbing malfeasance before it becomes scandalous. Most important among these checks are the standing

"THE 'DOUGH' BOY." Political cartoon referring to the alleged influence of arms and munitions manufacturers and traffickers on U.S. foreign policy. In 1933 and 1934 House and Senate committees investigated these allegations. Some Americans believed that an "international munitions racket" was at least partially responsible for drawing the United States into World War I. Pencil drawing by Harold M. Talburt.

LA FOLLETTE COLLECTION, MANUSCRIPT DIVISION, LIBRARY OF CONGRESS committees of Congress, with their control over the budget, their subpoena powers, and other points of leverage. In their day-to-day interaction with men and women of power—ever liable to abuse in human hands, Madison warned—the standing committees are in a good position to guard against violations of the public trust.

Studies of congressional oversight indicate, however, that the devotion of legislators to this aspect of their duties has often been uneven. Failure to conduct serious routine legislative review of government programs ironically may be the most important trigger of congressional investigations, as legislators are finally forced to confront a full-blown scandal that the preventive of careful systematic oversight might have scotched.

[*See also* Investigations, Senate Permanent Subcommittee on; Investigative Power; McGrain v. Daugherty; Watkins v. United States; Witnesses, Rights of. *For discussion of particular investigations, see* Army-McCarthy Hearings; Iran-Contra Committee; Pearl Harbor Investigation; Pecora Wall Street Investigation; Pujo Investigation; St. Clair Investigation; Un-American Activities Committee, House; Watergate Committee.]

BIBLIOGRAPHY

Cohen, William, and George Mitchell. *Men of Zeal.* 1989.
Davidson, Roger H. "The Political Dimensions of Congressional Investigations." *Capitol Studies* 5 (1977): 41–63.
Fulbright, J. W. "Congressional Investigations: Significance for the Legislative Process." *University of Chicago Law Review* 18 (1950–1951): 440–448.
Johnson, Loch K. *A Season of Inquiry: The Senate Intelligence Investigation.* 1985.
Rovere, Richard. *Senator Joe McCarthy.* 1959.
Schlesinger, Arthur M., Jr., and Roger Bruns, eds. *Congress Investigates, 1792–1974.* 1975.

LOCH K. JOHNSON

INVESTIGATIONS, SENATE PERMANENT SUBCOMMITTEE ON. One of the more enduring congressional investigative bodies, the Permanent Subcommittee on Investigations of the Senate Committee on Governmental Affairs was formed in 1948 to succeed the Senate Special Committee to Investigate the National Defense Program. The Special Committee had been established early in 1941 on the initiative of Sen. Harry S. Truman (D-Mo.), who became the panel's first chairman. Popularly known as the Truman Committee, it examined various aspects of the growing national

defense program to ensure that appropriated funds were spent wisely, efficiently, and equitably.

The Truman Committee functioned until 1948, when the Senate abolished all special committees. (Its progenitor had left the Senate three years earlier to become president.) To preserve the panel's investigative expertise, many of its resources were vested in a new permanent investigative subcommittee of the Senate Committee on Expenditures in the Executive Departments on the initiative of that committee's chairman, Sen. George D. Aiken (R-Vt.). The Expenditures Committee, mandated to probe inefficiencies throughout government, later became the Committee on Government Operations, subsequently renamed the Committee on Governmental Affairs.

During its first two years (1949–1950), the Permanent Subcommittee on Investigations, under the leadership of Sen. Clyde R. Hoey (D-N.C.), unmasked influence peddling in Washington, which was found to involve aides to President Truman.

With the 1952 elections, the Republican party captured the White House and gained majorities in both houses of Congress. Consequently, a new chairman took control of the permanent subcommittee—Sen. Joseph R. McCarthy (R-Wis.). During his tenure (1953–1954), McCarthy committed the subcommittee's resources to identifying and probing the influence of communists in government. His investigative style, characterized by bullying tactics, disregard for witnesses' civil liberties, and unsupported charges of disloyalty, came to be known as McCarthyism. Late in 1954, the Senate approved 67 to 22 a resolution condemning McCarthy for abusing and obstructing the Subcommittee on Privileges and Elections and for attacking the Select Committee to Study Censure Charges concerning their respective examinations of his conduct as a senator.

When the Democrats recaptured control of the Senate in 1955, the permanent subcommittee came under the chairmanship of Sen. John L. McClellan (D-Ark.). For the next eighteen years (1955–1972), he led the panel in scrutinizing labor-management racketeering, fraud in the government purchase of military uniforms, improprieties in the Foreign Operations Administration's contracting for the construction of grain storage elevators in Pakistan, inefficiencies in the Department of Agriculture's grain storage program, interstate gambling, the structure of organized crime, traffic in stolen and bogus securities, urban civil disorder, and bombings and other terrorist acts.

Following Senator McClellan's death in 1972, the permanent subcommittee came under the successive chairmanships of Henry M. Jackson (1973–1978), Sam Nunn (1979–1980), William V. Roth, Jr. (1981–1986), and, once again, Nunn (1987–). Among the matters probed by the panel during these two decades were undercover drug enforcement methods, fraudulent insurance schemes, weapons development and procurement cases, corruption in U.S. post exchanges and servicemen's clubs in Southeast Asia, organized crime, various aspects of government waste, enforcement of the Employee Retirement Income Security Act, Soviet grain sales, East-West technology transfer, and federal security clearance programs. In recent years, the permanent subcommittee has been composed of about a dozen senators supported by a staff of approximately two dozen individuals.

BIBLIOGRAPHY

Nunn, Sam. "The Impact of the Senate Permanent Subcommittee on Investigations on Federal Policy." *Georgia Law Review* 21 (1986): 17–56.

Wallace, H. Lew. "The McCarthy Era, 1954." In vol. 5 of *Congress Investigates: A Documented History, 1792–1974*. Edited by Arthur M. Schlesinger, Jr., and Roger Bruns. 5 vols. 1975.

HAROLD C. RELYEA

INVESTIGATIVE POWER. Congress's famous investigations, such as Watergate in 1973 and Iran-contra in 1987, make use of one of the institution's most important and historic powers. By investigating, Congress has served as the U.S. public's eyes and ears on important economic and social issues and national controversies in every era from the earliest days of the Republic to the present. Although Supreme Court cases have highlighted Congress's investigative power, investigations have never failed to raise numerous controversial and complex questions, ranging from executive privilege for presidents to immunity for witnesses.

Definition and Importance. In the 1957 case of *Watkins v. United States*, the Supreme Court gave a classic definition of the congressional investigative power:

The power of the Congress to conduct investigations is inherent in the legislative process. That power is broad. It encompasses inquiries concerning the administration of existing laws as well as proposed or possibly needed statutes. It includes surveys of defects in our social, economic or political system for the purpose of enabling the Congress to remedy them. It comprehends probes into departments of the Federal Government to expose corruption, inefficiency or waste.

This *Watkins* definition refers to the various possible subjects of investigation, which some famous examples illustrate. When the Court referred to "inquiries concerning the administration of existing laws" (often called oversight), it meant the type of investigative power involved, for example, when House committees in 1982 examined whether the Reagan administration's Environmental Protection Agency was carrying out environmental cleanup laws. "Surveys of defects" include investigations of financial or social problems such as the 1933–1934 investigation into the causes of the 1929 stock market crash. "Probes [of] corruption, inefficiency or waste" include the 1990 House committee investigation of influence peddling in housing grants by the Department of Housing and Urban Development.

The congressional investigative power can also be defined by the ways in which investigations are carried out. Typically, Congress exercises its investigative power through committees. For special problems it may use select committees, such as, for example, the Senate Select Committee on Improper Activities in the Labor or Management Field, better known as the McClellan Committee after its chairman, Sen. John L. McClellan (D-Ark.), which in 1959 investigated connections between labor unions and racketeers, or the Special Committee to Investigate Organized Crime in Interstate Commerce, chaired by Sen. Estes Kefauver (D-Tenn.), which in 1950 and 1951 traveled to cities around the United States holding hearings on organized crime. Standing committees such as the House and Senate Judiciary committees regularly investigate the Justice Department. The committees hold hearings in which members of Congress question witnesses, usually in public session and, in important investigations, with television coverage, though sensitive testimony may sometimes be taken in closed (also called "executive") session.

Congress's many investigative tools for handling witnesses have generated the court cases that have developed and defined the law governing the investigative power. Witnesses may be required to take an oath, so that if they testify falsely they can be prosecuted for perjury. Witnesses, including government officials, who are reluctant to appear (or to provide documents) may be subpoenaed; if they fail to appear when subpoenaed, or refuse to answer questions, the committee may hold them in contempt, for which they may also be tried in court.

History and Constitutional Basis. The British Parliament, particularly the House of Commons, began to use the investigative power in the early 1600s. It developed the power in its struggles with the Tudor and Stuart monarchs, struggles that culminated in the Glorious Revolution of 1688. As William Pitt the Elder wrote of the House of Commons in 1742, "We are called the Grand Inquest of the Nation, and as such it is our duty to inquire into every Step of publick management, either Abroad or at Home, in order to see that nothing has been done amiss." In America the colonial legislatures exercised similar investigative power in their tussles with the royal governors. State legislatures continued to exercise this power after independence.

When the Framers drafted the Constitution, they therefore understood the investigative power to be a fundamental aspect of a legislature. Article I of the Constitution provided in its first section that "All legislative Powers herein granted shall be vested in a Congress," and this included the power of investigation. Article I, section 5 provided that the House of Representatives and the Senate shall each "determine the Rules of its Proceedings," from which came the power to establish committees and determine the procedures for committee investigations. Parliament's power of impeachment had long been understood to be one of the ultimate outcomes of investigations; the Constitution, Article I, sections 2 and 3, prescribed a vigorous power and procedure for impeachment of the president or other officers, signaling the continuing importance in the Framers' minds of congressional inquiries.

The House first exercised the investigative power in 1792, during President George Washington's first term. After a major military disaster in which an Indian confederacy in the Ohio River valley defeated the U.S. Army under Gen. Arthur St. Clair, the House established a select committee to investigate. The committee extracted documents from the Washington administration that elucidated the problems that underlay the disaster, and then it forced changes in the military procurement system. The investigation of St. Clair's defeat cemented the eighteenth-century view that Congress fully possessed the investigative power, and the acquiescence of President Washington to the House's demands for documents established a precedent for executive obedience to congressional inquiries.

Key Court Cases. Congress conducted numerous investigations during the 1800s. From the earliest times on, Congress would punish witnesses' contempt—the refusal by witnesses to answer questions or to produce documents—by its power of "inherent contempt." With this power the House or Senate could summon an uncooperative witness to the floor of the chamber, try the witness for contempt without involving the courts, and, on finding him guilty, imprison the witness. (As recently as 1972, in a case involving state legislatures, the Supreme Court confirmed the validity of the procedure of inherent contempt, so long as the legislature affords the witness basic due-process protections.) In 1857 Congress enacted a statute that sent trials of contempt charges to the judiciary. The power of inherent contempt remains, but Congress last used it in 1935; since then Congress has used the statutory system for judicial trials in all its contempt cases.

The first Supreme Court case about congressional investigations, *Kilbourn v. Thompson* (1881), dealt the investigative power a temporary setback. The Court held that a House committee investigation of a defunct banking firm involved a judicial, not legislative, subject because the bankruptcy courts had jurisdiction over the bankrupt firm. Although the decision cast a shadow over congressional inquiry power, Congress continued to investigate. The 1912 House investigation of the Rockefeller and Morgan interests, conducted by the so-called Pujo Committee (for its chairman, Democratic representative Arsène P. Pujo of Louisiana), held the nation's rapt interest on the concentration of banking power and led to the laws establishing the modern Federal Reserve System.

During the 1920s the Senate investigated the Harding administration's Teapot Dome scandal. Two key Supreme Court cases arising out of the Teapot Dome inquiries removed the shadow of *Kilbourn* and firmly upheld the congressional investigative power. In *McGrain v. Daugherty* (1927) the Court held that congressional committees could issue subpoenas, compel witnesses to appear, and punish them for contempt if they disobeyed. Also, in *Sinclair v. United States* (1929), the Court held that a witness who lied under oath to a congressional committee could be convicted of perjury. Both *McGrain* and *Sinclair* recognized two central purposes of the investigative power: to provide information needed for new laws and to determine whether the executive branch—the president and the departments and agencies—is adequately enforcing existing laws.

Major congressional investigations during the 1930s laid the groundwork for New Deal legislation. In particular, the Senate's 1933–1934 investigation of the causes of the stock market crash of

1929, conducted by the so-called Pecora Committee (for its chief counsel, Ferdinand Pecora), prepared the way for modern laws regulating the securities industry. Similarly, during World War II a Senate committee chaired by Sen. Harry S. Truman received widespread credit for investigating wartime waste and fraud.

During the late 1940s and then more intensively during the 1950s, congressional committees generated major controversy with their investigations of alleged domestic communist conspiracies. These committees—especially the House Un-American Activities Committee and the Senate Subcommittee on Investigations chaired by Sen. Joseph R. McCarthy (R-Wis.)—held numerous witnesses in contempt for refusing to say whether other people they knew had ever belonged to the Communist party, an association that was legal but, once publicized, likely to be ruinous. In *Watkins v. United States* (1957) the Supreme Court initially reversed the conviction of a witness for contempt in such an investigation; the Court's opinion made broad statements that such inquiries must not run afoul of the Bill of Rights.

When Congress reacted sharply against the *Watkins* decision, the Court retreated. In *Barenblatt v. United States* (1959), the Court moderated its language, permitting Congress full power of investigation. Congress may not violate a witness's Fifth Amendment right against self-incrimination or the Fourth Amendment right against excessively broad subpoenas, but Congress has rarely transgressed these limits. The Supreme Court indicated it would reverse convictions for contempt only when a congressional committee has made some procedural error violating a witness's rights under statutes, congressional rules, or the Constitution.

In 1973, a Senate committee investigated the Watergate scandal, which involved the Nixon administration's bugging of the Democratic party headquarters and the subsequent coverup. The Senate Watergate Committee (officially, the Senate Select Committee on Presidential Campaign Activities) made the first use of an important investigative tool, "use immunity." Use immunity prohibits prosecutors by statute from using a witness's testimony against himself or herself, thereby permitting the witness to testify freely to the investigative committee without fear of self-incrimination, even when parts of the testimony are evidence of the witness's guilt. The witness can still be convicted, but only on the basis of evidence unconnected to his or her own testimony (for example, testimony by another witness with an independent recollection). The committee conferred use immunity on John Dean, President Richard M. Nixon's former counsel and the key witness to the Watergate conspiracy. Dean then told his story in hearings on national television. Subsequently, such top officials as White House Chief of Staff H. R. Haldeman and Attorney General John Mitchell, whose testimony before the Watergate Committee disagreed with Dean's, were convicted of perjury.

During the 1970s and 1980s reluctant congressional witnesses, both private individuals and government officials, tried to use the courts as an offensive weapon against congressional investigations. In 1975 the Supreme Court in *Eastland v. United States Servicemen's Fund* ruled that a congressional committee is immune to such suits. In 1983 a lower court rejected a famous suit by the Reagan administration, *United States v. House of Representatives*, by upholding the House's insistence on its power to investigate free of executive and judicial intrusion.

The congressional Iran-contra committees of 1987 again used use immunity, this time to investigate the Reagan administration's trading of arms to Iran in exchange for the release of American hostages and the related resupplying of the Nicaraguan Contras, right-wing rebels fighting that country's Marxist government. The committees conferred use immunity on the two central figures, Col. Oliver North, a White House aide, and John Poindexter, the national security adviser. In subsequent trials in 1989 and 1990, juries convicted North and Poindexter, respectively, for taking gratuities and lying to Congress. Subsequently, an appellate court of judges appointed by the Reagan administration reversed both convictions. This court decision made it all but impossible for Congress to employ use immunity to obtain testimony and still hold a witness responsible for pretestimony crimes.

Contemporary Issues. A major issue of the congressional investigative power has concerned attempts by a president or his subordinates to cover up a scandal. Starting in the 1950s, presidential orders to government witnesses not to testify, or to withhold records, came to be known as executive privilege. Claims of executive privilege culminated in 1973 when Richard M. Nixon attempted to withhold from Congress and the courts a set of audiotapes recorded in the White House. The Supreme Court's rejection of his claim of executive privilege in *United States v. Nixon* (1974) led directly to his resignation in August 1974.

THOUSANDS OF PAGES OF TRANSCRIPTS. From the deliberations of the Army-McCarthy hearings, piled high for the benefit of the television cameras on the last day of the hearings, 17 June 1954. Beginning on 22 April 1954, the hearings investigated Sen. Joseph R. McCarthy's (R-Wis.) allegations of communist influence in the U.S. Army and the army's allegation that McCarthy's charges represented a misuse of the congressional investigative power to improperly pressure the U.S. Army to give preferential treatment to Pvt. G. David Schine, a friend of McCarthy's aide Roy M. Cohn.   LIBRARY OF CONGRESS

Thereafter, government officials, including presidents, still periodically attempted to withhold evidence from Congress. They argued for the need for secrecy so that government officials would feel free to discuss and deliberate without their debates becoming public. Congress, however, often rejected such arguments. In 1981 and 1982, President Ronald Reagan claimed executive privilege twice, in House investigations involving, respectively, Secretary of the Interior James Watt and Environmental Protection Agency Administrator Anne Gorsuch. In each instance the House overcame the claim of executive privilege and compelled the witnesses to provide evidence.

Sometimes presidents have argued for withholding from Congress information about national security subjects such as intelligence agency matters or foreign affairs. From the 1940s to the early 1970s Congress mostly avoided investigating intelligence matters. But after a series of scandals—including CIA assassination plots and the Federal Bureau of Investigation's electronic eavesdropping on civil rights leader Martin Luther King, Jr.—Congress created select committees to investigate the intelligence agencies. Standing intelligence committees were established in the late 1970s and given full power and ability to receive highly classified information. In the Iran-contra investigation in 1987 Congress again looked into highly classified matters, this time involving secret negotiations with Iran and other foreign countries.

An unresolved issue of congressional investigative power concerned members of Congress who placed classified records about executive abuses in the public record. Sen. Mike Gravel (D-Alaska) put the so-called Pentagon Papers in the public record in 1970, producing a Supreme Court case, *Gravel v. United States* (1972), which found that the senator was immune from questioning or prosecution. In 1992 Rep. Henry B. Gonzalez (D-Tex.) placed in the public record numerous classified records about the Bush administration's friendly dealings with Iraqi dictator Saddam Hussein before Iraq invaded Kuwait. Both the Gravel and Gonzalez incidents provided fertile material for debate about the public's right to know, effectuated through the congressional investigative process, versus the interest every administration has in keeping secrets.

[*See also* Investigations *and entries on particular court cases:* Gravel v. United States; Kilbourn v. Thompson; McGrain v. Daugherty; Watkins v. United States.]

BIBLIOGRAPHY

Berger, Raoul. *Executive Privilege: A Constitutional Myth.* 1974.
Grabow, John C. *Congressional Investigations: Law and Practice.* 1988.
Hamilton, James. *The Power To Probe: A Study of Congressional Investigations.* 1976.
Schlesinger, Arthur M., Jr., and Roger Bruns, eds. *Congress Investigates: 1792–1974.* 1975.
Van Cleve, George W., and Charles Tiefer. "Navigating the Shoals of "Use Immunity" and Secret International Enterprises in Major Congressional Investigations: Lessons of the Iran-Contra Affair." *Missouri Law Review* 55 (1990): 43–92.

CHARLES TIEFER

IOWA. Iowa became U.S. territory as a result of the Louisiana Purchase of 1803. Between 1834 and 1838, Congress included Iowa in the Michigan and Wisconsin territories, and in 1838 it created the Iowa Territory. Boundary disputes bedeviled and delayed Iowa's admission to statehood. Settlers in southern Iowa contested Missouri's claim to their territory, and when Congress admitted Iowa to the Union it directed the two states to take their case to the Supreme Court, which in 1849 upheld Iowa's claim. Meanwhile, in 1845, Iowans had rejected admission after Congress had restricted the would-be state's northern and western boundaries. When Congress accepted their western claim, Iowans adopted a constitution and started a state government two months before President James K. Polk signed the enabling legislation on 28 December 1846.

At first, Iowans elected to Congress Democrats who favored compromise with the slave states. But the slavery controversy soon fractured the Democrats and produced a vigorously antislavery Republican party that swept Iowa in 1856 and dominated the state for most of the next century.

During the Civil War era the voting of Iowa's congressional delegation revealed a complex pattern of personal, state, regional, and national interests, favoring cheap land and improved transportation but differing over establishing land-grant colleges and national banks. Congressmen such as Josiah B. Grinnell (1863–1867) were abolitionists who favored equal rights for blacks. Sen. James W. Grimes (1859–1869) enraged Iowa Republicans when he voted to acquit President Andrew Johnson on impeachment charges because he feared enlarging the powers of Congress over the president.

After the Civil War Iowa's typical congressman was Sen. William B. Allison (1873–1908). A legislative craftsman who was adept at forming coalitions and balancing national Republican principles against Iowa's interests, Allison represented a centrist conservatism that made him a powerful ally of high-tariff reactionary Sen. Nelson W. Aldrich, chairman of the Finance Committee, and in President Theodore Roosevelt's struggle against Aldrich for railroad regulation. Also in the Allison mold was Rep. David B. Henderson (1883–1903) who served two terms as the first Speaker of the House from west of the Mississippi River.

Allison was succeeded by progressive reformer Albert B. Cummins (1908–1926), who campaigned for low tariffs and railroad regulation. In the 1920s Iowa's agricultural interests dominated as the state's delegation in Congress formed the "farm bloc" to pass laws to aid farmers, including the McNary-Haugen bill to support farm prices, sponsored by Rep. Gilbert N. Haugen (1899–1933). The Great Depression temporarily interrupted Iowa's Republican domination, but the elections of 1938 restored the pattern. Not until the 1960s did Iowa's congressional delegations begin to change with national voting trends.

Iowa's House delegation declined from a high of eleven at the beginning of the twentieth century to five at its end. Its influence was sustained by the seniority system, which made Rep. Neal Smith, elected as Democrat in 1958, a high-ranking member of the Appropriations Committee.

BIBLIOGRAPHY

Sage, Leland L. *A History of Iowa.* 1974.
Larew, James C. *A Party Reborn: The Democrats of Iowa, 1950–1974.* 1980.

GEORGE MCJIMSEY

IRAN-CONTRA COMMITTEES.

On 2 November 1986, *Al-Shiraa*, an obscure Lebanese magazine, reported that the United States had been selling weapons to Iran, which the United States had declared a terrorist nation, to ransom Americans held hostage by terrorists in Lebanon. It also asserted that Robert McFarlane, national security adviser to President Ronald Reagan, had led a secret mission to Iran in the spring of 1986 to negotiate a missiles-for-hostages swap.

This tale initiated the unraveling of what became known as the Iran-contra affair, which, in the words of historian Theodore Draper, "threatened the constitutional foundations of the country." Investigations showed that the Reagan administration had lied to and deceived Congress and the public; scorned the constitutional rights and responsibilities of Congress in the conduct of foreign policy; abdicated the conduct of that policy to private, profit-seeking persons; and, through "tin-cup diplomacy," solicited from wealthy foreign potentates and rich Americans money for the U.S.-financed Nicaraguan rebels (Contras)—aid that Congress had refused to furnish.

At first, the administration denied the arms sales. But on 13 November, Reagan conceded the McFarlane trip and the sales, which were contrary to public policy against arms to Iran. He denied, however, that the sales were a swap of missiles for hostages, a ransom effort that would have repudiated his oft-stated, vehement avowals that he would never do such a thing. He insisted, instead, that he was selling arms to try to establish relations with moderates in Iran. (No such faction existed, however.)

Days later, Attorney General Edwin Meese opened an inquiry into the arms sales. It was a hurried, haphazard effort carried out by Reagan political appointees. It failed to use the professional investigators of the FBI and the criminal division of the Justice Department. And it gave Adm. John Poindexter, Reagan's national security adviser, and an aide, Col. Oliver North, time and opportunity to destroy or falsify documents relating to the sales. Despite this obstruction, on 22 November, Meese's aides stumbled onto a memorandum in North's files that indicated that millions of dollars in proceeds from the sales had been secretly channeled to arm the Contras fighting the Soviet-supported Sandinista government. At this time, a congressional ban on aid to the Contras was in effect, and Reagan avowed that he was abiding by the ban. Meese announced his findings on 25 November.

On 26 November, Reagan appointed a Special Review Board to investigate Iran-contra. And, at the request of Meese, an independent counsel was named to launch a criminal investigation. Early in January 1987, the Senate and House established separate investigating committees.

On 26 February, the Special Review Board issued its report. It criticized Reagan's lackadaisical management style but found him uninformed and blameless in the funds' diversion. By that time, the congressional investigation had begun.

To avoid duplication, the House and Senate merged their efforts. The two staffs reviewed more than 300,000 documents and interviewed, deposed, or publicly interrogated more than five hundred witnesses. There were forty days of televised hearings and several closed sessions.

Despite this historic effort, the committees' final report, issued on 18 November 1987, acknowledged that the record was marred by inconsistent testimony, failed memories, and the death of a key witness, William J. Casey, director of the Central Intelligence Agency. In addition, it noted, National Security Council (NSC) staff members destroyed "objective evidence that could have resolved the inconsistencies and the failures of memory. . . ." It might have added that the committees' own work was hampered by their decision to set short deadlines and not to subpoena agencies and officials of the executive branch.

Whatever its merits, the merging of the efforts of

the Senate and House committees created problems. The twenty-six members sat towering above the witnesses in the televised sessions. The day-after-day questioning of witnesses by committee lawyers, followed by hour-after-hour interrogation by committee members, sometimes lent an aura of inquisition to the proceedings and produced an often rambling and repetitive record.

In addition, there was procedural disagreement between the outside lawyers, mostly former federal prosecutors, hired to take charge of the investigation, and the congressional staff lawyers asked to assist the outside counsel. The latter, experienced in congressional oversight operations, were skeptical of the executive branch's pledge of full cooperation with the investigation, while the outside counsel was more trustful of that pledge.

The investigation did, however, expose in detail administration policies rooted in nearly paranoid secrecy and poisoned by deception and disdain for the law. The report stated that

a small group of officials believed they alone knew what was right. They viewed knowledge of their objectives by others in the Government as a threat to their objectives. They told neither the Secretary of State, the Congress nor the American people of their actions. When exposure was threatened, they destroyed official documents and lied to Cabinet officials, to the public, and to elected representatives in Congress. They testified that they even withheld key facts from the President.

The report detailed how North and his NSC staff allies solicited foreign and private funds for the Contras, with more than half of the millions collected going to the fund-raisers. Furthermore, they turned over to private profiteers the procurement, sale, and delivery of arms to Iran and the Contras in an enterprise that was accountable to no one in the U.S. government.

Who was responsible for this breakdown in constitutional government? The president set the policy but shunned responsibility for it. The six most powerful men in the administration—the president, the vice president, the secretary of State, the secretary of Defense, the attorney general, and the White House chief of staff—all professed ignorance of the Contra diversion. Secretary of State George P. Shultz and Secretary of Defense Caspar Weinberger strenuously opposed the arms deal with Iran, and Shultz was doubtful about getting foreign money for the Contras. But once Reagan had decided in favor of the arms deals, they, in Draper's words, "folded their tents and stole away."

In the report, the Democratic majority upheld the constitutional role of Congress in the setting of foreign policy, a role denigrated by some witnesses and members of the committees. It was, however, uncritical of Congress's failure to fulfill its role in Iran-contra, and its twenty-seven recommendations primarily called for the strengthening of the oversight capabilities of the intelligence committees. It acknowledged that the recommendations were "not remarkable."

The minority report mostly emphasized the need to patch congressional leaks, which it cited as an excuse for administration secrecy. It, too, was uncritical of Congress's failure to live up to its constitutional duty to share foreign-policy powers with the executive branch.

The report's recommendations, although unremarkable, did not fare well in subsequent Congresses. Furthermore, in 1990 President George Bush pocket-vetoed rules for executive-branch reporting to Congress on covert activities—rules the House Democrats thought too weak but nevertheless approved.

In August 1991, four years after the end of the televised hearings, Bush signed into law rules purportedly requiring for the first time that the executive branch report to Congress all covert intelligence activities and authorize such actions in advance in writing. (In 1985 Reagan had clandestinely approved in writing—after the fact—a shipment of arms to Iran, the questionable legality of which much concerned the administration.)

The 1991 *Congressional Quarterly Almanac* called the reporting requirement the "most significant byproduct of the Iran-Contra scandal." However, one Democratic House member complained that a loophole in the law "allows the President to still claim that he can withhold whatever information he wants."

For his part, Bush, in his statement upon signing the legislation, refused to commit to prompt notification about all covert operations in all cases. Sen. Sam Nunn (D-Ga.) said Bush's definition of when and what he would withhold "would virtually cover everything the CIA has done that I know anything about in covert activity." He called this a "fundamental difference" from what Congress intended.

BIBLIOGRAPHY

Draper, Theodore. *A Very Thin Line: The Iran-Contra Affairs.* 1991.

U.S. Congress. *Report of the Congressional Committees Investigating the Iran-Contra Affair, With Supplemental,*

Minority and Additional Views. 100th Cong., 1st sess., 1987.

U.S. Congress. *Report of the Congressional Committees Investigating the Iran-Contra Affair,* Appendix C: *Chronology of Events.* 100th Cong., 1st sess., 1988.

ROBERT J. HAVEL

IRON TRIANGLE.

The term *iron triangle* metaphorically refers to a relatively closed and stable policy-making system with three participants. Also known as the "power triad" or "cozy triangle," the iron triangle links three primary political actors: congressional committees, interest groups, and executive bureaus and agencies. The triangle is a fixed, closed, autonomous system for making policy. The relationships between the congressional committees and the other two actors tend to resist disturbances, thus the "iron" nature of the system. The iron triangle metaphor posits that the parent chambers of Congress, the general public, the president, and political appointees have little influence on the three actors in the system. Political scientist Hugh Heclo has rejected the iron triangle metaphor as a paradigm for policy-making and replaced it with the "issue network" concept. In issue networks, policy-making is more open to scrutiny by the public, power is disaggregated, and many participants flow in and out of decision making.

Neither the iron triangle nor the issue network is a complete description of the policy-making process, and in recent years the more complex "policy subsystem" idea has gained ascendance. In the policy subsystem, congressional committees are not as prominent as political actors; instead the visibility of the policy, the amount of conflict it generates, and the number of political actors who are interested in the policy tend to determine the latitude of congressional committees in setting policy.

BIBLIOGRAPHY

Heclo, Hugh. "Issue Networks and the Executive Establishment." In *The New American Political System.* Edited by Anthony King. 1978.

Thurber, James A. "Dynamics of Policy Subsystems in American Politics." In *Interest Group Politics,* 3d ed. Edited by Allan Cigler and Burdett Loomis. 1991.

JAMES A. THURBER

IRRECONCILABLES.

The League of Nations Covenant was President Woodrow Wilson's most treasured contribution to the Treaty of Versailles after World War I. When in 1919 and 1920 the Senate refused to approve the treaty, the outcome was due in part to the irreconcilables, the label attached to the treaty's most obdurate opponents. There were sixteen of them, fourteen Republicans and two Democrats. They were William E. Borah, Frank B. Brandegee, Albert B. Fall, Bert M. Fernald, Joseph I. France, Asle J. Gronna, Hiram W. Johnson, Philander C. Knox, Robert M. La Follette, Joseph Medill McCormick, George H. Moses, George W. Norris, Miles Poindexter, James A. Reed, and Lawrence Y. Sherman. Borah, Johnson, and Reed, the three most vocal of the group, were isolationists who warned against straying from the isolationist advice of George Washington, Thomas Jefferson, and James Monroe by involving the nation in foreign wars. Others, headed by former secretary of State Philander C. Knox, were willing to assume limited international obligations in cooperation with the wartime Allies. All of the irreconcilables rejected Article Ten of the Covenant, the ambiguous obligation to defend any member state. And they warned of League intervention in the Western Hemisphere in defiance of the Monroe Doctrine.

Irreconcilables undermined the treaty by a long campaign of speech making in the Senate and outside and by their tactics in committee and on the floor. Implacably against the treaty, they supported crippling amendments. To defeat these, Republican friends of the treaty put forth as alternatives stern reservations that required no renegotiation yet limited U.S. international commitments. When Wilson rejected them, the pro-treaty forces divided. Compromise efforts ensued, but Borah and Johnson threatened to bolt the Republican party if too much was conceded to those who sought to involve the United States in greater international obligations. No successful compromise was reached.

[*See also* League of Nations.]

BIBLIOGRAPHY

Maddox, Robert James. *William E. Borah and American Foreign Policy.* 1969.

Stone, Ralph. *The Irreconcilables: The Fight against the League of Nations.* 1970.

HERBERT F. MARGULIES

ISOLATIONISM.

The term *isolationism* is conventionally used to denote the foreign relations that the United States nurtured in its early national period and pursued effectively until U.S. entry into World War II. The proponents of isolationism did not advocate hermitlike seclusion from the rest of the world. Rather, they espoused a form of diplomatic detachment so as to protect the nation from becoming entangled in international quarrels that might subvert U.S. autonomy and uniqueness.

Congress, especially the Senate, sought to preserve the isolationist tradition in the twentieth century even as world circumstances made it less and less viable. Isolationist members invoked a heritage with roots in the belief of Thomas Paine that the nation could only pursue its ordained mission if it separated itself from the corrupt politics and dynastic wars of the Old World. Although the ideal of isolation, enshrined in George Washington's Farewell Address, often ran up against the reality of external involvement, Americans barely questioned its time-honored maxims until World War I, and many sought to preserve them thereafter.

Only during debate over U.S. involvement in the Great War did isolationism become a matter of pointed public controversy. The war triggered isolationist fears, and if most in Congress managed to overcome them in 1917, the peace, threatening to perpetuate and codify U.S. ensnarement in diplomatic intrigue, led to the reassertion of isolationism. Starting with defeat of the Treaty of Versailles—a defeat that blocked U.S. entry into the League of Nations—isolationists in the Senate succeeded for two decades in halting all attempts to join in collective action against potential or actual aggressors. They emasculated the Four-Power Treaty of 1922; blocked U.S. membership on the World Court; ensured that the Kellogg-Briand Pact for the outlawing of war was merely an "international kiss"; severely circumscribed the use of sanctions against those who breached the peace in the 1930s; and legislated a determined neutrality as the world again catapulted toward war.

Leading the isolationist cause were many of the nation's most prominent senators, including William E. Borah, Hiram W. Johnson, Robert M. La Follette, Robert M. La Follette, Jr., Gerald P. Nye, Robert A. Taft, Arthur H. Vandenberg, Burton K. Wheeler, and for most of the interwar period, George W. Norris. Often branded as reactionary, ill-informed, and parochial—and even, on the eve of World War II, pro-Nazi—isolationists, although far from homogeneous, were in fact often progressive in domestic outlook, far from indifferent to world affairs, and by no means sympathetic to the Axis. A minority whose views faced increasing challenge, they brought immense commitment and forensic ability to legislative contests and used political

leverage and parliamentary skills to prolong their success.

The coming of war in 1939 impugned isolationism as no abstract counterargument could have. Despite strenuous efforts, isolationists saw public sentiment and a majority of their colleagues back away from strict neutrality to endorse repeal of the arms embargo, Lend-Lease, and other measures "short of war." Finally, Pearl Harbor, as Vandenberg acknowledged, "ended isolationism for any realist."

A few of the faithful carried an essentially isolationist stance into the Cold War era, but most, even when reaction against excessive global interventionism resurrected some of the arguments the isolationists had used, accepted that the experience of the 1930s had destroyed isolationism as a respectable credo.

[See also Irreconcilables; League of Nations; Neutrality Debates.]

BIBLIOGRAPHY

Adler, Selig. The Isolationist Impulse: Its Twentieth Century Reaction. 1957.
Cole, Wayne S. Roosevelt and the Isolationists. 1983.

THOMAS N. GUINSBURG

ITEM VETO. Proposals to amend the Constitution to assign the president line-item veto authority respecting appropriations bills have been introduced, and occasionally considered, in various Congresses for more than a century. The item veto, in its simplest form, would augment the president's general veto power by permitting a veto of a "line-item" provision within a larger appropriations bill.

The basic concept of the item veto first appeared in the 1861 constitution of the Confederate States of America. After the Civil War, a number of states adopted a variation of this concept, a trend that continued through 1991, by which time governors of forty-three states had some form of item veto. A number of presidents, including Presidents Ronald Reagan and George Bush, have requested Congress to pass a constitutional amendment giving the executive authority similar to that which is believed to prevail among the majority of states (though in fact there is a wide variety of item-veto provisions among the several states). Thus far, Congress has declined to pass such an amendment.

The principal argument given in favor of the line-item veto is that it would permit the president to "get inside" appropriation bills and eliminate those particular expenditure items believed to be wasteful and products of congressional pork-barrel spending. The line-item veto process is often depicted as a simple, politically neutral device to bring about economy and efficiency in government. It would permit, according to its sponsors, the president to reassert some lost discipline over the budget. Proponents further contend that state experience demonstrates the savings that could be achieved by more sophisticated forms of the item veto, such as the amendatory and item-reduction vetoes.

Critics of the item veto at the national level argue that such a change in the Constitution, far from being a neutral, good-government provision, would in fact profoundly alter the relationship of the Congress to the president, to the advantage of the latter. The item veto would require the detailed segmentation of appropriation bills, which by consent of both Congress and the president are now lump-sum in character, in order to facilitate both preenactment negotiations and postenactment renegotiations. The details of appropriations are presently found in committee reports and, as such and as presently understood, would not be subject to the line-item veto. For the line-item veto to work, all budgetary details would have to be spelled out in law, thus making for exceptionally long appropriations bills. The item veto would compel a subtle political change in that the critical negotiations would tend to shift from the preenactment stage to the postenactment, or veto consideration, period. The latter process would largely be conducted outside public scrutiny. Other likely consequences of the item veto would be an increase, possibly exponential, of presidential vetoes accompanied by extensive litigation. Critics maintain that states' experi-ence with the item veto, insofar as it may have relevance to the federal government, has been far from salutary. Conflict resolution, they argue, becomes more, not less, difficult; pressure to expand the scope of the item veto is virtually inevitable, and, as a consequence, political authority and accountability become further dispersed.

The line-item veto tends to be favored by presidents not so much for its observable and measurable impact but rather for the subtle influence and leverage it gives the chief executive during the long budgetary and appropriations processes. Congress, on the other hand, tends to be wary of the item veto in part because the Constitution does not permit the impact of the veto power, whether general or item, to be softened by extraconstitutional practices (e.g., bill recall procedures) used in the states. Thus, the item veto is seen by many as a process that would further rigidify the expenditure phase of the budgetary process.

Whatever else may be said about an item-veto amendment to the Constitution, it cannot be described as simple cosmetic surgery to correct a flaw made visible by institutional age. The only predictable aspect of giving the line-item veto power to the president is that it would have unpredictable consequences.

[*See also* Deferral; Impoundment; Rescission.]

BIBLIOGRAPHY

Moe, Ronald C. *Prospects for the Item Veto at the Federal Level: Lessons from the States.* 1988.
Spitzer, Robert J. *The Presidential Veto: Touchstone of the American Presidency.* 1988.

RONALD C. MOE

J

JACKSON, ANDREW (1767–1845), representative and senator from Tennessee, seventh president of the United States, strong advocate of democracy, vigorous opponent of nullification, secession, and the Bank of the United States. Jackson was born on 15 March 1767 in the Waxhaw Settlement, South Carolina, the son of Andrew and Elizabeth Hutchinson Jackson. His father died two weeks prior to his birth and he was raised by his mother with his two older brothers. His early education came under the tutelage of James White Stephenson, a Presbyterian minister.

Jackson left school at the age of thirteen, during the Revolutionary War, to join a regiment taking part in the Battle of Hanging Rock. He was captured by the British and interned in Camden, South Carolina, where he contracted smallpox. His mother won his release by assisting in an exchange of prisoners. Jackson was orphaned at the age of fourteen.

He lived with relatives for a few years and in 1784 decided to move to Salisbury, North Carolina, to study law with Spruce MacCay. He completed his legal training in the office of Colonel John Stokes and on 26 September 1787 was licensed to practice as an attorney in the several courts of pleas and quarter sessions in North Carolina. Offered the position of public prosecutor for the western district of the territory that is now Tennessee, Jackson headed west in the spring of 1788 and settled in Nashville, where he met and later married Rachel Donelson.

Having married into one of the territory's most prominent families, and with the support of William Blount, the territorial governor, he moved

ANDREW JACKSON. *PERLEY'S REMINISCENCES, VOL. 1*

swiftly up the social and political ladders. In 1795 he was elected a delegate to the constitutional convention that drew up Tennessee's first constitution prior to its admission into the Union as the sixteenth state. In 1796 he was elected Tennessee's sole representative to the U.S. House of Representatives, where he distinguished himself by being

BORN TO COMMAND.

OF VETO MEMORY.

HAD I BEEN CONSULTED.

KING ANDREW THE FIRST.

ANDREW JACKSON. Political cartoon depicting the president as a monarch in royal regalia, 1833.

one of the very few to vote against extending a tribute to President George Washington on the occasion of his farewell from office. He believed that Washington had dishonored the country by agreeing to the Jay Treaty with Great Britain. A Jeffersonian Republican, Jackson served on five House committees, chaired a select committee on claims, presented two petitions, introduced one resolution, made five speeches (mostly about western claims and problems with the Indians), and voted twenty-four times with the House majority out of a total of thirty-nine votes.

In 1797 Jackson was elected to the U.S. Senate, but he hated the brief time he spent there. Vice President Thomas Jefferson recalled that "his passions are terrible" and he could never speak because of "the rashness of his feelings." It is true that Jackson had a violent temper, but he frequently feigned anger to frighten his adversaries. He could be gentle and generous with family and friends, but those who opposed or disobeyed him, whether soldier, slave, or politician, felt the brunt of his wrath. He treated opponents as enemies.

Jackson's senatorial record for 1797 is undistinguished: he did not participate in debates; he chaired one committee; he introduced one bill; and he voted with the majority only thirteen times out of a total of thirty-four votes. He resigned his seat in 1798 to accept election as a judge on the Superior Court of Tennessee, the state's highest tribunal. He served in this office for six years but left little record of his accomplishments as a justice. He had extensive business interests, from Philadelphia to New Orleans, in tobacco, cotton, and horses, as well as slaves. Over the years he acquired a large plantation.

In 1802 Jackson was elected major general of the Tennessee militia, a position filled by the field officers of the three divisions within Tennessee. It was as a military commander that he found his true calling. When the Creek Indians attacked Fort Mims during the War of 1812, Blount, the governor of the state, summoned Jackson to lead the militia to put down the uprising. In a series of engagements, "Old Hickory," as his troops called him, defeated the Creeks at the Battle of Horseshoe Bend on 27 March 1814. He then proceeded to New Orleans in time to stop an invasion by the British from the Gulf of Mexico. The Battle of New Orleans, on 8 January 1815, made Jackson a permanent hero of the American people, for he proved to the world that the United States had the will and ability to successfully defend its freedom, even against Europe's most powerful nation. Jackson reinforced his popularity in 1818 by seizing Florida from Spain after he had been ordered to repel the attacks of Seminole Indians along the Alabama-Georgia frontier. Spain agreed to sell Florida to the United States, and Jackson became the first governor of the newly acquired territory.

Jackson's celebrated status around the country resulted in his unanimous nomination for the presidency by the Tennessee legislature on 20 July 1822. To advance his candidacy, he was elected to the U.S. Senate on that same date, a position he did not want but felt "compelled to accept." This time he conducted himself with a dignity and bearing befitting the office. He served on the Senate Foreign Relations Committee and chaired the Committee on Military Affairs. But he was not active in debate, nor did he initiate any important legislation. Whenever he was required to report the business of the Military Affairs Committee, he did so in short, staccato phrases. He delivered four speeches on the floor, none of which took more than a few minutes, dealing with fortifications and road construction. His voting record is noteworthy because he did not avoid controversial issues, such as internal improvements and the tariff, both of which he supported, even though he was a presidential candidate. He recorded his position on every question that required a vote.

Although Jackson won a plurality of electoral and popular votes in the presidential election of 1824, he failed to win the required majority, and the House of Representatives chose John Quincy Adams as president. Feeling himself cheated, he resigned from the Senate on 12 October 1825, returned to his home, and prepared for the next election. He won a tremendous victory over Adams in 1828.

Jackson served two terms as president (1829–1837) and dominated the Democratic party, through which he attempted to control Congress. He used his veto power more than all his predecessors combined, thereby forcing Congress to give him the legislation he wanted. His Maysville veto, opposing an extension of the national road within Kentucky, questioned the constitutionality of federally sponsored internal improvements. He faced stiff opposition in the Senate, where Henry Clay, Daniel Webster, and John C. Calhoun—the so-called Great Triumvirate—regularly denounced him as a dictator whose actions violated the Constitution. When Congress passed a bill to recharter the Bank of the United States for an additional twenty years, Jackson vetoed it, citing reasons the opposition found unacceptable. The Senate failed to override the veto, and Jackson won reelection to the presidency in 1832 largely on this issue. He then removed the government's deposits from the Bank of the United States and placed them in selected state banks. Clay introduced and won passage of two resolutions censuring the president and the secretary of the Treasury, something never done before or since. Jackson responded with a protest message in which he publicly declared himself the head of the government and the representative of the people, to whom he was responsible. Again the Great Triumvirate denounced his pretensions as a violation of the Constitution. The hostile Senate responded by rejecting many of his appointments, including Roger B. Taney as secretary of the Treasury, Andrew Stevenson as minister to Great Britain,

four appointees to the governing board of the Bank of the United States, and many others. Consequently, Jackson held off submitting nominations to the Senate as long as the law allowed. At one time a majority of the cabinet was unconfirmed, as well as a long list of ministers to foreign nations. Not until 1836, when Democratic strength in the Senate increased, was Jackson able to get his appointments approved, including Taney as chief justice, Amos Kendall as postmaster general, and Stevenson as minister to Great Britain. Jackson had better relations with the House because of its large Democratic majority, although he sometimes failed to get a Speaker elected whom he had approved.

Jackson succeeded in killing the Bank of the United States, removing the Five Civilized Tribes from the southern portion of the country, and limiting the number of appropriations for internal improvements. He paid the national debt and by executive order (Specie Circular) decreed that gold and silver were to be used for the purchase of public lands. When South Carolina nullified the tariffs of 1828 and 1832 and threatened secession, Jackson warned the people of South Carolina that "disunion by armed force is *treason*" and "nullification . . . means insurrection and war." Passage of the Compromise Tariff of 1833 prevented secession and civil war. At the conclusion of his two terms of office, Jackson retired to his plantation, where he died on 8 June 1845.

BIBLIOGRAPHY

Remini, Robert V. *Andrew Jackson and the Course of American Empire, 1767–1821.* 1977.
Remini, Robert V. *Andrew Jackson and the Course of American Freedom, 1822–1832.* 1981.
Remini, Robert V. *Andrew Jackson and the Course of American Democracy, 1833–1845.* 1984.
Schlesinger, Arthur M., Jr. *The Age of Jackson.* 1945.

ROBERT V. REMINI

JACKSON, HENRY M. (1912–1983), Democratic representative and senator from Washington. "Scoop" Jackson, who was elected to the U.S. House of Representatives from Washington's 2d Congressional District in 1940 and then to the U.S. Senate in 1952, was a proponent of organized labor, civil rights, military preparedness, and the Vietnam War. Jackson distrusted the policy of détente with the Soviet Union and coauthored the so-called Jackson-Vanik amendment, which denied most-favored-nation trading status to the Soviet

HENRY M. JACKSON.
OFFICE OF THE HISTORIAN OF THE U.S. SENATE

Union. He also strongly supported Israel and the rights of Jews living in the U.S.S.R.

Jackson was one of the first senators to oppose the anticommunist fearmongering of Wisconsin senator Joseph R. McCarthy. Jackson won a seat on the Armed Services Committee in 1956, eventually chairing the Subcommittee on Arms Control. An early supporter of the presidential aspirations of John F. Kennedy, Jackson was bitterly disappointed when Kennedy chose Lyndon B. Johnson rather than him as his running mate in 1960. A member and ultimately chairman of the Committee on Energy and Natural Resources, Jackson helped write the National Environmental Policy Act of 1960. Additionally, Jackson served on the Joint Atomic Energy Committee, where he favored the development of nuclear power, and the Select Committee on Intelligence. Jackson unsuccessfully ran for the Dem-

ocratic nomination for president in 1972 and again in 1976.

Jackson's ideological significance lies in his having combined a liberal position on domestic issues with a conservative position on national security and international relations. His example exerted an influence on the neoconservatives of the 1980s, including Jeanne Kirkpatrick and Richard Perle, the latter of whom had worked for Jackson as a legislative assistant.

BIBLIOGRAPHY

Ognibene, Peter J. *Scoop: The Life and Politics of Henry M. Jackson.* 1975.
Reeves, Richard. *Old Faces of 1976.* 1976.

JAMES A. THURBER

JACKSON-VANIK AMENDMENT.

Under pressure from American Jews, Congress in 1974 enacted legislation requiring the Soviet Union to relax restrictions on Jewish emigration to Israel as the price for receiving U.S. trade preferences. This amendment to the Trade Act of 1974 (P.L. 93-618) was sponsored by Sen. Henry M. Jackson (D-Wash.) and Rep. Charles A. Vanik (D-Ohio). It required the president to impose extra import tariffs and credit constraints on any communist country that denied citizens the right to emigrate freely. The president could waive the penalties, with Congress's approval, only by showing that the country was moving toward free emigration.

Both houses overwhelmingly supported the measure over the Nixon and Ford administrations' opposition. Secretary of State Henry A. Kissinger warned that the amendment would anger the Soviets, impair U.S.-U.S.S.R. détente, and possibly lead to an even more restrictive Soviet emigration policy. The Trade Act's final passage was delayed for months while Kissinger sought a compromise that would satisfy Congress and the Jewish community without alienating Soviet leaders. That effort failed, and his warning about the amendment's unintended consequences proved accurate.

The Soviets rejected the amendment's terms and, in addition, refused to implement an earlier trade agreement that had paved the way for improved U.S.-U.S.S.R. relations. Soviet Jewish emigration, which had grown from around two hundred in 1968 to some thirty-five thousand in 1973, sank below one thousand in 1976 and remained at a trickle for a decade.

The impasse between Soviet leaders and Jackson-

Vanik supporters was finally resolved during the decline of communism and the resultant lowering of travel barriers in the late 1980s. Jewish emigration soared to 180,000 in 1990. In response, President George Bush waived the Jackson-Vanik mandate in December of 1990. Granting most-favored-nation trade status to the former adversary, Bush closed the book on a congressional foreign policy initiative that had addressed a bad situation and made it worse.

BIBLIOGRAPHY

Drachman, Edward R. *Challenging the Kremlin: The Soviet Jewish Movement for Freedom, 1967–1990.* 1991.

Robson, John S. P. "Henry Jackson, the Jackson-Vanik Amendment, and Détente: Ideology, Ideas, and United States Foreign Policy in the Nixon Era." Ph.D. diss., University of Texas, Austin, 1989.

DONALD C. BACON

JAVITS, JACOB K. (1904–1986), Republican representative and senator from New York, defender of Congress's war power, and combative advocate for liberal causes. Jacob Koppel Javits was born and raised on the Lower East Side of New York City. After attending New York University Law School, he was admitted to the bar in 1927 and joined his brother's law firm. He began his political career in 1946, becoming the first Republican since 1923 to win a seat from the 21st Congressional District in New York City. Reelected three times, he spent eight years in the House of Representatives, where he served on the Foreign Affairs Committee and became chairman of the subcommittee on Foreign Economic Policy.

In 1954, Javits ran for attorney general of New York State and was the only statewide Republican candidate to win that year. Two years later, he won election to the U.S. Senate; his senatorial career was to last twenty-four years.

Although a junior member of the Senate, Javits was one of the leaders of the successful fight to pass the Civil Rights Act of 1957, the first such legislation in eighty years. Always a champion of liberal causes, Javits was one of the first members of Congress to introduce legislation to provide day care for children of working parents and was a leading advocate in 1957 of the National Defense Education Act, passed in 1958.

During the Vietnam War, Javits was the first member of Congress to question the right of the president to wage war without congressional approval. His efforts resulted in the passage of the War Powers Resolution, which gave Congress rather than the president the authority to commit U.S. armed forces overseas when a war had not been declared. Congress overrode President Richard M. Nixon's veto, and the resolution became law in 1973.

Javits was also the author of the Pension Reform Act of 1974. In 1978, he led the fight to pass the Age Discrimination in Employment Act Amendments, which raised the mandatory retirement age from sixty-five to seventy.

In 1980, while battling amyotrophic lateral sclerosis (Lou Gehrig's disease), Javits sought reelection as a Liberal party candidate after losing the Republican nomination to Alphonse D'Amato. D'Amato went on to defeat Javits in the general election.

BIBLIOGRAPHY

Javits, Jacob K. *Order of Battle: A Republican's Call to Reason.* 1964.

Javits, Jacob K., with Rafael Steinberg. *Javits: The Autobiography of a Public Man.* 1981.

MICHAEL P. KELLY

JAY'S TREATY. Jay's Treaty of 1794–1795 between the United States and Great Britain resolved a war crisis and settled long-standing problems involving both nations. Ratification and implementation of the treaty led to a major clash over Congress's role in the treaty-making process, while political conflict between Federalists and Democratic-Republicans over foreign policy accelerated the development of the two-party system.

The treaty, negotiated by President Washington's envoy, Supreme Court Chief Justice John Jay, and British foreign minister Lord Grenville, addressed violations of the Treaty of Paris of 1783 and commercial issues. Jay's Treaty, more favorable to Great Britain than to the United States, provided for British evacuation of the northwestern military posts and permitted American trade in India but severely restricted it in the British West Indies. Joint commissions were established to adjudicate disputes over debts, boundaries, and British seizures of American ships. Impressment of American seamen and neutral-nation trading rights were ignored.

Signed on 19 November 1794, the treaty was to be kept secret until the Senate could act, but hostile Republican senators leaked its terms. The Republican press fanned public furor against John Jay and

JOHN JAY. As Chief Justice of the United States. Engraving by H. B. Hall.   LIBRARY OF CONGRESS

British influence; the treaty did not guarantee maritime neutral rights, and southern planters failed to win compensation for British removal of slaves during the Revolution. Senate opposition, mostly from southern Republicans, could not prevent a 20 to 10 majority in favor of ratification.

President Washington delayed placing the treaty before the House until March 1796. Democratic-Republican representatives called on the president for documents relating to Jay's negotiations. This triggered a struggle that Federalist representative Fisher Ames described as a "fierce war." Washington refused to release the papers, asserting that it would "establish a dangerous precedent," thereby raising the issue of executive privilege.

The intense House debate dealt largely with the legislative-executive relationship with respect to foreign policy. Republican representatives, especially Albert Gallatin, attacked the treaty on constitutional grounds and asserted that the House, through its power over appropriations, had a basic right to consider the expediency of executing a treaty. Despite James Madison's cogent argument that the House had the right to obtain executive documents in order to judge the viability of Jay's

Treaty, the Republican majority melted away. Federalists mobilized 10,200 pro-treaty petitioners, deluging Congress with demands to support the treaty, and by 23 April Republicans had only an eight- or nine-vote majority.

The climax of the House debate came on 28 April when Fisher Ames overcame a debilitating illness to present a brilliant defense of Jay's Treaty, condemning exaggerated Republican claims of the powers of the House and portraying the terrors of a British-incited Indian war, which he predicted would follow rejection of the treaty. Speaker of the House Frederick A. C. Muhlenberg broke a tie vote to support the treaty, and on 30 April the crisis ended with a 51 to 48 victory for the pro-treaty forces. Jay's Treaty can be seen as a vivid test of partisan power in Congress.

BIBLIOGRAPHY

Bernhard, Winfred E. A. *Fisher Ames: Federalist and Statesman, 1758–1808.* 1965.

Combs, Gerald A. *The Jay Treaty: Political Background of the Founding Fathers.* 1970.

Sharp, James Roger. *American Politics in the Early Republic: The New Nation in Crisis.* 1993.

WINFRED E. A. BERNHARD

JEFFERSON, THOMAS (1743–1826), vice president (1797–1801) and third president (1801–1809) of the United States. Jefferson established important precedents for the coming to power of an opposition party, helped prevent the destruction of the national judiciary, doubled the size of the United States by obtaining the Louisiana Territory from France, provided a process by which the newly acquired territory became self-governing, and brought about the adoption of his ill-fated embargo policy.

Jefferson never was elected to Congress, but as vice president under John Adams he was presiding officer of the Senate. The position turned out to be mainly ceremonial. His most significant accomplishment as vice president was in the area of legislative procedure: Jefferson ran the Senate in an unusually fair, systematic, and efficient manner and compiled the *Manual of Parliamentary Practice* (1801), which continues to influence the operations not only of the Senate but also the House of Representatives and many state legislatures.

During his tenure as vice president, Jefferson assumed active leadership of the Jeffersonian Republican party. Operating behind the scenes, he drafted

THOMAS JEFFERSON. As secretary of State. Medallion portrait in a mural by Constantino Brumidi on the wall of the President's Room, Senate wing of the Capitol.

LIBRARY OF CONGRESS

the Kentucky Resolutions of 1798, protesting the Alien and Sedition Acts, and circulated political tracts that systematically spelled out his opposition to Alexander Hamilton's financial plan and the Federalist party's anti-French bias. He also formed an organization on both the national and state levels to support his bid for the presidency in 1800. Yet, like most members of his generation Jefferson did not really believe that the existence of a permanent, organized, legitimate opposition was a good thing. Instead, he justified his leadership of the Jeffersonian Republicans on the grounds that Federalist policies were undermining the Constitution and destroying the republican heritage of the Revolution. After his victory in 1800, Jefferson generally followed a policy of conciliation toward the Federalists that came to fruition in the period of one-party rule, known as the Era of Good Feelings, that followed the end of the War of 1812.

As president Jefferson generally got what he wanted from Congress, but it took a substantial amount of behind-the-scenes maneuvering and personal involvement in legislative politics to achieve his aims. Many members of the Jeffersonian Republican party retained the fear, inherited from the days of the Revolution, of undue executive influence. An important source of the problem was that the administration lacked an effective spokesman to represent its interests in Congress. Early in the nineteenth century, congressional leaders were neither elected nor chosen on the basis of seniority. Instead, the positions went either to those who were assertive or who had the confidence of the administration. During the 1790s, when he was a leader of the opposition, Jefferson worked most closely with James Madison and Albert Gallatin, both of whom served in the House of Representatives. When Jefferson became president, he gave them cabinet appointments. This meant that in 1801 John Randolph of Virginia, chairman of the Ways and Means Committee, became the most important member of Congress. Jefferson tried to develop a working relationship with him. But Randolph was an independent and combative individual, hostile to executive prerogatives, and at odds with Jefferson on a number of policy questions. In particular, he wanted to see Hamilton's entire financial program dismantled, Federalist influence in the national judiciary eliminated, and fundamental changes made in the Constitution. Although Jefferson had some sympathy for these demands, he opted instead for a policy of moderation and reconciliation. As Jefferson put it, "What is practicable must often control what is pure theory."

To influence congressional outcomes Jefferson had to work around Randolph, especially in his first administration. He quietly enlisted individual members of Congress to work behind the scenes with him to obtain the adoption of specific pieces of legislation. In a number of cases, Jefferson himself drafted the bills that he wanted to be passed. He encouraged trusted supporters to run for Congress, among them Caesar A. Rodney of Delaware and Wilson C. Nicholas of Virginia, and his Virginia sons-in-law John W. Eppes and Thomas M. Randolph. Jefferson frequently entertained members of Congress from both parties in small groups to get a better sense of what was happening in Congress and perhaps to influence the proceedings. He made it a rule to consult with individual members before he used his extensive powers of patronage or made appointments in their local districts. Finally, Jefferson used his cabinet to influence congressional developments. Gallatin, the secretary of the Treasury, was the most active in this regard. He maintained informal contacts with many legislators, constantly providing advice and information for friends of the administration, making recommendations for changes in specific pieces of legislation, and, like the president, actually drafting a number of the bills that were adopted. Because Jefferson's popularity remained high with the voters until the last year of his second term, getting along with the president clearly had its advantages for most members of Congress.

Jefferson was especially successful in the area of domestic legislation. Although he accepted Hamilton's system for funding the national debt and did not try to repeal the charter of the Bank of the United States, he, with Congress's help, sharply reduced expenditures, cut internal taxes, and started to pay off the national debt. He also took the country in a very different direction from the Federalists in terms of economic development. He rejected their reliance on U.S. participation in the Atlantic economy and their belief in the all-importance of the mercantile and financial communities. Instead, he emphasized western expansion, a cheap land policy, the primacy of the agricultural community, and the growth of the internal economy of the United States. Jefferson's approach to U.S. economic development was much more popular than Hamilton's, because it recognized the overwhelmingly rural nature of American society and its enthusiasm for the growth of the West.

Jefferson's leadership played a key role in containing the struggle over the federal judiciary, which dominated his first administration. Like most Republicans he was concerned about Federalist domination of the national court system, where judges held their positions during good behavior. He was especially annoyed at the rash of "midnight appointments" John Adams had made under the Judiciary Act of 1801. But he was inclined to move cautiously and did not support those Republicans who wished to eliminate the federal judiciary and who favored a broad interpretation of the impeachment clause of the Constitution to allow the removal of judges for political reasons. In particular, he did not want the attack on the judiciary to spill over into an assault on the Constitution itself. Instead, Jefferson brought about the repeal of the Judiciary Act of 1801, which had increased the numbers of federal judgeships and expanded the jurisdiction of the circuit courts, and reinstituted the federal court system that had been created in 1789. Nor did Jefferson overreact to the Supreme Court's decision in *Marbury v. Madison* (1803), although he did not like its tone. He ignored it because he had gotten his way: in its decision the Court did not order the administration to deliver the commissions to Adams's appointees. To be sure, Jefferson helped initiate impeachment proceedings against John Pickering, an alcoholic and insane district court judge from New Hampshire, and lobbied behind the scenes for his conviction. But he did not lobby Congress or enforce party discipline in the impeachment proceedings against Associate Justice Samuel Chase of the Supreme Court, thus allowing Republican senators to vote for acquittal in 1805, which brought to an end the Republican assault on the federal judiciary.

Jefferson had an important legislative success when he convinced Congress to adopt the Louisiana Government Act of 1804. He strongly believed that the inhabitants of the newly acquired territory lacked the experience to self-govern successfully. A delay would therefore be necessary before they could be given their full political rights. To this end, Jefferson drafted an act that gave the president the power to appoint most key local officials (including the governor, the secretary, and the judges) and the governor the power to appoint a legislature. Opposition came from the Federalists for partisan reasons but also from many Republicans who viewed the measure as tending toward the despotic. Jefferson, however, refused to back down on his opposition to immediate self-government for Louisiana. Working closely but clandestinely with Sen. John Breckinridge of Kentucky and other trusted members of Congress, he made some minor concessions but retained the key parts of his bill, which was adopted with little change in March 1804. Less than a year later, convinced that sufficient progress had been made, Jefferson helped initiate a more liberalized plan for self-government in Louisiana.

Congress did not give Jefferson everything he wanted. A number of the president's nominees for appointments were turned down by the Senate, but most were approved. He also was unable to convince Congress to adopt legislation creating a uniform national militia system. And he failed to get an amendment to the Constitution authorizing the federal government to undertake a national plan of internal improvements that would include the building of roads, canals, and various educational, scientific, and literary institutions. Jefferson suffered a major defeat in 1804 and 1805 on the Yazoo controversy. This involved a series of land frauds by the Georgia legislature in 1795 (overturned by a succeeding legislature when it was found out) in which large amounts of land, in what are today Alabama and Mississippi, were sold to unsuspecting second and third parties. The matter became a federal issue when Georgia transferred its western claims, along with the attendant legal problems, to the federal government in 1802. Jefferson appointed a special commission, made up of his cabinet and other important advisers, and they recommended a compromise that Jefferson supported. The measure was killed by Congress, because it sought to protect the interests of speculators. It was an embarrassing defeat for the administration, and it came at the hands of Randolph and other purists in the Jeffersonian Republican party who believed that Jefferson had already made too many compromises with the Federalists.

The Jefferson administration's most spectacular achievement in foreign affairs was the Louisiana Purchase. The president at first had reservations, because the Constitution, which he tended to interpret strictly, did not provide for the acquisition of foreign territory. He therefore urged that a constitutional amendment, granting this power, be adopted. But his closest advisers in the cabinet and in Congress warned that this would take too much time and that Napoléon Bonaparte might change his mind and withdraw the offer. Although he remained deeply concerned about the constitutional issues involved, Jefferson proved flexible because of the immense advantages of the acquisition, and he submitted the Louisiana Purchase to the Senate for its approval. It quickly and easily passed by a vote of 27 to 7. Only the New England Federalists opposed it, fearful that America's continued development in a southern and western direction would reduce even further the little influence they had left.

Jefferson was much less successful in other areas of foreign affairs. He never adequately came to terms with the renewal of war between France and England in 1803. Preoccupied by domestic concerns, he failed to pay sufficient attention to developments in Europe. Then, when circumstances demanded some kind of action on his part, he asserted a doctrine of neutral rights that claimed for the United States the right to trade unhindered with all belligerents. But England and France, now engaged in what amounted to total war, ignored this claim. Jefferson responded by asking Congress, which was almost always deferential to his requests on foreign policy issues, to adopt a nonimportation law on a number of significant items in 1806. But the law did not have the effect he desired, and he

quickly suspended it. Then, in 1807, a British warship fired on a U.S. naval vessel and seized several seamen. Jefferson resisted the popular outcry for war. Instead, he sought and quickly got the Embargo Act of 1807, which virtually eliminated all commerce with foreign nations.

It soon became clear that Jefferson had badly miscalculated. The embargo hurt the United States more than it did Great Britain, its primary target. Domestic opposition became intense and widespread. The embargo proved virtually unenforceable because of heavy smuggling, particularly along the Canadian-American border. The economic difficulties created by the embargo led to a Federalist revival in New England and in a number of the Mid-Atlantic states, and this, along with considerable constituency pressure for its repeal, weakened and divided the Republicans in Congress. In the end, Jefferson recognized that his embargo policy could not be sustained, and he agreed to allow Congress to repeal the act in early 1809. Dispirited and weary of criticism, he failed to develop an alternative policy, rationalizing that he did not want to limit the options of his successor.

Despite the failure of his embargo policy, Jefferson was a strong and successful leader of Congress. He effectively isolated his opponents, the Federalists and the Old Republicans around Randolph, and kept them disunited. He never had to use his veto power. Among other things, he was the first president to accomplish the difficult job of combining the presidency with being a party leader. The policies he advocated, and that Congress adopted, profoundly affected the future development of the United States.

BIBLIOGRAPHY

Cunningham, Noble. *The Process of Government under Jefferson*. 1978.
Ellis, Richard E. *The Jeffersonian Crisis: Courts and Politics in the Young Republic*. 1971.
Johnstone, Robert M. *Jefferson and the Presidency: Leadership in the Young Republic*. 1978.
McDonald, Forrest. *The Presidency of Thomas Jefferson*. 1976.

RICHARD E. ELLIS

JEFFERSONIAN REPUBLICANS. The Jeffersonian Republican party emerged early in George Washington's first administration (1789– 1793). The party was led by Thomas Jefferson and James Madison, who opposed Alexander Hamilton's financial plan, which mainly consisted of the funding of the national debt, the assumption of the state debts, the chartering of the first Bank of the United States, and the levying of a variety of taxes. Foreign policy and personality conflicts deepened the division during Washington's second administration (1793–1797). Hamilton and his Federalist followers favored an alliance with Great Britain in the wars of the French Revolution, while Madison in Congress and Jefferson in the cabinet assailed this policy; Madison and Jefferson were anti-English and believed the United States should live up to its treaty obligations with France. With the exception of the Third Congress (1793–1795), when the Republicans gained control of the House of Representatives, they were a minority party throughout the 1790s.

When Washington retired from politics in 1796, the first contested election for the presidency took place. Jefferson was the standard-bearer for the Republicans, but Federalist candidate John Adams won by 71 electoral votes to 68. Jefferson did, however, become vice president (1797–1801) and presided over the Senate, because the Constitution (before the Twelfth Amendment) required that the vice presidency go to the person with the second-highest number of electoral votes. From this position, with the help of Albert Gallatin in the House, Jefferson continued to lead the Republican opposition.

The Republicans gained control of Congress in the election of 1800, which also saw Jefferson capture the presidency. His support was located mainly in the areas south of New England and consisted of former Anti-Federalists, planters, artisans and skilled laborers, small backcountry farmers, and commercial and trading interests who opposed the Federalist financial system. From that point on, despite sharp internal differences over such issues as whether to repudiate Hamilton's domestic policies, what to do about Federalist control of the national judiciary, the diplomatic problems leading up to and the actual fighting of the War of 1812, the need for a protective tariff, the chartering of the second Bank of the United States, and questions about the constitutionality and desirability of a federal program of internal improvements, the Republicans retained their hegemony over Congress during the administrations of Jefferson (1801–1809), Madison (1809–1817), and James Monroe (1817–1825).

Perhaps the most important function of the party was the congressional nominating caucus. Consisting of Republicans from both houses of Congress, it selected the party's presidential candidate. The practice started with the election of 1800 and continued through 1824. The congressional nominating caucus played a key role in 1808 in selecting Madison over Monroe, despite opposition by a number of important Old Republicans led by John Randolph, John Taylor, Nathaniel Macon, and George Clinton, who feared Madison's constitutional nationalism and believed he had not been sufficiently extreme in his opposition to the Hamiltonian-inspired financial system after Jefferson's election. Monroe received the caucus nomination in 1816, defeating William H. Crawford, the candidate of the younger, more aggressive members of the party, by a vote of 65 to 54. Monroe went on to an easy victory in the presidential election of 1816, because the Federalists were no longer a viable opposition party on the national level. Crawford served eight years as Monroe's secretary of the Treasury and his heir apparent. But by 1824 when he received the caucus nomination, it did not mean very much. By then the Jeffersonian Republican party had begun to disintegrate from the pressures created by the panic of 1819 and the depression that followed, the states' rights reaction to the nationalist decisions of the U.S. Supreme Court, the sectional debate over slavery and the Missouri Compromise, and the emergence of Andrew Jackson as a national political figure. By 1828 the Jeffersonian Republicans had irrevocably split into two different parties: the National Republicans, who eventually became the Whigs, and the Jacksonian Democrats.

The Jeffersonian Republicans were sometimes referred to as Democratic-Republicans or simply Republicans. There is no connection between the Jeffersonian Republicans and the Republican party that emerged in 1854. There are, however, important organizational and intellectual links between the Jeffersonian Republicans and the Democratic party of today, although they have come to differ sharply on such issues as the role of the central government in the economy.

[*See also* Anti-Federalists; Federalists.]

BIBLIOGRAPHY

Cunningham, Noble E., Jr. "The Jeffersonian Republican Party." In vol. 1 of *History of U.S. Political Parties*. Edited by Arthur M. Schlesinger, Jr. 4 vols. 1973.
White, Leonard. *The Jeffersonians*. 1951.
Young, James S. *The Washington Community*. 1966.

RICHARD E. ELLIS

JEFFERSON'S MANUAL. Thomas Jefferson's *Manual of Parliamentary Practice* is a treatise on parliamentary procedure in the English parliamentary tradition. Jefferson completed the Manual

JEFFERSON'S MANUAL. Page of the original draft of the *Manual of Parliamentary Practice*, published in 1801.

son's lifetime, the Manual was also published in French, Spanish, and German editions.

Pertinent sections of Jefferson's Manual are today the foundation of many House procedures. In fact, pursuant to House Rule XLII, adopted in 1837, the House adheres to the rules of parliamentary practice contained in Jefferson's Manual in all cases where they are applicable and where they are not inconsistent with the standing rules and orders. The Senate has no similar rule, nor does the presiding officer of the Senate, in modern practice, cite the Manual to support rulings of the chairman. Because of its standing as a cornerstone of House procedure, the House prints Jefferson's Manual with the House Rules every Congress in a publication called *Constitution, Jefferson's Manual, and Rules of the House of Representatives.*

BIBLIOGRAPHY

Howell, Wilbur Samuel, ed. *Jefferson's Parliamentary Writings*. 1988.

U.S. House of Representatives. *Constitution, Jefferson's Manual, and Rules of the House of Representatives, 103d Congress*. Compiled by William Holmes Brown. 102d Cong., 2d sess., 1992. H. Doc. 102–405.

MUFTIAH McCARTIN

JOHNSON, ANDREW (1808–1875), representative and senator from Tennessee, governor of Tennessee, seventeenth president of the United States, became embroiled in a controversy with Congress over reconstruction policy that resulted in his impeachment. Born in Raleigh, North Carolina, in poverty and lacking formal education, Johnson moved to Greeneville, Tennessee, in 1826. He quickly became involved in local politics and served in the state legislature before moving to the U.S. House for five terms beginning in 1843. By the late 1830s, Johnson was a staunch Jacksonian Democrat with a fiercely independent and populist streak, remarkable demagogic political skills, and abiding faith in states' rights and a strictly interpreted Constitution.

During his service in the House, Johnson generally voted with fellow southerners. His special interest was a homestead bill that he first sponsored in 1846 and doggedly pursued until the Republicans finally enacted it during the Civil War. He left Washington in 1853 to serve two terms as governor of Tennessee; in 1857 the state legislature elected him to the Senate. He denounced radicals on both sides for precipitating the sectional crisis of the late 1850s. But when secession came, maintaining the

in its earliest form in 1800 and first published it in 1801. The Manual, the first treatise of its kind in the United States, is based on Jefferson's *Parliamentary Pocket-Book*, which he began preparing in the 1760s. Jefferson relied heavily on the *Pocket-Book* while presiding over Senate proceedings from 1797 to 1801, calling it his "pillar." Yet he also found the *Pocket-Book* inadequate to answer the many parliamentary situations that arose, and he thus embarked on drafting the more complete Manual.

Jefferson's original intention was to give the Manual, in handwritten form, to the Senate at the end of his vice presidency to show what his own standards as presiding officer had been and to suggest guidelines to be followed in the future. He later decided to have the Manual published. During Jeffer-

ANDREW JOHNSON.   LIBRARY OF CONGRESS

Union proved to be more important than slavery to Johnson, and he was the only southerner from a seceded state to remain in the Senate.

Courted by the Republicans, Johnson accepted President Abraham Lincoln's request to serve as the military governor of Union-occupied Tennessee in 1862. With Lincoln's influence, Johnson reluctantly came to support emancipation, but he maintained his deep-seated belief in the innate inferiority of blacks. In an effort to broaden the party's appeal to War Democrats, he was chosen to be Lincoln's running mate on the National Union (Republican) ticket in 1864, and was thus thrust into the presidency when Lincoln was assassinated in April 1865.

Although Johnson initially seemed to be in accord with congressional Republicans on handling the defeated South, it soon became clear that he viewed reconstruction as an executive responsibility and was interested in a quick and lenient restoration. Beginning in late May, with Congress out of session, Johnson outlined his own plan in proclamations of amnesty and reconstruction. He required southerners to take an oath of future loyalty to vote and hold office, although high-ranking ex-Confederate leaders and wealthy southerners had to appeal to him personally for pardons. For every state that had not established wartime Unionist governments, Johnson appointed a provisional governor to register loyal voters and call a constitutional convention to abolish slavery, nullify the state's ordinance of secession, and repudiate the Confederate war debt. Following new elections, the "restored" legislatures were to ratify the Thirteenth Amendment, which abolished slavery. Most states had completed the process to Johnson's satisfaction by the time Congress came back into session in December 1865.

Congressional Republicans, moderate and Radical alike, watched with growing unrest as some southern states balked at fulfilling even Johnson's modest requirements. Thanks to Johnson's liberal pardoning policy, ex-Confederates filled many political positions, and unrepentant southern legislators passed black codes that severely restricted the freed people's liberties. Distressed about the situation, Congress refused to seat the southern representatives and senators.

The Republican majority initially hoped to work with the president to offer more protection to the freed slaves. Johnson, however, stubbornly resisted even moderate congressional proposals on strict-constructionist grounds, and he insisted that the blacks' future was best left to southern whites acting at the state level. When Congress passed a bill extending the life of the Freedmen's Bureau in February 1866, Johnson responded with a sharply worded veto and harshly denounced leading congressional Radicals as traitors. In March he vetoed a moderate-sponsored civil rights bill as an unconstitutional extension of federal powers, but Congress overrode his veto (the first override on a major bill in American history) and later did the same in passing a new Freedmen's Bureau bill. After Congress submitted the proposed Fourteenth Amendment as a tentative plan of reconstruction, only Republican-controlled Tennessee ratified it; the other ex-Confederate states, with Johnson's encouragement, turned it down.

Johnson attempted to rally northern support for his reconstruction policy in his famous "swing around the circle" tour in late summer 1866, but the North returned an even stronger anti-Johnson majority to Congress in the fall elections. The breach with Johnson widened beyond repair, and Congress took full control of the reconstruction process in December. During Johnson's remaining years in office, his relationship with Congress was a sequence of vetoes and veto overrides of major legislation, including four acts defining the final congressional plan of reconstruction and a Tenure of Office Act requiring Senate approval for Johnson's removal of appointed officials.

Led by Radical Republicans in the House, efforts to find grounds to impeach Johnson as an impediment to reconstruction foundered because of insufficient evidence. In August 1867, however, Johnson suspended Secretary of War Edwin M. Stanton, the solitary remaining Radical voice in his cabinet, and named Gen. Ulysses S. Grant as an interim replacement. When the Senate refused to concur with Stanton's suspension in January 1868, Johnson replaced Stanton with Gen. Lorenzo Thomas, in violation of the Tenure of Office Act. The House immediately voted (126 to 47) to impeach, and then formulated eleven articles of impeachment centering on Johnson's defiance of the Tenure of Office Act and impeding the will of Congress. His trial before the Senate began on 13 March; on 16 May that body acquitted him by failing to cast a two-thirds vote in support of the catch-all Article 11. Ten days later, after similar votes on Articles 2 and 3, the Senate abandoned the process.

Johnson remained obstructionist and obstinate to the end. Even after leaving the presidency in March 1869, he fought congressional reconstruction and was accorded some retribution when Tennessee returned him to the Senate in March 1875. He served for a brief period before dying of a stroke on 31 July of that year. Although Johnson was in many ways a shrewd and successful politician, his inability to grow beyond his Jacksonian background and his resolute refusal to work with the Republican moderates on reconstruction doomed his presidency to failure.

BIBLIOGRAPHY

Benedict, Michael Les. *The Impeachment and Trial of Andrew Johnson.* 1973.

Bowen, David Warren. *Andrew Johnson and the Negro.* 1989.

McKitrick, Eric. *Andrew Johnson and Reconstruction.* 1960.

Trefousse, Hans L. *Andrew Johnson: A Biography.* 1989.

TERRY L. SEIP

JOHNSON, HIRAM W. (1866–1945), progressive Republican senator from California and prominent opponent of the League of Nations. In 1910, Hiram Warren Johnson won the Republican nomi-

nation for governor of California in the state's first direct primary. He ran on a single issue: kicking the Southern Pacific Railroad out of the state's politics. In 1912, Johnson was Theodore Roosevelt's running mate on the losing ticket of the Progressive (Bull Moose) party. Four years later, Woodrow Wilson carried California by less than 4,000 votes, but Johnson won the first of five elections to the Senate by a margin of almost 300,000 votes.

A firm believer in democracy, the balance of power, and the Senate as an institution coequal with the presidency, Johnson eventually clashed with five of the six presidents who served during his twenty-eight years in the Senate. He was too ill in his final year to clash with Truman. His first vote as senator in 1917 was to support Wilson's declaration of war. He noted at the time that "the first casualty when war comes is truth" and vigorously fought the president's attacks on free speech at home. After the war, when Johnson saw Wilson violate the principles of open diplomacy, he followed

HIRAM W. JOHNSON. As progressive candidate for the Republican presidential nomination, c. 1924. Johnson was known as the "poor" candidate because he was not backed by moneyed interests.   LIBRARY OF CONGRESS

in Wilson's wake as the chief executive toured the country to garner support for his ideals. But it was Johnson—the most vigorous orator of the "irreconcilables" in the Senate—who packed the halls and stirred the people to defeat U.S. entry into the League of Nations. Worried that too great a focus on Europe meant overlooking the rise of Japan, Johnson became an advocate of a stronger navy and merchant marine.

The three leading contenders for the 1920 Republican presidential nomination asked Johnson to accept the vice presidency. He declined. Each of them, including the successful candidate, Warren G. Harding, died within four years. In 1924, Johnson began a half-hearted effort to challenge President Calvin Coolidge that ended in the California presidential primary, which Coolidge delegates won. It was Johnson's only defeat in his native state.

Urged by fellow former Bull Mooser Harold L. Ickes to challenge President Herbert Hoover in 1932, Johnson declined and ultimately endorsed Democratic presidential nominee Franklin D. Roosevelt. Offered the secretaryship of the Interior by an appreciative Roosevelt, Johnson rejected it and recommended Ickes for the post; Roosevelt complied. Johnson enthusiastically supported the domestic New Deal. In 1936, illness kept him out of the campaign, but he cast an absentee ballot for Roosevelt. However, the president's Court-packing attempt; his seeming quest to be, in Johnson's words, "an absolute dictator"; and his desire for a third term drove Johnson to support Wendell Willkie in 1940.

During his Senate career, Johnson diligently protected California agricultural interests against foreign competition. In 1926, he steered the authorization of the Boulder Canyon Reclamation Project (Hoover Dam) through the Senate over the objections of the private power interests. As a key member of the Foreign Relations Committee, Johnson advocated a neutral foreign policy to keep the United States out of European wars. The Johnson Debt Default Act of 1934, reflecting his ongoing wariness of international bankers, prohibited nations owing money to the United States from defaulting and selling bonds and securities in this country.

Ten days before Johnson's death on 6 August 1945, the Senate approved the United Nations Charter, 89 to 2. True to his isolationist principles, Johnson sent word from the hospital that he would have opposed joining the U.N.

BIBLIOGRAPHY

Burke, Robert E., ed. *The Diary Letters of Hiram Johnson, 1917–1945.* 7 vols. 1983.

Fitzpatrick, John James. *Senator Hiram W. Johnson: A Life History, 1866–1945.* 1976. Microfilm.

Levine, Lawrence W. "The 'Diary' of Hiram Johnson . . ." *American Heritage*, August 1969, 64–76.

Weatherson, Michael A., and Hal Bochin. *Hiram Johnson: A Bio-Bibliography.* 1988.

STEPHEN HORN

JOHNSON, LYNDON B. (1908–1973), Democratic representative and senator from Texas, minority and majority leader of the Senate, vice president, thirty-sixth president of the United States. Born on 27 August 1908, Lyndon Baines Johnson spent his childhood on an impoverished Texas hill-country farm near the banks of the Perdenales River. Lyndon's parents, Rebekah and Sam Johnson, sparked their son's lifelong interest in politics. While Rebekah devoted much of her free time to reading biographies of governors and presidents and to discussions of politics and ideas, Sam Johnson became a direct participant in the political process, serving as a member of the Texas house of representatives intermittently over ten years. Lyndon's enthusiasm for politics manifested itself during his years at Southwest Texas State Teachers College, where he participated in student government and became one of the most skilled members of the debating team.

In the House. Although he did not become a member of the House of Representatives until 1937, Johnson began his illustrious congressional career in 1931 as a secretary to Texas representative Richard M. Kleberg. But Johnson was no ordinary secretary. Working for an often absent congressman, he quickly took control of Kleberg's office, handling constituent requests, contacting federal agencies, establishing relations with other members of Congress, and sometimes determining Kleberg's vote on New Deal legislation. In September 1934, Johnson met Claudia Alta (Lady Bird) Taylor; on 17 November, they married, forging a relationship that would last until his death. The next year, President Franklin D. Roosevelt appointed him head of the Texas division of the National Youth Administration.

In May 1937, after Rep. James Buchanan from Texas's 10th Congressional District died, Johnson declared his candidacy for the seat. He succeeded in distinguishing himself from his opponents by his unqualified support of Roosevelt, who was much admired in the district, which included Austin. This support included his backing of Roosevelt's controversial plan to pack the Supreme Court with justices favorable to his New Deal reform programs. With Postmaster General James Farley and Roosevelt's son, Elliott, quietly boosting Johnson's candidacy, the young politician from Blanco, Texas, defeated his older, more seasoned opponents with a 28-percent plurality.

As a freshman congressman, Johnson wasted little time in establishing himself as a shrewd political operator eager to advance his own career while serving the needs of his constituents. President Roosevelt interceded with House leaders to secure Johnson a seat on the House Naval Affairs Committee. Impressed with Johnson's drive and determination, the president also gave him access to powerful administration officials.

Soon after his arrival in Washington, Johnson established equally strong ties to members of Congress. He convinced House leaders that he was a reliable Democrat and an effective legislator. Rep. Carl Vinson (D-Ga.), chair of the House Naval Affairs Committee, and newly elected Speaker of the House Sam Rayburn (D-Tex.) became important supporters.

Johnson's unwavering support of President Roosevelt during his first two terms in the House and his strong ties to senior House leaders allowed him effectively to address the needs of his district. A firm believer in the measured use of government to alleviate human suffering, Johnson secured loans for farmers who had no collateral, helped provide federal funds for paving farm-to-market roads, and played a role in starting a long-term relief program for farmers suffering from declining cotton prices. Johnson also helped secure for his district millions of dollars in Works Project Administration grants for, among other things, federal buildings, school renovations, and public health services. In addition, he enabled Austin to become one of the first cities to receive federal money for the construction of low-income housing under the U.S. Housing Authority. Perhaps most important, Johnson persuaded President Roosevelt and Texas municipalities to provide public power and rural electrification to south-central Texas in the hope of raising living standards for hill country inhabitants still without basic electricity.

Always careful to avoid identification with the more liberal elements in the House so as to retain his seat, Johnson nevertheless worked behind the scenes to help disadvantaged Texans and minorities obtain a larger share of New Deal largess. Although, for example, Johnson voted with his southern colleagues against 1940s civil rights measures, he worked quietly with the administration to ensure that black farmers received small loans from the Farm Security Administration and to include blacks in provisions of the 1938 Agricultural Adjustment Act.

In 1940, when President Roosevelt feared the Democrats would lose their House majority, he appointed Johnson unofficial chair of the Democratic Congressional Campaign Committee. Working around the clock to raise money, win endorsements for congressional candidates, and secure federally funded projects for incumbents' districts, Johnson surpassed all expectations when, on election day, the Democratic party actually gained three seats in the House.

Having always set his sights on higher office, Johnson jumped at the opportunity to run for the U.S. Senate in 1941. When senior Texas senator Morris Sheppard died, Johnson ran in a special election against three better known politicians, including Texas governor W. Lee ("Pappy") O'Daniel. Well financed by Brown & Root, a Texas construction company that Johnson had helped win federal contracts, Johnson violated campaign spending laws through excessive spending. He preached support for Roosevelt, national unity, and military preparedness and hired a radio personality and a traveling road show to help him win the hotly contested race. Unofficially Johnson had five thousand more votes than Governor O'Daniel. However, Texas beer and liquor interests were eager to see O'Daniel, a supporter of prohibition, leave Austin for Washington; therefore, they stole the election from Johnson by having ballot boxes stuffed in East Texas.

In 1945, Roosevelt, Johnson's longtime ally, died. As World War II came to a close, the country turned more conservative. Johnson now identified himself with southern antilabor, anti–civil rights, and anticommunist sentiment in preparation for another statewide race. From 1945 to 1948, he voted with conservative members of Congress against antilynching and anti–poll tax legislation, against bills granting federal authority over tidelands oil, and for the Taft-Hartley bill, which limited the power of labor unions. But while Johnson adopted conservative positions on such highly visible issues, he remained staunchly liberal on matters that were less controversial in Texas.

In the Senate. In 1948, Johnson again ran for the U.S. Senate. His principal opponent, Texas governor Coke Stevenson, campaigned on a strongly anticommunist platform that also emphasized less government, lower taxes, and states' rights. Johnson countered by campaigning in a helicopter and denouncing Stevenson as a do-nothing, old-style, parochial politician. Remembering his defeat in 1941, Johnson had his campaign personnel scrutinize county ballot boxes to prevent opposition tampering. At the same time, Johnson's campaign used county bosses to manipulate election returns in Johnson's favor. The final tally gave Johnson an eight-to-seven-vote victory, and with it the nickname "Landslide Lyndon."

Johnson quickly established himself in the Senate as a national figure who could effectively serve the needs of his constituents and the nation at large. On civil rights, federal control of oil refineries, and the communist threat, he sided with his Texas and southern counterparts, calling the first two issues matters better left to the states and describing the third as a grave and menacing danger. When the Korean War broke out in 1950, Johnson presided over a Senate subcommittee designed to increase the efficiency of the United States' war machine. The subcommittee not only advanced the war effort but also served Johnson's political ambitions, winning him favorable national press and enhancing his status within the Democratic party. In 1951, Senate colleagues elected Johnson party whip.

During his first six-year term, Johnson's conservatism was balanced by his efforts to preserve and expand liberal New Deal economic programs, such as Social Security and unemployment compensation. In 1953, after a number of prominent Democratic senators lost their seats, Johnson won election as Democratic minority leader. A moderate striving to balance the concerns of conservative and liberal Democrats, he stressed and generally achieved party harmony. After winning reelection in 1954, Johnson worked behind the scenes to orchestrate the downfall of Sen. Joseph R. McCarthy (R-Wis.). McCarthy faltered after Johnson persuaded ABC television to broadcast the senator's unseemly interrogation of U.S. Army personnel in the Army-McCarthy hearings.

Majority Leader. In 1954, the Democrats won a two-vote majority in the Senate, and Johnson was elevated to majority leader. Although that position was then seen as a dead-end job for aspiring politicians, Johnson turned it into a powerful office. As a moderate southern Democrat, he effectively bal-

"THE BIG TWISTER STRIKES AGAIN." Political cartoon commenting on President Lyndon B. Johnson's reputation as a master in the art of "twisting arms," particularly among members of Congress. Gib Crockett, *Washington Star*, 1967. LIBRARY OF CONGRESS

anced the interests of fellow southern, anti–civil rights senators with those of his northern, liberal colleagues.

Equally important to Johnson's success as majority leader was his ability to persuade senators to vote with him on a given bill. Armed with extensive files on every colleague, Johnson knew the personal interests and habits of each. In addition, Johnson understood which issues were important to which senators. He also used his forceful personality to deal with uncooperative colleagues. Using an approach that was popularly known as the Johnson Treatment, he would cajole, supplicate, praise, and threaten fellow senators, all the while touching and needling them. The result was usually that the senator was overwhelmed and soon ready to follow the larger-than-life majority leader. Johnson was able to assert control over the Senate as no majority leader had before or has since in U.S. history.

In 1955, Johnson's efforts as majority leader translated into passage of more than thirteen hundred bills, nearly two hundred more than during the entire previous Congress. In his five years as majority leader, Johnson helped pass, among other measures, the first civil rights bill in eighty-two years, a Social Security reform act, and a bill creating the National Aeronautics and Space Administration (NASA).

As majority leader, Johnson's principal concerns were the advancement of his own political career and the nurturing of a unified Democratic party that would work in a bipartisan way to pass legislation beneficial to the nation. On foreign affairs, he remained throughout most of his Senate career a staunch anticommunist supportive of a strong national defense. When it came to domestic matters, he saw the maintenance and expansion of federal New Deal programs as vital to economic prosperity and social justice. On civil rights, he became one of the few southern senators in the 1950s to strike a balance between intense southern opposition to integration and strong northern support of civil rights. In 1958, when liberals became the dominant force in the Democratic-controlled Senate, Johnson recognized that, as a moderate southerner, his effectiveness as majority leader would be undermined. Two years later, when Democratic presidential nominee Sen. John F. Kennedy asked him to run for vice president, Johnson accepted, leaving behind one of the most accomplished congressional records in U.S. history.

Vice President. As vice president, Johnson played a negligible role in steering legislation through the Congress. President Kennedy was reluctant to have Johnson, the more experienced legislator, eclipse him as the administration's leading advocate of major bills. Instead, Johnson headed the Committee on Equal Employment Opportunity (EEOC), the principal executive agency under Kennedy working for black equality, and chaired the National Aeronautics and Space Council. As a consequence of his EEOC chairmanship and his extensive legislative experience, Johnson had a role in designing the Kennedy administration's tactics for promoting the 1963 civil rights bill in Congress and for persuading Congress to appropriate funds for the Apollo program to land a man on the moon by the end of the 1960s.

President. When Johnson became president after the assassination of President Kennedy in November 1963, he set his sights on three things: the passage of pending bills as a tribute to his fallen predecessor; the enactment of his own Great Society legislative program, which would include a "war on poverty"; and the garnering of a record in both domestic and foreign affairs that would

eclipse Franklin Roosevelt's and make Johnson the greatest reform leader in U.S. history.

Johnson's domestic legislative record was more far-reaching than any other president's. A list of the bills passed during his tenure from 1963 to 1969 would go on for pages. The more important included the tax reform act, the Civil Rights Act, and the Economic Opportunity Act of 1964; the Public Works and Economic Development Act, the Voting Rights Act, and the Housing and Urban Development Act of 1965; the first major change in immigration restrictions since the 1920s; legislation creating two new cabinet departments, the Department of Transportation and the Department of Housing and Urban Development, various pieces of social legislations, including acts creating Medicare and Medicaid and providing federal aid to elementary, secondary, and higher education; legislation creating the National Endowment for the Arts and the National Endowment for the Humanities; and the Freedom of Information Act.

Johnson's success as a presidential legislator rested to some extent on techniques he had used as majority leader. He relied on a store of knowledge about individual representatives and senators, paying special attention to how he could reward key congressional figures for their votes. But his success is only partly explained by the promises he

CAMPAIGN SIGN. Urging voters to go to the polls for the November 1948 elections. The poster makes reference to Lyndon B. Johnson's exceedingly narrow eighty-seven-vote victory over Coke Stevenson in the Texas Democratic senatorial primary.

COLLECTION OF DAVID J. AND JANICE L. FRENT

MAJORITY LEADER LYNDON B. JOHNSON. Counseling freshman senator Robert C. Byrd (D-W.Va.), c. 1959.
OFFICE OF THE HISTORIAN OF THE U.S. SENATE

made to members of Congress to help them with pork-barrel measures and his commitments to appoint people they recommended to federal jobs and judicial posts. The mandate Johnson achieved with his landslide victory over Arizona senator Barry Goldwater in the presidential election of 1964 and the huge Democratic majorities that rode Johnson's coattails into the House and Senate were also essential components of his success. In addition, Johnson's personal style of directly pressuring members of Congress with his appeals to their patriotism and their sense of duty was highly effective.

Johnson's failure in Vietnam, however, ultimately undercut his success in domestic affairs. From the start of his presidency, Johnson vowed not to lose Vietnam, believing that a communist victory there would eventually lead to nuclear conflict with the Soviet Union and China. He also thought that a U.S. defeat in Vietnam would ensure a Republican presidential victory in 1968—and with it the repeal of his domestic programs.

To escalate U.S. involvement in Vietnam, Johnson pressed Congress into passing the Tonkin Gulf Resolution in the summer of 1964. Although evidence that North Vietnamese torpedo boats had attacked U.S. warships in the gulf was open to question, Johnson persuaded Congress that such an attack had occurred and won a near-unanimous endorsement for his policy of saving South Vietnam from a communist takeover. Between 1965 and 1968, as Johnson expanded U.S. involvement through an air campaign and an increase of U.S. ground forces in Vietnam to more than half a million, he won congressional appropriations for the war through intensive lobbying and public appeals to American patriotism. By 1968, however, events in Vietnam, in particular the so-called Tet Offensive staged by communist forces at the end of January, into February, belied Johnson's assertions about a timely U.S. victory. Growing congressional opposition to the conflict—most notably that of Sen. J. William Fulbright (D-Ark.), chairman of the Foreign Relations Committee, and of a number of other Democrats in the House and Senate—helped convince Johnson to withdraw from the 1968 presidential campaign.

Johnson's presidency combined great successes and great failures, especially in his dealings with Congress. Many items in his domestic reform program, such as civil rights legislation, Medicare, and the Head Start preschool program for young children, remain fixtures on the national scene. By contrast, his Vietnam policy ultimately antagonized many in Congress and deepened divisions and suspicions between the executive and legislative branches. Whatever else historians may ultimately say about Johnson, he will surely be remembered as one of the most important representatives, senators, and presidents of the twentieth century.

BIBLIOGRAPHY

Caro, Robert. *The Years of Lyndon Johnson: Means of Ascent.* 1990.

Caro, Robert. *The Years of Lyndon Johnson: The Path to Power.* 1982.

Dallek, Robert. *Lone Star Rising: Lyndon Johnson and His Times, 1908–1960.* 1991.

Dugger, Ronnie. *The Politician: The Drive for Power from the Frontier to Master of the Senate.* 1982.

Kearns, Doris. *Lyndon B. Johnson and the American Dream.* 1976.

ROBERT DALLEK

JOINT COMMITTEE. *For discussion of the nature and function of congressional joint committees, see* Committees, *article on* Joint Committees. *For particular joint committees, see* Atomic Energy Committee, Joint; Conduct of War Committee, Joint; Congressional Operations Committee, Joint; Economic Committee, Joint; Library Committee,

Joint; Printing Committee, Joint; Reconstruction Committee, Joint; Taxation Committee, Joint.

JOINT SESSIONS AND MEETINGS.

Joint sessions and joint meetings of Congress occur when members of the House and Senate gather together to transact congressional business or to receive addresses from the president or other dignitaries. The first such gathering was a joint session held on 6 April 1789 to count electoral votes for the nation's first president and vice president.

Of the two types of gatherings, a joint session is the more formal and occurs upon adoption of a concurrent resolution passed by both houses of Congress. Congress holds joint sessions to receive the president's annual State of the Union address and other presidential addresses, and to count electoral votes for president and vice president every four years.

A joint meeting, on the other hand, occurs after both houses, by unanimous consent or by resolution, declare themselves in recess for such a joint gathering in the Hall of the House of Representatives. Because the Hall of the House of Representatives has more seats than the Senate chamber, both joint sessions and joint meetings have nearly always been held in the Hall of the House. Congress holds joint meetings for such matters as receiving addresses from dignitaries (e.g., foreign heads of state and famous Americans such as astronauts and military leaders) and for commemorating major events. The Speaker of the House of Representatives usually presides over joint sessions and meetings; however, the president of the Senate presides over counts of the electoral votes, as required by the Constitution.

Between 1913 and 1993, every president from Woodrow Wilson to Bill Clinton has delivered an annual State of the Union address before Congress. During this period presidents gave over 120 addresses before Congress. These included Woodrow Wilson's 1917 request for a declaration of war against Germany and his request for Senate approval of the Versailles treaty in 1919; Franklin D. Roosevelt's 1934 speech on the 100th anniversary of Lafayette's death and the 1941 declaration of war; Harry S. Truman's submission of the United Nations charter in 1945 and his speech on the railroad strike in 1946; Lyndon B. Johnson's voting rights speech in 1965; Richard M. Nixon's Vietnam policy address in 1969; Jimmy Carter's Middle East speech in 1978; Ronald Reagan's U.S.-Soviet summit address in 1985; George Bush's speech on the invasion of Kuwait by Iraq in 1990; and Bill Clinton's address on health reform in 1993.

According to Seymour H. Fersh, "With President Roosevelt taking advantage of radio, the annual address more than ever before was directed at a national and world audience, rather than merely to Congress." Using the broadcast media of first radio and then television, presidents have been able to deliver their messages not just to Congress, but directly to the voters.

The Marquis de Lafayette, French hero of the American Revolution, in 1824 became the first foreign dignitary to address a joint meeting of Congress. More than seventy-five foreign dignitaries have since addressed joint meetings. Sir Winston Churchill addressed three joint meetings (in 1941, 1943, and 1952), the most by a non-American. Congress upon occasion has declined requests by foreign dignitaries to address a joint meeting because of the volume of such requests, a busy legislative schedule, or differences of opinion surrounding the proposed speaker. Among the more controversial requests were those by Soviet leaders Nikita Khrushchev (1959) and Mikhail S. Gorbachev (1987), who were never invited to address a joint

PRESIDENT DWIGHT D. EISENHOWER. Addressing a joint session of Congress, 10 January 1957.

LIBRARY OF CONGRESS

meeting of Congress. However, with the collapse of the Union of Soviet Socialist Republics, Boris Yeltsin, president of Russia, addressed a joint meeting of Congress in 1992.

For a foreign dignitary to address Congress, a formal agreement must be reached by the Senate and House. The Speaker then sends a formal letter of invitation to the foreign dignitary. Parallel to these formalities, however, informal efforts are usually undertaken to prepare the way for extending the formal invitation.

After the two chambers have recessed, the senators and representatives assemble in the House in a joint meeting to receive the foreign dignitary's address. When the House next convenes after a joint meeting, it usually agrees to a unanimous consent request by the majority leader or his designee permitting the proceedings and remarks of the foreign dignitary made during the recess to be printed in the Congressional Record.

From the first joint meeting to receive Lafayette's address to the present time, the process has been simplified. Congress typically approves the unanimous consent request, thus eliminating the need to bring the matter up by resolution, joint resolution, public bill, or appropriation. When the matter is controversial, however, or involves the expenditure of public funds, a joint resolution or public bill is the legislative vehicle used.

Other American citizens below the level of U.S. president also address the Congress in joint meeting, or in the Senate or House separately. These speakers have included Generals Douglas MacArthur and Norman Schwarzkopf, astronauts, and others.

[See also State of the Union Message.]

BIBLIOGRAPHY

Byrd, Robert C. The Senate, 1789–1989. Vol. 4: Historical Statistics, 1789–1992. 1992.

Kerr, Mary Lee, ed. Foreign Visitors to Congress: Speeches and History. 2 vols. 1989.

Pontius, John Samuels. Addresses by Foreign Dignitaries, 1789–1986. Congressional Research Service, Library of Congress. 1986.

Wellborn, Clay. Joint Sessions and Joint Meetings of Congress. Congressional Research Service, Library of Congress, CRS Rept. 87-244. 1987.

JOHN SAMUELS PONTIUS

JORDAN, BARBARA (1936–), Democratic representative from Texas, civil rights advocate, and member of the Judiciary Committee during its hearings on the impeachment of President Richard M. Nixon. Barbara Charline Jordan represented the 18th District of Texas in the 93d through 95th Congresses (1973–1979). She was the first black woman elected to Congress from a southern state. Previously she had been the first black woman to be elected to the Texas senate, a post she held from 1967 to 1972.

A member of the Judiciary Committee, Jordan is perhaps best known for her participation in the 1974 hearings on the impeachment of President Richard M. Nixon for his role in the Watergate scandal. Her emotional speech expressing faith in the principles of the U.S. Constitution was a highlight of the House impeachment hearings. It catapulted her into the national spotlight and led to much speculation that she would hold higher elected or appointed office. However, in 1979, after three terms in the House, illness forced her retirement and she returned to Texas. She subsequently became a professor at the Lyndon B. Johnson School of Public Affairs at the University of Texas at Austin, a job she still held in 1994.

BARBARA JORDAN. In January 1975.

A protégé of President Lyndon B. Johnson, Jordan preferred to be known as a worker rather than a crusader. She viewed herself as a professional politician and focused on crafting legislative solutions to "people" issues that extended beyond race and gender. During her tenure in the House, she did not actively align herself with the Black Caucus or the informal organization of women members. Instead, as a freshman, she sought and obtained appointment to the Judiciary Committee, where she helped write the laws that shaped the direction of civil rights in education and employment. She was also a member of the Democratic Steering and Policy Committee.

BIBLIOGRAPHY

Broyles, William. "The Making of Barbara Jordan." *Texas Monthly*, October 1976.

Jordan, Barbara, and Shelby Hearon. *Barbara Jordan: A Self-Portrait*. 1979.

Kelin, Norman, and Sabra-Anne Kelin. *Barbara Jordan*. 1993.

MARY ETTA BOESL

JOURNALS. The Constitution (Art. 1, sec. 5) provides that "Each House shall keep a Journal of its Proceedings, and from time to time publish the same, excepting such Parts as may in their Judgment require Secrecy." The House maintains one *Journal* and the Senate keeps two: the *Journal of the Senate of the United States of America*, which reports Senate legislative action, and the *Executive Journal*, which records Senate actions on matters requiring the Senate's advice and consent (i.e., treaties and nominations). Actions taken by the Senate in secret session or when it sits as a court of impeachment are kept separate and are published only by Senate order as separate journals.

The journals are the formal, official record of House or Senate action. They differ from the *Congressional Record* in that the journals do not include transcripts of floor debate prepared by the official reporters of debate. The journals merely summarize chamber activity: the number and title of bills, the sponsors and texts of floor amendments, the results of all yea-and-nay votes in the chamber, and the text of resolutions and conference reports. Any discrepancies between a journal and the *Congressional Record* are decided in favor of the journal. The House *Journal* does not include detailed descriptions of actions taken in the Committee of the Whole (or indeed in any committee) because technically these actions do not occur in the House. In early Congresses, the journals were kept personally by the Clerk of the House or the Secretary of the Senate, but journal clerks in both houses now prepare the journals under the supervision of the Clerk or Secretary.

Approval and correction of these documents is accorded high parliamentary standing. In earlier years, approving the journal in the House and Senate caused substantial delay because members could demand the reading of the journal in full. During the Jackson administration, the Senate passed a resolution censuring President Andrew Jackson for removing government funds from the Bank of the United States; later, the Senate voted to expunge the resolution from the original, handwritten *Journal*, and a black box was then drawn around the offending language with an inscription noting the later action to expunge the censure resolution.

Under current House and Senate rules, the journal is not read. In the House, the Speaker announces that he has found the *Journal* for the previous day to be accurate. In the Senate, the majority leader offers a nondebatable motion to approve the journal. Votes on approving the journal in the House or Senate are usually attendance checks by the parties and not serious attempts to reject the journal.

BIBLIOGRAPHY

Byrd, Robert C. *The Senate, 1789–1989: Addresses on the History of the United States Senate*. Vol. 1, chap. 8. 1988.

Tiefer, Charles. *Congressional Practice and Procedure: A Reference, Research, and Legislative Guide*. 1989.

PAUL S. RUNDQUIST

JUDICIAL REVIEW. The Supreme Court and the lower federal courts have the power to review any federal or state legislation or other official governmental action and to invalidate it if they deem it inconsistent with the Constitution or federal law. The constitutional language (Article III) simply provides that "the judicial Power of the United States, shall be vested in one supreme Court, and in such inferior Courts as the Congress may from time to time ordain and establish." Aside from the enumeration of the kinds of cases and controversies that the Court may hear on original jurisdiction, the judiciary's power is not further defined. Instead, Article III gives Congress the authority to define the Court's appellate jurisdiction and the structure of, as well as the types of cases to be heard by, the lower federal courts.

Congress's power to define the Court's appellate jurisdiction and the kinds of cases that may be raised in federal courts significantly conditions the exercise of judicial review. The Judiciary Act of 1789 initially defined the Supreme Court's appellate jurisdiction and created the basic structure of the federal judiciary: federal district courts are the trial courts of the federal judicial system, and situated between them and the Supreme Court are the circuit, or regional, courts of appeals. But Congress did not authorize any appellate court judgeships in 1789. Rather, Supreme Court justices were required to "ride circuit," sitting with district court judges as circuit courts of appeals. Appellate court judgeships were not authorized until the Circuit Court of Appeals Act of 1891. In response to growing caseloads, Congress subsequently increased the number of circuit courts of appeals from three to thirteen and the number of district courts to ninety-four, together staffed by more than seven hundred judges.

The business of the federal judiciary also changed as a result of congressional legislation. Congress greatly expanded the jurisdiction of all federal courts by extending it to include civil rights, questions of federal law decided by state courts, and all suits of more than five hundred dollars arising under the Constitution or federal legislation. In the post–World War II era, Congress enacted major legislation regulating health, safety, and the environment as well as greatly expanding federal criminal law. That legislation in turn dramatically increased the number of administrative appeals and regulatory and criminal cases confronting the federal judiciary.

Shaping the Supreme Court's Caseload. Besides defining federal courts' jurisdiction, congressional legislation indirectly affects the work of the federal judiciary. During its first decade, the Supreme Court had little of importance to do. Over 40 percent of its business consisted of admiralty and prize cases (disputes over captured property at sea). About 50 percent raised issues of common law, and the remaining 10 percent dealt with matters such as equity. But in the early years of the Republic, Congress did not undertake to broadly regulate social and economic conditions. When it began regulating railroads, corporations, and working conditions in the late nineteenth century, the Court's business evolved with challenges to that legislation. The number of admiralty cases dwindled

to less than 4 percent by 1882. Almost 40 percent of the Court's decisions still dealt with either disputes of common law or questions of jurisdiction and procedure. More than 43 percent, however, involved interpreting congressional statutes. The increase in statutory interpretation registered the impact of the Industrial Revolution and growing regulation of social and economic relations. In the 1990s, about 47 percent of the cases annually decided by the Court involve matters of constitutional law. Another 40 percent deal with the interpretation of congressional legislation. The remaining cases involve issues of administrative law, taxation, patents, and claims.

As the Court's caseload grew, its discretionary jurisdiction was expanded by Congress. Congress thus enabled the Court not only to manage its work load but to set its substantive agenda for exercising judicial review. In its first few decades, the Court annually heard fewer than one hundred cases. Its docket then steadily grew throughout the late nineteenth and twentieth centuries. Whereas in 1920 there were only 565 cases on its docket, the number rose to more than 1,300 by 1950, 2,300 by 1960, 4,200 by 1970, to more than 5,000 cases a year in the 1980s. By 1990, the Court docket annually exceeded 6,000 cases.

For most of the nineteenth century, Congress required the Court to decide every appeal. But because the Court could not stay abreast of its caseload, Congress incrementally enlarged the Court's discretionary jurisdiction by eliminating mandatory rights of appeal in narrow though important areas. Then, in the Judiciary Act of 1925, Congress basically established the jurisdiction of the modern Court. That act replaced many provisions for mandatory review of appeals with discretionary review of petitions for writs of certiorari (requests that the Court review the record and judgment of a lower court), which the Court may deny. In 1988, the Act to Improve the Administration of Justice eliminated virtually all of the Court's remaining nondiscretionary appellate jurisdiction. As a result, the Court has virtually complete discretion over what cases it reviews and how it exercises its power of judicial review.

The Supreme Court and Congressional Statutes. Because judicial review is not expressly defined in Article III, the Court was initially reluctant to assert that power. Chief Justice John Marshall provided the classic justification for judicial review in the landmark ruling in *Marbury v. Madison* (1803). There, the Court struck down a section of the Judiciary Act of 1789 that Marshall in his opinion construed as having unconstitutionally expanded the Court's original jurisdiction under Article III by giving it the power to issue writs of mandamus—court orders directing a government official to take some action. While that decision was controversial, the Marshall Court further legitimated its power of judicial review by overturning a number of state laws, although it did not again challenge Congress's power. Indeed, the Court did not strike down another act of Congress until *Scott v. Sandford* (1857), which invalidated the Missouri Compromise of 1820.

Since the late nineteenth century, the Court has more frequently asserted its power to overturn congressional legislation, as can be seen in table 1.

Note, though, that when invalidating a congressional statute, the Court sometimes throws into question many other statutes as well. In *Immigration and Naturalization Service v. Chadha* (1983), for instance, the Court struck down a provision for a one-house legislative veto in the Immigration and Naturalization Act and effectively declared all legislative vetoes unconstitutional. While *Chadha* is counted in table 1 as a single declaration of the unconstitutionality of a statute, more than two hundred provisions for legislative vetoes were affected by the Court's decision.

Major confrontations between Congress and the Court have occurred a number of times over the exercise of judicial review. The Marshall Court generally approved the expansion of national govern-

TABLE 1. *Acts of Congress Overturned by the Supreme Court*

COURT	YEARS	NUMBER OF ACTS OVERTURNED
Pre-Marshall Court	1789–1800	0
Marshall Court	1801–1835	1
Taney Court	1836–1864	1
Chase Court	1865–1873	10
Waite Court	1874–1888	9
Fuller Court	1889–1910	14
White Court	1910–1921	12
Hughes Court	1921–1930	14
Stone Court	1941–1946	2
Vinson Court	1947–1953	1
Warren Court	1953–1969	25
Burger Court	1969–1986	34
Rehnquist Court	1986–1992	7

mental power, but because of the states' opposition to the Court's rulings Congress in the 1820s and 1830s threatened to remove the Court's jurisdiction over disputes involving states' rights. After the Civil War, Congress repealed the Court's jurisdiction over certain denials of writs of habeas corpus—orders commanding that a prisoner be brought before a judge and that cause be shown for his imprisonment. In *Ex parte McCardle* (1869), the Court upheld that repeal of its jurisdiction, thereby avoiding a controversial case attacking Reconstruction legislation.

Congressional Restraints on the Court. Progressives in Congress unsuccessfully sought to pressure the economically conservative Court at the turn of the century. They proposed requiring a two-thirds vote by the justices when striking down federal statutes and permitting Congress to overrule the Court's decisions by a two-thirds majority. The confrontation escalated with the Court's invalidation of much of the early New Deal program in the 1930s. The Senate refused to go along with President Franklin D. Roosevelt's Court-packing plan to increase the number of justices from nine to fifteen; but in order to secure a majority on the bench in support of the New Deal, Congress passed legislation allowing justices to retire with full rather than half salary, thus making retirement more financially attractive to the sitting justices and giving Roosevelt openings to appoint justices who shared his political philosophy.

Congress may pressure the Court in a number of ways. It has tried to do so when setting the Court's terms and size and when authorizing appropriations for salaries, law clerks, secretaries, and office technology. Only once, in 1802, in repealing the Judiciary Act of 1801 and abolishing one year's session, did Congress actually set the Court's term in order to delay and influence a particular decision.

The size of the Court is not constitutionally ordained, and changes in the number of justices generally reflect congressional attempts to influence the Court's exercise of judicial review. The Jeffersonian Republicans' quick repeal of the act passed by the Federalists in 1801, an act that reduced the number of justices, was the first of several such attempts to influence the Court. Presidents James Madison, James Monroe, and John Adams all claimed that the country's geographical expansion warranted enlarging the size of the Court. But Congress refused to do so until the last day of Andrew Jackson's term in 1837. During the Civil War, the number of justices was increased to ten, ostensibly because of the creation of a tenth circuit in California. This gave Abraham Lincoln his fourth appointment and a pro-Union majority on the bench. Antagonism toward Andrew Johnson's Reconstruction policies led to a reduction from ten to seven justices. After General Ulysses S. Grant was elected president, Congress again authorized nine justices, the number that has prevailed.

Under Article III, Congress is authorized "to make exceptions" to the Court's appellate jurisdiction. That authorization has been viewed as a way of denying the Court review of certain kinds of cases. Although Congress once succeeded in doing so, with the 1868 repeal of jurisdiction over writs of habeas corpus, Court-curbing legislation has generally failed to win passage. Furthermore, the Court has suggested that it would not approve repeals of its jurisdiction that are merely attempts to dictate how particular kinds of cases should be decided.

Reversal by constitutional amendment. Congress has had somewhat greater success in reversing the Court by constitutional amendment. Four decisions have prompted this approach. *Chisholm v. Georgia* (1793), holding that citizens of one state could sue another state in federal courts, was reversed in 1795 by the Eleventh Amendment, which guaranteed sovereign immunity for states from suits by citizens of other states. In 1865 and 1868, the Thirteenth and Fourteenth Amendments abolished slavery and made African Americans citizens of the United States, thereby overturning *Scott v. Sandford*. With the ratification in 1913 of the Sixteenth

Amendment, Congress reversed *Pollock v. Farmers' Loan & Trust Company* (1895), which had invalidated a federal income tax. In 1970, an amendment to the Voting Rights Act of 1965 lowered the voting age to eighteen years for all elections. But within six months, the Court held in *Oregon v. Mitchell* (1970) that Congress had exceeded its power by lowering the voting age for state and local elections. Less than a year later, the Twenty-sixth Amendment was ratified, extending the franchise to eighteen-year-olds in all elections.

In addition, two other amendments effectively overrode two prior rulings. In 1920, the Nineteenth Amendment extended voting rights to women and basically nullified *Minor v. Happersett* (1874), which had rejected the claim that women could not be prohibited from voting under the Fourteenth Amendment's equal protection clause. The Twenty-fourth Amendment, ratified in 1964, prohibits the use of poll taxes as a qualification for voting. It technically invalidated the Court's rejection of a challenge to poll taxes in *Breedlove v. Suttles* (1937).

Finally, several leaders in the Reconstruction Congress maintained that the Fourteenth Amendment would override *Barron v. Baltimore* (1833) and apply the Bill of Rights to the states as well as to the federal government. Shortly after that amendment's ratification, however, the Court rejected that interpretation of the amendment in the *Slaughterhouse Cases* (1873). Yet in the twentieth century, the Court selectively incorporated the major guarantees of the first eight amendments

TABLE 2. *Congressional Reversals of Supreme Court and Lower Federal Court Decisions*

Congress	Number of Statutes	Supreme Court Decisions Overridden	Lower Federal Court Decisions Overridden	Total Reversals
90th (1967–1969)	14	6	10	16
91st (1969–1971)	8	2	13	15
92d (1971–1973)	7	8	4	12
93rd (1973–1975)	10	7	7	14
94th (1975–1977)	17	12	22	34
95th (1977–1979)	14	19	24	43
96th (1979–1981)	20	8	23	31
97th (1981–1983)	17	8	16	24
98th (1983–1985)	16	15	29	44
99th (1985–1987)	25	18	27	45
100th (1987–1989)	24	12	27	39
101st (1989–1991)	15	9	18	27
Total	187	124	220	344

TABLE 3. *Landmark Legislation Affecting the Jurisdiction of the Supreme Court and Federal Judiciary*

TITLE	YEAR ENACTED	REFERENCE NUMBER	DESCRIPTION
Judiciary Act	1789	1 Stat. 73	Provided basic appellate jurisdiction; instituted a three-tier federal judicial system staffed by justices and district court judges; required the justices to ride circuit.
Act of 24 February 1807	1807	2 Stat. 420	Added seventh circuit and justice.
Act of 3 March 1837	1837	5 Stat. 176	Divided country into nine circuits and increased the number of justices to nine; expanded the Court's jurisdiction to include appeals from new states and territories.
Act of 2 March 1855	1855	10 Stat. 631	California added as tenth circuit.
Act of 3 March 1863	1863	12 Stat. 794	Increased the number of justices to ten.
Act of 23 July 1866	1866	14 Stat. 209	Reorganized the country into nine judicial circuits and reduced the number of justices to seven.
Act of 5 February 1867	1867	14 Stat. 385	Expanded the Court's jurisdiction over writs of habeas corpus and state court decisions.
Act of 10 April 1869	1869	16 Stat. 44	Created nine circuit court judgeships and fixed the number of justices at nine.
Circuit Court of Appeals Act of 3 March 1891	1891	26 Stat. 826	Established nine circuit courts and broadened the Court's review in criminal cases.
Act of 20 July 1892	1892	27 Stat. 252	Provided for *in forma pauperis* (indigents') filings.
Act of 9 February 1893	1893	27 Stat. 434	Established circuit for the District of Columbia.
Judiciary Act of 13 February 1925	1925	43 Stat. 936	Greatly expanded the Supreme Court's discretionary jurisdiction.
Act of 28 February 1929	1929	45 Stat. 1346	Reestablished tenth circuit.
Act of 25 June 1948	1948	62 Stat. 869–870	Revised, codified, and enacted Judicial Code into law; established eleventh circuit.
District of Columbia Court Reform Act and Criminal Procedure Act	1970	84 Stat. 473	Reorganized the judicial system in the District of Columbia and expanded the Court's discretionary jurisdiction.
Act of 2 January 1971	1971	84 Stat. 1890	Repealed the right of direct federal government appeals.
Act of 12 August 1976	1976	90 Stat. 1119	Eliminated most other jurisdiction from three-judge courts and rights of direct appeals, with the exception of voting rights and reapportionment.
Federal Courts Improvement Act	1982	28 U.S.C. 41	Created Court of Appeals for the Federal Circuit by joining the appellate division of the Court of Claims with the Court of Customs and Patent Appeals.
Act to Improve the Administration of Justice	1988	102 Stat. 662	Eliminated virtually all of the Court's nondiscretionary appellate jurisdiction.

into the Fourteenth Amendment and applied them to the states.

Reversals by statute. More successful than amending the Constitution have been congressional revisions of legislation in response to Court rulings. For example, the Court held in *Pennsylvania v. Wheeling and Belmont Bridge Company* (1852) that a bridge built across the Ohio River obstructed interstate commerce and violated a congressionally approved state compact. Congress immediately passed a statute declaring that the bridge did not obstruct interstate commerce.

Congressional reversals usually relate to nonstatutory matters involving administrative policies.

But in *Zurcher v. The Stanford Daily* (1978), the Court held that there was no constitutional prohibition against police searching newsrooms without a warrant for "mere evidence" (in this case, photographs) of a crime. Congress reversed that ruling by passing the Privacy Protection Act of 1980 and prohibiting warrantless searches of newsrooms.

Congressional reversals of the Court's statutory interpretations are less frequent, since Congress is usually constrained by the lobbying efforts of beneficiaries of the Court's rulings. Still, the modern Congress has tended to reverse a growing number of the federal judiciary's statutory decisions. The Civil Rights Act of 1991, for instance, reversed twelve rulings of the Court. Between 1967 and 1990, Congress overrode 121 of the Court's statutory decisions; by contrast, between 1945 and 1957 only twenty-one rulings were overridden. Moreover, Congress has increasingly overruled lower federal court decisions, as indicated in table 2.

Notably, 73 percent of the decisions overturned were handed down by the Court less than ten years earlier. Almost 40 percent were conservative rulings while 20 percent were liberal holdings, and in slightly over 40 percent there was no clean liberal-conservative split. The decisions reversed by Congress most commonly involved civil rights, followed by criminal law, antitrust law, bankruptcy, federal jurisdiction, and environmental law.

The Court may invite Congress to reverse its rulings when legislation appears ambiguous. It suggested as much in *Tennessee Valley Authority v. Hill* (1978) when holding that a TVA dam could not be put into operation because it would destroy the only habitat of a tiny fish, the snail darter, protected under the Endangered Species Act of 1973. Congress later modified the act by authorizing a special board to decide whether to allow federally funded public works projects when they threaten endangered species.

Defying the Court. Congress cannot overturn the Court's interpretations of the Constitution by mere legislation. But Congress can enhance or thwart compliance with the Court's rulings. After the Warren Court's landmark decision in *Gideon v. Wainwright* (1963) that indigents have a right to counsel, Congress provided attorneys for indigents charged with federal offenses. By contrast, in the Crime Control and Safe Streets Act of 1968, Congress permitted federal courts to use evidence obtained from suspects who had not been read their rights under *Miranda v. Arizona* (1966) if their testimony appeared voluntary based on the "totality of the circumstances" surrounding their interrogation. In 1977 Congress passed the so-called Hyde Amendment, sponsored by Republican representative Henry J. Hyde of Illinois. That amendment registered opposition to the Court's abortion ruling in *Roe v. Wade* (1973) and to federal funding of abortions. The Hyde Amendment to appropriations bills bars Medicaid coverage of abortions except where the life of the mother would be endangered were the fetus carried to full term.

Congress may openly defy the Court in other ways. After *Chadha*, Congress passed no fewer than two hundred new provisions for legislative vetoes, in direct defiance of *Chadha*. Congress indubitably has the power to delay and undercut implementation of the Court's rulings. For example, Congress delayed implementation of the Court's watershed school desegregation ruling in *Brown v. Board of Education* (1954) by not authorizing the executive branch to enforce the decision until the Civil Rights Act of 1964. Then, by cutting back on appropriations for the departments of Justice and of Health, Education and Welfare, Congress registered the growing opposition to busing and other attempts to achieve integrated public schools.

In sum, on major issues of public policy, Congress is likely to prevail or at least to temper the impact of the Court's rulings and its exercise of judicial review.

[*See also* Constitution, *article on* Congress in the Constitution; Immigration and Naturalization Service v. Chadha; Judiciary Act of 1789; Judiciary and Congress; Marbury v. Madison; Scott v. Sandford.]

BIBLIOGRAPHY

Craig, Barbara. *Chadha: The Story of An Epic Constitutional Struggle.* 1988.

Eskridge, William N., Jr. "Overriding Supreme Court Statutory Interpretation Decisions." *Yale Law Journal* 101 (1991): 331–445.

Fisher, Louis. *Constitutional Conflicts between Congress and the President.* 3d ed. 1991.

Katzman, Robert, ed. *Judges and Legislators: Toward Institutional Comity.* 1988.

Keynes, Edward, with Randall K. Miller. *The Court vs. Congress: Prayer, Busing, and Abortion.* 1989.

O'Brien, David M. *Constitutional Law and Politics: Struggles for Power and Governmental Accountability.* 1991.

DAVID M. O'BRIEN

JUDICIARY ACT OF 1789 (1 Stat. 73–93).

"An Act to establish the Judicial Courts of the United States" was enacted by the First Congress on 24

September 1789. Commonly known as the Judiciary Act of 1789, the statute created a judicial system for the United States.

Although Article III, section 1 of the Constitution stipulated a single Supreme Court, section 2 sharply limited the Court's original jurisdiction, and its appellate jurisdiction was subject to exceptions and regulations made by Congress. Otherwise, section 1 called for "such inferior Courts as the Congress may from time to time ordain and establish," thereby leaving the nature and organization of the judiciary to the legislature.

As soon as a quorum was reached in April 1789, the Senate established a committee, with a representative from each state, to organize the judiciary. Its outstanding members were Oliver Ellsworth of Connecticut, William Paterson of New Jersey, and Caleb Strong of Massachusetts, all of whom had been members of the Constitutional Convention. (In 1793 Paterson became a justice of the Supreme Court; in 1796 Ellsworth became chief justice.)

The nature of a federal judiciary had been a hotly debated issue in the state ratification debates; those who feared threats to the independence of the individual states and the role of the state courts opposed a powerful system of federal courts. Conversely, nationalists welcomed the centralizing potential of a federal judicial system. These differences persisted in the Senate debates over the draft bill on the judiciary. The committee rejected proposals that the state courts serve as inferior federal courts and offered instead a novel structure of federal courts. The act as passed represented a compromise by various political factions, mitigating some of the fears of a powerful federal judiciary.

The Judiciary Act created a system of separate courts, with original and appellate jurisdiction arranged in a hierarchical manner. It divided the nation into districts generally matching state boundaries, each with a district court and a resident judge to sit four times a year at specified times and places. The districts were grouped into three circuits; a circuit court was to convene in each twice a year. The circuit courts were composed of the district judge and two Supreme Court justices who traveled the circuits.

In general, the district courts served as admiralty courts, with limited jurisdiction over minor criminal offenses. The circuit courts were the primary trial courts in the new system, given exclusive jurisdiction over federal criminal offenses and original jurisdiction (although concurrent with the state courts) over civil suits involving citizens of differ-

ent states, those to which an alien was a party, and those in which the United States was plaintiff. The amount in controversy in such cases was limited to $500. No jurisdiction was given to supplement Article III's grant of judicial power over cases in private civil litigation arising under the Constitution, laws, or treaties of the United States. The circuit courts were also given appellate authority over specified decisions of the district courts. The Supreme Court capped the system. The act provided for a chief justice and five associate justices, fleshed out details of that Court's original jurisdiction, and provided it with appellate jurisdiction over the federal circuit courts and over the highest courts of the states in certain categories of cases.

From time to time the number of Supreme Court justices, the number of federal courts, the scope of federal jurisdiction, and the relationship of state and federal courts all would be altered by Congress. In 1891 the Everts Act (26 Stat. 826) created circuit courts of appeal as intermediaries between the federal district courts and the Supreme Court, but in its essential form the federal judicial system established by Congress in 1789 persists today.

BIBLIOGRAPHY

Goebel, Julius, Jr. *History of the Supreme Court of the United States.* Vol. 1: *Antecedents and Beginnings to 1800.* Edited by Ray Roberts. 1971.
Ritz, Wilfred J. *Rewriting the History of the Judiciary Act of 1789.* Edited by Wythe Holt and L. H. LaRue. 1990.
Warren, Charles. "New Light on the History of the Federal Judiciary Act of 1789." *Harvard Law Review* 37 (1923): 49–132.

KATHRYN PREYER

JUDICIARY AND CONGRESS. The federal judiciary has become a critical element in the legislative process because what the courts decide can have significant consequences for Congress. At the same time, Congress affects in vital ways the structure, function, composition, and well-being of the judiciary (Katzmann, 1986). Indeed, the character of relations between the two branches has ramifications not only for each, but for the shape and development of policy (Shapiro, 1988; Melnick, 1985; Katzmann, 1988a).

The Constitution. Article III, section 1 of the Constitution states that "the judicial Power of the United States, shall be vested in one supreme Court, and in such inferior Courts as the Congress may from time to time ordain and establish." The article further asserts that "the Judges, both of the supreme and inferior Courts, shall hold their Offices during good Behaviour, and shall, at stated Times, receive for their Services, a Compensation, which shall not be diminished during their Continuance in Office." Apart from establishing the Supreme Court, the Constitution says nothing about the subject of federal court organization; that matter is left to Congress.

Congress's power to punish individual members of the judiciary is limited, but recent impeachment proceedings reaffirm that all federal judges are "civil officers of the United States" within the meaning of Article II, section 4 of the Constitution and can be removed from office for the commission of "high crimes and misdemeanors" in the constitutional sense. Commission of, and conviction for, a criminal offense are not preconditions for impeachment (Kastenmeier and Remington, 1988, p. 56).

With respect to the classes of cases and controversies to which the judicial power of the United States extends, Article III, section 2 delineates nine categories, including controversies between citizens of different states and cases arising under the Constitution and federal laws. In cases affecting ambassadors, public ministers, and consuls, and those in which a state is a party, the Supreme Court has original jurisdiction. In all other cases, the Supreme Court has appellate jurisdiction, both as to law and as to fact, with such exceptions and under such regulations as the Congress shall make. Article VI declares that the Constitution, treaties, and laws of the United States shall be "the supreme Law of the Land" and that "the Judges in every State shall be bound thereby, any Thing in the Constitution or Laws of any State to the Contrary notwithstanding."

With regard to the selection of the federal bench, the Constitution states that the president shall nominate, "and by and with the Advice and Consent of the Senate" shall appoint judges of the Supreme Court and all other officers of the United States "whose Appointments are not herein otherwise provided for, and which shall be established by Law."

Article I, the legislature's guide, provides in section 8 that "Congress shall have the Power . . . To constitute Tribunals inferior to the supreme Court." In accordance with that article, Congress, beginning with the creation of the Court of Claims shortly before the Civil War, has established many specialized courts. These tribunals, known as legislative courts, which include the bankruptcy courts, the Tax Court and the Court of Military Appeals, do not provide judges with lifetime tenure. Congress thus has the flexibility to "modify or abolish the tribunal at any time in response to changing societal, legal, or political conditions" (Kastenmeier and Remington, 1988, p. 58).

How the Judiciary Affects Congress. The judiciary affects Congress when it passes on the constitutionality of laws and interprets statutes.

Judging constitutionality. The Framers of the Constitution, having established the fundamental ground rules for the evolution of the new republic, left for succeeding generations the task of developing the character of relationships among institutions. Alexander M. Bickel wrote that

Congress was created very nearly full blown by the Constitution itself. The vast possibilities of the presidency were relatively easy to perceive and soon, inevitably materialized. But the institution of the judiciary needed to be summoned up out of the constitutional vapors, shaped and maintained. And the Great Chief Justice, John Marshall—not single-handed, but first and foremost—was there to do it and did. (Bickel, 1962)

Accordingly, the Supreme Court soon settled the question of whether it could invalidate an act of Congress.

In *Marbury v. Madison* (5 U.S. [1 Cranch] 137 [1803]), William Marbury asked the justices to order Secretary of State James Madison to deliver to him his commission as a justice of the peace for the District of Columbia. Marbury had been appointed to the position by outgoing president John Adams, but acting secretary of State John Marshall failed to deliver the commission before the Adams administration left office at midnight on 3 March. Marbury filed suit, asking that the Supreme Court issue a writ of mandamus to Secretary of State James Madison of the new Jefferson administration, pursuant to the Judiciary Act of 1789. Chief Justice Marshall recognized that the Jefferson administration was virtually certain to ignore any order directing Madison to deliver the commission, and such a consequence would undoubtedly have been ruinous for the Court. Thus, as Louis Fisher says: "Marshall chose a tactic he used in future years. He would appear to absorb a short-term defeat in exchange for a long-term victory" (Fisher, 1983, p. 55). The Court held that Marbury was entitled to his commission, but that it lacked authority to order its delivery. Chief Justice Marshall concluded that section 13 of the Judiciary Act of 1789 expanded the original jurisdiction of the Court, and

CHIEF JUSTICES OF THE UNITED STATES. From 1789 through 1873. Center figure is Salmon P. Chase, who died in 1873.

HARPER'S PICTORIAL HISTORY OF THE GREAT REBELLION

thus violated Article III of the Constitution. The highest tribunal held that Congress could change only the appellate jurisdiction of the court. Asserting that the law conflicted with the Constitution, and that judges took an oath to support the Constitution, the chief justice wrote that the Court had the power to declare such an act void. The opinion, Robert G. McCloskey observes, is a "masterwork of indirection, a brilliant example of Marshall's capacity to sidestep danger while seeking to court it, to advance in one direction, while his opponents are looking in another" (McCloskey, 1960, p. 40).

Since 1803, the Supreme Court, according to one account, has voided, in whole or in part, some 120 pieces of legislation. Of these, several have figured especially prominently in U.S. history (Baum, 1985). For instance, in the Dred Scott case (60 U.S. [19 How.] 393 [1857]), the Court struck down provisions of the Missouri Compromise of 1820 having to do with slavery in the territories; in *Hammer v. Dagenhart* (247 U.S. 251 [1918]) and *Bailey v. Drexel Furniture Co.* (259 U.S. 20 [1922]), the Court invalidated laws designed to protect child labor; the Court overturned New Deal legislation in such decisions as *Carter v. Carter Coal Co.* (298 U.S. 238 [1936]) and *Schechter Poultry Corp. v. United States* (295 U.S. 495 [1935]); in *Buckley v. Valeo*, (424 U.S. 1 [1976]), the Court invalidated provisions of the Federal Election Campaign Act relating to campaign financing; in its 1982 decision *Northern Pipeline Construction Co. v. Marathon Pipe Line Company* (458 U.S. 50 [1982]), it declared unconstitutional the bankruptcy court system Congress had created in 1978; and in *Immigration and Naturalization Service v. Chadha* (462 U.S. 919 [1983]), as well as some other related cases decided in 1983, the Court struck down the legislative veto.

On average, the Court overturns legislation, in whole or in part, more than once every two years (Baum, 1985, p. 169). In one sense, that activity affects only a fraction of the more than sixty thousand pieces of legislation Congress has enacted. In another sense, the real measure is the significance of the legislation under review and the consequences of the Court's action.

Lawrence Baum has reviewed historical patterns of judicial review and has identified periods in which the Court has been in "major" conflict with Congress as a legislator. The most conflictual period lasted from 1918 to 1936, when the Court overturned twenty-nine laws. That time period included the attack on the New Deal, which lessened with the Court's retreat in 1937. "Only in a single period,

REPLACING OLIVER WENDELL HOLMES. This political cartoon, which appeared shortly after Justice Holmes announced his retirement on 12 January 1932, ridicules progressive Republican senators, who expressed doubts about all the leading contenders to replace Holmes. Bearing *Who's Who in America*, the billygoat, cartoonist Clifford K. Berryman's symbol for the insurgents, suggests to President Hoover that nobody rises to the progressives' ideal. *Washington Evening Star*, January 1932.

LIBRARY OF CONGRESS

then, has the Court's power to review federal legislation been used to disturb a major line of federal policy" (Baum, 1985, p. 172).

Interpreting statutes. The judiciary touches the legislative branch not only when it renders a constitutional decision, but also when it interprets statutes in the quest to discern legislative intent (a subject to which we will later return). Indeed, in this age of statutes, the task of interpreting statutes has become a critical part of the legislative process (Mikva, 1987; Eskridge and Frickey, 1988). The courts are called upon to reach such decisions on matters of varying significance, ranging from the Standard Apple Barrel Act (1912), which set the dimensions for a standard barrel of apples and provided for penalties recoverable in federal court, to major legislation that affects every facet of American life, such as civil rights, the economy, and air and water pollution. Apart from diversity cases, Congress has vested jurisdiction in federal courts in legislation covering over three hundred subjects.

How Congress Affects the Judiciary. Just as the judiciary affects Congress, so the legislature touches the courts in a variety of ways.

Confirmation. The president "shall nominate, and

by and with the Advice and Consent of the Senate, shall appoint . . . Judges of the supreme Court." With these words, Article II of the Constitution sets forth the formal order of the appointment process, but little else. The charter of nationhood is silent about the bases for nomination and approval and about the balance of authority between the president and Congress in the confirmation process. Nor has the nation since prescribed exactly what criteria a nominee must meet to guarantee approval. Throughout the two-hundred-year history of the United States, the standards for confirmation have been the assertions of the Senate at the particular moment it considers a nominee. Altogether, twenty-eight nominees to the Supreme Court—nearly one out of five—have been rejected or have otherwise failed to take their seats on the Court (Katzmann, 1988b; Abraham, 1992).

Although the Senate has a formal role in the confirmation of all federal judges, the influence of individual senators is perhaps greatest in the choice of district court nominees. Appointments to the lower court are made following discussions between the executive branch and individual senators who belong to the same political party as the president, from the state where the appointment is being made. Senatorial courtesy allows a senator from the president's party to block a nomination. Senators from a particular state also can reach some agreement between them as to the allocation of appointments. For example, in New York, where the senators are of different parties, Daniel Patrick Moynihan (D) and Alfonse M. D'Amato (R) agreed that the senator whose president is in power has responsibility for recommending three out of every four nominees; the other senator makes the fourth recommendation (although the White House has not felt bound to follow that recommendation). The president exercises more authority over appellate judgeships, and even more over Supreme Court nominees. Even there, however, the White House consults with key senators and takes into account the likelihood of confirmation when making nominations.

Controversy surrounding confirmations is not a new development, nor is change in the confirmation process itself. Although the confirmation hearing is a standard practice today, it was not until 1925 that a Supreme Court nominee—Harlan Fiske Stone—testified before the Senate Judiciary Committee. Fourteen years and five confirmation proceedings elapsed before Felix Frankfurter became the second nominee to testify. As late as 1949, a nominee, Sherman Minton, could refuse to appear,

asserting that his "record speaks for itself," and still be confirmed.

However standard the hearings have become, it was, at least until the 1987 hearings on Robert L. Bork, generally considered inappropriate to probe into a nominee's views about specific areas and doctrines. Since the Bork proceedings, senators have viewed ideology as an acceptable subject for questioning. The Bork nomination involved a change not only in the nature of the hearings, but also in lobbying techniques. In addition to trying to influence senators directly, several groups sought to mobilize public opinion. To defeat his nomination, Bork's opponents undertook an extensive media campaign that included advertisements on radio and television and in the newspapers.

Structure, function, procedure, and institutional health. The legislative branch not only has a role in determining who becomes a judge; it also shapes the structure of the judiciary. That has been true since the passage of the Judiciary Act of 1789 (24 September), which established a three-tier system: apart from the constitutionally created Supreme Court, it consisted of district courts and intermediate appellate bodies (circuit courts). Supreme Court justices and district court judges were the members of the intermediate courts. Little more than a century passed before Congress enacted the Evarts Act (1891), which established regional courts of appeals, with full-time judges. Congress has created thirteen circuits—twelve are regional; the other, the Court of Appeals for the Federal Circuit, has special jurisdiction over such cases as patents and government contracts.

Congress also sets the number of judges in the federal judiciary. In 1994, in addition to the 9 Supreme Court judges, there are 168 circuit judges, 575 district judges, 284 bankruptcy judges, and 280 magistrates. In expanding the judiciary, Congress generally responds to the requests of the judicial branch through its Judicial Conference, the policy-making arm of the courts. The Judicial Conference is an outgrowth of the Judiciary Act of 1922 (which in no small measure bore the imprint of Chief Justice William Howard Taft).

Congress not only affects the structure and size of the judiciary, but also has the power to regulate practice and procedure in the federal courts. The legislature in the first instance delegates to the courts the power to prescribe rules that regulate evidence, bankruptcy, appellate proceedings, and criminal and civil procedures, but retains the authority to veto those rules. Through its appropriations power, Congress has a significant effect on the financial health of the judiciary (in 1994, the judicial branch represented about 0.1 percent of the federal budget). Congress, through its legislative committees and the authorizations, oversight, and investigation processes, directly affects the administration of justice (Kastenmeier and Remington, 1988, pp. 65–70). The Judicial Conduct and Disability Act of 1980, the Speedy Trial Act of 1974, the Judicial Improvements and Access to Justice Act of 1988, and the Judicial Improvements Act of 1990 are examples of such legislative activity. The first created mechanisms within the judicial branch to assess complaints against judges; the second regulated the conduct of trials; the third (among other things) established within the Judicial Conference a Federal Courts Study Committee to study and report on the future of the federal judiciary; and the fourth created a national commission to examine judicial discipline and removal.

Legislation that affects judicial administration is the product of the Judiciary committees, in particular their subcommittees: the House Subcommittee on Intellectual Property and Judicial Administration and the Senate Subcommittee on Courts. The two Judiciary panels receive more bills and resolutions than any other committees in the House and Senate (Davidson, 1988, pp. 104–105), but interest in judicial administration tends to be restricted to the two subcommittees. Despite the fact that virtually all legislation affects the courts charged with interpreting statutes, few committees are cognizant of the consequences on the judiciary.

Congress is, of course, central to the determination of judicial pay, survivors' annuities, and travel expenses. With respect to salaries, the Commission on Executive, Legislative, and Judicial Salaries makes its report to the president by 15 December every four years, and the president then accepts, changes, or rejects its proposals. The president's recommendations take effect unless disapproved by a joint resolution of Congress, not later than thirty days following the transmittal of the recommendations.

Congressional responses to judicial decisions. In response to judicial decisions, Congress can take a variety of actions (Fisher, 1988, pp. 200–230). Four times, the legislative branch was a partner in the effort to overturn the Court through constitutional amendments. The Eleventh Amendment sought to reverse *Chisolm v. Georgia* (2 U.S. [2 Dall.] 419 [1793]), which held that a state could be sued in federal court by out-of-state plaintiffs; the Thirteenth, Fourteenth, and Fifteenth Amendments

overturned *Scott v. Sandford* (60 U.S. [19 How.] 393 (1857]), which ruled that blacks as a class were not citizens protected by the Constitution; the Sixteenth Amendment overturned *Pollock v. Farmers' Loan and Trust Co.* (157 U.S. 429 [1895]), which voided a federal income tax; and the Twenty-sixth Amendment reversed a court decision, *Oregon v. Mitchell* (400 U.S. 112 [1970]), which had nullified a congressional attempt to lower the minimum voting age in state elections to eighteen.

Congress also occasionally passes legislation in reaction to judicial interpretations of its statutes (Henschen, 1983; Mikva and Bleich, 1991). Between 1967 and 1990, Congress overrode 121 of the Court's statutory decisions, compared with only 21 such reversals between 1945 and 1957 (Eskridge, 1991). One such example was legislation, passed over President Reagan's veto, responding to *Grove City College v. Bell* (464 U.S. 555 [1984]). In that case, the Supreme Court ruled that Title IX of the Education Amendments of 1972, which prohibited sex discrimination in any education program or activity that received federal financial assistance, applied only to those specific programs tainted by the discrimination. Congress's 1988 legislation essentially holds that federal funds would be terminated for the entire institution, not simply the specific program.

In another important instance, Congress overturned twelve rulings of the Court with the Civil Rights Act of 1991. Thus, it reversed *Wards Cove Packing, Inc. v. Atonio* (490 U.S. 642 [1989]) and returned the burden to employers (sued for discrimination) of proving that their hiring practices are "job-related to the position in question and consistent with business necessity." Congress, in that same act, reversed eight other decisions that had made it more difficult for women and African Americans to prove discrimination in employment—*Crawford Fitting Co. v. J. T. Gibbons, Inc.* (482 U.S. 437 [1987]); *Price Waterhouse v. Hopkins* (490 U.S. 228 [1989]); *West Virginia University Hospitals v. Casey* (111 S. Ct. 1138 [1991]); *Independent Federation of Flight Attendants v. Zipes* (491 U.S. 754 [1989]); *Evans v. Jeff D.* (474 U.S. 717 [1986]); and *Marek v. Chesney* (473 U.S. 1 [1985])—and less difficult for whites to challenge court-ordered affirmative-action programs—*Lorance v. AT&T* (490 U.S. 900 [1989]) and *Martin v. Wilks,* (490 U.S. 755 [1989]). Congress broadened the coverage of the 1866 Civil Rights Act to forbid discrimination in all phases of employment, not only in hiring practices, as the Rehnquist Court ruled in *Patterson v. McClean Credit Union* (485 U.S. 617 [1988]). Overturning *Equal Employment Opportunity Commission v. Arabian American Oil* (111 S.Ct. 1227 [1991]), Congress provided protection against discrimination based on race, religion, gender, and national origin to employees of American companies who are stationed abroad. Last, Congress overrode a 1986 decision, *Library of Congress v. Shaw* (478 U.S. 310 [1986]), to allow winning parties in cases against the federal government to recover interest payments as compensation for delays in securing awards for past discrimination. Through these various means, Congress thus engages in what Louis Fisher has called a "dialogue" (Fisher, 1988), or as Alexander Bickel put it, "a continuing colloquy" (Bickel, 1962, p. 240; Murphy, 1986, p. 401). Some in Congress have attempted to remove the Supreme Court from the decision-making process by withdrawing the Court's jurisdiction to hear appeals in such cases as school prayer, abortion, and school busing, but these endeavors have thus far failed.

Present and Future State of Relations. If Congress and the judiciary affect each other in fundamental ways, each also feels that the other needs to better understand its institutional workings. From the judiciary's perspective, Congress seems often unaware of the courts' institutional needs. In this view, the legislative branch consistently adds to the judiciary's burdens without concomitant resources. Apart from the Judiciary committees and Appropriations committees of Congress, the sense is that few in the legislative branch focus on the problems of the courts. From the legislature's vantage point, the judiciary often seems unattuned to the critical nuances of the legislative process. Using strong words, Judge Frank M. Coffin, a former House member, described the state of affairs between the branches as one of "estrangement." Former Rep. Robert W. Kastenmeier and Judiciary Committee staff member Michael Remington commented that "as participants in the legislative process, we are struck by the simple fact that few in Congress know much about or pay attention to the third branch of government" (Kastenmeier and Remington, 1988, p. 54). Judge Deanell R. Tacha lamented that the "complexities of the law-making and law-interpreting tasks in the third century of this republic cry out for systematic dialogue between those who make and those who interpret legislation" (Tacha, 1991, p. 281). Yet many in each branch are uncertain about how and under what conditions they can interact with members of the others.

To some extent, the judiciary is hesitant to maintain a greater presence because of constitutional barriers against rendering advisory opinions and the need to avoid prejudging issues that might come before it. Even regarding nonadjudicatory matters, some of which directly affect the administration of justice, there is unease that Congress might view such involvement as improper. To be sure, the perception that the courts are above the political fray reinforces the judiciary's legitimacy, although such a stance is not without costs.

Members of Congress might be more sensitive to the problems of the courts if they were more knowledgeable about the courts' problems. In addition, Congress generally does not draw upon judicial experience when it revises laws. Courts that have had to grapple with statutes may have something useful to contribute when Congress considers changing them; they may, for example, be able to identify parts of legislation that need legislative review. The gap between the branches, however, has inhibited such input.

Even more fundamentally, perhaps, distance has fostered among some on Capitol Hill a feeling of hostility toward the "Third Branch." Judges, according to this view, are unelected, imperial beings who mangle legislation to impose their preferences on society. But this perception ignores the irony that judicial action is often a function of legislative directives. Not infrequently, Congress passes the buck to the courts to avoid controversial choices and then blames judges for rendering decisions that it in fact mandated.

In recent years, efforts have been made by the judiciary and by some in Congress to bridge the gulf between the branches. The Administrative Office of the U.S. Courts, the Federal Judicial Center, and some of the committees of the Judicial Conference, particularly the Committee on the Judicial Branch, have all devoted attention to improving relations between the branches. More generally, Chief Justice William Rehnquist focused on improving interbranch relations as the theme of his 1992 end-of-the-year report. Within Congress, the Subcommittee on Intellectual Property, Civil Liberties, and the Administration of Justice of the House Committee on the Judiciary, and the Joint Committee on the Organization of Congress, have held hearings on problems of interbranch relations. Private organizations such as the Brookings Institution and the Governance Institute have also sought to work with both branches in an attempt to increase understanding between Congress and the courts. At the invitation of the U.S. Judicial Conference Committee on the Judicial Branch, the Governance Institute has undertaken a major project with two principal themes. The first examines the sorts of ground rules for communication and patterns of relationships that are proper. The second explores how the judiciary can better understand the legislative process and legislative history, how Congress can better signal the intent of its legislation, and how the courts can make the legislature better understand its decisions that interpret statutes. The objective is to devise or refine mechanisms to ameliorate relations between the branches. One product of that effort is a pilot project, begun with the participation of both chambers of Congress, in which the opinions of various courts of appeals, which identify problems in statutes, are sent to the legislative branch for consideration. This is but one more step that could help bridge the gulf between Congress and the courts.

No one should harbor any illusions about the ease with which some of the problems in judicial-congressional relations can be resolved. Indeed, some may simply be an inevitable part of the political system. But to the extent that one branch better appreciates the processes of the other, unnecessary tensions may be avoided.

[*See also* Advice and Consent; Confirmation; Constitution; Court-Packing Fight; Eleventh Amendment; Fourteenth Amendment; Impeachment; Judicial Review; Judiciary Act of 1789; Judiciary Committee, House; Judiciary Committee, Senate; Legislative Courts; Legislative Intent; Senatorial Courtesy. *For discussion of particular Supreme Court cases, see* Baker v. Carr; Bowsher v. Synar; Buckley v. Valeo; Davis et al. v. Bandemer et al.; Gravel v. United States; Immigration and Naturalization Service v. Chadha; Kilbourn v. Thompson; McCulloch v. Maryland; McGrain v. Daugherty; Marbury v. Madison; Morrison v. Olson; Myers v. United States; Powell v. McCormack; Scott v. Sandford; United States v. Curtiss-Wright Export Corp.; Watkins v. United States; Wesberry v. Sanders; Youngstown Sheet and Tube Co. v. Sawyer.]

BIBLIOGRAPHY

Abraham, Henry J. *Justices and Presidents*. 3d ed. 1992.
Baum, Lawrence. *The Supreme Court*. 1985.
Bickel, Alexander M. *The Least Dangerous Branch*. 1962.
Davidson, Roger H. "What Judges Ought to Know about Lawmaking in Congress." In *Judges and Legislators*. Edited by Robert A. Katzmann. 1988.
Eskridge, William N., Jr. "Overriding Supreme Court Statutory Interpretation Decisions." *Yale Law Journal* 101 (1991): 331, 338.
Eskridge, William N., Jr., and Philip Frickey. *Cases and Materials on Legislation: Statutes and the Creation of Public Policy*. 1988.
Fisher, Louis. *Constitutional Dialogues: Interpretation as Political Process*. 1988.
Henschen, Beth. "Statutory Interpretations of the Supreme Court: Congressional Response." *American Political Quarterly* 11 (1983): 441.
Kastenmeier, Robert W., and Michael S. Remington. "A Judicious Legislator's Lexicon to the Federal Judiciary." In *Judges and Legislators*. Edited by Robert A. Katzmann. 1988.
Katzmann, Robert A. "Approaching the Bench: Judicial Confirmation in Perspective." *Brookings Review* 6 (Spring 1988): 42–46.
Katzmann, Robert A. *Institutional Disability: The Sage of Transportation Policy for the Disabled*. 1986.
Katzmann, Robert A. *Judges and Legislators: Toward Institutional Comity*. 1988.
McCloskey, Robert G. *The American Supreme Court*. 1960.
Melnick, R. Shep. "The Politics of Partnership." *Public Administration Review* 45 (November 1985): 653–660.
Mikva, Abner J. "Reading and Writing Statutes." *University of Pittsburgh Law Review* 48 (1987): 627.
Mikva, Abner J., and Jeff Bleich. "When Congress Overrides the Court." *California Law Review* 79 (1991): 729.
Murphy, Walter F. "Who Shall Interpret? The Quest for the Ultimate Constitutional Interpreter." *Review of Politics* 48 (1986): 401.
Shapiro, Martin M. *Who Guards the Guardians? Judicial Control of Administration*. 1988.
Tacha, Deanell. "Judges and Legislators: Renewing the Relationship." *Ohio State Law Journal* 52 (1991): 279, 281.

ROBERT A. KATZMANN

JUDICIARY COMMITTEE, HOUSE.

The House Committee on the Judiciary has been a permanent standing committee since 1813. Its formal jurisdiction has come to include all matters dealing with federal courts and judges; federal crimes and prisons; civil rights and liberties; the Federal Bureau of Investigation; immigration and the naturalization of citizens; bankruptcy; patents, copyrights, and trademarks; antitrust law and monopolies; and administrative law. In addition, it is the only House committee that has jurisdiction over proposed constitutional amendments. Thus, the Congress has entrusted the committee with some of its most important constitutional and judicial issues.

According to Richard Fenno's book *Congressmen in Committees* (1973), House Judiciary is a prototypical policy-oriented committee that draws members because they want to make good public policy. In recent history the committee members have tended to be ideologically polarized, in that the

Democrats tend to be much more liberal than their colleagues in the full House, and Republicans tend to be much more conservative than their colleagues. Its policy-oriented members are almost all experienced lawyers who are interested in producing policies that deal directly with the legal system in general and with the courts in particular.

In the 1960s and 1970s, the House Judiciary Committee handled very significant legislation dealing with the burning civil rights and civil liberties issues of the day. It was at that time a much desired and highly visible committee for policy-oriented members, especially liberals. After the election of Ronald Reagan to the White House in 1980, however, the committee's Democratic leadership changed the focus of the committee in an attempt to kill the president's conservative social agenda. The committee became a graveyard for many conservative initiatives, including proposed constitutional amendments. Many House members, liberals and conservatives alike, were often privately pleased that the committee did not act on the many emotionally charged issues before it, because they were thereby protected from difficult votes. Nevertheless, membership on House Judiciary became less desirable because of the committee's inactivity, and because members had to face difficult and divisive issues such as abortion, crime control, school prayer, busing, balanced budget amendments, and flag burning.

Committee Leadership. The Judiciary Committee has experienced very little turnover in its leadership. In fact, only three powerful individuals have chaired the committee in the post–World War II era: Emanuel Celler (D-N.Y.) during the 81st and 82d Congresses (1949–1952) and again from the 84th through 92d Congress (1955–1972); Peter W. Rodino, Jr. (D-N.J.), from the 93d through 100th Congress (1973–1988); and Jack Brooks (D-Tex.) from the 101st Congress (1989–). Thus, the committee has had a history of leadership by powerful senior members of the House.

Celler was a true liberal who was instrumental in helping President Lyndon B. Johnson get the landmark Civil Rights Act of 1964 enacted. After he had chaired the committee for the better part of two decades, Celler's reign ended in 1972 when he was defeated in the Democratic primary in his Brooklyn district, in part because of his advanced age. Also a northeastern liberal, Rodino presided over the Watergate investigations and hearings of 1973–1974 and encouraged the enactment of the landmark compromise Immigration Control and Reform Act

of 1986. Rodino, who represented a district in Newark with a black majority, retired at the age of seventy-nine rather than face a possible primary challenge. Brooks, the former chair of the House Government Operations Committee, was somewhat less liberal than his predecessors, but the nature of the committee did not change drastically under him. This may be because Brooks is one of the most partisan Democrats in the House today. Even when disagreeing with his liberal Democratic colleagues on many issues, Brooks hated to allow the Republicans to gain even the slightest victory. Under Brooks, the committee approved almost annual crime control bills; a statute that unsuccessfully attempted to prohibit flag burning following the Supreme Court's decision in *Texas v. Johnson* (1989), which declared that flag burning is a form of protected political speech; and the Civil Rights Act of 1991, which overturned more than a dozen Supreme Court decisions dealing with proving discrimination in the workplace.

From 1983, the ranking Republican on the committee was Hamilton Fish, Jr. (R-N.Y.), much less conservative than his fellow Judiciary Republicans. When Fish joined the committee as a freshman in 1969, he was part of a numerous group of moderate Judiciary Republicans who supported civil rights and other liberal causes. By 1992, he was the only moderate-to-liberal member remaining on the Republican side of the committee.

The Committee of Lawyers. The House Judiciary Committee is often referred to as the "committee of lawyers," because traditionally only lawyers have served on it. Perhaps this is because attorneys feel more comfortable with the highly legalistic subject matter of the committee. Roughly half of all House members since the First Congress have been lawyers, while nearly all the Judiciary Committee members have been attorneys. In addition, the vast majority of Judiciary members had practiced law for at least five years before being elected to political office. For example, during the 101st Congress (1989–1991), almost 60 percent of House Judiciary members had practiced law for more than five years before election to either a state legislature or the House.

Due to the fact that the House Judiciary Committee attracts so many attorneys, its deliberative style is very much like that of the courts. Judiciary is the only House committee with a formally designated parliamentarian, and its hearings and markup sessions often look and sound more like courtroom proceedings than political events. The members utilize formal markup sessions in which the exact language of legislation is hotly debated. They rarely delegate the drafting of final legislative language to staff. Judiciary staff function much like law clerks for judges or like junior associates in a large law firm, and they are hired for their legal skills as well as for their political savvy. Staff are generally prohibited from talking to the press and are very cautious in talking with academics.

Hearings on House Judiciary are designed to bring out both sides of any controversy, and they serve to build a record in support of legislative action. Judiciary hearings are thorough and workmanlike, with a level of questioning often much higher intellectually than on other committees. In addition, the committee's oversight of executive agencies tends to be relatively slow and methodical. In their oversight role, Judiciary Committee members seem to act more like judges than prosecutors.

Judiciary members spend a great deal more time than members of other committees debating the constitutionality of the legislation that they approve. Judiciary members and staff pride themselves on their ability to anticipate how the federal courts will read the legislative language produced by the committee. Unlike most House committees, Judiciary also has formal rules against interfering in any way with ongoing litigation, and a committee norm prescribes that no bills should take effect retroactively.

Interaction with the Courts. The Judiciary Committee often interacts with the federal courts, both because it has jurisdiction over judicial salaries and the creation of new judgeships and because lobbyists and others often ask it to overturn court decisions that are unfavorable to their interests. Because they are lawyers, Judiciary members are very likely to read the actual court opinions themselves, while members of other committees are more likely to rely on interpretations of staff or interest groups. Recent research has found that the Judiciary Committee is somewhat more hesitant than other committees to overturn controversial federal court decisions. The committee will move to overturn court decisions when appropriate, but only after careful study and analysis of the ramifications of such action. In recent years, the committee has approved legislation to overturn various antitrust, criminal procedure, and civil rights decisions from federal courts.

The legal training and outlook of the members have probably fundamentally influenced their view of the proper role and decision-making style of the committee. One also suspects they have greatly marked the substantive decisions that the committee is willing to make. In many ways, the Judiciary Committee functions in a manner analogous to that of a large law firm or a court. The members of the committee (the judges or senior partners) react to the important issues before them. They leave the lesser issues to the committee staff (analogous to law clerks or junior associates). The work of other committees is occasionally influenced by the legal training of some of their members, but lawyer-legislators on other committees are likely to have acquired law degrees as a matter of political expediency. Many of them do not have extensive law practice experience. The lawyers on Judiciary are different, however, in that they are mostly experienced lawyers who bring a unique mix of politics and law to their work.

[*See also* Judiciary Committee, Senate.]

BIBLIOGRAPHY

Cohodas, Nadine. "House Judiciary Looks to Post-Rodino Era." *Congressional Quarterly Weekly Report*, 7 June 1986, p. 1307.

Perkins, Lynette P. "Influence of Members' Goals on Their Committee Behavior: The U.S. House Judiciary Committee." *Legislative Studies Quarterly* 5 (1980): 373–392.

Perkins, Lynette P. "Member Recruitment to a Mixed Goal Committee: The House Judiciary Committee." *Journal of Politics* 43 (1981): 348–364.

Ralph Nader Congress Project. *The Judiciary Committees: A Study of the House and Senate Judiciary Committees.* 1975.

MARK C. MILLER

JUDICIARY COMMITTEE, SENATE.

The Committee on the Judiciary is one of the oldest committees in the U.S. Senate, with a jurisdiction that encompasses some of the most important and divisive issues in American politics, including abortion, busing, the death penalty, crime and gun control, habeas corpus reform, and school prayer. The Judiciary Committee is also one of the busiest committees in Congress. During the 101st Congress (1989–1991), more than 21 percent of the measures referred to Senate committees were sent to the Committee on the Judiciary—the greatest committee workload in the chamber. The Judiciary Committee is also highly visible. For instance, the committee's hearings on the nominations to the U.S. Supreme Court drew intense public scrutiny in the 1980s and 1990s, making the committee a potentially important forum for the public discussion of pressing social and constitutional issues.

The Judiciary Committee was created in 1816, when the Senate first developed a system of standing committees with fixed jurisdictions. Since that time, the panel has played a significant role in many of the key political issues of U.S. history. During the Civil War, for example, Chairman Lyman Trumbell of Illinois helped ensure that President Abraham Lincoln had the emergency powers necessary to pursue the war effort. In 1889 the Judiciary Committee reported what became the landmark Sherman Antitrust Act. In 1937 the Judiciary Committee blocked President Franklin D. Roosevelt's infamous attempt to pack the Supreme Court. And throughout its long history, the Judiciary Committee has been a potentially important arena for the consideration of civil rights measures.

Jurisdiction. Since the creation of the panel the jurisdiction of the Senate Judiciary Committee has centered on law enforcement and the courts. The early Judiciary Committee also considered the admission of new states into the Union, overseeing, for example, the landmark Missouri Compromise of 1820.

The committee has jurisdiction over seventeen distinct areas: (1) apportionment of representatives; (2) bankruptcy, mutiny, espionage, and counterfeiting; (3) civil liberties; (4) constitutional amendments; (5) federal courts and judges; (6) access to governmental information; (7) holidays and celebrations; (8) immigration and naturalization; (9) interstate compacts; (10) civil and criminal judicial proceedings; (11) local courts in the territories and possessions; (12) claims against the United States; (13) federal penitentiaries; (14) patents, copyrights, and trademarks; (15) antitrust policy; (16) revision of the criminal code; and (17) state and territorial boundary lines.

The Judiciary Committee also considers a wide range of nominations by the president, including nominations to the U.S. Supreme Court. Before 1868, there was no requirement that Supreme Court nominations be referred to the Committee on the Judiciary, and only one-third of Supreme Court nominees were formally considered in committee. Since then, however, the Judiciary Committee has been central to the confirmation process. The committee is also responsible for initial scrutiny of executive branch nominees for the U.S. district and circuit courts, high Justice Department officials, and U.S. attorneys across the country. During the 101st Congress, the Judiciary Committee deliberat-

ed on 171 executive nominations, of which 162 were eventually confirmed by the full Senate.

Political Environment. Judiciary Committee deliberations are swayed by a larger political environment comprised of interest groups, executive branch officials, judges, and public opinion. These elements of the political environment vary in their degree of influence, depending on the issue at hand.

Interest groups are crucial in certain areas of the committee's jurisdiction. Antitrust policy, for instance, is of concern primarily to affected economic interests and to consumer groups. Patent and copyright policy also activates economic interests. Immigration issues tend to energize a range of competing interests, including organized labor, industry, and groups representing ethnic minorities. The legal community is active on most major bills considered by the Judiciary Committee.

Similarly, agencies in the executive branch of the federal government can shape the Judiciary Committee's agenda, as well as the behavior of committee members. The most important of these is the Justice Department: the committee tends to take very seriously the views of high Justice Department officials on committee legislation, and significant opposition from the Department of Justice can signal a potential presidential veto unless substantive changes are made in a bill.

The Judiciary Committee's agenda is also influenced by Court decisions. For example, in *Texas v. Johnson* (1989), the Supreme Court overruled a statute that prohibited physical desecration of the American flag. The general public was outraged, and as a result, a constitutional amendment to overturn the decision was introduced in the Senate and considered by the Judiciary Committee. Other Supreme Court decisions have also sparked a legislative response in the Judiciary Committee.

Above and beyond these influences, however, public opinion is the single most important component of the environment in which the committee operates. Members of the public often have strong policy preferences, particularly on the more controversial social issues considered in the panel's Subcommittee on the Constitution. On such issues, despite the role played by interest groups and the executive and judicial branches, the mood of the voters tends to dominate committee deliberations.

Structure. Because members' preferences on so many Judiciary Committee issues are very intense, participation in committee deliberations is relatively broad. As a result, the resources and prerogatives

ATTORNEY GENERAL ROBERT F. KENNEDY. *Right,* appearing before the Senate Judiciary Committee during hearings on civil rights, July 1963.   LIBRARY OF CONGRESS

that facilitate such participation are also widely distributed, making the Senate Judiciary Committee one of the most decentralized committees in Congress.

During most of the 1970s, there were as many as seventeen subcommittees on the Judiciary Committee. In 1977, however, the Senate subcommittee system was streamlined, and the number of subcommittees on Judiciary fell to six or seven, where it has remained.

Most of the committee's areas of jurisdiction are parceled out to one or more subcommittees. The major exception during the chairmanship of Republican Strom Thurmond of South Carolina (1981–1987) was antitrust policy, which was held at full committee. When Thurmond became chairman, he chose not to recreate the Subcommittee on Antitrust, reportedly because an antitrust subcommittee would have been chaired by liberal Republican Charles McC. Mathias, Jr., of Maryland, whose

policy preferences differed from Thurmond's. When Democrat Joseph R. Biden, Jr., of Delaware became chairman in 1987, he did create a subcommittee on antitrust but opted to retain many criminal law issues at full committee. On most issues considered by the panel, however, members are able to participate at both the full and subcommittee levels.

The Judiciary Committee staff is large and very decentralized. Each subcommittee has its own staff, hired and fired by the subcommittee chair and ranking minority member. Besides being expert on issues related to their own subcommittee, these aides also tend to follow other Judiciary Committee issues for their bosses. Consequently, most members of the committee have the staff assistance necessary to participate in committee decision making on a broad range of issues.

Decision Making. Legislative work in the Judiciary Committee reflects legislative work in the Senate as a whole. Deliberations in the committee can be highly polarized and ideological, with many members taking an active role in debate and the amendment process. And as the minority sometimes does on the Senate floor, members of the minority on Judiciary have been known to use dilatory tactics in committee to stall or block items they oppose. For example, during the early 1980s, when Republicans were in the majority, liberal Democrats Howard M. Metzenbaum of Ohio and Edward M. Kennedy of Massachusetts occasionally extended debate in the panel. Similarly, Strom Thurmond and other conservative Republicans used delaying tactics in the late 1970s, when Democrats controlled the chamber.

Throughout most of the 1960s and 1970s, the Judiciary Committee was chaired by Democrat James O. Eastland of Mississippi. Eastland, for most of his career an archsegregationist, usually led a solid working majority of conservative Democrats and Republicans. As a result, he was able to block or delay civil rights legislation, as well as other initiatives favored by liberal Democrats but opposed by the conservative coalition. Committee liberals were forced to circumvent the panel entirely to pass many of the landmark civil rights measures of the 1960s. The Civil Rights Act of 1964, for example, was not considered by the Senate Judiciary Committee, and the Voting Rights Act of 1965 was automatically reported to the full Senate when Eastland refused to schedule the necessary meetings.

The ideological preferences of the chair shifted substantially when Edward M. Kennedy became chairman of the Judiciary Committee in 1978. With Kennedy in the chair, liberal legislation was placed on the panel's agenda, but the membership of the committee remained split along ideological lines. As a result, Kennedy and other committee liberals were forced to compromise with Republicans and conservative Democrats to pass legislation in committee.

In 1981 the committee shifted back to the right with the election of a Republican Senate majority and the elevation of South Carolina's Strom Thurmond to the chairmanship. Thurmond generally had a conservative majority, but on certain issues the committee split, giving the balance of power to swing voters Arlen Specter (R-Pa.), Dennis DeConcini (D-Ariz.), and Howell Heflin (D-Ala.).

Thurmond's major interests as chairman concerned criminal law, where a degree of cooperation between committee liberals and conservatives was often possible. For example, after many years of effort, in the 98th Congress (1983–1985) the Judiciary Committee reported to the full Senate a major reform of the nation's criminal code. The measure became law in 1984.

Thurmond also advocated the social agenda of the so-called New Right, much of which fell under the Judiciary Committee's jurisdiction. On these issues, however, Thurmond generally deferred to fellow Republican Orrin G. Hatch of Utah, who chaired the Constitution Subcommittee and was more concerned than Thurmond about such matters. Although the committee considered and reported measures relating to abortion and school prayer during the Thurmond chairmanship, these initiatives died either in the full Senate or in the Democratically controlled House.

The Judiciary Committee shifted somewhat to the left when Democrats regained control of the Senate in 1987, although on close votes, the balance of power was still held by the swing voters— Specter, DeConcini, and Heflin. Chairman Joseph R. Biden, like Thurmond, was primarily interested in criminal law issues. Consequently, during the 101st Congress, for example, the committee reported measures relating to sentencing procedures, bail reform, habeas corpus, violence against women, and child abuse.

The potential for ideological polarization on the Judiciary Committee continued to exist under Democratic control of the Senate. In 1989, for instance, the panel was deeply divided over whether to report to the floor the proposed constitutional amendment to prohibit flag burning. And in October 1991, after a weekend of anguished testimony before a national television audience, the Judiciary Committee split 7 to 7 on the confirmation of Judge Clarence Thomas to the U.S. Supreme Court.

The Senate Judiciary Committee was the target of significant criticism in the 1980s and early 1990s. By most accounts, the committee's handling of the Thomas nomination in 1991 seriously damaged its reputation with the general public. Further tainting its reputation is the fact that the Judiciary Committee has only rarely produced major legislation subsequently passed by Congress and signed into law. Particularly in the highest-profile areas of the committee's jurisdiction—issues such as abortion, busing, gun control, and school prayer—committee recommendations have seldom prevailed. Those Judiciary Committee measures that have become law have tended to fall instead in the area of criminal law or the less controversial portions of the committee's jurisdiction, such as juvenile justice and administrative law.

The uneven performance of the Senate Judiciary Committee should be evaluated from the perspective of the political constraints within which the panel must operate. The areas over which the committee has jurisdiction are rife with conflict, and the committee membership traditionally has been deeply divided over policy. Because of these constraints, the committee's most important role may be to provide a national forum for regular discussion of some of the most contentious issues in U.S. politics. This alone is a valuable contribution.

[*See also* Judiciary Committe, House.]

BIBLIOGRAPHY

Biskupic, Joan. "Thomas Hearings Illustrate Politics of the Process." *Congressional Quarterly Weekly Report,* 21 September 1991, pp. 2688–2692.

Evans, C. Lawrence. *Leadership in Committee: A Comparative Analysis of Leadership Behavior in the U.S. Senate.* 1991.

Schuck, Peter. *The Judiciary Committees.* 1975.

U.S. Senate. Committee on the Judiciary. *History of the Committee on the Judiciary, 1816–1981.* 99th Cong., 1st sess., 1985. S. Doc. 97-78.

C. LAWRENCE EVANS

GEORGE W. JULIAN.   LIBRARY OF CONGRESS

JULIAN, GEORGE W. (1817–1899), representative from Indiana, Radical Republican leader. Elected to the 31st Congress (1849–1851) as a Free-Soiler from Indiana's Fourth Congressional District, comprising four eastern border counties with large Quaker and antislavery populations, Julian opposed the Compromise of 1850 as too favorable to slaveholders, and as a land reformer he supported the Homestead Act. This combination of antislavery fervor and concern for land reform set the pattern for Julian's congressional career.

Returning as a Republican to the 37th Congress in 1861, he served five consecutive terms. A leader of the Radical faction, he became a member of the Committee on the Conduct of the War, working with Senators Benjamin F. Wade, Zachariah Chandler, and others for the removal of generals such as George B. McClellan who refused to wage a war against slavery while fighting to preserve the Union. Although Julian remained personally friendly to Abraham Lincoln, he opposed the president's relatively moderate wartime reconstruction policies, especially his refusal to confiscate the real property of rebels beyond the owners' natural lifetimes. But Julian withdrew from the Radical plot to deny Lincoln the Republican nomination in 1864.

As chairman of the House Committee on Public Lands from 1863 on, Julian was untiring in his ef-

forts to protect the public domain from speculators, monopolists, and railroads and to provide homesteads for settlers, white and black. Most of his projects failed, but he succeeded in winning passage of the Southern Homestead Act in 1866.

On reconstruction, Julian was as radical as Thaddeus Stevens. He wanted Jefferson Davis tried and hanged if found guilty, was outraged by the "spared life" of Robert E. Lee, and condemned the nation's "sickly magnanimity and misapplied humanity . . . in dealing with its leading traitors." Julian detested Andrew Johnson and wanted to be one of the managers of impeachment, but he received only a membership on the committee that drew up the articles of impeachment. The Reconstruction acts of 1867 were too mild for Julian, and he objected to their provision for military occupation of the South.

Unwelcome in the Republican party of Ulysses S. Grant and contending that the ratification of the Thirteenth, Fourteenth, and Fifteenth Amendments to the Constitution made the existence of the party unnecessary, Julian joined the Liberal Republicans in 1872 and the Democratic party in 1876. By that time he had abandoned his crusade for freedmen's rights.

BIBLIOGRAPHY

Clarke, Grace Julian. *George W. Julian.* 1923.
Julian, George W. *Political Recollections, 1840 to 1872.* 1883.
Riddleberger, Patrick W. *George Washington Julian, Radical Republican: A Study in Nineteenth-Century Politics and Reform.* 1966.

PATRICK W. RIDDLEBERGER

JUNKETS. *See* Perquisites; Travel.

JURISDICTION. *See* Committees, *article on* Committee Jurisdictions.

JUSTICE. *See* Crime and Justice.

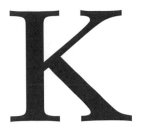

KANSAS. The Kansas Territory was established in the midst of growing tensions concerning the expansion of slavery—tensions that culminated in the Civil War. The Kansas-Nebraska Act became law on 30 May 1854, and the territory officially opened for settlement. It soon became a verbal, and occasionally literal, battleground for anti- and proslavery forces, as the territory's residents were to decide if the new state would allow or prohibit slavery. Legal and extralegal territorial governments were established; each side recruited militia; residents voted four different constitutions; elections were disputed, with one side often refusing to vote in elections sponsored by the other; and several outbreaks of violence occurred. In 1856 a congressional investigating committee toured Kansas and issued a lengthy report on its findings concerning numerous counts of electoral fraud and violence. The merits of the various constitutions were vigorously and acrimoniously debated in Congress, and "Bleeding Kansas" became the focal point for the slavery debate. Kansas finally entered the Union on 29 January 1861 under the Wyandotte constitution, which banned slavery and had been approved overwhelmingly by voters in 1859.

Over the years, Kansans have elected a number of prominent and colorful people to serve in the U.S. House of Representatives and the Senate. Republicans James H. Lane and Samuel C. Pomeroy served as the state's first senators, and Martin F. Conway was elected the first representative. Lane had been a leader among the most radical antislavery forces, and when the Civil War began in April 1861, Senator Lane organized the so-called Frontier Guard, which camped out in the East Room of the White House to protect President Abraham Lincoln. The guard remained in service for three weeks until sufficient Union troops reached Washington, D.C. Lane's successor, Republican Edmund G. Ross, is credited with casting the deciding vote in President Andrew Johnson's impeachment proceedings, as his place in the roll call provided the necessary votes for acquittal. Ross's decision to vote against the stand taken by the Republican party, and most Kansans, cost him his Senate seat.

In 1890, as an agrarian depression continued across the nation, discontented farmers in Kansas organized a statewide People's party that became part of the Populist movement. The Populists proposed a variety of reforms aimed at assisting workers and farmers: government ownership of all means of transportation and communication as a way of regulating the power of railroads over farmers; unlimited coinage of silver and other currency reform; direct election of senators; and adoption of the secret ballot, the initiative, and referendum. During the 1890s, Kansans elected twelve Populists to the House and one, William A. Peffer, to the Senate.

A number of the Kansas representatives and senators have concentrated on serving the agrarian interests of their constituents. Sen. Arthur Capper (1919–1949) and Rep. Clifford R. Hope (1927–1957), both Republicans, were leaders in the development of agricultural policies in the first half of the twentieth century, as was Rep. Frank Carlson (1935–1947; later senator, 1950–1969), also a Republican. Another Republican, Charles Curtis, who was part Kansa Indian, also served in the House (1899–1907) and then the Senate (1907–1913; 1915–1929), after which he was elected Herbert Hoover's vice president. Sen. Bob Dole was first elected to the House in 1961 and served until his election to the Senate in 1969. Dole was majority leader from 1985 to 1987, then minority leader (1987–) when the Republicans lost their briefly held Senate majority.

Until well into the twentieth century, most of the Kansas delegation in Congress were Republicans, with the exception of the Populists and an occasional Democrat. The state had one House member until 1873, the beginning of a period of rapid expansion in the delegation's size. The delegation reached a high of eight from 1893 until 1933 and gradually decreased thereafter. Kansas lost one seat after the 1990 census, reducing its House delegation to four. Kathryn O'Loughlin McCarthy was the first Kansas woman to be elected to the House (1933–1935), and Nancy Landon Kassebaum became the state's first woman senator after her election in 1978.

[See also Kansas-Nebraska Act.]

BIBLIOGRAPHY

Bright, John D. *Kansas: The First Century.* 1956.
Clanton, O. Gene. *Kansas Populism: Ideas and Men.* 1969.
Richmond, Robert W. *Kansas: A Land of Contrasts.* 1974.

PATRICIA A. MICHAELIS

KANSAS-NEBRASKA ACT

(1854; 10 Stat. 277–290). A major cause of the escalating sectional conflict before the Civil War, the Kansas-Nebraska Act opened the northern portion of the Louisiana Purchase to slavery. The bill had a complicated legislative history. Introduced by Sen. Stephen A. Douglas (D-Ill.) in January 1854, it met southern resistance for not repealing the Missouri Compromise of 1820, which had prohibited slavery in this region. Rewritten in a series of caucuses, the bill in its final form divided the area into two territories, Kansas and Nebraska, explicitly repealed the Missouri Compromise, and declared that the residents of each territory could decide the status of slavery there (an idea known as popular sovereignty).

Despite the protests of northerners opposed to the expansion of slavery, the bill easily passed the Senate in March 1854, and after a strenuous two-month struggle the House approved it in May by a vote of 113 to 100. The act drove a deep sectional wedge through both parties, as all northern Whigs and half the northern Democrats opposed it in the House, while all but nine southern representatives favored it. President Franklin Pierce quickly signed it into law.

Contrary to the promises of its supporters that it would peacefully resolve the slavery controversy, the law had a disastrous political impact. It severely weakened both parties, led to the formation of the sectional Republican party, deepened suspicions between the two sections, and produced unusual turmoil in Kansas, where fighting soon broke out between proslavery and antislavery factions. The Kansas-Nebraska Act was a major event in the coming of the Civil War.

BIBLIOGRAPHY

Johannsen, Robert W. *Stephen A. Douglas.* 1973.
Potter, David M. *The Impending Crisis, 1848–1861.* 1976.

WILLIAM E. GIENAPP

KEFAUVER, ESTES

(1903–1963), Democratic representative and senator from Tennessee best known for his investigations into organized crime and monopolies. Born into a rural middle-class family, Kefauver earned a law degree from Yale and entered practice in Chattanooga. In 1939 he won a special election to the U.S. House of Representatives. His courtship of the press and tireless campaigning proved the key to his subsequent reelections and to his stunning upset victory in a 1948 Senate race. That year, to symbolize his independence from bossism, Kefauver first donned the coonskin cap that would become his political trademark. A moderate on civil rights, he would win two subsequent Senate campaigns even while losing races for the Democratic presidential nomination in 1952 and 1956. He did, however, defeat Sen. John F. Kennedy to win his party's vice presidential nomination in 1956.

Kefauver took a particular interest in congressional reform. He displayed considerable impatience with the clubby protocol and the seniority system, publicly advocating limitations on the filibuster and the curbing of the powers of committee chairs. Congressional leaders frequently found Kefauver too publicity-conscious, overly ambitious, and unwilling to reciprocate favors. His style foreshadowed the more individualistic approaches to advancement that many legislators would follow in the late twentieth century.

Senator Kefauver's highly publicized investigations reflected his interests in antimonopoly activity. In 1950 and 1951, he chaired a special committee that exposed to fascinated television viewers the "cartel" of organized crime. During hearings of the Judiciary Subcommittee to Investigate Juvenile Delinquency, the Senator linked teenage crime to irresponsible behavior by the mass media. As chairman of the Judiciary Antitrust and Monopoly Subcommittee, he presided over controversial hearings into price-fixing in the steel, automobile, and pharmaceutical industries. The subcommittee's lengthy investigation of drug industry prices and practices, begun in 1957, culminated in passage of the Drug Amendments of 1962, which significantly tightened regulations under the Federal Food, Drug, and Cosmetic Act.

BIBLIOGRAPHY

Fontenay, Charles L. *Estes Kefauver: A Biography.* 1980.
Gorman, Joseph Bruce. *Kefauver: A Political Biography.* 1971.

WILLIAM HOWARD MOORE

KEFAUVER CRIME COMMITTEE. The Senate Special Committee to Investigate Organized Crime in Interstate Commerce, better known as the Kefauver committee of 1950 and 1951 after its chairman, Sen. Estes Kefauver (D-Tenn.), set the stage for almost two generations of highly publicized congressional hearings into the structure of the American criminal underworld.

The committee sprang from fears of a crime wave. Various citizens' crime commissions and a number of newspaper reporters had anticipated that gang warfare would mushroom in the unsettled postwar environment. Amid growing allegations that powerful national gambling syndicates were subverting local law enforcement, federal officials became increasingly concerned. The Truman administration launched a series of grand jury investigations and began auditing the income-tax returns of well-known racketeers, but some civic leaders found these efforts too limited and called for a broadly based congressional probe into organized crime in America.

Congress debated several alternative suggestions for such an investigation. Sen. Joseph R. McCarthy (R-Wis.) urged that the work be done by the Special Investigations Subcommittee of which he was a member. Senator Kefauver, a liberal Democrat with presidential ambitions, proposed a study by the Judiciary Committee on which he served. Others suggested that, because the problem involved interstate activities, the Senate Commerce Committee was the appropriate vehicle. In general, however, the discussions pivoted as much around who would serve on the investigating panel as they did on proper jurisdiction. Given the politically explosive nature of the subject, both the White House and congressional figures were concerned that it not be mishandled. The assassination of a Kansas City politician and gambling entrepreneur in a Democratic clubhouse (beneath a large wall photograph of Harry S. Truman) in April 1950 finally broke the congressional logjam. In May, the Senate created a special committee of five members drawn from both Judiciary and Commerce to conduct the investigation. Kefauver was made chairman, while two other Democrats and two Republicans served as members.

Kefauver generally dominated the committee. He established the principle that witnesses could be accompanied by attorneys and decided that television coverage would be permitted. Drawing from evidence collected by grand juries, citizens' crime commissions, journalists, and the Federal Bureau of Narcotics, he focused on allegations concerning the influence of nationwide gambling combines and on the sinister activities of an Italian-American syndicate, the Mafia. The committee and its staff visited some fourteen major cities in fifteen months, attracted unprecedented press and television coverage, and tried to balance the partisan damage done by its hearings. Kefauver proposed several remedial laws, including the creation of a Federal crime commission, but little legislation flowed from the committee's labors. This stemmed in part from the complexity of Senator Kefauver's proposals and in part from resentment of his publicity-seeking direction of the committee.

In addition to establishing Kefauver as a serious presidential possibility, the Kefauver committee molded public perceptions of organized crime as a highly centralized conspiracy of Italian-American gangsters. While criticized by academics, this interpretation has generally shaped the work of subsequent congressional investigations and the law enforcement community in general.

The unexpected presence of television at the New York hearings certainly dramatized the committee's conclusions. While not the first congressional committee to be televised, the Kefauver hearings were clearly the most spectacular. Able to capitalize on a sharp increase in the number of home TV sets, the committee captured in unforgettable fashion the furtive behavior and answers of underworld figures and their political allies. An estimated 30 million people viewed the Kefauver hearings and approximately 250,000 wrote directly to the committee. The unprecedented public reaction prompted a vigorous debate over the propriety of television in congressional hearings.

BIBLIOGRAPHY

Moore, William Howard. *The Kefauver Committee and the Politics of Crime, 1950–1952.* 1974.

Moore, William Howard. "Was Estes Kefauver 'Blackmailed' during the Chicago Crime Hearings?: A Historian's Perspective." *The Public Historian* 4 (1982): 5–28.

WILLIAM HOWARD MOORE

KELLEY, WILLIAM D.

KELLEY, WILLIAM D. (1814–1890), Republican representative from Pennsylvania who acquired the nickname "Pig-Iron" for his consistent support of high protective duties, especially on iron and steel. First elected to Congress in 1860 from the urban wards of the 4th District in Philadelphia, Kelley was reelected fourteen times. While in the House, he served on various committees, including Agriculture, Naval Affairs, and Indian Affairs. For twenty years Kelley served on the prestigious Ways and Means Committee, chairing it from 1881 to 1883.

A prominent supporter of Radical Reconstruction and an early advocate of civil rights for African Americans, Kelley was one of the first Republicans to call for nationwide black suffrage. The wording of his 1868 proposal for a constitutional amendment on that issue closely paralleled that of the 1870 Fifteenth Amendment. His meager formal education (he left school at age eleven) and his subsequent career as a young apprentice jeweler convinced him of the primacy of the laboring class over the economic elite. As an ardent advocate of labor's social and economic welfare, Kelley supported high tariffs (to protect American wages), the eight-hour workday, woman suffrage, a ban on foreign contract labor, homestead legislation, reclamation of public lands from domestic and foreign capitalists, a government-managed inflationary currency (paper greenbacks and, later, free silver), and arbitration of labor disputes. His daughter Florence Kelley (1859–1932) was a prominent social worker and reformer, who worked to improve life in the slums and championed protective labor legislation, especially for women and children. When William Kelley died in January 1890, as the oldest member in both years and service, he had earned the title bestowed on him: "Father of the House."

BIBLIOGRAPHY

Brown, Ira V. "William D. Kelley and Radical Reconstruction." *Pennsylvania Magazine of History and Biography* 85 (July 1961): 316–329.

Nicklas, Floyd William. "William Kelley: The Congressional Years, 1861–1890." Ph.D. diss., Northern Illinois University, 1983.

ROBERT S. SALISBURY

KENNEDY, JOHN F.

KENNEDY, JOHN F. (1917–1963), Democratic representative and senator from Massachusetts, thirty-fifth president of the United States (1961–1963). The first president born in the twentieth century, John Fitzgerald Kennedy became one of the most admired and popular chief executives in U.S. history. His "New Frontier" administration stressed youth and vigor, reason and eloquence, and wit and courage in seeking to end the Cold War with the Soviet Union abroad and racial inequality at home. He was assassinated on 22 November 1963, in Dallas, Texas, by a hidden rifleman identified as Lee Harvey Oswald.

As a young man, Kennedy was thoughtful, introspective, and physically somewhat frail. He aspired vaguely to a modest career in journalism. But he was pushed to the presidency by his father, Joseph Patrick Kennedy, a New Dealer and ambassador to England (1938–1940) during Franklin D. Roosevelt's second term. Joseph Kennedy was determined that one of his four sons would be the country's first Irish-Catholic president. When the eldest, Joseph Patrick, Jr., died in combat in World War II, the mantle fell on second son John.

Jack Kennedy was a war hero, too. A U.S. Navy lieutenant in the Pacific, he was hurt when a Japanese destroyer rammed and sank the torpedo-firing patrol boat he commanded, PT 109. He kept his crew together, saving one from drowning, until rescue came. In 1946, a brace on his injured back, he began his run for the White House as a twenty-nine-year-old candidate for the House of Representatives in Massachusetts' 11th District. His victory was a family affair. Brothers, sisters, cousins—the whole energetic, attractive clan—combined to create "the Kennedy mystique" that served him well again in 1952, when he ran for the Senate against the popular Republican incumbent, Henry Cabot Lodge, Jr., and won by seventy thousand votes. It was a harbinger of his defeat of Republican nominee Richard M. Nixon in the 1960 presidential race, a victory attributed to what many called "the smooth-running, well-oiled Kennedy machine," a description more myth than fact.

Kennedy's three two-year terms in the House lacked distinction. He backed the Truman Doctrine and the Marshall Plan for containing communism, reflecting the view, expressed in his 1940 book, *Why England Slept*, that "we must be prepared to take our part in setting up a world order that will prevent the rise of a militaristic dictatorship."

In the Senate, Kennedy gravitated even more toward national and international issues. His actions often were more conservative than his words seemed

JOHN F. KENNEDY. *Right*, with Robert F. Kennedy, on the Senate Select Committee on Improper Activities in the Labor or Management Field, March 1957.

to indicate. He raised no public objection, for instance, to the freewheeling, communist-hunting investigations of Republican senator Joseph R. McCarthy of Wisconsin, whom his father admired and on whose committee staff his brother Robert F. Kennedy served until he quit in protest against its tactics.

Kennedy spoke out on a wide spectrum of issues, honing a recognizable style marked by self-deprecating witticisms, historical and literary quotations, and elegant language, all mingled with detailed data. He gambled with the support of organized labor by serving on a Senate select committee that investigated union embezzlement, with brother Robert as chief counsel. In two years, the committee heard fifteen hundred witnesses over nearly three hundred days of public hearings (which produced 20,432 pages of testimony),

helped jail corrupt labor leaders, and led to laws requiring honest union elections and financial reports (Kennedy-Ives and Landrum-Griffin).

In September 1953, Jack Kennedy married the elegant, striking Jacqueline Bouvier. The match secured the Kennedy mystique, further enhanced in time by children Caroline and John, Jr. Kennedy's next book, *Profiles in Courage*, won the 1957 Pulitzer Prize for biography.

When Kennedy lost a bid for the vice presidential nomination at the Democrats' 1956 convention, his 1960 campaign for the presidential nomination began the next day, with brother Robert again his manager. Kennedy won first-ballot nomination by a bare majority and picked Sen. Lyndon B. Johnson of Texas as his vice presidential running mate. A Roman Catholic, he pledged his private religious views would never interfere with his presidential duties. He challenged voters to join his New Frontier, proclaiming that "the torch has been passed to a new generation of Americans." He came from behind to nose out Nixon, 34,227,096 to 34,108,546 at the polls (303 to 219 in the Electoral College). His inaugural address commanded: "Ask not what your country can do for you, ask what you can do for your country."

He drew heavily on his alma mater, Harvard, in assembling a young, intellectual, politically savvy, well-to-do, industrious, somewhat-liberal administration that included brother Robert as attorney general and closest confidant on all matters. Kennedy had a strong interest in foreign policy, seeking to stabilize U.S.-Soviet relations and maintain a strong U.S. economy in the Cold War. His national agenda embraced the unfinished business of the New Deal. In his first three months, he called on Congress for legislation to improve health and hospital care, education, natural resources, highways, housing and community development, agriculture, and regulatory agencies. Other messages soon followed on civil rights, transportation, public welfare, consumer protection, mental illness, the elderly, and youth. During his three years as president, Kennedy sent up a record 1,054 legislative requests.

However, his legislative proposals had hard going in a Congress more conservative than his administration. Kennedy's narrow victory over Nixon was mirrored in the 87th Congress (1961–1963). The Democrats maintained control in the 1960 elections but failed to gain appreciably over Republicans, winding up with a 263 to 174 House majority and a 64 to 36 Senate majority. Moreover, the balance of power was held by a coalition of Republicans and Democratic conservatives. The latter included ninety-nine representatives and twenty-one senators from the old Confederacy, most of whom, by virtue of seniority, held critical committee chairmanships. A handful of votes often was decisive, and close fights were frequent in the House Rules Committee, which controlled the flow of bills.

Kennedy moved quickly but gingerly. He created a strong congressional liaison group headed by Lawrence O'Brien, his chief campaign strategist, and hosted weekly White House meetings with congressional leaders. He inspired Speaker Sam Rayburn's fight to expand the Rules Committee so his legislative program could get to the floor. Rayburn won, by five votes, after a personal plea from the well of the House. Twenty-two Republicans voted with him. Sixty-four southern Democrats were opposed.

Lyndon Johnson, a superb wheeler-dealer in winning votes as Senate majority leader, went largely unused on Capitol Hill as Kennedy's vice president. Johnson at first sought to continue running the Senate Democratic caucus, but seventeen senators rejected him as an executive-branch intruder, and Kennedy was wary anyway of giving Johnson too much control over his program. Johnson sulked but remained steadfast in public. Kennedy, despite fourteen years in the House and Senate, had no lasting ties and was uneasy with Congress. He vowed to make loyalty a test when he sought reelection in 1964 and "deal with those who failed to support the ticket."

Congress handed Kennedy early setbacks on his Medicare bill to assure medical care for all citizens and on economic proposals for curbing inflation and recession. He was blocked, too, on measures for hospital construction, medical school expansion, mental health assistance, air and water purification, and creation of a Department of Urban Affairs within his cabinet. However, he devised techniques for bypassing Congress. For example, the Peace Corps, which put Americans to work helping people in developing countries, operated by executive order for six months before Congress was asked for enabling legislation. After Kennedy's death, Congress adopted many of his programs in health, education, tax reduction, trade expansion, and, most notably, civil rights.

Kennedy was plagued by a series of crises, at home and abroad, during the thousand days of his tenure. He took full responsibility for the 1961 Bay of Pigs fiasco in Cuba, in which fifteen hundred anti-Castro exiles fell captive in a U.S.-backed assault on Cuba. Its 1962 aftermath, the Cuban Missile Crisis, threatened nuclear war until the Soviet Union withdrew its missiles from Cuba. Also in 1961, the Soviets provoked the Berlin Crisis by threatening to bar the West from the city and erecting the Berlin Wall to halt the flight of refugees from the communist East, causing Kennedy to call up military reserves. In Indochina, he saw U.S. involvement in Vietnam escalate, from a few hundred Americans in 1960 to fifteen thousand by 1963, with aid totaling over $500 million. Yet Kennedy's foreign policy legacy also included the Peace Corps, the Alliance for Progress to strengthen U.S. bonds with Latin America, and his several peace overtures made to the Soviets, which resulted in the 1963 nuclear test ban treaty, hailed as the first arms control accord of the Cold War.

At home, he struggled with civil rights unrest, clashing with Deep South governors, mayors, and police, often amid bloodshed, in backing freedom riders and blacks who wanted to vote, have equal public accommodations, and enter white schools, as laws and court rulings provided. He sent three thousand troops to enroll James Meredith in 1962 as the first black student at the University of Mississippi and used troops again in 1963 in desegregating the University of Alabama. Kennedy at first opposed as potentially inflammatory and then welcomed the August 1963 March on Washington of a quarter-million peaceful civil rights demonstrators, who heard black leader Martin Luther King, Jr., declaim his "I Have a Dream" speech at the Lincoln Memorial. Kennedy drew up a civil rights package, but he never got it through a Congress increasingly balky with him. Successor Lyndon Johnson, invoking Kennedy's name as that of a fallen martyr, won its passage as the Civil Rights Acts of 1964. On the economic front, Kennedy fought and won a pitched battle over wage-price stabilization with big steel companies. In space research, with congressional backing, Kennedy launched a program to overtake the Soviets, vowing to put an American on the moon by 1970, a goal achieved on 20 July 1969.

Kennedy's stylish grace inspired many to enter politics, which he called an "honorable profession." Yet his tenure was far more difficult and painfully real than the "one brief shining moment that was known as Camelot," as his young widow fancifully described it, using words from the song of the Broadway musical he loved to hear.

BIBLIOGRAPHY

Bergquist, Laura, and Stanley Tretick. *A Very Special President.* 1965.

Donovan, Robert J. *PT 109: John F. Kennedy in World War II.* 1961.

Kunhardt, Philip B., Jr. *Life in Camelot: The Kennedy Years.* 1988.

Schlesinger, Arthur M., Jr. *Robert Kennedy and His Times.* 1978.

Schlesinger, Arthur M., Jr. *A Thousand Days: John F. Kennedy in the White House.* 1966.

Sorensen, Theodore C. *Kennedy.* 1965.

Sorensen, Theodore C., ed. *"Let the Word Go Forth": The Speeches, Statements, and Writings of John F. Kennedy, 1947 to 1963.* 1988.

WARREN ROGERS

KENNEDY, ROBERT F. (1925–1968), counsel to Senate committees (1953–1959), senator from New York (1965–1968). His congressional initiation began in 1953 as assistant counsel for Sen. Joseph R. McCarthy's Permanent Subcommittee on Investigations of the Government Operations Committee. Sympathetic to the committee's anticommunist objectives, Kennedy was disquieted by the chairman's reckless methods and resigned after six months. Returning as Democratic counsel in 1954, he wrote the minority report condemning McCarthy's investigation of the army.

After the 1954 election produced a Democratic majority, Kennedy became the subcommittee's chief counsel. Investigations now concentrated on fraud and waste in government; one forced the resignation of Harold Talbott, Eisenhower's secretary of the Air Force. Kennedy's reputation as a relentless prosecutor grew from 1957 to 1959, when he served as chief counsel for the Senate Select Committee on Improper Activities in Labor-Management Relations, otherwise known as the Senate Rackets Committee, inves-

ROBERT F. KENNEDY. Speaking at a civil rights demonstration in Washington, D.C., outside the Department of Justice, June 1963.   LIBRARY OF CONGRESS

tigating the penetration of the labor movement by organized crime.

The work on committee staffs enlarged the outlook of a young man already marked by a capacity for growth. Appointed attorney general when his brother John won the presidency in 1960, Robert Kennedy remained in close contact with Congress, especially on civil rights issues. After his brother's assassination and an antagonistic relationship with President Lyndon B. Johnson, Kennedy decided in 1964 to run for the Senate from New York. Overcoming charges that he was ruthless, arrogant, and a carpetbagger, Kennedy defeated the Republican incumbent, Kenneth Keating, by 719,693 votes.

His Senate committees—Labor and Public Welfare, Government Operations, and the District of Columbia—gave Kennedy an outlet for his increasing concerns with racial justice, welfare, poverty, and juvenile delinquency. He excelled in hearings, and committee assignments permitted him to expose hunger and squalor in the Mississippi Delta, among California grape growers, in migratory labor camps, and on Indian reservations. His activism on behalf of the poor and powerless led him to organize the community development of Bedford-Stuyvesant in Brooklyn. "Today in America," he said in 1967, "we are two worlds," and he made himself in effect the tribune of the dispossessed.

In rough-and-tumble floor debate, Robert Kennedy was well prepared and articulate but in his intensity sometimes seemed unduly blunt and cutting. His colleagues considered him a more effective senator than his older brother John but less a "senator's senator" than his younger brother Edward, the senator from Massachusetts.

A strong supporter of Johnson's domestic initiatives, Robert Kennedy broke with the administration on foreign policy, first over the support of military dictatorships in Latin America and later, more decisively, over Vietnam, when the president's obsession with the war threatened to swallow his Great Society. By 1967 Kennedy had emerged as a leading Senate "dove." "Can we ordain to ourselves," he cried, "the awful majesty of God—to decide what cities and villages are to be destroyed, who will live and who will die?"

At first he declined to challenge Johnson for the presidency in 1968. Then, after Eugene J. McCarthy's success in the New Hampshire primary, he entered the contest. His passion, eloquence, and wit appealed to both white and black working-class voters, as well as to many intellectuals and the young, and carried him to victory in a series of primaries. He seemed well on the road to the nomina-

tion when he was killed in Los Angeles on 4 June 1968, the night he won the California primary.

BIBLIOGRAPHY

Kennedy, Robert F. *The Enemy Within*. 1960.
Schlesinger, Arthur M., Jr. *Robert Kennedy and His Times*. 1978.
vanden Heuvel, William, and Milton Gwirtzman. *On His Own: RFK 1964–1968*. 1970.

ARTHUR M. SCHLESINGER, JR.

KENTUCKY. Kentucky followed a tortuous and lengthy path to statehood. At the time of the Declaration of Independence, most of the state was still part of Fincastle County, Virginia, and had been settled by Euroamericans only the year before. As the first area west of the Alleghenies to achieve statehood, Kentucky would be a testing ground for the new nation.

From 1784, when formal debate on the issue of separation began among the first settlers, until 1792, when Kentucky entered the Union, different groups pursued various options. Some leaders wanted total independence as a nation in the West; others suggested breaking away from Virginia, whether the Old Dominion acquiesced or not. In

SEN. HENRY CLAY (WHIG-KY.).   LIBRARY OF CONGRESS

the end, the majority worked with the parent state toward separation. In 1788, a committee of the Second Continental Congress recommended admission of Kentucky, effective 1 January 1789, but the full body voted to postpone the action until the new U.S. Constitution took effect. After further debate in Virginia, Kentucky, and the new Congress, an act of admission was signed by President George Washington in February 1791, effective 1 June 1792. After eight years and ten statehood conventions, Kentucky became the fifteenth state.

The commonwealth quickly arose as an important force in the nation. Firmly Jeffersonian Republican in its early political years, with Sen. John Breckinridge as spokesman, Kentucky soon followed a new leader into new party paths. With the formation of the Democratic and Whig parties, the state generally supported its chief political figure, Henry Clay. As presidential candidate, Speaker of the House, and outstanding Whig senator, Clay dominated Kentucky politics until his death in 1852. In the same era, John White served one term as Whig Speaker of the House, while John J. Crittenden, who in 1842 succeeded Clay in the Senate, inherited the Clay mantle of compromise. Party uncertainty, the growth of the state Democratic organization under leaders like House Speaker Linn Boyd and vice president and presidential candidate John C. Breckinridge (the grandson of John Breckinridge), and then the Civil War all confused the political scene through 1865.

From 1865 to 1895, the Democratic Party ruled supreme in the state, winning virtually every important election. The selection of Kentucky Democrat John G. Carlisle as Speaker of the House in the 48th through 50th Congresses exemplified the Commonwealth's prominence in Democratic party circles on the national level. Kentucky became part of the solid South, but yielded that place as Republicans made inroads between 1895 and 1930. In those years the two parties almost evenly divided the governorship and the U.S. Senate seats. However, the Hoover administration, the Depression, and the successful presidency of Franklin D. Roosevelt reversed the trend. Eastern Kentucky miners and African Americans gradually turned from the Republicans, and since 1947 the Republican party has won the governor's office only once. Reflective of the Democratic resurgence was Sen. Alben W. Barkley's key role as Roosevelt's majority leader, while Democratic senators Albert B. "Happy" Chandler and Earle C. Clements also strode to the forefront for brief periods. Barkley later served as vice president under President Harry S. Truman.

Since the 1950s, Kentucky has had two political faces. At the state level, Democrats have continued to dominate—in registration, legislative seats, and the governorship. Yet since 1980, the commonwealth has voted Republican much more often than Democratic in presidential elections. U.S. Senate seats have been almost evenly divided, which has allowed Republicans, such as Sen. John Sherman Cooper, to become established leaders. Still, it has remained easier for Kentucky Democrats to win election, develop seniority, and gain places of importance in Congress.

BIBLIOGRAPHY

Harrison, Lowell H. *Kentucky's Road to Statehood.* 1992.
Klotter, James C., ed. *Our Kentucky: A Study of the Bluegrass State.* 1992.
Miller, Penny M. *Kentucky Politics and Government.* 1994.

JAMES C. KLOTTER

KENTUCKY AND VIRGINIA RESOLUTIONS.

Opening Thomas Jefferson's presidential campaign of 1800, the Kentucky and Virginia resolutions of 1798 and 1799 were a political response to the Alien and Sedition Acts and made ideological statements about constitutional limits of federal power. Attacking Federalist legislation as a threat to civil liberties and freedom of the press, Jefferson secretly drafted resolutions to be adopted by state legislatures, urging Congress to repeal the "obnoxious" legislation. He argued that the Constitution was a compact among states that relinquished only specific powers to the general government. If Congress went beyond its constitutional authority, its actions had no force. Every state should judge "the mode and measure of redress," Jefferson contended, although he did not advocate outright nullification. Originally intended for North Carolina's consideration, the nine resolutions were submitted by John C. Breckenridge to the Kentucky assembly, which adopted them on 10 November 1798.

James Madison's more moderate Virginia Resolutions, adopted by the legislature on 24 December 1798, denounced the Alien and Sedition Acts and asserted that the "compact" (i.e., Constitution) limited federal powers. States were duty-bound to intervene in maintaining their "rights and liberties" if undelegated powers were exercized by the federal government.

Federalist opposition and a muted response from the politically divided southern states undermined the impact of the resolutions, but the "principles of 1798" were central to the Republican party and remained an important expression of states' rights theory of the Union. They would later influence John C. Calhoun's arguments for states' rights and nullification.

BIBLIOGRAPHY

Cunningham, Noble E., Jr. *The Jeffersonian Republicans: The Formation of Party Organization, 1789–1801.* 1957.

Elkins, Stanley, and Eric McKitrick. *The Age of Federalism.* 1993.

Koch, Adrienne, and Harry Ammon. "The Virginia and Kentucky Resolutions: An Episode in Jefferson's and Madison's Defense of Civil Liberties." *William and Mary Quarterly,* 3d ser., 5 (1948): 145–176.

Smith, James Morton. "The Grass Roots Origins of the Kentucky Resolutions." *William and Mary Quarterly,* 3d ser., 27 (1970): 221–245.

WINFRED E. A. BERNHARD

KERN, JOHN WORTH (1849–1917), Democratic senator from Indiana, arguably the Senate's first majority (or floor) leader. Prior to the early twentieth century, when both parties established a formal floor leadership, party control in the Senate depended on the personal talents and abilities of individual lawmakers. Kern's important contribution was to give credibility to the new party post and to establish precedents that all floor leaders have since followed.

Kern grew up in Indiana and after law school joined the state's Democratic organization. Aligned with the party's progressive wing, he won election to local and state legislative offices but twice (in 1900 and 1904) lost contests for Indiana's governorship. In 1908 he was nominated by the Democratic national convention to be its vice presidential candidate on the ticket headed by William Jennings Bryan.

Although the Bryan-Kern ticket was defeated by Republican William Howard Taft, Kern's long party service and admirable political reputation stood him in good stead when, two years later, the Democrat-controlled Indiana state legislature elected him to the U.S. Senate. After the 1912 election, progressive Senate Democrats outnumbered their conservative partisan colleagues, and they wanted one of their own to lead the Senate. On 5 March 1913, Kern was unanimously elected floor leader by the Democratic caucus.

Kern's initial actions as majority leader involved organizational issues. He named the party panel that assigned Democrats to the standing committees and ensured that important committees were

JOHN WORTH KERN. Photograph by Waldon Fawcett, c. 1908.   LIBRARY OF CONGRESS

filled with colleagues sympathetic to Woodrow Wilson's New Freedom program. He negotiated committee party ratios with Republican leaders and influenced the selection of the Senate's administrative officers. Kern played an important role in organizing both the Senate and his party, still the responsibilities of his successors as floor leader.

The rejuvenated Senate was largely and willingly led by President Wilson. As one scholar said of the Kern-Wilson alliance, "Never before had the president's party in the Senate intentionally elected a floor leader for the primary purpose of implementing an executive-initiated legislative program," which included banking reform (the Federal Reserve Act of 1913) and antitrust legislation (the Federal Commission Act of 1913). Kern's efforts on Wilson's behalf highlight another continuing role for floor leaders: to consult regularly with the president (especially if they are of the same party) on procedural, substantive, and political matters.

As majority leader, Kern took on two other important tasks. He defended the administration against partisan attacks on the Senate floor. This responsibility is now an informal part of any floor leader's job description. In addition, he initiated innovations to assist him in carrying out such floor responsibilities as scheduling, maintaining a quorum, and ensuring that party colleagues were present for votes. In 1913, the Democratic caucus created the position of party whip. The whip's job, in part, was to assist Kern in ensuring Democratic attendance on the Senate floor.

While President Wilson's advocacy of party and legislative leadership may have enhanced Kern's role as majority leader, the Senate itself seemed ready to augment the floor leader's duties, given the growing complexities of the era. Kern ran for reelection but failed in November 1916 to win another term from Indiana's voters. Several factors accounted for Kern's defeat, including the disunity of Indiana's Democratic party, the skill of Republican state leaders in attracting voters to their senatorial candidate, and Kern's ill health, which limited his reelection effort. He died nine months after leaving the Senate.

BIBLIOGRAPHY

Haughton, Virginia Floy. "John Worth Kern and Wilson's New Freedom: A Study of a Senate Majority Leader." Ph.D. diss., University of Kentucky, 1973.

Oleszek, Walter J. "John Worth Kern: Portrait of a Floor Leader." In *First among Equals: Outstanding Senate Leaders of the Twentieth Century.* Edited by Richard A. Baker and Roger H. Davidson. 1991. Pp. 7–37.

WALTER J. OLESZEK

KERR, ROBERT S. (1896–1963), Oklahoma governor, Democratic senator, known by the early 1960s as the "uncrowned king" of the Senate. Elected to the Senate's renowned Democratic class of 1948, Robert Samuel Kerr quickly allied with powerful southern committee chairmen. As the protégé of Georgia's Richard B. Russell, he learned early that the path to legislative influence was effective committee work. The Public Works Committee was his power base, but before the end of his first term he had secured membership on the Finance and Democratic Policy committees as well.

A self-made oil millionaire from an energy-producing state, Kerr never shed the stereotype that he was a parochial, special-interest politician. He attended to the needs of the Oklahoma voters, but he also shaped national policies to broaden So-

cial Security coverage and spurred the development of the manned space program.

From the helm of the powerful Aeronautics and Space Sciences Committee in the early 1960s, Kerr became indispensable to the enactment of the Kennedy legislative program, especially its crucial tax and trade legislation. His legislative prowess as President John F. Kennedy's shadow leader resulted from a peculiar combination of nominal congressional leadership, a politically unattractive legislative program, and Kerr's own institutional power and dominating personality. At the height of his power and influence, he died suddenly of a heart attack on 1 January 1963 in Washington, D.C.

BIBLIOGRAPHY

McPherson, Harry. *A Political Education.* 1972.

Morgan, Anne Hodges. *Robert S. Kerr: The Senate Years.* 1977.

ANNE HODGES MORGAN

KILBOURN V. THOMPSON (103 U.S. 168 [1881]). The Supreme Court case of *Kilbourn v. Thompson* marked the first major judicial test of Congress's investigative power and its immunity from lawsuits. In 1876 a House committee investigated the bankruptcy of Jay Cooke's banking firm. The House voted to arrest Hallet Kilbourn, an associate of the firm, for defying the committee's inquiries. In turn, Kilbourn sued House members and the House sergeant at arms, John G. Thompson, for false imprisonment.

The Supreme Court's opinion found that House members are immune from suit. Their voting and reporting are protected by the Constitution's speech or debate clause (Article I, section 6, clause 1). However, the Court held that the clause did not protect the sergeant at arms from a lawsuit for having conducted the actual arrest. The Cooke bankruptcy case was a matter "in its nature clearly judicial," the Court said, and thus not for Congress to probe.

Kilbourn cast a temporary shadow on Congress's investigative power, which the Supreme Court lifted with the 1927 case of *McGrain v. Daugherty* (273 U.S. 135). In *Hutcheson v. United States* (1962) the Supreme Court subsequently described the antagonism to congressional investigations in *Kilbourn* as "severely discredited." Today, some condemn *Kilbourn* as misguidedly interfering with Congress; others celebrate it as protecting individual rights, because it established the precedent that an individual investigated by Congress, like Kilbourn, could sue to protect his rights and win.

[*See also* McGrain v. Daugherty.]

BIBLIOGRAPHY

Grabow, John C. *Congressional Investigations: Law and Practice.* 1988.
Taylor, Telford. *Grand Inquest: The Story of Congressional Investigations.* 1955.

CHARLES TIEFER

KING, RUFUS (1755–1827), Federalist senator from New York and signer of the Constitution. King represented Massachusetts in the Confederation Congress (1784–1787), but his 1786 marriage to the wealthy Mary Alsop shifted his allegiance to New York. In 1789 New York governor George Clinton sought him out for a Senate appointment.

King, a Federalist, was a leader in the work and deliberations of the early Senate. Involved in the negotiations leading to the compromise of 1790, he actively supported both the financial plans of Secretary of the Treasury Alexander Hamilton and the choice of New York as temporary or permanent federal capital. After being reelected by small majorities of both houses of the state legislature in January 1795, he ably advocated the Senate's consent to Jay's Treaty later that year. When war with France threatened, King supported reestablishment of a navy. In 1796 he resigned to become minister to Great Britain.

Returning to the Senate in 1813, King initially opposed the War of 1812, but the British threat soon caused him to advocate strong prosecution of the war effort. King opposed the second Bank of the United States. When the Senate reorganized its committees in December 1816, he was appointed to the Finance and Foreign Relations committees.

King considered that authoring the protective Navigation Act of 1818 was his greatest legislative accomplishment. His abilities, not his political viewpoints, persuaded New York's legislature to reelect him in 1820. While debating Missouri statehood that year, he insisted that Congress had the power to forbid the extension of slavery. He left the Senate in 1825.

BIBLIOGRAPHY

Ernst, Robert. *Rufus King: American Federalist.* 1968.
King, Charles, ed. *The Life and Correspondence of Rufus King.* 1894–1900. Repr. 1971.

CHARLENE BANGS BICKFORD

KING OF THE HILL RULE. *See* Rule, Special.

KITCHIN, CLAUDE (1869–1923), Democratic representative from North Carolina, House majority leader (1915–1919), widely recognized expert on tax and finance legislation. A member of a prominent Democratic family, Kitchin was born in Scotland Neck, North Carolina. He graduated from Wake Forest College in 1888 and won admission to the bar two years later. For a time in the 1890s he crisscrossed the state as a bank examiner, a position that enabled him to meet many prominent North Carolinians. In 1900, grasping the opportunity offered by the state's virulent white supremacy campaign, he ran successfully for the congressional seat that for two terms had been occupied by Republican George H. White, a black lawyer. Republicans were never again a threat in his district, and only in 1916 did he have significant primary opposition.

Until World War I, Kitchin's career differed little from those of most of his southern Democratic associates: he stood against tariffs, twitted Republicans, and loyally supported the party leadership.

RUFUS KING.   *PERLEY'S REMINISCENCES,* VOL. 1

CLAUDE KITCHIN.   LIBRARY OF CONGRESS

He also developed into an unrivaled debater. Having won appointment to the Ways and Means Committee, he helped mold the Underwood tariff in 1913. His seniority brought him the majority leadership in February 1915 after Oscar W. Underwood of Alabama was elected to the Senate.

Kitchin's assumption of majority leadership came as the nation began to experience the impact of the war in Europe and as President Woodrow Wilson was moving toward endorsing "a wise preparedness." Outwardly the two Democrats got along well, with Kitchin supporting the president's stand on the torpedoing of the *Lusitania*. But he resisted Wilson's plan to enlarge the army and navy. Unable to sidetrack the program, he used his position as chairman of Ways and Means to ensure that it was paid for by taxes that the administration opposed. While Wilson plumped for excise levies, Kitchin successfully piloted increased income and inheritance taxes and a special tax on munition makers through the House.

After Wilson requested a declaration of war on 2 April 1917, Kitchin took the floor in opposition, dramatically arguing that "nothing in [the Allies'] cause, nothing in that quarrel, has or does involve a moral or equitable or material interest in or obligation of our Government or our people." His courage swelled the antiwar vote in the lower chamber to fifty but left him tagged as a renegade. After war was declared, Kitchin usually supported the president even though he had serious reservations about conscription. He did break with the administration over war taxes, which he wanted imposed on those profiting from the conflict. In the Revenue Act of 1918 he inserted what he termed an "equalizer," a corporate excess-profits tax. A Treasury official complained to Congress, however, that the tax was an attack on the wealthy and "goes to the very root of the social and economic problem." Still, the war had to be financed, and Wilson signed the bill. It remained a major achievement, though it later fell victim to the normalcy of Republican Warren G. Harding's administration.

Kitchin suffered a stroke in 1920 and died three years later, while still serving in the institution where, despite his occasionally unpopular stands, he was one of the most widely admired members.

BIBLIOGRAPHY

Arnett, Alex M. *Claude Kitchin and the Wilson War Policies.* 1937.

Ingle, H. Larry. "The Dangers of Reaction: Repeal of the Revenue Act of 1918." *North Carolina Historical Review* 44 (1967): 72–88.

Ingle, H. Larry. "Pilgrimage to Reform: A Life of Claude Kitchin." Ph.D. diss., University of Wisconsin, 1967.

H. LARRY INGLE

KNOWLAND, WILLIAM F. (1908–1974), senator from California and Republican leader of the Senate following the death of Robert A. Taft; a leading opponent of communist expansion in Asia. After his 1929 graduation from the University of California at Berkeley, William Fife Knowland was elected to the state assembly at age twenty-four, and the state senate at age twenty-six. By age thirty-three, he had become the youngest executive committee chairman of the Republican National Committee.

With Sen. Hiram W. Johnson's death in 1945, Governor Earl Warren appointed Knowland to the U.S. Senate. Knowland was then serving as a major in the U.S. Army in Europe. He read of his appointment in the army newspaper *Stars and Stripes* and returned to be sworn in on 26 August 1945.

Knowland took a major interest in American policy in the Far East. He made five Asian tours while a senator and successfully fought the Truman administration policy that had placed Korea beyond the U.S. defense perimeter. He advocated an Asian alliance resembling the North Atlantic Treaty Orga-

WILLIAM F. KNOWLAND. *At left,* with, *left to right,* Rep. Joseph W. Martin (R-Mass.), Sen. Lyndon B. Johnson (D-Tex.), and Rep. Sam Rayburn (D-Tex.).

OFFICE OF THE HISTORIAN OF THE U.S. SENATE

nization a year before the Southeast Asia Treaty Organization (SEATO) was organized in 1954. For his support of the Chinese Nationalist government on Taiwan and his opposition to seating the mainland communist government in the United Nations, his critics dubbed him "the Senator from Formosa."

In 1953 Majority Leader Robert A. Taft, ill with terminal cancer, designated Knowland to succeed him as leader of the one-vote Republican majority carried in by the 1952 presidential victory of Dwight D. Eisenhower. Knowland saw his role as speaking "to the President for the Senate, not to the Senate for the President." Although Knowland did help Eisenhower sidetrack the proposed Bricker amendment, which would limit the effect of treaties on domestic law, he could also be "a deadly serious lone wolf." On one occasion, he left his leadership seat to stand by a desk at the rear of the chamber and vigorously voice his disagreement with an administration budget because of what he saw as its irresponsibility.

Knowland decided to leave the Senate and seek the governorship of California in 1958 to position himself for the presidential nomination in 1960 or 1964. Abandoning a safe Senate seat to which he had been overwhelmingly reelected in 1952 (after receiving both the Republican and Democratic nominations under the state's cross-filing system), he was in effect squeezing aside the popular Republican governor, Goodwin J. Knight. A switch was arranged, with Knight running for the Senate and Knowland for the governorship. Knowland lost, however, by a million votes. His strong support for a right-to-work law elicited the wrath of organized labor. Republicans were tossed out of state offices that the party had held since 1896.

The former senator returned to California and eventually succeeded his father as publisher and editor of the *Oakland Tribune.* He took his own life on 23 February 1974.

BIBLIOGRAPHY

MacNeil, Neil. *Dirksen: Portrait of a Public Man.* 1970.
McPherson, Harry. *A Political Education.* 1972.
Mooney, Booth. *The Politicians, 1945–1960.* 1970.

STEPHEN HORN

KOREAN WAR. The decision to resist aggression in Korea was strictly an executive decision based on controversial analogies of the 1930s and a desire to "save" the United Nations. Members of Congress were not involved. Two bipartisan meetings did take place with congressional leaders during the critical week of 24 to 30 June 1950, but these meetings were held only to inform them of the events and decisions that had already taken place.

A major military involvement in the nuclear age, the Korean War lasted thirty-seven months and two days. More Americans actively participated in the Korean War than were active in seven of the eight major wars that preceded it in United States history. It was a limited war in the sense that it had a limited objective and the battle was confined to a specific geographic area and was directed against selected targets. It also permitted American economic, social, and political patterns to continue without serious disruption. Indeed, the term *limited war* came into fashionable use during the Korean hostilities; on the domestic scene there was a sense of business as usual.

Despite the magnitude of American involvement, Congress was not officially asked for a resolution of approval or a declaration of war. On the contrary, Secretary of State Dean Acheson counseled against the idea, fearing that a partisan debate in Congress would undermine the morale of the American people and the American military. President Truman agreed, and added that the constitutional power of the president as commander in chief was also at stake. That Truman erred in deciding not to seek an action by Congress soon became apparent as the Korean Conflict, as it was officially termed, quickly became known as "Mr. Truman's War."

Congress debated the issues related to the con-

FUNERAL SERVICES. For unknown soldiers of World War II and the Korean War, in the Great Rotunda of the Capitol, May 1958.
LIBRARY OF CONGRESS

duct of the war throughout the duration of the conflict. Some issues were partially clarified, some were confused and blurred, some issues were exploited for partisan political purposes, while some nonissues were given such attention that they were perceived as legitimate issues by the general public. There were four major categories of debate over the conduct of the war in Congress: (1) problems related to the American response; (2) definition of objectives and strategy; (3) circumstances related to the Chinese intervention in the "new war"; and (4) domestic consequences of the war. In each instance Congress failed to rise above partisan sniping. For the president's policy to succeed in Korea it had to have a foundation of legitimacy that typically emanates from Congress and ultimately the American people; Congress did not allow this to develop.

The Truman administration added to the policy confusion by altering the objectives as the circumstances of the conflict changed. The initial policy was to punish North Korean aggression and drive the invaders back above the 38th parallel, a status quo ante bellum policy. After the successful Inchon invasion in September, the policy quickly evolved into one that advocated unification of Korea by force; that is, the U.N. decided to do what it had said North Korea had attempted illegally to do. By November 1950, the Chinese communists had entered the war and U.N. forces were in retreat. The policy changed again by mid June 1951, when the goal was to obtain a negotiated settlement that would end the hostilities along a line that divided the North and the South at the approximate boundary separating the two nations prior to the invasion. While negotiations for peace commenced, the battle took on a World War I style of trench warfare, a stalemated condition that was to last a little more than two years.

During this period members of Congress coalesced around three basic policy positions. One group believed that the only way to prevent World War III was to use all the power necessary to win the conflict. This victory group wanted to use the entire military and naval forces of the United States and the resources of the United States to prosecute the war against North Korea and communist China. A second group supported a negotiated settlement and an effort to limit the conflict geographically to Korea. This group's views were based on three assumptions: (1) America should save its resources for a war with the Soviet Union, (2) the war would be fought in Europe, and (3) Europe was more strategically important than Asia. The third group,

which advocated withdrawal, was split between those who adhered to the concept of a Fortress America in the Western Hemisphere and those who wanted to limit America's commitments to Europe and "other strategic areas," which meant Greece, Turkey, and Japan.

Four events during this period gave each group a forum for expression and demagoguery. First was the November off-year election in 1950; next was the first "Great Debate" in 1951, which concerned sending four combat divisions to Europe; this was followed by the second "Great Debate," also in 1951, on the controversy that surrounded Truman's recall of General Douglas MacArthur, commander of the U.N. forces in Korea; and fourth, the 1952 election, with its infamous formula—K1-C2—which translated into Korea, communism, and corruption. These four events were superimposed over what was becoming known as the McCarthy era in American politics, named for the junior senator from Wisconsin, Joseph R. McCarthy, and his charges of communists in government, corruption in high places, "treason" at the Yalta Conference of 1945, and the "fall" of China to the communists in 1949.

The general public gradually began to share the dissatisfactions and frustrations associated with the complexity of limited war. The Democratic majorities in Congress were reduced in the 1950 election, and in 1952 the voters elected a five-star general, Republican Dwight D. Eisenhower, president of the United States, and gave the Republicans a majority of eight in the House and one in the Senate.

On 27 July 1953, six months after Eisenhower took office, a cease-fire was negotiated in Korea. The terms were essentially the same as Truman's. In signing the treaty, Eisenhower gave an aura of bipartisan legitimacy to the dual policy of containment and limited war, which Congress had been unable to do.

Throughout the Korean War the sensitivity to public opinion caused members of Congress friendly to the Truman and Eisenhower administrations to apologize and defend the key policies of containment and limited war, although their critics lacked viable alternatives. The debates and the political rhetoric of the era made it easy to become a critic of congressional involvement in foreign policy decisions, but the consensus among scholars is that in this instance it was deserved. Critics of Congress's performance argue that the institution failed to confront the long-term policy consequences of the role America was to play in the post–World War II international arena. The body also has been faulted for shortsightedness and an obsession with sniping at day-to-day policy during the Korean War.

Within two years of the end of the conflict in Korea, Congress gave President Eisenhower complete authority to do whatever he deemed necessary to prevent communist China from taking the islands of Quemoy and Matsu from Nationalist China—an indication to many Congress watchers that the myopia of policy implications continued to grip the legislative branch.

BIBLIOGRAPHY

Acheson, Dean. *Present at the Creation: My Years in the State Department.* 1969.

Burns, James MacGregor. *The Deadlock of Democracy: Four-Party Politics in America.* 1963.

Caridi, Ronald J. *The Korean War and American Politics: The Republican Party as a Case Study.* 1968.

Paige, Glenn D. *The Korean Decision: June 24–30, 1950.* 1968.

Rees, David. *Korea: The Limited War.* 1964.

Spanier, John W. *The Truman-MacArthur Controversy and the Korean War.* 1959.

JAMES R. RIGGS

L

LABOR. Congressional labor policy may be treated under three interrelated headings. First, Congress has occasionally adopted laws that directly govern the employment relationship. Second, and more common, Congress has promoted labor standards (wages, hours, and working conditions), either directly through determinative legislative or administrative regulation or indirectly through promotion of collective bargaining. Third, Congress has shown growing interest in legislation intended to influence the disposition, composition, and quality of the labor force in accordance with national economic goals.

Congressional activity on the second and third fronts is primarily a modern phenomenon, largely resting on the expansive reinterpretation of the national government's domestic responsibilities that dates from the 1930s. Even within the more restricted conception of federal jurisdiction prevailing prior to the twentieth century, however, one finds significant instances of congressional "labor" legislation in all three of the senses cited.

Beginnings, 1790–1860. For the eighteenth century and much of the nineteenth century, federal jurisdiction over "interstate and foreign commerce" meant jurisdiction over oceanic and coastwise trade. From the outset, congressional exercise of that authority included a recognition of the instrumental importance of regulating labor. The Constitution supplied three distinct bases for that regulation: the commerce power itself (Art. I, sec. 8); the specific power "To define and punish Piracies and Felonies committed on the high Seas, and Offenses against the Law of Nations" (Art. I, sec. 8); and the reservation of "admiralty and maritime Jurisdiction" to the federal courts (Art. III).

Congressional interest in the maritime employment relationship dates from the earliest years of the Republic. In the Crimes Act (1790), capital punishment was prescribed for acts of piracy, mutiny, revolt, absconding with goods, and assault on the ship's commander, or for assisting in any such crime. Later that year, Congress passed general legislation "for the government and regulation of seamen in the merchant service." The act required masters and seamen to execute shipping agreements; prescribed criminal penalties for nonperformance or abandonment of work; punished the harboring of deserters; and established procedures for recovery of unpaid wages. Subsequent legislation extended regulation to fisheries and the "government of the fishermen employed therein" (1792); gave consuls jurisdiction over master-sailor disputes in foreign ports (1792); and levied sailors' wages to fund a marine hospital system (1798).

These acts controlled maritime employment for most of the next century. Little new legislation was passed before the Civil War. Two acts deserve mention. The first (1835) amended the 1790 Crimes Act by replacing capital punishment for mutiny or revolt with imprisonment and made the unjustifiable beating or mistreatment of a crew member by the master an offense. Second, midcentury campaigns against corporal punishment brought abolition of disciplinary flogging at sea (1850). In debates over these matters, northern members of Congress espoused "free labor" principles: self-discipline over physical coercion and voluntary acquiescence to authority over constraint. Southern members defended flogging as an effective means of maintaining authority and as a "manly" and "honorable" punishment.

Deepening Involvements, 1860–1920. The "free labor" theme was sounded with added force after the Civil War, particularly in Congress's Reconstruction debates and in the Anti-Peonage Act (1867). But "free" labor did not mean toleration of labor indiscipline. Particularly for workers commonly thought improvident and shiftless—notably sailors and former slaves—free labor excluded only physical force as a constraint. Thus, while the Thirteenth Amendment (1865) banned involuntary servitude along with slavery, the Freedmen's Bureau (created in 1865, its powers expanded in 1866) saw nothing wrong in enforcing freedom on its charges with what its chief, Gen. Oliver Otis Howard, called "wholesome constraint." And while the Civil Rights Act (1866) and the Fourteenth Amendment (1868) helped ensure nullification of the postwar South's "black codes," it was the codes' discriminatory singling out of black labor that was the target, not their disciplinary substance.

Congress took the same tack with maritime labor. In the Shipping Commissioners Act (1872), it targeted "crimps"—port agents who enmeshed sailors in debt and consigned them to ships needing crew in return for a share of their wages—by requiring the validation of all seamen's shipping contracts in American ports before appointed commissioners. This created a form of protection of "freedom in contract" in maritime hiring like that exercised by the Freedmen's Bureau. But the act also affirmed a wide range of statutory punishments—fines, imprisonments, loss of wages and effects—for refusals to work or other labor indiscipline. Once employment was voluntarily entered, criminal sanctions would enforce performance.

Maritime employment followed this course well into the twentieth century. The Dingley Act (1884) prohibited peremptory discharge overseas and made "cruel or unusual treatment" a defense in cases of desertion, but it did not touch the bedrock of maritime labor law's criminal sanctions. The Maguire Act (1895) gave coastwise sailors immunity from imprisonment for desertion, and the White Act (1898) extended immunity to any sailor in an American port. But premature departure remained a statutory offense, and desertion overseas continued to be punishable by imprisonment. Not until the La Follette Act (1915) was arrest and imprisonment for desertion comprehensively outlawed. Even then, the departing sailor still lost all rights to accrued wages. Disobedience at sea, meanwhile, remained a crime.

Outside maritime employment, Congress's jurisdiction in labor regulation was limited to the affairs of federal employees, the District of Columbia and the territories, clearly interstate enterprises such as railroads, and immigration. By the early twentieth century, its involvement in these areas was extensive. Thus, in 1868 legislation declared a workday of eight hours in federal employment; in 1892 the standard was extended to employees of public works contractors with the federal and District of Columbia governments and in 1913 to all persons employed on U.S. and District river or harbor improvements. In 1895 Congress required that seating be made available for female employees of District stores, shops, and factories for use "when not actively employed"; in 1914 it limited the hours of female employment in the District; and in 1918 it established a District minimum wage for women. Finally, in 1920 Congress passed legislation requiring the inclusion of certain labor standards—an eight-hour day, wage-payment regulations, restrictions on the employment of juveniles and women—in public domain mining leases ("provided, that none of such provisions shall be in conflict with the laws of the state in which the leased property is situated").

The Adamson Act (1916) set an eight-hour standard for employees on interstate, District of Columbia, and territory railroads. Congress had first legislated on interstate railroad safety in 1893 (requiring automatic couplers and brakes) and in 1907 (prescribing initial limitations on hours of service) and on railroad liability in cases of employee injury or death in 1906 and 1908. But the Adamson Act was its first foray into direct prescription of labor standards in domestic nongovernment employment. Also in 1916, Congress passed the Kern-McGillicuddy Act, which established workers' compensation schedules for all federal employees, and the Keating-Owen Child Labor Act, which invoked the commerce power to ban juvenile labor from extractive and manufacturing industries. As to immigration, Congress took steps in the 1880s to extend federal control over its flow, culminating in the creation of a federal superintendent of immigration in 1891. Immigration remained generally open until after World War I, although restrictionist sentiments had sufficient support in Congress to win particular curbs—notably, the exclusion of convicts and paupers in 1882 and of labor imported under contract in 1885.

The courts gave all this activity a mixed reception. Hours and safety legislation passed scrutiny, but the District minimum-wage act was ruled an unconstitutional deprivation of employee and employer contractual freedom. Now that women could vote, said the Supreme Court (*Adkins v. Children's Hospital*, 1923), their civic inequality was no longer at issue and hence could no longer be cited to justify protection. Laws protecting children, who were not full citizens, were less vulnerable to due process arguments. Nevertheless, in *Hammer v. Dagenhart* (1917), the Court voided the Keating-Owen Child Labor Act on the grounds that manufacturing was not commerce. Regulation of the conditions of production was a state responsibility, it ruled. Congress tried again in 1919, using the federal revenue power to impose a 10 percent excise tax on businesses using child labor, but the outcome was the same (*Bailey v. Drexel Furniture* [1921]).

The stirring of congressional interest in labor standards, particularly evident during Woodrow Wilson's presidency, reflected the Progressive era's impulse to national efficiency through social improvement, along with a dawning perception of labor (or "the labor force") as a national resource, properly subject to national management. Such arguments were used by the La Follette Act's proponents among organized labor; state protection of seamen's conditions, they believed, would enhance the quality of the maritime labor force. They can also be found in the era's debates over immigration restriction, touching, for example, on the quality of labor attracted through mass immigration. Here, organized labor's interest in immigration restriction intersected with progressives' desire to improve the "human capital" of the United States.

The same shift in perspective can be seen in early congressional investigations of "labor problems" and the creation of administrative structures to manage the labor resource. In 1884 the Bureau of Labor was established to collect information about labor, labor-capital relations, hours, and wages. The bureau became a noncabinet department in 1888, part of the new cabinet-level Department of Commerce and Labor in 1903, and finally, in 1913, a separate cabinet-level department. The Women's Bureau was added in 1920 "to formulate standards and policies which shall promote the welfare of wage-earning women."

Yet the progressives' emphasis on labor as a human resource did not yet dominate congressional labor policy. Older, "free labor" ideas remained potent. Looking at labor, Congress saw not a "force" or a "resource" but freely contracting individuals. This view had particularly important repercussions for Congress's response to labor organizations. Their attempts to press collective rather than individual bargaining, and the intense union-employer struggles that resulted, were in many ways the supreme challenge to the reigning free labor idea.

Industrial Relations Policy, 1880–1930. Initially, congressional attention to industrial relations took the form of recurrent investigations of "the labor problem" and spasmodic attempts to draft a policy addressing the legality of collective action. The investigations were reactions to strikes, usually on the railroads. The first investigation was set up by the House of Representatives in 1878 after the strike wave of the previous year. Nothing came of it. Then, in 1882 the Senate authorized its Committee on Education and Labor to conduct a study of labor-capital relations. Testimony was published in 1885, without recommendations. In 1886 Congress passed a federal incorporation act for trade unions, but no union ever utilized it, and the act was repealed in 1932.

In 1888, the Burlington Railroad strike prompted Congress to pass a voluntary arbitration measure that had languished for two years, but it did not grant unions legal status in arbitration proceedings. It was used only once, when the U.S. Strike Commission was appointed to examine the causes of the 1894 Pullman strike. Meanwhile, the 1890 Sherman Antitrust Act, which outlawed "every contract, combination in the form of trust or otherwise, or conspiracy in restraint of trade or commerce," became a potent judicial weapon against strikes, particularly in the tempestuous years 1892 through 1894.

The U.S. Strike Commission's report on the Pullman strike recommended a major federal commitment to enforceable conciliation and arbitration of disputes and a strong endorsement of union recognition, preparing the ground for the Erdman Act (1898). But the act itself, while making provision for the enforcement of decisions, did not make arbitration mandatory. Railway unions gained some legitimacy from this legislation, but its section 10 provisions protecting union members from discriminatory discharge fell afoul of the Supreme Court in 1908 *(Adair v. United States)*. The act was used little through 1907 but more frequently thereafter, until it was superseded in 1913. Also in 1898, Congress created the U.S. Industrial Commission "to collate information and to consider and recommend legislation to meet the problems presented by labor, agriculture, and capital." Its activities and reports helped to bring about the creation of the Department of Commerce and Labor.

Industrial conflict continued to influence congressional labor relations policy throughout the Progressive era. Some responses seemed conciliatory. In 1912, for example, the U.S. Commission on Industrial Relations was appointed to inquire into "the general condition of labor in the principal industries of the United States." Also that year, Congress passed the Lloyd-La Follette Act, acknowledging the right of federal employees to organize unions. In 1913 the Newlands Act replaced the Erdman Act's voluntary arbitration with a permanent Board of Mediation and Conciliation vested with interventionist powers.

However, accommodation had its limits. Federal employees might join unions but not strike. Nor would Congress go along in 1914 when the American Federation of Labor (AFL) tried again to obtain the antitrust exemption for unions that it had failed to get in the Sherman Antitrust Act. The Clayton Antitrust Act (1914) included some grand language—for example, "the labor of a human being is not a commodity or article of commerce"—and AFL president Samuel Gompers christened it "labor's Magna Charta." But overall it simply reconfirmed the status quo ante: unions were not illegal per se under the antitrust laws, nor were they exempt. What counted was whether in any particular labor dispute courts construed a union's activities to constitute unlawful restraint upon commerce.

Preparedness and mobilization during World War I led to a break in the status quo. Unions were a formidable presence in key sectors of the war economy—mining, transport, construction—and could not be ignored. But conduct of the war was an executive rather than a legislative enterprise, and so few of the administration's wartime labor policies translated into peacetime legislation. For example, the wartime Railroad Administration explicitly guaranteed an employee's right to join a labor organization. But Congress's postwar Esch-Cummins Transportation Act (1920), which returned the railroads to private control, was conspicuously silent on the matter. The act kept unions at arm's length in other ways, creating a Railway Labor Board with final decision-making power over unresolved disputes. By 1923, union disenchantment with the board's performance had rendered the legislation a dead letter.

Esch-Cummins was eventually superseded by the 1926 Railway Labor Act, in which nonfederal employees for the first time gained the statutory right to organize. The act imposed no bargaining obligation on railroad employers, nor did it distinguish between company and independent unions. However, it backed recognition of employee rights with prohibitions against company "interference, influence, or coercion" (though without a remedy for violation). The Supreme Court upheld the law in 1930 (*T. & N.O.R.R. Co. v. Brotherhood of Railway Clerks*), acknowledging that Congress could, if it chose, seek industrial peace "by promoting labor organizations and creating mechanisms in which they could function as full, free and relatively equal partners." In 1934 Congress amended the Railway Labor Act to create a substantive federal collective bargaining policy on the railroads.

The New Deal, 1930–1940. In the 1930s, Congress had more to worry about than the railroads. The surface buoyancy of the 1920s had hidden major dislocations in the economy. Overall income returns to labor were increasingly out of balance with returns to capital. Chronic overcapacity and chaotic price competition in particular industries—bituminous mining, textiles, clothing—had produced severely depressed regional labor market conditions. When the downturn struck, these problems became universal. The result was a nationally depressed labor market and renewed (and politically threatening) labor-capital conflict over income shares.

During the 1930s, congressional attention to labor policy focused on the two fronts we have seen slowly opening up since the late nineteenth century: labor as a human resource, leading to employment, welfare, and standards policies; and industrial dispute resolution, resulting in further guarantees of employee organization rights. For a period, however, a third front combining elements of these transcended them both in importance: the encouragement of collective bargaining as the central element of a mildly redistributive incomes policy.

Congressional concern over the Depression predated the New Deal. The Employment Stabilization Act (1931) provided for "advance planning and regulated construction of public works" as a spur to employment. The Davis-Bacon Act (1931) specified that prevailing local wage rates be paid to all employees working under federal and District of Columbia public building contracts. After the 1932 election, New Deal labor policies rapidly expanded beyond this cautious beginning, though in a somewhat ad hoc manner. Establishment of the U.S. Employment Service as a national system of public employment offices early in June 1933 was a modest start. But the National Industrial Recovery Act

AMERICAN LABOR PARTY CAMPAIGN POSTER. Emphasizing the advances for workers gained under the Roosevelt administration. The poster was for the 1936 reelection campaigns of President Franklin D. Roosevelt and Herbert H. Lehman, Democratic governor of New York. In 1949 Lehman was elected to the Senate to fill a vacancy.   COLLECTION OF DAVID J. AND JANICE L. FRENT

(NIRA), passed a few days later, was a real departure, for it claimed comprehensive federal responsibility for the national economy. NIRA sought to bring labor and product markets under federal supervision for purposes of planning wage, hour, and employment stabilization, delegating the detail to industry participants working under suspended antitrust constraints to develop codes of "fair competition." Two years later, the Social Security Act's national system of old-age insurance, federal-state unemployment insurance, and aid to dependent mothers and children offered another package of measures that, though cautiously framed, indicated further congressional acceptance of a national interest in, and responsibility for, the labor force's long-term social and economic welfare.

Congress also approved several huge appropriations to sustain short-term public employment programs—the Public Works Administration, the Federal Emergency Relief Administration, the Civil Works Administration, and, largest of all, the Works Progress Administration. And in 1936 Congress passed the Merchant Marine Act, the first of a series of significant labor standards measures. It was followed by the much more important Walsh-Healey Government Contracts Act (1936), which required all federal and District of Columbia government contractors to be in compliance with prescribed wage, hour, and safety standards; by an apprenticeship labor standards act (1937); and by the Fair Labor Standards Act (FLSA) of 1938. In the name of the "health, efficiency and general well-being of workers" (but with numerous exceptions), the FLSA introduced nationwide wage and hour standards and prohibited child labor.

All of these labor policies demanded a radical expansion of federal authority. As such, they became the principal terrain on which the New Deal's bitter constitutional wars were fought. The first battle came in 1935, when the Supreme Court held the

NIRA unconstitutional *(Schechter Poultry Corp. v. United States)*, depriving the administration of its central stabilization policies. The following year, the Court *(Carter v. Carter Coal)* threw out the Bituminous Coal Conservation Act's attempt to reestablish those policies within the framework of a single industry. Labor market conditions, said the Court, were indelibly local. Then, just a month later, the Court ruled *(Morehead v. New York)* that state minimum-wage laws were also unconstitutional. Labor policy had been rendered a "no-man's land," the administration protested, off-limits to government at all levels. Social security suddenly seemed vulnerable, and federal labor standards, completely beyond the pale.

President Franklin D. Roosevelt's response was the 1937 Court-packing plan. Although not adopted, the pressure that the plan applied, along with changes in the Court's membership, pushed the Court into a less confrontational stance on matters of economic regulation. Federal courts would continue to review the substance of regulatory action, but due deference would be accorded legislative intent in considering the actual constitutionality of statutes. The change of tack could be seen in decisions like *West Coast Hotel v. Parrish* (1937), where the Court finally bowed to the concept of the minimum wage, clearing the way for the FLSA.

Labor policy was the chief beneficiary of the New Deal's constitutional upheaval. Federal social security and labor standards legislation were secured. So too was collective bargaining, the strand of incomes policy that had come to overshadow all others during the previous five years.

Collective bargaining attained this status largely by default. Roosevelt and Labor Secretary Frances Perkins preferred to pursue labor market reform through standards legislation. And they did not have any reason, in the early 1930s, to think that organized labor might have potential as a policy vehicle. On the defensive since the early 1920s, the unions' position had weakened steadily since the onset of the Depression. To be sure, administration policy accorded labor's right to organize some recognition but geared it to piecemeal intraindustrial "peacekeeping" and dispute resolution rather than to market reform. Roosevelt and Perkins supported comprehensive collective bargaining legislation only belatedly, in 1935, after the *Schechter* decision wiped out the NIRA and left the administration scrambling for a recovery policy.

Congress took a somewhat more sympathetic view. During the second half of the 1920s, minorities in both houses had been willing to listen to labor's protests against the courts' straitjacket of injunctive restraints on collective action. In 1932 they proved strong enough to pass the Norris-LaGuardia Act restricting the use of injunctions in labor disputes. Further measures endorsing collective bargaining soon followed: section 7(a) of the NIRA, which required that codes of fair competition include guarantees of organization and bargaining rights; the joint resolution (P.R. 44) of June 1934, which authorized the president to create administrative boards to oversee implementation of 7(a) rights; and, finally, the National Labor Relations Act (NLRA) of 1935.

The NLRA expressed two policy trends. One was the willingness to acknowledge that working people had a social right to organize and bargain collectively for current security, just as they had a social right to security in old age. But it also stood for something more. Proponents of the Norris-LaGuardia Act had chosen to justify it not as a belated acknowledgment of labor's "rights," but as a policy decision based on the discovery of a "public purpose" for organized labor. Under "prevailing economic conditions" of increasingly concentrated ownership, the individual unorganized worker was helpless to exercise actual liberty of contract. Collective organization was hence endorsed as the most practical means whereby workers could obtain "acceptable terms and conditions of employment" for themselves. Over the next three years, that public purpose came increasingly to be defined as securing a greater "equality of bargaining power" between labor and capital in order to augment returns to labor and thus lessen destabilizing maldistributions of income and purchasing power. This, precisely, was the NLRA's express policy justification. With the fall of the NIRA, the passage of the NLRA made collective bargaining the principal means of establishing and enforcing labor force standards and benefits above the modest minimum set by the Fair Labor Standards Act.

To the chagrin of its numerous opponents, the act was upheld in 1937 by the newly moderate Supreme Court, and for two years it was implemented with determination. Yet the vision behind the act was vulnerable to changing political fortunes. Conservative resurgence in the 1938 elections confirmed that the impetus of the New Deal was winding down. The NLRA and its administrators at the National Labor Relations Board (NLRB) became the subject of major conservative attacks; these climaxed with hostile hearings during 1939 and 1940 by a House

TEAMSTERS UNION PRESIDENT JIMMY HOFFA. Appearing before the Senate Permanent Subcommittee on Investigations (McClellan Committee), 24 January 1961. LIBRARY OF CONGRESS

special investigative committee chaired by conservative southern Democrat Howard W. Smith of Virginia. Crippling amendments recommended at the conclusion of the hearings failed of enactment, but the investigation discouraged the NLRB from pursuing "equality of bargaining power." Roosevelt quickly moved to place the administration of the NLRA in more cautious, orthodox hands.

After the New Deal, 1940–1990. Congress passed two significant pieces of labor legislation during World War II. The first, adopted over Roosevelt's veto, was the Smith-Connally War Labor Disputes Act (1943). The act required the authorization of strikes by ballot on thirty days' notice in any dispute threatening war production, banned strikes completely in any government-operated plant, and outlawed political contributions by unions. It was the first legislative success of the conservative reaction against the New Deal's labor policy.

The second bill, the Servicemen's Readjustment Act (1944), better known as the GI Bill, was very different. One of the most far-reaching pieces of employment assistance legislation in American history, the act provided job counseling and employment placement services for returning veterans and created a Veteran's Employment Service within the U.S. Employment Service. Together with its famous education provisions, the GI Bill represented a major commitment of federal resources to the enhancement of employment opportunity and to ensuring the quality of the postwar labor force.

Peacetime saw moves to expand each of these commitments. The Murray-Wagner full-employment bill (1945) attempted to imbue the economy at

Landmark Labor Legislation

TITLE	YEAR ENACTED	REFERENCE NUMBER	DESCRIPTION
An Act for the government and regulation of seamen in the merchants service	1790	1 Stat. 131, Chap. 29	Established federal code for government of maritime employment.
Erdman Act	1898	30 Stat. 424, Chap. 370	Provided for mediation and arbitration of labor disputes on railroads; protected employees against discrimination on account of union membership.
An Act to create a Department of Labor	1913	37 Stat. 736, Chap. 141	Cabinet-level department created.
La Follette Act	1915	38 Stat. 1164, Chap. 153	To promote the welfare of American seamen: abolition of arrest and imprisonment as a penalty for desertion; promotion of safety at sea; regulation of crew composition and training; further regulation of wage payment; confirmation of abolition of flogging and other corporal punishment.
Adamson Act	1916	39 Stat. 721, Chap. 436	Established an 8-hour day for employees of carriers engaged in interstate and foreign commerce.
An Act to protect . . . women and minor workers in the District of Columbia . . .	1918	40 Stat. 960, Chap. 174	D.C. Minimum Wage Board created to investigate wages of women and minor workers, declare minimum wage standards for them, and secure compliance.
Railway Labor Act	1926	44 Stat. 577, Chap. 347	Repealed Newlands Act (1913) and Title III of the Transportation Act (1920). Substituted a voluntaristic dispute-settlement procedure for latter's compulsions, returning federal role to mediation. Established a duty on the part of carriers to make and maintain agreements and to settle grievances, and to consider and if possible decide all disputes in conference with representatives designated by employees.
Norris-LaGuardia Act	1932	47 Stat. 70, Chap. 90	Promulgated a series of exceptions to federal courts' capacity to issue injunctions: (a) to enforce any contract requiring abstention from membership as a condition of employment; or (b) to enjoin any of the following: refusal to continue in employment; becoming or remaining a member of a labor organization; giving money to or otherwise lawfully assisting those involved in a labor dispute; publicizing a dispute; assembling peaceably in connection with a labor dispute; advising, urging, or causing or inducing, without fraud or violence, any of these acts.
National Industrial Recovery Act	1933	48 Stat. 195, Chap. 90	Declared the policy of Congress to be to provide for the general welfare through promotion of the organization of industry for "cooperative action among trade groups," to induce "united action of labor and management" under "adequate governmental sanctions and supervision," to eliminate unfair competitive practices, to promote full use of productive capacity, to increase consumption by increasing purchasing power, to reduce and relieve unemployment, to improve labor standards, to rehabilitate industry, and to conserve natural resources. Guaranteed employees the right to organize and bargain collectively through their chosen representatives.
An Act to amend the Railway Labor Act	1934	48 Stat. 1185, Chap. 691	Forbade limitations upon employees' freedom of association, or denial, as a condition of employment, of their right to join a labor organization; provided for "complete independence" of carriers and employees in self-organization; provided for prompt and orderly settlement of disputes and grievances. Strengthened Railway Labor Act's bargaining provisions.

Landmark Labor Legislation (Continued)

TITLE	YEAR ENACTED	REFERENCE NUMBER	DESCRIPTION
National Labor Relations Act (Wagner Act)	1935	49 Stat. 449, Chap. 372	Cited the denial by employers of employees' rights of self-organization and collective bargaining as the cause of strikes and unrest burdening commerce; cited the inequality of bargaining power between employees and employers as a burden upon commerce, depressing wage rates and purchasing power and preventing stabilization of competitive wage rates and working conditions within and between industries; proclaimed collective bargaining an essential component of public policies addressing economic recovery. Created a National Labor Relations Board (NLRB) to implement the policy of the act.
Social Security Act	1935	49 Stat. 620, Chap. 531	Established a system of federal old-age authorized grants to the states to assist in the relief of aged persons, blind persons, dependent and crippled children, and in services such as maternal and child welfare and public health.
Fair Labor Standards Act	1938	52 Stat. 1060, Chap. 676	Specifying numerous exceptions, act established 25-cent minimum hourly wage in industries engaged in or producing for interstate commerce, with graduated increase to 40-cent minimum over 7 years; maximum 44-hour work week, falling to 40 hours after two years, with overtime at time and a half; also prohibited child labor. Established a Wage and Hour division in the Department of Labor to oversee implementation.
Servicemen's Readjustment Act of 1944 (GI Bill; Title IV) ("Employment of Veterans")	1944	58 Stat. 284, Chap. 268	Declared a federal government commitment to effective job counseling and employment placement services, maximizing access to employment, and created a Veterans' Placement Service Board within the U.S. Employment Service.
Labor Management Relations Act (Taft-Hartley Act)	1947	61 Stat. 136, Chap. 120	An omnibus multi-titled statute amending and supplementing the structure of federal labor relations law established in the National Labor Relations (Wagner) Act (1935) as administered by the National Labor Relations Board (NLRB). Title I amended the administration and content of the Wagner Act. Among other provisions, it reorganized NLRB; introduced union "decertification" provisions; specified union unfair practices; defined "good faith" in bargaining; banned closed shops; gave the NLRB authority to determine jurisdiction and demarcation disputes and required unions to register with the secretary of Labor, file annual financial reports, and certify that none of their officers were Communists. Title II endorsed federal conciliation, encouraged parties to develop grievance procedures, and established national emergency strike procedures. Title III specified categories of unlawful union and employer behavior (certain employer payments to employee representatives, certain boycotts and combinations by unions), decreed labor agreements legally enforceable, and restricted unions' political expenditures. Title IV established a joint committee of Congress to investigate labor relations.

Landmark Labor Legislation (Continued)

Title	Year Enacted	Reference Number	Description
Labor-Management Reporting and Disclosure Act (Landrum-Griffin Act)	1959	P.L. 86-257	Declared Congress's continuing responsibility to protect employee organization and bargaining rights; declared Congress's concern at instances of breach of trust, corruption, and disregard of rights of individual employees on the part of unions. Title I specified a "bill of rights" for members of labor organizations similar in respects to those prescribed in the U.S. Constitution's Bill of rights: equality (but not extending to racial or gender discrimination); freedom of speech and assembly; intraorganizational due process; right to sue. Title II required extensive reporting by labor organizations and employers (of aspects of their relations with labor organizations). Title III regulated union trusteeships. Title IV regulated union elections. Title V established requirements of fiduciary responsibility and bonding in officers. Title VI covered implementation and listed miscellaneous proscriptions on unions. Title VII closely regulated secondary boycotts and picketing (both for recognition and organization purposes) and outlawed hot cargo clauses in collective bargaining agreement.
Equal Pay Act	1963	P.L. 88-38	Amended FLSA to prohibit employers from discriminating between employees on the basis of sex "by paying wages to employees . . . at a rate less than the rate at which he pays wages to employees of the opposite sex in [the same] establishment for equal work on jobs the performance of which requires equal skill, effort, and responsibility, and which are performed under similar working conditions, except where such payment is made pursuant to (i) a seniority system; (ii) a merit system; (iii) a system which measures earnings by quantity or quality of production; or (iv) a differential based on any other factor other than sex."
Civil Rights Act	1964	PL 88-352	Title VII specified unlawful employment practices; established enforcement procedures to prohibit discrimination in hiring, firing, wages, terms, and conditions or privileges of employment on the grounds of race, color, religion, sex, or national origin. Title VII permitted differentials in pay within terms of Equal Pay Act. Created an Equal Employment Opportunity Commission to administer the law.

large with something of the spirit of the GI Bill by authorizing federal investment and expenditures sufficient to ensure a "full employment" volume of production. But the measure was diluted by congressional conservatives. Passed as the watered-down Employment Act (1946), the legislation instead committed the federal government to maximize employment opportunity "for those able, willing and seeking to work" and created the Council of Economic Advisers. The next year, after a decisive conservative majority had been elected to Congress in 1946, two more measures resculpted other key elements of New Deal labor policy. The first, the Portal-to-Portal Act (1947), excluded traveling and

preparation from the definition of compensable working time under federal statutes and imposed a two-year limit on employees' opportunities to recover back wages owed for any violation of federal labor standards legislation. Far more important, however, was the Taft-Hartley Labor-Management Relations Act (1947).

The Taft-Hartley Act set a course for federal labor relations policy that has since been followed with few deviations. Like much of the labor and employment legislation that would come after it, the act's complexity defies easy description. Essentially, it replaced the New Deal's economic and social rationale for assistance to labor organizing with a policy

Landmark Labor Legislation (Continued)

TITLE	YEAR ENACTED	REFERENCE NUMBER	DESCRIPTION
Age Discrimination in Employment Act	1967	P.L. 90-202	Banned discrimination based on age, whether by employers, labor organizations, or employment agencies; protected employees defined as those aged 40–65. Amended 1974 (P.L. 93-259): protection extended to employees of state and federal governments. Amended 1978 (P.L. 95-256): protected employees redefined as those aged 40–70; exceptions allowed to permit mandatory retirement of certain executives and tenured academics at age 65. Amended 1986 (P.L. 99-592): protected employees redefined as those aged 40 and over; statutory retirement age removed; exceptions allowed to permit mandatory retirement of certain executives at age 65 and tenured academics at age 70, the latter exception to terminate 31 December 1993.
Occupational Safety and Health Act	1970	P.L. 91-596	Gave secretary of Labor authority to set mandatory safety and health standards and created procedures for enforcement of the standards. Programs created to assist states in their efforts to assure safe and healthful working conditions; provision made for research, information, education, and training in the field of occupational safety and health.
Equal Employment Opportunity Act	1972	P.L. 92-261	Title VII of the 1964 Civil Rights Act amended to create Equal Employment Opportunity Commission to hear complaints of unlawful employment practices and enforce compliance.
Worker Adjustment and Retraining Notification Act	1988	P.L. 100-379	Required employers of 100 or more full-time employees to provide 60 days' advance notification of any employment loss affecting at least 33% of such employees (which shall be at least 50 employees). Employment loss meant termination other than disciplinary or voluntary departure or retirement; or layoff exceeding 6 months; or reduction in hours of more than 50% during each month of a six-month period.

of grudging toleration, coupled with formidable administrative obstacles to union extension. Over the course of the long postwar period, the result was to confine organizing to those sectors of the economy where it had already put down deep roots.

In the short term, Taft-Hartley's restrictions seemed to many no more than a necessary counterweight to a labor movement grown too powerful, too "irresponsible." Unions in the 1950s did not seem unduly confined. The economy expanded; collective bargaining flourished; and FLSA amendments in 1949, and again in 1955 and 1956, kept the minimum wage moving upward and expanded mandated standards. But whenever organized labor attempted to gain amendments loosening Taft-Hartley's strictures—in 1949, in the early 1950s, in the late 1950s—it failed. Indeed, the last attempt became a rout, as conservative Republicans and southern Democrats capitalized on the illegality

and corruption uncovered by the racketeering investigation of the Senate's McClellan committee and passed the Landrum-Griffin Labor-Management Reporting and Disclosure Act (1959), adding a new round of restrictions on unions.

Landrum-Griffin completed the edifice of federal labor relations law. Laws passed since—for example, the Labor-Management Cooperation Act (1978)—have had only minimal impact.

While federal support for collective bargaining has lessened substantially in comparison to the pre–Taft-Hartley period, involvement in other areas—employee protections and labor standards, employment access and discrimination, and employment training—has burgeoned. Periodic FLSA amendments have continued to raise the minimum wage (1955, 1961, 1966, 1974, 1977, 1989). Other standards legislation has included the Service Contract Act (1965) and the Federal Pay Comparability Act

(1971). Workplace safety has been fostered by attempts at comprehensive occupational safety legislation—the Coal Mine Safety and Health Act (1969) and the Occupational Safety and Health Act (1970) are the outstanding examples. New forms of employee protection have appeared, as in the Polygraph Protection Act and the Worker Adjustment and Retraining Notification Act (both 1988). Under this heading, one may also include the formidable Employee Retirement Income Security Act (1974, amended 1980), which recognized the critical importance of private pension plans to the economy and to individual welfare and for the first time attempted to regulate the detail of their administration.

Employment opportunity and discrimination has become a densely legislated field, largely as a result of the civil rights movement of the 1960s. Landmark legislation included the Equal Pay Act (1963), Title VII of the 1964 Civil Rights Act, the Age Discrimination in Employment Act (1967, amended 1978), the Equal Employment Opportunity Act (1972), the Rehabilitation Act (1973), and, most recently, the Americans with Disabilities Act (1992).

Since the early 1970s, U.S. economic performance has become increasingly exposed to trends in international competition. Resultant upheavals in comparative advantage have caused major dislocations in the distribution of employment among the economy's various sectors. As a consequence, job training and retraining has become an increasingly prominent feature of congressional debate, exemplified in measures such as the Comprehensive Employment and Training Act (1973, amended twice in 1978). Throughout the 1970s, however, policy formation in this field took place in the context of an economy suffering slowing growth and increasingly stubborn structural unemployment, particularly among minority youth. Through most of the decade, Congress responded by funding short-term emergency programs (for example, the Emergency Jobs and Unemployment Assistance Act of 1974), by offering incentives (for example, the Youth Employment and Demonstration Projects Act of 1977), and by making declarations (for example, the Humphrey-Hawkins Full Employment and Balanced Growth Act of 1978). However, Congress was never able to develop the necessary measure of consensus to approve a comprehensive measure. The Humphrey Hawkins bill is a good example. Beginning as a proposal for a massive federal jobs and planning program to reduce unemployment and lift the economy, the bill was so extensively amended by Senate conservatives that when enacted, even its most committed adherents could describe it only as "a small, symbolic step."

Into the 1990s. Discrimination and access, labor standards, employment promotion, education and training, collective bargaining—the areas that dominated post–World War II labor policy debates—all came under increasing assault from free-market advocates during the 1980s. By the end of the decade, each of the mechanisms successively invoked over the previous fifty years to moderate market movements—first organization and bargaining, then public regulation—had been thoroughly denounced. Government, like unions, was portrayed as an institutional inefficiency preventing markets from operating properly.

Market reasoning has not supplanted governmental oversight in the labor policy paradigm of the United States, and the chances of it doing so in the 1990s are receding. The dominant domestic policy themes of the early 1990s have been shaped by popular perceptions of profound economic uncertainty and gathering social crisis, both stemming from continued globalization of competition and the resulting rapid attrition of high wage–high benefit jobs in traditional manufacturing industries. As a result, the 1992 elections turned almost entirely on competing proposals for enhancing real incomes, promoting employment, and job training.

Yet government oversight is no more assured of ascendancy. The victory of a Democratic presidential candidate and a Democratic Congress in 1992 elections promised policies that favored interventionist over market solutions. Even a renewed role for collective bargaining seemed conceivable, if the Democratic Congress and the administration chose to respond to organized labor's campaign for labor law reform to reverse the erosion of union strength. But in its first two years the Clinton administration has encountered determined Republican opposition that has delayed or defeated the Democrats' grandest plans—the striker replacement ban, universal employer-funded health care—and threatens to replay 1980s policy gridlock. Ironically, the North American Free Trade Agreement (NAFTA), which organized labor sees as a threat to domestic labor standards and long-term manufacturing job growth, was the administration's clearest political success.

The labor policy issues with which Congress must continue to grapple in the 1990s and beyond are no different in essence from those that have dominated the labor policy agenda since the 1930s:

the capacity for collective bargaining to play a significant role in incomes policy and its wider macroeconomic impact; protecting and enhancing employees' access to job opportunities through antidiscrimination, occupational safety, and labor standards laws; and the role of government in managing the labor force as a national resource.

In the 1990s, however, one circumstance is very different. Congress confronts major problems in labor policy—stagnant manufacturing employment, inadequate retraining, falling real incomes—while its budgetary options are tightly constrained by massive public-sector debt. The situation requires unusual inventiveness in policy-making. After a decade in which policy "debate" meant little more than a competition of alternating dogmas—"market" solutions arrayed against "government" solutions—the times demand a pragmatic and intelligent canvassing of all possible options. Otherwise the 1990s threaten to become a decade of gnawing political failure, failure that could prove socially devastating to the many fragile worlds of human relations that are touched by labor policy to an extent unexperienced since the 1930s. This must be a time when all sides in labor policy elevate realism over hype.

[*For discussion of related public policy issues, see* Child Labor; Civil Service; Commerce Power; Social Welfare and Poverty; Women's Issues and Rights. *See also* Coxey's Army; Education and Labor Committee, House; Labor and Human Resources Committee, Senate; New Freedom. *For discussion of related legislation, see* Disability Legislation; Employment Act of 1946; Fair Labor Standards Act; GI Bill of Rights; Occupational Safety and Health Act of 1970; Social Security Act; Taft-Hartley Labor-Management Relations Act; Wagner-Connery National Labor Relations Act.]

BIBLIOGRAPHY

Eggert, Gerald G. *Railroad Labor Disputes: The Beginnings of Federal Strike Policy.* 1967.

Epstein, Richard W. "A Common Law for Labor Relations: A Critique of the New Deal Labor Legislation." *Yale Law Journal* 92 (1983): 1357–1408.

Forbath, William E. *Law and the Shaping of the American Labor Movement.* 1991.

Gross, James. *The Making of the National Labor Relations Board: A Study in Economics, Politics, and the Law.* 1974.

Gross, James. *The Reshaping of the National Labor Relations Board: National Labor Policy in Transition.* 1981.

Lee, R. Alton. *Eisenhower and Landrum-Griffin: A Study in Labor-Management Politics.* 1990.

Lee, R. Alton. *Truman and Taft-Hartley: A Question of Mandate.* 1966.

Rogers, Joel. "Divide and Conquer: Further 'Reflections on the Distinctive Character of American Labor Laws.'" *Wisconsin Law Review* (1990): 1–148.

Tomlins, Christopher L. *The State and the Unions: Labor Relations, Law, and the Organized Labor Movement in America, 1880–1960.* 1985.

Vittoz, Stanley. *New Deal Labor Policy and the American Industrial Economy.* 1987.

Zakson, Laurence S. "Railway Labor Legislation 1888 to 1930: A Legal History of Congressional Railway Labor Relations Policy." *Rutgers Law Journal* 20 (1989): 317–391.

CHRISTOPHER L. TOMLINS

LABOR AND HUMAN RESOURCES COMMITTEE, SENATE.

Initially known as the Committee on Education (1869), then the Education and Labor Committee (1870), this committee was labeled Labor and Public Welfare by the Legislative Reorganization Act of 1946. The Committee Reorganization Amendments of 1977 redesignated it the Committee on Human Resources, and in 1979, the Senate renamed it Labor and Human Resources.

Developmental Years, 1869–1935. The committee had little to do in its early stages. The 1862 Morrill Act had established land grant colleges, but they came under the jurisdiction of the Committee on Public Lands. Much of the legislation under the purview of the Committee on Education and Labor concerned increases in federal control and thus was viewed as a threat to states' rights. As a result, committee activity was sporadic, and its jurisdiction fluctuated until 1947. Beginning in the 1870s a number of ideas were proposed to expand the federal role in improving labor conditions, health, education, and the general welfare of the population. Many of these ideas took root in national policy in the 1930s when the federal role in these arenas increased.

Role Expansion, 1935–1969. The New Deal emphasis on long-term federal approaches to promote the general welfare increased momentarily the salience of the committee's jurisdiction. Most emergency relief bills went to other committees, but beginning in the 73d Congress (1933–1935), several bills to increase federal participation in social welfare areas were referred to this committee. In 1935 there was a notable shift in federal action from emergency "relief" measures to long-term federal involvement. The committee considered bills to relieve unemployment and to extend the Civilian Conservation Corps and handled several landmark labor bills, including the Wagner-Connery National Labor Relations Act, which established the National Labor Relations Board and promoted equal bargaining power between labor and management. Committee bills also aided the disadvantaged (e.g., the blind and those who lacked adequate educational facilities). In 1938, the committee was instrumental in enacting the Fair Labor Standards Act, which set standards for minimum wage, child labor, and overtime pay. The same year, the Federal Food, Drug, and Cosmetic Act became law.

The committee's jurisdiction was codified in the Legislative Reorganization Act of 1946. As amended, it now covers measures related to education, labor, health, or public welfare, generally, and those related to aging. The education jurisdiction includes agricultural colleges, arts and humanities, and student loans. Labor comprises measures related to the mediation and arbitration of disputes, wages and hours, convict labor and the interstate commerce aspects of convict-made goods, regulation of foreign laborers, child labor, labor standards and statistics, private pension plans, railway labor and retirement, and equal employment opportunity. The committee also considers measures related to Gallaudet University, Howard University, Saint Elizabeth's Hospital, public health, occupational safety and health, miners' welfare, biomedical research and development, handicapped individuals, and domestic activities of the American National Red Cross. The committee also is responsible for nominations for the departments under its purview. Until the early 1970s the jurisdiction included veterans' legislation.

Following the social initiatives of the 1930s, however, the committee considered few major new proposals until issues under its jurisdiction hit the national agenda in the late 1950s. Committee legislation enacted in the late 1950s and 1960s provided the framework for federal involvement in education, employment, health, labor, and economic opportunity. In many areas, the committee was instrumental in adopting innovative approaches to social problems. The committee handled the National Defense Education Act of 1958, which was a response to the successful Soviet launch of the satellite *Sputnik I*. Committee bills included three landmark laws: the Vocational Education Act of 1963, the Elementary and Secondary Education Act of 1965, and the Higher Education Act of 1965. In labor, the committee was vital in the passage of the 1959 Landrum-Griffin Act, which regulated admin-

istration of welfare and pension funds to curtail abuses of the sort that had been disclosed in committee hearings. The committee also worked on employment and poverty bills, including the Manpower Development and Training Act of 1962 and the Economic Opportunity Act of 1964—the War on Poverty program. It was active in the Older Americans Act of 1965 and a variety of health programs, including the Community Health Services and Facilities Act of 1961 and the Mental Retardation Facilities Construction Act and Community Mental Health Center Act of 1963.

Retrenchment and Redirection, 1969–1990s.
Throughout the 1960s, the committee was a vehicle for a large part of the Kennedy and Johnson administrations' domestic agendas. By the end of the decade, the Vietnam War crowded out domestic spending, however, and the economy was sagging. A Republican administration came to power with objectives entirely different from those of the Great Society. Opposed to large social welfare programs, Republicans tried to abolish them or replace them with cash grants. In addition, they had a different goal for federal aid to education. Nixon favored a general revenue-sharing approach to revive state discretion over education spending. Federal spending also was increasing, and efforts were under way to balance the budget. These efforts resulted in reductions in spending for federal education and welfare programs.

Another factor that affected the committee was the weakening power of some of its constituent groups. Labor unions, among the strongest supporters of committee programs, were declining in membership, political and financial clout, and salience. With the loss of labor influence, education programs were more susceptible to attack. The education establishment maintained its strength, but it, too, was vulnerable to budget cuts.

Much committee activity shifted from innovation to a holding pattern. A primary goal of liberal Democrats was to preserve the gains in social programs that had been made in the 1960s. Republicans, on the other hand, set out to limit many of these programs (e.g., scholarships, guaranteed student loans, and Basic Educational Opportunity Grants [BEOGs]). Although education authorizations increased, there were large gaps between the amounts approved and the amounts appropriated. To compensate for such declines the committee broadened its scope, shifted toward issues new to the political agenda, and focused on the other aspects of its jurisdiction.

During the 1970s, most of the labor agenda concentrated on health and safety issues, minimum wage, and pension and welfare funds. Employment activity focused on vocational rehabilitation, antidiscrimination, and emergency jobs for the unemployed, disadvantaged, or handicapped. The committee also handled legislation concerning the training of health care professionals. Committee bills expanded prevention and treatment programs for various diseases, emphasized drug and alcohol abuse treatment and prevention programs, and promoted health maintenance organizations. In education, the committee considered various modifications and extensions of the Elementary and Secondary Education Act of 1965, education of the handicapped, library services, and guaranteed student loans. The committee ventured into child abuse prevention and treatment and several times extended and amended the Older Americans Act.

In the 1980s and early 1990s, while the committee still dealt with education, labor and employment, and the elderly, a large portion of its time was spent on health-related issues. New issues, such as AIDS, "orphan drugs," and reform of the health care system, rose to the top of the national agenda. (Used for treating rare diseases, orphan drugs have limited applicability and commerical potential, hence high developmental and production costs. Legislation encourages drug companies to produce such products.) Other prominent initiatives the committee has undertaken include family and medical leave, child abuse prevention and treatment, alcohol and drug abuse prevention and treatment, assistance to the homeless, and the Americans with Disabilities Act of 1990.

Membership and Ideological Character. Membership on the Labor and Human Resources Committee was most valued by senators when its issues topped the national agenda. As attention waned, and as funding for social programs was redirected, fewer members sought assignments to the committee.

Often labeled a policy committee, it appeals most to ideologically committed members who promote their personal policy preferences on divisive issues. Recently, Republicans have been reluctant to serve on the committee because its primary constituent groups are organized labor and organized education lobbies, among others. Liberal Democrats are still drawn to the committee, as can be seen by the presence of well-known liberals such as Chairman Edward M. Kennedy (D-Mass.), Tom Harkin (D-Iowa), and Paul Wellstone (D-Minn.); there was a dearth of southerners (only one, a Republican) on the committee in the 103d Congress (1993–1995). The importance of health care reform in the 1990s should improve its attractiveness to members.

The committee's reputation for being partisan, ideological, and contentious stems from the diverse and controversial issues before it. Democrats traditionally have favored labor unions and government intervention in the social arena, whereas Republicans have preferred state or local control of education and private solutions to unemployment.

Committee Operations. The committee operates in an intensely charged environment with a jurisdiction that includes issues of concern to many. Because of the increased salience of health issues in the 1990s and the other controversial subjects the committee confronts, the panel is seen as highly conflictual relative to other Senate committees. Conflict frequently spills over to the Senate floor.

This committee is subcommittee oriented, although not nearly to the extent that it was in the 1960s and 1970s. Contributing to that decrease may be full committee consideration of health bills and a general trend toward omnibus legislation. Health measures are kept at the full committee because of widespread interest among committee members and because the chairman as of 1994, Sen. Edward M. Kennedy, is a national leader in health policy. Most other committee business is conducted in subcommittees.

The most active and influential members are the full committee and subcommittee chairs and the corresponding ranking minority members. Particularly on this committee, however, subcommittee leaders in the 1980s were more active in shaping the content of legislation than were full committee leaders. Subcommittee leaders, unlike on some other committees, are allowed to appoint their own employees. The large staffs of both the full committee and the subcommittees reflect the tremendous workload.

Representatives of health-related interests now comprise a major part of the committee's clientele. Otherwise, committee members have interacted most frequently with labor unions and the education establishment.

Others who try to influence committee legislation include organizations that represent the interests of higher education, libraries, vocational education, public employees, minorities, children, women, the elderly, persons with disabilities, the poor and homeless, state and local governments, and various religious positions. Prior to the early 1970s, veterans' associations were among the primary clientele.

Primary executive agency contacts include the Departments of Labor, Education, and Health and

Human Services. The committee also deals with the Legal Services Corporation, the National Labor Relations Board, the National Endowment for the Humanities, the National Science Foundation, the Occupational Safety and Health Administration, and the Mine Safety and Health Administration. Between 1981 and 1990, 56 percent of the measures considered by this committee and reported to the Senate were enacted into public law.

[See also Education and Labor Committee, House.]

BIBLIOGRAPHY

Evans, C. Lawrence. "Influence in Congressional Committees: Participation, Manipulation, and Anticipation." In Congressional Politics. Edited by Christopher J. Deering. 1989.

Evans, C. Lawrence. Leadership in Committee: A Comparative Analysis of Leadership Behavior in the U.S. Senate. 1991.

Fenno, Richard F., Jr. The Making of a Senator: Dan Quayle. 1989.

Smith, Steven S., and Christopher J. Deering. Committees in Congress. 2d ed. 1990.

U.S. Senate. History of the Committee on Labor and Human Resources. 96th Cong. 2d sess. 1981. S. Doc. 96-71.

ANDRÉE E. REEVES

LABOR-MANAGEMENT RELATIONS ACT. See Taft-Hartley Labor-Management Relations Act.

LA FOLLETTE, ROBERT M. (1855–1925),
Republican representative and senator from Wisconsin, governor of Wisconsin, and national progressive leader. La Follette's most durable legacy was progressive government in Wisconsin, yet his congressional career was so significant that the Senate, in 1955, selected him as one of five outstanding former members whose portraits were to hang in its reception room. Unlike the other four (Daniel Webster, John C. Calhoun, Henry Clay, and Robert A. Taft), La Follette's fame was that of a principled, often self-righteous outsider. Such an honor would have been unlikely at La Follette's death thirty years earlier, when his bitterly offended foes dominated the Senate. Nevertheless, at that time, the Wisconsin legislature had voted to place La Follette's statue in one of the state's two allotted slots in the U.S. Capitol.

Born on a Wisconsin farm, La Follette came to nearby Madison to work his way through the University of Wisconsin. Graduating in 1879 and gaining admission to the bar in 1880, he almost immediately bypassed party leaders to win the Republican nomination and election as district attorney of the county that includes Madison. Reelected district attorney in 1882, La Follette quickly moved two years later, again on his own initiative and with characteristic personal intensity, to gain the Republican nomination and then election to his district's congressional seat.

When he entered the House of Representatives in 1885, at the age of twenty-nine, La Follette was its youngest member. Despite his disregard for Wisconsin party leaders and the strongly personal support that he built in his county and district, his next six years in the House were marked by fairly orthodox Republicanism. He delivered a well-prepared attack on a Democratic tariff bill in 1888, and his hard work and debating skill earned him a seat on the Ways and Means Committee in the next Congress. There he became an effective supporter of the McKinley tariff of 1890. His promising career in the House was abruptly terminated in 1890 by an unusual Democratic landslide that defeated most of Wisconsin's Republican congressional delegation along with many state officeholders.

Resuming legal practice in Madison, La Follette became openly hostile to Wisconsin's Republican leadership rather than merely independent of it. In 1891, La Follette publicly charged that Sen. Philetus Sawyer, a dominating figure in state politics and business, had tried to bribe him to influence the outcome of a case in a court whose presiding judge was La Follette's brother-in-law. That disputed charge contributed to the fervor with which La Follette began his long campaign against the perceived corruption of politics by corporations, railroads, and banks. Through prodigious effort, magnetic speeches, and a network of personal friendships, plus eventually the financial aid of a dissident and wealthy businessman named Isaac Stephenson, La Follette built a substantial statewide following. Organizing that following within the Wisconsin Republican party, "Fighting Bob" sought to use the existing caucus-convention system to win the party's nomination for governor. He was thwarted at nominating conventions in both 1896 and 1898 by what he regarded as corrupt tactics, but he did finally win nomination and then election as governor in 1900. By this time he had developed ideas about direct primaries, increased corporate taxes, and commissions of experts to reg-

ROBERT M. LA FOLLETTE. In the 1920s.

ulate railroads and other utilities. To enact these and other progressive reforms related to conservation, civil service, labor, and banking, La Follette secured not only his own reelection in 1902 and 1904 but also the election of progressive legislative majorities. Although portions of the progressive program owed something to an older agrarian populism, especially its anticorporate rhetoric, La Follette's support drew heavily on urban middle-class preferences for honest, effective, and professional government. Wisconsin progressivism attracted national attention, particularly after a favorable magazine portrait by Lincoln Steffens, and La Follette expanded his appeal outside Wisconsin by becoming a popular Chautauqua lecturer.

Consequently, La Follette was already a significant national figure when he returned to Washington as a senator in 1906. Elected in 1905 (a year before he left the governorship) and reelected in 1910 by the state legislature, he retained the seat by popular vote in 1916 and 1922. At first, La Follette stood alone as a progressive insurgent among Re-

publican senators, but within a few years he was joined by several converts and newly elected senators. La Follette's zealous purposiveness and well-informed, statistics-laden speeches made him their acknowledged leader. As early as 1908, he conducted a record-breaking filibuster against an emergency currency measure, and in 1909 he led the insurgents' attack on the Payne-Aldrich tariff. Battles lost in the Republican Senate served to publicize the progressive cause, and La Follette's speaking tours provided further opportunities for attacking both conservative senators and the Taft administration. In 1912, La Follette challenged President William Howard Taft for the Republican nomination, but his candidacy was soon overwhelmed by the more spectacular challenge of former president Theodore Roosevelt. The experience was embittering since, as La Follette saw it, progressive Republicans deserted him for a less rigorously devoted reformer.

Within the Senate, La Follette pursued a substantial legislative career along with his insurgency. In the two Congresses before 1913, he chaired the Census Committee, and he served afterward for many years on the Finance, Interstate Commerce, and Manufactures committees, chairing the last from 1919 to 1925. A major accomplishment, after persistent effort, was passage of the La Follette Seamen's Act of 1915. Notably, enactment occurred when Democrats controlled both the Congress and the presidency and when, in Woodrow Wilson's first term, La Follette shared considerable policy ground with the Democratic administration.

His relations with Wilson deteriorated sharply as the administration moved toward belligerence in World War I. Suspicious of U.S. financial ties to the Allies, La Follette strenuously opposed U.S. military involvement. Before Congress adjourned in March 1917, he organized and led a filibuster that prevented enactment of Wilson's proposal to arm merchant ships. A month later, La Follette spoke and voted (with five other senators) against the declaration of war. By this time, he was widely vilified as unpatriotic and pro-German. Even in Wisconsin, he was denounced both by old enemies and by some former supporters. After the war, however, as patriotic fervor gave way to disillusion, La Follette's fierce opposition to American entry made him a heroic prophet, especially in Wisconsin. The state's large German American population helped to produce an overwhelming reelection in 1922. At the same time, La Follette had become the voice of midwestern isolationism in the Senate as he proclaimed his hostility to U.S. participation in the League of Nations and the World Court.

On domestic as well as international issues, La Follette continued to lead insurgent Republicans in the early 1920s and, with occasional help from Democrats, to exert influence in the Republican Senate. In 1922, he introduced the resolution authorizing the famous Teapot Dome investigation that revealed the oil lease scandals of the Harding administration. La Follette's last hurrah in the progressive cause was his presidential candidacy against the Republican and Democratic nominees in the election of 1924. Though he carried only Wisconsin, he received a larger portion of the total popular vote (one-sixth) than any other independent or third-party candidate between Theodore Roosevelt in 1912 and Ross Perot in 1992. After the 1924 presidential election, La Follette returned to the Senate under his customary Republican label, but the conservative Republican majority treated him as an independent and deprived him of a seniority-based committee chairmanship shortly before his death in 1925.

ROBERT M. LA FOLLETTE, JR. *Left*, with Robert M. La Follette, Sr., 1920s.   LIBRARY OF CONGRESS

BIBLIOGRAPHY

Cooper, John Milton, Jr. "Robert M. La Follette: Political Prophet." *Wisconsin Magazine of History* 69 (1985–1986): 91–105.

La Follette, Belle Case, and Fola La Follette. *Robert M. La Follette.* 1953.

Thelen, David P. *Robert M. La Follette and the Insurgent Spirit.* 1976.

LEON D. EPSTEIN

LA FOLLETTE, ROBERT M., JR. (1895–1953), senator from Wisconsin and persistent champion of progressive causes. Working from 1916 in the Senate office of his father, the senior Robert M. La Follette, "Young Bob" was an old Washington hand by 1925 when, following his father's death, he won election to the Senate at the age of thirty. Elected as a Republican in 1925 and 1928, he joined insurgent senators whom his father had long led against the national Republican party. He was reelected on a new third-party Progressive ticket in 1934 and again in 1940, before returning to the Republican party in 1946. His failure to win its primary ended a twenty-two-year Senate career.

During his Republican years, he chaired the Committee on Manufactures (1929–1932) and became a member of other important committees, including Finance and Foreign Relations. As a Progressive in Democratic Congresses from 1935 to 1947, La Follette retained his old committee assignments, on the minority side. He became an influential member of the Committee on Education and Labor when he sponsored a resolution authorizing an investigation of violations of civil liberties in labor relations and then chaired the much publicized investigation of 1936 to 1940. Another major landmark in his Senate service was the Legislative Reorganization Act of 1946. Generally, his record displayed strong support for most New Deal legislation of the 1930s. But in the years just before Pearl Harbor, La Follette maintained an isolationist stance, as had his father, and thus broke with President Franklin D. Roosevelt's foreign policy.

BIBLIOGRAPHY

Auerbach, Jerold S. *Labor and Liberty: The La Follette Committee and the New Deal.* 1966.

Maney, Patrick J. *"Young Bob" La Follette: A Biography of Robert M. La Follette, Jr., 1895–1953.* 1978.

LEON D. EPSTEIN

LAGUARDIA, FIORELLO H. (1882–1947), representative from New York, mayor of New York City. Born in lower Manhattan to immigrant parents, Fiorello Henry LaGuardia grew up in the

manding attention to the poor, the exploited, and the unemployed. He offered legislation to regulate big business, lashed out at immigration restriction, and assailed the hypocrisies of prohibition. He supported equal rights for women, freedom of speech for socialists, old-age pensions, unemployment insurance, workmen's compensation, public housing, federal energy development, and an end to child labor. Together with Sen. George W. Norris (R-Nebr.) he helped pass the landmark Norris-LaGuardia Act (1932), which was intended to prevent the use of crippling anti-labor injunctions. In the age of Warren G. Harding and Calvin Coolidge, he was the closest thing to a radical that many Americans could identify, at different times running on the Republican, Socialist, and Progressive tickets, and once even winning the endorsement of the Democrats.

With the Depression, his insurgent programs finally won wide attention. Ironically, however, the Roosevelt landslide that swept Republicans from office across the nation also led to his defeat in 1932. In his last few months in Congress, he helped lay the legislative groundwork for the New Deal; subsequently he would work with the Roosevelt administration in carrying out his urban progressive policies as New York's most admired and effective mayor in modern times.

BIBLIOGRAPHY

Kessner, Thomas. *Fiorello H. LaGuardia and the Making of Modern New York*. 1989.

Mann, Arthur. *LaGuardia: A Fighter against His Times, 1882–1933*. 1959.

Zinn, Howard. *LaGuardia in Congress*. 1959.

THOMAS KESSNER

FIORELLO H. LAGUARDIA.   LIBRARY OF CONGRESS

West, where as the pugnacious son of an Austrian Jewish mother and Italian agnostic father he built his identity as an American.

In 1916 he defeated Tammany Hall's candidate to become the first Republican since the Civil War to represent New York's 14th Congressional District. Later he would espouse a progressive pacifism; but soon after assuming his seat, the United States entered World War I and LaGuardia joined only four other congressmen to enlist in the army, where he flew as a fighter pilot.

After returning to Congress in 1923, LaGuardia poured his energies into progressive causes, de-

LAMAR, LUCIUS Q. C. (1825–1893), representative and senator from Mississippi, secretary of the Interior, Supreme Court justice, a leader of southern sectional politics. Lucius Quintus Cincinnatus Lamar's career was divided into two parts by the Civil War. He advocated southern "rights" in the territories after his election to the House in 1857. In 1860 he was emissary for Jefferson Davis in an unsuccessful effort to keep the Mississippi delegation from leaving the Democratic national convention and seceding independently of other southern states. Afterward he wrote Mississippi's secession ordinance.

After a career as soldier and diplomat in the Confederate States of America, Lamar returned to the

LUCIUS Q. C. LAMAR.   LIBRARY OF CONGRESS

House in 1873 as the first postwar Democrat from Mississippi. He was particularly noted for his advocacy of an end to reconstruction and sectional antagonism. This advocacy gained particular fame when he pled, in 1874, for reconciliation in a eulogy of Sen. Charles Sumner of Massachusetts, who had been a leading critic of the South. Lamar pursued conservative fiscal goals, often voting with the Republican opposition. He also often voted for Republican internal improvement programs favorable to the South. He sought a workable, though unequal, relationship with black Republicans in Mississippi, asking for their support but acquiescing in and rationalizing the denial of black political rights.

In 1877 Lamar entered the Senate after a "home rule" election victory that marked the end of Republican power in Mississippi. In the Senate Lamar continued, despite bad health and poor attendance, to work for conservative fiscal policy, while at the same time chairing the Mississippi River Committee and supporting government-financed internal improvements.

In 1885 Lamar became secretary of the Interior during the first administration of Grover Cleveland, as part of Cleveland's policy of sectional reconciliation. Cleveland later appointed him to the Supreme Court. Lamar was the first former Confederate to join the Court, and he served until his death in 1893.

BIBLIOGRAPHY

Murphy, James B. *L. Q. C. Lamar: Pragmatic Patriot.* 1973.
Cate, Wirt Armistead. *Lucius Q. C. Lamar: Secession and Reunion.* 1935.

JAMES B. MURPHY

LAME DUCK SESSION. The term *lame duck session* refers to the time Congress is in session between the November congressional elections and the convening of the new Congress following those elections. The defeated members of Congress who remain in office during this time are the lame ducks. Lame duck, which has British origins in the early nineteenth century, originally described a bankrupt businessman. The expression found application in politics, where it is used to describe a defeated officeholder or a political party, or the time period between an incumbent's defeat at the polls and the beginning of the successor's term. Its usage in the United States dates from the 1830s according to some authorities. While the term can apply to state and local politics, most often it is used to characterize a president or a Congress.

The Continental Congress set 4 March 1789 as the date the First Federal Congress under the new Constitution would meet. In an age when the nation was largely agricultural and when transportation and communication over long distances consumed considerable time, the length of time between the fall elections and a 4 March beginning date did not seem particularly long. Furthermore, Congress, with some exceptions, convened a new session in December of the year following the elections, which meant that newly elected members had to wait thirteen months before taking office.

The ratification of the Twentieth Amendment of the Constitution (sometimes called the lame duck amendment) on 23 January 1933 addressed both the problem of shortening the time period between the election and the assumption of office and the long time period between election and the beginning of a new session of Congress, calling for Congress to convene on 3 January (unless another date close to this is selected by law). It also stipulates that the terms of the president and vice president begin on 20 January.

Prior to the adoption of the Twentieth Amendment critics pointed to the potential mischief of the lame duck session. On the rare occurrences when the House of Representatives was called upon to select a president, lame ducks took part in the process. Some questioned whether a lame duck could remain an effective member of Congress and represent the wishes of his or her district if they were more interested in voting to improve their chances for a job with the new administration or in private life.

[*See also* Twentieth Amendment.]

BIBLIOGRAPHY

Safire, William. *Safire's Political Dictionary.* 1980.
U.S. Congress. *Congressional Record.* 69th Cong., 2d sess., 3 March 1927. See Emanuel Celler, "Lame Ducks: Exclusively American," pp. 5673–5678.

RAYMOND W. SMOCK

LAND-GRANT COLLEGE ACT. *See* Morrill Land-Grant College Act.

LANGUAGE.

Throughout the history of Congress, the spoken word has occupied center stage. The written instruments of Congress—statutes, reports, studies, and recorded legislative histories—are also essential parts of the final work product; but, it was and is open and honest debate, along with the statement and the friendly informality of casual conversation, that are the lifeblood of the legislature.

At the core of congressional rhetoric is the code of comity. Congress can be a very contentious place from time to time, and rules and precedents were adopted long ago to prevent rudeness and to force the uncivilized to be civil.

Perhaps the Founders carefully studied the classics and noted how the legislative murders of the Gracchi in Rome led to civil war and tyranny. They learned from Plutarch about Cicero's assassination by Marc Antony's soldiers, followed by the placement of his head and right hand on a stake in the Roman Forum; a silver pin was thrust in his tongue, thus endowing our culture with the rhetorical question "How do you like that, you silver-tongued devil?"

Throughout U.S. history—in peace and in war—the Congress has suffered the abuse of rhetoric as well as the enforcement of comity and verbal courtesy. Sen. Charles Sumner of Massachusetts was caned and nearly killed by Rep. Preston S. Brooks of South Carolina shortly before the Civil War started, and in the 1990s, members are still periodically disciplined for insulting and intemperate remarks uttered in the heat of debate.

Thomas Jefferson captured the core of this aspect of congressional rhetoric in his Manual as follows:

No one is to disturb another in his speech by hissing, coughing, spitting, speaking or whispering to another; not stand up to interrupt him; nor to pass between the Speaker and the speaking Member, nor to go across the House or to walk up and down it, or to take books or papers from the table, or write there. Nevertheless, if a Member finds that it is not the inclination of the House to hear him, and that by conversation or any other noise they endeavor to drown his voice, it is his most prudent way to submit to the pleasure of the House and sit down; for it scarcely ever happens that they are guilty of this piece of ill manners without sufficient reason, or inattention to a Member who says anything worth their hearing.

While many observers besides Thomas Jefferson, some from within Congress and some from outside, have expressed their views about the meaning and function of Congress, two leap from the pages of history to demonstrate true affection for the institution. The first is former president and House minority leader Gerald R. Ford, who said:

I know well the coequal role of the Congress in our constitutional process. I love the House of Representatives. I revere the traditions of the Senate despite my too-short internship in that great body. As President, within the limits of basic principles, my motto towards the Congress is communication, conciliation, compromise, and cooperation. (*Public Papers of the Presidents of the United States*, 1974, pp. 6–7)

The other is humorist Will Rogers, who observed:

So when all the yielding and objections are over, the other Senator said, "I object to the remarks of a professional joker being put into the *Congressional Record*." Taking a dig at me, see? They didn't want any outside fellow contributing. Well, he had me wrong. Compared to them I'm an amateur, and the thing about my jokes is that they don't hurt anybody. You can say they're not funny or they're terrible or they're good or whatever it is, but they don't do no harm. But with Congress—every time they make a joke it's a law. And every time they make a law it's a joke. (P. J. O'Brien, *Will Rogers, Ambassador of Good Will, Prince of Wit and Wisdom,* 1935, pp. 156–157)

Enriching the Vocabulary. Congress has often enriched the public's vocabulary. Two memorable examples are the words *filibuster,* an analogy to pirateering, and *sequestration,* a new word for impoundment. For better or worse, these examples are now a part of American rhetoric, just as the suffix *gate* has come to indicate scandal, as in Watergate, Koreagate, and Rubbergate (the House bank episode). The Watergate investigation led to many new and distinct terms and phrases, but none was more rhetorically redundant than *at this point in time.* Future rhetoricians will always wonder "was it at this point? . . . or was it at this time?" Over the years, congressional debate has produced scores of terms that have become part of the political and general vocabulary of American English— words such as *omnibus bill, bunkum, grassroots, gag rule, lame duck, favorite son,* and *pork barrel.*

Humor in Debate. In a system that grants the majority the right to have its way and the minority the right to have its say and its pay (to paraphrase Speakers James C. Wright, Jr., and Thomas B. Reed), it often happens that good humor is used to ease a difficult dispute or prevent impatience or anger from destroying any prospects of conciliation or compromise, which are the bedrock of the legislative path. In the 1970s, for example, a severe frost in the San Francisco Bay area caused considerable damage to the indigenous eucalyptus trees. Federal relief was sought, and the House Agriculture Committee responded with a eucalyptus disaster bill designed to help tree owners pay for tree removal. When the bill came to the floor of the House, the eagle-eyed congressional purse-watcher, Rep. Harold R. Gross of Iowa, helped kill the bill by continually referring to it as the "you clipped us" bill.

Members of Congress also occasionally provide themselves with humorous rhetoric without realizing it. For example, in the 1992 debate on an amendment to the Constitution to balance the budget, one member shouted, "It's time for us to put our guts where our mouth is." Earlier, a member had urged broad-based action in "one swell poop" (later corrected in the *Congressional Record* to read "one fell swoop.")

Humor on the Stump. Much of the humor that is generated by members of Congress originates and is used in places far from the hallowed halls of Congress. The campaign trail, the rubber chicken circuit, banquets, weddings, anniversaries, and dozens of other social events that politicians attend generate a great deal of political rhetoric and humor.

On 19 June 1980 Rep. Silvio Conte observed that *Roll Call* and the *Congressional Record* were very similar, but that there was one important difference: "When the *Congressional Record* prints something a Congressman didn't say, they put a bullet next to it. Something for the press to think about," he chortled.

Conte, a Republican, didn't spare the Democrats as targets for his humor. He pointed out that Republican members of Congress usually win the annual charity baseball game because "Democrats play baseball the same way they try to balance the budget . . . they start out trying to keep things even, but always wind up short in the end."

Speaker Thomas P. O'Neill, Jr., a man not easily outshone on podiums in the House or in hotels, once opened his remarks to the assembled congressional horde with these words: "Distinguished guests at the head table including the paid ups and the freebies, big and little shots, the mucky mucks and the retreads, the ringers, friends, frauds, window dressing and heavy hitters, other specified and unspecified comedians on the dais; it's a great honor to be here and to speak to so many Congressmen."

As for Republicans, O'Neill contended that Democrats would always control the House because they marry young and sleep in double beds. Republicans, on the other hand, marry older and sleep in single beds and in different rooms, which explains why there are just more Democrats around.

The early days of the Republic were extremely contentious, and for a not too brief period it was a federal crime to criticize the government. Men were actually jailed under the infamous Alien and Sedition Acts for ridiculing President John Adams for being fat, referring to him as "His Rotundity." Before and during the Civil War, blood was spilled and hatreds hardened, but the good humor exhibited by Abraham Lincoln and the new congressional delegations of a reunited America helped heal the wounds of slavery and disunion. After two centuries of constitutional adventure, one hopes that the Congress of the United States will continue to be both a buyer and a seller of open and honest debate in a rhetorical atmosphere of due process of law, fair play, and a little fun.

[*See also* Congress, *article on* Customs and Mores; Debate and Oratory; Humor and Satire.]

BIBLIOGRAPHY

Boller, Paul. *Congressional Anecdotes.* 1989.
Boykin, Edward. *The Wit and Wisdom of Congress.* 1961.
Caldwell, Taylor. *A Pillar of Iron.* 1965.
Harris, Leon A. *The Fine Art of Political Wit.* 1964.
Murray, Hyde H. "Notes on *Roll Call*, Silver Anniversary Salute." 1980.
Wallace, Karl R. *Francis Bacon on Communications and Rhetoric.* 1943.

HYDE H. MURRAY

LATINO MEMBERS. *See* Hispanic Members.

LAWMAKING. [*The following article provides an overview of how a bill becomes a law. For further discussion of this process, see* Committees; Congress; House of Representatives, *articles on* Daily Sessions of the House *and* House Rules and Procedures; Leadership; Senate, *articles on* Daily Sessions of the Senate *and* Senate Rules and Procedures; Veto, *article on* Presidential Veto; Voting in Congress. *See also numerous entries on particular technical and procedural terms mentioned herein; such entries can be found within the body of the encyclopedia as well as in the glossary at the back of volume 4.*] The legislative process in practice is a complex maze through which measures must wind their way. The efficient assembly line portrayed in a typical legislative process flow chart may be true for some noncontroversial issues, but for more significant measures, a game of chess is a more accurate analogy. Most legislative moves can be met with a countermove. What is lost at one stage of the process can be reclaimed at another. The reverse is also true. Victory in an earlier phase may turn into defeat later. Until the stage of public law is reached, no game of legislative chess is truly over. A bill may clear the entire legislative labyrinth, only to be vetoed by the president. Conversely, there are instances in which bills are enacted without passing through all of the earlier legislative stages. Therefore, while the narrative that follows describes the usual route most measures travel, it does not encompass all the possible procedural side roads the legislative process permits.

Moreover, legislation is not processed solely in a procedural context. The need for a political consensus and the complexities of policy disputes also contribute to a measure's progress along the legislative path. Those measures that become public law reach that end only through a combination of political, policy, and procedural factors.

Development and Introduction. While only members of the House or Senate may introduce a bill, the idea for the measure can come from many different sources. The president, federal department or agency officials, state governors or legislatures, interest groups, lobbyists, constituents, or congressional staff may contribute to a member's decision to initiate a specific proposal.

The primary motive for introducing a bill is enactment into law. However, a bill may also be introduced for other reasons: for example, to establish a member's political position on an issue; to spur desired executive or judicial action; to serve as a basis for policy development; or as a vehicle to heighten public awareness of an issue.

The member who introduces a measure is known as that bill's sponsor. Other members who wish to associate themselves with the proposal are known as its cosponsors. Members strive to collect a large number of cosponsors prior to introducing a bill in the hopes that it will signal that the proposal has significant support and merits priority consideration. In the House chamber, members introduce their bills by dropping them into a deep wooden box located on the Speaker's dais, known as the hopper. In the Senate chamber, bills are handed to a clerk at the rostrum. The bills are printed and copies distributed to all members. Copies of bills are also available to the public through the House or Senate document rooms or the Government Printing Office.

Both the House and Senate provide the services of nonpartisan legislative counsels to assist members in drafting the legal language necessary to transform their legislative proposal into the text of a bill. Members may also choose to accept draft language for a bill from interest groups, or assign the drafting responsibility to their own staff.

The term *bill* is commonly used interchangeably with the term *measure* to refer to any piece of legislation. However, there are clear distinctions between bills, joint resolutions, and concurrent and simple resolutions. Measures designed to become public law must technically take the form of bills or joint resolutions. House bills are expressed as "H.R. 1000" (the actual numbers vary), while those that originate in the Senate are numbered "S. 1000." House joint resolutions are labeled "H.J. Res. 100," while those in the Senate are marked "S.J. Res. 100." While no rule stipulates whether a proposed law be drafted as a bill or a joint resolution, some traditions apply. For example, proposals to amend the Constitution are normally drafted as joint resolutions, as are some appropriation bills and commemorative measures. Bills and joint resolutions must pass both chambers and receive the president's approval or survive his veto to become law.

Concurrent resolutions do not make law but are used to take an action on behalf of the Congress as a whole, or to express congressional opinion on a matter. The House version is tagged "H. Con. Res. 100," while the Senate label is "S. Con. Res. 100." Concurrent resolutions must pass both chambers, but are not presented to the president.

Simple resolutions take action on behalf of one chamber alone, or express the opinion of only that body. They are classified as either "H. Res. 100" or "S. Res. 100." Because these proposals affect only one chamber, they are sent neither to the other body nor to the president.

The life span of a measure is limited to the two-year Congress in which it is introduced. Measures die at the end of a Congress unless they are enacted prior to its final adjournment. If passed by Congress and approved by the president, bills become either public or private law. Proposals that affect the nation at large become public laws, while proposals that seek relief for only one individual or legal entity become private laws.

Referral to Committee. After introduction, most measures are referred to a legislative committee for review. House and Senate rules establish the specific subject matter areas, known as jurisdiction, of each chamber's standing committees. In the House, the Speaker makes the referral decision based on advice from the House parliamentarian, a nonpartisan employee of the chamber. In the Senate, the presiding officer refers measures pursuant to the recommendations of its parliamentarian. In making their referral decisions, the parliamentarians rely on their chamber's jurisdiction rule, as well as past historical practice, known as precedents.

Some measures encompass subject matter that may fall within the purview of more than one legislative committee. Referral to more than one committee, known as multiple referral, is possible in both chambers. Multiple referrals come in three varieties. A "joint" referral sends an entire bill to two or more committees simultaneously. A "sequential" referral sends an entire bill first to one committee, and subsequently to a second or more committees. A "split" referral sends most of the measure to one committee but splits off a provision, usually an entire title, and sends just the designated portion to another committee. If a bill has been multiply referred, it is not eligible for floor consideration until all the committees involved have completed their work. As a result, a multiple referral tends to reduce a bill's chances of reaching the floor. The complexities of coordinating disparate political perspectives and committee schedules inherent in a multiple referral are sometimes enough to halt a measure's progress. At times, however, the presiding officer may impose a time deadline on each committee involved in a multiple referral. In such cases, a measure's progress may actually be speeded up.

Because most legislation that fails to become law fails to clear the committee process, the decision on committee referral can be crucial. Members sometimes employ creative drafting techniques to ensure that a bill is referred to a committee inclined to give it favorable consideration.

Committee Hearings. Once a committee receives a measure it may keep it at the full committee level for processing, or it may refer it to one of its subcommittees. Individual committee rules, which differ, govern this practice. Hearings on a measure are usually first held at the subcommittee level, although this is not mandatory. The full committee may accept the views developed during the subcommittee's review, or choose to hold its own hearings, which must be open to the public unless the committee, in open session, votes to close further proceedings. This is rarely done except in cases where national security issues or pending court cases are involved. Most hearings are held in Washington, D.C., although so-called field hearings are sometimes scheduled in localities across the country.

Hearings serve a variety of purposes. They may be planned to help a committee gain specific information and advice from expert witnesses in order to perfect the policies and the language of the legislation under consideration. Some hearings are designed to explore whether or not legislation in a given area is even necessary. Hearings can be devised to increase public awareness of an issue, or to simply provide a forum for interested individuals and groups to express their views or frustrations with certain federal policies. Hearings are also structured to investigate problems or to conduct a review of executive branch performance or programs, known as oversight.

Each committee has its own rules governing various aspects of hearing procedure, such as quorum requirements, calling of witnesses, scheduling, and

How a Bill Becomes a Law

This illustration shows the most typical way in which proposed legislation is enacted into law. There are more complicated as well as simpler routes, and most bills never become law. The process is illustrated with two hypothetical bills, House bill No. 1 (H.R. 1) and Senate bill No. 2 (S. 2). Bills must be passed by both houses in identical form before they can be sent to the president. The path of H.R. 1 is traced by a solid line, that of S. 2 by a dotted line. In practice, most bills begin as similar proposals in both houses.

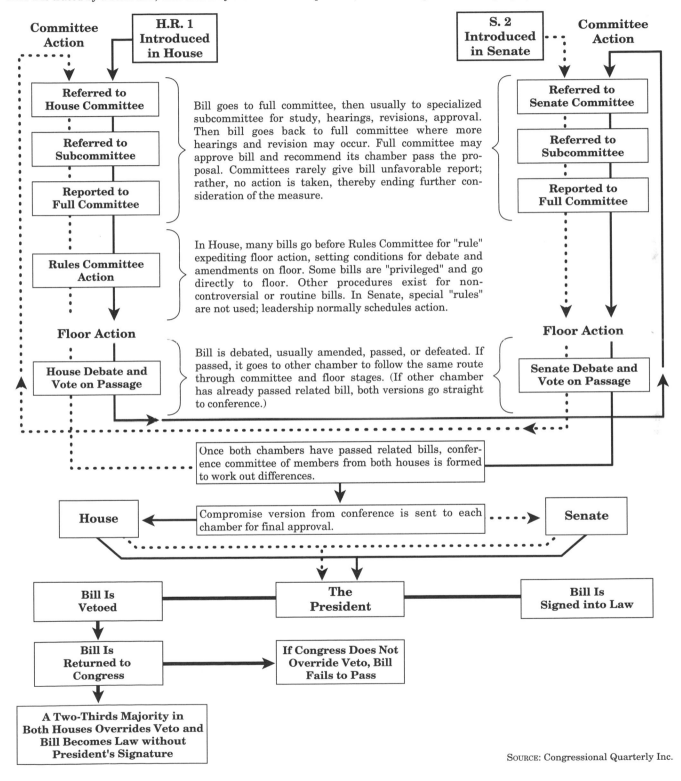

Committee Action

H.R. 1 Introduced in House

Referred to House Committee

Referred to Subcommittee

Reported to Full Committee

Bill goes to full committee, then usually to specialized subcommittee for study, hearings, revisions, approval. Then bill goes back to full committee where more hearings and revision may occur. Full committee may approve bill and recommend its chamber pass the proposal. Committees rarely give bill unfavorable report; rather, no action is taken, thereby ending further consideration of the measure.

S. 2 Introduced in Senate

Committee Action

Referred to Senate Committee

Referred to Subcommittee

Reported to Full Committee

Rules Committee Action

In House, many bills go before Rules Committee for "rule" expediting floor action, setting conditions for debate and amendments on floor. Some bills are "privileged" and go directly to floor. Other procedures exist for noncontroversial or routine bills. In Senate, special "rules" are not used; leadership normally schedules action.

Floor Action

House Debate and Vote on Passage

Bill is debated, usually amended, passed, or defeated. If passed, it goes to other chamber to follow the same route through committee and floor stages. (If other chamber has already passed related bill, both versions go straight to conference.)

Floor Action

Senate Debate and Vote on Passage

Once both chambers have passed related bills, conference committee of members from both houses is formed to work out differences.

House

Compromise version from conference is sent to each chamber for final approval.

Senate

Bill Is Vetoed

The President

Bill Is Signed into Law

Bill Is Returned to Congress

If Congress Does Not Override Veto, Bill Fails to Pass

A Two-Thirds Majority in Both Houses Overrides Veto and Bill Becomes Law without President's Signature

SOURCE: Congressional Quarterly Inc.

order of recognition. Copies of a committee's rules can be obtained from the committee or from the *Congressional Record*. Hearings usually consist of committee members making opening remarks, listening to prepared statements offered by witnesses, and posing questions to those witnesses. Witnesses are most frequently federal agency or department officials, members of Congress, representatives of interest groups or trade associations, technical specialists, or academic experts.

Committees are required to keep a verbatim transcript of hearings held, and these may be examined by the public. Most committees eventually publish a full record of the hearing, including the texts of witness statements not delivered and other related material inserted for the record. The hearing record becomes a part of a measure's legislative history, although it reflects only the preliminary explorations of that panel and does not necessarily indicate the entire chamber's perspective on the issue.

Hearings are a good, but not final, indicator that a measure will receive further legislative action. Legislative enactment is not the motivation behind all hearings; conversely, some legislation is enacted even though it was never the subject of committee hearings.

Committee Markup. Markups are committee meetings held to discuss and often revise the text of a particular bill. The term is derived from the practice of literally marking up the original text of the bill to reflect changes adopted by the committee. Committees may also decide not to alter the original bill at all, although this rarely happens.

Markups can be held on bills previously introduced and referred to the committee, or on informal drafts of bills not yet introduced. Such drafts are commonly referred to as the "chairman's mark" because it is the chairman of the committee who typically initiates the proposed text.

Markups are held at either the subcommittee or full committee level, or both. The full committee may choose to accept the subcommittee's proposed changes, or it may decide to revise the text further. Markups usually follow the completion of hearings, although hearings are not a required prerequisite to holding a markup. Markups are usually open to the public, but a committee or subcommittee may decide by majority vote to close a particular session, usually done if national or international security issues are involved.

Committees vary in their reliance on parliamentary procedure during a markup. Some panels require that proposals to change text be offered as formal amendments, each of which must receive a vote. Other committees prefer a more informal approach. Changes to the text are discussed and negotiated and committee staff are delegated the task of drafting the precise language to reflect these agreements. Committees may report a bill with one amendment that substitutes an entire new text for the original, or with a series of amendments that make lesser changes throughout the bill. At times, committees choose to report an entirely new measure, written in committee, for the original text. These are known as clean bills in the House, and original bills in the Senate.

Markup sessions normally end with a vote on whether or not to report the revised version to the House or Senate floor with a recommendation for passage by the chamber. This vote must be taken at the full committee level, with a quorum present, or the measure may later be ruled out of order.

Committee Reports. Committee reports explain the committee's actions on a bill and present the case for passage to the full chamber. Committee reports are required in the House, but are optional in the Senate. They accompany a reported bill to the floor and are filed along with it.

Reports must contain a section-by-section analysis of the measure and describe the changes the committee recommends to the original text. Reports must also contain a comparison with the text of existing law to show how the committee version proposes to alter it. Other content requirements include roll-call votes taken in committee, cost estimates of implementing the legislation, and regulatory impact statements, among others. Frequently comments received from federal agencies on the proposed legislation, known as executive comments, are included.

Committee members may also place their own individual views in the report. Statements essentially in agreement with the viewpoint expressed in the report are inserted as "supplemental" or "additional" views. Statements in opposition to the committee's perspective are incorporated as "minority" or "dissenting" views. These individual statements often signal possible floor amendments and debating points.

Committee reports serve as an essential part of a bill's legislative history. If the measure is enacted into law, the federal agencies responsible for its implementation will turn to the committee report for guidance on congressional intent. Courts of law also consult committee reports to aid in interpreting the meaning of the text.

Figure 2
From Bill to Law: House and Senate Statistics[1]
from the 102d Congress (1991–1993)

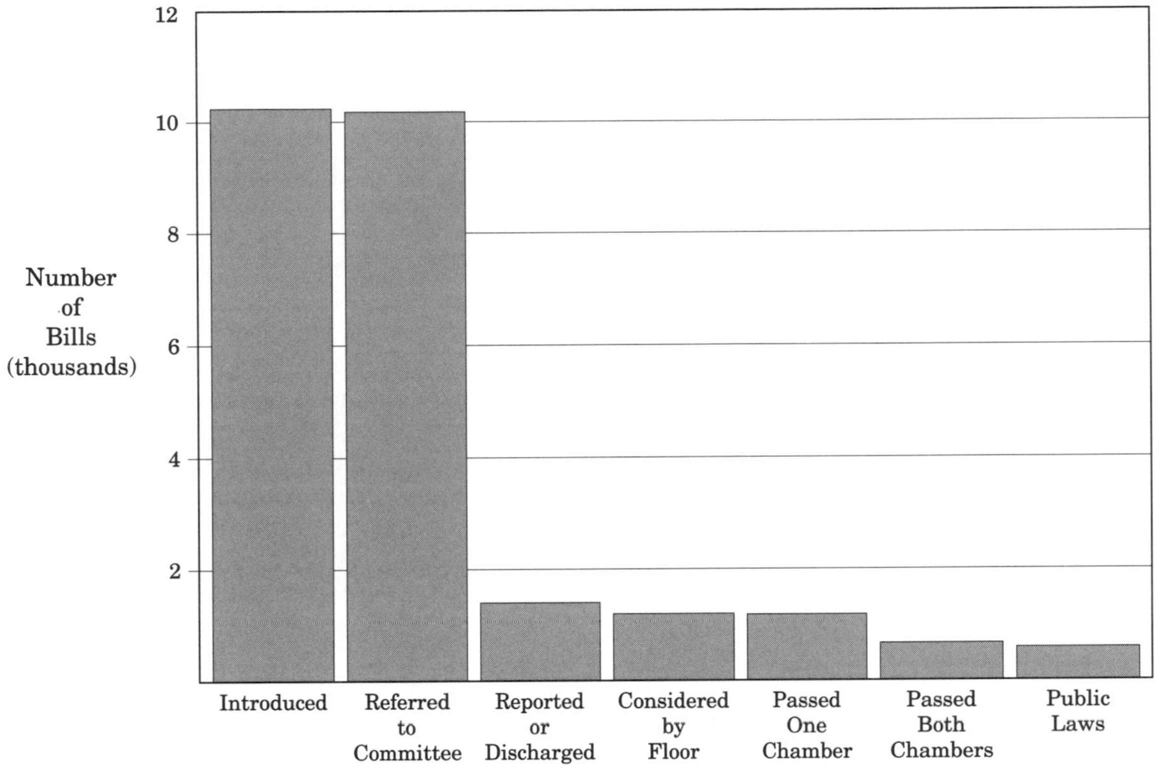

[1]Statistics represent only measures that can become public law (i.e., bills and joint resolutions). Simple resolutions, concurrent resolutions, and private bills are excluded.

SOURCE: Ilona B. Nickels, Congressional Research Service, Library of Congress, Washington, D.C.

Procedures exist in both the House and Senate that permit the chamber to consider a bill not yet reported from committee. When time constraints make expediting the legislative process necessary, committees often arrange for a friendly floor motion or a unanimous consent request to be discharged from further consideration of a measure. The effect of discharging a committee also supplants the House requirement for a committee report.

Getting to the Floor. Legislation reported from a House committee is placed on one of two primary calendars (House or Union) or on one of three specialized calendars (Consent, Private, or District of Columbia). In the Senate, all legislation is placed on the Calendar of General Orders (known as the Legislative Calendar). Executive branch business (nominations or treaties) reported from a Senate committee are placed on the Executive Calendar.

Placement on a calendar, however, does not guarantee that an item will receive floor consideration. The majority leadership in both chambers selects the floor agenda, basing their choices on a variety of political, procedural, and scheduling factors.

Once the decision has been made to turn to a specific measure, the chamber's leadership chooses from among several procedures available to call up a bill for floor consideration. The choice of procedure is crucial because it also determines the conditions under which the bill will be debated and amended. Some procedures allow for open-ended debate and amending, while others severely restrict the opportunity for legislators to discuss or change the measure before them.

House leaders call up most bills under a set of restrictions known as the "suspension of the rules" procedure. As its name connotes, the suspension procedure waives the regular rules of order. Measures brought up under the suspension procedure are debated for no more than forty minutes and may not be amended from the floor. Therefore, the vote on final passage occurs on the unaltered committee version of a bill.

Moreover, because the suspension procedure waives all normal rules of procedure, points of order against a measure are prohibited. This concept extends to the committee reporting requirements. Measures brought up under suspension of the rules need not have been formally reported by their committee of jurisdiction, nor is a committee report necessary. The suspension procedure is also useful for the consideration of conference reports that may contain rules violations. In a measure brought up under suspension, the fact that conferees may have inserted new language that was not in either the original House or Senate version or may have taken out language that appeared in both versions is not subject to challenge.

The most controversial measures in the House are called up under the auspices of a "special rule" from the House Rules Committee. A special rule temporarily replaces the regular rules of order, serving as a blueprint for a bill's consideration. It imposes upon the chamber uniquely crafted debate and amending conditions for the specified measure, taking into account the political factions and policy disputes that affect that particular bill. However, before it can take effect, a special rule must be adopted by a majority vote of the House.

Special rules typically have four routine provisions. The first makes it in order to call up the bill for consideration. The second provision sets a time limit on general debate and allocates that time between the majority and minority parties. The third structures the amending process by either allowing all amendments (a so-called open rule), no amendments except those reported by the committee (a closed rule), some amendments but only by specified individuals (a modified closed rule), or all amendments except those to certain portions of the bill protected from change (a modified open rule). In its final provision, a special rule may prohibit points of order, which means that technical violations in the text of the bill or in a designated floor amendment may not be challenged.

Special rules are frequently controversial and the subject of intense debate. Members of the majority party see special rules as a method of establishing priorities among the legislative agendas of 435 members, and of streamlining the consideration of conflicting policy perspectives. However, minority party members often view special rules as unduly restricting lawmaking by overly curtailing debate and excessively limiting amendments.

The House leadership calls up the least controversial bills under unanimous consent practices. In most instances, these measures attract little attention and receive no debate, no amendments, and passage "without objection" or by voice vote.

Finally, a very small number of bills are called up under either the Private, Consent, or District of Columbia calendars. Measures on those calendars are called up for floor consideration during two specified days per month, under the particular procedures prescribed by the individual rules governing that calendar.

In the Senate, measures most often are brought up by a simple request to turn to a specified bill's immediate consideration. If the request meets no objection, the Senate debates and amends the bill without any restrictions. A second method is a unanimous consent agreement, negotiated in advance by the Senate majority and minority leaders among all interested senators on their respective side of the aisle. Often called time agreements, these contracts for a bill's consideration impose time limitations on debate, restrict the offering of amendments and motions, and sometimes provide for a "vote certain" on final passage. The agreement takes effect unless an objection is registered at the time it is formally proposed by the majority leader on the Senate floor.

A motion to proceed to the consideration of a bill is the final method by which a measure can be raised for floor consideration in the Senate. The motion requires a simple majority vote for adoption. However, it is fully debatable and is often subjected to a filibuster. Ending a filibuster requires sixty votes, a super-majority. If the filibuster is ended and the motion to proceed is adopted, the measure called up is itself subject to another filibuster. Therefore, unless assured of the support of at least sixty senators, the Senate majority leader uses the motion to proceed sparingly.

Debate and Amending. The normal debate rule of the House is the "one-hour rule," which provides one hour of debate, equally divided between the majority and minority party, for any measure or matter brought up in the House. However, special rules or the suspension of the rules procedure frequently supersede the one-hour rule.

The House conducts debate on the most significant measures in another forum, the *Committee of the Whole*, the term used to describe the House when it meets as the Committee of the Whole House on the State of the Union. Debate is still conducted in the House chamber, with the full membership of the House, but under different procedures. To signal the change of forum, the Speaker leaves the podium and appoints a majority party member as chairman to preside over the Committee of the Whole. The mace is removed by its keeper, the sergeant at arms. When members wish to address the chair, they now forsake "Mr. or Madame Speaker" in favor of "Mr. or Madame Chairman." With these symbolic changes, the House has resolved itself into the Committee of the Whole.

The rules of procedure employed in the Committee of the Whole expedite the consideration of bills. As a result, it is the favored forum for all measures to which numerous amendments are expected. Instead of the one-hour rule, the five-minute rule operates in the Committee of the Whole. It provides for five minutes for the proponents and five minutes for the opponents of any amendment offered. However, the time for debate is frequently extended on more controversial amendments through unanimous consent or parliamentary devices known as pro forma amendments.

At the end of general debate on a bill, the Committee of the Whole begins the amending process. The bill is normally presented to the chamber for amendment section by section, and amendments must be offered at the right time in the sequence, or they will be ruled out of order. Amendments must also be germane, or relevant, to the subject matter of the bill. When all allowed amendments are disposed of, the Committee of the Whole "rises," transforming itself back into the House. Amendments adopted by the Committee of the Whole must also be approved by the House. Usually they are endorsed as a package with one vote. However, at times a member will insist on a separate vote on one or more of the amendments agreed to in the Committee of the Whole. As the parent chamber, the House has the last word, and, at times, has reversed the decision of the Committee of the Whole on an amendment.

The Senate's rules governing debate and amendment are in sharp contrast to the strictly regulated debate period and the sequential and orderly amending process in the House. The regular order in the Senate places no restrictions on debate time nor on the number or nature of amendments. As a result, it is always difficult to predict for how long the Senate will consider a particular measure. This emphasis in the Senate on deliberation, not on efficiency, is in keeping with the Founders' original concept for a bicameral Congress. The ability to force deliberation in the Senate was viewed as a check on decisions that might be taken too hastily and with insufficient examination by a House eager to respond to popular opinion.

Once recognized, senators may speak for as long as they wish on a bill. It is this right to extend debate that allows a senator to conduct a filibuster, the Senate's term for speaking at length to prohibit the chamber from coming to a vote on final passage. At times senators voluntarily cede their rights to unlimited debate by agreeing to a unanimous consent agreement that sets debate limitations.

Amendments in the Senate may be offered when any senator so desires. Bills are open to amendment at any point, and no chronological sequence is observed. In most circumstances, amendments in the Senate need not be germane to the subject matter of the bill under consideration. This allows senators the ability to bring to the floor of the Senate subject matter of their own choosing. Nongermane amendments, known as riders, are frequently offered with motives other than passage in mind. They may be used as devices to focus the attention of the Senate, and in dramatic cases, of the nation, upon topics a senator feels merit immediate attention. Nongermane amendments are integral to the concept of minority rights in the Senate. Such amendments serve as a method by which the decisions of the majority party concerning the agenda can be supplemented or even circumvented.

In the interests of hastening the legislative process, senators sometimes do permit unanimous consent agreements to establish a germaneness requirement for amendments. In a few specified circumstances, Senate procedure also requires amendments to be germane. However, these restrictions are often set aside. As a result, the amending process in the Senate is often complex in nature and extensive in reach.

Final Passage and Voting Procedures. The House may dispose of the question of final passage by one of four voting methods. The bill may pass "without objection" or by unanimous consent. If even one objection is heard, the chair will put the question of final passage to a voice vote. The yeas and nays are shouted aloud and the chair declares his or her judgment as to which side prevailed. Any member dissatisfied with the opinion of the chair may demand a division vote, a standing vote in which members are counted as they stand in support or opposition to the bill.

The final method of voting is the record vote, and it alone places members on record. A record vote requires a sufficient second. If it is ordered, members in the House vote by electronic device. Members are issued plastic identification cards, which are inserted into voting stations on the House floor. They press a button for their chosen position and their vote is instantly displayed on the chamber's vote tally board. Each record vote is also printed in the *Congressional Record*. The House has three forms of record votes: the yeas and nays, an automatic roll-call, and a recorded vote. They are each obtained differently, but all are conducted in the same way and have the same result—a member's position becomes a matter of public record.

In the Senate, the same four methods of voting are used. However, the Senate has only one form of record vote, known as the yeas and nays. No electronic machinery exists. Instead, a clerk reads each senator's name aloud and waits for a response. The call of the roll is repeated; thereafter, senators are recognized out of sequence as they appear in the chamber to signal their position. In both chambers, the period for a vote is established at a minimum of fifteen minutes. Sufficient time is allowed to give members the ability to reach the chamber from their offices and committee rooms. Bells ring throughout the Capitol complex to signal a vote. In addition, many members carry beepers to alert them of a pending vote. Often the voting period is held open in order to convince undecided members to change their votes when the margin is close.

Resolving Differences between the Houses. The House and Senate each must pass identical versions of a bill before it can proceed to the president for his signature or veto. Because the two chambers so often enact differing versions of the same bill, the differences must be fully resolved before the bill can progress. The two chambers use one of two methods to reconcile their versions: a conference committee or a procedure known as amendments between the houses. Although conferences are the better known method, more measures are reconciled using the amendments between the houses procedure.

In the latter method the House and Senate exchange the text of a bill back and forth, each further amending the changes last made by the other. The ping-pong match continues until one chamber concurs with the last amendment of the other body, making no further changes. The differences in text are thus resolved and the measure is cleared for the White House. This method is favored when the number of members interested in the final text of the measure is minimal, when no written reports are needed or required, or when

Resolving House and Senate Differences, 102d Congress

METHOD OF RESOLVING DIFFERENCES	PERCENT OF LAWS	NUMBER OF LAWS
Adoption of measure without change by second chamber	68	404
Exchange of amendments between the houses	20	118
Conference committees	12	68

time deadlines make it difficult to convene a conference committee.

The conference process begins when members of the House and Senate are appointed by their presiding officer to serve as their chamber's representatives on a conference committee. Known as conferees, they come primarily from the standing committees that initially reported the bill. The conference committee's responsibility is to negotiate a compromise text from the two differing versions. Their final agreement is known as the conference report. The conference report must be adopted by a majority in both the House and Senate. If one chamber defeats the conference report, the other body takes no action on it. Once the report has passed both the House and Senate, it is presented to the president for his review.

Presidential Action. The final version of a bill is prepared for formal presentation to the president by the enrolling clerk of the chamber where the measure originated. The president is given ten days to review the proposed law, not counting Sundays or the day on which the measure was received by the White House. Four options are available to the president. First, the president can sign the measure into law. Second, the president can permit the bill to become law without his signature, which occurs when ten days pass without his taking action, but only if Congress is in session. Third, the president can "pocket veto" the bill. If ten days pass and the president takes no action, the measure does not become law, but only if Congress *is not* in session due to an adjournment. Fourth, the president can veto the bill. If Congress is still in session, he may return the measure to the chamber that originated it with a veto message expressing his objections to the bill. Two-thirds of that chamber, with a quorum present, must vote to again pass the bill "the President's objections notwithstanding." If the vote (known as a veto override) is successful, the bill is sent to the other body, which also must pass the bill over the president's objections with a two-thirds vote of those present. If both chambers are able to override the veto, the bill becomes law.

The complexities of parliamentary procedure make it far simpler to block the progress of a bill than to secure its passage. Only those measures aggressively promoted and with sufficient political appeal will reach the ultimate goal of public law. In recent years, no more than 7 percent of all the legislation introduced in each Congress has become public law. This statistic reveals that the legislative process is truly "Darwinian," permitting only the survival of the fittest.

BIBLIOGRAPHY

Congressional Quarterly Inc. *How Congress Works*. 2d ed. 1991.

Green, Alan. *Gavel to Gavel: A Guide to the Televised Proceedings of Congress*. C-SPAN and the Benton Foundation. 1986.

U.S. House of Representatives. *How Our Laws are Made*. 101st Cong., 2d sess., 1990. H. Doc. 101-139.

ILONA B. NICKELS

LEADERSHIP. [*The following entry discusses leadership in two separate articles:*

House Leadership
Senate Leadership

For related discussions, see Caucus, *article on* Party Caucus; Committees, *article on* Assignment of Members; Discipline of Members; Floor Leader; Majority and Minority; Managers; Minority Rights; Political Parties; Seniority; Whips; *and biographies of particular members of Congress.*]

House Leadership

In 1959, political scientist David Truman described the complexity of congressional leadership: "Everyone knows something of leaders and leadership of various sorts, but no one knows very much. Leadership, especially in the political realm, unavoidably or by design often is suffused by an atmosphere of the mystic and the magical, and these have been little penetrated by systematic observation" (Truman, 1959, p. 94). House leadership remains a complex concept, but it has been defined more clearly and more systematically in the years since Truman's observation.

An explanation and evaluation of House leadership should incorporate at least four key elements: (1) the functions of the House of Representatives; (2) the context, or conditions under which those functions are performed; (3) a description of the various formal and informal leadership positions; and (4) the individual leaders themselves.

General Considerations. A general concept of House leadership can be developed with reference to the functions of the House, the conditions that affect House politics, and the role of individual leaders. After taking a look at these overarching considerations, the remaining sections of this article describe the tasks, styles, and strategies pursued by three types of House leaders: party, committee, and informal leaders.

Functions. All institutions are designed to perform certain functions, and leaders are expected to assist in those functions. The primary functions of the House of Representatives are lawmaking and representation; leadership can be defined in terms of those functions. "Leadership is an organizational condition facilitating the expression [i.e., representation] and integration [i.e., lawmaking] of opinions, facts, and conclusions among the extended membership (to include staff) at different stages of the lawmaking process" (Charles O. Jones, "House Leadership in an Age of Reform," in Mackaman, 1981, p. 119). Thus, a conception of House leadership should identify the specific tasks, strategies, and styles that leaders pursue as they attempt to facilitate lawmaking and representation.

Context. The actions of House leaders are influenced partly by the context, or the conditions under which the House attempts to make laws and represent interests. Ideally, leaders seek to facilitate both representation and lawmaking, but circumstances often limit their capacity to do so. Some conditions are conducive to lawmaking, while others favor representation. Under some circumstances neither representation nor lawmaking is easily served, making leadership extremely difficult. Political scientists are interested in understanding how the particular set of conditions at any given time affects the tasks, styles, and strategies of House leaders.

Context is defined by three categories of factors: institutional, political, and issue-agenda factors. Institutional factors include the organization, rules, and procedures of the House and the constitutional arrangements (bicameralism, separation of powers, and checks and balances) that define the House's role in the political system. Political factors include the outcomes of elections and the strength of political parties. Elections determine the relative numbers of Democrats and Republicans in the House and Senate as well as the party represented by the president. House leadership also depends on the strength of party organizations—specifically, their capacity to nominate candidates for office—and party unity within the Congress. The issue agenda consists of the policy issues debated and deliberated in the committees and on the floor of the House.

The variety of conditions that affect how leaders attempt to facilitate lawmaking and representation confirms the notion that House leadership is a complex phenomenon. While some conditions are very stable (e.g., bicameralism), others change occasionally with institutional reforms (e.g., reforms of the committee system) and still others change periodically (e.g., electoral outcomes). Thus, leadership depends on the enduring conditions that shape the general patterns of lawmaking and representation as well as the changing conditions that alter leadership tasks, styles, and strategies.

Enduring conditions support at least three general, complementary propositions about House leadership. Each proposition will necessarily be refined to fit specific leadership positions and particular circumstances, but together they provide a general framework for the concept of House leadership.

First, since leaders are elected by House members, leadership requires the leaders to pay attention to members' goals. The most difficult questions are determining what the members want and how their preferences relate to those of the leaders—questions that can be answered only by reference to specific leadership positions under a given set of conditions.

Second, there are limitations to strong, centralized leadership in the House of Representatives. Speaker of the House Joseph G. Cannon (R-Ill.) and Rules Committee Chairman Howard W. Smith (D-Va.) both exceeded the acceptable bounds of authority in the eyes of most members (see Jones, 1968). Although the degree of centralized power in the House has varied over time, there are always limitations to the power a leader can exercise.

Finally, leadership style typically, though not always, involves bargaining with other members and accommodating their preferences. With few exceptions, House leaders have lacked the power to dictate policy or procedure to the members.

These general tendencies of leadership stem from three relatively stable conditions that have defined representation and lawmaking in the House: constituency representation, weak parties, and a fragmented committee system. Perhaps the most enduring feature of House politics from the stand-

point of leadership is that members are obliged to pursue the interests of their constituents. A second important condition for understanding party leadership is that, with the exception of a brief period at the turn of the twentieth century, congressional parties generally have been weak, and party leaders have lacked the power to discipline members. The combination of strong constituency representation and weak parties normally gives members a certain degree of autonomy from leaders. And since leaders are ultimately selected by the members, they must be responsive to the members' goals and preferences. A third prevailing feature of House politics is its decentralized committee system. Except for the period of strong parties (1890–1910), power in the House has traditionally been dispersed among numerous committees. There have been circumstances under which members have tolerated centralized party leadership, but members accept such leadership only if it helps them satisfy their political and policy goals.

Personality. A third critical aspect of House leadership is the individual leader. Whereas political scientists tend to emphasize the context within which leaders operate, journalists and the leaders themselves tend to view leadership from the perspective of individual personalities. Biographies by journalists (e.g., John Barry's book on Speaker James C. Wright, Jr. [D-Tex.], *The Ambition and the Power*, 1989) and autobiographies by political leaders (e.g., Speaker Thomas P. [Tip] O'Neill, Jr.'s book, *Man of the House*, 1987) furnish rich insights into the personalities of individual leaders. These studies describe a leader's upbringing and personal experiences as they relate to leadership style. By definition, biographical studies furnish the least general theoretical claims about House leadership, since their central purpose is to account for the peculiarities of individuals and their influence on the House. Most biographies of House leaders have focused on Speakers, and they are too numerous to list here (see Donald Kennon's *Speaker of the U.S. House of Representatives: A Bibliography, 1789–1984*, 1986). Perhaps the most thoroughly developed biography of a Speaker is *Rayburn: A Biography* by D. B. Hardeman and Donald C. Bacon (1987).

Some studies conceptualize leadership in terms of both context and personal factors (see Peters, 1990; Rohde, 1991, and Palazzolo, 1992). These studies argue that institutional, political, and issue-agenda conditions set the constraints within which leaders operate, but leaders can define their styles within those constraints. For example, both Speakers Tip O'Neill and Jim Wright acted under roughly similar conditions during the 1980s, but Wright pursued a more aggressive leadership style.

In sum, institutional functions, context, and individual personalities are all essential to understanding House leadership. In general, leaders operate within a context that places limitations on power, demands responsiveness to House members, and typically requires leaders to bargain with members and accommodate their preferences. Yet these general propositions take us only so far in understanding the complex phenomenon of House leadership: even relatively stable conditions are subject to change, which in turn may create new opportunities for leadership or place greater constraints on leaders. Institutional reforms have occasionally altered the committee system, legislative procedures, and the formal powers of leaders. Changes in the party system have at times strengthened and at other times weakened the powers of party leaders. Furthermore, individual leaders have made special contributions to House leadership. The general conception of leadership will be elaborated here by assessing the evolution of specific leadership positions in the House.

Party Leaders. House leadership by party differs according to whether the party is in the majority or the minority. Also, the styles and strategies employed by party leaders in the House have changed over time.

Majority party leadership. The majority party leadership is headed by the Speaker of the House, who fills the only constitutionally mandated leadership position in the House. In addition to representing a congressional district, the Speaker essentially performs two leadership roles: leader of the majority party and presiding officer of the House. As presiding officer, the Speaker is expected to administer the rules and procedures of the House in a fair, impartial, and consistent manner. The Speaker also refers bills to committees and is in charge of allocating office space to members. As party leader, the Speaker aims to advance the priorities of the majority party in the House. His role depends partly on the president. If the president is of the same party, the Speaker's primary task is to build coalitions in support of the president's legislative priorities. If the president is of the opposing party, the Speaker acts as the leading spokesperson of the majority party and will more likely be involved in setting the party's legislative priorities. In both roles—presiding officer and party leader—the Speaker is responsible for managing conflict in the House. Conflict can be managed in a variety of ways: from helping to draft fair rules for floor debate, to appointing members to special committees or task forces, to building camaraderie among members.

The Speaker's role as party leader is shared by several other party leaders. Barbara Sinclair (1983) divides the party leadership into two groups: the core leadership and the extended leadership. The core leadership includes the majority leader (who assists the Speaker with scheduling legislation, conducting business on the floor, and mediating intraparty conflict) and the majority whip (who is in charge of collecting and distributing information about member preferences and plotting strategy to build coalitions in support of the leadership). From the late 1970s to the early 1990s, the chief deputy whip and the chairman of the Democratic Caucus were also considered part of the core leadership. The extended leadership refers to the auxiliary resources the party leadership uses to carry out its basic functions: the whip system, the party's steering and policy committee, and the House Rules Committee.

Minority party leadership. The House minority party is headed by the minority leader, the minority whip, the party caucus (or conference) chairman, and the steering and policy committee chairman. Like majority leaders, minority leaders seek to manage intraparty conflict and to build coalitions, a task that includes attempting to win the support of some members in the majority party. Minority party leadership may also involve obstructing the majority party from advancing its agenda, though obstructive tactics became less common after the late 1800s and early 1900s. In the late twentieth century, minority party leaders were more likely to offer alternative programs to the majority party or to help members of their party initiate programs. A common strategy of Republican minority leaders in the 1980s was to blame the Democratic party for policy failures and procedural unfairness.

History of party leadership. The styles and strategies of party leadership have varied with conditions and the individuals occupying formal positions. At least five conceptions of party leadership have evolved over time: (1) parliamentary, (2) centralized party leadership, (3) leadership by commission, (4) middleman leadership, and (5) conditional party leadership. In her 1896 work *The Speaker of the House,* Mary Parker Follett found that the Speaker had always been a parliamentary and party leader.

The Speaker had the power to appoint committees and committee chairmen and to recognize members on the floor. Yet, as Ronald Peters (1990) argues, conditions before the Civil War prevented Speakers from exercising strong party leadership. The federal government had a limited role in American society, the nation was divided over the slavery issue, and the House was just beginning to develop as a representative and lawmaking institution. Under those conditions, the Speaker concentrated primarily on the tasks associated with the presiding officer role. The speakership was not a highly sought-after position and was generally occupied by "second rate men," according to Follett.

Henry Clay of Kentucky (Speaker, 1811–1814, 1815–1820, and 1823–1825) represented the one major exception to the parliamentary leadership model of the pre–Civil War era. Clay made several unique contributions to the status and power of the Speaker's office. He added a third component to the Speaker's theretofore twofold role of party leader and presiding officer—that of exercising the privileges of a House member (specifically, participating in floor debate and regularly casting roll-call votes). As Peters points out, Clay was popular and famous for his oratory skills; he was one of the only Speakers in history to be elected on the basis of the programs he advocated; and he was instrumental in developing the committee system in the House.

After the Civil War, the Speaker's office developed into a strong party leadership position. By the end of the nineteenth century, House leadership was virtually defined by the centralized power wielded by the Speaker. From 1890 to 1910, the House saw the rise of "boss," or "czar," Speakers. Two notable Republican Speakers of this period—Thomas B. Reed (R-Maine, 1899–1891 and 1895–1899) and Joseph G. Cannon (R-Ill., 1903–1911)—epitomized strong, centralized party leadership. In addition to appointing committees, the Speaker chaired a five-person Rules Committee, which controlled the scheduling of bills for debate on the floor and the length of floor debate. The Speaker also had unprecedented power on the House floor, including the ability to recognize members and suspend House rules.

The Speaker's vast power was supported by conditions that encouraged strong, centralized party leadership. A stable and cohesive party system enabled the Speaker to set the congressional agenda and discipline members. State and local party organizations controlled nominations for office and encouraged party loyalty and conformity to the Speaker's demands. Most important, the members within each party were unified on most issues because they represented similar constituencies and therefore shared many interests (Cooper and Brady, 1981). Finally, the seniority rule had not yet developed as the standard for career development. Thus, the Speaker could use committee assignments to sanction or reward members, depending on their loyalty to the party's position on issues that came to the House for a vote.

Although centralized party leadership expedited lawmaking, it limited representation in the House. Ultimately, members concluded that Speaker Cannon had abused his powers and too greatly restricted their ability to participate in the process. The period of centralized party leadership ended in 1910 with the famous revolt against Speaker Cannon. A faction of progressive Republicans coalesced with Democrats to pass a resolution that called for enlarging the Rules Committee from five to fifteen members, electing the Rules Committee's members by House vote, removing the Speaker from the committee, and having the members of the committee select its chairman. The revolt against Cannon demonstrated the limitations to centralized leadership in the House (see Jones, 1968).

After 1910, centralized party leadership was never fully restored to the Speaker. The concept of leadership evolved in important ways, however, as conditions changed and new leaders defined their roles. For a brief period, until 1916, party leadership continued under the auspices of a highly disciplined party caucus. As Chang-wei Chiu observed (*The Speaker of the House of Representatives since 1896*, 1928), in contrast to the strong centralized leadership exercised by the czar Speakers, caucus government relied more on leadership by "commission"—a group of leaders who collaborated on strategy. The commission typically included the Speaker, majority floor leader, chairmen of the Rules and Appropriations committees, and the chairman and members of the Ways and Means Committee. The Democrats were the majority party during the period of caucus government, and Oscar W. Underwood (D-Ala.), floor leader and chairman of the Ways and Means Committee, emerged as a prominent figure.

After only a few years, though, party factionalism undermined the binding caucus and the House proceeded through a long period of "committee government." Powerful, autonomous committee chairmen, protected by seniority, emerged as the leaders of a fragmented committee structure. As noted in the following section, committee chairmen wielded most of the lawmaking power and exercised constraints on representation. While party leadership was not totally ineffectual, it was undermined by weak parties and the dispersion of power among the committees. The Speaker continued to exercise scheduling powers, participated in committee assignments, and could extend small favors to members, but his primary function was to act as a mediator of the various factions within the majority party.

According to Truman (1959) the conditions of the committee government era were conducive to a "middleman" concept of party leadership. The middleman concept comes from the nature of the congressional party itself, which lacked sufficient cohesion to formulate and enact a party program. Party leaders were expected to be ideological moderates who avoided siding with any factions in the party and acted as brokers of competing interests within the party. Sam Rayburn, Speaker of the House for eighteen years during the committee government era (1940–1947, 1949–1953, and 1955–1961), skillfully implemented the middleman style of leadership. Lacking the formal powers of the czar Speakers, Rayburn developed informal relationships with committee chairmen and led by bargaining, compromise, and persuasion.

Finally, "conditional party leadership," a term developed by David Rohde (1991), reflected the role of party leaders in the period following the extensive reforms passed by the House in the 1970s. Although party leaders in the late twentieth century lacked the power of the czar Speakers, they did have the resources to exercise strong leadership on issues that enjoyed a consensus among party members. In fact, the key condition of "conditional" party leadership was consensus among party members: when members of the majority party agreed on an issue, they wanted leaders to exercise the authority to advance the party's interests.

Conditional party leadership is rooted in the peculiar mix of institutional reforms passed during the 1970s, which seemed to serve contradictory purposes. Some reforms aimed toward decentralization—weakening the power of committee chairmen and enhancing opportunities for all members to participate in the policy process. Others sought to centralize power in the Speaker, who was given the authority to refer bills to more than one committee, appoint members to the Rules Committee, and chair the party's steering and policy committee, which has responsibility for nominating members to appointments on standing committees.

The reforms make sense from the perspective of members who wanted to improve Congress's capacity to perform the functions of lawmaking and representation. The reforms created a context within which members of the majority party could pursue their individual interests but also bind together when they agreed on specific issues. The first impulse of party leaders in the reform period was to involve members in the policy process as much as possible and to accommodate the diverse preferences of party members (Sinclair, 1983). In the 1980s, members continued to participate actively in the policy process, but with increased party unity. House Democrats enjoyed a greater consensus—greater than at any other time since the turn of the twentieth century—on many issues because the preferences of their constituents were more alike. Strong party unity combined with the reforms that strengthened the party leadership enabled party leaders to exert strong leadership when members thought it was necessary for collective action.

Committee Leaders. Committee chairmen also hold important leadership positions in the House. The workload of the House is divided up by standing committees, which have traditionally served as the primary source of deliberation and lawmaking in the House of Representatives. Each committee has jurisdiction over a particular set of policy issues: agricultural, armed services, foreign affairs, and the like. Almost all committees further divide up their work by subcommittees. Committee leadership involves the actions taken by the chairman of each committee and each subcommittee. Conceptions of committee leadership evolved as the committee system developed and as political scientists conducted more systematic study of committees.

Woodrow Wilson gave the first description of committee leadership in *Congressional Government* (1885). He argued that if Congress possessed any leadership at all, it resided in the standing committees. House leadership reflected the incoherent, fragmented committee system, which produced a "multiplicity of leaders"—the committee chairmen.

There are in Congress no authoritative leaders who are recognized spokesmen of their parties. Power is nowhere concentrated; it is rather deliberately and of set policy scattered amongst many small chiefs. It is divided up, as it were, into forty-seven seigniories, in each of which a Standing Committee is the court-baron and its chairman lord-proprietor. (Wilson, p. 92)

The feudal nature of this initial conception of committee leadership suggested a general lack of leadership in the House as a whole. The committee chairmen were "petty barons," despotic in their narrow spheres of policy-making but incapable of acting responsibly on behalf of the House as an institution. The committees were autonomous and unconnected, and their leaders were generally selfish, unruly, and uncooperative. In Wilson's view, the committee system's supposed virtues of limiting centralized power and permitting members to become experts on specific policies were outweighed by the "irresponsible" leadership that inevitably surfaces when power is divided. The emergence of seniority in the post–World War I period reinforced the general conception of the narrow-minded, all-powerful, despotic committee chairmen described in Wilson's account of the late 1800s. Seniority made committee chairmen even more powerful, enshrining them as the permanent leaders of their respective committees and giving them a sense of invincibility.

Analysts eventually challenged the generalizations about committee politics and refined the concept of committee leadership. Later studies found that committees and committee chairmen were not all alike. Those studies also drew distinctions between "power" and "influence" in the exercise of committee leadership. A description of Chairman Wilbur D. Mills (D-Ark.) of the Ways and Means Committee (1958–1974) underscores the notion that committee leadership encompasses far more than the simplified conception of chairmen as "petty barons" (Manley, 1969). While formal power was indeed centralized in the chairman of the Ways and Means Committee, Mills's personal leadership style was very informal. Mills was not a dictator who sought to advance a particular policy agenda but was, in fact, an ideological moderate who worked to build consensus on the committee and to ensure that the committee's bills would be approved by large margins on the House floor. Such leadership required compromise and bargaining. Thus, belying the notion that committee chairmen ruled by intimidation and coercion, members of Ways and Means praised Mills as a cooperative, fair, and persuasive leader.

Richard F. Fenno (*Congressmen in Committees*, 1978) develops a broader theoretical context for committee leadership in his comparative study of six House committees (Appropriations, Education and Labor, Foreign Affairs, Interior and Insular Affairs, Post Office and Civil Service, and Ways and Means) from the 84th through the 89th Congresses (1955–1967). Fenno argues that committee leadership, as with committee decision making, will differ according to several variables: member goals,

external constraints (the expectations of external groups), and strategies for pursuing member goals within the context of external constraints.

Committee leadership has also changed as a result of institutional reforms. Reforms passed in the 1970s further decentralized committee power and encouraged wider participation by junior members. Specifically, reforms increased the number of subcommittees and enhanced their autonomy, opened committee hearings to the public, facilitated floor amendments to committee bills, and empowered the party caucus to elect committee chairmen. Of course, Fenno's central argument still held in the 1990s—leadership continued to vary from one committee to the next. But committee chairmen generally had less control over subcommittees; the chairmen were more responsive to members' preferences; and they depended more upon party leaders to pass bills on the floor.

Informal Leadership. Besides the formally designated party and committee leaders, House leadership includes "informal leaders"—leaders who lack formal authority in the House. Informal leaders typically are characterized as independent, hardworking policy experts. Yet, as Roger H. Davidson indicates, informal leaders perform a wide variety of roles: as "procedural experts," who are skillful at facilitating or delaying action with parliamentary tactics; as "brokers," or mediators, among competing interests; as ideologues or publicists, who use the media to try to build external support; as leaders of regions or special caucuses; and as "policy entrepreneurs," who formulate and build support for specific issues ("Congressional Leaders as Agents of Change," in Mackaman, 1981). Susan Hammond divides informal leaders into two categories: leaders with portfolio and leaders without portfolio ("Committee and Informal Leaders in the U.S. House of Representatives," in Kornacki, 1990). Leaders with portfolio include all formal leaders plus informal leaders who act on behalf of an informal organization (a caucus or discussion group). Leaders without portfolio are members who act individually or without any organizational base.

The number and type of informal leaders increased under the conditions of the House prevailing in the late twentieth century. Informal leadership was promoted by the expanded subcommittee system, changes in rules and informal norms that encouraged members to participate more actively in the policy process, and increases in staff and information sources (the Congressional Budget Office, the Congressional Research Service, and the Office of Technology Assessment). As Burdett

Loomis illustrates in *The New American Politician* (1988), many members who came to the House in the 1970s exercised informal leadership. Unwilling to wait patiently for a formal leadership position in order to affect policy decisions, these members built their own informal enterprises through caucuses or personal staffs. Eventually, many informal leaders expanded their influence through formal subcommittee chairmanships, and came to constitute the group from which committee chairmen and party leaders were recruited.

Of course, in any institution there are clear limitations to influence without a formal position of power. Still, the ambitious, independent, entrepreneurial style of informal leaders broadened the concept of House leadership and placed particular emphasis on representation. As Loomis warns, however, the rise of the new American politician may undermine prospects of collective leadership and lawmaking with respect to the nation's most pressing problems. Since the informal leaders of yesterday and today are the formal leaders of tomorrow, the future of House leadership—specifically, the capacity of leaders to balance lawmaking and representation—will depend on how the self-styled politicians of the 1990s respond to the conditions of the future.

[*See also* Cannon Revolt; Clerk of the House; Speaker of the House; *table under* Floor Leader.]

BIBLIOGRAPHY

Cooper, Joseph, and David W. Brady. "Institutional Context and Leadership Style: The House from Cannon to Rayburn." *American Political Science Review* 75 (1981): 411–425.

Follett, Mary Parker. *The Speaker of the House of Representatives.* 1896.

Jones, Charles O. "Joseph G. Cannon and Howard W. Smith: An Essay on the Limits of Leadership in the House of Representatives." *Journal of Politics* 30 (1968): 617–646.

Jones, Charles O. *The Minority Party in Congress.* 1970.

Kornacki, John J., ed. *Leading Congress: New Styles, New Strategies.* 1990.

Mackaman, Frank H., ed. *Understanding Congressional Leadership.* 1981.

Manley, John F. "Wilbur Mills: A Study in Congressional Influence." *American Political Science Review* 63 (1969): 442–464.

Palazzolo, Daniel J. *The Speaker and the Budget.* 1992.

Peabody, Robert L. *Leadership in Congress.* 1976.

Peters, Ronald M., Jr. *The American Speakership.* 1990.

Ripley, Randall B. *Party Leaders in the House of Representatives.* 1967.

Rohde, David W. *Parties and Leaders in the Postreform House.* 1991.

Sinclair, Barbara. *Majority Leadership in the U.S. House.* 1983.

Truman, David. *The Congressional Party.* 1959.

DANIEL J. PALAZZOLO

Senate Leadership

The Senate leadership refers collectively to the top Democratic and Republican leaders, called the "majority leader" or "minority leader," depending on which party controls the Senate. Both are elected to their position for every new Congress by their party's caucus. Both the majority leader and the minority leader are responsible for developing their party's procedural and political strategy, typically in collaboration with their top lieutenants (e.g., the whips and committee leaders), and for acting as their party's chief spokesperson, both on the Senate floor and with the press and media. Because the Senate's procedures and practices grant large influence to individual senators, the majority leader's fundamental prerogative of agenda setting is done in consultation with the minority leader.

In June 1990, one Democratic senator described Majority Leader George J. Mitchell thusly: "This poor guy who gets here before us in the morning and leaves after we are all back home at night in our pajamas . . . is supposed to keep on standing here subject to all this abuse." Mitchell, the Senate's top institutional and party leader, was in this instance struggling to speed up the pace of Senate business.

Mitchell, a Maine Democrat, faced a common dilemma, because the Senate is unique among legislative assemblies worldwide. The principle of minority rule undergirds the Senate's rules; its customs grant large authority to every senator, with each lawmaker having the right of unlimited debate (filibuster) and of offering unlimited and even nongermane floor amendments to legislation. No wonder Senate leaders find it difficult to set firm schedules or to move legislation, especially near the end of a legislative session, when time is at a premium. Only in the Senate and "only in the last few days of a session," stated Majority Leader Mitchell, "can 85 Senators vote one way: Yes, for this bill; 12 Senators vote another way, No, against the bill—and the noes prevail." The noes prevailed because there were so many opportunities for opponents to filibuster the measure and insufficient time to bring them all to an end.

From virtually the beginning, senators recognized that two "rules" broadly characterize their chamber's deliberative processes: unanimous consent and exhaustion. In 1893, for example, Sen. Orville H. Platt (R-Conn.) said, "There are just two ways under our rules by which a vote can be obtained. One is by getting unanimous consent—the consent of each Senator—to take a vote at a certain time. Next comes what is sometimes called 'sitting it out,' that is for the friends of a bill to remain in continuous session until the opponents of it are so physically exhausted that they can not struggle any longer." Daily, Senate leaders confront something akin to institutionalized anarchy: the reality or threat (the "silent" filibuster) of talkathons that can frustrate decision making. To be sure, the right to engage in endless debate gives a minority protection against majority steamrollers, but it also gives the minority a steamroller power of its own.

Although the modern Senate has Rule XXII, the cloture rule, to curtail filibusters, cloture requires an extraordinary majority of sixty votes to invoke. There are also many informal ways to achieve compromises and accommodations that facilitate the lawmaking process, yet the Senate's emphasis on freedom of expression and individual prerogative means that Senate leaders dread hearing the words "I object" to their unanimous consent requests. Such an objection may forecast blocking action. Patience, persistence, and perseverance are among the important qualities of Senate leaders; these virtues are essential to the leadership's ability to overcome frustrating circumstances and to guide and manage the chamber's legislative business.

Emergence of Senate Leadership. Leadership in a formal sense came belatedly to the Senate. During the nineteenth century, Senate leadership was informal and individual. The Senate's small size and its tradition of viewing members as "ambassadors" from sovereign states promoted a style of leadership linked to the personal talents and abilities of individual lawmakers. Scores of senators were regarded as "leaders": some were sectional or factional leaders; some were committee leaders (by the 1840s committees and their chairmen had become important centers of power); and still others (Henry Clay, Daniel Webster, John C. Calhoun) exercised wide influence because of their special political, oratorical, or intellectual gifts. As late as 1885, Woodrow Wilson could write in *Congressional Government,* "No one is *the* Senator. . . . No one exercises the special trust of acknowledged leadership."

This situation changed, however. By the late nineteenth and early twentieth centuries, officially designated party leaders began to take charge of the Senate's business. They emerged because senatorial

parties became more coherent, stable, structured, and active. Party caucuses assumed important roles in debating legislation and promoting party unity. Caucus committees were created to assign party members to committees and to assist in scheduling the Senate's business. Called by various names—Policy Committee, Steering Committee, or Committee on Committees—these caucuses' descendants still exist today. The senators who chaired the partisan gatherings acquired levers of authority, shaped the Senate's agenda, and mobilized party majorities behind issues. By the early 1900s, the official position of floor (majority or minority) leader had evolved from the post of caucus leader.

Not every floor leader is automatically the "real" leader of his or her party. The majority leadership has had its ups and downs since the office came into formal existence at the turn of the twentieth century. Democrat Scott W. Lucas of Illinois, who served as floor leader (1949–1951) of fifty-four Democrats during the Truman administration, was often blocked in trying to enact the president's programs by a shifting coalition of Republicans and southern Democrats. After his one term as majority leader of a "paper" majority, Illinois voters ended Lucas's political career. His successor, Ernest W. McFarland of Arizona, met the same fate, losing his reelection bid after serving only two years (1951–1953) as majority leader.

Many members by this time viewed the majority leader's position more as a liability than an asset. All this changed when Republican Robert A. Taft of Ohio became majority leader in 1953 and Democrat Lyndon B. Johnson of Texas assumed the leadership of his party, first as minority leader (1953–1955) and then as majority leader (1955–1961).

Until 1953, Taft had dominated his party behind the scenes through the force of his character, his intellect, his partisan zeal, and his chairmanship of the Republican Policy Committee. After losing the presidential nomination to Dwight D. Eisenhower in 1952, Taft decided to run for the leadership post and was unanimously elected majority leader at the beginning of the 83d Congress. He died less than a year after becoming majority leader, but his occupancy of that office enhanced its stature and underscored its potential as an independent source of authority.

Johnson was elected minority leader in 1953 after only four years of Senate service. Supported by Sen. Richard B. Russell of Georgia, the de facto leader of the Democratic party, Johnson possessed a winning combination of personal attributes that helped him gain the top party office. "He doesn't have the best mind on the Democratic side," remarked Russell. "He isn't the best orator; he isn't the best parliamentarian. But he's the best combination of all of these qualities." Johnson transformed the Democratic leadership post into one of immense authority and prestige and made it the influential office that it has remained.

The styles of party leaders are broadly shaped by personal inclinations and institutional context. Factors such as leaders' view of their roles, their colleagues' expectations, the size of their party's (or the other's) majority in the Senate, whether the White House is controlled by the opposition party, workload demands, and the national mood define leadership opportunities and constraints.

Duties of the Majority Leader. Elected, not formally by the Senate, but by partisan colleagues at closed party caucuses that meet prior to the start of a new Congress, the majority leader is the head of his or her party in the Senate, its leader on the floor, and the leader of the Senate. Several important functions are part of the floor leader's responsibilities. How the leader conducts these diverse responsibilities and employs available resources influences both the effectiveness of leadership and legislative decision making. Other Senate leaders— the minority leader, the party whips, and committee chairmen—have a hand in carrying out or influencing the majority leader's functions, such as scheduling floor business, promoting party unity, conducting liaison with the White House, consulting with House leaders, and managing the leader's senatorial party.

Scheduling floor business. Scheduling is the bedrock on which the majority leader's authority rests. The Senate's floor activities are essentially scheduled by the majority leader in consultation with the minority leader. The majority leader, by using scheduling power aggressively, can transform this procedural responsibility into one with significant programmatic overtones. Legislation can be scheduled to suit party or White House initiatives, to expedite policies supported by the bipartisan leadership, to coordinate policy-making, or to dramatize the majority party's differences from the minority.

Each party's policy committee might help identify legislative priorities and formulate strategies and tactics appropriate to each measure's consideration on the floor: when it should be taken up, what amendments might be offered, or who should offer them. The leadership may also try to accommodate the personal scheduling preferences of individual lawmakers. Scheduling involves other elements as well, such as formulating the annual calendar of recesses and adjournments.

Promoting party unity. The majority leader tries to persuade colleagues to support priority legislation and to mobilize winning coalitions. With the assistance of the whip and other senators, the leader works to ascertain how lawmakers might vote on given pieces of legislation and to make sure that senators who favor the leadership's views are on the floor at the right time. Being on the winning side enhances a leader's reputation, while too many losses may tarnish his or her record. Careful use of resources—scheduling an important colleague's favorite bill, for example, or helping someone win a coveted committee assignment—can strengthen the leader's persuasive abilities.

Liaison with the White House. Traditionally, the majority leader is the central person communicating Senate views to the president and, conversely, informing members of executive preferences and intentions. At least since the days of President Franklin D. Roosevelt, House and Senate leaders have collectively or individually met regularly with the presidents to discuss a wide range of policy and political issues. If the majority leader and the president are of the same party, it is expected that the Senate leader will assist the president whenever their policy views coincide.

Consulting with House leaders. House and Senate party leaders commonly communicate and cooperate closely on legislative and political matters. The preeminent examples of such cooperation during the mid-twentieth century were the close personal relationship between Speaker Sam Rayburn (D-Tex.) and Senate Democratic leader Lyndon B. Johnson and the "Ev and Charlie Show" of Senate minority leader Everett M. Dirksen (R-Ill.) and House minority leader Charles A. Halleck (R-Ind.). House and Senate leaders, as well as their key aides, meet regularly and keep in touch on important matters so that interchamber efforts can be coordinated and unnecessary delays avoided.

Managing the party organization. Leaders help to organize, manage, and guide their senatorial party. They can appoint members to party committees, facilitate the election of other party leaders, choose administrative officers, revamp party rules, influence the assignment of party colleagues to committees, and appoint party task forces to study and recommend substantive changes to legislation or procedural changes to Senate rules. In 1992, for example, Majority Leader Mitchell appointed the Democratic Defense Transition Task Force to identify ways to ease defense employment disruptions in the post–Cold War era. Two years earlier, Minority Leader Bob Dole (R-Kans.) had named the Republican Health Care Task Force to study and develop health care reform legislation. And in the 102d Congress both leaders appointed a bipartisan task force to clarify acceptable constituent service by members to people who contribute to their campaigns. Majority Leader Mitchell named Majority Whip Wendell Ford (D-Ky.) to chair the bipartisan task force. Party leaders may also use task forces or their party conferences (once called caucuses) to develop an agenda highlighting their parties' substantive goals or identifying areas of potentially fruitful cooperation between the Senate and White House.

A variety of resources augments the majority leader's influence in the legislative process. By custom, law, and Senate rules, the leaders have gained a number of useful prerogatives: they occupy a front row, center aisle seat; they are accorded priority in recognition by the presiding officer, which better enables them to control floor actions; they are recognized first at the beginning of each day's session; they possess additional staff resources and office space; they usually offer the motion to recess or adjourn each daily session; and they may, with the concurrence of minority leaders, waive certain Senate rules.

The Senate leaders also participate in committee work while discharging their leadership duties. Several Senate majority and minority leaders have made notable, substantive policy contributions: Lyndon Johnson on space policy, Mike Mansfield (D-Mont.) on international affairs, Bob Dole on tax policy, and George Mitchell on environmental protection.

The Minority Leader. Minority leaders, like their majority party counterparts, are the principal spokespersons on the floor for their political parties. They, or their designees, are always on or near the Senate floor to protect the party's substantive and political interests or to take the floor to address important issues. By long-standing custom, the minority leader receives preferential recognition (after the majority leader) from the presiding officer, which facilitates the minority leader's ability to advance party priorities on the floor.

Minority leaders possess an array of formal and informal prerogatives that mirror those of majority leaders. Formally, for example, Senate rules prohibit most standing committees from meeting after the first two hours of a daily session. The majority leader and minority leader are authorized jointly to waive that rule. Informally, the Senate operates largely through the unanimous consent of the membership. The minority leader plays an instrumental role in advancing the Senate's business by securing, with the assistance of key staff aides, the consent of party colleagues to move legislative issues. To be sure, the minority leader is strategically positioned to block legislation as well. Depending on issues and circumstances, then, the minority leader may function in diverse capacities: to oppose the majority party, to promote alternatives to majority party initiatives, or to cultivate a cooperative relationship with the majority leader to maximize the Senate's legislative performance.

An important determiner of the minority leader's job is the president. If the president is of the same party, the minority leader typically defends the administration from partisan attacks and mobilizes support for presidential initiatives. By contrast, if the president is of the opposite party, the minority leader has leeway to function between two poles: partisan critic or presidential ally. Of utmost concern to the minority leader is devising legislative and political strategies to win the Senate back for the party.

Setting and Personality: Two Cases of Leadership. Different circumstances produce different kinds of Senate leaders. Donald Matthews, the noted scholar of the 1950s Senate (*U.S. Senators and Their World*, 1960), wrote that "Democrats incline toward a highly personalized rule by the floor leader." Matthews was referring to Sen. Lyndon Johnson, whose persuasive techniques and manipulative skill as Democratic leader are legendary. Mike Mansfield, Johnson's successor as floor leader, had a very different personal style and operated under contrasting circumstances. Table 1, which lists but a few characteristics of the Senate during Johnson's time and Mansfield's time, illuminates how different were the environments in which they worked.

Table 1 shows not only that Johnson and Mansfield operated in dissimilar political environments but that each had a different conception of the majority leader's role. Johnson utilized every fragment of power (scheduling, committee assignments, office space) to run the Senate personally. He had an extensive intelligence-gathering network of trusted aides and colleagues. As a result, he was better informed about more issues than any other senator. The power of persuasion was Johnson's forte, and he was famous for the face-to-face method dubbed

TABLE 1. *The Senate under Johnson and under Mansfield*

UNDER LYNDON B. JOHNSON (1955–1961)	UNDER MIKE MANSFIELD (1961–1977)
Southern Democrats dominate	Northern and midwestern Democrats dominate
Small Democratic majorities (until 1959)	Large Democratic majorities
Opposition party controls the White House	Democratic and Republican presidents
Power centralized in majority leader	Majority leader viewed as first among equals
Senate activities dominated by majority leader	Majority leader encouraged participation of all senators on an equal basis
Aggressive leadership style	Relaxed leadership style
Staff resources concentrated in senior members	More staff resources available to all senators
Contained work load	Expanded work load
Senate passive in relation to the president	Senate assertive in relation to the president

the "Johnson treatment." As Rowland Evans and Robert Novak described it in their book *Lyndon B. Johnson: The Exercise of Power* (1966),

> The Treatment could last ten minutes or four hours. It came, enveloping its target, at the LBJ Ranch swimming pool, in one of LBJ's offices, in the Senate cloakroom, on the floor of the Senate itself—wherever Johnson might find a fellow Senator within his reach. Its tone could be supplication, accusation, cajolery, exuberance, scorn, tears, complaint, the hint of threat. It was all of these together. It ran the gamut of human emotions. Its velocity was breathtaking, and it was all in one direction. Interjections from the target were rare. Johnson anticipated them before they could be spoken. He moved in close, his face a scant millimeter from his target, his eyes widening and narrowing, his eyebrows rising and falling. From his pockets poured clippings, memos, statistics. Mimicry, humor, and the genius of analogy made the Treatment an almost hypnotic experience and rendered the target stunned and helpless. (p. 104)

Reinforcing the effectiveness of the Johnson treatment was an "inner club" of powerful senior senators as well as an internal, informal system of norms that rewarded rank-and-file deference to "club" leaders. Johnson also enjoyed the solid backing of more than twenty southern Democrats. This regional group, many members of which held committee chairmanships, often voted as a bloc. Johnson could usually count on them for solid, consistent support.

Johnson's effectiveness as majority leader was also facilitated by the opposition party's control of the White House. Under no obligation to support President Eisenhower's legislative program, Johnson could pick which policies to favor and choose the strategies to get them enacted. He had the luxury of independence, discretion, and a small Democratic majority for most of his tenure. In sum, Johnson's dominating personality, persuasive skills, and mastery of both details and broad strategies, centralized his control over practically every phase of senatorial policy-making.

Mansfield exercised his leadership in a completely different way. He worked diligently to decentralize authority, sharing power with colleagues and committees. He encouraged greater participation by junior senators and substantially did away with the informal norm of apprenticeship. New senators were not expected to sit back for months, listening to their elders, before they became actively involved in the Senate's business. As one freshman of that period, Sen. William D. Hathaway (D-Maine), explained to his colleagues in 1973:

> Being a freshman senator in 1973 is very different from being a freshman senator in 1953. The freshmen of that year were expected to listen and learn, but not to be heard. That ancient tradition no longer holds. Freshmen are encouraged to speak out, to play an active and vocal role in formulating legislation and policy. Indeed, one freshman was mildly chastised by Mike Mansfield, the majority leader, for not speaking up and making his views known at a Democratic caucus.

Unlike Johnson, Mansfield limited his role as majority leader. He permitted his colleagues a larger piece of the action. A number of party groups—the Conference, the Policy Committee, and the Steering Committee—were revamped, granted genuine responsibility, and utilized more frequently. Majority Leader Mansfield worked quietly behind the scenes, permitting floor managers and individual Senators to handle substantive issues on their own and to take public credit when measures were enacted. He relied heavily on Majority Whip Robert C. Byrd of West Virginia to manage floor activities. For exam-

TABLE 2. *Senate Majority and Minority Leaders*

MAJORITY			MINORITY		
Congress	(Dates)	Leader	Congress	(Dates)	Leader
63d	(1913–1915)	John Worth Kern, D-Ind.	63d	(1913–1915)	Jacob H. Gallinger, R-N.H.
64th	(1915–1917)	John Worth Kern, D-Ind.	64th	(1915–1917)	Jacob H. Gallinger, R-N.H.
65th	(1917–1919)	Thomas S. Martin, D-Va.	65th	(1917–1918)	Jacob H. Gallinger, R-N.H.
				(1918–1919)	Henry Cabot Lodge, R-Mass
66th	(1919–1921)	Henry Cabot Lodge, R-Mass.	66th	(1919)	Thomas S. Martin, D-Va.
				(1920–1921)	Oscar W. Underwood, D-Ala.
67th	(1921–1923)	Henry Cabot Lodge, R-Mass.	67th	(1921–1923)	Oscar W. Underwood, D-Ala.
68th	(1923–1924)	Henry Cabot Lodge, R-Mass.	68th	(1923–1925)	Joseph T. Robinson, D-Ark.
	(1924–1925)	Charles Curtis, R-Kans.			
69th	(1925–1927)	Charles Curtis, R-Kans.	69th	(1925–1927)	Joseph T. Robinson, D-Ark.
70th	(1927–1929)	Charles Curtis, R-Kans.	70th	(1927–1929)	Joseph T. Robinson, D-Ark.
71st	(1929–1931)	James E. Watson, R-Ind.	71st	(1929–1931)	Joseph T. Robinson, D-Ark.
72d	(1931–1933)	James E. Watson, R-Ind.	72d	(1931–1933)	Joseph T. Robinson, D-Ark.
73d	(1933–1935)	Joseph T. Robinson, D-Ark.	73d	(1933–1935)	Charles L. McNary, R-Oreg.
74th	(1935–1937)	Joseph T. Robinson, D-Ark.	74th	(1935–1937)	Charles L. McNary, R-Oreg.
75th	(1937)	Joseph T. Robinson, D-Ark.	75th	(1937–1939)	Charles L. McNary, R-Oreg.
	(1937–1939)	Alben W. Barkley, D-Ky.			
76th	(1939–1941)	Alben W. Barkley, D-Ky.	76th	(1939–1941)	Charles L. McNary, R-Oreg.
77th	(1941–1943)	Alben W. Barkley, D-Ky.	77th	(1941–1943)	Charles L. McNary, R-Oreg.
78th	(1943–1945)	Alben W. Barkley, D-Ky.	78th	(1943–1945)	Charles L. McNary, R-Oreg.
79th	(1945–1947)	Alben W. Barkley, D-Ky.	79th	(1945–1947)	Wallace H. White, Jr., R-Maine
80th	(1947–1949)	Wallace H. White, Jr., R-Maine	80th	(1947–1949)	Alben W. Barkley, D-Ky.
81st	(1949–1951)	Scott W. Lucas, D-Ill.	81st	(1949–1951)	Kenneth S. Wherry, R-Nebr.
82d	(1951–1953)	Ernest W. McFarland, D-Ariz.	82d	(1951)	Kenneth S. Wherry, R-Nebr.
				(1952–1953)	H. Styles Bridges, R-N.H.
83d	(1953)	Robert A. Taft, R-Ohio	83d	(1953–1955)	Lyndon B. Johnson, D-Tex.
	(1953–1955)	William F. Knowland, R-Calif.			

ple, Byrd refined and expanded the use of unanimous consent agreements designed to impose debate limitations on amendments and motions and to bring more control and predictability into floor sessions.

The power of individual senators was enhanced as a result. Members found it easier to exercise initiative in legislation and oversight, to have their amendments adopted on matters reported by other committees, to influence the scheduling of measures, and in general to participate more equally and widely in all Senate and party activities. None of these developments occurred overnight, yet their cumulative effect wrought fundamental changes in the Senate and on its leadership.

Mansfield bequeathed to the party leaders who followed him a Senate that was more democratic,

more assertive, more independent, and more open to public view. It became an institution where individualism and freedom of action were widely shared norms and where there was wider participation in the many phases of policy-making. The Senate was transformed from being a clublike institution to an individualistic legislative body in which senators' personal agendas must be accommodated if the collective enterprise is to achieve its goals and deadlines. Senate leaders must constantly negotiate with their colleagues—on both sides of the aisle—if they are to achieve their objectives with reasonable dispatch. As congressional scholar Richard F. Fenno put it:

The relevant distinction in [a Senator's life] is not between the Senate and the rest of the political

TABLE 2. *Senate Majority and Minority Leaders (Continued)*

MAJORITY			MINORITY		
Congress	(Dates)	Leader	Congress	(Dates)	Leader
84th	(1955–1957)	Lyndon B. Johnson, D-Tex.	84th	(1955–1957)	William F. Knowland, R-Calif.
85th	(1957–1959)	Lyndon B. Johnson, D-Tex.	85th	(1957–1959)	William F. Knowland, R-Calif.
86th	(1959–1961)	Lyndon B. Johnson, D-Tex.	86th	(1959–1961)	Everett M. Dirksen, R-Ill.
87th	(1961–1963)	Mike Mansfield, D-Mont.	87th	(1961–1963)	Everett M. Dirksen, R-Ill.
88th	(1963–1965)	Mike Mansfield, D-Mont.	88th	(1963–1965)	Everett M. Dirksen, R-Ill.
89th	(1965–1967)	Mike Mansfield, D-Mont.	89th	(1965–1967)	Everett M. Dirksen, R-Ill.
90th	(1967–1969)	Mike Mansfield, D-Mont.	90th	(1967–1969)	Everett M. Dirksen, R-Ill.
91st	(1969–1971)	Mike Mansfield, D-Mont.	91st	(1969)	Everett M. Dirksen, R-Ill.
				(1969–1971)	Hugh Scott, R-Pa.
92d	(1971–1973)	Mike Mansfield, D-Mont.	92d	(1971–1973)	Hugh Scott, R-Pa.
93d	(1973–1975)	Mike Mansfield, D-Mont.	93d	(1973–1975)	Hugh Scott, R-Pa.
94th	(1975–1977)	Mike Mansfield, D-Mont.	94th	(1975–1977)	Hugh Scott, R-Pa.
95th	(1977–1979)	Robert C. Byrd, D-W.Va.	95th	(1977–1979)	Howard H. Baker, Jr., R-Tenn.
96th	(1979–1981)	Robert C. Byrd, D-W.Va.	96th	(1979–1981)	Howard H. Baker, Jr., R-Tenn.
97th	(1981–1983)	Howard H. Baker, Jr., R-Tenn.	97th	(1981–1983)	Robert C. Byrd, D-W.Va.
98th	(1983–1985)	Howard H. Baker, Jr., R-Tenn.	98th	(1983–1985)	Robert C. Byrd, D-W.Va.
99th	(1985–1987)	Bob Dole, R-Kans.	99th	(1985–1987)	Robert C. Byrd, D-W.Va.
100th	(1987–1989)	Robert C. Byrd, D-W.Va.	100th	(1987–1989)	Bob Dole, R-Kans.
101st	(1989–1991)	George J. Mitchell, D-Maine	101st	(1989–1991)	Bob Dole, R-Kans.
102d	(1991–1993)	George J. Mitchell, D-Maine	102d	(1991–1993)	Bob Dole, R-Kans.
103d	(1993–1995)	George J. Mitchell, D-Maine	103d	(1993–1995)	Bob Dole, R-Kans.

world but between himself (plus his staff) and everything else. With the help of the media, he knows he can cultivate a visible national image for himself. With the help of the Senate's formal rules, he knows he can bring the collective business to a halt. He can be a force to be reckoned with whenever he wants to be. Among these prima donnas there are always leaders, people who think about the collectivity and tend to its common business. But they lead only so long as they indulge the individualism of their colleagues and obtain unanimous consent for their actions. (1986)

Current and Future Leadership Challenges. Scores of diverse developments influence the activities and functions of Senate leaders. Some of these changes are beyond the floor leader's control (the country's mood, technological breakthroughs, and

so on), yet they affect his fundamental responsibilities of agenda-setting and coalition-building. For example, today's video politics (C-SPAN began to televise the Senate's floor proceedings gavel-to-gavel in 1986) has added another requirement to leadership: the ability to project well on television and to articulate Senate and party positions to the viewing public. To illuminate how contemporary circumstances have altered the floor leader's work, three trends are discussed below. They reflect the outside dimensions (changes in the electorate), electoral perspectives (pursuit of campaign funds), and institutional dimensions (floor amendment activity) that affect how the floor leader operates.

Changes in the electorate. Many interests compete for influence on Capitol Hill, but *constituents*—not the president, the party, or the congressional leadership—are the ones who grant and can take away a senator's job. A lawmaker who is popular back home can defy the president, the party, and the leadership in ways unthinkable in a parliamentary system, where the executive, the party, and the legislative leadership are the same.

To maintain popularity back home is not always easy, however. Lobbyists and their political action committees (PACs) employ sophisticated techniques to generate grassroots pressure campaigns; they can combine with other state-based groups to form potent electoral coalitions. Further, senatorial actions are subject to close scrutiny by the press and media. The intensity of such pressures means that the majority leader encounters more difficulty in brokering necessary compromises because senators may be unable or unwilling to change or modify their positions once they have expressed them publicly.

Constituents are better informed than ever before. Voters learn about their senators largely from media accounts. Political parties no longer act as the main mediators between elected officials and voters. Senators make up their minds about constituency opinion not simply on what local political leaders say but on what their statewide polls and surveys reveal. Small wonder, then, that senators create their own personal party organizations back home. Like House members, senators travel to their states frequently to meet with constituents: most senators now go home nearly every weekend of the year. The consequence of this trend is some loss of collegiality, which complicates the floor leader's job of coalition-building.

Heightened attentiveness to constituents and the almost permanent campaign that senators now engage in to ensure their reelection affect the floor leader's scheduling responsibilities in many ways. Senate leaders must regularly resolve conflicting demands as they strive to process the Senate's essential business yet accommodate senators who may want votes delayed or business postponed or who must leave the chamber by a certain time. The conflicting pressures of working on legislation and handling constituents' needs even prompted a scheduling innovation. The majority leader, with the concurrence of the other Senators, established a "three-week, one-week" scheduling system in which the Senate is in session three weeks (Monday through Friday) every month and then off for one week. Senators can thus plan with greater certainty and conduct their constituency-related business without fear they will miss votes.

The money chase. It costs a lot to win and hold a Senate seat. Election expenditures have escalated enormously (inflation and the cost of television ads account for part of these increases). In 1976 the winner of a Senate seat spent an average of $610,000 on his or her campaign; by 1992 the average cost was more than $4 million. This financial reality affects the majority leader's job in several connected ways.

First, it influences the scheduling of the Senate's business. Members' fund-raising activities take up more of their time and have increasingly led to scheduling conflicts. Members cannot "chase money" and debate and vote on measures at the same time. Floor leaders, as a result, commonly provide windows in the Senate schedule—periods when no votes will be taken. These windows often occur from around 6:00 P.M. to 8:00 P.M. to allow senators to attend fund-raising events near Capitol Hill. Some senators worry that they are becoming part-time legislators and full-time fund-raisers.

The ongoing need to raise funds affects the party leader's job in another important way. To the qualities of intelligence, parliamentary shrewdness, and so on that influence who is chosen party leader can be added fund-raising capability. Party leaders are expected to raise money for their partisan colleagues. They and other senators often establish their own personal political action committees and distribute financial contributions to party officeholders. It is worth noting that Majority Leader Mitchell headed the Democrats' campaign committee in 1986, before he became floor leader. He reportedly won the support of many Democrats elected that year, and he succeeded in his bid for the job of majority leader in the 101st Congress. According to the *Washington Post*, Senator Mitchell "became an overnight Democratic hero when he led the 1986 campaign that resulted in his party regaining Senate control."

Floor amendments. Given the contemporary Senate's individualistic and entrepreneurial culture, it should come as no surprise that the floor has become a more active arena for decision making. In the 1950s, most Senators specialized in their own committee work and generally deferred to other committee experts on the floor. "The [floor] consideration of matters not previously studied by a committee," Donald Matthews wrote of the 1950s Senate, "is frowned upon." Today, it is commonplace for senators who are not members of the committees originally evaluating legislation to offer floor amendments. Scores of such amendments may be offered, immensely compounding the floor leader's problems in processing senatorial business. Because the Senate has no general germaneness rule, extraneous issues are often raised on the floor. "We seem to create amendments," remarked one senator, "by reading yesterday's headlines so that we can write today's amendments so that we can gather tomorrow's headlines."

Scheduling is no easy assignment for the majority leader when senators are increasingly willing to offer amendments to whatever appropriate "vehicle" is pending on the floor. Not only do many senators want to be involved in scores of issues; they are often under pressure from outsiders (interest groups, the White House, the media, and so on) to employ their resources to shape or frustrate the Senate's agenda. Floor amendments are offered not only to affect policy changes but for a variety of other purposes, such as making friends in outside constituencies and embarrasing partisan foes. When Democrats recaptured control of the Senate following the 1986 elections, assistant Republican leader Alan K. Simpson of Wyoming told the *New York Times*, "We'll be standing there with our little score cards, waiting for them to jump over the cliff." Party leaders must be ready to respond quickly to partisan amendments and statements, especially now that Senate floor proceedings are televised.

The connection between lawmaking and campaigning adds to the majority leader's responsibilities. Inevitably, members' reelection concerns affect their decisions. "Don't make us vote on that or it will kill me" is a refrain party leaders regularly hear. Thus, decisions may sometimes be postponed if Senators fear electoral retribution. Or leaders may innovate, for example, by encouraging the use of megabills (legislation that may be thousands of pages in length), outside commissions, ad hoc panels, or legislative-executive summits to provide political cover for colleagues and to diffuse sensitive political issues, such as changes in Social Security eligibility or benefits. Matching good politics with effective governance is an ever-present challenge for leaders in today's individualistic Senate.

Howard H. Baker (R-Tenn.), who served as majority leader from 1981 to 1985, once said: "Every majority leader reinvents the role. He does it in his own image." Both George Mitchell and Bob Dole, the Democratic and Republican leaders of the Senate in the early 1990s, were forced to reinvent their roles when divided government ended after the 1992 election. As leader of the opposition, Minority Leader Dole lacked the leverage provided by a Republican president and was now forced to decide whether and on what issues to cooperate with or to confront Democratic president Bill Clinton and to strategize about how to advance and publicize Republican policy alternatives now that his party had been deprived of the "bully pulpit" of the White House. Majority Leader Mitchell, too, faced a new situation; he had to develop a new relationship with the White House and determine how best to advance President Clinton's agenda in the Senate.

It is plain that its unique method of operation makes it difficult for anyone to "lead" the Senate. Given the large authority accorded every Senator, the ever-present partisan and ideological divisions, and the participatory nature of senatorial decision making, Senate leaders must work constantly to achieve compromise, to gain consensus, and to forge winning coalitions. Their tasks have become even more arduous in an era of fiscal scarcity and growing complexity of policy issues. Ironically, as issues have become more intricate and globally interdependent, the Senate's hectic schedule gives senators less time to study and think about policy matters. "There is no shortage of information," declared Majority Leader Mitchell. "There is a shortage of time."

Senate leaders are expected to meet the needs and expectations of their colleagues (leadership, after all, depends on followership) and to process and structure the Senate's business with reasonable dispatch and coherence. These objectives often conflict. How to reconcile the tension between individual senators' prerogatives and institutional obligations is something that confronts Senate leaders virtually every day. As Senate Republican leader Everett Dirksen (1959–1969) so aptly put it, "There are one hundred diverse personalities in the U.S. Senate. O Great God, what an amazing and dissonant one hundred personalities they are! What an amazing thing it is to harmonize them. What a job it is." Ultimately, the Senate leaders are responsible for focusing and framing the actions of these "one hundred diverse personalities."

[*See also* President Pro Tempore of the Senate; Secretary of the Senate.]

BIBLIOGRAPHY

Baker, Richard A., and Roger H. Davidson. *First among Equals: Outstanding Senate Leaders of the Twentieth Century.* 1991.

Davidson, Roger H. "The Senate: If Everybody Leads, Who Follows?" In *Congress Reconsidered.* 4th ed. Edited by Lawrence Dodd and Bruce Oppenheimer. 1989. Pp. 275–305.

Ehrenhalt, Alan. "In the Senate of the '80s, Team Spirit Has Given Way to the Rule of Individuals." *Congressional Quarterly Weekly Report*, 4 September 1982, pp. 2175–2182.

Evans, Rowland, and Robert Novak. *Lyndon B. Johnson: The Exercise of Power.* 1966.

Fenno, Richard F. "Adjusting to the U.S. Senate." In *Congress and Policy Change.* Edited by Gerald Wright et. al. 1986. Pp. 123–147.

Foley, Michael. *The New Senate.* 1980.

Kornacki, John J. *Leading Congress: New Styles, New Strategies.* 1990.

Mackaman, Frank. *Understanding Congressional Leadership.* 1981.

Matthews, Donald. *U.S. Senators and Their World.* 1960.

Peabody, Robert L. *Leadership in Congress.* 1976.

Sinclair, Barbara. *The Transformation of the U.S. Senate.* 1989.

Stewart, John G. "Two Strategies of Leadership: Johnson and Mansfield." In *Congressional Behavior.* Edited by Nelson W. Polsby. 1971. Pp. 61–92.

Smith, Steven S. *Call to Order: Floor Politics in the House and Senate.* 1989.

WALTER J. OLESZEK

LEAGUE OF NATIONS.

The idea of the League of Nations, an international organization to preserve peace, developed during World War I. As head of the U.S. delegation to the Paris Peace Conference in 1919, President Woodrow Wilson became the League's main architect, and the League Covenant was incorporated in the Treaty of Versailles with Germany. But by 10 July 1919, when Wilson presented the treaty to the Senate, Republicans, who held a 49 to 47 advantage, agreed that at the least the treaty must include reservations that would express the U.S. understanding of certain provisions and limit some obligations. Since two-thirds of the Senate was needed to approve the treaty, they could not be ignored. There was little objection to provisions for consultation and arbitration among nations to maintain peace. But Republicans insisted, above all, on a reservation to Article Ten. That article, as they construed it, would commit the United States, on the recommendation of the League Council, to come to the aid of any member state under attack. Reservationists were unwilling to commit either Congress or the nation to so broad an obligation or to make promises that might not be fulfilled.

Dissatisfied with compromise discussions with the Senate in August 1919, Wilson closed negotiations and embarked on a speaking tour. Before it ended his health failed, and on 2 October he suffered a severe stroke. For months Wilson was out of touch with events, and he became more stubborn than before. Democrats had no mandate from Wilson to negotiate, and pro-League Republicans had to make compromises on a program of reservations with the strong reservationists and irreconcilables of their own party. The resulting fourteen reservations were stronger than they might have been had the Democrats negotiated. Wilson, in a decision that remains controversial, rejected them, and on 19 November most Democrats joined the Republican irreconcilables to defeat, 39 to 55, a ratification resolution that embodied the reservations.

In January 1920 a bipartisan treaty conference failed to reach a satisfactory compromise. Nevertheless, a new slate of reservations was developed in the Senate. However, Wilson suggested converting the 1920 presidential and congressional elections into a "solemn referendum" on the League. During the 19 March vote on a resolution of ratification with these reservations, twenty-one Democrats deserted the president and voted for approval. But the 49 to 35 vote fell seven short of the required two-thirds. The election results were ambiguous regarding the issue, and President Warren G. Harding did not again submit the treaty.

VERSAILLES TREATY. Political cartoon published on the day President Woodrow Wilson presented the treaty to the Senate. The drawing portrays a puzzled figure, representing the Senate, who is examining the lengthy treaty document deposited on his desk by Wilson. Clifford K. Berryman, *Washington Evening Star,* 10 July 1919.

LIBRARY OF CONGRESS

THE ACCUSER. Political cartoon referring to the U.S. Senate's failure to approve the Versailles treaty. The cartoonist suggests that the Senate, portrayed as a thug, perpetrated a crime against humanity when it rejected the treaty, depicted as a slain woman. Rollin Kirby, *New York World*, 22 March 1920.

OFFICE OF THE CURATOR, U.S. SENATE

BIBLIOGRAPHY

Ambrosius, Lloyd E. *Woodrow Wilson and the American Diplomatic Tradition: The Treaty Fight in Perspective.* 1987.

Ferrell, Robert H. *Woodrow Wilson and World War I, 1917–1921.* 1985.

Margulies, Herbert F. *The Mild Reservationists and the League of Nations Controversy in the Senate.* 1989.

HERBERT F. MARGULIES

Rejection of the League reflected policy disagreements, political factors, including objection by some Irish-Americans and other ethnic groups, and personality conflicts. In addition, it sprang from institutional and constitutional quarrels. Many senators felt that Wilson had exalted and misused the presidency at the expense of Congress. They blamed him for persistent vagueness about the treaty, for absenting himself from the country for months during the Paris Peace Conference, for naming no senator or any prominent Republican to the conference delegation, for going over their heads during his tour, and for insulting senators in some of his statements. They found in the League Covenant no adequate recognition of Congress's powers respecting war, appropriations, and the making of international policy. When a new world organization, the United Nations, was created in 1945, President Franklin D. Roosevelt showed an awareness of this historical legacy, especially by naming Republican senator Arthur H. Vandenberg to the peace delegation.

[*See also* Irreconcilables; Isolationism.]

LEGISLATIVE BRANCH. [*This article provides a brief overview of the legislative branch of the U.S. government. For overviews of the other branches of government, see* Executive Branch; Judiciary *and* Congress.] One of the three branches of the federal government of the United States, the legislative branch includes the United States Congress and several research and administrative agencies that provide support services to the Congress.

The legislative branch functions within a system of checks and balances prescribed by the Constitution and designed to keep power from becoming concentrated in any one person or any one branch of government. Most basically, Article I of the Constitution provides for a legislative branch, the Congress, to make the laws; Article II provides for an executive branch, the president, to enforce the laws; and Article III provides for a judicial branch, the Supreme Court, to interpret questions about the law.

The legislative branch has several unique powers that separate it from the executive and judicial branches. These include the power to collect taxes, pay debts, and provide for the general welfare of the United States; to borrow money; to coin money and regulate its value; to regulate commerce; to establish a postal system; to declare war; to maintain the armed forces; to enact patent and copyrights laws; and to establish federal courts below the Supreme Court.

In practice, however, powers of the three branches sometimes overlap and are shared rather than separated. For example, in addition to listing specific powers, the Constitution also provides Congress with generalized authority to make all the laws that are necessary to carry out its specified powers. This "elastic clause" may be broadly interpreted to justify a wide range of congressional activity.

There are a number of additional ways in which the three branches share powers and are interdependent. For example, the Supreme Court can declare unconstitutional a law enacted by Congress;

the vice president of the United States acts as president of the Senate; and the president can veto congressional legislation.

Organizationally, Congress is a bicameral institution; that is, it is divided into two distinct chambers, the House of Representatives and the Senate. The two chambers have very different characteristics. The House has 435 members who serve two-year terms; the Senate has 100 members who serve six-year terms. In the House, states are represented according to their population; they may have one representative, as does Alaska, or fifty-two representatives, as does California. In the Senate, each state is represented by two senators, regardless of population.

The House and Senate have equal legislative power; both bodies write and pass laws and have executive oversight responsibilities. However, each chamber also has some specific responsibilities the other chamber does not have. Only the Senate can approve treaties and presidential appointments. The House of Representatives alone has the authority to initiate tax bills.

In addition to the House and the Senate, the legislative branch includes the following congressional support agencies: the Congressional Budget Office, the Library of Congress, the General Accounting Office, the Office of Technology Assessment, the Government Printing Office, the Architect of the Capitol, the United States Botanic Garden. Although these support agencies are a part of the legislative branch and exist primarily to support Congress, some perform wider service. For example, the Government Printing Office is responsible for all federal printing, the Library of Congress registers all copyrights, and the General Accounting Office sets governmentwide accounting standards and resolves disputed claims by or against the United States.

[See also Bicameralism; House of Representatives; Senate. For further discussion of congressional support agencies, see Architect of the Capitol; Botanic Garden; Congressional Budget Office; Congressional Research Service; General Accounting Office; Government Printing Office; Library of Congress; Office of Management and Budget; Office of Technology Assessment.]

BIBLIOGRAPHY

Congressional Quarterly Inc. "Origins and Development of Congress." In Congressional Quarterly's Guide to Congress. 4th ed. Edited by Mary Cohn. 1991.

Silbey, Joel H., ed. The First Branch of American Government: The United States Congress and Its Relations to the Executive and Judiciary, 1789–1989. 1991.

MARY ETTA BOESL

LEGISLATIVE COUNSEL. The Office of the Legislative Counsel of the House of Representatives and the Office of the Legislative Counsel of the Senate are the bill-drafting arms of Congress. They were established in 1919, after two young staff assistants from the Legislative Drafting Research Fund at Columbia University, Middleton Beaman and Thomas I. Parkinson, came to Washington at the invitation of congressional leaders and demonstrated the benefits that the provision of professional drafting services on an organized basis could confer.

The following people have served as legislative counsels of the House:

Middleton Beaman (1919–1949)
Allan H. Perley (1949–1962)
Edward O. Craft (1962–1972)
Ward M. Hussey (1972–1989)
David E. Meade (1989–).

In the Senate, those holding the position include:

Thomas I. Parkinson (1919–1920)
John E. Walker (1921–1922)
Frederic P. Lee (1922–1930)
Charles F. Boots (1930–1936)
Henry G. Wood (1936–1943)
Charles F. Boots (1943–1945)
Steven Rice (1945–1950)
John H. Simms (1950–1966)
Dwight J. Pinion (1967–1969)
John C. Herberg (1969–1971)
Harry B. Littell (1971–1980)
Douglas B. Hester (1980–1990)
Francis L. Burk, Jr. (1991–).

The original purpose of the two offices was to aid committees in drafting legislation, but there was no statutory enumeration of their specific functions, and in practice the bulk of their work (in quantitative terms if not in terms of time spent) has been done for individual members. The functions of the House office were eventually spelled out more fully by Title V of the Legislative Reorganization Act of 1970 (2 U.S.C. 281 et seq.), which directed the office "to advise and assist the House of Representatives, and its committees and Members, in the achievement of a clear, faithful, and coherent expression of legislative policies," and then went on to describe its specific functions in their approximate order of priority:

1. To assist conference committees in the preparation of conference reports, at the request of the House conferees
2. To assist standing committees of the House (and joint committees), at their request, in the drafting of bills, amendments, and reports
3. To advise and assist members on the floor in appropriate cases
4. To assist individual members in the drafting of bills and amendments
5. To perform other legal services on behalf of the House, at the direction of the Speaker.

The legislative counsels are appointed by the presiding officers of their respective chambers, and they appoint their own staffs with the approval of those officers; all appointments are made solely on the basis of fitness to perform the work. Both offices are totally nonpolitical and nonpartisan, and all the members of their professional staffs are attorneys occupying career positions. At the beginning of the 103d Congress the House office had a professional staff of thirty-six with a supporting staff of thirteen, and the corresponding staffs of the Senate Office numbered twenty-four and nine.

[*See also* Beaman, Middleton.]

BIBLIOGRAPHY

Jones, Harry W. "Bill-Drafting Services in Congress and the State Legislatures." *Harvard Law Review* 65 (January 1952): 441.
Kofmehl, Kenneth. *Professional Staffs of Congress.* 1962.
Lee, Frederic P. "The Office of the Legislative Counsel." *Columbia Law Review* 29 (April 1929): 381.

LAWRENCE E. FILSON

LEGISLATIVE COURTS. The Constitution plainly vests the judicial power of the United States in independent courts staffed by judges with security of tenure and compensation. But early on—in an 1828 opinion by Chief Justice John Marshall—the Supreme Court approved giving judicial power to bodies not having that security. At times, the practice was based on necessity, providing courts for the territories, the District of Columbia, and the military, but the broadest justification is in the doctrine of public rights. Tracing to an 1856 opinion, the doctrine holds that in matters involving the enforcement of statutory rights and benefits—whether between government and individual or between individuals—Congress may recognize tribunals other than those set forth in Article III, which describes the judicial branch. Judicial bodies owing their provenance to the doctrine are the Tax Court, Court of Veterans Appeals, Court of Military Appeals, Court of Federal Claims, bankruptcy courts (adjuncts of federal district courts), and local courts in the District of Columbia and the territories. Congress has also given judicial powers to executive branch and independent regulatory agencies, such as the Federal Trade Commission and the Interstate Commerce Commission, so that they may adjudicate certain matters within their jurisdiction.

The Supreme Court has intermittently sought to limit the power of courts established by Congress. Could the values intended to be protected by Article III—generally, the rule of law—be undermined when Congress gives jurisdiction to unprotected entities that may bend to the popular will? Subjecting these entities to review by Article III courts is the only security against abuse, and it is not yet established that the Constitution requires Congress to provide such review.

BIBLIOGRAPHY

Fallon, Richard S. "Of Legislative Courts, Administrative Agencies, and Article III." *Harvard Law Review* 101 (1988): 916.
Bator, Paul. "The Constitution as Architecture: Legislative and Administrative Courts under Article III." *Indiana Law Journal* 65 (1990): 233.
Young, Gordon. "Public Rights and the Federal Judicial Power: From *Murray's Lessee* through *Crowell* to *Schor.*" *Buffalo Law Review* 35 (1986): 765.

JOHNNY H. KILLIAN

LEGISLATIVE DAY. In the Senate a legislative day is the period beginning with Morning Hour and ending with adjournment. It may involve one or more calendar days; in an extreme case, one legislative day ran for 162 calendar days (from 3 January to 12 June 1980). Alternatively, two legislative days may occur within a single calendar day.

At the end of each calendar day, the Senate adjourns or recesses pursuant to either a unanimous consent request or a motion. The decision of whether to adjourn or to recess is significant because Senate Rule VII provides for a two-hour period called Morning Hour at the beginning of each legislative day, during which routine morning business is transacted before any unfinished business may be considered. If the Senate recesses, the legislative day remains the same and the Senate may turn immediately to any unfinished business. In addition, the general practice of the Senate is to interpret the use of the word *day* in the rules to mean legislative day (unless calendar day is specified), as in the requirement under Rule XVII that committee reports lie over one day or in the prohibition against speaking more than twice on the same question during a legislative day under Rule XIX.

This distinction between legislative and calendar days is not as significant in the House, where the motion to recess is not highly privileged and the practice accordingly is to adjourn at the end of each day's session. On occasion, however, the House has had two legislative days on a single calendar day by reconvening immediately after an adjournment to comply with the requirement that resolutions reported by the Rules Committee lie over for one day.

[*See also* Adjournment and Recess.]

BIBLIOGRAPHY

U.S. Senate. *Precedents, Decisions on Points of Order with Phraseology in the United States Senate.* Compiled by Henry H. Gilfry. 61st Cong., 1st sess., 1909. S. Doc. 129.

U.S. Senate. *Senate Procedure, Precedents, and Practices,* by Floyd M. Riddick. 97th Cong., 1st sess., 1981. S. Doc. 97-2.

JAMES V. SATURNO

LEGISLATIVE INITIATIVE. During the 101st Congress (1989–1991), members of the House of Representatives introduced 6,683 bills and joint resolutions, averaging more than fifteen legislative initiatives per member. Although the Senate introduced fewer (3,669), senators were individually more active, submitting an average of nearly thirty-seven initiatives each. In past Congresses members of both chambers were often even more prodigious, averaging as many as fifty initiatives per member (Norman J. Ornstein, Thomas E. Mann, and Michael J. Malbin, eds., *Vital Statistics on Congress, 1991–1992,* 1991, pp. 151–153). What is the source of such active legislative initiative in Congress, intending everything from the most modest adjustments in existing law to sweeping reforms of the nation's economic, health care, welfare, educational, environmental, and defense establishments?

First, these numbers admittedly overstate the actual amount of independent legislative activity. Numerous initiatives are "companion" bills introduced in both chambers with nearly or completely identical wording. Dozens of bills in the same house may share quite similar themes or approaches. Indeed, on Capitol Hill, legislative plagiarism is the highest form of flattery, as whole paragraphs, sections, and parts of previously introduced initiatives are mixed and matched for inclusion in another member's "new" proposal. Further, a significant number of bills entail routine and recurring legislative business, from reauthorizations of expiring programs to mandatory annual appropriations. However, even discounting companion legislation, common frameworks, word-for-word copying, and repetitive routines, Congress displays a striking propensity to initiate legislation. This activity requires a close examination of the contributions made by presidents and their administrations, members of Congress themselves aided by their staffs, interest groups, constituents, and policy entrepreneurs.

Presidents and Their Administrations. Ever since George Washington took the oath of office in 1789, presidents have demonstrated the capacity to be legislative initiators. It was not until early in the twentieth century, however—when Theodore Roosevelt forged national policy on railroads and conservation and Woodrow Wilson developed the first systematic party program—that the chief executive of the Constitution became identified in common practice as the "chief legislator" (under the Constitution, the president cannot formally introduce bills; actual submission must be done by a sympathetic representative or senator). By the time of Franklin D. Roosevelt's New Deal in the 1930s, actual legislative language was routinely drafted by the executive, and the president's announced policy agenda became the primary legislative agenda of Congress. As Dwight D. Eisenhower entered office in 1953, law and custom, as well as congressional expectations, granted enduring institutional means for presidents to identify and convey a formal program of legislative initiatives to Congress. The Constitution provided for the State of the Union address; the Budget and Accounting Act of 1921 mandated a unified federal budget under executive leadership as expressed in the president's annual budget message; the Employment Act of 1946 required the president's annual economic report; and the practice of sending special messages to Congress to transmit additional administration proposals had become fully accepted. Eisenhower added a formalized White House office of congressional liaison to help further the president's legislative interests.

The president in the modern era has emerged as the single most influential agenda setter in Congress, although the executive's clout over what issues the legislature deliberates is far greater than over which particular policy alternatives it enacts. The vast majority of bills introduced in Congress do not receive serious legislative attention. In the House, almost seven times as many bills are submitted as enacted; in the Senate, more than three bills are introduced for every one that passes. A mere fraction survive in both chambers and make it to the statute books. But three-quarters of the legislative initiatives proposed by presidents from Eisenhower to Reagan, for example, and 85 percent of their most consequential initiatives, were acted upon by Congress. Over half were passed into law. Successful legislative initiative in Congress is closely associated with legislative initiative by the president.

Policies that presidents propose, therefore, have particular significance. Where do they come from? Presidents may have ideas of their own for legislative initiatives, and their campaigns for office often identify issues of priority for their administrations, but U.S. chief executives most often select ideas and alternatives from the reservoir of options generated by others inside and outside of government. Since Harry S. Truman standardized the process by which the Bureau of the Budget (now the Office of Management and Budget, OMB) solicits legislative recommendations from federal departments and agencies, political appointees and career officials in the executive branch have customarily participated in shaping legislation sponsored by the president. However, because presidents typically become frustrated by the perceived inertia and absence of imagination in the bureaucracy, and fear the lack of responsiveness by the permanent government to their own political needs, they often turn to more reliable and creative sources of ideas. Major legislative initiatives are frequently drafted by trusted aides in the Executive Office of the President, or White House personnel coordinate policy alternatives that are developed by presidentially appointed task forces and commissions composed of specially selected external policy experts, group representatives, administration officials, and possibly members of Congress and civil servants. At times, the ideas of outside policy entrepreneurs find their way into the president's legislative initiatives. In making their legislative choices, presidents and their staffs generally also keep a watchful eye on current events, public opinion, and the media.

The most important source of ideas for presidential legislative initiatives, however, is Capitol Hill. Dozens of careful qualitative and quantitative studies of legislative initiatives, beginning with Lawrence Chamberlain's classic work, *The President, Congress, and Legislation* (1946), reveal the extent to which even the most important presidential proposals can be traced to bills previously introduced in Congress. Only rarely are presidential proposals truly new legislative initiatives. For example, core facets of Franklin D. Roosevelt's New Deal and many of the social welfare programs of the Kennedy and Johnson administrations (such as Medicare) all were derived from legislation in play on Capitol Hill before these presidents entered the White House. The 1981 income tax cuts of Ronald Reagan's economic recovery plan began as the Kemp-Roth bill, which was defeated in 1980. Chief executives usually choose policy options that comport with their policy preferences, and the presidential imprimatur unquestionably transforms the politics of initiatives, but as Nelson Polsby put it: Congress, especially the Senate, is an "incubator" of policy ideas.

Congress as Initiator. Congress is quite unlike legislatures in parliamentary systems, where the cabinet, representing the majority party or multiparty coalition, develops almost all legislative initiatives and individual members of the parliament possess little of the institutional resources necessary to formulate, or even evaluate, complex policy proposals. With its constitutional separation from the executive (reinforced by the absence of strong party organizations with clear policy agendas), independent electoral base, decentralized structure, powerful committee and subcommittee system, vast professional staffs, and analytically mature support agencies, the U.S. Congress provides its entrepreneurial members with myriad opportunities to nurture the ideas that ultimately appear in presidential initiatives and to grant independent judgment to recurring program reauthorizations and appropriations. Congress also affords members the discretionary resources needed to challenge presidential initiatives and to fill in proactively the policy gaps not addressed by presidential agendas. Despite the well-recognized rise of the president as chief legislator, empirical research by Lawrence Chamberlain and subsequent scholars has consistently found that Congress is responsible for most proposed legislation and a large share of enacted programs, either on its own or working in conjunction with the president.

Where do members of Congress get their ideas? Sometimes they arise from personal experience—their own or that of constituents. Members also react to and build upon the previous legislative efforts of others, especially those programs that trigger popular expansions of federal activity. Usually congressional staff operating within the guidelines established by their bosses, particularly the committee and subcommittee professional staff, are instrumental in generating (sometimes), receiving, soliciting, shaping, and advocating various policy options. Issue and program evaluation reports distributed by the Congressional Budget Office (CBO), General Accounting Office (GAO), and Office of Technology Assessment (OTA) commonly furnish ready-made proposals that are picked up and introduced by members.

Innumerable external sources of ideas are also directed at Congress, primarily through this conduit of congressional staff. In the complex, intermixed world of legislative initiative, a major source of ideas for members of Congress, usually those in the president's party, are the broader reaches of the executive branch. Federal agencies constantly generate legislative proposals that are not included in the president's agenda but that are determined by OMB to be "in accordance" (i/a) with administration policy and available for introduction. On occasion, too, executive-branch officials take proposals that were rejected by the administration and surreptitiously promote their introduction by agency supporters in Congress.

Interest groups and their lobbyists, both individually and in coalitions, enjoy far more open access to the legislature than to the executive and are another significant source of policy options. As representatives of important constituent groups, distributors of campaign financing, and disseminators of valuable policy information, they are uniquely situated to provide legislators with needed political intelligence and technical expertise.

Academics, independent policy specialists, and members of think tanks and consulting firms also contribute ideas for legislative initiatives through both the circulation of their writings and personal contact with members of Congress and their staffs. Taken together, in any given policy area Congress taps into a broad network of idea merchants and managers in the executive and legislative branches of government, the interest group community, the business world, as well as universities and other research settings.

BIBLIOGRAPHY

Chamberlain, Lawrence C. *The President, Congress and Legislation.* 1946.

Kingdon, John W. *Agendas, Alternatives, and Public Policies.* 1984.

Light, Paul C. *The President's Agenda: Domestic Policy Choice from Kennedy to Carter.* 1982.

Neustadt, Richard E. "The Presidency and Legislation: Planning the President's Program." *American Political Science Review* 49 (1955): 980–1021.

Peterson, Mark A. *Legislating Together: The White House and Capitol Hill from Eisenhower to Reagan.* 1990.

Polsby, Nelson W. *Political Innovation in America: The Politics of Policy Initiation.* 1984.

MARK A. PETERSON

Sources of Ideas for the President's Domestic Agenda

SOURCES MENTIONED	PERCENTAGE OF RESPONDENTS
EXTERNAL SOURCES	
Congress	52
Events and crises	51
Executive branch	46
Public opinion	27
Party	11
Interest groups	7
Media	4
INTERNAL SOURCES	
Campaign and platform	20
President	17
Staff	16
Task forces	6

Note: Respondents were 118 officials who had served in the Executive Office of the President from the Kennedy through the Carter administrations. They were asked the following question: "Generally speaking, what would you say were the most important sources of ideas for the domestic agenda?"
SOURCE: Paul C. Light, *The President's Agenda: Domestic Policy Choice from Kennedy to Carter* (1982), p. 86.

LEGISLATIVE INTENT. Legislative intent is the meaning that Congress imbues in a statute as a guide to its purposes and direction. How that intent is to be discerned has been the subject of ongoing debate. What should the balance of authority be between those political institutions, the agencies and the courts, charged with interpreting legislative intent? What should constitute the materials by which legislative intent is divined? How should the courts, the ultimate interpreters of legislative intent, approach their task?

The first question, the balance to be struck between agencies and courts in determining legislative intent, goes to the heart of power relations in an administrative state. In the case of *Chevron v. Natural Resources Defense Council, Inc.* (467 U.S. 837 [1984]), the Supreme Court determined that if Congress has not spoken directly to an issue, courts should defer to an agency's interpretation of a statute if it is based on a permissible construction. The effect of that ruling, in the view of many, has been to shift power to the executive branch in administrative policy.

Ultimately, courts become involved in a large number of cases that seek to ascertain legislative intent. In this age of statutes, interpretation has become for courts an increasingly significant, difficult, and time-consuming duty. Consider the typical pattern. Congress passes a law; the statute becomes the subject of legal action. The court must interpret the meaning of the words of the statute. But the language is often unclear. As the judiciary looks for clues to congressional intent, it delves into the legislative history—the basis on which judges have traditionally sought to interpret statutory meaning. In so doing, the court must first determine what constitutes legislative history and how to assess its various parts—such as committee reports, conference committee reports, floor debates, and votes. It may have to delve into layers of rules and procedures. At times, the legislative history is virtually nonexistent. In other situations, the legislative history is ambiguous. To be sure, in particular cases Congress may deliberately not deal with difficult issues. In other circumstances, the legislature might well have chosen to deal with the issue if it had been made aware of the problem.

Sometimes, the problem results not from legislative ambiguity but from silence: Congress simply has not addressed the issue. The court is then asked to fill in the gaps, not only with respect to the meaning of statutory language but also with regard to a whole host of commonly overlooked issues—for example, those bearing on preemption, attorney's fees, civil statutes of limitation, constitutional severability provisions, private right of action, exhaustion of administrative remedies, and the nature of the administrative proceedings.

The difficulty of discerning the legislative will has increased as Congress has changed. In some ways, fragmentation has increased—staffs have grown substantially, subcommittees have proliferated—and the opportunities for legislative entrepreneurship, in ways unobserved by the entire house, have expanded as well.

Courts have traditionally relied on the "canons of statutory construction" in interpreting statutes (Sutherland, 1972, p. 5). The canons allow courts to use generic rules to resolve cases. Whatever their utility, the canons, as Karl Llewellyn wrote, are not definitive guides to construction. Equal and opposite canons may be invoked to support virtually every outcome possible. No canon exists for ranking or choosing among canons.

Other approaches, based on assumptions about how the legislative process works, seek to provide judges with more direction as they interpret statutes. One influential perspective—a "public interest" approach, advocated by Henry Hart and Albert Sacks (1958), among others—claims that "every statute and every doctrine of unwritten law developed by the decisional process has some kind of purpose or objective" (pp. 166–167). Thus, a judge who seeks to understand unclear wording identifies the purpose and policy it embraces and then deduces the result most consonant with that purpose or policy. This approach, much like the vision of James Madison, assumes that the legislative process and legislative decisions are deliberative, informed, and efficient.

The perspective provides an important antidote to the canons of statutory construction. Its thrust is to try to understand the meaning of statutes in context, with appropriate resort to the process that produced the law, which encompasses relevant legislative history. The flexible nature of the inquiry means that judges can extend the underlying rationale of the policies of the statute to cover new circumstances, even those not envisioned when the legislature enacted the law.

Other perspectives deny the validity of the public interest conceptions, offering startlingly different assumptions about the way Congress works, although not necessarily a shared view about how courts should interpret statutes. One such challenge, the public-choice school, uses principles of market economics to explain decision making. Like many schools, its scholars are not all of one mind and cannot be characterized simply. Generally, however, its proponents depict the legislative process as driven by rational, egoistic legislators whose primary motivation is to be returned to office. Legislators will pass laws that tend to transfer wealth and reduce efficiency, at the expense of society, to satisfy cohesive special interest groups that lobby the legislature. Laws that benefit the public will be scarce, because of the "collective action" problem—that is, the difficulty of mobilizing the wider public not directly affected by a policy.

But public-choice theory hardly explains the universe of the legislative process. The motivations of legislators are complex and cannot be reduced to simple formulas. The view that legislators simply respond to interest groups, that their behavior, votes, and agenda are dictated by those interest groups, and that they simply transfer wealth to those groups in return for campaign support is askew. As studies have shown, Congress can respond without much interest-group support and often despite powerful and intense interest-group opposition. To be sure, legislators are responsive to the need to be reelected. But they are also affected by a desire to affect policy in ways that they think are in the public interest. The twentieth century saw a wide variety of legislation to protect the environment, health, and safety of the public—legislation that the various economic theories of regulation would not have predicted.

Even if the theories of public choice succeeded in explaining legislative outcomes, they do not—indeed, could not—lead to a single prescriptive view about how judges should construe statutes. Any theory of statutory interpretation inevitably is based upon some conception of the judicial role in society, a subject not central to most public-choice explanations.

Still another conception of how to discern legislative intent maintains that judges should generally restrict themselves to the words of the statute, to the "plain meaning" of the statute. This "textualist approach" regards legislative history as susceptible to distortion and manipulation. Supreme Court Justice Antonin Scalia is the most prominent proponent of this view, and thus what was once an argument conducted in the halls of academia has become a viable assault on traditional modes of statutory construction that draw upon legislative history.

Intellectually, at least three prongs appear to underlie the textualist attack on legislative history. The first is the idea that the only appropriate law, according to the Constitution, is that which both houses of Congress and the president have approved (or in some cases enacted over the chief executive's veto). It is a perspective that draws strength from the Supreme Court's interpretation of Article I, section 7 in *Immigration and Naturalization Service v. Chadha* (462 U.S. 919 [1983]), in which the high tribunal struck down legislative vetoes, because they effectively legislated without securing the affirmation of both legislative chambers and the president. According to this view, because it is unlikely that all members of Congress are familiar with the hearings, floor debates, and committee reports surrounding a bill, those documents cannot be thought of as dispositive of legislative intent.

A second prong of this critique is that when judges rely on legislative history, they perforce increase their discretion at the expense of elected representatives. The textualists argue that when judges go beyond the words of the statute and choose from a wide range of (often conflicting) materials that comprise legislative history, they increase their capacity, however unconsciously, to enforce their own policy preferences. According to this view, the responsibility for making policy belongs to those in the elected branches, not to usurping jurists.

A final prong holds that focusing attention on the words of a statute will compel legislators to do their jobs with greater care—to write laws with precision and with a clarity that would offer direction to the executive and judicial branches.

Textualists have quite rightly pointed to some of the excesses of legislative history. But to acknowledge the value of their challenge is not necessarily to accept their analyses of the problem or their prescriptions. As to the causes of the problem, it is undoubtedly true that at times laws are ambiguous because of sloppy drafting; certainly, one can point to examples of a conscious strategy of drafters to put the contentious aspects of statutory meaning in committee reports in order to obscure controversy. However, it is also the case that legislation is often ambiguous because the problems confronted are not simply defined and Congress lacks the expertise to resolve them; given the complexities and uncertainties that the problem presents, it might be more prudent to cast the legislation in more general terms and leave difficulties to administrative agencies to resolve. The committee reports can thus provide important policy guidance for agencies as they seek to implement legislative intent. That Congress does not foresee problems arising from the statutory scheme may not always be a failure of legislative will or precision; sometimes it is too much to expect Congress to foresee all manner of developments. In such situations, exhorting the legislative branch to write unambiguous legislation will have little effect.

It is not at all clear, moreover, that a judiciary that refrains from using legislative history is less likely to impose its preferences. If the courts simply stick to the statutory text, and if that text is ambiguous, arguably courts will have considerable discretion to interpret the statute, perhaps in ways that Congress did not intend.

Context thus becomes important, particularly when it takes into account the legitimate historical record. The task, given some of the criticisms of legislative history, is to find ways to make the legislative history more authoritative, to find ways that Congress can more clearly signal its meaning and the judiciary better interpret statutes.

Clarifying statutory meaning has at least three parts. The first is in some sense preventative; that is, it seeks to anticipate potential difficulties and to deal with them before a bill becomes a law. As such, it goes to the heart of the drafting process. The second component focuses on the materials that constitute legislative history and is geared toward finding ways for Congress to signal its meaning more clearly. The third part entails developing routinized means so that, after the enactment of legislation, courts that have experience with particular statutes can transmit their opinions to Congress, identifying problems for legislative consideration. In fact, a major project, sponsored by the Governance Institute with the support of representatives of both branches, was under way in the mid 1990s; it sought to bridge the gap between legislators who make legislative history and those who digest it.

BIBLIOGRAPHY

Eskridge, William N., Jr. *Statutory Interpretation. Virginia Law Review* 74 (1988): 275, 320.

Eskridge, William N., Jr., and Philip P. Frickey. "Legislation Scholarship and Pedagogy in the Post-Legal Era." *University of Pittsburgh Law Review* 48, no. 3 (Spring 1987): 691–731.

Hart, Henry M., Jr., and Albert Sacks. *The Legal Process: Basic Problems in the Making and Application of Law.* 1958.

Katzmann, Robert A. "Bridging the Statutory Gulf between Courts and Congress: A Challenge for Positive Political Theory." *Georgetown Law Journal* 87 (1992): 653–669.

Katzmann, Robert A., ed. *Judges and Legislators.* 1988.

Landis, James. "A Note on Statutory Interpretation." *Harvard Law Review* 43 (1930): 886–901.

Llewellyn, Karl N. *The Common Law Tradition: Deciding Appeals.* 1960.

Llewellyn, Karl N. "Remarks on the Theory of Appellate Decision and the Rules or Canons about How Statutes Are to Be Construed." *Vanderbilt Law Review* 3 (1950): 395–410.

Sutherland, J. G. *Statutes and Statutory Construction.* 4th ed. 1972.

ROBERT A. KATZMANN

LEGISLATIVE REORGANIZATION ACTS. [*This entry includes two separate discussions of the acts of 1946 and 1970. For related discussion, see* Reorganization of Congress.]

Act of 1946

The Legislative Reorganization Act of 1946 (P.L. 79–601; 60 Stat. 812-852) reduced the number of standing committees from 48 to 19 in the House and from 33 to 15 in the Senate. The act codified committee jurisdictions, set rules for how committees should function, directed committees to maintain "continuous watchfulness" over the executive branch, and put in place procedures for regulating lobbyists. The act also initiated a new congressional budget process through which the appropriations committees of both chambers would jointly prepare budgets. These fiscal reforms, never completely implemented, were abandoned within three years.

The most significant and unanticipated impact of the act was on congressional staffs. Largely because of processes that the act set in motion, the number of congressional staffers doubled from 1946 to 1956 and then doubled again by 1966. This expansion of the Capitol Hill work force put Congress on a more even footing with the president following two decades of rapid growth in the executive branch.

In response to hostile public criticism of Congress, the Joint Committee on the Organization of Congress was formed in 1945. Cochaired by Sen. Robert M. La Follette, Jr. (Prog.-Wis.), and Rep. A. S. Mike Monroney (D-Okla.), the Joint Committee hired George Galloway, a policy analyst associated with the Brookings Institution, as staff director. Galloway, La Follette, and Monroney crafted the act.

Impetus for the act came from widespread concern among lawmakers that the balance of power was tilting toward the president. While the federal government's executive branch grew dramatically in the 1930s and 1940s, at the close of World War II Congress was making do with staffing levels and committee jurisdictions that were legacies of the 1800s. In 1946, all House and Senate committees combined had just 356 employees, including janitors and stenographers. Meanwhile, public opinion polls berated a "do-nothing Congress" for obstructing the president.

The Joint Committee held hearings during the spring of 1945, and in testimony before the panel many legislators complained of being overworked by an ostensibly archaic and fragmented committee system. It was often said that House members were on as many as eight standing committees, but this actually held true for only one person, a member who wanted to be on all the committees related

CONGRESSIONAL REFORM. Democratic leadership in Congress had hoped that reform and reorganization of Congress would be popular with voters and improve the public's outlook on the legislature. This political cartoon presents Senate majority leader Alben W. Barkley (D-Ky.) and House Speaker Sam Rayburn (D-Tex.) wooing the public with the Legislative Reorganization bill. John Q. Public's reply reveals the cartoonist's skepticism over the political gains the Democrats would reap from the reform. In the November elections after the bill was passed, the Democrats were in fact voted out of power. Clifford K. Berryman, *Washington Evening Star*, 28 July 1946.

U.S. SENATE COLLECTION, CENTER FOR LEGISLATIVE ARCHIVES

to the one he chaired. Of Democrats who were not also committee chairs, 77.8 percent served on only one standing committee. The problem was not multiple committee memberships but the failure to provide legislators with staff sufficient to keep up with the expanding scope of the one or two committees on which they served. Again, the lasting legacy of the act was the rapid growth of professional staff that followed. In 1946, however, "committee reorganization" became a rallying cry that was pushed onto the editorial pages of leading newspapers.

Even though the number of committees was cut by two-thirds, the act should not necessarily be seen as marking the birth of the modern committee system. For the most part, the act did not, as advertised, realign jurisdictions. In the House, ten of the nineteen postreform committees were carried over untouched. The remaining committees were consolidated along lines that reinforced prereform coalitions. For example, before the reform act the Public Lands, Irrigation, Mining, Indian Affairs, and Insular Affairs committees coordinated activities and shared many members. They were, for all intents and purposes, behaving like subcommittees, and it was no surprise that these five committees were combined in the act to create one Committee on Interior and Insular Affairs.

As for clarifying committee jurisdictions by writing them into the House and Senate rules, the act did little more than copy into the rules what had long been in the books of precedents maintained by the House and Senate parliamentarians. To alter the committee system radically would have been tantamount to overhauling Congress's internal power structure. Instead, that power structure was consolidated by reducing the number of committee chairs and by encouraging expanded oversight of the executive branch.

In debates about the act on the House and Senate floors, controversy surrounded a 25 percent pay increase included in the measure. The bill also extended the Civil Service Retirement Act to cover lawmakers. Committee sizes were adjusted to give most committees twenty-five or twenty-seven members (numbers easily inflated by later Congresses), and the bill-drafting service and Legislative Reference Service were greatly expanded. The final version of the 1946 Legislative Reorganization Act passed the Senate overwhelmingly (by voice vote) on 26 July 1946 after clearing the House 229 to 61 a day earlier.

When President Harry S. Truman signed Public Law 79-601 on 2 August 1946, congressional reformers had high hopes that the consolidation of committees and the new budget process would stand the test of time. However, the budget process was scrapped within three years, loopholes were quickly found in the act's lobbying regulations, and committee reforms were undermined by the growing number of subcommittees. By the early 1970s, the number of subcommittees in the House and Senate had nearly doubled, spurring calls among subcommittee chairs for more autonomy. Furthermore, by reducing the number of committee chairs in 1946, the power of remaining committee chairs was strengthened, which helped set the stage for new reforms in the 1970s.

BIBLIOGRAPHY

Byrd, Robert C. "Congressional Reform: The Legislative Reorganization Act of 1946." In vol. 1 of *The Senate,*

1789–1989: Addresses on the History of the United States Senate. 1988.

Davidson, Roger H. "The Advent of the Modern Congress: The Legislative Reorganization Act of 1946." *Legislative Studies Quarterly* 15 (1990): 357–373.

DAVID C. KING

Act of 1970

The Legislative Reorganization Act of 1970 (P.L. 91-510; 84 Stat. 1140–1204) was the first major legislative reform bill enacted after the Legislative Reorganization Act of 1946. The 1970 act encouraged open committee meetings and hearings, required that committee roll-call votes be made public, allowed for television and radio broadcasting of House committee hearings, and formalized rules for debating conference committee reports. Many of these reforms were adopted in the name of opening up the legislative process to the public eye. The reform of longest-lasting significance provided that House votes in the Committee of the Whole be recorded on request, which ended the secrecy often surrounding members' votes on important measures.

Within a decade after the 1946 reorganization act, a handful of reform-minded legislators had begun calling for revisions to deal with the act's unanticipated consequences. By reducing the number of committee chairmen while strengthening congressional oversight of the executive branch, the act greatly expanded the chairmen's power. In party caucuses, seniority was the guiding rule for appointing committee chairmen. A disproportionate number of chairmen were long-serving southern Democrats who effectively vetoed a more liberal social welfare and civil rights agenda throughout the 1950s and much of the 1960s.

In 1965, Congress established the Joint Committee on the Organization of Congress headed by Sen. A. S. Mike Monroney (D-Okla.) and Rep. Ray J. Madden (D-Ind.). The joint committee's final report in 1966 recommended limiting the powers of chairmen, reducing the number of committee assignments, improving committee staffs, and expanding the Legislative Reference Service (later renamed the Congressional Research Service). In 1967, the Senate passed a bill (S. 355) largely based on the joint committee's recommendations, but the bill languished in the House in the face of fierce opposition from committee chairmen.

In a move that surprised most observers, two House Rules Committee members, B. F. Sisk (D-Calif.) and Richard W. Bolling (D-Mo.), pushed for a special subcommittee to consider legislative reform in 1969. The result was House Report 91-1215, which became the basis for the 1970 Legislative Reorganization Act. Most of the provisions in the 1970 bill opened up the legislative process through what are called sunshine provisions (i.e., measures that increase public access by "letting the sunshine in" on legislative proceedings). Very few of the proposals to limit the powers of committee chairmen and to weaken seniority that had been discussed by the 1969 joint committee survived in the bill.

In ten days of floor debate, 65 amendments were considered. A package of ten amendments (nine of which passed) was presented on the House floor by a bipartisan coalition of reformers. The House passed its version of the reorganization act 326 to 19 on 17 September 1970. The Senate made minor changes, passing the bill 59 to 5 on 6 October, and the House accepted the Senate's modifications on 8 October.

The Legislative Reorganization Act of 1970 was a harbinger of things to come. While limitations on seniority were modest, within a year the House and Senate had passed resolutions stating that the selection of committee chairmen need not be based solely on seniority. In 1973, the House "Subcommittee Bill of Rights" mandated that legislation be referred to subcommittees, further weakening the power of the chairmen of full committees.

[*See also* Government in the Sunshine Act.]

BIBLIOGRAPHY

Davidson, Roger H. "Inertia and Change: The Legislative Reorganization Act of 1970." In *On Capitol Hill.* Edited by John F. Bibby and Roger H. Davidson. 2d ed. 1972.

Kravitz, Walter. "The Advent of the Modern Congress: The Legislative Reorganization Act of 1970." *Legislative Studies Quarterly* 15 (August 1990): 375–399.

DAVID C. KING

LEGISLATIVE SERVICE ORGANIZATIONS.

A special type of informal caucus created under House regulations, a legislative service organization (LSO) is a congressional caucus, committee, coalition, or similar group that "operate[s] solely to provide legislative services or other assistance to . . . members . . . in the performance of their official duties." Such groups must (a) consist solely of House members or members of both bodies; (b) receive support from the House (office

Legislative Service Organizations of the 103d Congress

LSOs[1] CERTIFIED AND OPERATING	Former LSOs Operating as CMOs[2]	LSOs No Longer Operational
Arms Control and Foreign Policy Caucus	Long Island Congressional Caucus	Clearinghouse on the Future, Congressional[3]
Arts Caucus, Congressional	Military Reform Caucus	Export Task Force[3]
Automotive Caucus, Congressional		New England Congressional Caucus[4]
Black Caucus, Congressional		
Border Caucus, Congressional		Ninety-fifth [Democratic] Caucus[5]
California Democratic Congressional Delegation		Ninety-sixth [Democratic] Caucus[5]
Children and Families Caucus		
Democratic Study Group		Ninety-seventh [Democratic] Caucus[6]
Environmental and Energy Study Conference		Ninety-eighth [Democratic] Caucus
Federal Government Service Task Force		
Hispanic Caucus, Congressional		Science and Technology, Congressional Caucus for[3]
House Wednesday Group		Senior Citizens Caucus, Congressional[5]
Human Rights Caucus, Congressional		
Hunger Caucus, Congressional		Territorial Caucus, Congressional[6]
Narcotics Abuse and Control Caucus		
New York State Congressional Delegation		
Northeast-Midwest Congressional Coalition		
Older Americans Caucus		
Pennsylvania Congressional Delegation		
Populist Caucus		
Republican Study Committee		
Rural Caucus, Congressional		
Space Caucus, Congressional		
Steel Caucus, Congressional		
Sunbelt Caucus, Congressional		
Textile Caucus, Congressional		
Travel and Tourism Caucus, Congressional		
Women's Issues, Congressional Caucus for		

[1]Legislative service organizations
[2]Congressional member organizations
[3]No longer operational for the 103d Congress (1993–1995)
[4]Not reorganized for the 100th Congress (1987–1989)
[5]Not reorganized for the 99th Congress (1985–1987)
[6]Inactive since the 101st Congress (1989–1991)

SOURCE: Richardson, Sula P. *Caucuses and Legislative Service Organizations of the 103d Congress, Second Session: An Informational Directory.* Congressional Research Service, Library of Congress. CRS Rept. 94-707 GOV. 1994.

space, furniture, telephone service, and the like) or from members' office allowances; and (c) accept no substantial income or contributions from outside sources. As of 1994, only 28 of the 130 or more informal caucuses (also known as congressional member organizations) were designated as LSOs (see accompanying table).

Informal caucuses such as the liberal House Democratic Study Group, formed in the late 1950s, developed the practice of assessing "dues" from their members' clerk-hire and official expense allowances. For example, a number of representatives could donate a small portion of their office

funds and pool them to hire one or more caucus staffers. House office space, supplies, and services were also made available to such groups. After complaints that some groups receiving such support from public funds also undertook public fundraising and charged fees to outsiders for their publications, the House Administration Committee in 1981 devised the LSO concept (revising the guidelines in 1994) to designate organizations entitled to official support.

LSO status assists groups that seek to assess dues or fees from their members' official accounts, and that maintain a separate staff and office space. Not all such groups have sought LSO status, however. Congressional member groups that are not LSOs operate from the offices of one or more members, whose staff manage the group's activities as part of their regular duties.

[See also Caucus, article on Special Interest Caucus.]

BIBLIOGRAPHY

Richardson, Sula P. *Caucuses and Legislative Service Organizations of the 103d Congress, Second Session: An Informational Directory.* Congressional Research Service, Library of Congress. CRS Rept. 94-707 GOV. 1994.

ROGER H. DAVIDSON

LEGISLATIVE VETO. *See* Veto, *article on* Legislative Veto.

LEND-LEASE ACT (1941; 55 Stat. 31–33). Signed into law by President Franklin D. Roosevelt on 11 March 1941, the Lend-Lease Act was the most important step that the United States took to aid Adolf Hitler's enemies before entering World War II in December 1941. It authorized the president to sell, transfer, exchange, or lease military and other aid to any country whose defense he deemed vital to American interests.

By early 1941, Britain's plight was desperate. President Roosevelt proposed his lend-lease plan "to eliminate the dollar sign" in aid to Britain and said that America "must be the great arsenal of democracy." The legislation was drafted in the Treasury Department and debated heatedly in both houses of Congress. People across the country inundated Congress and the White House with letters and telegrams expressing their views. Proponents said that if Britain fell, America could be next on Hitler's list. Opponents insisted that the Axis could not successfully invade America and that steps short of war would become steps to war. They charged that the bill would give the president dictatorial powers.

A clear majority of Americans favored the proposal. It passed in the House 260 to 165 and in the Senate 60 to 31. The strongest support came from Democrats in the South and the urban Northeast, while the strongest opposition came from Republicans in the Middle West, Great Plains, and Far West. By the time World War II ended, the United States had extended fifty billion dollars in lend-lease aid to countries warring against the Axis. The

REPUBLICAN PARTY DISAGREEMENT. House minority leader Joseph W. Martin (R-Mass.) and Senate minority leader Charles L. McNary (R-Oreg.) held opposing opinions on the Lend-Lease bill. The political cartoon depicts the Republican elephant torn between the differing stances of the two party leaders. Clifford K. Berryman, *Washington Evening Star,* 8 March 1941.

U.S. SENATE COLLECTION, CENTER FOR LEGISLATIVE ARCHIVES

largest amount went to Britain, but substantial assistance also reached the Soviet Union. It was an important part of the process by which the United States helped defeat the Axis powers.

BIBLIOGRAPHY

Cole, Wayne S. *Roosevelt and the Isolationists, 1932–1945.* 1983.
Kimball, Warren F. *The Most Unsordid Act: Lend-Lease, 1939–1941.* 1969.

WAYNE S. COLE

LIBERALISM. A worldview that emphasizes individual freedom, liberalism is usually defined in terms of universal rights based in divine or natural law. It rests on an optimistic view of human nature as fundamentally rational and thus disposed toward tolerance and the enlightened pursuit of self-interest.

In its earliest incarnation, liberalism was largely a reaction against despotic state power. Its enumeration of rights stressed representative government, protection against arbitrary arrest or imprisonment, and the affirmation of free speech and religious belief. It advocated small, localized government close to the people and favored the legislative branch over the executive or judicial branches. It stood for free economic activity, as unhindered as possible by state grants of monopoly and special privilege. Regarding standing armies as instruments of oppression and war as an irrational activity, liberalism from the beginning possessed an antimilitary, near-pacifist bias.

Jeffersonian and Jacksonian Democracy. In the Congresses of the early Republic, the Jeffersonian Republicans were the principal exponents of this tradition. Envisioning small-scale agriculture as the basis of social stability, the Jeffersonians celebrated the agrarian way of life and feared the growth of class-ridden cities. They were suspicious of capitalism and big finance. In Congress, this philosophy was dogmatically espoused by Virginia's John Taylor of Caroline and John Randolph of Roanoke and North Carolina's Nathaniel Macon. Known as the Old Republicans, they and their followers considered their principles moral absolutes and criticized even Presidents Thomas Jefferson and James Madison for departing from them.

Jacksonian Democracy largely restated Jeffersonian liberal principles while adding a less restrained celebration of the virtues of majoritarian democracy, about which Jeffersonians had been somewhat ambivalent. Perhaps its most eloquent congressional spokesman was Sen. Thomas Hart Benton of Missouri. Jacksonian liberalism had special appeal to the West, but it also drew support from hard-money radicals who distrusted modern finance, from "workingmen's" organizations in the cities, and from the lower classes in general. The financial panic of 1837 and the consequent economic depression, a fairly direct outcome of Jacksonian policy, largely ended the democratic and libertarian phase of Jeffersonian-Jacksonian ideology. Thereafter, advocates of states' rights, agrarianism, and the compact theory of the Constitution were largely identified with the interests of the South and the defense of slavery, the most profoundly antiliberal institution of the United States.

Republicanism, Patrician Reform, and Populism. In the mid-nineteenth century, liberalism in its more authentic meaning as faith in individual freedom and natural rights was represented primarily by a growing antislavery movement that found its political identity first in the Free Soil party and then the Republican party. The Republicans successfully combined opposition to the extension of slavery with a program of positive government—internal improvements, a homestead act, and a pro-

tective tariff. Although indelibly linked with the memory of Abraham Lincoln, the Republican cause had been pioneered in Congress by others, notably Sen. William H. Seward of New York and Rep. Thaddeus Stevens of Pennsylvania—men who mixed antislavery zealotry with interest-group politics and a positive concept of government.

The upsurge of industrialism in post–Civil War America created a society of growing cities, big business, and unequal distributions of power, all of which had the effect of making old definitions of liberalism seem unsatisfactory. Some claimants to the liberal tradition, primarily patrician influentials, argued for restoration of the old ethic of small, frugal, honest, responsible government to be run by men very much like themselves through a professional civil service. Mostly Republicans, they dominated the Liberal Republican movement of 1872. Their major achievement was the Pendleton Act of 1883, which established the beginnings of a merit civil service system.

Other dissenters, not yet prone to use the term *liberal*, advocated a range of programs designed to aid farmers and small enterprisers, groups that increasingly felt themselves being pushed by corporate power to the margins of society. These programs included monetary inflation, low tariffs, antitrust legislation, farm price stabilization mechanisms, and regulation (or outright government ownership) of the railroads. The major legislative achievements of the late-nineteenth-century reform impulse were the Bland-Allison Act (1878), the Interstate Commerce Act (1887), the Sherman Silver Purchase Act (1890), and the Sherman Antitrust Act (1890)—all more impressive in appearance than in actual impact. They set the stage for the angry People's (Populist) party movement of the 1890s.

Progressivism. In the early twentieth century, Congress was increasingly affected by a drive for "progressive" reform to regulate the economy, provide rudimentary welfare benefits for the working class, protect consumers, support farmers, and curb the power of big capital. "Insurgent" Republicans in Congress, including Robert M. La Follette, Sr., of Wisconsin and George W. Norris of Nebraska, spearheaded the movement on Capitol Hill. They enjoyed their greatest success in cooperation with neopopulistic Democrats from the South and West, who shared their resentment of the railroads, large corporations, Wall Street, and the high tariff. A small but growing group of urban-oriented Democrats and Republicans worked effectively for legis-

"CUTTING THEMSELVES OFF FROM THE PARTY." Political cartoon commenting on the Liberal Republicans—the supporters of Horace Greeley's failed 1872 candidacy for president—who continued to distance themselves from the Republican party. The illustration bears the caption: "Full deep is the pit and all ragged the edge / Where are stuck these unfortunate elves; / For they find that to cut a great party in two, / They receive the worst gashes themselves." 10 June 1875.

OFFICE OF THE HISTORIAN OF THE U.S. SENATE

lation on behalf of the city working classes. The election of Woodrow Wilson as president in 1912 all but ensured that congressional Democrats would be a reform force as a matter of party loyalty as well as ideology. In fact, acting as nearly coequal partners in the passage of a major series of reform programs during Wilson's first term, they frequently nudged the president farther than he might otherwise have traveled.

Wilson's decision to bring the United States into World War I in 1917 brought the surge of progressivism to an end by dividing progressives who previously had been substantially united on domestic issues. Many of Wilson's liberal supporters, by nature ambivalent about war, were disillusioned by the inevitably less-than-perfect compromises of the peace settlement. The peace controversy, domestic turmoil, and economic recession ensured a serious defeat for the Democrats, by now the primary advocates of liberal reform.

The New Deal. The Great Depression and the Democratic return to power under Franklin D. Roosevelt were accompanied by a resurgence of the old progressive coalition in Congress and provided liberalism with its greatest moment of the twentieth century. Once again, the Democrats provided most of the votes for reform. But by the end of the 1930s, they were more the party of labor and the urban masses than of the rural South and West; their most important figure was Sen. Robert F. Wagner of New York. They were allied with a significant number of dissenting Republicans in the old insurgent mold, led by Norris and Robert M. La Follette, Jr. Other leading congressional liberals, by chamber (and roughly in order of importance), were as follows: in the Senate, Burton K. Wheeler (Mont.), Alben W. Barkley (Ky.), Hugo L. Black (Ala.), Joseph F. Guffey (Pa.), Harry S. Truman (Mo.), and Claude Pepper (Fla.); in the House, Sam Rayburn (Tex.), John W. McCormack (Mass.), Maury Maverick (Tex.), and Fred M. Vinson (Ky.). These Democrats were joined, ideologically, by Republican representative Tom Amlie of Wisconsin.

Once again, congressional liberals (the term had supplanted "progressive") frequently pushed a cautious president farther than he expected to go, making Roosevelt's New Deal a creation of Congress as well as of the presidency. The result was to identify liberalism more clearly than ever with labor and minority groups politically and with social democracy intellectually. But after the election of 1938, Congress came under the control of an informal but potent "conservative coalition" of Republicans and southern Democrats that more frequently acted as a barrier to reform.

World War II, the Great Society, and Beyond. World War II effectively ended the drive for liberal reform; the war effort required the support of ideological conservatives and created a politics focused on winning a military struggle. Persuaded that American self-interest was best expressed in the global defense of fundamental freedoms against totalitarian regimes, many liberals found it intellectually consistent to move from the struggle against fascism to the Cold War against Soviet communism.

From 1945 to 1963, the overriding demands of the Cold War and de facto conservative control of Congress made liberalism more a matter of conceptualization and proposal than of accomplishment, despite the efforts of Sen. Hubert H. Humphrey (D-Minn.) and other neo–New Deal liberals. President Lyndon B. Johnson, an experienced veteran of Congress and a master legislator benefiting from the public sentiment that followed the assassination of John F. Kennedy, secured a pathbreaking series of Great Society measures—civil rights acts, a multifaceted war on poverty, and numerous spending programs, some aimed at increasing the quality of life, others at enhancing federal benefits for large segments of the population. In this case, far more than in earlier reform epochs, Congress largely reacted to presidential initiatives.

The Great Society, perhaps because it was aimed primarily at a narrow segment of the population—the urban poor—never developed the broad support that the New Deal had achieved. Johnson's commitment to the Vietnam War, moreover, led to increasing opposition on the Hill and disrupted liberalism. Many congressional liberals, supportive of the Great Society, saw the war as possessing no urgent moral purpose (at best) and serving no compelling national interest.

Beginning with the 1960s, moreover, liberals would find themselves increasingly forced to deal not simply with questions of economic distribution or basic constitutional rights but also with a wide range of cultural controversies, among them black militancy, feminism, homosexuality, illegal drug use, the rituals of patriotism, abortion, government and religion, and crime and punishment. Instinctively, they embraced the libertarian side of such issues, a stance that rarely enjoyed broad public support.

The cultural controversies that began in the 1960s continued in one form or another into the 1990s, leaving liberalism, once a popular movement with mass political appeal, heavily dependent on favorable rulings in the courts. Nonetheless, it remained dominant within the Democratic party, which in turn controlled at least one house of Congress during the Republican presidencies of Richard M. Nixon, Gerald Ford, Ronald Reagan, and George Bush. With the election of Bill Clinton in 1992, liberal Democrats once again came to the ascendancy with ambitious programs of social welfare and economic development.

[See also Great Society; New Deal; Progressive Movement.]

BIBLIOGRAPHY

Foner, Eric. *Free Soil, Free Labor, Free Men: The Ideology of the Republican Party before the Civil War.* 1970.

Hamby, Alonzo L. *Liberalism and Its Challengers: F.D.R. to Bush.* 1992.

Hofstadter, Richard. *The Age of Reform: From Bryan to F.D.R.* 1955.

Matusow, Allen J. *The Unraveling of America: A History of Liberalism in the 1960s.* 1984.

Schlesinger, Arthur M. *The Age of Jackson.* 1946.

ALONZO L. HAMBY

LIBRARIES OF THE HOUSE AND SENATE.

As early as the Second Congress, meeting in Philadelphia in 1791 and 1792, both the Senate and House of Representatives adopted resolutions directing each of their respective officers "to procure, and deposit in his office, the laws of the several states" for the use of members. These actions are regarded as the foundation of the present-day libraries of the two chambers, which serve primarily as legislative libraries.

The modern United States Senate Library was formally established as a department under the jurisdiction of the secretary of the Senate in 1870 and 1871, when a suite of rooms in the Capitol was designated for such use and a Senate librarian was appointed. Since then, the library's collections and range of services have gradually expanded to include comprehensive sets of congressional, governmental, legal, and periodical materials as well as both traditional and technology-based information resources. Its staff specializes in compiling legislative histories and in answering legislative and general reference inquiries from the chamber during debates and from senators' and committee offices. In addition to its normal hours of daily operation, the library is open whenever the Senate is in session. Its core holdings are a complete collection of the printed documents of the Senate and House of Representatives that have been produced from the earliest Congresses to the present time. As a government depository library, it also has an extensive collection of publications of the executive branch. Its book holdings consist primarily of political biographies and the published papers of senators, presidents, and other key political figures, along with works of history, political science, international relations, economics, and general reference.

The Library of the House of Representatives, in part because of its physical proximity to the Library of Congress, is a smaller facility than its Senate counterpart. Its collection, while similar to that of the Senate Library, is confined for the most part to materials generated by the House itself. It has few commercially published works and only a lim-

SENATE LIBRARY AT THE CAPITOL. *Left to right,* Senators Harold H. Burton (R-Ohio) and Carl Hayden (D-Ariz.) studying in the library in 1945.

ited number of Senate documents. It is oriented specifically toward directly supporting the House's legislative activities, both those related to the ongoing preparation and development of legislation and those involving the immediate needs of floor, committee, and other legislative operations. The House library is by far the older of the two, as it has evidently been in continuous existence since its origin in 1792; it is known to have been burned by the British in 1814, and a designated librarian has been on the rolls since at least 1824. It is under the jurisdiction of the clerk of the House of Representatives.

Both the Senate and House libraries act as the official internal libraries of record of their respective houses and as such are reserved for the exclusive use of the members of the two chambers and their staffs, committees, and leadership and administrative offices. Both are also distinct from and independent of the Library of Congress, although they often work in close cooperation with the latter's Congressional Research Service.

BIBLIOGRAPHY

DeMaggio, Janice A., ed. *Directory of Special Libraries and Information Centers.* Vol. 1, pt. 2. 1991.
Lewis, E. Raymond. "The House Library." *Capitol Studies* 3 (1975): 107–128.

ROGER K. HALEY and E. RAYMOND LEWIS

LIBRARY COMMITTEE, JOINT. The Joint Committee on the Library is one of five joint committees in the 103d Congress. The panel is a permanent committee that continues to exist from one Congress to the next, but it does not have legislative authority.

Membership on the Joint Committee on the Library includes an equal number of legislators from the House and from the Senate. In the 103d Congress (1993–1995) five senators and five representatives serve on the joint committee. The chairmanship of the committee is rotated; a senator is the committee chair in one Congress, and a member of the House of Representatives is the chair in the next Congress. The committee also has a vice chairman, who is a member of the legislative body that does not hold the chairman position in that Congress.

Congress organized temporary library committees as early as 1800. A permanent Joint Committee on the Library was established on 7 December 1843 and was given the authority to manage the Library of Congress.

In modern times, the Joint Committee on the Library remains an administrative unit that handles routine internal housekeeping matters. Much of the work of both the librarian of Congress and the architect of the Capitol falls under the general direction of the committee.

The jurisdiction of the committee in the 103d Congress includes: (1) management of the Library of Congress; (2) development and maintenance of the Botanic Gardens; (3) receipt of gifts for the benefit of the Library of Congress; and (4) matters related to receiving and placing statues and other works of art in the U.S. Capitol.

BIBLIOGRAPHY

U.S. House of Representatives. Commission on Information and Facilities. *Organizational Effectiveness of the Congressional Research Service.* 95th Cong., 1st sess., 1977. See Paul S. Rundquist, "Congressional Committee Jurisdiction over the Library of Congress," pp. 108–115.

MARY ETTA BOESL

LIBRARY OF CONGRESS. A unit of the legislative branch of the federal government, the Library of Congress is also the national library of the United States. While not designated as the national library by law, it has attained this position through almost two centuries of growth of its collections, facilities, functions, and services.

The library's fundamental mission is to assemble, organize, maintain, and promote access to and use of a general collection of information and human ex-

pression. Its collection of materials in 1992 consisted of 101,395,257 items, including 15,700,905 classified books; 41,467,185 manuscripts; 15,744,298 visual materials, including photographs, posters, prints and drawings, moving images (motion pictures, videotapes, and videodiscs), and other visual media; 9,350,504 microforms; and 4,156,896 maps. The collection contains materials in 470 languages. The library also registers claims to copyrights in the United States filed by individual authors, artists, and composers and by the motion picture, music, computer software, and other industries. In 1992, 605,322 claims were filed.

In addition, the library provides extensive services to many local, national, and international clients. Services include processing and preservation of material; organization and dissemination of information and references; consultation and technical assistance; education; and conduct of artistic, cultural, and ceremonial events. These functions can be classified into eight categories by the primary constituency served:

1. Providing materials, information, research, and technical assistance and consultation to members and committees of the Congress in support of their legislative, oversight, and representational functions, particularly through the Congressional Research Service, a department of the library;

2. Operating reference centers in House and Senate office buildings for the public, twenty-two public reading rooms in the library's three buildings on Capitol Hill, and the public Performing Arts Library at the John F. Kennedy Center for the Performing Arts in Washington, D.C.;

3. Providing books and other informational materials to the executive and judicial branches of the federal government and to state and local governments on request or under cooperative agreements and contracts;

4. Exercising leadership in the professional library community and providing services and assistance to other libraries through the establishment of national and international cataloging standards, original cataloging of books and other materials in systems used by other libraries, distribution of cataloging and reference data, and other methods;

5. Administering the National Library Service for the Blind and Handicapped, a national program serving 750,000 people with more than twenty million materials in braille or recorded form

INTERIOR VIEWS OF THE LIBRARY OF CONGRESS. *Left,* main hall, c. 1900, showing disarray and overcrowded conditions. *Right,* main reading room, April 1991, after renovation; photograph by Reid S. Baker.

LIBRARY OF CONGRESS

available through a network of 160 affiliated libraries in 1993;

6. Conducting educational and cultural activities through The Center for the Book, the American Folk Life Center, the Global Library Project, and the American Memory project;

7. Responding to requests for reference material from organizations and the public at large through the National Reference Service and other services, requests that totaled 1,362,490 in 1991;

8. Conducting international activities, such as acquisition and exchange of informational materials with other countries, in which are involved permanent offices in Rio de Janeiro, Cairo, New Delhi, Karachi, Jakarta, Nairobi, and Moscow, as well as providing limited-term assistance to institutions in other countries, including the emerging democratic parliaments and libraries in Central and Eastern Europe in the early 1990s.

In addition to these functions, the library pursues innovation in information technology to improve access to its collections and to data held by other organizations. It promotes the development of electronic networks among organizations, such as the Linked Systems Project, a computer-to-computer system that is a cooperative effort between the Library of Congress and other research libraries. The library also undertakes special initiatives with congressional approval, as when it assisted the library of the Russian Academy of Sciences in Saint Petersburg in preserving materials damaged by a disastrous fire in 1988.

Origins and Development. The Library of Congress was created as a unit of Congress by the law establishing Washington, D.C., as the site of the federal government. The law, signed by President John Adams in 1800, provided "$5000 for the purchase of such books as may be necessary for the use of Congress . . . and for fitting up a suitable apartment for containing them."

From its inception, many factors have affected the library's development. These have included the personalities and leadership qualities of the thirteen librarians of Congress; the changing needs and priorities of Congress; the interests of members serving on the principal congressional committee with jurisdiction over the library, the Joint Committee on the Library of Congress, established early in the library's history; developments in the library profession and the community of libraries in the United States and abroad; and changing national needs and priorities in domestic and international affairs.

The early period of the library's history (1800–1864) was marked by notable advances and notable disasters. The disasters included fires in 1814, 1825, and 1851 that destroyed many of the library's holdings, then housed in rooms of the Capitol. The 1814 fire resulted from the British attack on Washington. The most notable advance in this period was the acquisition in 1815 of Thomas Jefferson's library of 6,487 volumes (many of which were destroyed in the fire of 1851). Jefferson's cataloging system was used by the library throughout the nineteenth century. The second major advance was the appropriation by Congress in 1853 of $150,000 to replace the books destroyed by the 1851 fire and to construct extensive space and facilities for the library on the west side of the Capitol.

The second period of development, from 1864 to 1897, was a time of extensive expansion of library holdings and facilities. Librarian Ainsworth Rand Spofford dramatically shaped the library during this thirty-three-year period. Spofford, a Cincinnati publisher and writer, was serving as first assistant librarian when he was appointed librarian of Congress by President Abraham Lincoln in 1864. A lover of books, he also proved to be an adept politician and institution builder. With Congress's support, he transformed the library from a small government agency into an important national institution.

During Spofford's tenure, the library was assigned copyright functions by law. Laws required the deposit in the library of free copies of each copyrighted work, greatly increasing the library's holdings. In 1866, the Smithsonian Institution transferred its approximately forty-thousand-volume library to the Library of Congress, and in 1867 the Library of Congress purchased the collection of Peter Force, a Washington publisher, which consisted of 22,529 books on the early history of the United States. In 1886, legislation was enacted authorizing the construction of a library building adjacent to the Capitol grounds, and the building was completed in 1897, the last year of Spofford's term. (He was succeeded by John Russell Long, who served as librarian from 1897 to 1899.)

The massive Italian Renaissance–style building was designed by John L. Smithmeyes and Paul J. Pelz. Dozens of skilled craftsmen and artisans worked on the project, creating one of the most ornate and majestic structures in Washington. Its centerpiece is the dome of the main reading room, 125 feet high and 100 feet in diameter. Now renamed the Thomas Jefferson Building, it was extensively renovated in the late 1980s and early 1990s. An annex, now called the John Adams Building, was opened in 1939, and a third building, the James Madison Building, was added in 1980. The Madison Building contains a total of 1,560,582 square feet of floor space, making it the third-largest building of the federal government and the largest library building in the world.

While the second era of the library was marked by expansion of holdings and facilities, the third period (1899–1939) was distinguished by increased professional leadership of the library community; systemization and professionalization of cataloging and other operations; extension of services to the Congress and others; and diversification of holdings to include musical manuscripts, musical instruments, many additional rare documents and books, and other items.

In this period of consolidation, further expansion, and diversification, the library was led by Herbert Putnam, who served as librarian of Congress from 1899 to 1939. Putnam, a lawyer, was director of the Boston Public Library before he took office on 5 April 1899. He replaced the Jeffersonian classification system with an alphanumeric system (e.g., world history is classified under the letter D, and, under that general category, modern history is classified under the numerals 204 to 725). This system is still used by large libraries in the United States. Putnam exercised strong leadership in the library community by developing centralized services for other libraries, such as the printing and selling of catalog cards at cost and a program of interlibrary loans.

To meet Congress's increasing needs for information and technical, legal, and other services, Putnam worked with interested members in developing the Legislative Reference Service, which was formally established as a department of the library in 1915.

Putnam also attracted more gifts from private

Figure 1. Organization of the Library of Congress

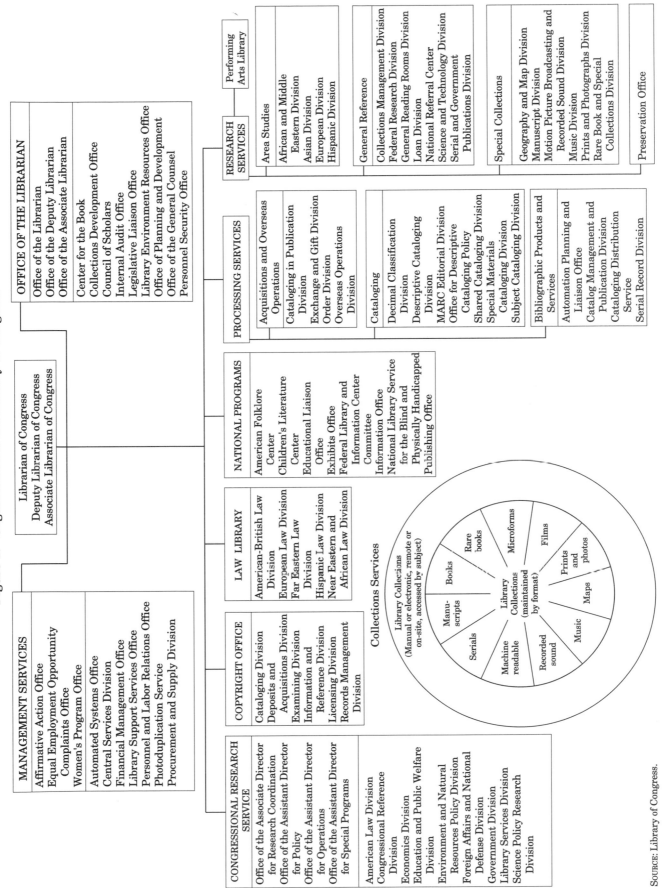

SOURCE: Library of Congress.

donors than did his predecessors, and he proposed creating the Library of Congress Trust Fund to receive them. Congress enacted this proposal into law in 1925. The largest gift received was from Elizabeth Sprague Coolidge, who donated funds to construct an auditorium for the performance of chamber music. Gertrude Clarke Whittall provided perhaps the most unusual gift—five Stradivarius instruments, with an endowment to cover the cost of concerts using the instruments. In this period, the Hispanic Division reading room was donated to the library by the Hispanic Society of America and its president, Archer M. Huntington. Putnam initiated several special divisions, such as the program for acquisition of American folk songs, now part of the library's American Folk Life Center. He also was the first librarian to name a consultant in poetry to the library. This position was the predecessor to the poet laureate.

In the most recent period, 1939 to 1992, five librarians provided leadership that especially emphasized increasing service to Congress and strengthening the library's national and international roles. Archibald MacLeish (1939–1945) developed a strong fiscal and administrative structure. Luther Evans (1945–1953) stressed increased foreign acquisitions and established the Science Division. L. Quincy Mumford (1954–1974) developed automation in cataloging. One of his most notable accomplishments was his defense of the location of the library in the legislative branch against an effort by the Kennedy administration to transfer the library to the executive and to designate it officially the National Library of the United States. In 1970 he oversaw conversion of the Legislative Reference Service into the Congressional Research Service (CRS) through the Legislative Reorganization Act of 1970.

Daniel Boorstein (1975–1987) emphasized making the library accessible to readers and researchers. He created the Council of Scholars to advise the library on developments in scholarship and was instrumental in establishing The Center for the Book, which promotes public interest in the history and culture of the book. James H. Billington (1987–) has emphasized the potential of technology to make the Library of Congress a "library without walls." In Billington's vision, the library will expand its service to people nationwide through electronic links to local libraries and other initiatives.

Governance and Organization. As a unit of the legislative branch, the Library of Congress is governed by the Congress through the Joint Committee on the Library. The committee consists of five representatives and five senators. Appropriations are made by the legislative branch subcommittees of the House and Senate Appropriations committees. Other committees, such as the Joint Committee on Printing, also oversee certain aspects of the library's operations.

The librarian of Congress is nominated by the president and confirmed by the Senate. The librarian submits an annual report, which constitutes an official record of the activities of the library, to the president of the Senate and the Speaker of the House. The Trust Fund of the library is overseen by a board composed of the librarian of Congress, the secretary of the Treasury, the chairman of the Joint Committee on the Library, and ten private citizens (two appointed by the U.S. president, four by the House Speaker, and four by the Senate majority leader).

In 1990, the Library of Congress established the James Madison Council, the library's first general-purpose private-sector advisory body. The council's mission is to support the library's outreach efforts to the public, which include conferences, exhibits, and fellowships. In 1991, the fifty council members each made contributions of $10,000 to $100,000 to the library's public outreach efforts. The National Film Preservation Board advises the librarian on the selection each year of twenty-five films for the National Film Registry, designed to preserve prints of notable films at least ten years after their release. An eight-member board of trustees oversees the American Folk Life Center, and other committees and individuals advise the library from time to time on other aspects of its operations.

Following his 1987 appointment as librarian of Congress, James Billington initiated a broad strategic management and planning review process to examine the library's goals, objectives, and operations on a continuing basis and to develop a dynamic and flexible approach to the library's structure and operations. Billington's initiatives are designed to make the library a future-oriented institution open to opportunities for organizational, technological, and other forms of change in the twenty-first century.

As of 1992, the Library of Congress employed 5,050 people. For fiscal year 1992, the Library of Congress received appropriations that totaled $322,228,000; this represented a 9 percent increase over 1991. Appropriated funds are supplemented by reimbursements and receipts for goods and services, gifts, trusts, service fees, and other funds resulting in a total of almost $400 million under the library's control in 1992.

Librarians of Congress

John Beckley, 1802–1807
Patrick Magruder, 1807–1815
George Watterston, 1815–1829
John Silva Meehan, 1829–1861
John C. Stephenson, 1861–1864
Ainsworth Rand Spofford, 1864–1897
John Russell Young, 1897–1899
Herbert Putnam, 1899–1939
Archibald MacLeish, 1939–1944
Luther Harris Evans, 1945–1953
Lawrence Quincy Mumford, 1954–1974
Daniel J. Boorstein, 1975–1987
James H. Billington, 1987–

With pressure on the federal budget generated by the deficit, the library in the 1990s has struggled to resolve competing claims for allocations of the limited increases in its funding. These claims included reductions in backlogs of unprocessed materials; modernization of the library's computer systems; installation of new technologies to improve and enlarge its data base; and special initiatives in response to congressional concerns, such as increasing the library's resources on the relationship of science and technology to business.

Assessment. The competing demands and pressures faced by the Library of Congress are a product not of failure but of its success in responding to and initiating change over two centuries. The diversity and plurality of the library's operations are an expression of the pluralistic nature of American democracy, the rate and magnitude of changes in information technology, and the changing role of the United States in the international economic and political order. Somewhat ironically, the implicit tension between the library's role in serving Congress and its role as a national library has increased its influence in national life. The materials, information, analysis, research, and consultation and advice the library provides Congress through the CRS are indispensable to the national legislature. Because Congress appropriates funds and authorizes agency activities, the library has benefited from Congress's involvement and support. This support has allowed the institution to remain responsive to shifting historical currents, sometimes at the cost of orderly development. At the same time, the library's development as a national institution with ties to the community of libraries, scholars, publishers, and artistic and cultural groups has deep-

ened its expertise and capacity to serve Congress, other clients, and the public.

The strength of the Library of Congress lies in the plurality as well as in the expertise of its operations. In a period of budget constraints, tension from competing priorities—assembling, processing, and preserving knowledge; serving Congress; and serving other constituencies—will persist. This tension has strengthened the library for almost two centuries.

[*See also* Library Committee, Joint.]

BIBLIOGRAPHY

Annual Report of the Librarian of Congress. 1991.
Cole, John Y. *For Congress and the Nation: A Chronological History of the Library of Congress.* 1979.
Dalrymple, Helen. *The Library of Congress.* 1992.
Goodrum, Charles A. *Treasures of the Library of Congress.* 1991.
Goodrum, Charles A., and Helen W. Dalrymple. *The Library of Congress.* 1982.
Library of Congress. *Librarians of Congress: 1802–1974.* 1977.
Nelson, Josephus, and Judith Farley. *Full Circle: Ninety Years of Service in the Main Reading Room.* 1991.
Simpson, Andrew. *The Library of Congress.* 1989.
Small, Herbert. *The Library of Congress: Its Architecture and Decoration.* 1982.

JAMES D. CARROLL

LIMITED TEST BAN TREATY (14 U.S.T. 1313–1387). The Treaty Banning Nuclear Weapons Tests in the Atmosphere, in Outer Space, and Under Water was signed in 1963 by the United States, the Soviet Union, and Britain and was generally viewed as a positive contribution to ecological safety and to arms control and also (just one year after the Cuban missile crisis) as a new and positive development in East-West relations.

The treaty also signaled an important compromise between (U.S. decision makers who favored a total ban on all nuclear testing and those who, either because of the needs of weapons development or because of fears that the Soviet Union might cheat on any test ban by means of clandestine underground detonations, favored continued nuclear weapons testing. Several congressional committees played important roles in sorting out these contending positions and in developing a consensus supporting the compromise represented by this partial test ban. The Joint Committee on Atomic Energy tended to endorse and voice the attitudes of the Atomic Energy Commission, which stressed the unfinished business in weapons design that could

"I GUESS THE FINE PRINT'S BEEN READ CAREFULLY!" Political cartoon by Gib Crockett, *Washington Star*, 19 August 1963.   LIBRARY OF CONGRESS

be completed only by further testing and which worried about the risks of Soviet cheating. The Senate Foreign Relations Committee, and in particular its Subcommittee on Disarmament, tended instead to reflect the strong feelings of Sen. Hubert H. Humphrey (D-Minn.) about the potential political and geophysical benefits of a cessation of nuclear testing, and thus agreed more with the views of the State Department and the Arms Control and Disarmament Agency (ACDA) within the executive branch. The hearings of these committees provided important forums for the development of the arguments. Some gaps were bridged by important members of Congress, for example, Sen. Albert A. Gore, Sr. (D-Tenn.), and Sen. Bourke B. Hickenlooper (R-Iowa), who served on both committees (and also as congressional advisers attached to the U.S. delegation in Geneva negotiating the test ban).

The idea of tolerating underground testing (where compliance with a ban would be most difficult to monitor) while banning other kinds of tests emerged from many different sources, not the least important of which had been suggestions for such a compromise made by Senator Gore in 1958 and Senator Humphrey in 1959.

The national consensus behind President John F. Kennedy's decision to sign the 1963 partial test ban

was demonstrated by the ease with which the Senate ratified it, by a vote of 80 to 19.

BIBLIOGRAPHY

Goldblat, Jozef, and David Cox, eds. *Nuclear Weapons Tests: Prohibition or Limitation?* 1988.
Jacobson, Harold Karan, and Eric Stein. *Diplomats, Scientists, and Politicians: The United States and the Nuclear Test Ban Negotiations.* 1966.

GEORGE H. QUESTER

LINCOLN, ABRAHAM (1809–1865), representative from Illinois and sixteenth president of the United States. Lincoln served one term in the U.S. House of Representatives. In 1846 he ran as a Whig in Illinois's 7th Congressional District, beating Democrat Peter Cartwright, a Methodist minister. Illinois was an overwhelmingly Democratic state, and competition among ambitious Whigs to be the party's candidate in this, the state's lone Whig district, was fierce. Lincoln had left the Illinois state legislature in 1842 but for four years had been forced to bow to the ambitions of other Whigs.

Term in Congress. Lincoln was elected on 3 August 1846; by mid-month he had chosen to answer charges, circulated during the campaign, that he was irreligious. The resulting statement proved to be the only public pronouncement on his religious convictions that Lincoln ever made. He affirmed that he had never been a member of "any Christian Church" but denied that he had ever spoken disrespectfully of religion or stated that the Scriptures were untrue. He admitted "that in early life" he "was inclined to believe in . . . the 'Doctrine of Necessity,'" a sort of village skeptic's fatalism, but he said that he had given up arguing for it more than five years before. "I do not think I could myself," Lincoln added, "be brought to support a man for office, whom I knew to be an open enemy of, and scoffer at, religion."

The timing of elections for Congress was then quite irregular, and Lincoln now waited sixteen months before going to Washington to assume his place in the 30th Congress. Most of the Whigs who would be his colleagues ran in opposition to the Mexican War, which had begun in the spring of 1846. Lincoln himself had spoken at a bipartisan rally in Springfield to recruit volunteers for the war on 30 May, but he was not otherwise on public record on the issue. He did follow events closely and feared that President James K. Polk and the

ABRAHAM LINCOLN. Photograph by Mathew Brady, 27 February 1860. LIBRARY OF CONGRESS

Democrats would attempt to elevate Democratic generals over the highest-ranking generals, Winfield Scott and Zachary Taylor, who were not known to be Democrats. Such partisan "rascality" in military appointments proved to be a practice that Lincoln, when he became president himself fifteen years later, would scrupulously avoid.

By the time Congress convened on 6 December 1847, all fighting in Mexico had ceased. But Lincoln, whose Illinois friends were eager to see him distinguish himself, introduced a series of resolutions on 22 December demanding to know the spot where American soldiers had been attacked on U.S. soil—the ostensible reason for starting the war. Then, on 12 January 1848, he gave a formal speech arguing that the controversial "spot" lay in territory not clearly belonging to either Texas or Mexico.

Lincoln franked copies of the speech to his district, as was customary.

The young representative's stand on the war made William H. Herndon, his law partner back in Springfield, uneasy, and there ensued between them a private correspondence in which Lincoln made clear that he would vote for supplies for the troops in the field, that the Whig leaders fighting in the war nevertheless did not believe the Democratic president's explanation of its cause, and that the Constitution gave the "war-making power to Congress" and that support for President Polk's position was tantamount to surrendering that power to one man and putting "our President where kings have always stood."

In sum, Lincoln considered the war unconstitutional and unnecessary. Polk, he thought, had started it to distract voters from the president's surrender to Great Britain's demands in a recent dispute over the Oregon boundary. Although he lived in Washington at Mrs. Sprigg's boardinghouse, known as a residence of antislavery Whigs, Lincoln "did not believe with many . . . fellow citizens that this war was originated for the purpose of extending slave territory." It was, rather, "a war of conquest brought into existence to catch votes." Thus Lincoln did not agree with the abolitionist interpretation of the Mexican War, nor did he oppose the war because of an internationalist outlook. Years later, when talking about the discovery of gold on land acquired as a result of the Mexican War, Lincoln boasted that "yankees, almost instantly, discover[ed] gold in California, which had been trodden upon, and over-looked by indians and Mexican greasers, for centuries."

Though not eager for territorial expansion, Representative Lincoln assumed a compromise position on that question. He endorsed the "defensive-line" strategy devised by General Taylor to hold the territory in northern Mexico he had taken but not to campaign for more. Lincoln voted against a resolution that would have demanded no territorial indemnity from Mexico.

Lincoln's stand on the Mexican War was the most important aspect of his experience as a member of Congress. In dealings with other Whigs, he repeatedly pressed his position on the Texas boundary and the origins of the war. Fortunately for him, he handled the issue carefully, because he had to defend his record on it in future political campaigns.

Lincoln otherwise devoted his attention to the presidential election of 1848. He became an enthusiastic supporter of war hero Zachary Taylor's nom-

INAUGURATION OF ABRAHAM LINCOLN. On the steps of the Capitol, 4 March 1861.

LIBRARY OF CONGRESS

ination, telling Herndon that it took the Democrats "on the blind side. It turns the war thunder against them." He attended the convention in Philadelphia at which Taylor was nominated.

During the congressional recess in the late summer and autumn of 1848, Lincoln campaigned for Taylor in Maryland, Massachusetts, and Illinois. Meanwhile, on 20 June 1848, he delivered a speech on internal improvements for the underdeveloped West, of which he had long been an enthusiastic advocate. President Polk had vetoed a rivers and harbors bill, partly on constitutional grounds, and Lincoln's speech was unusual for its attention to the question of constitutionality. Lincoln argued that the "question of improvements is verging to a final crisis; and the friends of the policy must now battle, and battle manfully, or surrender all." His next speech, delivered on 27 July, was a purely political one meant to be printed and circulated as a

campaign pamphlet. It concerned the presidential question and asserted that Taylor's lack of platform or record constituted no problem for voters, because the candidate was pledged to follow the will of Congress in such matters as internal improvements and the tariff. In deriding Democratic candidate Lewis Cass's claim of having a distinguished military record, Lincoln took the unusual step of ridiculing his own fruitless experience as a volunteer in the Black Hawk Indian War and likening it to Cass's military career. (Ambitious first-term congressmen were not usually given to making light of their own military records.)

Lincoln decided not to run for reelection, essentially obeying the principle he had attempted to establish in the past, that the district should be rotated among Whig leaders. He returned to Congress for the session that began on 7 December 1848 as a lame duck—as was, in fact, President Polk.

Now Lincoln openly exhibited his antislavery sentiments. He voted to exclude slavery from territory acquired as a result of the Mexican War. He even drafted a bill to abolish slavery in the District of Columbia. Its provisions included government compensation to masters who freed their slaves and a gradual approach to freeing the rest. He would have declared free all children born to slave mothers resident in the District after 1 January 1850, though they were to serve an apprenticeship to their current masters. Members of Congress temporarily resident in the District were exempted, and the whole scheme was contingent upon majority approval of the white males over twenty-one who had resided in the District for a year. Lacking significant support from his colleagues, Lincoln never formally introduced the measure as a bill. He did, however, vote for a bill to abolish the slave trade in the District of Columbia. It failed.

Lincoln was a diligent representative who sought patronage appointments for his constituents (though without much success during a Democratic administration) and sent them the government documents—mainly congressional speeches—they were eager to see. The work, however, proved ungratifying. He compared making speeches in the halls of Congress to speaking in court in Illinois. His wife, Mary Todd Lincoln, who came to Washington with him, went home after about four months. Lincoln afterward wrote her a revealing letter:

When you were here, I thought you hindered me some in attending to business; but now, having nothing but business—no variety—it has grown exceedingly tasteless to me. I hate to sit down and direct documents, and I hate to stay in this old room by myself. You know I told you in last sunday's letter, I was going to make a little speech during the week; but the week has passed away without my getting a chance to do so; and now my interest in the subject has passed away too.

It made him "a little impatient" when Whig newspapers in his district failed to publish speeches dutifully sent to them from Washington. When his political associate and friend David Davis wrote him near the end of his term, Lincoln responded wearily, "Out of more than three hundred letters received this session, yours is the second one manifesting the least interest for me personally."

After Congress adjourned, Lincoln returned home without much regret and applied himself more diligently than ever to his law practice. He was aroused to run for office again only after the passage of the Kansas-Nebraska Act in 1854, and then he vied—twice—for the U.S. Senate.

Lincoln's political career in Illinois and his single term in Congress are often viewed as failures and thus an astonishing prologue to his success as president. But such a view is distorted. Lincoln enjoyed as successful a political career in Illinois as any Whig could in so overwhelmingly Democratic a state. The Whig party never elected a governor or senator there, and for much of the time, the single Whig congressional district had to be shared to maintain party harmony.

Lincoln's term in Congress was not a failure either, though he opted not to run for reelection and though the district went Democratic in the next election. Historians have often pointed to the local unpopularity of Lincoln's opposition to the Mexican War as the cause of these developments. But the Whig candidate in 1848, Stephen T. Logan, a former law partner of Lincoln's, proved a hopelessly inept campaigner. As for reelection, Lincoln had many reasons not to seek it, the most powerful being his own belief in rotating the seat among Whig hopefuls.

Presidency. As president of the United States from 1861 to 1865, Lincoln, now a Republican, enjoyed what every president hopes for, a Congress dominated by his own political party. This circumstance, as well as Lincoln's Whig political heritage, dictated that he would seldom interfere with Congress. He rarely used the veto and generally consulted the relevant members of Congress on appointments to office, as was customary.

President Lincoln did develop a belief in the very considerable powers of the executive branch in wartime. Less than two weeks after the firing on Fort Sumter, he suspended the privilege of the writ of habeas corpus around Washington, a power most authorities had assumed to belong to Congress. Though at first Lincoln thought Congress might have some power to legislate against slavery in wartime, he decided by 1862 that the powers of the commander in chief, the so-called war powers, were the only constitutional authority for attacking slavery in order to damage an enemy in war. Democrats complained that the Emancipation Proclamation, announced by him on 22 September 1862 and justified as a military measure, was unconstitutional, but Republicans, overjoyed by this blow against the rebellion and slavery, did not raise the question of presidential authority. Lincoln also assumed the power to appoint governors of conquered Confederate states. On 3 March 1863, Congress endorsed suspension of the writ of habeas corpus without making clear whether the president's previous unilateral suspensions were legal in the absence of such endorsement.

But many members of Congress from the president's own party came into conflict with him over his exercise of power to reconstruct Confederate states. The Wade-Davis bill, passed by Congress on 2 July 1864, insisted on a different approach to reconstruction, imposing a loyalty threshold for the population of any state hopeful of being readmitted—which surely could not be met until the war was over—and requiring the abolition of slavery in any restored state. Lincoln refused to sign the bill, in effect giving it a pocket veto. The struggle between the president and Republicans who supported the bill was as much over who was to lead reconstruction as over specific features of restoration plans, though Lincoln was more eager to restore the states quickly than many Republicans in Congress. On 8 July the president issued a proclamation explaining his refusal to sign the bill. He insisted that he was "unprepared . . . to be inflexibly committed to any single plan of restoration," but he also refused "to declare a constitutional competency in Congress to abolish slavery in States." In a response called the Wade-Davis Manifesto, Lincoln's proclamation was described as a "studied outrage on the legislative authority of the people." President Lincoln and some members of Congress were struggling over the issue at the time of his murder in April 1865.

STEPHEN A. DOUGLAS. Proponent of the Kansas-Nebraska Act and Democratic candidate in the 1860 presidential election.   NATIONAL ARCHIVES

BIBLIOGRAPHY

Basler, Roy P., et al., eds. *The Collected Works of Abraham Lincoln.* 9 vols. 1953–1955.
Riddle, Donald W. *Congressman Abraham Lincoln.* 1957.
Riddle, Donald W. *Lincoln Runs for Congress.* 1948.
Thomas, Benjamin P. *Abraham Lincoln: A Biography.* 1952.

MARK E. NEELY, JR.

LINCOLN-DOUGLAS DEBATES. On the afternoon of 16 June 1858, the Republican state convention meeting in Springfield, Illinois, declared unanimously that Abraham Lincoln was "its first and only choice for the United States Senate, as the successor of Stephen A. Douglas." Thus began an exhausting campaign, in which Lincoln delivered sixty-three major speeches and Douglas fifty-nine, in addition to countless lesser appearances. At the end of July, arrangements were made

for the two candidates to "divide time" on the same platform at seven different locations in the state.

The historic role of these debates is ultimately to be found in the fact that they were between the men who would become the two principal candidates for president in 1860. In 1858, however, their importance lay in the fact that they marked the first great turn toward the popular election of senators. Before the Seventeenth Amendment (1913), senators were elected by joint sessions of the state legislatures. Candidates for the Senate lobbied the legislators, not the voters. Now, five months before the fall elections, Illinois voters were being presented with the rival candidates, and the choice of senator became a leading consideration in determining which party a voter would follow in choosing a state representative or senator. The 1858 Illinois popular vote was close, with the Republicans holding a slight edge in statewide totals. But thirteen state senators were not up for election; eight of them were Democrats, and Douglas was reelected.

The central issue that divided Lincoln and Douglas—the only one under serious discussion—was that of slavery in the territories. As chairman of the Senate Committee on Territories, Douglas in 1854 had sponsored a bill repealing the Missouri Compromise prohibition of slavery in Kansas and Nebraska. Douglas replaced the exclusion of slavery with a provision that allowed the settlers in the territories to decide the question for themselves. Over and over, Douglas professed in the debates that he did not care whether slavery was "voted up or voted down" in Kansas (or any other territory). He cared only for the sacred right of the people to decide for themselves.

Underlying this point of contention was the more fundamental question of whether blacks were included in the proposition of equality in the Declaration of Independence. Lincoln repeatedly pointed out that if an exception could be made of blacks, why not of others—for example, Roman Catholics or foreigners, as the Know-Nothings would have done. In the end, no one's rights would be safe, and government by the consent of the governed would be an absurdity. Lincoln denied Chief Justice Roger B. Taney's assertion in the 1857 Dred Scott decision that "the right of property in a slave is distinctly and expressly affirmed in the Constitution." Even if, as Douglas argued, Taney was right, then, as Lincoln pointed out, the constitutional obligation of Congress to guarantee police protection to slaveowners in the territories would rest upon the same foundation as the constitutional obligation to provide for the return of fugitive slaves. "Popular sovereignty" would in fact be a device for nullifying a constitutional right and, ironically, would put Douglas into the camp of the abolitionists, who called for the nullification of the fugitive slave law.

Lincoln's relentless exploitation of the incompatibility of "popular sovereignty" with the Dred Scott decision became the rock upon which Douglas's political career foundered. In May of 1860, the seven states of the Deep South seceded from the Democratic National Convention in Charleston, South Carolina. They did so because the majority in the convention, which was about to nominate Douglas, refused in the name of popular sovereignty to grant their demand for a slave code for the Territories. This was what Lincoln had said they were entitled to, if the Dred Scott decision was correct. It was this secession that split the Democratic Party and contributed decisively to Lincoln's election to the presidency. It could be said to mark the true beginning of the Civil War.

BIBLIOGRAPHY

Angle, Paul M., ed. *Created Equal? The Complete Lincoln-Douglas Debates of 1858.* 1958. Repr. 1991.

Fehrenbacher, Don E. *Prelude to Greatness: Lincoln in the 1850s.* 1962.

Jaffa, Harry V., and Robert W. Johannsen, eds. *In the Name of the People: Speeches and Writings of Lincoln and Douglas in the Ohio Campaign of 1859.* 1959.

Johannsen, Robert W. *Stephen A. Douglas.* 1973.

HARRY V. JAFFA

LINE ITEM VETO. *See* Item Veto.

LITERATURE ON CONGRESS. [*This article focuses on fictional literature. For comparable treatment of motion pictures, see* Movies on Congress. *For discussion of academic research on Congress and an analytic bibliography of publications about Congress, see* Congress, *articles on* Bibliographical Guide *and* The Study of Congress.] Congress as an institution and members of Congress as individuals were slow to gain a place in American fiction. Early American writers such as Hugh Henry Brackenridge, Washington Irving, and James Fenimore Cooper had strong political opinions—Irving observed of Congress in 1833: "The grand debate in the Senate occupied my mind as intensively for three weeks, as did ever a dramatic representation." But their fiction (reflecting the taste of their audience) dwelt rather on more exotic places, people, and times: Indians and the frontier, Moorish Spain, and an earlier America that already seemed to be part of a golden past.

Nor did prominent successors such as Nathaniel Hawthorne and Herman Melville turn to the halls of Congress, although theirs was the era of the great legislative struggle over slavery and states' rights. Only in the wake of the Civil War did members of Congress become conspicuous protagonists in novels that gained wide public attention, two of which won a lasting place in American literature: Mark Twain and Charles Dudley Warner's *The Gilded Age: A Tale of To-day* (1873) and Henry Adams's *Democracy* (1880, published anonymously). Less well known is John W. De Forest's series of congressional novels, *Playing the Mischief* (1875), *Honest John Vane* (1875), and *Justine's Lovers* (1878).

TWO ILLUSTRATIONS FROM MARK TWAIN'S *THE GILDED AGE*. Both depicting Sen. Abner Dilworthy. 1902 edition.

OFFICE OF THE HISTORIAN OF THE U.S. SENATE

These political satires had a common subject—the American political process—and a common theme: its grossness and venality. Sen. Abner Dilworthy in *The Gilded Age* was modeled on Kansas Radical Republican senator Samuel C. Pomeroy (who was caught buying a vote in the state legislature for his reelection but was cleared by a Senate select committee). The character of Illinois senator Silas P. Ratcliffe in *Democracy* in good part resembled James G. Blaine (R-Maine), with more than a dash of Roscoe Conkling (R-N.Y.) thrown in. Blaine was incensed by the portrayal but apparently never learned the identity of *Democracy*'s author.

Twain's biographer Justin Kaplan has called *The Gilded Age* "an angry and reactionary book about Americans . . . a novel of reaction and despair" (Kaplan, 1966, p. 166). It reflected Twain's pessimistic view of humanity, inflated (as was the case with many writers and intellectuals of his generation) by a sense of idealism and hope betrayed in the wake of the great moral crusade for the Union and against slavery. As he bitterly put it, "This nation is not reflected in Charles Sumner, but in Henry Ward Beecher, Benjamin Butler, Whitelaw Reid, Wm. M. Tweed. *Politics* are not going to cure moral ulcers like these, nor the decaying body they fester upon."

Democracy is a comparably powerful assault on the venality of American politics. Madeleine Lee, the novel's heroine, in fact represents Henry Adams himself, and the book is full of contempt for a political process in which an Adams could find no place. He later told his brother Brooks, "I bade politics good-bye when I published *Democracy*."

De Forest had been a Civil War officer and a district commander for the Freedmen's Bureau and

Novels about Congress

LATE NINETEENTH CENTURY

Curtis, George W. *Trumps*. 1861.

Twain, Mark, and Charles Dudley Warner. *The Gilded Age*. 1873.

De Forest, John W. *Honest John Vane*. 1875.

De Forest, John W. *Playing the Mischief*. 1875.

Adams, Henry. *Democracy*. 1879.

Crawford, F. Marion. *An American Politician*. 1885.

Hamlin, Myra. *A Politician's Daughters*. 1886.

Locke, David R. *The Demagogue*. 1891.

Garland, Hamlin. *A Member of the Third House*. 1892.

Garland, Hamlin. *A Spoil of Office*. 1892.

Tarkington, Booth. *The Gentleman from Indiana*. 1899.

EARLY TWENTIETH CENTURY

Atherton, Gertrude. *Senator North*. 1900.

Grant, Robert. *Unleavened Bread*. 1900.

Whitlock, Brand. *The Thirteenth District*. 1902.

Lewis, Alfred Henry. *The President*. 1904.

Phillips, David Graham. *Joshua Craig*. 1909.

MID- AND LATE TWENTIETH CENTURY

Fergusson, Harvey. *Capitol Hill*. 1923.

Hackett, Francis. *The Senator's Last Night*. 1924.

Adams, Samuel. *Revelry*. 1926.

Huston, McCready. *Dear Senator*. 1928.

Stribling, Thomas S. *The Sound Wagon*. 1935.

Kimbrough, Edward. *From Hell to Breakfast*. 1941.

Dos Passos, John. *District of Columbia*. 1952.

Chatterton, Ruth. *The Betrayers*. 1953.

Drury, Allen. *Advise and Consent*. 1959.

Vidal, Gore. *Washington, D.C.* 1967.

Vidal, Gore. *1876*. 1976.

Truman, Margaret. *Murder on Capitol Hill*. 1981.

Hart, Gary, and William S. Cohen. *The Double Man*. 1985.

Wicker, Tom. *Donovan's Wife*. 1992.

---

unsuccessfully sought a diplomatic post under President Rutherford B. Hayes. His flawed hero, the initially innocent representative John Vane, who quickly turned into a spoilsman, had gone to Congress believing that "general legislation was the big thing, reform, foreign relations, sectional questions, constitutional points, and so on." A more experienced colleague soon set him right: "All exploded, my dear sir! All gone out with Calhoun and Webster, or at the latest, with Lincoln and Stanton.

All dead issues, as dead as the war. Special legislation—or, as some people prefer to call it, finance—is the sum and substance of Congressional business in our day."

For all the emphasis on political corruption during the Progressive period of the early twentieth century, Congress—and indeed politics in general—did not figure largely in the imaginative literature of the time. The major novelists—Theodore Dreiser, Stephen Crane, Frank Norris, Jack London—were more interested in exploring individual crises of conscience and capacity, or the systemic problems of American society and a capitalist economy, than they were in the halls of Congress. What went on in the legislature attracted muckraking journalists such as Lincoln Steffens and David Graham Phillips, whose exposé "The Treason of the Senate" (1906) was an acerbic portrait of that "rich men's club."

The late twentieth century has seen more congressional novels than at any time since the late nineteenth century. The pattern was set by Allen Drury's enormously successful *Advise and Consent* (1959). Its subject matter and moral stance differ in interesting ways from its Gilded Age predecessors. Far from focusing on the individual foibles and weaknesses of members of Congress in order to make a point about corruption in the democratic process, *Advise and Consent* sees Congress rising above the strengths and weaknesses of its characters, as it weathers the ideological, political, and personal storms over the confirmation of a secretary of State. In this the novel echoes its near contemporary, *The Caine Mutiny* (1952), and the general post–World War II confidence in American institutions.

Gore Vidal's political novels, *Washington, D.C.* (1967), *Burr* (1973), *1876* (1976), and *Lincoln* (1984), are just as representative of the disillusionment with American institutions that became endemic from the mid 1960s on. They are chockablock with public figures drawn (or caricatured) from life, but their real theme is a distaste for the democratic process similar to that of Twain and Adams almost a century before.

Most congressional novels since the 1950s have been essentially entertainments capitalizing on the drama inherent in that institution. Murder, sex, and power are sure-fire fuel for popular fiction. Examples of the genre include Margaret Truman's *Murder on Capitol Hill* (1981), and *The Double Man* (1985), coauthored by senators Gary Hart and William S. Cohen. As Sen. Robert C. Byrd observed,

"If you put a senator in a whodunit, he probably did it."

Newspaper columnist Tom Wicker's *Donovan's Wife* (1992) suggests that the congressional novel has inherent limitations. The book appeals to contemporary taste by detailing a senatorial campaign plagued by all the ills of contemporary politics: dirty (right-wing) politics, a hero (as it happens, a political columnist like the author), and his (of course sexy) crusading consort. But contemporary fiction about Congress appears to be unable to convey what it is really like to live and work in that complex social institution.

BIBLIOGRAPHY

Blotner, Joseph. *The Modern American Political Novel, 1900–1960.* 1966.

Byrd, Robert C. *The Senate, 1789–1989: Addresses on the History of the United States Senate.* Vol. 2. Chap. 21, "The Senate in Literature and Film."

Kaplin, Justin E. *Mr. Clemens and Mark Twain: A Biography.* 1991.

Kemme, Tom. *Political Fiction, the Spirit of the Age, and Allen Drury.* 1987.

Milne, Gordon. *The American Political Novel.* 1966.

MORTON KELLER

LOBBYING. Lobbying is a technique in the political process of advocacy and persuasion. As applied to Congress it is the practice of convincing individual members or groups of members to take a particular course of action to the benefit of the interest or interests represented by the lobbyist.

Perhaps the most important feature of lobbying in the American system is its status as a constitutionally protected freedom. The First Amendment guarantees every citizen the rights of free speech and assembly, and the right "to petition the Government for redress of grievances." Court decisions have consistently upheld this principle, but have also determined that lobbying is not a totally unfettered right and is subject to certain prohibitions, limitations, and disclosures.

Because lobbying is both protected under the Constitution and encouraged by the democratic nature of American politics and society, the role of interest groups and lobbyists has been pivotal in the history of the republic. The Founders considered as a matter of first importance the question of balancing self-interested "factions" with what would be best for the new nation. Lobbyists were prominent in the economic expansion of the new nation and in the social upheavals of the late nineteenth and mid-twentieth centuries, and they are conspicuous in the current era of postindustrial change.

A number of considerations make it important to understand the role of interest groups and lobbyists today. First, the interest group system has grown extremely large and shows no signs of slowing down (although this does not mean that lobbyists are more effective or successful); more diverse and different types of interests are represented than ever before; and the techniques of interest representation have multiplied, causing confusion for policymakers, who struggle to separate the honest voices from the clamor. Second, attitudes and beliefs among leaders and the public about lobbying are complex and paradoxical; some blame the interests for policy stalemate or even national decline. Third, federal regulation of lobbying appears to have gained ground as a strategy to mitigate the stresses caused by interest group activities. Finally, the explosion of interest group activity does not seem to be a uniquely American occurrence: other democracies are now considering strategies to contend with special interest pressures.

Origins. The term *lobbying* is English in origin. Its common usage dates from the mid-seventeenth century and derives from the large public room off the floor of the House of Commons where members of Parliament could be approached by special pleaders.

In the United States, the political and philosophical justification for interest group lobbying can be traced to the nation's formative years. In *Federalist* 10, James Madison discussed how the new Constitution proposed to treat the role of "faction"—today, the term is *interests*—in the new democracy. Factions, he wrote disapprovingly, "are united and actuated by some common impulse of passion, or of interest, adverse to the rights of other citizens, or to the permanent and aggregate interests of the community." In one respect, he believed that factions should be constrained because they represent only the interests of the few at the expense of the larger common good. But in another respect, they are a natural and unavoidable part of democratic governance; to constrain them would be to deny them their liberty, an unacceptable consequence. Control of the "mischief of faction" in a democratic republic, Madison concluded, could best be accomplished by promoting competition among groups and by devising a system of procedural checks and balances to reduce the power of any single group, majority or minority.

The Founders' concerns were realized as the new Constitution was implemented: factional groups within Congress coalesced almost immediately, soon leading to an embryonic party system. So, too, individuals and groups appeared at the convening of the First and all subsequent Congresses to press their claims, causes, and interests before the legislature.

Indeed, Madison, Alexander Hamilton, George Washington, and their Federalist colleagues had themselves orchestrated one of the most successful lobbying campaigns in American history. They promoted the idea of a revised national charter, guided the deliberations of the Philadelphia Convention of 1787, and secured state ratification of the Constitution in a campaign that would have been the envy of any modern lobbyist.

Lobbying in the Nineteenth Century. Early lobbying activities had several features. Lobbying was usually conducted by individuals or ad hoc coalitions established for specific purposes and carried forward for a limited duration. Most lobbyists represented commercial or business interests: Congress had the ability to grant concessions, to enact tariffs on foreign goods, to extend patents, to grant railroad right-of-ways, to grant subsidies, licenses, and charters, and in general to encourage commercial and industrial growth. Lobbying techniques included familiar methods of advocacy: legal and technical arguments, the planting of news stories (some reporters were hired by lobbyists or combined the two vocations), the pursuit of personal contacts with influential lawmakers, and appearances at committee proceedings.

By standards that today would be found intolerable, lobbyists offered and lawmakers accepted—and sometimes solicited—money and gifts as bribes and payments for services rendered. One of the better-known cases involved Sen. Daniel Webster of Massachusetts and his relationship with Nicholas Biddle, president of the second Bank of the United States. In 1833, when the question of rechartering the bank was before Congress, Webster was in Biddle's employ. His letter to Biddle soliciting the "usual retainers" to ensure his support is often cited in criticisms of lobbying.

In the explosion of economic and industrial growth following the Civil War, individual lobbyists—who could be retained to promote any bill—began to be replaced by permanent representatives of established interests. In addition to the rail lobby, industrialists' agents successfully lobbied for high tariffs on imported manufactures (a basic element of Republican party platforms) and veterans' organizations sought to expand Civil War pension coverage. Likewise, the Women's Christian Temperance Union and similar groups launched a persistent, and ultimately successful, campaign for prohibition.

Abuses and ethical improprieties, especially during and just following the Grant administration—the Gilded Age—were common during this period, depicting a view of Washington as scandalous, corrupt, and decadent. The poet Walt Whitman characterized "lobbyers" as "crawling serpentine men, the lousy combings and born freedom sellers of the earth." In 1873, an author of a Washington exposé wrote of lobbyists: "Their plan is to rob the public treasury." An 1888 *Dictionary of American Politics* defined *The Lobby* as "a term applied collectively to men that make a business of corruptly influencing legislators."

Although political corruption and lobbying abuses were significant features of late-nineteenth-century politics, recent scholarship (for example, Margaret Susan Thompson, *The "Spider Web": Congress and Lobbying in the Age of Grant,* 1985) suggests that the depiction of lobbyists as a principal cause of governmental ineptitude does not tell the whole story. In the post–Civil War era, both Congress and the executive branch struggled to cope with an ever greater work load caused by increasing responsibilities undertaken by the government. The institutional mechanisms of both branches, however, were still better suited to the less complicated days of the antebellum period. Lobbyists' knowledge of substance and process, this interpretation argues, helped focus legislators' attention on demands that might otherwise have gone unnoticed in a legislature characterized by clogged agendas, obsolete procedures, amateurism, and a lack of professional staff.

Progressive Reaction. By the latter part of the century, the excesses of the Gilded Age gave way to the reforms of the Progressive Era, which included among its aims a frontal assault on lobbying. One element of this assault consisted of the work of the "muckrakers," journalists and writers who exposed social, economic, and political corruption and injustice. Their exposés were enormously influential, and many of them targeted the power of special interests in Washington.

A second point of attack came from reform-minded politicians, the best known of whom was President Theodore Roosevelt. Roosevelt's drive against big corporate interests—oil, railroads, banking, and drugs (at the time, patent medicine

"THE LOBBY: A MEMBER AND HIS CONSTITUENTS." Lobbyists waiting in the corridors of the Capitol, making appeals to passing members of Congress. *The Century Illustrated Monthly Magazine,* May 1902.

manufacturers whose products often did more harm than good)—was one of the hallmarks of his presidency and helped account for his enormous popularity. As president, Woodrow Wilson also clashed with the industrial and commercial interests; as early as 1885, in his classic *Congressional Government,* he had warned against "the power of corrupt lobbyists to turn legislation to their own purposes."

In 1913, the Senate launched the first full-scale investigation of lobbying ever undertaken by either house. The impetus was the disclosure in a New York newspaper that a lobbyist for the National Association of Manufacturers (NAM) had his own office in the Capitol, had the chief House page in his employ, and influenced appointments to House committees and subcommittees. Senate Judiciary Committee hearings disclosed a pattern of abuses by Washington lobbyists. The investigators eventually recommended passage of a bill requiring regis-

tration of all lobbyists with the clerk of the House. The bill passed the House of Representatives but failed in the Senate. This investigation, however, set the pattern for Congress's treatment of egregious lobbying abuses—investigation, recommendations for remedial legislation, most often in the form of disclosure requirements, and eventual collapse of the legislative initiative.

The years of the Wilson administration also witnessed an accelerating trend toward institutionalized interest group representation. When the United States entered World War I in 1917, the federal government faced an unprecedented challenge of mobilizing the private sector to participate in the war effort. Federal agencies officially requested the establishment of trade associations in many industries that had not previously been served by such groups. Organized to promote cooperative planning and standardization of products during wartime, new associations, such as the National Coal Association, were established in many segments of American society and remained in existence after 1918, acquiring the peacetime mandate of promoting the interests of their members.

The number of interest groups grew as government became increasingly occupied with the lives of its citizens. As programs were enacted, as statutes created classes of citizens entitled to special treatment, as industries and sectors of the economy fell under governmental regulation, groups arose to monitor governmental actions and to seek to influence governmental decisions. For example, the American Farm Bureau Federation, established in 1919, was energized by laws passed to improve food production during World War I. The United States Chamber of Commerce found itself responding to a number of measures, such as a 1921 law to prevent unfair trade practices in the livestock, poultry, and dairy industries. Hostility toward the interests, especially those engaged in commerce and industry, increased. In 1927, Sen. Thaddeus Caraway, the sponsor of a lobby regulation bill, noted that "nearly every activity of the human mind has been capitalized by some grafter with headquarters established for this activity in Washington."

The growth of government activity created by the New Deal brought a legion of lobbyists to Washington. Before the decade of the 1930s was over, Congress had investigated and passed laws regulating lobbying by public utility holding companies, shipping firms, and propagandists for the fascist and Nazi cause. By 1936, as the result of an investigation by Alabama senator Hugo Black (later a Supreme Court justice), the House and Senate both passed broad lobbying disclosure bills, but attempts to reconcile differences between the bills failed in conference.

In 1946, with the support of President Harry S. Truman—who as a senator had chaired an investigation into waste and mismanagement in wartime production and so had firsthand experience with the lobbying efforts of defense contractors—Congress passed a broad lobby disclosure bill, which came under almost immediate criticism and was rendered generally ineffective a few years later. A 1954 Supreme Court decision, *United States v. Harriss* (347 U.S. 612), found the 1946 Federal Regulation of Lobbying Act to be vague and overly broad. The Court's narrow interpretation has meant that reports filed under the act rarely portray an accurate picture of lobbying.

Interest Group Explosion. Prior to the mid 1960s, the Washington interest group community was relatively limited in numbers and in scope, "a closed-door marketplace of political influence by a few established interests," observed Norman J. Ornstein and Mark Schmidt ("The New World of Interest Politics," in *Governing*, edited by Roger H. Davidson and Walter J. Oleszek, 1991). Most trade associations were headquartered in New York City, and few corporations kept Washington offices. On broad public policy matters business relied on the presence of the United States Chamber of Commerce and the National Association of Manufacturers. For specific representation, they called on their own legal departments or Washington law firms. Labor and agriculture had several large pressure groups. Other interests included veterans' groups, churches and religious organizations, and professional groups like the American Medical Association (AMA).

Congressional operations at the time favored insider lobbying. Power was centralized in the committee chairmen, the "barons"; staffs, who might act as a buffer between members and lobbyists, were small. Lobbyists were thus able to concentrate their efforts on a few individuals. Grassroots lobbying campaigns, when undertaken, were generally unsophisticated letter-writing, telephone, or telegraph campaigns. Many interests, especially those inexperienced or with few resources, were either underrepresented or not represented at all. Individuals could make large campaign donations with little or no accountability.

Interest representation during this period could be viewed as "iron triangles" of interest groups, congressional subcommittees, and government regulatory agencies. The cast of political and policy actors was limited and stable, the policy debates contained, and the outcomes largely predictable. Organizations had a relatively limited and manageable set of policy concerns, and could participate effectively in a narrow range of institutional arenas.

In a few years, this changed dramatically. The size of government continued to grow into the 1980s, but more important, the scope of government involvement expanded; even during Nixon's administration, the Democratic Congress enacted and the Republican president signed legislation—for example, creating a Consumer Product Safety Commission—that invested the national government with new and far-reaching responsibilities. To an unprecedented degree, Washington came to be seen as a place where, if one's interests involved a government component, a physical presence was essential.

Congress changed as the result of procedural reforms, and the locus of policy-making expanded from the committees to the subcommittees and to the floor. Lobbyists had to increase their activities to cover the large number of members who could influence legislative outcomes. Open-meeting rules lowered some of the barriers that separated members of Congress from group pressures, and lobbyists were permitted to attend markup sessions and conference committee sessions that used to be held behind closed doors.

Political parties also changed. No longer did they act to mediate and aggregate citizen and interest group demands; they left that for the interest groups. The relative rise in national affluence and education meant that Americans had more opportunities for social and economic mobility, and luxury of choice about ideas and values that were often expressed in political terms, that is, in the number and types of organizations people joined. Advances in technology, especially in telecommunications, allowed rapid mobilization of group resources, including capabilities for soliciting contributions and directing communications to the offices of government officials.

While the power of the political parties and the power of the vote declined in this period, direct involvement in political decision making in the form of interest group membership grew. Beginning in the 1950s, civil rights groups, groups who protested the Vietnam War, and environmental, consumer, and public interest groups all became components of the new interest group universe. Many protest groups, for example, were transformed from loosely knit gatherings concerned with short-term goals through the use of confrontational techniques to legitimized, permanent interests with long-term goals whose lobbying strategies and techniques were indistinguishable from those of their more established counterparts.

Groups continued to use protests and demonstrations as a tactic for getting a point across, attracting media attention, and promoting group cohesion. Various groups have massed on the steps of the Capitol, protesting issues such as abortion policy or U.S. intervention abroad. In one notable demonstration in 1979, farmers who were unhappy with U.S. agriculture policy drove their tractors to Washington, paraded in "tractorcades" around the Capitol, camped on the Mall, and announced their intention to stay until Congress passed the legislation they sought. Confrontations with police and property damage to the Mall in excess of a million

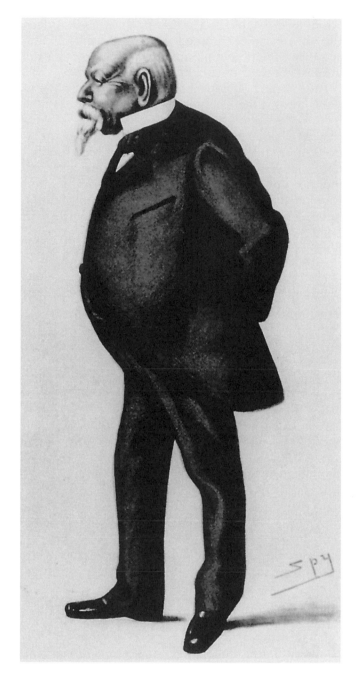

SAM WARD. Originally hired by Secretary of Treasury Hugh McCulloch to influence Congress to retire the $450 million in greenbacks issued during the Civil War, Ward, known as King of the Lobby, extravagantly wined and dined members of Congress to promote the interests of individuals, corporations, and foreign governments that were his clients. Active on Capitol Hill during the administrations of Andrew Johnson and Ulysses S. Grant, Ward remained largely free of suspicion during the many lobbying scandals of the Gilded Age. Caricature by Sir Leslie Ward (pseudonym, Spy), *Vanity Fair,* 10 January 1880.

OFFICE OF THE HISTORIAN OF THE U.S. SENATE

dollars turned the protest into a public relations disaster; the farmers eventually left without achieving their goals.

By 1993, interest group and lobbying activity had exploded. For example, the membership of the American Association of Retired Persons (AARP)—a group with an interest in protecting old-age benefits such as Social Security and Medicare—grew from 4.5 million in 1973 to 33 million in 1993. This made the AARP twice the size of the AFL-CIO and, after the Roman Catholic Church, the nation's largest organization.

The number of organizations with an interest in health care policy and with Washington offices grew from slightly more than one hundred in 1979 to more than seven hundred in 1991. The proportion of national trade and professional associations headquartered in Washington rose from 19 percent to 32 percent between 1971 and 1990. The total number of national associations grew from 4,900 in 1956, to 8,900 in 1965, to 12,900 in 1975, and to 23,000 by 1989, in effect doubling every fifteen years. Further, the number of registered, active lobbyists increased from slightly more than 3,000 in 1976 to more than 8,500 in 1992, although because

of flaws in the lobbyist registration statute, this number greatly underestimates the total number of Washington lobbyists.

The increase in the diversity of interests is also striking, in large part the result of technological achievements and scientific advancements in the late twentieth century. An example is the system of interest groups that developed around public policy issues of organ transplantation. In the early 1980s, development of the drug cyclosporine greatly mitigated the problem of organ rejection, and transplant success rates improved dramatically. Thus, transplantation of organs other than kidneys became possible and practical, and in 1984 Congress enacted the National Organ Transplant Act (which established the Division of Organ Transplantation within the Department of Health and Human Services to administer programs under the act) to encourage donation and to regulate the allocation of donor organs. As the field of organ transplantation experienced rapid growth, a network of groups (including National Transplant Action, the Transplant Foundation, and others) emerged to represent interests within the field and to participate in setting government policies.

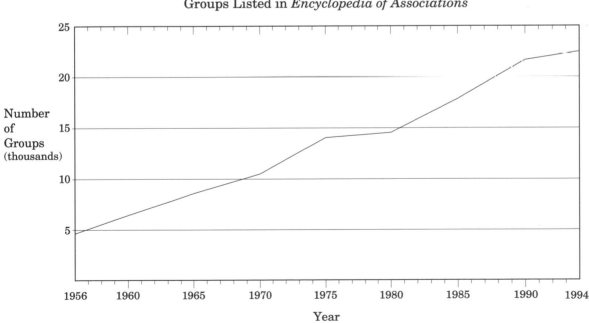

Figure 1
Groups Listed in *Encyclopedia of Associations*

Note: Figures prior to 1975 are estimates by the American Society of Association Executives.

SOURCES: Gale Research, Inc.; American Society of Association Executives; Jonathan Rauch, *Demosclerosis* (Random House, 1994).

Figure 2
Number of Health Groups in Washington, D.C., 1979–1991

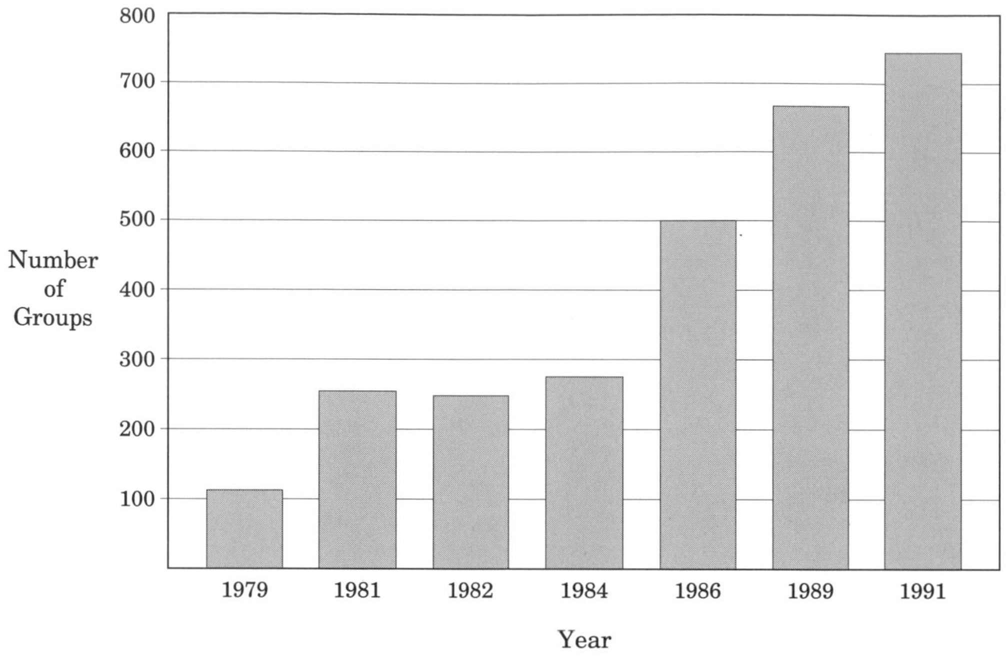

SOURCE: National Health Council, *Health Groups in Washington*, various editions; Jonathan Rauch, *Demosclerosis* (Random House, 1994).

Another recent distinguishing characteristic of lobbying since the 1980s is the growth of foreign interest activity, especially foreign corporate and commercial lobbying. In 1994, about 750 individuals or organizations representing about 1,400 foreign governments, political parties, or private interests were registered with the Department of Justice as foreign agents under a 1938 statute meant originally to disclose the activities of fascist propagandists in the United States. These numbers, however, underestimate the actual degree of activity because, like other lobbyist disclosure rules, the 1938 act is ineffective in reliably portraying lobbying activities.

The growth in foreign interest lobbying can be attributed, in addition to the forces discussed above, to the trend toward economic and trade globalization. In the last twenty years, international trade has become a major element in the U.S. economy. Congress's passage of the 1988 Omnibus Trade and Competitiveness Act, the 1988 Canada Free Trade Agreement and Implementation Act, and the 1993 North American Free Trade Agreement (NAFTA) are an indication of the changing relationship of the United States and its trading partners. For some, who perceive the lobbying activities of countries such as Japan to be overly aggressive, this growth is a cause for apprehension. Similarly, analysts are troubled by the so-called revolving door by which U.S. government officials leave federal service to work on behalf of foreign interests.

Responding to these concerns in one of his first actions after taking office in 1993, President Bill Clinton issued an executive order that added to and expanded upon postemployment restrictions for certain high-level political appointees in the executive branch. The Clinton rules expanded the one-year ban on working for a foreign entity to five years. High executive-branch officials were barred for life from employment as lobbyists for foreign governments or political parties (but, significantly, were not excluded from foreign corporations or other private entities). Similar rules to cover members of Congress have been introduced in legislation. A new lobby disclosure law under consideration in 1994 would provide more effective reporting of foreign lobbying activities, and Congress was also considering legislation to prohibit foreign interest lobbyists from providing members and staff with gifts such as vacations, tickets to sporting events, and expensive dinners. Finally, in 1993 Congress ended the tax breaks available to lobbyists for lobby-related expenses.

While traditional lobbying techniques—testifying at hearings, meeting with members of Congress and their staff, drafting legislation, making campaign contributions, and activating letter-writing campaigns—show no signs of becoming outdated, modern communications technology provides new avenues for access to congressional offices. In recent years, interest groups have delivered video tapes, have created computer-generated letters designed to look as though they were personally written by group members, and have set up free "800" telephone numbers that connect directly with a member of Congress's office or the Capitol switchboard. As a result it is increasingly difficult to tell the difference between manufactured public opinion and genuine expressions of popular sentiment.

One of the most controversial techniques used by interest groups is that of giving financial contributions to political campaigns, seen by many as a form of institutional bribery. According to this view, political action committees (PACs), the legally established organizations that funnel interest group money into political campaigns, heavily favor incumbents and put challengers at a disadvantage; moreover, contributions make legislators more beholden to contributors than to their constituents. Defenders of PACs, on the other hand, argue that campaign contributions encourage participation and broaden the base of the political system. In 1976, the Supreme Court decided (*Buckley v. Valeo*, 424 U.S. 1) that campaign contributions comprised a form of protected free speech. Where detractors claim that PAC contributions influence legislators' voting decisions, other analysts point out that legislators make voting decisions for a multiplicity of reasons, including ideology, party, constituency, and individual conscience. The many issues associated with political money, especially the question of whether moneyed special interests benefit unfairly, continue to confound reformers in and out of Congress, and the search for a solution that satisfies the diversity of opinions remains elusive.

The Case against and the Case for Lobbying. Madison's belief that interest groups (factions) were an inherently disruptive force in society remains a compelling theme. It surfaces in attitudes reflected in public opinion surveys, in attacks on lobbyists by governmental officials and others, and in journalistic accounts.

Public attitudes toward lobbying are complex and often paradoxical. Opinion surveys consistently indicate that people believe government officials and institutions are beholden to special interests. But responses are different when people are asked about interests to which they belong or in which they have a personal stake. For example, an older American may decry the power of the special interests in general, but also may see no contradiction in supporting the public policy objectives of the AARP.

Congress's attitudes are similarly complex. It is often both a willing suitor and an unhappy victim of pressure groups. Depending upon time, place, and circumstance, it welcomes the assistance that groups provide, such as research and political support, or it assails them for selfishness and obstructionism. Likewise, government leaders see no contradiction in assailing lobbyists while seeking their support for favored policies. For example, in 1993 and 1994, the Clinton administration, with one hand, conducted an aggressive campaign against the special interests, and with the other hand, solicited from the same interests campaign contributions and support for its budget, jobs program, and other policies, including campaign finance reform.

From the muckrakers to the present, journalists have found special interest lobbying a fertile field. Often, their focus is on the shady, dubious aspects of lobbying. The introduction to *Wall Street Journal* reporter Jeffrey Birnbaum's book *The Lobbyists* (1992) is illustrative: "[This book] is an insider's glimpse at a process that is usually cloaked in darkest secrecy. It will attempt to shed light on the trials and triumphs, the foibles and failings of a little understood but increasingly important group. It lays bare the brazen manipulation of both lawmakers and the public by the entire lobbying industry."

Arguments against lobbying are easily summarized: groups exercise influence far beyond the numbers of their membership; their influence runs counter to what is perceived as the public interest; their activities are conducted in secret and are unavailable to public scrutiny; their techniques, involving campaign contributions and social relationships with officials, are unsavory if not improper or illegal; and their activities undermine public confidence in the institutions of government. Issues surrounding campaign contributions and the belief of many that this type of political giving and spending is corrupt has cast particular doubt on the political activities of groups.

These perceptions have been bolstered by the research of some political scientists and analysts who have found that lobby groups tend to represent the interests of the well-to-do at the expense of the poor, that campaign contributions have influenced policymakers' decisions, and that interest groups in general are an inherently divisive force in society.

The arguments that lobbying is an important, necessary, and useful force can also be summarized: significantly, lobbying is a tangible manifestation of the First Amendment freedom of petition for redress of grievances. Lobbyists bring information to the government and take away information from the government; in this way, they facilitate the flow of knowledge and understanding. Lobbying is a check on governmental power; without the input lobbyists provide, decisions would be based entirely on the information developed by government officials—information that may or may not be sufficient, accurate, complete, or fair. Lobbying is a representational activity that supplements the electoral process. It permits citizen participation not only in legislative affairs but also in administrative matters. Lobbying legitimizes emerging groups; the move from protest group to interest group signifies political maturity and commitment. Lobbying contributes to political socialization by educating group members about government and keeping them informed about governmental decisions. More often than not, lobbying is a self-regulating activity; when a group arises to support or oppose an issue, another group appears to take the opposite position.

The debate on whether interest groups and their lobbyists are harmful or helpful turns, in part, on how successful they are judged in shaping legislation to their own benefit. As in other facets of this subject, informed observers disagree sharply. Some cases demonstrate that interest group pressure is effective; many of these depend on showing a relationship between political campaign contributions and decision making. Other cases demonstrate the power of grassroots action. For example, in 1988, Congress passed the Medicare Catastrophic Coverage Act, a plan developed with the endorsement of the AARP. But a year later, Congress was forced to repeal the act after a grassroots uprising among AARP's membership objected to the higher Medicare premiums some senior citizens would be required to pay.

Other observers contend that interest groups are not very powerful, are concerned more with information gathering and monitoring government activities than with influencing them, and that when they do seek to influence policymakers, they are only marginally effective. A 1972 study by Harmon L. Zeigler and G. Wayne Peak concluded that most lobbyists accomplish little except to convince their own membership to continue payment of dues. A large-scale study, reported in 1993 (Heinz, et al.), found that the contemporary system of interest representation presented a paradox: although attempts to shape national policy were at a historic high, there was little tangible evidence to show that these efforts were successful.

Disagreement over the effectiveness of lobbying raises a broader question about its ultimate objectives. Lobbyists themselves argue that the techniques of influence—from straightforward activities such as testifying at hearings (a technique that lobbyists rank as one of their most important) to campaign contributions to social relationships—are meant to help gain access to decision makers in order to present information. The degree to which legislators are influenced or persuaded by lobbyists depends primarily, according to practitioners, on both the merits of the case presented and the skill of the presenter—not on a sinister capacity to cloud the minds of decision makers. To others, "access," "influence," and "persuasion" are synonymous, especially in cases where moneyed interests are perceived to dominate interests that cannot draw competitively on similar resources, either financial or political. In this view, access is influence, since only one side of the issue will reach the decision maker.

Impact of Size. Of perhaps greater significance than lobbyist effectiveness is the impact of the expanding size of the interest group system. As the number of interest groups has increased, groups with similar concerns have sought to position themselves in the marketplace of ideas, and Congress must now contend with a dynamic of intergroup competition. Entrepreneurial leadership groups—formed from the top down, often with little or no rank-and-file membership—also contribute to Congress's difficult task of sorting out who speaks for what and for whom. Finally, the rate of interest group growth suggests that in the future Congress may need to develop new strategies to manage interest group demands.

Beyond the narrow problem of how Congress manages its relations with this large system are the broad social and political implications of the interest group explosion. Three perspectives can be identified. At one extreme are theorists who believe the interest group system dooms Congress to gridlock and the nation to decline. These theorists (Olson, 1982) argue that in a stable democracy interests develop and accumulate over time; their long-term effect is to inhibit economic innovation and growth, and further stifle the economy through permanent subsidy arrangements with government. These beliefs are popular with those who see the United States in a broad period of decline. But the theory is also controversial, and analysts have produced research that questions its assumptions and conclusions.

Another view is held by those who, far from conceding the certainty of decline, view the proliferation of interests as a positive indication of the vitality of pluralism in American society. However, the vast array of political choices available bring with them certain social consequences, namely that the traditional institutions and support systems one looks to for stability in an era of rapid change are themselves subject to the same laws of change responsible for the benefits of pluralism. The result, according to Nelson W. Polsby (1984), is that "we are doing better and feeling worse."

Finally, a middle perspective between the extremes are those who worry that the interest group explosion has introduced "a potentially dysfunctional particularism into national politics." But they acknowledge, as James Madison articulated, that restraints on interest groups as a remedy are more pernicious than the cure for the disease. The interests, no matter how difficult they may make life for Congress and other governmental decision makers, conclude Kay Lehman Schlozman and John T. Tierney (1986), are the price of a free society. Other analysts such as Jeffrey Berry (1984) take a more reformist position, emphasizing the need for renewal of the party system and the usefulness of campaign reform as one way to level the playing field between well-represented and underrepresented interests.

Regulation as a Coping Mechanism. In 1993 and 1994, statutory regulation of lobbying seemed to be the strategy chosen by Congress and the Clinton White House to reduce the stress of the interests on the political system. In addition to the overarching dynamic of the interest group explosion, the immediate antecedents for this effort were several: the tradition, articulated by all three candidates in the 1992 presidential campaign, of blaming the interest groups for the failures of government; reformist unhappiness with present laws controlling interests—especially campaign finance laws but also postemployment and lobbyist disclosure laws; and the public perception of the Reagan-Bush years as a period when lobbyists, especially those representing corporate and foreign interests, were able to hold sway over policies that ran counter to the public interest.

The 1993 and 1994 offensive against the interests included the following elements: by executive order, postemployment rules were changed to require a five-year wait before a senior executive-branch official could become a lobbyist; and senior executive-branch officials were barred entirely from ever becoming lobbyists for foreign political or business interests. Legislation was introduced to make similar standards apply to members of Congress and senior staff. Congress considered a measure to rewrite several lobby disclosure laws and fold them into a single statute; its sponsors hoped this new law would provide more useful information about lobbying activities. President Clinton's deficit reduction package ended the policy of allowing businesses to deduct lobbying expenses. Campaign reform legislation proposed prohibiting political contributions by lobbyists. Other legislation would bar members of Congress from accepting gifts from lobbyists and others.

These initiatives could provide a measure of relief from the perception that lobbyists have undue influence over the governmental process, although some may have to survive a constitutional challenge first. Restoring the political parties' former role of mediating interest group demands would also reduce some of the pressure. But the structural dilemma of growing numbers of interests, expanding varieties, and increasing demands from all will remain. In whatever way they are regulated, interest groups and their lobbyists will continue to be major actors in governmental decision making; the debate as to their merit will not diminish; and government policymakers will seek new strategies to curb their perceived excesses.

[*See also* Interest Groups.]

BIBLIOGRAPHY

Berry, Jeffrey M. *The Interest Group Society.* 1984.

Birnbaum, Jeffrey H. *The Lobbyists: How Influence Peddlers Get Their Way in Washington.* 1992.

Cigler, Allan J., and Burdett A. Loomis. *Interest Group Politics.* 3d ed. 1991.

Crawford, Kenneth G. *The Pressure Boys: The Inside Story of Lobbying in America.* 1939.

Deakin, James. *The Lobbyists.* 1966.

Heinz, John P., Edward O. Laumann, Robert L. Nelson, and Robert H. Salisbury. *The Hollow Core: Private Interests in National Policy Making.* 1993.

Herring, Pendleton. *Group Representation before Congress.* 1928.

Olson, Mancur. *The Rise and Decline of Nations.* 1982.

Ornstein, Norman J., and Mark Schmidt. "The New

World of Interest Politics. In *Governing*. Edited by Roger H. Davidson and Walter J. Oleszek. 1991.

Polsby, Nelson W. "Prospects for Pluralism in the American Federal System: Trends in Unofficial Public-Sector Intermediation." In *The Costs of Federalism*. Edited by Robert T. Golembiewski and Aaron Wildavsky. 1984.

Rauch, Jonathan. *Demosclerosis: The Silent Killer of American Government*. 1994.

Salisbury, Robert H. *Interests and Institutions: Substance and Structure in American Politics*. 1992.

Schlozman, Kay Lehman, and John T. Tierney. *Organized Interests and American Democracy*. 1986.

Thompson, Margaret Susan. *The "Spider Web": Congress and Lobbying in the Age of Grant*. 1985.

U.S. Senate. Committee on Governmental Affairs. Subcommittee on Intergovernmental Relations. *Congress and Pressure Groups: Lobbying in a Modern Democracy.* 99th Cong., 2d sess., 1986. 5. Prt. 99-161.

Zeigler, L. Harmon, and G. Wayne Peak. *Interest Groups in American Society*. 1972.

RICHARD C. SACHS

LODGE, HENRY CABOT

LODGE, HENRY CABOT (1850–1924), representative and senator from Massachusetts and leader of the Republican party during the League of Nations controversy. An old-stock Bostonian, Lodge honored his Anglo-Saxon, Federalist heritage. After receiving a Ph.D. from Harvard in 1876, Lodge wrote history and biography from a Federalist standpoint. He was a staunch Republican and stayed in the party in 1884, when his social peers rejected the presidential candidacy of James G. Blaine, and again in 1912, when his best friend, Theodore Roosevelt, ran for president as a Progressive.

Lodge served in the House of Representatives from 1887 to 1893 and in the Senate thereafter. In the House, he cosponsored the 1891 force bill to establish federal supervision over all polling places at national elections in order to protect black voters in the South, and he also supported immigration restriction. As a senator, on domestic matters he was a conservative, but he was also adaptable. Thus, he supported regulatory reform and conservation measures during the presidencies of fellow Republicans Roosevelt and William Howard Taft. No friend to the direct popular election of senators, he nevertheless adjusted to passage of the Seventeenth Amendment of 1913 and won two terms from the electorate.

Lodge served on the Senate Foreign Relations Committee and also became his party's main spokesman on foreign policy. In 1900 he ardently

HENRY CABOT LODGE.   LIBRARY OF CONGRESS

defended an imperialist U.S. policy toward the Philippines. When, through an exchange of notes with imperial powers in 1899 and 1900, the United States secured for itself equal trading rights in China and hard-to-defend promises not to abridge China's independence, Lodge approved. But after popular enthusiasm for U.S. imperialism and the open door in China waned, Lodge developed a lasting sense of caution about international commitments. Since sound foreign policy required the fulfillment of all obligations, caution seemed warranted if the public would not give enduring support to its periodic political enthusiasms. Thus, in 1911 and 1912 Lodge led the way in supporting the exemption of vital questions like immigration policy in arbitration treaties with Britain and France. On the other hand, sure of public support, he was assertive in espousing the Monroe Doctrine. In 1912 the Senate adopted as a resolution the Lodge Corollary disapproving of the transfer of strategic places in the Americas to companies not from the Americas which might serve as agents for their nation of origin. His resolution was prompted by a Japanese corporate initiative in Mexico.

When war broke out in Europe in 1914, Lodge favored the Allies. In the Senate, he spoke out for military preparedness and for firm defense of the United States' neutrality rights against German violations. On these and other issues, Lodge differed markedly from President Woodrow Wilson, and so a strong and mutual antipathy developed.

When in December 1918 Wilson went to France to implant a League of Nations charter in the Versailles treaty with Germany, Lodge feared the result and began counteraction against Senate approval of the League. As the prospective Republican majority leader and chairman of the Foreign Relations Committee in the new Congress, Lodge would prove to be a key figure in the League controversy, though far from alone in determining the outcome.

Publication of preliminary and then final versions of the League Covenant confirmed Lodge's fears about the organization. Above all, he objected to the equivocal obligation in Article Ten requiring all League members to defend other member states under attack. It was, to him, an open-ended promise that would not be fulfilled and therefore should not be made. To meet the challenge, he sought to keep his party unified to serve as an instrument in the League battle and to maximize chances for Republican victory in the 1920 election. Such a victory, he felt, was needed to restore foreign policy to steady hands. As to membership in the League, he sought either to accompany approval of the League Covenant with certain reservations that would make U.S. membership a tolerable option or to reject the organization altogether. His call for reservations served to unify his party against pro-League Democrats: Republican senators, ranging from pro-League mild reservationists to anti-League irreconcilables, could agree at least on the need for reservations, though irreconcilables wanted more. Wilson, meanwhile, discouraged Democrats from engaging in realistic compromise negotiations.

Lodge played his cards well. He enlisted the prestigious former secretary of State Elihu Root in unifying the Republicans behind the idea of reservations. He also packed his committee with anti-League members and delayed matters in committee while the public heard more about the covenant and grew wary. In September 1919 Lodge acted as mediator among Republicans in forging agreement on the key reservation, to Article Ten. He then strongly encouraged Republicans to agree among themselves on other reservations. After his resolution of ratification with the reservations failed largely at the hands of Democrats, Lodge yielded to the demand for further compromise effort. At a bipartisan conference in January, he made concessions to pro-League members but broke off the negotiation over issues on which his party was united, Article Ten and the Monroe Doctrine. Then, encouraging independent Democrats and mollifying mild reservationists, he again reported the treaty and accepted the reservation changes agreed to at the bipartisan conference. He even acceded to a change in the wording, though not the substance, of the Article Ten reservation. Wilson rejected the compromise, however, and it failed by seven votes. Lodge shed no tears over its defeat.

BIBLIOGRAPHY

Garraty, John A. *Henry Cabot Lodge: A Biography.* 1953.
Margulies, Herbert F. *The Mild Reservationists and the League of Nations Controversy in the Senate.* 1989.
Widenor, William C. *Henry Cabot Lodge and the Search for an American Foreign Policy.* 1980.

HERBERT F. MARGULIES

LOGAN, JOHN A. (1826–1886), representative and senator from Illinois and leader of the Republican party's "stalwart" faction. Elected as a Democrat to the 36th and 37th Congresses (1859–1863), he served until his resignation on 2 April 1862, to enter the Union Army. After the Civil War, he returned to the House as a Republican in the 40th, 41st, and 42d Congresses. He resigned in 1871, when he was elected to the U.S. Senate, where he served until his defeat for a second term in 1877. Elected again to the Senate in 1879 and 1885, Logan was a member of that body until his death on 26 December 1886.

JOHN A. LOGAN. A post–Civil War opponent of the South, Logan, as reported in *Perley's Reminiscences*, "seemed as ready to meet his political opponents as he had been at the head of his brigade to charge the enemy" (p. 362).

PERLEY'S REMINISCENCES, VOL. 2

Despite his lifelong aversion to the professional military, which he viewed as elitist, Logan remained a staunch proponent of veterans' pensions. His election for three terms as national commander in chief of the Grand Army of the Republic and his 1868 original conception of Memorial Day further attest to his political support among Union veterans. His abrasive personality and wartime experience made Logan one of the strongest anti-southerners in the post–Civil War Congress. He denounced southern white violence against blacks during Reconstruction and was a great proponent of using the emotional cause of the Civil War as a Republican weapon against the Democrats: "waving the bloody shirt," in the phrase of the time.

Logan advocated inflation, women's suffrage, federal aid to public education, African American civil rights, and party patronage (he opposed civil service reform and the merit system). He was one of seven Republican managers of the 1868 impeachment trial of President Andrew Johnson and was the unsuccessful Republican candidate for vice president in 1884, indicators of his standing in the Republican party.

BIBLIOGRAPHY

Jones, James Pickett. *John A. Logan: Stalwart Republican from Illinois.* 1982.

Paxson, Frederic Logan. "John Alexander Logan." In *Biographical Dictionary of the United States Congress, 1774–1989.* 1989.

ROBERT S. SALISBURY

LOGROLLING. Logrolling, or vote trading, is a means of organizing legislative majorities by coupling similar or, at times, disparate legislative initiatives that separately would have difficulty passing at various stages of the legislative process, but combined, would garner support of a majority of numbers, either at the committee level or when a bill reaches the floor for a vote of all members. According to congressional scholars Roger Davidson and Walter Oleszek, logrolling "is a bargaining strategy in which the parties trade off support so that each may gain its goal. The term originated in the nineteenth century when neighbors helped each other roll logs into a pile for burning. In its most visible form, trading is embodied in a something-for-everyone enactment—known as *pork barrel.*"

Logrolling is utilized in two basic ways. First, a logroll effort may be applied to a single omnibus bill working its way through the legislative process. In this context, a member or group of members supporting a particular program or project in an omnibus bill that lacks majority support at the outset of the process would seek out members in similar situations. These blocs of members supporting various district- or state-based programs would join forces in a "horse-trading" fashion. Members from an alliance that may be enduring or last as long as it takes to cast a single vote. The end result is the passage of a legislative measure that contains the programs of the members of the logrolling coalition.

A frequently cited example of this type of logrolling involves the inclusion of the authorization for and funding of Food Stamp programs within the Department of Agriculture. Basically the inclusion of the Food Stamp program in the Agriculture budget provided a supportive voting bloc of members representing traditionally nonagricultural constituencies; because the Food Stamp program provided assistance to these nonagricultural areas, urban members became more likely to support farm subsidies that had no benefit to their districts or states. This logroll has endured for three decades.

PRESIDENT GROVER CLEVELAND. Political cartoon bearing the caption, "Cleveland steps on the log-rolling Congressmen who traded tariff favors at the expense of American consumers."

The second type of logroll involves the trading of votes on different bills. Due to rules of germaneness in the House of Representatives, it is difficult to include unrelated programs in the same omnibus bill. Therefore, members may construct coalitions that involve two or more unrelated bills. Obviously this type of vote trading is more difficult to administer and is most often very short lived. Vote trading in this manner implicitly involves a quid pro quo on the part of individual legislators. Such interactions are tenuous and have led to broken deals and tarnished relationships among members.

Logrolling exists, in large part, to facilitate the often cumbersome process of making laws in Congress. It results from the perception that members of Congress serve dual roles as lawmakers and as constituent servants; logrolling facilitates the perceived need of legislators to "deliver the goods" to their constituents.

In recent years, Congress has acknowledged its inability to overcome logrolling tendencies when addressing various policy issues. In an effort to break the deadlock surrounding the closing of U.S. military bases, Congress in October 1988 passed the Defense Base Closure and Realignment Act. This act established a bipartisan commission to make recommendations to Congress and the secretary of Defense on closures and realignments of military bases. Since then, the commission's recommendations have resulted in the closure of more than one hundred bases and the realignment of an equal number of bases. While this approach has circumvented the traditional logrolling strategy in an isolated policy area, without the discipline of strong party leadership in Congress, logrolling will continue to be an inevitable component of the legislative process.

[*See also* Bargaining; Pork Barrel.]

BIBLIOGRAPHY

Ferejohn, John. "Logrolling in an Institutional Context: A Case Study of Food Stamp Legislation." In *Congress and Policy Change.* Edited by Gerald C. Wright, Jr., et al. 1986.
Stratmann, Thomas. "The Effects of Logrolling on Congressional Voting." *American Economic Review* 82 (December 1992): 1162–1176.
Kau, James B., and Paul H. Rubin. "Self-Interest, Ideology, and Logrolling in Congressional Voting." *Journal of Law and Economics* 22 (October 1979): 365–384.
Davidson Roger H., and Walter J. Oleszek. *Congress and Its Members.* 4th ed. 1994. Pp. 375–378.

RONALD G. SHAIKO

LONG, HUEY P. (1893–1935), Democratic senator from Louisiana (1932–1935), governor (1928–1932), and fiery populist who rallied the dispossessed during the Great Depression. Huey Pierce Long, Jr., dominated politics in Depression-era Louisiana while serving as governor and senator. A product of northern Louisiana's agrarian populist tradition, Long was born in Winn Parish on 30 August 1893. After promising but brief careers as a traveling salesman and an attorney, Long turned to politics. He won a seat on the state's Railroad Commission at the age of twenty-five. In 1928 Long seized the governorship by mobilizing rural voters against the conservative New Orleans establishment. Two years later he defeated the incumbent, Sen. Joseph E. Ransdell, in the Democratic primary, which guaranteed him the seat in this Democrat-controlled state. Unwilling to cede the governor's office to a hostile successor, Long delayed taking his Senate seat for fourteen months until one of his lieutenants was elected as the state's chief executive. But even as senator, the Kingfish,

HUEY P. LONG.

as he was called, continued to run the state through his notorious political machine.

A potent mixture of shrewd political instincts, compelling oratory, and colorful antics propelled Long onto the national scene. In defiance of party discipline, he resigned from his Senate committees and accused Democratic majority leader Joseph T. Robinson of conflicts of interest. Long even invaded Robinson's home state of Arkansas, pioneering the use of the sound truck in a successful bid to return Hattie W. Caraway to the Senate. The Caraway campaign gave Long an opportunity to demonstrate his political strength outside Louisiana, while aiding a progressive ally and embarrassing the majority leader. Although Long supported Franklin D. Roosevelt in 1932, the New Deal soon proved too conservative for the Kingfish, who obstructed administration measures with colorful filibusters. The White House retaliated by giving federal patronage to his political opponents in Louisiana and by withholding public works funds. "I came here a clown," Long observed, "but now I'm a menace because someone is paying attention to me."

Long's own prescription for the ailing economy was a sweeping redistribution of wealth. He proposed to tax wealth as well as income and to place ceilings on both. Although these radical measures were defeated in the Senate, a more progressive income tax structure, social security legislation, and a steeper inheritance tax became law. While Long succeeded in pushing the New Deal to the left, some of his thunder was stolen in the process.

Long garnered fans in all regions of the country as a result of the Depression. With his national Share Our Wealth movement, Long appealed to the discontented, whom he mobilized through his radio addresses, his own newspaper, and an extensive mailing list. This grassroots organization was intended to carry him to the White House, but he died from an assassin's bullet on 10 September 1935. His legacy included a political dynasty, as both his wife, Rose McConnell Long, and his son, Russell B. Long, succeeded him in the Senate, while his brother, Earl, became governor and other Long relatives served in Congress.

BIBLIOGRAPHY

Brinkley, Alan. *Voices of Protest: Huey Long, Father Coughlin, and the Great Depression.* 1982.
Long, Huey P. *Every Man a King.* 1933.
Williams, T. Harry. *Huey Long.* 1969.

MICHAEL L. GILLETTE

LONG, RUSSELL B. (1918–), senator from Louisiana, chairman of the Committee on Finance, the most durable officeholder of his state's colorful Democratic dynasty. The son of populist governor and senator Huey P. Long, nephew of Gov. Earl Long and Rep. George S. Long, Russell Billiu Long had not quite reached the constitutional age of thirty when, without previous political experience, he first ran for the Senate in 1948. A narrow winner, he was then reelected six times on the strength of his family name and attention to state interests, especially oil. He retired in 1987.

Long's folksy mannerisms—"putting his arm around a senator and talking in his ear"—were reminiscent of his father's brief time in the Senate, said West Virginia's Robert C. Byrd (*The Senate*, 1988). In his family's populist tradition, Russell Long fought mostly losing battles to retain public control of communications satellites and of patents

RUSSELL B. LONG. *Right,* conferring with Sen. Spessard L. Holland (D-Fla.), as Long prepared to make his first speech in the Senate, protesting a proposed rule designed to end filibusters, 2 March 1949.   LIBRARY OF CONGRESS

resulting from government-financed research. His main legislative base was the Finance Committee, which he chaired from 1965 through 1980. At times Long aspired to rival his dominant House counterpart, Wilbur D. Mills, chairman of the Ways and Means Committee, in generating broad tax-policy ideas, but his Finance Committee was better known for amending tax bills with narrow-interest benefits. The chairman was a frequent drawing card for Democratic fund-raising dinners attended by corporate lobbyists.

Long could be an effective handler of complex legislation when his attention was fully engaged, as with the Medicare bill in 1965. That year Democratic colleagues chose him as assistant floor leader, but he was replaced in 1969 after not showing enough diligence to daily details.

BIBLIOGRAPHY

Mann, Robert. *Legacy to Power: Senator Russell Long of Louisiana.* 1992.

ARLEN J. LARGE

LONGWORTH, NICHOLAS (1869–1931), representative from Ohio, Republican floor leader (1923–1925), Speaker of the House (1925–1931). Son of a wealthy, socially prominent Cincinnati family, Longworth was one of the most urbane and popular leaders ever to serve in the House. He was

first elected to Congress in 1902, lost his seat in the Democratic sweep of 1912, was reelected two years later, and thereafter remained a House member until his death.

His congeniality, moderately conservative politics, and fierce party allegiance won him quick acceptance on Capitol Hill. He led an active social life and became a frequent visitor to the White House, where he met President Theodore Roosevelt's daughter Alice, whom he married in 1906. He also established himself as a skilled legislator. A member of the Foreign Affairs Committee, he championed a law for the purchase of residences for U.S. diplomats living abroad. In 1907 he was appointed to the Ways and Means Committee and there earned recognition for his work on revenue and tariff issues. Upon his election as majority floor leader in 1923, he resigned from Ways and Means to devote his full time to House Republican affairs and management of the House's legislative business.

As majority leader, Longworth demanded party loyalty, which he said was necessary for an effective

HOUSE SPEAKER NICHOLAS LONGWORTH. In 1928, Republicans swept many normally Democratic districts. In this political cartoon, Speaker Longworth predicts that the Democrats will reclaim many of those seats in 1930. He was right; they picked up fifty-three House seats, only two seats short of a majority. Before the next Congress convened, twelve representatives-elect died, Longworth among them, giving the Democrats control of the House. Clifford K. Berryman, *Washington Evening Star,* 11 October 1930.

U.S. SENATE COLLECTION, CENTER FOR LEGISLATIVE ARCHIVES

Congress. He surprised colleagues in 1924 with his firmness in denying important committee assignments and the right to vote in party caucuses to thirteen insurgent Republicans who had often sided with the Democrats on partisan issues. At the same time, he pleased Democrats by stressing bipartisan cooperation on scheduling and other routine matters.

The speakership, stripped of many of its powers in the Cannon Revolt of 1910, held only limited authority when Longworth was elected to that office in December 1925. He methodically set about enhancing the Speaker's role, announcing candidly that he intended to be more than a presiding officer and that he would retain the political control he had exercised as majority leader. He soon proved effective in the new job. In his first act as Speaker, he engineered an increase in the number of signatures required for discharge petitions, greatly restricting that method of bringing bills to the floor without the approval of House leaders. He won bipartisan praise for his impartiality as a presiding officer and respect for his ability to command his own party while making private accommodations with the Democrats. A comfortable Republican majority and a dearth of divisive issues prior to 1930, when political debate shifted abruptly to the Great Depression, made his job easier. Still, Longworth proved that even a diminished speakership could be powerful and effective in the hands of an experienced, respected, and innovative leader.

Longworth's death of lobar pneumonia on 9 April 1931 closed a period of unusual civility in the House. From the spirited adjournment parties that he hosted in the chamber to his remarkable friendship with his rough-hewn Democratic rival for Speaker, John Nance Garner of Texas, the fun-loving Ohio aristocrat showed that making laws need not be a joyless endeavor. His place in history rests not only on his record of success as Speaker and party leader but also on the salubrious effect of his personality on the generation of Republicans and Democrats with whom he served.

BIBLIOGRAPHY

Cheney, Richard B., and Lynne V. Cheney. *Kings of the Hill.* 1983. Pp. 138–159.

De Chambrun, Clara Longworth. *The Making of Nicholas Longworth.* 1933.

Peters, Ronald M., Jr. *The American Speakership: The Office in Historical Perspective.* 1990. Pp. 102–105.

DONALD C. BACON

LOUISIANA. First a French colony (1699–1769), then a Spanish colony (1769–1801), the territory of the Louisiana Purchase (1803) can be considered the first "colony" of the United States. The area now called Louisiana is one of the thirteen states ultimately carved from this territory.

On 26 March 1804, the U.S. Congress divided Louisiana into the Territory of Orleans and the District of Louisiana. On 2 March 1805, Congress passed additional legislation providing for a greater measure of representative government in the Orleans Territory. Finally, Congress passed the Orleans Territory Act of 1811, which authorized a state constitution, and on 20 February 1811, President James Madison signed the bill permitting Louisiana's statehood. On 30 April 1812, Louisiana joined the Union as the eighteenth state.

The Pelican State has had more constitutions than any state in the Union. The secession convention held in Baton Rouge on 23 January 1861 allowed the state briefly to become an independent nation (26 January–21 March 1861) until it joined the Confederate States of America. The U.S. Congress refused to recognize the state's fifth constitution in 1864, even though Louisiana ratified the Thirteenth Amendment. Finally, after Gen. Philip H. Sheridan ordered another constitutional convention and the state ratified the Fourteenth Amendment and permitted expansion of suffrage to former slaves, Louisiana was formally readmitted to the Union on 25 June 1868.

Louisiana's senators and representatives had little impact on Congress until the early twentieth century, when the traditionally Democratic state began to benefit from Congress's seniority system. The first to mark the growing importance of Louisiana's Democratic delegation in Congress was Joseph E. Ransdell, who served in the House (1899–1913) and Senate (1913–1931). Known as the father of the National Institutes of Health, Ransdell eventually lost his seat to Huey P. Long, a Democratic populist with presidential aspirations, who served in the Senate from 1932 until his assassination in 1935. Long's widow, Rose McConnell Long, served out the remainder of his term as the state's first woman senator. When their son Russell B. Long was elected to the Senate in 1948, he became the first senator whose parents had both served in the Senate. A senator for nearly forty years (1948–1986), Russell Long was sometimes referred to as the "fourth branch of the U.S. government" in his role as the chairman of the Finance Committee. Gillis W. Long, a distant relative of the other Longs, wielded influence as chairman of the House Democratic caucus in the early 1980s.

Hale Boggs, representative of New Orleans (1940–1942 and 1946–1972), served as Democratic whip (1962–1970) and later as majority leader (1971–1972). His widow, Corinne C. (Lindy) Boggs, took over his House seat, holding it until her retirement in 1990, for a total of fifty years' service by the Boggses in Congress.

Yet these nationally known (and often liberal) Democrats were the exception in the Louisiana delegation. The state's conservative tradition is perhaps best reflected in the career of Rep. F. Edward Hébert from southern Louisiana, who served in the House from 1940 to 1977. His autocratic abuse of power led to his ouster from the chairmanship of the Armed Services Committee in January 1978. Another prominent conservative, whose career marked the state's transition from segregation, was Rep. Joe D. Waggonner, Jr., the unofficial leader of the House conservative coalition in the 1970s. By the early 1990s the Louisiana House delegation included African American representatives and Republicans as well as Democrats.

[See also Louisiana Purchase.]

BIBLIOGRAPHY

Howard, Perry H. *Political Tendencies in Louisiana*. 1969.
Pederson, William D., and Vincent J. Marsala, eds. *Louisiana's Political Leaders: Ratings and Case Studies*. 1993.

WILLIAM D. PEDERSON

LOUISIANA PURCHASE. In early 1803 Napoleon Bonaparte of France, ever needful of money to continue his wars in Europe, offered to sell the Louisiana Territory to the United States for approximately $15 million. Although the proposed cession did not define exact boundaries, it consisted of about 828,000 square miles, stretching from western Florida to the eastern slopes of the Rocky Mountains. Most Americans viewed it as a spectacular opportunity. It would remove the threat of a major imperial power establishing a colonial empire on the nation's western boundary, double the size of the United States, ensure the continued commercial expansion of the South and West, and guarantee U.S. domination of the North American continent.

President Thomas Jefferson fully recognized the benefits. But he also had some qualms, because the U.S. Constitution, which he was inclined to interpret strictly, had no provision for acquiring foreign territory. Before signing a treaty with France he wanted a constitutional amendment granting this power. Jefferson's closest advisers and a substantial number of Republican members of Congress, fearful that the ever-mercurial Napoleon might change his mind, opposed this approach because they believed it would consume too much time. In the end, Jefferson capitulated to the pressure and submitted the Louisiana Purchase Treaty directly to the Senate, which quickly and easily approved it by a vote of 27 to 7 on 26 October 1803. The main opposition came from New England Federalists who feared that continued expansion westward would diminish even further the little influence that remained to them. The acquisition of territory by means of a treaty was later upheld by the Supreme Court in *American Insurance Company v. Canter* (1828).

There still remained the problem of incorporating the Louisiana Territory into the Union. Both the president and a majority of Congress were reluctant to grant too much self-government to the newly acquired territory, because they believed the French and Indian inhabitants to be insufficiently Americanized. In a series of acts they created the Orleans Territory (the present state of Louisiana) from the more densely populated lower section of the purchase and temporarily attached the vast but sparsely inhabited area north of it to the Indiana Territory for administrative purposes. In 1805 this became the Louisiana Territory. Power to govern was vested in an appointed governor and legislative council. Unhappy with these developments, which they viewed as autocratic, the inhabitants of the Orleans Territory asked for immediate statehood. The request was denied, but an 1805 law provided for the election of a representative legislature, and the Orleans Territory was increasingly allowed self-government on the model of the Northwest Ordinance of 1787. Louisiana became a state in 1812. Out of the Louisiana Purchase also came the entire states of Missouri (1821), Arkansas (1836), Iowa (1846), and Nebraska (1857) and large portions of Minnesota (1858), Kansas (1861), Colorado (1876), South Dakota (1889), North Dakota (1889), Montana (1889), Wyoming (1890), and Oklahoma (1907). Congress thus fulfilled America's ongoing commitment to incorporating acquired territory into the Union as equal self-governing states.

BIBLIOGRAPHY

Brown, Everett S. *The Constitutional History of the Louisiana Purchase*. 1920.

Dargo, George. *Jefferson's Louisiana: Politics and the Clash of Legal Traditions.* 1975.

RICHARD E. ELLIS

LUCE, CLARE BOOTHE (1903–1987), Republican representative from Connecticut; controversial international figure characterized by one journalist as "friend or foe of nearly every major political thinker" from 1920 to 1980. Clare Boothe Luce was elected to represent the 4th District of Connecticut in the 78th and 79th Congresses (1943–1947), running on a Republican ticket in a traditionally Democratic district that included New York City bedroom communities as well as small working-class towns. A nationally known playwright, author, lecturer, war correspondent, and managing editor of a major magazine, Luce was already a public figure when she entered the House, where her outspokenness and quick wit attracted great media attention.

Luce's legislative work defies label. She sought and received appointment to the prestigious House Military Affairs Committee, where she worked in the areas of foreign policy, war production, and racial equality in the armed services. While a representative, she toured World War II battlefronts and was one of the first to see the Buchenwald concentration camp after its liberation. A staunch anticommunist, she was one of the first representatives to warn against Soviet domination of Eastern Europe.

On the domestic front, Luce frequently backed legislation that would benefit her working-class constituents, including measures to establish a minimum wage, subsidized housing, and the right to strike, and she sponsored a full employment plan. Though she supported the principles of many New Deal programs, she was an outspoken critic of President Franklin D. Roosevelt and his administration. Some saw her as a Republican "hatchet man," particularly after 1944, when she was the first woman to address a Republican national convention. Her reelection to a second congressional term became one of the most hotly contested partisan battles of the 1944 election year.

Clare Boothe Luce voluntarily retired from Con-

CLARE BOOTHE LUCE.   LIBRARY OF CONGRESS

grcss in 1947. From 1953 to 1957 she served as U.S. ambassador to Italy, the first American woman ambassador to a major power. In 1964 she announced her candidacy for the U.S. Senate, running on the New York State Conservative Party ticket, but withdrew after Sen. Barry Goldwater, the Republican presidential candidate, urged her not to split the Republican vote. Although she sought no further elected positions, she remained politically active; at the time of her death in 1987 she was completing her eighth year as a member of the president's Foreign Intelligence Advisory Board.

BIBLIOGRAPHY

Lyons, Joseph. *Clare Boothe Luce.* 1989.
Shadegg, Stephen C. *Clare Boothe Luce: A Biography.* 1970.
Sheed, Wilfrid. *Clare Boothe Luce.* 1982.

MARY ETTA BOESL

M

MACARTHUR FIRING. At a tumultuous moment in American history, a joint session of the 82d Congress gathered on 15 April 1951 to hear an address by Gen. Douglas A. MacArthur eight days after he had been relieved by President Harry S. Truman for insubordination as commander of United Nations forces in the Korean War. In a memorable peroration, MacArthur said, "'Old soldiers never die; they just fade away.' And like the old soldier of that ballad I now close my military career and just fade away—an old soldier who tried to do his duty as God gave him the light to see that duty. Goodbye."

MacArthur's performance, broadcast on national television, was one of the great historic spectacles of Capitol Hill. The decisive point of the controversy over Truman's dismissal of MacArthur, however, was not reached until May, when the Senate Armed Services Committee and the Senate Foreign Relations Committee held joint hearings to assess the firing of MacArthur.

Trouble between Truman and MacArthur had flared after November 1950, when Chinese forces had entered the Korean War against U.N. troops and hurled them back across the Chinese–North Korean border. Truman had approved the U.N. advance into enemy North Korea, but MacArthur sought approval to pursue Chinese forces into Chinese territory and permission to bomb China and blockade the Chinese coast. Truman refused. In effect, MacArthur went over Truman's head by writing to House Republican leader Joseph W. Martin, Jr., to plead his case. Martin read the letter to the House, and Truman was outraged. Finally, in an unauthorized public statement, MacArthur undermined an effort by the United Nations to arrange a truce. On 11 April 1951, Truman fired him, arousing fierce hostility from Republican conservatives and others of MacArthur's admirers. In the Senate hearings, Secretary of Defense George C. Marshall and the Joint Chiefs of Staff supported the president. In time, MacArthur did fade away.

BIBLIOGRAPHY

Donovan, Robert J. *Tumultuous Years: The Presidency of Harry S Truman, 1949–1953.* 1982. Chaps. 25, 32, 33.
James, D. Clayton. *Years of MacArthur: Triumph and Disaster, 1945–1964.* Vol. 3. 1985.
McCullough, David. *Truman.* 1992.

ROBERT J. DONOVAN

MCCARRAN, PATRICK A. (1876–1954), Democratic senator from Nevada, chairman of the Committee on the Judiciary and the Joint Committee on Foreign Economic Cooperation, important critic of President Harry S. Truman's foreign and internal security policies. Pat McCarran was Nevada's first native-born senator. He rose to prominence as an attorney specializing in criminal defense and divorce cases. McCarran served on the Nevada Supreme Court from 1913 to 1918 but was otherwise excluded from statewide office by George Wingfield's bipartisan political machine. He was elected to the U.S. Senate in 1932 and was reelected in 1938, 1944, and 1950.

He chaired the District of Columbia Committee from 1941 to 1944, the Judiciary Committee from 1944 to 1946 and 1949 to 1952, and became a high-ranking member of the Appropriations Committee.

He also chaired the Senate Internal Security Sub-committee of the Judiciary Committee during its investigation of the Institute of Pacific Relations and was responsible for the government's prosecution of sinologist Owen Lattimore, whom he believed to be consciously advancing communist interests in China.

Sen. Richard B. Russell of Georgia had it right when he called McCarran "an able and effective legislator." According to Russell, no senator had ever "sponsored the passage of more legislation, in wider and more varied fields, than he did." McCarran was responsible for the Civil Aeronautics Acts of 1938, the Airport Act of 1946, the McCarran Internal Security Act of 1950, and the McCarran-Walter Immigration and Nationality Act of 1952, the last two enacted over Truman's veto. He was a critic of President Franklin D. Roosevelt's Court-packing plan in 1937. In the late 1940s he was a forceful opponent of the influx of postwar refugees from Europe. At that time McCarran also took strong positions on international aviation, advocating the "All American Flag Line," a federally chartered airline that would have had sole responsibility for all American passenger aviation overseas. After 1950, he and Sen. Joseph R. McCarthy (R-Wis.) were close political associates, though McCarran was far more successful than McCarthy in getting his way in the Senate.

His political strength in Nevada arose from his assiduous attention to the needs and desires of his constituents, who included such interest groups as

GEN. DOUGLAS MACARTHUR. Making his farewell address to a joint session of Congress. Behind him sit Vice President Alben W. Barkley (D-Ky.), *left,* and House Speaker Sam Rayburn (D-Tex.). Photograph by Mark Kauffman, April 1951. *(See preceding page.)*   LIBRARY OF CONGRESS

PATRICK A. McCARRAN. A supporter of Sen. Joseph R. McCarthy, McCarran delivered a speech in the Senate charging that the Army-McCarthy hearings had brought "ridicule" and "decline in the respect in which the Congress is held," 22 June 1954.   LIBRARY OF CONGRESS

ranchers, miners, and casino owners. Since at that time Nevada had the smallest population by far of all the states, McCarran was able to deal with its voters on a close, personal basis. By skillful use of patronage, he built up the strongest political organization in the history of the state, in the process becoming the dominant force in both major parties there. McCarran demanded full loyalty from the people he rewarded and could be quite vindictive toward his political enemies.

Within the Senate, McCarran's power derived from his keen understanding of the legislative process, his close attention to detail, and his willingness to use his position within Congress's institutional structure in the most forceful way possible. A lone wolf, McCarran was not particularly well liked by his colleagues, but he understood how to get things done.

BIBLIOGRAPHY

Edwards, Jerome E. *Pat McCarran, Political Boss of Nevada.* 1982.

Newman, Robert P. *Owen Lattimore and the "Loss" of China.* 1992.

JEROME E. EDWARDS

MCCARRAN INTERNAL SECURITY ACT OF 1950 (64 Stat. 987–1031). On 23 September 1950, the Internal Security Act was passed by Congress over President Harry S. Truman's veto. The lengthy and complex measure, more popularly known as the McCarran Act, was designed to "protect the United States against certain un-American and subversive activities by requiring registration of Communist organizations, and for other purposes."

Title I, the Subversive Activities Control Act of 1950, contained controversial communist registration provisions originally sponsored in 1948 by Rep. Karl E. Mundt (R-S.D.) and Rep. Richard M. Nixon (R-Calif.), and later by Sen. Homer Ferguson (R-Mich.) and Rep. John S. Wood (D-Ga.). To carry out the registration of "Communist-action" and "Communist-front" organizations, a five-member Subversive Activities Control Board was established. Other portions of the measure amended existing espionage and sabotage laws, alien exclusion and deportation laws, and immigration and nationality laws. These changes were sponsored by Sen. Patrick A. McCarran (D-Nev.), Rep. Sam Hobbs (D-Ala.), and other Democrats.

Title II, the Emergency Detention Act of 1950, was added to the law after much debate in Congress. It had been offered as a last-minute substitute for the McCarran bill by several Democratic senators from the so-called Liberal Caucus. They were Harley M. Kilgore of West Virginia, Paul H. Douglas of Illinois, Hubert H. Humphrey of Minnesota, Herbert H. Lehman of New York, Frank P. Graham of North Carolina, Estes Kefauver of Tennessee, and William Benton of Connecticut. Title II provided for the detention of suspected spies, saboteurs, or subversives under certain conditions and only after a presidentially proclaimed "internal security emergency."

Called a "chamber of horrors bill" by one White House aide, Truman vetoed the Internal Security Act on the grounds that it would be ineffective, unworkable, and dangerous to civil liberties, and would "give Government officials vast powers to harass all of our citizens in the exercise of their right of free speech." Without debate, the House overrode his veto 286 to 48. After a futile filibuster attempt by a few Democrats, the Senate voted 57 to 10 to override. Many members of Congress did not bother to vote.

The Internal Security Act was a product of Cold War fears of external aggression, internal subversion, and political maneuvering. Confrontations with the communist world in Berlin and Korea, cases of domestic spying investigated by the House Committee on Un-American Activities, and the reemergence of the bipartisan conservative coalition to roll back New Deal programs and resist Truman's Fair Deal congealed in 1950 to help produce anticommunist demagogues, such as Sen. Joseph R. McCarthy (R-Wis.), and legislation, such as the McCarran Act.

The McCarran Act was only minimally effective. Government employees were intimidated and immigrants were harassed. However, no communist organizations were ever registered. Although money was appropriated to rehabilitate Japanese relocation camps from World War II for purposes of detaining suspected subversives, the Emergency Detention Act was never implemented. Much of this legislation was declared unconstitutional in the 1960s, and the Detention Act was repealed in September 1971.

BIBLIOGRAPHY

Kirshen, H. B. "The Internal Security Act of 1950." *American Association of University Professors Bulletin* 37 (1951): 260–275.

Tanner, William R., and Robert Griffith. "Legislative Politics and 'McCarthyism': The Internal Security Act of 1950." In *The Specter*. Edited by Robert Griffith and Athan Theohasis. 1974. Also in vol. 3 of *The Congress of the United States, 1789–1989*. Edited by Joel Silbey. 1991. Pp. 709–726.

WILLIAM R. TANNER

MCCARRAN-WALTER IMMIGRATION AND NATIONALITY ACT (1952; 66 Stat. 163–282). At the end of World War II, Congress enacted legislation to permit displaced persons (refugees from Europe) to enter the United States. Such laws were needed because the national origins quota acts of the 1920s, which allocated the 150,000 European immigration slots available annually on the basis of each nation's proportion of the U.S. population as of 1920, favored northern and western European nationals. The 1920s quotas applied only to European nations and their colonies and excluded nearly all Asians. During the 1940s, Congress also repealed the ban dating from the 1880s on immigrants from China, India, and the Philippines and set small quotas for these nationals. The changes prompted Congress to take a broad new look at immigration policy. A Senate committee under Patrick A. McCarran of Nevada held hearings and reported to Congress. In the

House Francis E. Walter of Pennsylvania assumed leadership; the resulting Immigration and Nationality Act of 1952 became known as the McCarran-Walter Act.

The McCarran-Walter Act kept the national origins quotas of the 1920s intact. The new law repealed the remaining bans on Asians and permitted South and East Asian nationals to have small immigration quotas. Senator McCarran, like many of his colleagues, worried about communists and subversives entering the United States; hence the final act contained provisions barring suspected subversives and communists.

The 1952 law, like its 1920s predecessors, did not have quotas for immigrants from the Western Hemisphere. But those nationals came under bans on communists and people likely to become public charges and others Congress considered undesirable.

Patriotic groups such as the Daughters of the American Revolution, some labor leaders, and conservatives argued that the law was needed to protect the nation from radicals and to keep out immigrants who might depress the U.S. standard of living. They also defended the national origins quotas as a means of selecting people who they believed would easily assimilate into U.S. society. Liberals opposed the McCarran-Walter Act, and President Harry S. Truman vetoed it. Truman insisted that the act's quotas discriminated against the nations of southern and eastern Europe, including some of America's NATO allies. In a close vote Congress overrode the president's veto.

The McCarran-Walter Act had scarcely become law when Congress passed another refugee bill to get around the small quotas for some nationals. And President Dwight D. Eisenhower established an important precedent when he authorized the attorney general to use the "parole" power to admit about 30,000 Hungarian refugees from the abortive Hungarian Revolution of 1954. As a result increasing numbers of immigrants were able to enter without regard to the national origins quotas.

Liberals, ethnic groups, and civil rights and church organizations called for a major overhaul of the 1952 immigration act. But they lacked the necessary votes and presidential initiative until the 1960s. President John F. Kennedy proposed a new policy, as did his successor, Lyndon B. Johnson. Finally, in 1965, Congress abolished the national origins quotas and established a new immigration system based on family unification, the economic needs of the United States, and safe haven for political refugees. The limits on potential subversives were not repealed until 1990, when Congress passed a new immigration law.

BIBLIOGRAPHY

Divine, Robert A. *American Immigration Policy, 1924–1952.* 1957.
Reimers, David M. *Still the Golden Door: The Third World Comes to America.* 1985, 1992.

DAVID M. REIMERS

MCCARTHY, EUGENE J. (1916–), Democratic representative and senator from Minnesota, a founder of the Democratic Study Group, and a leader of liberal causes in the 1950s and 1960s.

A college professor before entering Congress in 1949, Eugene Joseph McCarthy organized a group of fellow liberals to counter the 1956 "southern manifesto" and its denunciation of civil rights; in January 1957 the group announced a legislative program for the 85th Congress. Known as "McCarthy's Mavericks," the group later became formalized as the Democratic Study Group. In the late 1950s the DSG promoted a progressive legislative agenda, and during the 1960s it led the ultimately successful fight to reform the archaic rules and procedures of the House.

"The House is not a home," McCarthy, known for his wit, remarked before running for the Senate and unseating incumbent Republican Edward J. Thye in 1958. As Democratic senator from Minnesota from 1959 to 1971, McCarthy served on the Finance Committee (1959–1971) and the Public Works Committee (1959–1961); as chairman of the Senate Special Committee on Unemployment Problems (1959–1960); and on the Agriculture Committee (1961–1965), the Foreign Relations Committee (1965–1969), and the Government Operations Committee (1969–1971).

As chairman of the Senate Special Committee on Unemployment Problems in 1959 and 1960, McCarthy held hearings, and thereafter the committee outlined many of the economic development and social welfare programs later enacted during the Kennedy and Johnson administrations. On the Ways and Means and Finance committees of the House and Senate, respectively, McCarthy pushed for additional benefits and minimum wage coverage for migrant workers. In the early 1960s he led the fight to give Medicare coverage to the mentally ill and was also a leader in efforts throughout the 1960s to extend unemployment compensation. Be-

ginning in 1954 and subsequently for more than fifteen years in both House and Senate, McCarthy called for congressional oversight of the Central Intelligence Agency.

McCarthy, who with Senators Wayne L. Morse, Ernest Gruening, and J. William Fulbright was an early opponent of the Vietnam War, in November 1967 challenged President Lyndon B. Johnson for the 1968 Democratic presidential nomination. His unexpected success in the New Hampshire primary and elsewhere nudged President Johnson out of the race and brought in Sen. Robert F. Kennedy of New York. McCarthy retired from the Senate in 1971. He ran for president as an independent in 1976, successfully challenging numerous state laws limiting ballot access to independent and third-party candidates. At McCarthy's initiative, in 1975 and 1976 a challenge to the constitutionality of the Federal Election Campaign Act Amendments of 1974, joined by Sen. James L. Buckley (R-N.Y.) and others, was carried to the Supreme Court, which acted to protect basic freedoms of speech.

McCarthy has written numerous books on American politics and institutions, including *A Liberal Answer to the Conservative Challenge* (1964); *America Revisited: 150 Years after Tocqueville* (1976); *The Ultimate Tyranny: The Majority over the Majority* (1980); and *Up 'Til Now: A Memoir of the Decline of American Politics* (1987). In 1992 McCarthy ran for president as a Democrat; he called for a tax on capital gains to eliminate the national debt and for a shorter working day to reduce chronic unemployment. Although he was on the primary ballot in major states, the networks and the Democratic party excluded him from televised debates.

BIBLIOGRAPHY

Eisele, Albert. *Almost to the Presidency.* 1972.
Herzog, Arthur. *McCarthy for President.* 1969.
McCarthy, Eugene J. *Up 'Til Now: A Memoir of the Decline of American Politics.* 1987.

JOHN F. CALLAHAN

MCCARTHY, JOSEPH R. (1908–1957), Republican senator from Wisconsin, chairman of the Senate Committee on Government Operations and its Permanent Subcommittee on Investigations; gained notoriety for his inflammatory allegations of communist infiltration in the U.S. government, U.S. Army, and elsewhere in American society. Joseph Raymond McCarthy was born on a 142-acre dairy farm near Appleton, Wisconsin, on 14 November

THE END OF THE LA FOLLETTE DYNASTY. Joseph R. McCarthy beat three-term incumbent Robert M. La Follette, Jr., in the 1946 Republican primary in Wisconsin, ending the forty-year La Follette legacy that began in 1906, when Robert M. La Follette, Sr., entered the Senate. The cartoon alludes to McCarthy's campaign claims of heroic war exploits. Clifford K. Berryman, *Washington Evening Star*, 15 August 1946.

U.S. SENATE COLLECTION, CENTER FOR LEGISLATIVE ARCHIVES

1908. His trademark—reckless ambition—was apparent from the start. He quit school at fourteen, began a poultry business, went bankrupt, returned to high school, crammed four years of work into two semesters, and entered Marquette College, a Jesuit school in Milwaukee. After earning his law degree in 1935, McCarthy returned to Appleton, ran for circuit judge, and pulled off a stunning upset by campaigning furiously and smearing the incumbent's good name.

At twenty-nine, Judge McCarthy attracted much attention. The press roasted him for providing "quickie" divorces to political supporters, and the state Supreme Court censured him for destroying crucial evidence in a price-fixing case. In 1942, McCarthy joined the Marines. He spent World War II as an intelligence officer in the Pacific, although he later claimed to have been a tailgunner who suffered a war wound when his plane crash-landed under fire. In fact, his only war injury occurred during a hazing incident aboard a troopship, when he fell down a stairwell and broke his foot.

In 1946, McCarthy took on three-term incumbent Robert M. La Follette, Jr., a member of Wisconsin's leading political family, in the Republican senatorial primary. La Follette did not bother to campaign; McCarthy never stopped. Having no record to run on, the thirty-eight-year-old challenger bragged about his war exploits and berated La Follette, then fifty-one, for failing to enlist. McCarthy beat La Follette by five thousand votes. A few months later, he defeated his Democratic opponent by making numerous baseless allegations.

McCarthy, an erratic freshman senator known mainly for raucous behavior, angered his colleagues, who accused him of lying, insulting senior members, and disregarding the Senate's cherished rules and folkways. Before long, his political career was in trouble, and his reelection chances looked grim. He needed a big issue, a major theme, to energize his faltering career.

In February 1950, Senator McCarthy discovered the issue that would restart his political career. "I have here in my hand a list of 205 [Communists] who were known to the secretary of State and who nevertheless are still working and shaping the policy of the State Department," he told a startled Republican audience in Wheeling, West Virginia. In fact, McCarthy had no list. He knew nothing about "Reds" in the State Department or anywhere else. But the newspapers printed his charges, and the public was aroused. In the weeks before his Wheeling speech, China had fallen to the Communists and the Soviet Union had successfully tested an atomic bomb; Alger Hiss had been found guilty of perjury; and Klaus Fuchs, a physicist on the Manhattan Project, had confessed to funneling atomic secrets to the Soviet Union. Now a U.S. senator had stepped forward with a simple explanation for America's troubles in the world: the Communists were "winning" the Cold War because traitors in the U.S. government were aiding their cause.

McCarthy's charges about treason in high places made him an instant celebrity. The cartoonist Herblock coined a new word—McCarthyism—to describe his reckless charges, but prominent Republicans rallied to McCarthy's side. Sen. Robert A. Taft of Ohio, known as Mr. Republican, privately dismissed McCarthy's allegations as "nonsense," but told McCarthy to keep punching: "If one case doesn't work out, try another." Taft shrewdly viewed McCarthy as the man who could turn fear and distrust into Republican votes.

In March 1950, the Senate formed a special committee, chaired by Democrat Millard E. Tydings of

Maryland, to evaluate McCarthy's allegations. By this time, however, McCarthy had rearranged both his numbers and his charges: the 205 "Communists" had been reduced to 81 "fellow travelers" and "security risks." But the senator now claimed to have uncovered the "top Russian spy" in the United States, an obscure Johns Hopkins professor named Owen Lattimore. The charge was preposterous; the headlines were spectacular. After bitter debate, the Tydings Committee split along party lines. The Democrats' majority report claimed that McCarthy had perpetrated "a fraud and a hoax" upon the Senate, but the Republican members refused to sign it.

The Tydings report was quickly overshadowed by news of North Korea's invasion of South Korea. With U.S. troops battling communist forces in Asia, McCarthy's message took on special force. In the 1950 elections, the Republicans gained five seats in the Senate and twenty-eight in the House. As the presidential campaign approached, McCarthy's attacks grew bolder. He called Secretary of Defense George C. Marshall a traitor, mocked Secretary of State Dean Acheson as the "Red Dean of Fashion," and described President Harry S. Truman as a drunkard, adding, "The son-of-a-bitch should be impeached." During the campaign, McCarthy claimed, falsely, that the Communist *Daily Worker* had endorsed Democrat Adlai E. Stevenson II for president. And he made the intentional slip "Alger . . . I mean Adlai" on several occasions.

McCarthy was easily reelected in the Republican landslide of 1952. With his own party in control of Congress, he became chairman of the Committee on Government Operations and its powerful Subcommittee on Investigations. Filling key staff positions with ex–FBI agents and former prosecutors such as Roy M. Cohn, an abrasive young attorney from New York, McCarthy began to track down "communist influence" throughout the federal bureaucracy. His early targets included the Voice of America, the Government Printing Office, and the Foreign Service.

McCarthy's hearings uncovered no Communists. They did, however, ruin numerous careers, undermine government morale, and make the United States look ridiculous in the eyes of the world. Not surprisingly, however, Republican criticism of McCarthy began to build because he was now attacking a bureaucracy within his own party's administration. Before long, his sternest opponents included Republican senators such as Arthur V. Watkins of Utah, Ralph E. Flanders of Vermont, and Margaret Chase Smith of Maine.

Many expected Dwight D. Eisenhower to put McCarthy in his place, but the new president was slow to respond, believing that a brawl with the senator would divide Republicans into warring camps and seriously demean the presidential office. Time and again he told his aides, "I just will not—I refuse to get into the gutter with that guy."

Eisenhower changed his mind in the fall of 1953, when Cohn and McCarthy began to investigate the U.S. Army. The two men charged, among other things, that a communist spy ring was operating at Fort Monmouth, New Jersey, headquarters of the Army Signal Corps. Army officials responded that Roy Cohn was harassing the service in order to win preferential treatment for a close friend and part-time McCarthy staff member named G. David Schine, who had recently been drafted into the army. President Eisenhower was furious. At long last, McCarthy had attacked the one institution guaranteed to pit the Republican White House against him.

Early in 1954, the Senate decided to investigate the running feud between the U.S. Army and McCarthy. At Eisenhower's insistence, Republican lead-

JOSEPH R. MCCARTHY

ers agreed to allow televised coverage of the hearings. The president wanted the American people to see McCarthy in action, and it proved to be a wise move. The cumulative impression of McCarthy—his windy speeches, his frightening outbursts, his crude personal attacks—was truly devastating. The highlight of the hearings came in June 1954, when McCarthy questioned the loyalty of a young lawyer who had worked on the staff of army counsel Joseph Welch. "Have you no sense of decency, sir? At long last, have you left no sense of decency?" Welch responded in a voice rich with sorrow. The spectators burst into applause.

A few months later, the Senate censured McCarthy for bringing that body "into dishonor and disrepute." The vote was 67 to 22, with only the most conservative Republicans opposed. Many believed that McCarthy's censure was linked to the easing of Cold War tensions at home. The Korean War was over, Stalin was dead, and the radical right was in disarray. For McCarthy himself, things came apart rapidly. Reporters and colleagues ignored him, and his influence disappeared. Unable to get his message across, McCarthy spent his final days drinking in private, railing against those who had deserted his cause. He died of acute alcoholism in 1957, virtually alone, at the age of forty-eight.

BIBLIOGRAPHY

Caute, David. *The Great Fear: The Anti-Communist Purge under Truman and Eisenhower.* 1978.

Fried, Richard. *Nightmare in Red: The McCarthy Era in Perspective.* 1990.

Oshinsky, David M. *A Conspiracy So Immense: The World of Joe McCarthy.* 1983.

Whitfield, Stephen J. *The Culture of the Cold War.* 1991.

DAVID M. OSHINSKY

MCCLELLAN, JOHN L. (1896–1977), Democratic representative and senator from Arkansas, chairman of the Senate Committee on Government Operations. John Little McClellan was elected to the House of Representatives in 1934 and reelected in 1936. An unsuccessful candidate for the Senate in 1938, he was subsequently elected to that body in 1942 and reelected in 1948, 1954, 1960, 1966, and 1972.

In 1962, while serving as chairman of the so-called Senate Rackets Committee, he wrote a book, *Crime Without Punishment,* which disclosed and discussed the anatomy of organized crime and earned him the nickname of "America's number-

one crime-buster." He chaired the Senate Government Operations Committee and its famed subsidiary, the Permanent Subcommittee on Investigations, better known as the McClellan Committee.

Toward the end of his tenure and his life, McClellan served as chairman of the Senate Committee on Appropriations. As chairman, he pumped billions of federal dollars into his home state in the form of economic development and flood control and drainage projects, most notably the Kerr-McClellan Arkansas River Navigation System, a $1.2 billion project.

Nationally, his legislative focus was on fighting crime. Long-term results of his work included the Organized Crime Control Act of 1960, the Omnibus Crime and Safe Streets Act of 1968, the Organized Crime Control Act of 1970, and the new Criminal Code of 1974.

As ranking Democrat on the Senate Judiciary Committee, he participated in all the confirmation hearings during the Nixon administration. His was the decisive voice in blocking the selection of L. Patrick Gray III as the director of the Federal Bureau of Investigation.

He occasionally ventured outside these primary areas of concern, as was the case in his involvement in the funding of the Elementary and Secondary Education Act of 1965. Teaming up with chairman Carl D. Perkins of Kentucky in the House, he led the defeat of the Senate Education Committee's funding proposal that would have given a financial edge to large city schools. Twenty-eight states, including Arkansas, benefited from his successful fight.

BIBLIOGRAPHY

McClellan, John L. *Crime Without Punishment.* 1962.

McClellan, John L. Public Papers. Onachita Baptist University, Arkadelphia, Arkansas.

KAY C. GOSS

MCCORMACK, JOHN W. (1891–1980), Democratic representative from Massachusetts, majority leader, minority whip, Speaker of the House of Representatives. For thirty years (1941–1971), McCormack occupied a major leadership post among the Democrats of the House. He was majority leader during all of Sam Rayburn's seventeen years as Speaker and was minority whip during the Democrats' last two stints in the minority (80th and 83d Congresses). Following Rayburn's death in November 1961, McCormack became Speaker and served for nine years, the second-longest period of consecutive service in House history.

Born in Boston, John McCormack was an Irish American whose father, a bricklayer, died when he was thirteen. His native intelligence and ambition led him to read for the law in a Boston lawyer's office. As a young man he embarked almost immediately on a political career, one of the major routes of social advancement for the Boston Irish.

McCormack served in both houses of the Massachusetts legislature. In 1928 he filled the vacant U.S. House seat of Democrat James A. Gallivan and was reelected to the following twenty-one Congresses.

After the Democrats gained control of the House following the deaths of a number of Republican members, McCormack was invited by Speaker John Nance Garner of Texas to run for one of the five newly open seats on the influential Ways and Means Committee. McCormack finished second in the caucus balloting and began his service on the committee in his third year in the House—a remarkable feat for the time.

Garner's early support led to a lifetime link between McCormack and the Texas House delegation—often called the "Austin-Boston" alliance. Throughout the 1930s, McCormack regularly voted for conservative southern candidates in the Democratic caucus. His most valuable service to the southern Democrats was rendered in the 1937 battle for the majority leader post between Rules Committee chairman John O'Connor of New York City and Commerce Committee chairman Rayburn. With the votes of other northern urban Catholic members, McCormack tilted the election for Rayburn, 184 to 127.

Rayburn's election as Speaker in 1940 after the death of Speaker William B. Bankhead (D-Ala.) led to another majority leader election. In this contest, a more southern-dominated House Democratic caucus elected McCormack to the post. He was the first New Englander to hold a House Democratic leadership position in more than a century.

Apart from staunch anticommunism and a generalized commitment to federal entitlement programs, McCormack had little in the way of a legislative agenda. No major bills bore his name. He saw himself as a facilitator of party proposals, not as an architect. He preferred his floor leadership role, with its interparty give-and-take, to his later role of presiding over the House as Speaker.

As Speaker, McCormack served for seven of nine years under presidents John F. Kennedy and Lyn-

JOHN W. MCCORMACK. As Speaker of the House, January 1963.　LIBRARY OF CONGRESS

don B. Johnson, fellow Democrats who were also products of the Austin-Boston alliance. Although both Kennedy and McCormack were Boston Irish, they were often rivals. Johnson's ascendancy to the presidency in 1963 provided a more hospitable atmosphere for McCormack. For fourteen months following Kennedy's death, McCormack was first in the order of presidential succession, after Johnson. In the 89th Congress (1965–1967), McCormack worked closely with the president to push Great Society legislation through the House. The escalating war in Vietnam, however, derailed the Great Society legislative agenda, and McCormack's loyalty to Johnson's war aims led to a caucus challenge to his speakership in 1969. Although McCormack easily withstood the challenge from Morris K. Udall (D-Ariz.), charges of influence peddling against key members of his staff and the less congenial Republican presidency of Richard M. Nixon led to his retirement in 1971. On 22 November 1980 McCormack died at the age of eighty-eight.

BIBLIOGRAPHY

O'Neill, Thomas P., Jr., and William Novak. *Man of the House: The Life and Political Memoirs of Speaker Tip O'Neill.* 1987.
Peabody, Robert L. *Leadership in Congress: Stability, Succession, and Change.* 1976.
Peters, Ronald M., Jr. *The American Speakership in Historical Perspective.* 1990.

GARRISON NELSON

MCCULLOCH V. MARYLAND (17 U.S. [4 Wheat.] 316 [1819]). In the twentieth century, *McCulloch v. Maryland* has permitted the federal government's increasing involvement in the economy and has provided the constitutional basis for the New Deal and for numerous federal educational, scientific, and social programs. The case originated in a Maryland law that required all banks not created by the authority of the state to pay an annual tax of $15,000. James W. McCulloch, cashier of the Baltimore branch of the Second Bank of the United States, protested the tax as unconstitutional and sued the state. The case was ultimately appealed to the U.S. Supreme Court, where Chief Justice John Marshall, speaking for a unanimous court, declared the Maryland tax unconstitutional and void.

The decision is one of Marshall's most important pronouncements, a careful and vigorous exposition of the Constitution that stressed nationalist principles and greatly enlarged the powers and discretion of Congress. The central issue in the case was whether Congress had the power to incorporate a bank. Marshall justified the creation of the Bank of the United States on the grounds that the Constitution, which emanated from the people of the United States, had delegated certain specified powers to the federal government, including the right to lay and collect taxes and to borrow money. He argued that the bank was a convenient, useful, and essential instrument for implementing these powers. Because the Constitution in Article I, section 8 had given Congress the power to "make all Laws which shall be necessary and proper for carrying into Exe-cution the foregoing Powers," the bank was constitutional, the Court reasoned.

Marshall elaborated further on the need for a loose and expansive interpretation of the powers of the federal government, especially those of Congress. He rejected the idea of a strict interpretation of the Constitution, then espoused by states' rights Jeffersonian Republicans; that approach would make the Constitution unworkable. Marshall argued that the necessary and proper clause had been included among the powers of Congress, not among its limitations, and was meant to enlarge, not reduce, its ability to execute enumerated powers. Marshall declared, "Let the end be legitimate, let it be within the scope of the Constitution, and all means which are appropriate which are plainly adapted to that end, which are not prohibited, but consist with the letter and spirit of the Constitution, are constitutional." Congress was to have broad discretion in applying a loose interpretation to the Constitution.

The decision was controversial and aroused much criticism. Opponents denounced Marshall's strong endorsement of a broad interpretation of the power of the federal government; among other things, the decision seemed to sanction an all-encompassing federal program of internal improvements. Nor did they accept Marshall's view of the bank primarily as an agency of the federal government; for they pointed out that the bank was essentially a private profit-making corporation. The critics argued that the decision had not adequately dealt with the myriad constitutional problems involved in creating national corporations and took the Court to task for giving the bank the power to establish branches in the different states without the states' permission.

The victory of the Bank of the United States in *McCulloch* was only temporary. In 1832 President Andrew Jackson vetoed its recharter, primarily on constitutional grounds. However, on a more important level, Marshall's broad interpretation of the powers of the federal government was ultimately triumphant, reflected in the wide reach of federal programs of the twentieth century.

[*See also* Bank of the United States.]

BIBLIOGRAPHY

Ellis, Richard E. "The Path Not Taken: Virginia and the Supreme Court, 1789–1821." In *Virginia and the Constitution.* Edited by A. E. Dick Howard and Melvin I. Urofsky. 1992.
Gunther, Gerald, ed. *John Marshall's Defense of McCulloch vs. Maryland.* 1969.

White, G. Edward. *History of the Supreme Court of the United States.* Vols. 3, 4: *The Marshall Court and Cultural Change, 1815–1835.* 1988.

RICHARD E. ELLIS

MACE. One of the oldest symbols of the U.S. government, a mace was chosen in 1789 by the first Speaker of the House of Representatives as the proper symbol for the sergeant at arms, to be used in carrying out the duties of the office. The tradition of using a mace in a legislative chamber came to the United States from Great Britain, where the ceremonial mace symbolized the authority of the House of Commons.

THE MACE.   *PERLEY'S REMINISCENCES,* VOL. 1

The design of the House mace derives from the ancient battle weapon of the same name and the Roman fasces. The mace consists of a shaft of thirteen ebony rods, bound together by silver bands and surmounted by a silver globe and solid silver eagle. Made by New York silversmith William Adams, it was first used by the House in 1841. It replaced both the original mace, destroyed when the British burned the Capitol in 1814, and a temporary wooden substitute.

The mace must be in the chamber whenever the House is in session. Carried by the sergeant at arms, it is placed on a pedestal at the Speaker's right. When the House resolves itself into the Committee of the Whole House on the State of the Union, the mace is removed to a lower pedestal.

In accordance with the Rules of the House, whenever an individual member or group of members becomes disorderly, the sergeant at arms, on order of the Speaker, presents the mace before the offenders to restore order in the chamber.

BIBLIOGRAPHY

U.S. House of Representatives. Office of the Sergeant at Arms. *The Mace of the United States House of Representatives.* 1992.
Wilding, Norman, and Philip Laundy. *An Encyclopaedia of Parliament.* 1961.

CYNTHIA PEASE MILLER

MCFARLAND, ERNEST W. (1894–1984), Democratic senator from Arizona and Senate majority leader. Raised in frontier Oklahoma, McFarland graduated from the University of Oklahoma in 1917 and from Stanford University, where he earned degrees in law (1921) and political science (1922). He held several county and state legal and judicial posts in Oklahoma in the 1920s and 1930s. In 1940 he won a seat in the U.S. Senate, defeating twenty-eight-year-incumbent Henry F. Ashurst in the Democratic primary.

He gained assignments on the Senate's Irrigation, Indian Affairs, and Interstate Commerce committees, posts that reflected Arizona's pressing legislative interests. For his entire Senate career, he fell under the legislative shadow of his state's senior senator, Carl Hayden. Nonetheless, he saw enacted much of his own legislative agenda in the areas of water resources, veterans' benefits, Indian rights, and mineral development. McFarland easily won reelection in 1946.

In the November 1950 election, the Senate's majority leader and Democratic party whip, along with three other Democratic incumbents, were turned out of office. The most likely successors to those posts among senior party leaders feared that further defeat would come to those charged with defending the policies of the increasingly unpopular Truman administration. Persuaded by de facto party leader Richard B. Russell (Ga.), they selected as majority leader the easygoing McFarland, who had only two years left in his term and faced a difficult reelection contest. Though lacking in evident leadership skills, McFarland had consistently supported the administration. To balance him, the Democrats named as party whip the energetic and ambitious Lyndon B. Johnson. Unsuited to the post, and unhappy defending the programs of an administration more liberal than he was, McFarland failed to tend to his constituency and lost the 1952 election to Republican Barry Goldwater.

BIBLIOGRAPHY

McFarland, Ernest. *Mac: The Autobiography of Ernest McFarland.* 1979.

RICHARD A. BAKER

GEORGE MCGOVERN. On 20 April 1971.

LIBRARY OF CONGRESS

MCGOVERN, GEORGE (1922–), Democratic representative and senator from South Dakota, leading opponent of U.S. involvement in Vietnam, and Democratic presidential nominee in 1972. After serving in World War II as a B-24 bomber pilot and flying thirty-five missions over Europe, McGovern studied for a doctorate in history at Northwestern University. While teaching at Dakota Wesleyan University in Mitchell, South Dakota, he undertook to rebuild his state's moribund Democratic party. In 1956 he defeated Republican incumbent Harold O. Lovre in the 1st Congressional District, benefiting in the race from the midwestern farm revolt against Secretary of Agriculture Ezra Taft Benson. He was reelected in 1958.

In 1960 he challenged two-term senator Karl E. Mundt but was defeated. President John F. Kennedy later named him director of the Food for Peace program. After South Dakota's other Republican senator, Francis H. Case, died in June 1962, McGovern was elected to the Senate by a margin of 246 votes. This narrow margin led to a major political career. McGovern was reelected in 1968, defeating former governor Archie Gubbrud, and in 1974, defeating Vietnam War veteran Leo Thorsness. McGovern was an early, outspoken, and persistent critic of expansion and continuation of the war in Vietnam under Presidents Kennedy, Lyndon B. Johnson, and Richard M. Nixon. His Senate speech in September 1963 brought him world attention.

McGovern finished third behind Hubert H. Humphrey and Eugene J. McCarthy in convention balloting for the 1968 Democratic presidential nomination, but in 1972 won his party's nomination only to be resoundingly defeated in the fall by President Nixon. McGovern's campaign was plagued by wrangling in the Democratic party hierarchy, debilitating primary clashes with Hubert Humphrey and other Democratic hopefuls, the unfortunate choice of Sen. Thomas F. Eagleton as his running mate (he was subsequently replaced by Sargent Shriver), and Nixon's financial advantage. McGovern received only 37.5 percent of the 1972 popular vote and, carrying only Massachusetts and the District of Columbia, won a total of seventeen electoral votes, the lowest of any Democratic presidential candidate since 1860. In 1980 McGovern made a bid for a fourth Senate term, but lost to Republican representative James Abdnor.

In his early Senate years, McGovern served on the Agriculture and Interior committees. For several years he chaired the Select Committee on Nutrition and Human Needs. During his final Senate term he served on the Agriculture and Foreign Relations committees. Although neither a top party leader nor chairman of a standing committee during his twenty years in Congress, McGovern became an internationally known spokesman for peace, disarmament, and more effective world food distribution. He continued to be a popular political commentator into the 1990s, and was often mentioned as a possible presidential nominee after he left the Senate; he made a weak and short-lived bid for the presidency in 1992.

BIBLIOGRAPHY

Anson, Robert Sam. *McGovern: A Biography.* 1972.
Clem, Alan L. "George McGovern." In *South Dakota Leaders.* Edited by Herbert Hoover and Larry Zimmerman. 1990.
Hart, Gary W. *Right from the Start: A Chronicle of the McGovern Campaign.* 1973.
McGovern, George S. *Grassroots: The Autobiography of George McGovern.* 1977.

ALAN L. CLEM

MCGRAIN V. DAUGHERTY (273 U.S. 135 [1927]).

The Supreme Court case of *McGrain v. Daugherty,* deemed "perhaps the most important in the constitutional history of congressional investigations" by Telford Taylor (*Grand Inquest: The Story of Congressional Investigations,* 1955), first firmly established Congress's investigative power. A Senate committee in 1924 examined why the attorney general had not prosecuted the officials implicated in the Teapot Dome scandal. A witness, the attorney general's brother Mally S. Daugherty, challenged the Senate's investigation.

In its scholarly opinion, written by Justice Willis Van Devanter, the Court traced the long history of legislative investigative power, from the precedents of the British Parliament and the states through the many congressional examples. The Court reasoned, in phrases that have since been quoted countless times, that a "legislative body cannot legislate wisely or effectively in the absence of information"

and that "some means of compulsion are essential to obtain what is needed." Therefore, the Court deemed the matter—"whether the attorney general and his assistants were performing or neglecting their duties"—a "plainly" appropriate subject for congressional inquiry.

Since *McGrain* firmly established the general power of congressional committees to compel testimony, subsequent cases have considered only whether committee has violated some particular right of a witness. Congress has relied on *McGrain* as giving it authority to investigate the Justice Department numerous times, as in the Watergate hearings in 1973 and the Iran-contra hearings in 1987.

BIBLIOGRAPHY

Grabow, John C. *Congressional Investigations: Law and Practice.* 1988.
U.S. House of Representatives. *The Attorney General's Refusal to Provide Congressional Access: Hearing Before a House Subcommittee on the Judiciary.* Testimony by Charles Tiefer. 101st Cong., 2d sess., 1990.

CHARLES TIEFER

MCKELLAR, KENNETH D. (1869–1957),

Democratic representative and senator from Tennessee, chairman of the Senate Committee on Appropriations (1945–1946, 1949–1952). Kenneth Douglas McKellar graduated from the University of Alabama and earned a law degree there in 1892. He began practicing law in Memphis the same year. Interested in politics even as a youth, he soon established the connections necessary for political success. He was chosen as a delegate to the national Democratic convention in 1908 and two years later was elected to the House, where he served for three terms before being elected to the Senate.

By 1916 the Democratic party in Tennessee, after nearly a decade of division and defeat chiefly over the prohibition question, was sufficiently united to elect McKellar senator over the popular Republican governor, Ben Hooper. McKellar embarked on a Senate career that continued for thirty-six years. As a freshman, he supported President Woodrow Wilson in the war effort and in the president's struggle to bring the United States into the League of Nations.

In 1922 McKellar won reelection, although the Republican party held both the presidency and the governorship in Tennessee. Six years later he encountered only nominal opposition and was easily

KENNETH D. MCKELLAR.
OFFICE OF THE HISTORIAN OF THE U.S. SENATE

reelected again. During the 1920s he was on friendly terms with President Warren G. Harding, although he did not hesitate to criticize Republican policies, particularly the tax program of Treasury Secretary Andrew Mellon. He faced no serious opposition in 1934 and 1940, and his basically liberal philosophy enabled him to give wholehearted support to President Franklin D. Roosevelt and the New Deal, although he did develop some differences with the chief executive late in Roosevelt's second term. A member of many Senate committees during his long tenure, he gave careful attention to the Senate Appropriations Committee, which he chaired during the postwar recovery and the implementation of the Marshall Plan. McKellar also served as president pro tempore of the Senate from 1945 to 1947 and from 1949 to 1952.

In 1946, although opposed by some veterans groups, McKellar defeated challenger Ned Carmack, son of a former senator whom McKellar had warmly supported decades earlier. Six years later, at the age of eighty-three—ill, at times disoriented,

and weakened politically—he was defeated by Albert A. Gore, Sr.

Early in his political career McKellar had established a close alliance with Edward H. Crump, who was the leader of the Democratic political machine in Memphis and Tennessee. Although neither was subservient to the other, they worked closely together for mutual benefit. The Crump machine was a waning power by the time of McKellar's loss to Gore.

McKellar was a strong supporter of the New Deal, and especially of the Tennessee Valley Authority, although his frequent quarrels with TVA management and particularly with Director David Lilienthal caused some to view him as a foe of the TVA. But even in the House he had favored the building of a dam and nitrate plant at Muscle Shoals, and he continued to promote development of the area after becoming senator. Many referred to him as the TVA's "rich uncle."

BIBLIOGRAPHY

Pope, Robert D. "Senatorial Baron: The Long Political Career of Kenneth Douglas McKellar." Ph.D. diss., Yale University, 1976.
Tindall, George B. *The Emergence of the New South, 1913–1945.* 1967.

ROBERT E. CORLEW

MCKINLEY, WILLIAM (1843–1901), Republican representative from Ohio, twenty-fifth president of the United States. McKinley was first elected to the House of Representatives in 1876 by the 18th Congressional District in northeastern Ohio. He was a Civil War veteran who had seen active and heroic service and then had practiced law in Canton, Ohio. In this he was a typical member of his congressional generation.

During McKinley's years in the House, his seat was never safe. He represented an ethnically diverse district with a mixed economic base of farming, coal mining, and railroading. The Democrats gerrymandered his district to try to defeat him, but he nevertheless usually emerged victorious. In 1882, however, the Democrats contested his victory in the House and he was unseated. The voters reelected him in 1884.

From the beginning of his House service, McKinley identified himself with the doctrine of the protective tariff. His constituency wanted governmental protection from foreign competitors for its growing industrial enterprises. He soon mastered this controversial issue and became recognized as one of the chief Republican spokesmen for the tariff. He favored "a wise discrimination in favor of American manufactures." McKinley took a leading part in the 1882 House debates over the revision of the tariff that culminated in the so-called Mongrel tariff of 1883. He had an even more prominent role among Republicans in opposition to the Democrat-sponsored Mills Bill of 1888, which sought limited tariff reductions.

When the Republicans gained control of the House after the presidential election of 1888, McKinley ran for Speaker but lost to Thomas B. Reed of Maine. Reed then named McKinley to the Committee on Rules and to the chairmanship of the Ways and Means Committee. In the latter capacity McKinley set about shaping the new tariff bill that the Republicans had promised in their campaign platform. He presented the tariff legislation to the House on 16 April 1890 with the argument that it was for "the better defense of American homes and American industries."

The McKinley bill, as it soon became known, was a protective measure that raised tariff duties on such articles as tin plate, wool, iron, and steel. McKinley also supported James G. Blaine's idea of tariff reciprocity that would lower United States duties in exchange for similar concessions from trading partners. (Reciprocity would later become a theme of the McKinley administration's economic policy.) The McKinley bill passed the House on 21 May 1890 by a partisan vote of 164 to 142. The Senate passed it in the fall. But the Democrats won a sweeping national victory in the congressional elections of 1890, and McKinley was among the Republicans who lost their seats.

After leaving the House, McKinley was elected governor of Ohio in 1891 and again in 1893. He became a candidate for the Republican presidential nomination in 1896 and was chosen on the first ballot. He defeated the Democratic nominee, William Jennings Bryan, and was inaugurated as the twenty-fifth president on 4 March 1897.

McKinley's fourteen years in Congress had instilled in him a deep knowledge of the way the House and the Senate operated. The experience had a significant influence on how McKinley approached Congress while he was president. During his administration, he enjoyed excellent relations with Congress. He consulted lawmakers frequently and avoided public criticism of their performance. He enlisted senators for specific tasks, such as service on the commission that negotiated a treaty with Spain in 1898. When necessary he wielded the veto threat to push action on Capitol Hill. By the end of his presidency, one editorial writer concluded, "No executive in the history of the country . . . has given a greater exhibition of his influence over Congress than President McKinley."

The results of these techniques were evident early in McKinley's term. Calling Congress into special session in 1897, he secured passage of the Dingley Tariff Act, which raised rates at no cost to Republican unity. When a crisis with Spain over Cuba threatened in the spring of 1898, McKinley staved off efforts to recognize the Cuban rebels and to limit his executive authority. Rather than yield to congressional cries for war with Spain, McKinley pursued a diplomatic solution until it became clear that Madrid would not accept any reduction in its sovereignty over Cuba. The president set the terms

WILLIAM MCKINLEY. As a U.S. representative, with his wife Ida, 1881.
STARK COUNTY HISTORICAL SOCIETY OF CANTON, OHIO

under which the United States went to war in April 1898. He exercised his influence with Capitol Hill to obtain the annexation of Hawaii through joint resolution during the Spanish-American War.

The peace treaty with Spain especially illustrated McKinley's effective dealings with Congress. Once an armistice had been reached in August 1898, the president enlisted Democratic and Republican senators to serve on the delegation to negotiate a peace treaty. While that process was going forward, McKinley made a speaking tour of the Midwest to rally public support for the acquisition of the Philippines. After the treaty was signed, he made a similar swing through the South to woo Democratic senators to support the pact. During the deliberations in the Senate, he used patronage, personal negotiations, and quiet pressure to win ratification—by one more vote than the necessary two-thirds—in February 1899.

McKinley's only serious difficulty with Congress came in 1900 over two issues: a tariff for Puerto Rico and a treaty with Great Britain to make possible a canal across Central America. In both cases, the president retreated once it was clear that his original position would not be sustained. Following the election of 1900 and his victory for a second term, McKinley demonstrated his usual mastery when he obtained enactment of the Platt amendment to govern relations with Cuba and the Spooner amendment to provide a civil government for the Philippines. He then intended to use his influence with Congress to obtain ratification of reciprocal trade treaties that had been negotiated with foreign governments during his first term. When he traveled to Buffalo, New York, in September 1901, he did so as part of a campaign to induce Congress to act on reciprocity.

McKinley was assassinated during a public reception in Buffalo on 6 September 1901, and he died eight days later. As president, he never forgot the lessons in consultation and collegiality that he had taken from his years in the House. Few presidents have been more successful in their ability to work with Congress and to maintain good relations with Capitol Hill.

BIBLIOGRAPHY

Gould, Lewis L. *The Presidency of William McKinley*. 1980.

Morgan, H. Wayne. *William McKinley and His America*. 1963.

LEWIS L. GOULD

MCKINLEY TARIFF ACT (1890; 26 Stat. 567–625). The McKinley Tariff Act of 1890 was one of the most important congressional enactments in the ongoing "tariff wars" of the late nineteenth century. From the nation's founding, parties in Congress had argued the merits and constitutionality of protective tariffs. In the post–Civil War decades, when sectional issues began to yield to economic questions, the debate reached a crescendo. By the 1880s the tariff issue had become the chief point of contention between Republicans and Democrats in election campaigns and in Congress.

Republicans, faithful to their ideological origins in the Whig party, supported a protective tariff. They stressed the importance of protection to domestic producers, both factory owners and laborers. Drawing on their history as defenders of free labor in the 1850s and 1860s, Republicans argued that import duties protected U.S. workers from competition with "pauper" labor abroad. Further, they proposed to use tariff-generated revenues to pay for internal improvements, veterans' pensions, defense, and other programs.

Democrats, following party traditions dating to the early days of the Republic, favored low tariffs or free trade. They blamed high import duties for high consumer prices and for a growing surplus in the Treasury that led to wasteful spending. They also emphasized that reduced tariffs on raw materials would lower manufacturing costs and make U.S. producers more competitive in overseas markets, hence bringing greater returns to factory owners and workers alike.

The issue dominated the 1888 elections won by Benjamin Harrison and the Republicans, as a result of which the Republicans controlled the presidency and both houses of Congress for the first time in a decade and a half. They proceeded to enact their program. In the House, Ways and Means Committee chairman William McKinley led the effort to write new tariff legislation. McKinley conducted public hearings for several months and worked closely with committee members to recast the nation's customs duties, schedule by schedule. The resulting bill placed many items on the free list and raised the tariff on many others so high as to discourage their importation, thereby also reducing revenues and the Treasury surplus. The expanded free list, especially sugar, appealed to consumers, while the high rates on other items afforded protection to U.S. producers. Secretary of State James G. Blaine appeared before congressional committees to argue successfully for a reciprocity provision that would permit the administration to negotiate agreements to open foreign markets to U.S. products, especially agricultural goods. Harrison also worked on behalf of the bill, which finally passed on 1 October 1890.

But passage came too late to benefit the Republicans in the 1890 congressional elections. Democrats charged that the legislation would bring high prices, and, to underscore the point, they allegedly paid itinerant peddlers to raise prices on common household items, including those made of tin, on which the tariff rates had been raised to prohibitive levels. Moreover, sugar was not to be put on the free list for half a year, thus delaying the benefit to consumers. Thanks to the McKinley act and other issues, the Democrats took 235 seats in the House and reduced the Republicans to just 88. After regaining the presidency as well as the Senate in 1892, Democrats replaced the McKinley act with the Wilson-Gorman Tariff Act of 1894.

BIBLIOGRAPHY

Morgan, H. Wayne. *William McKinley and His America.* 1963.
Williams, R. Hal. *Years of Decision: American Politics in the 1890s.* 1978.

CHARLES W. CALHOUN

MACLAY, WILLIAM (1737–1804), Federalist senator from Pennsylvania.

Maclay holds the distinction of having been the first person elected to the United States Senate. On 30 September 1788, the Pennsylvania Assembly elected him by a vote of 66 to 1. Maclay drew a two-year term when the Senate divided itself into two-, four-, and six-year classes in 1789.

Most significantly, Maclay stood against those who wished to empower the presidency. He led the important and successful fight against an honorary title for the president and against those who wished to turn the Senate's advice-and-consent power into a mere rubber stamp. He was unsuccessful in efforts to locate the federal capital on the Susquehanna River, where he resided at Sunbury, Pennsylvania, and to block Alexander Hamilton's proposals for funding the public debt. Historian Charles Beard called Maclay the "first Jeffersonian." This was true in the sense that he was the first of several members of the Federalist party who broke away before James Madison did so. Pennsylvania Federalists helped ensure that Maclay was not reelected when his short term ended.

Maclay was reserved, pessimistic about human nature, and Calvinistic in his morality. Analytical and introspective, he was also self-assured, proud, self-conscious, and quick to take offense. Perhaps for these reasons, he spent his evenings transferring to a diary the notes he had taken while on the Senate floor. The diary included extensive reports on the Senate's closed debates as well as comments on the manner and motives of various federal officials, social life at the capital, and his own role as a legislator.

Maclay's diary stands just behind Madison's notes from the Federal Convention as the most important journal in American political and constitutional history. Selections from it were first published in 1880, but a complete edition did not appear until 1988.

BIBLIOGRAPHY

Bowling, Kenneth R., and Helen E. Veit, eds. *Documentary History of the First Federal Congress, 1789–1791.* Vol. 9: *The Diary of William Maclay and Other Notes on Senate Debate.* 1988. This edition also contains a biography of Maclay, his anonymous newspaper pieces, and a list of his First Congress correspondence.

KENNETH R. BOWLING

MCMAHON ACT. *See* Atomic Energy Act.

MCNARY, CHARLES L. (1874–1944), Republican senator from Oregon, minority leader, vice presidential candidate.

Born into a pioneer family and orphaned at nine, Charles Linza McNary was raised by older sisters and a brother in Salem, Oregon. He attended Salem public schools and Stanford University, read law and went into practice with his brother John. In 1904 he managed his brother's successful campaign for district attorney, then served as chief deputy. He was later dean of the Willamette University law school and, at thirty-eight, was appointed to the state supreme court. Justice McNary's populism was reflected in the opinions he wrote on workmen's compensation and the eight-hour workday. Organized labor supported McNary throughout his political career. Defeated for renomination to the court by a single vote in the 1914 primary, McNary thought his public career was over. But three years later he was appointed to the U.S. Senate after the death of Sen. Harry Lane. McNary won a full term in 1918; reelected four times, he served in the Senate until his death.

During the League of Nations fight, McNary was among the Republican "mild reservationists" who favored ratifying President Woodrow Wilson's Versailles treaty. Though Senate majority leader Henry Cabot Lodge (R-Mass.) differed with McNary on the League, he was impressed with McNary's efforts to achieve a compromise. McNary became Lodge's protégé and his chief link with the western progressives.

Skill in building personal relationships was a large factor in McNary's rise to Senate leadership. Several times his colleagues voted him the most popular senator. In an era of polarization, he was a force for moderation, serving as a link between the Republican party progressives and the old guard and also maintaining close ties with key Democratic senators.

McNary gained national prominence in the 1920s as a leader of the farm bloc and the sponsor of legislation that sought to lift farmers out of a depression by subsidizing the sale of surplus crops abroad. The legislation was twice approved by both houses of Congress, then vetoed by President Calvin Coolidge. McNary said that what Coolidge "doesn't know about such things would fill a great big library." President Herbert Hoover, who opposed McNary's farm legislation, later also opposed McNary's elevation to majority leader.

In the wake of Hoover's defeat for reelection in 1932 and Republican losses in the Senate, McNary was unanimously elected as Senate minority leader. Believing that Franklin D. Roosevelt's election was a popular mandate, he supported most of the early New Deal initiatives. Roosevelt and McNary developed a close friendship and working relationship. McNary obtained funding for huge public works projects in his home state, including Bonneville Dam. McNary, though, was no rubber stamp. In 1937, he worked with Democratic and other Republican senators to plot the strategy that blocked Roosevelt's Court-packing plan. Five years later, Roosevelt offered to name McNary to the Supreme Court, but he declined.

Reluctantly, McNary accepted the 1940 Republican nomination for vice president. As an insider, he was chosen to balance a ticket headed by political newcomer Wendell L. Willkie. McNary, who campaigned indifferently for a job that he did not really want, was not disappointed by Roosevelt's election to a third term.

Seriously underestimating the threat posed by Nazi Germany and imperial Japan, McNary opposed Roosevelt's attempt to repeal the arms embargo. But he provided Roosevelt with key support for the nation's first peacetime draft and for lend-lease emergency aid of war matériel for western allies. Privately he suggested that Roosevelt move ahead with the 1940 destroyers-for-bases deal with British prime minister Winston Churchill without seeking legislative approval.

Harry S. Truman placed McNary on his short list of "good old work horses who really cause the Senate to function." Democratic counterpart Alben W. Barkley once described McNary as the only real leader in the Senate. "His popularity with his colleagues," said Sen. Arthur H. Vandenberg, "was matched only by their granite confidence in him."

BIBLIOGRAPHY

Neal, Steve. "Charles L. McNary—The Quiet Man." In *First among Equals: Outstanding Senate Leaders of the Twentieth Century.* Edited by Richard A. Baker and Roger H. Davidson. 1991.

CHARLES L. MCNARY.   LIBRARY OF CONGRESS

Neal, Steve. *McNary of Oregon: A Political Biography.* 1985.

STEVE NEAL

MCNARY-HAUGEN FARM RELIEF BILL.

The most controversial and best-known agricultural relief measure proposed during the 1920s, the McNary-Haugen bill sought "equality for agriculture." Congress twice passed the exhaustively debated measure, which President Calvin Coolidge forcefully vetoed in 1927 and 1928.

Introduced in 1924 by Sen. Charles L. McNary (R-Oreg.) and Rep. Gilbert N. Haugen (R-Iowa), the bill twisted the tariff in favor of farmers, in a plan conceived by George N. Peck and Hugh S. Johnson, the president and general counsel of the Moline Plow Company. The bill called for government dumping of surpluses abroad at the world price but also the sale of commodities in the tariff-protected domestic market at a "fair-exchange" ratio between what farmers bought and sold (the "parity" concept). An "equalization fee" levied on commodities so benefited would defray losses on government sales overseas.

Viewed as harmful to consumers and business, with objectionable price-fixing, bureaucratic, and equalization-fee features, the bill was defeated on a vote that ruptured the farm bloc and aligned the East and South against the Corn Belt and the West. Congress, however, continued to consider this politically tempting bill in many versions. Enough southern votes for passage were attracted by including cotton and tobacco among the benefited commodities. Cooperative marketing enthusiasts were lured by providing for a farm board charged to aid them in limiting production and disposing of surpluses abroad. The McNary-Haugen episode set the stage for the adoption of parity in later agricultural policy, swung American society to the principle of government farm aid, and contributed to altering the partisan loyalties of farmers.

BIBLIOGRAPHY

Fite, Gilbert C. *George N. Peck and the Fight for Farm Parity.* 1954.

Kelley, Darwin N. "The McNary-Haugen Bills, 1924–1928." *Agricultural History* 14 (1940): 170–180.

PATRICK G. O'BRIEN

"THE SINGING SONS OF THE SOIL." Cartoon alluding to differences between Sen. Charles L. McNary (R-Oreg.) and Rep. Gilbert N. Haugen (R-Iowa) that cropped up as their controversial farm relief measure moved slowly through the legislative process. Clifford K. Berryman, *Washington Evening Star,* c. 1924–1927.

U.S. SENATE COLLECTION, CENTER FOR LEGISLATIVE ARCHIVES

MACON, NATHANIEL

(1758–1837), Revolutionary patriot, representative and senator from North Carolina, Speaker of the House, conservative Jeffersonian Republican leader. Macon, after serving in the Revolutionary War, was a North Carolina state senator from 1781 to 1786. He subsequently declined an appointment to the Continental Congress but became the representative from the Hillsboro district in the Second Federal Congress, taking his seat on 26 October 1791. Reflecting the interests of southern small farmers, he opposed Alexander Hamilton's financial plans. Macon was hostile to all aspects of Federalist pro-British foreign policy. He supported the Kentucky and Virginia resolutions, which developed the states' rights theory of the Constitution as protection against encroachments by the national government.

Thomas Jefferson's presidency brought Macon to power in the House. As Speaker of the House between 1801 and 1807, he promoted Jeffersonian Republican party programs. Ultimately he rejected Jefferson's drift away from strict construction of the Constitution, joining John Randolph of Roanoke and "Old Republicans" opposing the Democratic-Republican leadership. Macon consequently lost the speakership but in 1807 rejoined the party. Still staunchly Republican, Macon supported the 1807 embargo, and as chairman of the Foreign Relations Committee, he gave his name to Macon's

NATHANIEL MACON.   LIBRARY OF CONGRESS

Miller, Zane. "Senator Nathaniel Macon and the Public Domain, 1815–1828." *North Carolina Historical Review* 38 (1961): 482–499.

WINFRED E. A. BERNHARD

MADISON, JAMES (1751–1836), representative from Virginia, architect of the Constitution, cofounder of the Jeffersonian Republican party, and fourth president of the United States. By the time James Madison took his seat in the House of Representatives of the First Congress at age thirty-eight, he had already had a long and distinguished legislative career. Born into the Virginia gentry, a graduate of the College of New Jersey at Princeton, and from an early age intensely interested in public affairs, he entered political life virtually as a matter of course.

Madison began his national legislative career at age twenty-nine when he was elected a Virginia delegate to the Continental Congress, then sitting in Philadelphia. From March 1780 until October 1783 Madison served continuously in Congress, dealing with problems of war and peace and reaching his firm conviction that the union of the states needed to be strengthened. After three years in the Virginia legislature Madison returned to the Continental Congress in January 1787, but by then it was nearly moribund. One of fifty-five delegates to the Constitutional Convention, which gathered in May, he became its leading figure. Another delegate summed up Madison's legislative style:

[H]e blends together the profound politician with the scholar. In the management of every question he . . . took the lead. . . . From a spirit of industry and application . . . he always comes forward the best informed man of any point in debate. . . . Of the affairs of the United States, he perhaps, had the most correct knowledge of any man in the Union.

Madison returned to Congress, by then sitting in New York, where with Alexander Hamilton and John Jay he worked for ratification of the new Constitution by writing twenty-nine of the essays collected in *The Federalist*, including all the pieces on the federal system and the House of Representatives and the most important ones on the Senate. Madison's leading role in the Virginia ratifying convention (June 1788) completed his pre-Constitution legislative experience. At age thirty-seven he was universally regarded as the nation's preeminent theorist and practitioner of representative government.

bills No. 1 and 2, part of the intricate legislative efforts of 1810 to curb British and French intrusions into American commerce.

As a senator after 1815, he strongly opposed moves to expand national powers, fearing in 1825 that "Congress now stopped almost at nothing, which it deemed expedient to be done." In the debates of 1819 to 1821 on federal land policies, Macon wanted settlers protected from land speculators but did not favor civic improvements at public expense. During the Missouri controversy, he emphatically supported state sovereignty, contending that any attempt to restrict slavery was unconstitutional. In 1826 Macon was elected president pro tempore of the Senate but retired two years later. Described as "the real Cincinnatus of America," Macon was chosen president of the North Carolina constitutional convention of 1835, two years before his death.

BIBLIOGRAPHY

Cunningham, Noble E., Jr. "Nathaniel Macon and the Southern Protest against National Consolidation." *North Carolina Historical Review* 32 (1955): 376–384.
Dodd, William E. *The Life of Nathaniel Macon.* 1903.

Before Madison could take part in the new government he had to survive the efforts of Patrick Henry to make the Virginia delegation to the new Congress antifederalist. Henry, in firm control of the Virginia legislature, first prevented Madison from being one of the state's federal senators and then placed his home county in a congressional district otherwise strongly antifederal. Though Madison found electioneering exceedingly distasteful, he realized he had to return to Virginia to face the antifederal candidate, his close friend James Monroe. After making clear to Baptists and other "dissenters" that he favored a bill of rights and especially a clause guaranteeing liberty of conscience, Madison confronted Monroe in a series of debates around the district. The result was an impressive victory for Madison, the last time he was ever challenged seriously for any election in his home district.

When Madison took his seat in the first House of Representatives in April 1789, he was President George Washington's closest political confidant and the acknowledged legislative leader in Congress. Madison prepared Washington's inaugural address, wrote the reply of the House of Representatives to it, and then drafted Washington's responses to Congress. He introduced an impost plan for raising revenue, sought to limit British domination of American trade, opposed "princely titles" for American officeholders, supported the executive responsibility of the president for subordinates, and drafted and introduced a bill of rights. In these measures and in advising Washington on appointments, etiquette, diplomacy, and other matters, Madison took the initiative and exerted strong influence on all questions facing the new government. In this session he was perhaps the only nonpartisan floor leader in the history of the House of Representatives.

In the second session of the First Congress, with both Hamilton and Thomas Jefferson in Washington's cabinet, Madison began to emerge, with great personal reluctance, as a party leader. Three issues dominated the session: Hamilton's plans for "a sound public credit," relations with France and Great Britain, and the location of the national capital. Much to Hamilton's anguish, Madison believed that Hamilton's proposals to fund the national debt at full face value created an unearned windfall for speculators, who had acquired the debt at very low prices, and at the same time was unfair to the original creditors. He also thought that full federal assumption of the states' Revolutionary War debts was unfair to Virginia and other states that had made some provision for their debts and that it shifted power unduly from the states to the national government.

But Madison's general agreement on the need to ensure a sound public credit caused him to acquiesce in a compromise: After the assumption plan was modified to relieve inequities suffered by Virginia and some other states, Madison tacitly supported it in exchange for Hamilton's accepting a move of the federal capital temporarily to Philadelphia and after ten years to a new city to be built on the banks of the Potomac.

Madison's disagreement with Hamilton became more profound over the latter's proposal for the Bank of the United States. This, he thought, not only strengthened the dangerous power of speculators and (mostly northern) financiers but threatened the very idea of constitutional government.

JAMES MADISON. As president.

Castigating the "chain [of reasoning] that will reach every object of legislation . . . within the whole compass of political economy," Madison declared that the constitutional doctrine of broad construction and implied powers, on which the national bank was based, struck "at the very essence of the Government as composed of limited and enumerated powers." Though Madison lost the fight against the bank, the struggle further defined a deepening division. Madison believed that the debt assumption and bank bills put at risk the ideal of limited republican government, attentive to the needs of all the people, which was at the center of his political philosophy.

The split with the Hamiltonians (who termed themselves *Federalists*) became an open party division when it coincided with bitter foreign policy disputes. Like many Americans, Madison hoped that a republican France might be both an ideological ally of the United States and a help to the new nation in resisting the omnipresent power and influence of Great Britain. But Hamilton and those preoccupied with U.S. commercial and development needs sought to strengthen ties with the former mother country, whose economy was the most advanced in the world. When war broke out between France and Great Britain in 1792, Madison supported commercial restrictions against Great Britain and other moves to keep the United States at least neutral in the growing conflict. Madison led the Jeffersonian Republicans in Congress in a long struggle against the Federalists' Jay's Treaty with England and its seeming acquiescence in British commercial hegemony. This losing fight dominated Madison's last two terms in the House of Representatives (1793–1797).

Madison in fact moved slowly and reluctantly from being the creative, nonpartisan legislative leader of 1789 to becoming the leader (with Jefferson) of the Jeffersonian Republican party, which functioned as a broad opposition party to the dominant Federalists. He built coalitions in Congress; wrote (mostly anonymous) polemics in the newspapers and in pamphlets; supported Republican candidates in local, state, and federal elections; and with Jefferson, Monroe, Albert Gallatin, Aaron Burr, and others was a member of the party's informal leadership group.

After serving briefly in the Virginia legislature (1798–1800), Madison returned to federal service as secretary of State under President Jefferson from 1801 to 1809. As a member (with Jefferson and Gallatin) of the "triumvirate" that directed the Republi-

can administration, Madison worked closely, though informally, with Congress. He discussed dispatches and other diplomatic papers with members of Congress, prepared lengthy documents setting forth administration positions, and took part in intricate negotiations seeking congressional approval of treaties, appointments, and legislation. Perhaps because he aroused envy as Jefferson's heir apparent, Madison earned the hostility not only of Federalists in Congress but also of increasingly large groups of dissident Republicans.

By the time of Madison's own presidency, 1809 to 1817, his relations with Congress had become frayed indeed. Opposition to the failed Jeffersonian Republican diplomacy that led up to the War of 1812 and then opposition to the war itself greatly strengthened the Federalists, especially in New England. And the mixed group of Republican dissidents in Congress, who had promoted Monroe's intraparty opposition to Madison's election to the presidency in 1809, persistently intrigued against his administration. Madison's efforts at reconciliation or even coexistence with them failed. So he worked increasingly with Henry Clay, John C. Calhoun, William H. Crawford, Jonathan Roberts, Felix Grundy, and other, younger members of Congress who supported the War of 1812 and the often nationalistic measures that went with it. The successful conclusion of the war, with the attendant eclipse of the Federalists and rise of the "National Republicans" who looked to Madison as their leader, left him with strong backing in Congress for such measures as a national bank, a mildly protective tariff, and internal improvements. But Madison believed the last of these required a constitutional amendment, so he vetoed legislation providing for them.

This veto, on Madison's last day as president, symbolized his nearly forty years of experience in and with Congress. He had been throughout an advocate and practitioner of active national legislative efforts by a self-governing people. As a drafter and ratifier of the Constitution he had insisted on the dignity and authority of the legislative branch. Then, as the leading member of the first four Congresses, 1789 to 1797, he had been a nearly model legislator, at first backing measures to ensure the effective inauguration of the federal government and then forming a principled partisanship in the legislative branch. Finally, as secretary of State and president he offered leadership that was fully willing to offer executive guidance but also deferential to the will of the people as expressed in Congress.

At the same time, he insisted that Congress pay careful attention to the limits on its powers imposed by the Constitution. Madison thus played a leading role in defining the place of Congress in U.S. constitutional government.

BIBLIOGRAPHY

Brant, Irving. *James Madison.* 6 vols. 1941–1961. See especially vol. 3, *James Madison: Father of the Constitution, 1787–1800* (1950) for Madison's career in Congress.

Ketcham, Ralph. *James Madison: A Biography.* 1971. 2d ed. 1991.

Stagg, J. C. A. *Mr. Madison's War: Politics, Diplomacy, and Warfare in the Early American Republic, 1783–1830.* 1983.

RALPH KETCHAM

MAGNUSON, WARREN G. (1905–1989), Democratic representative and senator from Washington. First elected to the U.S. House of Representatives in 1936 and to the Senate in 1944, "Maggie" Magnuson described himself as a "progressive New Dealer." He was a noted pork-barrel politician whose pet projects included the National Institutes of Health in Maryland in the D.C. area, the Hanford Nuclear Reservation in Washington State, and the Health Services Center in Seattle, Washington. Magnuson was a member, and ultimately chairman, of the Senate Committee on Appropriations, where he focused his energies on the development of hydroelectric power, on reform of land-reclamation law, and on increasing funding for fisheries, military construction, and the environment. Senator Magnuson was the author of major legislation concerning civilian satellite technology, consumer protection, civil rights, worker and consumer safety, and the merchant marine, and he coauthored books on health-care finance and consumer rights. Magnuson was also chairman of the Commerce Committee and served on the Committee on Aerospace and Science and the Committee on the Budget. He was a close friend of President Lyndon B. Johnson and an advocate of Johnson's legislative agenda. As chairman of the Commerce Committee during the 1976 Senate committee reorganization, Magnuson brought all of his political power to bear before the Rules Committee to keep "his" oceans within the jurisdiction of the Commerce Committee. This helped him control fishing policy for his constituents in Washington State. Magnuson was defeated in his bid for a seventh consecutive Senate term in 1980.

WARREN G. MAGNUSON.   LIBRARY OF CONGRESS

BIBLIOGRAPHY

Magnuson, Warren G., and Jean Carper. *The Dark Side of the Marketplace: The Plight of the American Consumer.* 1968.

Magnuson, Warren G., and Elliott A. Segal. *How Much for Health?* 1974.

JAMES A. THURBER

MAHON, GEORGE H. (1900–1985), Democratic representative from Texas and chairman of the House Appropriations Committee. Tall, lean, and courtly, Mahon entered politics soon after receiving his law degree in 1925. He served as county attorney and district attorney before his election to the U.S. House of Representatives in 1934. A Democrat who described himself as "the hired hand" of his constituents, he represented the 19th Congressional District in sparsely populated West Texas for forty-four years.

Service on the Appropriations Committee was the height of his political ambitions, and for twenty years he proved quietly effective as chairman of its powerful Subcommittee on Defense and, from 1964 through 1978, as committee chairman. In contrast to his predecessor, the autocratic Clarence Cannon (D-Mo.), Mahon believed in sharing power. He continued a process, begun hesitantly by Cannon shortly before his death, of delegating to subcommittees the prime responsibility for examining budget requests and drafting most appropriations bills, subject to final review by the full committee.

Mahon, respected by his peers and known for his simple and economical way of life, was a conservative whose gentle demeanor belied his aggressive pursuit of a strong national defense and economy in government. When his friend and fellow Texan Lyndon B. Johnson became president in 1963, Mahon emerged as a key proponent of most Johnson defense policies. He provided crucial support for administration requests for funds to finance the Vietnam War. He balked, however, at many Johnson domestic proposals, including the civil rights acts of 1964 and 1965 and most Great Society programs that required substantial federal expenditures.

In spite of his vast power over the nation's purse strings, Mahon maintained close ties to his district. He believed that voters did not care about issues or whether their representative wielded power in Washington. What they wanted, he said, was someone in office whom they liked and trusted. When he left Congress in 1979, he returned to West Texas.

BIBLIOGRAPHY

Barone, Michael, Grant Ujifusa, and Douglas Matthews, eds. *Almanac of American Politics 1978.* 1977. Pp. 841–842.

White, William S. *Home Place: The Story of the U.S. House of Representatives.* 1965. Pp. 64–69.

ANTHONY CHAMPAGNE

MAIDEN SPEECH. *See* Debate and Oratory.

MAINE.
The twenty-third state, Maine entered the Union in partial settlement of one of the most ominous political disputes in U.S. history. But the Missouri Compromise, by which Maine was admitted as a free state on 15 March 1820 and Missouri as a slave state the following year, marked only a temporary suspension of the sectional dispute over the expansion of slavery that would eventually tear the nation apart.

From the 1650s until 1820, with one short interlude late in the seventeenth century, Maine was a part of Massachusetts. During the Confederation and

WILLIAM P. FESSENDEN. Representative (1841–1843) and senator (1854–1869) from Maine, he was a Whig until 1859 and thereafter served as a Republican. He was scorned by his party and his constituents for opposing Radical Reconstruction and for voting not guilty in the impeachment trial of President Andrew Johnson.

HARPER'S PICTORIAL HISTORY OF THE GREAT REBELLION

very early constitutional periods, a separation movement led by Federalists failed to gain popular support. After a huge influx of new settlers into the backcountry in the 1790s, however, the tide in favor of statehood began to turn. The leadership of the movement now shifted to the Democratic-Republicans (also called the Jeffersonian Republicans) under William King, who eventually became the new state's first governor. The final referendum in favor of statehood, on 26 July 1819, carried overwhelmingly. At that point, however, having won the day in Maine and secured the approval of Massachusetts, the proponents of statehood had to face a divided Congress—and were forced to agree to what many of them considered a moral compromise with slavery—in order to gain admission to the Union. Five of the seven Massachusetts members from Maine, in fact, voted against the compromise, which Congress nevertheless approved.

During the early decades of statehood, Maine voters usually favored Jeffersonian Republicans and Jacksonian Democrats over Federalists and Whigs, though not invariably. Beginning in 1854, however, the new Republican party attracted consistent support in Maine—support that extended well into the twentieth century. Hannibal Hamlin, senator and former governor of Maine, was Abraham Lincoln's running mate on the first winning Republican presidential ticket in 1860 and served as vice president during most of the Civil War. In 1884 James G. Blaine, who had served as a representative, senator, and, briefly, secretary of State, was the Republican presidential nominee. In 1936 Maine's political obstinacy became something of a national joke. At the height of the popularity of the New Deal, it was one of only two states to cast its electoral votes for Alfred M. Landon, prompting political wags to alter the old saying "As Maine goes, so goes the nation" to "As Maine goes, so goes Vermont." Republican supremacy continued through the era of Margaret Chase Smith, who was the first woman to serve in both houses of Congress and who gained special prominence and respect in 1950 after speaking for the seven Republican senators who issued the Declaration of Conscience against their party colleague Joseph R. McCarthy.

The Republican monopoly on high office ended with the election of Edmund S. Muskie to the governorship in 1954 and 1956 and to the first of four terms in the U.S. Senate in 1958. Muskie's prominence in the Senate, and as Democratic vice presidential candidate in 1968 and secretary of State in the last year of the Carter administration, was undoubtedly a factor in providing what has been essentially a level playing field for the two parties since about 1960. Former governor Kenneth M. Curtis served as Democratic national chairman in the 1970s, and George J. Mitchell as Democratic majority leader of the U.S. Senate in the 1980s and early 1990s.

Maine's delegation to the U.S. House of Representatives has diminished almost steadily since 1830, when there were eight congressional districts. By 1860 the districts numbered five, and by 1960 only two.

BIBLIOGRAPHY

Banks, Ronald F. *Maine Becomes a State: The Movement to Separate Maine from Massachusetts, 1785–1820.* 1970.

Clark, Charles E. *Maine: A History.* 2d ed. 1990.

CHARLES E. CLARK

MAJORITY AND MINORITY. The U.S. constitutional order is, above all else, a sophisticated joining of majority power and minority rights. Congress is an essential and often conflicting part of that joining.

While sovereignty rests in principle with the people, its expression is shared by Congress, the judiciary, and the president. Within Congress, governing power is shared between House and Senate, and among the members of each. The specific rights of individual representatives and senators are protected by the American speech or debate clause, which grants immunity for any critical speech or debate. This essential provision is the direct descendant of the British House of Commons speech and debate clause. As in the original British case—protecting members of Parliament against a king claiming sedition for their criticism of his profligate spending—this provision helps guarantee Congress's independence from executive tyranny. This protection is essential to the larger division of power in its adjudication of majority and minority rights.

The Constitution provides for rule by a simple majority of the members of the House or Senate except in five cases, which require more than a majority. To protect the minority from elimination, a two-thirds vote is required to expel a member. Two-thirds is also necessary to advise and consent to a treaty, to convict for impeachment in the Senate, to pass a constitutional amendment, and to override a veto in both houses.

The House of Representatives, with members now elected from equally populated districts, approximates majority rule. In the Senate, however, small states are vastly overrepresented. For example: the twenty-one smallest states have forty-two senators (with a combined population no greater than California, with its two senators). Fully half the people in the United States live in nine states, which have only eighteen of one hundred seats. These biases are reinforced by two internal privileges of minorities. First, on the five topics that require two-thirds majorities, it is possible that thirty-four negative votes might come from the seventeen smallest states with just 7 percent of the country's people. Second, there is the filibuster, initially prevented by Jefferson's Manual but now a robust institution that can be arrested only by a vote of sixty senators to limit debate. The filibuster, never approved by the Founders, has been a creature of slavery and segregation, and the Senate can become a graveyard even for legislation that enjoys overwhelming national support. The major effect of these practices has been to canonize the rights of geographic minorities, clusters of small states who with their allies historically and ironically have denied voting and equal protection rights to ethnic and political minorities.

Majority power in both houses has been obstructed from time to time by a powerful Speaker, by authoritarian committee chairmen, by seniority rules, by the mere threat of filibuster, and by the Senate practice of honoring the power of a single member to put a "hold" on a bill to which he or she objects. A 1973 revolt of junior members in both the House and Senate brought reform of many obstructionist practices by establishing subcommittees and by enhancing the powers of party caucuses.

Because of the two-house structure, the Senate's malapportionment, the filibuster, the presidential veto, and the great influence of already advantaged interest groups, the capacity of negative minorities to prevent or delay change is greater than the ability of affirmative majorities to induce change by the enactment of new laws. It also, of course, exceeds the power of affirmative minorities to generate change.

With respect to party majorities and minorities, the Democratic party controlled the House of Representatives for more than sixty years: from 1931 through the mid 1990s, except for four years during the 80th and 83d Congresses. The same circumstances prevailed in the Senate, although the Republicans organized that body for an additional six years (1981 to 1987) during the Reagan administration. Party majority figures, however, can be misleading: except for a few years during the Kennedy and Johnson presidencies, effective control of the Congress was actually in the hands of the bipartisan southern Democratic (or Dixiecrat) and conservative Republican coalition from the end of World War II through the Nixon presidency.

In more recent years the House Democratic leadership has centralized its control of the House through the Democratic Steering and Policy Committee (which controls both committee appointments and the House agenda) and by appointment of a disproportionate number of Democrats to the House Rules Committee, which determines debate procedures on the House floor, and the Ways and Means Committee, the most powerful committee in the House. House Republicans have complained bitterly about House floor procedures, including the closed rule, which limits both debate and the opportunity to offer amendments to major legislation on the floor.

In the Senate the minority has often prevailed through the use of either the filibuster (or threat of the filibuster) or the veto (or threat of the veto) by the executive when the president is of the minority party.

In summary, the majority party can and does control legislation in the House. In the Senate, where legislation needs an outsized majority of sixty votes (required to limit debate) in order to prevail, the minority party has the upper hand on issues it chooses to thwart. Because of the two-thirds vote needed in both houses to override a veto, neither Democrats nor Republicans can prevail against a determined president strongly opposed to congressional legislation. Presidents Ronald Reagan, George Bush, and Bill Clinton all learned that, while they can kill legislation they oppose, they cannot pass legislation they propose without the support of a supermajority of sixty votes in the Senate on any item not passed under the Budget Act procedures.

BIBLIOGRAPHY

Davidson, Roger H., and Walter J. Oleszek. *Congress and Its Members*. 3d ed. 1990.
Fisher, Louis. *The Constitution between Friends*. 1978.
Wilson, Woodrow. *Congressional Government*. 1885.

HOWARD E. SHUMAN and DOUGLAS RAE

MANAGEMENT AND BUDGET OFFICE.
See Office of Management and Budget (OMB).

MANAGERS.
Managers are members of Congress who serve as floor leaders during a bill's consideration, as negotiators during conference deliberations, or as prosecutors during an impeachment trial.

The chairman and ranking minority member of the committee (or subcommittee) that reported a measure act as its floor managers. The majority floor manager has the responsibility to defend the committee text, while the minority floor manager seeks to either alter the bill's language prior to passage or to defeat the bill altogether. Floor managers explain their party's position on the measure and control the debate time allotted their party. They take the lead in defending against or offering amendments to the bill, and are responsible for handling the parliamentary motions or points of order that may arise.

Members who represent their chamber in conference committee negotiations seek to resolve the differences between House and Senate versions of a bill. Although officially known as managers on the part of the House or Senate, they are more commonly called "conferees." Conferees are expected to uphold their chamber's version to the maximum extent possible without jeopardizing the ultimate goal of achieving agreement with the other body. They are appointed by their chamber's presiding officer, upon the recommendation of the chairman or ranking member of the original committee(s) of jurisdiction.

House members serve as the managers in an impeachment proceeding and are elected by House resolution. They present to the Senate the articles of impeachment against the accused official and conduct the prosecution during the Senate trial.

BIBLIOGRAPHY

Beth, Richard. *Senate Floor Managers: Functions and Duties.* Congressional Research Service, Library of Congress. CRS Rept. 87-328. 1987.

Oleszek, Walter. *Congressional Procedures and the Policy Process.* 3d ed. 1989. Pp. 148–151, 246–252.

U.S. House of Representatives. *Deschler's Precedents of the United States House of Representatives*, by Lewis Deschler. 94th Cong., 2d sess. 1977. H. Doc. 94-661. Vol. 3, chap. 14.

ILONA B. NICKELS

MANHATTAN PROJECT. The story of Congress's crucial role in the development of the atomic bomb during World War II has never been fully told. None of the handful of representatives and senators who shared the war's best-kept secret ever discussed the episode in detail. What is known is that a few lawmakers, acting on their own authority and with scant knowledge of the weapon or its implications, circumvented the usual appropriations process to provide some $2.3 billion for the project, which was code-named the Manhattan Engineer District.

"The Manhattan Project in which the money was provided by Congress in such complete confidence was one of the best examples of the functioning of our democratic processes in an emergency," political scholar Roland Young observed in 1956. H. Styles Bridges (R-N.H.), the Senate Military Appropriations Subcommittee's ranking minority member and one of four senators apprised of the secret project, later described the manner of the funding as "extremely interesting and probably one of the most unusual things which has ever occurred in our nation insofar as Congress is concerned."

Scientists involved in the endeavor, which was approved by President Franklin D. Roosevelt in 1939 but not begun until 1942, believed they were in a race with Germany to develop a superweapon that would determine the war's outcome. They also believed that the success of the United States depended largely on keeping Germany, which had a head start in atomic research, from learning it was in a race at all. The project was in its third year and had consumed $800 million covertly taken from other war appropriations before Secretary of War Henry L. Stimson and Army Chief of Staff George C. Marshall decided to inform key members of Congress of the deception. Influencing their action was the fact that Rep. John Taber and other lawmakers had begun to question unexplained large expenditures in the War Department budget.

On 18 February 1944, Stimson, accompanied by Marshall and Vannevar Bush, director of U.S. scientific research and development, met with House Speaker Sam Rayburn, Majority Leader John W. McCormack, and Minority Leader Joseph W. Martin, Jr. Stimson convinced the trio of the project's vital importance and of the need for utmost secrecy. Told that another $1.6 billion might be required, Rayburn agreed to seek the help of Appropriations Committee chairman Clarence Cannon in hiding the funds in the overall War budget. Martin, meanwhile, implored Taber to go along. Taber, the committee's senior Republican and a fervent critic of government waste, was known for demanding a strict accounting for every expenditure. In this case he remained silent, acting "on faith," he later said.

Stimson then gained the cooperation of key senators, namely Majority Leader Alben W. Barkley, Minority Leader Wallace H. White, Jr., Military Appropriations Subcommittee chairman J. W. Elmer Thomas, and Bridges. The secret remained so tightly held that not even Vice President Harry S. Truman learned of it until he became president in 1945.

Experts still debate the morality of developing the weapon and whether Truman erred, militarily and morally, in ordering its use against Japan with U.S. victory already looming as inevitable in August 1945. Congress's role has been less thoroughly examined. For their part, lawmakers who financed the program showed a surprising lack of curiosity about it. Apparently few asked questions, particularly about the weapon's long-term implications. Fewer still accepted the administration's invitation to visit project laboratories at Oak Ridge, Tennessee. As Rayburn told Vannevar Bush when invited to visit the labs: "No . . . I would see a lot of buildings and pots and pans and jars that nobody could explain to me. But if you say you've got it, it is all right."

The lawmakers' biggest worry appeared to be that the effort might fail and that they would look foolish for having embraced an expensive program on trust alone. Arguably, there is basis for the charge that Truman's momentous decision to drop the bomb was influenced in part by a need to justify to Congress the project's high cost and extraordinary secrecy. Cannon perhaps spoke for many of his colleagues in revealing after the war that he had had "great doubts as to the eventual success of the experiment" and had greeted the news that the bomb had fallen as "a great relief."

BIBLIOGRAPHY

Groves, Leslie R. *Now It Can Be Told: The Story of the Manhattan Project.* 1962. Pp. 359–366.

Hardeman, D. B., and Donald C. Bacon. *Rayburn: A Biography.* 1987. Pp. 289–291.

Martin, Joe. *My First Fifty Years in Politics.* 1960. Pp. 100–101.

Young, Roland. *Congressional Politics in the Second World War.* 1956. Pp. 44–46.

DONALD C. BACON

JAMES R. MANN.   LIBRARY OF CONGRESS

MANN, JAMES R. (1856–1922), Republican representative from Illinois, parliamentarian, legislative expert, and minority floor leader (1912–1919). Born near Bloomington, Illinois, and educated at the University of Illinois and the Union College of Law, Mann established his political reputation as an advocate for the Chicago neighborhood of Hyde Park. As the district's representative on the Chicago Common Council (1892–1896) he proved to be a tenacious, incorruptible, yet "regular" Republican. Hyde Park voters promoted Mann to the U.S. House of Representatives for the 55th Congress (1897–1899) and, impressed by his industry and fidelity to the party, returned him to his seat every two years until he died in office on 30 November 1922.

Once in Congress Mann attached himself to the conservative Republican faction loyal to House Speaker Joseph G. Cannon. Mann's parliamentary ability and dogged attention to detail won him appointment as the Republican monitor of legislation under Cannon. Never a reformer, Mann's legislative skills nevertheless assured him a prominent role in the formulation of the era's most important regulatory acts, including the 1906 Pure Food and Drug Act, the 1910 Mann-Elkins Act (which strengthened the Interstate Commerce Commission), and the 1910 Mann Act (which attempted to regulate prostitution).

Mann became minority leader when the Democrats took control of the House after the 1912 election. His mastery of legislative detail impressed and frustrated his opponents. Mann's sometimes arrogant style and his connection to the deposed Cannon cost him the Republican nomination for Speaker in 1919. Ill health and a reduced role in Congress marked the remainder of his tenure.

BIBLIOGRAPHY

Clark, Champ. *My Quarter Century of American Politics.* 2 vols. 1920.

Ellis, Lewis Ethan. "James Robert Mann: Legislator Extraordinary." *Journal of the Illinois State Historical Society* 46 (Spring 1953): 28–44.

THOMAS R. PEGRAM

MANN ACT. *See* White Slave-Trade Act.

MANSFIELD, MIKE (1903–), representative and senator from Montana, Democratic floor leader in the Senate (1961–1977), and U.S. ambassador to

Japan (1977–1989). Born in New York City in 1903, Mansfield was raised in Montana, where, after serving in the navy, army, and the marines during and after World War I, he had a remarkably varied career as a miner, mining engineer, and professor of history and political science before entering politics.

After several unsuccessful attempts, Mansfield was elected to the House in 1942 and spent four terms there, staying until 1952, when he ran for the U.S. Senate against an opponent supported by Sen. Joseph R. McCarthy (R-Wis.). He became a lieutenant to the Democratic floor leader, Sen. Lyndon B. Johnson of Texas, and in 1957 became Democratic whip. On Johnson's accession to the vice presidency in 1961, Mansfield was chosen majority leader by the Senate Democratic Conference.

Mansfield's elevation was controversial. It was believed that Johnson would attempt to control the Senate Democrats from the vice presidency and that the soft-spoken Mansfield would be merely a figurehead. Johnson's move to exert control was re-

MIKE MANSFIELD. On 5 January 1967.

buffed, but Mansfield suffered for a time from the perception that he was Johnson's handpicked candidate. His early influence was also blunted by the fact that the newly elected Kennedy administration was setting the Democratic agenda. Mansfield, who was personally fond of John F. Kennedy, acted as an important intermediary between the White House and Congress and continued this role after Johnson became president following Kennedy's assassination.

Mansfield's quiet and deferential style of leadership was strikingly different from Johnson's hard-driving, muscular persuasion. Johnson had directed the Senate with the help of a bipartisan group of senators that came to be known as "the inner club." Mansfield, in contrast, believed in the equality of all senators and rarely presumed to impose his own views on his colleagues. Mansfield's detractors complained that his laissez-faire approach to lawmaking permitted excessive delay and obstruction, but the record of the Senate in enacting the major legislation of the Kennedy and Johnson administrations undercuts that argument. In the case of the landmark Civil Rights Act of 1964, Mansfield's willingness to let southern senators state their case against the bill probably promoted a greater amount of compliance than if they had been coerced into early surrender.

Mansfield presided over a large, predominantly liberal contingent of Senate Democrats throughout the 1960s. The growth since 1958 in the percentage of northern and western Democratic senators proportionately weakened the long-dominant southern wing. The newer senators were more independent and Mansfield acknowledged this by deferring to their initiatives. He stood aside for Hubert H. Humphrey (D-Minn.) to floor-manage the 1964 Civil Rights Act and yielded a major role to the minority leader, Everett M. Dirksen of Illinois, on the same bill.

Although a political protégé of President Johnson, Mansfield harbored deep misgivings about the role of the United States in Southeast Asia. He never openly opposed the Vietnam War while Johnson was president, but privately Mansfield attempted to convince Johnson of the folly of the war.

With the election of Richard M. Nixon in 1968, Mansfield's opposition to the war became bolder. He left the authorship of antiwar bills to other senators, but his reputation as an Asia expert gave strength to the antiwar group in the Senate. While Mansfield felt drawn to foreign affairs, his most conspicuous policy interest was in reducing U.S. troop commitments to NATO.

In the Watergate investigation, Mansfield won praise for his shrewd selection of senators to serve on the panel that conducted the hearings. He earned the gratitude of senators for his fairmindedness and political judgment.

BIBLIOGRAPHY

Baker, Ross K. "Mike Mansfield and the Birth of the Modern Senate." In *First among Equals: Outstanding Senate Leaders of the Twentieth Century.* Edited by Richard A. Baker and Roger H. Davidson. 1991.

Hood, Charles Eugene, Jr. *China Mike: The Making of a Congressional Authority on the Far East.* 1980.

Stewart, John G. "Two Strategies of Leadership—Johnson and Mansfield." In *Congressional Behavior.* Edited by Nelson Polsby. 1971.

ROSS K. BAKER

MANUALS OF PROCEDURE.

[*This entry includes two separate discussions of congressional manuals of procedure, the first on House manuals and the second on Senate manuals. See also* House of Representatives, *article on* House Rules and Procedures; Precedents; Senate, *article on* Senate Rules and Procedures.]

House Manuals

The Rules and Manual of the House of Representatives is revised each Congress by the House parliamentarian and printed as a House document for the information of members, staff, and the public. The Manual contains the fundamental source material for parliamentary procedure used in the House of Representatives: the Constitution of the United States; applicable provisions of Jefferson's Manual (written by Thomas Jefferson when he was vice president); standing rules of the House as they have been amended and adopted by the current Congress (together with citations to earlier dates of adoption and previous amendments to those rules); provisions of law and resolutions having the current force of a rule of the House; and pertinent decisions of the Speakers and other presiding officers of the House and of the Committee of the Whole that have interpreted the rules and other procedural authority used in the House, with citations to permanent *Congressional Record* pages or volumes of House Precedents in which those decisions are carried in full.

Other manuals of House procedure include *Cannon's Procedure in the House of Representatives* by

Clarence Cannon, former member and clerk at the Speaker's Table, last printed in 1963 as House Document 610 of the 87th Congress, and *Procedure in the United States House of Representatives* (4th ed., 1982) by Lewis Deschler and William Holmes Brown, past and present parliamentarians of the House of Representatives. *Cannon's Procedure* is an alphabetical summary of rules, forms, practices, and precedents of the House through 1959. Cannon, in his forward to that work, states that

the purpose of this book is to provide a synopsis of such decisions (on questions of procedure) and of the procedure of the House for use on the floor where the authorities and sources, because of their bulk and diversity, are not always immediately available. While comprehensiveness and detail have been sacrificed to brevity and accessibility, no notable decision has been omitted, and each topic is for practical purposes a complete résumé of the procedure on that subject.

Procedure in the United States House of Representatives is a compilation of modern precedents and practices of current use of the House from 1959 through 1987. Together, these Manuals can serve as handbooks for understanding and effectively participating in floor and committee proceedings. Precedents of historical importance only and nonprocedural precedents, such as ceremonies of the House, are excluded from these Manuals.

BIBLIOGRAPHY

U.S. House of Representatives. *Constitution, Jefferson's Manual, and Rules of the House of Representatives, 103d Congress.* Compiled by William Holmes Brown. 102d Cong., 2d sess., 1992. H. Doc. 102–405.

CHARLES W. JOHNSON

Senate Manuals

The parliamentary procedures of the Senate can be understood either by studying the rules and the individual precedents established under those rules, or by reading a narrative of those procedures prepared by someone who has already studied the rules and precedents. The Senate has focused on the former by preparing compilations of precedents and practices under the chamber's rules; very few narratives on parliamentary procedure have been prepared by the Senate.

The Standing Rules of the Senate, which provide only a limited guide to the Senate's parliamentary procedure, can be found in *Rules and Manual of the United States Senate.* This work also contains the orders, laws, documents, and statistical information that affect the business of the Senate. Of the forty-two numbered rules, only twenty-eight contain mandates or prohibitions that directly concern procedures on the floor of the Senate. The rules are also printed separately as a pamphlet.

Precedents, Decisions on Points of Order with Phraseology (known as *Gilfry's*) was the first digest of Senate parliamentary practice. The volume was prepared by Chief Clerk Henry H. Gilfry and is a compilation of Senate precedents from the First through the 60th Congress (1789–1907). The second edition of *Gilfry's* contains precedents through the 62d Congress (1789–1913); that volume was supplemented in 1915 and 1919. The second edition and the 1919 supplement comprise a complete set of the significant precedents from the First Congress through the 65th Congress (1789–1919).

Gilfry's contains only representative samples of precedents sufficient to indicate the practice of the Senate in a given circumstance. The volume is arranged in chapters corresponding to major issue areas, with the precedents in each chapter further grouped by subtopic. Many of the precedents in *Gilfry's* include excerpts from the records of proceedings where the precedent was considered significant or where the text enhances the reader's understanding of the decision.

Senate Procedure, Precedents and Practices, the successor to *Gilfry's*, is a compilation of precedents from the 48th Congress (1884) through the present. The 1958 and 1964 editions were prepared by Charles L. Watkins and Floyd M. Riddick, former parliamentarians of the Senate. The 1974 and 1981 editions were authored by Riddick. The 1992 edition, retitled *Riddick's Senate Procedure*, updated the compilation through the 101st Congress (1990) and was coauthored by Riddick and Parliamentarian Alan S. Frumin.

Riddick's is arranged by chapter, each of which covers a procedural issue area. Chapters are divided in sections by subtopic, with further subdivisions where necessary for clarity and ease of perusal. Precedents are typically one-sentence statements of the decisions reached on a procedural issue; excerpts from the proceedings are not included. At least one precedent for each unique decision is contained in *Riddick's;* the proceedings as recorded in the *Senate Journal* and the *Congressional Record* are referenced in an accompanying footnote. Similar precedents are noted only in the footnote.

The best narrative of the Senate's parliamentary procedures is contained in the third chapter of the *Congressional Handbook*, which explains in detail the procedural issues that arise on the Senate floor, providing the context in which individual precedents and the actions of the Senate may be understood.

BIBLIOGRAPHY

U.S. Senate. Committee on Rules and Administration. *Rules and Manual of the United States Senate.* 102d Cong., 1st Sess., 1992. S. Doc. 102–1.

U.S. Senate. *Precedents, Decisions on Points of Order with Phraseology in the United States Senate from the First to the Sixty-second Congress Inclusive, 1789–1913,* by Henry H. Gilfry. 62d Cong., 3d Sess., 1914. S. Doc. 62-1123.

U.S. Senate. *Precedents, Decisions on Points of Order in the United States Senate, 63rd to 65th Congress, Inclusive (1913–1919),* by Henry H. Gilfry. Vol. 2. 1919.

U.S. Senate. *Riddick's Senate Procedure, Precedents and Practices,* by Floyd M. Riddick and Alan S. Frumin. 101st Cong., 2d sess., 1992. S. Doc. No. 101–28.

U.S. Senate. Committee on Rules and Administration. *Congressional Handbook.* 102d Cong., 2d Sess., 1992. S. Prt. 102–113.

JENNIFER L. SMITH

MARBURY V. MADISON (5 U.S. [1 Cranch] 137 [1803]). In transcending its origins as a political battle, *Marbury v. Madison* has become the foremost precedent for judicial review. The case began when President Thomas Jefferson ordered his secretary of State to withhold the signed and sealed but undelivered commissions of William Marbury and several other justices of the peace who had been appointed under an 1801 federal law creating local government for the District of Columbia. This law was passed by the Federalist-controlled Congress after it had become clear that the Jeffersonian Republicans had captured the presidency in 1800, but before Jefferson took office. It was not the law itself but outgoing President John Adams's decision to take advantage of the patronage opportunities it offered that upset the incoming administration. Marbury and other appointees sued for a writ of mandamus from the U.S. Supreme Court to compel delivery of their commissions. In rendering his decision for a unanimous court, Chief Justice John Marshall dismissed Marbury's suit on the grounds that the Court lacked jurisdiction.

This case was the first in which the Supreme Court ruled an act of Congress unconstitutional. Marshall found that section 13 of the Judiciary Act of 1789, which granted the Supreme Court the power to issue writs of mandamus, conflicted with the Constitution, which gave the Supreme Court original jurisdiction in only limited areas, not including the issuing of writs of mandamus. Therefore, the Court reasoned, the Judiciary Act was invalid.

The Jeffersonian-dominated Congress in 1803 did not protest the decision. For one thing, the practical effect of *Marbury* was to limit the power of the Supreme Court without taking any power away from Congress. For another, while the decision contained a long discourse on why Marbury and the other petitioners deserved their commissions, the actual decision did not order the Jefferson administration to deliver them. To be sure, the decision involved the concept of judicial review, but nothing in it was inconsistent with what is known as coordinate branch judicial review (to which most Jeffersonians subscribed), which allows each branch of the federal government the power to rule on the constitutionality of matters before it but denies that the decision of one branch of the federal government is in any way binding on the other two branches. In *Marbury* the Supreme Court claimed the right to oversee the Constitution but did not declare that its powers to do so were either exclusive or supreme.

Over time, *Marbury* has taken on a different and considerably broader meaning. The Marshall Court never declared any other federal law unconstitutional, and the Supreme Court did not do so again until 1857, when it held the 1820 Missouri Compromise invalid in the Dred Scott decision. Since the Civil War the view has prevailed that the Supreme Court should have final say in interpreting the Constitution. In justifying this claim, the Supreme Court in *Cooper v. Aaron* (1958) cited *Marbury v. Madison* as the key precedent. Although the idea of judicial supremacy has occasionally been disputed, Congress and the public accept it today.

[*See also* Judiciary Act of 1789.]

BIBLIOGRAPHY

Clinton, Robert L. Marbury v. Madison *and Judicial Review.* 1989.

Ellis, Richard E. *The Jeffersonian Crisis: Courts and Politics in the Young Republic.* 1971.

RICHARD E. ELLIS

MARCANTONIO, VITO (1902–1954), representative from New York, often called the most radical member ever to serve in Congress. Marcanto-

nio was so liberal that many suspected and accused him of being a communist, but there is no evidence to suggest he had any formal ties to the Soviet Union. He was first elected to the House in 1934 as a Republican–City Fusion candidate, claiming Fiorello H. LaGuardia's seat after LaGuardia's election as New York City mayor. Marcantonio's East Harlem district was ethnically diverse, with a large population of African American, Hispanic, and Jewish voters.

Marcantonio was defeated for reelection in Franklin Roosevelt's landslide year of 1936. In 1938, he was returned to Congress, running on the American Labor party ticket as well as that of the Republican party, despite having been officially expelled by the Republicans earlier in the year.

In 1942, he also secured the Democratic nomination, which allowed him to run unopposed for reelection that year. He continued on the tickets of his district's three major parties through the 1940s, prompting the New York State legislature to pass a

VITO MARCANTONIO. At the Mecca Auditorium, New York City, addressing delegates of the American People's Meeting, 6 April 1941. LIBRARY OF CONGRESS

law prohibiting a candidate from entering a party primary without that party's permission. Allowed to run only on the American Labor party ticket in 1948, he was still reelected. In 1950, at the height of the red scare, Marcantonio was defeated.

Marcantonio could never shake allegations that he was associated with the Communist party, although his voting record was similar to that of many others in the House. He voted faithfully for the measures of the New Deal and he supported U.S. involvement in World War II. His critics later attacked him for his opposition to U.S. aid to Greece, Turkey, and China as well as the Marshall Plan.

On domestic issues, Marcantonio was a strong advocate of anti–poll tax and antilynching legislation. He also opposed granting permanent status to the House Un-American Activities Committee. These liberal ideas, and his apparent acceptance of communists in the American Labor party, led to renewed accusations of communist leanings. These were charges he always denied, stating that his greatest concern was to fight fascism and that he supported building a united front, including communists, against it.

Despite his defeat in 1950, Marcantonio remained popular with many East Harlem voters. He had earned their trust and spoke Italian, Spanish, and Yiddish. He was planning a comeback when he died in 1954.

BIBLIOGRAPHY

Meyer, Gerald. *Vito Marcantonio: Radical Politician, 1902–1954.* 1989.
LaGumina, Salvatore. *Vito Marcantonio: The People's Politician.* 1969.

DONNA GIORDANO

MARINE CORPS. Congress and the U.S. Marine Corps have enjoyed an association of mutual respect and collaboration for almost two centuries. Certainly the Marine Corps expects Congress to protect it from its detractors within the executive branch and to respect its military professionalism, combat valor, and affectionate ties with the American people. In almost every challenge to the existence and functions of the Marine Corps, Congress has emerged as the marines' savior.

Matters concerning the Marine Corps and the navy were within the jurisdiction of the Senate and House Naval Affairs committees until 1947, when they were shifted to the unified Armed Services committees. The military budget subcommittee of the two Appropriations committees also reviews marine policies.

Although it approved of the navy's plan to place marines on warships in the Frigate Act of 1794, Congress made its first real contribution when it passed the Marine Corps Act of 11 July 1798. This act created a "Corps of Marines" distinct from the army and navy and established the marines' right to maintain a separate headquarters and staff, headed by the commandant of the Marine Corps, at the seat of the federal government. Congress allowed the Corps to be governed by either the Naval Regulations or the Articles of War, depending on whether the marines were serving at sea as ships guards or ashore as a navy-yard security force or performing "such other duties as the President may direct." This arrangement gave the commandant special flexibility in managing the Corps so long as he had congressional support. No commandant missed that lesson.

Establishing its headquarters and barracks in Washington in 1804, the Marine Corps cultivated Congress by providing the services of its exceptional band, by training a ready force close to the Capitol that was available to protect Congress, and by ingratiating itself by drawing officers from the sons (often failed entrants to the service academies) of the Washington political-professional elite. Its social and political elitism caused it some trouble in the Jacksonian period, when the Treasury and Navy departments found officers at the marine barracks in several navy yards involved in financial irregularities. The serving commandant, Archibald Henderson, had some responsibility for the situation, since he encouraged creative interpretation of both the Articles of War and Naval Regulations, focusing on whichever provisions favored marines in authority, pay, and living conditions.

Congress rushed to the rescue with the Marine Corps Act of 1834, which made the marines clearly an independent military service within the Navy Department. According to the act, however, marine officers fell under the command of navy officers ashore (yard commanders) and at sea (ships captains) and would conduct their affairs under Navy Department instructions, unless the marines were specifically attached to the army for temporary duty (e.g., strike duty or land defense of the Capitol). This legislation stood the test of a Supreme Court decision in *U.S. vs. Freeman* (1845), a case in which a marine barracks commander challenged the authority of a navy-yard commander.

Congress again proved itself a friend of the Corps when it forced President Theodore Roosevelt to withdraw his executive order removing marine ships guards from navy warships. Acting on behalf of navy officers who saw no need to have marines enforce ship regulations, Roosevelt abolished the ships guards in 1908; but Congress, responding to marine officers' claims that such an act would destroy the Corps, refused to fund any new battleships unless Roosevelt reversed his decision, which he did.

After 1898, the marines assumed a new function, providing colonial infantry and civil administrators in the Caribbean and the Pacific. Marines performed in combat with admiring press attention at Guantánamo Bay, Cuba (1898); Beijing, China (1900); and Veracruz, Mexico (1914). But derring-do in the tropics also imperiled relations between the Corps and Congress. In its 1902 investigations of affairs in the Philippines, members of the Senate found evidence of atrocities by marines against Filipinos, and in 1921 and 1922 the Senate Select Committee on Haiti and Santo Domingo concluded that similar abuses had occurred during the occupation of those Caribbean countries by two marine brigades.

World War II brought the Marine Corps to a new peak of congressional and media popularity. The new bonds of affection were put to their ultimate test in the years 1945 to 1947, when Congress considered the question of postwar defense organization and management. The Truman administration advocated centralized control of the armed forces by a single cabinet secretary and a joint general staff headed by a powerful military chief of staff. This plan would have allowed the executive branch to determine service roles and missions, negating the similar function performed by Congress in the budget process. Dogged Marine Corps opposition to this plan, with equivocal support from the navy, produced the National Security Act of 1947, which provided legislative protection of service roles and missions. The functions written into law covered all the services, but they were especially important to the Marine Corps. The authors of the provisions were marine officers then advising the House Committee on Government Expenditures, which had reviewed the legislation because the Senate managers of the original legislation were afraid to refer it to the pro-Marine House Armed Services Committee.

Impressed by the performance of the First Marine Division and the First Marine Aircraft Wing in the Korean War, Congress exercised its right to determine field organization structure as well as roles and missions by passing the Douglas-Mansfield Act of 1952. This act required the Department of Defense to maintain three divisions and three aircraft wings in the Fleet Marine Force (the largest part of the Marine Corps operating forces), even in peacetime. The sense of Congress was that the Fleet Marine Force would provide a "force in readiness," deployed to trouble spots on amphibious ships and ready to spearhead almost any form of military intervention, large or small. The law also provided that the commandant of the Marine Corps might attend meetings of the Joint Chiefs of Staff (JCS) on all issues that he decided affected the Corps. This provision was expanded in 1979 to make the commandant a full statutory member of the JCS and, thus, eligible to become chairman.

Congress also proved the depth of its commitment to the Fleet Marine Force in the 1970s and 1980s. In the face of civilian and military opposition in the Department of Defense, it supported a number of weapons and equipment innovations for the Marine Corps. In personnel matters, Congress cooperated from 1975 to 1980 with two favorites, Commandants Louis H. Wilson, Jr., and Robert H. Barrow, to purge the Marine Corps of those whom they grouped together as undesirables—malcontents, drug addicts, thugs, homosexuals, racial agitators, and the mentally deficient. Congress made the crusade to restore a quality enlisted force possible by stating it would not penalize the Corps for failing to maintain its budgeted enlistment strength. The only issues on which Congress questioned the Corps involved its conduct of recruiting and recruit training in the mid 1970s and the conduct of the Lebanon intervention in 1983. Congress may, however, have loosened its support for the Marine Corps with the Goldwater-Nichols Defense Reorganization Act of 1986, which gave the chairman of the Joint Chiefs of Staff power to influence interservice affairs well beyond the boundaries envisioned in 1947. The Marine Corps cast a wary eye at the new law and urged Congress to do so, too, since a forceful chairman might use his power, especially during a budgetary or an international political crisis, to change roles and missions—for instance, by not supporting funding for a particular function. The Marine Corps thus serves as a watchdog for Congress within the armed forces while exploiting its ties with Congress to preserve its own identity and functions.

BIBLIOGRAPHY

Millett, Allan R. *Semper Fidelis: The History of the United States Marine Corps.* Rev. ed. 1990.

Millett, Allan R., ed. *Commandants of the Marine Corps.* Forthcoming.

Heinl, Robert D., Jr. *Soldiers of the Sea: The United States Marine Corps, 1775–1962.* 1962.

Keiser, Gordon W. *The U.S. Marine Corps and Defense Unification, 1944–1947.* 1982.

ALLAN R. MILLETT

MARKUPS. *See* Committees, *article on* Markups.

MARSHALL PLAN. The Marshall Plan became the popular name for the program for post–World War II European economic recovery submitted to Congress by President Harry S. Truman in December 1947. The basis for the specific request for economic assistance had been supplied by the Committee for European Economic Cooperation, which was set up by sixteen European countries in response to a speech by Secretary of State George C. Marshall at Harvard University on 5 June 1947. Marshall had been the U.S. Army chief of staff from the day World War II began, 1 September 1939, until after the end of the war in the Far East in October 1945. He was called the "organizer of victory" by Winston Churchill. In his speech he had addressed the invitation to all countries willing to work in good faith for the success of his proposal, but the Soviet Union denounced the plan as imperialistic and forbade its satellites to participate.

The time was not favorable for a Democratic president campaigning for a second term to ask a Republican-controlled Congress for a large sum for European foreign aid. Success came from remarkable cooperation between President Truman, Secretary of State Marshall, and Republican senator Arthur H. Vandenberg of Michigan, chairman of the Senate Foreign Relations Committee. Vandenberg, once strongly isolationist, became internationalist and neutralized much of the rigid conservatism of Ohio senator Robert A. Taft and helped to kill crippling amendments to the legislation in both houses of Congress.

Marshall won Vandenberg's support by stressing the nonpartisanship of the State Department; he and his undersecretary, Robert A. Lovett, consulted frequently with the Republican senator. Vandenberg proclaimed the importance of reducing the postwar

BIPARTISAN INTERNATIONALISTS, 1948. Senators Tom T. Connally (D-Tex.), *left,* and Arthur H. Vandenberg (R-Mich.) were initiators of bipartisanship in post–World War II foreign affairs.

OFFICE OF THE HISTORIAN OF THE U.S. SENATE

economic chaos in Europe that encouraged communist takeovers there. He persuaded the administration to allow the aid program to be controlled by an independent agency, the Economic Cooperation Administration, rather than by the State Department, and insisted that a Republican businessman, Paul G. Hoffman, be named program administrator instead of Dean Acheson, Truman's first choice. The result was sufficient Republican support to ensure an impressive majority of votes for the plan in both houses of Congress in April 1948. The program enacted was for a four-year period (1948–1952), with authorized expenditures of $15.5 billion. Seven-eighths of the amount was to consist of grants, the remainder of loans.

In later years revisionists have argued that the European Recovery Program was designed to promote U.S. interests by imposing U.S. views on Europe. But improvements in trade and industry were widely hailed in the 1950s and won Marshall a Nobel Prize for Peace. Forty years later, congressional leaders seeking solutions for various global economic problems still called for the adoption of other "Marshall Plans," as for example in eastern Europe and the former Soviet Union.

BIBLIOGRAPHY

Hogan, Michael J. *The Marshall Plan: America, Britain, and the Reconstruction of Western Europe, 1947–1952.* 1987.

Pogue, Forrest C. *George C. Marshall: Statesman.* 1987.

Wexler, Imanuel. *The Marshall Plan Revisited. The European Recovery Program in Economic Perspective.* 1983.

FORREST C. POGUE

MARTIN, JOSEPH W., JR. (1884–1968), representative from Massachusetts, Republican floor leader, Speaker of the House. From blacksmith's helper to newspaper publisher, Martin sampled a variety of occupations before entering politics as a state representative in 1912. He served as a Republican legislator for forty-five years, rising from 1947 to 1949 and again from 1953 to 1955 to the speakership of the U.S. House.

A friendly, low-key, shrewd bachelor who spoke with an Irish brogue, Martin came to politics riding the Republican tide of the first third of the twentieth century. As early as 1896, when he was twelve years old, Martin marched in a torchlight parade for William McKinley, and he ever remained part of the Republicans' old guard until retiring from Congress at the end of 1966.

Martin's motto was "Vote your district," and no one ever practiced the precept more sedulously. From boyhood through his years as a journalist and eventually publisher of the Republican *Evening Chronicle* in his hometown of North Attleboro, Massachusetts, he cultivated hundreds of friends. In the Massachusetts legislature (1912–1917) and in the U.S. House (1925–1966) he worked tirelessly for the interests of his constituents.

When in 1939 a Massachusetts colleague in the House nominated him for Republican leader, he said, "We are doing more than electing a floor leader. We are chosing a symbol of the Republican party." "Symbol" was the right word. During the 1930s Martin's was one of the most persistent voices attacking the New Deal. In the years before Pearl Harbor he sided with the isolationists. Nevertheless, he was more of a spokesman for than an author of Republican policy.

In Franklin D. Roosevelt's 1940 presidential campaign he famously lampooned Martin and his fellow isolationist representatives Bruce Barton and Hamilton Fish. In citing instances of their obstruction to his internationalist foreign policy Roosevelt chanted, "Martin, Barton, and Fish" to the cadence of "Wynkin, Blinkin, and Nod." Over a national radio broadcast the audience joined him in chanting, "Martin, Barton, and Fish."

To most Americans Martin was probably most familiar wielding the gavel as permanent chairman at the Republican national conventions of 1940, 1944,

1948, 1952, and 1956. In 1940 he was Republican national chairman and manager of Wendell L. Willkie's losing campaign against Roosevelt. On three occasions Martin was himself a dark-horse candidate for the presidential nomination.

With their landslide victory in the 1946 off-year elections, the Republicans moved into control of both houses of Congress for the first time since 1931. They viewed their triumph as a sure step toward defeating President Harry S. Truman in 1948. Elected Speaker by virtue of his seniority, Martin presided over the party's efforts in the House. But the Republicans' success evaporated when Truman defeated Thomas E. Dewey and the Democrats recaptured Congress.

In April 1950, when Martin was again serving as House Republican leader, he deliberately stepped into the middle of a historical conflict, with explosive results. The Korean War was at its darkest point, Communist Chinese troops having invaded North Korea to battle United Nations forces there. Truman and Gen. Douglas A. MacArthur, commander of the U.N. forces, were increasingly at odds over strategy. Martin, who was on MacArthur's side, wrote to the general on 5 April, asking whether MacArthur thought the Chinese Nationalist govern-

JOSEPH W. MARTIN, JR. *Right,* as newly elected Speaker of the House, receiving the gavel from his predecessor, Sam Rayburn (D-Tex.), January 1953.

ment on Taiwan (then Formosa) should open a second front on the Chinese mainland to harass the Chinese Communists and divert them from their incursion into North Korea. Such a strategy had been ruled out by Truman and his advisers, but MacArthur replied to Martin's letter endorsing the idea of a second front. Martin read MacArthur's reply to the House. MacArthur's action was clearly insubordinate, and it set the Truman administration ablaze. On 10 April, the president relieved MacArthur of his command.

When Dwight D. Eisenhower was elected in 1952 the Republicans also captured the 83d Congress, and Martin was again chosen Speaker. Although he was identified more with the conservative wing of the party, led by Sen. Robert A. Taft, than with the moderate Eisenhower faction, Martin liked Eisenhower and cooperated with him on legislation. On the other hand, Eisenhower's internationalist views were far from Martin's nationalist outlook, and the two men were not close.

On 6 January 1959, at the age of 75, Martin was overthrown as Republican leader in a coup that established Rep. Charles A. Halleck of Indiana as his successor. After Republican losses in the 1958 elections, Halleck took advantage of growing restlessness among younger members over Martin's tiring leadership. After losing the position of minority leader, Martin remained in Congress for another eight years.

BIBLIOGRAPHY

Martin, Joseph W., Jr., with Robert J. Donovan. *My First Fifty Years in Politics*. 1960.

ROBERT J. DONOVAN

MARYLAND. The seventh state to ratify the Constitution, Maryland made significant contributions to the cause of national union. Nationalist sentiment in Maryland grew after the Revolutionary War as troops returned from fighting on the soil of neighbors from Georgia to New York. Maryland withheld ratification of the Articles of Confederation until 1781, insisting that the western lands be granted to the Union as national domain for the support of the central government. In 1785 Maryland and Virginia demonstrated the benefits of interstate cooperation by meeting at the Mount Vernon Conference to improve navigation on the Potomac.

Maryland's delegation to the Constitutional Convention was vocal but not united, with James

McHenry, Daniel of St. Thomas Jenifer, and Daniel Carroll signing the document, while Luther Martin and John Mercer abstained.

Martin, the most influential Marylander, opposed a strong central government. He supported equal state representation in Congress in the New Jersey plan and, after that failed, served on the committee that drafted the compromise providing for equal representation in the Senate and proportional representation in the House. He believed the Constitution could only be perfected through periodic amendment and argued against ratification of the document as it was written.

John Mercer believed that separation of powers would obviate usurpation of power by the legislature, advocated landholding qualifications for electors, and argued against a residency requirement for voters.

Daniel Carroll, who had served in the Continental Congress with Daniel of St. Thomas Jenifer, argued that the salaries of members of Congress should be paid by the federal treasury and not by the states. He supported a last-minute move by Nathaniel Gorham of Massachusetts that increased the size of the House of Representatives by reducing the number of people per member from 40,000 to 30,000.

Samuel Chase and William Paca were among the Maryland Anti-Federalists to oppose ratification without amendment. A spirited and sometimes violent debate ensued. Federalists saw dangers in delay and the appointed convention agreed that the Constitution should be examined and ratified as a whole without changes to its parts. The Maryland vote of 63 to 11 to ratify came at a crucial point in the ratification struggle, leaving no question of sentiment in the state and encouraging Federalists in Virginia and South Carolina, who quickly followed suit.

Maryland's original allotment of six representatives was increased to eight in 1790, nine in 1800, and thereafter ranged between five and nine. Since 1960 it has been eight.

The Democratic party and its predecessors have long been a dominant force in Maryland. The roots of Maryland's Democratic party can be traced as far back as 1776, when voters favored reduced government expenses and taxes, a strong executive, paper money, and debtor relief. After the election of 1796 the Democrats took the name Republicans and Democratic-Republican societies formed across the state.

Federalists sent majorities to the House and Senate until 1803, when Jeffersonian Republicans, who identified with suffrage for all white men and other liberal causes, gained ascendancy. The Jeffersonian Republicans dominated or shared power in Maryland's delegation until the demise of Maryland's Federalist party in 1821.

There followed a turbulent eight-year period when independents, then Jacksonians and Anti-Jacksonians controlled the House (1829–1837), an eighteen-year period when House seats were shared by Democrats and Whigs (1837–1855), and three Congresses when the House delegation was split between Democrats and Know-Nothings (1855–1861). From 1825 to 1859 Maryland was represented in the Senate by at least one Whig, and by two Whigs from 1839 to 1857.

During the Civil War Maryland sent Unionists, Unconditional Unionists, and Democrats to the House and split Senate seats between Democrats and Republicans. Democrats have dominated Maryland's delegation to the House since the Civil War, with Republicans electing a majority in only eight of the sixty-three elections since 1865. During the same period Maryland sent Democratic senators to Washington for fifty-two Congresses and Republican senators for thirty Congresses.

Notable among Maryland's members of Congress is Gen. Samuel Smith, Revolutionary War hero, commander of the Maryland Militia in the Whiskey Rebellion, and defender of Baltimore during the War of 1812. Smith served in Congress for forty years; from 1793 to 1803 as a member of the House, 1803 to 1815 in the Senate, 1816 to 1822 again in the House, and again in the Senate from 1822 to 1833. He was chairman of the Senate Committee on Finance during the 18th and the 20th through the 22d Congresses. He ended his career in public life as mayor of Baltimore from 1835 to 1838.

Millard E. Tydings, a Democrat, served as a representative from 1923 to 1927, when he was elected to the Senate, where he served until 1951. He was chairman of the Committee on Territories and Insular Possessions from 1933 to 1946 and the Armed Services Committee from 1949 to 1951. His son Joseph D. Tydings was a Democratic senator from Maryland from 1965 to 1971.

BIBLIOGRAPHY

Brugger, Robert J. *Maryland: A Middle Temperament, 1634–1980.* 1988.

Walsh, Richard, and William Lloyd Fox, eds. *Maryland: A History, 1632–1974.* 1974.

CHARLES EDWARD SCHAMEL

MASSACHUSETTS. The second colony settled by immigrants from England, Massachusetts shared with Virginia and Pennsylvania a preeminent role in the American colonies prior to the Revolution. Massachusetts leaders such as John Hancock, Samuel Adams, and John Adams played important roles in the Continental Congress that shaped the nation's destiny. At the Constitutional Convention, Massachusetts leaders were less prominent.

Massachusetts was the sixth state to enter the Union, and at the time of the first census in 1790, it was second in size only to Virginia and held eight House seats in the First Congress. The state's congressional delegation eventually grew to twenty, but in 1820 the Missouri Compromise led to Maine's separation from Massachusetts and seven Massachusetts seats became Maine's. The Bay State's proportion of the House would never again be as high. The twentieth-century peak for Massachusetts was sixteen members (1913–1933), but its decline has been steady. Six seats have been lost following the postcensus reapportionments of 1930 (one), 1940 (one), 1960 (two), 1970 (one), and 1990 (one). Massachusetts will have only ten seats upon the close of the twentieth century.

House. The most prominent of the early House members from Massachusetts were Federalist Fisher Ames (1789–1797), whose trenchant observations about the House have long been quoted, and Elbridge Gerry (1789–1793), for whom the "gerrymander" was named and who later served as vice president under James Madison (1813–1814).

From 1797 to 1987, Massachusetts provided the House of Representatives with eight Speakers: Theodore Sedgwick (1797–1801); Joseph B. Varnum (1807–1811); Robert C. Winthrop (1847–1849); Nathaniel P. Banks (1855–1857); Frederick H. Gillett (1919–1925); Joseph W. Martin, Jr. (1947–1949, 1953–1955); John W. McCormack (1962–1971); and Thomas P. (Tip) O'Neill, Jr. (1977–1987).

The Federalist party dominated House elections in Massachusetts until the 1820s. When the Federalists collapsed, the most conservative remnant of National Republicans and later the Whigs captured the loyalty of Massachusetts voters.

The most notable of the Whig House members was former president John Quincy Adams (1831–1848), who led the fight against the gag rule, which was intended to prohibit antislavery petitions from coming to the House floor.

When the Whigs fell into disarray in the 1850s, the newly formed Republican party emerged with almost all of the state's House seats. Republican

MASSACHUSETTS CAMPAIGN POSTER. For the 1892 candidates for president, vice president, governor, and lieutenant governor.

domination of the delegation continued for most of the next century. Among post–Civil War Massachusetts Republicans who gained prominence in the House were: Oakes Ames (1863–1873), whose infamous Crédit Mobilier scheme implicated a number of House members in the selling of railroad leases, and Gen. Benjamin F. Butler (1867–1875, 1877–1879), whose oppressive Civil War occupation of New Orleans gained him the title of "Beast" Butler.

Republican control of the Massachusetts delegation began to wane in the twentieth century, but the party still provided prominent national figures, including two of the last three Republican Speakers of the House, Frederick Gillett and Joseph Martin.

Democratic House victories were confined to the Irish Catholic enclaves of Boston. From these enclaves came the singing mayor of Boston, John F. ("Honey Fitz") Fitzgerald, whose three grandsons would all serve in the U.S. Senate: John F. Kennedy (Mass., 1953–1960), Robert F. Kennedy (N.Y., 1965–1968), and Edward M. Kennedy (Mass., 1963–). James M. Curley also served in the House (1911–1914, 1943–1947). The most distinctive feature of Curley's second term was that he ran from a district that was adjacent to the one in which he lived, thereby demonstrating that constitutional residency requirements were limited to states and not districts of residence.

It has been in the past fifty years that Massachusetts Democrats have exercised their greatest power in the House. Two Bostonians, John McCormack and Tip O'Neill, his protégé, served successively for forty-six years in the House Democratic leadership (1941–1987). McCormack served as majority floor leader (1941–1947, 1949–1953, 1955–1961), minority whip (1947–1949, 1953–1955), and Speaker (1962–1971). Upon McCormack's retirement in 1971, O'Neill began his ascent up the House leadership ladder, serving first as majority whip (1971–1973), then majority leader (1973–1977), and ultimately as Speaker of the House (1977–1987). O'Neill's ten consecutive years and McCormack's nine consecutive years are the two longest continuous terms in the history of the speakership.

Senate. John Adams, the first vice president, was the Senate's initial presiding officer. Also seated from Massachusetts in that original Congress were Federalists Caleb Strong and Tristram Dalton. In 1791, George Cabot, the great-grandfather of Henry Cabot Lodge and the great-great-great grandfather of Henry Cabot Lodge, Jr., was seated.

It was the Whig party that gave pre–Civil War Massachusetts senators their greatest prominence. Daniel Webster was born in New Hampshire and represented that state in the House (1813–1817, 1823–1827), but in the Senate he served from Massachusetts (1827–1841, 1845–1850). Both of his Senate departures were due to his being named secretary of State. Webster, considered one of the five greatest U.S. senators, led the rhetorical fight for the Union on the Senate floor in heated debates with John C. Calhoun and Robert Y. Hayne of South Carolina.

As the battle shifted to questions of the extension of slavery, it was Boston's Charles Sumner (1851–1874) who emerged as antislavery's most eloquent voice. He suffered for his beliefs; while he wrote at his Senate desk, he was beaten senseless by Rep. Preston S. Brooks of South Carolina. Massachusetts voters left the seat open during Sumner's prolonged recuperation as a testament to his beliefs.

Sumner's Senate seatmates included Edward Everett (1853–1854), who succeeded Webster as Fillmore's secretary of State, and Henry Wilson (1855–1873), who served as President Grant's second vice president.

Late in the nineteenth century, Henry Cabot Lodge (1893–1924) emerged as a major force among the Senate Republicans. Lodge chaired the Republican Conference, served as floor leader (1918–1924), and contributed greatly to the defeat of President Woodrow Wilson's Treaty of Versailles with its League of Nations provision. Lodge's grandson, Henry Cabot Lodge, Jr., also served in the Senate (1937–1944, 1947–1953) and spent seven and one-half years (1953–1960) as U.S. ambassador to the United Nations, this century's most successful multinational forum, prior to his selection as Richard M. Nixon's vice presidential running mate in 1960.

The junior Lodge lost his seat to John F. Kennedy in 1952, which presumably atoned for the Senate defeat of Senator Kennedy's grandfather, John F. Fitzgerald, to the senior Lodge in 1916. In 1960 Kennedy, running for president, defeated Nixon, thus denying Lodge his bid for vice president. Two years later, Edward Kennedy, the president's youngest brother, defeated George Lodge, the son of Henry Cabot Lodge, Jr., for the vacant Senate seat, ending the nation's longest ethnopolitical family feud.

Two other recent Massachusetts senators with national reputations were Republican Edward W. Brooke (1967–1979), the only African American to serve in the U.S. Senate between 1881 and 1993, and the man who defeated him in 1978, Paul E. Tsongas (1979–1985), who ran unsuccessfully for the 1992 Democratic presidential nomination.

BIBLIOGRAPHY

Barbrook, Alex. God Save the Commonwealth: An Electoral History of Massachusetts. 1973.
Huthmaker, J. Joseph. Massachusetts: People and Politics, 1919–1933. 1969.
Litt, Edgar. The Political Cultures of Massachusetts. 1965.
Lockard, Duane. New England State Politics. 1959.
Peirce, Neal R. The New England States: People, Politics, and Power in the Six New England States. 1976.

GARRISON NELSON

MASS TRANSPORTATION. See Transportation; Urban Mass Transportation Act of 1964.

MAVERICKS. The term *maverick* first arose in the 1840s, initially referring to an unbranded stray, after a Texas rancher named Samuel Maverick who did not brand his cattle. By the Civil War, however, it had begun to be used more generally as a description for an independent person. Although the term may refer to a person in any walk of life, its most common usage has been political. As the power of political parties grew throughout the nineteenth century, the label *maverick* was applied to some legislators who resisted the constraints that partisanship imposes on individual judgment. The label reflected admiration for a frontier-style independence that seemed to be vanishing as the decades passed.

No single political style can be identified as maverick. Some mavericks, such as Rep. John Quincy Adams of Massachusetts in the 1840s and Sen. Wayne L. Morse of Oregon a century later, have been genuinely intellectual. Others, like New Deal senator Huey D. Long (D-La.), have been noted for thumbing their noses at staid Washingtonians. Still others, such as Sen. Joseph R. McCarthy (R-Wis.) in the 1950s, won fame for belligerence and invective. Whatever the style, however, maverick politicians have always been outspoken and often stridently individualistic in their rhetoric.

No common ideology unites maverick politicians. Behind some have stood constituencies with goals unpopular in the mainstream. Others have been pioneers for new values. Before the Civil War, many mavericks took extreme sectional stances, exacerbating tensions that divided the major parties. Ohio representative Joshua R. Giddings, for example, was expelled by the House for his radical antislavery tactics. In the decades after the Civil War, mavericks were associated with troubled groups such as western farmers or industrial workers. On the other hand, the mugwumps, dissident elite Republicans of the 1880s, were also described as mavericks.

By the early twentieth century, as more regular organization of the procedures for lawmaking gave parties—or the powerful groups within them—still greater control over legislation, the term increasingly conveyed the image of someone outside the machinery of the government as well as of parties. A case in point is Sen. William Proxmire (D-Wis.), for many years portrayed as the conscience of a bloated executive and a profligate Congress. As government has steadily grown in size, the image of maverick has become a political asset deliberately cultivated by men and women who may be privately at ease with partisanship.

The studied individualism of maverick politicians can be politically effective. By appealing to the spirit of principled independence, the politician may be able to move the legislature to action. Interested constituencies or influential outsiders may be persuaded to exert pressure in support of a maverick's position. Yet maverick politicians can also become destructive. In his essay "Civil Disobedience," perhaps the most famous personal declaration of independence ever written in the United States, Henry David Thoreau attacked legislators who could not see beyond the procedures and policies of the Congress, and he urged right-thinking men to "stop the machine" of government. In a pluralistic society, mavericks who follow the dictates of conscience and disdain the practical methods that reconcile differences within the Congress may stop government when it needs to act. Whether seen as heroes or villains, however, maverick politicians seem inseparable from the consensus politics that has dominated the United States since the rise of the two-party system.

BIBLIOGRAPHY

Huitt, Ralph K. "The Outsider in the Senate: An Alternative Role." In *Congress: Two Decades of Analysis.* Edited by Ralph K. Huitt and Robert L. Peabody. 1969.

Shields, Johanna Nicol. *The Line of Duty: Maverick Congressmen and the Development of American Political Culture, 1836–1860.* 1985.

JOHANNA NICOL SHIELDS

MC-. *Names beginning with this prefix are alphabetized as if spelled Mac.*

MEDAL OF HONOR. *See* Congressional Medal of Honor.

MEDIA. *For discussion of Congress and the news media, see* Press. *For discussion of coverage of congressional proceedings, see* Broadcasting of Congressional Proceedings; C-SPAN.

MEDICARE. A federal health insurance program passed by the 89th Congress in 1965, Medicare covers practically all Americans over sixty-five and technically consists of two separate trust funds. Part A, the Hospitalization Insurance program (HI), pays for acute hospital services. Part B, Supplemental Medical Insurance (SMI), finances a major share of the expenses of physician services, and almost all of the elderly enroll in it. The HI fund is financed by a payroll tax; the SMI fund draws from the general revenues of the federal government and from premiums charged to the elderly. Medicare operates on a pay-as-you-go basis (i.e., money collected from those in the work force today pays for the health insurance of those already retired). In 1990 Medicare spent over $100 billion, and estimates are that its expenditures will be $150 billion in 1995, making it one of the fastest-growing federal programs.

Medicare is uniquely American. It coexists with a variety of private funding schemes, making America's health insurance arrangements more complex than those of other comparable countries. No other industrial democracy began compulsory health insurance with its elderly citizens alone; most other comparable societies have universal health insurance (i.e., all citizens are covered, regardless of age or income).

Medicare's origins date back to Theodore Roosevelt's unsuccessful attempt to introduce universal health insurance in 1912. During the 1930s, Franklin D. Roosevelt wanted to include health insurance in his social insurance legislation, but advisers convinced him that it would jeopardize the chances of passing the Social Security Act of 1935. During the 1948 election, President Harry S. Truman also urged the enactment of national health insurance. His bill was defeated by a combination of opponents among Republicans, conservative southern Democrats, and groups like the American Medical Association, which popularized the pejorative phrase *socialized medicine* in one of the most expensive lobbying campaigns in U.S. history.

In the 1950s, proponents of government health insurance adopted a new strategy. As a first step, they sought health insurance only for those eligible for Social Security retirement benefits. Considered poor risks by private insurance, the elderly included many needy citizens but were still regarded as a particularly deserving social group. In addition, the elderly's medical problems regularly came to the attention of both their children and the media. This combination of factors made older Americans an attractive political target for government health insurance.

From 1951 to 1964, Congress considered Medicare legislation without passing any bill, despite public opinion polls that showed two out of three Americans supported the reform. This failure partly reflected the ideological objections of the conservative coalition within Congress, a mix of Republican critics and southern Democrats who, through long seniority, controlled the chairmanships of key congressional committees (House Ways and Means and Senate Finance, for example). But congressional resistance to Medicare reflected intense pressure-group activity as well, particularly that of physicians, who were strategically placed in the districts of every member. Resisting that pressure were crusaders like Aime J. Forand, the Rhode Island Democrat who took the legislative lead in the House in the late 1950s, joined in the 1960s by Rep. Cecil R. King and Sen. Clinton P. Anderson in sponsoring the King-Anderson bill.

During the 1964 presidential race, Lyndon B. Johnson made the passage of Medicare a central theme of his campaign. His electoral mandate was considerable. (Johnson received 61 percent of the popular vote and 90 percent of the electoral college vote.) This, combined with the Democrats' sweeping congressional victory (adding thirty-eight to their majority in the House and gaining two seats in the Senate), gave President Johnson the votes needed to enact Medicare overwhelmingly. But, while popular with the elderly, Medicare's operation, along with U.S. medical care in general, became increasingly controversial as costs rose faster than national income in the late 1960s and the problems of "stagflation" became chronic in the 1970s and early 1980s.

In the late 1970s, President Jimmy Carter changed Medicare's politics by transferring it from the Social Security Administration to the Health Care Financing Administration. As a result, Medicare could no longer rely on Social Security's local administration or its near sacrosanct political status. This increased vulnerability was reflected in the Reagan administration's budget cuts of 1981. Although these "reforms" were prompted by claims that Medicare was itself a cause of medical inflation, the primary effect was to transfer costs from the federal budget to Medicare recipients and to other payers.

In 1983, the 98th Congress adopted a more serious and sophisticated approach to cost containment, legislating the prospective method of hospital payment known as diagnosis-related groups, or DRGs. This meant paying fixed rates for specific diagnoses, with reimbursement amounts known in advance. Despite some success, DRGs have several worrisome side effects: they induce hospitals to shift whatever costs they can to non-Medicare patients to make up for lost revenue; they restrict the access of some elderly to medical care; and they endanger the financial stability of some hospitals as payments have lagged behind medical costs.

Another recent change in Medicare took place between 1987 and 1989, when catastrophic care provisions were added, extending coverage for chronic illnesses. The new program was to be financed by charges concentrated on the wealthiest Medicare beneficiaries. But the legislation was quickly repealed in response to intense protests by the more affluent elderly and by pressure groups that were mobilized.

Popular with the elderly, Medicare experienced several recurring problems in its first two decades. The program originally paid for treatment retrospectively, financing what had been delivered, with little control over what was done or how much was spent. In addition, Medicare from the start used private insurance firms as financial intermediaries, increasing both overhead costs and the complexity of the bureaucracy. For most of its first two decades, Medicare's costs grew rapidly, rising from 9.2 percent of national health expenditures in 1967 to 16.7 percent in 1984. Since the mid 1980s, however, the Medicare program has grown far less rapidly than medical care in general.

Medicare's future is now entwined with the fate of general health reform. Not only is overall health reform uncertain, but President Bill Clinton's health care reform bill, and most of the alternatives, do not include Medicare, which would continue to operate as a separate federal program. Despite its reduced rate of increase in spending, Medicare still appears a voracious consumer of public dollars and, if unreformed, seems certain to defeat hopes for deficit reduction. On the other hand, integrating Medicare into health reform is a precondition for both the program's longer-term stability and the ability of the country to control costs while expanding access to the economic security of universal health insurance.

BIBLIOGRAPHY

Brown, Lawrence D. "Technocratic Corporatism and Administrative Reform in Medicare." *Journal of Health Politics, Policy, and Law 10* (1985). 579–599.
Marmor, Theodore R. "Coping with a Creeping Crisis: Medicare at Twenty." In *Social Security: Beyond the Rhetoric of Crisis.* Edited by Theodore R. Marmor and Jerry L. Mashaw. 1988.

Marmor, Theodore R. *The Politics of Medicare.* 1973.

Smith, David G. *Paying for Medicare: The Politics of Reform.* 1992.

THEODORE R. MARMOR

MEDICINE. *See* Health and Medicine.

MEMBERS. [*The eight separate articles in this composite entry focus on personal aspects of serving as a member of Congress:*

For more detailed discussion of the careers of particular members, see numerous biographical entries.]

Daily Life and Routine in the House

Long, unpredictable days are a fact of life for all members of Congress, representatives and senators alike. Time constraints are a constant source of difficulty for those with families as well as for those single members who would simply like their lives to have some semblance of normalcy. In fact, the lack of free time is one of the commonest reasons leading some members to decide after a few terms to return to private life. "I need to spend more time with my family" is the reason lawmakers give most often when announcing they will not seek reelection.

Being a member of Congress not only means working long days in Washington, D.C., when the House and Senate are in session; it also means having to travel back home at least several times a month to keep in touch with constituents. Dividing their time between Washington and their home districts frequently undermines members' family life. Some members leave their spouses and children back home and visit them on weekends and holidays. Ironically, many of those who move their families to Washington so that they can be close to them find that their duties back in their home districts cause them to be away too often. There is, in fact, no perfect solution to the dilemma.

Of course, the conflict between private life and public duty is only one of the multiple conflicts a member faces, day in and day out. Each day presents its own wealth of pressures. A good idea of how a member of the House spends a legislative day can be gained by following a typical representative through that day. The legislator, in this case study, was Rep. Robert T. Matsui (D-Calif.). The day was 29 July 1992—one of the final days of the 102d Congress.

Morning. When Representative Matsui showed up for work at 8:00 A.M. on the morning of 29 July 1992, he knew he was in for a long day. His schedule listed a dozen appointments. He did not anticipate, however, that his day would not end until 12:08 A.M. the following morning, when the House finally recessed. Matsui's sixteen-hour workday included at least a dozen private meetings, fifteen recorded floor votes, a committee markup session, several minor crises, numerous telephone conversations, a fund-raiser for a House colleague, and a banquet.

Like most of his colleagues, Matsui knew well the inconveniences and occasional heartache caused by the crowded, hectic nature of congressional life. When Matsui had first moved to Washington after his 1978 election, he and his wife, Doris, were the parents of a six-year-old boy, Brian. He moved his family into a house in the Washington suburbs but had to spend many long weekends by himself back in their hometown of Sacramento. Now, thirteen years later, Brian Matsui was attending college in California, and his father was still regretting how much his enjoyment of his son's childhood years had been diminished by the strenuous demands of his own political career.

And just a year before, in 1991, Matsui had been sadly forced to choose between politics and family obligations. He had already committed himself to a campaign for the Senate when he learned that his father was dying of cancer. His duties as a House member and the frantic fund-raising schedule for his Senate campaign left him no time to spend with his ailing father, whom he loved dearly, so Matsui quit the Senate race, deciding to remain a House member for the foreseeable future.

On 29 July, as Matsui began his marathon sixteen-hour day, family matters had weighed heavily on him as he had driven to the Capitol from his home in Chevy Chase, Maryland. Doris was in California, visiting her sick father, and Matsui found himself making mental contingency plans to return to California himself if Doris's father were to take a turn for the worse. He was also planning a memorial service for his own father, who had died a few weeks after Matsui dropped out of the Senate race in 1991. As usual, he also found himself missing Brian, who was attending summer school in California.

Competing with these personal thoughts were concerns about a number of pressing political matters. As cochairman for finance of the Democratic National Committee, Matsui was deeply involved in raising money for presidential candidate Bill Clinton, and he hoped to arrange his schedule to allow him to be on hand when Clinton visited California on 15 August. Also on his mind was his commitment to winning repeal of a Civil War–era law establishing what is known as the Special Occupational Tax on Alcohol, levied against businesses that manufacture, distribute, or sell alcohol. In addition, he was one of many House Democrats involved in intensive efforts to fashion a Democratic proposal for health-care reform in the upcoming 103d Congress.

Like most energetic members of Congress, Matsui became involved in numerous issues and political causes. But he insisted that he had become better at focusing his energy than he had been during earlier stages of his congressional career. He claimed to have learned how to say no to interest groups pressing him to champion their cause in Congress: "I've learned to take on just a few big issues that I want to develop and to say to people who come to me with other matters, 'I may be sympathetic, I will vote for you, but I'm not going to carry your water,'" he said.

Matsui had little reason to be concerned about his own chances in the upcoming November election. (His Republican opponent, Robert Dinsmore, ultimately received less than 25 percent of the vote.) But other members of Congress were growing anxious about getting home to campaign. It was, after all, late July, and many incumbents were facing tough challenges mounted by candidates trying to capitalize on the anti-incumbent sentiment among voters across the nation. As July wore on, the House was meeting for longer hours each day in an effort to adjourn as early as possible.

On the small printed scheduled that Matsui received from his staff when he arrived at the office on 29 July were twelve scheduled events, beginning at 8:00 A.M. and ending at 8:00 P.M. He was aware that there were several other tentatively scheduled meetings that he might be called on to attend as the day progressed.

"The most difficult part of this job is the competing scheduling demands," confided Matsui. "For each scheduled appointment, there are usually five [others] that come in."

Members of Congress seldom strictly adhere to the schedules that their staffs work so hard to prepare. Perhaps because members tend to overbook themselves, many find it necessary—or simply desirable—to skip even some scheduled appointments throughout the day. Indeed, Matsui began this day by deciding to skip the first three meetings on his printed schedule: a breakfast with the California delegation, a Democratic budget study group meeting led by Majority Leader Richard A. Gephardt of Missouri to discuss health-care legislation, and a smaller meeting of Democratic members on the health-care issue. He instead decided to remain in his office and catch up on reading and letters that had accumulated during a recent trip to California.

Finding sufficient time to do necessary reading is difficult. Members accumulate piles of reading material each day and often take it home to read in the evening. Many members use airplane travel time to catch up on newspapers. It is hardly unusual to see a member of Congress boarding an airplane carrying a huge shopping bag of unread periodicals.

As Matsui learned later in the day, the early-morning health-care meetings he missed had actually been canceled because too many other members, with their own pressing and overbooked schedules, had also decided not to attend.

Matsui particularly hated to miss the weekly California delegation breakfast, because its members often used that occasion to make important decisions affecting the whole group. He vividly remembered how unhappy some of his fellow Californians had been after missing a similar meeting a year earlier—and finding out afterward that the group had decided that each member would contribute $25,000 from his or her campaign fund to win a state reapportionment plan favorable to the Democrats. Despite the absent members' complaints, that decision was never reversed.

After a brief meeting with five members of his staff, who reviewed the issues that he was likely to encounter that day, Matsui headed off to a House Ways and Means Committee markup accompanied by Dianne Sullivan, his adviser on tax and trade issues. By design, Matsui arrived at the committee room at 10:15, fifteen minutes after the markup had been scheduled to begin. Since most members do not arrive at markups on time, it is a waste of time to be punctual. As it turned out, though, Matsui was still early; the committee meeting did not convene until 10:25. For congressional workaholics, late-convening hearings and meetings inflict enormous frustration. Many complain bitterly that they waste too much time waiting for their colleagues to show up for meetings, hearings, and floor votes.

The irony is that these complainers are often the very same people who regularly show up late.

The meeting finally got under way, and while the committee marked up a minor bill on international trade—the last piece of legislation the committee would report out during the 102d Congress—Matsui talked privately with a number of other members, including Representatives J. J. (Jake) Pickle (D-Tex.) and Don J. Pease (D-Ohio), hoping to secure their support for repeal of the special occupational tax on alcohol. It is not unusual for a member of Congress to use a committee meeting as a place to conduct other business. In most cases, every member of the committee knows in advance how the voting will come out, so they often pay only scant attention to the formal proceedings.

The Ways and Means Committee adjourned at 10:45 A.M., and members were summoned to a vote on the House floor. On the way to the Capitol from the committee room, Matsui encountered Rep. Barbara B. Kennelly (D-Conn.), who pleaded with him to relinquish a room that he controlled adjacent to her office suite. The two had discussed this subject many times before.

"Tip gave that to me," said Matsui, referring to former House Speaker Thomas P. O'Neill, Jr.

"I understood why you didn't want to give it up during your Senate race," Kennelly countered. "But now, you don't use it."

"My staff doesn't want to give it up," Matsui replied.

With the proliferation of staff over the past few decades, office space available to members of the House is now at a premium. House staffers often work in very cramped quarters, and members are constantly on the lookout for ways to gain more space.

While casting his vote, Matsui did what House members regularly do during floor votes: he cornered a number of members and asked for their support on a matter of special concern, in his case the repeal of the occupational alcohol tax. Among others, he persuaded Ed Jenkins (D-Ga.) to talk to other House members about it. It is always easier to contact a member on the floor than to reach him or her on the telephone during a busy legislative day.

Back in his office at 11:12 A.M., Matsui sat down with a group of lobbyists representing child welfare agencies to discuss the dubious fate of certain provisions of the Family Preservation Act. It was a short meeting, the first of a series of face-to-face encounters with lobbyists during the day. Matsui expressed support for the child welfare legislation and promised to contact several of the Democratic leaders on its behalf.

At 11:30 A.M., Matsui welcomed an old friend, lobbyist Howard Paster, into his office. Paster, who worked for the lobbying firm of Timmons & Co., was accompanied by a new client, Maura Melley, vice president of Phoenix Home Mutual. Melley was concerned about how her firm would fare under health-care reform legislation. During the discussion, Paster bluntly noted that Matsui had received financial support for his campaign from Phoenix Home Mutual.

Afternoon. At 12:20 P.M., traveling to the Capitol on the congressional subway, Matsui ran into Rep. Robert A. Roe (D-N.J.), chairman of the Committee on Public Works and Transportation, and Rep. Vic Fazio (D-Calif.), Matsui's colleague from Sacramento. Matsui and Fazio seized the opportunity to lobby Roe on behalf of a local project, the Auburn Dam. Roe listened, but he gave them no encouragement that the dam would be approved by his committee.

After a quick lunch in the House dining room, Matsui returned to his office to chair a meeting of lobbyists favoring repeal of the Special Occupational Tax on Alcohol. The group included representatives of grocers, truck-stop operators, distillers, vintners, and convenience store owners. Although the measure was scheduled to appear on the suspension calendar, the lobbyists feared that House members might balk and demand a recorded vote on what might appear to be a special interest tax break. Matsui pledged to redouble his efforts on their behalf.

Matsui's 3:00 P.M. meeting with Richard G. Austin, administrator of the General Services Administration (GSA), was delayed. Therefore, Matsui agreed to meet briefly with Joyce Ride, mother of astronaut Sally Ride, who had come to encourage Matsui to continue using summer interns from Santa Monica College on his staff.

On his way to another floor vote, Matsui was briefed by an aide in preparation for his meeting with Austin, which began at 3:43 P.M. Matsui wanted to persuade the GSA to build a new federal courthouse in Sacramento rather than at a possible site outside the city, and, in inviting Austin to his office, Matsui was trying to smooth over a dispute between the GSA and local officials.

His next visitors, arriving at about 4:15 P.M., were lobbyists from two big insurance companies, Aetna and CIGNA, who wanted to explain their views on health-care reform. At about 4:45 P.M., he received a visit from two lobbyists for Pacific Telesis who had come to urge him to oppose a bill to prevent telephone companies from getting into the information services business. Matsui made no commitment to either the insurance or the telephone company lobbyists.

Between meetings, Matsui was on the telephone with the office of Majority Leader Gephardt in an effort to determine when his tax-repeal bill would appear on the House calendar.

After his last scheduled meeting of the day, Matsui learned from an aide that although the House had been scheduled to recess at 6:15 P.M., floor proceedings were likely to stretch late into the evening. Matsui observed that although many members go to the House gym around 5:00 P.M., he cannot. "I can't imagine putting on a gym outfit at this time of day," he said.

Evening. At 6:00 P.M., Matsui walked down New Jersey Avenue to the Democratic Club, where he attended a fund-raiser for Rep. William J. Coyne (D-Pa.). Matsui seldom accepted evening invitations, preferring to go straight home when his work was done. But with Mrs. Matsui in California tending to her father, there was no reason to reject Coyne's invitation. And, as it turned out, he could not have left Capitol Hill anyway, because the House was still in session.

After Coyne's party, Matsui stopped by the annual House Gym Dinner, which was attended by President George Bush. Matsui had earlier told the organizers of the dinner that he did not intend to come, but it proved to be something for him to do between floor votes.

As the evening wore on and the House continued to meet, Matsui stayed on the House floor, chatting with friends and continuing to ask colleagues to support repeal of the alcohol tax (which later was defeated on the House floor). It was past midnight when the House finally adjourned, and Matsui was exhausted as he drove home through the empty Washington streets.

Never once during his sixteen-hour day did Matsui ever sit down at the massive mahogany desk that dominated his office. As his day demonstrates, being a member of Congress is not a desk job. "If you're working at your desk," he observed, "you are not really working."

BIBLIOGRAPHY

Miller, Clem. *Member of the House: Letters of a Congressman.* Edited by John W. Baker. 1962.
Price, David E. *The Congressional Experience: A View from the Hill.* 1992.
Tacheron, Donald G., and Morris K. Udall. *The Job of the Congressman.* 2d ed. 1970.

SARA FRITZ

Daily Life and Routine in the Senate

The Framers of the Constitution conceived of the Senate as a reservoir for deliberation and reflection. Public opinion was to play little or no role in shaping the institution or its members' activities, for under Article I, section 3 senators were to be appointed by state legislatures, not elected by the public. Further shielded by its members' staggered six-year terms, the Senate was perpetually to have a majority that would not be standing for reappointment.

These provisions, placing the Senate at arm's length from the popularly elected, shorter-termed House, were clearly designed to protect the institution from a volatile public. Daily life in the Senate was to be centered on the great debates of the day, leavening the popular instincts of the House. And so it was for much of the nation's first century, with senators witnessing great debates led by orators like Daniel Webster and Henry Clay and having ample time for deliberation.

Changing Climate of Senate Life. Yet because of its representational structure, daily life in the Senate was destined to be filled with crosspressures. As political scientist Richard Hall suggests, "Elected from larger and more heterogeneous areas, senators must represent a wider range of interests; they receive greater media and interest group attention; and, given the relative size of the two chambers, individual senators face both greater obligations and greater opportunities for legislative involvement" (Dodd and Oppenheimer, 1989, p. 203). These organizational pressures have existed from the beginning, but, in addition, five more recent political factors have reshaped the daily life of the Senate, transforming it into an arena of nearly unending stress.

Electoral pressure. First, senators now face immense electoral pressure. Directly elected since the ratification of the Seventeenth Amendment in 1913, senators have lost much of the protection from public passions that they once enjoyed. The decision to expose one-third of the body to electoral scrutiny every two years has taken its toll, forcing the Senate to accustom itself to increasingly expensive, highly visible campaigns. In contrast to the local issues that dominate House races, Senate contests are now national in nature, with better-funded challengers; thus, senators have lower reelection rates than representatives. Senators therefore invest great amounts of time and energy planning for future contests, reserving large blocks of their days for campaign-oriented efforts. With spending for the average Senate race reaching almost $6 million in 1992—more than ten times the cost of the average House campaign—fund-raising is a major component of that activity. Even spread over six years, an average senator must now raise almost $3,000 every day to meet the average spending level.

Work load. Second, the 100 members of the Senate must handle the same work load as the 435 members of the House—all thirteen annual appropriations bills, all reauthorizations, and so on—with arguably less institutional support. Although the Senate has fewer committees than the House (16 versus 22 in 1989–1990) and subcommittees (86 versus 138 in 1989–1990), it actually produces a larger number of bills introduced per member (33 versus 14 in 1987–1988). Even though the total number of bills introduced in the Senate has declined from 4,500 in the late 1950s to just over 3,300 in 1989–1990, the average length of each bill has increased substantially. Personal staffs are larger in the Senate (50 staff members versus 17 in 1987), but so, in most cases, is the geographic area that a senator must cover back home.

Further, as senators have engaged in more casework for their constituents, this time-honored source of incumbency advantage has come to occupy a significant portion of the average day. Moreover, because senators serve on nearly twice as many committees and subcommittees as their House colleagues (11.1 versus 6.8 in 1989–1990), and because these committees have somewhat broader jurisdictions than the corresponding bodies in the House, senators spend more time shuttling between hearings and legislative markups and cover a wider agenda. Every day therefore begins with the need to make choices between competing priorities and opportunities.

Floor debate. Third, Senate floor debate is rife with opportunities for the consideration of new and old issues alike; every bill is a potential vehicle for amendment. Unlike the House, whose Rules Committee structures and limits debate, the Senate can be in session longer and offer more conduits for indirect influence. This greater flexibility is a product of the natural individualism of the Senate. According to political scientist Steven Smith's 1989 analy-

sis of floor politics in the House and Senate, "Senators view deliberation as central to their chamber's collegial process, with its minimal restraints on floor participation and relatively weak procedural safeguards for committee recommendations." Floor amendments have become more likely in the Senate than the House as the norms of apprenticeship and deference to committees have evaporated. Vigilance is therefore the watchword, as senators must dedicate significant amounts of staff and personal energy just to monitor the unpredictable course of each legislative day.

Presidential ambitions. Fourth, the Senate has long been an incubator of future candidates for the presidency. Although the vice presidency has more recently become the preeminent launching post for successful party nominees (nine out of the eighteen nominees between 1960 and 1992 were sitting or former vice presidents), the Senate is still a time-honored institution for producing presidential candidates.

The fact that a large number of senators may harbor presidential ambitions clearly shapes the institution's daily routines. Many senators maintain crushingly heavy speaking agendas, traveling widely outside their home states in search of national exposure and potential campaign financing.

Thus, as the number of print and electronic journalists covering Congress roughly doubled over the 1960-1990 period, members had more outlets for their stories. Further, as the number of political action committees (PACs) that provide campaign dollars grew from roughly 600 in the mid 1970s to 4,500 plus today, so, too, did the number of contact points for senators, for both incoming lobbying and outgoing fund-raising. Members had to find time on the daily schedule for these new lobbyists, too. As a result of PACs, writes political scientist Gary Jacobsen in *Congress Reconsidered*, "More time and attention is devoted to politics outside the institution, and outside influences on internal politics have become stronger and more pervasive." Whether or not those PACs have undue influence in the Senate, they have certainly reshaped daily life in the body, demanding an increasing share of a finite commodity, time.

Decline of consensus. Fifth, like the House, the Senate has experienced growing difficulty in achieving consensus on policy. Facing an unyielding budget deficit, tempers have flared more frequently as the once-contemplative Senate has struggled to balance its entrepreneurial instincts with budget realities. Senators have noted the decline in comity among members, reporting that their greatest frustration is with the budget process and its series of seemingly meaningless votes.

This growing anger over sessions that are too long and too often crowded with trivia, coupled with the election of increasingly younger members—who come to Washington with their young families—has led the Senate leadership to promise shorter sessions and, consequently, more time for family life. Despite that promise, the average Senate day remains frenetic, driven by endless scheduling conflicts, comings and goings, and nearly interminable waiting.

Overlong days, fragmented schedules, and member frustration have resulted in increasing committee truancy, as Richard Hall characterizes it. Absenteeism became such a serious obstacle to legislative productivity in the mid 1980s that the Senate created a select committee to hold hearings on possible reforms. It was therefore rather ironic when nine of this select committee's twelve members had scheduling conflicts during the first two days of hearings. Only three attended both days of the opening hearings, while five never appeared at all.

Senators' Major Activities. The average day in the Senate has become increasingly fractured as electoral pressures, a growing casework burden, constant media scrutiny, and an increasingly complex policy agenda threaten to overwhelm members. Although every day has its own contours—the days at the beginning of a session, for example, being vastly different and more relaxed than the days just before adjournment—most senators divide their time between four sometimes competing kinds of activity.

Constituent service and contact. Senators invest significant amounts of time in traditional casework and constituent contact, amounts that appear to be relatively constant across the six-year term. According to a 1988 study, senators not running for reelection were almost as likely as those who were running to make contact with voters through mail, television, radio, print media, or personal meetings. All of these points of contact with constituents must be squeezed into a schedule already crowded with the normal legislative business of the Senate. Although most Senate casework is performed by staff, whether in Washington, D.C., or back in the home state, senators must be kept posted; furthermore, they occasionally intercede on particularly difficult or visible issues.

Publicity seeking and credit claiming. Media interviews present senators with opportunities to claim credit for the public service they have performed and the benefits their work has created, both in their home states and, when a senator has presidential ambitions, in the key states of an upcoming presidential campaign. A senator's ability to claim credit for a particular piece of legislation, however, depends on a long trail of actions: his or her work in shaping an appropriations bill, for example, or participation in an oversight hearing or in fashioning new rules for a federal agency, or the committed way in which he or she backed a presidential initiative. That is, to claim credit, a senator has to have done a lot of work. True, staff often lay the groundwork, but there is no substitute for the kind of individual, personal lobbying that only a senator can perform. And no matter what form that personal contact takes—composing a note, making a phone call, arranging for a face-to-face meeting—the senator must clear the time needed to do it. Added to this time pressure is the fact that a senator must often personally lobby the media to make sure that he or she gets the credit due.

Agenda setting and policy advancement. Ultimately, senators may care the most about setting the policy agenda. Becoming known as a national expert and spokesperson on an issue such as health care is one route to a presidential candidacy. Thus, the Senate's role as a presidential incubator has long gone hand in hand with its role as an incubator of policy agendas. Individual senators often invest great energy in developing ideas that bear their mark and that ultimately become statutes. No matter how pressured by the exigencies of the budget deficit or other time-consuming matters, many senators make sure they reserve at least a portion of each day to learn more about the policy areas in which they have chosen to become experts.

Enterprise management. Finally, all senators must dedicate time merely to keeping track of their staffs, staff assignments, and schedules. Although this management function is often overlooked when the sources of constraint are enumerated, a significant portion of an average day is dedicated to making choices regarding how time will be allocated. The calendar itself can be a source of conflict among staffers representing different concerns, such as constituent demands, publicity seeking, and policy development. Some senators resolve this pressure by appointing strong chiefs of staff; others reserve the adjudicatory role for themselves. At least one recent senator has handled the problem electronically, setting up a command center in his Senate hideaway office from which he monitored his personal staff by phone and electronic mail.

The Stresses of an Average Day. Given all these activities, it is hardly surprising that daily life in the Senate is extraordinarily stressful. The average day starts long before the opening prayer by the Senate chaplain. Usually, it begins with an early breakfast, then continues with the first of several committee and subcommittee appearances. These are normally marked by quick opening statements, which can be inserted for the record, and short rounds of questions and answers for particularly important witnesses. More often than not, several hearings are scheduled simultaneously, so senators conduct a good deal of business as they run from one to the other and back again. Such is a normal morning when Congress is in session.

The already frantic day continues with trips to the Senate television studio for short interviews and longer satellite feeds to television stations back home, speeches to and meetings with assorted lobbying groups, occasional stops at Capitol hideaway offices, subway rides to and from the Senate office buildings, staff briefings, quorum calls and votes on the Senate floor, constituent contacts, quick lunches and dinners, caucus meetings, interviews with local and national reporters, strategy sessions, scheduling conferences to sort out invitations, and further business until late into the evening. Now that Senate floor debate is televised, rare is the senator who does not make at least one appearance a day to speak on the floor. Although every senator's schedule is different, it is safe to say that the average day allows little or no time for reflection and debate as meetings and quick contacts merge into a strobe light of activity. The schedule rarely eases, even during the most contentious floor debates (which merely make the day longer).

Ironically, the greater collegiality of the Senate as compared to the House can actually contribute to the frustrations of the daily routine. Senators do possess a much greater potential to exert individual influence than do their House colleagues, but the atmosphere in which conversation and dealings go on has a claustrophobic, small-townish intensity. Senators strive to keep personal conflict at a minimum through, for example, the time-honored practice of seeking unanimous consent for all business. But while the search for unanimity does smoothe the rough edges of policy disputes, it also often delays progress, adding to the time needed for passing even the most routine legislation. The sources of delay are many and varied—ranging from the full-blown filibuster to personal requests for delays on pending legislation—and they are available to even the most junior member.

In the search for ways to resolve disputes, individual senators, particularly committee chairmen, have few of the levers that allow for quick action in the House. The norm of committee deference is long forgotten, and committee chairmen may find that even the most strongly supported committee measure can be all too easily replaced on the floor by an alternative crafted by a single member. Such unpredictability adds to the demands on already pressured members, who must allocate time for scouting the potential opposition and for crafting the bargains that will make progress possible.

A House in Senate Clothing? The notion that the Senate has become a House of Representatives in more collegial, less rule-bounded clothing has clear implications for daily life. Unanimous consent does provide at least some semblance of predictability in the daily floor schedule, but the rest of the process, including floor amending, is often anything but predictable. The Senate's lack of the tight rules that guide procedure in the House, combined with the ever-greater electoral tension felt by all its members, have made the Senate the antithesis of what the Framers envisioned—at least in terms of the daily routine. Time to think and reflect has become exceedingly rare.

BIBLIOGRAPHY

Davidson, Roger H., ed. *The Post-Reform Congress.* 1992.
Deering, Christopher. *Congressional Politics.* 1989.
Dodd, Lawrence, and Bruce I. Oppenheimer. *Congress Reconsidered.* 4th ed. 1989.
Light, Paul. *Forging Legislation.* 1992.
Loomis, Burdette. *The New American Politician: Ambition, Entrepreneurship, and the Changing Face of Political Life.* 1988.
Sinclair, Barbara. *Transformation of the U.S. Senate.* 1989.
Smith, Steven. *Call to Order: Floor Politics in the House and Senate.* 1989.

PAUL C. LIGHT

Qualifications

The Constitution clearly and starkly enumerates the qualifications for serving in the House of Representatives and the Senate. In the qualifications clauses (Article I, sections 2 and 3), the basic requirements of age, citizenship, and residency are set out. House members must be twenty-five years old, U.S. citizens for at least seven years, and inhabitants of the state (not the district) that they represent. Senators must be thirty years old, citizens for at least nine years, and inhabitants of their states.

A series of court rulings and two hundred years of congressional decisions have established that these constitutional criteria represent an exclusive list of qualifications for members of Congress. States have been barred from imposing additional requirements; for example, ex-felons cannot be barred, nor can those rare individuals who reside outside the congressional districts in which they run and are elected.

Still, the two houses have traditionally served as the judges of the qualifications of their own memberships. In the past, the chambers have excluded members-elect on the basis of polygamy and disloyalty. Like the Senate, the House has the uncontested capacity to expel one of its members for actions committed after election, but this power has been exercised only four times in its history, three times in the 1860s in connection with members from border states who were accused of treason and in 1981 in connection with one representative found guilty of accepting bribes in the Abscam corruption case. On occasion, members have resigned rather than face possible expulsion, as did two other members involved in the Abscam affair. But there is no question that actions committed prior to their election cannot be used to bar members-elect from taking their seats.

In 1969 the Supreme Court clarified the qualifications criteria with its landmark decision in *Powell v. McCormack*. In 1967 the House voted to deny Rep. Adam Clayton Powell, Jr. (D-N.Y.), the seat he had won in the 1968 election. Powell stood accused of the misuse of official funds and unauthorized travel by staff members; in addition, he had refused to pay a judgment in a highly publicized libel case. After the Democrats stripped him of his Education and Labor Committee chairmanship, the full House refused to seat him. Powell sued the House, and the Supreme Court somewhat surprisingly agreed to hear the case. Powell's congressional seat remained vacant through 1968, and he once again won the office in the 1968 election. In January 1969 he was seated, although he had been stripped of his seniority. But the 1967 House decision remained before the Court, which ruled in June 1969 that the House had exceeded its constitutional limits by imposing additional qualifications for its membership. Only a constitutional amendment could impose further restrictions.

Directly related to the question of qualifications is that of contested elections. While the qualifications issue has rarely generated much internal congressional turmoil, this has not been the case with contested elections. Almost six hundred such cases have come before the House and its Elections Committee (or, after 1947, a subcommittee of the House Administration Committee). In the nineteenth century, highly partisan decisions were regularly rendered; more recently, however, the winner of a contested seat has generally been decided on the merits of the case, as a substantial body of precedent has been established. Still, only very rarely have contested elections turned on matters of formal qualification. For example, one issue of residence was resolved in 1807 when the House decided that the current residence in Maryland of representative-elect William McCreery met the inhabitancy qualification and that the state could not require a twelve-month residence for eligibility.

Advocates of term limitations contest past rulings and congressional practice; they argue that there is no explicit constitutional prohibition of such state-imposed limits. With Colorado leading the way in 1990 by mandating twelve-year limits for both U.S. senators and representatives (1991 counted as the first year), and with many other states having since passed similar requirements, this argument will surely come before the Supreme Court, unless a constitutional amendment renders the issue moot.

There have been some apparent state limitations on would-be candidates. Some defeated congressional primary candidates have been refused ballot access as independents in the general election. When write-in votes have been permitted, this restriction has not generally been interpreted as an additional qualification; rather, the states have been seen as carrying out their constitutional duty to conduct the elections of senators and representatives. More common have been various states' attempts to regulate ballot access to independents and to sitting state officeholders. Independents can be forced to comply with stringent provisions for gaining ballot status. Current state officeholders can be forced to resign their positions in order to run for the Congress; the Ninth District Court of Appeals ruled in an Arizona case (*Joyner v. Mofford* [1983]) that such restrictions are within the state's province of regulating state officials. *Joyner* ruled that no new qualifications are considered to have been imposed on such individuals; rather, they are being required to comply with the conditions of service that apply to the state offices they hold.

In sum, the constitutional qualifications of age, citizenship, and residency have stood solidly as the major formal restrictions on congressional service. In the wake of the *Powell* decision, other prior qualifications have little chance of standing up to the scrutiny of the House, the Senate, or the Supreme Court. The term limitation movement, while presenting the most serious set of qualifications issues in more than two hundred years, will probably need a constitutional amendment to triumph in its attempt to restrict congressional service.

[*See also* Contested Elections; Elections, Congressional; Ethics and Corruption in Congress; Term Limitation.]

BIBLIOGRAPHY

Benjamin, Gerald, and Michael Malbin, eds. *Limiting Legislative Terms*. 1992.
Galloway, George B. *History of the House of Representatives*. 1961.
Jacobs, Andrew. *The Powell Affair: Freedom Minus One*. 1973.

BURDETT A. LOOMIS

Demographic Profile

An interest in the backgrounds of political leaders stems from both normative and positive concerns. From a normative perspective, democratic theorists are concerned that government should represent the will of the people. If leaders come from higher social strata, have different occupations, and go to different places of worship than the masses, the broader interests of the people may not be served. The positive perspective evolved in American political science in the 1950s and 1960s. In a break with previous institutional studies, scholars such as Donald R. Matthews, Heinz Eulau, Herbert Jacob, and many others argued for a focus on individual politicians; for the study of members of Congress rather than the study of congressional rules and institutions. Many behavioralists, as they came to be known, shared the democratic theorists' normative concern that representatives should reflect the broader population, although this assumption generally was left unspoken.

The Founders recognized the impact that the backgrounds of leaders could have on representation. In creating a bicameral legislature, they envisioned a different type of leader and function for each body. The Senate was to be an elite institution that was removed from the public to serve as a check on the more popularly based and responsive House. The House, on the other hand, was to replicate the population at large in terms of demographic characteristics. John Adams said that a legislature "should be an exact portrait, in miniature, of the people at large, as it should think, feel, reason, and act like them." This essay will examine the extent to which Congress is an "exact portrait" of the broader public and offer explanations for the demographic profile of Congress that exists today.

Racial and Ethnic Background. The composition of Congress does not reflect the diverse image of America. Ethnic and minority groups have always been underrepresented in Congress, although the situation has improved in recent years. No African Americans served in Congress between 1901 and 1929 and no more than two served until 1955. Twenty blacks served in the House and two in the Senate between 1869 and 1901; all of them were from the South, and most served during the Reconstruction era. In the 1960s, black representation in Congress slowly increased (see figure 1), and by 1991, blacks comprised about 5 percent of Congress, although this is far short of their 12 percent of the U.S. population. Similar patterns hold for other minorities. Only 3.6 percent of the members of Congress are Hispanic, while Hispanics comprise about 7 percent of the population. Seven members of Congress (1.3 percent) are Asian Americans, which is less than a third of their proportion in the population. Ben Nighthorse Campbell (D-Colo.) was elected to the Senate in 1992, becoming the first Native American to serve in Congress.

Similarly, despite the success of Italian, Polish, and Irish Americans in urban political machines, immigrant groups have never had proportionate representation in Congress. Lacking the necessary resources to become easily integrated into the new society, immigrants turned to political machines that offered them patronage and the means for social mobility. However, two factors limited their numbers in Congress: (1) like blacks, new immigrants were victims of discrimination outside of their areas of urban concentration and (2) the machines that channeled their political activity were primarily interested in state and local politics rather than in Congress. Matthews (1954) shows that in the periods of peak immigration in the early twentieth century, 12 to 15 percent of the population but only 3 to 5 percent of senators were foreign born. In 1940, only six House members were foreign born. In contrast, 75 percent of urban machine bosses were either foreign-born or second-generation Americans. Today most members of Congress with European backgrounds are third and fourth-generation Americans, rather than first and second- (however, there were still five foreign-born members of the House in 1991).

Women in Congress. For many decades, women have been the most seriously underrepresented group in Congress. However, the 1990 elections continued a decade-long trend of increasing the number of women in politics. In 1991 women held a record 17 percent of statewide offices (including three governorships) and 18 percent of state legislative seats (2,063 women ran for state legislatures in 1990). In 1993 women held a record thirty-one seats in Congress, forty-eight in the House and six in the Senate (twenty-three more than in the 102d Congress).

It has taken a long time for women to be thus represented. From the mid 1940s until 1970, the proportion of women in Congress was about 2 percent. Through the 1970s it reached 3.5 percent, but many women were still being elected to Congress by replacing their deceased husbands. From 1920

to 1979, 41 percent of all women who reached Congress did so through this "widow's mandate," but, with notable exceptions like Margaret Chase Smith, these women typically did not have long or distinguished careers. By the mid 1980s, most women were elected in their own right, and their proportion in Congress reached 4.5 percent and jumped to 10 percent in 1993 (see figure 1).

Religious Backgrounds. There are two distinctive features of the religious affiliations of members of Congress. First, 99 percent of them claim some religious affiliation (although 5.6 percent label themselves "unspecified Protestant" or "other Christian," which implies inactive involvement), compared with roughly two-thirds of the general population. Second, there has been a gradual but significant shift in the denominational distribution of congressional religious affiliations. In the 1940s, Protestant denominations associated with high social status (Episcopalian, Congregational, and Presbyterian) were very overrepresented in Congress. Between 1941 and 1946 about 29 percent of all members of Congress

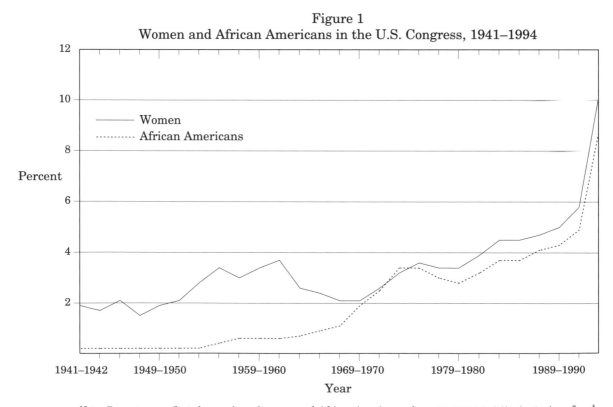

Figure 1
Women and African Americans in the U.S. Congress, 1941–1994

Note: Percentages reflect the number of women and African Americans who were serving at the beginning of each Congress.

SOURCE: Norman J. Ornstein, Thomas E. Mann, and Michael J. Mablin, eds., *Vital Statistics on Congress, 1993–1994*, Washington, D.C.: Congressional Quarterly Press, 1994.

were affiliated with these three denominations, compared with about 7 percent of the U.S. population. The proportion of House members and senators from other Protestant denominations was about the same as their proportion in the population in the 1940s. Jews and Catholics were severely underrepresented; Jews comprised 3 percent of the population, but represented only 1 percent of the members of Congress; Catholics represented about one-fourth of the population, but only about 12 percent of the members (Matthews, 1954).

Several shifts are evident in the 103d Congress (see figures 2 and 3). Jews are one of the most overrepresented groups (they comprise 2.5 percent of the population, but 7.9 percent of Congress), and there are slightly more Catholics in Congress than would be proportional. At the same time the representation of high-status Protestant churches has fallen, although they remain very overrepresented.

Episcopalians and Presbyterians each comprise about 2 percent of the population, but they made up 9.4 and 10.1 percent, respectively, of the members of the 102d Congress. However, the all-time high for overrepresentation goes to the 2,748-member Schwenkfelder church of Pennsylvania, which was overrepresented by a ratio of about 800 to 1 during the twenty years of Republican Richard Schweicker's membership.

Social Background. No myth dies harder in American politics than the log cabin, rags-to-riches notion that anyone can be elected president or a member of Congress. Although there are exceptions to the normal patterns, age, father's occupation, family connections, and education are significant determinants of who is elected to Congress.

At least at a superficial level, age restricts entry into Congress: few people under the age of thirty or over the age of sixty-five are elected. The average

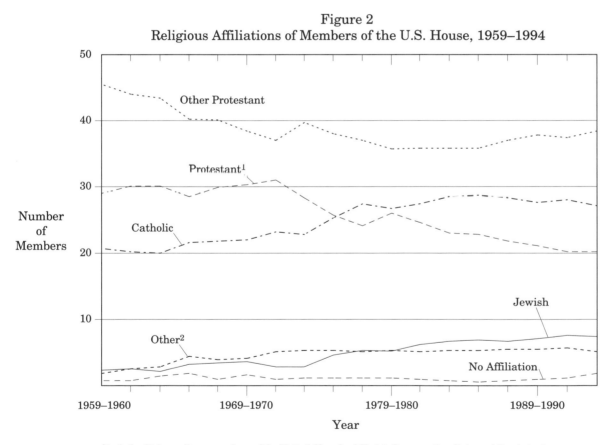

Figure 2
Religious Affiliations of Members of the U.S. House, 1959–1994

[1]Includes Episcopalians, members of the United Church of Christ, Congregationalists, and Presbyterians.
[2]Includes Christian Scientists, members of the Eastern Orthodox Church, Mormons, and Unitarian-Universalists.

SOURCE: Norman J. Ornstein, Thomas E. Mann, and Michael J. Mablin, eds., *Vital Statistics on Congress, 1993–1994*, Washington, D.C.: Congressional Quarterly Press, 1994.

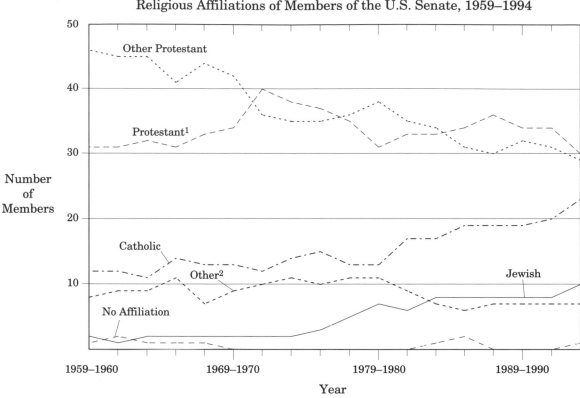

Figure 3
Religious Affiliations of Members of the U.S. Senate, 1959–1994

[1]Includes Episcopalians, members of the United Church of Christ, Congregationalists, and Presbyterians.
[2]Includes Christian Scientists, members of the Eastern Orthodox Church, Mormons, and Unitarian-Universalists.

SOURCE: Norman J. Ornstein, Thomas E. Mann, and Michael J. Mablin, eds., *Vital Statistics on Congress, 1993–1994*, Washington, D.C.: Congressional Quarterly Press, 1994.

age of members in the 103d Congress (1993–1995) is 53.1 years; it was 47 years in the 98th Congress (1983–1985). Father's occupation, a typical indicator of social class and social mobility, reveals the upper-class tilt of members of Congress; very few fathers of members of Congress have been of the working class.

Family connections may also help gain a seat in Congress. There are sixteen American "dynasty" families that have produced eight presidents, three vice presidents, thirty senators, twelve governors, fifty-six House members, and nine cabinet officers. One study revealed that 54 percent of one group of eighty-five members of Congress said they had relatives in politics. However, the proportion of representatives who have had a close relative in the House fell from between 20 and 24 percent in the first five Congresses to between 5 and 6.8 percent in the 86th Congress (1959–1961) (Czudnowski, 1975).

Higher education is another factor that can affect one's chances for election to Congress. Although higher education is not a requirement, no senator and only 3 percent of members of the House did not attend college at all. Eighty-seven percent of House members and 92 percent of senators hold a college degree, compared with 70 percent of the general population who never attended college and 17 percent who have a degree.

Occupation. Members' occupations provide more evidence of the upper-class bias of Congress: blue-collar workers, the service sector, and farmers are underrepresented. About three-fourths of the members of Congress come from banking, business, or law activities. In the 1993 Congress there were more doctors than engineers (six and five, respectively), one actor in the House (Fred Grandy, R Iowa, "Gopher" from the television show "The Love Boat"), and two professional athletes (former basketball star Bill Bradley, D-N.J., and former major league pitcher Jim Bunning, R-Ky.).

Special note must be made of lawyers in Congress, if for no other reason than the amount of attention the topic has drawn from political observers for 150 years. Elite theorists searching for the "ruling class" in the military-industrial complex, the business world, or the halls of the Ivy League need look no further than their local American Bar Association. Lawyers, quite literally, have ruled the nation since its inception. The "high priests of politics" comprised 37 percent of Congress in 1790, 70 percent in 1840, 54 percent in 1957, and 45.6 percent in 1993 (while they comprise only 0.1 percent of the work force). The downward trend has been more apparent in the House than in the Senate from 1973 to 1993 (see figure 4). The proportion of lawyers in the Senate, although it has decreased from its peak of 68 percent in 1977–1978, has remained relatively stable.

Data on occupations must be viewed with caution because members of Congress have an incentive to misreport their backgrounds. A member from a farm state may call himself a farmer, even though he has not been on a tractor since he was seventeen. More significant, most members of Congress refuse to admit they are politicians, even if they have been in politics most of their adult lives.

Running for Congress by running against the "Washington establishment" is a time-honored tradition, but it reached new heights in the 102d Congress (1991–1993). In the wake of the savings and loan crisis and anti-incumbency sentiment, forty-nine fewer incumbents were willing to admit that "public service or politics" was their career. In the 101st Congress, ninety-four House members and twenty senators said politics was their career; two years later these numbers fell to sixty-one and four. This change cannot be explained by the election of freshman members, 16 percent of whom named politics, compared with 12 percent of Congress as a whole. However, in the 103d Congress eighty-seven House members and thirty-six senators named politics as their career.

Ironically, the most important aspect of occupational data, in terms of explaining who is elected to Congress and who is not, is whether or not the congressional aspirant is a current officeholder. Candidates with previous political experience have many advantages: an existing voter base that leads to higher name recognition, a campaign organization and fund-raising network in place from previous races, and greater attention from the media. As a result, from 1972 to 1978, the average experienced

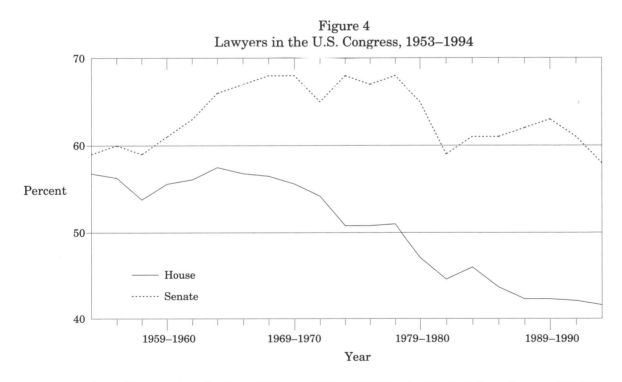

Figure 4
Lawyers in the U.S. Congress, 1953–1994

SOURCE: Norman J. Ornstein, Thomas E. Mann, and Michael J. Mablin, eds., *Vital Statistics on Congress, 1993–1994*, Washington, D.C.: Congressional Quarterly Press, 1994.

challengers received 7 percent more of the two-party vote than inexperienced candidates (Jacobson and Kernell, 1983).

Most inexperienced candidates run poorly funded campaigns that have almost no chance of success. Amateurs are hindered not only by their lack of campaign experience and (with the exception of celebrities) low name recognition, but also by a general preference among voters for candidates who have prior experience. Newcomers are thus at a distinct disadvantage, but the obstacles are not insurmountable. Successful amateur campaigns have been waged with large expenditures on consultants, staff, and advertising. In general, the political career structure in the United States is relatively open. Compared to nations with stronger party systems, the United States requires little in the way of party or office apprenticeship even for the highest offices.

Indeed, as can been seen in figures 5 and 6, previous experience has never been a requirement for service in the House or Senate. Amateurs comprise about 25 percent of the membership of the House and between 5 and 15 percent of the Senate (Canon, 1990).

Geographic Representation. All of the indicators thus far have described an unrepresentative, upper-class, highly educated, white, male institution. But the geographic backgrounds of members of Congress show that they have stronger local roots than the people they represent. *Federalist* 56 argues that this is the way it should be; that House members should have a "considerable knowledge of state laws and a local knowledge of their respective districts."

Members of Congress often tout their local roots during campaigns. In many districts, being an outsider can be a political liability. Since the Reconstruction era, the charge of "carpetbagger" has brought down many candidates (most recently Pete Dawkins in the 1988 New Jersey Senate race;

Figure 5
Amateurs in the U.S. Senate, 1913–1994

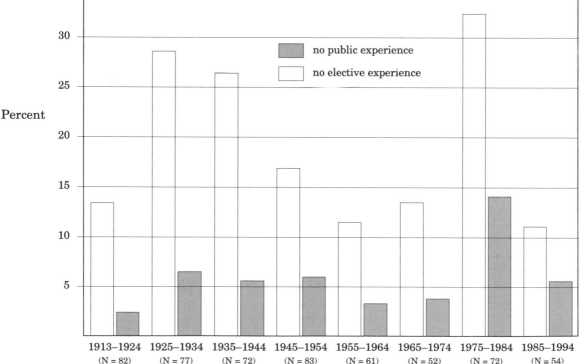

Year (N = Total Number of Senators Considered Amateurs)

SOURCE: Data collected by the author from *Biographical Directory of the American Congress: 1774–1971* and various editions of *Almanac of American Politics.*

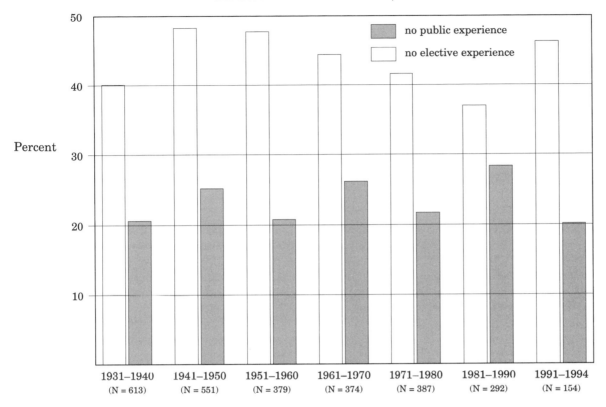

Figure 6
Amateurs in the U.S. House, 1931–1994

Dawkins, who did not have strong roots in the area, apparently had been shopping for a state in which to run for the Senate).

Only 6 percent of senators and 7 percent of House members in the 96th Congress (1979–1981) were outsiders (i.e., people who were not born in the state and did not go to college or serve in elective office in the state). Approximately three-fourths of the members of that Congress were born in their home states, compared with 68 percent of the U.S. population (as of the 1980 census). In the 102d Congress (1991–1993) this proportion dropped to only sixty-five of one hundred senators who were born in their home states. The pattern is stronger in the South, where 80 percent had local roots (compared with 61 percent outside the South).

Explaining Representational Patterns in Congress. The two most important patterns of representation outlined above concern the place of women and minorities in Congress. Why are there so few minorities and women, and what are the prospects for change? Until the 1960s, the under-representation of minorities in Congress could largely be explained by overt discrimination and racism, especially true for blacks in the South. Poll taxes, racially applied literacy tests, grandfather clauses, and whites-only primaries disenfranchised blacks for nearly a century after they had the constitutional right to vote (black men were given the right to vote in 1870, women in 1920). With a majority of blacks living in the South, it was not surprising that only a handful were elected to Congress between the Reconstruction era and the Voting Rights Act of 1965.

Today, the number of blacks in Congress is limited by voting along racial lines, electoral laws, and redistricting. Racial voting makes it almost impossible for blacks to win in white-majority districts. Politicians such as Gov. L. Douglas Wilder of Virginia and Rep. Alan Wheat of Missouri are evidence that this is not an ironclad rule, but the proportion of minority population is the best indicator of success for minority office-seekers.

Runoff elections, which exist only in the South, have also limited opportunities for blacks. In some instances the black candidate wins the first election with 40 to 45 percent of the vote against two white candidates, only to lose in the runoff. Rev. Jesse Jackson and other black leaders have lobbied to abolish runoff elections or to weaken their bias by reducing the winning percentage from 50 to 40.

The 1991–1992 redistricting process was another target of the black leadership, who wanted more black-majority districts created. In the past, redistricting has limited black representation in Congress by disenfranchising blacks and diluting their voting power. In 1986, the Supreme Court ruled in *Thornburg v. Gingles* that racial votes cannot be diluted, even if there is no demonstrable intent to discriminate. This case has been widely interpreted as a mandate for the creation of more black-majority districts. An unlikely alliance to pursue this mandate has been forged among black leaders in the NAACP and the Congressional Black Caucus, who want to increase their representation, and Republicans, who are willing to sacrifice a few districts to dilute Democratic strength in many others. This strategy was quite successful as thirteen of the newly elected African Americans in the 103d Congress had districts that were intentionally drawn to increase black representation.

Hispanics have been affected by many of the same conditions that limit African American representation in Congress. Hispanics are an important group in American politics, partly because the Hispanic population, which is growing faster than the general population, is concentrated in states that are pivotal in presidential elections (Florida, Texas, California, and New York). In the 1980s this concentration served as a ceiling for the potential impact of Hispanic representation in Congress. The greatest potential for Hispanic representation occurred in less than 2 percent (eight) of all districts where Hispanics comprised at least half the population. Only 6 percent (twenty-seven) of all congressional districts in the 1980s had constituencies that are at least one-fourth Hispanic. However, creative cartography in redrawing congressional district lines in 1992 led to the election of six new Hispanic members of the House.

Women have also faced overt discrimination and structural barriers in their attempts to be elected to Congress. Early studies indicated that voters, the media, contributors, and parties all discriminated against women candidates. Gallup polls in the 1970s revealed that between 9 and 13 percent of all voters said they would refuse to vote for a qualified woman candidate in their party. Another national poll in 1983 showed that only 87 percent of the public still would vote for a woman nominee of their party for president.

Some recent studies, however, show that there is no evidence of discrimination by voters against women running for office at the state or local level (Darcy, Welch, and Clark, 1987) or for national office (Gertzog, 1984). In fact, in House races, women tend to be viewed more favorably than men by voters, and voters perceive themselves closer to women on the issues than to men. In a 1991 poll, women still were not viewed favorably for executive offices, although they had a distinct advantage for legislative positions.

The media and campaign contributors are other potential sources of discrimination. The media often perpetuate stereotypical female roles, as when Geraldine Ferraro was asked about her favorite recipes on the campaign trail in 1984. Evidence from the early 1970s indicated that contributors discouraged women from running for office by refusing to support them, but more recent studies show this is no longer true. Several studies have found that women do as well as men in raising money for congressional campaigns, even after taking into account campaign context and the strength of the opponent. Women in the Democratic party, in an attempt to make sure this trend continues, have established their own fund-raising network called EMILY's List (Early Money Is Like Yeast—it raises the dough).

The characteristics of the women candidates also help explain the dearth of women in Congress. Women running for Congress are handicapped by their lack of previous elective experience. Women's political base, appointive office or local political activism, are better stepping-stones to state and local office than to the U.S. House or Senate. Women are also hurt by their underrepresentation in the two occupations that are the dominant base for political service: law and business. Only 10 percent of all women members of Congress are attorneys compared with half of the men. Women are also hampered by societal expectations concerning families and children. Although traditional roles are slowly changing, women still have primary responsibility for childrearing, which often forces them to postpone careers.

The most important barriers to women and minorities in Congress are structural: the incumbency advantage, the problems of raising money as a challenger, the infrequency of open seats and the intense competition when an incumbent does retire, fickle voters, and weak parties. These roadblocks to office are equally obstructive to both men and women, whites and minorities, but because the barriers protect the status quo, which is a male-dominated white institution, women and minorities are still disproportionately disadvantaged. The best hope for these groups to gain access to Congress has been to concentrate their efforts in years such as 1992, when there were a large number of open seats, and to continue to build a base in state and local offices that serve as springboards to Congress. This strategy was quite successful in 1992, when forty-eight women were elected to the House and four new women senators were elected, bringing their total to six.

Conclusions and Significance. That members of Congress are not representative of the broader public is well established, but the significance of this is more difficult to demonstrate. First, knowing that 41.6 percent of all House members are lawyers, and that 27.1 percent are Roman Catholics, and that all but a few have college degrees does not indicate why the hundreds of thousands of other people who are similarly situated did not pursue a career in politics, or why the handful who are elected to Congress every two years did.

Second, nearly every study on this question has failed to demonstrate a link between members' backgrounds and their behavior. Theorists such as Floyd Hunter and C. Wright Mills maintain that the ruling class serves its own interests, but systematic tests of this theory have provided mixed results. The link between socioeconomic background and legislative behavior seems obvious. Politicians such as Thomas P. (Tip) O'Neill, Jr. (D.-Mass.), who represented a working-class ethnic constituency, and William O. Lipinski (D.-Ill.), a product of a political machine, are likely to have very different outlooks on politics than Rudy Boschwitz (R.-Minn.), who became a millionaire by selling plywood and then was elected to the Senate. However, it is difficult to separate the influence of constituency from personal background variables. Was Tip O'Neill a supporter of the "common man" because his father was a bricklayer, or because his district shared his ethnic, working-class background? The difficulty in sorting and calculating the effects of these various influences has led most political scientists to avoid trying to explain legislative behavior on the basis of social backgrounds.

However, whether sanctioned by political scientists or not, practitioners of politics care about descriptive, or symbolic, representation. African American leaders push strongly for redistricting that would create more black-majority districts. The National Women's Caucus and other women's groups urge more women to get involved in politics and run for office. The media pay attention to the backgrounds of our leaders, and every textbook on Congress has the obligatory chapter on its members. Thus, social background data are useful primarily in providing information about varying levels of symbolic representation, for setting the broad parameters within which recruitment operates, and perhaps giving some clues about substantive representation.

[*See also* Asian American Members; Black Members; Elections, Congressional, *article on* Becoming a Candidate; Hispanic Members; Women in Congress.]

BIBLIOGRAPHY

Canon, David T. *Actors, Athletes, and Astronauts: Political Amateurs in the United States Congress.* 1990.
Czudnowski, Moshe M. "Political Recruitment." In vol. 2 of *Handbook of Political Science.* Edited by Fred I. Greenstein and Nelson W. Polsby. 1975.
Darcy, Robert, Susan Welch, and Janet Clark. *Women, Elections, and Representation.* 1987.
Gertzog, Irwin. *Congressional Women: Their Recruitment, Treatment, and Behavior.* 1984.
Jacobson, Gary C., and Samuel Kernell. *Strategy and Choice in Congressional Elections.* 1983.
Matthews, Donald R. "Legislative Recruitment and Legislative Careers." *Legislative Studies Quarterly* 9:4 (November 1984): 547–585.
Matthews, Donald R. *The Social Backgrounds of Political Decision-Makers.* 1954.

DAVID T. CANON

Congressional Careers

For nearly a century, careerism among members of Congress has been the defining feature of legislative life. Typically, politicians acquire political experience before entering Congress and expect to serve there for many years. They are consequently ambitious for personal power and skillful at keeping themselves in office. These aspirations shape both the internal organization of Congress and lawmakers' behavior in their constituencies. Consideration of the institution's performance as a lawmaking and representative institution thus leads us to an examination of how members get to Congress and what they hope to achieve on Capitol Hill.

Evolution of Careerism. Legislative careers take shape in relation to political and institutional contexts. When politicians find particular offices rewarding, when they are able to secure reelection and acquire genuine influence, they are likely to view their jobs as long-term investments. All these stimulants to careerism—motive, means, and opportunity—are present in the U.S. Congress. As this mix of incentives has evolved over the institution's history, it has produced four distinct career patterns in the following periods: 1789 to the Civil War; the 1860s to the end of World War I; the 1920s to the mid 1960s; and 1965 to the present. For each era the pattern varies in terms of length of service, levels of leadership and partisanship, complexity of the legislative agenda, and availability of institutional resources.

During the earliest Congresses, members tended to be experienced officeholders in their states or localities who served only brief stints on Capitol Hill. Representatives commonly shunned reelection and senators often resigned in the middle of their first term. Until the Civil War, the average lawmaker served roughly four years; typically the majority of members in both chambers were freshmen. Legislative business—dominated by private bills, tariffs, and slavery—was conducted a few months a year without benefit of staff or offices. The members' lack of commitment to Congress was reflected in the institution's unstable rules, highly conflictual selection of leaders, and voting coalitions based on regional ties forged among colleagues living in the same boardinghouses. Legislators called the Congress "Babbletown," deploring the sectionalism and lack of discipline that left the nation open to British invasion during the War of 1812 and stymied resolution of the slavery question.

After the Civil War, however, tenure lengthened, first in the Senate, then in the House, and particularly among southerners. Although the Congress remained only a part-time institution with limited staff and perquisites, it had begun to acquire policy expertise through an expanded committee system. The institution also developed strong party leaders who appointed members to committees, designated committee chairs, and enforced a high degree of party-line voting. Its policy agenda, too, broadened to include economic development, foreign affairs, and business regulation. But however appealing members found the more orderly and challenging decision-making environment in Congress, most lacked the means to pursue a career there. Strong party organizations in the state legislatures and local counties controlled nominations for the Senate and House, respectively, and they tended to enforce a system of rotation for both offices.

At the turn of the century, membership turnover declined rapidly as lawmakers gained greater lee-

way in seeking reelection. The introduction of ballot reforms and primaries, as well as direct election of senators after 1913, diminished the party bosses' ability to designate congressional candidates. In addition, the rise of safe seats for Republicans in the North and Democrats in the South after the realigning election of 1896 heightened the probabilities of electoral success.

As both the motive and means for securing reelection increased, members of both chambers promoted opportunities for advancement inside Congress. Senators adopted seniority as the criterion for selecting committee chairs. Representatives overthrew an autocratic Speaker in 1911, lodging power initially in their party caucus and subsequently selecting the seniority rule as the basis for allocating chairmanships. A well-defined ladder of advancement after a long apprenticeship became the norm for selecting party leaders. Members added staff, improved their offices and pay, and settled into year-round sessions that were punctuated by trips home.

By the 1920s the parameters of the congressional career were firmly in place. The mean length of service in both houses hovered between eight and nine years. First-term lawmakers represented about 20 percent of members, although political crises swept large freshmen classes into office in 1932, 1946, and 1958. Congress was ruled by a powerful oligarchy of committee chairmen and occasional masterful party leaders, such as House Speaker Sam Rayburn (1940–1947; 1949–1953; 1955–1961) and Senate Majority Leader Lyndon B. Johnson (1955–1960). Junior members deferred to those with seniority in the expectation that eventually they themselves would have a turn at wielding power.

As the Depression, World War II, and the Cold War created pressures for a more activist government, the congressional workload exploded. Although party discipline was fairly strict, roll-call votes on domestic issues often prompted the alliance of southern Democrats and Republicans in what came to be known as the conservative coalition. Congress became a complex, stable institution whose members enjoyed secure, predictable careers and enough autonomy to pursue a conservative agenda when their constituents demanded it.

In the 1960s, however, the emergence of new social issues and the decline of local and national party organizations created a climate favorable to "entrepreneurial" candidates who cultivated their constituencies more intensively and sought greater power inside the institution. This new generation of lawmakers proved particularly adept at securing their seats, and reelection rates climbed from 80 percent in the early 1960s to more than 90 percent in the 1980s. All members spent more time at home in their constituencies, while dramatically expanding personal and committee staffs in Washington. At the same time, many more subcommittees, and thus more chairmanships, were created, bringing the total to 135 in the House and 87 in the Senate. As junior and minority-party members gained autonomy and broadened their policy agendas, the committee chairs lost some control over the organization and resources of their fiefdoms. Committee chairs also had to be more accountable to the majority party, because reforms in the House required that the party caucus approve their selection by secret ballot.

Retirement among senior lawmakers increased during the late 1970s, as Democrats reacted to the constraints imposed on their personal power and Republicans lost hope of ever chairing committees. By the mid 1980s the rate of retirements had dropped to record lows, but the hectic schedules reflecting the demands of constituency service at home and subcommittee work in Washington made congressional careers more demanding than they had been a generation earlier. New pressures arose with numerous new interest groups that strove for positions on the legislative agenda or established groups that fought to preserve earlier policy gains. Members also found themselves increasingly frustrated by budget constraints imposed by record deficits, increased defense spending, escalating entitlements, and partisan battles with the president. Careers in Congress during the 1990s, members grumbled, were less rewarding than in the past. So it was not surprising that redistricting, a scandal involving the House bank, and general voter disaffection produced a record number of 66 retirements in the House in 1992.

The difficulties confronting career-minded legislators prompted them to relinquish some independence and turn to party leaders to negotiate comprehensive legislative packages. These omnibus bills provide protection from constituency groups as well as greater leverage with the president, but they have concentrated power in the hands of a few top legislators. Party-line voting, which had shrunk to historical lows in the 1970s, averaged better than 80 percent in both chambers in the 1980s. Thus, members' careers in Congress today seem more secure electorally, but they are more constrained politically.

Patterns of Entry. How do members launch their careers in Congress? Most hold public office prior to their election to the House or Senate. As of the early 1990s, nearly 50 percent of all House members had served in their state legislatures, up from 35 percent forty years before; 15 percent had served in local government; about 5 percent had been congressional staffers; and a similar percentage had held appointive or party positions. Among House members, apprenticeship in state legislatures had increased across the nation as state governments became more professionalized. In the Senate, fully 40 percent of the members had come from the House, a proportion representing a significant increase over the previous two decades. Roughly 15 percent of senators had been former governors. These patterns have developed because voters like experienced candidates, because ambitious individuals imitate their successful predecessors, and because party leaders prefer to recruit seasoned politicians to run for Congress. In states with strong party organizations, candidates with prior office-holding experience are more likely to be nominated, although Republicans nationwide have a greater penchant than Democrats for choosing political amateurs.

However, significant numbers of representatives and senators have held no previous public position. On average, about 25 percent of representatives and 20 percent of senators lack experience in public office prior to their election to Congress. In 1980, fully 40 percent of the successful Senate candidates were political neophytes. The number of inexperienced legislators varies over time, but they are elected most frequently during periods of political upheaval—when, for example, voter realignments or presidential landslides occur or when an incumbent has been involved in scandal or weakened by changes in local partisan conditions.

Except during the 1970s, the number of voluntary retirements from Congress in the postwar era has been quite low—roughly thirty-three in the House and five in the Senate. Senior lawmakers are most likely to leave the House when reapportionment alters their districts, whereas junior members are more likely to retire in order to run for the Senate or sometimes for governor. Those who demonstrate ambition to advance to the Senate typically contest open or marginal seats and come from smaller states where constituencies of the two congressional chambers overlap considerably. Between 1972 and 1992, nineteen incumbent senators sought the presidency—all unsuccessfully—

and since 1968 only one Democratic senator has challenged a sitting president. The typical senator with presidential ambitions has served more than one term, is not up for reelection, and belongs to the opposite party of the president.

Careers inside Congress. Inside the Congress, career-minded members pursue power and influence through the committee system. Typically, House members serve on two committees and four subcommittees, while senators average three full committee and seven subcommittee assignments. Through the expansion of the whip system and the party caucus, the number of party leadership positions has increased in recent years. Nevertheless, a chairmanship of one of the most prestigious committees, such as Ways and Means in the House or Finance in the Senate, is more coveted than all but the very top party leadership posts—the speaker and majority leader. Leadership of powerful subcommittees, particularly those within Appropriations, rivals most full committee posts in perceived influence.

Reforms enacted during the 1970s democratized the distribution of leadership posts, particularly in the House. Prior to the 1970s, members normally waited four or five terms for a subcommittee chairmanship or lower-level party position. The reforms made House members eligible for such posts in their second or third term. Yet the large, stable Democratic majority in the House so constrained lawmakers' access to the most important positions that career patterns among senior representatives in the 1990s do not greatly differ from those of several decades before. The movement to distribute influence in the Senate began much earlier—in the 1950s under Lyndon Johnson. Because this chamber is smaller, nearly all majority-party senators chair at least one subcommittee, even in a freshman term.

Despite the greater opportunity for leadership in both chambers, junior members still tend to serve a period of apprenticeship, particularly in the House. Opportunity for legislative activity of all sorts—bill sponsorship, delivery of floor speeches, proposal of amendments—is closely related to the number of terms a member has served. It also depends on the degree of political experience the member brings to Congress. Those who have held office previously clearly advance more rapidly and become more active at an earlier stage in their careers.

Larger Effects of Careerism. As career patterns in the contemporary Congress continue to evolve, careerism itself has become a source of controversy. Many political observers view the long tenure and perquisites of office associated with careerism as obstacles to responsive and responsible government. They often charge legislators with avoiding difficult policy choices in order to protect their careers. They also see members' careful attention to their constituencies as deterrents to competition, because strong candidates, who could offer the voters an alternative to the status quo, avoid challenging seemingly invulnerable incumbents. The resulting increase in the number of uncompetitive races and uncontested seats also perpetuates divided party control of the federal government, because popular presidential candidates cannot carry their partisans into Congress on their coattails. Critics further decry the personal influence exercised by individual lawmakers, because they view it as fostering clientele-based politics within the committee system and impeding presidential control of the bureaucracy. Their remedy for such ills is to limit the number of terms of service, which by eliminating lengthy careers would presumably remove many of the incentives for pursuing personal power.

On the other hand, many analysts oppose such limitations on the grounds that careerism creates incentives for members to develop the leadership capabilities and policy expertise required in a modern democracy. In their view, members' desire for long tenure keeps them accessible to their constituents and counterbalances the demands of special interests. At the same time, they argue, the prospect of influence obtained through the committee system creates incentives for members to become specialists in particular policy areas and master the intricacies of legislative procedure. These senior members, through their expertise, are more able to prevent executive agencies from abusing their authority and better equipped to withstand the imperial tendencies of the modern presidency. At the heart of this dispute, then, is a fundamental difference about the kind of Congress that will best serve the country's interest in the future: an institution that opens itself to constant change or one that emphasizes continuity and experience.

[See also Seniority.]

BIBLIOGRAPHY

Canon, David T. *Actors, Athletes, and Astronauts.* 1990.

Fowler, Linda L., and Robert D. McClure. *Political Ambition: Who Decides to Run for Congress.* 1989.

Hibbing, John R. *Congressional Careers: Contours of Life in the U.S. House of Representatives.* 1991.

Kernell, Samuel. "Toward Understanding Nineteenth Century Congressional Careers: Ambition, Competition and Rotation." *American Journal of Political Science* 11 (1977): 669–693.

Matthews, Donald R. "Legislative Recruitment and Legislative Careers." In *Handbook of Legislative Research.* Edited by Gerhard Loewenberg et al. 1983.

Price, H. Douglas. "The Congressional Career: Then and Now." In *Congressional Behavior.* Edited by Nelson Polsby. 1971.

LINDA L. FOWLER

Spouses and Families

A visitor to the office of a House Democrat was surprised to find a baby basket on the congressman's desk. When asked to explain, the lawmaker responded, "You see, I'm a recent father, but my wife has to work, so I keep the kid with me two afternoons a week."

While few members of Congress actually watch their infant children during working hours, this exchange underscores the difficulty that many members experience in trying to contend with the competing obligations of career and family life.

Late night sessions, weekends away from home, heavy social obligations, and the high cost of maintaining two homes make it difficult for members of Congress to maintain a stable family life. The unusual working hours and conditions intrude on time that a member of Congress would normally spend with the family, and economic pressures often demand that the member's spouse work long hours as well. Under those circumstances, children can be transformed from being a joy to being a burden.

The result in many such cases is divorce, separation, or dysfunctional families in which the spouse and children become alienated from their prominent absentee breadwinner. Congress is widely believed to have a higher divorce rate than the general population, although the precise numbers have never been calculated. Indeed, Washington has witnessed some celebrated marital breakups. In the late 1980s, for example, Sen. David F. Durenberger (R-Minn.) was embarrassed when many news stories recounted his separation from his wife and stormy affair with a secretary.

In 1988, a study of Congress by the Center for Responsive Politics—which recounted the conversation with a member whose family duties included caring for an infant two days a week—found that 80 percent of the members were dissatisfied, because their work left them little time for family life. "I remember how a representative asked another representative's son what he wished to be when he grew up," a congressional staffer told the center. "When the boy said a pilot or a fireman, the congressman asked why he didn't want to be a congressman like his dad. The boy said you can't be a congressman and a daddy."

Efforts to remedy this situation have been tried, without success. In 1987, a bipartisan group of senators with young children formed a "quality of life" task force that pressed the leadership for changes in scheduling that would allow them to have more time at home. Their efforts brought a few changes, which were quickly forgotten when pressing political matters arose. In 1993, a similar movement was under way in the House.

But in the era of two-wage-earner families, the difficulties for congressional families far surpass simple time pressures. Many members of Congress find that the source of a spouse's income can cause trouble. In 1984, when Rep. Geraldine A. Ferraro (D-N.Y.) was chosen as the Democratic vice presidential nominee, she learned that she could not draw a line between her political career and her husband's business activities.

Indeed, the difficulties of maintaining a personal life for members of Congress are so great that even the unmarried ones are complaining. In 1993, a number of single lawmakers told the *New York Times*

HOUSE SPEAKER NICHOLAS LONGWORTH (R-OHIO). With his wife Alice, seated on the Capitol steps watching a snake dance performed by Native Americans from Arizona, May 1926.   LIBRARY OF CONGRESS

CONGRESSIONAL BASEBALL. Margaret Speaks, *left*, daughter of Rep. John C. Speaks (R-Ohio), *not shown*, sells peanuts to Rep. Edith Nourse Rogers (R-Mass.) and Sen. Frederick H. Gillett (R-Mass.) at a baseball game between the Democratic and Republican teams of the House of Representatives, May 1926.   LIBRARY OF CONGRESS

that they were so skittish about negative publicity that they hesitated even to date.

BIBLIOGRAPHY

Center for Responsive Politics. *Congress Speaks: A Survey of the 100th Congress.* 1988.

Dowd, Maureen. "Single in Congress: No Time for Love, No Time for Laundry." *New York Times*, 30 March 1993.

MacPherson, Myra. *The Power Lovers: An Intimate Look at Politics and Marriage.* 1975.

SARA FRITZ

Retirement

In January 1942, Public Law 77-411 extended to members of Congress coverage under the Federal Civil Service Retirement System (CSRS), the pension plan established in 1920 for executive-branch personnel. However, that law was repealed two months later because of adverse public opinion. In 1946, Public Law 79-601 extended CSRS coverage to members again, at their option, with somewhat more generous benefits than those of regular federal employees. In support of that legislation, Senate

Report 79-1400 (31 May 1946) explained that a retirement plan for members

would contribute to independence of thought and action, [be] an inducement for retirement for those of retiring age or with other [sic] infirmities, [and] bring into the legislative service a larger number of younger Members with fresh energy and new viewpoints concerning the economic, social, and political problems of the Nation.

Originally, members contributed 6 percent of their salary to the CSRS. Annuities ranged from about 15 percent of a member's final annual pay if the member had at least 6 years of service and was age 62 or over to a maximum of 75 percent at age 60 after 30 years. As of 1992, members have been contributing 8 percent of their salary; benefits at the time of retirement range from about 12.5 percent of pay if the member has 5 years of service and is age 62 or over, to 80 percent after 32 years if the member is at least age 60. A member can retire with a reduced annuity if he or she is not reelected and is at least age 50 with 20 years of service.

In 1983, Public Law 98-21 required social security coverage for federal civilian employees entering the civil service. All incumbent members were included, regardless of when they entered Congress. Those participating in the CSRS before 1984 could elect to stay in that plan in addition to social security, but the CSRS was closed to new employees and members, and the plan will end when all enrolled are deceased.

Public Law 99-335 established the Federal Employees' Retirement System (FERS) to coordinate with social security for those entering federal service or Congress after 1983. Again, FERS benefits for members are more generous than those of most other federal employees because of the uncertain tenure of congressional service and to compensate for the interruption of retirement benefits members might otherwise accrue in private careers. As of 1992, members covered by the FERS pay 1.3 percent of their salary into that system (plus social security taxes). Starting annuities range from about 8.5 percent of final annual pay after 5 years of service to 34 percent after 20 years plus 1 percent for all years of service beyond 20, with no maximum. To be eligible to retire, members must be age 50 with at least 20 years of service, age 62 with 5 years, or may be any age with at least 25 years.

Congressional pensions, like those of other federal employees, are largely financed by general revenues; participant contributions cover only a small portion of the cost. As of September 1992, there were 336 former members of Congress receiving a pension. Their federal service averaged 20.7 years,

REP. JAMES G. BLAINE (R-MAINE). Retiring from the speakership in 1875.

their average age was 75, and the average monthly payment they received was $3,502.

Members' pensions have been criticized as being more generous than those for private-sector workers. However, studies show that members' benefits are comparable to or less than benefits paid to high-level managers or executives in private business. Although the terms of the congressional pension plans (particularly the CSRS) may be more generous than typical private plans, private-sector executives are generally paid more, which is reflected in their pensions, and may receive retirement benefits in addition to a pension. However, since 1962, civil-service and members' pensions have been indexed to reflect inflation, a feature seldom found in private plans.

BIBLIOGRAPHY

Merck, Carolyn L. *Retirement for Members of Congress.* Congressional Research Service, Library of Congress. CRS Rept. 93-421 EPW. 1993.

U.S. Congress. General Accounting Office. *Need for Overall Policy and Coordinated Management of Federal Retirement Systems.* GAO Doc. FPCD-78-49. 1978.

U.S. Senate. *Report to Accompany S. 2177, the Legislative Reorganization Act of 1946.* S. Rept. 79-1400. 1946.

CAROLYN L. MERCK

Tenure and Turnover

As applied to Congress, tenure and turnover are closely related concepts. Tenure refers to the length of time members serve in the House of Representatives or Senate. Turnover refers to the rate at which the membership "turns over," or changes. Tenure is usually reported as the mean number of years the current membership has served. Turnover is usually measured as the percent of the membership entering the body for the first time. Tenure and turnover are thus different ways of measuring the relative stability of the congressional membership. A stable membership is one in which new members rarely enter, because those already in the body are willing and able to stay. This results in small entering classes, a lengthy mean tenure, and a relatively consistent and experienced membership.

Desirability of Long Tenures. Historically, there has been much discussion of the optimal length of congressional service. Under the Articles of Confederation, the length of a stay in Congress was limited to "only three out of every six years." But during the summer of 1787, when the current U.S. Constitution was being debated, mandatory limits on length of service were proposed (in the Virginia Plan) and then rejected. It seems clear from several sources that most of the delegates assumed that congressional service, even without formal limits, would be brief. In recent years, the idea of limiting the tenure of senators and representatives has resurfaced. States have passed laws limiting service, and amendments to the Constitution have been floated. Public opinion polls indicate that approximately 70 percent of the American people feel term limits are a good idea. The most commonly mentioned figure is twelve years (two six-year terms) in the Senate and eight years (four two-year terms) in the House.

The debate over limits on length of service reveals deep differences as to the ideal nature of a legislature. Supporters of term limits prefer representatives to serve briefly and never lose sight of the views possessed by ordinary citizens. Opponents of term limits prefer representatives who are sophisticated and experienced in complex public issues and the nature of the legislative process. Supporters want a legislature that is a mirror of the American people, opponents a prism. Supporters want a legislature that is as good as the American people; opponents want a legislature that is better than the American people. Thus, squabbles over the proper length of congressional service can quickly turn into fundamental disagreements over approaches to governance.

Actual Tenure. The absence of a restriction on length of congressional service was of little consequence for quite some time. In the early days of the Republic few members of either the House or the Senate were eager to stay for more than a year or two. Indeed, members often did not even serve out their terms, instead choosing to resign before a session was complete. Even in the 1830s the membership was surprisingly fluid. Of the 242 members in the 24th Congress (1835–1837), 128 were not in the 25th Congress. Gradually, however, the mean length of stay in the House and the Senate increased and the number of first-termers diminished. Still, the pace of change should not be overstated. As recently as one hundred years ago, the mean length of service in the House was approximately five years. In 1893, 44 percent of the House membership were new to their positions.

Why, in the nineteenth century, did members leave Congress so quickly? Most of the turnover was voluntary (that is, members were not defeated in an election but instead simply decided to quit). The federal government did not then have nearly the clout it does now. Many state legislatures were more important than Congress, and Washington was viewed by some politicians as a mosquito-infested outback. In addition, some states followed a tradition of rotation, whereby after a few years of congressional service the incumbent would step aside to make room for someone else. In a restricted sense, then, departures for reasons other than electoral defeat may not all have been entirely voluntary. Finally, there was a high level of electoral volatility. Partisan tides would occasionally sweep out large numbers of members. In 1874, for example, the Republicans lost 96 seats in the House, and in 1894 the Democrats lost 116.

All this combined to create substantial turnover. In the first half of the twentieth century, however, things began to settle down. The United States was becoming a world power; the New Deal expanded the domestic role of the federal government; Washington was becoming more livable (some say the introduction of air-conditioning was a factor here); and the custom of rotation had long since faded. As a result, the rate at which members of Congress were retiring voluntarily declined sharply and by the 1960s had reached very low levels; only eighty people left the House voluntarily (and did not pursue another political office) during that decade.

Electoral volatility also diminished. The previously mentioned partisan swings in the range of one hundred seats were replaced by swings in the range of ten, twenty, or perhaps, in an unusual election year, forty to fifty. Incumbent senators and, especially, incumbent representatives became much more adept at winning reelection. On average, in the last thirty years, nearly 95 percent of all House incumbents and 80 percent of all Senate incumbents who wanted to secure reelection were able to do so. Most of these incumbents won quite easily. During the late 1960s, the mean percentage of the vote received by incumbents went up more than 5 percent. Thus, since 1970 not only have 95 percent of House incumbents won, but they have also received on average two votes to every one for the increasingly outgunned challengers.

In the 1970s, although incumbents continued to do well electorally, there was an increase in voluntary retirements, due largely to an improved pension plan and congressional reforms which devalued the seniority of older members who were already predisposed to voluntary retirement. But by the 1980s both the desire and the ability of incumbents to secure reelection were present in force. In percentage terms, fewer new members entered the Congress in the 1980s than in any previous decade. Each new Congress of the decade (in other words, every two years) brought in less than fifty new representatives, or only about 12 percent of the House.

In light of this, it may not be surprising that some recent careers in Congress have been remarkably long. Carl Vinson (D-Ga.) served for fifty consecutive years in the House of Representatives before retiring in 1965. Emanuel Celler (D-N.Y.) also served five full decades in the House before he was defeated in 1972. And in January of 1992 Jamie L. Whitten (D-Miss.) passed both of them by beginning his fifty-first consecutive year of House service. In terms of combined House and Senate service, the record is held by Carl Hayden (D-Ariz.) who served fifteen years in the House and forty-two years in the Senate prior to 1969.

While intriguing, these record-length careers are not typical. The average stay is about twelve years in the House and eleven years in the Senate. As of 1990, nearly 60 percent of the congressional membership had begun their service sometime in the 1980s and thus had served less than ten years. In the 102d Congress (1991–1993) there were as many representatives who had served less than four years as had served more than twenty, and about one-third of all senators were in their first terms. The atypically high House turnover in the 1992 elections (110 new members) lowered the mean length of service even more. Nevertheless, congressional career length is longer than it has ever been, on average, but is still not as long as some people imagine—and it is not as long as average length of service in many other national legislatures.

Still, the low (by historical standards) current level of membership turnover has prompted concern. As happened fleetingly in the 1960s, much was written in the late 1980s about a stale, ossified, and out-of-touch Congress. By the early 1990s such concerns had coalesced around the issue of term limitations. Highly visible failures in dealing with budget matters, unpopular pay raises that members had voted themselves, and various scandals and revelations about congressional barbershops, restaurants, and banks all contributed to the sentiment.

Of course, the key feature in the debate over the merits of congressional experience is whether senior legislators are assets or liabilities. Advocates of term limits feel that senior members are susceptible to "Potomac fever"—that their concerns shift from the home district to Washington—and that they become too chummy with interest groups and big contributors. Opponents of term limits are more likely to see the value of expertise and experience and to worry about the tendencies of inexperienced junior members (whose numbers would increase under term limits) to rely on unelected staffers and bureaucrats and to put forward an unfocused and unrealistic legislative agenda.

Evolving Bicameralism. One of the more instructive changes in turnover rates over the years has to do with the relationship of the House and the Senate. The authors of the Constitution clearly intended for the Senate to be less influenced by short-term changes in personnel and political mood. The six-year term, staggered elections, and indirect elections were designed to put a little distance between senators and the people. The House was to be more electorally sensitive. But something unexpected happened as the years passed. In recent

decades, the House has become the less changeable body, largely due to the overwhelming advantage of House incumbents over their challengers. As figures 1 and 2 indicate, the Senate once had a much more stable membership than the House, but around the time of World War I the patterns merged, and during some recent periods the stability of House membership has actually exceeded that of the Senate. Even though individual terms are three times longer in the Senate, careers in the Senate are not currently any longer than careers in the House. For the most part, Senate tenure and turnover are about equal to House tenure and turnover.

This new bicameral equality of tenure was underlined recently when the partisan majority in the Senate switched twice (in 1980 and 1986) while the House remained dominated by the same party (the

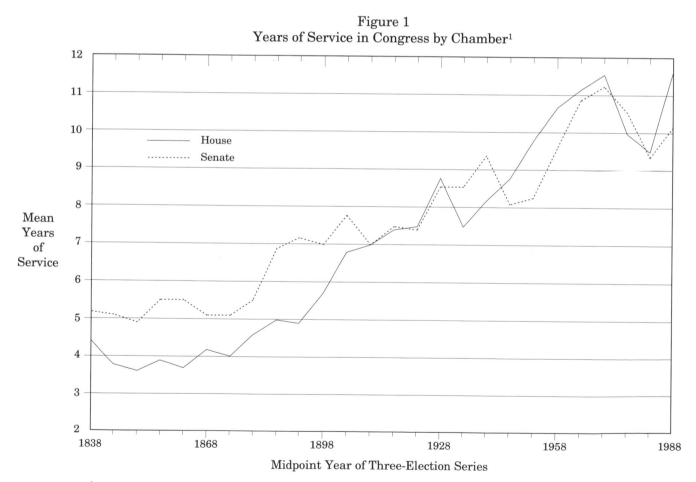

Figure 1
Years of Service in Congress by Chamber[1]

[1]Based on averages for three successive Congresses.

SOURCE: John R. Hibbing and John R. Alford, "Electoral Sensitivity in the United States Congress," paper presented at the annual meeting of the Western Political Science Association, Salt Lake City, March–April 1989.

Figure 2
New Members in Congress by Chamber[1]

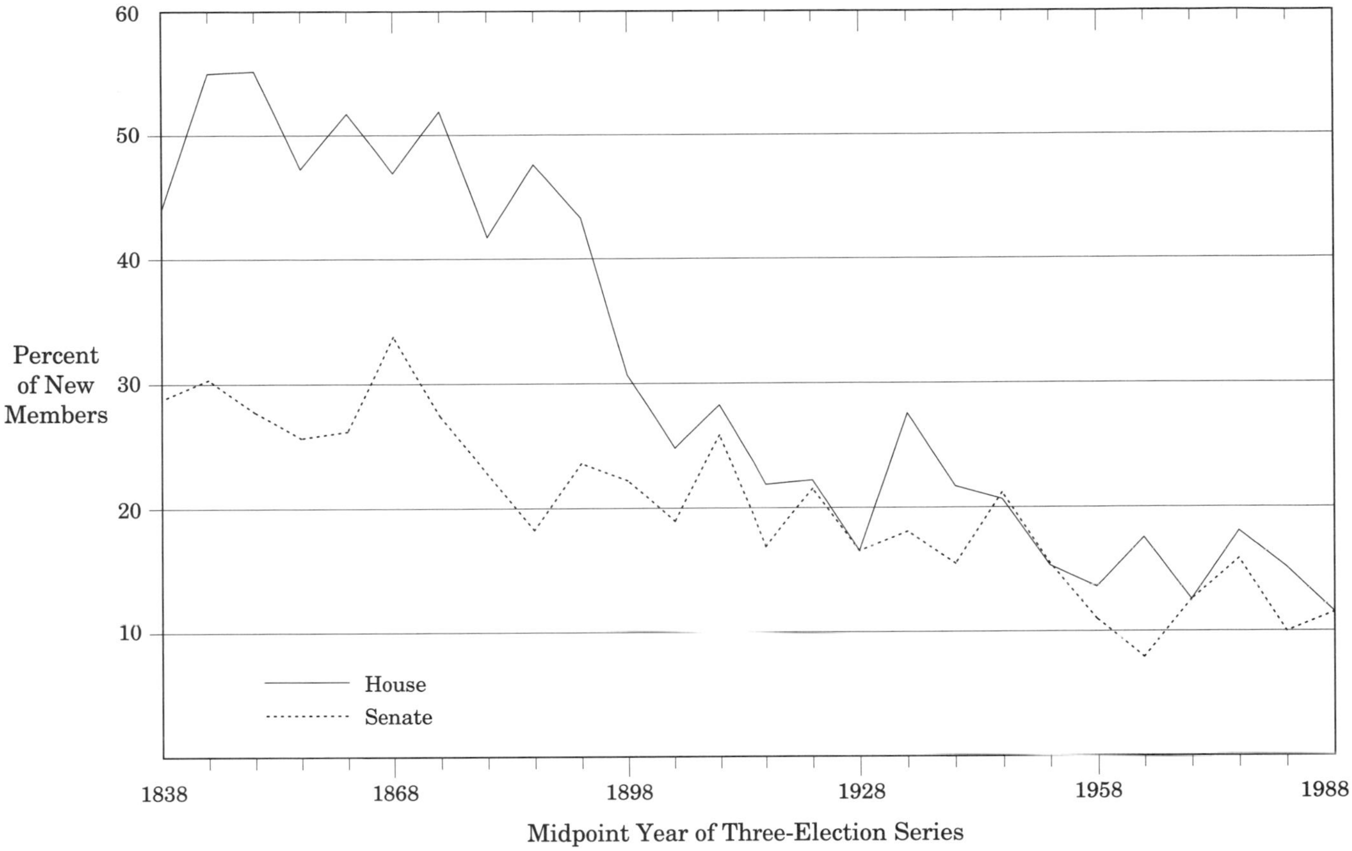

Midpoint Year of Three-Election Series

[1]Based on averages for three successive Congresses.

SOURCE: John R. Hibbing and John R. Alford, "Electoral Sensitivity in the United States Congress," paper presented at the annual meeting of the Western Political Science Association, Salt Lake City, March–April 1989.

Democrats). Senate membership has become every bit as fluid as House membership, and U.S. politics may even have experienced an inversion of the bicameral relationship intended by the Framers. This situation makes it less likely the Senate will serve as the "saucer" that cools the passions of the House. Whether this is ultimately for the better or the worse is a question beyond the scope of this essay.

Three points about congressional tenure and turnover are worth underscoring. First, compared to two hundred years ago, congressional tenure has increased and congressional turnover has decreased. The changes are substantial. By 1990, the annual infusion of new members constituted, on average, about 6 percent of the overall membership (or 12 percent every two years) and the average representative or senator had been in the body a little over eleven years. The range of service ran from a few months to fifty years. Second, Senate turnover is now virtually equal to House turnover despite the Framers' desire for the Senate to be the more stable and sedate body (*Federalist* 62). Finally, as the ongoing debate over term limits would point up, changes in levels of turnover and length of tenure have serious political implications. Views as to the optimal level of each are generally determined by larger convictions about the kind of legislators most desirable as the U.S. political system enters the next century.

[*See also* Elections, Congressional, *articles on* Election Results *and* Voting; Incumbency; Term Limitation.]

BIBLIOGRAPHY

Hibbing, John R. *Congressional Careers: Contours of Life in the U.S. House of Representatives.* 1991.

Matthews, Donald R. *U.S. Senators and Their World.* 1960.

Polsby, Nelson W. "The Institutionalization of the U.S. House of Representatives." *American Political Science Review* 62 (1968) : 144–168.

Price, H. Douglas. "The Congressional Career: Then and Now." In *Congressional Behavior.* Edited by Nelson W. Polsby. 1971.

JOHN R. HIBBING

MEMORIALS. *See* Petitions and Memorials.

MERCHANT MARINE. Legislative interest in the U.S. merchant marine is as old as the Republic. Acts in 1789 and 1790 supported building and operating merchant ships under the American flag. In the early nineteenth century, however, there was no need for government support of U.S. foreign-trade shipping. It was the time of clipper ships, a technology in which American shipbuilders and shipowners excelled. Domestic ocean trade was reserved for U.S. ships by the Act of 1817 and reaffirmed in the Merchant Marine Act of 1920.

The second part of the nineteenth century was less kind to merchant marine fortunes. Steam propulsion and iron hulls made sailing ships less competitive, while always-higher American wages could no longer be offset by smaller crews. The United States had become a high-cost producer of shipping services.

Between 1850 and 1935, Congress passed a number of merchant marine support measures, including mail subsidies, cargo preference in moving U.S. military supplies, mortgage guarantees for shipowners, construction loans, favorable terms in purchasing the 1,792 government-owned ships contracted for in World War I, and various forms of indirect aid. However, the impact of this legislation was marginal. In 1910, U.S. ships were carrying less than 10 percent of America's foreign trade. And while American ships did somewhat better in the interwar years, primarily because of assistance provided by the Merchant Marine acts of 1920 and 1928, their long-term future was not promising.

By 1935, neither Congress nor President Franklin D. Roosevelt was satisfied with the condition of American foreign-trade shipping. The result was enactment of the most comprehensive maritime bill in the nation's history, the Merchant Marine Act of 1936. This legislation effectively bound together the interests of shipowners, shipbuilders, and seagoing labor, while affirming merchant shipping's role in national defense.

Key provisions provided construction subsidies for shipyards and operating subsidies for ship operators. The act was the legislative base on which the world's largest fleet of merchant vessels, some five thousand in number, was built and manned in World War II.

Immediately following the war, American ships played a major role in world trade. However, the high cost of providing shipping services again took its toll. Neither the Cargo Preference Act of 1954, requiring that 50 percent of all government-impelled cargo move on American bottoms, nor the Merchant Marine Act of 1970, which began the process of disciplining wages and crew sizes, was able to stem the decline. One result was the transfer of many American-owned vessels to lower-cost foreign registries. In 1979, ships flying the American flag were carrying less than 6 percent of total U.S. imports and exports.

The 1980s saw the number of American ships and their share of foreign commerce continue to fall. In 1981, subsidized operators were allowed to purchase their vessels at world prices, and the Shipping Act of 1984 deregulated American liner firms with respect to shipping conference participation. These measures helped stem but did not reverse the decline.

Since 1865, higher-cost American ships have depended on government support to remain competitive in foreign commerce. Yet in six conflicts since 1865—the Spanish American War, World Wars I and II, the Korean War, the Vietnam War, and the Persian Gulf War—it was this high-cost merchant marine that provided the greater part of ocean-going logistical support for U.S. forces overseas.

In the 1990s, the same issue—the need for a merchant marine versus the cost to taxpayers to maintain one—confronted Congress. Specific questions involved the number and type of U.S. flag ships needed for national defense; whether U.S.-registered ships in the protected domestic trades were of sufficient national security value to warrant continued exclusion of lower-cost, American-owned, foreign-flag vessels; whether U.S.-owned, foreign-registered and -manned vessels had any national security value; and whether the national security need for shipyards should be closely tied to the need for ships, as set out in the Merchant Marine Act of 1936. Congress, when considering defense expenditures, was also faced with the task of making meaningful comparisons between the cost of keeping a given number of merchant ships at sea and the cost of keeping a given number of bombers, frigates, or tanks operational.

Congressional committees charged with merchant marine oversight are the Subcommittee on the Merchant Marine of the House Committee on Merchant Marine and Fisheries and the Subcommittee on the Merchant Marine of the Senate Commerce, Science, and Transportation Committee.

BIBLIOGRAPHY

Commission on Merchant Marine and Defense. *Recommendations: A Plan for Action.* Fourth Report. 20 January 1989.

Whitehurst, Clinton H., Jr. *The U.S. Merchant Marine: In Search of an Enduring Maritime Policy.* 1983.

Whitehurst, Clinton H., Jr. *The U.S. Shipbuilding Industry: Past, Present, and Future.* 1986.

CLINTON H. WHITEHURST, JR.

MERCHANT MARINE AND FISHERIES COMMITTEE, HOUSE.

The merchant marine, and maritime issues generally, have occupied a central location in U.S. history since the First Congress in 1789 enacted a law keeping foreign ships out of the new nation's ports. As the maritime industry grew, so did the need for a formal panel in Congress to address issues related to it. To that end, the Merchant Marine and Fisheries Committee was created on 21 December 1887 by an amendment to the Rules of the House of Representatives. This rule change established a committee "on the merchant marine and fisheries, to consist of thirteen members," which replaced the Select Committee on American Shipbuilding and Shipowning Interests.

From its beginning the committee exercised jurisdiction over a host of matters, including shipping legislation, shipbuilding, the admission of foreign-built ships to U.S. ports, registering and licensing of vessels, and tonnage taxes, fines, and penalties on vessels. The committee also had responsibility for setting standards for ocean navigation, shipping wages, and the treatment and health of sailors.

Partly as a result of a series of battles with the Committee on Interstate and Foreign Commerce in the first half of the twentieth century, the committee's jurisdiction expanded to include control over all transportation by water, the Coast Guard, all lifesaving or navigational services, the Coast and Geodetic Survey, lighthouses, lightships, ocean derelicts, and the Panama Canal.

Since 1959, when the maritime industry started to decline, the committee has become more active in environmental and oceanographic affairs in a broad context. Marine science and the preservation, protection, and enlightened use of the sea have increasingly come to the forefront of national attention. The 1960s witnessed the rapidly escalating use, exploitation, and exploration of ocean resources made possible by new technology. Accordingly, the committee's work promoting the protection of marine wildlife and the wise use of water resources has increased.

During the 93d Congress (1973–1975), the House of Representatives undertook to reduce the number of House committees and to streamline jurisdictions. At that time, a bid was made to abolish the Merchant Marine and Fisheries Committee. A draft plan to eliminate the panel prompted protests from shipyards, labor unions, and recreational boating groups, which saw their voice in Congress threatened. This lobbying effectively saved the committee and even increased its areas of influence. After the reorganization, the jurisdiction of the committee was formally enlarged by granting it control over oceanography and marine affairs, including coastal zone management and the U.S. Coast Guard and Merchant Marine academies. The committee also gained jurisdiction over international fishing agreements, which reflected a shift of jurisdiction over those matters from the House Committee on Foreign Affairs.

The majority of the committee's work is handled through its legislative subcommittees. At the beginning of the 103d Congress (1993–1995), there were five subcommittees: Merchant Marine; Fisheries Management; Environment and Natural Resources; Coast Guard and Navigation; and Oceanography, the Gulf of Mexico, and the Outer Continental Shelf. The regular subcommittee structure has remained largely unchanged since its establishment during the 93d Congress. Also, at various times the committee has created temporary and select committees to address special issues. Most notable among these was the Special Subcommittee on Maritime Education and Training (89th–92d Congresses) and the Ad Hoc Select Subcommittee on Maritime Education and Training (93d, 95th–96th Congresses).

In the face of declining emphasis on maritime issues the committee moved into the area of environmental protection. Major legislation in the 1980s and early 1990s dealing with ocean engineering, the regulation of offshore oil and gas matters, and the establishment of marine sanctuaries reflects this new focus. During this time the committee was responsible for producing the Endangered Species Act Amendments of 1982, the National Fish and Wildlife Foundation Establishment Act, and the Coastal Barrier Resources Act.

Legislative activity on the Merchant Marine and Fisheries Committee has ebbed and flowed. After a dramatic rise in the number of measures handled by the committee in the 1960s and 1970s, the panel saw a decline in its workload. This was due in part to changes in the structure of the House committee system and in part to agenda shifts faced by other standing committees. Since the mid 1970s, the workload has been fairly stable. Figures for the 101st Congress are representative of the trend. During this period (1989–1991), 371 measures were referred to the committee. Of these, 57 bills were reported to the House and 29 were passed. By session's end the committee could be credited with 21 laws. These resulted from measures reported by the Merchant Marine and Fisheries Committee that became law or were incorporated into others that became law or measures, such as Senate companion legislation, that became law in lieu of those considered by the committee.

For more than one hundred years legislation considered by the committee has done much to maintain the U.S. Merchant Marine. For supporters the committee has been a strong and vocal advocate for protection of the U.S. maritime industry. Others, however, have criticized the close relationship between committee members and the groups affected by its work. The concerns of opponents were bolstered during the late 1970s and early 1980s by the indictment of four subcommittee chairs on charges of criminal links between those members and maritime industry figures. Three of the four were later convicted.

Since then, criticism has focused on whether there is a need for a standing committee to address the concerns of a steadily declining industry. That question is similar to those raised by the Committee on Committees (known as the Bolling Committee) in the mid 1970s. In 1974 this group, charged with examining committee jurisdictions, recommended that the Merchant Marine and Fisheries Committee be abolished. Indeed, the Senate does not even have a corresponding committee; most of the maritime and environmental issues that the House committee deals with are divided, in the Senate, between the Commerce, Science and Transportation Committee and the Environmental and Public Works Committee. But, with solid support from the relevant industries, the Committee on Merchant Marine and Fisheries seems likely to maintain its control over maritime issues while expanding its role in environmental concerns.

BIBLIOGRAPHY

Starobin, Paul. "Merchant Marine: Too Close to Its 'Clients'?" *Congressional Quarterly Weekly Report* 46 (11 June 1988): 1559.

U.S. House of Representatives. Committee on Merchant Marine and Fisheries. *History of the House Committee on Merchant Marine and Fisheries,* by Carol Hardy Vincent. 101st Cong., 2d sess., 1990. Committee Document.

U.S. House of Representatives. Committee on Merchant Marine and Fisheries. *Report on the Activities of the Merchant Marine and Fisheries Committee.* 101st Cong., 2d sess., 1990. H. Doc. 101-1018.

KATHLEEN A. DOLAN

MEXICAN WAR. Once President James K. Polk decided that the United States had to acquire California and other Mexican lands, war was inevitable. Among its consequences were the loss of half of Mexico's territory and the collapse of the Jacksonian party system.

One of the principal causes of war with Mexico was the 1836 revolt in Texas. U.S. involvement was critical to the rebels' success. Most Texans desired to join the United States, but Andrew Jackson, fearing war with Mexico and domestic controversy, delayed annexation.

By the 1840s, however, many U.S. citizens believed that the continent was preordained for their expansion. The rationale behind U.S. policy was Manifest Destiny, which asserted that God had blessed the United States, that U.S. pioneers represented the triumph of democracy, and that the Republic required more land. Support for expansionism was fueled by various regional concerns, including New England's desire for trade markets and southern interest in increasing the number of slave states. The only questions were how far the United States would expand and whether Congress would utilize diplomacy or sanction war.

Polk favored annexing Texas and triumphed in the 1844 presidential election by articulating Manifest Destiny. Concerned that the Union was shaky, he assumed that expansionism would unify the country. As if to underline his views, Congress annexed Texas shortly after Polk's inauguration. Many members of Congress saw expansionism as a means to unite the country, acquire wealth, and reaffirm America's institutional success—thereby diverting attention away from the sectional conflict at hand.

Polk and Congress assumed an aggressive stance toward Mexico. A claims commission instituted by Mexico and Congress could not satisfy U.S. claimants who demanded payment from Mexico. When Mexico refused to recognize the credentials of John Slidell, a New Orleans lawyer dispatched to obtain agreement on the Rio Grande border and to purchase California and New Mexico, tensions increased. Polk sent Gen. Zachary Taylor to Corpus Christi, Texas, as part of a continued effort to claim the Rio Grande boundary. In an obvious attempt to intimidate Mexico, Taylor moved his troops toward the Rio Grande. Finally provoked into fighting, Mexican forces attacked in April 1846. Polk then called for war, claiming that American blood had been shed upon American soil, even though it was a disputed area at best.

Congress responded to events uncritically, a re-flection of the patriotic fever that gripped the United States that spring. On 11 May the House listened to Polk's address for more than an hour. After merely thirty minutes of debate, the representatives voted by the lopsided margin of 173 to 14 in favor of war. The Senate approved Polk's request by 40 to 2. Congress authorized the government to call up fifty thousand volunteers. Both houses approved a generous war bill despite the opposition of fourteen abolitionists. Although most Whigs condemned the manner in which Polk had provoked hostilities, they still voted to fund the war, mindful of the Federalists' mistake in opposing the War of 1812.

But the Mexican War released much tension over the sectional slavery conflict. In August 1846, just as Congress was preparing to adjourn, Polk requested that $2 million be placed at the government's disposition to pay for territorial concessions that he assumed Mexico would make in order to obtain peace. As Congress debated the measure, Democratic representative David Wilmot of Pennsylvania introduced his famous proviso. By this

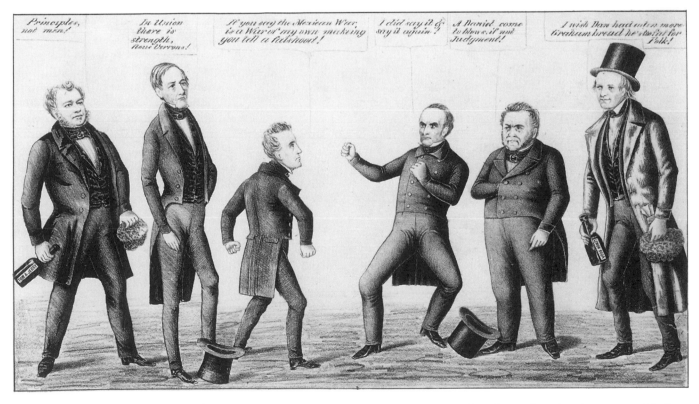

"THE ISSUE JOINED." President James K. Polk, *center, left,* confronts Sen. Daniel Webster (W-Mass.), *center, with fists raised,* who had publicly condemned Polk's Texas policy. The two are flanked, *on the left,* by newspaper editors Watson Webb and Thomas Ritchie and, *on the right,* by an unidentified figure. Horace Greeley, editor of the *New York Tribune,* stands, *at far right.* Lithograph on wove paper, 1846.
LIBRARY OF CONGRESS

means, Polk would receive his $2 million with the condition that any territory acquired from Mexico would not be permitted to maintain slavery. The $2 million measure passed the House by a narrow margin but fell victim to a filibuster in the Senate, an indication that the Whigs had begun to criticize the Mexican War in sectional terms.

Congress became less generous as the war continued. In January 1847 it passed an authorization bill to continue the war but objected to Polk's crude request to establish a new rank of lieutenant general. Everyone knew that Polk intended to give it to Thomas Hart Benton, an administration ally. Polk, a highly partisan politician, disliked the fact that the army's four generals, including Taylor, were Whigs.

Congress also objected when Polk attempted to incorporate the Mexican state of Yucatán. When Yucatán's white elite faced disaster at the hands of Maya rebels in early 1848, its leaders requested that the United States annex the peninsula. Polk urged Congress to accept the Yucatecan offer and proposed that troops be sent immediately. But Congress wisely voted against Polk's proposal when word reached Washington that the Maya rebels had finally agreed to a peace treaty.

The war, which ended in 1848, was an almost continuous string of U.S. victories. As military success undercut the popular base for continued Whig opposition, Polk anxiously awaited peace terms and contemplated annexing all of Mexico. He recalled Nicholas Trist, his personal emissary, and prepared for negotiations in Washington, D.C.

At this point Trist ignored Polk's recall and hammered out a harsh treaty. The United States took over California, New Mexico, Arizona, and parts of Colorado as well as Wyoming in exchange for paying $15 million and assuming $3.25 million in claims by U.S. citizens against Mexico. The treaty also promised to stop Indian raids into Mexico and pledged protection of those Mexicans who decided to remain in the southwest. Although the agreement was ratified in Mexico, Congress attempted to weaken the clauses that protected Mexicans who stayed in the United States.

The Mexican War and the ensuing treaty created distrust that remains. Mexican Americans became economically inferior and politically impotent. After state governments expropriated many of their lands, Mexican Americans sank into poverty. Native Americans discovered that although the Treaty of Guadalupe confirmed thirty-five Spanish land grants, local courts would not protect their holdings. Most Mexicans believed that the war was an invasion that allowed the United States to steal their northern frontier.

[See also Wilmot Proviso.]

BIBLIOGRAPHY

Eisenhower, John S. D. *So Far from God: The U.S. War with Mexico, 1846–1848*. 1989.

Richmond, Douglas W., ed. *Essays on the Mexican War.* 1986.

Sellers, Charles. *James K. Polk, Continentalist: 1843–1846*. 1966.

DOUGLAS W. RICHMOND

MEXICO. After conflict throughout most of the nineteenth century, including an expansionist war from 1846 to 1848, Congress established peaceful relations with Mexico in the 1880s. Thereafter, relations grew increasingly harmonious, stabilizing over the next sixty years.

Early congressional policy with Mexico emphasized trade. Because the United States was competing strongly with Great Britain for the Mexican market as well as for Mexican silver imports, Congress decided to admit Mexican silver and gold on a duty-free basis. But the loss of Texas in 1836 encouraged Mexico to divert more of its trade to Great Britain. Mexico angered Congress by dragging its feet over consideration of a treaty of reciprocity in 1829. Congress became particularly irritated when Mexican tariffs targeted finished U.S. cottons, excluding them in 1837 and at various times thereafter.

The genesis of free trade arrived with the fall of Santa Anna in 1855. The 1883 commercial treaty created lists of duty-free goods as part of a congressional movement to establish a customs union embracing all the Americas. Trade increased from a mere $7 million in 1867 to more than $117 million by 1900.

Overborrowing in the early twentieth century created an overwhelming debt obligation in Mexico. The suspension of debt payments in 1927 virtually precluded economic assistance until World War II, when Congress needed Mexico's cooperation. Negotiations finally moved Congress to discharge all accrued interest and over 60 percent of the principal. U.S. economic assistance increased when Congress declared Mexico eligible for Lend-Lease aid in 1942.

Congress began to devise an immigration policy toward Mexico in 1903, when Congress prohibited the entry of Mexican anarchists. The Immigration Act of 1917 was more restrictive, insisting that all aliens be literate and pay a head tax of eight dollars. Faced with a high demand for labor throughout the Southwest, Congress responded months later by allowing Mexican workers (braceros) to stay for six-month periods under the supervision of state governments. After World War I, the Southwest obtained more Mexican laborers because the immigration quota acts of 1921 and 1924 did not apply to Mexico. Establishment of the Border Pa-

BENITO JUÁREZ. President of Mexico during the U.S. Civil War. Although Juárez's government favored the Union, his administration made no effort to curtail commerce between Mexico and the Confederacy.

trol in 1924 was the only congressional victory for nativists who wished to restrict Mexican migrants.

Against this background, Congress in 1942 approved the Bracero Program, which established guidelines for treatment of Mexican migrant workers. About 200,000 Mexican braceros worked in the United States from 1942 to 1946 and several million thereafter. Hailed as a success, the program was renewed by Congress in 1947. The Bracero Program seemed permanent when President Harry S. Truman in July 1951 signed Public Law 78, which made the Department of Labor the labor contractor of braceros. Growers prevented Congress from passing further legislation that would have punished those growers who hired illegal migrants. Pressured by public outcries against abuses suffered by migrant workers, Congress nearly defeated the program's renewal in 1960. President Lyndon B. Johnson ended the Bracero Program in 1964 as part of his initiative to secure Mexican-American votes and the loyalty of the AFL-CIO.

By means of a 1907 treaty, the United States and Mexico agreed to share water on an equal basis. But Mexico resented U.S. citizens who pumped over 70 percent of Rio Grande waters for their use even though these waters for the most part originate in Mexico. The United States never established a national water law and thus allowed private citizens to take water without restriction.

The Rio Grande's rapid currents eventually pushed the U.S. border southward, generating a century-long dispute known as the Chamizal controversy. Arbitration committees could not resolve the affair until President John F. Kennedy agreed to return the land to Mexico.

As local Mexican authority diminished during the Mexican Revolution (1910–1920), enterprising individuals made drug smuggling a multimillion-dollar business. Congress responded by enacting the Harrison Narcotics Act in late 1914. As amended in 1916, the legislation attempted to regulate opiates to the extent that only licensed people could sell them.

Congress has been actively involved in relations between the United States and Mexico since 1964, the most prominent issue being the large number of undocumented Mexican workers who have illegally entered the United States. As communities and public figures confronted the high educational, medical, and legal expenses brought on by illegal immigration, Congress took action, and in 1986 passed the Immigration Reform and Control Act. This legislation imposed sactions on employers

1396 MICHEL, ROBERT H. (BOB)

who knowingly hired undocumented workers. It also provided amnesty for immigrants who could establish continued residence in the United States since 1982.

Drugs and criminal activity were other issues that mobilized Congress. After the murder of U.S. Drug Enforcement Administration agent Enrique Camarena near Guadalajara, Congress conducted hearings on terrorism and drug traffic in 1986 and 1987. As a result, the Senate declined to certify Mexico for economic assistance, based on the conviction that Mexico did little to interdict drug shipments across the border. Nevertheless, Congress later decided that conditions in Mexico had improved considerably under the leadership of Carlos Salinas de Gortari and in 1993 ratified the North American Free Trade Agreement. This comprehensive act gradually reduces or eliminates tariff charges on goods moving between Canada, Mexico, and the United States.

BIBLIOGRAPHY

Craig, Richard. *The Bracero Program. Interest Groups and Foreign Policy.* 1971.
Reisler, Mark. *By the Sweat of their Brow.* 1976.
Salvucci, Richard. "The Origins and Progress of U.S.-Mexican Trade, 1825–1884: Hoc Opus, Hic Labor Est." *Hispanic American Historical Review* 71 (1991): 697–735.
Sandos, James A. "Northern Separatism during the Mexican Revolution: An Inquiry into the Role of Drug Trafficking, 1910–1920." *The Americas* 45 (1984): 191–214.

DOUGLAS W. RICHMOND

MICHEL, ROBERT H. (BOB) (1925–), representative from Illinois, longest-serving minority leader (1980–1994) in the history of the House of Representatives. Robert H. Michel was born in Peoria, Illinois, in 1925 to a French-immigrant working-class family. He was educated in the Peoria public schools and fought in World War II. He was wounded and was decorated for bravery, and he returned to graduate from Bradley University, and then in 1949 went to work for the local U.S. representative, Republican Harold H. Velde, who had succeeded the legendary Everett M. Dirksen. When Velde retired in 1956, Michel ran for the seat, won, and was repeatedly reelected.

Michel's skills, affability, and close relationship with Dirksen, who was by 1956 a leader in the Senate, led to Michel's appointment to the Appropriations Committee after only one term. Michel became known as a talented consensus-builder and

vote counter. His sonorous baritone voice and strong pitching arm made him a favorite for both patriotic luncheons and congressional baseball games, adding popularity to his growing reputation as one of the most skillful legislators in the House Republican Conference.

In 1973, he was elected chairman of the House Republican Congressional Campaign Committee and elevated to House minority whip soon thereafter. When House minority leader John J. Rhodes retired in 1980, Michel became leader just as Ronald Reagan was swept into office with, for the first time in nearly thirty years, a Republican Senate. Michel quickly forged a working coalition of House Republicans and conservative Democrats to help pass the Reagan budget initiatives of 1981.

Although the number of Republicans in the House decreased after 1982, Michel was still able to block or pass key bills for Presidents Reagan and Bush. Perhaps the most significant was the passage of the Michel-Solarz resolution, which authorized the use of force against Iraq during the Persian Gulf crisis in 1991.

Over time, however, Michel's style of midwestern pragmatic leadership became less appealing to the younger, more ideological and impatient southern and western conservatives, who were quickly becoming the dominant force among House Republicans. His attempt to fashion a budget compromise in 1990, for example, failed when significant numbers of the conservative group, led by the new minority whip, Newt Gingrich of Georgia, abandoned the plan.

In October of 1993 Michel announced he would not run for reelection in 1994. Describing his own leadership, Michel once said "It's one thing to be out there on the stump flapping your gums, and it's another thing trying to put something together." The Michel legacy of leadership was built on things put together.

BIBLIOGRAPHY

Broder, David S. "Bob Michel and the Virtues of Moderation." *Washington Post,* 10 October 1993.
Clymer, Adam. "Michel, GOP Leader, to Retire." *New York Times,* 5 October 1993.

JOHN J. KORNACKI

MICHIGAN. In December 1833, Congress received the first formal petition from the Michigan Territory seeking admission into the Union. The following year Congress rejected the request, despite a census that showed the Michigan Territory had met the minimum population requirement for statehood under the provisions of the Northwest Ordinance of 1787.

On 12 January 1835 acting territorial governor Stevens T. Mason announced to the territorial legislative council that Congress had denied Michigan's request to call a constitutional convention. Mason declared that Michigan had a right to be admitted to the Union, and twelve days later the council called a constitutional convention. Delegates elected in April gathered in Detroit in early May to write a state constitution.

Michigan's actions precipitated the Toledo War, a bloodless conflict with Ohio over less than five hundred square miles of land dominated by the port of Toledo at the mouth of the Maumee River. Ohio responded to Michigan's call for a constitutional convention by annexing the disputed territory. In February 1835 Michigan retaliated with legislation that threatened Ohioans exercising official jurisdiction in the Toledo Strip with fines and imprisonment.

President Andrew Jackson's firing of Governor Mason in August 1835 ended the Toledo War but not Michigan's quest for statehood. On 5 October, Michigan voters chose a congressional delegation, elected Mason governor, and approved the state constitution. When Congress convened in December 1835, Michigan's congressional delegation—Senators John Norvell and Lucius Lyon and Rep. Isaac E. Crary—were not permitted to take their seats.

For six months Congress debated Michigan's admission. The most vocal opponents included the Whigs, who disliked Michigan's strong Democratic ties; Ohio delegates, who feared the loss of Toledo; and the Indiana and Illinois delegations, who worried about losing their states' Lake Michigan ports if Michigan retained Toledo. On 15 June 1836 the House of Representatives concurred with an earlier Senate decision and passed the Northern Ohio Boundary bill. The act gave the Toledo Strip to Ohio and offered Michigan the western Upper Peninsula and immediate statehood. It also required that Michigan hold a convention to approve the compromise measure.

The Northern Ohio Boundary bill asserted Congress's claim that no measure, including the Northwest Ordinance, could prevent it from altering the boundaries of a territory. Congress also contended that it was "expedient" to give Ohio the mouth of the Maumee River to guarantee the completion of a canal connecting Lake Erie with the Ohio River.

Underlying this logic, however, was the fact that 1836 was a presidential election year and that Ohio, Indiana, and Illinois, which would all be offended if Toledo were given to Michigan, had a total of thirty-five electoral votes—more than ten times the number Michigan would have if it became a state by election day.

During the fall of 1836, after much debate and "a great diversity of opinion," Michiganites gathered once in September and once in December to discuss the Northern Ohio Boundary bill. The elected delegates at the first convention rejected the measure, but in December a different set of delegates—chosen in a controversial election—approved the compromise. On 27 December 1836, President Jackson sent the proceedings of both conventions to Congress, recommending that the results of the later gathering be accepted and that Michigan be admitted into the Union. Throughout January 1837, Congress was again immersed in debate over Michigan's admission. The primary concern was the extralegal nature of the December convention; because that convention had not received the sanction of the state legislature, the results might not withstand legal scrutiny at a later date.

Nevertheless, on 5 January 1837 the Senate voted 25 to 10 to recognize the December election results and admit Michigan into the Union. Twenty days later, the House concurred by a margin of 132 to 43. On 26 January President Jackson signed the bill making Michigan the nation's twenty-sixth state.

Despite the state's shaky entrance into the United States, two Michigan senators enjoyed positions of recognized national leadership during the mid-nineteenth century. Governor of the Michigan Territory from 1813 to 1831, Lewis Cass was first elected to the Senate in 1844. In 1848 he became the Democratic party's presidential nominee, losing to Zachary Taylor. He remained in the Senate until 1857, when he became President James Buchanan's secretary of State.

Zachariah Chandler became Michigan's first U.S. senator from the Republican party, a position he used to resolutely oppose southern slavery. Chandler is credited with shaping the Committee on the Conduct of the War in 1862. Following his defeat for reelection in 1875, he served as President Ulysses S. Grant's secretary of the Interior. Michigan returned Chandler to the Senate in March 1879, but he died suddenly the following November.

Between the Civil War and the Great Depression, the Republican party dominated Michigan's congressional delegation, except for a brief period during the early 1890s. Franklin D. Roosevelt's election to the presidency in 1932 allowed Michigan Democrats to capture ten of the state's seventeen House seats, but in the mid 1930s the Republicans regained their congressional majority, which they held until the 1960s. In 1964 the Democrats elected twelve of the state's nineteen representatives. They have retained a majority of Michigan's congressional delegation into the early 1990s.

Michigan's best-recognized mid-twentieth-century congressional leader was Arthur H. Vandenberg, who was elected to the Senate in 1928. In 1936, and again in 1940, he received serious consideration for his party's presidential nomination. In 1945 President Roosevelt appointed Vandenberg as a delegate to the conference to organize the United Nations; despite his prewar isolationism, Vandenberg is credited with persuading Republican isolationists to support the formation of the U.N. After becoming chairman of the Foreign Relations Committee in 1946, he helped secure Senate approval for the Marshall Plan, which provided funds for the postwar reconstruction of western Europe.

During the 1960s and early 1970s Democrat Philip A. Hart was the most influential member of Michigan's congressional delegation. Elected to the Senate in 1958, Hart was particularly concerned with antitrust and antipoverty matters. He served as floor manager and chief strategist for passage of the Voting Rights Act of 1965. Hart was reelected twice with overwhelming majorities. He died in Washington, D.C., on 26 December 1976. In 1987 the newest Senate office building in Washington was named for Hart, whose high ethical standards and commitment to public service had earned him the unofficial title of "Conscience of the Senate."

BIBLIOGRAPHY

Rosentreter, Roger. "Michigan's Quest for Statehood." In *Michigan: Visions of Our Past*. Edited by Richard Hathaway. 1989.

ROGER L. ROSENTRETER

MILITARY. *See* Defense. *See also* Air Force; Army; Coast Guard; Marine Corps; Navy.

MILITARY JUSTICE, UNIFORM CODE OF.

Military law is a legitimately unique system designed to meet the needs of the military establishment. Its uniqueness is grounded on the oft-cited language from Supreme Court opinions that "it is the primary business of armies and navies to fight and be to ready to fight wars should the occasion arise" (*Toth v. Quarles*, 350 U.S. 11, 17 [1955]). The purpose of military law is to "promote efficiency and effectiveness in the military establishment, and thereby to strengthen the national security of the United States" (preamble to 1984 *Manual for Courts-Martial*). The ultimate responsibility for ensuring that the primary purpose of the armed services is met rests in Congress, which has promulgated a variety of statutory provisions addressing military law.

Congress is explicitly empowered under Article I, section 8, clause 14 of the Constitution to "make Rules for the Government and Regulation of the land and naval Forces." Although that provision is the most frequently cited as authority for congressional actions, other provisions in section 8 provide for declaring war, raising and supporting armies and a navy, and calling and regulating the militia. Together, they provide expansive powers for Congress to regulate the military.

Most of the legislation promulgated under this authority rests in Title 10 of the United States Code, which includes the Uniform Code of Military Justice (UCMJ), a broad statutory outline for the operation of the branch of military law that deals with military justice (i.e., nonjudicial and judicial procedures [courts-martial] for dealing with offenses committed by servicemembers). While the formal citation to the UCMJ is 10 U.S.C. secs. 801–946, most references are to specific articles in the code.

The Uniform Code of Military Justice was first enacted by Congress in 1950 in an attempt to provide uniform statutory guidance to all the services. Before 1950, Congress had enacted various Articles of War (in 1806, 1874, 1916, and 1920), which were patterned after the British Articles of War. The periodic changes in the Articles of War generally reflected Congress's concern that the due process rights available to servicemembers being tried by court-martial parallel the rights available to civilian defendants. Since 1950, Congress has amended the UCMJ several times; the most recent major changes occurred in the Military Justice Act of 1983. Congress's role in overseeing operation of the Uniform Code of Military Justice was highlighted in its consideration in 1993 of the issue of gays in the military. Although Congress made no amendments to the code, it carefully considered potential criminal justice issues in adopting a policy of limited accommodation for allowing homosexuals to serve in the armed forces.

The UCMJ includes both procedural rules and protections and specifies substantive crimes. Articles 1 through 76 address jurisdictional and procedural aspects of military justice. Those articles include statutory recognition of various procedural rights. For example, Article 31 includes a requirement that suspects be warned of their right to remain silent when questioned about an offense. A statute of limitations is set out in Article 43. Article 45 prohibits double jeopardy, and Article 46 provides that the defense shall have an equal opportunity with the prosecution to obtain witnesses and other evidence.

Substantive offenses are set out in Articles 77 through 134, which are usually referred to as the "Punitive Articles." Some have no civilian counterpart. For example, Article 86 prohibits the familiar offense of AWOL, or "absent without leave." Article 133 prohibits "conduct unbecoming an officer and a gentleman." Still other offenses are very similar to those recognized in the civilian criminal legal system. Larceny and robbery, for instance, are prohibited by Articles 121 and 122, respectively.

In regulating military justice, Congress has delegated certain powers to the president. Article 36 of the UCMJ specifically authorizes the president to prescribe "[p]retrial, trial, and posttrial procedures, including modes of proof, for cases arising under this chapter triable in courts-martial." An exercise of that executive authority is found in the *Manual for Courts-Martial*, which provides more detailed guidance on military criminal procedures.

When an offense is reported, the unit commander is required to conduct a thorough and impartial inquiry. If it appears that an offense has been committed and that the accused committed it, the commander may begin nonjudicial punishment proceedings under Article 15, UCMJ; begin administrative discharge procedures under the appropriate service regulations; or prefer court-martial charges.

If charges are preferred, a convening authority may ultimately refer the charges to a particular court-martial, a temporary tribunal, for trial. There are three types of courts-martial: summary, special, and general. More serious charges are referred to general courts-martial, following a pretrial "Article 32 hearing" to determine if the charges appear to be supported by the evidence.

Throughout the process, the servicemember is entitled to free legal representation from a uniformed lawyer (i.e., a "JAG," an officer in the Judge Advocate General's Corps), broad discovery rights, and other due process and constitutional protections available in civilian criminal trials. The presiding officer at the court-martial is a military judge, an armed forces lawyer with many years of experience. The accused has the option of requesting trial by judge alone (a bench trial) or with "members" (the equivalent of a jury trial). If the latter option is exercised, the convening authority selects the court members who will decide the case.

Civilian control of the military justice system is exemplified in provisions in the UCMJ that address appellate review of courts-martial convictions. Under Article 66, the accused may appeal to a Court of Military Review, consisting of panels of senior uniformed lawyers. Appeals from the Courts of Review go to the U.S. Court of Military Appeals, which sits in Washington, D.C., and consists of five civilian judges appointed by the president and confirmed by the Senate for fifteen-year terms. In 1983, Congress provided that a military accused could seek direct review by the Supreme Court of the United States.

In reviewing challenges to military justice decisions, the Supreme Court and lower federal courts are extremely deferential to Congress's exercise of authority. In *Rostker v. Goldberg* (453 U.S. 57 [1981]), the Court stated that its deference to Congress is at its "apogee when legislative action under the congressional authority to raise and support armies and make rules and regulations for their governance is challenged." In *Solorio v. United States* (483 U.S. 435 [1987]), the Court compared Congress's powers under the Commerce Clause with its plenary authority over the military and noted that it defers to Congress, even where the individual rights of servicemembers were implicated. The Supreme Court's deference rests in large part on the Court's recognition that the judiciary lacks expertise in military affairs. But the deference is not limitless. In a series of decisions, including *Reid v. Covert* (354 U.S. 1 [1957]), the Supreme Court rejected attempts by Congress to extend court-martial jurisdiction over civilians in peacetime.

BIBLIOGRAPHY

Morgan, Edmund M. "The Background of the Uniform Code of Military Justice." *Vanderbilt Law Review* 6 (1953): 169–185.

Schlueter, David. "Gays and Lesbians in the Military: A Rationally Based Solution to a Legal Rubik's Cube." *Wake Forest Law Review* 31 (1994).

Schlueter, David. *Military Criminal Justice: Practice and Procedure.* 3d ed. 1992.

Schlueter, David. "Military Justice in the 1990's: A Legal System Looking for Respect." *Military Law Review* 133 (1991): 1–29.

DAVID A. SCHLUETER

MILLS, ROGER Q.

MILLS, ROGER Q. (1832–1911), representative and senator from Texas, Democratic leader in the House (1887–1889). Born in Kentucky, Roger Quarles Mills migrated to Texas in 1849, studied law, and settled in Corsicana. In 1859 and 1860, Mills represented Navarro County in the state legislature. From 1861 to 1865 he fought for the Confederacy, enlisting as a private and rising to the rank of colonel.

Mills served for twenty-six years in Congress, nineteen in the House (1873–1892) and seven in the Senate (1892–1899). Although an outspoken critic of the Electoral Commission, which accepted Rutherford B. Hayes over Samuel J. Tilden in 1877, he remained in relative obscurity. He primarily pushed for frontier defense in Texas and for the construction of a deep-water ship channel from Galveston to Houston.

From the early 1800s on, Mills figured prominently in Democratic policies and the national agenda. He was a leader among the "Confederate Brigadiers" who gained great influence in the House of Representatives during the post-Reconstruction decades. In particular he became identified with the tariff-for-revenue-only position, which was a defining Democratic party policy in this period. From the 46th to the 51st Congresses—except for the 47th, in which he served on the Committee on Claims and the Committee on the Territories—Mills was a member of the powerful Ways and Means Committee; and in the 50th Congress (1887–1889) he became its chairman. In this position he led the Cleveland administration's attack against a high protective tariff by pushing the so-called Mills bill through the House in the summer of 1888.

In December 1891, Mills ran for the speakership of the House in the 52d Congress. He was the odds-on favorite to win because, as James Beauchamp (Champ) Clark reflected, "he was, next to [former Speaker John G.] Carlisle, the most popular man in America with the rank and file of Democrats." But Mills was perceived as a Cleveland man by silver Democrats, and after a lengthy contest in the House Democratic caucus he was narrowly defeated by Charles F. Crisp of Georgia, the result of a bargain struck by Crisp and Democratic prosilver representatives from the West.

After the resignation of Sen. John H. Reagan of Texas in 1891, Mills was elected as his replacement. He was then reelected for a six-year term beginning in 1893. In the Senate he served on three committees: Coast Defenses; Mines and Mining; and Post Offices and Post Roads. Mills continued to support legislation for a lower tariff and advocated free and unlimited coinage of silver. At the same time he vigorously opposed a federal income tax. Because of formidable opposition by Gov. Charles A. Culberson (who was backed by former governor James S. Hogg), Mills decided not to seek reelection and retired at the end of his term on 3 March 1899.

BIBLIOGRAPHY

Acheson, Sam Hanna. *Joe Bailey, The Last Democrat.* 1932.

Clark, Champ. *My Quarter Century of American Politics.* 2 vols. 1920.

Roberts, Myrtle. "Roger Quarles Mills." Master's thesis, University of Texas, 1929.

Webb, Walter Prescott, and H. Bailey Carroll, eds. *The Handbook of Texas.* 2 vols. 1952.

BEN PROCTER

MILLS, WILBUR D.

MILLS, WILBUR D. (1909–1992), representative from Arkansas, chairman of the Committee on Ways and Means (1957–1975), and one of the most effective legislators ever to serve in Congress. Born in the agricultural community of Kensett, Arkansas, Wilbur Daigh Mills graduated from Hendrix College in 1930 and attended Harvard Law School from 1931 to 1933, where he studied under Felix Frankfurter. A Democrat, he served for four years as county and probate judge in White County, Arkansas, and in 1938 was elected to the U.S. House of Representatives.

After first serving on the Committee on Banking and Currency, he was assigned in 1942 to the Committee on Ways and Means. He rose to become chairman of the prestigious tax-writing panel in 1958. When he retired from Congress in January 1977 he held the records for tenure as a Ways and Means member and for uninterrupted service as chairman.

A protégé of Speaker Sam Rayburn, Mills immersed himself in committee work. He brilliantly mastered the intricacies of taxation, Social Security, welfare, trade, and other committee matters and was without peer in Congress in those areas. As chairman, his mild, congenial demeanor belied the firmness with which he ruled. He relied on a small,

WILBUR D. MILLS. During an interview at *U.S. News & World Report* offices, 4 June 1956.

LIBRARY OF CONGRESS

gifted professional staff that reported only to him, and he abolished subcommittees, thus centralizing decisions. He cultivated a close bipartisan relationship with Republicans on the committee and in the House, while encouraging junior members to participate in committee affairs. He sought geographical and political balance on the committee, believing it would help him assure support in Congress and across the country for bills he brought before the House. Ever protective of his own and the committee's reputation and authority, Mills shunned any legislative battle that he might lose. He deployed various tactics to delay bills until he developed a broad, favorable consensus, then sent bills to the floor only under protection of closed rules, which restricted debate and the possibility of amendments. He had no hard and fast personal agenda, allowing him adequate flexibility to construct bills with the best chance of passing. He personally presented his committee's legislation to the House, providing, without notes, a well-organized, convincing summation of the proposals. His ability to change votes sheerly through the power of his presentation was legendary.

Under Mills's direction, Ways and Means compiled a productivity record unmatched in the committee's history. Major tax legislation included the Revenue acts of 1962, 1964, 1969, and 1971; the Excise Tax Reduction Act of 1965; the Revenue and Ex-

penditure Control Act of 1968, tying federal income tax increases directly to decreases in expenditures; and the Tax Reform Act of 1969, removing 5.5 million low-income taxpayers from the rolls. Its keystones in social legislation were Medicaid, providing medical benefits for welfare recipients and certain other low-income people, and Medicare—which Mills called his proudest achievement—providing health care insurance under Social Security for the elderly and disabled. The Social Security statutes saw dramatic change during Mills's tenure on Ways and Means: age requirements were lowered, benefits rose sharply, and disability coverage was developed and significantly broadened. Mills designed the Highway Trust Fund to support the Interstate Highway System. The committee also dealt with a wide range of other issues, including aid to dependent children, welfare and workfare programs, trade expansion, recession measures, unemployment compensation, retirement savings, and pension reform.

In his last years in Congress, Mills was weakened by institutional frustration, political disappointment, painful physical ailments, and personal trauma. The Legislative Reform Act of 1970 stripped the Ways and Means Committee and its chairman of many crucial powers, undermining his ability to secure consensus in the committee and in the House. He was disappointed in 1972 when a Draft Mills for President movement, which he had endorsed reluctantly, failed to catch fire, his first political defeat after twenty-one primary elections and twenty-one general election victories. In 1973, he suffered painfully from a slipped disk, requiring surgery, pain relievers, and a long period of recuperation.

Mills's heavy drinking became apparent on 7 October 1974, when the press reported that his car had been stopped at 2 A.M. by U.S. Park Police. Mills was not driving, but one of the other four passengers, a striptease dancer who performed as "Fanne Foxe the Argentine Firecracker," made a dramatic leap into Washington's Tidal Basin—making front-page news and creating a major embarrassment for the normally reserved congressman. Two months later, after a second widely publicized episode, Mills issued a public apology, acknowledged his addiction to alcohol, and resigned as Ways and Means chairman. He then entered a treatment program, served the remaining two years of his term, retired from politics, and began a successful private career as a tax lawyer and a popular lecturer-counselor on alcoholism.

BIBLIOGRAPHY

Manley, John. *The Politics of Finance.* 1970.

Mills, Wilbur D. Public Papers. Hendrix College, Wilbur D. Mills Center, Conway, Arkansas.

Smith, Steven S., and Christopher J. Deering. *Committees in Congress.* 1984.

U.S. House of Representatives. Committee on Ways and Means. *The Committee on Ways and Means: A Bicentennial History, 1789–1989,* by Donald R. Kennon and Rebecca M. Rogers. 101st Cong., 1st sess., 1989. H. Doc. 100–244.

Witte, John F. *The Politics and Development of the Federal Income Tax.* 1985.

KAY C. GOSS

MINNESOTA. Minnesota, the thirty-second state, was admitted to the Union on 11 May 1858. The Territorial Act approved on 3 March 1849 was championed by Sen. Stephen A. Douglas of Illinois. To win approval of the Minnesota bill, congressional Democrats agreed to support the Whig-sponsored bill calling for the creation of the U.S. Department of the Interior, and to permit the incoming Whig administration of Zachary Taylor to name territorial officers.

The Minnesota Enabling Act, which Congress approved on 26 February 1857, specified the present state boundaries, which were generally favored by Minnesota's Democrats and opposed by its Republicans, who preferred a long and narrow state extending from the Mississippi to the Missouri rivers. Such an east-west state with a northern boundary slightly north of the present-day Twin Cities would have opened the way for removing the capital southward from St. Paul to a site in an area dominated by Republicans. In early 1858 the Minnesota statehood bill precipitated sharp congressional debate, because it was considered with the issue of statehood for Kansas. Southerners, especially, contended that "free state" Minnesota had to be counterbalanced by the admission of Kansas as a slave state. However, because of the English Compromise, by which Congress agreed that the voters of Kansas had to approve their state's constitution, Kansas statehood was deferred and Minnesota was admitted.

The size of the state's representation in the House increased from two to a high of ten in the elections held from 1912 to 1930. It then remained at nine for three decades but after the census of 1960 was reduced to the present eight.

After wresting control from the Democrats in the second state election, held in 1859, the Republicans dominated Minnesota's congressional delegation until the 1920s. William Windom (House, 1859–1869; Senate, 1870–March 1881, November 1881–1883) and Cushman K. Davis (Senate, 1887–1900) were particularly noteworthy. Between his Senate terms, Windom served as James A. Garfield's secretary of the Treasury, a position he held again in the Benjamin Harrison administration. Davis chaired the Senate Foreign Relations Committee that drafted the Spanish-American War resolution and later served as a member of the peace commission.

The traditional Republican control was seriously challenged in 1922 by the recently formed Farmer-Labor party. This party, with socialistic leanings, briefly held both Senate seats and launched the career of the isolationist Henrik Shipstead, who remained in the Senate for four terms (1923–1947).

After Republican successes in the elections of 1938, 1940, and 1942, the Farmer-Laborites merged with the Democrats to create Minnesota's Democratic-Farmer-Labor (DFL) party in 1944. The DFL made startling advances in the election of 1948, when Hubert H. Humphrey was elected to the Senate and Eugene J. McCarthy to the House. Humphrey distinguished himself during the first phase of his Senate career, which ended in 1964 with his election as vice president. He served as Democratic whip from 1961 to 1964 and, as one of the nation's most prominent liberals, championed civil rights and organized labor. In 1968 Humphrey was the Democratic candidate for the presidency and in 1970 was reelected to the Senate. He served there until his death on 13 January 1978.

When Humphrey was elected to the vice presidency in 1964 he was replaced in the Senate by another DFL member, Walter F. Mondale. Mondale resigned from the Senate on 30 December 1976 to assume the vice presidency. In 1984 he was the Democratic candidate for president.

Despite its liberal image Minnesota's later congressional delegation has had a strong conservative component. The Republican party held both Senate seats from 1979 to 1991. In 1992 each party controlled one senatorship, but members of the DFL held six of the House seats.

BIBLIOGRAPHY

Blegen, Theodore C. *Minnesota: A History of the State.* 1975.

Lass, William E. *Minnesota: A History.* 1983.

White, Bruce M., et al. *Minnesota Votes: Election Returns by County for Presidents, Senators, Congressmen, and Governors, 1857–1977.* 1977.

WILLIAM E. LASS

MINORITY. *See* Majority and Minority.

MINORITY RIGHTS. The allocation of procedural rights in Congress has long been a contentious issue in both the House and the Senate. Although the Constitution grants each chamber the power to make its own rules, there are no constitutional guidelines for determining the appropriate balance between the rights of the political majorities and minorities in the House and the Senate. Instead, over the course of congressional history, minority rights have alternately been extended and suppressed as a result of both partisan and other factors. Moreover, the House and Senate have taken distinctly different paths: majority rule is entrenched today in the House, while minority rights are fiercely protected in the Senate.

Minority rights can be defined as procedural advantages guaranteed to individuals and minority coalitions. Such rights can be used to amend, delay, or obstruct the majority's agenda. Some minority rights apply to committee operations. For example, since 1970 the minority party in both chambers has been guaranteed the right to call witnesses to testify at congressional committee hearings. Other minority rights concern floor procedure, such as the right of the minority to offer a motion to recommit a bill to committee. Many minority rights are codified in the formal rules of the House and Senate; others exist only as accepted practices. For example, individual senators can place "holds" on measures to obstruct their progress, even though the formal rules do not recognize that practice. Also, many rules regarded by the minority party as minority rights do not explicitly mention the minority

TABLE 1. *Significant House Minority Rights*

RULE	YEAR ADOPTED	STATUS
Two-thirds vote required to suspend the rules	1822	Right still protected
Disappearing quorum	c. 1832	Eliminated 1890
Guaranteed five minutes to explain or debate amendment	1847	Right still protected
Guaranteed debate on suspensions and previous question	1880	Right still protected
Calendar Wednesday provisions	1909	Right still protected
Two-thirds vote required to suspend Calendar Wednesday	1909	Right still protected
Motion to recommit secured for minority	1909	Right still protected
Party committee slates are not divisible	1917	Right still protected
Discharge petitions require 150 signatures	1924	Signatures raised to 218 in 1925
Rules Committee must report to the House three days after reporting a bill	1924	Right still exists
Two-thirds vote required to waive layover of special rules	1924	Right still exists
Discharge petitions require 145 signatures	1931	Signatures raised to 218 in 1935
Equal majority and minority representation on Committee of Standards of Official Conduct	1967	Right still protected
Minority party guaranteed right to call witnesses	1970	Right still protected
Minority party guaranteed one-third of permanent committee staff	1970, 1974	Revised 1971, 1975
Ban on proxy voting in committee	1974	Eliminated 1975
Minority party guaranteed debate time for amendments, motions to recommit, and conference reports; submission of minority committee views guaranteed	1970	Rights still exist
Joint majority and minority appointment of House administrator; joint approval of House General Counsel litigation	1992	Rights still exist
Equal majority and minority representation on House Administration oversight subcommittee	1992	Right still exists
Discharge petition signatures may be made public	1993	Right still exists

party. For example, House Republicans since the 1960s have been fighting to ban voting by proxy in committee deliberations because they believe proxy voting benefits the minority party.

Origin and Historical Development. Individuals and minority coalitions in the first Congresses after 1789 faced few restrictions on their rights of expression. Although no member in either chamber could speak more than once per day on any topic, there were few other restrictions. Within decades, however, as the size and work load of each chamber increased, pressures built to curtail minority participation. The emergence of party organizations brought, by the 1830s, obstruction by partisan minorities, as well as by maverick individuals. In the House, the "disappearing quorum"—when minority members would refuse to answer "present" on a roll call, thereby preventing further floor votes—was the key tool used by the minority to obstruct the majority's agenda for most of the nineteenth century. In the Senate, the absence of a previous question motion—the Senate having eliminated the rule in 1806—meant that majorities had no way to restrict debate or amendments. Thus, prior to the twentieth century, the balance of power in both chambers was strongly tilted toward the rights of minorities and against majority rule.

Two events in Congress's history bear special notice for their effect on minority rights. The adoption of Reed's Rules in 1890, named for Speaker Thomas B. Reed (1889–1891, 1895–1899), eliminated the disappearing quorum and reduced to one hundred the number of members required to make a quorum in the House's Committee of the Whole. Combined with other rules changes, Reed's Rules granted the Speaker and the majority party control over the legislative process. Although minority parties in subsequent years have on occasion been able to wrest procedural concessions from weakened majority parties, the balance of power in the House has since been lodged strongly in the hands of the majority party.

In the Senate, no such dramatic change occurred to limit obstruction and the expression of minority views. In 1917, however, the Senate adopted Rule XXII, which allows an extraordinary majority to invoke cloture to bring a matter to a vote. The rule was adopted after a successful filibuster against President Woodrow Wilson's plan to arm merchant ships during World War I. Lacking other rules to limit debate and amendments, Senate leaders must seek unanimous consent to structure floor action. The reliance on unanimous consent in the Senate strongly enhances the power of individuals and minorities to shape or obstruct the majority's agenda.

Interchamber Differences. The disparate treatment of minority coalitions in the House and Senate is due in part to chance and in part to historical accident. For example, the Senate eliminated the previous question more out of happenstance than from a philosophical commitment to individual expression. Differences between the House and Senate are also the result of institutional and political factors. Senators' larger and more heterogeneous constituencies encourage them to be active across a broader range of issues than are House members. This factor, coupled with the smaller size of the Senate, where the participation of minority members can be accommodated, has made individual senators in both parties far less willing to cede parliamentary rights to the majority party. Further, unlike the House, where simple majorities must adopt a set of rules every two years, the Senate is considered a continuing body: Rule XXII is always in operation, making rules changes in the Senate subject to filibuster and requiring a two-thirds vote to invoke cloture. Not surprisingly, rules changes in the House have a distinctly partisan cast, while bipartisan compromise is almost always necessary to alter Senate procedure.

Allocation of Committee Seats. House and Senate minority parties are allocated a share of committee seats roughly proportionate to the chamber-wide party ratio. A House minority party holding 42 percent of chamber seats, for example, would be allocated roughly the same percentage of seats on the Education and Labor Committee. The right of the minority party to a share of committee seats, however, is not dictated in House or Senate standing rules. Instead, majority and minority party leaders generally negotiate the size of each party's committee rosters at the start of each Congress. Because minority party senators can obstruct the majority in many ways, it is difficult for the Senate majority to deny the minority a proportionate share of seats. In the House, however, the majority party has stacked the Appropriations, Rules, and Ways and Means committees in its favor, reducing the minority party's ratio on those panels.

Current Debates. Many members and observers of Congress believe that an acceptable balance between majority rule and minority rights has yet to be struck in the modern House or Senate. At issue is how to balance the majority's capacity to act efficiently with the minority's right to be heard and to offer alternatives. In the House, where the Demo-

TABLE 2. *Significant Senate Minority Rights*

RULE	YEAR ADOPTED	STATUS
No germaneness restriction on floor amendments	1789	Right to offer nongermane amendments still exists, except under certain conditions
Unlimited debate secured (previous question motion eliminated)	1806	No previous question motion currently exists
Any member can appeal a decision of the presiding officer	1828	Right still exists
Unlimited debate unless two-thirds of the Senate present and voting invokes cloture	1917	Revised in 1949, 1959, 1975, 1979
Unlimited debate secured on motions to proceed	1917	Protection eliminated in 1949
Unlimited debate secured on motions to consider rules changes	1949	Protection eliminated in 1959; threshold or cloture raised to two-thirds of the Senate present and voting in 1959
Minority party guaranteed equal debate time for conference reports, right to call witnesses at committee hearings, submission of minority committee views, and one-third of increase in committee staff and funding	1970	Rights still exist
Unlimited debate unless three-fifths of the entire Senate votes to invoke cloture	1975	Revised in 1979 to impose postcloture debate restrictions; additional debate and germaneness restrictions imposed as part of budget reform acts in 1974, 1985, and 1990

cratic party has been in control continually since 1955, minority Republicans object to practices such as the stacking of key committees in the majority's favor and the majority's reliance on restrictive rules, which Republicans claim foreclose their ability to participate meaningfully in floor debate. In the Senate, changing political conditions and existing rules have combined to yield a chamber of individualism and obstruction, and as a result, the Senate is sometimes unable to act on bills favored by sizable majorities. Periodically, proposals surface to enhance minority protections in the House and to reduce minority rights in the Senate. House Democrats, for example, recently conceded to minority demands to revise the committee discharge process. In the Senate, Majority Leader George J. Mitchell (D-Me.) has proposed limiting debate on motions to proceed to legislation and reducing the use of legislative

"holds." The Joint Committee on the Organization of Congress, which convened in the 103d Congress (1993–1995), considered these and other procedural reforms affecting minority rights.

[*See also* House of Representatives, *article on* House Rules and Procedures; Majority and Minority; Senate, *article on* Senate Rules and Procedures.]

BIBLIOGRAPHY

Binder, Sarah A. "A Partisan Theory of Procedural Change: The Creation of Minority Rights in the House of Representatives, 1789–1991." Paper presented at the annual meeting of the Midwest Political Science Association, Chicago, April 1992.
Dion, George Douglas. "Removing the Obstructions: Minority Rights and the Politics of Procedural Change in the Nineteenth-Century House of Representatives." Ph.D. diss., University of Michigan, 1991.

Polsby, Nelson. "The Institutionalization of the House of Representatives." *American Political Science Review* 62 (1968): 144–168.

Sinclair, Barbara. *The Transformation of the U.S. Senate.* 1989.

Smith, Steven S. *Call to Order.* 1989.

Smith, Steven S., and Christopher J. Deering. *Committees in Congress.* 2d ed. 1990.

SARAH A. BINDER

MISSISSIPPI. In the 1795 diplomatic agreement known as Pinckney's treaty, the United States and Spain resolved a long-standing dispute over control of the Natchez, Mississippi, area. U.S. acquisition of the region ended nearly a century of colonial rule under France, England, and Spain. On 7 April 1798, Congress established the Mississippi Territory from the disputed area. The territory originally lay between 31° and 32°28′ north latitude and extended westward from Georgia's western border to the Mississippi River. The territorial government was largely organized under the provisions of the Northwest Ordinance of 1787.

Attractive to cotton growers, the frontier region grew rapidly, especially after Andrew Jackson defeated the Creek Indians in 1814 in the area that is now Alabama. The so-called Great Migration of 1816 into the eastern counties accelerated an existing statehood movement, but not without controversy. An east-west rivalry, largely influenced by economic and social factors, had long disrupted territorial politics. The disruptive statehood issue, which centered on the question of unified versus divided admission, was ultimately resolved by a Congress heavily influenced by territorial delegate William Lattimore, who supported the interests of the Mississippi river district. In 1817, Congress gave the eastern region territorial status as the Alabama Territory and provided for admission of the western area as the state of Mississippi. President James Monroe signed the admission bill on 10 December 1817, making Mississippi the twentieth state in the Union.

Former territorial delegate to Congress George Poindexter was elected the state's first representative. Thomas Hill Williams, formerly a superior court judge, and Walter Leake, previously a territorial secretary, were the first U.S. senators. These leaders and their immediate successors served uneventfully. Not until the emergence of the antebellum sectional controversies did several of Mississippi's congressional delegates achieve regional acclaim and national recognition. Perhaps no leader was more notable than states' rights champion Jefferson Davis, who, before serving as president of the Confederacy during the Civil War, represented Mississippi in both congressional houses.

Democrats have dominated the congressional delegations throughout most of the state's history. Only during the brief era of Republican Reconstruction in the 1870s, and in the years since the early 1970s, have Magnolia State Republicans consistently won congressional elections. During Reconstruction, two black Republicans, Hiram R. Revels and Blanche K. Bruce, served in the U.S. Senate; another African American Republican, the respected former slave John R. Lynch, was twice elected to the House of Representatives.

Through much of the twentieth century, Mississippi's members of Congress supported conservative regional interests. Staunch segregationists, they were among the nation's most controversial leaders. Rep. John E. Rankin, and Senators Theodore G. Bilbo and James O. Eastland were prominent and ardent opponents of civil rights legislation. Establishing long tenures of seniority, Eastland and Senate colleague John C. Stennis exercised considerable influence as powerful committee chairs; Representatives Jamie L. Whitten and G.V. (Sonny) Montgomery, achieved similar status.

In 1992, Mississippi had five congressional districts—down from a high of eight between 1903 and 1933—all represented by Democrats, including one African American. Population trends through the late twentieth century make additional districts unlikely.

BIBLIOGRAPHY

McLemore, Richard Aubrey, ed. *A History of Mississippi.* 2 vols. 1973.

Skates, John Ray. *Mississippi: A History.* 1979.

ROBERT L. JENKINS

MISSOURI. On 20 October 1803, the U.S. Senate ratified the Louisiana Purchase, an expanse of 828,000 square miles in the trans-Mississippi West acquired from France for $15 million. From that land, Congress created in 1805 one territory above and one below the thirty-third parallel. The surge of American migration into the new territories led Congress in 1812 to admit Louisiana as the eighteenth state and to reorganize the region above the thirty-third parallel into the Territory of Missouri. By an act of Congress on 4 June 1812, the territorial legislature was designated the General Assembly. The increase of population after the War of 1812 spurred the movement for statehood throughout Missouri.

In 1819, John Scott, territorial delegate to Congress, presented a petition for Missouri to be admitted to the Union as a slave state. A heated controversy erupted as northern antislavery and southern proslavery forces collided over the issue of slavery's expansion into the rest of the Louisiana Purchase. Congressional deadlock was broken by the Missouri Compromise of 1820, which admitted Missouri as a slave state and Maine as a free state and outlawed slavery in the Louisiana Purchase above the line 36°30″ north latitude. In 1821, Missouri took its place as the twenty-fourth state.

As Missouri's first U.S. senator, Thomas Hart Benton (Democrat, 1821–1851) championed the cause of Jacksonian democracy, the economic concerns of western states, westward expansion, and laid the foundations of the Democratic party in Missouri. Appointed to an interim term and then elected, Democrat Lewis F. Linn (1833–1843) joined Benton in the Senate and urged American occupation of the Oregon country in the 1840s. His successor, David R. Atchison (1843–1855), became a leader in the pro-southern faction of the Democratic party in Missouri that divided the party and ended the senatorial career of Thomas Hart Benton. Following the Civil War, Sen. Charles D. Drake (1867–1870) supported the policies of the Radical Republicans until his appointment to the U.S. Court of Claims. Republican senator Carl Schurz (1869–1875) was a prime mover in the Liberal Republican party (1870–1872) that supported civil service reform and a more temperate reconstruction policy toward the South. Rep.

"The Battle of Boonville; or, The Great Missouri 'Lyon' Hunt." Northern satire of the defeat of Missouri troops at Boonville, Mo., 17 June 1861, when Gen. Sterling Price's state militia forces opposed federal forces led by Union army captain Nathaniel Lyon. The cartoon depicts Missouri's secessionist governor Claiborne F. Jackson (in women's clothing) and General Price fleeing in terror from a lion with the head of Captain Lyon. Attributed to Currier & Ives, New York, 1861.   Library of Congress

James Beauchamp "Champ" Clark (1893, 1895–1921) narrowly lost the 1912 Democratic presidential nomination to Woodrow Wilson but is the only Missourian to have served as Speaker of the House (1911–1919). Democratic representative Clarence G. Cannon (1921–1963) took Clark's seat in the House and served for more than four decades. The Cannon House Office Building was named in his honor. A loyal supporter of Franklin D. Roosevelt and the New Deal, Sen. Harry S. Truman (1935–1945) was chosen Roosevelt's running mate in the 1944 presidential election and became president on Roosevelt's death in 1945. In the postwar era, Democratic senators Stuart Symington (1953–1976) and Thomas F. Eagleton (1968–1987) provided strong national leadership. Missouri has sent two women, Leonor Kretzer Sullivan (1952–1976) and Joan Kelly Horn (1990–1992) and two African Americans, William L. Clay (1968–) and Alan Wheat (1982–), all Democrats, to the House. Historically, Missouri has been Democratic in local and national politics. Today Missouri Democrats enjoy a majority in the congressional delegation. However, a Republican resurgence led to the election of Senators John C. Danforth (1977–) and Christopher S. Bond (1987–).

BIBLIOGRAPHY

March, David D. *The History of Missouri.* 4 vols. 1967.
Parrish, William E., Charles T. Jones, and Lawrence O. Christensen. *Missouri: The Heart of the Nation.* 2d ed. 1992.

CHARLES T. JONES

MISSOURI COMPROMISE. The Missouri Compromise of 1819–1820 was the first major sectional compromise in U.S. history. In the 1780s the policy had evolved of dividing the national domain between freedom and slavery, and when the United States acquired the Louisiana Purchase in 1803, slavery, in the absence of any legal prohibition, spread into the southern portion, including the Missouri Territory. Since adoption of the Constitution the expansion of slavery had not been a major issue in Congress, and little difficulty was anticipated when Missouri applied in 1819 for admission as a state.

When the Missouri enabling bill came before the House in February 1819, however, James Tallmadge, Jr., a New York representative, introduced an amendment prohibiting the further importation of slaves into the state and providing that slave children born after the admission of Missouri would become free at age twenty-five. Subsequently divided into two separate amendments, Tallmadge's proposal constituted a program of gradual emancipation that if enacted would eventually convert Missouri into a free state.

In the wake of a severe depression that began in 1819, northern representatives, alarmed at growing southern complaints against the tariff and federal aid to internal improvements, rallied to Tallmadge's amendment. They were convinced that a new slave state was contrary to the economic and political interests of the North and West. With northern members of Congress denouncing the South's national political dominance and the three-fifths rule (which counted the slave population three-fifths in apportioning the House of Representatives), southerners demanded that Missouri be admitted without restriction as to slavery. Maine, which had previously been part of Massachusetts, was awaiting admission as a free state, and without Missouri's admission as a slave state, the sectional balance in the Senate would shift in favor of the northern states, 12 to 11. As the 1820 census soon confirmed, the South was slipping behind the North in population, and thus the Senate, with its equal representation for each state, stood as the bastion of protection for southern interests.

Congress deadlocked over the issue in 1819. The House approved Tallmadge's proposal by an almost straight sectional vote, but the Senate rejected the antislavery amendment, and the Missouri bill died. Debate resumed with increased intensity when a new Congress assembled in December 1819. With southern members threatening disunion, the House approved Maine's admission and passed an even stricter antislavery amendment to the Missouri bill—freeing slave children at birth. The Senate rejected these bills in favor of a three-part compromise fashioned by sectional moderates: Maine would be admitted as a free state; Missouri would be admitted without restriction, which meant that it would be a slave state; and in the remainder of the Louisiana Purchase, with the exception of Missouri, slavery would be forever prohibited north of the line 36°30' (Missouri's southern boundary). Under this proposal the bulk of the Louisiana Purchase would be reserved for freedom.

Endorsing this approach, Speaker Henry Clay of Kentucky held the admission of Maine hostage to gain the votes in the House to pass this compromise piecemeal in March 1820. Free state representatives, however, voted 87 to 14 against dropping the antislavery amendment; slave state representatives narrowly supported the 36°30′ line, with the Virginia delegation leading the opposition. After consulting his cabinet, President James Monroe hesitantly signed the compromise legislation, and supporters breathed a sigh of relief, convinced that the Union had weathered a dangerous sectional storm.

A new problem surfaced, however, when Missouri's proposed state constitution, which Congress had to approve, included a clause requiring the state legislature to prohibit free blacks and mulattoes from entering the state. Some northern members charged that this clause violated the Constitution's provision that citizens of a state were entitled to equal privileges and immunities. Southerners denied that blacks could be citizens under the Constitution. In February 1821 Clay engineered a face-saving solution. Missouri was admitted with a resolution stipulating that this clause was never to be used to restrict the privileges of a citizen of any state. After Missouri formally joined the Union in August, finally ending the crisis, the state legislature repudiated this resolution.

The Missouri Compromise was a major event in American history. It temporarily settled the question of slavery's status in the territories, foreshadowed the development of the argument among southerners that slavery was a positive good, and marked the emergence of the South as a conscious minority. In the aftermath of this crisis, southerners began to feel that they were a permanent minority whose safety depended on retaining control of the Senate. With time the compromise came to be viewed as a special compact between the sections, and its repeal by the Kansas-Nebraska Act in 1854 caused a dangerous escalation of the sectional crisis. Despite its repeal, in 1857 the U.S. Supreme Court, in the *Scott v. Sandford* decision, declared the Missouri Compromise unconstitutional, proclaiming that Congress had no power to prohibit slavery from a territory. As Thomas Jefferson had prophesied, the compromise of 1820 was merely a reprieve for the Union.

[*See also* Kansas-Nebraska Act.]

BIBLIOGRAPHY

Brown, Richard H. "The Missouri Crisis, Slavery, and the Politics of Jacksonianism." *South Atlantic Quarterly* 65 (1966): 55–72.

Dangerfield, George. *The Awakening of American Nationalism, 1815–1828.* 1965.

Moore, Glover. *The Missouri Compromise, 1819–1821.* 1953.

WILLIAM E. GIENAPP

MITCHELL, GEORGE J. (1933–), Democratic senator from Maine (1980–), Senate majority leader (1988–). The political career of George J. Mitchell has been marked by remarkable advances to and equally unpredictable retreats from power. Longtime aide to Maine senator Edmund S. Muskie and former chair of the state Democratic committee, Mitchell surprised many by winning his party's gubernatorial primary in 1974, but he lost the general election to an independent. President Jimmy Carter appointed Mitchell a U.S. attorney and later a Federal District Court judge; he earned widespread praise in each office. But he stepped back from a promising judicial career and gave up life tenure on the bench to accept appointment to the U.S. Senate seat vacated when Muskie became secretary of State in 1980. Mitchell's loss in the race for governor in 1974 led many to believe that he also would lose the 1982 senatorial election. However, Mitchell overcame a forty-point deficit and won a landslide victory, completely reversing his reputation as a stiff and unappealing campaigner.

Mitchell established himself as a conscientious and studious senator, and as an expert on environmental and Finance Committee issues. As a member of the Iran-contra Committee he confronted Oliver North over definitions of patriotism, thereby gaining the attention of the national media and the public and further strengthening his colleagues' opinions of him. As chair of the Democratic Senatorial Campaign Committee (DSCC) in 1986, he was credited with aiding the Democrats to regain majority status. He demonstrated that he was not only a scholarly former judge working in the Senate but also a formidable politician as well. Mitchell's work on the DSCC benefited him in his successful bid to succeed Robert C. Byrd of West Virginia, who stepped down as majority leader in 1988. Mitchell defeated two more experienced colleagues, Daniel K. Inouye of Hawaii and J. Bennett Johnston of Louisiana, with the aid of all save one of the freshmen he had helped to elect two years earlier.

Mitchell's years as Democratic leader transformed that office. Unlike his immediate Democratic predecessors, Mike Mansfield of Montana and Robert Byrd, who led the Senate from the inside, Mitchell became a national media spokesperson for all Democrats. He did this without neglecting the "inside" role, fulfilling the promise he had made as he campaigned for majority leader to make the Senate a more livable workplace. Mitchell's power was not based on dominance by parliamentary tactics, as was the case with Byrd, nor on browbeating and fear, as was the case with Lyndon B. Johnson. Rather, if there was a "Mitchell treatment," it combined patience, understanding the needs and desires of independently powerful colleagues, reasoning, and persuasion. Because of his own prominent national role, he convinced numerous senators that what he wanted them to do was in their own best interest as well. During the Bush administration, he did this by standing as the symbol of Democratic opposition to the Republican president. During the first Clinton years, he convinced his colleagues that it was in their best interest to support their party's president.

Mitchell surprised Washington and the nation when in 1994, at the peak of his power, he announced his plan to retire from the Senate. He added to that surprise when he later rejected President Clinton's reputed offer of a nomination to the Supreme Court. But while retreating from the national stage, Mitchell made it clear that he was not closing the door on future public service should other offers be forthcoming.

BIBLIOGRAPHY

Clymer, Adam. "Quietly, and Off the Air, Mitchell Cuts the Deals." *New York Times*, 9 August 1993.

L. SANDY MAISEL

MONROE, JAMES (1758–1831), senator from Virginia, governor, diplomat, and fifth president of the United States. Elected to the Senate in 1790, Monroe rapidly became a leading figure, serving on nearly all select committees and acting as the spokesman for the Jeffersonian Republican party, which he founded with Thomas Jefferson and James Madison to oppose the fiscal and foreign policies of the Washington administration. Soon after entering Congress he voted against the bill chartering the Bank of the United States. In the following session he vigorously attacked the bill apportioning representation in the House (vetoed by Washington) because it favored New England. He opposed the nomination of Gouverneur Morris as minister to France because of Morris's promonarchical views and speculation in public securities. Later in the session George Washington sought Monroe's approval before nominating the controversial Anthony Wayne as commander of the armies in the West. Monroe reluctantly promised not to raise objections although he personally disliked the choice. He led the opposition to a bill for enlarging the army, which nevertheless passed by a narrow majority. During his years in

JAMES MONROE. As president. Stipple engraving, after a painting by C. B. King, 1817.   LIBRARY OF CONGRESS

the Senate, Monroe repeatedly introduced bills to open the proceedings of that chamber to the public, a measure not adopted until 1794, when he was no longer a member.

Between sessions Monroe and Madison collaborated on anonymous letters to the newspapers defending Jefferson from charges that Alexander Hamilton (also anonymously) was making in the press. Monroe organized public meetings denouncing Washington's foreign policy as pro-British and hostile to the French revolutionary government. In the spring of 1793 he again organized meetings to protest Washington's proclamation of neutrality issued after the arrival of the French chargé d'affaires Edmond Genét. Both in Congress and out, Monroe thus contributed significantly to the development of the first American two-party system.

Monroe continued his attacks on the administration in the Congress of 1793 to 1795, putting through a resolution that called on the president to let Congress see the correspondence of America's minister to France, Gouverneur Morris, hoping to expose Morris's antirepublican views. Monroe was able to secure passage of his resolution because of a one-vote Jeffersonian Republican majority, which was soon eliminated when the Federalists successfully challenged the legality of the election of Albert Gallatin as senator from Pennsylvania. Later in the session, Monroe managed to prevent the seating of Federalist Kensey Jones of Delaware on technical grounds.

By the spring of 1794, Monroe's influence was sufficient to block consideration of Hamilton for appointment as special envoy to Great Britain. He considered John Jay no more acceptable but was unable to prevent Jay's confirmation. In an effort to mollify the Jeffersonian Republicans, Washington appointed Monroe minister to France in the spring of 1794; Monroe remained there until 1796, when his open sympathy with the revolutionary government led to his abrupt recall.

In his relations with Congress during his presidency (1817–1825) Monroe worked in the framework of the strict but simplistic interpretation of the Constitution established by his Jeffersonian Republican predecessors. They had defined the legislature as the central branch of the government and saw the role of the executive as primarily that of carrying out laws enacted by the people's representatives. Monroe did depart from previous usage in several instances. He did not, as Jefferson had done, rely on semiofficial spokesmen in Congress to introduce administration measures. He also departed from Jeffersonian Republican precedent by outlining in his annual messages matters that he felt Congress should consider.

With the advent of the one-party system of the Era of Good Feelings, Monroe could not rally party loyalty to gain political support. But he enjoyed an excellent working relationship with many members of Congress that dated from his service as secretary of State (1811–1817). Most important, he relied on the influence of his cabinet members, who had significant blocks of supporters in Congress. As in the past, bills were drafted by the administration in response to requests from congressional committees. This system of leadership proved effective until Monroe's second term, when rivalry over the presidential succession brought House Speaker Henry Clay and cabinet members John Quincy Adams and William H. Crawford into conflict.

It was in the context of this struggle for succession that Adams pushed for, and Monroe put forward in his December 1823 annual message to Congress, the declaration against European involvement in the Western Hemisphere that came to be known as the Monroe Doctrine—the most notable accomplishment of his presidency.

Monroe conducted foreign affairs as an independent function of the executive, submitting treaties for Senate approval only after they had been negotiated. He was also adamant in defending the presidential power of appointment against senatorial interference.

BIBLIOGRAPHY

Ammon, Harry. *James Monroe: The Quest for National Identity.* Rev. ed. 1991.

Cunningham, Noble E. *The Jeffersonian Republicans: The Formation of Party Organizations, 1789–1800.* 1957.

Swanstrom, Roy. "The United States Senate, 1789–1801." Ph.D. diss., University of California, 1959.

HARRY AMMON

MONROE DOCTRINE. President James Monroe used the occasion of his 2 December 1823 annual message to Congress to set out the two basic principles that came to be known as the Monroe Doctrine: "The American continents are henceforth not to be considered as subjects for future colonization by any European power," and any effort by European states "to extend their political system to any portion of this hemisphere" would be regarded by the United States "as dangerous to our peace and safety."

The Monroe Doctrine was rarely mentioned in congressional debates on foreign policy through most of the nineteenth century. But around the turn of the century, as the economic and strategic interest of the United States in Latin America grew, so did the doctrine's utility and importance. In his 1905 annual message to the Congress, President Theodore Roosevelt proposed what came to be known as the Roosevelt Corollary to the Monroe Doctrine: that while it would not be used "as a cloak for territorial aggression," the United States reserved the right to intervene when a Western Hemisphere nation misbehaved. Some congressional Democrats spoke out against this extension of the executive power, but their complaints had little effect on U.S. intervention in Latin America between 1905 and 1916.

The fight over the League of Nations at the end of

"A True American Rough Rider." Poster showing Theodore Roosevelt on horseback in his Rough Rider uniform riding toward South America, knocking aside figures representing various international powers. Ribbons on the horse's bridle are marked: "Monroe Doctrine." The streamer on the American flag reads: "Europe take notice. Keep off American Soil. Roosevelt." Lithograph, 1902.

Collection of David J. and Janice L. Frent

World War I gave the doctrine an importance that it had not had since the 1820s. Opponents such as Senators Henry Cabot Lodge (R-Mass.) and William E. Borah (R-Idaho) played on the fear that the League Covenant would allow European powers to intervene in a conflict between two Western Hemisphere nations. To quiet these concerns, President Woodrow Wilson secured an article in the Covenant that explicitly forbade the League from

overriding the Monroe Doctrine. Lodge argued (accurately enough) that the doctrine was a unilateral declaration of policy by the United States and thus outside the League's jurisdiction. He offered a resolution—accepted by the Senate—that said as much.

This approach to Latin America came under growing criticism by U.S. liberals. After taking office in 1933, President Franklin D. Roosevelt and his secretary of State, Cordell Hull, put forward the Good Neighbor policy, renouncing U.S. intervention in Latin America. In June 1937, without a roll call or a dissent from the floor, the Senate ratified a protocol that made nonintervention a general principle in the relations between Western Hemisphere states. In effect, this action repudiated the Roosevelt Corollary.

Monroe's original concept of the United States standing guard against threats from Europe took on new significance when Nazi Germany sought to extend its influence in Latin America. But the congressional (and American diplomatic) response in that case emphasized collective security rather than unilateral action by the United States. The Cuban missile crisis of 1961, with its implicit threat to U.S. national security, gave the Monroe Doctrine a brief new lease on life in the halls of Congress and in public discourse.

In the 1990s, with the evaporation of communism's power worldwide, the Monroe Doctrine might appear vestigial. Still, though cited in no treaty or act of Congress, it remains obscurely in force, ready to be resurrected if the winds of change (or congressional rhetoric) should so require.

BIBLIOGRAPHY

Dozer, Donald M., ed. *The Monroe Doctrine: Its Modern Significance.* 1965.
May, Ernest R. *The Making of the Monroe Doctrine.* 1975.
Perkins, Dexter. *A History of the Monroe Doctrine.* Rev. ed. 1955.

Morton Keller

MONRONEY, A. S. MIKE (1902–1980), Democratic representative and senator from Oklahoma, advocate of congressional reorganization; known as "Mr. Aviation" for his work to advance commercial air travel. Born in Oklahoma City, Monroney graduated from the University of Oklahoma in 1924 with a B.A. in economics. After college he served as state capitol reporter for the (Oklahoma City) *Oklahoma News.* He made his first political race in 1937, seeking to fill the unexpired term of the late

Robert P. Hill. Placing third in that race, he won the seat in 1938 and continued to represent Oklahoma's 5th Congressional District (consisting largely of Oklahoma City) through six terms.

In the House, Monroney managed legislation establishing price controls during World War II and served on the select committee authorizing the Marshall Plan. Most notable, however, was his cosponsorship (with Sen. Robert M. La Follette, Jr., of Wisconsin) of the Legislative Reorganization Act of 1946, the first systematic restructuring of Congress since 1893. In tribute to such work, he was the first recipient of *Collier's* magazine's Distinguished Congressional Service Award.

In 1950 Monroney defeated J. W. Elmer Thomas, a four-term incumbent, for the Senate. Chairing the Interstate and Foreign Commerce Committee's subcommittee on aviation, he authored legislation providing federal aid to airport construction as well as the Federal Aviation Act of 1958, which established the Federal Aviation Administration.

In 1966 Monroney served as cochairman of a new Joint Committee on the Organization of Congress, modeled after the reorganization committee on which he served as vice chairman in 1946. Like the earlier panel, the 1966 committee made numerous recommendations for changes in Congress's operations. Unlike in 1946, however, none of these recommendations was adopted by the two houses.

Defeated by Republican Henry L. Bellmon in 1968, Monroney remained in Washington, where he died. He is buried in Washington's National Cathedral.

BIBLIOGRAPHY

Davidson, Roger H. "The Office of Mike Monroney." In *On Capitol Hill: Studies in the Legislative Process.* Edited by John F. Bibby and Roger H. Davidson. 1967. Pp. 94–112.

DANNEY GOBLE

MONTANA. Following a gold rush (1862–1864), Montana Territory was created on 26 May 1864; it had been divided between Dakota Territory and Washington Territory from 1861 to 1863, and most of it had been placed in the new Idaho Territory in 1863. Montana petitioned for statehood as early as 1866, but low population and national political considerations delayed the success of these efforts. Neither national party wanted to admit a state that had regularly voted for the opposition party. Democratic leaders in Congress were supportive of statehood for Montana and New Mexico because Democrats were dominant in both territories, while Republican leaders looked with favor on the applications of Republican-dominated Washington and Dakota, and went so far as to advocate splitting Dakota Territory in half in the hope that statehood would produce four new Republican senators. In the presidential campaign of 1888, both national parties adopted planks calling for the admission of Montana, Dakota, Washington, and New Mexico, with the Republicans adding Idaho, Wyoming, and Arizona. (Neither party was ready to accept Mormon Utah.)

The 1888 election produced a new Republican president, Benjamin Harrison, and gave the Republican party control of both chambers of Congress. Acknowledging reality, the lame duck 50th Congress in early 1889 passed an omnibus act admitting Washington, Montana, North Dakota, and South Dakota that was signed by outgoing President Grover Cleveland on 22 February 1889. Montana was formally admitted to the union on 8 November 1889.

Montana presents interesting cultural and political contrasts. Silver and copper attracted early white settlement, and the mining economy produced sharp and enduring class and political divisions. On one side of the class cleavage were mining interests, led by the Anaconda Company, and the many newspapers, utilities, and politicians they dominated, combined with the stockmen's association, the railroads, and the Farm Bureau. On the other side were the labor unions and small farmers who formed the nucleus of the Populist and Progressive movements.

Accusations of political bribery were common in the early years of statehood, most notably in the campaigns of mining and banking magnate William A. Clark, who served one term in the U.S. Senate (1901–1907). These charges were partly responsible for Montana's following the example set by Oregon by adopting the direct primary and popular election of U.S. senators early in the twentieth century.

Leading in Progressive reform efforts were Democratic senators Thomas J. Walsh (1913–1933) and Burton K. Wheeler (1923–1946). Walsh, a Senate liberal on national issues but a conservative on most matters having to do with Montana itself, was credited with a major role in breaking the Teapot Dome scandal in the Harding administration. Both were early supporters of Franklin D. Roosevelt. Walsh was to be appointed attorney general by Roosevelt but died suddenly while en route to Roosevelt's inauguration in March 1993. Wheeler broke with Roosevelt over the Court-packing plan and the neutrality issue, and he became increasingly isolationist in his final two terms.

Democrat Mike Mansfield, the most eminent member of Montana's delegation, was the popular, consensual Senate majority leader from 1961 to 1976—through the Kennedy, Johnson, Nixon, and Ford administrations. His ten years in the House (1943–1952) and twenty-four years in the Senate (1953–1976) overlapped the service of Wheeler as well as of Democrat James E. Murray (1935–1960), who chaired the Senate Interior Committee; Republican Wesley A. D'Ewart (1945–1954), who left the House to become secretary of the Interior under President Dwight D. Eisenhower; and Democrats Lee Metcalf (1953–1978), John Melcher (1969–1988), and Max Baucus (1975–), who became chairman of the Senate Environment and Public Works Committee in the 103d Congress.

Mansfield served in Congress longer than any other Montanan. His length of service is followed by that of Murray (26 years), Metcalf (25 years), Wheeler (24 years), and Baucus, Melcher, and Walsh (20 years each).

Republican representative Jeannette Rankin was the first woman to be elected to the U.S. House of Representatives. Serving only two widely separated terms (1917–1919 and 1941–1942), Rankin voted against U.S. entry into both World War I and World War II.

From Montana's admission to the Union through 1993, Democrats controlled Montana's congressional seats 69 percent of the time; Republicans, 31 percent. When the state was divided into eastern and western congressional districts (1919–1992), Democratic candidates in the western mountainous region enjoyed a 32-to-5 margin in victories, while in the eastern plains region Republicans won twenty-five races and lost twelve.

BIBLIOGRAPHY

Malone, Michael P., Richard B. Roeder, and William L. Lang. *Montana: A History of Two Centuries.* Rev. ed. 1991.
Spence, Clark C. *Montana: A Centennial History.* 1978.
Toole, K. Ross. *Montana: An Uncommon Land.* 1959.

ALAN L. CLEM

MORGAN, JOHN T. (1824–1907), Democratic senator from Alabama and aggressive advocate of territorial expansion and southern economic independence. John Tyler Morgan achieved public

"THE VERDICT." Caricature of John T. Morgan that alludes to his interests in developing a Nicaraguan canal to achieve Southern economic independence, February 1899.   LIBRARY OF CONGRESS

prominence by helping lead Alabama's secession from the Union, by serving as a brigadier general in the Confederate cavalry, and by opposing Republican Reconstruction. These activities resulted in his election to the Senate in 1876. His zealous defense of the South's racial codes and economic and political autonomy accounted for his unassailable standing in Alabama's cotton belt and his five reelections. He died in office in 1907.

Virtually all of Morgan's senatorial work derived from his conviction that the North and Great Britain held the South in colonial bondage. While supporting domestic remedies such as a reduced tariff and the free coinage of silver, he advocated an expansionist foreign policy as the key to southern autonomy. From his positions on the Foreign Relations and Interoceanic Canals committees, he tirelessly championed a Nicaragua canal as the crucial link to Asian and South American markets. He believed that southern economic independence would accompany access to foreign markets for the region's cotton, coal, and timber. Similarly, he endorsed territorial expansion with the hope that new acquisitions might become southern states and augment Dixie's voting strength in the Senate.

A political maverick, Morgan disagreed with most Republicans on domestic policy and with most Democrats on foreign relations. This independence, together with his disdain for political bargaining and his party's minority status through most of his tenure, accounts for Morgan's failure to sponsor significant legislation. Still, his twenty-five-year campaign for the Nicaragua waterway earned him general recognition as the "father" of the isthmian canal.

BIBLIOGRAPHY

Fry, Joseph A. *John Tyler Morgan and the Search for Southern Autonomy.* 1992.
Radke, August C. "Senator Morgan and the Nicaraguan Canal." *Alabama Review* 12 (1959): 5–34.

JOSEPH A. FRY

MORRILL, JUSTIN S. (1810–1898), representative and senator from Vermont, known for the Morrill Tariff Act of 1861 and the Morrill Land-Grant College Act (1862). Justin Smith Morrill, a lifelong resident of Strafford, Vermont, ended his formal education at fifteen. Success at business and farming enabled him to retire at thirty-eight and, shortly thereafter, to enter politics. Elected to the House of Representatives in 1854, Morrill served six terms before moving to the Senate, to which he was also elected six times, dying in office in 1898.

On first coming to Congress, Morrill was immediately plunged into the slavery controversy. Firmly opposed to slavery, he took an active part in the battle against its extension. A moderate protectionist, Morrill's first major legislative achievement was drafting a new tariff to fulfill a major Republican party goal. Soon after the party's electoral triumph of 1860, his tariff, which had been a campaign issue, passed in Congress. Besides significantly increasing rates, it was landmark legislation because it changed the basic system from one that used ad valorem rates to one that imposed specific duties. The Morrill tariff became the base for the much larger tariff increases of the Civil War.

Morrill's name is also attached to the Land-Grant College Act of 1862. Always regretting his lack of formal schooling, Morrill had a lifelong commitment to education. He felt the need to expand high-

JUSTIN S. MORRILL. Painting by Eastman Johnson, 1884. OFFICE OF THE ARCHITECT OF THE CAPITOL

er education beyond the professions to farmers and other workers. There is still debate over how the act originated. Some claim that the idea for land grant colleges originally belonged to Professor Jonathan Baldwin Turner of Illinois College at Jacksonville, Illinois. But Morrill was familiar not only with Turner's work but with that of others espousing similar ideas, so he was probably inspired by a number of sources. Regardless, without Morrill's considerable legislative skills, the bill, which never received a favorable committee recommendation, might never have passed. Morrill watched over the resulting land grant colleges for the rest of his life.

Because of his outstanding parliamentary skills, Morrill was given responsibility in 1861 for Civil War finance bills. He played a major role in securing the internal taxes and tariff revisions passed to support the major war loans. So skilled was Morrill that only rarely was a finance bill significantly altered.

In his last House term (1865–1867), Morrill became chairman of the Ways and Means Committee.

He quickly began the process of repealing wartime taxation. Most internal taxes were gone by the time Morrill went to the Senate in March 1867.

When Morrill began his distinguished senatorial career, most of his legislative goals had already been accomplished. No more landmark legislation carried his name, even though Morrill served in important positions. He chaired both the Finance Committee and the Public Buildings and Grounds Committee. In the latter role, he continued to make a lasting contribution. His interest in this new realm of policy had begun in the House, where he had offered the resolution to create the Capitol's National Statuary Hall. In the Senate, Morrill pushed through legislation to complete the Washington Monument, construct the Library of Congress, and purchase the site for the Supreme Court Building.

BIBLIOGRAPHY

Hoyer, Randal L. "The Gentleman from Vermont: The Career of Justin S. Morrill in the United States House of Representatives." Ph.D. diss., Michigan State University, 1974.

Parker, William B. *The Life and Public Services of Justin Smith Morrill.* 1924.

RANDAL L. HOYER

MORRILL LAND-GRANT COLLEGE ACT

(1862; 12 Stat. 503–505). The proposal to distribute federal lands to the states for the benefit of higher education was hardly new in 1862. Republican representative Justin S. Morrill of Vermont had been pushing the idea for five years, and a bill embodying this proposition had been passed by Congress during the Buchanan administration, only to be vetoed by the president. On 16 December 1861, Morrill once again introduced a proposal to grant public lands to such states as would establish colleges "for the benefit of agriculture and the mechanic arts."

But the House Committee on Public Lands, to which it was referred, contained a majority opposed to the proposal and, consequently, Morrill asked Republican senator Benjamin F. Wade of Ohio to introduce the measure in the Senate, which he did on 5 May 1862. The bill moved quickly through the Senate Committee on Public Lands and onto the Senate floor. The measure came to a vote on 10 June, after weathering opposition from western senators, who feared (correctly) that the eastern states would sell their land warrants to speculators who would inhibit population growth in the territories and the states containing large amounts of federal lands. The westerners managed to prohibit land companies from taking more than one million acres of land in a single state. All other limiting amendments were beaten back, and the bill passed the Senate by a vote of 32 to 7 on 10 June 1862. Action was exceptionally swift in the House, which passed the measure by a vote of 91 to 25 on 17 June. Opposition came largely from the Midwest.

The act provided for a grant of public lands in the amount of thirty thousand acres (valued for preemption at $1.25 per acre) for each representative and senator from any state that should establish at least one college "where the leading object shall be (without excluding other scientific and classical studies, and including military tactics) to teach such branches of learning as are related to agriculture and the mechanic arts." Enticed by these promises of extensive blocks of land that could be converted into cash, the states established or adopted institutions to be beneficiaries of the federal government's largess. They introduced a public component into American higher education heretofore dominated by private (and largely religious) institutions, and also became the avenues for the expansion of technical training on the collegiate level.

BIBLIOGRAPHY

Curry, Leonard P. *Blueprint for Modern America: Nonmilitary Legislation of the First Civil War Congress.* 1968.

Simon, John Y. "The Politics of the Morrill Act." *Agricultural History* 37 (April 1963): 103–111.

LEONARD P. CURRY

MORRIS, GOUVERNEUR

(1752–1816), Federalist senator from New York. During the 1787 Constitutional Convention, Morris polished the Constitution's final draft, but a decade-long European residence denied him a firsthand role in the new government until his April 1800 election to the last three years of an unexpired Senate term. A determined Federalist, he entered Congress just as his party's dominance passed. Morris, unlike most high Federalists, accepted this prospect calmly, opposing schemes to exploit the electoral tie of 1800 by placing a Federalist president of the Senate in the White House. Still, in the closing weeks of the sixth Congress, Morris supported the Judiciary Act of February 1801 and John Marshall's appointment as

GOUVERNEUR MORRIS. LIBRARY OF CONGRESS

chief justice, tactics designed to perpetuate Federalist influence.

Jeffersonianism, however, proved less congenial in practice than in theory. When the seventh Congress convened in December 1801, Morris denounced Thomas Jefferson's call for repeal of the Judiciary Act as a "victory meditated over the Constitution," while Jefferson's demand for repeal of internal taxes seemed to him fiscal heresy. In the spring of 1802 New York's Jeffersonian Republican legislature denied Morris another term, and he returned to the Senate in December a lame-duck legislator with nothing to lose as the administration's gadfly. When Federalist circuit judges who were appointed under the Judiciary Act (and then denied office by the act's repeal) petitioned the Senate for redress, Morris disingenuously recommended that the Federalist-controlled Supreme Court decide the question. He next supported bellicose resolutions on the "Mississippi Question"—the issue of American rights in the Mississippi Valley—speaking his own political epitaph: "This, I believe, is the last

scene of my public life." As Morris foresaw, his remaining years were spent as a private citizen.

BIBLIOGRAPHY

Fischer, David H. *The Revolution of American Conservatism: The Federalist Party in the Age of Jeffersonian Democracy.* 1965.

Swiggett, Howard. *The Extraordinary Mr. Morris.* 1952.

MARY-JO KLINE

MORRISON V. OLSON (487 U.S. 654 [1988]). The Supreme Court in *Morrison v. Olson* upheld the independent counsel provisions of the 1978 Ethics in Government Act, which provides for court appointment at the behest of the attorney general of an independent counsel to investigate and prosecute criminal violations by certain government and campaign officials. The statute gives the counsel full authority to investigate and prosecute in such cases, and he or she is only removable by the attorney general for stated causes.

The Court held that the appointment provision is not unconstitutional under the appointments clause. Court appointment of officers, it asserted, is contemplated by the clause, and, given the appointing court's involvement in the work of the counsel, vesting the appointment in the court does not constitute an incongruous interbranch appointment. Such appointment power and oversight were also held not to violate Article III of the Constitution, which limits courts to judicial functions. Since the independent counsel is a temporary office whose court-defined jurisdiction is confined to specific circumstances, *Morrison* concluded that the court's powers neither encroach significantly on executive power or the counsel's prosecutorial discretion nor threaten impartial adjudication of cases.

The statute was also held not to be inconsistent with separation of powers. The removal restrictions and the act as a whole were seen as not unduly interfering with executive authority. The Court held that Congress was not attempting to aggrandize its powers at the executive's expense and that there was no judicial interference with executive functions. While the counsel is independent from the executive to a degree greater than other prosecutors, the act was held to provide sufficient limits and control to ensure the proper exercise of the executive's constitutional functions.

The *Morrison* case was an important articulation of a functional approach to separation of powers. It rejected the categorization in earlier cases of those officers who could be made removable for cause, while at the same time it recognized that there are officers who may be essential to the performance of executive functions and whose removal must remain at the will of the president. The counsel's office, while performing clearly executive functions, was not seen as carrying the potential to undermine the executive's constitutional role; therefore, the post could be structured by Congress with a degree of independence from presidential control.

BIBLIOGRAPHY

Pierce, Richard E. *"Morrison v. Olson,* Separation of Powers and the Structure of Government." In *1988 Supreme Court Review.* 1988. Pp. 1–41.

Carter, Stephen L. "The Independent Counsel Mess." *Harvard Law Review* 102 (1988): 105–141.

RICHARD EHLKE

MORSE, WAYNE L. (1900–1974), liberal Republican turned Democratic senator from Oregon (1945–1968) and vociferous early critic of the war in Vietnam. Born on a farm in Wisconsin, Morse was imbued with the political principles of Robert M. La Follette, who once counseled the young Morse that, in debating public issues, one could choose either to win the contest or to educate the public. In the course of his long Senate career, Morse frequently took uncompromising stands that served primarily the latter purpose.

After earning a degree in law from the University of Minnesota, Morse was appointed dean of the law school at the University of Oregon. By 1938 Morse had been selected as Pacific coast labor arbitrator by the administration of Franklin D. Roosevelt, and in 1942 he won appointment to the National War Labor Board. Although sympathetic to the interests

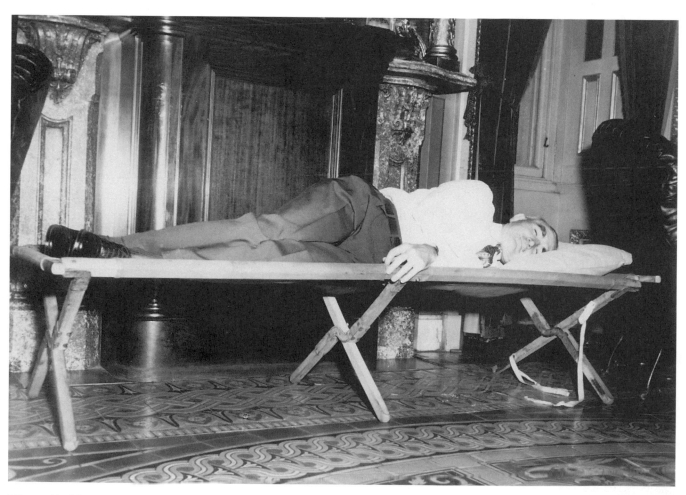

WAYNE L. MORSE. Resting on a cot before returning to the floor during a Senate debate. In 1953, Morse held the floor for more than twenty-two hours, filibustering in opposition to an offshore oil bill.   LIBRARY OF CONGRESS

of labor, Morse resigned in 1944 in the face of administration concessions made to the United Mine Workers' president, John L. Lewis. Shortly thereafter Morse won election to the U.S. Senate as a Republican, defeating incumbent Rufus C. Holman.

Regarded as a renegade liberal in the conservative Republican caucus of the postwar Congresses and scornful of his critics, Morse quickly established a maverick "outsider" role in the Senate. Espousing legislative reform even while using the filibuster, Morse antagonized Republican leader Robert A. Taft over both labor and foreign policy issues. As a member of the labor committee, Morse sought to weaken the restraints placed on labor unions in the evolving Taft-Hartley Act, although he was soundly defeated on the floor. Often accused of having shallow Republican loyalty, in 1952 Morse withdrew his support for Dwight D. Eisenhower's presidential candidacy, citing the party's lack of moral principles.

Resigning from the Republican party caucus at the start of the 83d Congress (1953–1955), Morse requested reassignment to his seats on the Labor and Armed Services committees as an Independent. Spurned by both parties, Morse was instead assigned to the low-ranked District of Columbia and Public Works panels. At the beginning of the 84th Congress in 1955, Morse finally joined the Democrats when his vote gave them a one-man majority. As a reward for his party switch, Majority Leader Lyndon B. Johnson provided Morse with a long-coveted seat on the Foreign Relations Committee. Morse remained a harsh critic of the Eisenhower administration.

With the election of a Democratic administration in 1960, Morse managed the most extensive postwar federal aid-to-education bill through Congress, securing its passage in 1965. Even as Morse continually supported the Johnson administration's domestic policies, he increasingly inveighed against the administration's "extraconstitutional" military aid to South Vietnam and other rightist regimes. When Johnson sought direct congressional approval for stepped-up intervention in Southeast Asia through the Gulf of Tonkin resolution in 1964, only Morse and Sen. Ernest Gruening (D-Alaska) stood in dissent on Capitol Hill. An indefatigable and irascible opponent of the war, Morse questioned the soundness of U.S. involvement in the escalating conflict, thus legitimizing the peace movement that had sprung up on college campuses and had by 1968 led to widespread public disaffection with the administration's policy. That year, Morse

was defeated for his Senate seat by the youthful, moderate Republican Bob Packwood. Seeking to return to the Senate in 1972 and again in 1974, Morse died during his final campaign.

BIBLIOGRAPHY

Huitt, Ralph K. "The Morse Committee Assignment Controversy: A Study in Senate Norms." In *Working within the System.* 1990.
Smith, A. Robert. *The Tiger in the Senate.* 1962.
Wilkins, Lee. *Wayne Morse: A Bio-Bibliography.* 1985.

RICHARD C. BURNWEIT

MOTIONS. [*This entry includes separate articles on motions in the House and in the Senate. For related discussion, see* Adjournment and Recess; Amending; House of Representatives, *article on* House Rules and Procedures; Lawmaking; Manuals of Procedure; Senate, *article on* Senate Rules and Procedures; Tabling.]

In the House

The term *motion* refers generally to any formal proposal made before a deliberative assembly. However, its use here is confined only to the general and more frequently used motions, called *secondary motions*, which are used to dispose of the main proposition under consideration.

Secondary motions are outlined in clause 4 of Rule XVI of the House Rules, where they are given the following order of priority: to adjourn, to lay on the table, for the previous question, to postpone to a specified day (day certain), to refer, to amend, and to postpone indefinitely.

The motion to adjourn not only has the highest precedence when a question is under consideration but, with certain restrictions, has the highest privilege under all other conditions. The motion to lay on the table is used in the House for a final, adverse disposition of a matter.

The motion for the previous question, explained in Rule XVII, is used to close debate or to foreclose further amendments and bring the pending matter to a vote. Defeat of this motion not only throws the main question open for further consideration but also transfers the right of recognition to those members who opposed the motion.

There are two distinct, debatable motions to postpone: to postpone to a day certain and to postpone indefinitely. The adoption of a motion to postpone indefinitely constitutes a final, adverse disposition of the underlying measure.

There are four motions to refer, which send a measure to a specific committee or committees, with or without instructions as to the actions the committee is to take: the ordinary motion to refer when a question is "under debate" (clause 4 of Rule XVI), the motion to recommit after the previous question has been ordered on a bill or joint resolution to final passage (clause 4 of Rule XVI), the motion to commit pending the motion for or after the ordering of the previous question (clause 1 of Rule XVII), and the motion to refer pending a vote in the House on the motion to strike the enacting clause (clause 7 of Rule XXIII). The terms *refer, commit,* and *recommit* are sometimes used interchangeably; when used in the precise manner contemplated in each rule, they reflect certain procedural differences.

The motion to amend (under Rule XIX and under Section XXXV of Jefferson's Manual) and motions to dispose of amendments between the houses (under Section XLV of Jefferson's Manual) are discussed elsewhere in this work.

[*See also* Previous Question; Recommital.]

BIBLIOGRAPHY

U.S. House of Representatives. *Constitution, Jefferson's Manual, and Rules of the House of Representatives, 103d Congress.* Compiled by William Holmes Brown. 102d Cong., 2d sess., 1992. H. Doc. 102-405.

U.S. House of Representatives. *Deschler's Precedents of the United States House of Representatives,* by Lewis Deschler. 94th Cong., 2d sess., 1977. H. Doc. 94-661. Vol. 7, Chap. 23.

MUFTIAH MCCARTIN

In the Senate

The Senate operates largely by unanimous consent of its members. When that fails, there are a number of motions that can be used to avoid the requirement of unanimous consent. The two most commonly used motions are the motion to proceed and the motion to invoke cloture.

It is in order to move to proceed to bills on the calendar if the bill has complied with the requirement of being on the calendar for one legislative day and a written report on the bill has been printed and available for forty-eight hours. The motion to proceed is a prerogative of the majority leader. Such a motion is debatable, however. While it is pending, Rule XXII allows senators to make a second motion that would end debate on the motion to proceed. The second motion is a motion to invoke cloture, or limit debate. Cloture motions are also the prerogative of the majority leader.

A motion to invoke cloture is automatically voted on after one intervening day of session. Unlike the motion to proceed, which is carried by a majority vote, a cloture motion requires a three-fifths majority of the total membership. Under the rules of the Senate, thirty hours of consideration are allowed once a cloture motion passes.

If a motion to proceed is agreed to, several other motions are in order under Rule XXII. For example, it is then in order to move that the pending matter be referred to a Senate committee. It is also in order to move to postpone a pending matter either to a certain day or indefinitely (this latter is a "killing" motion).

All these motions are debatable in the Senate. Several other kinds of motions, however, must be decided without debate. The motion to table, which is commonly used when amendments are pending, is not a debatable motion, and, if it is adopted, it kills the item that is tabled. Certain procedural motions are also not debatable under Rule XXII. These include motions to recess and adjourn.

With rare exceptions, motions in the Senate do not require seconding. The motion to go into closed session does require one senator to second the motion, and the motion to discharge a particular kind of bill—the so-called rescission bill—requires a second by one-fifth of the members. A senator's request that a vote be a recorded vote also requires a second by one-fifth of the members.

[*See also* Cloture.]

BIBLIOGRAPHY

Tiefer, Charles. *Congressional Practice and Procedure.* 1989.

U.S. Senate. *Riddick's Senate Procedure, Precedents, and Practices,* by Floyd M. Riddick and Alan S. Frumin. 101st Cong., 2d sess., 1992. S. Doc. 101-28.

ROBERT B. DOVE

MOTION TO RECONSIDER. *See* Reconsider, Motion to.

MOVIES ON CONGRESS. Fictional portrayals of Congress and its members in feature films are more common than one would imagine. The congressional election campaign, political ambition

THE CANDIDATE. Actor Robert Redford, *center,* in a scene from the film.

within Washington, the legislative process, and congressional committees in action (especially the House Committee on Un-American Activities) have all made their cinematic appearances.

The Campaign. The best movie about political campaigns is *The Candidate* (1972). Written by Jeremy Larner, a speech writer for Sen. Eugene J. McCarthy in the 1968 presidential campaign, it stars Robert Redford as an altruistic legal aid attorney who is asked to run for the Senate against an entrenched incumbent. He wins by modifying his principles and giving up control of the campaign to his handlers, who concentrate on style and image. A related film, *Power* (1986), traces the activities of a political campaign strategist (Richard Gere) in his work for various candidates. Earlier films, such as *Washington Merry-Go-Round* (1932) and *The Farmer's Daughter* (1947), portrayed elections as controlled by party political machines.

The year 1992 saw *Bob Roberts*, a faux documentary, directed by and starring Tim Robbins as an extreme right-wing senatorial candidate devoted to greed and power, who wages a slick campaign, featuring his singing of ersatz folksongs with conservative themes, against a liberal opponent played by the writer Gore Vidal. What Roberts lacks in sincerity he more than makes up in expert packaging, wealth, and his talent as an entertainer. Roberts wins a close race after he feigns that a shooting has partially paralyzed him.

The movie is a virulent attack on conservatives—insubstantial candidates who wage campaigns based on people's fears, invoking patriotism and championing drug-fighting—and on the system that enables them to win election to the Senate. But it may undermine its credibility and effects by exaggerating Roberts to the point of unbelievability.

Political Ambition. A recurring character is a senator who wants to become president. These include the dimwit in the 1947 farce *The Senator Was Indiscreet* (he is "against inflation, against deflation, for flation"), the unscrupulous conservative senator vying for the nomination at the presidential convention in *The Best Man* (1964, adapted by Gore Vidal from his stage play), and the stop-at-nothing senator in *A Fever in the Blood* (1961).

The Seduction of Joe Tynan (1979), written by and starring Alan Alda, offers the most sympathetic portrait, focusing on the conflicts between the senator's personal and political lives. Even this film, however, shows senators as variously lecherous, immoral, or senile, and the legislative process as characterized by manipulation and frustration. This treatment is mild compared to the portrayals of senators in the extraordinary political thriller *The Manchurian Candidate* (1962). The conservative is an ignorant buffoon (loosely modeled on the late senator Joseph R. McCarthy) controlled by his evil wife; the liberal is hopelessly ineffectual. Both end up dead.

Congressional Processes. The best-known movie on Congress is *Mr. Smith Goes to Washington* (1939). James Stewart stars as the idealistic Jefferson Smith, appointed to complete the term of a deceased senator. His first action on arriving in Washington, D.C., is to visit its monuments, most notably the Lincoln Memorial. He is spiritually lost in a Senate of practical politicians. His one legislative effort, to establish a boys' camp in his state, falls prey to the scheme of the boss of his state, abetted somewhat unwillingly by the state's senior senator, Joseph Paine, for a personally beneficial and machine-enriching federal dam project. Framed by the schemers, Smith is about to flee Washington in despair but is inspired to return to the Senate by his once cynical, now redeemed (by Smith) and loving secretary, played by Jean Arthur. To fight his impending expulsion, Smith stages a one-man filibuster on the Senate floor (the chamber was meticulously re-created for the film). Although the state boss uses his control of the media to inflame the public against Smith, the senator's sincerity, grit, and natural eloquence begin to persuade the senators, particularly the presiding officer. After twenty-three hours Smith collapses, his cause apparently lost. But the guilt-ridden Senator Paine, failing in a suicide attempt, declares his own guilt and Smith's innocence.

With its paean to American ideals, its theme of a Christ-like Smith redeeming a Senate whose members have forgotten their heritage, memorable per-

MR. SMITH GOES TO WASHINGTON. The character Jefferson Smith, played by actor Jimmy Stewart.

formances from its stars and supporting players, and fast-paced direction by Frank Capra, *Mr. Smith* was a financial and critical success. But it outraged many members of Congress, for its portrayal of the Senate is ambiguous at best. As Senator Paine tells Smith, the Senate is "a man's world and you've got to check your ideals outside the door like you do your rubbers."

Advise and Consent (1962), based on the best-selling novel by Allen Drury, follows the congressional process as the Senate majority leader tries to achieve confirmation of the president's controversial nominee for secretary of State, Robert Leffingwell, played by Henry Fonda. Opposition comes from within the party in the person of a conservative southern senator (incarnated with relish by the English actor Charles Laughton), who uses the testimony of a mentally unbalanced clerk to brand the nominee a communist. Leffingwell denies the accusation to the committee but confesses its partial truth to the president, who dismisses it as a youthful indiscretion. The subcommittee chairman learns about the perjury, but the president rejects his demand that the nomination be withdrawn. The chairman, blackmailed by a liberal peace-activist senator (the film's most obnoxious character) over a past homosexual indiscretion, commits suicide. The nomination is brought to the Senate without

the perjury being revealed, and the vote ends in a tie. Before it can be broken, news arrives of the president's death. The formerly docile, now assertive vice president announces that he will appoint his own secretary of State. This is a film full of archetypes, sometimes degenerating into stereotypes, and of plausible individual events that become incredible in combination.

In 1992 the comedian Eddie Murphy starred in *The Distinguished Gentleman*, directed by Jonathan Lynn (of *Yes, Minister* fame) from a screenplay by experienced Washington hand Marty Kaplan. Murphy plays Thomas Jefferson Johnson, a con artist elected to Congress because he shares the name of a recently deceased member. Johnson finds Congress to be a con man's cornucopia, with lobbyists and corporate interest groups eager to bestow

ADVISE AND CONSENT. Actor Charles Laughton, *lower left, in a white suit,* being filmed on location outside the Russell Senate Office Building.   OFFICE OF THE HISTORIAN OF THE U.S. SENATE

Movies on Congress

Advise and Consent, 1962	*Louisiana Purchase,* 1941
The Best Man, 1964	*The Man,* 1972
Big Jim McClain, 1952	*The Manchurian Candidate,* 1962
Billy Jack Goes to Washington, 1977	*The Man from Oregon,* 1915
Bob Roberts, 1992	*Mr. Smith Goes to Washington,* 1939
The Candidate (also called *Party Girls for the Candidate*), 1964	*Moonlight and Honeysuckle,* 1921
	No Way Out, 1987
The Candidate, 1972	*On the Waterfront,* 1954
Deliverance, 1928	*Power,* 1986
The Distinguished Gentleman, 1992	*The Price of Silence,* 1917
The Eagle's Wing, 1916	*Protocol,* 1984
Fail Safe, 1964	*The Seduction of Joe Tynan,* 1979
The Farmer's Daughter, 1947	*The Senator,* 1915
A Fever in the Blood, 1961	*The Senator Was Indiscreet,* 1947
First Monday in October, 1981	*Seven Days in May,* 1964
A Foreign Affair, 1948	*State of the Union,* 1948
The Front, 1976	*Tucker: The Man and His Dream,* 1988
Gabriel over the White House, 1933	*The Velvet Paw,* 1916
A Gentleman from Mississippi, 1914	*The Washington Masquerade,* 1932
The Godfather, Part II, 1974	*Washington Melodrama,* 1941
Guilty by Suspicion, 1991	*Washington Merry-Go-Round,* 1932
The Happy Hooker Goes to Washington, 1977	*Washington Story,* 1952
High Noon, 1952	*The Way We Were,* 1973
A King in New York, 1957	*Wild in the Streets,* 1968
The Life of Big Tim Sullivan; Or, From Newsboy to Senator, 1914	

largess upon him. But his conscience is stirred by the possible link between a child's cancer and an electric power line in his district, and he exposes a powerful and corrupt committee chairman (persuasively portrayed by Lane Smith). But whereas Jefferson Smith was honest and naive, Jefferson Johnson, befitting the 1990s, is streetwise and savvy, qualities that allow him to win.

The Distinguished Gentleman is visually and aurally authentic in some details (aspects of staff influence, of lobbying, of committee processes), while caricaturing others (election campaigns, members' motives, and the power of lobbyists). Overall, it depicts Congress, despite the presence of a few good public-spirited members, as a corrupt and cynical forum for farce.

Congressional Committees. Much of the congressional work-load is undertaken by committees. Most committee work—slow, complicated, and undramatic—makes unpromising material for fiction films. The major exceptions are committee hear-ings, with their potential for confrontation and conflict. No wonder fictional movies on Congress often feature dramatic hearings as effective devices, as in *Mr. Smith* and *Advise and Consent*. In *First Monday in October* (1981) a tense moment comes with the testimony before a Senate committee of the first woman Supreme Court nominee (Jill Clayburgh). *Seven Days in May* (1964) depicts a committee hearing involving a confrontation with the chairman of the Joint Chiefs of Staff. In *Protocol* (1984) a congressional hearing enables the heroine (Goldie Hawn) to root out corruption and deliver a patriotic speech.

More often than not the hearings are unrealistic, the senators portrayed negatively. *The Happy Hooker Goes to Washington* (1977) revolves around the title character's testimony upstaging the hypocritically prudish member of a Senate committee investigat ing the supposed danger and damage of sex to America. The Senate investigating committee in *The Godfather, Part II* (1974), containing one member beholden to the godfather and its counsel controlled by a mob boss, is shown as ineffectual against organized crime.

The House Un-American Activities Committee (HUAC). During the late 1940s and early 1950s the committee investigated alleged communist activities in Hollywood. Individuals who refused to testify before or to cooperate with the committee, or who were named as communists, usually lost their jobs and were blacklisted, thus becoming unemployable under their own names in the movie industry.

The committee soon began appearing in feature films. Praise came first, as in the inadvertently hilarious *Big Jim McClain* (1952), starring John Wayne, which features a simulated hearing of the committee, replete with some actual members.

Allegorical treatments followed. In *On the Waterfront* (1954), a movie directed and written by men who had cooperated with the committee, the protagonist chooses to testify before a state investigative committee concerning corrupt union activities. Superb acting, most notably by Marlon Brando and Rod Steiger, and Boris Kaufman's superb cinematography make this an outstanding American movie. Similarly allegorical, and almost as compelling, is *High Noon* (1952), starring Gary Cooper as a sheriff who ends up essentially alone, having to defend a western town against the villains (the committee).

Movies subsequently took on the HUAC more directly. Charlie Chaplin literally hoses down its members in *A King in New York* (1957). *The Way We Were* (1973) condemns the committee's methods and effects, but less so than originally intended by its screenwriter, Arthur Laurents. Deleted at the last moment was a scene in which Robert Redford tells Barbra Streisand: "The studio says I have a subversive wife and they'll fire me unless you inform." She replies, "We get a divorce. Then you don't have a subversive wife" (Pat McGilligan, *Backstory 2*, 1991, p. 152). An emphasis on romance at the expense of politics no doubt contributed to the film's enormous commercial success.

Next came *The Front* (1976) starring Woody Allen as a front man for blacklisted writers. Directed by, written by, and featuring supporting actors who had all been blacklisted, the film's point of view is best expressed by Allen's character, who when called to name names states that he does not recognize the committee's right to "ask those kinds of questions and furthermore you can all go f—— yourselves."

In *Guilty by Suspicion* (1991) the main character, played by Robert DeNiro, has his directing career ruined by false rumors that he is a communist. Given the opportunity to save himself by testifying about others, he too preserves his integrity by defying the committee.

Members of Congress outside the Institution. Members of Congress occasionally appear outside the institution other than as candidates for office. Some portrayals are favorable, others negative. An Iowa congresswoman is humanized while in Berlin to investigate corrupting moral influences on American occupation troops in Billy Wilder's droll *A Foreign Affair* (1948). In *Fail Safe* (1964), an apocalyptic military drama, a congressman present in the central military control center presciently voices his concern about the dangers of U.S. nuclear policy. Two senators, one honest and the other corrupt, appear in *State of the Union* (1948). In *Seven Days in May* (1964) one senator participates in an attempted military coup, another helps rescue the country. In *Tucker* (1988), Francis Ford Coppola's film about Preston Tucker (who in 1948 challenged the Detroit automakers by producing his own innovative car), a Michigan senator causes Tucker's plant to be taken away from him.

Sometimes plots and portrayals go to extremes. In the sexploitation film *The Candidate* (1964, also known as *Party Girls for the Candidate*), senators are involved with women of dubious reputation; in *Wild in the Streets* (1968), with hallucinogens.

Conclusion. Depictions of Congress and its members from the 1930s through the early 1950s were relatively benign *(Washington Merry-Go-Round, The Farmer's Daughter,* and *Washington Story).* Even *Mr. Smith Goes to Washington* is ambiguous. The 1960s brought cynicism *(The Best Man, A Fever in the Blood, The Manchurian Candidate).* The movies of the 1970s depicted character, election campaigns, and legislative processes with greater complexity and a more critical eye *(The Candidate, Power, The Seduction of Joe Tynan).* After that Congress was virtually absent from, and congressional characters were peripheral to, American movies. Members who did appear usually came off badly, as in *The Godfather Part II* and *Tucker.* Meanwhile, portrayals of the House Un-American Activities Committee went from attempts to curry favor to condemnation, the latter culminating with *Guilty by Suspicion.*

There is an axiom in Hollywood that politics is box office poison. As the notable director and writer Billy Wilder told George Axelrod early in the latter's screenwriting career: "My dear boy, you and I will leave political satire to others. You and I will write about screwing and become very rich" (cited by Axelrod in an interview in *Sight and Sound,* Autumn 1968, p. 165). Nonetheless, their country's government and politics, its institutions and processes, seem to exert a perennial fascination for American filmmakers inside and outside Hollywood. Thus the early 1990s saw films about a candidate, *Bob Roberts,* and about lobbying and influence in Congress in *The Distinguished Gentleman.*

In sum, Congress as seen on the screen is not a pleasant place, especially in recent times. Its processes are misrepresented and overdramatized, its members portrayed as egocentric and expedient. Some of these characterizations are partially valid. What is usually missing is the positive and workaday side.

[*For comparable treatment of novels, see* Literature on Congress.]

BIBLIOGRAPHY

Axelrod, George. "Interview." *Sight and Sound* 37 (Autumn 1968): 165.
Christensen, Terry. *Reel Politics.* 1987.
Ryan, Michael, and Douglas Kellner. *Camera Politica.* 1988.
Thompson, Robert. "American Politics on Film." *Journal of Popular Culture* 20 (Summer 1986): 27–47.

DAVID L. PALETZ and DANIEL LIPINSKI

MUCKRAKING. Muckraking magazine journalism grew out of publisher S. S. McClure's claim that the exposés of business, government, and labor corruption by Lincoln Steffens, Ida Tarbell, and Ray Stannard Baker in the January 1903 issue of *McClure's* magazine constituted a general indictment of American society. The journalistic movement that he touched off dominated the new popular magazine world for the next decade and played an important role in the reform politics of the Progressive Era. New presses, linotype, and photoengraving processes enabled highly energetic entrepreneurial editors to produce cheap, dramatic, brightly illustrated magazines such as *McClure's, Colliers's, Cosmopolitan, American,* and *Everybody's,* which featured detailed, factual accounts and high moral criticism of the widespread corruption and growing social problems of the newly industrialized America. Popularizing terms such as *high finance, frenzied finance, the trusts, the interests,* and *the system,* they maintained that an apathetic society was being corrupted by concentrated wealth. It is that focus on the role of concentrated economic power

"TREASON OF THE SENATE." When novelist David Graham Phillips's series in *Cosmopolitan* began in March 1906, a sinister portrait of Sen. Chauncey Depew (R-N.Y.) was published on the magazine cover.

LIBRARY OF CONGRESS

that separates them from many later journalists to whom the term *muckraker* has since been applied.

The term *muckraker* came from a speech by President Theodore Roosevelt. On 14 April 1906, at the laying of the cornerstone of a new House of Representatives office building, he took the image from John Bunyan's seventeenth-century puritan morality story, *The Pilgrim's Progress,* to criticize these journalists. Fearing that they might stir up dangerous socialistic public discontent, Roosevelt claimed that they were too negative and likened them to Bunyan's "Man with the Muck-Rake," who refused to stop raking the filth and lift up his eyes to see what was good about the world.

Roosevelt's ire was raised by David Graham Phillips's "Treason of the Senate" series in William Randolph Hearst's *Cosmopolitan* magazine. The series profiled twenty-one leading senators as having sold out to the big financial "interests." The senators Phillips denounced were Nelson Aldrich (R-R.I.), William B. Allison (R-Iowa), Joseph W. Bailey (D-Tex.), Joseph R. Burton (R-Kans.), Winthrop Crane (R-Mass.), Shelby M. Cullom (R-Ill.), Chauncey Depew (R-N.Y.), Stephen B. Elkins (R-W.Va.), Charles W. Fairbanks (R-Ind.), Joseph B. Foraker (R-Ohio), William P. Frye (R-Maine), Arthur Pue Gorman (D-Md.), Eugene Hale (R-Maine), John Kean (R-N.J.), Philander C. Knox (R-Pa.), Henry Cabot Lodge (R-Mass.), Knute Nelson (R-Minn.), Boies Penrose (R-Pa.), Thomas C. Platt (R-N.Y.), John C. Spooner (R-Wis.), and William Stone (D-Mo.). Muckraking journalism provided popular support for the growing Progressive Era attack on Senate conservatism and corruption. By the time the "direct election" Seventeenth Amendment, passed by Congress in 1911, went into effect in 1913, death, retirement, and defeat had removed all of Phillips's Senate targets except Lodge, Penrose, Nelson, and Stone.

Series of articles about railroad power and corruption by Charles Edward Russell, Ray Stannard Baker, Lincoln Steffens, Ida A. Tarbell, Will Irwin, Burton Hendrick, G. K. Turner, and C. P. Connolly paralleled a decade of congressional regulatory struggles. The exposés of the patent-medicine industry in the *Ladies Home Journal* and *Collier's* by Mark Sullivan and Samuel Hopkins Adams, aided by E. W. Kemble's devastating cartoons, helped pass the 1906 Pure Food and Drug Act. In 1911, muckraking environmentalism focused on the fight over Alaskan lands, and *Collier's* editor Norman Hapgood hired Louis D. Brandeis to represent the Pinchot side at the joint congressional investigation of the Pinchot-Ballinger controversy.

While the muckrakers focused more on the Senate, the Meat Inspection Act struggle, which was prompted by Upton Sinclair's 1906 packinghouse novel, *The Jungle*, was fought in the House of Representatives, and journalists Mark Sullivan and William Hard urged on the effort that curtailed the power of House Speaker Joseph G. Cannon in 1910.

The journalists of exposure relied upon an awakened public to effect necessary reforms. For all the fierceness of their criticism, their proposals for change, even those of the muckraker-socialists, were generally limited and seldom detailed. However, they did influence municipal and state elections, and helped pass legislation for insurance industry reform, for railroad regulation (Hepburn Act), and for the direct election of senators, as well as the Meat Inspection and Pure Food and Drug acts. Although by 1912 many of the writers had turned to other concerns, and most of the magazines had gone out of business or been bought by business interests, the muckraking journalists had helped arouse concern over social conditions and set the political agendas of the Progressive Period.

BIBLIOGRAPHY

Buenker, John, and Edward Kantowicz, eds. *Historical Dictionary of the Progressive Era*. 1988.
Chalmers, David. *The Muckrake Years*. 1974.
Filler, Louis. *Crusaders for American Liberalism*. 1939.
Phillips, David Graham. *The Treason of the Senate*. 1906.
Steffens, Lincoln. *The Autobiography of Lincoln Steffens*. 1937.

DAVID CHALMERS

MUHLENBERG, FREDERICK A. C.

(1750–1801), Revolutionary War patriot, Pennsylvania politician, first Speaker of the U.S. House of Representatives. Frederick Augustus Conrad Muhlenberg, a Pennsylvania-born, German-trained Lutheran minister, became a delegate to the Continental Congress, where he served until 1780. Strongly supported by German constituents, he was elected to the state assembly from Philadelphia and became Speaker of the House. In 1787 he was president of the convention that ratified the Federal Constitution.

Muhlenberg was elected to the First Congress over Anti-Federalist opposition. He was immediately chosen Speaker of the House, defeating Elias Boudinot of New Jersey, and presided until 3 March 1791. A nonpartisan Speaker, he used his influence to choose experienced members for committees.

Usually silent in House debates, Muhlenberg sided with the Federalists on the assumption of state debts and opposed Virginia representative William B. Giles's anti-Hamilton resolutions. But he lost Federalist support for reelection as Speaker in the Second Congress. He resumed the Speakership in 1793 with Republican support, defeating Federalist Theodore Sedgwick; yet in 1795 in the Fourth Congress he lost to Jonathan Dayton. As chair of the Committee of the Whole during the intense Jay's Treaty debate, he broke a tie vote to support appropriations to carry out the treaty. His Republican constituents abandoned him, ending his congressional career in 1797. He allied with Pennsylvania's Republicans in the late 1790s. Even so, just before his death in 1801, Federalists wanted him to oppose Thomas McKean for the governorship. His political career reflected the vacillations of the early local and national party system.

BIBLIOGRAPHY

Brunhouse, Robert L. *The Counter-Revolution in Pennsylvania, 1776–1790.* 1942.

Christman, Margaret C. S. *The First Federal Congress, 1789–1791.* 1989.

Seidensticker, Oswald. "Frederick Augustus Conrad Muhlenberg, Speaker of the House of Representatives, in the First Congress, 1789." *Pennsylvania Magazine of History and Biography* 13 (1889): 184–206.

WINFRED E. A. BERNHARD

MUSKIE, EDMUND S. (1914–), senator from Maine who made his mark as an environmental and budget legislator while aspiring to executive office. Edmund Sixtus Muskie entered the Maine legislature after naval duty in World War II. Projecting himself as a steady centrist, he helped build the Democratic party in that Republican state and was elected governor in 1954, serving four years.

He arrived in the U.S. Senate with the "class of '58" and quickly showed an independent streak that antagonized Majority Leader Lyndon B. Johnson. Muskie wanted to be more than just "a Senate man," his faintly disparaging term for Johnson. Yet the former governor proved an adept legislator in producing from his Senate Public Works subcommittee a series of major bills regulating air and water pollution. His victories owed much to a collegial spirit fostered by the full-committee chairman, Jennings Randolph of West Virginia. Challenges on the Senate floor to antipollution compromises struck at the committee level usually met a stout bipartisan defense from Randolph's members.

By 1973 Muskie's seniority and internal stature had won him the initial chairmanship of the new Senate Budget Committee. His leadership of the committee put it on a firm footing and garnered bipartisan support for its work.

Muskie was Senate floor manager for the 1973 War Powers Resolution enacted over President Richard M. Nixon's veto. However, he continually

EDMUND S. MUSKIE. During a press conference, 18 January 1971.   LIBRARY OF CONGRESS

regarded executive office as a better outlet for his strong foreign policy interests. After running for vice president on the losing Democratic ticket of 1968, Muskie entered the 1972 primaries as the party's presidential front-runner. However, he could not match the appeal of rivals with various protest messages, and he was hurt by widely published pictures of him choking up during a speech in New Hampshire. In 1980 Muskie resigned from the Senate to become secretary of State in President Jimmy Carter's cabinet.

BIBLIOGRAPHY

Muskie, Edmund. *Journeys.* 1972.

ARLEN J. LARGE

MYERS V. UNITED STATES (272 U.S. 52 [1926]). The Supreme Court's opinion in *Myers v.*

United States was a broad articulation of presidential power to control executive officials pursuant to the president's constitutional responsibility to see to the faithful execution of the laws. Writing for the majority, Chief Justice (and former president) William Howard Taft declared that a provision for Senate approval of the removal of postmasters was unconstitutional. The Court viewed Senate participation in the removal of an executive officer as undermining the constitutional obligation of the president to see to the faithful execution of the laws. Accompanying this holding was the proposition that the Constitution demanded recognition of the president's power to remove at will those officers in whose appointment he participated.

Less than a decade later, the Court in *Humphrey's Executor v. United States* (1935) retreated from its position in *Myers*, upholding the removal for cause provision for commissioners of the Federal Communications Commission. The Court now limited the *Myers* rationale to so-called purely executive officers. In *Humphrey's Executor*, the Court saw independent regulatory agencies as performing quasi-legislative or quasi-judicial functions. Therefore, the Court held, their officers could be insulated from at-will presidential removal. The Court revisited the issue in 1988 in *Morrison v. Olson* and dispensed with such categories, adopting instead a functional approach that examined whether removal restrictions interfered with the constitutionally assigned duties of the executive. *Morrison* recognized that there might be a class of purely executive officers whose removal may not be limited by Congress. As a result of both *Morrison* and *Bowsher v. Synar* (1986), *Myers* has been essentially confined to its precise holding: Congress itself may not participate in the removal of officers performing executive functions.

[*See also* Bowsher v. Synar; Morrison v. Olson.]

BIBLIOGRAPHY

Corwin, Edward S. "Tenure of Office and Removal Power under the Constitution." *Columbia Law Review* 27 (1927): 353–399.

Parker, Reginald. "The Removal Power of the President and Independent Agencies." *Indiana Law Journal* 36 (1960): 63–74.

RICHARD EHLKE

N

NARCOTICS ABUSE AND CONTROL COMMITTEE, HOUSE SELECT. Created on 26 July 1976 to conduct a "continuing comprehensive study and review of the problems of narcotics abuse and control," the House Select Committee on Narcotics Abuse and Control was further charged with reviewing any recommendations made by the president or any agency of the executive branch of the federal government relating to narcotic-drug programs or policies. Members were appointed by the Speaker, with at least one member to be chosen from each of the following standing House committees with jurisdiction over some major aspect of the drug issue: Agriculture (added in the 95th Congress), Armed Services, Government Operations, Foreign Affairs, Energy and Commerce, Judiciary, Merchant Marine and Fisheries, Veterans' Affairs (added in the 98th Congress), and Ways and Means. Later resolutions of reconstitution made clear that abused non-narcotic drugs were included within the committee's purview. Original membership consisted of twelve Democrats and six Republicans; in the 102d Congress, the committee consisted of twenty-one Democrats and fourteen Republicans.

The committee's establishment reflected the growing significance of the drug problem during the 1970s. Sponsors argued that it was impossible, given the increasing complexity of the issue, for standing committees to supply adequate oversight. Although provided a narrower mandate, the committee could be viewed as continuing the work of the House Select Committee on Crime, created in 1969 and abolished in 1973.

From its inception through the 102d Congress, the committee was led by only three chairmen, all Democrats from New York City: in the 94th through 96th Congresses by Lester L. Wolff, in the 97th Congress by Leo C. Zeferetti, and in the 98th through 102d Congresses by Charles B. Rangel. Of the two representatives who served as ranking minority members, one represented a surburban New York district and the other a portion of Philadelphia and the surrounding area.

With the exception of President Jimmy Carter, the White House was occupied by Republicans during the committee's lifetime, and much of the group's agenda developed in reaction to administration initiatives and management. However, some Reagan and Bush administration initiatives received its solid support. For the most part, the stance of Select Narcotics was characterized by calls for increases in federal resources devoted to antidrug purposes.

Although without legislative authority, the committee was directed to provide guidance to the appropriate standing committees of the House. While its influence on the development of legislation is difficult to measure, most analysts see it as having been a major factor in keeping drug abuse a priority issue. Furthermore, some qualified observers credit the committee and its chairmen with playing a key role in persuading other governments to cooperate with U.S. antidrug policies.

The committee's continued existence was periodically challenged, principally on the ground that a select committee should be a temporary entity, created for specific purposes and not reauthorized indefinitely. However, it was always reconstituted by a comfortable vote margin until the opening of the

103d Congress when, along with other select committees in the House, it fell victim to a movement for congressional reform and was abolished.

BIBLIOGRAPHY

U.S. Congress. *Congressional Record.* 94th Cong., 2d sess., 29 July 1976. See "Providing for the Establishment of a Select Committee on Narcotic Abuse and Control," vol. 122, pt. 19, pp. 24422–24440. See also floor debates and House Rules Committee reports on committee reconstitution in subsequent Congresses.

U.S. House of Representatives. Committee on House Administration. *Providing for the Expenses of Investigations and Studies to be Conducted by the Select Committee on Narcotics Abuse and Control.* Report to accompany H. Res. 174. 96th Cong., 1st sess., 1979. H. Rept. 96-85. See also similar reports in subsequent Congresses.

U.S. House of Representatives. Select Committee on Narcotics Abuse and Control. *Annual Report for the Year 1977.* 95th Cong., 1st sess., 1978. H. Rept. 95-841. See also subsequent annual reports.

HARRY HOGAN

NARCOTICS AND OTHER DANGEROUS DRUGS.

Prior to the twentieth century, responsibility for public health, including the regulation of drug commerce and medical practice, was for the most part left to the states. Enactment of the Food and Drugs Act of 1906 marked the beginning of a new era of federal activism, however, and efforts aimed specifically at the nonmedical use of narcotics quickly followed. From that time until the 1960s, federal interest lay for the most part in "supply reduction" as opposed to "demand reduction." Since then, involvement in prevention and treatment efforts has grown steadily, as has the funding of new, nonfederal activities. Congress has played a key role in this expansion.

Despite the added dimensions of more recent years, the history of U.S. drug control policy is essentially about the development of restrictions on commerce in and use of narcotics and similar substances that, although they give pleasure and are therefore attractive for recreational use, produce significant dependency. Although criticized from time to time, this basic orientation has not met a serious challenge since it was established. Battles over priorities and funding levels have, however, been a feature of congressional drug control debate since the 1960s.

Before 1914. Drug misuse began to be perceived as a public policy problem in the mid-nineteenth century. A new sophistication about drugs, first in the medical community and then among laypeople, brought about the gradual spread of recreational consumption. Public reaction, gathering strength over a period of some fifty years, was instrumental in securing regulation in a number of states and cities. It also led to the search for a system of international controls to limit the availability of abused drugs, at that time principally opiates. These developments coincided with other humanitarian reform movements of the nineteenth century: for example, the antiwar, temperance, and public health movements.

The first significant federal moves toward drug control other than taxation measures came in the early years of the twentieth century. The Food and Drugs Act, although not focused on abuse and dependency, established federal authority over certain basic aspects of drug commerce. Subsequently, the abuse problem itself was addressed through separate and more restrictive statutes.

Interest at first centered on international control. The pivotal Shanghai Opium Commission, meeting in 1909, was created mostly through U.S. efforts. A fact-finding body, the commission was empowered only to make recommendations, but it led to a larger international conference in 1911 and to the adoption of the Hague Opium Convention, which called on signatories to enact restrictive domestic antinarcotics legislation.

Pressure from the Hague Convention led in the United States to the 1914 enactment of the Harrison Narcotics Act (38 Stat. 785). Such a pattern runs through the history of U.S. drug control: first an international forum in which certain conclusions are reached or resolutions taken, then the application of those conclusions at home, and especially before Congress, in an appeal to national honor or a plea that America set a good example.

1914 to 1960. The form the Harrison Act took was influenced by such interests as the commercial drug trade, the medical profession, and the Bureau of Internal Revenue, which was assigned enforcement responsibility. To avoid constitutional pitfalls, the law was written as a tax measure. Under its provisions, anyone other than the ultimate user who dealt in narcotics was required to be registered. All transactions that involved a controlled drug, except direct administration by a physician, were subject to taxation and order-form requirements.

The Harrison Act was not a law of outright prohibition, but it contained elements that made it possible to achieve virtual prohibition where desired. As in the case of alcohol prohibition, adopted several years later under a constitutional amendment, the act's implementation came to be colored more by a law enforcement than a public health emphasis.

The system of international regulation continued to develop. The Geneva Conferences of 1924 and 1925 resulted in the creation of the Permanent Central Opium Board, shifting the focus of drug control from domestic regulation to international mechanisms. Another major step came in 1961, when previous international concords were consolidated into one governing multilateral treaty, the Single Convention on Narcotic Drugs.

Domestically, the progress of drug control policy during the first fifty years after the Harrison Act was essentially an elaboration of that statute's themes, all viewed as elements in a scheme of worldwide controls. Highlights were passage of the Marihuana Tax Act of 1937, almost a replica of the Harrison Act, and, in the 1950s, a series of substantial penalty increases for drug violations. A special enforcement unit, the Federal Bureau of Narcotics, was created in 1930.

1960 to 1983. In the early 1960s, growing dissatisfaction with drug policy along with an increased interest in mental health issues led to a movement in Congress for greater federal commitment to treatment and rehabilitation of the addict. Later in the decade, the country's drug problem began to take on new dimensions—not only a rapid increase in users and in the number of new drugs available but also, perhaps most significantly, in the age range of the using population. The development of a "drug culture" among young Americans, middle-class suburban as well as inner-city poor, further alarmed the public and energized policymakers.

The operation of two federal addict "farms" established in the 1930s, in Lexington, Kentucky, and Fort Worth, Texas, had been based on the medical research mandate of the Public Health Service. Proponents of a larger federal role argued that those facilities were inadequate to the country's needs three decades later. They sought a network of treatment and rehabilitative services throughout the country so that addicts need not leave their home communities.

Under the Community Mental Health Centers Act of 1963 (P.L. 88-164), "mental illness" was redefined to include narcotic addiction. In 1968, the act was amended to establish a program of grants specifically for the treatment of drug addicts and alcoholics (P.L. 90-574); the program rapidly expanded during the early 1970s. Also during those years, Congress added another facet to drug policy by funding various programs to prevent the initiation of use or to intervene before the development of dependency. In 1981, in a major initiative of the Reagan administration, legislation was passed that replaced many of the categorical grants for treatment and prevention of drug abuse, alcoholism, and mental illness by a single block grant to the states (P.L. 97-35).

The major development in regulatory law after 1960 was the passage in 1970 of the Controlled Substances Act and its companion, the Controlled Substances Import and Export Act (P.L. 91-513, Titles II and III). While these statutes were at first intended only to consolidate the many laws passed since 1909—covering not only narcotics and marijuana but also such "dangerous" drugs as amphetamines and barbiturates—they ended up making major changes in existing penalty structures and strengthening federal regulation of the pharmaceutical industry. In their final form, the two acts contained a number of provisions whose provenance—the executive branch or Congress—is difficult to trace, so complex were the behind-the-scene maneuvers leading to their passage.

Other significant legislative developments of the period included, first, the establishment under the Foreign Assistance Act of an aid program designed to encourage the reduction of overseas drug production and to foster the international control of narcotics generally (P.L. 92-226); and, second, the clarification of the Posse Comitatus Act to permit appropriate assistance by the armed forces in civilian enforcement of drug laws, particularly outside the United States (P.L. 97-86). The first represented a major shift of policy on drug-control efforts overseas, away from relying principally on international treaties and the various efforts of agencies of the United Nations and toward greater emphasis on bilateral arrangements with producer countries. Bringing the armed forces into the antidrug campaign showed Congress's willingness to reverse long-held military policies because of the drug problem's persistence.

Important administrative actions taken during this period (and subsequently provided with statutory backing by Congress) include the establishment of the Special Action Office for Drug Abuse Prevention (1971); the Drug Enforcement Administration in the Justice Department, a merger of five existing agencies (1973); and the Alcohol, Drug Abuse, and Mental Health Administration in the Department of Health, Education, and Welfare (1974). The overall structure of contemporary federal antidrug strategy took shape during the late 1960s and early 1970s. That strategy embraces five

Landmark Enactments and Treaties

TITLE	YEAR ENACTED	REFERENCE NUMBER	DESCRIPTION
Act of 23 February 1887	1887	24 Stat. 409	Prohibited importation of opium into the United States by subjects of the emperor of China and prohibited the trafficking in opium in China by U.S. citizens.
Pure Food and Drugs Act	1906	34 Stat. 768	Prohibited the movement of adulterated foods and drugs in interstate commerce and required accurate labeling.
Opium Exclusion Act	1909	35 Stat. 614	Banned the importation of opium into the United States except for medicinal purposes.
Hague Opium Convention	1912	1 Bevans 855	Drawn up by an international conference called for by the Shanghai Commission in 1909; required signatories to "enact efficacious laws or regulations for the control of production and distribution of raw opium."
Harrison Act	1914	38 Stat. 785	Provided for the licensing and taxation of all individuals or groups producing, importing, manufacturing, selling, or dispensing opium, cocaine, or their derivatives.
Narcotic Drugs Import and Export Act	1922	42 Stat. 596	Strengthened the import and export controls initiated by the Opium Exclusion Act by extending the earlier statute's ban against trade in smoking opium to cover other narcotics (including coca leaves and derivatives), except for those to be used for medical or other legitimate purposes.
Act of 19 January 1929	1929	45 Stat. 1085	Established two "narcotic farms" for the confinement and treatment of persons addicted to narcotic drugs, convicted of federal offenses or voluntarily submitting themselves for treatment.
Act of 14 June 1930	1930	46 Stat. 585	Established the Bureau of Narcotics in the Treasury Department, provided for cooperation with the states in the suppression of narcotics abuse, and directed the surgeon general to conduct research on narcotic drug use.
Marihuana Tax Act	1937	50 Stat. 551	Made marijuana subject to controls substantially similar to those imposed by the Harrison Narcotics Act.
Act of 8 March 1946	1946	60 Stat. 38	Provided for an administrative process for controlling newly discovered synthetic drugs determined to possess habituating qualities similar to those of morphine or cocaine.
Durham-Humphrey Amendment	1951	65 Stat. 648	Made it unlawful to dispense a drug bearing the ℞ legend without a prescription and defined the kinds of drugs for human use that may be dispensed only with the prescription of a "practitioner licensed by law to administer such drugs," including hypnotic or habit-forming drugs.
Boggs Act	1951	66 Stat. 767	Established mandatory minimum penalties for narcotic and marijuana offenses and denied probation or suspended sentence for a second offense.
Narcotics Control Act	1956	70 Stat. 567	Outlawed heroin and further increased penalties for marijuana smuggling and narcotics violations. Singled out the transfer of heroin by adults to minors for especially severe treatment, allowing the death penalty.
Single Convention on Narcotic Drugs	1961	T.I.S. 6298	Consolidated existing treaties relating to narcotics (including coca) and cannabis (marijuana).
Community Mental Health Centers Act	1963	P.L. 88-164	Established a program of construction (and later, staffing) grants for community centers treating mental illness, defined to include narcotic addiction.
Drug Abuse Control Amendments	1965	P.L. 89-74	Amended the Food, Drug, and Cosmetic Act to place special restrictions on depressant and stimulant drugs.

Landmark Enactments and Treaties (Continued)

TITLE	YEAR ENACTED	REFERENCE NUMBER	DESCRIPTION
Narcotic Addict Rehabilitation Act	1966	P.L. 89-793	Provided for possibility of civil commitment, for treatment, of narcotic addicts charged with federal law violations and provided for possible civil commitment to federal treatment centers of addicts not charged with a criminal offense.
Narcotic Addict and Acoholic Treatment Amendments	1968	P.L. 90-574	Amended the Community Mental Health Centers Act to establish programs of specialized grants for treatment of narcotic addiction and alcoholism.
Comprehensive Drug Abuse Prevention and Control Act	1970	P.L. 91-513	Under Titles II and III, the Controlled Substances Act and the Controlled Substances Import and Export Act, consolidated federal controls on narcotics and other dangerous drugs; in general, moderated penalties except for "continuing criminal enterprise" offenders; strengthened regulation of the pharmaceutical industry. Under Title I, extended and expanded treatment efforts and authorized a new program of grants for drug abuse education (to be administered by the National Institute of Mental Health).
Drug Abuse Education Act	1970	P.L. 91-527	Authorized new grant programs for drug abuse education in elementary and secondary schools and for community-oriented education projects (the forerunner of the Drug-Free Schools and Communities Program).
Foreign Assistance Act Amendments	1972	P.L. 92-226	Established an aid program designed to encourage efforts by producer and transiting countries to curb drug production and traffic, providing for cutoff in other assistance to uncooperative countries.
Drug Abuse Office and Treatment Act	1972	P.L. 92-255	Established Special Action Office for Drug Abuse Prevention, headed by the first drug czar; program of grants to states for drug abuse prevention; National Institute on Drug Abuse; National Drug Abuse Training Center; and a council to develop national drug abuse strategy.
Convention on Psychotropic Substances	1972	T.I.S. 9725	Supplemented the Single Convention on Narcotic Drugs by providing for similar restrictions on depressant, stimulant, and hallucinogenic substances not subject to the earlier treaty. Later supported by domestic legislation, the Psychotropic Substances Act of 1977 (P.L. 95-633).
Reorganization Plan No. 2 of 1973	1973	—	Administrative reorganization created the Drug Enforcement Administration in the Justice Department by merging four other agencies with the Bureau of Narcotics and Dangerous Drugs.
International Security Assistance and Arms Export Control Act	1976	P.L. 94-329	Instituted the requirement that the president determine and certify to Congress that a country receiving assistance under the International Narcotics Control program is "significantly reducing the amount of illegal opiates entering the international market." Prohibited participation by any U.S. official in any "direct police arrest action" in a foreign country with respect to narcotics control efforts.
Omnibus Budget Reconciliation Act	1981	P.L. 97-35	Made major changes in the way the federal government provides assistance for a variety of health and social services, including those dealing with treatment and prevention of drug abuse—principally by replacing the existing categorical grants with block grants to the states. Assistance for the prevention and treatment of drug abuse was combined with alcoholism and mental health assistance into a single block grant, but requirements governing allocation were set forth.

Landmark Enactments and Treaties (Continued)

TITLE	YEAR ENACTED	REFERENCE NUMBER	DESCRIPTION
Department of Defense Appropriation Authorizations, Fiscal Year 1982	1982	P.L. 97-86	Amended the Posse Comitatus Act of 1878 to allow the U.S. military to provide specified kinds of drug control support to civilian law enforcement authorities.
Comprehensive Crime Control Act	1984	P.L. 98-473, Title II	Contained many provisions aimed at drug trafficking, featuring preventive detention of certain arrestees, forfeiture of trafficker assets, and trafficking penalty increases, and strengthened procedures to prevent diversion of drugs from legal commerce.
Anti–Drug Abuse Act of 1986	1986	P.L. 99-570	Attacked drug trafficking and abuse at virtually every stage—authorizing expanded enforcement efforts in drug-producing countries, increasing interdiction efforts, strengthening antismuggling provisions, proscribing money laundering, increasing criminal sanctions against drug offenders, establishing the Department of Education's Drug-Free Schools and Communities Program, creating the Office of Substance Abuse Prevention (in ADAMHA), and authorizing large increases in funding for treatment and rehabilitation.
Anti–Drug Abuse Act of 1988	1988	P.L. 100-690	Dealt with new and increased penalties for offenses related to drug trafficking, the creation of new federal offenses and regulatory requirements, changes in criminal procedures, and general increases in funding authorizations for federal drug control; organization and coordination of federal antidrug efforts (providing for creation of a so-called national drug czar); increased treatment and prevention efforts; "user accountability" measures; and efforts to reduce overseas drug production and international trafficking in illicit drugs. Authorized additional appropriations of $2.7 billion for these purposes in fiscal year 1989.
Comprehensive Crime Control Act	1990	P.L. 101-647	Doubled appropriations authorization for drug law enforcement grants to states and localities; expanded regulation of precursor chemicals used in manufacturing illicit drugs; called for additional measures aimed at seizure and forfeiture of drug traffickers' assets; and authorized $220 million in matching grants to states for development of alternatives to criminal incarceration.
Alcohol, Drug Abuse, and Mental Health Administration Reorganization Act	1992	P.L. 102-321	Reconstituted ADAMHA as the Substance Abuse and Mental Health Services Administration (SAMHSA), with the former agency's research functions transferred to the National Institutes of Health. Changed block grant concept so that substance abuse and mental health services were to be funded by separate grants and revised formula whereby funds were to be apportioned among the states.

general areas of activity: regulation and enforcement (including interdiction), treatment, prevention, international control, and research.

After 1983. Beginning in 1984, a new legislative pattern emerged: the enactment every two years of an omnibus, far-ranging bill for the purpose of either drug control specifically or crime control generally. These lengthy measures have added substan-

tially to federal criminal and drug laws as well to the scope and level of federal efforts to effect demand reduction and U.S. participation in international efforts to control the drug trade. The impact of the Comprehensive Crime Control Act of 1984 (P.L. 98-473, Title II), the Anti–Drug Abuse Act of 1986 (P.L. 99-570), the Anti–Drug Abuse Act of 1988 (P.L. 100-690), and the Comprehensive Crime

Control Act of 1990 (P.L. 101-647) may in part be judged by the great increase in federal antidrug spending in subsequent years, especially after the 1986 law. Other significant features include an increased emphasis on financial curbs on trafficking, such as seizure and forfeiture of assets and deterrents to money laundering. Also of note is the inclusion of user accountability measures in the 1986 and 1988 statutes. One provision of the 1988 act particularly exemplifies the frequent triumph of Congress over the executive branch: despite long-standing White House resistance to a concept that would seem to threaten the logic of executive departmental structure, the statute created a separate agency to coordinate all federal drug control efforts, headed by a so-called drug czar.

Among important measures of federal interest in the drug problem are the funding levels for related programs and activities. Since fiscal year 1969, the first year such estimates were compiled, budget authority allocated to all such functions has risen from $82 million to an estimated $12 billion (fiscal year 1994). As of 1994 approximately 65 percent of that total is allocated to supply reduction and 35 percent to demand reduction.

The development of a federal role in efforts to curb nontherapeutic drug use has always been conditioned by current interpretations of the authority of Congress with respect to police and relevant regulatory powers. Changing views on the meaning of the Tenth Amendment and the commerce clause have permitted a great expansion of that role over the past thirty years.

Considering the complex, give-and-take, sometimes sub-rosa nature of the lawmaking process, it is not always possible to separate the roles that the legislative and executive branches have taken in developing any given policy. Nevertheless, it can probably be said that, until the 1960s, federal policy on narcotics and dangerous drugs resulted for the most part from executive rather than congressional initiatives. In the 1960s the legislative branch began to take a more active part. In 1976 a special oversight group was established on the House side, the Select Committee on Narcotics Abuse and Control; though this committee was eliminated by the 103d Congress at the beginning of 1993, as of that year more than seventy-five committees or subcommittees claiming some share of jurisdiction over drug control matters were identified.

[See also Health and Medicine; Narcotics Abuse and Control Committee, House Select; Pure Food and Drugs Act.]

BIBLIOGRAPHY

Morgan, H. Wayne. *Drugs in America: A Social History, 1800–1980.* 1982.
Musto, David F. *The American Disease.* 1973.
Taylor, Arnold H. *American Diplomacy and the Narcotics Traffic, 1900–1939.* 1969.
Terry, Charles E., and Mildred Pellens. *The Opium Problem.* 1925.
U.S. National Commission on Marihuana and Drug Abuse. *Drug Use in America: Problem in Perspective.* 1973. Vol. 3, appendix: "The Legal System and Drug Control."

HARRY L. HOGAN

NATIONAL AERONAUTICS AND SPACE ACT OF 1958

(72 Stat. 426–438). The National Aeronautics and Space Act of 1958 emerged out of the Cold War rivalry of the United States and the Soviet Union for the allegiance of the nonaligned nations of the world. The Soviets gained the upper hand in the competition over space exploration on 4 October 1957, when they launched *Sputnik I,* the first artificial satellite, from the rocket-testing facility in the desert near Tyuratam in the Kazakh Republic. The launch was part of a larger scientific effort associated with the International Geophysical Year.

Many Americans thought this Soviet achievement represented a tremendous coup for the communist system at U.S. expense. The event had a Pearl Harbor–like effect on U.S. public opinion and induced the illusion of a technology gap, thereby providing the impetus for the 1958 Space Act.

During the furor surrounding these events, many people accused the Eisenhower administration of neglecting the American space program. The *Sputnik* crisis reinforced for many people the popular image of President Dwight D. Eisenhower as a smiling incompetent; the Soviet lead in space was widely seen as the fault of a "do-nothing," golf-playing president. G. Mennen Williams, the Democratic governor of Michigan, even released a poem about it:

> Oh little Sputnik, flying high
> With made-in-Moscow beep,
> You tell the world it's a Commie sky
> and Uncle Sam's asleep.
>
> You say on fairway and on rough
> The Kremlin knows it all,
> We hope our golfer knows enough
> To get us on the ball.

More seriously, Sen. Lyndon B. Johnson (D-Tex.) opened hearings by the Senate Armed Services Committee on 25 November 1957 to review the whole spectrum of U.S. defense and space programs. His investigation found serious underfunding and fragmented and diffuse organization in the Department of Defense for the conduct of space activities. One of Johnson's concerns, of course, was that a nation capable of orbiting satellites was also probably capable of developing accurate nuclear missiles. He threw his considerable political skills behind a measure to create an independent government organization to manage the U.S. space program.

Early in 1958 the principal issues concerning a new space agency revolved around whether it should be civilian or military in orientation and organization, whether it should be part of an existing agency or newly created entity, and how aggressively it should pursue space exploration. Congress first considered assigning the space mission to the Department of Defense and then to the Atomic Energy Commission. But in March 1958 President Eisenhower proposed the creation of a civilian agency to handle an expanded space exploration effort; it would be known as the National Aeronautics and Space Administration (NASA) and would be cobbled together from several existing organizations.

The president's staff drafted legislation that set forth a broad mission for the agency to "plan, direct, and conduct aeronautical and space activities"; to involve the nation's scientific community in them; and to disseminate widely information about these efforts. The NASA administrator, to be appointed by the president, would work closely with a "space council" including the vice president and key members of the cabinet. The National Aeronautics and Space Act was passed by Congress and signed into law on 29 July 1958, and NASA began functioning on 1 October of that year.

BIBLIOGRAPHY

Bulkeley, Rip. *The Sputniks Crisis and Early United States Space Policy: A Critique of the Historiography of Space.* 1991.

Divine, Robert A. "Lyndon B. Johnson and the Politics of Space." In *The Johnson Years: Vietnam, the Environment, and Science.* Edited by Robert A. Divine. 1987. Pp. 217–253.

Griffith, Alison. *The National Aeronautics and Space Act: A Study of the Development of Public Policy.* 1962.

Rosholt, Robert L. *An Administrative History of NASA, 1958–1963.* 1966.

ROGER D. LAUNIUS

NATIONAL ANTHEM. Francis Scott Key was inspired to write the words to *The Star-Spangled Banner* after witnessing a sustained shelling of Baltimore's Fort McHenry by British warships on 13 and 14 April 1814. Borrowing the tune of *To Anacreon in Heaven,* an old British drinking song, Key fashioned a stirring composition that soon won popular acceptance as the best musical representation so far of the American patriotic ideal. The army and navy accepted Key's song as the national anthem in 1890, and President Woodrow Wilson likewise designated it by executive order in 1916.

In 1918, at the request of the Maryland Chapter of the National Society of the United States Daughters of 1812, Rep. J. Charles Linthicum (D-Md.) introduced a bill to make the designation official. The proposal languished for twelve years while opposing sides debated the song's merits and Congress probed for a national consensus. Writer Marshall Kernochan argued that the song's exceptional range of an octave and a fifth precluded popular singing and its words were mediocre and hard to impress on the casual reader's memory. Others faulted its warlike and dated language. Several groups, led by the American Legion and the Veterans of Foreign Wars, defended the tune in hearings before the House Judiciary Committee. They pointed out that it had endured as the unofficial anthem for more than a century and had no serious competitor.

Congress formally adopted *The Star-Spangled Banner* as the national anthem in 1931. In so doing, it ignored the Judiciary Committee's recommendation that the words but not the music be adopted. The two houses acted without enthusiasm, reflecting the private view of many lawmakers that, despite heavy lobbying in its behalf, the composition failed key tests of a great national song. President Herbert Hoover signed the legislation (P.L. 71-823) on 3 March 1931.

BIBLIOGRAPHY

Blake, John Henry. *American National Anthem.* 1912.

Kernochan, Marshall. "Our National Anthem." *Outlook* (19 March 1930): 473.

Noble, Hollister. "Many National Anthems of Doubtful Standing." *New York Times,* 9 February 1930, sec. XX, p. 10.

DONALD C. BACON

NATIONAL ARCHIVES. *See* Archives.

NATIONAL BANKING ACT (1863; 12 Stat. 665–682). Believing that a uniform currency was essential to the prosecution of the Civil War and the development of the nation's economy, Secretary of the Treasury Salmon P. Chase urged Congress on 9 December 1861 to pass a law establishing a national banking system. He favored a system based roughly on the New York Free Banking Act of 1837, which mandated government bonds as security for note issues. However, in 1862 Congress, instead of passing the banking bill, authorized an additional $100 million issue of greenbacks—legal tender Treasury notes.

By January 1863, Chase and his allies had won more support outside of Congress for the national banking scheme. On 26 January Republican John Sherman of Ohio introduced the banking bill in the Senate. On 9 February the measure was brought to the floor. After three days of debate, it passed by a vote of 23 to 21. The narrow victory was achieved only through heavy political pressure; several Republican senators who had earlier opposed the bill cast affirmative votes because they viewed it as a Lincoln administration measure (because of Chase's active support and Lincoln's late endorsement), and other Republican opponents failed to vote. On 19 February the House passed the bill 78 to 64.

The act was long and complex, but its intent was relatively simple. Groups of individuals or existing state-chartered banks that met certain capital requirements could obtain charters as national banks. These banks were required to deposit with the treasurer of the United States federal bonds equal in value to not less than one-third of the paid-in capital and would receive in return national bank notes amounting to 90 percent of the market value of such bonds. No more than $300 million in such notes were to be issued. To oversee the system, a commissioner of currency was created.

Perhaps because of the speed with which it was passed or the determination of its supporters to permit no amendments, the measure was reenacted in the summer of 1864. Numerous changes were incorporated into the 1864 act, but there were no substantial modifications to the basic concepts and primary provisions.

Not until 1865 was a 10 percent tax placed on other bank notes, essentially ending note issue by non-national banks and forcing most of them into the national system.

BIBLIOGRAPHY

Curry, Leonard P. *Blueprint for Modern America: Nonmilitary Legislation of the First Civil War Congress.* 1968.

Hammond, Bray. *Sovereignty and an Empty Purse: Banks and Politics in the Civil War.* 1970.

LEONARD P. CURRY

NATIONAL BUDGET AND ACCOUNTING ACT. *See* Budget and Accounting Act.

NATIONAL CEMETERIES, MONUMENTS, AND BATTLEFIELDS. Congress, since the Declaration of Independence, has sought to commemorate on-site battles vital to the nation's establishment and survival, and to honor and provide landscaped and solemn cemeteries for its heroic dead. The concept of battlefield commemoration began on 29 October 1781, when the Continental Congress, upon news of the surrender by Lord Cornwallis of his army at Yorktown ten days before, voted to erect "at York, Virginia, a marble column, adorned with emblems of the alliance between the United States" and France. No money was appropriated and Congress took no further action on this measure until the centennial of the surrender, in 1881, when it appropriated $100,000 to erect the Yorktown column in accordance with the resolution of the Continental Congress. The column is today a centerpiece of Colonial National Historical Park.

Battlefield commemoration achieved its first significant breakthrough in Massachusetts, with the chartering of the Bunker Hill Battle Monument Association in 1823, the construction of the monument, and its dedication on 17 June 1843 by Sen. Daniel Webster. He had also delivered a moving oration in front of thousands at the laying of the cornerstone for the 220-foot obelisk eighteen years before.

During the centennial years of the American Revolution (1875–1883) Congress appropriated Federal moneys to supplement local contributions for Revolutionary War monuments. Beginning with Bennington, Vermont, in 1881, Congress voted moneys ranging from $5,000 to $100,000 to support construction of tributes to Revolutionary War patriots at Saratoga, Newburgh, and Oriskany, New York; Kings Mountain, South Carolina; Monmouth, New Jersey; and Groton, Connecticut.

Revolutionary War commemorations represented by these monuments—shared by the North and the South—helped bind Civil War wounds. In 1875, former Confederate soldiers from South Carolina and Virginia traveled to Boston and together participated in celebrating the centennial of the Battle of

Bunker Hill. This was the first occasion at which men in faded blue and gray publicly fraternized. Since 1864, land had been set aside at Gettysburg, Pennsylvania, and administered by the Gettysburg Battlefield Memorial Association, which was chartered by Pennsylvania to commemorate "the great deeds of valor . . . and the signal events which render these battle-grounds illustrious." But the memorials and lands administered by the association honored only the Union Army of the Potomac and its heroes. In 1889 a committee had been formed by veterans to work for the establishment of a park at Chickamauga, Georgia, to preserve the battlefield and commemorate both armies that had fought there. With such interest and support, Congress went well beyond the measures it had taken to commemorate the Revolutionary War. By 1900 Congress had authorized the nation's first four national military parks—Chickamauga, Georgia, and Chattanooga, Tennessee (1890); Shiloh, Tennessee (1894); Gettysburg, Pennsylvania (1895); and Vicksburg, Mississippi (1899)—and the Antietam National Battlefield Site in Maryland (1890).

Land acquisitions for Gettysburg National Military Park resulted in a Supreme Court decision vital to the expansion of the government's role in the creation of battlefield parks. A local interurban railway company challenged the condemnation of its right-of-way across the battlefield, protesting that preserving and marking battle lines were not public uses justifying the taking of private property. The Supreme Court, on 19 January 1896, determined unanimously that such action was "within the powers granted Congress by the Constitution for the purpose of preserving the whole country."

Congress's 1907 authorization of the Chalmette Monument, which commemorated the War of 1812's Battle of New Orleans, was a step away from the previous decade's focus on the Civil War. Guilford Court House National Military Park, authorized in 1917, contained the first Revolutionary War battlefield preserved by the United States. By 1933, when administration of the national battlefields was transferred from the War Department to the National Park Service, a bureau within the Department of the Interior, Congress had authorized nineteen national battlefields or sites. In 1993 the National Park System included forty-six military parks, battlefields, battlefield sites, memorials, and historical parks commemorating and interpreting on-site battlefields and forts from all of America's wars, from the French and Indian War through World War II, except World War I.

The nation was in its eighth decade before Congress, in 1850, took action toward the establishment of a national cemetery system for members of the armed services who fell in battle or died from other causes when campaigning against the enemy. In that year, Congress appropriated money for the establishment of a cemetery in Mexico City as a final resting place for those who "fell in battle or died in and around the said city." This provided a precedent for creation of permanent military cemeteries outside the United States more than a decade before legislative sanction would be given for a national cemetery system within the country.

It was not until 17 July 1862 that Congress provided a legal mandate for creation of a national cemetery system by authorizing the president "to purchase cemetery ground . . . to be used as a national cemetery for soldiers who have died in the service of the country." This was fifteen months after the beginning of the Civil War, a conflict in which 621,000 would lose their lives. In accordance with the vague interpretation by Congress of the term, twenty-seven burial grounds bore the designation of national cemetery by 31 December 1864. There were seventy-three by 1870, when the consolidation and reinterment program, begun in 1865 with funds appropriated by Congress, was completed. Not included in this number were Soldiers National Cemetery at Gettysburg, the Antietam Cemetery, the post cemetery at West Point, and numerous cemeteries for Confederate soldiers established by the United Daughters of the Confederacy and other patriotic and memorial organizations.

The difficulties encountered in acquisition and development of lands for use as cemeteries, on a scale unforeseen at the beginning of the reburial program, required amplification of the 1862 statute. This led to a congressional initiative, and on 22 February 1867, the president approved an Act to Establish and Protect National Cemeteries, vesting this authority in the secretary of War. The legislation provided a legal basis for a national cemetery system and committed Congress to support the system with public funds.

By 1880, Congress had authorized the War Department to create a national cemetery system, with administrative control vested in the quartermaster general. By executive order in 1933, eleven national cemeteries associated with federal Civil War battlefield parks were transferred to the jurisdiction and care of the National Park Service, Department of the Interior. The War Department, until 1947, and its successor agency, the Department of the Army, from then until 1973, continued to be responsible for administration and maintenance of more than eighty national cemeteries located within the United States. On 18 June 1973, President Richard M. Nixon signed legislation transferring to the Veterans Administration responsibility for administration of eighty-two national cemeteries managed by the Department of the Army. Not included in the transfer were the fourteen national cemeteries then administered by the National Park Service; Army post cemeteries such as West Point; Arlington and Soldiers Home National cemeteries; and the cemeteries located on foreign soil overseen by the American Battle Monuments Commission (ABMC). In the years since becoming the lead agency for management of national cemeteries, the Veterans Administration has overseen the establishment of eleven regional cemeteries to provide honored resting places for additional millions of military veterans, their spouses, and dependent children.

World War I confronted Congress, the War Department, and the nation with the awesome tasks of returning three-fifths of the war dead to the United States, as had been the practice in all U.S. wars or police actions fought on foreign soil since 1848, and planning and preparing suitable burial places for those dead whose next of kin chose for them to remain in Europe. Much of this was accomplished by the American Graves Registration Service (AGRS), a special organization constituted within the army's Quartermaster Corps. The return program culminated with the entombment of the Unknown Soldier at Arlington National Cemetery in 1922. Eight permanent cemeteries were established in Europe. In 1923 Congress enacted legislation creating the independent ABMC. The first chairman was Gen. John J. Pershing, who served until his death in 1948.

World War II led to the death of more than 360,000 U.S. sailors, marines, airmen, and coast-guardsmen. In the postwar years, some 171,000 casketed remains were delivered to next of kin in the United States. Of this total, 37,000 were interred in national cemeteries. In accordance with a Pentagon decision, the responsibility for military cemeteries abroad was kept separate from responsibility for national cemeteries at home. In addition, World War II dead were identified and kept separate from those who had died in World War I. In keeping with this logic, fourteen permanent cemeteries were developed abroad by AGRS and then transferred to ABMC. Like those of World War I, each of these is steeped in association, ranging from St. Laurent, overlooking the Normandy beaches; to Nettuno, recalling bloody Anzio; to Fort McKinley, in the Manila suburbs.

The bodies of American heroes who fell in Korea, Vietnam, the Persian Gulf War, and other actions subsequent to World War II have been returned to the United States for burial in family plots, in national cemeteries, or in the post cemetery at West Point. Since 1979, the Tomb of the Unknown Soldier at Arlington has come to represent unknown servicemen and -women from World War II and the Korean and Vietnam conflicts who have been buried with appropriate ceremonies alongside their comrades from Flanders Field.

[See also Congressional Cemetery.]

BIBLIOGRAPHY

Holt, Dean. *American Military Cemeteries.* 1992.
Lee, Ronald F. *The Origin and Evolution of the National Military Park Idea.* 1973.
Mackintosh, Barry. *The National Parks: Shaping the System.* 1991.
Steere, Edward. *Shrines of the Honored Dead: A Study of the National Cemetery System.* 1960.

EDWIN C. BEARSS

NATIONAL DEFENSE EDUCATION ACT OF 1958 (72 Stat. 1580–1605).

The National Defense Education Act (NDEA) of 1958 (P.L. 58-864) was a response to the Cold War and most immediately to the launching of the Sputnik satellite by the Soviet Union in October 1957. In addition, the early and mid 1950s had witnessed growing criticism of progressive education and the lack of emphasis on academic achievement in the public schools. This criticism by traditional academics, such as the historian Arthur Bestor, had laid the groundwork for the legislation. Nonetheless, congressional advocates of aid to education needed the missile crisis to overcome long-standing opposition to federal involvement in local school districts. Adm. Hyman G. Rickover testified repeatedly about the superiority of Soviet schools, and Dr. Vannevar Bush of M.I.T. urged strong federal aid. Senate Majority Leader Lyndon B. Johnson declared, "We are in a race for survival, and we intend to win that race." Elliot Richardson, assistant secretary of Health, Education, and Welfare, and Alabama representative Carl A. Elliott of the House Education and Labor Committee were the key figures in a series of negotiations and compromises on issues of general aid for school construction (which was deleted), aid to religious schools (which was included, though limited), and desegregation (which was left vague by the administration).

NDEA followed the precedent of the Smith-Hughes Act for vocational education (1917) in providing categorical aid. It provided loans and fellowships for college and graduate students, with a preference for those in math, science, and modern languages. It offered grants to elementary and secondary schools to improve instruction in those subjects, as well as testing and counseling services to identify talented students and guide them in desired directions. NDEA also supported area studies at universities through the creation of centers and language institutes. In addition, it supported research and development on the use of media in education, improvements in highly technical vocational education, the enhancement of communication among scientists, and the upgrading of state education agencies. In August 1958 the Senate passed the bill by 65 to 15, and the House voted in favor, 212 to 85. President Dwight D. Eisenhower signed the NDEA on 2 September. Various provisions of NDEA were reenacted in subsequent Congresses without major changes of purpose until the Elementary and Secondary Education Act of 1965, which shifted the primary federal concern in elementary and secondary education from issues of technical excellence and international competition to issues of poverty, discrimination, and equality.

BIBLIOGRAPHY

Clowse, Barbara Barksdale. *Brainpower for the Cold War: The Sputnik Crisis and the National Defense Education Act of 1958.* 1981.
Sufrin, Sidney C. *Administering the National Defense Education Act.* 1963.

CARL F. KAESTLE

NATIONAL ECONOMIC COMMITTEE, TEMPORARY. *See* Temporary National Economic Committee (TNEC).

NATIONAL ENDOWMENT FOR THE ARTS. *See* National Foundation on the Arts and the Humanities Act of 1965.

NATIONAL ENDOWMENT FOR THE HUMANITIES. *See* National Foundation on the Arts and the Humanities Act of 1965.

NATIONAL ENVIRONMENTAL POLICY ACT OF 1969 (83 Stat. 852–856). Congress passed the National Environmental Policy Act (NEPA), one of the first environmental protection statutes, late in 1969. The act, a harbinger of what is often called the "environmental decade," was signed into law by President Richard M. Nixon on New Year's Day, 1970. NEPA quickly became controversial when the federal courts used it to halt a number of federal projects.

NEPA declares that it is the U.S. government's policy "to use all practical means" to "create and maintain conditions under which man and nature can exist in productive harmony." It created a cabinet-level Council on Environmental Quality (CEQ) to collect information on the environment, to advise the president, and to help coordinate environmental policy. Most important, NEPA requires federal agencies to complete a detailed environmental impact statement (EIS) before taking any major action "significantly affecting the quality of the human environment." This section of the law also requires agencies to consider alternatives that do less harm to the environment.

The law does not specify who shall interpret and enforce the EIS requirement. Although the CEQ has issued guidelines on preparation of impact statements, it is the federal judiciary that has given teeth to the act. The courts opened their doors to hundreds of suits brought by environmental groups and abutters seeking to block action by such prodevelopment agencies as the U.S. Army Corps of Engineers, the Federal Highway Administration, the Atomic Energy Commission, the Department of Housing and Urban Development, the Tennessee Valley Authority, and the Department of the Interior. Between 1970 and 1980 federal agencies filed more than ten thousand full environmental impact statements. Nearly two thousand of these were scrutinized by the courts.

The courts have declared that NEPA is an "environmental full disclosure law." The EIS process should not only bring to light as much information about the environment as possible but should also provide the various interested groups with the opportunity to make their views known and should ensure that the agency places adequate weight on environmental values.

While individual members of Congress were often angered when judges enjoined projects within their districts, Congress as a whole has made few changes in the law. It exempted the Alaskan pipeline from the law but rebuffed efforts to exempt the Atomic Energy Commission. Gradually, federal agencies learned how to write impact statements that were acceptable to the courts.

The impact of NEPA on agency decision making is a matter of some dispute. According to one school of thought, agencies simply learned to jump through all the procedural hoops without making significant changes in their ultimate decisions. According to a second view, however, the act and judicial interpretation of it have given project opponents a potent weapon for delaying government action, thus intensifying what is often called the NIMBY ("not-in-my-back-yard") syndrome. A third view is that by bringing new "environmental impact" specialists into the federal bureaucracy NEPA has had a significant and beneficial effect on agencies, promoting a more integrative and long-range approach to policy-making.

[See also Clean Air Act; Endangered Species Act of 1973.]

BIBLIOGRAPHY

Anderson, Frederick. NEPA in the Courts. 1973.
Taylor, Serge. Making Bureaucracies Think: The Environmental Impact Statement Strategy for Administrative Reform. 1984.

R. SHEP MELNICK

NATIONAL FLORAL EMBLEM.

Efforts to designate a national flower span nearly a century of U.S. history. A formal movement to achieve this goal began at an 1889 floral convention in Athens, Georgia. It reached fruition on 7 October 1986, when President Ronald Reagan signed Public Law 99-449 designating the rose as the national floral emblem of the United States.

Congress first considered the idea in December 1892, when Rep. Walter H. Butler of Iowa recommended the pansy. By far the most popular choices of the 134 congressional proposals subsequently offered were the rose, which prompted more than one-third of the bills, and the American marigold, which accounted for approximately 17 percent. Other recurring selections included the carnation, corn tassel, laurel, and Luther Burbank shasta daisy. More than three-quarters of the bills were introduced between 1955 and 1986.

Congress held hearings on the question in 1917, 1958, 1964, and 1986. Several million Americans also had the opportunity to participate in the debate through public opinion polls, in all of which they favored the rose by a wide margin. Popular publications such as Arena, Household, the Independent, the Journal of Education, Life, Nature Magazine, the New Republic, the New York Times, Parade, and Science News Letter also contributed to the discussion.

The 1960s speeches of Sen. Everett M. Dirksen of Illinois on the yellow marigold became part of the folklore of the U.S. Senate. However, after "decades of sniffing marigolds," as Congressional Quarterly quipped, the Senate on 15 September 1985 decided to make the rose the official flower of the United States. The House followed suit on 23 September 1986.

BIBLIOGRAPHY

U.S. House of Representatives. Post Office and Civil Service Committee. Subcommittee on Census and Population. Designation of a National Floral Emblem. 99th Cong., 2d sess., 1986. Hearing Serial No. 99-63.

STEPHEN W. STATHIS

NATIONAL FOUNDATION ON THE ARTS AND THE HUMANITIES ACT OF 1965

(79 Stat. 845–855). On 29 September 1965, President Lyndon B. Johnson signed the National Foundation on the Arts and the Humanities Act (P.L. 89 209). Under the original terms of the act, the National Foundation on the Arts and the Humanities (NFAH) was composed of two independent grant-making agencies—the National Endowment for the Arts (NEA) and the National Endowment for the Humanities (NEH). The act also provided for the Federal Council on the Arts and Humanities to facilitate coordination between the foundation's operating agencies as well as between the foundation and other federal programs affecting the arts and humanities. In 1976, Congress established an independent Institute for Museum Services (IMS), which was brought under the statutory umbrella of the NFAH in 1984.

Four main developments influenced the passage of the NFAH Act. First, a few key legislators, including Senators Claiborne Pell (D-R.I.) and Jacob K. Javits (R-N.Y.) and Rep. Frank Thompson, Jr. (D-N.J.), had cultivated congressional support of the arts for over a decade. Second, August Heckscher, special consultant on the arts to President John F. Kennedy, issued a report in 1963 that provided a philosophical basis and offered practical recommendations for federal support of the arts. Third, a National Advisory Council on the Arts was established in June 1963 by executive order of President Kennedy. Fourth, the efforts of arts advocates coincided and combined with those of the humanities community, which included a 1964 report of the National Commission on the Humanities, chaired by Barnaby Kenney, urging the establishment of a national humanities foundation. All these efforts came together in the NFAH Act, a component of Johnson's Great Society education initiatives.

The act constructed the arts and humanities endowments similarly, outlining two major structural components for each: a chairman and a national council.

The chairman of each endowment is appointed for a four-year renewable term by the president, with Senate confirmation. The chairmen approve all grants, establish agency procedures and policy, serve as national spokespersons for the arts and the humanities, and chair the councils of their respective endowments.

The councils each consist of twenty-six members appointed by the president and confirmed by the Senate. The members serve six-year terms that are staggered. Council members are private citizens widely recognized for their broad knowledge or expertise. Collectively, they provide comprehensive representation of the arts and the humanities. The councils review grant applications and advise each chairman on policy issues. Although they are similarly structured, the NEH has fewer legislatively specified guidelines and requirements than the NEA.

The IMS is headed by a director and a fifteen-member National Museum Services Board appointed by the president and confirmed by the Senate. IMS administers grant programs to aid museums in three general areas: general operating support, conservation projects support, and museum assessment. The Museum Assessment Programs (MAP) are administered by the American Association of Museums and provide museums with management tools to evaluate their institutional operations and collections management, and the public's perceptions of and involvement with the museums.

Congress sets general policy guidelines and projected funding levels during periodic reauthorizations of the foundation and its component operating agencies. Initially, the foundation had a biennial authorization cycle that gradually lengthened until it became a five-year schedule in 1985, an indication of growing congressional support for the endowments. The return to a triennial schedule in 1990 reflected a period of prolonged controversy surrounding the NEA that affected the NEH and IMS as well.

The 1990 reauthorization of the foundation was marked by heated controversy over the purposes, procedures, and standards of federal funding for the arts and the operations of the NEA. The debate expanded to encompass discussions about allegedly obscene, pornographic, and offensive artwork as well as charges of censorship, homophobia, and unaccountability. Indeed, reauthorization of the NEA was seriously jeopardized by the controversy. Congressional supporters of the NEA were the targets of negative campaign tactics. In 1990, twenty-one House Democrats who voted in support of the NEA found that the National Republic Congressional Committee had sent press releases to their home districts accusing them of supporting "sexually explicit and anti-religious works of art that are offensive to millions of Americans." During the congressional elections of 1992, NEA supporters such as Sen. Dale Bumpers (D-Ark.) confronted criticism from conservative religious groups, while Rep. Pat Williams (D-Mont.) was attacked as "Porno Pat" by his opponent in a close election for a redistricted seat.

Only a hard-won compromise secured reauthorization and resulted in significant changes in the terms of the NFAH Act in 1990. One change that affected all three component agencies (NEA, NEH, and IMS) was a shortened reauthorization term of three years, meaning that the NFAH was due for renewal again in 1993. A de facto two-year extension moved full reauthorization hearings to 1995.

Congress also outlined a number of new conditions for the NEA. In an effort to make the NEA more accountable for its grants, Congress added a requirement for interim and final reports from all grant recipients. The NEA chairman was also given more explicit control over grants awards decisions, even though he or she cannot approve applications rejected by the council. In addition, new reauthorization language required the NEA chair to take "into consideration general standards of decency" when awarding grants. On 9 June 1992, the U.S. District Court for the Central District of California ruled that this provision was unconstitutionally vague. Although in June of 1993 the NEA agreed to pay the artistic plaintiffs an out-of-court settlement of $252,000, the Clinton administration's Justice Department filed an appeal against the district court's ruling regarding the decency clause.

Congress also stipulated that grant review panels should be more diverse with regard to artistic, geographic, ethnic, and minority representation; that panel members must not have a conflict of interest; and that no panel member serve for more that three consecutive years. It also stipulated that all panels include a knowledgeable "layperson"—someone neither engaged in the arts as a professional nor a member of either artists' or arts organizations.

Congress also redistributed the allocation of NEA funds. Under the new legislation, 50 percent of all funds exceeding $175 million were earmarked for arts education. Additionally, between 1991 and 1993, the proportion of endowment program funds allocated directly to state art agencies was increased from 20 percent to 35 percent.

BIBLIOGRAPHY

Bolton, Richard, ed. *Culture Wars: Documents from the Recent Controversies in the Arts.* 1992.

Miller, Stephen. *Excellence and Equity: The National Endowment for the Humanities.* 1984.

Mulcahy, Kevin V., and Margaret Jane Wyszomirski, eds. *America's Commitment to Culture: Public Policy and the Arts.* 1994.

MARGARET JANE WYSZOMIRSKI

NATIONAL HOLIDAYS. *See* Federal Holidays.

NATIONAL HOUSING ACTS. *See* Federal Housing Acts.

NATIONAL INDUSTRIAL RECOVERY ACT (1933; 48 Stat. 195–211).

Congress enacted the National Industrial Recovery Act (NIRA) in June 1933, during the depth of the Great Depression, as the keystone of the First New Deal. The act created the National Recovery Administration (NRA) to work with the nation's industries in drafting codes, exempt from antitrust prosecution, to regulate competitive practices and hours and wages. It also guaranteed, in section 7(a), labor's right to collective bargaining. Finally, it provided for $3.3 billion in public works spending to be administered by a Public Works Administration (PWA).

To a great extent, the NIRA was a response to demands long made by many businessmen for liberalization of the antitrust laws. During the Depression, business leaders such as Gerard Swope of General Electric had popularized the concept of combining antitrust liberalization with labor benefits to achieve recovery. Other recovery ideas, how-

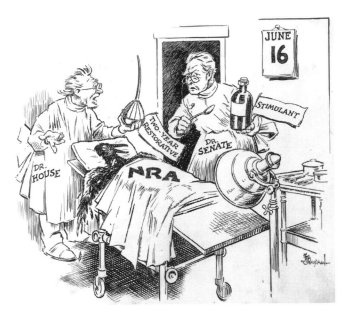

THE SICK BIRD. A comment on Congress's efforts to extend parts of the National Industrial Recovery Act prior to 16 June 1935, the date the act was due to expire. The ailing bird represents the much criticized National Recovery Administration. Even as Congress debated whether to extend the NIRA, the Supreme Court, on 27 May 1935, issued its landmark decision invalidating the statute. Jim Berryman, *Washington Evening Star.*

U.S. SENATE COLLECTION, CENTER FOR LEGISLATIVE ARCHIVES

ever, competed with these business proposals. A group of key liberal senators, led by Robert F. Wagner of New York, pressed for huge "pump-priming" public works expenditures. A measure proposed by Sen. Hugo L. Black of Alabama and backed by the American Federation of Labor limiting the workweek to thirty hours appeared likely to be enacted. President Franklin D. Roosevelt, wishing to initiate an effective recovery plan but anxious to avoid excessive spending or radical limitation of the workweek, instructed several of his key advisers to create a workable measure.

The recovery act was a compromise that appeared to concede as much to labor as to business. There is general agreement, however, that because business was better organized and its viewpoint favored by the NRA's administrators, the codes better served the interests of business than of labor. Roosevelt appointed Hugh Johnson, a partisan of the concept of business self-government, to head the NRA. Johnson worked with immense energy during the summer of 1933 to bring every industry immediately under an emergency code providing for increased wages, believing that this would initiate recovery. Employers who signed were eligible to

NATIONAL RECOVERY ADMINISTRATION (NRA) MARCH-ING SONGS. In 1933 and 1934 parades took place in various U.S. cities to encourage participation in the NRA program. COLLECTION OF DAVID J. AND JANICE L. FRENT

display the Blue Eagle, the symbol of compliance with NRA codes. Within a few months, Johnson succeeded in completing individualized codes with nearly all the major industries.

Though initially acclaimed, the NRA soon began to founder. Critics, including influential senators, denounced the codes, claiming that they fostered price-fixing. In mid 1934, Roosevelt replaced Johnson with a three-person board that tried to reform the codes. However, not wishing to alienate business support and uncertain about its legal powers, the board made little progress. Before Congress decided whether to renew the NRA's charter, perhaps in amended form, the agency's history abruptly ended in May 1935, when the Supreme Court ruled, in *Schechter Poultry Corp. v. United States*, that the NIRA was unconstitutional because it excessively delegated legislative authority to the president.

Most commentators believe that the NRA experience was unfortunate because it tended to raise prices and limit production rather than promote economic expansion and recovery. However, the act did introduce certain reforms, such as federal protection of collective bargaining, which though not effectively enforced by the NRA, were fulfilled later in the New Deal era.

BIBLIOGRAPHY

Bellush, Bernard. *The Failure of the NRA.* 1975.
Hawley, Ellis W. *The New Deal and the Problem of Monopoly.* 1966.
Himmelberg, Robert F. *The Origins of the National Recovery Administration.* 1976.

ROBERT F. HIMMELBERG

NATIONALISM. *See* History of Congress, *article on* Sectionalism and Nationalism.

NATIONAL LABOR RELATIONS ACT (1935). *See* Wagner-Connery National Labor Relations Act.

NATIONAL LABOR RELATIONS ACT (1947). *See* Taft-Hartley Labor-Management Relations Act.

NATIONAL PARKS AND FORESTS. According to the Constitution, "Congress shall have the Power to dispose of and make all needful Rules and Regulations respecting the Territory or other Property belonging to the United States" (Article IV, section 3). Arguably the most important public-land decisions Congress has made concern the federal government's retention, use, and protection of some public lands as national parks and national forests. Today, the system of national parks and forests, which has resulted from more than a century of decision making by Congress and the executive branch, provides diverse benefits and opportunities to the people of the United States. In an ongoing, dynamic process, the executive and legislative branches have, by turns, played the roles of defender and developer of these lands.

The first national park, Yellowstone, was authorized by Congress in 1872 after a government-funded expedition reported on the area's great natural wonders and recommended that it be set aside as a public preserve. The Yellowstone legislation set a dual, seemingly contradictory, mandate: it required not only that Yellowstone's resources be preserved substantially unchanged for future generations, but also that Yellowstone serve as a public recreation area. This dual mandate has framed the debate on the establishment and use of national parkland ever since.

All the national parks established after Yellowstone—including Yosemite, Sequoia, Mount Rainier, and Crater Lake—were designated to preserve various outstanding natural or scenic resources on federally owned lands. But the first federal dollars actually spent to acquire land for parks went to the army. During the 1890s Congress authorized the secretary of the Army to purchase a number of major Civil War battlefields (including those at Vicksburg, Mississippi, and Gettysburg, Pennsylvania) for preservation and use as military training grounds. These were variously designated as national parks or battlefield parks. The authorizing legislation contained provisions, such as purchase and leaseback of lands, that remained innovative as late as the 1980s.

Public and congressional concern over the loss or damage of archaeological and cultural resources on public lands led to passage of the Antiquities Act of 1906. This act ended mining on some public lands that were designated as national monuments. More important, the act allowed the president as well as Congress to make such designations.

Until 1916 each park or monument was administered independently, sometimes by a civilian superintendent appointed by the secretary of the Interior and with protection provided by army cavalry or engineer units. Then Congress authorized the establishment of the National Park Service within the Department of the Interior to provide central management and guidance for a national park system and the training of professional park managers.

Congress gave the Park Service new responsibilities with the Historic Sites and Buildings Act of 1935 and the Park, Parkway, and Recreation Area Study Act of 1936. President Franklin D. Roosevelt also increased the Park Service's responsibilities by placing all the army's military and battlefield parks under its management in 1933.

Most of the national forests were created from the public domain; Congress transferred ownership of the forests from the Department of the Interior to the Agriculture Department in 1905. The first step came in 1891, when Congress authorized the president to set aside as forest reserves any part of the public lands, whether the forest cover was of commercial quality or not. Congress enacted more restrictive criteria for such reservations in 1897,

limiting new establishments. By 1907, Congress reacted to the continuing extensive establishment of forest reserves by President Theodore Roosevelt by requiring that, thereafter, the establishment or expansion of national forests occur only through an act of Congress.

National forests came east in 1911, despite the absence of public lands in the eastern United States. That year, the Weeks Act authorized the secretary of Agriculture to purchase lands at the headwaters of navigable streams to ensure the rivers' continued navigability.

To emphasize the fact that national forests are meant to play many roles, Congress enacted the Multiple Use Sustained Yield Act in 1960. This legislation notes that national forests are established and are to be administered for "outdoor recreation, range, timber, watershed, and wildlife and fish purposes." During the 1970s, Congress enacted additional legislation to ensure adequate planning and management of the national forests to meet these manifold purposes.

The outdoor-recreation opportunities offered by the national parks and forests were enhanced by the 1962 enactment of the recommendations made by the Outdoor Recreation Resources Review Commission. Under these laws, national recreation areas, wild and scenic rivers, and national trails are administered by the Park Service and the Forest Service. Congress continues to ensure preservation of extensive areas on federally owned lands by authorizing new wilderness areas.

In the late twentieth century, controversy touched many legislative proposals affecting the national parks and forests. Property rights groups opposed the establishment and acquisition of many new park or recreation areas because, they argued, federal acquisition of land often violated constitutional safeguards against the taking of property. Environmental groups fought logging operations in national forests in the Northwest because of loss of habitat for endangered species.

While congressional action on natural-resource issues has often been controversial, the problems had changed setting; public lands no longer seemed vast enough to accommodate all the uses proposed for them. The generally opposing views of the legislative and executive branches, especially during the Reagan and Bush administrations, on many issues of resource use versus protection made consensus elusive.

Private-sector environmental and preservation groups have had strong and effective advocates

Landmark Legislation concerning National Parks and Forests

TITLE	YEAR ENACTED	REFERENCE NUMBER	DESCRIPTION
Yellowstone National Park Act	1872	17 Stat. 32	Authorized the first national park.
Preservation of American Antiquities Act	1906	34 Stat. 225	Allowed congressional or presidential withdrawals of public lands from mining use to protect ancient cultural resources.
National Park Service Organic Act	1916	39 Stat. 535	Established an agency to manage national parks and monuments.
Chickamauga and Chattanooga National Military Park Act	1890	26 Stat. 333	Authorized first military park, to be acquired and administered by the secretary of War.
Forest Reserve Act	1891	26 Stat. 1103	Authorized the president to reserve lands from the public domain, retaining them for federal ownership.
Weeks Act	1911	36 Stat. 961	Authorized the Agriculture secretary to acquire lands at the headwaters of navigable streams; brought national forests to the East.
Multiple Use Sustained Yield Act	1960	P.L. 86-517	Provided legislative authority for the Forest Service to manage national forests for a variety of purposes and benefits.
Wilderness Act	1964	P.L. 88-577	Designated 9 million acres of national forests as wilderness and set process for further review and possible congressional designation of forest and national parklands.

within the Congress. An interesting development in the 1980s and 1990s was the clustering of private groups with opposing views: commodity user groups, property rights advocates, and the "wise use" school of resource management forged a common position and sought broader public support. This coalition was analogous to that formed by various conservation and environmental groups in the late 1960s, which effectively garnered both public and governmental support, particularly in Congress. The question was whether congressional consensus on park and forest issues would begin to change, moving strongly in favor of economic over environmental concerns in the years to come.

[*See also* National Cemeteries, Monuments, and Battlefields; Public Lands.]

BIBLIOGRAPHY

Clawson, Marion, and Burnell Held. *The Federal Lands.* 1957.

Ise, John. *Our National Park Policy: A Critical History.* 1961.

U.S. Senate. *History of the Committee on Energy and Natural Resources, United States Senate.* 100th Cong., 2d sess., 1989. S. Doc. 100-46.

GEORGE H. SIEHL

NATIONAL PROHIBITION ACT (1919; 41 Stat. 305–323). Ratification of the Eighteenth Amendment in January 1919 compelled Congress to devise plans for the nationwide enforcement of the new constitutional prohibition of "the manufacture, sale, or transportation of intoxicating liquors . . . for beverage purposes." Impressed by the strength of prohibitionist sentiment reflected in the 1914 and 1916 congressional elections and the quick, widespread approval of the new amendment by state legislatures, a bipartisan majority in each house readily accepted the enforcement bill drafted by Anti-Saloon League general counsel Wayne B. Wheeler and submitted by Rep. Andrew J. Volstead (R-Minn.). The bill established stiff penalties for the manufacture or sale of intoxicants but did not make their purchase or use a crime. It created a federal enforcement bureau of about 1,500 agents but left the main policing burden to state and local officials. Of critical importance, the bill defined intoxicating beverages as any that contained more than 0.5 percent alcohol (thus banning beer and wine as well as distilled liquors, an unexpectedly severe step that went beyond most earlier state prohibition laws). President Woodrow Wilson, who disagreed with various provisions and believed that the public would more easily give up distilled liquor if beer continued to be permitted, vetoed the bill. Congress overrode the veto by a House vote of 176 to 5 and a Senate vote of 65 to 20 on 27 October 1919. Modified by stricter penalties in 1929 after more than 500,000 arrests had failed to discourage its violation, the National Prohibition Act, also known as the Volstead Act, remained the basic prohibition enforcement law until the repeal of the Eighteenth Amendment on 5 December 1933.

BIBLIOGRAPHY

Blocker, Jack S., Jr. *American Temperance Movements: Cycles of Reform.* 1989.
Kerr, K. Austin. *Organized for Prohibition: A New History of the Anti-Saloon League.* 1985.

DAVID E. KYVIG

NATIONAL SECURITY ACT (1947; 61 Stat. 495–510). The blueprint for the modern U.S. defense establishment is the National Security Act of 1947 (P.L. 80-253). Attempting to apply the lessons of World War II to the circumstances of the early Cold War, the act incorporated hard-fought compromises within both the executive and legislative branches.

The act established numerous enduring institutions, among them the National Security Council (NSC), the Central Intelligence Agency (CIA), the secretary of Defense, and the Joint Chiefs of Staff (JCS). As conceived in the legislation, these offices

and organizations reflected a complex set of policy and political balances. Striving to achieve overall "integration of domestic, foreign, and military policies relating to the national security," Congress directed that the NSC be chaired by the president and include the secretaries of State, Defense, and the military services. To assure civilian control of what it designated as the National Military Establishment, the act gave the secretary of Defense "general direction, authority, and control" over the several military services, but it severely limited the staff resources available to perform those tasks. To perpetuate intelligence functions that the United States had largely neglected until wartime, the act charged the CIA with supporting the NSC with evaluations and coordination of the several agencies conducting intelligence activities; the Director of Central Intelligence (DCI) was vested with exceptional powers to fire employees at his discretion and with the responsibility "for protecting intelligence sources and methods from unauthorized disclosure."

In creating a separate Department of the Air Force, the law preserved and strengthened the traditional role of service secretaries, not only by assigning them slots in the NSC but by authorizing them to deal directly with the president and the budget director. Indeed, in language reminiscent of the Tenth Amendment to the Constitution, the act reserved to the service secretaries "all powers and duties . . . not specifically conferred upon the Secretary of Defense."

Bureaucratic logrolling among the services and their congressional patrons tempered the impulse to centralize; the JCS was to be a relatively weak committee, with a staff limited to one hundred officers drawn from the services and a director "junior in grade to all members of the Joint Chiefs of Staff." Although the JCS's duties included creating "unified commands in strategic areas" where needed, the act paid clear deference to the separate military services and resisted any notion of merger. The Joint Chiefs were to retain dominance in planning, equipping, training, and commanding military forces. The act implicitly relied on interservice rivalry to counter any tendencies toward formation of the kind of military general staff that Americans viewed as dangerous to liberty.

The act addressed most of the central requirements of national security architecture, but its provisions underwent repeated revision, beginning with the 1949 amendments that set up the Department of Defense, removed the service secretaries from the NSC, and began to expand the size of the JCS staff. Some of the agencies created by the act—the National Security Resources Board, the War Council, the Munitions Board—would fade from view. Others, notably the JCS, would gain stature, as through the 1986 Goldwater-Nichols Act (P.L. 99-433), which strengthened the powers of the JCS chairman, added a statutory vice chairman, and obliged officers to gain experience in joint commands to qualify for senior promotions. What was not anticipated was that the director of the NSC staff, a presidential assistant for national security affairs not subject to Senate confirmation, would emerge as a power comparable to the statutory offices specified by the law.

BIBLIOGRAPHY

Clifford, Clark, with Richard Holbrooke. *Counsel to the President.* 1991.
Patterson, Bradley H., Jr. *The Ring of Power.* 1988.

ALTON FRYE

NATIVE AMERICANS. *See* Indian Policy.

NATURALIZATION ACT. *See* Alien and Sedition Acts.

NATURAL RESOURCES COMMITTEE, HOUSE. In 1803, the purchase by the United States of the Louisiana Territory doubled the size of the new nation overnight and brought with it new and expansive responsibilities. As a consequence, in January 1805, a proposal was offered in the House of Representatives to establish a Committee on Public Lands. Later that year, on 17 December, Rep. William Findley of Pennsylvania moved to establish a "committee respecting the lands of the United States" as a new standing committee of the House. The House agreed, and the Public Lands Committee was created.

A number of closely related committees were created during the nineteenth century to reflect the increasingly complex issues facing the nation: the Committee on Private Lands Claims on 16 April 1816; the Committee on Indian Affairs, 17 December 1821; the Committee on Territories, 13 December 1825; the Committee on Mines and Mining, 19 December 1865; the Committee on Irrigation of Arid Lands, 18 December 1883; and the Committee on Insular Affairs, 5 December 1899.

The jurisdictions of these committees generally remained unchanged (although the name of the Irrigation of Arid Lands Committee was changed in 1924 to the Irrigation and Reclamation Committee) until World War II, which served as the impetus to reorganize the committees of Congress to help it function more effectively. As a result of these efforts, the Legislative Reorganization Act of 1946 consolidated the jurisdictions of the Committees on Indian Affairs, Territories, Mines and Mining, and Irrigation and Reclamation into a newly established Committee on Public Lands. This committee also acquired jurisdiction over military parks and battlefields and national cemeteries, which formerly had been assigned to other House committees.

The broad new jurisdiction of the Public Lands Committee was formally incorporated into the Rules of the House with the beginning of the 80th Congress in 1947. The committee's name was changed in 1951 to the Committee on Interior and Insular Affairs to reflect the growing importance of legislation affecting overseas U.S. territories in the work of the committee.

The jurisdiction of the Interior Committee comprised these subjects as enumerated in Rule X:

(1) Forest reserves and national parks created from the public domain; (2) Forfeiture of land grants and alien ownership, including alien ownership of mineral lands; (3) the U.S. Geological Survey; (4) Interstate compacts relating to the apportionment of waters for irrigation purposes; (5) irrigation and reclamation, including water supply for reclamation projects, and easements of public lands for irrigation projects, and acquisition of private lands when necessary to complete irrigation projects; (6) Measures relating to the care, education, and management of Indians, including the care and allotment of Indian lands and general and special measures relating to claims which are paid out of Indian funds; (7) Measures relating generally to Hawaii, Alaska, and the insular possessions of the United States, except those affecting revenue and appropriations; (8) Military parks and battlefields, and national cemeteries; (9) Mineral land laws and claims and entries thereunder; (10) Mineral resources of the public lands; (11) Mining interests generally; (12) Mining schools and experiment stations; (14) Petroleum conservation on the public lands and conservation of the radium supply in the United States; (14) Preservation of prehistoric ruins and objects of interest on the public domain; (15) Public lands generally, including entry, easements, and grazing thereon; (16) Relations of the United States with the Indians and Indian tribes.

The jurisdiction of the Interior and Insular Affairs Committee was formally changed or clarified three times between 1974 and 1980, as part of a series of reorganization studies undertaken by Congress. In 1974, the Select Committee on Committees, chaired by Rep. Richard W. Bolling of Missouri, proposed a sweeping modification of House committee jurisdictions that would have made a revised Interior Committee one of the key environmental committees in the House. However, the House on 8 October 1974 adopted a less radical alternative developed by a Democratic caucus panel chaired by Rep. Julia Butler Hansen of Washington.

As a result of this reorganization, the Interior and Insular Affairs Committee assumed jurisdiction over parks in the District of Columbia, and it received new oversight jurisdiction over nonmilitary nuclear energy and nuclear research and development (including nuclear waste disposal). At the same time, the Committee's shared jurisdiction over energy and environmental research and development was transferred to the exclusive legislative authority of the Science and Technology Committee (now the Committee on Science, Space, and Technology). In addition, the Interior Committee's jurisdiction over population, demography, and Indian education programs was transferred to other House committees.

All House committees were, under the Hansen proposal, directed to "review and study on a continuing basis, the application, administration, execution, and effectiveness of the laws . . . the subject matter of which is within each committee's jurisdiction." The committees were additionally directed to review "the organization and operation of the Federal agencies and entities having responsibilities . . . for the administration and execution of those laws." These provisions marked a strong shift in the emphasis of House rules to encourage all committees to devote substantial time and effort to the oversight function.

In 1977, the House and Senate acted to dissolve the Joint Committee on Atomic Energy, which had been for nearly thirty years the primary focus of nuclear policy legislation in the Congress and the only joint committee to have legislative jurisdiction. The Senate that year, as part of its own committee-system reorganization, initiated the action by recommending the abolition of the Atomic Energy Joint Committee; the House later concurred.

Several House committees acquired portions of the legislative and oversight jurisdiction of the Joint Committee on Atomic Energy. The Interior Committee gained jurisdiction over the "regulation of the domestic nuclear energy industry." Through a memorandum of understanding agreed to by the chairmen of the relevant House committees, the jurisdiction of the Interior Committee was clarified to include regulation of nuclear reactors and commercial nuclear power plants, and other aspects of nuclear power production and regulation.

In 1980, the House established another Select Committee on Committees chaired by Rep. Jerry M. Patterson of California. To a resolution reported from that committee to establish a new committee on energy, an amendment offered by Rep. Jonathan Bingham of New York proposed to designate the Committee on Interstate and Foreign Commerce as the leading energy committee in the House and to rename it the Committee on Energy and Commerce. As with the abolition of the Joint Committee on Atomic Energy, a series of written agreements among the concerned committees was entered into the *Congressional Record* as part of the legislative history. These agreements stipulated that the formal jurisdiction of the Interior Committee was not changed, but provisions designed to guide the parliamentarian in the referral of future bills reiterated that the Interior Committee was to remain the primary committee of jurisdiction over measures relating to commercial nuclear power, nuclear regulatory research, the Nuclear Regulatory Commission, and related matters. The House agreed to the Bingham amendment (and by implication the terms of the written agreements) on 25 March 1980, and it went into effect with the beginning of the new Congress in 1981.

At the request of committee leaders, the new name of the Committee on Natural Resources was adopted at the beginning of the 103d Congress. It reflects the view of the current primary focus of the committee's work.

Legislative Accomplishments. The Committee on Natural Resources and its predecessor committees produced legislation of substantial scope and diversity. During the 1800s, the Public Lands Committee oversaw the disposition through sales, auctions, and grants of over 1.2 billion acres of the 1.8 billion acres of public domain lands owned by the United States at that time.

In 1862, the Homestead Act was enacted after southern members of Congress departed as their states seceded from the Union. This act's provisions were expanded by the Desert Land Act of 1877, which provided 160 acres of land if the grantee agreed to irrigate the land. In 1909, this figure was increased to 320 acres. These two desert acts resulted in the distribution of over 288 million acres of land to private landowners.

The Natural Resources Committee and its predecessors have considered virtually every measure directed at the admission of a territory to statehood. Indeed, it was the controversy surrounding whether to admit the Missouri Territory as a slave or free state that led to the creation of the Territories Committee in 1825. With the admission of Alaska and Hawaii to statehood in the 1950s, the work of the committee was refocused on legislation affecting overseas territories of the United States, including recommendations permitting these territories to represented by delegates or resident commissioners in Congress. In recent Congresses, the Natural Resources Committee has considered legislation authorizing the Commonwealth of Puerto Rico to hold a plebiscite to determine its future political relationship with the United States.

In 1832, Congress enacted legislation to protect access to forty-two hot springs in what was then the Arkansas Territory. This action is generally acknowledged as the forerunner of the national park system. Forty years later, in 1872, Congress enacted legislation to "set aside certain lands near the headwaters of the Yellowstone River as a public park." This marked the establishment of the first U.S. national park. The Natural Resources Committee has been instrumental in obtaining massive enlargements of the national park system—a system that has been copied in legislation enacted in more than one hundred other nations.

In 1891, the public lands and national park systems led to the creation of a national forest system under the jurisdiction of the Natural Resources Committee. Presidents Benjamin Harrison and Grover Cleveland in that decade set aside over 39 million acres of public lands as forest reserves, and President Theodore Roosevelt added an additional 125 million acres. The committee has primary responsibility for legislation affecting timber harvesting and reforestation projects on lands that are in the public domain.

In the twentieth century, the Natural Resources Committee and its predecessors expanded their areas of responsibility as the role of the federal government also increased. Territorial legislation became more complex as the United States acquired through war, purchase, or international mandate responsibility for many overseas possessions and protectorates. Governmental legislation affecting Native Americans became both more complex and contentious as policymakers sought to establish a more equitable relationship between the federal government and tribal organizations. Public awareness of the environmental consequences of resource development and exploitation put additional pressure on the Natural Resources Committee and its predecessors for appropriate remedial legislation.

The legislative work load of the Natural Resources Committee has grown as the policy areas within its purview have become the focus of greater public attention. Since the early 1980s, the committee has generally ranked among the top House committees in terms of bills referred to committee, bills reported, and measures enacted into law.

The membership composition of the Natural Resources Committee has changed as well. Traditionally, the predecessor committees were dominated by members drawn from western states. These members were forceful advocates for increased exploitation of natural resources on the public lands, and were instrumental in gaining enactment of timber, grazing, and other related legislation that greatly benefited ranchers, farmers, and business interests in the West.

By the 1960s, however, the western and developmental focus of the committee began to change. In part, this change resulted from a new pro-environment consciousness among some members of Congress from the western states. Moreover, the broader policy focus of the committee on such other issues as nuclear power regulation and national mining policy made an assignment to the Interior Committee or the Natural Resources Committee more attractive to urban and eastern lawmakers. Within this changed political environment, the committee reported landmark legislation on surface mining reclamation, development of mineral resources on the Outer Continental Shelf, and the establishment of vast public land tracts designated as protected wilderness areas.

This more diverse membership had many policy consequences. When the Subcommittee Bill of Rights increased the autonomy of House subcommittees in the 1970s, major policy disputes occurred between Interior's subcommittees and the parent committee on environmental policy, surface mining and reclamation, and the protection of wilderness areas. Rep. Morris K. Udall of Arizona, chairman of the Interior Committee from 1977 through 1991, provided strong leadership and advocacy for a progressive conservation and environmental policy to the committee. He frequently found himself at odds with other committee members who did not share his policy commitments. His successor, Rep. George Miller of California, continued this strong advocacy tradition. The addition of newer, more pro-environment members to the Natural Resources Committee appears to have overcome the intracommittee policy disputes that were common during Udall's tenure.

[*See also* Atomic Energy Committee, Joint; Energy and Commerce Committee, House; Energy and Natural Resources Committee, Senate; Indian Affairs Committee, Senate Select.]

BIBLIOGRAPHY

Cohen, Richard. "The New Barons." *National Journal* 26 (1994): 940–945.

Fenno, Richard F., Jr. *Congressmen in Committees.* 1973.

Ralph Nader Congress Project. *The Environment Committees: A Study of the House and Senate Interior, Agriculture, and Science Committees.* 1975.

ROY STAPLETON JONES, JR., and
PAUL S. RUNDQUIST

THE SPIRIT OF NAVY DAY, 1927

NAVY DAY. Political cartoon commemorating the founding of the navy, with Uncle Sam and figures representing the House and Senate. Clifford K. Berryman, *Washington Evening Star*, c. 13 October 1927.   LIBRARY OF CONGRESS

NAVY. Beginning in November 1775, a committee of the Continental Congress supervised a wartime Continental Navy. That navy was liquidated after the Revolutionary War, and no attempt was made to rebuild it until Barbary piracy on U.S. ships and the violation of American neutrality during the French Revolution necessitated the construction of U.S. warships. While Vice President Thomas Jefferson's followers in Congress preferred to have the Department of War administer naval affairs, partisans of Secretary of the Treasury Alexander Hamilton demanded a separate small navy to support maritime interests and national honor. The result was a compromise: six large superfrigates—including the forty-four-gun *Constellation, Constitution,* and *United States*—would be built, but construction would stop if peace was obtained with the Barbary powers. Because of Barbary and British intransigency and continued French spoliations, on 30 April 1798 Congress enacted legislation creating a separate, cabinet-level Navy Department under the direction of a secretary of the Navy.

The first change in naval organization was the creation by Congress of a Board of Navy Commissioners in 1815 to advise the secretary of the Navy. In 1842 Congress again revised the navy's management system by establishing five bureaus, each with responsibility over a different part of the navy's operations. The bureau system remained largely unchanged until the office of Chief of Naval Operations was added in 1915. In 1942 Congress established the Joint Chiefs of Staff to improve coordination between the services and to advise the president and secretary of Defense. In the 1960s the bureaus became commands. Since the end of World War II, geographical unified commands have included all operating forces within a certain geographical area, with command exercised by the senior officer present, regardless of the officer's service.

The navy has long been known on Capitol Hill as a staunch protector of its traditions and independence. During World War II, demands for an independent air force that would assume control of all airborne military activities and for a Department of Defense came from the U.S. Army Air Forces and those who believed that unifying the services would save money. The navy disputed the air forces' assertion that strategic air bombing would reduce the will of an enemy, citing experiences of World Wars I and II. It also opposed demands for a single chief of staff, a proposal to shift control of the Marine Corps from the navy to the army (Congress had created the Marine Corps and placed it under the navy's jurisdiction on 11 July 1798), a plan for the air forces to take over naval aviation, and a movement toward reliance solely upon atomic bombs—a single weapons system that, for example, could not be tailored to amphibious operations or defense of ocean trade. On the other hand, over the opposition of the air forces, the navy sought authority from Congress to build aircraft carriers capable of handling aircraft that would carry nuclear weapons.

Largely following the suggestions of Secretary of the Navy James V. Forrestal, the National Security Act of 1947 eschewed a single chief of staff and created a civilian secretary of Defense, a National Military Establishment of three coordinated service departments, and various supporting agencies. The Defense secretary replaced the navy and army secretaries in the cabinet. The navy retained its aviation corps and the Marine Corps. In March 1948 Forrestal also revised roles and missions by assigning the services primary and collateral functions, the latter being ways in which each service can help the others. The navy, however, received the broad mandate to "attack any targets, inland or otherwise, which appear necessary for the accomplishment of its missions." Roles and missions have not basically changed since then, but the air force especially has had to be reminded several times to carry out missions designed to help the army and navy.

In 1949 Forrestal obtained amendments to the National Security Act that changed the name of the National Military Establishment to Department of Defense, of which he became its secretary. When his naval secretary sought to build a large carrier to serve strategic bombers, the army and air force objected. At hearings held by the House Armed Services Committee, chaired by Carl Vinson (D-Ga.), a staunch navy defender, the air force's best bomber, the B-36, was deemed inefficient because it lacked the range to strike Soviet targets. Although the new secretary of Defense, Louis A. Johnson, scrapped the building of a supercarrier, Vinson's report, dated 12 March 1950, recommended that one be built when funds became available. With the first *Forrestal*-class carrier in 1952, the navy verged upon breaking the air force's monopoly on strategic air power.

Congress often opposed a large navy, as from 1801 to 1815, 1865 to the days of Theodore Roosevelt, and during the 1920s, 1930s, and 1970s. Congress supported four naval disarmament conferences in the 1920s and 1930s, especially the one held in Washington in 1921 and 1922, which reduced capital ships by about half. Congress fully funded wartime expenses, but with peace restored, it customarily cut back quickly and hard. For ex-

ample, the 700-ship navy of the Civil War had been reduced to 63 wooden steamers, 48 monitors, and 29 sailors by 1873. An exception was the funding of President Ronald Reagan's requests between fiscal year 1980 and fiscal year 1985 for a 600-ship navy to counter the Soviet Union during the Cold War. That navy played significant roles during the conflicts in Vietnam, Panama, Grenada, and the Persian Gulf and in other emergencies. In fiscal year 1987, however, Congress began to reduce the defense budget. The defense budget for fiscal year 1992 was 24 percent lower than that for fiscal year 1985 and represented only 3.6 percent of the gross national product, the lowest since before World War II. Early in 1993, the Clinton administration asked Congress for cuts in defense expenditures that, if approved, would shrink the navy from a 450-ship, 13-carrier fleet to 340 ships and 12 carriers by 1998.

Until 1946 a naval affairs committee in each house of Congress oversaw naval matters, but funding was entrusted to the Appropriations committees. In 1946 the military and naval committees were merged into House and Senate Armed Services committees. The House Armed Services Committee in 1994 had fifty-five members, a professional staff of forty-eight, and a clerical force of twenty-four. The most important subcommittees are Procurement and Military Nuclear Systems, Seapower and Strategic and Critical Materials, Research and Development, Military Installations and Facilities, Military Personnel and Compensation, Investigations, and Readiness. The Senate committee, twenty strong, has subcommittees substantially parallel to those of the House panel. The annual cost of each committee is about $3 million. In the 103d Congress (1993–1995), Ronald V. Dellums (D.-Calif.) became the chairman of the House committee, and Sam Nunn (D-Ga.) became chairman of the Senate committee. These committees help shape military policy, and the Senate passes nominations onto the officer corps and also to those selected for flag rank, that is, for admiral and general.

BIBLIOGRAPHY

Albion, Robert G. "The Naval Affairs Committees, 1816–1947." *Proceedings* 78 (1952): 1227–1237.

Coletta, Paolo E. *The United States Navy and Defense Unification, 1947–1953.* 1981.

Coletta, Paolo E., Robert G. Albion, and K. Jack Bauer, eds. *American Secretaries of the Navy.* 2 vols. 1981.

PAOLO E. COLETTA

NEBRASKA. The territory of Nebraska was officially opened to settlement by the Kansas-Nebraska Act in 1854. Championed by Sen. Stephen A. Douglas of Illinois, this measure was designed to populate the northern plains in order to pave the way for a transcontinental railroad. To secure southern support for the bill, Douglas agreed to a clause that repealed the Missouri Compromise (which prohibited slavery in the northern plains) and substituted popular sovereignty, which allowed people living in the territory to decide for themselves whether or not to permit slavery. The bill was one of the most fiercely debated measures ever taken up by Congress, and it created a firestorm of controversy that helped bring on the Civil War. Nevertheless, Douglas's tireless efforts to line up votes, coupled with the unswerving support of President Franklin Pierce's administration, ultimately bore fruit, and the measure became law.

After the adoption of the Kansas-Nebraska Act, people poured into Nebraska. Although the territory escaped the bloodshed that tore Kansas apart, the question of statehood deeply divided Nebraskans along party lines. By 1864, Republicans (who favored statehood) controlled the territorial legislature and asked Congress for authority to organize a state government. Congress responded with a bill directing the territorial governor, Alvin Saunders, to summon a constitutional convention. Although hostile Democrats dominated the convention and voted to adjourn without taking any action, leading Republicans in the territory met privately to draw up a constitution. This document was rammed through the territorial legislature and then approved by the people of Nebraska in a closely contested and disputed referendum held in early 1866.

In July of 1866 Republicans in Congress pushed through a bill that admitted Nebraska to the Union, but President Andrew Johnson, who knew that Nebraska would elect Republicans to Congress, killed the measure with a pocket veto. In February of 1867 Congress passed another statehood bill, this time over Johnson's veto, though as a condition for admission Nebraska had to repudiate a state constitutional provision that denied the vote to black people. The territorial legislature responded with a law that extended the franchise to black citizens, and on 1 March 1867, President Johnson reluctantly issued a proclamation announcing Nebraska's admission to the Union as the thirty-seventh state. Nebraska is the only state to be admitted to the Union over a presidential veto and one of the few to be admitted conditionally.

Because of its rapid growth in the late nineteenth century, Nebraska had six representatives by 1893. This number declined to five in 1933, to four in 1943, and to three in 1963. Over the years the vast majority of the state's representatives and senators have been moderate or conservative Republicans, but there have been many exceptions. The most notable Nebraskans to sit in Congress—William Jennings Bryan, a Democrat who served in the House from 1891 to 1893, and George W. Norris, a Republican-turned-Independent who served in the House and Senate from 1903 to 1943—were both liberal reformers who favored using the machinery of government to help the disadvantaged and the poor.

[*See also* Kansas-Nebraska Act.]

BIBLIOGRAPHY

Hickey, Donald R. *Nebraska Moments: Glimpses of Nebraska's Past.* 1992.
Olson, James C. *History of Nebraska.* 1966.

DONALD R. HICKEY

NEPA. *See* National Environmental Policy Act of 1969.

NEPOTISM. The most common form of nepotism, the practice of showing favoritism or unfair preference to relatives, is hiring or promoting a member of one's family because of the relationship rather than merit. Federal law enacted in 1967 generally prohibits any official in the three branches of government, including a member of Congress, from appointing, promoting, or recommending for appointment or promotion any relative of the official to any agency or department over which the official exercises control or authority. The law specifies twenty-seven categories of relationships that fall within the definition of "relative."

The statute does not prohibit members of Congress from having relatives as unpaid staff or prevent their relatives from being employed by other members or committees on which the related member does not serve. These practices are often criticized by the press as violating the spirit if not the letter of the law, and legislation has been introduced from time to time to bar the practice.

The statute allows staff who become relatives of their employing official in Congress to remain on staff, although the individual may not receive promotions or raises other than cost-of-living or other across-the-board adjustments. The antinepotism law also does not prevent an official of one house of Congress from advocating the employment or advancement of a relative in the other body.

In the House of Representatives, all employing authorities must certify on monthly payroll information each employee's relationship, if any, to a member of Congress. When new employees are hired in the Senate, they must swear that they are not related to the appointing official.

Before 1967 nepotism in the federal government was not illegal. It had, in fact, been practiced for years. Relatives had routinely assisted members of Congress before the late 1880s, when the first personal staffers were authorized. After Congress provided funds for staff, many members retained and paid their relatives. J. McIver Weatherford, in his *Tribes on the Hill* (1981), pointed out that even after World War II "nepotism was the rule in Congress, not the exception." Defenders of nepotism pointed out that relatives had a special interest in their boss and were therefore likely to work harder and be more loyal. Besides, having a relative on the payroll was a way to supplement the family income, necessary because of inadequate congressional salaries.

Legislation making it unlawful for members of Congress, cabinet officers, and other employees of the government to practice nepotism was introduced as early as 1923. On 20 May 1932, following allegations that a majority of members of Congress had relatives on government payrolls, the House passed an antinepotism resolution to make payroll records available to the public. The next day, the *New York Times* published a list of some one hundred members whose staffs included individuals with names the same as theirs, insinuating that they employed their relatives.

Antinepotism legislation was introduced periodically during the next thirty years. In early 1959 the *New York Times* published damaging accounts of congressional hiring practices, including nepotism. Daniel Berman, in *In Congress Assembled* (1964), said that continuous needling by the press convinced the Senate in 1959 to follow the House and publish detailed payroll information.

In the early 1960s, press accounts revealed that a member of the House had retained his wife on his payroll even though she was not living in the United States. Ultimately, Congress in 1967 wrote the current ban on nepotism in the three branches of government as an amendment to the Postal Revenue and Salary Act of 1967 (P.L. 90-206, 81 Stat. 613–648). However, this restriction did not apply to relatives already employed.

BIBLIOGRAPHY

Congressional Quarterly Inc. "Questionable Hiring Practices." In *Congressional Quarterly's Guide to Congress.* 4th ed. Edited by Mary Cohn. 1991. Pp. 493–494.
"Fight on Nepotism Renewed in the Capital." *New York Times,* 18 December 1932, sec. II, p. 2.

MILDRED LEHMANN AMER

NEUTRALITY DEBATES. Seeking to insulate the United States against the danger of war, Congress passed so-called neutrality legislation in 1935, 1936, 1937, and 1939.

In 1935, the administration of Franklin D. Roosevelt sought authorization from Congress for a discretionary embargo on the sale of arms to belligerents. Under the influence of revelations produced by the Nye Committee's investigation of the munitions industry and with pressure provided by powerful isolationists, Congress instead passed a bill that provided for a mandatory arms embargo whenever war broke out anywhere. Proponents of the embargo argued that arms shipments to the Allies during World War I had been a major cause of American involvement in the war and that prohibiting such shipments would do much to keep the country out of future wars.

Roosevelt invoked the new law in the Italo-Ethiopian War on 5 October 1935 but noted that it was not neutral in its effect. Ethiopia was denied access to American arms it needed desperately, while well-armed Italy operated its tanks and planes with increasing quantities of American oil. Still anxious to use neutrality laws as a foreign policy tool, Roosevelt then sought to gain discretionary embargo powers for war materials other than arms. But the Neutrality Act of February 1936 simply extended the mandatory arms embargo for a year and added a ban on loans to belligerents.

The Neutrality Act of 1937 was the ultimate effort to prohibit the activities allegedly responsible for America's entry into war in 1917 and thus to insulate the United States against future conflicts. It applied even to civil wars (because the Spanish Civil War seemed to pose a threat of U.S. involvement) and required the president to embargo arms and implements of war, to ban loans and American travel on belligerent ships, and to forbid the arming of U.S. merchant ships trading with warring states. Its "cash-and-carry" clause, moreover, allowed the president to limit trade in contraband other than arms by requiring that it be paid for before it left the country and that it not be carried on U.S. ships.

In the spring of 1939, Roosevelt proposed scrapping the arms embargo and putting all trade with belligerents on a cash-and-carry basis, thereby making military aid to Great Britain and France possible. But the "selling arms means war" mood in Congress remained strong enough to prevent passage. Only after World War II broke out in Europe in 1939—and Hitler's forces overran Poland in less than a month—was Congress persuaded that attempts at insulation no longer served America's needs. Still, the Neutrality Act of 1939, which Roosevelt signed on 4 November, retained all the provisions of the earlier law except the arms embargo.

Over the next two years the Neutrality Act was circumvented in various ways, most spectacularly by the president's destroyers-for-bases deal with Great Britain in September 1940 and by congressional passage of the Lend-Lease Act in March 1941. Not until October 1941, however, did the president formally request revision and possible repeal of the Neutrality Act. Congress responded in November by voting to permit the arming of U.S. merchant ships and the entry of U.S. ships into war zones and belligerent ports. Although only a small minority held to the basic concept behind neutrality legislation, the debate nonetheless continued until the Pearl Harbor attack.

BIBLIOGRAPHY

Divine, Robert A. *The Illusion of Neutrality.* 1962.
Guinsburg, Thomas N. *The Pursuit of Isolationism in the United States Senate from Versailles to Pearl Harbor.* 1982.
Jonas, Manfred. *Isolationism in America, 1935–1941.* 1990.

MANFRED JONAS

NEVADA. As part of the Compromise of 1850 most of what is today Nevada became a part of the Utah Territory. The local population's ties with Utah largely ended in 1857 when Brigham Young recalled the region's Mormon settlers to Salt Lake City. Two years later the discovery of gold and silver at the Comstock Lode near present-day Virginia City led to a rapid growth of population and local demands for establishment as a separate territory. Congress responded, after the withdrawal of legislators from seceding Southern states, by creating the Nevada Territory on 2 March 1861.

Despite the Nevada Territory's small size—a census of July 1861 showed it to have a population of 16,374, which excluded transients and an estimated ten thousand Indians—in March 1864 the Republican-controlled Congress approved an enabling act, which delegated to the president the power to proclaim Nevada a state if its proposed constitution met his scrutiny. This Abraham Lincoln did on 31 October 1864. Eight days later Nevada voters chose Republican presidential electors and, with two exceptions, an all-Republican state legislature. The state's present boundaries date from 1866, when Congress added lands from the Utah and Arizona territories to Nevada.

Much of the state's 109,395 square miles is arid land of the Great Basin held as public domain by the federal government. Not until the 98th Congress (1983–1985) did Nevada cease being a single at-large congressional district.

Nevada sent only Republicans to Congress until the 47th Congress (1881–1883). During these years and well into the twentieth century, support for silver mining was an overriding concern for Nevada's senators and representatives. Democratic senator Francis G. Newlands (1909–1917) was first elected to the House in 1893 by the Nevada Silver party. Although Newlands as author of the Reclamation Act of 1902 deserves credit for the development of desert irrigation policy, Nevada's national legislators played only a secondary role in the key follow-up measure, the 1928 authorization of the construction of the Boulder (or Hoover) Dam on the Colorado River.

In addition to Newlands, Nevada's two most influential twentieth-century senators, also Democrats, have been Key Pittman (1913–1941) and Patrick A. McCarran (1933–1954). Pittman served as chairman of the Foreign Relations Committee (1933–1941). McCarran's dominant interests were promotion of aviation and protection of the United States against communist subversion. The 1950 hearings in Las Vegas on allegations of crime and racketeering in Nevada's gambling industry were held not by the Judiciary Committee, of which McCarran was chair, but by Estes Kefauver's Special Committee to Investigate Organized Crime in Interstate Commerce. The Republican representative Barbara F. Vucanovich is the only woman who has served Nevada in Congress.

Beginning with World War II Nevada's great open spaces took on new significance, first with the establishment of Nellis Air Force Base and then with the use of Yucca Flat as a test site for nuclear bombs. In 1987 under provisions of the Nuclear Waste Policy Act, Congress paved the way for Yucca Mountain to become the one permanent repository in the United States for the nation's radioactive waste.

BIBLIOGRAPHY

Elliott, Russell R. *History of Nevada.* 1973.
Ostrander, Gilman M. *Nevada: The Great Rotten Borough, 1859–1964.* 1966.

RODNEY A. ROSS

NEW DEAL.

NEW DEAL. On 4 March 1933, with the economy devastated by four years of depression and with the entire national banking system in collapse, Franklin D. Roosevelt took the presidential oath of office. During the campaign, the New York governor had promised "a new deal for the American people," and the public responded by giving him a landslide victory and a sympathetic Congress. Yet on inauguration day, the details of that "new deal" were vague, since FDR had run on an anti-Hoover platform, promising action but offering only sketchy details of his recovery plan.

Roosevelt launched his New Deal by calling Congress into special session for a burst of legislative activity that crafted fifteen major programs in the first hundred days. Five years of reform followed, years that fundamentally altered America's politics and political economy. FDR enjoyed a mostly compliant and cooperative Congress during the first New Deal (1933–1935) owing to the climate of national emergency and the Democrat-controlled House and Senate that he brought into office with him (60 Democrats to 35 Republicans in the Senate, 310 Democrats to 117 Republicans in the House). Frustrated by a conservative opposition that had emerged by 1935, the administration shifted its emphasis from partnership between government and business-agriculture to reform. The energies of this second New Deal (1935–1938) ensured Roosevelt's reelection and produced major reform measures in labor-management relations, old age pensions, taxation, a revived interest in antimonopoly activity, and a more militant rhetoric on matters of economic class. Yet despite the landslide Roosevelt victory in 1936, the second New Deal's labor and urban alliances also produced an entrenched anti-Roosevelt coalition of conservative Democrats and Republicans. Consequently, major New Deal legislation had ceased by 1938.

The Early Years. After his March 1933 inauguration, Roosevelt quickly called Congress into special session, launching a hectic and exciting three-month burst of creative activity. A stream of mes-

"THE TROJAN HORSE AT OUR GATE." Political cartoon depicting the conservative belief that the New Deal programs, in violation of the Constitution, delegated too much authority to the executive. The cartoon was published a few months after the Supreme Court declared the National Industrial Recovery Act unconstitutional in *Schechter Poultry Corp. v. United States.* Cartoon by Orr, *Chicago Tribune,* 17 September 1935.

LIBRARY OF CONGRESS

sages and legislative proposals flowed from the White House to Capitol Hill. Unemployment relief programs—the Federal Emergency Relief Administration (FERA) and the Public Works Administration (PWA)—and new banking legislation were put in place.

The heart of the early recovery plan was a pair of planning experiments in industry and agriculture, and in both cases the legislation was drafted in the executive branch, with Congress agreeing to laws conferring a broad set of tools on the president. The National Recovery Administration (NRA) displayed the New Deal's initial strategy of producer-oriented planning that emphasized voluntary compliance. The hope of spurring recovery through government-negotiated codes granting both higher wages and higher prices led instead to a tangle of complaints, but Roosevelt urged patience with the NRA experiment. Agriculture was hit hard by the depression, and the Agricultural Adjustment Administration (AAA) attempted to organize and empower farmers to collectively control production levels, thereby raising farm income and retiring submarginal land. One of the boldest New Deal agencies had deeper congressional roots. Born of Nebraska senator George W. Norris's lengthy 1920s battle to save the hydroelectric facility at Muscle Shoals on the Tennessee River, the Tennessee Valley Authority (TVA) was created to promote an extensive plan of reforestation, land-use management, retirement of submarginal land, and provision of cheap and abundant hydroelectric power. These beginnings made up the core of the first New Deal, backed up by innovative agencies such as the Civilian Conservation Corps (CCC) and experimental actions such as taking the United States off the international gold standard and reforming the stock markets and the banking system.

Despite the enthusiastic atmosphere, the first New Deal was plagued with problems. The NRA met its demise at the hand of the Supreme Court, which also tampered with the AAA. The TVA's larger scheme for regional planning was soon eclipsed by a more popular objective, generation of cheap electricity. The economy did improve, with the gross national product slowly climbing from $65 billion in 1933 to $72 billion in 1935, but ten million Americans still stood on unemployment lines that year. And, of course, not everyone liked the New Deal. By 1935, a conservative congressional coalition, led by southern Democrats Sen. Carter Glass, Sen. Harry Flood Byrd, Sr., and Rep. Howard W. Smith of Virginia and Republicans Sen. Charles L. McNary of Oregon and Rep. Bertrand H. Snell of New York, created problems for Roosevelt. As the 1936 election grew nearer, mass movements on the radical left sprang up, led by such controversial figures as Louisiana senator Huey P. Long, who pledged a plan, called Share Our Wealth, that guaranteed a minimum standard of living, Dr. Francis E. Townsend of California, who promoted a pension plan, and Socialist Norman Thomas, who saw the New Deal as a well-meaning failure. The radical right produced the American Liberty League, which thought the New Deal went too far—imposed too much government intervention and spent too much.

The Reform Agenda. In the summer of 1935, Roosevelt seized the initiative. He urged more congressional action, including an expansion of the relief and public works programs of the first New Deal and the creation of a new Works Progress Ad-

ministration (WPA), which offered jobs for construction workers, school teachers, artists, writers, and even college students. He also pushed a new agenda of progressive taxation, a collective bargaining labor law, and a new social insurance program to aid the elderly.

The measures of 1935 were radical in tone but moderate in outcome and were usually shaped by influential senators and special interest groups to be something less than the original conception. Social security, although the boldest move into social insurance in the nation's history, was altered under pressure from powerful southern senators so that it excluded many agricultural workers and was financed by a regressive tax. New York senator Robert F. Wagner's vigorous sponsorship of the National Labor Relations Act brought a hesitant administration to endorse it, cementing organized labor within the New Deal coalition. Hailed as the definitive statement of governmental support for unions and despised by management, the Wagner-Connery Act of 1935 would in time be seen as stabilizing the industrial-capitalist order.

FDR's popular support was so strong by the 1936 election that he buried Republican candidate Alfred

NEW DEAL REMEDIES. Published during the first New Deal, the cartoon makes reference to the flurry of programs proposed by the Roosevelt administration and rapidly approved by Congress. The drawing portrays President Franklin D. Roosevelt as a doctor treating an ailing Uncle Sam with his legislative remedies. Clifford K. Berryman, 5 January 1934.   LIBRARY OF CONGRESS

WPA PROJECT. Workers loading a truck with flood debris, Louisville, Kentucky, February 1937.

M. Landon. The president's popularity also packed Congress with the greatest Democratic majority to date; his party controlled 331 seats in the House and 76 in the Senate. Regardless of its critics, the vast majority of Americans obviously approved of the New Deal.

As Roosevelt entered his second term, he still saw "one-third of a nation ill-housed, ill-clad, ill-nourished." In the next four years, he hoped to extend regional development, further improve conditions for labor, and, most important, overhaul the executive branch itself. Despite these hopes, however, 1937 marked the beginning of the end of New Deal reform, for in that year FDR also decided to tackle the conservative Supreme Court, further angering his congressional opposition.

Rising Opposition. Since 1935 the Supreme Court had systematically blocked key New Deal programs. Roosevelt responded in 1937 by proposing a fundamental restructuring of the Court itself, or what the press called his Court-packing scheme. This plan was a serious political mistake, giving substantial ammunition to Roosevelt's conservative critics. Even many loyal Democrats, such as Sen. Tom T. Connally of Texas, balked at the scheme. The Senate Judiciary Committee refused to support the plan, and the conservative coalition stopped it in debate. When a recession that same year fueled pessimism not only in Congress but among depression-weary Americans, the subsequent loss of support prevented Roosevelt from completing his agenda.

One of the casualties of this 1937 debacle was Roosevelt's attempt to restructure the executive office, including the creation of twelve cabinet departments, an executive office with adequate staff, and a permanent national planning board. If accomplished, such a plan would have shifted the balance of power decisively to the executive.

Congressional opposition to such a shift was immediate and bipartisan. The political uproar over reorganization and Court reform stalled the third New Deal, and Roosevelt's hand was also weakened when the economy slumped into recession in the fall of 1937. Four million jobs were lost before the "Roosevelt Recession" ended in mid 1938, and a disgruntled electorate sent many Republicans back to Congress in the November elections, strengthening the conservative coalition. Congress passed a weak reorganization bill that fell far short of Roosevelt's intentions and did not include a permanent planning board. Throughout the 1938 session, the conservative coalition dictated congressional action. Conservative Democrats and prominent Republicans gained control of important positions, especially the House Rules Committee.

In the 1938 midterm election, Roosevelt tried to use his influence to realign Congress itself, actively campaigning for liberal supporters in an effort to "purge" conservative incumbents. The plan backfired. Few of his chosen candidates won, and the president further alienated lawmakers on the Hill. The Democratic majority remained but was reduced to 69 in the Senate and 261 in the House. By 1939 the conservative coalition controlled Congress, dictating policy and channeling funds into specific congressional districts, especially in the South, to satisfy local constituent demands. As the administration's attention began to shift toward the threats posed by expansionist fascist regimes abroad, the legislative phase of the New Deal gave way to consolidation.

The New Deal in Perspective. With the passage of the years, a clearer picture has emerged of the New Deal's achievements as well as its failures. The nation was steered through an immense crisis with its political and economic systems intact, though revised. "Positive government," in historian Arthur M. Schlesinger, Jr.'s phrase, had relieved unemployment and launched innovative programs in industrial and regional planning, resource conservation, and support for the arts. But the administration's New Deal aims were often defeated. The main goal of economic recovery eluded Roosevelt until wartime mobilization forced the government to undertake vast spending programs. The New Deal did not significantly redistribute wealth, nor find a strategy to solve the problem of business monopolies, nor adequately address the situation of racial minorities, nor successfully install national planning. The liberal impulse toward reform was thus significantly frustrated in Roosevelt's era, to the regret of some and the relief of others. Congress

acted mostly as a facilitator of the New Deal through 1936—and as a restraint thereafter. Despite Roosevelt's popularity and large Democratic majorities in both houses, the weak American party system allowed an emergent conservative coalition on Capitol Hill to shape and often to curb the New Deal.

[*See also* Agricultural Adjustment Acts; Banking Act of 1933; Court-Packing Fight; Emergency Banking Relief Act; Fair Labor Standards Act; Federal Anti–Price Discrimination Act; National Housing Acts; National Industrial Recovery Act; Securities Acts; Social Security Act; Tennessee Valley Authority; Wagner-Connery National Labor Relations Act; Wheeler-Rayburn Public Utility Holding Company Act.]

BIBLIOGRAPHY

Leuchtenburg, William E. *Franklin D. Roosevelt and the New Deal.* 1963.
Patterson, James T. *Congressional Conservatism and the New Deal: The Growth of the Conservative Coalition in Congress, 1933–1939.* 1967.
Porter, David L. *Congress and the Waning of the New Deal.* 1980.

OTIS L. GRAHAM, JR., and ELIZABETH KOED

NEW FREEDOM. Originally a phrase uttered by Democratic presidential candidate Woodrow Wilson in a speech in Indianapolis on 3 October 1912, "New Freedom" became the campaign slogan of the Democratic party that year. The phrase symbolized a political position that Wilson had formulated with the advice of Louis D. Brandeis. It was a response to the so-called New Nationalism of Theodore Roosevelt and his Progressive party, which held that business trusts should be legitimized and controlled by the federal government through regulatory agencies. The New Freedom, in contrast, insisted that genuine competition had to be restored through legislation forbidding the practices that had encouraged the creation of monopolies, thus gradually destroying the trusts by making them economically unviable. Both the New Nationalism and the New Freedom envisioned much wider legislative programs than the control or elimination of trusts. The former called for a host of social and economic reforms, while the latter stressed reforms that would free individuals to pursue their economic and social interests.

After the election, "New Freedom" was generally employed to describe the entire domestic legisla-

CONGRESS AND THE PRESIDENT. President Woodrow Wilson was the first president since Thomas Jefferson to deliver his addresses personally to Congress rather than through written messages. Published on the day after the opening of the first regular session of Congress, the cartoon depicts Theodore Roosevelt, former president and losing 1912 presidential candidate, expressing regret over not having done the same. Clifford K. Berryman, *Washington Evening Star,* 8 April 1913.

U.S. SENATE COLLECTION, CENTER FOR LEGISLATIVE ARCHIVES

tive program of the Wilson administration until 1917. The three major legislative achievements of 1913 and 1914—the Underwood Tariff Act, which substantially lowered or removed duties on many imported products; the Federal Reserve Act, which reformed the nation's banking system and placed it under federal government control; and the Clayton Antitrust Act, which prohibited many monopolistic business practices—represented the New Freedom of the 1912 campaign in that they sought to remove barriers to individual enterprise and initiative. The Federal Trade Commission Act of 1914, however, in its creation of a strong, independent regulatory agency, represented a shift in the thinking of Wilson, Brandeis, and others in the direction of Roosevelt's New Nationalism. In 1916, faced with the need to form a political alliance with for-

mer supporters of the Progressive party in order to ensure reelection, Wilson and his legislative leaders pushed through most of the program of the New Nationalism, including laws prohibiting the interstate shipment of the products of child labor, establishing a system of workmen's compensation for federal employees, creating banks to extend loans to farmers, and setting up a commission to recommend new tariff rates.

Wilson is often credited with being the first president to take the lead in initiating legislation in Congress, but it is more accurate to say that he and Congress had a shared, dynamic relationship in the passage of the New Freedom program. Congressional leaders such as Oscar W. Underwood (D-Ala.), Carter Glass (D-Va.), and Henry D. Clayton (D-Ala.) played crucial roles in the drafting and enactment of the tariff, Federal Reserve, and antitrust acts. Members of Congress, not Wilson, were the ones who added the first progressive income tax to the Tariff Act of 1913 and who imposed a more steeply graduated income tax to pay for war preparations in 1916. The Federal Farm Loan Act of 1916 was passed only after congressional leaders overcame strong opposition from Wilson and members of his cabinet. Wilson used the power and prestige of the presidency to help secure the enactment of much of the New Freedom, but members of the Democratic party majority in Congress were responsible for many of the specific details of the legislation. The legislative procedure remained largely unchanged, but it was energized by the alliance between the president and his party in Congress.

[*See also* Clayton Antitrust Act; Federal Reserve Bank Act; Federal Trade Commission Act.]

BIBLIOGRAPHY

Cooper, John Milton, Jr. *Pivotal Decades: The United States, 1900–1920.* 1990.

Link, Arthur S. *Woodrow Wilson and the Progressive Era, 1910–1917.* 1954.

JOHN E. LITTLE

NEW HAMPSHIRE. New Hampshire entered the Union as the ninth state and received three seats in the original 1789 apportionment of the House. From 1813 to 1833, New Hampshire sent six members to the House, but it lost single seats following the 1830, 1840, 1850, and 1880 censuses. By 1883, the state delegation was reduced to two representatives, its present allocation.

House. The Federalist party won most of New Hampshire's House seats from 1789 to 1817, but the Jeffersonian Democratic-Republicans claimed all six seats in the 1816 election. During the transitional period from 1824 through 1856, New Hampshire's was the most consistently Democratic House delegation from New England; Whig party successes were infrequent.

Representative Nicholas Gilman (1789–1797) was the initial chair of the House Select Committee on Rules in the First Congress (1789–1791) and Samuel Livermore (1789–1793) chaired Elections, the House's oldest standing committee in the Second Congress (1791–1793). New Hampshire's best-known early House member was Federalist Daniel Webster (1813–1817), the eloquent lawyer who argued the Dartmouth College case but who gained his greatest prominence as a U.S. senator from Massachusetts. Franklin Pierce, who would win the presidency in 1852, represented New Hampshire in the House for four years (1833–1837).

After the 1856 elections, the Republicans gained control of New Hampshire's House delegation and dominated it from 1856 through 1974. Democratic breakthroughs were relatively uncommon; the party won all the House seats only in 1874, 1890, and 1912.

New Hampshire was divided into two districts after the 1880 census. The eastern 1st District, which borders Maine and includes Manchester, the state's largest city, has been won by Republicans forty-four times in fifty-six elections (79 percent). The western 2nd District, which shares the Connecticut River Valley with Vermont, has been won by Republicans fifty-two times in fifty-six elections (93 percent).

Senate. New Hampshire's first U.S. senator, John Langdon (1789–1801), was an active delegate at the Constitutional Convention and was chosen as the Senate's first president pro tempore. Langdon was the first of six U.S. senators from New Hampshire to hold this post.

The two most prominent of New Hampshire's antebellum senators were Democrat Franklin Pierce (1837–1842), the state's only native to be elected president, and Levi Woodbury, who served as a Democratic-Republican (1825–1831) and as a Democrat (1841–1845). The best-known of New Hampshire's Civil War era senators was John P. Hale (Anti-Slavery, 1847–1853, 1855–1865) the Free Soil party's candidate for president in 1852.

The post-1932 Democratic dominance of Congress led to a diminished role for New Hampshire's predominantly Republican congressional delegation. Moderate Republican Charles W. Tobey (1939–1953) chaired the Senate Banking and Currency Committee (1947–1949) and the Interstate and Foreign Commerce committees (1953). However, the dominant Senate personality from post–New Deal New Hampshire was the archconservative Republican H. Styles Bridges (1937–1961), who emerged as a major force in opposition to liberal spending programs during his many years on the Appropriations Committee. Bridges also served as president pro tempore of the Senate and as majority floor leader (1953–1955). Republican senator Warren B. Rudman (1981–1993), a co-author of the 1985 Gramm-Rudman-Hollings deficit-reduction law, continued New Hampshire's tradition of fiscal conservatism.

BIBLIOGRAPHY

Hill, Ralph Nading. *Yankee Kingdom: Vermont and New Hampshire.* 1966.
Lockard, Duane. *New England State Politics.* 1959.
Squires, James Duane. *The Granite State of the United States.* Vols. 1 and 2. 1956.

GARRISON NELSON

NEW JERSEY. One of the thirteen original states, New Jersey played a central role at the Constitutional Convention in 1787. The goal of the New Jersey delegation, the first to be appointed to attend the Philadelphia gathering, was to create a more powerful central government without surrendering control of national affairs to the most populous states.

New Jersey consistently opposed that part of James Madison's Virginia Plan, debated and adopted in the opening weeks of the Convention, that proposed to base representation in both houses of the legislative branch on population alone. On 15 June, William Paterson, former attorney general of New Jersey, presented the alternative New Jersey Plan, a creation of small-state nationalists from New Jersey, Connecticut, and Maryland and anti-nationalists from New York. The New Jersey Plan suggested a return to the confederation form of government under the Articles of Confederation but with the delegation of additional powers to the national government. Although voted down on 19 June, the New Jersey Plan alerted the convention to the continued and adamant opposition of the small states to the system of representation embodied in the Virginia Plan.

After weeks of debate with little progress, on 16 July the Convention found a solution to the basic and divisive issue of representation. In the aptly named Great Compromise, the delegates proposed that representation in the first house be based on population, while each state would enjoy an equal vote in the second house, a distinct advantage for the small states. Thus New Jersey and the small states prevailed by forcing the delegates to fashion a compromise that preserved the power of the individual states in the Senate. On 18 December 1787, the state convention in New Jersey unanimously ratified the Constitution; the state thereby became the third to ratify.

New Jersey's delegation to the House of Representatives has grown from the four assigned in 1789 to fourteen in 1990. The Democratic party and its predecessors have had a long, but not unrivaled, run of success in New Jersey, excepting the era of Federalist party control in the 1790s and during the War of 1812; the Republican party's ascendancy immediately following the Civil War; and Republican party control in the 1890s, when New Jersey's liberal incorporation laws made it a favored haven for corporate headquarters. The second half of the twentieth century has witnessed a more vigorous competition between the two parties in New Jersey.

Prominent members of Congress from New Jersey have included Jonathan Dayton, who at twenty-six had been the youngest delegate at the Constitutional Convention; Dayton, a Federalist, served as both a representative and a senator and was Speaker of the House for the Fourth and Fifth Congresses. Also notable are the five members of the Frelinghuysen family who represented New Jersey over two centuries. More recently, Peter W. Rodino, Jr., as chairman of the House Judiciary Committee, presided over the July 1974 committee vote to impeach President Richard M. Nixon on three counts stemming from the Watergate break-in and attempted cover-up.

BIBLIOGRAPHY

Fleming, Thomas J. *New Jersey: A Bicentennial History.* 1977.
Rossiter, Clinton. *1787: The Grand Convention.* 1966.

RICHARD HUNT

NEWLANDS, FRANCIS G. (1848–1917), representative and senator from Nevada, primarily responsible for the National Reclamation Act of 1902.

After marrying into great wealth in California and failing to win the Democratic nomination for the U.S. Senate there, Newlands sought a Senate seat from Nevada as a Republican after his move to the state in 1888. Unwilling to outspend a determined opponent, however, he chose instead to serve as Nevada's lone representative from 1893 to 1903. Although he had entered Nevada politics as a Republican, Newlands became a bimetallist silver advocate in the state's Silver party and returned to the Democratic party when it embraced the silver standard in the presidential campaign of 1896. After urging state aid to irrigation development, Newlands took up the cause of national support for western irrigation. In the process he won the support of President Theodore Roosevelt for the passage of a National Reclamation Act, often known as the Newlands Reclamation Act, in 1902. With it the federal government extended an aid package with the benefits of the original 1862 Homestead Act to the arid West, where it had been ineffective. Newlands pressed for and achieved provisions establishing a 160-acre restriction on farms that received water from federal projects.

While a member of the Senate from 1903 until his death in 1917, Newlands was a modernizer and nationalizer within the Democratic party. He embraced a progressivism more in harmony with the emerging New Nationalism of the Roosevelt wing of the Republican party than with his own party's New Freedom approach to reform. While the New Freedom stressed antitrust policy and limited government, Newlands favored the regulation of large monopolistic corporations by government commissions. In 1913, with the election of a Democratic majority, he became chairman of the Interstate Commerce Committee. He supported legislation creating the Federal Trade Commission, a tariff commission, and a rivers and harbors commission, and he backed federal incorporation of the railroads. Newlands favored delegating the power of Congress to boards of experts in order to eliminate politics from and increase the efficiency of government oversight. After the outbreak of World War I, Newlands, in the last months of his life, could observe with satisfaction that the Wilson administration was moving in the direction of using the power of the federal government to mobilize the economy.

BIBLIOGRAPHY

Darling, A. B., ed. *The Public Papers of Francis G. Newlands.* 2 vols. 1932.

Pisani, Donald. *To Reclaim a Divided West: Water, Law, and Public Policy, 1848–1902.* 1992.

Rowley, William D. "Francis G. Newlands and the Promises of American Life." *Nevada Historical Society Quarterly* 22 (1989): 169–180.

WILLIAM D. ROWLEY

NEW MEXICO. New Mexico struggled longer than any state of the "lower forty-eight" to win admission to the Union. Settled by the Spanish in 1598, this region, home of the advanced Pueblo Indian culture, became a part of the United States following its conquest by U.S. troops during the Mexican-American War.

Even before the war's end, however, the American commander, Gen. Stephen Watts Kearny, proclaimed New Mexico a U.S. territory. President James K. Polk disallowed his proclamation, however, insisting that only Congress had the power to create a territory. Nevertheless, hopes were heightened in 1848 by the ratification of the Treaty of Guadalupe Hidalgo, which provided that New Mexico could "be admitted, at the proper time (to be judged by the Congress of the United States)." Still, the first major attempt to achieve statehood—a constitutional convention assembled in Santa Fe in 1850—ended in rejection: southern members of Congress objected to the antislavery provision in the constitution presented. Later that year, New Mexico was made a territory as part of the Compromise of 1850, receiving its new status on 9 September.

New Mexicans continued to strive unsuccessfully for admission for the next sixty-two years. The sectional issue frustrated them even after the Civil War; Territorial Delegate Stephen B. Elkins's eager handshake of a Michigan representative who had lambasted southern resistance to Reconstruction in 1875 again alienated southern support. Later, New Mexico, in frustration, agreed to join Arizona as a single state in order to placate Sen. Albert J. Beveridge (R-Ind.), who felt that New Mexico was out of step with the nation's budding Progressive movement; Arizona's refusal, in 1904, to be a part of this plan put an end to it. President William Howard Taft finally granted the territory its long-cherished wish when he signed New Mexico's statehood bill on 6 January 1912.

The long delay in New Mexico's admission was due in part to prejudice against its predominantly Spanish-speaking, Roman Catholic population. Opponents of statehood, however, usually offered different reasons for their resistance. In 1902, for example, Senator Beveridge insisted that the territory's estimated population of 246,700 was inadequate for statehood, even though Wyoming had been admitted a decade earlier with only half that population.

Historically, a majority of Hispanics within the territory had been politically disadvantaged; most of New Mexico's territorial delegates were Anglos or wealthy Hispanics who had won Anglo favor. But statehood ultimately elevated the political role of New Mexico's Hispanics. Democratic senator Dennis Chavez's twenty-seven years of service (1935–1962) are testament not only to the changed attitudes of New Mexico voters, but also to his political savvy. New Mexico has produced other prominent members of Congress, including Albert B. Fall, a Republican whose influential Senate career (1912–1921) was later eclipsed by his involvement in the Teapot Dome Scandal; Bronson M. Cutting, a Republican senator (1927–1928, 1929–1935) who was a more radical New Dealer than many Democrats; Clinton P. Anderson, a secretary of Agriculture under Harry S. Truman who sponsored significant social and economic legislation while serving in Congress (House, 1941–1945; Senate, 1949–1973); and Carl A. Hatch, a Democratic senator (1933–1949) who championed the important 1939 Hatch Act, which limited the political activities of federal employees. Two other New Mexicans of achievement are Republican representative Manuel Lujan, Jr. (1969–1989), who was George Bush's secretary of the Interior, and Pete V. Domenici (1973–), a Republican on the Senate Budget Committee who significantly influenced a number of congressional budgets.

BIBLIOGRAPHY

Beck, Warren A. *New Mexico: A History of Four Centuries.* 1962.

Larson, Robert W. *New Mexico's Quest for Statehood, 1848–1912.* 1968.

ROBERT W. LARSON

NEWSPAPERS. *See* Press.

NEW YORK. One of the original thirteen states, New York was the eleventh state to ratify the Constitution. Although New York's delegation to the Constitutional Convention, which included Alexander Hamilton, made only minor contributions to

FEDERAL HALL. At the corner of Wall and Nassau Streets, New York City, seat of the First Congress of the United States.   LIBRARY OF CONGRESS

the nation's founding document, the state's central location and large population made it a key player in the campaign for the Constitution's ratification. In 1789 New York City became the first seat of the new United States government, hosting the president and Congress until the capital was shifted to Philadelphia the following year.

The Congress established by the Constitution convened in New York's Federal Hall on 4 March 1789. The state was allocated 6 of the 65 seats in the House of Representatives, and the number was increased to 10 after the census of 1790. New York had the largest delegation in the House subsequent to the census of 1810, which condition prevailed until it was displaced by California following the census of 1970. The state's slow rate of growth relative to several other states has led to a steady decrease in the number of seats—from 45 in 1942 to 43 in 1952 to 34 in 1982 to 31 in 1992.

The state has produced few leaders of the houses of Congress. Vice President George Clinton pre-sided as president of the Senate (1805–1812). Aaron Burr was a senator (1791–1798) and contested Thomas Jefferson for the presidency in 1800. Because they received equal numbers of electoral votes, the election was transferred to the House, which chose Jefferson as president and Burr as vice president and ex officio president of the Senate. John W. Taylor, a ten-term member, was Speaker of the House (1820–1821 and 1825–1827), the only New Yorker to serve as such.

Millard Fillmore served four terms (1833–1834 and 1837–1843) in the House, was chairman of the Ways and Means Committee, was elected vice president in 1848, and became president in 1850 when Zachary Taylor died.

Benjamin B. Odell, Jr., served in the House (1895–1899) and was elected governor in 1900 and 1902. David B. Hill became a senator in 1891 after serving as governor (1885–1890), and William Sulzer served in the House for nine terms (1895–1912) before being elected governor in 1912. Similarly,

Hugh L. Carey served seven House terms (1961–1975) and became governor in 1975, and Stanley N. Lundine served five House terms (1977–1985) before his election as lieutenant governor in 1984.

Geraldine A. Ferraro, a three-term Democratic representative (1979–1985) was the first woman to be nominated for vice president (1984) by a major party. Colorful New York City mayor Fiorello H. La-Guardia (1934–1945) served in the House (1917–1919 and 1923–1933) and was cosponsor of the Norris-LaGuardia Act of 1932, which restricted issuance of court injunctions in labor disputes.

Rufus King, formerly of Massachusetts, was elected senator from New York in 1789 and set a precedent followed by Robert F. Kennedy of Massachusetts, who was elected senator from New York in 1964.

Robert F. Wagner was sponsor of the Wagner-Connery National Labor Relations Act (1935) and the Relief Act for the Unemployed of 1932 and cosponsor of the Social Security Act (1935).

In recent decades a majority of the New York members of the House have been Democrats. Twenty-seven Democrats and 15 Republicans served from 1969 to 1971, and 25 Democrats, 13 Republicans, and 1 Conservative served from 1979 to 1981. The delegation of 1991–1993 was composed of 21 Democrats and 13 Republicans. Fourteen members represent districts totally or partially in New York City.

The failure of New Yorkers to occupy leadership positions in the Congress is partly attributable to Congress's seniority system and New York's high turnover rate for senators and representatives.

BIBLIOGRAPHY

Alexander, DeAlva S. *A Political History of the State of New York.* 1906.

Brodhead, John R. *History of the State of New York.* 2 vols. 1853, 1871.

Ellis, David M., James A. Frost, Harold C. Syrett, and Harry J. Carman. *A Short History of New York State.* 1957.

Richards, Clay, and Carol Richards. "New York's Helpless Giant on Capitol Hill." *Empire State Report,* April 1975.

Salant, Jonathan D. "Clout." *Empire State Report,* July 1989.

JOSEPH F. ZIMMERMAN

NINETEENTH AMENDMENT. In 1848, when Elizabeth Cady Stanton first proposed that women seek the right to vote, it was a radical demand. Although the Constitution did not prohibit woman suffrage, it left voting requirements to the states, and virtually every state prevented women from exercising the franchise.

With much else to engage them, including the ignominy of slavery, women activists did not turn their attention to the vote until after the Civil War. Congress first addressed the issue of women suffrage in 1866 when Sen. Edgar Cowan, a Pennsylvania Republican, introduced a woman suffrage amendment to a bill to enfranchise African Americans in the District of Columbia. The Cowan proposal failed by a vote of 37 to 9. On 28 January 1867 the House of Representatives defeated a corresponding measure by a vote of 74 to 48, with 68 abstentions. Though prospects thus looked bleak for federal action, in December 1868 suffrage ally Sen. Samuel C. Pomeroy (R-Kans.) nevertheless made the gesture of proposing an amendment to the Constitution.

The battle over post–Civil War amendments broke apart the women's movement. In 1869, Susan B. Anthony and Stanton created the National Woman Suffrage Association, open only to women and vociferous about the injustice of the Fourteenth and Fifteenth Amendments, enfranchising only black men. The American Woman Suffrage Association, organized by Lucy Stone and Henry Blackwell, supported the amendments despite the slight to women and sought suffrage for women on a state-by-state basis.

Congress continued to be hostile. In 1874, it refused to permit woman suffrage in the Pembina Territory (part of what is now North Dakota), and it rescinded woman suffrage in an 1887 bill designed to outlaw polygamy in Mormon Utah, where women had voted since 1870.

In 1878 Sen. Aaron A. Sargent (R-Calif.) introduced what came to be known as the "Anthony amendment": "The right of citizens of the United States to vote shall not be denied or abridged by the United States or by any state on account of sex." The Senate Committee on Privileges and Elections held hearings, and a phalanx of suffragists appeared before it. The committee members, however, displayed not merely indifference but disdain, reading newspapers and staring at the ceiling, and the committee ultimately rejected the bill.

Suffragists introduced the bill in each subsequent Congress, and in 1882 both houses appointed Select committees on Woman Suffrage and reported the legislation favorably to the floor. The Senate Select Committee continued to report the bill favorably for the next two Congresses and the Senate held floor debates in December 1886 and January 1887, when it voted. Sen. Henry W. Blair (R-N.H.)

VOTES FOR WOMEN. Political cartoon depicting men climbing aboard the women's suffrage bandwagon. Clifford K. Berryman, 1919.   LIBRARY OF CONGRESS

led its supporters. But opponents, citing among other drawbacks the resulting enfranchisement of black women as well as white ones, easily carried the day. Not a single southern senator voted in favor. For another decade, the amendment won the support of congressional committees, but no further action took place on the floor.

The suffrage movement reunited in 1890 under the rubric of the National American Women Suffrage Association (NAWSA), and for the next twenty years, suffragists aimed their efforts at the states, even resorting, when it seemed effective, to racist and nativist appeals. They met with limited success. By 1910, only four states—Colorado, Idaho, Wyoming, and Utah—gave women the vote in all elections. The much larger number of state campaigns ended in defeat, due in part to the identification of women with temperance and the resulting opposition of the liquor interests. Suffragists called the years between 1896 and 1910 "the doldrums."

But after 1907 the example of British suffragists inspirited their American counterparts. On 8 November 1910 a referendum in Washington state gave the suffrage movement its first victory in fourteen years. California followed in 1911; Arizona, Kansas, and Oregon in 1912; and Illinois (with presidential suffrage only) in 1913. Women now had full suffrage in nine states.

A federal amendment once again became a national issue when militant suffragists led by Alice Paul staged a parade the day before Woodrow Wilson's inauguration in 1913. On 31 July 1913 a group of suffragists presented senators with 200,000 signatures in support of a constitutional amendment.

Congress responded to the heightened pressure. Routine annual hearings in Congress had yielded no action since the Senate floor debate in 1887; the last favorable committee report had appeared in 1893; since 1896, there had been no committee report at all. On 19 March 1914 the Senate considered the measure for the first time in twenty-seven years. Although it failed in the Senate (35 to 34) and, on 12 January 1915, in the House (204 to 174), suffragists were cheered by the show of substantial support.

By 1916 differences over militant tactics divided the Congressional Union, now renamed the National Woman's party (NWP), and the major suffrage group, NAWSA. Carrie Chapman Catt, NAWSA's head, focused her attention on winning support from President Wilson. While Catt praised Democratic supporters of suffrage and lobbied the president, the NWP campaigned against the Democrats in the congressional elections.

In 1917, President Wilson finally yielded to the suffragist cause and asked Democrats in Congress to move on a federal amendment. The illegal arrests and brutal treatment of NWP picketers at the hands of the police produced a group of martyrs and won suffragists some sympathy. Perhaps more important, eight states, including New York in the East and Arkansas in the South, gave women voting rights in 1917. In September, the Senate Committee on Woman Suffrage issued a favorable report on the federal amendment. At its December annual meeting NAWSA promised to target candidates in the next congressional election if the 65th Congress declined to submit the federal amendment to the states for ratification.

On 9 January 1918, President Wilson made a public statement in favor of the amendment to Rep. John E. Raker (D-Calif.), who chaired the House Committee on Woman Suffrage. Everyone nonetheless anticipated a close vote, and on 10 January the amendment won exactly the two-thirds majority it required: 274 votes in favor, 136 opposed. Republicans proved to be the more enthusiastic party; their vote was 165 to 33, compared to an almost evenly split Democratic vote, 104 to 102, opposition coming primarily from southern members.

Counting on the measure's defeat, opponents called for a vote on the bill in the Senate in September 1918. On 30 September, President Wilson personally addressed the Senate, asking for a vote in favor of the amendment. But on the following day, 1 October, the Senate defeated the amendment by a vote of 62 to 34 against, two votes short of the two-thirds needed to send the amendment to the states.

NAWSA targeted four senators for defeat in the 1918 election; two of them, John W. Weeks (R-Mass.) and Willard Saulsbury (D-Del.), lost. Three of four 1918 state referenda were successful; by early 1919, a majority of states would permit women to vote in the next presidential election.

President Wilson convened the 66th Congress in special session on 20 May 1919, and the House, with 117 new members, repassed the suffrage amendment on its opening day by a generous margin of 304 to 89. Senate opponents insisted on a two-day debate, during which they futilely repeated their claims of states' rights. Three amendments—stalling tactics—were offered and failed. Finally, the vote was taken. Absent opponents insisted on being paired, with the result that every senator went on record. The final vote, on 4 June 1919, went as planned, 56 to 25 (with 10 paired for it and 5 against). Three states acted on 10 June to ratify, Wisconsin being the first to file its ratification resolution, with Illinois and Michigan close behind.

Suffragists did not anticipate an easy ratification battle. The opposition needed only thirteen states to prevent its success, and twelve southern and border states seemed likely candidates to fail to ratify. Ratification campaigns went on simultaneously, straining suffragist energies. In June of 1920, a Supreme Court decision related to the ratification of the Prohibition amendment opened the way for a special session of the Tennessee legislature. Under pressure from the national Democratic party, Gov. Albert H. Roberts convened a special session of the Tennessee legislature for 9 August. Tennessee's Senate ratified generously, 25 to 4, on the opening day of the session. In the Tennessee House, the vote was delayed until 18 August, when, in a vote dramatic to the last moment, it ratified 49 to 47. With the signature of the secretary of State on August 26, the Nineteenth Amendment to the Constitution now enfranchised American women.

The adoption of the Nineteenth Amendment to the Constitution generated a flurry of activity on the part of Congress. Between 1920 and 1925, laws were passed ameliorating disabilities affecting women who married aliens, offering money for maternal and infant health, and equalizing pay in the federal

civil service. By 1925, though, Congress members had breathed a sigh of relief: women were not voting as a bloc and politics could go on as usual. Almost half a century passed before Congress again felt the pressure of an organized women's movement.

[See also Voting and Suffrage.]

BIBLIOGRAPHY

Buhle, Mari Jo, and Buhle, Paul, eds. *The Concise History of Woman Suffrage: Selections from the Classic Work of Stanton, Anthony, Gage, and Harper.* 1978.
Flexner, Eleanor. *Century of Struggle: The Woman's Rights Movement in the United States.* 1972.

CYNTHIA HARRISON

NIXON, RICHARD M.

NIXON, RICHARD M. (1913–1994), Republican representative and senator from California, vice president, thirty-seventh president of the United States, whose cover-up of the Watergate scandal led to congressional impeachment proceedings and ultimately the fall of his administration.

The second of five sons, Richard Milhous Nixon was born in Yorba Linda, California, to hardworking, lower-middle-class Quakers, Hannah Milhous and Frank Nixon. His marriage to Thelma Catherine (Pat) Ryan on 21 June 1940 produced two daughters, Patricia (Tricia) and Julie. Nixon, a determined and diligent student and class leader, advanced from Whittier College through Duke Law School.

On Capitol Hill. After serving with the U.S. Navy from 1942 until 1946, he became the Republican candidate to represent California's 12th Congressional District outside Los Angeles. His subsequent campaign against veteran liberal incumbent H. Jerry Voorhis began his reputation for "rock 'em, sock 'em" tactics when he linked Voorhis with communist and other left-wing elements. Nixon took his seat in the Republican-dominated 80th Congress by winning 56.7 percent of the vote against Voorhis. This campaign later became associated in the public mind with the one he ran in 1950 to defeat Rep. Helen Gahagan Douglas for one of California's senatorial seats. The candidates traded "soft on communism" charges. Nixon advanced to the Senate with 59.2 percent of the total vote, the largest margin of any senator elected that year.

As a freshman representative, Nixon became a member of the Education and Labor Committee and the House Un-American Activities Committee, commonly known as HUAC. He helped organize the Chowder and Marching Society, which was designed to bring together Republican freshmen to formulate strategy and legislation. As a conservative who did not share the traditional isolationist views of many Republican colleagues, he became a member of the special committee under the chairmanship of Rep. Christian A. Herter (R-Mass.), known as the Herter Committee, which investigated the feasibility of the Marshall Plan to spur postwar European economic recovery. In 1947, he went on a fact-finding mission to Europe. Despite his constituents' resistance to foreign aid, Nixon voted for the Economic Cooperation Act of 1948.

Unlike many red-baiters of his day, Nixon was relatively centrist in other ways. His vote in support of the Taft-Hartley Labor-Management Relations Act of 1947 (the Taft-Hartley Act) to rein in labor union power that had been granted by the Wagner-Connery National Labor Relations Act of 1935 was entirely consistent with the feelings of his district and the mood of the nation.

Nevertheless, Nixon became most noted for attacking ostensible left-wing subversion, and his name became synonymous with anticommunism. As a member of HUAC, he was associated with some of the most ardent communist headhunters in Congress. He began to become well known through his sponsorship of the Mundt-Nixon bill of 1948, which was designed to compel the registration of both individual communists and their organizations. Although the bill was buried by the Senate in 1948, much of Mundt-Nixon lived on in the McCarran Internal Security Act, passed two years later.

Nothing he ever did in Congress gave Nixon as much recognition as the Alger Hiss case. Hiss, who had worked in government during the 1930s and served with the State Department through 1946, was accused by a former communist, Whittaker Chambers, of having passed secret documents to a communist cell in Washington. Hiss's denials were not believed by Nixon, whose initiative led to House Un-American Activities hearings in August 1948 that undermined Hiss's denials about having known Chambers, which resulted in a federal indictment and two trials. The first ended in a hung jury; the second convicted Hiss on two counts of perjury (the statute of limitations on espionage committed in the 1930s had expired). The outcome had mixed results for Nixon; it established his credentials as a communist hunter, which helped bolster his career in Cold War America, but it also compounded his image as an unscrupulous fighter.

Nixon's criticism of the Truman administration was unrelenting. He denounced the president and the State Department for the "loss" of China when the communists forced Chiang Kai-shek's nationalists to withdraw to Formosa. Nixon backed the Korean intervention, but his excoriation of the Democratic president escalated when Truman relieved General Douglas MacArthur of his command in April 1951.

By the age of thirty-nine, Nixon was the party's most sought-after speaker. He was also ideally placed to become Dwight D. Eisenhower's running mate in 1952. By choosing Nixon, the Republicans not only achieved geographic and generational balance (Eisenhower turned sixty-two before that year's election) but also tied someone who was prominent among vehement anticommunists while also acceptable to the party's moderate internationalists. All such advantages almost came to naught when a New York City tabloid newspaper accused Nixon of being the beneficiary of a so-called secret fund donated by supporters to underwrite his extra congressional office expenses. Nixon's televised defense, the so-called "Checkers speech," was an effective early use of television's power to convey a folksy human interest story about Nixon's acceptance of the dog Checkers as a gift for his daughters. It succeeded in eliciting enough popular sympathy to force Eisenhower to keep him on the ticket.

The Vice Presidency. In terms of vice presidential activism, Nixon's tenure became a model for the modern conduct of the vice presidency. Statutory changes, such as the creation of the National Security Council in 1947, gave him a specific function. Since the president was reluctant to take on Sen. Joseph R. McCarthy himself, Nixon was assigned the task of making a televised speech in March 1954 critical of the senator's methods—methods that involved charges about supposed adherence to communism or associations that suggested actual or potential disloyalty to the United States. In that fall's congressional campaign, however, Nixon adopted the McCarthyesque theme of denouncing Democrats for their "softness" toward communism. He began the 85th Congress in early 1957 with a ruling, as presiding officer of the Senate, that later made him anathema to many anti–civil rights conservatives; a simple majority of senators, he stated, could in effect eliminate the filibuster by adopting new rules for that body. The Senate, however, failed to modify the long-standing filibuster rule, Rule XXII. Eisenhower, who suffered three major health scares while in office, signed an agreement with the vice president that, in the absence of an appropriate constitutional provision (the Twenty-fifth Amendment was not ratified until 1967), provided for his succession in the event of presidential disability.

Defeat and Comeback. Nixon was sidetracked en route to his own presidency. The Republican presidential nominee in 1960, he lost to John F. Kennedy by little more than 100,000 popular votes out of the 69 million cast and by 303 to 219 in the electoral college; it was one of the closest elections in U.S. history. That defeat was then compounded by an embarrassing loss to Gov. Edmund G. (Pat) Brown in the 1962 California gubernatorial race that seemed to confirm the end of his political career. He and his family soon after moved to New York City.

Restless and eager for a return to political life, he defied conventional analyses by achieving a comeback. His tireless campaigning in 1964 for Barry Goldwater against President Lyndon B. Johnson, in what he knew was a hopeless cause, served his purpose by reestablishing his standing with fellow Republicans. So did his work for the party during the congressional elections of 1966, a year when conservatives staged a resurgence.

By 1968, his potential Republican rivals had been weakened for a variety of reasons. Furthermore, the nation was dissatisfied with Johnson's conduct of the war in Vietnam and with Great Society management of social unrest and disorder at home. And so the public was receptive to Nixon's "practical liberalism" and his emphasis on the "traditional" values whose erosion, he argued, had undermined entrepreneurial initiative and hurt the new middle class. A split Democratic party, further crippled by the tumultuous events that surrounded its convention in Chicago, was unable to coalesce in time behind its candidate, Vice President Hubert H. Humphrey, and Nixon became the thirty-seventh president.

In the White House. As president, Nixon's relations with his three Congresses, the 91st through the 93d, approximated the contentiousness of President Andrew Johnson's congressional relations during Reconstruction. Nixon was the first president since Zachary Taylor in 1849 to be inaugurated with Capitol Hill controlled by opposing majorities in each house. Furthermore, the Democratic congressional leadership was facing a Republican president with a long history of engaging in partisan warfare. Nixon's focus on foreign policy and conservative spending policies created additional tensions, as did the ongo-

RICHARD M. NIXON. As president, in the House chamber, being applauded by members of Congress on the occasion of an appearance before a joint session of Congress.   OFFICE OF THE HISTORIAN OF THE U.S. SENATE

ing Vietnam War. Congressional-presidential relations were finally utterly spoiled by the scandal known as Watergate. Mounting revelations about Watergate wrongdoing coincided in October 1973 with the resignations of Nixon's vice president, Spiro T. Agnew, who pleaded nolo contendere in the face of bribery charges. The atmosphere between Capitol Hill and the White House had become so poisoned that Nixon chose as vice president the popular House Republican leader Gerald R. Ford, because the expected ease of his confirmation under the provisions of the Twenty-fifth Amendment would avoid compounding Nixon's already substantial difficulties.

At the beginning of his administration, Nixon stated that his inaugural objective was "to bring America together." The new administration, however, sensing that Washington was full of enemies and facing crises in Asia and Europe as well as in the streets of the United States, turned inward. Instead of establishing an activist legislative liaison team,

Nixon placed control chiefly in the hands of the White House staff, and in particular John Ehrlichman, head of the Domestic Affairs Council.

Early on, citing his responsibility to what he was later to call the "silent" or "forgotten" majority, he announced his New Federalism program on 8 August 1969, with welfare reform as its centerpiece. But that reform ultimately fell under criticism from both left and right and Nixon's own reluctance to push against the tide. He was, however, able to introduce his concept of "black capitalism" with passage of the Philadelphia Plan in late 1969. The plan aimed at desegregating the highly exclusionary construction industry by promoting the hiring of minority workers. Nixon also won a narrow victory that year by turning back an amendment to stop deployment of the Safeguard ABM (antiballistic missile) system. Although unwilling to spend as much as congressional liberals would have liked, the administration backed and won approval for the National Environmental Policy Act, which Nixon signed on 1 January 1970. His reorganization plan, sent to Congress in July, established an independent Environmental Protection Agency (EPA) that represented a consolidation of major antipollution programs. The 92d Congress denied his efforts to fund a supersonic transport (SST) and to increase foreign aid.

Nixon had long advocated the sharing of federal revenues among states and localities. In 1971, he had listed as one of his "great goals" the establishment of a federal revenue sharing program. This he achieved in 1972, with the passage of the State and Local Fiscal Assistance Act (which expired in 1986). In 1973 he proposed two plans for executive-branch reorganization, with which Congress went along. The objective was a leaner bureaucracy; the reality, however, was an enlarged White House staff during the Nixon years. This happened despite his announced second-term program, which he called the New American Revolution, to do something about a government he called "too fat, too bloated."

Nixon's primary absorption, however, was in the area of foreign policy. He teamed up with Henry Kissinger, who first served as national security adviser and then as secretary of State, to capitalize on the constitutional prerogatives that can be exploited by an activist president. His broad hint about having a "secret plan" (a phrase not actually spoken) to end the Vietnam War struck a chord with a nation already exasperated by being bogged down in what some called "the big muddy." A plan for disengagement did emerge, although it involved expanding hostilities into neighboring Cambodia and intensifying the air war over North Vietnam. Nixon's "Vietnamization" combined increased firepower from the skies with greater responsibility for indigenous forces, constituting the so-called Nixon Doctrine. Finally, after continued protests at home and massive bombing of the North in late 1972, he succeeded in disengaging the U.S. military through a peace accord in January 1973.

Already under way were such initiatives as his "opening" to the People's Republic of China and the dramatic presidential trip to that communist behemoth in February 1972, followed by a visit to Moscow. There, with Soviet leader Leonid Brezhnev, Nixon signed the first Cold War arms limitation agreements, the SALT I agreements. Nixon, with his accommodation with Moscow and the reversal of his longstanding hostility toward the government in Beijing, thereby took significant steps toward the achievement of détente. At the same time, Nixon and Kissinger maintained U.S. military as well as diplomatic muscle by the use of covert tactics to thwart the success of the leftist government of Salvador Allende in Chile and hostile threats to the Middle East. Most dramatic was the administration's declaration of a worldwide emergency to safeguard U.S. interests by protecting Israel during the Yom Kippur War of 1973. His strength in the world arena would later make it hard for much of the world to understand how such a "mere" scandal as Watergate could topple him from power.

The administration became more conservative with the passage of time, particularly as the Democratic opposition shifted to the left. By the advent of the 93d Congress, after his landslide victory over George McGovern in 1972, Nixon was fighting to dismantle a centerpiece of the Great Society, the Economic Opportunity Act. Another instance of the rightward shift was his impoundment of funds authorized by Congress, which resulted in battles that disrupted relations with Capitol Hill. Even more contentiousness was generated by Nixon's increasing use of the veto. One such veto aimed at the War Powers Act of 1973, which was a congressional attempt to limit presidential authority to deploy U.S. forces to a combat zone. Congress overturned this veto in the most significant of its five veto overrides of the Nixon era. Of Nixon's forty vetoes, twenty-eight coincided with the second session of the 92d Congress compared to just twelve during the first three years of his presidency.

Bitterness also surrounded some of Nixon's

Supreme Court nominees. The 1969 nomination of Warren Burger to succeeded the retiring Earl Warren as chief justice was routinely approved. Thereafter, the battle centered on Nixon's efforts to redesign the Court, which had been under bitter attack from conservatives for over a decade. He encountered strong hostility from congressional liberals and failed to secure approval for the successive nominations of Clement E. Haynsworth, Jr., of South Carolina and G. Harrold Carswell of Florida. He did manage to move the Court away from Warren liberalism by eventually proposing three nominees acceptable to Congress: Harry A. Blackmun of Minnesota; Lewis F. Powell, Jr., of Virginia; and William H. Rehnquist of Arizona.

With increasing evidence of high-level administration involvement in the break-in at Democratic party headquarters in the Watergate complex in Washington on 17 June 1972, revelations about related scandals, and the controversy over presidential tapes revealing White House complicity, Nixon's standing with the American people and with Congress eroded. So did support for his continuing pursuit of the war in Southeast Asia, to which the Hill responded not only with the War Powers Act but also by cutting off funding for the bombing of Cambodia and continued military operations in Vietnam. Nixon always blamed Congress for turning its back on his promise to grant postwar economic assistance to President Nguyen Van Thieu of South Vietnam, which he regarded as essential for the armistice agreement of January 1973.

Watergate overwhelmed congressional relations from mid-1973, and activity within the administration was similarly paralyzed. A senatorial investigating committee headed by Sam Ervin (D-N.C.) during the summer of 1973 uncovered the existence of an Oval Office taping system. The battle over the release of these tapes was played out in the Senate and the courts and led to the so-called Saturday-night massacre, which resulted in the firing, among others, of Watergate special prosecutor Archibald Cox. Nixon, meanwhile, attempted to court key members of Congress in preparation for an impeachment trial, but such efforts were futile. In July 1974, the House Judiciary Committee voted for three articles of impeachment against Nixon: obstruction of justice, abuse of presidential power, and contempt of Congress. Nixon's own subsequent release of the so-called smoking-gun tape of 23 June 1972, which recorded his instructions to have the CIA block an FBI investigation of the Watergate break-in, led to his resignation on 9 August 1974.

The impeachment proceedings were scheduled to begin only ten days later, and there can be little doubt that he would have been impeached and convicted. In later years, Nixon's defenders would have to restrict themselves to praising his foreign relations achievements—especially his opening of dialogue with the People's Republic of China—when citing his presidential accomplishments.

Nixon died on 2 April 1994, four days after suffering a massive stroke. He had just returned from a trip to Russia, where he was snubbed by President Boris Yeltsin because of his meetings with opposition leaders. The outpouring of obituaries and assessments from around the world tended to de-emphasize the Watergate affair, praising his contributions to foreign policy, especially his initiatives to the People's Republic of China. Some called him the most commanding American political figure of the second half of the twentieth century.

BIBLIOGRAPHY

Ambrose, Stephen E. *Nixon.* 3 vols. 1987–1991.
Kutler, Stanley I. *The Wars of Watergate.* 1990.
Morris, Roger. *Richard Milhous Nixon.* 1990.
Parmet, Herbert S. *Richard Nixon and His America.* 1990.
Sundquist, James I. *The Decline and Resurgence of Congress.* 1981.

HERBERT S. PARMET

NON-LEGISLATIVE AND FINANCIAL SERVICES, DIRECTOR OF.

On 9 April 1992, in the wake of the House Bank and Post Office scandals, the House passed a sweeping internal reform package that created the job of financial administrator and greatly reduced the powers of the House's traditional officers. The package eliminated the position of House postmaster, an officer's position first created during the 21st Congress in 1829, and returned to the remaining officers—the sergeant at arms, the clerk of the House, and the doorkeeper—their original constitutional duties, relieving them of all financial responsibilities.

The position of director of Non-Legislative and Financial Services was created and charged with taking over all financial operations of the House, including the barber and beauty shops, internal mail operations, telephone exchange, office supply service, payroll, and placement office, among others. In taking over all internal money matters, the House director is expected to prevent such mismanagement and corruption problems as sparked the House Bank and Post Office scandals. After passage of the reform package by a vote of 269 to 81, House Speaker Thomas S. Foley (D-Wash.) called the legislation "the most far-reaching reorganization of nonlegislative activities of the House of Representatives in the history of this country."

Unlike the other officers, who are chosen by the majority party in the House, the director is mandated as a nonpartisan position jointly appointed at the beginning of every new Congress by the Speaker, majority leader, and minority leader. The director is paid the same salary as all other House officers. In 1993, that salary was $122,932.

The April legislation called for the appointment of the first director within ninety days of its passage, but the House leadership could not come to an agreement on a qualified candidate until October 1992, three months after the original deadline. On 23 October 1992, after hiring an outside headhunting firm, the House finally selected retired Lieutenant General Leonard Wishart, a thirty-four-year army veteran who served two stints in Vietnam. Wishart officially took over as the new director at the beginning of the 103d Congress in January 1993. Just one year later, however, following months of disputes with House leaders over which financial operations should be given to the director's control, Wishart announced his resignation from office on 10 January 1994. Wishart's deputy director, Randall Medlock, was quickly named as acting director by House leaders, but a permanent director had not been designated as of May 1994.

The director's personal office staff consists of only several assistants, including a receptionist and scheduler. The hundreds of workers in the financial operations transferred to the director, however, are also considered under the jurisdiction of that position, with the supervisors of those operations reporting directly to the director.

One of General Wishart's first, and perhaps most far-reaching, reforms was ending the use of patronage within all the financial operations under his control. When previously under the purview of the clerk or postmaster, many of those financial operations had hired workers who had been sponsored by members of Congress. Those workers were often guaranteed jobs, regardless of performance, because of their connections. In taking control of such operations as the House Post Office and Finance Office, Wishart vowed to hire and retain workers solely on the basis of their performance and abilities.

The director, however, is not completely free of member supervision. The reform package that es-tablished the director's office also created a House administration subcommittee on administrative oversight, split evenly between Republicans and Democrats, which has final say over the director's activities. The reform package also created the post of an inspector general, who is charged with conducting periodic audits of the House's financial operations. On 27 October 1993, nearly eighteen months after the position of inspector general was first created, House leaders appointed John Lainhart, a former assistant inspector general with the Department of Transportation, to the post.

[See also Inspector General of the House.]

BIBLIOGRAPHY

Burger, Timothy. "Wishart Quits Abruptly as First House Director." *Roll Call*, 13 January 1994, p. 1.

Foerstel, Karen. "House Finally Gets a Housekeeper." *Roll Call*, 13 April 1992, p. 1.

U.S. House of Representatives. *House Administrative Reform Resolution of 1992*. 102d Cong., 2d sess., 9 April 1992. H. Res. 423.

KAREN FOERSTEL

NON-PROLIFERATION TREATY. *See* Nuclear Non-Proliferation Treaty.

NONSTATUTORY CONTROLS. It is frequently claimed that "this is a government of laws," but many of the public policies decided by Congress and the president are not determined by laws at all. Rather, they are established by directives set forth in committee reports, committee hearings, floor debates, and correspondence from members of Congress. Although these nonstatutory controls are not legally binding, agencies and departments prudently abide by them. Flaunting nonstatutory controls can provoke serious retaliations from Congress.

Agencies have much to gain by demonstrating respect for nonstatutory controls. So long as they comply with these signals from Congress, they will continue to receive substantial discretion in administering programs and obtaining important flexibility in the course of a fiscal year. For example, the energy appropriations act for fiscal 1993 provided $1.2 billion for construction by the U.S. Army Corps of Engineers. It is basically a lump sum, although the statute indicates with a few earmarks how some of the money is to be spent. But the great bulk of congressional controls is found in the conference report, which identifies state by state exactly where the construction funds are expected to go. If the Corps of Engineers finds it necessary to depart from the nonstatutory schedule, because of delays in some projects and the need to expedite others, it may move money around within the construction account. Depending on the agreement established between the Corps of Engineers and its review committees in Congress, the shifts may require the prior approval of designated committees.

Nonstatutory controls clearly meet the needs of both branches. Neither Congress nor the agencies are always certain of the specifics to be included in a statute. Agency estimates are based on assumptions about matters that are a year or perhaps several years in the future. It is often better to appropriate on a lump-sum basis and trust in committee-agency adjustments as the year unfolds. In this way a change in spending does not require the passage of another statute. Placing guidelines and details in nonstatutory sources adds valuable flexibility to the legislative and administrative process.

The system of nonstatutory controls is fragile. Much depends on a "keep the faith" attitude among agency officials. In presenting their budget justifications they are identifying how they think a lump sum should be spent. Congress then alters those justifications through the regular legislative process. Maintaining the integrity of the adjusted justifications is essential in preserving a relationship of trust and confidence with congressional committees. Violation of that trust is likely to result in budget cutbacks, restrictive language in statutes, and an itemization of appropriations in the statutes. Agencies do what they can to avoid such retribution. In a committee report in 1973 the House Appropriations Committee conceded that agencies may by law ignore nonstatutory controls but only at great peril:

> In a strictly legal sense, the Department of Defense could utilize the funds appropriated for whatever programs were included under the individual appropriation accounts, but the relationship with the Congress demands that the detailed justifications which are presented in support of budget requests be followed. To do otherwise would cause Congress to lose confidence in the requests made and probably result in reduced appropriations or line item appropriation bills. (H. Rept. 93-662, 93d Cong., 1st sess., 1973, p. 16.)

A widely used form of nonstatutory controls is "reprogramming," which consists of shifting funds within an appropriation account. Control is exercised primarily through committee reports, agency directives, and a complex yet precise set of understandings between the two branches. Initially, in the 1940s and 1950s, Congress generally insisted only that it be notified of reprogrammings, but the legislative controls gradually stiffened; prior approval is needed from designated committees before proceeding with certain types of reprogrammings. Over the course of time, prior approval was required not only from the Appropriations committees but also from the authorizing committees having jurisdiction over an agency.

In 1988 James C. Miller III, director of the Office of Management and Budget (OMB), decided to confront Congress on its use of report language to control agency activities. Claiming that the reports had "no force of law," he advised agency heads that in implementing their programs they could ignore nonstatutory controls. The condemnation from Congress was swift and bipartisan. The chairman of the House Appropriations Committee, Jamie L. Whitten (D-Miss.), warned the administration that Miller's views were "unsound and must not be followed." Democratic and Republican leaders from both the House and the Senate warned President Ronald Reagan to repudiate Miller's policy. Miller quickly retreated, and subsequent OMB directors have not repeated his challenge to nonstatutory controls.

BIBLIOGRAPHY

Fisher, Louis. *The Politics of Shared Power: Congress and the Executive.* 3d ed. 1993. Pp. 62–64, 68–71, 81–84.

Fisher, Louis. *Presidential Spending Power.* 1975. Pp. 71–98.

Kirst, Michael W. *Government without Making Laws.* 1969.

LOUIS FISHER

NONVOTING DELEGATES. *See* Delegates, Nonvoting.

NORRIS, GEORGE W. (1861–1944), Republican representative and senator from Nebraska, leader in the 1910 "insurgency revolt" against the power of the Speaker, chiefly responsible for the Tennessee Valley Act (1933), author of the Twentieth Amendment, Senate sponsor of the Anti-Injunction Act (1932). Born on a farm near Clyde, Ohio, on 11 July 1861, George William Norris was the eleventh of twelve children. He attended Baldwin University (later Baldwin-Wallace College) and Northern Indiana Normal School and Business Institute (now Valparaiso University), from which he received a law degree in 1883. He launched his career as a lawyer after moving to Nebraska in 1885 and entered politics in the 1890s as the state's prosperity gave way to an extended period of drought and depression. In 1902 Norris won the Republican nomination for Congress and in the November election narrowly defeated the Democratic incumbent. Thereafter, he won every race he engaged in until 1942, when, seeking a sixth term as a United States senator and running as an independent, he was defeated.

As a representative, Norris initially recognized his indebtedness to railroad officials and to the party organization. However, as sentiment in Nebraska prompted legislation to curb the power of the brewers and the railroads and to modernize government by making it more responsible and efficient, Norris began to support congressional measures regulating railroads. In 1908 he allied himself with the House insurgents seeking to curtail the power of Speaker Joseph G. Cannon. As a result, though he supported William Howard Taft for president in 1908, neither the national nor the state Republican organizations supported his reelection campaign. He won by twenty-two votes but learned that he no longer could rely on his party in future elections.

This view was reinforced when Taft revoked the patronage of Norris and the other Republican insurgents. In doing so he exacerbated the tensions between them and the old guard, who in the House were led by Speaker Cannon. Norris, denied major committee assignments because of his support of the insurgents in 1908, precipitated the revolt on 17 March 1910, when he rose and asked for recognition to present a matter privileged by the Constitution. Cannon unwittingly acceded to this request. Norris's motion called for an elected Rules Committee on which the Speaker could not serve. Cannon declared the motion out of order but could not find the votes to sustain his position. After extended emotional debate, Norris's resolution prevailed by a vote of 191 to 156, thanks to the Democratic minority supporting the insurgents. Overnight, Norris became a national political figure and in 1910 handily won reelection to a fifth term.

He also gained recognition as a prominent progressive. When Robert M. La Follette of Wisconsin organized the National Progressive Republican League early in 1911, Norris was named its first vice president. He endorsed La Follette for the presidency in 1912 but switched to Theodore Roosevelt when he became convinced that La Follette could not win the nomination. He stayed out of Roosevelt's third-party campaign because he did not wish to return the Republican organization in Nebraska to the "stand-pat" faction and thereby jeopardize his effort to secure a Senate seat. He was successful on both counts. He defeated the incumbent, Norris Brown (who supported Taft), for the Republican nomination in the primary and was the only Nebraska Republican to win a major office in the Democratic landslide in Nebraska.

Norris was fifty-one when he was sworn in as a senator. He served in the Senate for the next thirty years, during which he emerged as one of that body's most constructive and independent members. While he objected to the Democratic use of the caucus during the first Wilson administration, considering it another form of "Cannonism," he nevertheless voted for most of the significant New Freedom measures. In 1916 he voted for Louis D. Brandeis's appointment to the Supreme Court, one of only three non-Democratic senators to do so. He was critical of Wilson's foreign policy, however, and in 1917 opposed the resolution that called for the arming of merchant vessels traveling through Atlantic war zones. In so doing he was bitterly denounced by the president and others as one of "the little group of willful men." He voted in April 1917 against the declaration of war (one of six senators to do so) because of his belief that powerful business and financial interests stood to gain at the expense of American lives. While he then endorsed the administration's prosecution of the war, including increased taxation and government operation of the railroads, he was unable to vote for the Treaty of Versailles because of what he considered grave inequities, particularly the diplomacy that sanctioned Japanese control of the Shantung Peninsula in China and continued British domination of colonial peoples. Unwilling to compromise, he became a member of the Senate "irreconcilables" in opposition to the treaty.

Republican ascendancy in the 1920s enabled Norris to serve as chairman of the powerful Senate committees on Agriculture and the Judiciary. During that decade he emerged as a leading critic of the complacency and business orientation of the administrations of Warren G. Harding, Calvin Coolidge, and Herbert Hoover. He opposed confirmation of Charles Evans Hughes and John J. Parker to the Supreme Court, of Charles B. Warren as attorney general, of Thomas B. Woodlock to the Interstate Commerce Commission, and of Truman H. Newberry, Frank L. Smith, and William S. Vare for Senate seats, all because he found them too closely tied to corporate wealth or corrupt interests. In for-

GEORGE W. NORRIS. Standing on the roadway on top of the Tennessee Valley Authority's Norris Dam, November 1938.
TENNESSEE VALLEY AUTHORITY

eign policy his views also ran counter to those of his party. He favored recognition of the Soviet Union, endorsed the goals of the Mexican revolution, and opposed the use of U.S. Marines and the activities of U.S. business interests in Nicaragua.

Norris gained wide recognition as an advocate of the depressed farmer and the oppressed laborer, a supporter of more efficient use of natural resources, and a proponent of the direct election of presidents. In 1924, through the Norris-Sinclair bill, he called for government purchase and overseas sale of agricultural surpluses, a proposal refined and incorporated into the McNary-Haugen bills for farm relief. He sponsored and prepared the 1932 Norris-LaGuardia Anti-Injunction Act, which curbed the use of injunctions in labor disputes, prohibited the use of "yellow-dog" (anti-union) contracts, and affirmed the rights of working people to organize and bargain collectively. In addition, he was the author of the Twentieth Amendment to the Constitution, which shifted presidential inaugurations from March to January, thereby dispensing with the holdover (lame-duck) session of the outgoing Congress. This amendment, the only one enacted primarily through the efforts of one individual, was ratified by the requisite two-thirds (thirty-two) states early in 1933.

Norris became the leading opponent of private utility development of facilities on major American waterways. He called for public generation, transmission, and distribution of hydroelectric power at Muscle Shoals, Alabama, a hydroelectric facility built by the federal government during World War I. His initial task was to prevent its sale, first to Henry Ford and then to private utility companies at sums not reflecting its actual value. By 1928 he had convinced Congress to approve a measure calling for government development of Muscle Shoals. President Coolidge vetoed the bill, as did Hoover when it again passed Congress in 1931.

Norris's ties to the Republican party further weakened during the 1920s. He endorsed Hiram W. Johnson's bid for the nomination in 1920, and favored La Follette's third party in 1924. In 1928 he campaigned for the reelection of progressive senators of both parties and publicly endorsed the Democratic presidential candidate, Alfred E. Smith, largely owing to Republican platform planks on agriculture and hydroelectric power. In 1932 he again endorsed the Democratic candidate, Franklin D. Roosevelt. Norris survived an effort two years earlier by Republican regulars to end his career by promoting a grocery clerk also named George W. Norris in the senatorial primary. The plot was thwarted by the courts, and he won a fourth term in the Senate.

Norris supported most New Deal measures. He was the chief author of the Tennessee Valley Authority (TVA) Act, which provided for the multipurpose development of the Tennessee River, and he was largely responsible for two other New Deal measures, the Norris-Rayburn Rural Electrification Act (REA) of 1936 and, the following year, the Norris-Doxey Farm Forestry Act. These measures reflected his deep commitment to the public development of natural resources. His relationship with President Roosevelt was close both personally and politically. In 1936 and again in 1942 Roosevelt endorsed Norris's reelection as an independent, and in 1940 Norris campaigned for Roosevelt in western states, where public power was a vital issue. Norris was hostile, however, to New Deal patronage policies and the intense partisanship of James A. Farley, postmaster general and Democratic National Committee chairman. Thanks to Norris's efforts the enabling acts of the TVA and the REA contained provisions that all appointments and promotions had to be considered on a merit basis. In 1937, while a critic of Roosevelt's Court-packing plan, he nevertheless endorsed it after recognizing that his more modest proposal to curb the power of the Court in declaring laws of Congress unconstitutional commanded little attention.

Norris's most difficult task was to support the administration's foreign policy after 1936. He reluctantly concluded that totalitarian aggression could be challenged only through the threat of force. But he could not find it within himself to vote, in 1940, for compulsory military service or, later, for the drafting of eighteen-year-olds. Always sensitive to matters affecting civil liberties, Norris was openly critical of the Justice Department and the Federal Bureau of Investigation for their treatment of aliens and suspect persons after the Japanese invasion of Pearl Harbor. He was the first member of Congress to publicly denounce J. Edgar Hoover, the head of the FBI. His last significant legislative concern revolved around an effort to repeal the poll tax in national elections.

Again seeking reelection as an independent in 1942, Norris failed to win a sixth senatorial term. He returned to his hometown of McCook, Nebraska, retained an active interest in public affairs, and prepared his autobiography, *Fighting Liberal*. In August 1944, several weeks before he would have completed it, he suffered a cerebral hemorrhage. He died at his house in McCook at the age of eighty-three and was buried in the town's Memorial Park Cemetery.

BIBLIOGRAPHY

Fellman, David. "The Liberalism of Senator Norris." *American Political Science Review* 40 (1946): 27–51.
Lowitt, Richard. *George W. Norris.* 3 vols. 1963–1978.
Nebraska History (June 1961). Entire issue devoted to Norris.
Norris, George W. *Fighting Liberal.* 1961.

RICHARD LOWITT

NORTH ATLANTIC TREATY (63 Stat. 2241–2253). Signed in Washington, D.C., on 4 April 1949 and ratified by the Senate on 21 July 1949, the North Atlantic Treaty linked the United States in a collective defense alliance with eleven nations. The pact marked the abandonment of the U.S. tradition of nonentanglement that had begun in 1800 with the termination of the French alliance of 1778. The treaty's origins lay in the Cold War that grew out of conflict between the communist and noncommunist victors in World War II. The breakdown of the Yalta agreement of 1945 over the restoration of Europe made it impossible for the new United Nations to fulfill the peacekeeping functions with which its founders had invested it in 1944.

It required two years and the propounding of diplomat George Kennan's containment thesis before the Truman administration came up with a coherent plan to cope with communist expansion. Kennan's so-called Long Telegram of 1946 ultimately convinced the nation that a diplomatic accommodation with the Soviet Union was impossible and that only American power stood in the way of

NORTH ATLANTIC TREATY. Sen. Robert A. Taft (R-Ohio) opposed interventionist foreign policies and objected to military buildups under NATO. This cartoon portrays Taft arguing over the North Atlantic Treaty with John Foster Dulles (R-N.Y.), delegate to various postwar European conferences, while internationalist senators Arthur H. Vandenberg (R-Mich.) and Tom T. Connally (D-Tex.) confer in the background, asserting their bipartisan cooperation. Clifford K. Berryman, *Washington Evening Star*, 14 July 1949.

the spread of communism in Europe. Acceptance of the containment policy, expressed in the Truman Doctrine and Marshall Plan of 1947, did not necessarily mean abandoning the isolationist tradition. These measures did not include a political or military commitment to allies.

After the failure of the Foreign Ministers' Conference of December 1947, Britain and France attempted to convince the United States of the importance of a long-term military-political commitment. As evidence of their willingness to bury old rivalries, Britain and France, along with the Low Countries and Luxembourg, entered into a fifty-year military alliance on 17 March 1948 (the Treaty of Brussels) and hoped that the United States would join. The Truman administration, concerned about congressional reaction, was not prepared to take that step but in late March 1948 did allow secret conversations at the Pentagon with British and Canadian representatives to take place—conversations that recognized the inevitability of an Atlantic security pact.

No public move was made until Sen. Arthur H. Vandenberg (R-Mich.), chairman of the Foreign Relations Committee in the 80th Congress, led the Senate in a resolution on 11 June 1948 supporting collective security in Europe. While this was not a guarantee of American membership, it opened the way for negotiations with the signatories to the Brussels treaty. These negotiations were conducted in Washington from July to December 1948. Fears of opposition from both traditional isolationists and new partisans of internationalism contributed to postponing a decision until after the presidential election in November.

Even after the election the Foreign Relations Committee, now under Sen. Tom T. Connally (D-Tex.), had difficulty with the promise, contained in article 5 of the treaty, that an attack against any signatory nation would be considered an attack against all. The Brussels pact governments in turn had difficulty with American insistence that the membership be widened to include Denmark, Norway, Iceland, Portugal, and Italy. Most were stepping-stone countries included for the bases, to be negotiated bilaterally, that they would offer to U.S. military forces. Not until the end of March 1949 was the language of the treaty satisfactory to all partners. The Senate's overwhelming vote in favor of the treaty, 82 to 13, conceals the fact that the administration and Congress had intensely debated the wisdom of the new direction in American foreign relations.

Forty years later NATO could claim a share in the collapse of the Soviet Union and the Warsaw Pact bloc. The result of its success left the alliance seeking new missions for the 1990s.

BIBLIOGRAPHY

Ireland, Timothy P. *Creating the Entangling Alliance: The Origins of the North Atlantic Treaty Organization.* 1981.

Kaplan, Lawrence S. *The United States and NATO: The Formative Years.* 1984.

Reid, Escott. *Time of Fear and Hope: The Making of the North Atlantic Treaty.* 1977.

U.S. Senate. Committee on Foreign Relations. Hearings on North Atlantic Treaty. 81st Cong., 1st sess., 27 April–18 May 1949.

Vandenberg, Arthur H., Jr., ed. *The Private Papers of Senator Vandenberg.* 1952.

LAWRENCE S. KAPLAN

NORTH CAROLINA. On 8 April 1776, North Carolina's Provincial Congress authorized its delegates to the Continental Congress to join with the representatives of the other "United Colonies" in declaring independence from Britain. North Carolina thus became the first state to call officially for independence.

North Carolina sent delegates to the Constitutional Convention of 1787, but its representatives played only a small role in the debates over the Constitution. When the document produced by the Philadelphia gathering was presented for ratification in North Carolina, it was rejected at a convention dominated by Anti-Federalists opposed to the creation of a powerful central government. Following a vigorous campaign in favor of ratification, a second state convention ratified the Constitution on 22 November 1789. North Carolina thus became the twelfth state to enter the Union. The following year, North Carolina ceded to Congress the lands that later became the state of Tennessee.

The state's relationship with Congress was stormy in the new government. Most of North Carolina's representatives opposed the centralizing measures of the Washington administration and preferred the philosophy of limited government adopted by the Jeffersonian Republicans. North Carolina clung to the concept of federal union, however, and took no part in the efforts of neighboring South Carolina to nullify acts of Congress in 1831 and 1832. Though state leaders firmly supported the institution of slavery, most resisted the secessionist movement and did not view the election of Abraham Lincoln in 1860 as a sufficient reason to leave the Union. However, when President Lincoln called for troops to restore the Union by force after the attack on Fort Sumter, state leaders sided with their fellow Southerners. On 20 May 1861, a state convention repealed North Carolina's ratification of the federal Constitution, and the state joined the Confederate States of America the following day. After the Civil War, Congress readmitted the North Carolina delegation on 20 July 1868.

Following the census of 1790, North Carolina was allocated ten seats in the House of Representatives. It has retained about the same number ever since, dropping to a low of seven after the 1860 census and rising to thirteen after the censuses of 1810, 1820, and 1830. The state gained one seat from the census of 1990, giving it a House delegation of twelve in the 103d Congress (1993–1995).

Many of North Carolina's first members of Congress were nominal Federalists, but the state took on a strongly Jeffersonian-Republican cast after the election of Thomas Jefferson in 1800. After political parties reappeared during the administration of Andrew Jackson, North Carolina maintained a relatively strong two-party system through the secession crisis of 1860 and 1861. Republicans briefly governed the state during Reconstruction but lost power to the Democrats in 1876. A Populist-Republican insurgency prompted Democrats to seek the permanent disenfranchisement of blacks after 1898. Thenceforth, white Republicans from mountain districts continued to send some Republicans to Congress, but North Carolina otherwise belonged to the Democratic "Solid South" until after World War II. The increasing association of the national Democratic party with the civil rights movement led to a Republican resurgence.

Prominent congressional leaders from North Carolina have usually been conservatives. Nathaniel Macon, who served thirteen terms in the House and three terms in the Senate between 1791 and 1828, spent his career in opposition to measures for expanding federal power. During the 1930s, Josiah W. Bailey became a leader of the conservative coalition of Republicans and southern Democrats who curbed the reform agenda of the New Deal. Sam Ervin provided intellectual leadership to the southern lawmakers who resisted civil rights legislation in the 1950s and 1960s, but he later won liberal plaudits as chairman of the 1973 Senate committee that investigated the Watergate scandal. First elected in 1972, Sen. Jesse Helms became nationally prominent as a leader of the New Right.

BIBLIOGRAPHY

Boyd, William K. *History of North Carolina*. Vol. 2: *The Federal Period, 1783–1860*. 1919.

Powell, William S. *North Carolina through Four Centuries*. 1989.

Trenholme, Louise Irby. *The Ratification of the Federal Constitution in North Carolina*. 1932.

HARRY L. WATSON

NORTH DAKOTA. Dakota Territory, including the two Dakotas, northern Wyoming, and most of Montana, was established by Congress in 1861 from the northern part of what had been Nebraska territory. The Black Hills gold rush of the early 1870s, the advance of the railroads, and the gradual removal of Indians to fixed reservations contributed to steady population growth, somewhat earlier and heavier in the southern part of Dakota Territory, where a statehood movement was quietly started in 1879.

The removal of the territorial capital from Yankton to Bismarck in 1883 enhanced the southern separation movement. Southern leaders attempted to appropriate the unadorned name "Dakota" for their effort. But statehood for one Dakota or two Dakotas was delayed because of partisan divisions in the nation's capital.

The subsequent splitting of the sparsely populated territory into North Dakota and South Dakota was brought about by the decisive Republican victory in the November 1888 election, when the Republican party gained control of the White House, the Senate, and the House of Representatives. The outgoing 50th Congress passed an act providing for the admission of North Dakota, South Dakota, Montana, and Washington. They were formally admitted in late 1889—the two Dakotas on 2 November, Montana on 8 November, and Washington on 11 November.

Republicans dominated North Dakota politics from statehood in 1889 until 1960. After a twenty-year interlude in which each party won its share of elections, the Democrats have been dominant since 1980. The Republican party was never cohesive, having conservative and progressive wings from the early years of this century. In the World War I era, for example, Sen. Porter J. McCumber was an articulate Stalwart standard bearer, while Sen. Asle J. Gronna was a progressive and close friend of Senators George W. Norris of Nebraska and Robert M. La Follette of Wisconsin.

North Dakota's remoteness and dependence on grain markets have characterized the state's economy and, less directly, its politics. Wheat farmers have felt themselves to be at the mercy of the grain elevators and inspectors, banks, markets, and railroads. The Nonpartisan League (NPL), formed in 1915 to give voice to the farmers' grievances against these perceived nemeses, often dominated Republican party primaries. The direct primary and the absence of a voter registration requirement made this possible. The league called for state ownership of grain elevators, flour mills, packing houses, cold storage plants, and bank loans to farmers at cost. The league declined in the early 1920s but was resuscitated by William Langer, who served as governor in the 1930s and as senator from 1941 to 1959. Since Langer's time, the NPL has consistently supported Democratic congressional candidates.

In the first half of the twentieth century, the general perspective of North Dakota politicians in national politics was populist, socialist, pacifist, and isolationist, the latter two characteristics reflecting the state's strong German and Scandinavian population. In Washington they were long known for their adherence to a conspiracy theory of history and for their rustic, unsophisticated dress and manners.

Perhaps the most dramatic legislative initiative from North Dakota was the Frazier-Lemke Bankruptcy Act of the early New Deal years, which asserted that the rights of the user (borrower) are paramount to the rights of the owner (lender); the act was declared unconstitutional by the Supreme Court in May 1935, to the chagrin of Sen. Lynn J. Frazier and Rep. William Lemke, but to the relief of President Franklin D. Roosevelt. The persistent Lemke brought to the floor a weaker version of the bill to refinance burdensome farm mortgages, but it was defeated.

For the most part, the North Dakotans found themselves in political opposition to most of the country. Their agrarian, populist opposition to railroads and the grain trade put them at odds with national political leaders until the Depression descended upon the nation. Their spirit of isolationism arrayed most North Dakotans against President Woodrow Wilson's League of Nations. North Dakotans in Congress were at odds with the Republican administrations of Harding and Coolidge. When North Dakota senators Frazier and Edwin F. Ladd supported Progressive party candidate Robert La Follette for president in 1924, Senate Republican leaders banned them from the Republican caucus and stripped them of their committee seniority.

After World War II, Senator Langer was a fervent opponent of the United Nations. Langer, Lemke, and Rep. Usher L. Burdick adamantly opposed the Mundt-Nixon Anti-Subversive bill.

In recent decades, the rough edges of North Dakota's congressional reputation have been considerably softened by the more conventional, more consistent, and less colorful political styles of Republican senator Milton R. Young (1945–1980), Democratic representative (1981–1992) and Senator (1993–) Byron L. Dorgan, and Democratic senator Kent Conrad (1987–).

BIBLIOGRAPHY

Morlan, Robert L. *Political Prairie Fire: The Nonpartisan League, 1915–1922.* 1955.
Robinson, Elwyn B. *History of North Dakota.* 1966.
Wilkins, Robert P., and Wynona Wilkins. *North Dakota: A Bicentennial History.* 1977.

ALAN L. CLEM

NORTHERN PACIFIC RAILROAD ACT.
See Pacific Railroad Acts.

NORTON, MARY T. (1875–1959), representative from New Jersey (1925–1951) and chair of the Committee on Labor (1937–1947). The first Democratic woman elected to the House of Representatives and the first woman to represent an eastern congressional district, Norton had a political background very different from that of her Republican predecessors. She was a faithful lieutenant in Frank Hague's Jersey City political machine, and represented a working-class Catholic district.

Responding to the coming of woman suffrage, Hague put Norton on the Democratic state committee in 1921, and in 1925 she was elected to the U.S. House of Representatives. Longevity in office, her competence and self-possession, and her staunch support of issues that mattered most to her constituents—an end to prohibition (she was the first member of Congress to propose a bill to repeal the Eighteenth Amendment) and support of labor reform laws—helped her rise in the party's congressional hierarchy. When a member condescendingly agreed to "yield to a lady," she responded: "I'm no lady, I'm a member of Congress, and I'll proceed on that basis."

In 1931 she became chair of the Committee on the District of Columbia, the first woman to head a significant congressional committee; and in 1937 she became the chair of the Committee on Labor, a

MARY T. NORTON.   LIBRARY OF CONGRESS

position she held for the next decade. During that time she played an active role in the passage of the Fair Labor Standards Act of 1938 through Congress, and was a pioneering advocate of equal pay for women. She left the committee in 1947 in protest against her Republican successor as chair, fellow New Jerseyan Fred A. Hartley, Jr., and fought against the Taft-Hartley labor law of that year. She was perhaps the most influential of the women elected to Congress prior to World War II.

BIBLIOGRAPHY

Chambers, John Whiteclay, II. "Norton, Mary Theresa Hopkins." In *Dictionary of American Biography*, Supplement 6 (1956–1960). Edited by John A. Garraty. 1980. Pp. 479–481.
U.S. House of Representatives. *Women in Congress, 1917–1990.* Prepared by the Office of the Historian. 101st Cong., 2d sess., 1990. H. Doc. 101-238. Pp. 183–184.

MORTON KELLER

NOVELS. *See* Literature on Congress.

NUCLEAR NON-PROLIFERATION TREATY (21 U.S.T. 483–566). The Nuclear Non-Proliferation Treaty (NPT) of 1968 commits any signatory except the existing five nuclear powers to renounce the acquisition of nuclear weapons and to submit all their peaceful nuclear activities to inspection by the International Atomic Energy Agency (IAEA). The nuclear powers (the United States, the Soviet Union, Britain, France, and China) would be committed by the same treaty not to give such nuclear weapons to other states. The NPT reflected a growing concern that the continuing spread of nuclear weapons to additional national arsenals would greatly increase both the likelihood and destructiveness of future wars. Earlier concerns about preserving nuclear "secrecy" had been directed mainly at the Soviet Union and the People's Republic of China. But by the mid 1960s, with the Soviet Union joining the United States in favoring International Atomic Energy Agency (IAEA) safeguards as a way of keeping the by-products of civilian nuclear programs from being diverted to the manufacture of nuclear weapons, the nonproliferation issue transcended East-West rivalries. Concerns had broadened to include other nations capable of producing nuclear weapons, such as West Germany, Brazil, India, Sweden, Israel, or Japan.

Hearings of the Joint Committee on Atomic Energy and the Senate Committee on Foreign Relations were used to sort out the possible gains and losses of such an explicit focus on nonproliferation. The actual NPT, signed during the administration of Lyndon B. Johnson, was ratified in March of 1969 after President Richard M. Nixon had assumed office. While Nixon and his national security adviser, Henry A. Kissinger, were reputed to be unenthusiastic about the nonproliferation effort because they accorded more importance to alliance solidarity, the consensus that had already been developed in Congress made inevitable the submission of the NPT to the Senate and then its easy ratification.

BIBLIOGRAPHY

Brenner, Michael J. *Nuclear Power and Non-Proliferation.* 1981.
Willrich, Mason. *The Global Politics of Nuclear Energy.* 1971.

GEORGE H. QUESTER

NUCLEAR POWER. Congress played a critical role in the development of nuclear power as a major source of electricity in the United States during the 1950s and 1960s. It also played an important role in the controversy over nuclear technology that emerged as a prominent public issue during the 1970s and 1980s. The legislation enacted or considered by Congress and the activities of individual members and committees greatly influenced the history of nuclear power. They also reflected attitudes in the nation as a whole, from the soaring hopes of the 1950s to the growing reservations of later years.

The Atomic Energy Acts of 1946 and 1954. In the aftermath of World War II, when nuclear technology seemed esoteric, ominous, and at the same time potentially miraculous to most Americans, Congress enacted the first legislation to establish administrative control of nuclear energy. The Atomic Energy Act of 1946 created the U.S. Atomic Energy Commission (AEC) and a powerful congressional committee, the Joint Committee on Atomic Energy, to monitor its performance. Passed as postwar disputes with the Soviet Union were intensifying into the Cold War, the act emphasized the military applications of atomic energy. Although the legislation encouraged the AEC to investigate the civilian uses of atomic energy, it also imposed a tight government monopoly of the technology that effectively discouraged progress in exploring its peaceful benefits.

By the early 1950s, however, the joint committee, the AEC, and several utilities were seeking ways to foster the development of civilian nuclear power. The joint committee contributed to the efforts to spur the growth of a commercial nuclear power industry by holding extensive hearings in 1953. Witnesses stressed that atomic power would be important to the future economy of the United States and the world and that a cooperative venture by government and industry was needed to exploit the potential of the technology. Congress soon heeded that advice by passing a new law that superseded the 1946 act. The Atomic Energy Act of 1954 ended the government's exclusive control of technical information and made the development of a commercial nuclear industry an urgent national goal. This seemed of vital importance not because energy was in short supply but because of fears that the United States would fall behind the Soviet Union in demonstrating the peaceful applications of the atom. The 1954 act instructed the AEC both to promote the

Legislation concerning Nuclear Power

Title	Year Enacted	Reference Number	Description
Atomic Energy Act of 1946	1946	P.L. 79-585	Created the Atomic Energy Commission and the Joint Committee on Atomic Energy and established the first law to control the use of atomic energy.
Atomic Energy Act of 1954	1954	P.L. 83-703	Ended the government monopoly on technical information about atomic energy and encouraged the development of commercial nuclear power by assigning the AEC the tasks of promoting and regulating the private nuclear industry.
National Environmental Policy Act of 1969	1970	P.L. 91-190	Required that federal agencies consider the environmental impact of their activities.
Energy Reorganization Act of 1974	1974	P.L. 93-438	Divided the Atomic Energy Commission into the Nuclear Regulatory Commission and the Energy Research and Development Administration.
Nuclear Waste Policy Act of 1982	1983	P.L. 97-425	Established a schedule for building a federal repository for the geologic disposal of high-level radioactive waste.

civilian uses of atomic energy and to ensure their safety.

The Growth of Nuclear Power. The AEC acted to carry out its mandate by offering modest financial incentives to utilities that agreed to build demonstration nuclear plants. In light of high construction costs, technical uncertainties, and potential hazards, the AEC was surprised and gratified that by August 1955 five utilities, either singly or in consortia, had announced plans to construct nuclear plants. The joint committee, however, was not satisfied with the rate of progress. A bill introduced by Sen. Albert A. Gore, Sr. (D-Tenn.), and Rep. Chet Holifield (D-Calif.) proposed that the AEC be required to build six demonstration plants, each of a different design, to encourage development of nuclear power "at the maximum possible rate." The Gore-Holifield bill provoked a bitter clash between the joint committee and the AEC. Although the measure failed by a narrow margin on the floor of the House, it clearly signaled the impatience of the joint committee with existing programs and the emphasis it placed on the rapid expansion of nuclear power technology.

The joint committee's complaints ceased only after a boom in reactor orders, beginning in the mid 1960s, signaled the arrival of nuclear power as a technology that could compete with coal and other fossil fuels. The sudden and unexpected growth of nuclear power, described by one observer as the "great bandwagon market," came about because of intense competition among reactor manufacturers that drove down costs to utilities, the extension of interconnections among power systems, and widening concern about air pollution caused by coal plants.

The Nuclear Power Controversy. The bandwagon market, however pleasing to nuclear proponents, soon led to greatly increased antinuclear protests. For a time, the opposition to nuclear plants was sporadic and focused on matters related to specific sites. But by the late 1960s, expanding public concern over a number of broader questions, including thermal pollution, radiation protection, reactor safety, and radioactive waste disposal, had made nuclear power a major national issue. Several members of Congress spearheaded efforts to evaluate the hazards of nuclear power, to review the regulatory programs of the AEC, and in some cases to slow the growth of the technology. Sen. Edmund S. Muskie (D-Maine), for example, held well-publicized hearings on radioactive waste in 1966, on thermal pollution in 1968, and on other issues, hearings in which witnesses aired sharp criticism of the AEC. Rep. Jonathan B. Bingham (D-N.Y.) introduced legislation in 1969 to strip the AEC of its regulatory responsibilities, and Sen. Mike Gravel (D-Alaska) sponsored a bill in 1971 to impose a moratorium on the construction of nuclear plants. Although none of the antinuclear proposals advanced far, they suggested that the joint committee was no longer the unchallenged guardian of atomic energy affairs in Congress.

The growing attacks on nuclear power drove the joint committee and the AEC closer together in defense of their common interests. In 1969 and 1970, for example, the joint committee conducted hearings on the environmental effects of electrical production, which were designed to highlight the environmental advantages of nuclear power and the care with which AEC regulation guarded the public against its potential health dangers. Despite the efforts of the joint committee and other nuclear advocates, however, the controversy over atomic power continued to grow. The AEC, whose dual responsibilities for promoting and regulating nuclear power had long been a source of criticism, lost much of its credibility, largely because of the debates over its regulatory performance. In 1974, Congress passed the Energy Reorganization Act. It separated the AEC's functions by dividing the agency into the Nuclear Regulatory Commission and the Energy Research and Development Administration (which later became a part of the Department of Energy). Three years later, Congress abolished the joint committee, largely because it was viewed as a relic of bygone days. The demise of both the AEC and the joint committee symbolized the end of the boom years for nuclear power; since 1978, utilities have not ordered another nuclear plant.

The end of orders for nuclear plants did not signal an end to the controversy over nuclear power. Nuclear safety (particularly after the accident at the Three Mile Island plant in Pennsylvania in 1979), radioactive waste disposal, emergency planning, the authority of states, and energy supplies were only some of the issues that stirred debates, hearings, and speeches in Congress that reflected both sides, or all sides, of the arguments.

[*See also* Atomic Energy Act; Atomic Energy Committee, Joint; Energy and Commerce Committee, House; Energy and Natural Resources; Energy and Natural Resources Committee, Senate; Environment and Conservation.]

BIBLIOGRAPHY

Balogh, Brian. *Chain Reaction: Expert Debate and Public Participation in American Commercial Power, 1945–1975.* 1991.

Green, Harold P., and Alan Rosenthal. *Government of the Atom: The Integration of Powers.* 1963.

Hewlett, Richard G., and Jack M. Holl. *Atoms for Peace and War, 1953–1961: Eisenhower and the Atomic Energy Commission.* 1989.

Mazuzan, George T., and J. Samuel Walker. *Controlling the Atom: The Beginnings of Nuclear Regulation, 1946–1962.* 1984.

Walker, J. Samuel. *Containing the Atom: Nuclear Regulation in a Changing Environment, 1963–1971.* 1992.

J. SAMUEL WALKER

NUCLEAR TEST BAN TREATY. *See* Limited Test Ban Treaty.

NUCLEAR WEAPONS. Except for a few senior representatives and senators, Congress had no knowledge of the crash program, known as the Manhattan Project, under which the U.S. government developed an atomic bomb during World War II. President Harry S. Truman's announcement that the bomb had been dropped on Hiroshima, Japan, on 6 August 1945 broke the veil of secrecy and included a call for legislation on the proper public control of this new area of science.

The ensuing congressional debate on the handling of atomic energy began with the premise that this area of technology was more important than almost any other. The debate pitted advocates of a more exclusively military management of this technology, as exemplified in the May-Johnson bill, supported by the Pentagon and by the House Military Affairs Committee, against those concerned that such military management might stifle the development of civilian uses of atomic energy and, more generally, threaten civilian predominance. The principal opponent of military management was Brien McMahon (D-Conn.), whose position also had strong support from Sen. Arthur H. Vandenberg (R-Mich.), the Republican leader on foreign-policy issues. Ironically the argument that won, in the passage of the 1946 Atomic Energy Act, was that a military concern for preventing other countries from acquiring nuclear weapons would impose too much secrecy, thereby retarding the application of nuclear techniques to civilian needs. Exactly the reverse arguments were to acquire greater plausibility after India's detonation of a nuclear device in 1974, which led to the dismantling of the structures erected in 1946.

The Atomic Energy Act of 1946, otherwise known as the McMahon Act, established the Atomic Energy Commission (AEC), which was given substantial powers of management and regulation over all aspects of nuclear energy in the United States. Among other things, it virtually suspended the application of patent law in this field. Supporters of civilian supremacy and of congressional control had actually toyed with the idea of having members of Congress serve on the Atomic Energy Commission, but in the end they shifted to the creation of a separate congressional Joint Committee on Atomic Energy (JCAE), with nine members from the Senate and nine from the House of Representatives. Senator McMahon was elected the first chairman of the JCAE; after the Republican victory in the congressional elections of 1946, he was replaced by Sen. Bourke B. Hickenlooper (R-Iowa), with Rep. W. Sterling Cole (R-N.Y.) as vice chairman.

The JCAE was nearly unique as a joint committee (or as a congressional committee generally) in its powers and influence. For years, it was deferred to by Congress, the Atomic Energy Commission, and the rest of the executive branch as an important repository of expertise and guidance on all nuclear matters. The special nature of the JCAE's congressional role seemed to match the special nature of nuclear physics as a factor in international relations and U.S. public policy.

From 1946 to 1949, when the United States still possessed a monopoly on nuclear weapons, the JCAE was a little less assertive than it was to become. U.S. production of nuclear weapons was allowed to languish for a time. Rather than stockpiling dozens or even hundreds of such bombs with which to support some policy of nuclear dominance over the Soviet Union or any other foreign power, the United States by 1947 possessed no bombs at all that were ready for use. It took the Berlin crisis of 1948 to spur production.

The detection of a Soviet nuclear test in the fall of 1949 stepped up production even further. Thereafter the JCAE became actively involved in all aspects of policy, including the acceleration of atomic bomb production, the decision to produce the thermonuclear hydrogen bomb, the restraints on sharing nuclear secrets with Britain or France, and the post-1954 "Atoms for Peace" program, with its prospects for the production of electrical power by nuclear means.

Both the Atomic Energy Act and the congressional role of the Joint Committee on Atomic Energy were generally regarded as a great success for the first three decades of the nuclear age: civilian congressional control had been established and maintained over what had begun as a military secret, and some difficult passages of U.S. foreign policy were navigated.

The end of the 1950s, however, saw the emergence of new concerns about the proliferation of nuclear weapons to countries besides the United States, the Soviet Union, Britain, and France, amid fears that their spread could dramatically increase the destructiveness of war and even threaten the United States itself. While proliferation might always result from "dedicated" military projects like the original Manhattan Project, the worrisome possibility now loomed—realized in the Indian explosion of 1974—that bombs might also spread as a spin-off from the nuclear technology that was shared with other countries for civilian purposes.

Many in Congress believed that the entire structure of the 1946 McMahon Act was overcommitted to the promotion of nuclear power and nuclear industry and too little concerned with controlling and monitoring the uses to which nuclear technology was put. In the aftermath of the 1974 Indian explosion, the consensus in Congress was that the Nixon and Ford administrations, including Secretary of State Henry A. Kissinger, had not taken the proliferation risk seriously enough. This resulted in the Energy Reorganization Act of 1975 and the Nuclear Non-Proliferation Act of 1979. The 1975 act separated the Atomic Energy Commission into a management component, the Energy Research and Development Administration (ERDA; later the Department of Energy), and a regulatory component, the Nuclear Regulatory Commission (NRC). A year later, Congress abolished the Joint Committee on Atomic Energy and divided its responsibilities among all the committees dealing with defense and commerce.

All along, other components of nuclear weapons policy have, of course, involved the more traditional congressional committees. For the delivery systems that are coupled to nuclear warheads and for the broad policy choices and strategy behind the deployment of such weapons, the Appropriations committees of both houses had continuing roles, as did the committees on the Armed Services and the committees on Foreign Affairs and Foreign Relations. Yet after 1945, the most direct focus was on nuclear warheads and the technology behind them, and for a time this produced some unique congressional roles and mechanisms.

[See also Atomic Energy Act; Atomic Energy

Committee, Joint; Limited Test Ban Treaty; Manhattan Project; Nuclear Non-Proliferation Treaty; Strategic Arms Limitation Talks (SALT); Strategic Defense Initiative (SDI).]

BIBLIOGRAPHY

Gilpin, Robert. *American Scientists and Nuclear Weapons Policy.* 1962.

Green, Harold P., and Alan Rosenthal. *Government of the Atom.* 1963.

Hewlett, Richard G., and Oscar E. Anderson. *The New World: 1939–1946.* 1962.

Hewlett, Richard G., and Francis Duncan. *Atomic Shield: 1947–1952.* 1967.

Newman, James R., and Byron S. Miller. *The Control of Atomic Energy.* 1948.

Thomas, Morgan. *Atomic Energy and Congress.* 1956.

GEORGE H. QUESTER

NULLIFICATION. A position postulating states' rights, nullification was a step toward secession. The nullification controversy took place during the fall and winter of 1832–1833. It originated in the passage of the Tariff Act of 1828, the so-called Tariff of Abominations, which many South Carolinians believed to be unconstitutional. At first they hoped that President Andrew Jackson would bring about a reduction of the tariff, but when he failed to move on the issue, the state's Radicals, led by James Hamilton, Jr., and R. Barnwell Rhett, effectively enlarged their following to implement the doctrine of nullification. The idea had been forcefully developed by John C. Calhoun in the South Carolina Exposition and Protest of 1828, a report secretly drafted by a state legislative committee, whose ideas Calhoun elaborated on in several important speeches. The doctrine argued that the Union was a compact among the states, which had delegated only limited and clearly specified powers to the federal government under the Constitution. A state, it went on, had the right to determine whether the federal government had overstepped its authority and had violated the constitutional compact. Should a state declare a federal law null and void, the federal government had to abstain from enforcing the law unless or until it secured an amendment to the Constitution explicitly granting the nullified power. Should this occur, the state had either to recognize the authority of the federal government or to exercise its constitutional right to withdraw from the Union.

In November 1832 a South Carolina state convention declared the Tariff Act of 1828 and the recently adopted Tariff Act of 1832 (which lowered duties slightly but did not abandon the principle of protection) null and void and prohibited the collection of federal duties within the state beginning on 1 February 1833. It also prescribed a test oath for all military and civil officers of the state, forbade any appeal to the U.S. Supreme Court of cases arising from the action, and warned that any attempt by the federal government to use force would cause South Carolina to secede. The South Carolina legislature immediately adopted laws to enforce these decisions, which included establishing a military force and distributing weapons. Although President Jackson was a strong believer in states' rights, he strongly disliked nullification. On 16 January 1833, he sent a special message to Congress asking for a force law authorizing him to use the military to collect the federal revenues.

The great majority of Americans believed that South Carolina had acted precipitously. No other state formally endorsed the doctrine of nullification, and most condemned it. But a number of states specifically rejected or refused to endorse what they viewed as the extreme nationalist principles enunciated in the president's proclamation. Congress, under the leadership of Henry Clay (Whig-Ky.), formulated a compromise: a new tariff that abandoned the principle of protection and gradually reduced duties over a ten-year period, and (as a sop to Jackson) the adoption of the Force Bill. The president signed both into law on 2 March 1833.

When the radicals in South Carolina learned of the impending congressional compromise, they suspended the state's ordinance of nullification on 21 January. Shortly after the adoption of the compromise, the state reconvened its convention and rescinded its ordinance but in a final act of defiance nullified the Force Bill. Although both sides claimed victory, the most important result of the controversy was that over the following three decades the idea of secession became increasingly enmeshed with the doctrine of states' rights and the South's defense of slavery.

BIBLIOGRAPHY

Ellis, Richard E. *The Union at Risk: Jacksonian Democracy, States' Rights, and the Nullification Crisis.* 1987.

Peterson, Merrill D. *Olive Branch and Sword: The Compromise of 1833.* 1982.

RICHARD E. ELLIS

NYE, GERALD P. (1892–1971), progressive Republican senator from North Dakota and opponent of American entry into World War II. Born and reared in Wisconsin, Nye edited small-town newspapers in Wisconsin, Iowa, and North Dakota for fifteen years before being appointed in 1925 as an agrarian progressive Republican to the U.S. Senate, where he served for nearly twenty years. Strongly supportive of the interests of western farmers, he voted for much of President Franklin D. Roosevelt's New Deal program in the 1930s. Reflecting his western agrarian progressivism, however, Nye was most closely identified with efforts to keep the United States out of foreign wars. Like other western progressives, Nye thought that armaments races, imperialism overseas, and involvement in foreign wars were designed more to protect and expand eastern urban business and financial interests than to guard American security and freedom. From 1934 to 1936, he headed the Senate investigation of the munitions industry that probed roles of big financiers, shipbuilders, munitions makers, and, later, the executive branch of the government in involving the United States in armament races, imperialism, and wars. Though never a pacifist, he played a leading role in the drive for enactment of mandatory neutrality legislation designed to restrict the war-making and interventionist proclivities of urban business and the presidency. Nye helped win enactment of the neutrality laws of 1935, 1936, and 1937, but he was more effective in conducting investigations and in addressing public meetings than in accomplishing legislative goals.

With the eruption of war in Asia in 1937 and in Europe in 1939, Nye fought losing battles to prevent repeal of the neutrality legislation and to block enactment of Roosevelt's proposals to extend aid short of war to victims of Axis aggression. In 1941 he became a leading spokesman for the noninterventionist America First Committee, addressing public meetings around the country in opposition to American entry into World War II. He came under severe criticism for his so-called isolationism, however, and failed to defeat any of the administration's proposals for aid short of war.

When the Japanese attacked Pearl Harbor in Hawaii on 7 December 1941, Nye was addressing an America First meeting in Pittsburgh. With the Japanese attack, Nye and America First ceased their noninterventionist activities, and he joined his Senate colleagues in voting for declarations of war against Japan, Germany, and Italy. Nye supported the war effort against the Axis powers, but during the conflict he opposed committing the United States to internationalist policies after the war. In

1944 Nye went down to defeat at the hands of North Dakota voters after having served more than three terms in the Senate. His subsequent efforts to regain his Senate seat failed.

In his later years, Nye operated a record consultant business for a time and held appointive government positions concerned with housing for the elderly. He never repudiated or apologized for his noninterventionist efforts before Pearl Harbor and continued to believe that the United States could and should have stayed out of World War II. He died in suburban Maryland in 1971 at the age of seventy-eight.

BIBLIOGRAPHY

Cole, Wayne S. *Senator Gerald P. Nye and American Foreign Relations.* 1962.
Wiltz, John Edward. *In Search of Peace: The Senate Munitions Inquiry, 1934–1936.* 1963.

WAYNE S. COLE

NYE COMMITTEE. From its establishment in 1934, the Senate Special Committee Investigating the Munitions Industry was often identified with its colorful chairman, progressive Republican Gerald P. Nye of North Dakota. The committee and its investigation stemmed from widespread disillusionment with World War I and U.S. involvement in that conflict. Suspicion and distrust of big financiers, munitions makers, and so-called merchants of death were commonplace in the aftermath of the war and in the Great Depression of the 1930s. Pacifist Dorothy Detzer of the Women's International League for Peace and Freedom helped persuade Nye to initiate the probe.

At first the administration of Franklin D. Roosevelt supported the investigation, and it won widespread bipartisan support. Though Republicans were a minority in the Senate and on the seven-member committee, its members chose Nye as chairman. The most active members, in addition to Nye, were Republican Arthur H. Vandenberg of Michigan and Democrats Joel Bennett Clark of Missouri and Homer T. Bone of Washington. Most of the committee members were from farming states in the South and West, and most were progressives on domestic issues. None was a doctrinaire pacifist; all favored building military forces to guard U.S. security in the Western Hemisphere.

The committee began its investigation in September 1934 and held its final meetings in February 1936. Obtaining sensational press coverage, the panel questioned nearly two hundred witnesses, including such giants of big business and finance as J. P. Morgan and the du Ponts. Testimony and documents filled thirty-nine huge volumes. The committee issued seven reports and recommended legislation to put the munitions industry under government control or ownership and thus reduce the likelihood of involvement in foreign wars.

The Nye committee did not contend that munitions makers and financiers were solely responsible for U.S. entry into World War I. However, it did maintain that opportunities for private profit from war and preparation for war, shared by many more than big businessmen, made the task of keeping the United States out of war more difficult.

As the probe continued, the committee became persuaded that the executive branch of the government was a partner with big business in promoting war and preparation for war. When the committee's criticisms extended to include the late Democratic president Woodrow Wilson, it came under increasingly widespread attack, and its bipartisan support eroded.

The Nye committee was unable to win congressional adoption of any of the legislation it proposed. Working behind the scenes, however, its members and staff played important roles in the background and adoption of the neutrality acts of 1935, 1936, and 1937.

Some scholars contend that extreme allegations by committee members (much exaggerated and distorted by critics) helped discredit the antiwar movement. Others believe that the probe reinforced U.S. determination to stay out of foreign wars. In any event, the investigation was a spectacular expression of American opposition to involvement in foreign wars in the 1930s.

[*See also* Isolationism; Neutrality Debates; World War I.]

BIBLIOGRAPHY

Cole, Wayne S. *Senator Gerald P. Nye and American Foreign Relations.* 1962.

Wiltz, John Edward. *In Search of Peace: The Senate Munitions Inquiry, 1934–1936.* 1963.

WAYNE S. COLE

OATH OF OFFICE.

OATH OF OFFICE. Article VI, clause 3 of the U.S. Constitution requires that senators and representatives take an oath of office to support the Constitution. The language of the oath is set by statute (5 U.S.C. 3331) and has changed several times since 1789. In 1994 it reads:

> I do solemnly swear that I will support and defend the Constitution of the United States against all enemies, foreign and domestic; that I will bear true faith and allegiance to the same; that I take this obligation freely, without any mental reservation or purpose of evasion, and that I will well and faithfully discharge the duties of the office on which I am about to enter. So help me God.

The oath is administered to members-elect on the opening day of each new Congress. In the House, the most senior member (the "Dean" of the House) first administers the oath to the Speaker, who then administers it to all other members in the chamber en masse. Prior to 1929, the oath was administered by state delegation.

In the Senate, the oath is administered by the president of the Senate or a designated senator in his stead. Since 1927, senators have come forward to take the oath in alphabetical order in groups of four.

Members must be sworn before they can take their seats (2 U.S.C. 21, 25). Both chambers have at times authorized a member of Congress, one of their officers, or a justice to administer the oath to members necessarily absent on opening day.

BIBLIOGRAPHY

U.S. House of Representatives. *Deschler's Precedents of the United States House of Representatives*, by Lewis Deschler. 94th Cong., 2d sess., 1977. H. Doc. 94-661. Vol. 1, chap. 2.

U.S. Senate. *Riddick's Senate Procedure, Precedents, and Practices*, by Floyd M. Riddick and Alan S. Frumin. 101st Cong., 2d sess., 1992. S. Doc. 101-28. Pp. 699–710.

ILONA B. NICKELS

OBJECTORS. Objectors are members of the House of Representatives appointed to screen legislation considered under expedited floor procedures permitting passage with only minimal debate and no recorded vote. So that such measures are not adopted without some review, the majority and minority leaders appoint six members, three from each party, to serve as "official objectors" responsible for examining measures placed on the Consent Calendar. Another six members serve as objectors for Private Calendar measures.

Bills on the Private Calendar benefit one individual or entity, and do not become public law. Bills on the Consent Calendar must be so routine that they elicit no more than two objections to their passage.

During each new Congress, the official objectors issue criteria that legislation must meet to avoid an objection. The objectors are present on the House floor when Consent Calendar legislation is considered on the first and third Mondays of each month, and on the first and third Tuesdays when Private Calendar bills are called. The objectors decide if the legislation violates the announced criteria for their respective calendars, or is otherwise unacceptable. While other members are free to lodge an objection during these proceedings, the official objectors are responsible for doing so on behalf of their party.

The official objector system was first proposed in 1932, although several House members had been operating informally as objectors on their own initiative for years before that. The Senate abandoned objectors in the 1970s. The responsibility for reviewing routine legislation in the Senate now belongs to staff members of the two party policy committees.

BIBLIOGRAPHY

Congressional Quarterly Inc. *How Congress Works.* 2d ed. 1991. Pp. 46–48.

U.S. House of Representatives. *Deschler's Precedents of the United States House of Representatives,* by Lewis Deschler. 94th Cong., 2d sess., 1977. H. Doc. 94-661. Vol. 7, chap. 22.

ILONA B. NICKELS

OBRA (1981). *See* Budget Reconciliation Act.

OCCUPATIONAL SAFETY AND HEALTH ACT OF 1970 (84 Stat. 1590–1620).

Congress passed the Occupational Safety and Health Act (P.L. 91-596) after a three-year battle that pitted the AFL-CIO and congressional Democrats against business interests and their Republican allies. Regulation of health and safety risks on the job remained a contentious and partisan issue for many years.

The law created the Occupational Safety and Health Administration (OSHA) within the Department of Labor. Unions favored this administrative structure because they considered the department their strongest advocate within the federal government. The act authorized OSHA to promulgate health and safety rules, to inspect employment sites, and to fine businesses that fail to comply. The law specifies that OSHA must choose the standard that "most adequately assures to the maximum extent feasible, on the basis of the best available evidence, that no employee will suffer impairment of health or functional capacity even if such employee had regular exposure to the hazard dealt with by such standard for the period of his working life." The act allows OSHA to turn enforcement over to the states when it finds state programs fully adequate. About half the states have taken on this responsibility.

OSHA quickly became one of the federal government's most disliked regulatory agencies. Owners of small businesses protested that they were subject to voluminous, nit-picking rules and arbitrary inspections. Part of the problem was that soon after its creation OSHA adopted a wide variety of detailed "consensus standards" previously promulgated by trade associations, safety organizations, and federal agencies. Some of these rules were antiquated, making OSHA the object of ridicule and scorn.

Congressional committees held numerous hearings attacking OSHA. But the two committees with legislative jurisdiction, House Education and Labor and Senate Labor and Human Resources, opposed amending the law and refused to act. OSHA's critics responded by placing restrictions on the agency's annual appropriation. One appropriation rider, for example, exempted farmers with ten or fewer employees; another prohibited OSHA from fining employers for first-time violations.

In an effort to counter this criticism, OSHA eliminated a large number of its original safety rules and targeted the most dangerous workplaces for inspection. During the Carter administration it placed new emphasis on long-term health risks. Two notable examples were controversial rules limiting exposure to cotton dust and benzine. Both standards—like almost all those issued by OSHA—were challenged in court, and both ultimately reached the Supreme Court. The Court upheld the cotton-dust rule (*American Textile Manufacturers Association v. Donovan* [1981]) but invalidated the benzine standard, arguing that OSHA had failed to show that the health risk was significant (*Industrial Union Department, AFL-CIO v. American Petroleum Institute* [1980]).

In the 1980s the Reagan administration made a concerted effort to reduce the regulatory burden imposed on employees by OSHA. House committees, which had once attacked OSHA for overzealousness, now chided it for inaction. In several instances the federal courts ordered OSHA to promulgate new rules.

A variety of studies of occupational safety and health regulation in the United States and Europe show that policy-making is much more adversarial and contentious in the United States. Neither labor nor business has been willing to compromise, and both have important allies within the federal government. Although American standards tend to be more stringent than those issued by European nations, the United States regulates fewer substances.

BIBLIOGRAPHY

Wilson, Graham. *The Politics of Safety and Health: Occupational Safety and Health in the United States and Britain*. 1985.

Mendeloff, John. *The Dilemmas of Toxic Substances Regulation*. 1988.

R. SHEP MELNICK

OFFICE BUILDINGS. *See* Congressional Office Buildings.

OFFICE OF MANAGEMENT AND BUDGET (OMB).

The institutional memory and analytical arm of the president, the Office of Management and Budget evolved from the earlier Bureau of the Budget (BOB). Its role, its power, and even its organizational structure, however, have shifted through the years. In part, this is because presidents have differed in the balance they have sought between their personal staff and the permanent bureaucracy of the presidency. But such shifts have also occurred because the president's budget powers have been at the center of twentieth-century struggles between Congress and the president over the balance of power.

Bureau of the Budget. OMB in 1993 lay at the end of an evolutionary chain that began early in the twentieth century. Until that time, governmental budgeting—at the state and local as well as at the federal level—was primarily based on legislative decisions. Executives consolidated proposals and made recommendations, with some playing a far stronger role than others, but spending decisions were principally the prerogative of legislatures. The Progressive movement of the early twentieth century sought to improve government by making budgeting more analytical, comprehensive, and centralized. The Progressives believed that an executive budget was required. The states led the way, and the federal government followed with the 1912 report of President William Howard Taft's Commission on Economy and Efficiency, which argued that the federal government ought to establish a comprehensive executive budget. After much debate, Congress agreed, passing the Budget and Accounting Act of 1921.

As with all important policy decisions that have shaped the president's budgeting role, the 1921 act struggled to resolve two questions. The first of these concerned how much power should be given directly to the president. While some supporters argued that a budget bureau ought to be established under the president's direct control, others worried that such an office would lead to a dangerous concentration of power in the executive. Congress resolved the debate by establishing the new Bureau of the Budget as an agency of the Treasury Department, but with the bureau's director appointed by the president. The director would collect spending estimates from government agencies, revise them according to the president's wishes, and prepare them for the president to submit to Congress. The second question concerned how Congress would balance the new power given to the president. Congress responded by creating its own General Accounting Office (GAO), with authority to audit the accounts of executive agencies.

President Warren G. Harding appointed Charles G. Dawes, a former army general, as BOB's first director. With Budget Circular No. 1, Dawes defined the bureau's mission. He sought to build the bureau's behavior on an analytical foundation so strong as to be politically unassailable. He insisted that the staff be completely nonpolitical and that it pursue its job with neutral competence. This was the model followed by BOB until 1937, when President Franklin D. Roosevelt's Committee on Administrative Management (the Brownlow Committee) argued that the president required more help in managing the budget. The Brownlow Committee concluded that BOB ought to have a larger, stronger staff that would be directly responsible to the president. Although many members of Congress argued that the move would make the presidency too strong, the committee's recommendations were finally enacted into law in 1939. BOB was transferred from the Treasury to the new Executive Office of the President. Nevertheless, BOB continued to follow the tradition of neutral competence for the next thirty years.

Creation and Impact of OMB. President John F. Kennedy came into office committed to using the budget more actively to steer both the economy and the government, and a stronger policy role for BOB was an important part of his strategy. As the budget continued to grow in policy importance, President Richard M. Nixon appointed a study committee known as the Ash Council, headed by Roy Ash, a private sector executive. Following the Ash Council's recommendations, Nixon in 1970 renamed BOB, establishing the Office of Management and Budget as part of a broader reorganization that also created the

Domestic Council. The creation of OMB marked the last step in the agency's maturation. It raised OMB's visibility; it expanded the office's mission into management as well as budget, with the creation of new units to study government information systems and organization; and it added new staff and brought the agency even closer to the president at the time that the budget was becoming the president's preeminent policy tool. In 1974, Congress reacted to the growing power of the president's institutionalized budgeting power by creating its own budget process and establishing the Congressional Budget Office (CBO) as an analytical counterweight to OMB.

OMB performs several important roles, including legislative clearance, budget preparation, and management review. Legislation that executive branch agencies propose and testimony that their officials present to Congress must receive OMB's clearance. The legislative clearance function has helped to strengthen the president's control over the executive branch and to ensure that the branch speaks with one voice. Naturally, members of Congress have complained that OMB's legislative clearance role interferes with their prerogatives and information gathering responsibilities.

Preparing the president's budget has become an ever more demanding job, as the increasing size of the document itself testifies. OMB's career staff of budget examiners review the budgets submitted annually by executive branch agencies. Top-level political appointees make final recommendations to the president about the course of federal spending. OMB, furthermore, has become the nerve center of the executive branch's economic forecasting apparatus, coordinating projections and factoring them into spending and taxing decisions. This power has grown even greater since the adoption of successive versions of the Balanced Budget and Emergency Deficit Control Act (Gramm-Rudman-Hollings Act) in the late 1980s. OMB has become the executive branch's chief deficit and spending scorekeeper. If budget proposals threatened to push spending over the act's limits, OMB was empowered to force agencies to lower their targets. Finally, if mandatory spending cuts under the act were triggered, OMB was the executive branch's arbiter of where those cuts would fall.

During the 1980s, the rising federal deficit and the president's increasingly arduous battles with Congress over the deficit pushed OMB into a far more powerful position than ever before. It became the nerve center for devising the president's strategy and tactics. And as bargaining with congressional leaders over budget processes, forecasts, and de-tails became more important, OMB's top political officials became the president's chief negotiators.

Despite the agency's name, OMB's management function has always been overshadowed by its budget responsibilities. Short-term budget pressures have tended to squeeze out long-term management reviews. During the Reagan and Bush administrations, OMB's management arm briefly acquired a higher profile as it took on more responsibility for collecting information and reviewing government regulations. The movement reached its peak during the Bush administration when Vice President Dan Quayle's Competitiveness Council, supported by OMB, intervened to block several regulations proposed by executive agencies. Many Democrats in Congress vigorously contested the council's actions, arguing that the council was blocking the agencies from complying with laws that Congress had passed and that the president had signed. They saw the council's behavior as an unlawful shift in the balance of power.

In 1994, the Clinton administration tried a fresh approach by merging OMB's budget and management branches. Administration officials hoped to give greater weight to management by coupling it with budget review and to give the budget review broader perspective by incorporating management analysis. While critics suggested that linking the two would inevitably drive management out, proponents argued that only by linking them would either branch prosper. The reorganization was the biggest change in OMB since its creation.

In the wake of the management and budgetary battles of the 1980s, OMB was less sure of its mission. Its always uncertain management mission was further weakened by the budget squeeze and by the partisan controversies of the 1980s. Its importance in the budgetary process had grown vastly, but, as deficit politics and new budget-making procedures transformed top-ranking political OMB officials into key bargainers, the distance grew between them and the agency's career officials, who perform traditional budget reviews. Finally, because of the budget's higher political profile, OMB's top officials became a political lightning rod for the sometimes stormy conflicts between the president and Congress. The office's role and function were defined, as always, by what the president wanted, but the gap between its historic strengths and new missions created serious and ongoing tensions.

BIBLIOGRAPHY

Berman, Larry. *The Office of Management and Budget and the Presidency: 1921–1979.* 1979.

Mosher, Frederick C. *A Tale of Two Agencies: A Comparative Analysis of the General Accounting Office and the Office of Management and Budget.* 1984.

DONALD F. KETTL

OFFICE OF TECHNOLOGY ASSESSMENT (OTA).

During the years following World War II, technology increasingly became both the source of and the answer to public policy problems. The Office of Technology Assessment was created in response to this emergence of technology as a major force in twentieth-century society. By 1972, when the OTA was established, Congress was confronted with three immediate and compelling issues. First, it had become clear that technological innovation had unexpected environmental consequences—for example, the ecological devastation that had accompanied the widespread use of the insecticide DDT. Second, federal expenditures on technological research and development amounted to more than eighteen billion dollars, expenditures widely recognized as essential investments in the future. Third, struggles between President Richard M. Nixon and Congress over such issues as supersonic jet transport had convinced many members of Congress of the necessity of a specially designated source of scientific technical advice.

In retrospect, it is clear that Congress hoped that the OTA would act as an objective organization that could provide both Congress and the public with scientific and technical assessments in layman's terms. The OTA was seen as a body that could provide early identification of so-called second-order consequences of technology, such as negative environmental impacts. The OTA was intended as a support organization that could identify policy alternatives but that would not seek to substitute its judgments for those of the members of Congress.

In pursuit of these goals, Congress established a unique governance and advisory structure for the OTA. It is governed by the twelve-member Technology Assessment Board (TAB), divided equally between the House and the Senate and between the Democratic and Republican parties. In addition the Technology Assessment Advisory Council (TAAC), which is composed of eminent leaders from across the nation, the comptroller general of the United States, and the director of the Congressional Research Service, provides general advice. The OTA's director is chosen by the TAB and appointed for six years.

The OTA was a center of controversy throughout the tenure of its first two directors, Emilio Q. Daddario and Russell Petersen. During Daddario's term, some critics raised questions about perceived patronage on the part of TAB members in hiring OTA staff. The OTA was also seen by some as being too responsive to the short-term concerns of Congress (that is, its studies were too responsive to current legislative initiatives) and not concerned enough about major long-range issues, such as global warming. Some members of the press accused the OTA of being a research arm for the anticipated presidential campaign of Sen. Edward M. Kennedy (D-Mass.), who was TAB's first chairman. When Petersen took over as director, he had sole control over hiring; thus, any suspicion of patronage was eliminated. He also moved the OTA away from concern with short-term congressional interests toward what he perceived to be long-term issues. In so doing, however, he created the impression of being unresponsive to the needs of Congress.

John Gibbons's appointment, in June 1979, as OTA's third director was widely viewed as the OTA's last chance. Under Gibbons the OTA became what many believe to be Washington's most competent, unbiased, and valuable policy research organization concerned with science and technology issues. No longer a focus of controversy, the OTA was now a source of information, analysis, and insight used by a broad range of interests in the policy debates of the nation. Thus, when OTA's fourth director, Roger C. Herdman, was appointed in May 1993, he took over a highly regarded, well-established organization.

Over the years, the range of issues studied by the OTA has included the Strategic Defense Initiative (SDI), lie detector testing, and the preservation of books in the Library of Congress, as well as more general technological and environmental concerns. Key to the OTA's reputation is its ability to present clear characterizations of the uncertainty and controversy that frequently surround scientific and technical information relevant to public policy.

Recent OTA studies illustrate the diversity of its work. In a report entitled *Complex Cleanup*, OTA investigated the environmental management of nuclear waste materials stored at Department of Energy facilities. It noted that at some facilities technical solutions are not available and that for all sites there is a major need for establishing procedures that provide public credibility for the cleanup activities. The OTA has also devoted major attention to the health area recently. Reports have ranged from a focus on the efficacy and economics of various health-related technologies to the challenge posed by drug-resistant strains of tuberculosis.

Studies in the energy area have given particular attention to the many possibilities for increasing energy efficiency and within that focus have looked at the role that more efficient technologies might play in helping the new free-market economies of Eastern Europe. Studies in the international security area have ranged from reports on satellite-based remote sensing to reports on the proliferation of nuclear- and chemical-warfare capability. The diversity of topics treated by OTA reports is illustrated by, for example, an investigation of the efficacy of computers in improving American education and a report on crop substitution as a way to stop South American farmers from growing coca, the plant from which cocaine is made.

Many people believe the OTA's success is tied to its small size and the manifold expertise of its staff. It has less than two hundred employees and a budget of roughly $20 million. The OTA has a unique ability to tap diverse experts and interested parties through its contracting authority and its advisory panels.

The OTA's major studies have advisory panels of from twelve to twenty people, chosen to represent both the range of expert opinion and the range of interested parties. OTA advisory panel meetings sometimes contribute to the evolution of a consensus since they serve as a neutral meeting ground for such varied interests and experts.

The OTA uses outside expertise more than other congressional support organizations. OTA reports are written by the agency's staff, but it has great flexibility in contracting for specific expert support. Under Daddario, an effort was made to have all studies contracted out. Both because of the unique character of the OTA's assessments and the need to be sensitive to Congress's desires, the contracting approach failed.

OTA studies are normally completed in one to two years. The OTA responds only to study requests from committee chairmen, from the TAB, or from its own director. The OTA's relatively small size and budget means that it must do less than is requested and thus must negotiate with the requesting committees in establishing its priorities. This has resulted in a pattern of careful study development. Frequently, studies are defined in ways that serve the needs of multiple committees.

Information generated by the OTA flows to the Congress in a number of ways. OTA staff maintain informal (e.g., briefings) and formal (e.g., testimony and interim publications) contact with committee staff during the studies. The OTA produces highly readable reports that are of importance not only to Congress but to the research and policy community nationwide. Thus, information flows back to the Congress through interested parties who use the OTA's work.

For those who have observed the evolution of the OTA, there is a consensus that it is a striking success story. As scientific and technical issues become ever more important to U.S. policy-making, it seems clear that the OTA will continue to play a key role.

BIBLIOGRAPHY

Burby, Jack. "OTA Comes of Age." *Los Angeles Times*, 1 November 1987.

Jenkins, Chris. "The Office of What?" *San Diego Union*, 24 November 1992.

U.S. Congress. Office of Technology Assessment. *An Experiment in Technology Policy-Making: Fifteen Years of the U.S. Office of Technology Assessment*, by Mary Proctor. 100th Cong., 1st sess., 1987.

Walters, Rhodri. "The Office of Technology Assessment of the United States Congress: A Model for the Future?" *Government and Opposition* 27 (1992): 89–108.

Wood, Fred B. "The Status of Technology Assessment: A View from the Congressional Office of Technology Assessment." *Technological Forecasting and Social Change* 22 (1982): 211–222.

DON E. KASH

OFFICES, CONGRESSIONAL. Until the twentieth century, few members of Congress had official office space. The little space available in the Capitol building, which was constructed incrementally between 1793 and 1829 and not fully completed until the presidency of Abraham Lincoln, was reserved for the use of committees, officers, and leaders. During the nineteenth century, a member's boardinghouse room often served as his "office" away from the Hill. Senators did much of their work at their desks on the floor, as did representatives until they occupied the current House chamber in 1857, when desks were no longer provided on the floor. For the next half century, House members apparently worked from whatever space they could find.

As the size of the Union and, concomitantly, the membership of the House and Senate swelled by the end of the nineteenth century, House and Senate office buildings were needed. The House's Cannon Building, the first structure built for such purposes, was occupied in 1908; the Senate's Russell Building was ready for use in 1909 (prior to then, senators had space in the Maltby Building). As of 1993, exclusive of the Library of Congress's three buildings, the Capitol Hill complex included thirteen buildings: the Capitol and six buildings each for the House and Senate.

On the House side, each representative, delegate, or resident commissioner is entitled to a suite of offices in either the Cannon, Longworth, or Rayburn Building, with party leaders entitled to additional office space in the Capitol. Similarly, each senator is entitled to a suite of offices in the Russell, Dirksen, or Hart Building, with the leaders accorded additional space in the Capitol. For the most part, officers of the Congress and their employees are housed in the Capitol, while the almost three hundred congressional committees and subcommittees are scattered throughout the congressional complex. Including the 540 members and delegates, more than 15,000 congressional employees were housed in Capitol Hill office space by the 1990s.

Each representative, delegate, and senator receives annual funding to pay for staff salaries and office equipment and supplies, as do committees and subcommittees. In addition, members are provided funds to maintain one or more offices in their district or state. Furniture and equipment are provided at no charge.

Representatives in 1993 were allowed no more than eighteen permanent and four temporary staff, for which they could spend up to $558,000 per year. Of such employees, about 60 percent worked in Capitol Hill offices, while 40 percent were located in district offices. Senators receive an allowance for staffing based on the size of their state's population. Most senators were allotted approximately $1.4 million as of 1993, and the two senators from the most populous state (California) were entitled to $2.3 million annually. The size of Senate personal staffs in 1993, which averaged around forty, ranged from twenty-five to more than seventy; about one-third were located in state offices, the rest in Washington.

The 4,500 personal staff in district or state offices tend to focus on constituency services, while the 7,500 in Washington offices principally assist with members' legislative duties. The 4,000 committee staff assist committees in meeting their policy-making and oversight responsibilities, while the 5,000 staff of the officers of the House and Senate see to administrative and housekeeping tasks.

[See also Congressional Office Buildings; Offices, District; Staffing.]

BIBLIOGRAPHY

Congressional Quarterly Inc. *Congressional Quarterly's Guide to Congress.* 2d ed. 1976. "Capitol and Office Buildings," pp. 413–437.
U.S. Senate. *Congressional Directory.* 102d Cong., 1st sess., 1991. S. Doc. 102-4. "Capitol Buildings and Grounds," pp. 643–662.

FREDERICK H. PAULS

OFFICES, DISTRICT. Exactly when members of Congress began to maintain offices in their home district or state is not precisely known, but it was not a widespread practice before the mid-twentieth century. Prior to 1948 for the Senate and 1952 for the House, the federal government's General Services Administration was required to provide members with office space in government buildings, as available. As of these years, the Senate and House charged their respective sergeants at arms with securing such office space and authorized moneys for rent if suitable space was unavailable in government buildings.

District and state offices came into being for several reasons. Principally, they serve as a convenience to constituents desiring to contact their representative or senator. This is particularly so for constituents of members from Alaska, Hawaii, and the Mountain and Pacific Coast states whose members' Washington offices might well be closed by early to mid-afternoon local time. These offices also

TABLE 1. *Members' District and State Offices: 102d Congress*

NO. OF OFFICES MAINTAINED	NO. OF SENATORS	NO. OF REPS.
1	15	165
2	5	121
3	25	111
4	26	33
5	14	4
6	7	0
7	5	1
8	3	0
Total	100	435

SOURCE: Compiled by author from *1991–1992 Official Congressional Directory, 102d Congress.*

provide a workplace for members when they return to their district or state during periods of congressional recess or adjournment.

As communication and copying technologies have improved, such offices have facilitated the electronic transmission of correspondence to and from the members' Washington, D.C., offices. Increasingly, these offices have also become the locus for assisting constituents who seek congressional intervention and help with federal government agencies.

Representatives and senators are allowed a set amount of square footage for district or state offices; this amount has increased over time. As the table shows, one-fifth of senators in 1992 had 1 or 2 state offices, while two-thirds had 3, 4, or 5, and one-seventh had 6, 7, or 8. Area, geography, and population distribution of the home state roughly correlate with the number of offices individual senators maintain. A similar correspondence exists in

the House, although only 10 percent of members have more than three district offices. In recent years, members in some states have shared resources and work load in their local offices in order to serve constituents more efficiently and at less cost. Another development in major cities is the consolidation of district offices on a single floor in a single building.

Members from large rural districts or states sometimes have mobile offices that are driven from town to town as a courtesy and convenience to constituents. Funds are provided to pay for staff, equipment, supplies, and other operational expenses. In addition, members receive an allowance to enable them to travel to, from, and within their districts or states.

After 1970, members of Congress increased the number of local offices (in 1992, there were more than three hundred for senators and almost nine hundred for representatives) and transferred to

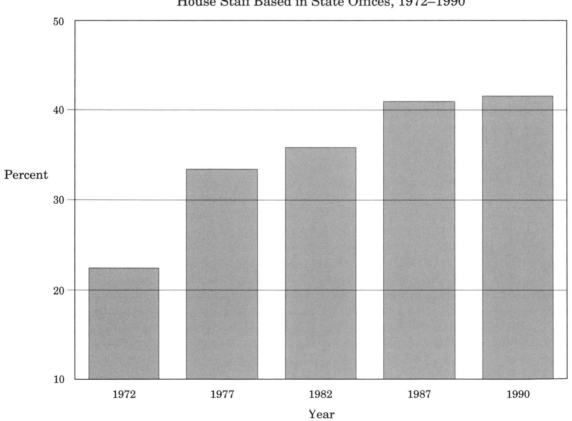

Figure 1
House Staff Based in State Offices, 1972–1990

Source: Norman J. Ornstein, Thomas E. Mann, Michael J. Malbin, eds., *Vital Statistics on Congress, 1991–1992*, Washington, D.C., Congressional Quarterly Press, 1992.

Figure 2
Senate Staff Based in State Offices, 1972–1990

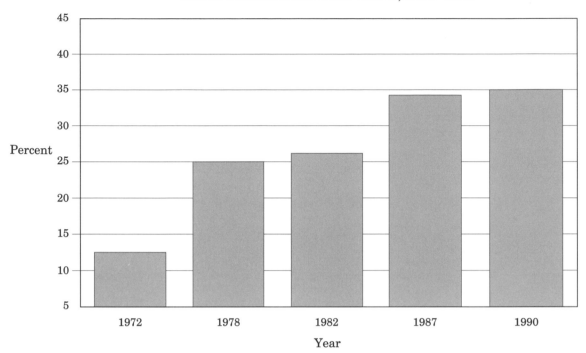

SOURCE: Norman J. Ornstein, Thomas E. Mann, Michael J. Malbin, eds., *Vital Statistics on Congress, 1991–1992*, Washington, D.C., Congressional Quarterly Press, 1992.

them increasing responsibility for constituent service and reelection politicking (e.g., scheduling political appearances during visits back to their district or state). Along with the transfer of these duties was the accompanying transfer of staff, including seasoned and senior staff, so that by 1992 about 40 percent of the almost eight thousand personal staff of House members were located in district offices and more than one-third of the four thousand personal staff of senators.

BIBLIOGRAPHY

Congressional Management Foundation. *Frontline Management: A Guide for Congressional District/State Offices.* 1989.

Tacheron, Donald G., and Morris K. Udall. *The Job of the Congressman.* 2d ed. 1970. Pp. 63–94.

FREDERICK H. PAULS

OHIO. Ohio entered the Union in 1803 as the first state admitted from the Northwest Territory. It was also the first state to be admitted through an enabling act—requiring a multistage admission procedure—rather than the simple, one-step admission act used previously for Vermont, Kentucky, and Tennessee. Ohio's Federalist officials encouraged a society based on orderly growth and the appointment of able officials, but a majority of the voters supported Jeffersonian Republican self-made surveyors and transplanted Virginians who favored rapid settlement and popular elections. Both parties tried to subdivide the Northwest Territory in ways that would produce at least one state favorable to them. Ohio's size was reduced through the creation of Indiana Territory in 1800, and in 1802, Federalist governor Arthur St. Clair tried to delay statehood by dividing Ohio along the Scioto River. A Jeffersonian Congress instead removed ostensibly Federalist lower Michigan from Ohio, and St. Clair unsuccessfully tried to persuade Ohio's constitutional convention to reject statehood. Congress gave Ohio land-sale revenues for road construction and set an imprecise Ohio-Michigan border that nearly produced interstate conflict in 1835.

A number of Ohioans became prominent in Congress. Territorial delegate William Henry Harrison

JAMES A. GARFIELD (R-OHIO).
HARPER'S PICTORIAL HISTORY OF THE GREAT REBELLION

promoted the liberal Land Act of 1800, and Sen. Thomas Worthington persuaded Congress in 1804 to allow 160-acre sales of frontier land. In 1809, Ohio's sole representative, Jeremiah Morrow, won a two-year extension on credit payments for federal land sales. By 1812 population growth had boosted Ohio's representation to six House seats, a number that grew to fourteen in 1822. Ohio's delegates favored rapid frontier development through easy land sales, federal tariffs, and aid to transportation. Ten of the state's fourteen representatives backed John Quincy Adams in the 1825 House presidential vote.

The Ohio delegation included both prodevelopment Whigs and anti-Bank Jacksonians, but voters often chose candidates opposed to the expansion of slavery. Former Whig senator Thomas Ewing became secretary of the Treasury in 1841, while Whig senator Thomas Corwin strongly denounced the Mexican War and Whig representative Joshua R. Giddings achieved national prominence for his antislavery stance. Senators Salmon P. Chase, Ben-

jamin F. Wade, and John Sherman and Rep. James M. Ashley all built Republican careers around opposition to slavery's expansion. Wade backed numerous reform causes, dominated the Union's Joint Committee on the Conduct of the War, and, as president pro tempore of the Senate, would have succeeded to the presidency if Andrew Johnson had been impeached. Ohio's southern-settled and Roman Catholic counties generally remained Democratic and strongly supported Rep. Clement L. Vallandigham and others who opposed the Civil War and Reconstruction.

Many postwar leaders ran for office on their war records, including Republican representatives Rutherford B. Hayes, James A. Garfield, and William McKinley. Garfield's career survived links to the Crédit Mobilier scandal. Ohio's identification with tariffs was symbolized by the McKinley tariff of 1890 and the selection of industrialist Republican leader Marcus A. Hanna as senator in 1897.

Several Ohioans, including Sen. Warren G. Harding and House Speaker Nicholas Longworth, achieved national prominence after World War I. Urban growth, the Depression, and increased ethnic participation in politics led to greater Democratic strength. Both parties remained competitive throughout the later twentieth century. Sen. Robert A. Taft dominated the conservative wing of the national Republican party from 1939 until 1953. The Taft-Hartley Act of 1947 sharply reduced labor-union power, but Taft also supported urban renewal programs. Leading Ohioans in Congress late in the century included Senators John Glenn and Howard M. Metzenbaum and black representative Louis Stokes, all Democrats. The Ohio congressional delegation, although reduced from twenty-three in 1960 to nineteen in 1992, remained one of the strongest groups in Congress.

BIBLIOGRAPHY

Wittke, Carl, ed. The History of the State of Ohio. 6 vols. 1941–1944.

JEFFREY P. BROWN

OKLAHOMA. Except for its long panhandle (which the United States acquired in the Adams-Oniz Treaty), Oklahoma was a portion of the Louisiana Purchase. Through much of the nineteenth century it was home to relocated Indian tribes. In the 1830s, the federal government relocated the so-called Five Civilized Tribes (the Cherokees, Creeks, Seminoles, Choctaws, and Chickasaws) there. After the Indian governments allied themselves to the Confederacy, the United States seized the western halves of their lands as penalty and proceeded to resettle Plains tribes in that section. Beginning in 1889, homesteaders settled the western lands as the reservations were broken up. In 1890, Congress created Oklahoma Territory—roughly the western half of the future state—to meet the needs of those homesteaders. The eastern portion remained as the Indian Territory, governed by five Indian republics. Well before 1900, however, the great bulk of its population consisted of white and black newcomers. Most of those who had settled in the west were of Republican stock from Kansas or other midwestern states. The great bulk of the new easterners were of Democratic southern ancestry.

These partisan circumstances were important elements in the timing and form of Oklahoma's eventual statehood. Although each territory soon had at least twice the population of any previous territory on its admission to the Union, Republican president Theodore Roosevelt and the Republican majorities in Congress had no intention to add sure Democratic votes to Congress and to the Electoral College. For that reason, they resisted all efforts to admit the two territories as separate states. In finally combining both territories into one state, they calculated that the Republicans in the west would have a fighting chance to hold their own against the Democrats of the east. In that form, Oklahoma became the forty-sixth state on 16 November 1907.

Most of Oklahoma's subsequent history has demonstrated the excessive optimism of that calculation. Only twice have the Republicans sent a majority of the delegation to the House, and nine times they have failed to win a single Oklahoma seat. Rarely have the Republicans won more than one or two seats, and those victors have almost always represented traditional pockets of party strength in the rural northwest. Similarly, Oklahoma Republicans have elected only six U.S. senators, four of whom served a single term each and one of whom (Edward H. Moore) was and remained a registered Democrat. In recent years, however, the Republicans have gained ground, largely by adding considerable strength in the state's two metropolitan centers, Oklahoma City and Tulsa, to their original base.

Not surprisingly, the Oklahomans who have had the greatest impact in Congress have been Democrats. Sen. Robert S. Kerr, who served from 1949 until his death in 1963, was a major figure in the Senate. Originally allied with Majority Leader Lyndon B. Johnson in the 1950s, Kerr used his positions on the Finance and Public Works committees to acquire great influence on Capitol Hill and great support at home. His personal organization was a dominant factor in state politics, and the Washington press designated him the "Uncrowned King of the United States Senate."

Easily the state's most notable member of the House of Representatives has been Carl B. Albert. First elected in 1946 from the 3d District—the state's extreme southeastern corner and the heart of so-called Little Dixie—Albert was Speaker Sam Rayburn's choice for Democratic party whip in 1955. On Rayburn's death in 1961, he was elected the majority leader, replacing the new Speaker, John W. McCormack. In 1971 Albert himself became Speaker. Before his retirement in 1977, he oversaw the House impeachment hearings against President Richard M. Nixon and the beginnings of the reform process that reshaped Congress in the 1970s and beyond.

BIBLIOGRAPHY

Albert, Carl, with Danney Goble. *Little Giant: The Life and Times of Speaker Carl Albert.* 1990.

Morgan, Anne Hodges. *Robert S. Kerr: The Senate Years.* 1977.

Scales, James R., and Danney Goble. *Oklahoma Politics: A History.* 1979.

DANNEY GOBLE

OLDER AMERICANS. Since the early days of the Republic, Congress has addressed specific needs of certain subsets of the nation's elderly population. Most of the Revolutionary War veterans who were granted pensions under an 1818 law were old men in need. The federal government instituted retirement plans piecemeal for such workers as soldiers, sailors, and some other classes of public employees, and in 1920 consolidated many of its programs in a civil service retirement system. Older people were prime beneficiaries of the 1935 Social Security Act. But the aged as a distinctive social group did not gain real political clout on Capitol Hill until the 1960s.

In 1958 Congress authorized (P.L. 85-908) a White House conference on aging to be held three years later. There were precedents for this meeting: decennial White House conferences on youth had been convened since 1909, and in 1950 the Federal Security Agency had brought together national experts to discuss the so-called problems of aging. In the last days of the Eisenhower administration, delegates to the 1961 conference urged the establishment of a federal agency to coordinate activities at the national level. John F. Kennedy on 21 February 1963 responded favorably to this suggestion in his "Special Message on Aiding Our Senior Citizens." In addition, he urged a five-year federal grant-in-aid to state and local officials under the oversight of the newly founded National Association of State Units on Aging (NASUA). During hearings three months later Rep. John E. Fogarty, a popular and well-respected Democrat from Rhode Island, declared that federal programs for the elderly were "without a central core of direction and coordination." Because Lyndon B. Johnson gave other civil rights issues higher priority during the election year, Fogarty's proposal for coordinating efforts languished.

House Resolution 3708, reintroduced by Fogarty on 27 January 1965, gained quick approval. The House passed the Older Americans Act (OAA) by a vote of 395 to 1 on 31 March. The measure went through the Senate without debate and passed by voice vote on 27 May. Small details were reconciled by 6 July, and the White House ceremony took place eight days later. July proved to be quite a month for senior citizens: on 30 July President Johnson flew to Independence, Missouri, to sign Medicare into law in the presence of Harry S. Truman.

Congressional leaders included older Americans in their plans for a Great Society on a scale that went far beyond anything envisioned before, even though organizations such as the American Association of Retired Persons/National Retired Teachers Association (AARP/NRTA) and the National Council on the Aging (NCOA) had not yet begun to engage in political activities. The American Medical Association and AFL-CIO did not lobby for OAA. Wilbur Cohen, then undersecretary of the Department of Health, Education, and Welfare (HEW), worried about how a special unit on aging might affect discipline within his department. But the selection of his Michigan friend William Bechill as the first commissioner on aging reduced his qualms. The fifteen-member Advisory Committee on Older Americans, picked in December 1965, ensured participation by labor, AARP/NRTA, NCOA, NASUA, the Social Security Administration, and academics.

In passing the Older Americans Act in 1965, Congress established a new social contract for the aged consonant with the prevailing politics and rhetoric of interest-group liberalism. Modeled on the Office of Employment Opportunity (OEO), the new Administration on Aging (AoA) was placed within HEW. AoA authorized financial grants for community planning, services, and university-based training programs and provided formula grants to states for community services and demonstration projects as well as for the establishment of state agencies on aging. The declaration of objectives in Title I of OAA enunciated its architects' high hopes:

> The Congress hereby finds and declares that the older people of our Nation are entitled to, and it is the joint duty and responsibility of the Governments of the United States and of the several States and their political subdivisions to assist our older people to secure equal opportunity to the full and free enjoyment of the following objectives:
>
> (1) an adequate income in retirement . . .
> (2) the best possible physical and mental health . . .
> (3) suitable housing . . .
> (4) full restorative services . . .
> (5) opportunity for employment . . .
> (6) retirement in health, honor, dignity . . .
> (7) pursuit of meaningful activity . . .
> (8) efficient community services, including access to low-cost transportation . . .
> (9) immediate benefit from proven research knowledge
> (10) freedom, independence and the free exercise of individual initiative in planning and managing their own lives. [P.L. 89-73]

This is an extraordinary statement, potentially more revolutionary in scope than any other measure in the war on poverty. The act went beyond matters of income and health and did more than simply extend OEO's community-action thrust. "The legislation is really the seed corn that provides an orderly, intelligent, and constructive program to help us meet the new dimensions of responsibilities which lie ahead in the remaining years of this century," observed President Johnson as he signed the measure into law. "The paid sum of this law will be modest in dollars but far reaching in results" (*Congressional Quarterly*, 23 July 1965, p. 1454). Perhaps this language was too grandiose: It had not yet become evident that implementing OAA's goals would entail difficult trade-offs far in excess of AoA's budget.

Having made big promises, the government seemed uncertain about what to do next. Annual budgetary authorizations under the act were minuscule. In the first year, 1966, only $7.5 million was allocated. Five years later, the figure was $33.6

million, still a paltry figure to cover the cost of administering the act and encouraging research, training, and social services for the elderly. Still, despite underfunding and frequent turnovers in leadership, OAA's mission has remained remarkably constant: by providing a wide array of services, AoA tries to enable—often, to empower—older persons to maintain maximum independence. Grassroots participation is a key part of the process.

AoA engaged in advocacy. The unit played an indispensable role in arranging state-level meetings to prepare for the 1971 White House Conference on Aging. But organizational constraints impeded AoA's efforts. Many major programs (including key aspects of Social Security, Medicare, and federal housing) bypassed state- and local-level administration and AoA. Governors periodically sponsored forums on aging, but most state agencies were minimally staffed and maintained a relatively low profile in the bureaucracy. County welfare departments typically dealt with elderly clients as part of their regular caseload. To be effective, AoA needed better linkages with other governmental units.

The Comprehensive Services Amendments to the Older Americans Act, enacted by Congress in 1973, sought to redress the balance of power. State agencies on aging gained considerable control over budgetary matters and more responsibility for planning and coordination. But in order to receive federal funds for their programs, states were required to establish a network of Area Agencies on Aging (AAAs) to act as brokers overseeing activities at the local level. The elaboration of this bureaucratic arrangement in later years created an extensive old-age advocacy network at all levels of government. By the mid 1970s, at least eighty different federal bureaus and commissions provided more than 135 programs designed to aid the nation's senior citizens.

The expansion of OAA activities reversed during the 1980s. President Ronald Reagan cut funding for research under Title IV, for instance, by more than 50 percent. Thus, while the elderly population's share of the total budget grew from 15 percent in 1960 to 30 percent in fiscal 1991, the portion covered under OAA actually declined, to less than 1 percent. When Congress repealed the year-old Medicare Catastrophic Coverage Act (P.L. 100-360) in 1989, many pundits predicted that the outcry over generational inequities and the financing of other public benefits presaged the end to giving "greedy geezers" everything they demanded. But, in the words of Fernando Torres-Gil, whom President

Bill Clinton named as the first assistant secretary in Health and Human Services for aging, "the Older Americans Act is the primary source of human and social services for the elderly." As the only national agency charged with overseeing federal policy, the Administration on Aging is bound to grow in administrative importance even if it operates under several financial constraints.

[*See also* Medicare; Social Security Act; Social Welfare and Poverty.]

BIBLIOGRAPHY

Achenbaum, W. Andrew. *Shades of Gray.* 1983.
Atchley, Robert C. *Social Forces of Later Life.* 3d ed. 1980.
Estes, Carroll. *The Aging Enterprise.* 1979.
Pratt, Henry J. *The Gray Lobby.* 1977.
U.S. Senate. Special Committee on Aging, et al. *Aging America.* 102d Cong., 1st sess., 1991.

W. ANDREW ACHENBAUM

OMB. *See* Office of Management and Budget.

OMNIBUS BUDGET RECONCILIATION ACT (1981). *See* Budget Reconciliation Act.

O'NEILL, THOMAS P. (TIP), JR. (1912–1994), representative from Massachusetts, Democratic whip (1971–1973), majority leader (1973–1977), and Speaker of the House (1977–1987). "All politics is local" is the phrase most often associated with Tip O'Neill, the Irish bricklayer's son from Cambridge, Massachusetts. O'Neill served for ten years as Speaker of the House and embodied the House's transition from a clubby, self-contained, and semi-anonymous body to a highly visible, major policy-making institution.

Born 9 December 1912 and educated in North Cambridge schools, O'Neill was a 1936 graduate of Boston College. His father, Thomas P. O'Neill, was the child of Irish immigrants. O'Neill was employed as an insurance salesman but quickly rose through the ranks of the city Democratic organization and was elected to the Massachusetts legislature (the Great and General Court) in 1936. In his sixteen years in the legislature (1936–1952), O'Neill moved rapidly up the leadership ladder and was chosen as minority leader in 1947. In 1949, he was elected the first Democratic Speaker of the Massachusetts house in more than a century.

In 1952, O'Neill sought and won election to the U.S. House of Representatives, replacing Democrat John F. Kennedy, who had relinquished the seat to run for the U.S. Senate. It was the first of O'Neill's seventeen elections to the House.

As a Boston Irish politician, O'Neill had to move gingerly between the tribal feuds that characterized the city. He was especially careful in his dealings with James M. Curley, Boston's four-time mayor and former governor and U.S. representative. Curley's hold on Boston politics at the time was legendary despite his two imprisonments, and O'Neill sought to be respectful of Curley without becoming enmeshed in his troubles. In 1946, the political clans led by U.S. ambassador Joseph P. Kennedy and U.S. House majority leader John W. McCormack had split over the fate of Curley, with McCormack urging the Massachusetts congressional delegation to rally behind the former mayor, while the Kennedys were trying to keep their distance lest the taint of corruption undermine the presidential dreams of the ambassador and his sons.

O'Neill demonstrated a remarkable ability to remain close to all of the key players in this intraparty dispute. These skills would serve him well in the 1962 Massachusetts U.S. Senate primary. By that time, Sen. John F. Kennedy had become president and Majority Leader John McCormack had become Speaker of the House. The tension between these two families erupted in a nomination contest between Massachusetts attorney general Edward J. McCormack, John McCormack's nephew, and Edward M. Kennedy, the president's youngest brother. O'Neill remained neutral, retaining the friendship of both camps. This was also the case in the 1980 presidential primary contests between President Jimmy Carter and Sen. Edward Kennedy.

O'Neill was initially assigned to the relatively minor Committee on Merchant Marine and Fisheries, but when the Democrats recaptured the House in 1954, he won assignment to the powerful Rules Committee along with Richard W. Bolling (Mo.). Bolling and O'Neill were to be "the eyes and ears" of Speaker Sam Rayburn (Tex.) and Majority Leader McCormack, respectively. The committee was dominated by two archconservative Southern Democrats, Howard W. Smith of Virginia and William M. Colmer of Mississippi, who confounded the Democratic leadership of the House by often voting with the committee's Republicans to prevent liberal legislation from coming to the House floor. Rayburn and McCormack gained access to the

THOMAS P. (TIP) O'NEILL, JR. As Speaker of the House, in front of the Capitol.

O'NEILL PAPERS, JOHN J. BURNS LIBRARY, BOSTON COLLEGE

committee through junior members Bolling and O'Neill.

O'Neill remained loyal to McCormack throughout the older man's leadership career and stuck with him during the House leadership battles that erupted in 1967 and 1969. However, during the Vietnam

War, O'Neill broke with the House leadership, which had supported President Lyndon B. Johnson's conduct of the war. In so doing, O'Neill earned not only the respect of his large college constituency in Cambridge, but national respect as well. This show of independence on a defining issue within his party helped him shed the label of "Boston Irish politician."

When McCormack left the speakership in 1970, he was succeeded by Majority Leader Carl B. Albert (Okla.). Hale Boggs (La.), the Democratic whip, replaced Albert as majority leader. Boggs had recommended Dan Rostenkowski (Ill.) to succeed him as Democratic whip, an appointment position at the time. However, Albert, nursing an old grudge against Rostenkowski, vetoed Boggs's choice and named O'Neill to the post, putting him third in the House leadership hierarchy.

When Boggs was declared dead after his plane disappeared over Alaska in 1972, House Democrats unanimously elected O'Neill to replace Boggs as majority leader. In 1977, following Albert's retirement, he was elected Speaker.

O'Neill's ascent to the speakership coincided with the election of a new Democratic president, Jimmy Carter. Speaker O'Neill expected to cooperate with the new administration, but Carter, who had maintained an "antipolitics" stance in his campaign, and his staff proved uncomfortable with O'Neill's old-style Boston politics image. O'Neill was unable to gain access to the White House and thus was unable to help President Carter salvage his troubled one-term presidency.

With the election of Republican Ronald Reagan in 1980 and the Republican capture of the Senate, Speaker O'Neill was left as the only major Democratic leader. Reagan worked closely with a coalition of Republicans and conservative southern Democrats (the so-called boll weevils) to pass his tax reduction plan and to undermine O'Neill's hold on the House. The 1982 congressional election featured a Republican-sponsored political TV advertisement with a clownish O'Neill "look-alike." The ad was meant to ridicule O'Neill and enable the Republicans to capture the House from a Democratic party that had won every House election since 1954. The strategy backfired, and Democrats, helped by favorable redistricting in California and an unemployment rate of 10 percent, gained twenty-six seats. This eliminated the voting leverage of the boll weevils and strengthened O'Neill's hold on the House.

From 1983 to 1987, O'Neill and Reagan wrestled for control of the legislative agenda, with O'Neill eventually gaining the upper hand. After Reagan's successful first year, never again was he able to mount House majorities in favor of either his economic agenda, which involved cutting capital-gains taxes, or his social agenda, which involved outlawing abortion, returning prayer to public schools, and limiting affirmative action programs.

O'Neill retired in 1987 after ten consecutive years as Speaker, the longest period of consecutive service ever attained in that post and the second-longest tenure of any Speaker, exceeded only by Sam Rayburn, who presided for seventeen years. Following his retirement, O'Neill remained in the public eye, publishing a best-selling autobiography, *Man of the House*, and parlaying his popularity into lucrative contracts for a series of television commercials. He died on 5 January 1994 at the age of eighty-one.

More than any Speaker in modern times, O'Neill learned how to move effectively from the "retail politics" of the House floor, where voting coalitions are put together member by member, to the "wholesale politics" of the mass media, where public images are shaped. He restored the integrity of the House and demonstrated anew the innate powers of the speakership.

BIBLIOGRAPHY

Clancy, Paul, and Shirley Elder. *Tip: A Biography of Thomas P. O'Neill, Speaker of the House.* 1980.
O'Neill, Thomas P., Jr. *Man of the House: The Life and Political Memoirs of Speaker Tip O'Neill.* 1987.
Peters, Ronald M., Jr. *The American Speakership in Historical Perspective.* 1990.

GARRISON NELSON

ONE-MINUTE SPEECHES. At the start of each day of session in the House of Representatives, members are normally recognized to address the House for one-minute on any subject they wish. These speeches are not a right accorded members under the Rules of the House of Representatives. Rather, they are a privilege granted under accepted House tradition. In order to give a one-minute speech, a member must first gain recognition by the chair and then must ask and receive the unanimous consent of the House to address it for one minute.

Members who wish to give a one-minute speech sit in the front row of seats on their respective party's side of the main aisle. The Speaker recognizes members in order from his right to his left. A majority member is recognized first, followed by a minority member, in an alternating pattern. There is no guarantee that each member seated will receive the opportunity to give a one-minute speech that day. The Speaker may decline to hold any one-minute speeches at all on a day when legislative business is pressing, or he may decide to hold only a minimal number.

One-minute speeches provide members with an outlet for expression and commentary, without the usual requirement to make only remarks relevant to pending legislative matters. In practice, members devote almost half these speeches to either national or international issues and approximately one-third to pending legislation, followed in descending order of frequency by eulogies or special tributes, items of local interest to their districts, commentary on internal House operations and procedures, and humorous topics.

One-minute speeches are very popular because of their brevity and variety. They are well suited for use as videotaped news releases to constituents and are widely viewed by congressional colleagues and staff. This makes them effective publicity tools for legislative initiatives.

Only a small number of members—less than 10 percent of any given Congress—choose to give no one-minute speeches at all. Invariably, one or two members gain reputations for giving many more one-minute speeches than their colleagues. The vast majority of members, whether they be majority, minority, junior or senior in tenure, fall between these extremes, giving occasional one-minute speeches.

The first one-minute speech was given in the House on 2 August 1937. By 1940, the strict one-minute limitation had been established as accepted practice, having been institutionalized by then-Speaker Sam Rayburn. In 1980, party leaders agreed that one-minute speeches would occur at the start of each day's proceedings unless advance notice is given that they will be shifted to a later time of day. In 1984, the Speaker instituted the practice of alternating recognition for one-minute speeches between majority and minority members. One-minute speeches are unquestionably an integral and valued part of House procedure.

BIBLIOGRAPHY

Nickels, Ilona B. *One-Minute Speeches: House Practice and Procedure.* Congressional Research Service, Library of Congress. CRS Rept. 90-47 GOV. 1990.

Tiefer, Charles. *Congressional Practice and Procedure.* 1989. Pp. 237–238.

U.S. House of Representatives. *Deschler's Precedents of the United States House of Representatives,* by Lewis Deschler. 94th Cong., 2d sess., 1977. Vol. 6, chap. 21, pp. 127–136.

ILONA B. NICKELS

ORATORY. *See* Debate and Oratory.

ORDERS. Orders grant authority for floor actions in both the House and Senate. Orders are used to govern a wide range of activities, from elaborately structuring a bill's consideration to simply permitting speeches not otherwise in order. Several specific types of orders exist.

A regular order consists of the normal standing rules of the chamber, taken together with its precedents (previous interpretive rulings of the chair). The regular order governs unless expressly waived.

A special order supplants the regular order, but usually only on a temporary basis. It is given the same respect as a standing rule while it is in force. A special order is also necessary to undertake an action on the floor on which the regular order is silent. In both chambers, special orders are most often agreed to by unanimous consent.

In the House, special orders are also created when the Rules Committee drafts a resolution establishing a procedure for floor action that does not otherwise fall within the regular order. Before this special resolution can become governing authority, the House must adopt it by majority vote. The Rules Committee has reported special orders as temporary authority for House floor actions since 1883.

In both chambers, a motion to suspend the rules and take a specified action implicitly creates a special order. If adopted by a two-thirds vote, the effect of a rules suspension is to temporarily waive the regular order for the purposes stated.

In the House special orders also mean those speeches delivered at the end of the day by members who have reserved time for this purpose in advance. Special order speeches may be given on any subject desired, and may range in length from five minutes to one hour. These speeches are not part of the regular order and unanimous consent is required for them to take place.

A standing order is a special order that applies for a specified duration of time. In the Senate, this is usually for the length of a two-year Congress but also can be for an open-ended period, with the order governing until retired or replaced. In the House, standing orders are quite infrequent, and usually govern only for the duration of one session.

In the Senate, the chamber will routinely agree to a list of requests for standing orders offered by its majority leader on the first day of a new Congress. For example, the majority and minority leaders are each granted ten minutes of floor time under their personal control on each day the Senate is in session. This so-called leader time occurs under the authority of a standing order, and is not addressed in the standing rules of the Senate. In the House, the chamber designates the hour of its daily meeting time by standing order on a yearly basis.

BIBLIOGRAPHY

U.S. House of Representatives. *Constitution, Jefferson's Manual, and Rules of the House of Representatives, 103d Congress.* Compiled by William Holmes Brown. 102d Cong., 2d sess., 1992. H. Doc. 102-405.

U.S. Senate. *Riddick's Senate Procedure, Precedents, and Practices,* by Floyd M. Riddick and Alan S. Frumin. 101st Cong., 2d sess., 1992. S. Doc. 101-28. P. 956.

ILONA B. NICKELS

OREGON. The Anglo-American Treaty of 1846 settled a long-simmering territorial dispute between Britain and the United States by extending the United States–Canada border along the 49th parallel to the Pacific. With stability in the Pacific Northwest came mounting appeals from American settlers for federal recognition and protection. In 1848, Congress passed the Organic Act establishing a vast area west of the Rocky Mountains as the Territory of Oregon. A few years later Congress removed from the territory areas covering what today are the state of Washington and parts of Idaho, Montana, and Wyoming.

In creating the Oregon territory, Congress validated all the legislation enacted up to that time by the area's informal but active provisional government, including its ban on slavery. This deference to local opinion was an important precedent for applying the principle of popular sovereignty to the Kansas and Nebraska territories in 1854. As to eventual statehood, the people of Oregon were divided. Many, having enjoyed self-government before Oregon achieved territorial status, were reluctant to trust their destiny to a distant government. From 1850 to 1857 several statehood petition efforts and three referendums failed. With no mandate from home, Oregon's territorial delegate, Joseph Lane, found little support for the enabling bills he introduced in Congress in 1855 and 1856.

Finally, in 1857, Oregonians did vote to petition Congress for statehood. A state convention was held and a constitution was adopted. Expecting early action on their request for statehood, voters rushed to elect their first state officials and a U.S. representative, La Fayette Grover, in June 1858. The "state legislature" convened and elected Joseph Lane and Delazon Smith as U.S. senators. The Oregon admission bill, however, languished in Congress for two years before it was finally passed in February 1859. Although irregular, the state legislature's premature actions, including the election of U.S. senators, were never officially challenged.

Congress's long delay on the Oregon bill resulted from northern opposition to a provision in the state constitution excluding the residence of free blacks and from southern objections to the state's constitutional prohibition of slavery. Republicans in Congress were also hesitant to admit a Democratic state.

Oregon's congressional delegation has included several national leaders. Republican senator George H. Williams served on the Joint Committee on Reconstruction (1865–1871); Republican senator Charles L. McNary was the minority floor leader from 1933 to 1944; Republican representative Willis C. Hawley was coauthor of the Hawley-Smoot Tariff Act of 1930; Democratic representative Edith S. Green led fights for federal aid to education and was the author of the Higher Education Act of 1965; and Wayne L. Morse (R-1945–1952; I-1952–1955; D-1955–1969) enlivened Senate debate with his independence and nonconformist views, particularly his early and outspoken opposition to U.S. involvement in the Vietnam War.

From one member in 1859 the state's delegation in the House has gradually risen to five. Oregon was a two-party state until about 1900, when Republicans came to dominate congressional elections. After World War II the two parties regained approximate parity.

BIBLIOGRAPHY

Dávilla-Colón, Luis R. *Breakthrough from Colonialism: An Interdisciplinary Study of Statehood.* Vol. 1. 1984.

Johannsen, Robert W. *Frontier Politics and the Sectional Conflict: The Pacific Northwest on the Eve of the Civil War.* 1955.

Onstine, Burton W. *Oregon Votes: 1858–1972.* 1973.

GORDON B. DODDS

ORGANIZATION OF CONGRESS COMMITTEE, JOINT

ORGANIZATION OF CONGRESS COMMITTEE, JOINT (1993). In 1993 the third joint effort to examine and recommend changes in congressional structures and procedures began in frustration and ended in disunity. The Joint Committee on the Organization of Congress emanated from the outburst of public criticism and demands for change that marked the early 1990s. On Capitol Hill, too, support for reorganization was mounting: more than twenty years had elapsed since committee jurisdictions had been assessed, for example. Four reform-minded members—Senators David L. Boren (D-Okla.) and Pete V. Domenici (R-N.Mex.) and Representatives Lee H. Hamilton (D-Ind.) and Bill Gradison (R-Ohio)—jointly introduced companion resolutions (S. Con. Res. 57; H. Con. Res. 192) to create the panel in the 102d Congress. Despite the mixed record of earlier reorganization panels, thoughtful critics saw the proposal as a credible effort that could address organizational problems and counteract the popular appeal of such schemes as term limits or wholesale staff cuts. Yet party leaders, fearful of losing power under reorganization, dragged their feet, finally yielding in spring 1992 to demands for the panel. The House approved the resolution on 18 June by a vote of 412 to 4; the Senate followed suit unanimously on 30 July.

The 28-member panel was directed to "make a full and complete study of the organization and operation of the Congress" and to recommend improvements to strengthen Congress's effectiveness, simplify its operations, and improve its relations with and oversight of other branches. It was to complete its task by the end of 1993, but the delay in authorizing the panel delayed the start of its formal activities until the 103d Congress convened in January 1993.

The Joint Committee's large membership—twelve from each house, divided equally by party—was chosen by the respective party leaders, four of whom (the Senate and House majority and minority floor leaders) held ex officio seats on the panel and played influential behind-the-scenes roles. Boren and Hamilton served as cochairmen; the vice chairmen were Domenici and David Dreier (R-Calif.), replacing Gradison, who resigned from the House in January 1993. Although the panel included some reform-minded members, these were especially lacking within the House Democratic contingent. House Democrats, who had controlled the chamber for nearly forty years, had the most to lose in a major reorganization: their party leaders wanted to protect their procedural prerogatives, and their committee chairmen would defend their jurisdictional domains.

The lack of consensus on reform directions surfaced in the opening hearings, which featured party leaders from both chambers. House Minority Leader Robert H. Michel (R-Ill.) voiced a lengthy list of complaints, declaring that the House was "in crisis," and that "legislative debate on the floor has degenerated into a majority monologue." He urged adoption of a Republican reform package that included reducing the numbers and sizes of committees, slashing staffs, curtailing restrictive special rules granted by the Rules Committee, ending proxy voting in committees, and applying federal laws to Congress. By contrast, Speaker Thomas S. Foley (D-Wash.) delivered an amiable defense of the status quo, and Rules Committee Chairman Joseph Moakley (D-Mass.) declared that ". . . it is the prerogative of the majority party leadership to both set the legislative agenda, and to provide for the orderly consideration of legislation in the House."

The most divisive Senate issue, which arose early in the hearings, was how to reconcile legislative efficiency with the chamber's cherished tradition of catering to the interests and schedules of each senator. Points of contention centered on (1) use of the filibuster and cloture; (2) the practice of senators placing holds on items on the calendars; and (3) scheduling conflicts. Majority Leader George J. Mitchell (D-Maine) proposed several procedural changes designed to expedite floor business, among them barring filibusters on motions to proceed (i.e., to take up measures on the floor) and reducing the number of allowable filibusters on a measure from six to two. But Republican Leader Bob Dole (R-Kans.) and several of his colleagues defended Senate practices as bulwarks for minority rights. Robert C. Byrd (D-W.Va.), the Senate's president pro tempore, held that "the root problem plaguing the Senate today [is] what I would term the 'fractured attention' of senators."

The panel's staff of sixteen struggled with these partisan and chamber divisions. Four staff members worked primarily for the four principals, whose divergent goals they mirrored. Staff Director G. Kim Wincup and Policy Director Dr. Walter Oleszek of the Congressional Research Service (CRS), assisted by nonpartisan CRS analysts, sought to keep deliberations on track and to knit the panel's work together.

Between 26 January and 1 July 1993, the committee held thirty-six public hearings comprising more than 114 hours of testimony. The committee heard more than 500 proposals from 243 witnesses. Most of the hearings focused on specific topics such as the budget process, committee operations, applying laws to Congress, or staffing and support agencies.

The committee commissioned numerous CRS studies and reports and consulted with various scholars, including participants in the joint Brookings Institution–American Enterprise Institute project on "Renewing Congress" and the Carnegie Commission on Science, Technology, and Government's study of information technology. Roundtable discussions tapped the views of current and former staff members, scholars, and other observers. Member and staff surveys were undertaken to gather suggestions as well as to gauge reactions to specific proposals.

As hearings drew to a close, behind-the-scenes negotiations among the committee's four principals and their staff representatives searched for consensus on recommendations that could be reported to the two chambers. Their efforts yielded few agreements. Eventually Boren and Domenici settled on an ambitious list of proposals, but the chasm that separated House Democrats and Republicans was too wide to be breached by Hamilton (taking his cues from Democratic leaders) and Dreier (pushing the Republican reformist agenda). As a result the committee's Senate and House members resorted to separate markup sessions, which neither the 1945 nor the 1965 joint committee had been forced to do.

The Senate members held their day-long markup session on 10 November. The Boren-Domenici package included committee assignment limitations, abolition of joint committees, biennial budgeting and appropriating, streamlined legislative-branch staffing, a two-hour limit for debate on the motion to proceed, limits on post-cloture delays, and committee oversight agendas. The unanimous vote to report out the final product was mainly symbolic, for many senators clearly opposed key portions and hoped to modify or eliminate them in the Rules and Administration Committee or on the Senate floor. Among those who held their fire were Wendell H. Ford (D-Ky.) and Ted Stevens (R-Alaska), chairman and ranking minority member, respectively, of the Rules panel, who would later have much to say about the fate of the reforms.

Not even symbolic consensus surrounded the House members' markup, which convened 16 No-vember and did not adjourn until 22 November, as Congress recessed for the year. Hamilton's markup draft included only items agreed upon by a majority of the House members (e.g., reduction in the number of subcommittees, committee and subcommittee assignment limits, revised handling of ethics complaints, biennial budgeting and multiyear authorizations, changes in bill referral procedures, oversight planning, and application of laws to Congress). "By design," the chairman explained, "the most controversial reforms . . . are not included in the markup draft."

Vice Chairman Dreier countered that "this bill is neither bipartisan nor comprehensive. . . . The culmination of seven months of hearings and two months of negotiations is a document that on most pressing issues recommends more studies and non-binding sense of the House resolutions." He noted that the report sidestepped such issues as committee jurisdictional realignment and major procedural changes (e.g., eliminating proxy voting in committees) and that it was too timid in cutting committees and staffs, moving to multiyear appropriations, and revising procedures for handling ethics charges.

The markup itself was an acrimonious affair during which thirty-five amendments were presented and voted on. Eight Republican amendments were accepted, including ones providing for biennial appropriations and for publishing committee voting records. However, more than twenty-five of the Republicans' amendments failed in partisan tie votes of 6 to 6, which Dreier denounced as "the attempts of a small but vocal faction of the Democratic caucus to derail this effort." Finally the members voted 8 to 4 to report the package. All Democrats voted to report, along with two Republicans—Dreier and Bill Emerson (Mo.)—who vowed to "keep the process moving forward" and to present amendments on the House floor, where members might fear to oppose bolder reforms.

When Congress reconvened in 1994, the House and Senate measures were taken up respectively by the House Rules and Senate Rules and Administration committees. House and Senate leaders who dominated these panels sensed that the reports would eventually have to be acted upon but were in no hurry to do so, hoping they could further dilute the recommendations before sending them to the floor. The hard-line reformers, for their part, struggled to keep the issue alive and to bring public and media pressure to bear on members during House and Senate floor deliberations.

BIBLIOGRAPHY

Mann, Thomas E., and Norman J. Ornstein. *Renewing Congress: A First Report.* 1992.

Mann, Thomas E., and Norman J. Ornstein. *Renewing Congress: A Second Report.* 1993.

U.S. Congress. Joint Committee on the Organization of Congress. *Business Meetings on Congressional Reform Legislation.* 103d Cong., 1st sess., 1993. S. Hrg. 103-320.

U.S. Congress. Joint Committee on the Organization of Congress. *Organization of the Congress. Final Report.* 3 vols. 103d Cong., 1st sess., 1993. H. Rept. 103-413; S. Rept. 103-215.

ROGER H. DAVIDSON

ORGANIZED CRIME CONTROL ACT. *See* Racketeer Influenced and Corrupt Organizations Act (RICO).

OTA. *See* Office of Technology Assessment.

OUTREACH. *See* Constituency Outreach.

OVERRIDE. *See* Veto, *article on* Presidential Veto.

OVERSIGHT. Congress is vested with the power not only to make laws but also to ensure that these laws are effectively executed. Thus the obligation to oversee—that is, to supervise and to monitor the bureaucracy—stems from the lawmaking function of Congress. Constitutional provisions reinforce this logic: the basic structure of the executive branch is determined by Congress; important policies concerning executive branch personnel are established in Congress; the money that the executive branch spends is appropriated by Congress; the laws that the bureaucracy applies come from Congress.

From a historical perspective, the task of overseeing the executive flows from an obligation to monitor the spending of money raised through the votes of the legislative assembly. From a more contemporary perspective, oversight results from the realization that public policy is created not only in the text of laws but also during the process of implementing them. Congressional interest in bureaucratic activity then emerges from a general sense of obligation to make certain that laws are faithfully car-

ried out and from specific concerns with implementation of particular policies. The former motive is general and diffuse; its impact is less than comprehensive. The latter motive is specific and pointed. Its power to stimulate oversight is considerable.

Congress has conducted oversight of the bureaucracy throughout U.S. history. There were congressional investigations of the conduct of war against the Indian tribes in 1792. Congress looked into the conduct of the Civil War. There were legislative inquiries into the Teapot Dome scandals in the 1920s. More recently, Congress investigated executive conduct in the Iran-contra scandal during the Reagan administration. Yet historically such oversight has not been frequent, comprehensive, or systematic.

The modern age of legislative oversight can be said to have begun in 1946, when Congress converted an assumed, traditional obligation to oversee into an explicit legal requirement. The Legislative Reorganization Act of 1946 required standing committees of the Congress to "exercise continuous watchfulness of the execution by the administrative agencies concerned of any laws, the subject of which is within the jurisdiction of such committee." Although this mandate seems all-inclusive, Congress has continued to write into law additional oversight authority, as in the Legislative Reorganization Act of 1970 and the Congressional Budget and Impoundment Control Act of 1974.

The legal mandate for oversight is substantial enough to permit Congress to look into just about any policy matter it desires. Therein lies the problem; the assigned task presents a broad agenda indeed. Moreover, oversight is only one of many congressional obligations. Because they are burdened with so many important tasks, members of Congress are constantly confronted with hard choices. Some of their obligations are given careful attention, some are generally attended to, and some are necessarily slighted. Members of Congress usually deny that any of their obligations are slighted, but the reality is clear. Where does oversight of the bureaucracy fit into the legislative workload?

Members of Congress set priorities in relation to their motives, the most prominent of which is the quest for reelection. Motivation for oversight of the bureaucracy soars if such activity leads to publicity for the member or benefits his or her constituency or persons, groups, or causes of special concern. Since much oversight involves hard, unglamorous work yielding little media attention and few direct benefits to the constituency, oversight tends not to be a high priority for members. Other motives are less prominent but surely relevant to oversight: the general desire to implement good policy and the desire to gain respect from one's peers. Members do not systematically oversee the bureaucracy because the law requires them to do so. If that were the dominant motive the quantity and quality of oversight would be vastly different than at present.

After motivation, resources are important. How much oversight is accomplished relates to the resources available. Adequately staffed committees and subcommittees with substantial investigative budgets can better oversee the bureaucracy when motivated to do so. Committees and subcommittees with inadequate resources are more predisposed to slight their obligations. In Congress, resources are largely adequate to support major, sustained oversight efforts. In some state legislatures, this is not the case. In Congress, staff numbers and committee budgets have been regularly augmented and auxiliary staff agencies, such as the Congressional Research Service, the General Accounting Office, the Office of Technology Assessment, and the Congressional Budget Office, provide significant additional support for oversight efforts.

So how is oversight conducted, and to what effect? The former question is amenable to extended discussion and serious analysis. Answers to the latter are fewer and less reliable.

Oversight Techniques. Congress conducts legislative oversight of the bureaucracy through a variety of techniques. Most obvious is the committee or subcommittee investigation where a particular program, agency, or policy area is subject to a formal on-the-record study. Congress may also require executive units to file periodic reports detailing their activities in specified areas. The assumption is that these reports will provide a solid base of information on which oversight can be built. Congress, more precisely the Senate, is called upon to confirm high-level executive branch appointments. Confirmation hearings may provide occasion for questions about departmental and agency behavior. To facilitate oversight, some congressional committees, about fifteen, have created subcommittees primarily dedicated to this task.

If oversight were limited to such formal procedures as investigations and reports, the oversight record would be easier to establish. In fact, much oversight occurs indirectly, as members of Congress pursue other tasks. Thus, in hearings held on proposed legislation, questions concerning what has been done before, by whom, and how well may arise. In appropriations hearings, how money previously requested was spent may become an issue. In pursuing casework (constituents' problems with the bureaucracy) congressional offices may identify patterns of abuse that require attention beyond solving the individual constituent's problem. Telephone calls, informal meetings, and luncheon sessions between congressional committee staff members and persons from the executive branch provide many occasions for the exchange of information and gossip useful for oversight.

In general, most members and staff persons prefer informal and unobtrusive methods of oversight. Regular communications removed from the public eye are commonplace. In fact, formal investigations sometimes signal that normal, informal methods have failed.

Each method, formal and informal, provides an opportunity for oversight. Not all opportunities are effectively pursued, however. For example, while Congress requires the president and executive departments and agencies to file annually thousands of reports detailing their activities, there is scant evidence that these reports are seriously attended to or even read. At times, report requirements are added to legislation simply to draw bureaucratic attention to specific constituent problems. While much daily casework takes place in Congress as members pursue constituents' requests, little attention is given to identifying from this activity patterns of problems that might require congressional attention. Confirmation hearings, an apt setting for oversight, are not often used for that purpose. Such sessions are often perfunctory, symbolic exercises.

Conditions for Oversight. Calculating the amount of oversight is difficult also because the degree of activity is not historically constant. Scholarly studies asserted in the 1950s and 1960s that little systematic oversight was being conducted, while more recent research argues that more congressional oversight is being conducted. While it is possible that some of these studies were simply wrong, it is more likely that the amount of oversight conducted did vary with time and context. If so, then what elements explain this variation?

Joel Aberbach has identified several possibilities. In eras when money is especially scarce, members of Congress may become more concerned with oversight partly because they lack resources to establish new programs and partly because of heightened concern with how scarce resources are actually used. Congressional staffs, grown larger over the years and not tied up in creating legislation, seek outlets for their creativity and energy and are on the prowl for good publicity vehicles for their members. Increased investigative journalism in the aftermath of the Watergate scandals has brought more information to Congress and has alerted members to new problems. Extended periods of divided government, where one political party controls the Congress and the other the executive, may also add incentive.

If congressional oversight has increased in recent years, attempts to assess the significance of the change generate controversy. Some scholars continue to suggest that Congress simply does not do its job of systematically and comprehensively overseeing the bureaucracy very well, even if it now does more than in the past. For others, the increase in oversight is seen as significant. Comprehensive and systematic oversight, they argue, is simply an unrealizable ideal. The fact that Congress is doing more is central. For still another group, any focus on comparative quantity is misplaced. What is central for these writers is how well members of Congress are using available time and energy. From this perspective, to oversee all bureaucratic activity or to try to do so is a waste of resources. What Congress should do and what it does is essentially to respond to problems. If programs are running well, why monitor them closely? If problems arise, look into them. Sometimes referred to as the "fire alarm model," this approach applauds the good sense of members of Congress in using their resources efficiently.

Impact. Even more difficult to assess firmly is the impact of congressional oversight. The clearest evidence is scattered and anecdotal, hardly a reliable base. Yet clearly specific efforts have resulted in changes in programs and bureaucratic behavior. Most bureaucratic units, most bureaucrats, and most programs are rarely the direct object of formal oversight. If oversight is effective it is not because it is comprehensive. It is more likely due to the possibility of its exercise.

The impact of the "law of anticipated reactions" is inordinately difficult to demonstrate. The argument here is that while comprehensive formal oversight is rarely conducted, much informal oversight does take place, and any executive branch structure, program, policy, or person is in principle an appropriate subject for inquiry. Thus the possibility of oversight, rather than its actual execution, may be the more potent congressional weapon. Executive units and members may be pressured to rethink what they might want to do by the threat of having to answer for their behavior in subsequent congressional investigations. Pushing the executive branch to anticipate possible questions from Congress and to be able to defend their actions and policies may be the most useful consequence of congressional oversight.

Political Considerations. The ostensible goal of oversight—more effective and responsible public policy and bureaucratic behavior—is not always attained. Abuse of congressional power is always possible. Members of the executive are not always wrong, and members of Congress are not always correct in executive-legislative disputes arising from oversight efforts. Executive departments are sometimes as capable as Congress of a broad perspective, just as members of Congress may adopt a parochial outlook. The ways in which the executive branch implements law may be more effective than the alternative actions pushed by Congress.

Moreover, the line between vigorous oversight and influence peddling is sometimes blurred. An apt illustration from the early 1990s is the case of the so-called Keating Five; it was charged that the efforts of several members of Congress, acting on behalf of substantial campaign contributors, were unduly vigorous in attempting to influence how regulators treated some savings and loan associations. What gave these legislative efforts particular clout was the potential for legislative reaction against nonresponsive regulators. The issue here is not whether the senators involved abused their power but rather that the power and influence legislators had may have led to questionable behavior by apprehensive bank regulators. Whether specific examples of legislative oversight, either formal or informal, promote efficient and responsible behavior and policy is always an open question.

One could argue that the executive branch should welcome congressional oversight in the hopes of improving performance and policy. This is, in fact, sometimes the case. More often, fears of congressional overmanagement, apprehensions concerning the clout of vested interests in Congress, and concerns over whether members of Congress have sufficient expertise usefully to challenge what the executive is doing probably predominate.

At the heart of the issue is the fact that oversight seldom concerns mere technical problems of management but more often is part of a wider process of building support or opposition to programs or agencies. This larger context is essentially political. Executive departments and agencies will react well to supportive oversight efforts from the Congress, just as committee members who largely agree with what an executive agency is doing are less likely to push oversight. When oversight is designed to support executive actions, there will be no resistance, only full cooperation, on the executive side.

When, as is more frequently the case, formal oversight results from someone in Congress thinking that something is wrong in the executive branch, guarded reactions from the executive are the norm. Delays and evasions are common in such circumstances. Few persons in or out of the executive branch gain joy in the exposure of their own errors of judgment, in revelations of failures to act expeditiously, or in disclosures seeming to show that they protected vested interests.

Executive Privilege. Perhaps the most extreme example of resistance comes when the doctrine of executive privilege is invoked. From the beginning of the republic, presidents and their subordinates have, at times, balked at congressional requests for information. Presidents argue that the advice they are given by assistants and some executive files should not be revealed to congressional investigators. In contrast, congressional committees regularly assert that, given their constitutional powers, they should be entitled access to any bureaucratic activity they find of interest. Neither position is totally without vested interest. Members of Congress may be trying to embarrass the president for partisan reasons. Assertions of executive privilege may relate to desires to hide ties to specific interests or to mask questionable decisions.

How, when, and by whom executive privilege can be invoked has never been resolved authoritatively. The Constitution is silent on this question. For most of U.S. history the courts have avoided grappling with the question of executive privilege. Only in the context of the Watergate incidents, subsequent court trials, and the strong possibility of the impeachment of President Richard M. Nixon did the Supreme Court directly confront the legality of the executive privilege doctrine. What the Court decided in *United States v. Nixon* (1974) was that there was a legal basis for the existence of the doctrine but that the limits of executive privilege were not to be decided by the president alone. In essence, this decision provides an astute political resolution of the problem cast in legal terms. Similarly, most disputes over executive privilege are resolved politically through intense negotiations and bargaining. Both executive and legislative positions are argued publicly in constitutional and legal terms. These conflicts are often resolved politically because problems with manifest political dimensions lend themselves to political solutions.

Congressional oversight of the bureaucracy is only one of many methods of promoting bureaucratic responsiveness. The personal values and professional norms of bureaucrats may stimulate responsive behavior. Presidents and their immediate associates try to impose on bureaucrats their view of what is appropriate. Interest groups monitor the executive just as they attempt to influence Congress. The courts on occasion impose standards of behavior on the bureaucracy. The executive branch, then, is accountable to institutions and groups other than Congress.

Moreover, Congress itself is not a single force when it comes to oversight. Oversight efforts normally come from committees and subcommittees in Congress. The fragmented nature of the congressional committee system is well known. Committees may work at cross-purposes. Some committees may be supportive of particular agencies or programs while others are hostile. What then does Congress want? The question almost answers itself. On many matters of legislative oversight of the bureaucracy, there is no single congressional voice. This fact further reinforces the proposition that an effective and responsive bureaucracy cannot be created by Congress alone.

[*See also* Bureaucracy; Executive Branch; Executive Privilege; President and Congress; Veto.]

BIBLIOGRAPHY

Aberbach, Joel D. *Keeping a Watchful Eye: The Politics of Congressional Oversight.* 1990.

Dodd, Lawrence C., and Richard L. Schott. *Congress and the Administrative State.* 1979.

Foreman, Christopher H., Jr. *Signals from the Hill: Congressional Oversight and the Challenge of Social Regulation.* 1988.

Harris, Joseph P. *Congressional Control of Administration.* 1964.

Ogul, Morris S. *Congress Oversees the Bureaucracy: Studies in Legislative Supervision.* 1978.

Ripley, Randall B., and Grace A. Franklin. *Congress, the Bureaucracy, and Public Policy.* 5th ed. 1991.

MORRIS S. OGUL

P

PACIFIC RAILROAD ACTS (1862, 1864). Providing land, rights-of-way, and funding through government bonds, the 1862 Pacific Railroad Act (12 Stat. 489-498) and the 1864 Northern Pacific Railway Act (13 Stat. 385-387) were enacted to provide federal financial support for the construction of a transcontinental railway. The notion of offering government aid for such construction was not a new idea in 1862. The territorial acquisitions of the Mexican War and the growth of population on the Pacific coast during the pre–Civil War decades made clear the desirability of a railroad to connect that region with the central United States. Moreover, the scope of the project and the undeveloped nature of the intervening area convinced many—even those normally strongly opposed to using federal funds to support internal improvements—that only with federal financial assistance would the completion of the railroad be possible. The Republican platform and both Democratic platforms in 1860 included planks favoring federal support for such construction.

Sectional interests had blocked the necessary legislation, though the Senate passed enabling bills in 1855 and 1859 and the House did so in 1860. But the removal of Southern representation—and, consequently, of the support for a southern route to the Pacific—in the Civil War Congresses opened the door to passage of Pacific railroad legislation. Special committees on the Pacific railroad were created in both houses of the 37th Congress in the summer of 1861. These panels worked out compromises between conflicting local and other interests to produce the proposals that came to the floor of the two houses.

After various postponements, the House committee released a bill for consideration on 8 April 1862. This measure provided for the transfer of huge amounts of public lands and more than $60 million in government bonds to half a dozen railroad corporations that were to construct the main transcontinental line and two eastern branches to connect with Iowa and Missouri railroads. An amendment was added providing that all work on the railroad would be forfeited to the federal government if the entire line were not completed by the beginning of 1876. On 6 May 1862, the House passed the measure 79 to 49. Solid support came from California, Missouri, Iowa, and Minnesota, the states that stood to profit most directly, while very little support came from Indiana and Illinois.

In the Senate, Democrat James A. McDougall of California, the chairman of the special committee, pushed the bill strongly but ran into opposition from the Finance Committee chairman, Republican William Pitt Fessenden of Maine, and from Lyman Trumbull of Illinois, chairman of the Judiciary Committee. The major change made in the Senate was the adoption of an amendment proposed by Republican Jacob Collamer of Vermont to withhold portions of the federal bonds partially financing the project until completion of the railroad. On 20 June the Senate passed the measure 35 to 5. The House quickly and overwhelmingly concurred with the Senate amendments.

The 1862 act chartered the Union Pacific Railroad Company, with a capital stock of $100 million controlled by a fifteen-man board of directors, two of whom were appointed by the president of the United States. This corporation and two preexisting

COMPLETION OF THE TRANSCONTINENTAL RAIL LINE. The ceremonial "wedding of the rails" at Promontory Point, Utah, 10 May 1869.

LIBRARY OF CONGRESS

railroad companies were to receive ten sections of public land per mile along the route, to be disposed of in three years, and additional support in the form of government bonds, subject to 15 to 25 percent withholding until the line was completed. In return, the federal government held a first mortgage on the property to the amount of the bonds issued.

Legislation was introduced in the 37th Congress to remove restrictions and attract more private investors, but the bill failed to clear both houses. In the 38th Congress (1863–1865), a second Pacific Railroad Act was passed that reduced the par value and increased the total number of shares of stock to be issued in the enterprise by ten times. The amount of public land granted was doubled, as was the width of the railroad right-of-way. The companies were authorized to issue first-mortgage bonds, reducing the federal government's claim to that of a second mortgage.

The Pacific Railroad acts initiated a series of financial and engineering actions that resulted in the linking of the West by rail to the rest of the nation. Thus, economic ties were formed across the United States that matched and strengthened existing political bonds. Equally important, it now became possible to live and carry on commercial agriculture in the Great Plains region. On the negative side, the opening of the Treasury doors to greedy corporate interests foreshadowed an era in which the representatives of such interests returned again and again to demand preferential treatment from Congress and freedom from oversight, corrupting government officials and procedures in the process. These acts had been framed in accordance with corporate demands, and it is perhaps not amiss to suggest that the corruption of the Grant era was sparked by (but not confined to) the activities of those companies (e.g., Crédit Mobilier) and individuals connected with the Pacific railway scheme.

BIBLIOGRAPHY

Curry, Leonard P. *Blueprint for Modern America: Nonmilitary Legislation of the First Civil War Congress.* 1968.
Haney, Lewis H. *A Congressional History of Railways in the United States, 1850–1887.* 1910.

LEONARD P. CURRY

PAGES. A group of high school juniors, known as pages, serve as messengers for members of the U.S. Congress. Numbering about one hundred young men and women, they come from all areas of the United States. Several current and former members and officials of Congress began their careers as pages.

Although the Senate employed older messengers from its beginning in 1789, it is believed that Sen. Daniel Webster arranged for the appointment of the first Senate page in 1829. The earliest record of pages in the House of Representatives dates from 1842. Not until 1971, however, were women first appointed as pages.

In 1983, following allegations of misconduct by pages and members of Congress, unfavorable press accounts of the system, and a desire to reform the program, Congress offered supervised housing near the Capitol for all pages, established a common age requirement, and made changes in the education provided.

The House page program is administered by the doorkeeper of the House and supervised by the House Page Board, composed of House members and officers. There were sixty-six House pages in 1992, all chosen through the patronage system administered by the majority party, then the Democrats.

In the Senate, both party secretaries supervise page appointments consistent with patronage positions given senior senators. The Senate sergeant at arms is in charge of the overall operation of the Senate page program. The Senate usually has thirty pages at a time. Customarily, members of Congress appoint pages from the areas they represent.

Pages are paid about one thousand dollars per month. Their salaries, which are subject to taxation, are expected to cover transportation costs to Washington, their living expenses, and uniforms.

Until 1983, when both houses required pages to be high school juniors (generally age sixteen or seventeen), ages had varied considerably and had been debated in and out of Congress. In the nineteenth century the youngest House and Senate pages were ten and twelve years old, respectively. For most of

SEN. WILLIAM A. PEFFER (PROG.-KANS.). Shown preparing an "oratorical eruption" for the Senate with the aid of two pages. Cover of *Harper's Weekly,* 20 February 1897.   OFFICE OF THE HISTORIAN OF THE U.S. SENATE

the twentieth century, however, they ranged in age from fourteen to eighteen.

Pages' duties have changed considerably over the years. Today, they no longer have ink boxes to fill or candles to light on members' desks, nor must they ride horseback to deliver urgent messages to the executive branch. Instead, the pages now serve principally as messengers on Capitol Hill, carrying documents between members' offices, committees, and the Library of Congress. They also help prepare the congressional chambers for each day's business, and they are present during sessions, seated near the members or in cloakrooms nearby, waiting to be summoned.

Pages live in housing provided by Congress and supervised by proctors and a full-time director. Since 1926, Congress has provided for the educa-

PAGE SCHOOL. Prior to the appointment of the first female page in 1971.

tion of pages who serve during the school year. Since 1983, the House and Senate have had separate school facilities located in the Library of Congress. The Senate Page School is operated by the District of Columbia school system, and the House operates and provides the staff for its school. Both facilities offer college preparatory courses and extracurricular activities unique to the Washington, D.C., area.

Prospective pages request appointment by contacting their representatives or senators. Members' eligibility to appoint pages is based primarily on the patronage system. While selection procedures vary in the House and Senate, all pages must be American citizens and are expected to have good scholastic records.

BIBLIOGRAPHY

"Groundless Page Sex Charges Prompt Reforms." *Congressional Quarterly Almanac* 38 (1982): 528–529.

Severn, Bill. *Democracy's Messengers.* 1975.

Springer, William. "Congressional Pages, Their Work and Schooling." In *We Propose a Modern Congress.* 1966. Pp. 183–184.

"Two Members Censured." *Congressional Quarterly Almanac* 39 (1983): 580–583.

MILDRED LEHMANN AMER

PAIRING. Pairing is a procedure available to members of Congress who wish to indicate their position with respect to a question even though they are not present when the vote is taken. In the House of Representatives, a pair is an agreement between members on opposite sides not to vote on a specified question or during a stipulated time. While pairing is authorized by clause 2 of Rule VIII and clause 1 of Rule XV, neither the House nor the Speaker exercises jurisdiction over pairs, and any interpretation of the terms of a pair rests with the contracting members. A member with a "live pair" with another member will first cast his vote on the question, and then withdraw the vote and vote "present" after announcing his agreement with an absent colleague who would have voted on the opposite side of the issue. This is the only type of pair that affects the outcome of a vote. A "definite" or "for and against" pair will appear in the *Congressional Record* immediately following the vote and will reflect specific instructions as to the preferences left by the contracting members that terminate automatically after the vote. An "indefinite" or "until further notice" pair does not indicate how either member would have voted if present. On constitutional amendments and other questions requiring a two-thirds vote it is customary to pair two affirmative votes with one negative.

Although its use is well established in the Senate, pairing is not mentioned in the Senate rules and therefore has no official standing. A senator who has a "live pair" merely refrains from voting and announces that he or she is paired with another senator who is absent. The process is not as simple as in the House because senators must have an acceptable excuse for not voting on a roll call, and pairing, about which the rules are silent, does not automatically qualify as an excuse. In practice, the Senate deals with this problem by ignoring it. The clerk and the presiding officer take no notice when pairs are announced and ignore them in calculating the results of a roll call. By custom, however, pairs are listed for informational purposes at the bottom of the roll-call tabulation.

BIBLIOGRAPHY

U.S. House of Representatives. *Constitution, Jefferson's Manual, and Rules of the House of Representatives, 103d Congress.* Compiled by William Holmes Brown. 102d Cong., 2d sess., 1992. H. Doc. 102-405.

U.S. House of Representatives. *Cannon's Procedure in the United States House of Representatives,* by Clarence Cannon. 87th Cong., 2d sess., 1963. H. Doc. 87-610.

U.S. Senate. *Riddick's Senate Procedure, Precedents, and Practices,* by Floyd M. Riddick and Alan S. Frumin. 101st Cong., 2d sess., 1992. S. Doc. 101-28.

THOMAS G. DUNCAN

PANAMA. The U.S. interoceanic canal across Panama has involved a parade of treaty ratifications and hefty sums of public money, making Congress a major player in relations with that Central American country. Since the first ship transit in 1914, U.S. policy has aimed at keeping the canal open and secure while gradually taking down the scaffolding of U.S. political control in Panama left over from the construction era. This retrenchment has followed a pattern in which presidents of both parties led the way while Congress concurred only grudgingly, reflecting the reluctance of many Americans to abandon a symbol of strength abroad.

As early as 1835, the Senate by resolution urged government protection for "capitalists" who might want to dig a commercial trans-isthmian canal. In 1855 an American company opened a railroad across Panama under terms of a treaty with Colombia (then the owner of the isthmus) ratified by the Senate in 1848. A French company headed by Ferdinand de Lesseps, builder of the Suez Canal, started work on a sea-level ditch in 1881, but the project died in Panama's malarial jungle.

The 1898 Spanish-American War spurred Washington's interest in a government-built naval shortcut between the oceans. President Theodore Roosevelt became its foremost advocate, along with such like-minded expansionists as Senators Henry Cabot Lodge (R-Mass.) and John T. Morgan (D-Ala.). Originally, Nicaragua was the preferred route. The way was cleared by the 1901 Hay-Pauncefote Treaty with Britain, which previously had claimed an interest. Here, the Senate put a lasting military stamp on the isthmian project, insisting before ratification on the U.S. right to fortify the canal.

In 1902 a House-passed bill authorizing the Nicaraguan canal was challenged in the Senate by John C. Spooner (R-Wis.), who offered an amendment favored by Roosevelt to switch to a shorter route through Panama. After intense debate in a chamber festooned with maps of Central America, the Senate in June chose Panama 42 to 34. The House concurred a week later.

In 1903 Colombia refused to accept U.S. terms for a canal in Panama. A group of Panamanians then declared independence from Colombia with open help from the U.S. Navy. Phillipe Bunau-Varilla, a Frenchman with shaky credentials as Panama's envoy to Washington, signed a treaty with Secretary of State John Hay awarding "in perpetuity" a ten-mile-wide zone through Panama for the United States to control as "if it were the sovereign."

The canal that opened on 15 August 1914 was a technological marvel of the age. Along its fifty-one-mile length, a flight of locks lifts ships eighty-five feet to artificial Gatun Lake and lowers them again to seaports at either end. Many of today's vessels, however, are too big to fit the locks.

Congressional Actions Relating to Panama

TITLE	YEAR ENACTED[1]	REFERENCE NUMBER	DESCRIPTION
Hay-Pauncefote Treaty (with Great Britain)	1901	T.S. 401[2]	Britain gave up rights to isthmian canal.
Spooner Act	1902	P.L. 57-183	Authorized land acquisition for canal through Panama.
Hay–Bunau-Varilla Treaty (with Panama)	1904	T.S. 431	Panama gave U.S. the Canal Zone "in perpetuity."
Hull-Alfaro Treaty (with Panama)	1939	T.S. 945	Panama regained police powers outside Canal Zone.
Eisenhower-Remon Treaty (with Panama)	1955	T.I.A.S. 3297[3]	Panama regained sanitation control outside Canal Zone.
Treaty for Canal Neutrality and Operation (with Panama)	1978	T.I.A.S. 10029	Set canal defense terms after 1999.
Panama Canal Treaty (with Panama)	1978	T.I.A.S. 10030	Abolished Canal Zone; transfers canal operations to Panama in 2000.
Panama Canal Act of 1979	1979	P.L. 96-70	Set terms carrying out canal transfer to Panama.

[1]For treaties, dates reflect Senate ratification.
[2]T.S. = Treaty Series, State Department
[3]T.I.A.S. = Treaties and other International Acts Series; it replaced T.S. in 1945.

The 1903 treaty gave the United States the right to maintain order and suppress disease outside the Canal Zone itself. Responding to Panamanian complaints, President Franklin D. Roosevelt negotiated a new treaty in 1936, restoring local police powers in Panama City and Colón. Senators fearful of insurrection delayed ratification until 1939. In 1955 the Senate agreed to an Eisenhower administration treaty giving up U.S. control of sanitation in the two cities.

Local unrest continued, however, prompting the Johnson administration in 1967 to negotiate three new treaties confirming Panama's sovereignty over the Canal Zone and authorizing construction of a new sea-level canal, possibly blasting with nuclear explosives. Rep. Daniel J. Flood (D-Pa.), a champion of American "Zonians" in Panama, threatened to lead a theatrical march of 150 House members on the Senate if ratification was even considered. The treaties were never submitted.

In the 1970s both the Nixon and Carter administrations agreed to terminate U.S. control as the best way of keeping the canal open. In ratifying the 1978 termination treaty, the Senate formally declared that the continuing duty of the United States to defend the canal would not include intervention in Panama's internal political affairs. Nevertheless, Congress generally applauded when President George Bush in December 1989 ordered an invasion of Panama to capture the country's dictator,

Manuel Noriega, who was convicted on U.S. drug-trafficking charges in April 1992.

The long-term U.S. grip on Panama, meanwhile, continued to erode in the early 1990s. Canal operations were being financed entirely from tolls, not congressional appropriations. Congress eventually may revisit the old idea of a sea-level canal, perhaps as a multinational project. In 1992 canal administrators began widening the Gaillard Cut through the Continental Divide, a twenty-year venture that will extend into the period of Panamanian operation after 1999. Whether a sea-level ditch could then compete with the lock canal's expanded capacity is being studied by a consortium of companies from the United States, Panama, and Japan.

[See also Panama Canal Treaty.]

BIBLIOGRAPHY

McCullough, David. *The Path Between the Seas: The Creation of the Panama Canal, 1870–1914.* 1977.
U.S. Senate. Committee on Foreign Relations. *Background Documents Relating to the Panama Canal.* 95th Cong., 1st sess., 1977. Committee Print.

ARLEN J. LARGE

PANAMA CANAL TREATY (T.I.A.S. 10030). Ratification in 1978 of the treaty relinquishing U.S. control of the Panama Canal forced senators to deal with two conflicting strains of U.S. opinion:

CANAL TREATY CONTROVERSY. Symbolized here by a giant sleeping tiger, the controversial Panama Canal treaties led to the second-longest ratification debate in Senate history. Cartoon by Garner, *Washington Evening Star*, 5 February 1978.   LIBRARY OF CONGRESS

recognition that the canal's colonial-era legacy could no longer be sustained and fear that the waterway's "surrender" would symbolize a decline in the United States' global strength.

The Senate's ratification debate lasted thirty-eight days, second only to the time consumed on the failed Versailles treaty in 1919–1920. The debate also was the first to be broadcast on live radio from the Senate chamber.

The canal agreement, signed 7 September 1977 by President Jimmy Carter and Panamanian dictator Omar Torrijos Herrera, actually involved two treaties. The main treaty turned control of the canal over to Panama beginning in the year 2000. It immediately abolished the ten-mile-wide Canal Zone across the isthmus that in 1904 had been granted "in perpetuity" to the United States by Panama. A second, "neutrality" treaty provided that the post-1999 waterway would remain open to all nations in peace and war, with Panama taking charge of the canal's defense installations.

Floor debate opened on 8 February 1978. Prominent supporters included Majority Leader Robert C. Byrd (D-W.Va.), Minority Leader Howard H. Baker (R-Tenn.), and floor manager Frank Church

(D-Idaho). They and others echoed White House arguments that it would be impossible to keep the canal open in the face of Panamanian hostility.

Among leading opponents were Senators Robert P. Griffin (R-Mich.), Bob Dole (R-Kans.), and James B. Allen (D-Ala.). They offered, unsuccessfully, a series of amendments that would have required renegotiation of treaty texts dealing with U.S. rights to defend the canal after Panama took control. On 16 March the Senate, with White House approval, agreed to a unilateral reservation to the neutrality treaty written by Dennis DeConcini (D-Ariz.) that asserted the U.S. right to defend the waterway with "military force" after 1999.

Beyond such tactical matters lay a broader issue of perceptions of the world prestige of the United States. Treaty opponents, argued Church, wanted to preserve a U.S. colony in Panama "in an age when colonies have disappeared elsewhere, gone with the empires of yesterday." But Dole warned that giving up the canal would be perceived as another U.S. setback following its failure in Vietnam: "There is this fear that we will turn tail and run."

On 16 March the Senate agreed to the neutrality treaty 68 to 32, one more vote than the required two-thirds majority. However, complaints by General Torrijos about the DeConcini language prompted a last-minute reservation to the main treaty disavowing any U.S. intention to encroach on Panama's political independence. With that, the canal treaty itself was ratified on 18 April by an identical vote of 68 to 32.

Though the House had no ratification role, treaty opponents there had some influence on a follow-up bill carrying out terms of the canal turnover. House amendments limited certain U.S. payments to Panama, though some restrictions were softened in conference with the Senate. The final implementation bill cleared Congress on 26 September 1979, five days before the treaties took effect.

[*See also* Panama.]

BIBLIOGRAPHY

Congressional Quarterly. "Panama Canal Treaties: Major Carter Victory." *Congressional Quarterly Almanac 1978.* 1979. Pp. 379–397.

U.S. Senate. Committee on Foreign Relations. *Senate Debate on the Panama Canal Treaties: A Compendium of Major Statements, Documents, Record Votes, and Relevant Events.* 96th Cong., 1st sess., 1979. Committee Print.

ARLEN J. LARGE

PARKS, NATIONAL. *See* National Parks and Forests.

PARLIAMENTARIAN. [*This entry includes separate discussions of the offices of House and Senate parliamentarian. See also* Manuals; Precedents.]

House Parliamentarian

The important office of the House parliamentarian has evolved from several earlier incarnations. In 1857 Speaker James L. Orr of South Carolina ap-

Parliamentarians of the House and their Predecessors

NAME	DATES OF SERVICE	CONGRESS	TITLE
Thaddeus Morrice	1857–1864	34th–38th	Messenger to the Speaker
William D. Todd	1865–1968	38th, 2d sess.–40th, 2d sess.	Messenger to the Speaker
William D. Todd	1869	40th, 3d sess.	Clerk to the Speaker
John M. Barclay	1869–1875	41st, 1st sess.	Clerk at the Speaker's Table
William H. Scudder	1875–1877	44th–45th, 1st sess.	Clerk at the Speaker's Table
J. Randolph Tucker, Jr.	1877–1879	45th, 2d and 3d sess.–46th, 1st sess.	Clerk at the Speaker's Table
George P. Miller	1879–1880	46th, 2d sess.	Clerk at the Speaker's Table
Michael Sullivan	1880–1881	46th, 3d sess.	Clerk at the Speaker's Table
J. Guilford White	1881–1882	47th, 1st sess.	Clerk at the Speaker's Table
J. Guilford White; Michael Sullivan	1882–1883	47th, 2d sess.	Clerk at the Speaker's Table
Nathaniel T. Crutchfield	1883–1890	48th–51st, 1st sess.	Clerk at the Speaker's Table
Edward F. Goodwin	1890–1891	51st, 2d sess.	Clerk at the Speaker's Table
Charles R. Crisp	1891–1895	52d–53d	Clerk at the Speaker's Table
Asher C. Hinds	1895–1911	54th–61st	Clerk at the Speaker's Table
Charles R. Crisp	1911–1913	62d	Clerk at the Speaker's Table
Bennett C. Clark	1913–1917	63d–65th, 1st sess.	Clerk at the Speaker's Table
Clarence C. Cannon	1917–1919	65th, 2d and 3d sess.–66th, 1st sess.	Clerk at the Speaker's Table
Lehr Fess	1919–1927	66th, 2d sess.–69th	Clerk at the Speaker's Table
Lehr Fess; Lewis Deschler	1927–1928	70th, 1st sess.	Parliamentarian
Lewis Deschler	1928–1974	70th, 2d sess.–93d, 2d sess.	Parliamentarian
William Holmes Brown	1974–1994	93d, 2d sess.–103d, 2d sess.	Parliamentarian
Charles W. Johnson	1994–	103d, 2d sess.–	Parliamentarian

pointed Thaddeus Morrice as "Messenger." Morrice was an adept young man whose memory for House precedents and other decisions of the Speaker quickly made him indispensable to the Speaker in his role as presiding officer of the House. When Morrice died in 1864, the position was continued, its title changed to clerk to the Speaker, then to clerk at the Speaker's Table, and finally in 1927 to House parliamentarian. Only seventeen individuals have held the position since its inception in 1857. The first person to be called by the title of parliamentarian was Lehr Fess, who served from 1927 to 1928. Lewis Deschler served as parliamentarian from 1928 to 1974 and was the author of the multivolume work *Deschler's Precedents of the United States House of Representatives*. His successor, William Holmes Brown, continued the practice of compiling and publishing volumes of House precedents, upon which many of the Speakers' parliamentary rulings are based.

The parliamentarian, or a member of his staff, sits or stands to the right of the Speaker when the House is in session and advises the Speaker or chairman of the Committee of the Whole on parliamentary procedure. A good portion of the parliamentarian's time is taken up by reading and referring, on behalf of the Speaker, the thousands of bills, resolutions, and executive communications that are introduced into the House in each session. The referral of bills to one or more committees of the House is often a routine matter, but in some instances it is a crucial step in the legislative process. The parliamentarian is also available for consultation with all members of the House on matters of procedure and legislative details related to the introduction or passage of a bill or resolution. The office functions in a nonpartisan manner, providing its services in an impartial manner to members of both political parties. The parliamentarian's office, just off the House chamber near the Speaker's lobby, can be a beehive of activity on a busy legislative day.

The parliamentarian also oversees a small operation known as the Precedents Office, which edits and publishes the precedents of the House, as well as the *Rules of the House of Representatives*, which is published every two years with each new Congress.

[*See also* House of Representatives, *article on* House Rules and Procedures.]

BIBLIOGRAPHY

Tiefer, Charles. *Congressional Practice and Procedure: A Reference, Research, and Legislative Guide.* 1989.

U.S. Congress. *Hearings before the Joint Committee on the Organization of Congress.* 103d Cong., 1st sess., 1993. S. Hrg. 103-119.

U.S. House of Representatives. *Deschler's Precedents of the United States House of Representatives,* by Lewis Deschler. 94th Cong., 2d sess., 1977. H. Doc. 94-661.

RAYMOND W. SMOCK

Senate Parliamentarian

The parliamentarian of the Senate is responsible for advising the presiding officer of the Senate on all matters affecting Senate procedure. The parliamentarian's role is most evident when the presiding officer must rule on formal points of order or give responses to informal parliamentary inquiries. Less evident, though equally important, is the parliamentarian's responsibility for ensuring that the consideration of all bills, resolutions, treaties, nominations, and trials of impeachment comply with the rules of the Senate and the applicable provisions of the Constitution and public law.

In the name of the presiding officer, the parliamentarian refers to the committee of jurisdiction all bills and resolutions introduced in the Senate or passed by the House of Representatives, all nominations and other communications received from the president, and all communications from other officers of the executive branch, as well as all communications to the Senate from state legislatures or from private citizens. The parliamentarian also advises senators and their staffs, the staffs of the Senate's committees, officers of the other branches of the federal government, state and local government officials, members of the press, and the general public on questions concerning Senate procedure.

The parliamentarian helps Senate leaders to formulate and interpret the numerous unanimous consent agreements that are indispensable to the daily operation of the Senate. When time for debate is limited by such agreements or by rule or statute, the parliamentarian serves as the Senate's official timekeeper. The parliamentarian is responsible for determining what amendments are in order at any given time, whether they are properly drafted, and whether they are subject to any points of order.

Another important part of the parliamentarian's job is to analyze all Senate proceedings and to maintain the precedents that are set, periodically publishing these in book form. Precedents were first published in their current format in 1958 as *Senate Procedure, Precedents, and Practices;* revised editions were published in 1964, 1974, and 1981.

Senate Parliamentarians

NAME	DATES
Charles L. Watkins	1937–1964
Floyd M. Riddick	1965–1974
Murray Zweben	1975–1980
Robert B. Dove	1981–1986
Alan S. Frumin	1987–

The current edition, which contains the Senate's precedents through the end of the 101st Congress, is entitled *Riddick's Senate Procedure, Precedents, and Practices*, in honor of the author of the previous three editions.

The parliamentarian frequently prepares replies on behalf of senators or other officers of the Senate to letters regarding the Senate's rules, precedents, and practices. The parliamentarian also participates in the orientation of newly elected senators and addresses groups interested in learning more about how the Senate operates.

The position of Senate parliamentarian was first recognized on 1 July 1935, when the title of the incumbent Senate journal clerk, Charles L. Watkins, was changed to that of parliamentarian and journal clerk. On 1 July 1937, the two positions were separated, and Watkins became the first parliamentarian of the U.S. Senate.

The parliamentarian is appointed by, and serves at the pleasure of, the secretary of the Senate. Every person who has become Senate parliamentarian has first served a lengthy apprenticeship as an assistant Senate parliamentarian. The parliamentarian or an assistant parliamentarian is always on duty when the Senate is in session, sitting just below and slightly to the right of the presiding officer.

BIBLIOGRAPHY

U.S. Senate. *Riddick's Senate Procedure, Precedents, and Practices,* by Floyd M. Riddick and Alan S. Frumin. 101st Cong., 2d sess., 1992. S. Doc. 101-28.
U.S. Senate. Committee on Rules and Administration. *Senate Manual, Containing the Standing Rules, Orders, Laws, and Resolutions Affecting the Business of the United States Senate.* 102d Cong., 1st sess., 1992. S. Doc. 102-1.

ALAN S. FRUMIN

PARTIES, POLITICAL. *See* Political Parties. *See also* Anti-Federalists; Democratic Party; Federalists; Jeffersonian Republicans; Republican Party; Whig Party.

PARTY COMMITTEES.

The congressional parties might well be described as structures of committees and leaders. Party government in Congress is, in important ways, government by committee. And yet, as significant as they are to the party organization of Congress, party committees have a rather vague and murky origin, and even today their role is often neglected in analyses of congressional politics. The committees of the four congressional parties—the House and Senate Democrats and the House and Senate Republicans—are creatures of the respective party conferences (or caucuses, as the House Democrats call theirs).

The congressional parties organize three major types of party committees: (1) committees to consider policy-related issues including policy formulation, scheduling, and strategy; (2) committees to work out the assignment of members to standing committees of the house and to recommend these assignments to the party caucus; and (3) committees to raise campaign money and provide campaign support in order to elect members of their party. In addition, House Democrats maintain a small personnel committee to oversee the appointment and operations of House patronage staff. The accompanying table provides a brief summary of the membership and functions of the congressional party committees of the 102d Congress.

Policy Committees. Policy committees have had a checkered history within the congressional parties. Originally, these committees were called steering committees. House Republicans first established such a committee in 1919 as part of the collegial leadership centering around Majority Leader Frank W. Mondell (R-Wyo.). The committee's purpose was to make day-to-day decisions about party policy and scheduling legislation. House Democrats developed a similar policy committee under the leadership of Speaker Henry T. Rainey (D-Ill.) when they won a majority in the 1932 election. But these party leadership entities were only irregularly effective for much of their early history.

In 1949, the House Republicans renamed the Steering Committee the Policy Committee and enlarged its membership. But it did not assume its modern form until 1959, when the committee was reconstituted by Minority Leader Charles A. Halleck (R-Ind.), who agreed that the leader should no longer chair it. In 1965 a subcommittee of the House Republican Policy Committee (called the Subcommittee on Special Projects) was spun off as a separate Research Committee. Consisting of thirty-four House Republicans and a small staff, the Policy Committee meets regularly and is actively involved in formulating policy positions and circulating policy statements on behalf of the Republican conference. Coordinating with the Policy Committee, the Research Committee establishes and manages task forces created to study salient issues and formulate position statements. During the 102d Congress, seven task forces were at work, concerned with criminal justice, defense, domestic policy, economic policy, the environment, foreign policy, and trade. They were, in turn, broken down into forty-six subcommittees, each focusing on a substantive policy area.

On the Democratic side, the contemporary Steering and Policy Committee came into being in 1973; the next year, it was given the task of recommending Democratic committee assignments. As a policy committee, it serves as an executive committee for the Democratic caucus, a forum for the exchange of information, and an apparatus for coordinating with standing committee chairmen. Occasionally, the committee has endorsed bills, especially budget bills. The chairmen of four important House committees—Appropriations, Budget, Rules, and Ways and Means—also serve ex officio on the Steering and Policy Committee. Moreover, among the Speaker's appointees to the committee have been leaders of the whip organization. (In the 102d Congress, three chief deputy whips and a floor whip were committee members.) Because the committee is chaired by the Speaker, who appoints nearly a third of its members, it is an important vehicle for majority party leadership in the House.

Senate party policy committees were created by law in the late 1940s, and their style and activities have, over the years, been shaped to the preferences and expectations of the party leaders. The policy committees of the Senate parties are important but not as central to party leadership as in the House. On the Democratic side, the Senate policy committee is chaired by the party's floor leader (in 1994, George J. Mitchell of Maine). On the Republican side, the party's floor leader is a member of the policy committee, but the chairman is a different senator (beginning in 1992, Don Nickles of Oklahoma). The Senate Democratic Policy Committee is a service agency, disseminating information about issues and provisions of legislation to Democratic senators and hosting a weekly luncheon meeting for the Democratic conference. The Policy Committee is essentially a staff operation, and the staff is, in effect, the staff of the Democratic conference. By the same token, the Senate Republican Policy Committee is largely a staff operation, providing information to Republican members and sponsoring a weekly luncheon meeting, but the Republican conference has its own separate staff.

Committees on Committees. All four congressional parties establish committees on committees. Their functions are to ascertain members' committee assignment preferences, to assemble a roster of committee assignments to propose to the party caucus, and to recommend committee chairmanships.

In 1910 and 1911, a bipartisan House coalition (the "insurgency") transferred the power to appoint standing-committee members and their chairmen from the Speaker to the majority party caucus. The Democratic caucus formed a committee on committees that consisted of the Democratic membership of the House Ways and Means Committee. A change in the committee assignment process occurred in the early 1970s as part of an effort to strengthen party leadership in the House. This function was vested in the Steering and Policy Committee, which was empowered to recommend Democratic committee assignments to the party caucus. Because party leaders and Speaker appointees make up a majority of the committee and the Speaker is the committee's chairman, House majority party committee assignments are largely in the hands of the party leaders, subject to caucus approval.

The House Republican Committee on Committees, first established in 1917, is chaired by the party leader (since 1981, Robert H. Michel of Illinois). This committee designates Republican members of standing committees and their ranking members (except that the Republican leader directly appoints the minority members on the Rules Committee), and these recommendations are not subject to approval by the Republican conference. The committee's processes are somewhat unusual. To provide representation on the committee from across the country, each Republican state delegation chooses a committee member. This selection process makes for quite a large committee, so for operating purposes it chooses an executive committee (in 1992 it had twenty-one members). In making committee assignments, a system of weighted voting is invoked, reflecting the varying sizes of the state delegations. The floor leader and whip are accorded extra votes in order to overweight their influence on committee assignments. While the approval of the Republican conference is not required for committee assignments to be made, the executive committee's decisions are contingent on ratification by the full membership of the Committee on Committees.

Party Committees of the 102d Congress

COMMITTEES	NUMBER OF MEMBERS	FUNCTION
HOUSE DEMOCRATS		
Steering and Policy	30[1]	Discusses and endorses party policy; recommends Democratic committee assignments to caucus; serves as an executive arm of the Democratic caucus.
Campaign	75[2]	Seeks to elect Democrats to the House.
Personnel	1	Oversees Democratic patronage appointments.
HOUSE REPUBLICANS		
Policy	34	Considers policy proposals and seeks consensus among Republicans.
Research	22[3]	Forms task forces to consider policy alternatives; conducts research.
Committee on Committees	21[4]	Makes Republican committee assignments.
Campaign	51[5]	Seeks to elect Republicans to the House.
SENATE DEMOCRATS		
Policy	21[6]	Considers party positions on legislation and assists the party leader in scheduling bills.
Steering	25	Makes Democratic committee assignments.
Campaign	30	Seeks to elect Democrats to the Senate.
SENATE REPUBLICANS		
Policy	22	Considers party policy positions, advises on party strategy.
Committee on Committees	4	Makes Republican committee assignments.
Campaign	11	Seeks to elect Republicans to the Senate.

[1]Includes nine members appointed by the Speaker, twelve members elected by regions, and nine ex officio members.

[2]Includes a chairman, a vice chairman, six cochairmen, four ex officio members, fifty elected members, eight Speaker's appointees, and six at-large members. Seventy-five members occupied seventy-six positions, with some members serving in more than one capacity.

[3]Executive committee; all Republican representatives are members.

[4]Executive committee; full committee includes one Republican from each state with Republican representation.

[5]Includes a chairman, forty-two elected members, three class representatives, and five ex officio members.

[6]Includes a chairman and cochairman, four vice chairmen, thirteen elected members, and two ex officio members.

Committees on committees, dating back to the Civil War period, were the first party committees to be created in the Senate. The Senate Democrats' committee on committees is called the Steering Committee. Until 1988, the Steering Committee was chaired by the Democratic leader, but that year, in an effort to widen participation in party decision making, Majority Leader Mitchell appointed Sen. Daniel K. Inouye (D-Hawaii) chairman. The Senate Republican Committee on Committees and its chairman are designated by the Republican conference chairman. The Democratic committee also nominates standing committee chairmen, subject to a conference vote if one-fifth of the conference members request it. Ranking Republican standing committee members are chosen by each committee's minority members, subject to conference approval.

Campaign Committees. Congressional campaign committees can be traced back to the midnineteenth century, but they have developed into substantial election enterprises only since the late 1970s. All four congressional parties create campaign committees to help recruit candidates capable of winning congressional seats for their party, to provide technical campaign advice and assistance to candidates, and, above all, to raise and dispense millions of dollars in campaign funds. Nowadays, these committees are well institutionalized—in the House, the Democratic Congressional Campaign Committee and the National Republican Congressional Committee, and in the Senate, the Democratic Senatorial Campaign Committee and the National Republican Senatorial Committee. Enjoying large and well-organized staffs, these campaign committees have a considerable direct influence on their parties' congressional campaigns and a substantial role in channeling and allocating campaign money flowing from political action committees.

Other Committees. The official party committee structure does not exhaust the party organization of the congressional houses. The conferences (caucuses) and their staffs, the leaders' staffs, unofficial organizations such as the Democratic Study Group and the House Republican Study Committee, task forces with special policy purposes, and the House Rules Committee all play parts in the organizational life of the four congressional parties.

One of the most active of these committees has been the House Democratic Committee on Organization, Study, and Review (OSR). This committee is explicitly provided for in the rules of the Democratic caucus. Its job is to consider proposed changes in the party rules. Working mostly behind the scenes, OSR has occasionally attracted notoriety. In the mid 1970s it became the center of controversy over the issue of committee reorganization, when the proposals of a Select Committee on Committees were referred to OSR for a fairly complete overhaul. Since 1991, the OSR has been chaired by Rep. Louise M. Slaughter (D-N.Y.). Following the November 1992 presidential election, the Democratic caucus considered and adopted a number of rules changes proposed by OSR. In its post-election report *Agenda for Change*, the committee developed the general outline of its reform plan, and its detailed recommendations were adopted by the caucus in December. Especially innovative among these was the creation of a working group on policy development, appointed by the Speaker, intended to advise the leadership about legislative priorities.

Speaker Thomas P. "Tip" O'Neill initiated the device of appointing "Speaker's task forces" in order to extend the reach of the party leadership and include more rank-and-file Democrats in consultation processes. Orchestrated by the caucus chairman and the task force coordinator, House Democratic party task forces have become a customary strategy for policy consideration. Nowadays, it is not unusual for eight or nine task forces to be working at a given time. Task force proposals can become centerpieces for both intraparty and interparty deliberation and conflict. For instance, in 1991, the caucus task force on campaign finance, chaired by Rep. Sam Gejdenson (D-Conn.), reported a controversial proposal providing public financing of House campaigns. In addition to these caucus task forces, ad hoc task forces may be es-tablished within the party whip system so as to involve backbenchers in the consideration of particular legislative proposals.

Republican task forces abound as well. The House Republican Research Committee now coordinates task forces on criminal justice, defense, domestic policy, economic policy, the environment, foreign policy, and trade. In the aftermath of President Bill Clinton's election, House Republicans revamped their organization, forming three standing advisory committees to develop party strategy (one to coordinate presentation of Republican partisans' arguments on the House floor, one to facilitate communication to the public, and one to coordinate with interest groups). In the spring of 1993, the House Republican conference created a special task force on restrictive rules strategy, chaired by Rep. Gerald B. H. Solomon (R-N.Y.). This task force's purpose is to attack proposals for rules that restrict amendments and debate when bills are considered by the House. Senate Republicans have found task forces useful as well. One of the most active has been the task force on health of Sen. John H. Chafee (R-R.I.), which gave shape to the Republican plan to restructure the national health system as an alternative to the much heralded Democratic health plan worked out during the early months of 1993 under the guidance of First Lady Hillary Rodham Clinton.

Party committees and other components of the congressional parties have grown stronger and more important since 1980. They provide significant forums for discussing and establishing agreement on policy positions; they constitute a "full-service organization," nurturing the informational, leadership, and political needs of members; and they help to stimulate intraparty cohesiveness in legislative decision making, thereby contributing to party government in Congress. By enlarging the number of leadership posts, and by creating a comprehensive system of task forces for both long-range and short-range planning, the congressional parties have widened member participation in their tactical and strategic deliberations. In so doing, the party leaderships have been able to involve themselves more fully in legislative decision making and have become more able to mobilize their members for concerted action. In short, congressional party organizations are stronger than they have been for at least a generation, and, notably in the House of Representatives, they provide conditions under which centralized party leadership can be exerted more effectively.

[*For general discussion of related issues, see* Caucus, *article on* Party Caucus; Campaign Committees; Campaign Financing; Committees, *article on* Assignment of Members; Leadership; Legislative Service Organizations; Political Parties. *See also* Democratic Study Group; Political Action Committees.]

BIBLIOGRAPHY

Dodd, Lawrence C., and Bruce I. Oppenheimer, eds. *Congress Reconsidered.* 5th ed. 1993.

Jones, Charles O. *The Minority Party in Congress.* 1970.

Ripley, Randall B. *Majority Party Leadership in Congress.* 1969.

Rohde, David W. *Parties and Leaders in the Postreform House.* 1991.

Sinclair, Barbara. *Majority Leadership in the U.S. House.* 1983.

SAMUEL C. PATTERSON

PATENTS. *See* Copyright, Trademarks, and Patents.

PATMAN, WRIGHT (1893–1976), Democratic representative from Texas, chairman of the Committee on Banking and Currency, and zealous advocate for populist ideas. Born to a family of impoverished farmers in northeastern Texas, Patman never forgot his populist roots. He entered Democratic politics soon after becoming a lawyer in 1916, serving successively as an assistant prosecutor, state representative, and district attorney. In 1928, he was elected to the U.S. House of Representatives, where he served for forty-seven years.

Patman's economic philosophy, particularly his unremitting support of inflationary policies and greater government economic planning, as well as his opposition to large banking interests, brought him a lifetime of controversy. He was a long-time critic of tax-exempt foundations and was concerned with financial conflicts of interest in the Treasury Department. He even attempted to impeach Herbert Hoover's secretary of the Treasury, Andrew W. Mellon. His mild appearance—a cherubic face framed by tiny, steel-rimmed glasses—belied an unusual tenacity in advancing his beliefs.

A champion of small business, he helped create the Small Business Administration and was coauthor in 1936 of the Robinson-Patman Act, which barred price discrimination and other anticompetitive practices. He was a lifelong advocate of low interest and other "easy money" policies, who blamed the Federal Reserve for much of the nation's economic ills. As chairman of the Banking and Currency Committee (1963–1975), he waged a one-man crusade against the Federal Reserve for its efforts to control inflation by tightening the money supply and boosting interest rates. When another of his frequent targets, the comptroller of the Currency who functions as administrator of the national banking system, sought in 1965 to ease controls on large commercial banks, Patman responded by introducing legislation to abolish the office.

Patman's autocratic style cost him popularity among his committee's members. He survived a committee rebellion in 1965. He continued as chairman until the election of a large number of reform-minded Democrats—and his advanced age—led the Democratic Caucus to remove him as chairman in January 1975.

BIBLIOGRAPHY

Schmelzer, Janet. "The Early Life and Early Congressional Career of Wright Patman, 1894–1976." Ph.D. diss., Texas Christian University, 1978.

Sherrill, Robert. "'The Last of the Great Populists' Takes on the Foundations, the Banks, the Federal Reserve, the Treasury." *New York Times Magazine,* 16 March 1969.

ANTHONY CHAMPAGNE

PATRONAGE. Although the number of traditional patronage positions has declined in recent years, giving way to qualification-based hiring, members of Congress may recommend candidates for certain jobs with House and Senate officers—the clerk of the House, sergeant at arms, and doorkeeper, and the secretary and sergeant at arms of the Senate—as well as with the architect of the Capitol, who is in charge of maintaining the Capitol complex.

Patronage employees include some Senate mail sorters and document room workers, elevator operators in both houses of Congress, and employees who run the two houses' cloakrooms and floor operations. Prior to 1992 the House post office was staffed almost exclusively by patronage workers, but that practice was abolished in the wake of an embezzlement scandal in which several counter clerks admitted having taken money from the cash drawers. Another hotbed of patronage was the nearly 1,300-member Capitol Police Department. In the late 1960s, however, it began using professional

OFFICE SEEKERS. Mobbing a member of Congress.
PERLEY'S REMINISCENCES, VOL. 1

standards for hiring, and only a handful of officers remain on the force from the days of patronage.

The House has gradually been placing its day-to-day administrative functions under the control of its director of nonlegislative and financial services, who has said he will hire based solely on qualifications and will require that patronage employees already in place retain their jobs through competence and not connections.

Members' success in getting people hired for patronage jobs depends on the members' seniority and relationship with those members of their party who control patronage appointments.

In the House, majority and minority patronage committees forward members' recommendations to the officers whose payrolls carry the jobs. The Senate handles this function through the majority and minority party secretaries, who forward recommendations to the majority and minority leaders for final approval.

Patronage in Congress has its most tangible manifestation in the more than 15,000 employees who work directly for representatives and senators, whether in the members' personal, committee, or leadership offices. These staffers all owe their positions solely to the member of Congress they work for, who has the power to unilaterally retain or remove them. All representatives and senators receive an allotment of payroll funds to hire staffers for "personal" staff in both their Washington, D.C., and home state offices. Members of the leadership and committee chairmen control substantial additional payrolls.

Congressional employees, particularly those who work directly for members, enjoy few of the specific job protections accorded executive branch civil service workers, who can be removed from their jobs only for egregious actions and after extensive disciplinary proceedings. Particularly demanding and temperamental members of Congress have been known to dismiss aides on a moment's notice and with what critics consider little or no justification.

Congressional exemption from job protection laws centers on the fact that members have been viewed by the constitution as empowered by popular election to represent their constituents however they see fit. With loyalty at a premium in the intense political atmosphere of Congress, members want to be free to replace staffers even if they suspect disloyalty.

Another argument was that allowing the executive branch to enforce employee protections in Congress as it does in the private sector would have violated the separation of powers doctrine—that, other than for criminal offenses, Congress must retain unto itself the power to judge and punish its members for misdeeds related to their official work. This was intended to avoid politically motivated executive branch investigations of Congress.

In recent years, however, Congress has been applying these laws to itself as internal rules, banning sex and race discrimination, among other offenses, and for the first time writing provisions into law that allow employees to sue. To avoid separation of powers questions, the House in 1988 and the Senate in 1991 established offices with which employees who feel they have been unfairly treated can file discrimination complaints.

In 1967, Congress passed a government-wide anti-nepotism law, offered by Rep. Neal Smith (D-Iowa), banning members from placing their relatives on their payrolls, until then a relatively common practice. An exception is made when a member marries a current staffer, in which case the spouse may remain on the payroll. Today, some members' spouses work without pay in their offices.

The House and Senate page programs also afford members an opportunity to wield prestigious patronage. Working with party leaders, who have final approval, the House Democratic Personnel Committee and Republican Patronage Committee and the Senate party secretaries allocate page slots to members, based largely on seniority, but also on who has most recently named pages and on members' relationships with the leadership. The sixty-six House pages and thirty Senate pages normally serve a semester each; some receive extensions to a full school year. House Democratic pages normally serve for a single semester, although they can be reappointed for a second, while Republican pages serve for a full school year. All pages attend the page school in the early morning and run errands and work on the House and Senate floors and for each body's leadership for the rest of the day. An abbreviated program operates two summer sessions for both the House and the Senate.

Another important aspect of congressional involvement in federal patronage is the power that members of both houses, particularly the Senate (which votes to confirm high-level nominees), wield in recommending candidates for executive and judicial branch appointments. The president, depending on his relationship with a state or region's congressional delegation, typically consults the senior senator of his own party on major regional positions, the senior representative in his party if both senators are members of the opposition, or local officials if a state's delegation is all of the other party. The positions traditionally subject to such consultation include U.S. attorney and U.S. marshal posts, some regional subcabinet and administrator jobs, and federal judgeships. By accepting or rejecting a member's recommendation, a president can forge or damage an important relationship, a consideration that is especially important in the Senate, where a single member can hold up legislation and other nominations.

Adhering to a practice that Senate president pro tempore Robert Byrd of West Virginia, a former Senate majority leader, refers to as "senatorial courtesy," that body normally will not confirm a regional nominee who is opposed by the senators representing the state in which the appointment is proposed.

The importance that some members attach to placing people in patronage posts was never more clearly demonstrated than in 1881, when Roscoe Conkling resigned his New York Senate seat to protest President James Garfield's insistence on naming William Robertson, a leader of Conkling's political rivals, collector for the Port of New York. The New York State legislature subsequently rejected the once-powerful Conkling's request that it promptly reelect him, thus ending his political career. But this dispute—and the subsequent assassination of Garfield by an unsuccessful patronage job seeker—led to the 1883 enactment of the Pendleton Act, the first substantial executive branch civil service law.

[See also Civil Service; Pendleton Act.]

BIBLIOGRAPHY

Byrd, Robert C. *The Senate, 1789–1989: Addresses on the History of the United States Senate.* Vol 2. 1991.
Hoogenboom, Ari. *Outlawing the Spoils: A History of the Civil Service Reform Movement, 1865–1883.* 1961.
Ornstein, Norman J., Thomas E. Mann, and Michael J. Malbin. *Vital Statistics on Congress.* 1992.

TIMOTHY J. BURGER

PEACE CORPS. Established in 1961 by President John F. Kennedy, the Peace Corps sends volunteers abroad to aid developing countries in education, agriculture, and health care. Until that time, the federal government had not, by and large, considered voluntary assistance programs to be its responsibility. The genesis of the Peace Corps was the 1933 establishment of the Civilian Conservation Corps (CCC) under President Franklin D. Roosevelt, a work program with a philosophy inherent in the Peace Corps.

The concept of an international corps of volunteers originated on Capitol Hill. Rep. Henry S. Reuss (D-Wis.) in January 1960 introduced the first Peace Corps bill to study the concept's practicability. The House Foreign Affairs Committee responded favorably in August 1960 when it added to its Mutual Security Act a rider that authorized $10,000 for a study of a Point Four Youth Corps, Reuss's name for the Peace Corps. Sen. Hubert H. Humphrey (D-Minn.) drafted a comparable bill in the spring of 1960 that first used the term *Peace Corps.* The legislation was passed the following year.

It was the Kennedy administration that created and organized the Peace Corps as it now exists. Advocating the program was part of Kennedy's New Frontier campaign platform to improve the quality of the nation and the world. Kennedy appointed his brother-in-law, R. Sargent Shriver, to head a task force to develop Peace Corps ideology and established the program by Executive Order 10924 on 1 March 1961. Kennedy assigned the Peace Corps to the Agency for International Development (AID), which incorporated all government economic and social development initiatives. Peace Corps advisers, however, did not want to lose the uniqueness and autonomy of the newly established program by including it in the government's traditional foreign aid establishment. With the assistance of Vice President Lyndon B. Johnson, they convinced Kennedy to place the Peace Corps in the Department of State. Once the Peace Corps was assigned to an agency, Kennedy requested legislation from Congress.

To Congress, the concept of a foreign assistance program was generally unpopular, and Kennedy's use of the executive order was seen by Congress as an indication of disdain for the constitutional division of powers. Many members were hesitant to approve Peace Corps legislation, their concerns ranging from the required amount of funding to the security of the volunteers sent abroad. Shriver and his team of lobbyists saturated the Hill with Peace Corps information to urge members to pass the legislation. Humphrey introduced a bill in the Senate on 1 June 1961. It passed in the Senate on 25 August 1961 and the House on 14 September 1961.

The Peace Corps gained popularity in the 1960s, when funding and the number of volunteers increased. In 1971 it was incorporated into a larger agency, ACTION (an agency combining the government's domestic and overseas voluntary organizations), as its popularity suffered from a lack of recruits and financial support. It was revived as an independent agency in 1983 during President Ronald Reagan's administration. Because of its status as a government agency, its budget and agenda have often been the focus of partisan disputes, but the Peace Corps remains an active volunteer program committed to helping people learn to help themselves.

BIBLIOGRAPHY

Rice, Gerard T. *The Bold Experiment: JFK's Peace Corps.* 1985.
Wingenbach, Charles E. *The Peace Corps: Who, How, and Where.* 1963.

KATHERINE A. COLLADO

PEARL HARBOR INVESTIGATION.

The surrender of Japan and the release of wartime army and navy reports on the Pearl Harbor attack dealing with the culpability of the local commanders, Adm. Husband E. Kimmel and Maj. Gen. Walter C. Short, set the stage for a public investigation in 1945. On 4 September, House Republicans called for a congressional hearing to fix responsibility for what Sen. Robert A. Taft called "the greatest disaster in our history." Coopting the issue, Majority Leader Alben W. Barkley offered his own resolution calling for a joint committee of the House and Senate to investigate the surprise attack.

The hotly partisan hearings of the Joint Committee Investigating the Pearl Harbor Attack, chaired by Barkley, produced forty-three public witnesses and resulted in sixty-seven volumes of testimony. The disclosure that Japanese high-level codes had been broken, with its implication that hostilities with Japan could have been predicted and prepared for, created a flurry of interest. Kimmel and Short, allowed to state their cases publicly for the first time, claimed that blame for the attack rested squarely on Washington, not the military command in Hawaii.

The majority report reflected the administration's position on the Pearl Harbor affair as stated in earlier investigations, that Kimmel and Short had committed errors of judgment but had not disregarded their obligations or been indifferent to their duties. Officials in Washington, including the president, escaped direct criticism. The Republican senators' minority report declared that while the record was incomplete, the committee had gathered enough evidence to demonstrate that, by late November 1941, Washington officials knew that an attack was imminent. Therefore, whatever errors in judgment the local commanders had committed, responsibility rested ultimately with their superiors. The reports did not end the controversy over the attack, but they did demonstrate that there was enough blame to go around.

BIBLIOGRAPHY

Beard, Charles A. *President Roosevelt and the Coming of the War, 1941.* 1948.
Melosi, Martin V. *The Shadow of Pearl Harbor: Political Controversy over the Surprise Attack, 1941–1946.* 1977.
Prange, Gordon W. *At Dawn We Slept: The Untold Story of Pearl Harbor.* 1981.
Toland, John. *Infamy: Pearl Harbor and Its Aftermath.* 1982.

MARTIN V. MELOSI

PECORA WALL STREET INVESTIGATION.

The Pecora Wall Street Investigation (1932–1934) explored the causes of the stock market crash of 1929 and the subsequent depression, exposed the malfeasance of prominent financiers, and led to major legislative reforms of U.S. banking and securities practices. In April 1932, the Senate Banking and Currency Committee launched an inquiry into Wall Street practices when President Herbert Hoover warned that "bear raiders" in the stock markets threatened his recovery program. The complex nature of the charges and the unwillingness of the New York Stock Exchange to cooperate with the inquiry overwhelmed the committee's first two chief counsels, who proved unable to mount effective investigations. In January 1933, the committee hired Ferdinand Pecora, an assistant district attorney in New York, to prepare its final report. In reviewing the files, Pecora concluded that further hearings were necessary. Armed with subpoenas, his staff examined the records of the National City Bank, where they uncovered evidence that the bank's securities division had unloaded stocks on customers to bail out the bank's bad loans. These revelations caused the president of National City Bank, Charles E. Mitchell, to resign.

The committee's new Democratic majority authorized Pecora to continue his probe. In May, the committee called banker J. P. Morgan, Jr., to testify and elicited information concerning how his bank's bookkeeping maneuvers had enabled Morgan to pay no income taxes in 1930 and 1931. The intense media publicity devoted to the Pecora hearings climaxed when a circus promoter slipped into the caucus room and placed a midget on Morgan's lap. Newspaper photographs broadcast the humbling of the nation's most prominent banker.

The Pecora hearings also stained the reputation of the "most popular banker on Wall Street," the retired chairman of Chase Manhattan Bank, Albert H. Wiggin. Pecora demonstrated how Wiggin had used family corporations to speculate in his own bank's stocks. Chase Manhattan responded by announcing plans to separate its banking and securities functions.

Pecora next turned the committee's attention to the workings of the New York Stock Exchange, subpoenaing records of its most active floor traders and investigating pool operations. Throughout these inquiries, Chairman Duncan U. Fletcher and other members of the Banking Committee regularly deferred to their remarkable chief counsel. "I looked with astonishment," wrote the journalist John T. Flynn, "at this man who, through the intricate maze of banking syndicates, market deals, chicanery of all sorts, and in a field new to him, never forgot a name, never made an error in a figure, and never lost his temper."

Pecora's headline-producing revelations of greed, excessive profits, and improper bank practices and stock sales contributed to the enactment of the Glass-Steagall Act of 1933, which divorced commercial and investment banking; the Securities Act of 1933, which required corporations to provide accurate information to stock purchasers; and the Securities and Exchange Act of 1934, which established federal regulation of the stock exchanges. Benefiting from bipartisan support, a shrewd chief counsel, and extensive press attention, the Senate Banking Committee's investigation provided the means for public scrutiny and supervision of previously private banking and stock market operations, and thereby significantly improved the nation's economic well-being.

[*See also* Banking Act of 1933; Securities Acts.]

BIBLIOGRAPHY

Pecora, Ferdinand. *Wall Street under Oath: The Story of Our Modern Money Changers.* 1939.
Ritchie, Donald A. "The Pecora Wall Street Investigation, 1934." In *Congress Investigates: A Documented History, 1792–1974.* Edited by Arthur M. Schlesinger, Jr., and Roger Bruns. 1974.

DONALD A. RITCHIE

PENDLETON ACT (1883; 22 Stat. 403–407). Also known as the Civil Service Act, the Pendleton Act established the legal foundation for much federal personnel administration until it was superseded by the Civil Service Reform Act of 1978. The 1883 act was promoted by civil-service reformers, who became a political force in the 1870s and continued to exert influence until the 1890s, when they were overshadowed by the Progressive movement for more comprehensive governmental and economic reforms. The act substituted merit for partisan patronage as the basis for hiring federal employees in what became known as the competitive, or classified, civil service. The competitive civil service, which comprised about 10 percent of the federal service in 1883, eventually rose to about 90 percent.

Enactment followed popular disgust at the assassination of President James A. Garfield by an office seeker in 1881. Further, the Republican party, having suffered a significant defeat in the midterm election of 1882, embraced civil-service reform as a means of denying the Democrats patronage in the future. Although the act's supporters emphasized the efficiency it would bring, it was a highly political measure because it reduced Congress's role in federal personnel matters and gave the president greater authority over the civil service.

Specific provisions included (1) a Civil Service Commission with rule-making authority for per-

GEORGE H. PENDLETON (D-OHIO). An 1864 presidential campaign banner bearing the portraits of vice presidential candidate Pendleton, *right*, and presidential candidate George B. McClellan. Pendleton served in the U.S. House from 1857 to 1865 and in the Senate from 1879 to 1885. Lithograph with watercolor, published by Currier and Ives, New York, 1864.   LIBRARY OF CONGRESS

sonnel administration and administrative responsibility for some aspects of federal personnel; (2) implementation of open, competitive, practical examinations for entrance into the classified service; and (3) development of rules to prevent partisanship in federal personnel administration. The act did not create significant legal barriers to the dismissal of federal employees.

[*See also* Civil Service Reform Act of 1978.]

BIBLIOGRAPHY

Hoogenboom, Ari. *Outlawing the Spoils*. 1961.
Skowronek, Stephen. *Building a New American State.* 1982.
Van Riper, Paul. *History of the United States Civil Service.* 1958.

DAVID H. ROSENBLOOM

PENNSYLVANIA. The colony of Pennsylvania originated in a grant in 1681 by England's King Charles II to William Penn of land extending five degrees west of the Delaware River between Maryland and New York. Although Penn's intentions included personal financial profit, he hoped also to establish a "holy experiment" in which people of diverse ethnic and religious backgrounds could worship freely and live together peacefully. Because so many of Penn's coreligionists in the pacifistic Society of Friends (Quakers) inhabited Pennsylvania, the colony was initially a reluctant participant in the revolutionary movement. In time, however, it became the "Keystone State" and on 12 December 1787 was the second to ratify the federal Constitution. Its capital, Philadelphia, served as the seat of the national government from 1791 until 1801, and Pennsylvanian Frederick A. C. Muhlenberg served as first and third Speaker of the House of Representatives.

Pennsylvania was a leader in the development of inclusive politics. Its constitution of 1776 made the state the first to abolish property qualifications and most religious qualifications for voting. Its Democrats were among the first in the nation to organize politically, in the late 1700s. Through so-called democratic clubs—forerunners of political parties—they were among the first to nominate a commoner, Simon Snyder, for governor, in 1808. They also were among the first to replace the exclusive legislative nominating caucus, conducting in 1817 a broader convention for selecting candidates to state and national offices. They used this technique to promote Andrew Jackson for the presidency, which he achieved in 1828. National political parties subsequently adopted this method of nominating candidates for president and vice president. Throughout this period most Pennsylvania senators and representatives supported such locally popular programs as federally funded roads, the protective tariff, and the second Bank of the United States, but they rarely achieved national fame. An exception was Democratic representative David Wilmot, who in 1846 presented to the House of Representatives a resolution specifying that no appropriations for the conflict with Mexico were to be used to acquire slave territory. Northern members of Congress supported the resolution strongly and southerners vigorously opposed it, and the Wilmot Proviso became a symbol of the widening breach between the North and South. In an unsuccessful attempt to ease sectional tension, James Buchanan a former Pennsylvania representative and senator, was elected president in 1856, fulfilling Pennsylvania Democrats' long-standing ambition to have a Pennsylvanian in the nation's highest office.

After the Civil War Pennsylvanians shifted their political allegiance from the Democrats to the relatively new Republican party, which dominated the state until the Great Depression of the 1930s. Its leaders, Simon Cameron, Matthew S. Quay, and Boies Penrose, represented the state in the U.S. Senate without distinction. The Republicans controlled the state's delegation to Congress, carried the state in every presidential election but one, and dominated the state legislature. During this period, all Pennsylvania governors but one were Republicans. The Republican party developed and maintained its control by skillful use of such issues as the suppression of former Confederates, the protective tariff, and "sound money" (currency based primarily on the gold standard), and through Republicans' arrogant implementation of extraordinarily corrupt political practices. So notorious were their misdeeds that when two of them attempted to take their seats in the Senate, their colleagues rejected them—Quay in 1900 and William S. Vare in 1926. The Republican machine began to lose power after Penrose's death in 1921. Hastening its end were new people, including the progressive governor Gifford Pinchot; new problems, such as severe unemployment; and new programs, especially the New Deal. Nevertheless Pennsylvania was one of only six states—and the only large industrial state—to vote Republican in the 1932 presidential election.

After World War II Pennsylvania became a two-party state. Although the Democrats built a significant lead in registered voters, especially in the cities of Philadelphia and Pittsburgh, neither party could count on winning elections. State government was normally divided, with the governor from one party and at least one house of the legislature dominated by the other. The state's congressional delegation also has been split almost evenly. Republican representative (later senator) Hugh Scott served as his party's national chairman in 1948. He also served as Senate minority leader from 1969 to 1977. Of Pennsylvania's later representatives, Republicans Richard S. Schweiker and John Heinz and Democrat Joseph S. Clark were the most capable and best known. In the House of Representatives, the state gradually lost seats because of comparatively slow population growth. From a high of thirty-six seats in 1910, the delegation dropped to twenty-one members following the 1990 census.

Nevertheless, the state's congressional team is still the fifth-largest in the nation.

BIBLIOGRAPHY

Beers, Paul B. *Pennsylvania Politics: Today and Yesterday.* 1980.

Cochran, Thomas C. *Pennsylvania: A Bicentennial History.* 1978.

Kehl, James A. *Boss Rule in the Gilded Age: Matt Quay of Pennsylvania.* 1981.

Klein, Philip S. *Pennsylvania Politics, 1817–1832: A Game without Rules.* 1940.

Klein, Philip S., and Ari Hoogenboom. *A History of Pennsylvania.* 1980.

JOHN B. FRANTZ

PENROSE, BOIES (1860–1921), senator from Pennsylvania (1897–1921) and the state's Republican boss (1904–1921). A brilliant, Harvard-educated member of a prominent Philadelphia family, Penrose entered Pennsylvania politics at age twenty-four, spent twelve years in the state legislature, where he steered Sen. Matthew S. Quay's political machine, and moved to the U.S. Senate after a bitter intraparty battle with reform forces headed by John Wanamaker. A large man (350 pounds) with a gargantuan appetite, Penrose could not sit in the regular Senate seats and, toadlike, occupied a special couch at the rear of the chamber.

He demonstrated little interest in the major legislative issues before the Senate except to defend the protective tariff and procure the patronage necessary to keep the party's state machine functioning smoothly. At various times he served on the Banking, Immigration, Education and Labor, Naval Affairs, Expenditures, Post Office, and Finance committees and once accepted the chairmanship of the Finance Committee.

A cynical, conservative patriarch, Penrose refused to allow the progressive reforms of his era to engulf either him or his state. He stood inalterably opposed to woman suffrage, the graduated income tax, Chinese immigration, the direct election of U.S. senators, prohibition, and the League of Nations. One of his severest critics, Theodore Roosevelt, attempted to defeat Penrose's Senate renomination in 1914; the former president "stormed and stomped" across Pennsylvania denouncing Penrose's character and tactics and proclaiming the virtues of his progressive challenger. But to no avail. The senator's patronage power carried his renomination and reelection by a wide margin; he served in the Senate longer than any other Pennsylvanian.

BIBLIOGRAPHY

Beers, Paul B. *Pennsylvania Politics: Today and Yesterday.* 1980.
Davenport, Walter. *Power and Glory: The Life of Boies Penrose.* 1931.

JAMES A. KEHL

CLAUDE PEPPER.   LIBRARY OF CONGRESS

PEPPER, CLAUDE (1900–1989), Democratic senator and representative from Florida, chairman of the House Committee on Rules, and advocate for the elderly. One of the few senators ever to serve in the House after failing to win reelection to the Senate, Pepper was born to impoverished parents in Alabama's rural red clay country. He worked his way through the University of Alabama. After a brief stint in the army he was awarded a disability grant that enabled him to attend the Law School at Harvard and afterward to launch a political career. His own experience in receiving government aid for his legal education convinced Pepper that the only chance for underprivileged Americans to be lifted out of their misery lay with the federal government. He thus became, as he expressed it in his autobiography, "a New Dealer before there was a New Deal."

Moving to Florida in the late 1920s, Pepper, a gifted and powerful orator, espoused liberalism and racial moderation as a young Democrat in the Florida legislature. When that body condemned Mrs. Herbert Hoover for inviting the wife of a black congressman, Illinois Republican Oscar De Priest, to the White House, Pepper refused to support the resolution. He was defeated for reelection after a single term.

As the Depression deepened, Pepper traveled throughout Florida, stressing the need for a federal minimum-wage law and other measures to aid the jobless akin to those initiated by Gov. Franklin D. Roosevelt of New York. In 1934, Pepper challenged an incumbent senator and lost narrowly. When both Florida incumbents died two years later, Pepper was elected without opposition to an unexpired two-year term. He was reelected in 1938 and 1944 before losing in 1950 to Rep. George A. Smathers in a vicious campaign now seen as a forerunner of McCarthyism. Berated as "Red Pepper" for his sympathy toward the Soviet Union and for New Deal measures (seen as antibusiness), Pepper never again won a statewide election in Florida, although he tried in 1958, losing to incumbent senator Spessard L. Holland in a Democratic primary. During his Senate years, he was an ardent supporter of the Roosevelt administration's foreign and domestic policies, including the president's interventionism in the earliest stages of World War II. In May 1940, Pepper cast the lone vote in the Senate Foreign Relations Committee in favor of "lend-lease" of battleships and war matériel to Great Britain, the first time this historic and eventually successful proposal was considered by an overwhelmingly isolationist Congress.

Pepper's landmark federal minimum wage law and his early advocacy of "socialized medicine" and equal pay for women earned him the undying enmity of corporate America. And his support for organized labor and civil rights did not go down well in the Florida of the 1950s. But when in 1962 a new congressional district was carved out including liberal Miami and other parts of Dade County, Pepper was urged to seek the seat. He won the first of fourteen elections, and wound up serving longer in the

House (twenty-six years) than he had in the Senate (fourteen years).

As a representative, Pepper was the foremost defender of Social Security in the Congress. He had been an early advocate of Medicare as a senator during the Roosevelt and Truman years, and as a representative saw it enacted into law in 1965. But he regarded his sponsorship of twelve federal institutes of health and passage of his bill to eliminate mandatory retirement at age sixty-five as his most satisfying legislative achievements. Only weeks before he died of cancer in 1989, his impassioned plea for passage of legislation to provide long-term health care for young and old alike won him an ovation—but not enough votes—from his colleagues in the House.

BIBLIOGRAPHY

Pepper, Claude, with Hays Gorey. *Pepper: Eyewitness to a Century.* 1987.

HAYS GOREY

PERQUISITES. Members' use, and abuse, of the taxpayer-financed perquisites of office (often termed *perks*) have historically fueled great public discontent. Even more than such volatile subjects as congressional salary, mail franking, and travel, controversies over perks have lent credence to deep-seated public cynicism toward members of an "imperial" Congress who have lost touch with their constituents.

Although each new conflict has appeared to place Congress in an increasingly adverse public light, some perquisites have been an object of public scorn virtually since the founding of the Republic. Whether the issue has been patronage slots that award high-ranking legislative or executive-branch jobs to political loyalists of powerful lawmakers, or the more mundane recreational and other private facilities available to members on the Capitol grounds, the public response has typically been the same: members of Congress improperly seek and acquire advantages not essential to their job performance and not available to private citizens in similar occupations. Office perks also have become a controversial issue during political campaigns, when challengers have claimed that their opponents have gained unfair advantage by using so-called incumbent-protection devices that can have an annual value of at least several hundred thousand dollars.

Defenders of Congress respond that the criticisms—for instance, the claim that office furniture and telephones are an official perk—are often exaggerated and distorted by journalists, public-interest groups, partisan opponents, and other critics of Congress. The benefits, they add, are necessary and appropriate for the people entrusted with managing the vast apparatus of the U.S. government. Public hostility to congressional perks has become especially severe when government is not performing well, as for example during a Washington scandal, an economic recession, or a period of high federal budget deficits.

The focus on official perquisites has acquired an added mystique owing to the secrecy and complexity that typically surround them. Partly because senior congressional leaders and officers are reluctant to disclose the details publicly, many members have found it difficult to determine what services are available to them and at what cost to the taxpayer. When reporters or citizen watchdog groups have sought to compile a list of the benefits, they have faced a seemingly indecipherable maze of figures and regulations.

WARTIME CONGRESSIONAL PRIVILEGES. Cartoon targeting Leon Henderson, the head of the Office of Price Administration. Already upset over OPA's handling of price controls and rationing, citizens grew even angrier upon learning that members of Congress had exempted themselves from the gasoline restrictions that held ordinary motorists to three gallons a week. Embarrassed lawmakers quickly exchanged their coveted "X" ration cards for "A" cards that accorded them no special privileges at the pump. Clifford K. Berryman, 13 May 1942.

LIBRARY OF CONGRESS

Official Allowances. In congressional jargon, most perquisites are labeled as official allowances essential to the operation of the lawmakers' duties. Historically, the Senate and House have maintained separate sets of practices, each with its own idiosyncracies.

The most costly allowance, by far, has been the expense of maintaining staff for members, their committees, and their varied support organizations. Each of the 435 House members annually receives the same "clerk-hire" allowance for office staff; in 1992, the inflation-adjusted figure was $537,480. The allowance for senators is based on a state's population, ranging in 1992 from slightly over $1 million for the smallest to $1.9 million for the largest (California). Any funds that are allocated but not used are typically returned to the Treasury. Committees have their own budgets, many of which run into millions of dollars. The support agencies in the legislative establishment, such as the Congressional Research Service and the General Accounting Office, have annual budgets that exceed several hundred million dollars, most of which goes for salaries to support thousands of staffers who provide the members with technical assistance.

Although congressional staffs have gradually become more professional, senators and representatives have complete control over their personal aides; there are no overall performance standards or reviews that must be met, as for example in the executive branch, nor do employees have civil service protection. Besides needing staff to help them meet the demands of the legislative process, lawmakers also hire aides for a host of other responsibilities: office managers, caseworkers to handle constituent-service demands, press aides, personal secretaries, mail processors, receptionists, and the like. Since the 1970s many have expanded their in-state offices to include responsibilities that had previously been performed in Washington.

In addition to staff salaries, lawmakers receive public funds to cover a variety of office services, including office equipment, telephones, postage, stationery, travel, and office rental and furnishings. For House members, the principal variable is the distance from the capital to their home district, which chiefly affects travel and communication costs. For senators, costs also are influenced by the size of their home state's population. In some cases where rules limit the amount for a particular allowance, lawmakers have been permitted to shift funds from one account to another. Both representatives and senators have also benefited financially from discounts on many items available to them from Capitol Hill operations—stationery and furniture, for example.

Despite occasional efforts to reduce these expenses, the efforts by members to stay in closer touch with their constituents have produced costly changes in the way many of them do their business. These increases have been spurred by technological improvements that make it easier for members to communicate. For example, mailing costs increased more than tenfold between 1970 and 1990, as members made more use of direct-mail services to send newsletters, often several times a year, throughout their home states and districts. Improved transportation also has allowed members to visit constituents on a regular basis, often weekly. Before the introduction of regularly scheduled airline services to many smaller cities in the 1960s, the House and Senate allowances compensated lawmakers for only a few visits each year. Now, with flexible official allowances, members are entitled to taxpayer-financed weekly trips home. Although foreign travel requires the approval of House and Senate officials, such permission is routine. Public reports of these trips, which critics deride as "junkets," are often disclosed months later and with sparse detail.

The cost and value of other congressional perks can be more difficult to quantify. Both the Senate and the House have, for example, their own gymnasiums and swimming pools, medical services, television and radio recording studios, photographers, restaurants, art and plant suppliers, and parking lots at the Capitol and nearby airports. Many of these services have been free or heavily subsidized, although there have been moves in recent years to reduce the cost to taxpayers.

As congressional salaries and other perquisites have grown, the total congressional budget has increased much faster than the inflation rate. According to the 1991–1992 edition of *Vital Statistics on Congress*, the legislative branch appropriation first exceeded $100 million in 1957; it reached $1 billion in 1978 and $2 billion in 1991. In the same thirty-four-year period, the consumer-price index increased less than fivefold. The relative growth in the congressional budget has slowed considerably, however, since the mid 1970s.

Much of those additional costs resulted from the doubling of House and Senate staffs between the mid 1960s and late 1970s (to totals of nearly eight thousand and four thousand aides, respectively), levels that subsequently have remained relatively unchanged. Some staff increases were made in response to demands from reformers seeking to allow members more access to information and more participation in legislative endeavors. Congress made other changes in response to Republicans' complaints that the minority party was entitled to a larger share of committee resources. Ironically, years later, other Republicans objected that committee staffs had grown too large.

Abuses and Reforms. Abuses of congressional perks have periodically triggered extensive public debate. These incidents have typically been followed by periods of intense legislative self-examination, which in turn have usually produced limited reforms that have fallen short of addressing the overall problems.

In 1976, for example, Rep. Wayne L. Hays (D-Ohio) was forced to give up his chairmanship of the House Administration Committee after reports that he put on his payroll a woman who provided him with services that were more personal than professional. With the departure of Hays, who kept a tight rein on the dispersal of favors to House members, Democratic leaders set up a study that overhauled the committee's power to fix allowances for members and gave the members greater flexibility in their office operations. But the House in 1977 defeated a key proposal that would have created a House administrator to coordinate and oversee most of its internal housekeeping.

A major controversy over House perks erupted in 1991, when the General Accounting Office reported that the House bank was allowing members to cash checks with insufficient funds in their accounts and that it did not charge them an overdraft fee. A few months later the House revealed the number of overdrafts by each member in a thirty-nine-month period. The angry public reaction resulted in an unusually high number of retirements and reelection defeats in 1992. In the wake of this controversy, the House agreed to close its private bank, created the administrator post that it had rejected fifteen years earlier, and cut back on other perks. "I think we should focus on what is needed to carry on the work of the institution," said House Speaker Thomas S. Foley (D-Wash.) in explaining why the House stationery shop no longer planned to sell cut-rate items that were used chiefly for personal gifts.

Reforms have proceeded more slowly in the Senate, which is less subject to public pressure because of the six-year term for senators. In 1976 a lengthy study prepared for the Senate-appointed Commission on the Operation of the Senate reached the following conclusion about the funding of senators' offices: "There does not appear to be any policy statement on use of the allowances as a funding device, nor is there a written rationale supporting the use of allowances or explaining why this means of funding is currently used for Senators." Little has changed in the Senate since that report was issued. Considerable overlap remains, for example, among the Senate's sergeant at arms, the secretary of the Senate, and the Architect of the Capitol in providing routine services to Senate offices.

When lawmakers reduce their perks, they are usually responding to elections showing a public desire for change—or anticipating bad electoral results should the perks continue. Often, however, once the pressure has subsided, members return to business as usual.

[*See also* Franking; House Bank; Salaries; Staffing; Travel.]

BIBLIOGRAPHY

Cohen, Richard E. "Congressional Allowances Are Really Perking Up." *National Journal*, 4 February 1978, 180–183.

Ornstein, Norman J., Thomas E. Mann, and Michael J. Malbin. *Vital Statistics on Congress, 1991–1992*. 1992.

Updegrave, Walter L. "What Congress Really Costs You." *Money*, August 1992, 128–140.

RICHARD E. COHEN

PERSIAN GULF WAR. The Persian Gulf War, a limited war in the Middle East, formally began on 16 January 1991 following Iraq's refusal to abide by a United Nations deadline to remove its invading military forces from neighboring Kuwait. The war ended on 27 February 1991, when President George Bush ordered a cease-fire and proclaimed victory for the allied forces.

A week after Iraqi troops invaded Kuwait in August 1990, President Bush notified Congress that he had deployed troops to the region (Operation Desert Shield). Although he neglected to consult with congressional leaders before acting, both chambers later adopted measures that endorsed the initial deployment and urged Iraqi dictator Saddam Hussein to withdraw from Kuwait. In an impressive diplomatic exercise, the Bush administration worked through the United Nations to assemble a broad military coalition against Iraq. Industrialized nations feared that Iraq, with the region's largest military force, might overwhelm the entire Arabian Peninsula and its vast oil reserves. The same fear persuaded Saudi Arabia to request aid in defending itself and to provide the main staging area for an assault to recapture Kuwait.

Prodded by the Bush administration and strengthened by U.S.-Russian post–Cold War cooperation, the U.N. passed resolutions that set a deadline of 15 January 1991 for Iraqi withdrawal and that authorized member states to use "all necessary measures" to restore peace and security to the area.

President Bush claimed he could launch the military action without congressional authorization, but leaders of both parties argued that positive action by Congress would strengthen the president constitutionally and politically. A week before the U.N. deadline, Bush asked Congress to pass a resolution supporting the use of all necessary means to implement the U.N. decrees.

This request resulted in the first major post–Cold War debate between activist "hawks" and cautious "doves." In votes on 12 January 1991, both chambers approved House Joint Resolution 77, a statutory authorization of military action under the 1973 War Powers Resolution. The House vote was 250 to 183, the Senate's 52 to 47. Although the vote was described as a unique vote of conscience, in fact it closely resembled military authorization votes of the period in that it was basically partisan: nearly all Republicans voted to authorize the president to use force in the Gulf, whereas a sizable majority of Democrats (68 percent in the House, 82 percent in the Senate) voted against it. Moreover, the force resolution commanded stronger support from the South and Rocky Mountain West than from the East and Midwest. Members of both parties who were troubled over their votes may have agonized unduly because six months after the congressional vote, only one-fifth of the public could recall whether their senators or representatives had favored or opposed the use of force.

Why did Congress not simply declare war on Iraq, inasmuch as lawmakers fully understood they were authorizing a war? Conceding that the resolution was militarily the same as declaring war, Speaker Thomas S. Foley (D-Wash.) later explained that "there is some question about whether we wish to excite or enact some of the domestic consequences of a formal declaration of war—seizure of property, censorship, and so forth, which the president neither sought nor desired."

Four days after the congressional vote, President Bush informed the nation that a military operation (Desert Storm) would be launched. A swiftly passed, virtually unanimous resolution stated that Congress "commends and supports the efforts and leadership of the president in the Persian Gulf hostilities" and "unequivocally supports the men and women of our Armed Forces."

The operation that forced Iraqi troops out of Kuwait proved a triumph of logistics and weaponry: more than half a million U.S. troops were deployed to the region; more than two dozen nations provided troops or financial aid.

The Gulf War, however, left a mixed legacy. Strategically, it temporarily arrested the Iraqi threat to destabilize the region. In the United States it was a political triumph: President Bush's job ratings soared to new (if short-lived) heights; everyone associated with the operation was lionized, especially Generals Norman Schwarzkopf, the field commander, and Colin Powell, chairman of the Joint Chiefs of Staff. It demonstrated the effectiveness of the U.S. military, whose post-Vietnam reforms embraced diverse volunteer-based personnel and high-technology weapons.

However, Saddam Hussein remained in power in Iraq, and final assessments revealed that his military machine, while damaged, was by no means destroyed. (The cease-fire was prematurely declared because Bush and his commanders worried that mounting Iraqi civilian casualties would erode public and congressional support for the effort.) Moreover, the war left unresolved the conflicts between president and Congress over the "war powers." Although Congress gave eleventh-hour support to the war, the president contended that his powers as commander in chief made such approval unnecessary.

BIBLIOGRAPHY

Atkinson, Rick. *Crusade: The Untold Story of the Persian Gulf War.* 1993.

Cook, Rhodes, Ronald D. Elving, et al. "Even Votes of Conscience Follow Party Lines." *Congressional Quarterly Weekly Report*, 19 January 1991, pp. 190–195.

Smith, Jean Edward. *George Bush's War.* 1992.

ROGER H. DAVIDSON

PETITIONS AND MEMORIALS. The right of citizens to petition for the redress of grievances is guaranteed in the First Amendment. Subsumed within that right in the federal system is a presumed corollary that state and local governmental

PETITION OF SUSAN B. ANTHONY. First page. Fined for voting, Anthony petitioned Congress to remit the fine, which would have been tantamount to recognizing women's right to vote. The petition was referred to the Judiciary Committee, 22 January 1874. NATIONAL ARCHIVES

ANTIDISCRIMINATION PETITION. Third page. This 28 January 1886 petition from the citizens of the District of Columbia requests measures to combat discrimination against persons of color in places of public entertainment and leisure, such as lunchrooms. Among the first signers was Frederick Douglass.

NATIONAL ARCHIVES

units possess a comparable right to call for action by the federal Congress.

The right to petition can be traced as far back as the Magna Carta. It evolved under the Norman kings of England as a means by which individual citizens, groups of citizens, and towns requested certain benefits from the Crown. With the evolution of Parliament, petitioners directed their requests to members of Parliament to present to the king. The practice was translated in roughly comparable form into the political life of the American colonies, although not without some variations. For example, the Massachusetts General Court in the early 1700s refused to accept citizen petitions on the ground that its members ought to remain apart from citizen agitation; but ultimately, in Massachusetts and elsewhere, the right of petition was firmly established. The petitions received asked for a variety of actions: passage or defeat of a pending bill, payment as compensation for various alleged administrative or judicial wrongs, enactment of new legislation, and action to ameliorate certain policy shortcomings. To commemorate the bicentennial of the Constitution and the Bill of Rights, the Office of the House Historian has undertaken to catalog and publish more than one thousand extant petitions received by the House of Representatives during the early years of the federal Congress.

The receipt of citizen memorials was at its most

controversial during the Andrew Jackson era. The Constitution had specifically banned any congressional action to restrict the slave trade in the original thirteen states prior to 1808, but even before the designated year, Congress received petitions calling for the abolition of slavery and the regulation of the slave trade. In this relatively tranquil environment, petitions were referred to committee, where they simply were not acted on.

Antislavery and sectional sentiment grew apace, and in the wake of several failed slave uprisings in the South, the issue of antislavery petitions became a more sensitive one to southern members of Congress and their political supporters. In December 1835, Rep. William Jackson, a Massachusetts Whig, presented a petition calling for the abolition of slavery in the District of Columbia. Rep. James H.

CITIZENS' PETITION. Petitions can take on cumbersome form, such as this one from 1924 bearing thousands of names and rolled on a giant spool.   LIBRARY OF CONGRESS

Hammond (D-S.C.) moved that the petition not be received. Lengthy House debate ensued (the one-hour rule had not yet been adopted), and an initial compromise was reached when the House decided to refer the issue of petition receipt to a select committee.

In May 1836, the select committee reported and recommended a new House rule requiring that all slavery- or abolition-related petitions received by the House be neither printed nor referred to committee, but that they automatically be considered tabled. This gag rule existed in some form until 1844, with John Quincy Adams of Massachusetts devoting most of his remaining years in Congress to fighting the rule. Attempts were made in 1842 to censure Adams (then chairman of the Foreign Affairs Committee) for his attempt to bring before Congress a petition calling for study of British and American foreign policies as they were affected by Britain's announced policy banning the slave trade. The censure attempt failed but also radicalized pro- and anti-slavery factions in the Whig and Democratic parties; two years later, anti-slavery Whigs and Democrats united to end the gag rule.

By the twentieth century, petitions had ceased to be a major source of policy input, and many members of Congress came to view them as outdated relics of a simpler time. Memorials from state legislatures seemingly increased in importance, however. In the early nineteenth century, memorials had been the vehicle in which state legislatures sent instructions to senators. Memorials from state legislatures were also instrumental in pressuring the Senate to act on the constitutional amendment providing for popular election of senators, and later, for unsuccessful attempts by the state legislatures to petition for the calling of a new constitutional convention.

BIBLIOGRAPHY

Higginson, Stephen. "A Short History of the Right to Petition Government for the Redress of Grievances." *Yale Law Journal* 96 (November 1986): 142–166.

Luce, Robert. *Legislative Principles.* 1930. Repr. 1971.

Parsons, Lynn. "Censuring Old Man Eloquent: Foreign Policy and Disunion, 1842." *Capitol Studies* 3 (Fall 1975): 89–106.

U.S. House of Representatives. *Cannon's Precedents of the House of Representatives of the United States*, by Clarence Cannon. 74th Cong., 1st sess., 1935. Vol. 7, chap. 217.

U.S. House of Representatives. *Hind's Precedents of the House of Representatives of the United States*, by Asher C. Hinds. 59th Cong., 2d sess., 1907. Vol. 4, chap. 40.

PAUL S. RUNDQUIST

PHILIPPINES. From 1898 to 1945, congressional policy toward the Philippines reflected a split between Republican members who wanted to fulfill the duties of empire and Democratic members anxious to protect constituencies injured by Filipino goods and labor. The executive branch in fact determined most aspects of Philippine policy, but Congress intervened at key junctures to establish a colonial government, to set trade policy, and to fix a timetable for independence. After 1945 members of both parties supported legislation establishing a neocolonial partnership under which the United States conferred trade advantages in return for military bases.

Under the terms of the 1899 Treaty of Paris, which ended the Spanish-American War, the United States purchased the Philippine Islands for $20 million. The question of whether, and on what terms, the Philippines should be annexed dominated the ratification debate in the Senate. The two Massachusetts senators, Theodore Roosevelt's friend Henry Cabot Lodge and the older George F. Hoar, both Republicans, took opposite sides in the debate, Lodge arguing for empire, Hoar advocating self-rule. Lodge fended off amendments pledging eventual independence, and assembled sufficient votes after what he called "the hardest, closest fight I have ever known." The Senate ratified the treaty on 6 February 1899.

Under Lodge's leadership the Senate Committee on the Philippine Islands enthusiastically drafted colonial legislation, but Congress as a whole remained ambivalent toward the Philippine venture. In the Organic Act of 1902, Congress established a government around the five-man commission dispatched earlier by President William McKinley. It provided for a popular assembly and for the appointment of two Filipino resident commissioners, who could speak but not vote in the U.S. House of Representatives. Congress, however, was anxious to prevent the exploitation of the Philippines by U.S. colonists and capital, and so placed strict limits on the amount of property and mineral claims that could be purchased by Americans. After 1902 Lodge pushed through a series of bills to liberalize Philippine-U.S. trade, culminating in the Payne-Aldrich Tariff of 1909, which allowed virtually unimpeded trade between the United States and the islands. Democrats opposed each of these measures on behalf of their agricultural and labor constituencies and obtained a modest victory in 1916 with the passage of the Jones Act, which pledged eventual independence (and the end of free trade) for the Philippines.

Legislation Affecting the Philippines

Title	Year Enacted	Reference Number	Description
Philippine Organic Act (Philippine Government Act)	1902	P.L. 57-235	Created a popularly elected assembly to legislate for the Philippines under the supervision of the Philippine Commission.
Philippine Tariff (Payne-Aldrich Tariff)	1909	P.L. 61-7	Provided for free trade between the Philippines and the United States.
Jones Act (Organic Act of the Philippine Islands)	1916	P.L. 64-240	Created a bicameral legislature and pledged the United States to grant independence once a stable government had been established.
Tydings-McDuffie Philippine Independence Act	1934	P.L. 73-127	Established a timetable leading to independence on 4 July 1946. Called for a constitutional convention, a self-governing commonwealth, and the end of free trade.
Philippine Rehabilitation Act	1946	P.L. 79-370	Provided $625 million in services and $400 million in direct payments for war damages.
Philippine Trade Act (Bell Trade Act)	1946	P.L. 79-371	In recognition of wartime sacrifices and the postwar military alliance, provided for eight years of free trade, followed by the gradual liquidation of tariffs over seventeen years.
Philippine Trade Agreement Amendments Act of 1946 (Laurel-Langley Agreement)	1955	P.L. 84-196	Extended the period in which Philippine goods could enter the United States free of duty, while allowing the Philippines to impose duties on U.S. goods.

When Democrats achieved majorities in both houses at the beginning of the 73d Congress in 1933, a coalition of interests seized the chance to press for Philippine independence. U.S. beet-sugar interests led this lobby, with help from the National City Bank of New York and other banks with investments in Cuban sugar. The American Federation of Labor, which opposed Filipino immigration, joined the lobby, as did societies with nativistic leanings such as the American Legion. In January 1933, Congress approved legislation by Sen. Harry B. Hawes (D-Mo.) establishing a ten-year timetable through which the Filipinos would draft a constitution, establish a self-governing commonwealth, and gradually lose their preferential tariff treatment. Meanwhile, U.S. exporters would continue to have duty-free access to the Philippine market. The act permitted the United States to retain naval stations, but paradoxically obliged the U.S. president to seek the "perpetual neutralization" of the islands.

President Herbert Hoover vetoed the bill, but Congress overrode the veto by a substantial majority. The legislation, however, required the approval of the Philippine assembly, which, mobilized by Philippine Senate leader Manuel L. Quezon, voted it down, principally because the act had been negotiated by Quezon's rival, Sergio Osmeña. Quezon himself then traveled to Washington to negotiate a nearly identical bill sponsored by Sen. Millard E. Tydings (D-Md.) and Rep. John McDuffie (D-Ala.).

The Japanese occupation of the Philippines in 1942 interrupted the timetable set by the Tydings-McDuffie Act. Moreover, the War Department's plans for postwar bases in the Philippines required legislation to assure that the islands did not fall into the economic orbit of Japan or the Soviet Union. In 1945, with encouragement from the Interior and War departments, Rep. C. Jasper Bell (D-Mo.) introduced legislation extending colonial tariff preferences for an addition eight years and then phasing them out over two decades. Bell pushed the legislation as a means of rehabilitating the Philippines through American investment, and he added a clause granting U.S. investors special privileges in the Philippines. The extent of war damage in the islands led Tydings to propose an additional Rehabilitation Act, which provided over $1 billion in services and payments to individuals.

The Bell Trade Act and the Tydings Rehabilitation Act served as the chief instruments for U.S. aid to the Philippines during the early years of the Cold War. In 1955, shortly after the Philippines renewed its alliance through the Southeast Asia Treaty Organization (SEATO) pact, Congress extended tariff preferences for another five years. The Revised Trade Act expired in 1973, but Congress continued to grant special preferences for Philippine goods until the United States began to withdraw from its Philippine bases in 1991.

BIBLIOGRAPHY

Cullather, Nick. *Illusions of Influence: The Political Economy of United States–Philippines Relations, 1941–1960.* 1993.

Friend, Theodore. *Between Two Empires: The Ordeal of the Philippines.* 1965.

Stanley, Peter W. *A Nation in the Making: The Philippines and the United States, 1899–1921.* 1974.

NICK CULLATHER

PICKERING, TIMOTHY (1745–1829), Federalist senator and representative from Massachusetts, secretary of State in the administrations of George Washington and John Adams. Pickering came to Washington in 1803 to finish the unexpired Senate term of Dwight Foster. Unreconciled to the Jeffersonian ascendancy, he soon gained a reputation for rudeness and intolerance; he was seldom appointed to committees and never chosen for important ones. Convinced that the Jeffersonians had formed a conspiracy to perpetuate their power indefinitely, Pickering hatched a plot to take New England and New York out of the Union. His secessionist plans, which reemerged periodically, went nowhere, however, for such drastic action had insufficient popular support.

During the crisis preceding the War of 1812 Pickering was unwaveringly pro-British. He defended the attack by H.M.S. *Leopard* on the U.S.S. *Chesapeake* and denounced Thomas Jefferson's embargo as part of a conspiracy between Jefferson and Napoleon Bonaparte to increase the economic pressure then being brought to bear on England by the French. In 1811 Pickering was denied another term in the Senate by a Massachusetts legislature controlled by the Jeffersonian Republicans. But from a seat in the House, to which he was elected in 1812, he did everything in his power to obstruct the war effort. He once again urged secession, and he longed to see the British attack on New Orleans succeed, hoping this would lead to the fragmentation of the Union.

In 1816 Pickering's record of obstructionism, his vote against the tariff of 1816, and his support for an unpopular congressional salary increase finally caught up with him. He was denied renomination to his House seat and sent into permanent retirement.

BIBLIOGRAPHY

Clarfield, Gerard. *Timothy Pickering and American Diplomacy, 1795–1800.* 1969.

Clarfield, Gerard. *Timothy Pickering and the American Republic.* 1980.

Upham, Charles W. *The Life of Timothy Pickering.* 4 vols. 1867–1873.

GERARD H. CLARFIELD

TIMOTHY PICKERING. Engraving by T. B. Welch from a drawing by J. B. Longacre after Gilbert Stuart.

LIBRARY OF CONGRESS

PIERCE, FRANKLIN (1804–1869), Democratic representative and senator from New Hampshire, fourteenth president of the United States (1853–1857). Pierce was born in Hillsboro, New Hampshire, into a wealthy and politically prominent family. He graduated from Bowdoin College in 1824 and later married Jane Appleton, the daughter of the college's president. He studied law, served in the New Hampshire legislature (1829–1833), and became speaker of the New Hampshire house of representatives. After two terms in the U.S. House (1833–1837), he was elected to the U.S. Senate. His wife hated politics, blaming it for his heavy drinking, and persuaded him to resign from the Senate in 1842. Pierce's congressional career was marked by loyalty to orthodox Democratic party principles, which usually coincided with the interests of the South. At one point he stated that not one person

FRANKLIN PIERCE.   LIBRARY OF CONGRESS

demned abolitionists and Free-Soilers for showing greater concern for the rights of Africans than for the constitutional rights of southern slaveholders.

Pierce's prosouthern attitudes and the strong influence of Jefferson Davis, his secretary of War, led him to offer concessions to the South. Most of Pierce's choice diplomatic appointments went to southerners or southern sympathizers. Pierce vetoed bills for internal improvements in the North, but signed bills providing improvements to rivers in North Carolina and Georgia. Pierce and Davis set aside twenty million acres of public land to subsidize a transcontinental railroad, and to make a southern route more feasible they engineered the Gadsden Purchase, buying 45,535 square miles of land from Mexico. Most important, Pierce was persuaded by Davis and Sen. Stephen A. Douglas (D-Ill.) to use every possible administration pressure to secure passage of the Kansas-Nebraska Act. The act repealed the Missouri Compromise, which had kept a vast area free from slavery since its enactment in 1820. Then, when Kansans created two governments, one proslavery and one free, Pierce recognized the proslavery government, and this triggered violence in Kansas and rage throughout the North. All these actions served to coalesce northern Whigs, Free-Soilers, and antislavery Democrats into the new Republican party.

On the positive side, Pierce's cabinet members managed their departments honestly, his administration expanded and tried to reform the army and navy, and an examination system was established for seven hundred federal jobs. The administration completed the opening of Japan to the west, an effort that had been initiated by President Millard Fillmore.

By 1856 sectional conflict had become so intense that Pierce stood no chance for renomination. He returned to New Hampshire after the end of his term. The 1860 election of Republican Abraham Lincoln filled him with despair, but he was incapable of recognizing his own role in helping to make it possible. He blamed the Civil War entirely on northern fanaticism, and he was (falsely) accused of membership in a secret pro-Confederate organization. He died in 1869.

in five hundred in New Hampshire sympathized with the abolitionists.

Pierce served as a brigadier general during the Mexican War. Apparently because of his alcoholism and his wife's poor health, Pierce declined appointment as attorney general by President James K. Polk, and in 1848 he refused both a senatorial appointment and a nomination for the New Hampshire governorship. In 1852 a deadlocked Democratic convention nominated him for president on the forty-ninth ballot. Although Pierce had wide appeal, his election to the presidency also resulted from the poor judgment of the opposing Whigs in nominating Gen. Winfield Scott, whose identification with the antislavery New York senator William H. Seward made him anathema to the South.

As president, Pierce personified the coalition between northern businessmen and southern planters. He had no moral objections to slavery and con-

BIBLIOGRAPHY

Gara, Larry. *The Presidency of Franklin Pierce.* 1991.
Hawthorne, Nathaniel. *Life of Franklin Pierce.* 1852. Repr. 1972.
Nichols, Roy F. *Franklin Pierce: Young Hickory of the Granite Hills.* 1931. Repr. 1938.

ELBERT B. SMITH

PITTMAN, KEY (1872–1940), Democratic senator from Nevada (1913–1940), chairman of the Senate Foreign Relations Committee (1933–1940), president pro tempore of the Senate (1933–1940). A loyal Democrat, Pittman supported President Woodrow Wilson's domestic, rearmament, and foreign policies and attempted to secure compromises that would bring the United States into the League of Nations. In the 1920s Pittman's legislative initiatives were confined to matters of most concern to his Nevada constituents—that is, the support of silver prices, the conservation of timber and mineral resources, and the protection of Nevada's water and power rights in the Boulder Dam project. On foreign policy matters, he took a moderate internationalist position. Within the Democratic party, he sought unity through his effort to secure compromise platforms and candidates at the nominating conventions in 1924, 1928, and 1932.

With the Democratic electoral landslide in 1932, Pittman became president pro tempore of the Senate. A member of the "inner club," he was a master of parliamentary procedure and legislative detail,

KEY PITTMAN.   LIBRARY OF CONGRESS

working behind the scenes to build coalitions for his program. His major initiatives included supports for the price of silver at the London Monetary Conference of 1933 and in the Silver Purchase acts of 1934 and 1939. He supported President Franklin D. Roosevelt's major New Deal legislation. In 1937, as presiding officer of the Senate, he backed the president's judiciary reorganization bill, resurrecting an obscure rule to limit debate.

As chairman of the Senate Foreign Relations Committee, Pittman worked with the administration on foreign policy issues. Most important were the U.S. neutrality laws passed in 1935–1937. The reasons for the failure to revise this legislation early in 1939 were complex. At Pittman's initiative the strategy agreed upon was the extension of the cash and carry formula of the 1937 bill to include arms and munitions as well as oil and steel, thus permitting, under guise of impartiality, the sale of arms to allies. Other senior internationalists on the committee, however, were preoccupied with domestic affairs, while the ultraisolationists on the committee, led by William E. Borah and Hiram W. Johnson, were intransigent. It was not until the Nazi invasion of Poland in September 1939 that Pittman was able to secure the revisions that would permit the shipment of arms to the Allies.

On Far Eastern issues Pittman thought in terms of balance of power. Beginning in 1936, he publicly warned of Japan's imperial ambitions, condemned its aggressive acts vis-à-vis China, and urged U.S. naval rearmament in the Pacific in response. As early as 1937, he urged an embargo on materials necessary to a Japanese war economy. The State Department finally embraced his suggestions that economic sanctions be used against Japan in the fall of 1940.

A brilliant and politically sophisticated man, Pittman was in some sense a tragic figure. A drinking problem that had been mild and sporadic in the 1920s gradually intensified in the 1930s, ultimately interfering with his work and undermining his credibility. These problems were due in part, to the stress he faced as chairman of the Senate Foreign Relations Committee. New foreign policies had to be devised within a very divided committee, often without clear guidance from the president or the secretary of State. Pittman was reelected to the U.S. Senate in 1940 and died five days later. His friend, Breckinridge Long, confided in his diary at the time, "The Senate has lost its ablest member. He had one of the keenest intellects and was one of the most resourceful men I have ever known."

BIBLIOGRAPHY

Glad, Betty. *Key Pittman: The Tragedy of a Senate Insider.* 1986.

Israel, Fred. *Nevada's Key Pittman.* 1963.

BETTY GLAD

PLATT, ORVILLE H.

PLATT, ORVILLE H. (1827–1905), senator from Connecticut and influential member of the Republican party in the last quarter of the nineteenth century. Platt was one of "The Four" with Nelson W. Aldrich, William B. Allison, and John C. Spooner, who set Republican policy in the Senate in the 1880s and 1890s.

Platt entered Connecticut politics in the 1850s, first as a Know-Nothing and then as a Republican. He became a member of the state House of Representatives in 1864 and its Speaker in 1869. When Republican lawmakers were deadlocked in their senatorial caucus of 1879, they selected Platt, then a state's attorney in New Haven, as a compromise choice.

Platt did not speak often in debate, but when he did, his speeches commanded respect. He rapidly established himself as an effective lawmaker, chairing the Patents Committee (on which he advocated international copyright laws), the Committee on Territories, and the Judiciary Committee. He played a significant role in shaping both the McKinley Tariff Act (1890) and the Dingley Tariff Act (1897).

When war with Spain threatened in 1898, Platt became a congressional spokesman for the McKinley administration. He advocated the annexation of Hawaii and the Philippines. Early in 1901, the president asked him to frame legislation that would allow U.S. intervention to preserve Cuba's independence and stability once occupation of that island ended. The result was the Platt amendment to the army appropriation bill of 1901. It barred Cuba from treaty alliances with foreign powers, limited its capacity to go into debt internationally, and allowed the United States to intervene "for the preservation of Cuban independence and the maintenance of a stable government." The amendment outlived its usefulness and was a major grievance in Cuban-U.S. relations until Franklin D. Roosevelt abrogated it in 1933.

Platt supported Theodore Roosevelt when he became president in September 1901 and was personally close to the young chief executive. He assured fellow conservatives that Roosevelt's policies posed

ORVILLE H. PLATT.   LIBRARY OF CONGRESS

no danger to business. The president consulted with him on tariff policy, and Platt reportedly advised him to make "few and moderate" changes after the 1904 election. In the spring of 1905, Platt contracted pneumonia, which led to his death. A strong conservative who disliked government regulation, Platt played a key role in most of the important economic legislation of his time and was a significant voice in the congressional response to the Spanish-American War and its imperial consequences. The Platt amendment was his most lasting achievement as a lawmaker.

BIBLIOGRAPHY

Coolidge, Louis A. *An Old Fashioned Senator: Orville H. Platt of Connecticut.* 1910.

Smith, Edwina Carol. "Conservatism in the Gilded Age: The Senatorial Career of Orville H. Platt." Ph.D. diss., University of North Carolina, 1976.

LEWIS L. GOULD

PLATT AMENDMENT

PLATT AMENDMENT (1901; 31 Stat. 897–898). The Platt Amendment served as the principal legal instrument of U.S. hegemony in Cuba from 1902 to 1934. The State Department, eager to end the U.S. Army's occupation of Cuba but unwilling to grant autonomy to the Cubans, proposed legislation in early 1901 permitting Cuba to form a government, provided its constitution contained an "ordinance" defining the country's relations to the United States. The Cuban government would promise to incur no additional external debts, to avoid alliances with foreign powers, to maintain laws enacted under the occupation, to lease naval stations to the United States, and to grant the United States "the right to intervene for the preservation of Cuban independence, the maintenance of a government for the protection of life, property, and individual liberty," or to enforce debts already incurred.

Introduced on 25 February 1901 by Sen. Orville H. Platt (R-Conn.) as a rider on the army appropriations bill of 1902, the legislation aroused the opposition of anti-imperialists like Sen. Joseph B. Foraker (D-Ohio), who foresaw that it would encourage Cuban oppositionists to create disturbances in order to provoke U.S. intervention. A generous rivers and harbors bill soothed Democratic opposition enough to prevent a filibuster. The amendment passed on party-line votes in the House and Senate and was signed into law by President William McKinley on 2 March and confirmed by subsequent agreement with Cuba. President Theodore Roosevelt used the amendment to justify the reoccupation of Cuba in October 1906. It was finally overturned by a Treaty of General Relations signed on 29 May 1934.

BIBLIOGRAPHY

Millett, Allan Reed. *The Politics of Intervention: The Military Occupation of Cuba, 1906–1909.* 1968.
Pérez, Louis A. *Cuba under the Platt Amendment, 1902–1934.* 1986.

NICK CULLATHER

POINTS OF ORDER

POINTS OF ORDER. A point of order is a claim from the floor by a member that a pending action violates a chamber rule or is procedurally improper in a specified way. Generally, the chair must entertain the point, at least if the member may be recognized, but no point of order may be raised against certain decisions of the chair or after the challenged action has been completed. The chair rules on the point of order (nowadays, on the basis of consultation with the parliamentarian); if the point is sustained, the proposed action is prohibited. Any debate on the point occurs for the information of the chair, who therefore controls it; under cloture in the Senate, no debate is permitted.

Any member may appeal the chair's ruling. The appeal is a debatable question, decided by vote; it may be viewed as an exercise of the body's constitutional power to say what its rules are. Rulings on points of order make precedents; those by the full body are held to be the most authoritative. Only the chamber, and not the chair, may decide a point of order raised on constitutional grounds.

In the House today, appeals are rare and reversals of the chair virtually unheard of, although before about 1930 the House seems to have addressed such questions more freely. The full Senate often settles points of order not only on appeal, but also by tabling, by waiving, by practices requiring it to do so, and, seldom nowadays, by suspending the rules. Some of these actions are available only on specific points of order, and some require a three-fifths or two-thirds majority.

In both chambers, points of order are frequently directed against amendments; perhaps the most common point raised is that an amendment to an appropriations bill constitutes legislation. In the House a point of order on an amendment must be raised (or reserved) before debate on the amendment begins.

[*See also* Amending.]

BIBLIOGRAPHY

U.S. House of Representatives. *Procedure in the United States House of Representatives,* by Lewis Deschler and William Holmes Brown. 4th ed. 97th Cong., 2d sess., 1982. Chap. 31, secs. 1–8, "Points of Order."
U.S. Senate. *Riddick's Senate Procedure, Precedents, and Practices,* by Floyd M. Riddick and Alan S. Frumin. 101st Cong., 2d sess., 1992. S. Doc. 101-28. Pp. 987–996.

RICHARD S. BETH

POLICE

POLICE. *For discussion of the security forces on Capitol Hill, see* Capitol Police.

POLITICAL ACTION COMMITTEES (PACS)

POLITICAL ACTION COMMITTEES (PACS). Political action committees, or PACs, as they are commonly known, are nonparty political committees that make campaign contributions to candidates for federal offices, particularly candidates for Congress. To qualify as a PAC under current law, a committee must receive contributions from more than fifty individuals and make campaign contributions to at least five candidates for federal office. Some PACs are formed by corporations, labor unions, and trade, membership, and health associations to complement the lobbying activities of their parent organizations, while other PACs are unaffiliated and are formed solely for the purpose of making campaign contributions. A political action committee may contribute up to $5,000 per election to an individual candidate, $15,000 per calendar year to a national party committee, and $5,000 per calendar year to any other political committee. There is no aggregate limit on the amount of money a PAC can contribute to different candidates and parties or to other PACs.

History. The first political action committee, CIO-PAC, was formed in 1943 by the Congress of Industrial Organizations. In 1955, when the CIO merged with the American Federation of Labor to become the AFL-CIO, CIO-PAC and the AFL's PAC, the League for Political Education, merged to form COPE, the Committee on Political Education. Individual unions followed suit, forming their own PACs. Although two large business-oriented PACs, BIPAC (the Business-Industry PAC) and AMPAC (the American Medical Association PAC), were formed in the 1960s, PACs were primarily a vehicle of labor unions until the mid 1970s. Business interests were more often voiced through campaign contributions from individuals with corporate ties.

In the early 1970s, a case making its way through the court system was threatening to destroy labor unions' use of political action committees. Because the Taft-Hartley Labor-Management Relations Act of 1947 prohibited labor unions from using members' dues to make campaign contributions to candidates for federal office, PAC activity had to be financed by voluntary contributions by union members. In 1968 the Justice Department had accused a local pipefitters' union PAC in St. Louis, Missouri, of coercing union members to contribute to the PAC and of using union dues to administer the PAC. The AFL-CIO feared that when the *Pipefitters* case (*Pipefitters Local Union No. 562 v. United States*, 434 F. 2d 1127, 8th Cir. [1970]) reached the Supreme Court, it would declare the organization and administration of political action committees in violation of the Taft-Hartley Act and thus illegal.

To protect PACs from an adverse Supreme Court decision the AFL-CIO drafted an amendment to the campaign finance reform legislation, the Federal Election Campaign Act (FECA) being considered by Congress in 1971. The amendment, which was passed by Congress, codified what had been the practice of political action committees since their inception by permitting corporations and labor unions to use corporate and union treasury funds for the "establishment, administration and solicitation of voluntary contributions to a separate segregated fund to be utilized for political purposes" (18 U.S.C. 610 [1972]).

The role of PACs in congressional campaigns remained more or less the same following the passage of FECA in 1972. But in 1974, when FECA was amended to place limits on campaign contributions from individuals, PACs, and parties, the role of PACs in congressional campaigns began to change. Before 1974 no limits were placed on the amount of money individuals and PACs could contribute to congressional candidates. By limiting the amount of money an individual could give to a candidate to $1,000 per election, the 1974 FECA amendments drastically curtailed the amount of money individuals—particularly wealthy individuals—could contribute to political campaigns. Because most business-related campaign contributions had come from individuals, the traditional avenue for business contributions was sharply restricted. As a result, corporations and trade associations began to form PACs. Between 1974 and 1976 the number of corporate PACs registered with the Federal Election Commission (FEC) increased fivefold, from 89 to 433. During the 1970s and early 1980s the number of PACs active in congressional elections continued to grow; by the mid-1980s more than four thousand political action committees were registered with the FEC.

The commission groups PACs into four major categories: corporate; labor; trade, membership, and health; and nonconnected. (Two other categories, cooperatives and corporations without stock, together comprise fewer than three hundred PACs). As of 1992 there were approximately two thousand corporate PACs; thirteen hundred nonconnected PACs; eight hundred trade, membership, and health PACs; and just under four hundred labor PACs.

Just as the number of PACs increased dramatically in the decade following their statutory recognition, so did the amount of money contributed to congressional candidates by PACs. PAC contributions increased from $12.5 million in 1974 to $188.7 million in 1992. The burgeoning number of PACs and the skyrocketing amount of money con-

Figure 1
Growth in Number of Political Action Committees, 1974–1994

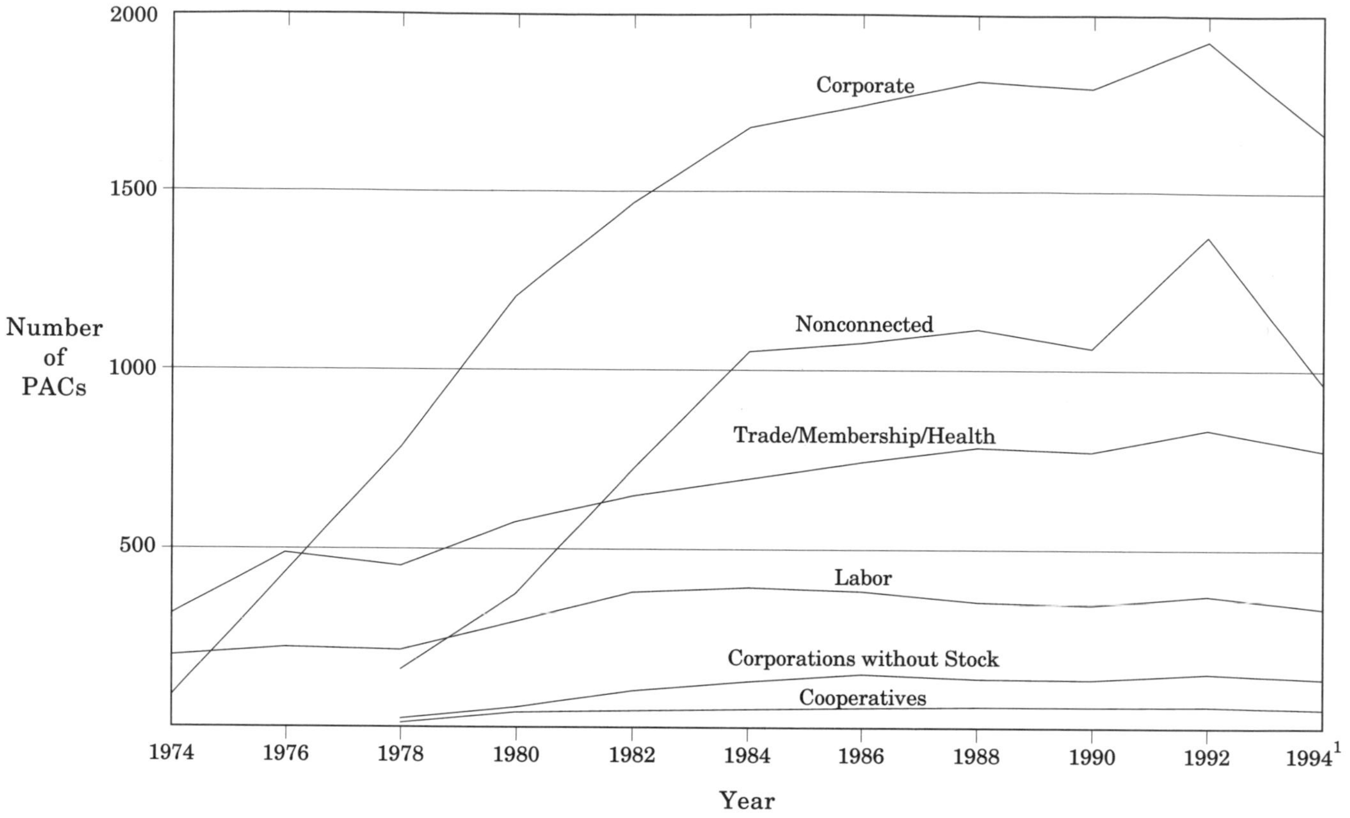

TABLE 1. *Growth in Political Action Committees, 1974–1994*

TYPE OF PAC	1974	1976	1978	1980	1982	1984	1986	1988	1990	1992	1994[1]
Corporate	89	433	785	1,206	1,469	1,682	1,744	1,816	1,795	1,930	1,666
Labor	201	224	217	297	380	394	384	354	346	372	336
Trade/ Membership/ Health	318	489	453	576	649	698	745	786	774	836	777
Nonconnected	NA	NA	162	374	723	1,053	1,077	1,115	1,062	1,377	963
Cooperatives	NA	NA	12	42	47	52	56	59	59	61	53
Corporations without Stock	NA	NA	24	56	103	130	151	138	136	153	138
Totals	608	1,146	1,653	2,551	3,371	4,009	4,157	4,268	4,172	4,729	3,933

[1]End-of-year figures are given for the years 1974 to 1992. Figures as of July 15 are given for 1994.

SOURCE: Federal Election Commission.

tributed by PACs raised questions about the role of PACs and, more generally, of organized (or "special") interests in congressional elections and congressional policy-making.

Contribution Patterns. As PACs became an important component of congressional campaign fi-

nancing it became clear that there were patterns to PAC contributions. Most PAC contributions went to incumbents; in 1992 PACs contributed two and a half times as much money to incumbents as to challengers and open-seat candidates combined. House incumbents were more dependent on PAC contributions than were Senate incumbents; almost half of all House incumbents' campaign contributions came from PACs, as against about one-fourth of Senate incumbents' campaign contributions. House Democratic incumbents received more than half their campaign contributions from PACs.

Different types of PACs also exhibit patterns in making campaign contributions. Labor PACs overwhelmingly give to Democrats: more than 90 percent of organized labor's PAC contributions go to Democratic candidates. Corporate PACs and trade, membership, and health association PACs divide their contributions more evenly between Democrats and Republicans. While most Republicans are philosophically closer to business and trade interests, the equitability of these PACs' contributions arose from the fact that, at least in the House, Democrats were in the majority during the first two decades of significant PAC activity.

PACs make contributions to congressional candidates both to influence the outcomes of congressional elections and to influence congressional policy making. By helping to elect candidates whose partisan and ideological interests are similar to its interests, a PAC seeks to elect a Congress that is sympathetic to the PAC's point of view. Campaign contributions can also help a PAC gain access to a member of Congress after an election, enabling the PAC to present its views on legislation of importance to the PAC or to the PAC's parent body.

Virtue or Vice? As PACs have proliferated and their campaign contributions have boomed, so have questions about the effect of PAC contributions on congressional policy making. Some applaud the growth in PACs as creating an opportunity for individual citizens, through small contributions to a PAC, to gain a collective influence over congressional decision making that they would not otherwise have. Others argue that PACs are vehicles enabling special interests to influence congressional debate unduly and, some suggest, even to determine the outcome of congressional voting.

Political scientists have done considerable research into the effects of PAC contributions on roll-call voting in the House and Senate. Some of these studies have found instances in which campaign contributions have appeared to have had an impact on voting, while other studies have found that other voting cues—such as party, ideology, or constituent interests—are more important influences on congressional voting.

Campaign Finance Reform. The debate over the role of PAC contributions in congressional decision making is reflected in the campaign finance reform proposals considered by the Congress in the late 1980s and early 1990s. Many of the bills introduced contained proposals to restrict PACs' operations or, in some cases, even to abolish political action committees. Those who believed too much special-interest money was being contributed to congressional campaigns were sufficiently active in promoting their anti-PAC view that many members of Congress began to feel that any legislation aimed at reforming the financing of congressional elections had to address the role of political action committees. Reform proposals either reduced the amount of money a PAC could contribute to a candidate in an election—from $5,000 per election to $3,000, for example, or $2,500, or $1,000—or prohibited congressional candidates from accepting PAC contributions.

Given the dependence of many members of Congress, particularly House Democrats, on PAC contributions, support for restricting PAC contributions was halfhearted at best. PACs were an easy target for proponents of campaign finance reform, but further restricting or prohibiting PAC contributions to congressional candidates would address only one aspect of congressional campaign finance practices.

Special interests have played a role in congressional elections since the earliest days of the United States. What did change in the decades following the passage of the Federal Election Campaign Act of 1972 was that, through a combination of restrictions on individual contributions and compulsory disclosure of all contributions, the amount of money contributed by special interests to members of Congress was now documented. Further limiting or prohibiting PAC contributions may cause some smaller PACs to stop operating, but larger PACs and organized interest groups will continue to play a role in congressional elections.

BIBLIOGRAPHY

Magleby, David B., and Candice J. Nelson. *The Money Chase: Congressional Campaign Finance Reform.* 1990.
Sabato, Larry J. *PAC Power: Inside the World of Political Action Committees.* 1984.
Sorauf, Frank. *Money in American Elections.* 1988.

CANDICE J. NELSON

POLITICAL DYNASTIES. Of the eleven thousand people to have served in Congress, 17 percent, or nearly one in five, have been related by blood or marriage. Most of these congressional families are of the two-person variety—father and

KENNEDY BROTHERS. *Left to right*, Attorney General Robert F. Kennedy, Sen. Edward M. Kennedy (D-Mass.), and President John F. Kennedy, 28 August 1963.

JOHN F. KENNEDY LIBRARY

son (such as Senators Albert A. Gore, Sr. and Jr., of Tennessee), father and daughter (Representatives Thomas D'Alesandro, Jr., of Maryland, and Nancy Pelosi, of California), husband and wife (Rep. Clyde H. Smith and Sen. Margaret Chase Smith, of Maine), or brothers (Rep. Sander M. Levin and Sen. Carl Levin, Michigan). But thirty families have contributed four or more members to the national legislature since the First Congress convened in 1789. There has been a Hamilton Fish in Congress from New York for four generations, starting in 1843; Delaware was represented in the Senate by two James A. Bayards, two Thomas F. Bayards, and a Richard H. Bayard between 1804 and 1929.

These are America's congressional dynasties and the states that sent them to Congress: Ashe (North Carolina, Tennessee), Bankhead (Alabama), Barbour (Virginia), Bayard (Delaware), Bell (New Hampshire), Breckinridge (Virginia, Kentucky), Byron (Maryland), Clark (Virginia, Kentucky, Missouri), Darlington (Pennsylvania), Fish (New York), Frelinghuysen (New Jersey), Harrison (Virginia, Ohio, Illinois, Indiana, Wyoming), Hawes (Virginia, Kentucky, Missouri), Hiester (Pennsylvania, Maryland), Hoar (Massachusetts), Johnson (Kentucky, Arkansas), Kennedy (Massachusetts, New York), King (New York, Massachusetts, New Jersey), Kitchin (North Carolina), Lee (Virginia, Maryland), Long (Louisiana), Marshall (Kentucky, Virginia), Muhlenberg (Pennsylvania, Ohio), Preston (Virginia, South Carolina, Kentucky), Roosevelt (New York), Tucker (South Carolina, Virginia), Washburn (Maine, Illinois, Wisconsin, Minnesota), Whittlesey (Ohio, New York, Connecticut), Williams (North Carolina, Tennessee), and Wise (Virginia). The record for most legislators from a single family, if one includes service in the Continental Congress, is held by the Lees—nine.

Since members of prominent families have a way of marrying each other, there are many more congressional dynasties when in-laws and collateral relations are counted. Sen. Claiborne Pell (D-R.I.) is only the second Pell in Congress, but he can claim three congressional Claibornes as ancestors; Sen. John D. Rockefeller IV (D-W.Va.), the first Rockefeller in the Senate, is related to the Aldrich family, which numbered three members of Congress, and his wife is the daughter of Sen. Charles H. Percy (R-Ill.). (Some of the other great political families, such as the Adamses, La Follettes, Lodges, and Tafts, did not produce four members of Congress. Alphonso Taft was Secretary of War and Attorney General; his son, William Howard, was president and chief justice of the United States. Neither served in Congress; three other Tafts, however, did.)

The early American dynasties tended to be English in origin, Protestant, and of the landed gentry, although there were some notable exceptions: the Carrolls of Maryland, of whom three served in the Continental Congress, were Catholics, and the Muhlenbergs, who sent six of their number to Congress, were initially impecunious German ministers. The second source of dynastic wealth, after landholding, was advantageous marriage. While the immensely rich, such as the Astors and Vanderbilts, steered clear of elective office, they were not averse to having their daughters marry politicians. Over time, dynasties moved into the professions, particularly law, which, of course, has a special connection with the business of lawmaking. The Tuckers, a family that included five members of Congress, were actually more distinguished for being legal scholars.

Although the dynasties are disproportionately found in the older states, especially the original thirteen, these families have been more footloose than might be expected of folks who need not seek greener pastures. The Harrisons of Virginia's upper crust kept moving west—to Ohio, then Indiana, Illinois, and Wyoming—electing two presidents along the way.

The phenomenon of an electorate in a democracy freely choosing a political nobility—the Constitution states, "No Title of Nobility shall be granted by the United States" (Art. I, sec. 9)—might appear anomalous. Partly it is a matter of supply and demand: these families have so often and with such determination sought public office, and with each step up the ladder it becomes easier for the succeeding generation (although some dynasties have borne a heavy emotional burden as well). As politics becomes the family business, its surname is turned into a brand name. If consumers like the product, they will come back for more. So the success of dynasties often reflects the talents of the dynasts—Richard Henry Lee, John C. Breckinridge, Robert A. Taft, and John F. Kennedy, among others.

Eventually some of the early dynasties stopped running for office. This often corresponded with a declining birthrate. There has not been a Lee in Congress since Blair Lee (of the Maryland branch) left the Senate in 1917; the last Lee of Virginia left the House of Representatives in 1891. But other families, some with remarkably different characteristics, have sprung up to take their places.

Huey P. Long, elected to the Senate in 1932, came from the poor hill country of north-central Louisiana. In 1985, when Cathy Long was elected to the House of Representatives to succeed her late husband, Gillis, she became the seventh Long of Louisiana to sit in Congress. Huey was succeeded by his wife, Rose, and subsequently their son Russell also made it to the upper chamber, thus becoming the only senator in history to be preceded in the Senate by his father and mother.

In Massachusetts in 1848, about ten years before the first Long arrived in Louisiana, Patrick Kennedy immigrated from Ireland. He worked in Boston making whiskey barrels. Of his descendants, three great-grandsons would sit in the U.S. Senate—John, Robert, and Edward (Ted)—and Robert's son Joe would hold the House seat that had once belonged to his uncle Jack, the president.

The rise of the Longs and the Kennedys together with the decline of such once powerful families as the Adamses and Bayards suggests the fluidity of the America's political aristocracy.

BIBLIOGRAPHY

Hendrick, Burton J. *The Lees of Virginia.* 1935.
Hess, Stephen. *America's Political Dynasties.* 1966.
Martin, Thomas. *Dynasty: The Longs of Louisiana.* 1960.
Ross, Ishbel. *An American Family: The Tafts, 1678 to 1964.* 1964. Repr. 1977.

STEPHEN HESS

POLITICAL PARTIES. Political parties in the United States are unique social institutions whose adherents are not normally formal card-carrying or dues-paying members. Party organization is highly decentralized, with power scattered among party officials, candidates' organizations, elected officials, fund-raisers, consultants, and professional staffs. In addition, American parties lack strong ideological and policy coherence and hence do not fit well under the often-quoted definition provided by the eighteenth-century English philosopher Edmund Burke, who described political parties as bodies "of men united, for promoting by their joint endeavors the national interest, upon some particular principle in which they are all agreed." Indeed, American political parties are in reality three-part social structures composed of the party in the electorate (voters with a sense of attachment to the party), the party organization (party officers, staff, and volunteer workers), and the party in government (party candidates and public officeholders).

The essence of political parties in the United States has been captured by Leon D. Epstein (*Political Parties in Western Democracies*, 1967), who defined parties as "any group, however loosely organized, seeking to elect governmental officeholders under a given label." This definition reflects the preoccupation of American parties with electoral activity and the fact that only parties nominate and run candidates under their own labels. The definition also allows for American parties' frequent disunity on policy and lack of hierarchical organization.

Unlike parties, other politically involved organizations, such as interest groups, do not have politics as their exclusive concern. Even the most politically active interest groups usually have significant nonpolitical activities. For example, labor unions engage in collective bargaining and manage pension funds. American parties also exhibit a level of durability and persistence that is not matched by cliques, campaign organizations, and most interest groups. Parties are also distinguished by the degree to which they serve as emotional symbols of voter loyalty. For millions of Americans, the party label is a potent cue in determining how they will vote on election day. Indeed, studies of voting behavior have determined that a voter's party identification is the single most important determinant of voter choice.

Evolution of Political Parties. The drafters of the Constitution deplored parties and factions and believed that by including provisions for federalism, separation of powers, and bicameralism they could prevent parties from dominating the government order. Initially, their goal of partyless politics seemed possible. The first national balloting under the Constitution (1788–1789) did not involve political parties. There was no formal nomination of candidates for president or Congress; George Washington was virtually the unanimous choice for president. Because the right to vote was restricted to property owners, electoral participation was low— only 5 to 8 percent of white males. As a result, there was little need for party organizations to mobilize masses of voters to contest elections.

The first party system: the emergence of parties (1790–1824). Parties began to emerge between 1790 and 1800 as Secretary of the Treasury Alexander Hamilton, a dominating figure in the Washington administration, proposed a controversial legislative program that called for funding of state debts, instituting a protective tariff, and creating a national bank. To gain congressional support for his program Hamilton called a legislative caucus of supporters, who called themselves "Federalists." Thomas Jefferson, a member of Washington's cabinet who opposed much of Hamilton's program, allied himself with other so-called Republican leaders in Congress, led by Rep. James Madison of Virginia.

Differences over foreign policy also fueled the development of partisan alliances within Congress. A major source of contention was Jay's treaty (narrowly ratified in 1796), designed to resolve differences between the United States and England arising from the treaty that had ended the Revolutionary War. Federalists and Republicans also divided over whether to support England or France in those nations' ongoing power struggle.

The early parties thus developed within Congress amid deep controversies over national, not state, policy issues, with Hamilton and Jefferson leading the two major clusters of interest. It was Jefferson's followers who first sought to broaden their operations by recruiting and endorsing candidates for Congress and presidential electors. The Republicans later ran slates of candidates for state offices. The Federalists were forced to follow the Republican example and compete for support within an electorate that was expanding as property restrictions on voting were eased. Reflecting their somewhat elitist orientation toward politics, the Federalists proved to be reluctant and less effective grassroots party organizers than their rivals.

Through aggressive local organizing efforts, the followers of Jefferson, operating under the Democratic-Republican label, swept the elections of 1800 as Jefferson won the presidency and his followers took control of Congress. After their disastrous defeat in 1800, the Federalists went into a precipitous decline and by 1816 disappeared as a party capable of contesting the presidency.

With the demise of the Federalists, partisan competition ceased, and the nation entered a period of partyless politics, characterized by factionalism within the dominant Democratic-Republican party. Thus, in 1811, House Speaker Henry Clay of Kentucky, leader of the party's War Hawks, sought to assert the power of the speakership and the supremacy of Congress over the other branches of government while pressuring President James Madison to declare war on Britain. Continuing intraparty factionalism during the administration of President James Monroe (1817–1825)—when most elected officials were members of one party—made it impossible for the president to exercise discipline over Congress; coherent policy-making suffered.

Intraparty factionalism within the dominant Democratic-Republican party also caused the downfall of the congressional caucus system for presidential nominations. In 1824, the congressional caucus nominated William H. Crawford for president, thereby bypassing the party's more prominent figures—John Quincy Adams, Andrew Jackson, and Clay. Each of these men then challenged Crawford in the general election, creating a four-way presidential race. When no candidate won a majority of votes in the Electoral College, the election was thrown into the House of Representatives, which chose Adams as president. Adams's administration was characterized by intense intraparty conflicts within Congress and between Congress and the president. The battles between the administration and the Jackson faction brought the first party system to a close.

The second party system: Democrats versus Whigs (1828–1854). Unlike the first party system, which emerged from the conflicts between the followers of Hamilton and Jefferson, the second party system was not closely linked to divisions within Congress nor was it the result of polarization on specific public policy issues. Rather, it developed between 1824 and 1840 out of successive contests for the presidency. And unlike the first party system after 1816, it did not lapse into one-partyism or partyless politics. Instead, two-party politics became a continuing feature of the American political system.

The election of Andrew Jackson in 1828 and 1832 marked a transitional period of bi-factional politics within the Democratic-Republican party, though by 1832 Jackson's faction was labeling itself the Democratic party. In 1834, midway through Jackson's second term, a loose amalgam of anti-Jackson forces (eastern manufacturers, southern planters, and westerners supporting higher outlays for internal improvements) sufficiently coalesced to form a new opposition party, the Whig party. For more than two decades between the 1830s and 1850s the Democrats and Whigs engaged in relatively close electoral competition. Both were truly national parties, though the Democrats were electorally the stronger of the two (the Whigs controlled both houses of Congress only during the 27th Congress, 1841–1843). The absence of highly salient national issues and the party leaders' skill in balancing diverse interests enabled the parties to compete in all regions. However, when the sectional conflicts between the North and the South intensified and slavery issues reached crisis proportions, the Whig party was eclipsed in the North by the new Republican party, and the Democrats, like the country as a whole, split along a North-South axis in the election of 1860.

The second party system arose during a period in which politics was being democratized: slates of presidential electors were being popularly elected, property restrictions on voting were being lifted, participation in elections was increasing, and party conventions were replacing caucuses as the means by which candidates were nominated. In this increasingly participatory environment, Democratic and Whig party organizations grew up across the country. Their development reflected the need for a way to mobilize the expanding electorate.

The third party system: Republicans emerge to challenge the Democrats (1856–1896). In the mid 1850s' sectional turmoil over slavery, the Republican party emerged to contest both congressional and presidential elections and established itself as the Democrats' principal electoral opposition. In 1854 and again in 1858 the Republican party won control of the House; in 1860 it elected its first

president, Abraham Lincoln. The new Republican party was composed of abolitionists, members of the old Free Soil party, and dissident northern Whigs and Democrats.

Between 1864 and 1874 the Republican party was electorally dominant, controlling both Congress and the presidency. The Civil War identified the party—at least in the North—with the Union, patriotism, and emancipation. The Republican electoral coalition was, however, broadly based. It gained rural voters for its support of the Homestead Act, which granted free land in the West, and it appealed to both business and labor with its high protective tariff policies.

During the immediate post–Civil War years the Republicans controlled the presidency and both congressional chambers, where their leaders exerted a dominating influence over policy-making. The House in particular was characterized by strong party leadership. For example, Speaker James G. Blaine of Maine (1869–1875) appointed loyal lieutenants to key committee posts, thereby controlling the flow of bills and producing a flood of Republican-sponsored probusiness legislation.

In the 1868 and 1872 elections, the Republicans swept the northern states, and with the benefit of Reconstruction, won the electoral votes of most of the southern states. The end of Reconstruction in 1874, however, enabled the Democrats to gain ascendency in the South, while the GOP's electoral support was confined to the North and West. The legacy of the war and of Reconstruction, along with regional economic differences, thus created a politics of sectionalism. Each party had its own sectional base of electoral strength. After 1874, the Republicans and Democrats competed nationally on a more even basis than in the immediate post–Civil War period, and they alternated control of the presidency and Congress.

During the post–Civil War era patronage-based party organizations (machines) emerged in many cities and states, particularly in the Northeast and Midwest. These organizations were capable of controlling the caucuses and conventions by which parties made nominations for elective offices. They also demonstrated a remarkable ability to mobilize voters. Indeed, party organizations of the period have been described as "militarist" (in Walter Dean Burnham's *Critical Elections and the Mainsprings of American Politics,* 1970) in the sense that they emphasized drill-like mobilization of their supporters. It is estimated, for example, that in Republican William McKinley's 1896 "front porch" campaign

TABLE 1. *Political Party Affiliations in Congress and the Presidency, 1789–1994*

YEAR	CONGRESS	HOUSE			SENATE			PRESIDENT
		Majority party	Principal minority party	Other (except vacancies)	Majority party	Principal minority party	Other (except vacancies)	
1789–1791	1st	Ad–38	Op–26	—	Ad–17	Op–9	—	F (Washington)
1791–1793	2d	F–37	DR–33	—	F–16	DR–13	—	F (Washington)
1793–1795	3d	DR–57	F–48	—	F–17	DR–13	—	F (Washington)
1795–1797	4th	F–54	DR–52	—	F–19	DR–13	—	F (Washington)
1797–1799	5th	F–58	DR–48	—	F–20	DR–12	—	F (John Adams)
1799–1801	6th	F–64	DR–42	—	F–19	DR–13	—	F (John Adams)
1801–1803	7th	DR–69	F–36	—	DR–18	F–13	—	DR (Jefferson)
1803–1805	8th	DR–102	F–39	—	DR–25	F–9	—	DR (Jefferson)
1805–1807	9th	DR–116	F–25	—	DR–27	F–7	—	DR (Jefferson)
1807–1809	10th	DR–118	F–24	—	DR–28	F–6	—	DR (Jefferson)
1809–1811	11th	DR–94	F–48	—	DR–28	F–6	—	DR (Madison)
1811–1813	12th	DR–108	F–36	—	DR–30	F–6	—	DR (Madison)
1813–1815	13th	DR–112	F–68	—	DR–27	F–9	—	DR (Madison)
1815–1817	14th	DR–117	F–65	—	DR–25	F–11	—	DR (Madison)
1817–1819	15th	DR–141	F–42	—	DR–34	F–10	—	DR (Monroe)
1819–1821	16th	DR–156	F–27	—	DR–35	F–7	—	DR (Monroe)
1821–1823	17th	DR–158	F–25	—	DR–44	F–4	—	DR (Monroe)
1823–1825	18th	DR–187	F–26	—	DR–44	F–4	—	DR (Monroe)
1825–1827	19th	Ad–105	J–97	—	Ad–26	J–20	—	C (John Q. Adams)
1827–1829	20th	J–119	Ad–94	—	J–28	Ad–20	—	C (John Q. Adams)
1829–1831	21st	D–139	NR–74	—	D–26	NR–22	—	D (Jackson)
1831–1833	22d	D–141	NR–58	14	D–25	NR–21	2	D (Jackson)
1833–1835	23d	D–147	AM–53	60	D–20	NR–20	8	D (Jackson)
1835–1837	24th	D–145	W–98	—	D–27	W–25	—	D (Jackson)
1837–1839	25th	D–108	W–107	24	D–30	W–18	4	D (Van Buren)
1839–1841	26th	D–124	W–118	—	D–28	W–22	—	D (Van Buren)
1841–1843	27th	W–133	D–102	6	W–28	D–22	2	W (W. Harrison)
								W (Tyler)
1843–1845	28th	D–142	W–79	1	W–28	D–25	1	W (Tyler)
1845–1847	29th	D–143	W–77	6	D–31	W–25	—	D (Polk)
1847–1849	30th	W–115	D–108	4	D–36	W–21	1	D (Polk)
1849–1851	31st	D–112	W–109	9	D–35	W–25	2	W (Taylor)
								W (Fillmore)
1851–1853	32d	D–140	W–88	5	D–35	W–24	3	W (Fillmore)
1853–1855	33d	D–159	W–71	4	D–38	W–22	2	D (Pierce)
1855–1857	34th	R–108	D–83	43	D–40	R–15	5	D (Pierce)
1857–1859	35th	D–118	R–92	26	D–36	R–20	8	D (Buchanan)
1859–1861	36th	R–114	D–92	31	D–36	R–26	4	D (Buchanan)
1861–1863	37th	R–105	D–43	30	R–31	D–10	8	R (Lincoln)
1863–1865	38th	R–102	D–75	9	R–36	D–9	5	R (Lincoln)
1865–1867	39th	U–149	D–42	—	U–42	D–10	—	R (Lincoln)
								R (A. Johnson)

Letter symbols for political parties: Ad—"Administration"; AM—Anti-Masonic; C—Coalition; D—Democratic; DR Democratic-Republican; F—Federalist; J—Jacksonian; NR—National Republican; Op—"Opposition"; R—Republican; U—Unionist; W—Whig. Figures are for the beginning of the first session of each Congress.

TABLE 1. *Political Party Affiliations in Congress and the Presidency, 1789–1994 (Continued)*

YEAR	CONGRESS	HOUSE			SENATE			PRESIDENT
		Majority party	Principal minority party	Other (except vacancies)	Majority party	Principal minority party	Other (except vacancies)	
1867–1869	40th	R–143	D–49	—	R–42	D–11	—	R (A. Johnson)
1869–1871	41st	R–149	D–63	—	R–56	D–11	—	R (Grant)
1871–1873	42d	R–134	D–104	5	R–52	D–17	5	R (Grant)
1873–1875	43d	R–194	D–92	14	R–49	D–19	5	R (Grant)
1875–1877	44th	D–169	R–109	14	R–45	D–29	2	R (Grant)
1877–1879	45th	D–153	R–140	—	R–39	D–36	1	R (Hayes)
1879–1881	46th	D–149	R–130	14	D–42	R–33	1	R (Hayes)
1881–1883	47th	R–147	D–135	11	R–37	D–37	1	R (Garfield)
								R (Arthur)
1883–1885	48th	D–197	R–118	10	R–38	D–36	2	R (Arthur)
1885–1887	49th	D–183	R–140	2	R–43	D–34	—	D (Cleveland)
1887–1889	50th	D–169	R–152	4	R–39	D–37	—	D (Cleveland)
1889–1891	51st	R–166	D–159	—	R–39	D–37	—	R (B. Harrison)
1891–1893	52d	D–235	R–88	9	R–47	D–39	2	R (B. Harrison)
1893–1895	53d	D–218	R–127	11	D–44	R–38	3	D (Cleveland)
1895–1897	54th	R–244	D–105	7	R–43	D–39	6	D (Cleveland)
1897–1899	55th	R–204	D–113	40	R–47	D–34	7	R (McKinley)
1899–1901	56th	R–185	D–163	9	R–53	D–26	8	R (McKinley)
1901–1903	57th	R–197	D–151	9	R–55	D–31	4	R (McKinley)
								R (T. Roosevelt)
1903–1905	58th	R–208	D–178	—	R–57	D–33	—	R (T. Roosevelt)
1905–1907	59th	R–250	D–136	—	R–57	D–33	—	R (T. Roosevelt)
1907–1909	60th	R–222	D–164	—	R–61	D–31	—	R (T. Roosevelt)
1909–1911	61st	R–219	D–172	—	R–61	D–32	—	R (Taft)
1911–1913	62d	D–228	R–161	1	R–51	D–41	—	R (Taft)
1913–1915	63d	D–291	R–127	17	D–51	R–44	1	D (Wilson)
1915–1917	64th	D–230	R–196	9	D–56	R–40	—	D (Wilson)
1917–1919	65th	D–216	R–210	6	D–53	R–42	—	D (Wilson)
1919–1921	66th	R–240	D–190	3	R–49	D–47	—	D (Wilson)
1921–1923	67th	R–301	D–131	1	R–59	D–37	—	R (Harding)
1923–1925	68th	R–225	D–205	5	R–51	D–43	2	R (Coolidge)
1925–1927	69th	R–247	D–183	4	R–56	D–39	1	R (Coolidge)
1927–1929	70th	R–237	D–195	3	R–49	D–46	1	R (Coolidge)
1929–1931	71st	R–267	D–167	1	R–56	D–39	1	R (Hoover)
1931–1933	72d	D–220	R–214	1	R–48	D–47	1	R (Hoover)
1933–1934	73d	D–310	R–117	5	D–60	R–35	1	D (F. Roosevelt)
1935–1936	74th	D–319	R–103	10	D–69	R–25	2	D (F. Roosevelt)
1937–1938	75th	D–331	R–89	13	D–76	R–16	4	D (F. Roosevelt)
1939–1940	76th	D–261	R–164	4	D–69	R–23	4	D (F. Roosevelt)
1941–1942	77th	D–268	R–162	5	D–66	R–28	2	D (F. Roosevelt)
1943–1944	78th	D–218	R–208	4	D–58	R–37	1	D (F. Roosevelt)
1945–1946	79th	D–242	R–190	2	D–56	R–38	1	D (Truman)

TABLE 1. *Political Party Affiliations in Congress and the Presidency, 1789–1994 (Continued)*

YEAR	CONGRESS	HOUSE			SENATE			PRESIDENT
		Majority party	Principal minority party	Other (except vacancies)	Majority party	Principal minority party	Other (except vacancies)	
1947–1948	80th	R–245	D–188	1	R–51	D–45	—	D (Truman)
1949–1950	81st	D–263	R–171	1	D–54	R–42	—	D (Truman)
1951–1952	82d	D–234	R–199	1	D–49	R–47	—	D (Truman)
1953–1954	83d	R–221	D–211	1	R–48	D–47	1	R (Eisenhower)
1955–1956	84th	D–232	R–203	—	D–48	R–47	1	R (Eisenhower)
1957–1958	85th	D–233	R–200	—	D–49	R–47	—	R (Eisenhower)
1959–1960[1]	86th	D–283	R–153	—	D–64	R–34	—	R (Eisenhower)
1961–1962	87th	D–263	R–174	—	D–65	R–35	—	D (Kennedy)
1963–1964	88th	D–258	R–177	—	D–67	R–33	—	D (Kennedy)
								D (L. Johnson)
1965–1966	89th	D–295	R–140	—	D–68	R–32	—	D (L. Johnson)
1967–1968	90th	D–246	R–187	—	D–64	R–36	—	D (L. Johnson)
1969–1970	91st	D–245	R–189	—	D–57	R–43	—	R (Nixon)
1971–1972	92d	D–254	R–180	—	D–54	R–44	2	R (Nixon)
1973–1975	93d	D–239	R–192	1	D–56	R–42	2	R (Nixon; Ford)
1975–1977	94th	D–291	R–144	—	D–61	R–37	2	R (Ford)
1977–1978	95th	D–292	R–143	—	D–61	R–38	1	D (Carter)
1979–1981	96th	D–276	R–157	—	D–58	R–41	1	D (Carter)
1981–1983	97th	D–242	R–189	—	R–53	D–46	1	R (Reagan)
1983–1984	98th	D–268	R–167	—	R–54	D–46	—	R (Reagan)
1985–1987	99th	D–253	R–182	—	R–53	D–47	—	R (Reagan)
1987–1989	100th	D–258	R–177	—	D–55	R–45	—	R (Reagan)
1989–1991	101st	D–260	R–175	—	D–55	R–45	—	R (Bush)
1991–1992	102d	D–267	R–167	1	D–56	R–44	—	R (Bush)
1993–1994	103d	D–258	R–176	1	D–56	R–44	—	D (Clinton)

[1]Excludes Hawaii; 2 senators (1-R, 1-D) and 1 representative (D) were seated in August.
SOURCES: Bureau of the Census, Historical Statistics of the United States, Colonial Times to 1957. Bureau of the Census, Statistical Abstract of the United States, 1985 and 1991 (1985, 1991).

for the presidency, 750,000 people (13 percent of the total Republican vote) visited the candidate in his hometown of Canton, Ohio.

The fourth party system: continuing Republican ascendancy and Progressive reforms (1896–1928). By the turn of the century, the United States had been transformed from an agrarian society into an industrialized and urban nation. The ethnic makeup of the country had also been changed by waves of immigrants from non-English-speaking European nations. The economic and social hardships caused by these changes reverberated through the party system. Agrarian protest movements spawned a major third-party movement, the People's party, or Populist party, of 1892. The discontent of urban

workers in the new industrial order stimulated the labor unions. Initially, neither the Republican party nor the Democratic party was responsive to these protest movements. However, in 1896 the Democratic party convention was captured by the populist forces of agrarian discontent, and their champion, William Jennings Bryan, became the party's presidential nominee.

Bryan appropriated many of the policy positions of the 1892 Populists by advocating free and unlimited coinage of silver along with a downward revision of the tariff. In contrast, McKinley, the Republican nominee, campaigned with a slogan advocating "Prosperity, Sound Money, Good Markets and Employment for Labor" while opposing calling for unlimited coinage of silver and retention of the gold standard and the maintenance of a high protective tariff.

The 1896 election, which the Republicans won, caused a major realignment of the electorate, which gave the Republican party an infusion of adherents, especially among urban residents of the Northeast. Indeed, this election so weakened the Democratic party that it was able to elect only one president, Woodrow Wilson, between 1896 and 1928, and his initial election was made possible by the 1912 split within the Republican party. The Republicans also controlled Congress from the election of 1896 until 1911, a period during which both the House and Senate were characterized by centralized and hierarchical partisan leadership. Both parties were internally homogeneous, with constituency interests in line with party policy. Republicans largely represented northern industrial constituencies and favored tariffs to protect domestic industries, the gold standard, and expansion of American interests abroad; the Democrats represented rural and southern areas and favored freer trade, coinage of silver at a ratio of 16 to 1 with gold, and an isolationist foreign policy. Strong party leadership was further enforced by machine-like organizations in many states, which sent to Congress loyal partisans prepared to bow to the wishes of congressional leaders.

It was during the fourth party system that the Progressive movement, with its emphasis on direct citizen control of the government, developed. Progressive-era reforms of the political system took root and weakened the capacity of party organizations to control nominations and mobilize voters. The most important of these reforms was probably the direct primary—the nomination of candidates via elections rather than by party conventions or caucuses. Presidential primaries were first instituted during this period. Parties also came under government regulation as states enacted primary laws that often contained provisions regulating the organization, operations, and financing of parties and campaigns.

The Progressive movement and the split it created within the Republican party between the conservative "stalwarts" and the Progressives had major consequences for the parties in Congress. In the House, the split within the Republican party led to a progressive Republican–Democratic revolt against Speaker Joseph G. Cannon of Illinois in 1910 and 1911 that deprived the Speaker of his membership on the Rules Committee and of the authority to appoint committees. The split also led to procedures (Calendar Wednesday and the Discharge Petition) that bypassed the leadership in scheduling legislation. The revolt against Cannon resulted in a severely weakened speakership as the constituencies represented by the two parties became less homogeneous and both parties became less cohesive in roll-call voting.

The fifth party system: from the New Deal to candidate-centered politics (1932–1992). The stock market crash of 1929 and Depression of the 1930s ended the era of Republican electoral dominance and made possible Franklin D. Roosevelt's 1932 election as president and the overwhelming Democratic majorities in the House and Senate. Roosevelt's New Deal program of economic reform and government social welfare programs, which Congress initially embraced with enthusiasm, forged a powerful electoral coalition composed of southern whites, blue-collar workers and union members, Catholics, Jews, urban dwellers, and African Americans. This electoral coalition gave the Democratic party electoral ascendancy from 1932 to 1964, except for 1952 and 1956, when the Republicans nominated a presidential candidate, Gen. Dwight D. Eisenhower, whose appeal extended beyond partisanship.

Ironically, Roosevelt's elections and his New Deal social welfare programs had long-term party-weakening consequences for the urban political organizations that had helped put him in office. New social programs (such as social security and unemployment compensation) and grant-in-aid programs, which emphasized professionalism in their administration, undermined the patronage base of the urban machines and robbed them of their traditional function of providing welfare services to deprived urban populations. Even so, the Democrats maintained their dominance of House and Senate elections. Between 1932 and 1995, the Republicans controlled both chambers only in the 82d Congress (1951–1953).

By the late 1960s, America had entered a post–New Deal political era. The electoral alignments of that period were still visible, but the New Deal Democratic coalition was suffering defections, particularly among white southerners, Catholics, and blue-collar workers.

The defection from the Democrats of white southerners was particularly significant because it helped the Republican party win five of six presidential elections between 1968 and 1988 and dramatically changed the composition of the congressional parties. As elections in the South became more competitive, Republicans began winning significant numbers of House and Senate seats in the region, making southerners a significant force within the Republican ranks in Congress. By 1993, for example, southerners constituted 23 percent of Senate Republican membership and 27 percent of House Republican members. This growth of southern influence gave the congressional Republicans a more conservative policy orientation. At the same time, the congressional Democratic party became less southern and less internally divided on policy.

Republican victories in presidential elections between 1968 and 1988 were not matched in elections to Congress and state offices, where the Democrats remained dominant. Instead of a major realignment and the emergence of a new Republican electoral majority, what seemed a partial realignment occurred. White southerners shifted to the Republicans, as did many Catholics, but the Democrats retained a plurality among those voters who identified themselves as belonging to a party and gained an overwhelming level of support among blacks.

Another major change was the tendency of voters to be less guided by partisan cues and to engage in substantial ticket-splitting in their votes for president and Congress. American politics had become more candidate centered, and as a result divided government became commonplace. Thus, between 1969 and 1992, one party controlled both the presidency and Congress only during the four years of the Carter administration, from 1977 to 1980. United party control of the executive and legislature was not restored until Bill Clinton's election as president in 1992.

Two-Party Dominance. While there have been transitional periods of one-party factionalism (e.g., 1824–1832, 1910–1912) and elections in which third parties or independent candidacies have constituted significant electoral forces (Progressives of 1912, Dixiecrats of 1948, George C. Wallace in 1968, John B. Anderson in 1980, and H. Ross Perot in 1992), the American political system has predominantly been a two-party system. Even when one party has disintegrated, as the Whigs did in the 1850s, the two-party character of the system has reestablished itself.

Causes of the two-party system. Political scientist V. O. Key, Jr., in *Politics, Parties, and Pressure Groups* (1964), offered three explanations for the creation and maintenance of the two-party system in the United States. The first focused on the institutional arrangements used to elect public officials.

National and state legislators are elected from single-member constituencies, with the candidate who receives a plurality of the vote being declared the winner. Unlike a proportional representation system, which rewards each serious party with a share of the legislative seats equal to its share of the popular vote, the single-member system is a winner-take-all arrangement. Such a system encourages the formation of broadly based parties that are capable of winning pluralities in a large number of districts. The single-member system tends to condemn third and minor parties to perpetual defeat—hardly a prescription for long-term political viability. The Electoral College system of electing the president also encourages two-party politics by requiring an absolute majority in the electoral vote (270 votes of 538) and by allocating individual states' electoral votes on a winner-take-all basis.

Key also noted that special historical circumstances played a role in producing the two-party system in the United States. The initial lines of political cleavage were built on a dualism of interests that prevailed when the economic and social structure of the country was far less complex than it is today. There was a split between agriculture and the interests of the mercantile and financial community.

The absence in American society of blocs of people irreconcilably attached to a particular ideology, creed, or class consciousness has also helped make two-party politics possible. Religious, racial, ethnic, and economic groups have not generally tended toward separatism. Most have found a niche in society. As a result of the broad consensus that exists regarding such fundamentals as maintenance of the constitutional order and a predominantly market-oriented economy, it is possible for one party to be slightly to the right and the other slightly to the left of center and still gain widespread voter support. Thus, while both the Democrats and Republicans have core support groups, both maintain a sufficiently centrist orientation to compete effectively for the votes of the majority of Americans who consider themselves moderates or middle-of-the-roaders.

While the American system is accurately described as a two-party system, that phrase masks substantial variation in the actual extent of interparty electoral competition. Two-party competition for the presidency clearly is intense, as it is in most states for major statewide offices such as governor or U.S. senator. In smaller and more socially homogeneous districts, however, such as those for members of the House and state legislatures, one party is frequently dominant, and meaningful interparty competition is therefore the exception rather than the rule.

One of the most striking features of electoral competition since 1856 has been the domination of electoral competition by the same two parties, the Democrats and Republicans. Only Democrats and Republicans have occupied the White House during this time, and only Republicans and Democrats have controlled the House and Senate.

In *Political Parties in American Society* (1982), Samuel Eldersveld attributed the persistence of Republican-Democratic electoral dominance to the parties' ideological eclecticism or nondoctrinaire approach to issues and changing conditions. This ideological flexibility makes it possible for both parties to harbor within their ranks leaders of widely varying policy viewpoints. In addition, both parties have exhibited an ability to attract significant levels of support from virtually every element of society.

The Republican and Democratic parties have also shown a capacity to absorb protests. Major third-party protest movements have arisen periodically since 1856, but none has been able to attract sustained voter, organizational, or financial support. Each has bloomed briefly and then withered as its remnants were absorbed into one or both major parties. Thus, the Populists of 1892 were taken over by the Democrats in 1896 through the nomination of Bryan, and the Progressive parties of Theodore Roosevelt (1912) and Robert M. La Follette, Sr. (1924), were absorbed back into the Republican fold.

The Republican and Democratic parties' success in absorbing protests owes much, in Leon D. Epstein's view (*Political Parties in the American Mold*, 1986), to the direct primary as the principal method of nominating congressional and state candidates. This uniquely American nominating procedure permits insurgents outside the ranks of the established party leadership to use an intraparty route to gain influence and public office, including seats in the U.S. Congress. By contesting and winning primaries, insurgents can gain access to the general election ballot without having to organize third parties. The availability of the direct primary as a means of achieving political change from within the major parties thereby reduces the incentive to create third parties.

Epstein has further observed that the direct primary contributes to Republican-Democratic domi-

nance because voters become accustomed to participating in party primaries and choosing among people competing for their party's nomination. Voters' partisan attachments are further encouraged by the requirement in most states that voters in a primary publicly declare their party affiliations or even register as Republicans or Democrats in order to participate in primary elections.

Federal campaign finance laws also work to the advantage of the two major parties. Under the Federal Election Campaign Act of 1974, the Republican and Democratic parties, the only parties that qualify as major parties under the law, receive the following governmental benefits: public funding for national conventions ($11.048 million in 1992), authority for national party committees to make expenditures in support of their presidential nominees ($10.332 million in 1992), public matching funds for candidates seeking presidential nominations, and public funding of general election campaigns for president ($55.240 million in 1992).

Third and Minor Parties. Although American politics has since the 1830s been characterized by two-party competition, third parties have at times had a major impact. The emerging Republican party, for example, helped focus national attention on the slavery issue and caused deep schisms within the Whig and Democratic parties during the 1850s. Third parties do not normally become major parties, but they can affect election outcomes and electoral alignments. The significant third-party movements in the twentieth century have been splinter parties—offshoots of the major parties—formed to protest policies of a party's dominant faction. Thus, Theodore Roosevelt's Progressive (Bull Moose) party reflected a split within the Republican party between the stalwart conservatives and the progressives. It caused the Republican vote in 1912 to be divided between Roosevelt and the Republican nominee, William H. Taft, enabling Democrat Woodrow Wilson to gain the presidency with less than a majority of the popular vote. In 1968 George C. Wallace, the antiestablishment, populist, and segregationist Democratic governor of Alabama, ran on the American Independent ticket and siphoned 13.5 percent of the popular vote from the major-party candidates, causing one of the closest elections in American history.

More significant, even, than Wallace's challenge was that mounted by H. Ross Perot in 1992. By capturing 19 percent of the presidential vote (though no electoral votes), he drew a larger share of the popular vote than any third-party or inde-

TABLE 2. *Party Development in the United States*

PARTY SYSTEM	DATES	COMPETING MAJOR PARTIES	SIGNIFICANT THIRD-PARTY MOVEMENTS	CHARACTERISTICS, MAJOR EVENTS
First	1790–1824	Federalists v. Democratic-Republicans	None	Parties emerge in Congress in 1790s; Jeffersonians organize at state and local levels; Democratic-Republican dominance (1800–1824); War of 1812 (1812–1815); one-party factionalism after 1816.
Second	1828–1854	Democrats v. Whigs	Anti-Masonic (1832) Free Soil (1848–1852) Know-Nothing (American) (1854)	Whigs emerge from Democratic-Republican factionalism; national two-party competition, with Democrats electorally stronger; intensification of sectional conflict (1850s); North-South schisms in both Whig and Democratic parties.
Third	1856–1896	Democrats v. Republicans	Republicans (1856) Southern Democrats (1860) Constitution Union (1860) Greenbacks (1880) Populists (1892)	Republicans emerge as a major party as Whigs dissolve; first Republican president (Lincoln) elected (1860); Civil War and Reconstruction; Republican electoral dominance (1864–1874); increasingly balanced electoral competition (1874–1896).
Fourth	1896–1928	Democrats v. Republicans	Progressive (Bull Moose) (1912) Socialist (1912) Progressive (La Follette) (1924)	Republican electoral dominance (1896–1910); Progressive movement develops, creating schism in Republican party and allowing election of Wilson (1912); direct primaries initiated; World War I (U.S. involvement, 1917–1918); "normalcy" of 1920s characterized by Republican dominance.
Fifth	1932–	Democrats v. Republicans	States' Rights Democratic (Dixiecrat) (1948) Progressive (Henry Wallace) (1948) American Independent (George Wallace, 1968; John Anderson, 1980; H. Ross Perot, 1992)	Depression of 1930s; World War II (U.S. involvement, 1941–1945); Democratic electoral dominance during New Deal era (1930s–1940s); Cold War and Korean War; Republican (Eisenhower) elected president (1952); civil rights movement; 1964 Democratic landslide and enactment of Johnson's Great Society; Vietnam War; Watergate scandal; Democratic electoral coalition weakens (1960s–1980s); divided government; candidate-centered politics.

pendent candidate since Theodore Roosevelt in 1912. Perot took votes from both major-party nominees, enabling Democrat Bill Clinton to be elected with 43 percent of the popular vote.

Third-party movements and major independent candidacies like Perot's are normally an indication of substantial voter discontent. When faced with such evident voter unrest and potential threats to their power, at least one of the major parties has usually sought to accommodate the protest group within its ranks.

Despite their occasional influence on presidential elections, third parties have not played a major role in congressional politics during the twentieth century. This was particularly evident during the century's last few decades. Between 1970 and 1992, only two people were elected to the House who were not Democrats or Republicans, and only one senator was elected on a third-party ticket. These numbers reflect the inability of third parties to overcome the problems associated with recruiting and running candidates in a sufficient number of constituencies to have even a chance of electing a bloc of representatives or senators. In a few states, however, third-party movements like Wisconsin's La Follette Progressives and the Farmer-Labor party of Minnesota were able briefly in the 1930s and 1940s to elect both senators and representatives. National political forces, however, caused these state-based parties to merge with the major parties.

Party Organization. Party organization at the national level illustrates the decentralized nature of party organizations in the United States. The national Republican and Democratic party organizations are composed of three major units—the national committees, the House campaign committees, and the Senate campaign committees.

National committees. National committees developed in the mid-1800s with the creation of the Democratic National Committee (DNC) in 1848 and the Republican National Committee (RNC) in 1856. They were created to serve as interim agents of the parties' supreme governing bodies, the national conventions. During the post–Civil War era, their principal function was the management of presidential campaigns. As a result, they were active for only a few months every four years. Not until the chairmanship of Will Hayes (1918–1921) did the RNC establish a year-round national headquarters with a full-time paid staff. The DNC followed the Republicans' example in 1928. Staffing through the 1930s and 1940s continued, however, to have a rather ad hoc quality, with party notables brought in temporarily to help with campaigns.

Gradually, the national committees became more institutionalized, with expanded full-time staffs that were characterized by specialization and professionalism. By the mid 1970s and 1980s the national committees had become highly sophisticated operations engaged in ongoing, large-scale fundraising, research, campaign training and consulting, and public relations. With multimillion-dollar budgets, the national committees provide technical and financial assistance to state and local party organizations across the country and to candidates. The national committees, however, do not manage presidential, congressional, senatorial, or gubernatorial campaigns. In America's candidate-centered system, campaigns are directed by the personal organizations of the nominees.

Presidents usually exert a dominating influence over the activities of the national committee of their party through designation of the national chairman and close liaison and supervision by the White House staff. For the "out" party, the national committee constitutes the party's most inclusive organization, and it is therefore an important intraparty force. The national committees tend to have a presidential and state-party focus. As a result, they involve themselves only limitedly in congressional and senatorial campaigns and operate quite autonomously from the party organizations within Congress. The autonomy of the national committees and the congressional parties reflects the effect of the constitutional separation-of-powers system and the electoral reality that representatives and senators are ultimately responsible for their own reelection.

Hill committees. On Capitol Hill, both Democrats and Republicans operate House and Senate campaign organizations; their official names are the Democratic Congressional Campaign Committee (DCCC), the Democratic Senatorial Campaign Committee (DSCC), the National Republican Congressional Committee (NRCC), and the National Republican Senatorial Committee (NRSC). These campaign units are organizationally autonomous from each other and the national committees. The so-called Hill committees are composed of incumbent representatives and senators, but the actual work of the committees is carried out by professional staffs. As their names suggest, the congressional (House) and senatorial campaign committees focus their efforts on holding their parties' marginal seats in Congress, assisting challengers with a realistic chance of being elected, and winning open-seat contests.

Although the national committees and Hill committees are separate and distinct entities, a good deal of interaction takes place between them. Coordination is encouraged by party expenditure limits imposed by the Federal Election Campaign Act, which restricts the amount that can be spent by Washington-based party committees in support of House and Senate candidates. The linked series of competitive races for president, senator, representative, and governor within each state also encourages coordination of activities. Relationships between a party's national-level committees, however, are not necessarily always harmonious because they compete for funds, professional staff, and the services of political consultants. Tensions also arise from the national-level committees' differing constituencies and electoral priorities. The national committees have as their principal constituencies the state party organizations, the president, and presidential candidates. They therefore tend to be primarily concerned with presidential politics and with assisting state organizations. By contrast, the Hill committees are composed of incumbent representatives and senators and therefore give priority to congressional and senatorial elections.

State parties. Each state has a state-level party committee, often operating under a title such as the Republican (or Democratic) State Central Committee. These state party groups, organizationally separate from the national parties, have tended to give priority to elections for state constitutional offices, especially the governorship and state legislature, rather than to U.S. House or Senate campaigns. Increasingly, however, state-party activities have been integrated into the programs of the national-level party committees. As the national committees have become more institutionalized and capable of raising larger and larger amounts of money, they have increasingly provided technical and financial assistance to their state affiliates. By transferring money to state parties for voter registration and get-out-the-vote drives, research, polling, fund-raising, and candidate recruitment, the national-level committees have strengthened the state parties while using them to achieve national party objectives. For example, the House and Senate party committees channel assistance to those states where there are highly competitive Senate or House races while largely ignoring other state parties. Similarly, in presidential election years the resources of the national committees flow primarily to states deemed critical to gaining an Electoral College majority for the party's presidential nominee.

In most states, there are state legislative campaign committees operating with autonomy from the state central committees. Legislative campaign committees, which are composed of incumbent legislators and operate in both the upper and lower legislative chambers, have become the principal party-support organizations for legislative candidates. These committees tend to focus their resources—money and technical services—upon competitive races and hence follow a strategy of seeking to maximize their parties' seats in legislative chamber. Because of their ability to raise campaign funds, legislative campaign committees in a number of instances have become the most effective party organizations in the state.

The Congressional Parties. While political parties in the United States emerged initially during the first Washington administration, the substantial organizational apparatus that now characterizes the congressional parties developed gradually. It was not until the twentieth century that an array of permanent party leadership positions, independent of the standing committee system, was established.

House party leadership. With the emergence of competing political parties in Congress, control of the position of Speaker of the House became a source of partisan contention. The early Speakers, however, were not party leaders. Instead, Federalist party leadership was in the hands of Treasury Secretary Hamilton until he left office in 1795. Similarly, Jefferson's Treasury secretary, Albert Gallatin, guided administration bills through the party caucus and House. During the Jefferson administration executive control of the congressional party even extended to the president's picking the chairman of the Ways and Means Committee as his floor leader and spokesman.

The era of executive dominance of the House ended during the Madison administration with Clay's election as Speaker in 1811. As leader of the War Hawks faction of the Democratic-Republican party, Clay eventually pushed a reluctant President Madison into war with England in 1812. Clay was a strong leader who stacked House standing committees with supporters of his policies. Clay's tenure marked the first time that the Speaker's prerogative to appoint committee members had been used independent of the president's designs. Clay also used his powers of recognition to limit the influence of his opponents.

For most of the nineteenth century, party leadership in the House, aside from the Speaker, was largely informal. The majority party floor leaders were informally designated for indefinite tenures. Often, the chairman of the Ways and Means Committee functioned as the chief lieutenant of the Speaker, though the chairman of the Committee on Appropriations occasionally assumed this role. It was not until the 1880s to early 1900s that the majority and minority leadership positions, along with the party whips, were established on a permanent basis.

The most elaborate leadership apparatus is found in the House of Representatives. Each party is ultimately governed by a party caucus (Republicans prefer the term *conference*) composed of all party members within the chamber. The caucus elects party leaders and determines party rules.

The House's most powerful figure is the Speaker, who serves as the leader of the majority party. Besides serving as the chamber's presiding officer, the Speaker influences committee assignments within the majority party, nominates party members to the Rules Committee, and refers bills to committee.

Working with the majority party members of the Rules Committee, the Speaker is able to influence profoundly the agenda of the House and to structure the conditions under which bills are considered on the House floor—conditions that frequently give advantage to the position of the Speaker's party.

The second-ranking leadership position in the House is the majority floor leader, who schedules bills, handles floor strategy, and serves as the principal party spokesperson on the floor. Assisting the Speaker and majority floor leader is a whip organization headed by a chief whip. The whip organization notifies members when key votes will occur, conducts head counts of members' sentiment on controversial issues, and attempts to whip up support for the party position on important roll-call votes.

Within the minority party, the highest-ranking official is the minority floor leader, who acts as its principal strategist and spokesperson. Like the majority floor leader, the minority leader has a whip organization to assist in measuring party sentiment and maintaining unity.

In addition to these formal leadership positions, both parties have a series of committees with specialized responsibilities. The Democratic Steering and Policy Committee assigns Democrats to standing committees and also discusses and endorses party policy positions. The Republicans divide these responsibilities between a Committee on Committees and a Policy Committee.

Senate party leadership. As in the House of Representatives, party leadership of the Senate emanated largely from the executive branch from the Washington through the Jefferson administration, with individual senators temporarily assuming the mantle of leadership. The vice president, an outsider imposed on the Senate by the Constitution, never served as its leader. Rather, in accordance with the precedent set by the first vice president, John Adams, the vice president served solely as a presiding officer. Throughout most of the nineteenth century, the Senate lacked strong, formal party leadership. It was, in the words of Sen. Daniel Webster (W-Mass.), a chamber "of equals" whose members "knew no master." Similarly, Woodrow Wilson observed in his classic treatise *Congressional Government* (1885) that in the Senate "no one exercises the special trust of acknowledged leadership."

Not until the 1890s did modern party leadership make its appearance in the Senate, when Republican William B. Allison of Iowa, the Senate Appropriations Committee chairman, was elected chair-man of the Republican caucus and that group assumed control of the chamber. By the end of the nineteenth century parties had assumed a dominant role in the Senate's deliberations. The parties named members to committees, made initial decisions on proposed legislation, and determined which bills would be considered for floor consideration. In the early 1900s the formal positions of majority and minority leader had been created.

In the Senate, an institution characterized by a high level of member independence and individualism, the formal powers of the party leaders are less extensive than in the House, and leaders are forced to rely more heavily on their skills of persuasion and negotiation.

The principal party leadership positions in the Senate are the majority and minority floor leaders, who are elected by their respective caucuses every two years at the beginning of each new Congress. Although the formal powers of the majority leader are limited, the leader does derive influence from the position's responsibility for scheduling legislative business in the Senate. As in the House, both parties have specialized committees. Each has a committee on committees (called the Steering Committee by the Democrats), which makes committee assignments, and a policy committee, which considers party positions on legislation. In the case of the Democrats the policy committee assists the floor leader in scheduling bills for floor consideration.

In both the House and Senate, party policy committees function mainly as mechanisms for gauging members' sentiment regarding legislation and for providing guidance on the party's position on an issue. The policy committees do not have the power to bind party members to support a particular position. They tend to enter the legislative process after bills have been considered in standing committee and hence do not function as agents for developing a party program.

Although virtually all representatives and senators are elected as Republicans or Democrats and also belong to a collegial entity in the House and Senate bearing one of those labels, the congressional environment is not usually conducive to high levels of intraparty unity or strong policy leadership by the parties. Party leaders in Congress are forced to adapt to the fact that their partisans are individually responsible for their own nomination and reelection. Since the congressional party cannot guarantee renomination, electoral safety in the general election, or extensive campaign resources to even its most able and loyal members, members frequently adopt relatively independent and constituency-oriented policy stances when voting on legislation. Party influence is also limited by decentralization of power through the standing committee system, which is Congress's principal means of ensuring specialized consideration of legislation.

Partisanship in Congress. Despite electoral forces and institutional arrangements that limit party influence, the congressional party is the primary integrative mechanism in both chambers and the primary means of achieving majority decision-making. Evidence of partisanship abounds in Congress.

Congress is organized on a partisan basis. Members of the majority party hold the most powerful leadership posts in each chamber—Speaker of the House, House majority leader, and Senate majority leader. A chamber's majority party controls all committee and subcommittee chairmanships and holds the majority on all the standing committees. With control of key leadership posts, a majority in the chamber, and the majority membership on committees, the dominant party's leadership largely determines which bills will be considered for floor action and under what conditions they will be considered.

Partisan influence is also apparent in House and Senate roll-call voting. Neither party is monolithic, and by the standards of most European parties the congressional Republican and Democratic parties are anything but unified. Even so, partisan influences on roll-call voting behavior are substantial. Since 1954 the level of unity in either party on roll calls has rarely dipped below 70 percent per session. Party unity is most commonly measured by computing the average number of party members voting with their party on roll calls that pit a majority of Democrats against a majority of Republicans.

By the late 1980s and early 1990s, party unity had increased in response to changes in the party system that affected each party's congressional membership. As the once solidly Democratic South gradually became more competitive between the parties and the Republicans came to win a significant share of the southern seats in the House and Senate, the composition of the parties within Congress underwent a substantial change. Republicans increasingly won election in many of the conservative districts of the region. This helped to create a more southern- and conservative-oriented Republican party in both chambers. At the same time, Democratic House and Senate candidates became increasingly dependent on African American and moderate-to-liberal white voters in both the primaries and general elections in the South. The Democrats who emerge from this milieu tend to be "national Democrats" whose policy views and constituencies have much more in common with their northern and western colleagues than was true in the 1950s and 1960s. The result has been heightened party unity in both parties, especially in the House, and a greater willingness on the part of the majority Democrats to accept firm leadership control of the policy agenda (David W. Rohde, *Parties and Leaders in the Postreform House,* 1991).

Partisanship also affects the relationship between the president and Congress. Presidents' success in achieving their legislative programs is heavily dependent on the number of their partisans serving in the House and Senate. Single-party control of both the White House and Congress does not ensure passage of a president's legislative program, but it can make the president's congressional leadership task substantially easier. Indeed, party leaders in Congress usually act as congressional spokespersons for the president's policies, and the president tends to work through them in seeking passage of policy initiatives.

The parties' role in Congress and the governing process is paradoxical. Party influence on the organization of Congress is pervasive, and partisan affiliation has been shown to be the best single predictor of how representatives and senators will vote on congressional roll calls. Shared partisanship can help bridge the gap between the president and Congress created by the constitutional separation of powers, just as divided partisan control of the executive and legislative branches tends to intensify conflict. Yet despite the evidence of strong party influence, there are constant reminders of the parties' limited capacity to control policy-making in government institutions like Congress. Given a committee system that makes coordinated party policy development difficult and given that senators and representatives are individually responsible for their own electoral survival, the congressional parties cannot impose strict discipline on their members. They periodically fragment on critical roll-call votes, and cross-party coalitions constantly form to pass legislation that either advances or impedes the president's program. Yet for all their weaknesses, which are so often on display in Congress, the American political parties have shown a remarkable capacity for adaptability, durability, and influence.

[*See also* Caucus, *article on* Party Caucus; Leadership; Party Committees. *For further discussion of particular political parties, see* Anti-Federalists; Democratic Party; Federalists; Independents; Jeffersonian Republicans; Radical Republicans; Republican Party; Whig Party.]

BIBLIOGRAPHY

Beck, Paul Allen, and Frank J. Sorauf. *Party Politics in America.* 7th ed. 1992.

Bibby, John F. *Politics, Parties, and Elections in America.* 2d ed. 1992.

Chambers, William Nisbet. *Political Parties in a New Nation.* 1963.

Epstein, Leon D. *Political Parties in the American Mold.* 1986.

Herrnson, Paul S. *Party Campaigning in the 1980s.* 1988.

Key, V. O., Jr. *Politics, Parties and Pressure Groups.* 5th ed. 1964.

Maisel, L. Sandy, ed. *Political Parties and Elections in the United States: An Encyclopedia.* 1991.

Mayhew, David R. *Placing Parties in American Politics.* 1986.

Reichley, A. James. *The Life of the Parties: A History of American Political Parties.* 1992.

Rohde, David W. *Parties and Leaders in the Postreform House.* 1991.

Rosenstone, Steven J., Roy L. Behr, and Edward H. Lazarus. *Third Parties in America: Citizen Response to Major Party Failure.* 1984.

JOHN F. BIBBY

POLK, JAMES K. (1795–1849), Democratic representative from Tennessee, Speaker of the House of Representatives, and eleventh president of the United States. A seven-term member of the House, James Knox Polk is the only Speaker ever to have been elected president. Polk was the son of a well-to-do North Carolina planter. In 1806 his family moved to Tennessee. Educated in Presbyterian academies, Polk graduated first in his class from the University of North Carolina at Chapel Hill in 1818. After legal study in Nashville under the tutelage of the distinguished Felix Grundy, he was admitted to the bar, opened a law office in Columbia, Tennessee, and became involved in politics. In 1823, Polk was elected to the lower house of the Tennessee legislature, and two years later, in the aftermath of Andrew Jackson's defeat for the presidency by John Quincy Adams, he took his seat in the U.S. House of Representatives.

Polk's political views were derived from the Jeffersonian beliefs of his family and the democratic convictions of his family's friend, Andrew Jackson. He never wavered in his deep and strong attachment to the Old Hero. Indeed, Polk's reputation as a loyal and orthodox Jacksonian earned him the title "Young Hickory." The freedom of the individual, the rights of the states in a confederation of sovereign states, a strict interpretation of the Constitution that would safeguard both individuals and the states against the centralizing power of the national government—these principles constituted the bedrock of Polk's political philosophy. He held in high regard what he called the "doctrines of '98," the Virginia and Kentucky resolutions written by Madison and Jefferson, respectively, and he strongly believed that government should reside with the plain people and be administered simply and economically in their interests.

Polk was one of the youngest members of Congress when he took his seat in December 1825. His maiden speech, a reaction against Adams's election to the presidency by the House of Representatives, was a forceful statement in favor of a constitutional amendment that would eliminate the House's role in presidential elections, thereby removing the possibility of "bargain and corruption" in the

JAMES K. POLK.   *PERLEY'S REMINISCENCES*, VOL. 1

choice of chief executive. Although lacking charisma and somewhat formal and stiff in his bearing, Polk quickly became known as an energetic and able debater. He relied on disciplined and documented argument, and his speaking style, like his personality, was thoughtful, reserved, and lacking in ornamentation.

Following Jackson's election in 1828, Polk became the president's spokesman and the leader of the Jackson forces in the House. He was a relentless opponent of the centralizing tendencies of Henry Clay's American System, repeatedly warning against the "splendid Government" and "consolidated empire" that he felt Clay's program fostered. Polk opposed funding internal improvements with federal money and questioned the constitutionality of such projects; he rejected the idea of tariffs for protection and worked for the reduction of tariff duties to revenue levels; and he was an implacable foe of the second Bank of the United States. Polk charged the bank with using its unbridled power and privilege to subvert the Republic and create a "despotism of money." If not checked, he declared, the power of money would one day "control your election of President, of your Senators, and of your Representatives." As a member of the Ways and Means Committee, in the spring of 1833 he submitted a minority report charging the bank with misuse of the people's money; several months later, as committee chairman, he wrote a report sanctioning Jackson's removal of the government's deposits from the bank.

In December 1835, Polk was elected Speaker of the House of Representatives, a post he held for two terms. It was a critical moment for both him and his party. Some Democrats had parted with Jackson over the national bank issue, while others refused to support Martin Van Buren as his successor. The abolitionist movement mounted a disruptive petition drive in Congress, while the Texas revolution raised the prospect of several new slave states being added to the Union. Polk's desperate effort to maintain order in the House was constantly challenged, but in the end his parliamentary skill and his calm, patient demeanor won out. It was Polk's first brush with the slavery issue. Although a slaveholder, he believed slavery was a "common evil." But he also thought that it was an institution "entailed on us by our ancestors" that could not be removed without doing irreparable damage to the South and to the Union.

Polk left the House in 1839 when, persuaded by Tennessee Democrats to redeem the state from Whig rule, he ran successfully for governor. The following year, Polk was an unsuccessful candidate for the vice presidential nomination on Van Buren's ticket; subsequently, he was defeated for reelection as governor in 1841 and 1843. With his political career apparently over, Polk made one more run for the vice presidential nomination in 1844. To his astonishment, he was nominated for the presidency instead. Polk was no less surprised when he was elected in a close contest over Henry Clay.

Polk's presidency has been judged one of the most successful in the nation's history. His long experience in Congress served him well in the discharge of his presidential responsibilities. Friendships made during his seven terms in the House provided a network of people on whom he could call for advice and support. He resisted pressures from the party's factions—Calhounites in the South, Van Burenites in the North, even Jackson himself—each of which expected to play a role in the administration. "I intend to be myself President of the United States," he declared. Polk reiterated his faith in America's republican system, warned against the divisiveness of sectional agitation, and promised a strict adherence to the Constitution and scrupulous regard for states' rights. To these, he added his devotion to the spirit of continental expansion that was alive in the land. Polk set certain limited objectives for his term: the annexation of Texas; the settlement of the Oregon boundary dispute with Great Britain; the acquisition of California; the reduction of the tariff to revenue levels; and the reestablishment of the independent treasury system. In the end, he achieved them all.

While the dispute with Great Britain was amicably resolved, relations with Mexico worsened over the Texas issue. Polk's efforts to settle the grievances between the two countries peaceably were unsuccessful, and the Mexican War was the result. He prosecuted the conflict with characteristic energy to a victorious end. Polk left the presidency in March 1849 (he had earlier vowed to serve only a single term), physically exhausted and in ill health. He died three months later, on 15 June 1849.

BIBLIOGRAPHY

Bergeron, Paul H. *The Presidency of James K. Polk.* 1987.

Sellers, Charles G. *James K. Polk: Continentalist, 1843–1846.* 1966.

Sellers, Charles G. *James K. Polk: Jacksonian, 1795–1843.* 1957.

ROBERT W. JOHANNSEN

POPULISM.

POPULISM. People's party delegations were represented in the House and Senate beginning with the 52d Congress of 1891 and continuing until the 57th Congress that adjourned in 1903. The labels *Populist* and *Populism* were coined by Kansan activists in the aftermath of the party's founding national convention held in Cincinnati in 1891 as a less cumbersome way of identifying party adherents. Before it was over, the party constituted the nation's most significant third-party, mass democratic movement since the creation of the modern-day Republican party in the 1850s. While always a tiny minority in Congress, the Populists' voice and influence belied the size of their delegations. Fusionists (individuals supported by one or more other parties) included, forty-seven men served in these congresses under the Populist banner. Forty of these were in the House of Representatives. A number were elected to more than one term; John C. Bell of Colorado heads the list with four terms. There were seven Populists in the Senate, with only Nebraska's William V. Allen exceeding one six-year term.

The Populist delegation in the 52d Congress (1891–1893) was made up of nine representatives and two senators; the 53d (1893–1895) counted ten representatives and three senators; the 54th (1895–1897) included nine representatives and four senators; the 55th (1897–1899) constituted the largest delegation, with twenty-three representatives and delegates and six senators; the 56th (1899–1901) declined to six representatives and five senators; and the 57th Congress (1901–1903), the last to include Populists, counted five representatives and four senators. William A. Peffer of Kansas, Allen of Nebraska, and Marion Butler of North Carolina were the party's outstanding senators; Thomas E. Watson from Georgia, Jeremiah Simpson from Kansas, and Bell from Colorado were party leaders in the House.

At the congressional level, Populism was primarily a western phenomenon. Only North Carolina, among southern states, managed to elect a significant Populist delegation to Congress. It was led impressively by Senator Butler, who also served as party chairman. During the 54th Congress, North Carolina's group of five was the largest Populist state delegation in Congress, and in the 55th Congress, the state's six-member delegation was second in size only to the one from Kansas.

Populists in the entire South, beyond North Carolina, managed to elect only three members of Congress: Watson of Georgia, to the 52d Congress, and Milford W. Howard and Albert T. Goodwyn, both from Alabama. Howard served in the 54th and 55th Congresses and was a genuine Populist; Goodwyn, because of a contested election, served only a fraction of a term in the 54th Congress and allied with congressional Republicans rather than with the Populists.

During the crisis of the 1890s, these Populist delegations pioneered a number of ideas and programs that would later come to have greater respectability and meaning for modern America, especially after the stock market crash of 1929. Particularly important were their repeated proto-Keynesian suggestions during the 1890s that government at the federal level had a responsibility to assume the initiative with respect to revitalizing the nation's troubled economy, if necessary by putting unemployed people to work on public work programs. Such suggestions earned for their creators merely a large dose of scorn in their own times.

BIBLIOGRAPHY

Bicha, Karel. *Western Populism: Studies in an Ambivalent Conservatism.* 1976.
Clanton, Gene. *Populism: The Humane Preference in America.* 1991.

GENE CLANTON

PORK BARREL. *Pork barrel* refers to the appropriation of public money for geographically defined projects that would not be funded in the absence of strong support from their local representatives. Such projects typically provide visible benefits to the geographic areas in which they are built while distributing their less visible costs across the entire nation. The term has its origins in the practice on southern plantations of distributing rations of salt pork to the slaves from large wooden barrels. The earliest known citation to a political use of the term was in 1863, but not until the turn of the century did pork barrel became a common political expression.

For some scholars the notion of pork barrel is reserved for projects that are inefficient, meaning that the costs outweigh the benefits. The term is used more generally to refer to a local project that is chosen because of the strong support of a local legislator rather than because it is the best way to achieve some national purpose. Pork barrel projects are part of a broader class known as particularized benefits (Mayhew, 1974), or benefits awarded to a specific individual, group, or geographic

THEODORE E. BURTON (R-OHIO). Chairman from 1899 to 1909 of the House Committee on Rivers and Harbors, the source of many pork barrel programs. The fictitious "Salt River" symbolizes the obscurity into which politicians may fall after political defeat; Burton had experienced a brush with such a fate after suffering an embarrassing loss in the Cleveland mayoral race. Clifford K. Berryman, *Washington Evening Star*, 13 November 1907.

U.S. SENATE COLLECTION, CENTER FOR LEGISLATIVE ARCHIVES

constituency in a case-by-case manner. The ad hoc nature of their distribution allows legislators to claim credit for obtaining these benefits, since unlike entitlement benefits, they are not awarded automatically.

Pork barrel arises because legislators are elected from geographically defined constituencies and are constantly looking for ways to demonstrate how effectively they serve their constituents' interests. "Bringing home the bacon" is a universal favorite among legislators because it involves few political risks. Most constituents consider federal spending a good thing; it stimulates the local economy and generates employment. Since most of the benefits of a project are locally concentrated, while most of the costs are incurred outside the district, on election day a legislator usually faces the beneficiaries of a local project rather than those who pay the costs.

The classic pork barrel program is rivers and harbors, a program that promotes water navigation and flood control by constructing a series of dams, levees, locks, and waterways across the nation. Legislators propose individual projects for their districts. These projects compete for funds in the House and Senate Public Works and Appropriations committees and again on the two floors; the funded projects are then constructed by the U.S. Army Corps of Engineers. Committees regularly obtain large supporting majorities for this program on the two floors, awarding virtually every representative and senator a project now and then. Legislators vote for rivers and harbors bills to guarantee that their districts will obtain their share of pork.

The standard criticism of rivers and harbors projects is that they are economically inefficient: they cost more to construct than they will deliver in benefits. For example, Congress approved and the corps constructed a $2 billion project to connect the Tennessee River to the Gulf of Mexico through Alabama (saving barge owners from taking the more natural route down the Mississippi), despite estimates that the project would yield only thirty-nine cents on the dollar. Congress has also built dams to control flooding when it would have been cheaper to buy all the land in the floodplain. Although some rivers and harbors projects fail to satisfy standard cost-benefit criteria, many projects do achieve that standard. They are still considered pork barrel projects, however, because they are chosen for political reasons rather than on the basis of the best use of national transportation funds.

Congress makes decisions about the geographic allocation of benefits for only a few programs, most notably the construction of large federal facilities and large transportation projects. Most decisions about geographic allocation are made by bureaucrats in federal agencies. However, the fact that Congress delegates direct authority over geographic allocation to agencies does not diminish legislators' interest in these allocations. The record shows that legislators work hard to obtain geographic benefits for their districts and that bureaucrats respond to their pressure. Bureaucrats work simultaneously to broaden the geographic distribution of benefits, and thereby attract the support of as many legislators as possible, and to concentrate generous shares in the districts of crucial supporters, most notably the members of the committees that oversee a program's funding. A famous example is the model cities program, which began as an effort to concentrate federal funds in a handful of large, troubled cities but quickly evolved into a program that spread funds among 150 cities. Some of the model cities were actually small villages that had the good fortune to be represented in Congress by influential legislators.

Journalists and scholars disagree about how much pork exists in the federal budget. Many journalists find pork everywhere they look and delight in recounting the worst examples. Most scholars conducting empirical studies find more modest amounts. Part of the reason for this disparity is that some journalists confuse correlation with causation. For example, after finding an association between representation on the military committees and military spending in the districts that are represented on the military committees, they presume that the former causes the latter. Most scholarly studies suggest that causation runs in the opposite direction; legislators seek to serve on the military committees because their districts already contain large military facilities. A second reason is that journalists often focus their attention on notorious pork barrel programs such as rivers and harbors and then incorrectly assume that this tiny part of the federal budget is representative of the whole. In actuality over half of the federal budget consists of interest on the national debt and transfer payments to individuals—expenditures unconnected to geographic concerns. Of the remaining programs, most geographic benefits are allocated by formula or in competitions where merit clearly dominates.

Most experts conclude that pork barrel spending constitutes a tiny and declining portion of the federal budget. Charles Schultze, former chairman of the Council of Economic Advisers, estimates that the amount of pork in the 1988 federal budget was "no more than $10 billion," less than 1 percent of annual expenditures (Ellwood and Patashnik, 1993). Pork barrel spending continues to decline as a share of federal spending because it is being squeezed by the steady growth in entitlement programs. Each year the federal government spends less and less on construction projects and more and more on health care, social security, and other transfer payments.

[See also Bargaining; Logrolling.]

BIBLIOGRAPHY

Arnold, R. Douglas. Congress and the Bureaucracy. 1979.
Ellwood, John W., and Eric M. Patashnik. "In Praise of Pork." The Public Interest 110 (1993): 19–33.
Hird, John. "The Political Economy of Pork." American Political Science Review 85 (1991): 429–456.
Mayer, Kenneth. The Political Economy of Defense Contracting. 1991.
Mayhew, David. Congress: The Electoral Connection. 1974.

R. DOUGLAS ARNOLD

POSSESSIONS. See Territories and Possessions.

POSTAL SERVICE. Article I, section 8 of the Constitution states: "The Congress shall have Power . . . To establish Post Offices and post Roads." For more than two centuries the application of this grant of authority has had significant consequences for the nation's economic and social development. From the first, its importance made the operation of the postal service a highly political matter, subject to strong economic, regional, and patronage interests. At the same time it is the most personal and universal of government services, daily touching almost every citizen. Yet it was assumed from the outset that the postal service would be a revenue-producing government activity. The resulting conflicts involving special interests, the general demand for universal and efficient delivery of the mail, and the pressure for economy have shaped the often turbulent history of congressional postal policy.

Creation and Development. In 1782 the Continental Congress made an effort to consolidate the scattered and disparate postal services that had developed during the colonial and revolutionary periods. For the first time a single set of regulations governed postal management, organization, routes, rates, and penalties for related offenses. The Continental Congress made it clear that the central government would have authority over both interstate and intrastate postal systems.

Although the federal legislature established the United States Post Office in 1789, it did not provide permanency of the service or define the place of the Post Office in the new government beyond prescribing a loose constituent relationship of the Post Office to the Treasury Department.

Congressional acts in 1792 and 1794 further consolidated the authority and responsibility of the service and established the Post Office as a permanent organization in the federal government. Its independence as a government department evolved gradually through changes in bureaucratic practice. Postmaster General John McLean began to report directly to the president instead of to the secretary of the Treasury in 1825 and to label his correspondence as coming from the "Post Office

To the Honorable, the members of the Senate and House of Representatives of the United States in Congress assembled:

The undersigned citizens of the Oak⬛⬛⬛ ⬛⬛⬛ State of *Illinois* would humbly represent to your honorable body, that, in their opinion, it would in a very great degree conduce to the Public good to have a MAIL ROUTE established from Danville Illinois, to Springfield Illinois, once in each and every week; that the mail be transported in stages from the first day of May to the first day of November in each and every year, on the route from Indiana gotte by way of Crawfordsville and Covington, Indiana—Danville Urbana and De⬛⬛⬛ Illinois, to Springfield, Illinois.

SUBSCRIBERS NAMES.

PETITION. For a new mail route in Illinois, referred to the Senate Committee on Post Offices and Post Roads, 1836; signed by Abraham Lincoln, then postmaster of New Salem.   LIBRARY OF CONGRESS

Department," instead of the "General Post Office." Andrew Jackson was the first president to include the postmaster general in the cabinet. Congress in 1873 finally recognized the Post Office formally as an executive department.

Over time Congress frequently enacted legislation affecting postal services. But the system established in the late 1790s was the basic framework for the organization until its decentralization in the 1950s.

Politics. The very nature of the postal service invites political association and involvement. The Post Office employed 78 percent of federal employees in 1816, 56 percent in 1881, and 57 percent in 1901. There were more than seventy-six thousand post offices in 1900, and the appointment of postmasters was the largest single source of party patronage in the nineteenth century. The Senate had to confirm appointments to some of the more important postmasterships, and members of the House assumed that they would be consulted on appointments in their districts.

Building post roads involved Congress not only in the appropriations for their construction but in the determination of locale and routes. Selection of those sites was the subject of intense debate. Post roads were the tracks over which the mail was carried from city to city, and they became the foundation for much of the country's early permanent highways. In later years, as railroads and airlines began to replace road carriers, lobbying for mail contracts was intense.

Personnel. For two hundred years Congress had considerable say over the numbers, pay, and working conditions of postal personnel. The legislature established categories of jobs such as postmasters, postal clerks, and letter carriers. Members of this work force became a constituency with considerable influence.

Congress on several occasions responded to pressures to establish a merit system in the postal service. Most positions other than postmaster were covered by the Pendleton Act of 1883. The Ramspeck-O'Mahoney Act of 1938 replaced postmasters' terms with lifetime appointments (dependent on good behavior). One consequence was an increasing number of appointments of postmasters from the career ranks.

Finances. From 1836 until 1971 Congress required that all postal revenues be deposited in the general treasury, that the postmaster general submit itemized budget estimates for the coming year, and that the Post Office secure annual congressional appropriations. These requirements were a serious source of friction between the Post Office and the legislature, because they enabled Congress to exert considerable influence over the policies of the department.

The setting of rates, levels of service balanced against revenue and deficits, and the issue of service priorities versus business practices are major themes in the rich history of Congress's relations with the Post Office. The legislature occasionally increased rates only to see revenues fall, because people were not using the service. Congress then would lower the rates, and revenues would increase, sometimes because service had expanded to new territories.

Post Office accounting methods became the subject of legislation. The Kelly Act (1930) provided for the separation of the expenses of direct postal services from ancillary activities such as private carrier subsidies, franked mail for government agencies (and Congress), the conduct of unemployment censuses, and the sale of migratory bird stamps.

Services. In its long history the Post Office has offered a variety of services, initiated either by or with the support of Congress. The Pony Express (1860) was a particularly dramatic example, although it was in place only for eighteen months. Other innovations have been postal money orders (1864), special delivery (1885), rural free delivery (1893, 1896), parcel post (1912), postal savings (1910–1966), and air mail (1918). Congress has imposed a number of other duties on the service, including the mail distribution and collection of census schedules.

Congress and the Corporation. The Postal Reorganization Act of 1970 converted the U.S. Postal Service into a government corporation. A nine-member board of governors, appointed by the president with the advice and consent of the Senate, elects the postmaster general. The Postal Rate Commission, established in 1970, is responsible for recommending postage rate adjustments. The salaries of postal service employees are established through collective bargaining. In short, Congress has divested itself of most of its traditionally close and highly political control over rates, personnel, and other management issues. Still, the postal service has not achieved full fiscal autonomy: Congress continues to legislate an annual subsidy through the Treasury, the Post Office, and general government appropriations acts. And Congress retains its constitutional prerogative in that it can legislate at any time to change the structure and duties of the system.

BIBLIOGRAPHY

Cullinan, Gerald. *The United States Postal Service.* 1973.
Daniel, Edward G. *United States Postal Service and Postal Policy, 1789–1860.* 1941.
Stewart, Alva W. *The U.S. Postal Service: Problems and Prospects.* 1985.
Tierney, John T. *The U.S. Postal Service: Status and Prospects of a Public Enterprise.* 1988.

SHARON STIVER GRESSLE

POST OFFICE AND CIVIL SERVICE COMMITTEE, HOUSE. The House Committee on Post Office and Civil Service was created in the Legislative Reorganization Act of 1946 (60 Stat. 812–852, effective 2 January 1947). The committee represents a consolidation of the jurisdictions of the 1808 Committee on Post-Office and Post Roads (except that post roads were transferred to the Committee on Public Works), the Committee on Civil Service (1893, formerly the Committee on the Reform of the Civil Service), and the Committee on the Census (1901). In addition, jurisdiction over the National Archives was transferred to the new committee from the Committee on the Library.

The Committee Reform Amendments of 1974 (H. Res. 988, 93d Cong., 2d sess., effective 3 January 1975) retained the Post Office and Civil Service Committee. Most of its jurisdiction remained intact, and several areas were expanded. Jurisdiction over the National Archives was transferred to the Committee on Government Operations in 1975.

The Post Office and Civil Service Committee in the House is responsible for census, population, and demographic issues as well as statistics; federal civil service matters covering all aspects of employment, including the Hatch Act (prohibitions on political activity by federal employees, formerly within the jurisdiction of the Committee on House Administration), compensation and benefits for officers and employees, the retirement system, classification of positions, and intergovernmental personnel policies; holidays and celebrations; and all matters relating to the U.S. postal system. Postal savings banks are still listed in Rule X; however, the banks were discontinued under statute in 1966.

In the 103d Congress, the committee had twenty-four members and five subcommittees: Oversight and Investigations; Civil Service; Census, Statistics, and Postal Personnel; Compensation and Employee Benefits; and Postal Operations and Services. A major change in the subcommittee structure was effected in 1971 in response to the changed status of the postal service.

Critics fault the committee for its clientele orientation—postal patrons, postal and civil employees, and their representative organizations. Further, the creation of the U.S. Postal Service took most direct influence away from those groups and thus diminished the appeal of the committee to members.

Throughout the history of the committee, in fact long in advance of the 1946 reorganization, certain issues came almost annually before the committee. These were postage rates and salaries and benefits, including retirement, for federal civilian employees, including post office staff. Among the early pieces of landmark legislation coming out of the committee was the Civil Service Classification Act of 1948, which established the general schedule grade system and remained almost unchanged until 1990. The committee has been instrumental in establishing other significant systemic changes that affect both the civil service system and the postal service system. In 1972, the federal wage system was provided with a statutory foundation. For almost one hundred years, the skilled labor, or blue-collar, work force had been working in a system of job classification and compensation not found in statute. The Government Employees–Prevailing Rate Systems Act did not significantly change the methods that determined compensation levels and grading. However, it basically codified the system that had been administratively established.

Historically, the issues of postal rates and postal employee compensation and appointment policies were among the most highly political areas of jurisdiction for the Post Office and Civil Service Committee and were virtually on the table annually. The Postal Reorganization Act of 1970 created a government corporation in lieu of the Post Office as an executive department. The president names a nine-member board of governors, with the advice and consent of the Senate, to the U.S. Postal Service. The Postal Service is responsible for managing the provision of mail and other related services. Postal Service employees do not have the right to strike but bargain for pay, benefits, and working conditions. The Postal Rate Commission, not Congress, is responsible for setting postage rates. The committee maintains an oversight function. However, while not fully self-supporting, the corporation is fundamentally autonomous, subject to amending legislation.

As early as 1962, the committee supported the principle of comparability of federal public- and private-sector pay. The Pay Act of 1967, the Pay Comparability Act of 1970, and the Federal Employee Comparability Act of 1990 are examples of efforts by committed members to create a progressively automatic environment in which pay for federal white-collar employees can be kept at a level reasonably close to that of private-sector employees in similar occupations in their communities.

Two other landmark pieces of legislation, relating to the federal civil service, were the products of the committee. The Civil Service Reform Act of 1978 created the Senior Executive Service, established a merit pay system for mid-level managers, and created both the Office of Special Counsel and the Merit Systems Protection Board. In 1984, the Federal Employees Retirement System was created as an alternative to the Civil Service Retirement System, allowing federal civil service pensions to tie into the Social Security system.

Finally, the Post Office and Civil Service Committee serves as the legislative point for such issues as the creation of holidays and the refinement and execution of the census by mail.

Despite the criticism leveled at the committee on the basis of lack of enthusiasm for the assignment, the perceived single dimension of its jurisdiction, and the clientele-oriented nature of the members and legislation, the Post Office and Civil Service Committee has its champions. Committee chairman William L. Clay (D-Mo.) responded to the clientele-orientation issue in his remarks before the Joint Committee on the Organization of the Congress (29 April 1993):

> [T]he clientele[s] of this Committee are special and deserve the attention they receive. After all, the Federal Government is the largest employer in the country. Its employees carry out the programs and policies established by the Congress and provide services that directly benefit two hundred fifty million Americans. The welfare of Federal employees and the terms and conditions of their employment directly affect their efficiency and productivity. The census is the basis by which we apportion representation in the House and also provides information essential to the development of private and public sector policies. And the Postal Service and its employees deliver one hundred sixty billion pieces of mail a year, keeping American citizens in touch with family, friends, businesses, and government.

[See also Governmental Affairs Committee, Senate.]

BIBLIOGRAPHY

Fenno, Richard F., Jr. *Congressmen in Committees.* 1973.

Ornstein, Norman J. "Changing Congress: The Committee System." *The Annals of the American Academy of Political and Social Science* 411 (1974): 1–175.

Smith, Steven S., and Christopher J. Deering. *Committees in Congress.* 1984.

Sharon Stiver Gressle

POWELL, ADAM CLAYTON, JR. (1908–1972), Democratic representative from Harlem (New York City) and prominent civil rights advocate. An African American, Powell was elected to Congress in 1944 and became chairman of the House Education and Labor Committee in 1961. Throughout his twenty-five years in the House he continued to serve as pastor of the large Abyssinian Baptist Church in Harlem; the congregation was also important as a political base.

Powell's career was characterized by controversy stemming from income tax evasion charges, overseas junkets, a high absentee record, misuse of committee funds, and legal problems involving a New York City constituent who sued him for libel. In 1967, as a result of these cumulative problems, the House excluded him from his seat following his reelection in 1966. He took his case to the Supreme Court, becoming the first member of Congress to challenge an exclusion vote. The Supreme Court ruled in his favor in June 1969, establishing the precedent that the House could not exclude a duly elected representative if the person met the three constitutional criteria of age, citizenship, and residence. The Court's ruling did not affect the House decisions to deny Powell his chairmanship, strip him of his seniority, and deduct the amount of misused committee funds from his salary. Powell returned to Congress in 1969 as a freshman but was defeated in a 1970 primary by Charles B. Rangel.

Prior to gaining his chairmanship, Powell had established a national reputation as "Mr. Civil Rights." In addition to his forceful speeches and constant prodding of the federal government to end racial segregation in the military and in federal facilities, over a ten-year period he introduced several amendments to social legislation to prevent federal funds from being allocated to any state or district that practiced racial discrimination. These "Powell Amendments" created considerable debate among liberal forces in Congress and throughout the country. Many felt such amendments would ensure the defeat of much-needed social legislation and were

Adam Clayton Powell, Jr. On 10 January 1967.
Library of Congress

therefore ill advised. Others supported Powell and applauded his unwillingness to compromise. The substance of the "Powell Amendments" was ultimately enacted into law in Title VI of the Civil Rights Act of 1964.

His seniority allowed Powell to assume the chairmanship of his committee despite the objections of some Democrats who resented his endorsement of President Dwight D. Eisenhower for reelection in 1956. Powell's defenders correctly countered that there had been other Democrats who had not supported the party in past elections but had not been punished. The issue of a racial double standard was constantly raised against those who attacked Powell throughout his controversial career.

The Education and Labor Committee led by Powell was responsible for much of the social welfare legislation enacted during the New Frontier and Great Society years of the 1960s. Powell was widely acknowledged to be effective in his role as chairman. Rather than create standing subcommittees, he assigned particular subjects to members. This approach was favored by his committee colleagues because it permitted them to concentrate on issues of particular interest to themselves and their constituents.

Throughout his career Powell enjoyed strong support in his Harlem district, whose lines were drawn in 1943 specifically to provide a likely seat for an African American. In 1970, the district was redrawn to include several hundred voters outside Harlem, who subsequently provided the margin for Powell's defeat.

BIBLIOGRAPHY

Hamilton, Charles V. *Adam Clayton Powell, Jr.: The Political Biography of an American Dilemma.* 1991.

Powell, Adam Clayton, Jr. *Adam by Adam, The Autobiography of Adam Clayton Powell, Jr.* 1971.

CHARLES V. HAMILTON

POWELL V. MCCORMACK (395 U.S. 486 [1969]). Writing in *Federalist* 60, Alexander Hamilton stated that "the qualifications of the persons who may . . . be chosen [to serve in Congress] . . . are defined and fixed in the Constitution, and are unalterable." The significance of *Powell v. McCormack* is that it made Hamilton's words judicially enforceable. The House of Representatives excluded Adam Clayton Powell from membership, after his election to the 90th Congress, on grounds that he had wrongfully diverted House funds in the previous Congress, had made false reports on expenditures of House funds, and had improperly asserted his congressional privileges to avoid litigation in New York courts. He and a group of voters in his district sued the Speaker of the House and other officials to invalidate his exclusion.

The Supreme Court first held that the issue of exclusion could be raised in court, that it was not a political question and was thus meet for judicial resolution, and second, that when the Constitution prescribed three qualifications for House members—age, citizenship, and residency—these were exclusive and could not be added to by the House or, necessarily, by the states. To support this conclusion, the Court reviewed the practice by which both House and Senate had denied the states the power to add to qualifications and the inconsistent post–Civil War practice in which the houses both asserted and denied the authority to add to qualifications. The House did have the power to police the

'THAT TAKES CARE OF THAT!'

A POTENTIALLY EXPLOSIVE PRECEDENT. The resolution of the *Powell* case is satirized for its future implications for Congress. Gib Crockett, *Washington Star*, 1967.
LIBRARY OF CONGRESS

behavior of its members, the Court stated, but if it wished to punish a member by denying the member a seat, it must expel the member, an action requiring a two-thirds vote, not exclusion by a majority.

Powell remains a potent precedent as successful efforts are made in the states to impose term limits on members by state action. The case provides a judicial avenue for challenging the efforts and a probable precedent for determining the results.

BIBLIOGRAPHY

McLaughlin, Gerald T. "Congressional Self-Discipline: The Power to Expel, to Exclude and to Punish." *Fordham Law Review* 41 (1972): 43.

Symposium. "Comments on *Powell v. McCormack.*" *UCLA Law Review* 17 (1969): 1.

JOHNNY H. KILLIAN

POWERS OF CONGRESS. *See* Congress, *article on* Powers of Congress.

PRECEDENTS. [*This entry includes two separate discussions of precedents in Congress, the first on the House and the second on the Senate. See also Manuals of Procedure.*]

House Precedents

The prefaces to Asher C. Hinds's, Clarence Cannon's, and Lewis Deschler and William Holmes Brown's Precedents of the U.S. House of Representatives all recite the overriding importance of precedent in assuring the stability of parliamentary bodies and protection of the rights of its various components: the majority, the minority, individual members, and the entire membership. Hinds describes the great majority of the rules of all parliamentary bodies as "unwritten law; they spring up by precedent and custom and are to this day the chief law of both Houses of Congress." However, he, Cannon, Deschler, and Brown all recognized the need to publish the precedents, not only to expedite the routine business of the House, but to enhance the concept of parliamentary equity and the prestige of the legislative branch of government.

The precedents of the House, while comprising the "unwritten law" in that they are not prescripted as standards of general applicability in advance of their establishment, fall into three main categories: (1) the rulings or decisions of the Speaker or chairman or Committee of the Whole, which are generally made in resolving a point of order or parliamentary inquiry (as distinguished from a situation that merely lurks in the *Record* and is never brought to the chair's attention); (2) the decisions or conclusions, express or implied, that emanate from the House itself without objection being made; and (3) precedents sub silento, that is, practices or procedures of the House that are never specifically ruled on but that have a tacit conceptual underpinning of procedural correctness and are thus more than mere "instances" or procedural aberrations. The definition of "precedent" as represented by these categories is to be distinguished from a routine substantive result that does not illuminate the procedure of the House, such as the regularity with which the House may vote for or against a particular bill.

A decision by the Speaker or chairman is a precedent in subsequent procedural dispute where the same point is again in controversy. Before applying a precedent, however, the chair must first be convinced that the pending factual situation—for example, the pending relationship between the underlying text and amendment offered thereto in the case of a germaneness question—does indeed comprise the same point.

On the theory that a government of laws is preferable to a government of men and women, the House has repeatedly recognized the importance of following its precedents and obeying its well-established procedural rules. In so doing, the House is applying a doctrine known to appellate courts as stare decisis, under which a judge in making a decision will look to earlier cases involving the same question of law. Determination of the will of the majority in an orderly and predictable way is to be desired, and thus parliamentary law as "common law" has come to be recognized as binding on the assembly and its members (except as it may be varied by the adoption by the membership of special rules).

BIBLIOGRAPHY

U.S. House of Representatives. *Cannon's Precedents of the House of Representatives of the United States*, by Clarence Cannon. 8 vols. 74th Cong., 1st sess., 1935.

U.S. House of Representatives. *Deschler's Precedents of the United States House of Representatives*, by Lewis Deschler. 10 vols. 94th Cong., 2d sess., 1977. H. Doc. 94–661.

U.S. House of Representatives. *Hinds' Precedents of the House of Representatives of the United States*, by Asher C. Hinds. 5 vols. 59th Cong., 2d sess., 1907.

U.S. House of Representatives. *Procedure in the United States House of Representatives*, by Lewis Deschler and William Holmes Brown. 4th ed. 97th Cong., 2d sess., 1982.

CHARLES W. JOHNSON

Senate Precedents

Since its Standing Rules provide only a skeletal framework for procedure, the U.S. Senate relies on recorded precedents to clarify and preserve its legislative practices. The historical development of Senate procedure has tended to enhance the legislative rights of individual senators and political minorities.

The absence of fundamental procedural constraints in the rules is striking. The rules do not, for example, impose a general germaneness requirement on amendments. Similarly, there is no limit to the time senators may consume in debate. Senators may, therefore, raise nonrelevant issues almost at will. Extensive, even exhaustive, debate may follow, often in face of the will of a large majority. Such freedoms dramatically affect the Senate's day-to-day consideration of legislation. The body has thus necessarily developed a mass of precedents addressing every conceivable aspect of procedure, and these have become essential to the Senate's ability to conduct business in an orderly manner. The precedents are the road signs on the Senate's legislative map.

Precedents are established in a variety of ways. The manner in which a precedent arises dictates its procedural weight in future Senate practice. The precedents of the greatest probative value are created when the Senate votes on a procedural question. In rare instances, such a vote occurs when the chair (the vice president, the president pro tempore, or a senator acting as presiding officer) submits a point of order to the Senate for consideration. More commonly, the Senate votes on an appeal from a ruling by the chair in response to a point of order. The Senate may vote to sustain or to reverse any ruling by the chair. A precedent is created regardless of the ultimate outcome of the vote.

Precedents of lesser weight are established when the chair rules on a point of order raised by a senator from the floor. The majority of the Senate's precedents are created in this manner. The chair's rulings, based on interpretation of Senate rules, precedents, and relevant statutes, are controlling in the Senate unless an appeal is taken.

Precedents of relatively limited probative value arise when the chair responds to a parliamentary inquiry from the Senate floor on some question of procedure. Responses to parliamentary inquiries are advisory opinions and are not necessarily dispositive statements of Senate practice or procedure. They do, however, provide guidance to the chair in the absence of precedents of greater weight.

Precedents occasionally arise when the chair itself calls a senator to order. This practice often springs from interpretations of the Senate's cloture rule. Cloture is the process by which the Senate determines, by supermajority vote, to limit debate on a question. Precedents initiated by the chair reflect the extraordinary significance of cloture within Senate procedure. The Senate always retains the right to reject the chair's rulings. Historically, the Senate has shown great deference to the chair within the cloture context.

Senate precedents are compiled and maintained by the Office of the Parliamentarian, a nonpartisan arm of the Office of the Secretary of the Senate.

BIBLIOGRAPHY

U.S. Senate. Committee on Rules and Administration. *Standing Rules of the Senate.* 1990. S. Doc. 101-25.

U.S. Senate. *Riddick's Senate Procedure, Precedents, and Practices,* by Floyd M. Riddick and Alan S. Frumin. 101st Cong., 2d sess., 1992. S. Doc. 101-28.

U.S. Senate. Committee on Rules and Administration. *Congressional Handbook.* 1990. S. Prt. 101-103.

JAMES P. WEBER

PRESIDENT AND CONGRESS. [*This entry includes two separate articles:*

An Overview

Legislative Success

The first describes patterns of interrelation between Congress and the president. The second examines presidential success concerning legislative initiatives. For further discussion of relations between Congress and the executive branch, see Advice and Consent; Bureaucracy; Cabinet and Congress; Checks and Balances; Constitution; Delegation of Powers; Emergency Powers; Oversight; Removal Power; Separation of Powers; War Powers. *See also* Executive Agreement; Executive Branch; Executive Communications; Executive Privilege; Executive Reorganization; Impeachment; Presidential Appointments; Presidential Assassinations and Protection; Presidential Transitions; Veto; *and biographies of particular presidents.*]

An Overview

One of the enduring conflicts in U.S. government is that between Congress and the presidency. At times Congress has been dominant; at other times the presidency has been in control; and at still other times the two branches have been roughly in balance. The Framers of the Constitution established the conflict in 1787 when they devised a government with Congress as the preeminent branch and the president as secondary to, but independent of, the legislature.

The Framers intensified the conflict when they combined a system of checks and balances with that of separation of powers. The Framers knew that separation of powers was a misnomer. The Constitution separates the three branches of government (legislative, executive, and judicial), but it fuses their functions, as each branch shares in the powers of another branch. For instance, Congress has the legislative power but the president has the power to veto congressional legislation. The

Framers further magnified the conflict by providing for a bicameral legislature. Friction arises not simply between the president and Congress but among the House, the Senate, and the president.

That the three institutions have separate electoral bases and terms of office makes matters worse. Presidents often face a Congress in which one or both houses are controlled by the opposite party. In seventeen of the forty-six Congresses from 1900 to 1994—thirty-four years—the majority party in one or both houses has been the party opposing the president. The Framers thus guaranteed an ongoing struggle between successive Congresses and presidents attempting to direct government action.

Theories of Presidential and Congressional Power. Three theories of power—one concerning congressional power and two concerning presidential power—have guided the conflict between Congress and the president. In the Constitution, the Framers offered a theory of congressional activism in which Congress, acting on behalf of the people, defines the scope and policies of the national government. "In republican government," wrote James Madison in *Federalist* 51, "the legislative authority necessarily predominates." The Congress enjoys a series of enumerated and implied powers that place it in charge of the very stuff of government: the authority to raise, borrow, coin, and spend money; the power to regulate the nation's interstate and foreign commerce; and the authority to oversee the national defense by declaring war, maintaining the army and the navy, and placing state militias in the service of the United States.

The Framers conceived of a theory of presidential restraint to complement their theory of congressional activism. Under this conception, the president acts as a true executive—carrying out the wishes of Congress and not initiating government action. The Framers did not wish the executive to be as powerful as the one they had known in the British monarchy, but they did wish to give the executive sufficient "energy" to counteract any congressional excesses. In the Constitution, the president has a series of enumerated powers, less

VIEW OF THE CAPITOL. From the White House, c. 1840. Engraving by H. Wallis from a sketch by W. H. Bartlett, in *Bartlett's History of America.*   LIBRARY OF CONGRESS

developed than those given to Congress, which include treaty making, appointing government officials, serving as military commander in chief, vetoing legislation, and executing the laws. By the logic of presidential restraint, the president acts only according to specified constitutional powers or others found in federal law.

The Framers' theory of congressional activism, coupled with that of presidential restraint, directed government action throughout most of the nineteenth century. After the turn of the century, however, two progressive presidents, Republican Theodore Roosevelt (1901–1909) and Democrat Woodrow Wilson (1913–1921), propounded a theory of presidential activism to replace the Framers' theory of presidential restraint. Roosevelt offered a twofold definition of presidential activism. First, in the absence of any specific prohibitions in the Constitution or in law, the president has an inherent grant of executive power to do whatever he feels is necessary to act in the public interest. Second, the president makes such claims, in Roosevelt's words, as the "steward of the people," or the people's representative. Wilson extended Roosevelt's claims of public leadership, maintaining that the link between the president and the public was the most significant feature of the office and not merely, as Roosevelt had maintained, a significant aspect of presidential power. Presidential activism turns presidential restraint on its head and makes the president at least as powerful as Congress.

With the introduction of presidential activism, the theory of congressional activism was not replaced by one of congressional restraint. Instead, throughout the twentieth century, as demands on government grew, both the president and Congress relied on notions of activism. These combinations of theories—congressional activism and presidential restraint in the nineteenth century and congressional activism and presidential activism in the twentieth century—have set the tone for the conflict between Congress and the president in four areas of power: legislation, war, executive action, and diplomacy.

Legislation. Most nineteenth-century presidents followed the lead of George Washington (1789–1797), who believed that the president's role was to execute the laws of Congress faithfully, not actively initiate legislation. Thomas Jefferson (1801–1809) proved an exception when he developed a disciplined party organization of Jeffersonian Republicans in Congress with the president as its leader. Yet, mindful of the precedent set by Wash-

THE PRESIDENTS OF THE UNITED STATES. Depicted on a printed French textile, c. 1827.

ington that the president should not directly guide the course of congressional events, Jefferson privately funneled proposals to Republican members of Congress. When Jefferson left office, the party apparatus he had established became a congressional, not an executive, tool. With the exceptions of Andrew Jackson (1829–1837), James K. Polk (1845–1849), and Abraham Lincoln (1861–1865), the remaining nineteenth-century presidents endorsed presidential restraint in legislation. Congress handled issues of slavery, western expansion, Reconstruction, tariffs, and industrialization with little help from presidents.

Not until the progressives championed the view that innovation should be expected from the president did presidential activism in legislative affairs emerge and remain. Theodore Roosevelt sent Congress his Square Deal initiatives, which included antitrust action, railroad regulation, consumer protection, civil service reform, and conservation. Woodrow Wilson's New Freedom crafted Progressivism to the traditions of the Democratic party, pushing for lower tariffs, an overhaul of the banking system, agricultural reform, and the adoption of a federal income tax. Although Warren G. Harding (1921–1923), Calvin Coolidge (1923–1929), and Herbert Hoover (1929–1933) were not as active as

Roosevelt or Wilson, they presented or supported initiatives before Congress on several occasions, thus continuing to move beyond the bounds of the nineteenth-century presidency. For instance, Harding endorsed the Budget and Accounting Act of 1921, which instituted a central comprehensive budget under presidential control.

Franklin D. Roosevelt (1933–1945) raised the legislative agenda-setting power of Theodore Roosevelt and Wilson to two new levels. First, the sheer quantity of his initiatives surpassed earlier presidential activism. New Deal legislation was adopted on a wide range of topics, including banking, securities, direct relief to states and localities, industrial codes, labor practices, farm relief, and social security. Second, much of the legislation required the delegation of power from Congress to the president to implement the programs. Roosevelt not only asserted power to propose programs but gained from Congress discretionary power to implement the programs. Presidents since Roosevelt have continued to offer policy packages. Harry S. Truman (1945–1953) announced the Fair Deal; John F. Kennedy (1961–1963) heralded the New Frontier; Lyndon B. Johnson (1963–1969) called for the Great Society; and Richard M. Nixon (1969–1974) announced the New Federalism. The initiatives of Ronald Reagan (1981–1989) were never officially titled because the nickname "Reaganomics" stuck so well.

To sell their legislative programs, presidents must "hit the ground running"—that is, they must present major policy initiatives with great public fanfare in the first months of their term. The honeymoon with the press, the public, and Congress, which almost all presidents enjoy upon taking office, provides presidents with the greatest opportunity to get what they want. To achieve success, presidents engage in three strategies: personally lobbying members of Congress, relying on the White House liaison staff to lobby Congress, and making appeals to the American public, which will itself lobby Congress.

Personal lobbying. Presidents can be their own best (or worst) liaison officers with congressional members. They use various mixes of accommodationist, combative, and detached legislative styles as events, bills, and members dictate. In adopting an accommodationist style, a president builds coalitions through bargaining and give-and-take. Lyndon Johnson frequently played the accommodationist by getting as many members of Congress as possible involved in legislation, keeping tabs on

support, using personal persuasion, and granting personal and political favors to convince members to join the coalition. Adopting the combative style, a president builds coalitions through threats and intimidation. Although Johnson often employed an accommodationist style, he also displayed a combative style by withdrawing support from a member's favorite bill if the member did not support the presidential initiative. In adopting a detached style, a president removes himself from lobbying efforts as much as possible and relies heavily on the formal congressional liaison staff to build a coalition. President Jimmy Carter (1977–1981), who had campaigned as a Washington outsider, adopted a detached style and did not personally court the Democratic leadership or membership. As criticism mounted, Carter's style began to shift to a more accommodationist approach.

White House liaison. Presidents since Dwight D. Eisenhower (1953–1961) have also relied on a staff of legislative liaisons to monitor the progress of their programs and other legislation through Congress. (Today, the liaison staff numbers nearly twenty people in the Office of Legislative Affairs.) Presidents Kennedy, Johnson, Nixon, Gerald R. Ford (1974–1977), Reagan, George Bush (1989–1993), and Bill Clinton (1993–) organized their liaison offices around key blocs in Congress, based on combinations of geography, ideology, and party. Some liaison staff members were assigned conservative Democrats; others courted their more liberal colleagues; still other staffers were assigned to Republicans. Carter initially reorganized the liaison office along issue lines because he felt members would support an issue on its merits. When members of Congress told Carter that he did not understand congressional factions, Carter switched to the approach taken by the other presidents.

Public appeals. Presidents also seek support for presidential programs before Congress by taking their case to the people. Theodore Roosevelt summed up this approach: "I achieved results only by appealing over the heads of the Senate and House leaders to the people, who were the masters of both of us." Presidents gamble that they will gain popular support by making public appearances throughout the country, delivering national radio and television addresses, and holding news conferences. If they are successful, they will use this new public support in bargaining with members of Congress.

Success and vetoes. How well have presidents done in Congress? Analyses of roll-call votes exam-

PRESIDENT RONALD REAGAN. *Left,* with Speaker Thomas P. (Tip) O'Neill, Jr. (D-Mass.), *right,* 1 July 1981. Vice President George Bush looks on. Photograph by Michael Evans, the White House.

COURTESY OF THE RONALD REAGAN LIBRARY

ine whether a majority of members concur with presidents' public stands on bills. Although this indicator is often referred to as presidential success, *presidential-congressional concurrence* is a better term. The measure merely shows the number of times presidents and Congresses agree on bills. It does not say anything about who influenced whom. Members of both parties will overwhelmingly support many roll-call votes regardless of whether the president has a position. The results show that the president and a majority of members of Congress often agree on legislation, especially early in the president's term, when the president and the Congress are of the same party and when the president's public approval is high.

This concurrence should not mask the difficulties many presidents have in getting their top-priority programs through Congress. Although people remember the early days of Roosevelt's New Deal, Johnson's Great Society, and Reagan's budget and tax cuts, some presidents have encountered problems in getting Congress to pass the main items on their policy agenda. In 1961, only one of Kennedy's high-priority items—rural development—was enacted; Nixon was unable to get his welfare reform plan through Congress intact; Ford's economic initiatives failed to win passage, as did Bush's capital gains tax proposal; Carter had difficulties with his energy, environment, and hospital-cost containment plans; and Clinton encountered opposition to his economic stimulus plan and health care reform. Members of Congress typically have their own ideas about what are major problems and how to solve them.

As the Framers intended, presidents do well in vetoing legislation. Woodrow Wilson observed in *Congressional Government* (1885) that a president's "power of veto . . . is, of course, beyond all comparison, his most formidable prerogative." Strategically, however, presidents recognize that vetoes are negative powers: by vetoing legislation a president stops what he does not want, but he does not get what he does want. According to the Constitution, a presidential veto automatically prevents a bill passed by both houses from becoming law unless two-thirds of both houses vote to override the veto. Getting two-thirds of all members of Congress to agree on a controversial action such as an override is almost always a herculean task. Congress has overridden presidents' vetoes just over one hundred times in more than two hundred years—a mere seven-tenths of 1 percent of all vetoes. This statistic applies only to regular vetoes. Congress cannot override so-called pocket vetoes, which occur when Congress adjourns before the elapse of the ten-day period that the Constitution gives the president to make up his mind. Between 1789 and 1991, presidents used the regular veto on 1,447 bills and the pocket veto on 1,055 bills. Actual vetoes are important items in a president's legislative bag of tricks, but veto threats may be just as compelling. Because overrides are usually unsuccessful, a president may exact compromises from Congress by threatening a veto. Congressional activism and presidential activism are pronounced in the legislative arena.

War. The Framers felt that the president's designation as commander in chief merely established that a civilian head would be in charge of the military. The commander would have the power to respond to surprise attacks but not to do much more without congressional authorization. Congress was expressly given the power to declare war and provide for the armed forces. Although Lincoln did not concur, all other nineteenth-century presidents acted as commanders in chief under the theory of presidential restraint. Jefferson made two requests to Congress to engage in offensive actions (against Tripoli in 1801 and Spain in 1805), both of which Congress denied. Although President Polk asked for and received a congressional declaration of war against Mexico in 1846, Congress, not the president, led the country to war against England in the War of 1812 and against Spain in the Spanish-American War of 1898.

Lincoln, however, asserted presidential activism in military affairs. He acted unilaterally during a three-month period at the outset of the Civil War when Congress was not in session to, among other things, call out state militias, expand the army and navy, spend $2 million from the Treasury without congressional appropriation, and issue the first Emancipation Proclamation. Congress approved some of the decisions (not all) after the fact.

Presidents' powers in the two declared total wars of the twentieth century—World War I and World War II—were as vast as those claimed by Lincoln and extended over the whole U.S. economy and social order, but Congress delegated many of these powers to the president. For instance, Congress gave Wilson the power to take over factories and railroads, fix prices in certain industries, declare certain exports unlawful, censor foreign communications, and operate the telephone and telegraph systems. Similarly, Congress gave Franklin Roosevelt the authority to establish and staff numerous emergency boards; to negotiate with other countries the sale, lease, or exchange of various items related to defense; and to evacuate and confine seventy thousand American citizens of Japanese descent residing on the West Coast.

Since World War II, presidents have effectively devised their own war-making power by expanding their authority as commander in chief and preempting Congress's power to declare war. This presidential war-making power involves presidents' ability to unilaterally commit U.S. troops anywhere on the globe. Presidents have unilaterally committed U.S. forces in two types of restricted military interventions: limited wars and emergency interventions.

Limited wars. So-called limited wars are limited in resources and goals. They involve specific initial commitments of troops, although the numbers have typically increased incrementally as such wars have gone on. The goal of a limited war often falls short of all-out victory. U.S. objectives have been to prevent communism in a vulnerable nation, for example, or to stop an aggressive dictator, not necessarily to bring the enemy to its knees. Limited wars are defensive military efforts confined to one country or one region. Today, however, because the United States is a world military and economic power, a president can determine that almost any nation at any moment in some way impinges on the security of the United States. Presidents have conducted three limited wars in the twentieth century: the Korean War, the Vietnam War, and the Persian Gulf War.

Truman took the most expansive view of the president's power to conduct limited war. When a senator asked Truman to seek a congressional resolution to authorize the U.S. intervention in Korea, Truman replied that he did not need one but instead could use his constitutional powers as commander in chief. As the war went on, Truman consistently relied on the commander-in-chief power to add more men, expand the theater of war into North Korea, and threaten the use of nuclear weapons.

Johnson agreed with Truman that the president already had full constitutional authority to send troops to foreign soil, but, unlike Truman, Johnson sought a resolution from Congress to support his decision to commit major ground troops in Vietnam after a reported attack on two U.S. destroyers by North Vietnamese gunboats in the Gulf of Tonkin in late July 1964. On 7 August 1964, Congress passed what became known as the Gulf of Tonkin Resolution, which read: "The Congress approves and supports the determination of the President, as Commander in Chief, to take all necessary measures to repel any armed attack against the forces of the United States and to prevent further aggression." In 1967, Johnson remarked, "We did not think the resolution was necessary to do what we did and what we're doing." Johnson sought the resolution as a matter of political insurance: through the resolution Congress gave the president full power to direct the war but it shared responsibility for the war in case something went wrong. When the Vietnam War turned ugly and Congress repealed the Gulf of Tonkin Resolution in January 1971, Nixon returned to Truman's exclusive reliance on the commander-in-chief power.

Congress attempted to reassert its war-making role with the War Powers Resolution of 1973. Passed over President Nixon's veto, the act requires that within forty-eight hours after committing U.S. troops into actual or "imminent" hostilities, the president must submit a report to Congress describing the reasons and the constitutional authority for the action. Once the notification has been given, a clock starts ticking. The president has sixty days to complete the military action, although he may request a thirty-day extension. The operation, however, must be completed in that ninety-day period unless Congress declares war or supplies specific authorization for the use of U.S. armed forces. The War Powers Resolution looks good on paper as a device by which Congress might reclaim some control over U.S. military efforts, yet presidents since Ford have brushed its requirements aside.

After Iraq invaded Kuwait in August 1990, Bush asserted that he had the sole authority to send first 120,000, then 200,000, and ultimately 560,000 men and women from all branches of the armed forces to fight Iraq. Bush, like Johnson, asked Congress to pass a resolution sanctioning the use of force. Bush, like Johnson, insisted that he had the authority to deploy troops without the resolution. "I don't think I need it," he said. The resolution was consistent with a United Nations declaration that asked member nations to use "all necessary means" to force Iraq out of Kuwait unless it ended its occupation by 15 January 1991. Several days before the deadline, a sharply divided Congress passed Bush's resolution. With the resolution in hand, Bush saw no need to follow the requirements of the War Powers Resolution.

Emergency interventions. Since the Vietnam War, presidents have favored the use of emergency interventions—the engagement of small numbers of troops for short periods of time in situations that purportedly involve threats to American lives. Emergency interventions are often the symbolic flexing of American military muscle that do not risk the large-scale entanglements of limited wars.

Presidents have consistently circumvented the requirements of the War Powers Resolution in ordering emergency interventions. They are loathe to have their hands tied by the act's consultation and report procedures. When Ford ordered the marines and navy to rescue a U.S. merchant ship, the *Mayaguez,* seized by Cambodia in May 1975, he did not report to Congress. Similarly, Carter did not tell Congress beforehand of the secret, ultimately unsuccessful, helicopter mission in March 1980 to try to free Americans held hostage in Iran. In October 1983, Reagan and Congress worked out a complex compromise regarding U.S. Marines in Lebanon. For the first time, a president invoked the imminent hostilities provision of the War Powers Resolution, but Congress gave Reagan eighteen months to complete the Lebanese mission (rather than the ninety-day maximum called for in the War Powers Resolution). In a separate letter, Reagan refused to recognize the constitutionality of the War Powers Resolution. In October 1985, Reagan informed congressional leaders that he was sending nineteen hundred troops to Grenada to protect the lives of American students on the island. But he expressly refused to comply with the notification requirements of the War Powers Resolution. Bush followed Reagan's lead when he ordered the invasion of Panama in December 1990. Truman had summed up presidential thinking about consulting Congress long before the War Powers Resolution was passed: "I do not have to unless I want to. But of course I am polite and I usually always consult them." Yet Truman did not consult Congress, nor have most presidents, with or without the War Powers Resolution.

Restricted military action, whether in the form of limited wars or emergency interventions, provides presidents unique opportunities to expand presidential activism. Congress today, weary because of Vietnam and wary of what many members perceive as a diminution of congressional activism, is plainly aware of this pattern. As the debates before the Persian Gulf War attested, Congress is no longer likely to be the silent partner of military affairs that presidents prefer. Instead, it will act as a watchdog. Its best weapon is not the War Powers Resolution but its appropriations power—its ability to give presidents money and to take it away. Although congressional efforts are often reactive and sporadic, post-Vietnam Congresses have consciously sought to avoid losing congressional power to activist presidents.

Executive Action. The Constitution instructs the president to take care that the laws be faithfully executed and to appoint executive officers to help in that execution. Ambiguities in these stipulations of the Constitution have, however, led to yet other conflicts between the legislative and executive branches.

Removal power. During the nineteenth century, the central debate in the arena of executive action stemmed from the Constitution's ambiguity concerning how executive officers can be removed from office. Although the Constitution gave the president the authority to make appointments with the advice and consent of the Senate, it was silent on the removal of such appointees. Congress narrowly defeated a bill opposed by Washington that would have made removal subject to Senate consent. As political parties grew, so did the practice of patronage whereby presidents gave government jobs to loyal party members. To maintain party unity, presidents accepted the names of job applicants from members of Congress, who took more and more interest in presidential appointments and, consequently, in presidential removals.

In 1867, Congress passed over Andrew Johnson's (1865–1869) veto the Tenure of Office Act, which required Senate consent for the president's removal of any executive official previously confirmed by the Senate, thus codifying presidential restraint. Johnson's resistance to the act led to his impeachment and near conviction. Congress denied President Ulysses S. Grant (1869–1877) his request to repeal the Tenure of Office Act. Presidents Rutherford

B. Hayes (1877–1881) and James A. Garfield (1881) fought against congressional efforts to block presidential nominations. After an eighteen-month battle, Hayes felt he had beaten top Senate leaders: "The contest has been a bitter one. It has exposed me to attack, opposition, misconstruction, and the actual hatred of powerful men. But I have had great success. No member of either house now attempts even to dictate appointments. My sole right to make appointments is now tacitly conceded." But senators continued to block executive appointments and removals until 1887, when Congress repealed the Tenure of Office Act. After a struggle of two decades, presidents regained their control over executive appointments and removals. Yet the victory did little more than recapture old ground. Presidents gained control of the executive action, but the action was decidedly restricted.

Congressional delegation and executive orders. In the twentieth century, the debate over executive power shifted from executive removals to congressional delegation of power. Congress has provided a dramatic expansion of executive power by its delegation of power to the president in two ways. First, Congress specifies that a law goes into effect when the president determines an event has occurred or a set of conditions has been met. Second, Congress gives the president authority to issue executive orders to carry out the substance of legislation. Executive orders carry the weight of law but do not require the approval of Congress. Executive orders allow presidents to act as legislators and in effect create a presidential lawmaking power.

Presidents since Franklin Roosevelt have used executive orders to shape policy. On civil rights, Roosevelt established the Fair Employment Practices Commission in 1943 to prevent discrimination in hiring by government agencies and military suppliers. Truman ended segregation in the armed services by executive order. Eisenhower and Kennedy issued executive orders to enforce school desegregation in Arkansas, Mississippi, and Alabama. In 1965, Johnson signed an executive order that required affirmative action (the active seeking of qualified minority applicants) in hiring by the federal government and government contractors. Reagan, who opposed affirmative action, sought to "repeal" Johnson's order, but public controversy swelled and he dropped the idea.

Reagan signed, and Bush continued, an executive order that prohibited federally funded family planning clinics from informing their clients about abortion. The Supreme Court in *Rust v. Sullivan* (1991) upheld the order. Congress tried several times to pass legislation that would have negated the executive order, but Bush vetoed one such attempt and threatened to veto others. Congress was unable to rally the two-thirds vote of both houses needed to override the Bush veto, and in October 1992 the executive order went into full effect. It did not last long. Also acting by executive order, President Clinton overturned this Reagan-Bush "gag order" as one of his first acts in office.

In an attempt to control presidential lawmaking, Congress has fashioned the so-called legislative veto. By means of this device, Congress may disapprove of executive orders designed to enforce legislation. In the most typical instance, Congress requires that the proposed executive action lie before Congress for a specified period of time. If, during the time period, either house disapproves the measure, it is void. In 1983, the Supreme Court held in *Immigration and Naturalization Service v. Chadha* that the legislative veto is unconstitutional because it is a violation of separation of powers. The Supreme Court's ruling against legislative vetoes has done little, however, to eliminate them as statutory and informal devices. In the year immediately following the Chadha case, Congress placed fifty-three legislative vetoes into bills that Reagan signed. As with legislation and war, congressional activism and presidential activism rival each other in matters of executive action.

Diplomacy. Although in legislation, war, and executive action, presidential restraint directed the actions of nineteenth-century presidents, presidents beginning with George Washington took an activist role in diplomacy and never lost the advantage to Congress. Although the Framers saw foreign relations as a joint presidential-senatorial venture, Washington moved the Senate to a subordinate role. He asserted that the negotiation of treaties was under the exclusive purview of the executive and that the president had a monopoly on the right to communicate with foreign governments. Members of Congress were willing to accept the president's central position in foreign affairs. The president was, according to Rep. John Marshall (later the chief justice of the United States), "the sole organ of the nation in its external relations, and its sole representative with foreign nations." In dicta the Supreme Court ratified the sole-organ doctrine in *United States v. Curtiss-Wright Export Corp.* (1936), stating that the president's power as the sole organ did "not require as a basis for its exercise an act of Congress."

Twentieth-century presidents have expanded their foreign policy role by the use of what are known as executive agreements. These are international agreements entered into by presidents; unlike treaties they do not require Senate consent. Presidents since Truman have entered into roughly seven times as many executive agreements as treaties. Truman both started and ended U.S. involvement in the Korean War by executive agreement, and Johnson and Nixon made key decisions to escalate the Vietnam War in the same way.

Treaties, however, have not been abandoned as a form of diplomatic exchange. In some instances, the importance of a diplomatic effort mandates a treaty, as did the creation of the North Atlantic Treaty Organization (NATO) after World War II and several Strategic Arms Limitation Talks (SALT) beginning in the Nixon administration. Presidents see political advantages to having the Senate on board. In other cases, tradition dictates that a treaty rather than an executive agreement be adopted. But presidents have few difficulties even with treaties. To be sure, presidents must keep an eye on Congress, especially the Senate, in negotiating treaties. Provisions of important treaties frequently evolve through informal consultation with senators. Senate ratification is usually pro forma, however. Since 1949, presidents have won approval of all but two treaties submitted to the Senate. If a treaty is in trouble, a president is more likely to withdraw it rather than face its defeat. In addition, the Supreme Court has held that presidents may unilaterally break treaties. The sole-organ doctrine espoused by presidents and approved by the Court gives presidents a broad, inherent claim of diplomatic power and plenty of room for unilateral action.

The presidents immediately before and after the Civil War are often depicted as prosaic, unhappy men unable to champion the office in which they served. In this view, they were too shy, too lazy, too inept, or too stupid to live up to the office's potential. Yet personality and talent hardly seem to explain why twenty of the twenty-five presidents during the eighteenth and nineteenth centuries were lords of passivity. Only Washington, Jefferson, Jackson, Polk, and Lincoln are clear exceptions to the nineteenth-century rule of presidential restraint. Nor does it seem possible that the restraint resulted from the charisma, energy, cunning, and intelligence of members of Congress. What stood in the way of nineteenth-century presidents were the ideas that the Framers had fashioned years before. The Framers offered a scheme of government dominated by Congress and characterized by presidential restraint. For the most part, the nineteenth-century presidency and Congress followed the Framers' philosophy. Woodrow Wilson declared in 1885 that "unquestionably, the predominant and controlling force, the center and source of all motive and all regulative power, is Congress."

Of the seventeen U.S. presidents of the twentieth century, only William Howard Taft (1909–1913) vigorously fought presidential activism. All the other presidents of this century have advanced, or at least have not opposed, activism in at least one, and often more than one, of the four areas of power. Helping twentieth-century presidents in their advocacy of presidential activism were different ideas, in part drawn from progressivism, that called for an expanded role of government and looked on the president as a representative of the people. Imbued with a public mandate and saddled with a government required to do more and more things for that public, the president's role expanded.

Yet congressional activism has not faded. While presidents today are far more active in the legislative process than any of their nineteenth-century (or even early twentieth-century) predecessors, the legislative process nevertheless remains firmly in congressional hands. The work of congressional committees and subcommittees, the power and autonomy of senior members, the electoral safety of many incumbents, and a complex budget process make it difficult for presidents to dominate Congress. Presidents realize that setting the agenda and getting one's way are two different things. Presidents may dominate, even determine, what problems are discussed, but they may have little control over the solutions that Congress takes seriously or the policy choices that are finally made. Similarly, presidents' command of television, the public's fascination with the president, and weak ties between the president and his party on Capitol Hill prohibit Congress from dominating the presidency. The twentieth-century conflict is not a zero-sum game in which one side wins and the other loses. Although in certain areas of policy, notably war and diplomacy, presidential influence has arguably grown at the expense of Congress, the overall influence of Congress on public affairs has not necessarily diminished. The conflict established by the Framers more than two hundred years ago is still a lively one.

BIBLIOGRAPHY

Davis, Eric. "Congressional Liaison: The People and the Institutions." In Both Ends of the Avenue. Edited by A. King. 1983. Pp. 59–95.
Fisher, Louis. The Politics of Shared Power. 3d ed. 1992.

King, Gary, and Lyn Ragsdale. The Elusive Executive: Discovering Statistical Patterns in the Presidency. 1988.
Light, Paul. The President's Agenda. Rev. ed. 1991.
Milkis, Stanley, and Michael Nelson. The American Presidency: Origins and Development, 1776–1990. 1990.
Ragsdale, Lyn. Presidential Politics. 1993.
Roosevelt, Theodore. Theodore Roosevelt: Autobiography. 1913.
Schlesinger, Arthur, Jr. The Imperial Presidency. 1973.
Shull, Steven, ed. The Two Presidencies. 1991.
Wayne, Stephen. The Legislative Presidency. 1978.
Wilson, Woodrow. Congressional Government. 1885. Repr. 1973.

LYN RAGSDALE

Legislative Success

Measuring the overall success in Congress of an administration's policy initiatives is difficult. The concept of presidential success involves subjective evaluation of the content and importance of the issues on which the president wins and loses. Any merely quantitative summary of presidential success, therefore, is imperfect.

Congressional Quarterly's calculation of presidential victories on all votes on which the president takes a clear-cut position, however, is a defensible and commonly used measure. Although this measure does not reveal how much of the president's program passes, it does provide an indication of the ebb and flow of relations between the president and Congress. Figure 1 shows the percentages from 1953 to 1991. Over the decades shown, Congress supported most of the president's publicly expressed positions on issues that come to the floors of the House and Senate. Only Ronald Reagan in 1987 and 1988 and George Bush in 1990 had success rates below 50 percent.

Yet presidential success is low compared to parliamentary systems, where prime ministers can expect to win over 90 percent of the votes. Only Lyndon B. Johnson in 1965 experienced a success rate exceeding 90 percent. The U.S. Congress remains an autonomous institution with the will and power to defeat the president's policy preferences.

As figure 1 also shows, legislative success varies substantially between presidents and over time within individual administrations. Four variables explain variation in presidential success in Congress: (1) political parties, (2) political ideology, (3) the president's popularity with the public, and (4) the president's leadership skills. Party and ideology are properties that members bring with them to Congress and over which presidents have little con-

Figure 1
Presidential Success on Roll-Call Votes in Congress, 1953–1991

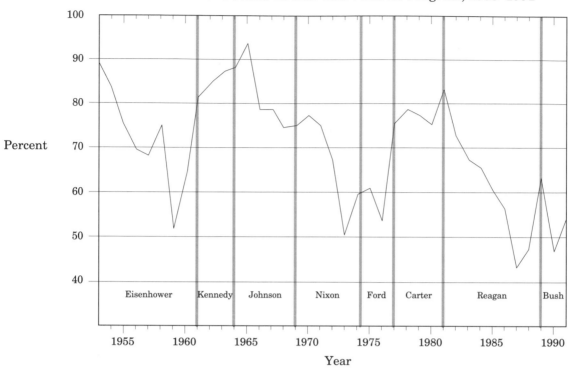

SOURCE: *Congressional Quarterly Weekly Report*, 28 December 1991, p. 3754.

trol. Presidential popularity and leadership skills, on the other hand, are factors directly concerned with the executive.

In addition, the institutional structure of Congress helps shape relations between the president and Congress. Committees and subcommittees, party and committee leaders, and congressional rules and norms all have the power to influence members' behavior.

Political Parties. Members of the president's party in Congress are more likely to support administration policy than are members of the opposition. Consequently, majority-party presidents win more often than minority-party presidents. For the period from 1953 to 1984, majority-party presidents won an average of 78 percent of House votes and 76 percent of Senate votes, while minority presidents won only 54 percent of the time in both chambers (Bond and Fleisher, 1990).

Why are members of the president's party predisposed to support his policy preferences? First, because members of the same political party must satisfy similar electoral coalitions, they share a wide range of policy preferences in common. Thus,

for many members of the president's party, constituency interests and presidential support do not conflict. Second, members of the president's party who seek reelection must run on his record as well as their own. Consequently, they have an incentive to help him succeed. Third, members of the same party share a psychological attachment to a common political symbol. Because American political parties are diverse and decentralized, disagreements between the president and members of his party are inevitable. But the conflicts within the president's party are ordinarily not as intense as those with the opposition.

Finally, the president has political resources that can be used to reward loyal party members and, more rarely, to punish those who stray. Presidents provide many types of favors for members of Congress (Edwards, 1984). These range from flattery from and social contact with the president to help with constituent problems and campaign aid. Presidential favors and attention go disproportionately to members of the president's party (Covington, 1988). Because most members of Congress can get reelected without the president's direct help, the effects of this activity are limited. But such favoritism does create a reserve of goodwill that may increase support on key issues.

Thus, parties provide the president with a base of support on which to build majority coalitions in Congress. Compared to political parties in other Western democracies, however, American parties are weak and undisciplined. Even when party voting in Congress was at a peak in the late nineteenth and early twentieth centuries, party loyalty among members of Congress barely reached the levels found in most other party systems (Brady and Althoff, 1974). The reforms of 1909–1911 and the rise of the seniority system in Congress limited party leaders' ability to command support from the rank and file.

Lax discipline in congressional parties means that majority presidents experience defections and defeats in Congress. But given the frequent periods of divided government in the United States, tighter party discipline could well lead to policy stalemate. The relatively loose discipline allows minority presidents to put together majority coalitions in support of their policy preferences fairly often.

Political Ideology. Because ideology is a major influence on lawmakers' roll-call votes, the president can attract support from members of both parties who have ideologies, and thus policy preferences, similar to his own. Party and ideology, of course, are related and usually mutually reinforcing. But each party embraces individuals with widely differing policy preferences that may be arrayed along a liberal-conservative continuum. Some members of each party will be pressured by beliefs that lie outside their party's mainstream. The weak party system allows individual members to cross party lines and vote their own ideological or policy preferences. Thus on most conflictual issues, the president can attract support from some members of the opposition for the same reasons, but he may lose some members of his own party.

Ideology influences roll-call decision making for several reasons. First, the electoral process brings individuals to Congress who have well-formed and strongly held attitudes on major policy issues. Second, a member's ideology may be reinforced by state or district preferences. Studies of House elections in the 1980s found that incumbents ideologically at odds with their districts were more likely to attract strong challengers (Bond, Covington, and Fleisher, 1985) and were more likely to be defeated (Johannes and McAdams, 1981). Finally, ideology figures in patterns of interaction and cue-taking in Congress. Members of Congress often must vote on roll calls about which they have either very little information or a wealth of undistilled, conflicting information. To make decisions in the limited time available, members turn to each other for information and advice. They tend to seek out knowledgeable colleagues—cue givers—with whom they agree on policy and ideology.

Thus, ideological forces often cause the formation of bipartisan coalitions to support or oppose the president's policy references. These ideological forces help explain why majority presidents have only a limited advantage over minority presidents in building support for their positions in Congress.

Although shared political values provide an important basis of support for the president, the effects of ideology are limited for several reasons. First, most members of Congress are pragmatic politicians whose views and preferences are not at the extremes of a liberal-conservative continuum. Because the typical American voter is not strongly ideological, most representatives try to avoid ideological extremes.

Second, many important votes do not have an ideological aspect. Distributive or pork-barrel programs, for example, typically do not produce ideological divisions. Even conservatives who want to cut domestic spending and liberals who want to re-

POLITICS IN WARTIME. Clifford K. Berryman's commentary on the running battle between Congress and the presidency over such wartime issues as taxes, price controls, and labor relations, 4 July 1943.

"GREAT POLITICAL FEUD" MECHANICAL COIN BANK. When a coin is inserted, Speaker Thomas P. (Tip) O'Neill, Jr. (D-Mass.) raps President Ronald Reagan on the head with his gavel.

COLLECTION OF DAVID J. AND JANICE L. FRENT

duce defense spending work to protect federal programs in their states or districts. Presidents who attempt to tamper with these programs are likely to find few friends in Congress, as Jimmy Carter discovered when he opposed several water projects in 1977 and as Ronald Reagan discovered when he vetoed the highway bill in 1987.

Finally, ideological voting blocs are relatively informal coalitions. The "conservative coalition" of Republicans and southern Democrats, for example, appears on certain votes and sometimes affects the outcome of floor votes. But this coalition has no formal organization or leadership. The formation of ideological coalitions remains relatively ad hoc.

Interaction of Party and Ideology. Both parties in Congress are ideologically diverse. Since the New Deal realignment of the 1930s, the Democratic party nationally has been generally liberal, while the Republican has been conservative. Because a majority in each party holds policy views consistent with their party's ideological mainstream, party and ideology are mutually reinforcing for most members of Congress. But each party has members outside their party's mainstream (i.e., conservative Democrats and liberal Republicans).

Presidents tend to be selected from the dominant ideological wing of their party. Hence, members of Congress can be grouped conceptually into four factions based on how the interaction of party and ideology affects their propensity to support the president's policy preferences. These factions are (1) the president's party base, (2) "cross-pressured" members of the president's party (i.e., those who experience a measure of conflict between their own ideology and that of the party's mainstream), (3) cross-pressured members of the opposition, and (4) the opposition party base.

The president's party base includes individuals who are most likely to support his policies because they share with him both party affiliation and ideological outlook. In Congress, liberal Democrats form the party base of Democratic presidents and conservative Republicans form the party base of Republican presidents. Presidents attract support from cross-pressured members of both parties (i.e., conservative Democrats and liberal Republicans), but partisan and ideological conflicts prevent these individuals from being considered part of the party base of any president. The opposition party base is the mirror image of the president's party base: conservative Republicans for Democratic presidents and liberal Democrats for Republican presidents. Because these members share neither party label nor ideological orientation with the president, they are the least inclined to support his preferences.

The relative size of the factions provides a new president with a more or less favorable mix of congressional members with whom he must interact. Every two years, however, elections change Congress's partisan and ideological mix. Although the president would like to expand the size of his political base, his capacity to do so is limited and appears to be decreasing over time. Incumbency advantage has been rising since the mid 1960s; it has tended to insulate congressional incumbents from national tides and to inhibit the coattails effect during presidential elections.

Although presidential success in Congress depends on the relative size of the party factions, these ratios do not tell the whole story. The number of members in the president's party base rarely constitutes a majority, and because Congress and the executive may have conflicting institutional perspectives on policy issues, even those members who are predisposed to support the president may occasionally fail to do so. Consequently, every president at times needs votes from members of other factions who are generally less inclined to agree with his preferences.

Presidents sometimes take positions that attract support from cross-pressured members and from the opposition. But such a strategy may be counterproductive. As the president takes positions that appeal to factions further and further from his base—from cross-pressured partisans to cross-pressured opponents to the opposition party base—he increasingly risks alienating that base.

Presidents, in short, attract the most support from their party base and the least support from the opposition's party base; support from the two cross-pressured factions falls somewhere in between. Analysis of the seven presidents from Dwight D. Eisenhower to Ronald Reagan indicates that members of the president's party base support him an average of 74 percent of the time, members of the opposition base support him about 30 percent of the time, and members of both party factions support him about 50 percent of the time (Bond and Fleisher, 1990).

Presidential Popularity and Leadership Skills. Because party and ideology are stable, their impact on congressional support for the president is relatively fixed between elections. Presidential popularity, in contrast, is highly variable. No president . since Franklin D. Roosevelt has avoided wide variation in public support while in office (see figure 2).

Presidential popularity is widely thought to affect support in Congress, but evidence supporting that belief is mixed and weak. The effects of presidential popularity are marginal at best. Liberal Democrats, for example, did not become solid supporters of President Reagan even at the zenith of his popularity. Systematic studies of the effects of presidential popularity (Bond and Fleisher, 1990; Edwards, 1989) suggest that presidential popularity does not greatly affect the decision making of members of Congress. Instead, its effects are likely to be indirect, operating through the electoral process to alter the distribution of partisan and ideological forces in Congress through changes in membership.

The study of presidential-congressional relations has been greatly influenced by Richard Neustadt's *Presidential Power* (1960). According to Neustadt, one of the most important sources of influence in Congress is the president's "professional reputation" as skilled or unskilled. Of all the forces that might link the president and Congress, the president's reputation as a leader is the one over which he has the most control. This reputation is defined largely by the perceptions of Washingtonians, but the president has the capacity to mold perceptions.

Students of presidential-congressional relations agree on the essential elements of leadership skill. Although such skills cannot be reduced to a checklist of items that will assure success with Congress, several activities, tactics, and resources seem to be associated with perceptions of skilled presidential leadership. Both interpersonal skills and structuring skills are involved (Bond and Fleisher, 1990).

Interpersonal skills. Interpersonal skills concern the president or his representatives in face-to-face contact with members of Congress. To be effective in these terms, presidents first need an intimate knowledge of Congress and its members. To gain this knowledge, they must spend time with members of Congress to learn their likes and dislikes, their needs and goals, and where the levers of power lie.

Second, presidents must consult with members of Congress, especially congressional leaders, and give them advance notice before initiating major policy proposals. Consultation indicates how proposals will be received and permits members to review the proposals and accommodate themselves to them.

Third, presidents must follow through, using their resources to persuade members to support, or at least not to oppose, their policies. In dealings with Congress, presidents should use their intimate knowledge of Congress to anticipate reactions and confront problems before they become unmanageable.

At the heart of the concept of follow-through is bargaining. Presidents may trade favors, supply members with services and personal amenities, and use personal appeals; they may enlist the aid of cabinet members, other members of Congress, or influential individuals in a member's constituency. If softer methods of persuasion fail, they may try arm-twisting, making implicit or explicit threats. If such tactics do not convert potential opponents or

Figure 2
Public Approval of the President[1]

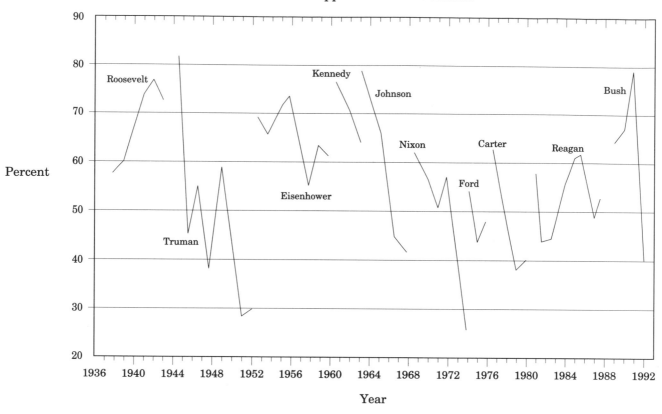

[1]Averaged by year. Respondents were asked, "Do you approve or disapprove of the way _____ (last name of president) is handling his job as president?"

SOURCES: *The Gallup Opinion Index*, October–November 1980, pp. 13–38; *The Gallup Report*, July 1988, pp. 19–20; The Gallup Poll, "Reagan Regaining Public Confidence," press release, 9 October 1988; Gallup Library; Harold W. Stanley and Richard G. Niemi, eds., *Vital Statistics on American Politics*, 3d ed., 1992, p. 279.

undecided members into supporters, at least they may convince members to "take a walk" and not vote against the president (Covington, 1987).

A final interpersonal skill is knowing when and how much to compromise. If the president gives in too soon, it may be seen as a sign of weakness, and he will lose more than necessary. If he waits too long, he may be viewed as stubborn, and resistance in Congress will harden.

Structuring skills. The notion of structuring skills deals with the president's success in manipulating the political environment in which followers operate or in taking advantage of any favorable conditions that might exist in that environment. Previous research has identified several activities associated with structuring skills.

Perhaps the most important structuring resource available to the president is his power to set the congressional agenda (see Edwards 1980; Christenson 1982; Jones 1983; and Malbin 1983). The president should carefully choose which issues to place before Congress and then present them so as to structure the situation to his advantage. Complex issues do not always readily reduce to clear partisan choices. The president, therefore, must frame issues so as to limit the choices open to members of Congress.

A second structuring skill is setting priorities. The president needs to determine which issues are most important, submit proposals to Congress in a measured way, and order his efforts in support of them. Setting priorities not only results in a more efficient use of the president's time but also increases the chances that Congress will focus attention on the issues about which he cares the most. Congress can deal with only a limited number of complex issues at a time. Asking for more attention than even a co-operative Congress is able to give may result in failure of key parts of the president's program.

There is also a strategic consideration in setting priorities. Presidents should consider the order in which proposals will be submitted to Congress. They should try to avoid sending highly divisive issues early in the term that might result in embarrassing defeats or victories that sow undue rancor and bitterness and sour future relations with Congress.

A final structuring skill is a good sense of timing. The president needs to read the mood of Congress and adjust his activities accordingly. Because Congress is more disposed to cooperate during the president's first year in office, the president can often benefit by acting fast, as was demonstrated during the administrations of Lyndon Johnson and Ronald Reagan. Further, unexpected events may give a president unforeseen opportunities for success. After the assassination of President John F. Kennedy in 1963, for example, Congress was ready to give Johnson the unfulfilled portions of his predecessor's program.

Evaluating presidential skills. Although these skills are widely thought to explain presidential success, the evidence toward such an assumption is mixed. Most supportive evidence consists of case studies that show how a president's skilled leadership led to passage of a bill he favored or how lack of skill led to defeat. Although such studies provide rich insights, they do not provide an adequate test of the effects of skills.

First, the empirical evidence offered in support of the skills explanation is based on a small number of cases selected because they were major proposals for which presidential interest and activity were high. But such cases are neither typical nor representative of presidential-congressional relations, and the conclusions should not be generalized.

Second, the cases appear to have been chosen because they are consistent with conventional views of what constitutes presidential skills. It is unlikely that every case will be consistent with any explanation, yet case studies of presidential skills provide no cases that run counter to theory. Social scientists will always worry about bias when all cases of failure are associated with poor skills and all cases of success are associated with high skills.

Finally, case studies are hard to interpret because they compare the success of different presidents without explicitly taking account of the particular balance of political forces facing each one. Was the outcome due to the president's skill or to the political conditions in which he operated? Evaluating the success of one president against another without accounting for different contexts is like trying to determine the winner of a race that did not have a common starting line.

Although no one has been able to measure leadership skills precisely, there appears to be general scholarly agreement on which presidents since Eisenhower were highly skilled and which were not. Presidents Johnson and Reagan are generally viewed as highly skilled in their dealings with Congress, while Presidents Richard M. Nixon and Jimmy Carter are viewed as unskilled. Presidents Eisenhower, Kennedy, and Gerald R. Ford are accorded mixed judgments (Bond and Fleisher, 1990).

To control for the different political contexts facing each president, Jon R. Bond and Richard Fleisher (1990) devised a statistical model to estimate the percentage of votes a president should win given the strength of his party in Congress, his popularity with the public, and the time of his term. If leadership skill is a major factor, then presidents viewed as highly skilled should win more often than predicted, and presidents viewed as unskilled should win less often than predicted. This analysis failed to produce the expected patterns. Skilled presidents won less often than predicted in at least one chamber, and unskilled presidents sometimes won more often than predicted.

The results suggest that the effects of presidential leadership skills, like the effects of presidential popularity, are marginal. Although presidential bargaining and lobbying sometimes change the outcome of votes, these cases are rare and unrepresentative of presidential-congressional relations generally. Members of Congress have their own political needs and predispositions. Presidents, however skilled, are unlikely to move members very far from their basic political predispositions. Thus, the parameters of presidential success in Congress are largely determined by the political and ideological mix of Congress.

Institutional Structure of Congress. Although party and ideology establish basic predispositions to support or oppose the president, members' decisions are not made in a vacuum. Instead, congressional decision making occurs within constraints imposed by the institutional structure of Congress.

Two of the most important institutional structures of Congress are (1) the party system, under the leadership of elected party leaders, and (2) the committee system, with each committee greatly influenced by committee leaders (the chair and ranking minority member), chosen on the basis of seniority.

Congressional leaders influence presidential-congressional relations for at least two reasons. First, they are the primary communication link between the president and Congress. Party and committee leaders transmit presidential preferences to Congress and congressional reactions back to the president. They influence the course of presidential initiatives and preferences through their control of the legislative schedule in committee and on the floor, and they serve as cue givers for rank-and-file members.

Second, congressional leaders are able to manipulate resources that directly affect members' careers. Compared to party leaders in parliamentary systems, those in the U.S. Congress are weak. But compared to the president, congressional leaders have more power to influence congressional behavior, through their parliamentary control over members' legislative proposals and through their power over committee assignments. Presidents cannot exercise such direct influence over members' careers; they are more likely to succeed by gaining the support of party and committee leaders in Congress.

Bond and Fleisher (1990) found that support from congressional leaders increases the chances that the president's position will win on floor votes. For majority presidents, support from the majority leader has the greatest effect. Support from the committee chair and the opposition party leader also has a significant influence. The same is true for minority presidents—they are more likely to win if they get support from the majority party floor leader and committee chair. This suggests that minority presidents are more successful if they compromise and avoid taking positions that provoke partisan coalitions.

Presidential success in Congress, therefore, is largely determined by the partisan and ideological predispositions of Congress. The partisan and ideological mix in Congress is set by election. If the president inherits a Congress dominated by members who share his partisan and ideological values, then he will win a large percentage of the time, as President Johnson did in 1965 and as President Reagan did in the Senate in 1981. If Congress is dominated by opposition party members who have ideological preferences different from the president, then he will suffer more defeats, as Reagan did in 1987 after Democrats won back control of the Senate (see figure 1). Skilled presidential lobby-

ing or high public popularity can contribute to a major presidential victory, but such cases are relatively unusual. In general, presidential leadership skills and popularity with the public have only a marginal effect; these forces cannot move members very far from their basic political predispositions.

BIBLIOGRAPHY

Bond, Jon R., and Richard Fleisher. *The President in the Legislative Arena.* 1990.

Bond, Jon R., Cary Covington, and Richard Fleisher. "Explaining Challenger Quality in Congressional Elections." *Journal of Politics* 47 (1985): 510–529.

Brady, David W., and Phillip Althoff. "Party Voting in the U.S. House of Representatives, 1890–1910: Elements of a Responsible Party System." *Journal of Politics* 36 (1974): 753–775.

Covington, Cary R. "Guess Who's Coming to Dinner?" *American Politics Quarterly* 16 (1988): 243–265.

Covington, Cary R. "Mobilizing Congressional Support for the President: Insights from the 1960s." *Legislative Studies Quarterly* 12 (1987): 77–95.

Christenson, Reo M. "Presidential Leadership of Congress." In *Rethinking the Presidency,* edited by Thomas E. Cronin. 1982. Pp. 255–270.

Edwards, George C., III. *At the Margins: Presidential Leadership of Congress.* 1989.

Edwards, George C., III. "Presidential Party Leadership of Congress." In *Presidents and Their Parties: Leadership of Neglect?,* edited by Robert Harmel. 1984. Pp. 179–214.

Edwards, George C., III. *Presidential Influence in Congress.* 1980.

Johannes, John R., and John C. McAdams. "The Congressional Incumbency Effect: Is It Casework, Policy Compatibility, or Something Else?" *American Journal of Political Science* 25 (1981): 512–542.

Jones, Charles O. "Presidential Negotiation with Congress." In *Both Ends of the Avenue,* edited by Anthony King. 1983. Pp. 96–130.

Malbin, Michael. "Rhetoric and Leadership: A Look Backward at the Carter Energy Plan." In *Both Ends of the Avenue,* edited by Anthony King. 1983. Pp. 212–245.

JON R. BOND

PRESIDENTIAL APPOINTMENTS. Disagreement prevailed among the Framers of the Constitution over the proper manner of selecting federal judges, ambassadors, and executive branch officials. Some, like Alexander Hamilton and James Wilson, believed that this was inherently an executive function and ought to be assigned to the president alone. In their view, this would minimize intrigue and cabal in the selection process and focus accountability on the person solely responsible for selection. Others, including John Rutledge and Luther Martin, argued that personnel selection was too important to be left to one person. To prevent an undesirable concentration of power, it was necessary, in their view, to assign appointment responsibility to the legislature, whose members would have a broad acquaintance with the leading citizens of the country and whose debates would ensure careful consideration of qualifications.

When neither view prevailed, the Constitutional Convention resolved the disagreement with the compromise that came to reside in Article II, section 2 of the Constitution: "[The President] shall nominate, and by and with the advice and consent of the Senate, shall appoint Ambassadors, other public Ministers and Consuls, Judges of the Supreme Court, and all other officers of the United States, whose appointments are not herein otherwise provided for, and which shall be established by Law." In sum, the president and the Senate would share the appointment power.

And so they have, with varying degrees of formality and informality, comity and hostility. The constitutional framework was only a starting point in defining the appointment process. It did not anticipate the emergence of political parties before the end of the eighteenth century, the development of standing congressional committees in the nineteenth, or the vast growth of the executive and judicial branches in the twentieth. Nor could it possibly have envisioned the extended period of divided party control of the federal government in the years since World War II. All of these factors have added new dimensions and new strains to the process.

Through much of U.S. history, the selection by the president of nominees for executive or judicial positions was without much structure and often without much rationality. For most of the thousands of positions that came to be executive appointments, presidents relied on their parties to propose nominees. Most of these were patronage appointments: local postmasters, customs collectors, revenue agents, and the like. They commanded little presidential attention. In the vast majority of cases, in fact, presidents nominated local candidates suggested by senators of their own party under a set of informal but rigidly followed procedures called senatorial courtesy.

For higher-level positions in the executive branch and for appointments to the courts of appeal and the Supreme Court, presidents often selected personal acquaintances or leading federal or state officeholders in their party. Through the early decades of the twentieth century, for example, it was a common practice for presidential cabinets to include representatives of all of the major factions of the president's party.

The Senate, for its part, adopted a dual posture toward presidential appointments. In accordance with senatorial courtesy, it expected to be consulted, and in most cases deferred to, on appointments to lower-level positions operating within the home states of individual senators. Over positions of this sort, it is fair to say, the Senate dominated. On the other hand, with a few notable exceptions, the Senate largely deferred to the president on cabinet and other top-level positions in the executive branch. From 1789 to World War II, only seven cabinet nominees were rejected by the Senate. Two more—Lewis Strauss to be secretary of Commerce in 1959 and John G. Tower to be secretary of Defense in 1989—have been rejected since then, for a total of nine rejected overall. The consensus in the Senate throughout much of U.S. history was that for those with whom he would be working closely the president was entitled to people of his own choosing.

The appointments about which the president and the Senate disagreed with some frequency were those to the Supreme Court. Recognizing that such appointees often served for very long terms and that their decisions directly affected the shape of public policy, the Senate objected more often to Supreme Court nominations than to any others. From 1789 through 1991, 106 individuals served on the Supreme Court. In that same period, the Senate rejected 27 nominees for the Court, more than one in five overall.

Systematizing the Process in the Executive. The enormous expansion that the New Deal and World War II wrought in the size and responsibilities of the government put new pressures on the appointment process. With more departments and agencies to staff, presidents could no longer rely on personal acquaintances for their nominees. And when political parties went into decline, they were no longer as effective a pipeline of candidates for appointment. In response, presidents began to construct new procedures for identifying, recruiting, clearing, and nominating candidates for appointment. The creation of the Executive Office of the President in 1939 also gave presidents, for the first time, resources of their own for use in the appointment process.

Harry S. Truman was the first president to assign one staff member, Donald Dawson, to work nearly full-time on appointments and to serve as his administration's principal overseer for recruitment. In the administration of Dwight D. Eisenhower, more staff were added to this function, and by 1958 Eisenhower had created an Office of Special Assistant for Executive Appointments, which formalized the personnel function in the Executive Office of the President.

John F. Kennedy, who came to office promising to establish a "ministry of talent," realized the need for a still more sophisticated personnel operation. He assigned to a young staff member, Dan H. Fenn, Jr., responsibility for assessing presidential needs and for setting up a White House personnel office to supply the administration with a steady stream of talented candidates for appointment. Under Fenn—and later, in the administration of Lyndon B. Johnson, under the leadership of John W. Macy, Jr.—the personnel office in the White House developed procedures for identifying candidates from many sources, some traditional and political, others not. The office took the lead in recruiting candidates, and it superintended the politically necessary task of clearing potential appointees with leading figures in the states and in Congress before their nominations were announced. From 1958 to 1970, the personnel selection process in the White House became increasingly formalized and institutionalized.

The administration of Richard M. Nixon was committed to getting control of the federal bureaucracy, many of whose employees it thought had enduring loyalties to the Democratic party. The Nixon administration regarded firm and efficient control of the appointment power as a critical aspect of this effort. Only by recruiting and appointing people who were loyal to the president and sufficiently competent to impose his policy preferences on recalcitrant bureaucrats could the Nixon imprimatur be placed on public policy.

In 1970, Frederic V. Malek was brought from the subcabinet to the White House to analyze and then reorganize the administration's personnel operation. What emerged was a comparatively large (more than sixty people at its peak), segmented, and functionally specialized professional recruiting operation. When a vacancy occurred, a position profile was prepared describing the functions of the office and the kinds of skills and experience it required. A staff of professional personnel recruiters would then reach out through carefully honed networks of contacts to identify candidates for the position. After this list was shortened, one or more of the candidates would be contacted and asked about

their interest in serving. When a favorite was identified, his or her name would be circulated in the White House and among relevant members of Congress to ensure that there were no strong objections to the nomination. After successful clearance and approval by the president and his top aides, the nomination would be announced.

This process, with minor variations, has remained essentially intact since the early 1970s. The Presidential Personnel Office, as it has been called in recent administrations, was a regular component of the White House by the early 1990s, and its director is usually an assistant to the president, the highest rank among presidential aides.

The Senate Expands Its Role. Change in the appointment process occurred in the Senate at the same time it was unfolding in the White House. The turning point came in the mid 1970s, during and immediately after the Watergate scandal. These were years of uncommon institutional and partisan hostility between the Congress and the White House. In this corrosive atmosphere, Senate committees, especially the Commerce Committee, became more aggressive than ever in their review of nominees. The tradition of deference to the president's choices no longer weighed so heavily in Senate deliberations.

Evidence of this new posture took several forms. Most obvious was the increased frequency with which the Senate rejected presidents' nominees. Both in committee and in votes on the floor, far more top-level nominees were denied confirmation from 1975 through 1990 than in any similar period in history. Even when Jimmy Carter was president, from 1977 to 1981, the only period during those years when one party controlled the White House and both houses of Congress, the Senate refused to confirm important nominations to ambassadorships, the federal judiciary, the Central Intelligence Agency, the Nuclear Regulatory Commission, and the Civil Aeronautics Board.

Equally notable is the growing extent to which Senate committees have used confirmation hearings to impose restrictions upon and to elicit promises from many of those nominees they do confirm. Since the early 1990s every Senate committee has had its own financial disclosure and other ethical requirements that nominees must satisfy before they can be confirmed. During hearings, individual senators frequently require nominees to make statements for the record that later restrict their latitude in policy decisions. The Foreign Relations Committee, for example, began in the 1970s to require nominees to indicate their support for a resolution that grants the Congress a role in all national commitments made by the United States to a foreign government. The Congress has also enlarged its role in the appointment process by extending the requirement for Senate confirmation to a number of high-level positions, such as the directors of the Office of Management and Budget and the Federal Bureau of Investigation, to which it had not previously applied.

As the size and scope of the federal government have grown, so too has the influence of the people who lead it. Because they have such a critical impact on the character of public policy and on the lives of individual Americans, appointments to the senior executive and judicial positions have become battlegrounds for fundamental political confrontations. That has raised the stakes of appointment decisions and consequently also the level of conflict that surrounds them.

In both the executive and legislative branches, new procedures have been established to channel and control that conflict. Nevertheless, more hostility pervades than ever before; the appointment process has become an increasingly institutionalized and formalized set of procedures aimed primarily at conflict resolution. In most cases, conflicts are resolved. Where they are not, as with Ronald Reagan's unsuccessful nomination of Robert Bork to the Supreme Court in 1987 and George Bush's unsuccessful nomination of John Tower as secretary of Defense in 1989, it becomes eminently clear that appointments matter and that, if necessary, the president and the Senate will fight intensely to control them.

[See also Advice and Consent; Bureaucracy; Cabinet and Congress; Confirmation; Executive Branch; Judiciary and Congress; Oversight; Senatorial Courtesy.]

BIBLIOGRAPHY

Fisher, Louis. *Constitutional Conflicts between Congress and the President.* 1985.
Mackenzie, G. Calvin. *The Politics of Presidential Appointments.* 1981.
Mackenzie, G. Calvin, ed. *The In and Outers.* 1987.
Pfiffner, James P. *The Strategic Presidency: Hitting the Ground Running.* 1988.

G. CALVIN MACKENZIE

PRESIDENTIAL ASSASSINATIONS AND PROTECTION. For the first century of the American presidency, presidential protection was provided haphazardly by the military, by local law enforcement, or by personal aides summoned at a president's discretion. Despite the violence that characterized that century and threatened the very existence of the United States, Congress was slow to acknowledge the need for presidential protection. Three of the eight presidents who served during the period from the Civil War to the end of the century were killed by assassins. Gunshots ended the presidencies of Abraham Lincoln (1865), James A. Garfield (1881), and William McKinley (1901) before Congress hesitantly acknowledged the need to provide authorization and funds to protect the president.

Although the issue was raised after each assassination, it was not until President Grover Cleveland's wife and his personal secretary requested protection in 1894 that the Secret Service became informally involved. When Congress discovered this, in 1898, it demanded the removal of Secret Service chief William P. Hazen, insisting that Hazen had overstepped the bounds of his authority and misused funds explicitly authorized to fulfill the Service's mission to "detect, arrest, and prosecute counterfeiters of coins of the United States." Three years later, however, after President McKinley was fatally shot greeting visitors to the Pan-American Exposition in Buffalo, a chastened Congress commended Hazen's replacement, John E. Wilkie, for his (unsuccessful) effort to provide the same unauthorized protection for the slain president. But it was not until five years after McKinley's funeral that Congress passed an appropriations bill, the Sundry Civil Expenses Act of 1906, that provided temporary authorization and funding to the Secret Service for presidential protection. McKinley's successor, Theodore Roosevelt, was the first president to receive such protection.

Roosevelt himself was to become the next target of a would-be assassin's bullet. After serving two terms in the White House he left office in 1908, only to run again as a third-party candidate in 1912. In the course of that campaign, he was shot as he stood greeting well-wishers in a touring car on a Milwaukee street. Roosevelt's life was spared only by a thickly folded speech in his breast pocket that absorbed most of the impact. This was the first attack on a presidential candidate.

Over the next decade following the Milwaukee incident, Congress slowly expanded the scope of presidential protection. The Treasury Department Appropriations Act of 1913 extended protection to presidents-elect; in 1917 legislation was enacted that made threats against a president's life a felony; and in the same year, another appropriations bill

PRIVATE BOX AT FORD'S THEATRE. The spot where Abraham Lincoln was assassinated on 14 April 1865.

NATIONAL ARCHIVES

extended protection to the president's immediate family. This last measure was augmented in 1922 by the creation of a uniformed White House police force to patrol and protect the executive mansion and grounds. In 1930 President Herbert Hoover transferred supervision of the White House police to the Secret Service.

The activities of the new police force remained routine and uneventful until 1950. Except for the shots fired in Miami in an unsuccessful attempt on the life of President-elect Franklin D. Roosevelt in 1933, the nation withstood the stress and tension of two world wars and a major economic depression without presidential bloodshed. That nearly changed on 1 November 1950, when two Puerto Rican nationalists tried to shoot their way into President Harry S. Truman's temporary residence at Blair House. An exchange of gunfire killed one of the would-be assassins and a White House policeman and left the other attacker and two policemen wounded. The president was not hurt.

The dramatic nature and the media coverage of that event led to the revelation that Congress had yet to provide the Secret Service with permanent statutory authorization to protect the president. The issue was finally resolved in 1951, when the House of Representatives unanimously passed, and

President Truman signed, Public Law 82-79, providing the Secret Service with permanent authority to protect the president, his immediate family, the president-elect, and the vice president (at the latter's request). In 1962 Congress expanded coverage to make protection of the vice president mandatory and to extend protection to the person next in the line of succession as well. In the same action, Congress authorized temporary (six-month) protection for former presidents (P.L. 87-829).

In the wave of emotion and concern following President John F. Kennedy's assassination on 22 November 1963, scores of bills on presidential security were introduced in Congress. The immediate response was legislation authorizing Secret Service protection for the president's widow and her children for the next two years (P.L. 83-195). This was followed in 1965 by a law making the assault, kidnapping, or assassination of a president or any person in the line of presidential succession a federal crime (P.L. 89-186). During the same period Congress supported many of the Warren Commission's recommendations to improve presidential security, appropriating funds to restructure and reorganize the Secret Service and expanding the number, training, and equipment of persons assigned to its protective mission. Family survivors' legislation was extended in 1967 and expanded in 1968 to cover a president's widow until death or remarriage and children to their sixteenth year (P.L. 90-145; P.L. 90-331).

Kennedy's assassination rekindled congressional interest in a constitutional amendment that would address the problem of governance during periods of presidential disability. Such an amendment had been discussed in Dwight D. Eisenhower's second term, after the president suffered a serious heart attack and a debilitating stroke. The issue seemed less pressing after Kennedy came to office in 1960, as at age forty-three, he was the youngest man ever elected to the presidency. But the sense of urgency returned after the assassination. What if Kennedy had survived his massive head wounds in an incapacitated state? What about the health of his successor, Lyndon B. Johnson, a man who had survived a heart attack in 1957? And what about the two frail, old men following him in the line of succession, House Speaker John W. McCormack, age seventy-five, and Senate president pro tempore Carl Hayden, in his eighties? Congressional concern had gone beyond simply protecting the president to the more fundamental issue of protecting the presidency itself. The answers to such questions were embodied in the Twenty-fifth Amendment. The amendment, which won congressional approval in 1965 and was ratified by the states in 1967, specified the circumstances and means required to replace an incapacitated president.

A year later, in 1968, the nation was stunned by the assassinations of two prominent Americans: civil-rights leader Dr. Martin Luther King, Jr., and the late president's brother, presidential candidate Robert F. Kennedy. As a direct response to Senator Kennedy's assassination, and with the urging of President Johnson, Congress in 1968 authorized Secret Service protection for all major presidential and vice-presidential candidates (P.L. 90-331).

Assassination attempts continued with alarming frequency during the 1970s. In 1971 Congress authorized Secret Service protection for visiting foreign heads of state and dignitaries. In the following year presidential candidate Gov. George C. Wallace was struck down and left permanently crippled by a would-be assassin at a Laurel, Maryland, shopping center. In 1974, in the midst of the Watergate scandal, an embittered, unemployed man chose Washington's Birthday to attempt assassination of President Richard M. Nixon. He failed, but in the process three people were shot, one fatally, before the assailant killed himself in an abortive attempt to hijack a commercial jetliner he intended to crash-dive into the White House. A year after Nixon's resignation in 1974, two separate unsuccessful attempts were made on the life of his successor, Gerald R. Ford. In the midst of Ford's reelection campaign of 1976, a concerned Congress extended Secret Service protection to the spouses of presidential and vice-presidential candidates (P.L. 94-408).

On 30 March 1981, President Ronald Reagan's life was saved by the courageous actions and quick thinking of his Secret Service detail and the skill of emergency room surgeons at the George Washington University Hospital. Reagan and three others in his party were shot and seriously wounded as they left the Washington Hilton. The subsequent acquittal of the president's assailant by reason of insanity stirred the first ripples of public outrage that swept into law the Insanity Defense Reform Act of 1984. Among its provisions the law includes a more narrowly defined standard for insanity as well as more restrictive release procedures for mental patients hospitalized for that reason. Secret Service protective procedures were also tightened, greatly restricting the president's mobility and exposure to crowds, even on Capitol Hill.

As a result of congressional responsiveness, combined with the diligence and skill of the Secret Service, presidents are now more thoroughly and better protected than at any time in history. But in a free, open, and heavily-armed society, the threat remains.

[See also Twenty-fifth Amendment.]

BIBLIOGRAPHY

Clarke, James W. *American Assassins: The Darker Side of Politics.* Rev. ed. 1990.

Clarke, James W. *On Being Mad or Merely Angry: John W. Hinckley, Jr., and Other Dangerous People.* 1990.

Kaiser, Frederick M. "Origins of Secret Service Protection of the President: Personal, Interagency, and Institutional Conflict." *Presidential Studies Quarterly* 18 (1988): 101–127.

JAMES W. CLARKE

JOHN WILKES BOOTH. President Lincoln's assassin.
NATIONAL ARCHIVES

PRESIDENTIAL CAMPAIGN ACTIVITIES COMMITTEE, SENATE SELECT.
See Watergate Committee.

PRESIDENTIAL ELECTIONS.

PRESIDENTIAL ELECTIONS. The constitutional role of Congress in presidential elections may be divided into two areas: its responsibilities for balloting, counting, and certification; and the requirement that the House choose a president if no candidate receives the required number (270) of electoral votes.

Balloting, Counting and Certification. Under Article II, section 1 of the Constitution, Congress determines the time for choosing presidential electors and the day on which they shall cast their votes—a day that must be uniform throughout the United States. After electors vote, they are constitutionally required to make a list of all persons voted for and the number of votes for each, and then to sign, certify, and transmit it, sealed, to the president of the Senate. Congress has since required that electors forward five additional lists: two must be sent to the secretaries of state of their respective states, two by registered mail to the administrator of General Services, and one to the federal judge of the district where the electors assemble to vote (see Title III, chapter 1, U.S. Code Annotated).

On 6 January, both houses of Congress must convene in joint session. As required by the Twelfth Amendment, the "President of the Senate shall, in the Presence of the Senate and House of Representatives, open all the Certificates, and the Votes shall then be counted." While this provision may appear fairly innocuous, the wording raises an important question: what import, if any, should be attached to the counting of votes? Is it a purely mechanical function, or does it give Congress the authority to determine the validity of those votes? The answer to this question generated considerable controversy in the nineteenth century. The noted political commentator Henry Luther Stoddard, writing in 1938, observed that the subject had been much discussed since the time of Thomas Jefferson—indeed, only slavery had been the object of more frequent debate. When Congress convened to count ballots after the elections of 1810, 1818, 1820, 1836, and 1856, votes were challenged. In no instance, however, would the challenged ballots have altered the outcome. Thus Congress was content to certify them without taking a position on whether it had the authority to rule on their validity. Finally, in 1865, a majority of the House and Senate adopted a joint rule that stipulated that a presidential ballot could be disallowed if either house objected. Although allowed to lapse by the Senate in 1876, this rule was used to invalidate electoral votes of some southern states in the elections of 1868 and 1872.

"MERRY GO ROUND FOR THE WHITE HOUSE BOUND." Satirical depiction of the candidates for the 1876 election. The figures in the front rank are *left to right*, New York governor Samuel J. Tilden, secretary of the Treasury Benjamin H. Bristow, Ohio governor Rutherford B. Hayes, Sen. Oliver P. Morton (R-Ind.), and Speaker James G. Blaine (R-Maine). Cover illustration, *The Daily Graphic*, 19 May 1876.

OFFICE OF THE HISTORIAN OF THE U.S. SENATE

In neither case, however, did the rejected ballots determine the election outcome. In contrast, the election of 1876 presented Congress with a unique set of circumstances involving disputed ballots, the resolution of which did indeed determine the winner.

On the day after this tightly contested election, Republican Rutherford B. Hayes had garnered 165 electoral votes, while Democrat Samuel J. Tilden was conceded to have 184 and the lead in the popular vote. An additional nineteen electoral votes from four states (South Carolina, Florida, Louisiana, and Oregon) were contested, with Democrats and Republicans accusing each other of fraud, bribery, and intimidation during the voting process. Consequently, in each of these four states the Republican and Democratic parties submitted their own set of election returns to Congress. (In the case of Oregon, only one electoral vote was in dispute.) This confusion was further complicated by the fact that Republicans controlled the Senate, and Democrats the House. Thus there was a distinct possibility that when both houses jointly assembled on 1 February 1877, the Republican Senate president would order the Hayes vote certificates counted and declare him president with 185 electoral votes, while the Democratic House Speaker would declare that no candidate had a majority, thereby requiring the House to retire and carry out its constitutional responsibility of choosing the next president. The House would no doubt have chosen Tilden, and the country would then have confronted the nightmarish prospect of two claimants to the office. While this scenario was predicted by some and urged by others, cooler heads prevailed, and both houses agreed to resolve the dispute by passing the Electoral Commission Law.

Signed into law by President Ulysses S. Grant just three days before the 1 February deadline for opening and counting electoral votes, this legislation was applied to the election of 1876 only. It established a fifteen-member commission—five House members, five Senate members, and five Supreme Court justices—to rule in those instances where a state had submitted double returns. The commission's rulings could be overturned only if both houses agreed. As it turned out, in the case of each disputed state, the commission voted 8 to 7 to accept the Hayes electors on the ground that they had been duly certified by the appropriate state officials. It was, therefore, inappropriate for Congress to second-guess their decision. Predictably, the Democratic House voted to reject each ruling, while the Republican Senate voted to uphold. Under the provisions of the Electoral Commission Law, therefore, the rulings of the commission stood. Thus, just two days before the next president was to assume office, and after deliberating for one month and a day, Congress certified Hayes as having won with a total of 185 electoral votes.

The use of the Electoral Commission for this purpose was not only awkward but almost certainly unconstitutional as well, in that it included members from another branch of government. Congress, understandably wanting to avoid a repetition of the 1876 election, passed legislation specifying procedures for raising and resolving challenges to presidential ballots. Known as the Electoral Count Act (1887), it provided that objections be made in writing and signed by at least one member of each house. Each house then separately considers the challenge, which prevails only if both houses concur. Furthermore, in a clear attempt by Congress to shift the burden of resolving disputed ballots to the states, the law stipulates that in any controversy arising over the appointment of a state's electors, a state's determination of that matter shall be final, provided that (1) a state has a law for determining such controversies; (2) the law was enacted prior to the date set for appointing electors; and (3) the ruling on such a controversy was made at least six

A TIPPECANOE PROCESSION. Supporters of William Henry Harrison roll a giant ball covered with campaign slogans in an election rally during the 1840 presidential race.   PERLEY'S REMINISCENCES, VOL. 1

days prior to the date when electors voted. Should a dispute arise over which state officials are authorized to certify electors, then both houses acting separately but concurrently will make the determination. Additionally, if double returns are submitted, as in 1876, and a state has made no determination as to which are valid, then both houses, provided they agree, will make the determination. If both houses do not agree, the votes certified by a state's executive will be counted.

It was not until 6 January 1969 that portions of this statute first came into play. Sen. Edmund S. Muskie (D-Maine) and Rep. James G. O'Hara (D-Mich.), joined by seven other senators and thirty-seven representatives, submitted an objection challenging the electoral vote of North Carolina elector Lloyd Bailey. Although he was an elector on the Republican slate of Richard M. Nixon and Spiro T. Agnew, Bailey nevertheless cast his vote for the third-party (American Independent) ticket of George C. Wallace and Curtis LeMay. The challenge to Bailey's vote was ultimately rejected by both the House (170 to 228) and the Senate (33 to 58), primarily on the ground that the Constitution does not impose any limitation on how an elector may vote.

In the absence of the Electoral Count Act, Congress might well have become embroiled in certification questions surrounding the 1960 election—the only one since 1887 in which widespread fraud and corruption were alleged. Two days after the voting, Republican National Committee chairman Thurston B. Morton asked party leaders in eleven states to inquire into charges of voter fraud. Of particular concern to the Republicans was the state of Illinois, which John F. Kennedy had won by only 8,858 votes. Repeated charges were made of voting irregularities in Cook County, where, according to the Republican county chairman, Kennedy was the beneficiary of approximately 100,000 fraudulent votes. Although three Cook County precinct workers would plead guilty to vote fraud some two years later, the political machine of Chicago mayor Richard J. Daley frustrated attempts to achieve an official recount. Republicans, moreover, were never able to demonstrate that the vote fraud in Illinois was substantial enough to alter the election outcome in that state. Thus, just six days before electors were due to assemble and vote, the five-member Illinois electoral board, four of whom were Republicans, certified the validity of the Kennedy electors. Once this action was taken by the electoral board, any attempt to challenge the Illinois ballots in Congress would have been fruitless.

Electing the President. In designing the executive branch, the Framers initially wanted the president to be chosen by the legislature. Indeed, they voted for this mode of selection four different times during their deliberations. But once the delegates decided to make the president eligible to run again, support for legislative selection began to erode as the Convention's most influential figures—James Madison, Gouverneur Morris, and James Wilson—argued that such an arrangement would render the executive overly dependent on the legislative branch. After protracted debate, they finally decided to have the president chosen by electors, but did not completely foreclose a role for the legislature. If no candidate received a majority of the electoral vote, the election would be referred to the outgoing House of Representatives (later changed to "incoming" by the Twentieth Amendment in 1933), where each state would have one vote and choose from among the five candidates having the highest number of electoral votes.

For those delegates who had consistently favored legislative selection, the prospect of referring the election to the House was very reassuring, particularly since several delegates were convinced that the size and diversity of the country would mitigate against a presidential candidate winning a majority of electoral votes. This belief, of course, failed to anticipate the rise of political parties and their ability to mobilize majorities. Indeed, on only two occasions (in 1800 and 1824) has the House been given the opportunity to choose a president.

The constitutional requirement that electors vote for two candidates for president had already produced one political oddity in the election of 1796—namely, a president (John Adams) and a vice president (Thomas Jefferson) from different political parties. Just four years later, it produced another. Jeffersonian Republican Thomas Jefferson and his running mate, Aaron Burr, challenged Federalist president John Adams and his new running mate, Gen. Charles Pinckney. Prior to the voting, the Jeffersonian Republicans neglected to instruct one of their electors to refrain from voting for Burr. Consequently, Jefferson and Burr tied with 73 votes each, followed by Adams (65), Pinckney (64), and John Jay (1). The election was forced into the outgoing House, where the Federalist party, with a ten-seat advantage over the Republicans, saw ample opportunity for mischief. The Federalists first entertained the idea of denying a majority of House votes to any candidate until 6 March 1801, at which time the offices of both president and vice president would become vacant. Under a statute passed in 1792, a dual vacancy would then have required a special election. This plan, however, was ultimately rejected as too cynical. Instead, the Federalists tried to deny the presidency to Jefferson, whom they viewed as highly capable but dangerously radical, by throwing their support behind the decidedly mediocre Burr. Jefferson's candidacy found an unlikely ally in Alexander Hamilton, who though an arch-Federalist and strong critic of Jefferson nevertheless believed Burr to be wholly unsuited for the presidency. His support, combined with growing skepticism that Burr could be persuaded to govern as a Federalist, enabled Jefferson to carry the day, winning ten states to Burr's four. But victory did not come easily. The House remained in continuous session for six days, and only on the thirty-sixth ballot was a majority achieved.

To ensure that there would be no repetition of the circumstances sending this election into the House, the Republicans pushed for and the states ultimately approved the Twelfth Amendment (1804), requiring electors to vote separately for president and vice president.

Nearly a quarter of a century later, the House was again called on to choose a president, but this time under very different political circumstances. Since the Federalist party had disintegrated, the 1824 election became a Jeffersonian Republican intraparty contest. Moreover, in the absence of an organized opposition party, the Republicans had much less incentive to submerge their differences. Thus six individuals were nominated, one by congressional caucus (Secretary of the Treasury William H. Crawford) and five by state legislatures, three of whom stayed in the race (Gen. Andrew Jackson, Secretary of State John Quincy Adams, and Speaker of the House Henry Clay). The major contenders proved to be Jackson and Adams. Jackson came in first, with 99 electoral votes and 152,933 popular votes, while Adams won 84 electoral votes and 115,696 popular votes. Crawford and Clay meanwhile accumulated only 41 and 37 electoral votes, respectively, but they nevertheless received enough support to force the election into the House. Under provisions of the Twelfth Amendment, the House was now required to choose from among the top three candidates—Jackson, Adams, and Crawford. Clay, having been eliminated, threw his support behind Adams, who won on the first ballot, garnering thirteen of twenty-four states. But the House election left a bitter aftertaste. Rumors circulated that Clay had thrown his support to Adams in return for a promise that he would be appointed secretary of State; these rumors gained greater credence when President Adams did precisely that. Even more unsavory, however, was the House's decision to deny the presidency to someone who had bested Adams not only in the electoral vote but, as Jackson supporters were quick to assert, in the popular vote as well. In actuality, it is not possible to determine which candidate commanded the most popular support, since electors in six states were chosen by state legislatures and turnout in several states was low. But the circumstances surrounding the 1824 House election continued to resonate over the next four years and played a significant role in Jackson's decisive defeat of Adams in 1828.

While the House has not elected a president since 1824, there have been three elections in this century (1948, 1960, 1976) where a relatively small shift of votes in a very few states would have prevented an electoral vote winner. Should political circumstances conspire to force some future election into the House, it may well be the last. Americans have, after all, become accustomed to popularly electing their presidents and even to determining their choices for president. Accordingly, they are likely to have little patience with a constitutional procedure that takes that decision out of their hands—particularly a procedure whereby every state has an equal vote and the opportunities for political intrigue remain considerable.

[*See also* Electoral College; Electoral Commission of 1877; Electoral Count Act; Twelfth Amendment.]

BIBLIOGRAPHY

Berns, Walter, ed. *After the People Vote.* 1983.
Peirce, Neil R., and Lawrence D. Longley. *The People's President: The Electoral College in American History and the Direct Vote Alternative.* Rev. ed. 1981.
Roseboom, Eugene H. *A History of Presidential Elections.* 3d ed. 1970.
Schlesinger, Arthur M., Jr., ed. *History of American Presidential Elections.* 1971.
Wilmerding, Lucius, Jr. *The Electoral College.* 1958.

ROBERT E. DiCLERICO

PRESIDENTIAL TRANSITIONS. One of a president-elect's important priorities is to lay the groundwork for good relations with members of Congress, who, collectively, can determine the fate of the new administration's policy agenda. A newly elected president often devotes significant time to "courting" Congress by meeting with members, individually and in groups. After the inauguration, the courting continues with invitations to the White House and with opportunities for members, particularly of the president's party, to appear with the president in photographs or in public.

A newly elected president may also work with the congressional leadership to plan an early legislative agenda. Because Congress convenes two and a half weeks before the inauguration, preparation for the change in administrations can begin on Capitol Hill even before the new administration takes office. This work may include staff preparations for Senate confirmation hearings on the president's cabinet nominations or the drafting of legislation.

The new president must move rapidly to establish a legislative liaison operation in the White House. The core of this operation should be set up before the inauguration so that the administration can react quickly to the large volume of correspondence that Congress inevitably directs to any new president and so that the White House can prepare to press the president's legislative agenda on the Hill. Much of the congressional correspondence will consist of recommendations of people to fill job openings in the executive branch. The legislative liaison staff must work closely with the Office of Presidential Personnel to coordinate action on these recommendations.

Recognizing the importance of a smooth transfer of power in an increasingly complex government, Congress in 1963 passed the Presidential Transition Act (P.L. 88-277), allowing outgoing and incoming administrations to use appropriated funds to facilitate the transition.

BIBLIOGRAPHY

Lauren, Henry. *Presidential Transitions.* 1960.
Pfiffner, James P. *The Strategic Presidency: Hitting the Ground Running.* 1988.

JAMES P. PFIFFNER

PRESIDENTIAL VETO. See Veto, *article on* Presidential Veto.

PRESIDENT PRO TEMPORE OF THE SENATE.

The Constitution designates the vice president of the United States as the president of the Senate and further provides that in the vice president's absence, the Senate may choose a president pro tempore to perform the duties of the chair. On 6 April 1789 the Senate elected New Hampshire senator John Langdon as its first president pro tempore. Langdon served until 21 April, when John Adams arrived to take his oath as vice president.

During the Senate's first century, vice presidents presided routinely, and the Senate chose a president pro tempore only for the limited periods when the vice president was ill or otherwise absent. Consequently, the Senate frequently elected several presidents pro tempore during a single session. Those individuals were selected on the basis of their personal characteristics, popularity, and reliability.

In 1890 the Senate established the policy, which continues today, of having its president pro tempore hold office continuously until the election of a successor, rather than just for the period of the vice president's absence. Since the end of World War II, the Senate has customarily elected the senior member of its majority party as president pro tempore.

That the Senate, from its earliest days, took the post of president pro tempore seriously can be seen in the Presidential Succession Act of 1792. Should

SEN. LAFAYETTE S. FOSTER (R-CONN.). Elected President pro tempore of the Senate on 7 March 1865.

HARPER'S PICTORIAL HISTORY OF THE GREAT REBELLION

Presidents Pro Tempore of the Senate

CONGRESS	NO.[1]	NAME	STATE	DATE ELECTED
1st	1	John Langdon	N.H.	6 April 1789
2d	2	Richard Henry Lee	Va.	18 April 1792
		John Langdon	N.H.	5 November 1792
				1 March 1793
3d	3	Ralph Izard	S.C.	31 May 1794
	4	Henry Tazewell	Va.	20 February 1795
4th				7 December 1795
	5	Samuel Livermore	N.H.	6 May 1796
	6	William Bingham	Pa.	16 February 1797
5th	7	William Bradford	R.I.	6 July 1797
	8	Jacob Read	S.C.	22 November 1797
	9	Theodore Sedgwick	Mass.	27 June 1798
	10	John Laurance	N.Y.	6 December 1798
	11	James Ross	Pa.	1 March 1799
6th		Samuel Livermore	N.H.	2 December 1799
	12	Uriah Tracy	Conn.	14 May 1800
	13	John E. Howard	Md.	21 November 1800
	14	James Hillhouse	Conn.	28 February 1801
7th	15	Abraham Baldwin	Ga.	7 December 1801
	16	Stephen R. Bradley	Vt.	14 December 1802
				25 February 1803
				2 March 1803
8th	17	John Brown	Ky.	17 October 1803
				23 January 1804
	18	Jesse Franklin	N.C.	10 March 1804
	19	Joseph Anderson	Tenn.	15 January 1805
				28 February 1805
				2 March 1805
9th	20	Samuel Smith	Md.	2 December 1805
				18 March 1806
				2 March 1807
10th				16 April 1808
		Stephen R. Bradley	Vt.	28 December 1808
	21	John Milledge	Ga.	30 January 1809
11th	22	Andrew Gregg	Pa.	26 June 1809
	23	John Gaillard	S.C.	28 February 1810
				17 April 1810
	24	John Pope	Ky.	23 February 1811
12th	25	William H. Crawford	Ga.	24 March 1812
13th	26	Joseph B. Varnum	Mass.	6 December 1813
		John Gaillard	S.C.	18 April 1814
				25 November 1814[2]
14th				6 March 1817

[1]Indicates the number of individuals who have held the post upon a senator's first election to the office. Thus, John Langdon was the first senator to serve as president pro tempore, Richard Henry Lee the second, and, following two more stints by Langdon, Ralph Izard became the third.
[2]Gaillard was elected after the death of Vice President Elbridge Gerry and continued to serve throughout the 14th Congress, as there was no vice president.

Presidents Pro Tempore of the Senate (Continued)

CONGRESS	NO.[1]	NAME	STATE	DATE ELECTED
15th				31 March 1818
	27	James Barbour	Va.	15 February 1819
16th				
		John Gaillard	S.C.	25 January 1820
17th				1 February 1822
				19 February 1823
18th				21 May 1824
19th				9 March 1825
	28	Nathaniel Macon	N.C.	20 May 1826
				2 January 1827
				2 March 1827
20th		Samuel Smith	Md.	15 May 1828
21st				13 March 1829
				29 May 1830
				1 March 1831
22d	29	Littleton W. Tazewell	Va.	9 July 1832
	30	Hugh Lawson White	Tenn.	3 December 1832
23d				
	31	George Poindexter	Miss.	28 June 1834
	32	John Tyler	Va.	3 March 1835
24th	33	William R. King	Ala.	1 July 1836
				28 January 1837
25th				7 March 1837
				13 October 1837
				2 July 1838
				25 February 1839
26th				3 July 1840
				3 March 1841
27th				4 March 1841
	34	Samuel L. Southard	N.J.	11 March 1841
	35	Willie P. Mangum	N.C.	31 May 1842
28th				
29th	36	Ambrose H. Sevier	Ark.	27 December 1845[3]
	37	David R. Atchison	Mo.	8 August 1846
				11 January 1847
				3 March 1847
30th				2 February 1848
				1 June 1848
				26 June 1848
				29 July 1848
				26 December 1848
				2 March 1849
31st				5 March 1849
				16 March 1849
		William R. King	Ala.	6 May 1850
				11 July 1850

[3]There was no actual election. Sevier was "permitted to occupy the chair for the day."

Presidents Pro Tempore of the Senate (Continued)

CONGRESS	NO.[1]	NAME	STATE	DATE ELECTED
32d				
		David R. Atchison	Mo.	20 December 1852
33d				4 March 1853
	38	Lewis Cass	Mich.	4 December 1854
	39	Jesse D. Bright	Ind.	5 December 1854
34th				11 June 1856
	40	Charles E. Stuart	Mich.	9 June 1856
	41	James M. Mason	Va.	6 January 1857
35th				4 March 1857
	42	Thomas J. Rusk	Tex.	14 March 1857
	43	Benjamin Fitzpatrick	Ala.	7 December 1857
				29 March 1858
				14 June 1858
				25 January 1859
36th				9 March 1859
				19 December 1859
				20 February 1860
		Jesse D. Bright	Ind.	12 June 1860
		Benjamin Fitzpatrick	Ala.	26 June 1860
	44	Solomon Foot	Vt.	16 February 1861
37th				23 March 1861
				18 July 1861
				15 January 1862
				31 March 1862
				19 June 1862
				18 February 1863
38th				4 March 1863
				18 December 1863
				23 February 1864
				11 April 1864
	45	Daniel Clark	N.H.	26 April 1864
				9 February 1865
39th	46	Lafayette S. Foster	Conn.	7 March 1865
	47	Benjamin F. Wade	Ohio	2 March 1867
40th				
41st	48	Henry B. Anthony	R.I.	23 March 1869
				9 April 1869
				28 May 1870
				1 July 1870
				14 July 1870
42d				10 March 1871
				17 April 1871
				23 May 1871
				21 December 1871
				23 February 1872
				8 June 1872

Presidents Pro Tempore of the Senate (Continued)

Congress	No.[1]	Name	State	Date Elected
42				4 December 1872
				13 December 1872
				20 December 1872
				24 January 1873
43d	49	Matthew H. Carpenter	Wis.	12 March 1873
				26 March 1873
				11 December 1873
				23 December 1874
		Henry B. Anthony	R.I.	23 January 1875
				15 February 1875
44th	50	Thomas W. Ferry	Mich.	9 March 1875
				19 March 1875
				20 December 1875
45th				5 March 1877
				26 February 1878
				17 April 1878
				3 March 1879
46th	51	Allen G. Thurman	Ohio	15 April 1879
				7 April 1880
				6 May 1880
47th	52	Thomas F. Bayard	Del.	10 October 1881
	53	David Davis	Ill.	13 October 1881
	54	George F. Edmunds	Vt.	3 March 1883
48th				14 January 1884
49th	55	John Sherman	Ohio	7 December 1885
	56	John J. Ingalls	Kans.	25 February 1887
50th				
51st				7 March 1889
				2 April 1889
				28 February 1890
				3 April 1890[4]
	57	Charles F. Manderson	Nebr.	2 March 1891
52d				
53d				
	58	Isham G. Harris	Tenn.	22 March 1893
	59	Matt W. Ransom	N.C.	7 January 1895
		Isham G. Harris	Tenn.	10 January 1895
54th	60	William P. Frye	Maine	7 February 1896
55th				
56th				
57th				7 March 1901
58th				
59th				

[4]In March 1890, the Senate adopted a resolution stating that presidents pro tempore would hold office continuously until the election of another president pro tempore, rather than being elected for the period in which the vice president was absent. The new system has continued to the present.

Presidents Pro Tempore of the Senate (Continued)

CONGRESS	NO.[1]	NAME	STATE	DATE ELECTED
60th				5 December 1907
61st				
62d				
	61	Charles Curtis	Kans.	4 December 1911
	62	Augustus O. Bacon	Ga.	15 January 1912
	63	Jacob H. Gallinger	N.H.	12 February 1912
	64	Henry Cabot Lodge	Mass.	25 March 1912
	65	Frank B. Brandegee	Conn.	25 May 1912
63d	66	James P. Clarke	Ark.	13 March 1913
64th				6 December 1915
	67	Willard Saulsbury	Del.	14 December 1916
65th				
66th	68	Albert B. Cummins	Iowa	19 May 1919
67th				7 March 1921
68th				
69th				
	69	George H. Moses	N.H.	6 March 1925
70th				15 December 1927
71st				
72d				
73d	70	Key Pittman	Nev.	9 March 1933
74th				7 January 1935
75th				
76th				
	71	William H. King	Utah	19 November 1940
77th	72	Pat Harrison	Mass.	6 January 1941
	73	Carter Glass	Va.	10 July 1941
78th				5 January 1943
79th	74	Kenneth D. McKellar	Tenn.	6 January 1945
80th	75	Arthur H. Vandenberg	Mich.	4 January 1947
81st		Kenneth D. McKellar	Tenn.	3 January 1949
82d				
83d	76	H. Styles Bridges	N.H.	3 January 1953
84th	77	Walter F. George	Ga.	5 January 1955
85th	78	Carl Hayden	Ariz.	3 January 1957
86th				
87th				
88th				
89th				
90th				
91st	79	Richard B. Russell	Ga.	3 January 1969
92d				
	80	Allen J. Ellender	La.	22 January 1971
	81	James O. Eastland	Mass.	28 July 1972

Presidents Pro Tempore of the Senate (Continued)

Congress	No.[1]	Name	State	Date Elected
93d				
94th				
95th				
96th	82	Warren G. Magnuson	Wash.	15 January 1979
	83	Milton R. Young	N. Dak.	4 December 1980
97th	84	Strom Thurmond	S.C.	5 January 1981
98th				
99th				
100th	85	John C. Stennis	Miss.	6 January 1987
101st	86	Robert C. Byrd	W. Va.	3 January 1989
102d				
103d				

SOURCE: Office of the Historian of the U.S. Senate

the offices of president and vice president both become vacant, the president pro tempore would then succeed to the presidency, followed by the Speaker of the House. The potentially serious consequences of this arrangement became clear after President Abraham Lincoln's assassination.

When Vice President Andrew Johnson succeeded him, the president pro tempore, Benjamin F. Wade of Ohio, became next in line for the White House. Had the Senate voted to remove Johnson during his impeachment trial in 1868, Senator Wade would have become president of the United States. Wade voted for conviction and President Johnson, after his acquittal, objected to placing the president pro tempore in the line of succession because he would therefore be "interested in producing a vacancy." In 1886 Congress removed the president pro tempore and Speaker of the House from the line of succession—only to return them in 1947. However, the Speaker of the House was placed ahead of the president pro tempore in order of succession.

The responsibilities of the office have changed significantly over the past two centuries. Between 1823 and 1863, presidents pro tempore appointed members of the Senate's standing committees, either indirectly or directly. Since 1820 the president pro tempore has had the power to name other senators to perform the duties of the chair in his absence. Various laws assign the president pro tempore authority to make appointments to an assortment of national commissions, usually with the advice of the appropriate party floor leader. In the absence of the vice president, the president pro tempore may administer all oaths required by the Constitution, may sign legislation, and may fulfill all other obligations of the presiding officer. Also, in the absence of the vice president, the president pro tempore jointly presides with the Speaker of the House when the two houses sit together in joint sessions or joint meetings.

The election of a senator to the office of the president pro tempore has always been considered one of the highest honors offered to a senator by the Senate as a body. That honor has been bestowed upon a colorful and significant group of senators during the past two centuries—men such as Richard Henry Lee (Va.), John Tyler (R-Va.), Arthur H. Vandenberg (R-Mich.), Carl Hayden (D-Ariz.), and Richard B. Russell (D-Ga.)—who stamped their imprint on the office and on their times.

[*See also* Presiding Officer.]

BIBLIOGRAPHY

Byrd, Robert C. *The Senate, 1789–1989: Addresses on the History of the United States Senate.* Vol. 2. 1991.

ROBERT C. BYRD

PRESIDING OFFICER. The presiding officer of the Senate is the vice president of the United States, an appointment imposed by Article I, section 3 of the Constitution. The Constitution further provides that in the absence of the vice president, the Senate elect a president pro tempore, usually the senior senator of the majority party, to carry out the duties of the chair. Given their numerous other responsibilities, neither the vice president nor the president pro tempore spends much time presiding over the Senate. In daily practice, the duties of the chair are carried out by the acting president pro tempore, usually first-term senators who rotate

SENATE GAVELS. *Left,* the old Senate gavel beside the new gavel, a gift from the government of India, presented on 17 November 1954. Silver disks were added to reinforce the old gavel.

OFFICE OF THE HISTORIAN OF THE U.S. SENATE

in the chair for shifts of one hour each. Since 1977, only majority party senators have been appointed to serve in the chair.

As a member of the executive branch, the vice president's role as presiding officer is viewed warily by the Senate, which has severely limited the powers of the position. For example, the presiding officer may not debate unless given the unanimous consent of the Senate, he may not vote except to break a tie, and he is instructed by the standing rules of the Senate to recognize the first senator addressing the chair, even without knowing the purpose for which the senator seeks recognition. (By precedent, however, the majority leader is given priority recognition over any other senator.) The presiding officer's procedural rulings in response to points of order are subject to appeal, and it is not unusual for the chair's rulings to be overturned by vote of the Senate. As a result, the duties of the chair in the Senate have become minimal, consisting mostly of preserving order and decorum, answering parliamentary inquiries, ruling on points of order, and enforcing voting and amending procedures.

The presiding officer of the Senate is assisted in performing his duties by the Senate parliamentarian, a nonpartisan employee of the chamber who is an expert on the Senate's rules, precedents, and procedures. The parliamentarian is always on duty when the Senate is in session, seated just below the presiding officer.

[*See also* Parliamentarian, *article on* Senate Parliamentarian; President Pro Tempore of the Senate; Vice President.]

BIBLIOGRAPHY

U.S. Senate. *Riddick's Senate Procedure, Precedents, and Practices,* by Floyd M. Riddick and Alan S. Frumin. 101st Cong., 2d sess., 1992. S. Doc. 101-28. Pp. 1025–1033.
U.S. Senate. *The United States Senate, 1787–1801,* by Roy Swanstrom. 100th Cong., 1st sess., 1988. S. Doc. 100-31. Pp. 253–260.

ILONA B. NICKELS

PRESS. Journalists alternately describe Congress as the "best beat" in Washington and as the "worst-reported part of our government." Historically, Congress earned its reputation as the "best beat" by being the most open of the three branches of the federal government. Throughout the nineteenth century, when the executive and judicial branches stood aloof, Congress debated in public, reserved special galleries for the press, and accommodated journalists with regular sources of news, quotable interviews, and political patronage. In the twentieth century, Congress remained the government's least-controlled news environment, even as news attention steadily shifted toward the presidency. "The President is an individual, while Congress is a group," the *St. Louis Post-Dispatch's* Washington correspondent, Paul Y. Anderson, explained in 1932. "His aims are more or less uniform, while the policies of Congress, until formed in legislation, are confused." The growth of the broadcast media further favored a singular, easily recognizable president over the more than five hundred disparate members of Congress with their myriad of committees and subcommittees, caucuses, and back-room negotiations and compromises over complex legislation. Yet while attracted to the White House, journalists still found that they could gather more substantive information, even about executive branch activities, from Capitol Hill.

Two hundred years of news gathering in Congress have resulted in a mix of adversarial and collaborative relationships between the press and the politicians. From the beginning, members of Congress have fluctuated between defending the freedom of the press and being offended by the press's license. On the day after the House of Representatives ap-

NATIONAL INTELLIGENCER. Editors Joseph Gales, *left*, and William W. Seaton.   PERLEY'S REMINISCENCES, VOL. 1

proved the First Amendment to the Constitution, with its fundamental guarantee of freedom of the press, House members debated expelling reporters from the floor for distorting and misrepresenting their debates. The Federalist majorities in the early Congresses subsidized party papers with printing contracts, set lower postal rates for newspapers, and allowed editors to exchange newspapers with each other free of postage. Yet the same Federalists enacted the Sedition Act of 1798, making "scandalous and malicious writing" against Congress or the president a federal crime, punishable by fine and imprisonment. The Sedition Act sent several journalists to prison, including one member of the House of Representatives. In 1800, Federalists in the Senate cited a Philadelphia editor for contempt of Congress for publishing information about legislation debated in secret and not formally released. And when Congress moved to Washington, the Federalist Speaker of the House denied reporters access to the House floor.

The Democratic-Republicans reversed this order, permitted the Sedition Act to lapse, and proved far more sympathetic to press needs. In 1819, the House and Senate elected as their official printers Joseph Gales and William Seaton, editors of the Republicans' official organ, the *National Intelligencer*. This patronage underwrote Gales and Seaton's reporting of the congressional debates, which they published in their newspaper and exchanged with other editors to be reprinted in papers nationwide. Gales and Seaton also collected the floor proceedings for publication in the *Register of Debates* and in a retrospective series called the *Annals of Congress*, both forerunners of the *Congressional Record*. At first, Washington editors like Gales and Seaton enjoyed a virtual monopoly on reporting the news from Congress. By the mid 1820s, such sectional issues as the tariff spurred newspapers in the North and South to send their own correspondents to spend the congressional session in Washington and to send back periodic letters highlighting and interpreting news of interest to their particular regions. Senators and representatives quickly came to distinguish between the reporters of debate for the *Intelligencer* and the Washington *Globe* on the one hand, "who gave a faithful historical account of the proceedings," and, on the other, the letter writers who sent their papers "partial and piquant accounts of such proceedings and debates as struck their fancy."

Press Galleries and Their Rules. Overcoming its suspicion of the correspondents, Congress sought to accommodate them. In July 1841, the Senate set aside the front row of the gallery immediately above the presiding officer's desk as the first reporters' gallery. The House also provided space, and when larger chambers were constructed in the 1850s, both the Senate and House chambers featured expanded press galleries with working space and telegraph offices for the exclusive use of the press. The leading Washington correspondents spent the largest share of their days in the congressional press galleries. In sharp contrast, the White House did not establish a press room until 1902. During the nineteenth century, no newspaper assigned a reporter solely to cover the president. Instead, reporters made the rounds of the city, stopping at the White House only when necessary to seek specific information and then often standing outside the building to interview the president's visitors.

The executive branch generated so little news throughout the nineteenth century that most newspapers kept their correspondents in Washington only for the months that Congress met in session, generally for about half the year. Benjamin Perley Poore, the veteran correspondent for the *Boston Journal*, observed that when Congress adjourned, Washington became as "silent as a theatre when the performances are concluded, and the spectators have gone home." Since newspapers only paid their correspondents for the months that Congress met, the journalists scrambled for additional sources of income. In the 1850s, when congressional committees began hiring clerks—who also were paid only for the duration of the congressional session—they regularly hired correspondents like Poore. Economics overwhelmed ethics, and journalists agreed to work for the same politicians whom they covered in their dispatches. Committee clerkships gave the correspondents privileged access to news but also restricted their freedom, since critical or indiscreet reporting could jeopardize their congressional salaries. One of Poore's newspaper colleagues commented that Poore felt "rather sensitive about speculating as to what the opinion of the Senate may be, as he himself is an officer of the Senate, and it might embarrass him." However, in the era of the partisan press, correspondents generally slanted their reporting to match their papers' editorial leanings, and so few journalistic scruples were raised by their dual employment. Only an occasional member of Congress objected to the practice "by which great men and heroes are manufactured here."

During the Civil War, some Washington correspondents discovered that their advance knowledge of the news could profit them both in stock speculations and in lobbying for business interests. In the Gilded Age that followed the war, journalists engaged in lobbying, and lobbyists posed as journalists to gain access to the congressional committees and inside sources of news. Reports spread that the Russian ambassador had paid members of the press as a means of generating favorable publicity for congressional appropriation of funds to purchase Alaska. Later, when members of Congress were bribed with stocks in the Crédit Mobilier company, the name of the *Philadelphia Inquirer's* Washington correspondent, Uriah Hunt Painter, also surfaced as a recipient of the stocks. In 1874, a congressional committee called several correspondents to testify about their influence peddling during Alexander "Boss" Shepherd's extravagant rebuilding of postwar Washington.

Leading Washington correspondents became concerned that lobbying scandals were undermining their working relationships with their political sources. They approached House Speaker Samuel J. Randall (D-Pa.) with a proposal that the correspondents themselves take charge of admission to the press galleries. Accordingly, the House in 1879 and the Senate in 1884 revised their rules to provide that a Standing Committee of Correspondents, elected by the correspondents, should judge press gallery accreditation. The new rules stipulated that reporters must earn the largest share of their income from newspaper correspondence, must send telegraphic dispatches to daily newspapers, and must not be employed by executive departments (although they could continue to clerk for the committees of Congress, a practice that persisted to the end of the nineteenth century).

The new rules not only eliminated lobbyists but barred women and minority journalists as well. Women correspondents had first gained access to the press galleries in 1850, when Jane Grey Swisshelm reported on Congress for the *New York Tribune*. Some twenty women had sat in the press galleries by 1879, the year before the new rules went into effect, but since they were hired chiefly to send social news via the mail rather than political news via telegraph, they were all banished to the public galleries. In the 1870s, Frederick Douglass and his sons had held press gallery passes for their newspaper, the *New National Era*, but since the entire black press consisted of weekly newspapers, no African American journalist sat in the galleries again until Louis Lautier was accredited in 1947—and then only because the Senate Rules Committee ordered the standing committee to admit him. In their exclusivity, press gallery rules created what amounted to a newspaper fraternity at the Capitol.

Accreditation to the congressional press galleries became essential for Washington reporting. By the 1930s, a reporter needed to meet the criteria of the Standing Committee of Correspondents to join the White House Correspondents Association, to attend the president's press conferences, and to get on the distribution lists for executive agency press releases. In addition, the standing committee and press

gallery superintendents allocated space for correspondents in the congressional committee rooms and at the national political party conventions. Elections for membership on the standing committee became hotly contested affairs, with the larger papers and magazines giving their reporters time off to campaign for themselves. Committee members justified their restrictive policies on the basis of the limited space in the press galleries and the need to exclude those representing organizations that lobbied Congress or that represented government news bureaus. Only after the Department of State intervened did the standing committee relent and admit reporters for TASS, the official Soviet news agency, and then only because the Soviet government had threatened to expel American correspondents from Moscow. Although TASS received accreditation, the United States Information Agency

"The Anteroom of the Reporter's Gallery during a Stupid Speech." From *Harper's New Monthly Magazine*, January 1874.

(USIA) was for years denied admission. A compromise finally granted USIA reporters press credentials if they agreed not to use the other services of the press galleries. The standing committee also rejected reporters for *Consumer's Report,* since its parent group, Consumer's Union, lobbied for consumer legislation.

Congress and the Changing Media. Technological changes constantly challenged whatever rules and relationships that the press and politicians established. During the early period, the pace of the news was determined by the mails. In the era before the railroad or the telegraph, Washington correspondents posted their news by fast rider, coach, or packet boat, knowing that it would be days or weeks before their stories appeared in print. Acts of Congress in 1790 and 1792 not only established that newspapers could be mailed, overriding the Post Office's preference to limit the mails to letters, but set low postage rates to encourage their widest circulation. When the Post Office Act of 1794 charged newspapers 1 cent for papers to be carried fewer than one hundred miles and 1.5 cents for anything going further, Virginia representative James Madison objected that even these modest costs were a "tax on newspapers." Over the following decades, whenever the Post Office moved to raise revenues, newspapers pressed Congress to retain their low postage. In 1851, Congress granted free postage for papers within their counties of publication, primarily to assist small rural weeklies. Rep. Abraham W. Venable (D-N.C.) described the rural press as an antidote to the "poisoned sentiments" of the metropolitan dailies. "We desire our country papers for our country opinions, our provincial politics, the organs of our conservative doctrines," he declared. But because the 1851 law penalized the long-distance mailing of newspapers, Congress in 1852 created a second-class mail category, which simplified newspapers' rates and made them more uniform while retaining their federal subsidy.

Even as Congress was solving the problems of mailing newspapers, the invention of the telegraph sped news past the mails and dramatically altered Washington reporting. When the first long-distance test of the telegraph between the Capitol Building and Baltimore, Maryland, was performed in May 1844, the new technology's news applications became immediately apparent. With bulletins going out by wire, the correspondents' longer, interpretive letters lost their "starch of novelty." Yet the high cost of telegraph tolls restricted the telegraph's universal adoption. To share costs and gain more control over the new medium, a group of New York publishers launched the Associated Press (AP). Before long, the AP's reporters at the Capitol had taken responsibility for all routine coverage of floor proceedings and committee actions. Since AP wire stories went to clients of all political hues, AP reporters had to develop a more straightforward, factual, and objective style of reporting. "My instructions do not allow me to make any comment upon the facts which I communicate," the AP's chief Washington correspondent, Lawrence Gobright, explained in 1861. Gobright tried to be "truthful and impartial" and described his reports as "dry matters of fact and detail." That left the more colorful, partisan, interpretive writing to the correspondents. Yet when they drafted the rules for press gallery membership, they used telegraph dispatches to a daily newspaper as the essential definition of their craft.

In the first decade of the twentieth century, the arrival of reform-minded magazine writers disrupted the comfortable, even cozy working relationship between the press and its congressional sources. For the most part, newspaper correspondents wrote under pseudonyms, such as "Perley," "Carp," and "S.M." (Sour Mash). But magazine writers signed their essays and earned national reputations. Unlike the correspondents, who painstakingly cultivated sources for daily reporting, the magazine writers, with their longer deadlines and diverse subjects, never lingered in one place long enough to need regular sources of information. Lincoln Steffens, for instance, developed his best news leads from local newspaper reporters who could not print what they knew. Over an eight-month period in 1906, David Graham Phillips published a series of articles in *Cosmopolitan* magazine attacking prominent senators for selling out to powerful special interests. Called "The Treason of the Senate," the series outraged both the politicians and the Washington press corps. When President Theodore Roosevelt responded by accusing Phillips and other magazine writers of "muckraking," he delivered the attack first to an enthusiastic audience of Gridiron Club members—Washington newspaper correspondents and their political guests—who encouraged him to deliver the speech again in public.

During the 1920s and 1930s, changing technology again disrupted the patterns of Washington reporting when radio began broadcasting the news. Although political leaders from Sen. William E.

Borah (R-Idaho) to President Franklin D. Roosevelt mastered the new medium, the Washington press corps did not take radio seriously. One Washington correspondent who spoke in error during a radio news program dismissed the matter with a shrug, saying, "What does it matter on radio?" When radio reporters applied for admission to the congressional press galleries, the Standing Committee of Correspondents repeatedly rejected them. Only radio reporters who also sent telegraph dispatches to daily newspapers received accreditation. The newspaper correspondents saw radio reporters as merely announcers and entertainers, not journalists. Finally, the radio reporters took their case to Congress, which in 1939 established separate radio galleries in the House and Senate. By 1953, they had become the radio-television galleries. At the same time that Congress established the radio galleries, it also authorized the creation of separate periodical press galleries for magazine writers, and the Senate set up a press photographers gallery. Members of these different media galleries elected their own standing committees of correspondents.

As the broadcast media expanded, Congress grew concerned over the eroding economic condition of newspapers. During the 1960s, House and Senate committees investigated ways of allowing a failing newspaper to merge with another paper in the same market without violating antitrust laws. Sen. Carl Hayden (D-Ariz.) introduced legislation to exempt newspapers from antitrust prosecution after the Justice Department filed suit against the Tucson, Arizona, *Citizen* and *Star*, which had been published under a joint operating agreement for nearly three decades. In 1969, the Supreme Court determined that the Tucson agreement had violated antitrust laws, a ruling that stimulated Congress to pass the Newspaper Preservation Act of 1970. While declaring it to be federal policy to preserve "a newspaper press editorially and reportorially independent and competitive," Congress exempted joint newspaper operating agreements from prosecution if one of the papers would otherwise have failed financially.

Congressional Secrets and Leaks. The collaborative nature of news gathering on Capitol Hill has long been epitomized by the leak, an act of mutual benefit to both the source of the information and the reporter who receives and publishes it while protecting the source's confidentiality. Correspondents received more notice from their editors and more column space in their newspapers when they reported "secret" information. Leakers got their

stories published and made friends among the press. Members of Congress leaked, as Benjamin Perley Poore explained in 1883, "in order that they and their political friends may be placed advantageously before the country." Poore further noted that a politician's willingness to cooperate with the press warmed in direct proportion to his presidential aspirations. Leaks occurred in both the executive and legislative branches, but the diversity of opinion on issues in a legislative body meant that those wanting to keep a secret would almost always have counterparts who wished to reveal that secret. Still, the tensions caused by frequent leaks produced many investigations into press violations of congressional secrecy; journalists were subpoenaed and even imprisoned within the Capitol. These investigations generally resulted in the further opening of the legislative process to public scrutiny.

In the First Congress, the House immediately opened its doors to the public and press, while the Senate met entirely in secret. House members would stand for reelection within two years and wanted their constituents to be aware of their legislative activities. Senators, who were elected for six-year terms by state legislatures, believed they could conduct business more productively if they were not tempted to speak to the galleries. Not until 20 February 1794 did the Senate hold a public session, during a debate on whether Albert Gallatin had the proper citizenship credentials to be seated as senator from Pennsylvania. Senators opposed to Gallatin did not wish to be seen as denying him a seat in a secret, "star chamber" proceeding. Having opened the doors once, they succumbed to newspaper pressure to open their debates on a regular basis, and by December 1794 the first public gallery was constructed. Even then, the Senate permitted the public and the press only for legislative business and continued to debate such executive business as treaties and nominations in closed session until 1929.

In 1800, the Senate summoned William Duane, editor of the Philadelphia *Aurora*, to explain how he had obtained information from a secret session of the Senate. Federalists still held the majority in the Senate, and Duane was a Jeffersonian Republican. Fortunately for Duane, Vice President Thomas Jefferson presided over the Senate session and granted his request for additional time to consult with counsel. Duane left the chamber and never returned. The Senate voted him in contempt but had no means of enforcing the contempt citation. Both the editor and the unidentified source of the leak

"The Reporter's Gallery." Half-tone engraving by R. C. Collins, c. 1890.

OFFICE OF THE HISTORIAN OF THE U.S. SENATE

went unpunished. Similarly, in 1812, when the Alexandria, Virginia, *Herald* published information about a secret House debate over war with Great Britain, the House cited editor Nathaniel Rounsavell for contempt for similarly refusing to divulge his sources but sought no other punishment. As the result of still another investigation of a journalist in 1857, prosecutions of contempt-of-Congress citations were turned over to the Department of Justice.

Twice the Senate censured members for leaking secret information. In 1811, Massachusetts senator and former secretary of State Timothy Pickering was censured for reading from confidential documents during an open session of the Senate. Pickering's mistake may have been an honest one, but as an arch-Federalist he had opened himself to retribution by the Jeffersonian Republican majority. In 1844, the Senate censured Benjamin Tappan (D-Ohio), an abolitionist, for releasing to the *New York Evening Post* a copy of President John Tyler's still-secret message to the Senate regarding a proposed treaty to annex Texas as a slave state.

The Senate also twice held newspaper reporters prisoner in the Capitol Building in efforts to force them to reveal their sources. In 1848, when John Nugent, the Washington correspondent of the *New York Herald*, refused to state where he had obtained a copy of the still secret Treaty of Guadalupe-Hidalgo, which ended the war with Mexico, he was confined in a Senate committee room. The *Herald*

continued to publish his dispatches under the dateline "Custody of the Sergeant-at-Arms" and doubled his salary during his captivity. As the Senate approached the end of its session, it finally had to let Nugent go. Again in 1871, the Senate imprisoned Zebulon White and Hiram Ramsdell, correspondents of the *New York Tribune*, for publishing the still-secret Treaty of Washington, which settled U.S. claims with Great Britain following the Civil War. White and Ramsdell were locked into a committee room, where they entertained family, friends, and senatorial visitors and dined in the Senate restaurant. They were eventually released without violating the confidentiality of their source.

Senators persisted in holding secret sessions long after it had become apparent that they could not hold secrets. When the galleries were cleared and the doors locked, senators unbuttoned their vests, lit up cigars, and debated nominations and treaties in private. At the conclusion of these sessions, newspaper correspondents awaited the senators outside the chamber. Resourceful reporters could quickly piece together what had been said and done in closed sessions. The press reported these executive sessions in such detail that some journalists suggested that Congress might get more publicity if it conducted all of its business in secret. In 1886, Sen. Orville H. Platt (R-Conn.) pointed out the obvious when he told his colleagues, "There is no secrecy possible. There never has been any secrecy possible in any matter about which the public desire information that took place in executive session."

The secret sessions of the Senate came to an abrupt halt as a result of an investigation into a leak regarding the nomination of former senator Irvine L. Lenroot to a seat on the U.S. Customs Court. The United Press's Senate reporter, Paul Mallon, published a lengthy account of the secret debate and vote on Lenroot's nomination. Sen. David A. Reed (R-Pa.) called for an investigation into the source of the leak, which he assumed came from anti-Lenroot senators. Robert M. La Follette, Jr. (R-Wis.), rose in Mallon's defense and cited the numerous other newspaper accounts of supposedly secret sessions. La Follette read an account of a secret session published the previous year under the byline of *Pittsburgh Post Gazette* reporter Theodore Huntley. "Where did the correspondent get that information? Who gave that out?" La Follette asked, before revealing that Huntley also served as Senator Reed's secretary. Such sarcasm exposed the vulnerability of every senator to charges of violating Senate rules and held up to ridicule their attempts to conduct public business in secret. Bowing to the inevitable, on 18 June 1929, the Senate changed its rules to transact all executive business in open session unless it specifically voted for a closed meeting. Since then, the Senate and House have closed their doors only on rare occasions to debate national security matters involving highly classified data.

Congressional committees also moved toward more open proceedings. "Sunshine" rules adopted in the 1970s required committees to hold hearings in public, including hearings of conference committees and committee mark-up sessions. Some committees, however, including the prestigious House Ways and Means Committee, have increasingly reverted to closed sessions. "It's just difficult to legislate," Chairman Dan Rostenkowski (D-Ill.) explained. "I'm not ashamed about closed doors." Little outcry came from the press, since reporters with reliable sources could still find out what happened in closed meetings without having to sit through them. "I am not an advocate of closed meetings," said *Wall Street Journal* bureau chief Albert R. Hunt, but his paper did better when meetings were closed, he stated, "because we knew the Hill, we worked it hard." Congressional investigations, because they stimulate great interest in the press, have also fostered considerable leaking. James Hamilton, assistant chief counsel to the Senate Select Committee on Presidential Campaign Activities (Watergate Committee), noted that leaks "made committee members and staff—including those *not* leaking—appear as publicity-grabbing buffoons incapable of keeping their own counsel and conducting conscientious investigations into serious matters."

Embarrassed over the leak of its report on an investigation of intelligence operations, the House Select Committee on Intelligence subpoenaed CBS correspondent Daniel Schorr and several editors of *New York* magazine in 1975. Similar chagrin over the leak from the Senate Judiciary Committee of sexual harassment charges against Supreme Court nominee Clarence Thomas in 1991 led the Senate to appoint a special prosecutor to identify the leakers. When the Senate Rules Committee declined to issue contempt citations or otherwise compel reporters Nina Totenberg of National Public Radio and Timothy Phelps of *Newsday* to testify, the investigation ended without disclosing the source of the leak. Some members worried that such investigations would lead to constitutional confrontations over the First Amendment rights of the press and the public's "right to know."

The Uneven Spotlight of the Press. Just as power has shifted back and forth among the separate branches of the federal government, the press has shifted its attention from the House, to the Senate, to the presidency, depending on which exerted the most influence at a given time. Initially, the House received far greater notice from the press than did the Senate. In 1804, when Rep. Samuel L. Mitchill of New York was elected to the Senate, he alerted his wife, "Henceforth you will read little of me in the Gazettes. Senators are less exposed to public view than Representatives." By the 1830s, during the Senate's "golden age of debate," newspaper attention followed legislators of the stature of Henry Clay, Daniel Webster, and John C. Calhoun from the House to the Senate, and the Senate tended to dominate the news from Washington for the remainder of the century. By the 1870s, newspaper correspondents recognized a handful of committee chairmen as sources of power and information on Capitol Hill. Junior senators might always be available for interviews, but they had few facts to report, and most House members were so far removed from their chamber's leadership that they seemed to learn what was happening only by reading the newspapers.

Newspaper correspondents cultivated committee chairmen and other "knowing ones" for regular sources of information on the scheduling of bills and other legislative matters. Correspondents found the powerful chairman of the Senate Finance Committee, Nelson W. Aldrich (R-R.I.), an especially useful source because he was always better informed than his colleagues about what had happened and was likely to happen. Although appearing "cold-blooded and unapproachable," Aldrich was willing to talk with reporters so long as they did not quote him directly. But the development and maintenance of such highly placed sources exacted a price. The Progressive era journalist Will Irvin charged that "Washington correspondence, viewed in bulk, tends toward the side of the powerful." Washington correspondent Louis Ludlow conceded that he and other reporters were a "graveyard of secrets," possessing information they dared not publish lest they violate confidences and jeopardize their influential sources.

During the nineteenth century, presidents rarely spoke to the press for attribution, preferring to reach the public through formal messages or party spokesmen in Congress. In the 1890s, presidential secretaries began delivering briefings to the press and promoting better press relations, but not until the dynamic presidencies of Theodore Roosevelt and Woodrow Wilson did press attention begin to shift dramatically from Congress to the president. Strong personalities made the presidency "a thing of flesh and blood" against the "aggregate of humanity" on Capitol Hill. "Broadly speaking," concluded New York Times Washington correspondent Richard Oulahan, who witnessed this evolution firsthand, "the people visualize the President of the United States as the Government."

The election of 1932 further accelerated the trend toward presidential domination of the news, and dramatic events from the New Deal through World War II made the White House the center of Washington reporting. Part-time reporting faded into history along with part-time government. Franklin D. Roosevelt's bold initiatives, numerous press conferences, fireside chats, and magnetic personality captivated the press as well as the public. Yet if the White House became the center of the story, Congress remained the most favorable grounds for collecting the news. Washington correspondents in the 1930s found that "it was far easier to break White House or departmental news from the Hill than from the White House itself or the department concerned."

During the 1950s, journalist James Reston observed that Congress and the press were natural allies. Members of Congress considered good press relations so essential to their reelection, Reston wrote, that "consequently they see reporters and some of them even read us." As the New York Times's Washington bureau chief, Reston assigned reporter Russell Baker to cover the White House, but Baker found it tedious to sit "in this awful lobby" waiting for the presidential press secretary to issue handouts. Transferring to Capitol Hill, Baker felt as if he were climbing out of a closed sewer and into the fresh air, since everyone in Congress "loved to talk." Members' willingness to be quoted was essential, since Washington reporting often worked on "reaction." When an event occurred, reporters contacted a variety of officials and requested comments, which reporters then passed along to the opposing side on that issue to gather counterbalance for their stories. Press-generated congressional reactions to presidential initiatives received more press attention than did members' remarks in floor debates. Rep. Bill Frenzel (R-Minn.) charged the press with using Congress to embarrass President Ronald Reagan: "I'm always expected to say something nasty about the President," Frenzel complained. "I am badgered; words are put in my mouth."

Despite the open availability of sources on Capitol Hill, statistical analysis showed a steady, unrelenting increase since the 1950s in news about the presidency at Congress's expense. As national news coverage of Congress eroded, regional reporting expanded on Capitol Hill. Both the Associated Press and United Press International divided their congressional staffs by state and region to provide specialized coverage for client papers. And by the 1970s, an estimated two-thirds of all Capitol Hill reporters covered news of interest to local and regional constituencies. Regional reporters were able to develop far more personal contacts with their congressional sources, but Washington Post correspondent and former regional reporter Lou Cannon charged that regional reporting created a congressional coverage "based on mutual needs and sometimes on mutual laziness." By focusing on the local angle of national news, regional reporters gave members visibility in their home states and districts, where it counted the most. In turn, regional reporters' dependence on senators and representatives from their regions for inside information, access to government agencies, and other well-placed tips moved their reporting, in Cannon's words, "beyond symbiosis to collusion." In addition to making themselves generally available to regional reporters, members of Congress wrote columns for local papers and prepared taped interviews for

SEN. HOWARD H. BAKER, JR. (R-TENN.). *Center,* meeting with the press.   OFFICE OF THE HISTORIAN OF THE U.S. SENATE

home state television and radio stations. With re-election in mind, members especially sought coverage in the local media—although national coverage elevated their prestige and influence in Congress.

Increasingly, television became the dominant medium on Capitol Hill. During the 1980s, the accredited membership of the radio and television galleries doubled in size, for the first time reaching parity with the newspaper press gallery. Television cameras on the Capitol lawn broadcast interviews and news reports with the familiar dome as a backdrop. Members viewed television as both a blessing and a curse. It enabled them to reach vast audiences and establish name recognition, but it also required them to reduce complex legislative issues to a few sections of explanation, preferably with a short, snappy sound bite.

Television first broadcast from the Capitol in 1947, carrying President Harry S. Truman's state of the union message. That same year, television covered Gen. George C. Marshall's testimony to the House Foreign Affairs Committee on the Marshall Plan. In 1949, however, when Sam Rayburn (D-Tex.) returned to the House speakership, he prohibited television in the hearing rooms to prevent committees such as the House Un-American Activities Committee from playing to the cameras. While the so-called Rayburn Rule banned the televising of House hearings, Senate committees welcomed the cameras. In 1950, live television coverage of the Senate investigation of organized crime made Chairman Estes Kefauver (D-Tenn.) a national figure and potential presidential candidate. In 1954, television's live broadcasts of the Army-McCarthy hearings helped to undermine public support for Sen. Joseph R. McCarthy (R-Wis.) by revealing his bullying tactics to a nationwide audience. Senators Barry Goldwater (R-Ariz.) and John F. Kennedy (D-Mass.) first came to national attention through the televised investigation of labor racketeering in 1957. In 1973, an enormous television audience followed the Senate Watergate hearings, turning its chairman, Samuel J. Ervin, Jr. (D-N.C.), from a "simple country lawyer" into a national folk hero.

During these years of televised committee hearings, the Senate and House chambers remained off-limits for television cameras. In 1974, in anticipation of an impeachment trial for President Richard M. Nixon, the Senate first investigated lighting its chamber for television. After Nixon resigned, the system was instead used to televise the swearing in of Vice President Nelson A. Rockefeller in the Senate chamber. The Senate in 1978 permitted radio broadcast of its debate over the Panama Canal treaties, but it was the House, in 1979, that first permitted its proceedings to be televised. Concerned in part that television was shifting attention back to the House, the Senate in 1986 abandoned its resistance and permitted gavel-to-gavel television broadcasts of the proceedings. Congressional employees worked the cameras, but the broadcasts were carried over C-SPAN, the private Cable Satellite Public Affairs Network. The major networks also broadcast segments of the debates.

Like that of newspapers and magazines, television coverage tended to focus on a small, powerful minority of members. "The print media exclude the powerless," media analyst Steven Hess observed. "The electronic media exclude the powerless and the inarticulate." Because most members expected little coverage on the national networks and only relatively brief appearances on local television, congressional offices continued to orient themselves primarily toward newspaper reporting. With the expansion of congressional staffs, members delegated more of their press relations to press secretaries and other staff, who routinely compiled, duplicated, and distributed newspaper clippings of the members' accomplishments.

Members of Congress grew increasingly sophisticated in their media relations. While twentieth-century senators and representatives no longer provided government subsidies for party papers or put Washington correspondents on their payrolls, they almost all employed press secretaries, many of whom had once been journalists. Congress also provided recording studios where members could tape radio and television programs for broadcast in their home states or for use in local news programs. Members used press releases, fax machines, and computers to generate a constant stream of publicity and meet the deadlines of their home-state papers. Despite their efforts, however, Congress constantly complained of negative coverage. The press coverage grew skeptical, if not cynical, about the national legislature. As correspondent Steven V. Roberts explained, "We have to tilt against the institution we cover, or risk being overwhelmed by the power of the political experts to manufacture and manipulate the message that voters receive from Capitol Hill."

[*See also* Bill of Rights; Broadcasting of Congressional Proceedings; C-SPAN; Press Galleries.]

BIBLIOGRAPHY

Hamilton, James. *The Power to Probe: A Study of Congressional Investigations.* 1976.

Hess, Stephen R. *Life from Capitol Hill: Studies of Congress and the Media.* 1991.

Hess, Stephen R. *The Ultimate Insiders: U.S. Senators in the National Media.* 1986.

Kielbowicz, Richard B. *News in the Mail: The Press, Post Office, and Public Information, 1700–1860s.* 1989.

Marbut, F. B. *News from the Capital: The Story of Washington Reporting.* 1971.

Ritchie, Donald A. *Press Gallery: Congress and the Washington Correspondents.* 1991.

Roberts, Steven V. "The Congress, the Press, and the Public." In *Understanding Congress: Research Perspectives.* Edited by Roger H. Davidson and Richard C. Sachs. 1991.

DONALD A. RITCHIE

PRESS GALLERIES. The openness of congressional proceedings and the collaborative nature of media coverage on Capitol Hill are represented by the congressional press galleries. The first reporters to cover Congress were stenographers who were admitted onto the floor of the House and Senate chambers and who recorded the speeches relatively verbatim. Beginning in the 1820s, correspondents for newspapers outside the capital began attending sessions of Congress—and had the effrontery not just to report the debates but also to interpret and criticize them. Consigned to the public galleries, the correspondents petitioned for equal access to the floor. Objecting vigorously, Sen. John M. Niles of Connecticut denounced all reporters as "hirelings, hanging on to the skirts of literature, earning a miserable subsistence for their vile and dirty misrepresentation of the proceedings here." However, on 8 July 1841 the Senate agreed to provide a "Reporters' Gallery" consisting of ten desks on the front row of the gallery immediately above the presiding officer's chair.

When the new House and Senate chambers were opened in 1857 and 1859, they included enlarged press galleries with equally spacious lobbies, fitted at government expense with writing tables, pens and ink, and telegraph offices. The doorkeeper assigned to each of these galleries eventually took the title of superintendent of the press gallery. The doorkeepers assisted reporters in following the floor proceedings and arranged interviews with members. By contrast, no press room existed inside the White House until 1902.

The vice president, Speaker of the House, and Rules committees of the Senate and House initially controlled admission to the press galleries. During the post–Civil War era, when lobbyists posed as reporters and some reporters supplemented their incomes by lobbying, congressional journalists urged the adoption of new rules and proposed electing a Standing Committee of Correspondents that would judge applicants' credentials for admission. The new standards required that correspondents draw their primary salary from reporting by telegraph to daily newspapers and that they have no personal involvement in legislation before Congress. These rules effectively eliminated lobbyists, but also all women and African American reporters, since they either wrote for weekly papers or sent their correspondence by mail. Women reporters had gained entrance to the press gallery as early as 1850, and twenty women were accredited at the time the House adopted the new rules in 1879 (the Senate followed in 1884). By 1880 there were no women in the press gallery, and not until World War II did they return in any appreciable numbers. No black reporters sat in the press galleries between 1874 and 1947, despite many applications for admission. The journalists' standing committees also rejected reporters for such government-sponsored news organizations as the U.S. Information Agency (although, at the State Department's request, they admitted the Soviet news agency, Tass) and reporters for the journals of advocacy groups, including *Consumer Reports*.

During the 1930s the press galleries similarly refused admittance to radio reporters, unless they also reported for a daily newspaper. Radio broadcasters took their case to Congress, which in 1939 established separate radio galleries in the House and Senate; in 1953 these became the radio-television galleries. Congress further established galleries for the periodical press (magazines, journals, and newsletters) and press photographers. Each gallery serves as a self-governing body of journalists, with superintendents and other costs and services underwritten by Congress.

BIBLIOGRAPHY

Byrd, Robert C. *The Senate, 1789–1989: Addresses on the History of the United States Senate.* Vol. 2. 1991.
Marbut, F. B. *News from the Capital: The Story of Washington Reporting.* 1971.
Ritchie, Donald A. *Press Gallery: Congress and the Washington Correspondents.* 1991.

DONALD A. RITCHIE

PREVIOUS QUESTION. The "previous question" is a motion used by the House of Representatives to end a debate and bring the House to a vote on the pending matter. This motion is not in order in the Senate.

Typically, the majority floor manager of a bill or resolution moves the previous question after the first hour of debate on it, but only if the House is considering the measure under its general rules. The motion to order the previous question is not debatable and requires a majority vote for adoption. If the motion is adopted, the measure is not subject to further debate or amendments. The House often proceeds to an immediate vote on the measure, although a motion to recommit may intervene. The previous question is not in order in the Committee of the Whole.

The most important practical effect of the previous question is to preclude amendments to a measure considered under the general rules of the House. Under these rules, the majority floor manager controls the first hour of debate, during which no other member can offer an amendment; only the member controlling the time for debate can propose an amendment to the measure. A member wishing to propose an amendment first must convince the House to vote against the previous question. If the motion to order the previous question is rejected, the Speaker then recognizes an opponent of the measure (in its present form) to control a second hour of debate, during which that member can offer an amendment to it.

BIBLIOGRAPHY

U.S. House of Representatives. *Deschler's Precedents of the United States House of Representatives,* by Lewis Deschler. 94th Cong., 2d sess. 1977. H. Doc. 94-661, Vol. 7, pp. 114–176.
U.S. House of Representatives. *Constitution, Jefferson's Manual, and Rules of the House of Representatives, 102d Congress.* Compiled by William Holmes Brown. 101st Cong., 2d sess., 1990. H. Doc. 101-256. Pp. 577–582.

STANLEY BACH

PRINTING COMMITTEE, JOINT. Prior to the establishment of the Government Printing Office, Congress had contracted with private firms for printing products and services, an arrangement that soon became corrupted. A congressional investigation in 1840 revealed profits of almost $470,000 for printers utilized by Congress during the previous seven years. Similar revelations in 1846 contributed to growing embarrassment and an outcry over the state of public printing.

In response, Congress approved a joint resolution, which became law on 3 August 1846, directing the principal officers of the House and the Senate to advertise and obtain sealed proposals for printing, with the lowest bid in each case receiving the contract. To oversee this new arrangement, Congress established the Joint Committee on Printing, composed of three senators and three representatives. Though legislative proposals were not referred to or directly acted upon by the joint panel, its members were to receive and report on motions to print extra copies of literature for their respective houses. The committee, however, was vested with "power to adopt such measures as may be deemed necessary to remedy any neglect or delay on the part of the contractor . . . and to make a pro rata reduction in the compensation allowed, or to refuse the work altogether, should it be inferior to the standard" (9 Stat. 114). The joint committee subsequently set printing and binding regulations, which it continues to do today. The panel's 1846 mandate also directed it to "audit and pass upon all accounts for printing."

Fourteen years later, the joint resolution of 23 June 1860, which established the Government Printing Office (GPO), effectively made the Joint Committee on Printing (JCP) the board of directors for the new entity. GPO physical plant and machinery purchases were subject to JCP approval, as were paper standards. The mandating of the JCP and its remedial and financial powers were reiterated in the Printing Act of 1895, which also gave the committee some additional oversight and management responsibilities.

The membership of the JCP was modified by the Legislative Reorganization Act of 1946 to include the chairman and two members of the Committee on Rules and Administration of the Senate and the chairman and two members of the Committee on House Administration. Later, in 1981, this structure was expanded to include the chairman and four members of each respective committee. The JCP chairmanship rotates in each Congress between the chairs of the Senate and House administration committees.

[*See also* Government Printing Office.]

HAROLD C. RELYEA

PRIVACY. Beginning in the 1960s, Congress considered the policy implications of various threats to personal privacy, especially from computerized data bases, wiretaps, psychological testing, and the polygraph. The policy problem was defined in terms of threats to individual privacy, and the appropriate policy solution was thought to be statutory rights giving individuals means to protect their privacy. Debates focused on the need to balance individual privacy against competing interests including effective law enforcement, efficiency of government operations, and reduction of employee theft. Numerous hearings, under the leadership of Sen. Samuel J. Ervin, Jr. (D-N.C.), and Rep. Cornelius E. Gallagher (D-N.J.), were held regarding various invasions of privacy, but these hearings did not result in legislation. In 1968, Congress passed the Omnibus Crime Control and Safe Streets Act, Title III of which required law enforcement agencies to obtain a special court order for wiretapping.

In the 1970s, Congress adopted additional statutes giving individuals rights to control information about themselves in a variety of situations. Each of these acts originated in a different congressional committee and reflected a balancing of somewhat different interests. Each, however, adopted a similar structure incorporating a "code of fair information practices" for the particular record-keeping relationship. These codes give individuals rights to gain access to their records, to correct or amend information in them, and to obtain copies. The codes also establish requirements for organizations to follow in collecting, using, and exchanging personal information; for example, information is to be timely, accurate, and complete, and information collected for one purpose is not to be used for another purpose without the consent of the person about whom the information has been compiled. The Fair Credit Reporting Act of 1970 was the first of these information privacy laws. Most important was the Privacy Act of 1974, passed in the wake of the Watergate revelations of government misuse of personal information. Information privacy laws also exist for a number of other kinds of information-gathering organizations, including educational institutions, banks, video rental stores, and cable companies.

Landmark Privacy Legislation

Title	Year Enacted	Reference Number	Description
Title III of Omnibus Crime Control and Safe Streets Act	1968	P.L. 90-351	Protects the privacy of wire and oral communications by prohibiting electronic surveillance of aural communications except for law enforcement surveillance under a court order, for specified telephone company monitoring for service purposes, and in cases where one participant consents to the surveillance.
Fair Credit Reporting Act	1970	P.L. 91-508	Requires credit investigations and reporting agencies to make their records available to the subject, provides procedures for correcting information, and permits disclosure only to authorized customers.
Family Educational Rights and Privacy Act	1974	P.L. 93-380	Requires educational institutions to grant students or parents access to student records, establishes procedures to challenge and correct information, and limits disclosure to third parties.
Privacy Act	1974	P.L. 93-579	Gives individuals rights of access to and correction of information held by federal agencies and places restrictions on federal agencies' collection, use, and disclosure of personally identifiable information.
Foreign Intelligence Surveillance Act	1978	P.L. 95-511	Establishes legal standards and procedures for the use of electronic surveillance to collect foreign intelligence and counter-intelligence within the United States.
Right to Financial Privacy Act	1978	P.L. 95-630	Provides bank customers some privacy regarding their records held by banks and other financial institutions and provides procedures whereby federal agencies can gain access to such records.

In the 1980s, various technological changes and the symbolically important year 1984—associated with George Orwell's novel of that name and its all-intrusive "Big Brother"—brought renewed public and congressional attention to privacy. Technological changes had obliterated or weakened many of the privacy protections contained in earlier laws. For example, Title III of the Omnibus Crime Control and Safe Streets Act required court orders for interception of communications transmitted by wire; by the 1980s, a number of transmission media not covered by Title III were being used, including microwave, satellite, and fiber optics. The information privacy laws of the 1970s dealt with discrete records and separate organizations, but the merging of computers and telecommunications in the 1980s allowed for the creation of massive record systems and regular exchanges of personal information. This led to what the congressional Office of Technology Assessment, in its 1986 report *Electronic Record Systems and Individual Privacy*, termed a de facto national data base using the social security number as an electronic identifier. In addition to press coverage and congressional hearings on the gaps in existing statutes, public opinion surveys indicated that a growing number of Americans were concerned about threats to their privacy and were supportive of stronger legislation and government involvement to protect privacy.

Landmark Privacy Legislation

TITLE	YEAR ENACTED	REFERENCE NUMBER	DESCRIPTION
Privacy Protection Act	1980	P.L. 96-440	Prohibits government agencies from conducting unannounced searches of press offices and files if no one in the office is suspected of committing a crime.
Cable Communications Policy Act	1984	P.L 98-549	Requires cable services to inform subscribers of the nature of personally identifiable information collected and the nature of its use; the disclosures that may be made of such information; the period during which such information will be maintained; and the times during which a subscriber may access such information. It also places restrictions on cable services' collection and disclosures of such information.
Electronic Communication Privacy Act	1986	P.L. 99-508	Extends the Title III protections and requirements of the Omnibus Crime Control and Safe Streets Act to new forms of voice, data, and video communications, including cellular phones, electronic mail, computer transmissions, and voice and display pagers.
Employee Polygraph Protection Act	1988	P.L. 100-347	Prohibits private-sector use of lie detector tests for employment purposes, except in certain circumstances.
Computer Matching and Privacy Protection Act	1988	P.L. 100-503	Requires agencies to formulate procedural agreements before exchanging computerized searching or record systems for purposes of comparing those records and establishes data integrity boards within each agency.
Video Privacy Act	1988	P.L. 100-618	Prohibits video stores from disclosing their customers' names, addresses, and the specific videotapes rented or bought by customers, except in certain circumstances.

SOURCES: Office of Technology Assessment, *Electronic Record Systems and Individual Privacy*, OTA-CIT-296 (June 1986); Robert Aldrich, *Privacy Protection Law in the United States*, NTIA report 82-98 (May 1982); and Sarah P. Collins, *Citizens' Control over Records Held by Third Parties*, CRS Rept. 78-255 (8 December 1978).

In response, Congress adopted three major laws providing new privacy protections. Each had the active support of a subcommittee chair and passed Congress with a large bipartisan majority. The Electronic Communications Privacy Act of 1986, introduced by Rep. Robert W. Kastenmeier (D-Wis.), expanded Title III protections to new communications techniques such as electronic mail. Vital to passage of this legislation was the support of the industries providing new communications services and equipment, which were concerned that consumers would not use new communication technologies unless the privacy of their communications was ensured. The Computer Matching and Privacy Protection Act of 1988, introduced by Sen.

William S. Cohen (R-Maine), established procedures for federal agencies to follow in exchanging their records with those of other federal or state agencies for the purpose of searching and comparing the records. Computer matching is generally used to detect fraud, waste, and abuse—for example, in the case of federal employees who have defaulted on their federal student loans. The Computer Matching and Privacy Protection Act also required agencies to establish data integrity boards to provide agency-level oversight of computer matching. Finally, the Employee Polygraph Protection Act of 1988, introduced by Rep. Pat Williams (D-Mont.), banned private-sector use of the polygraph in screening potential or current employees. Although privacy threats from the polygraph had been identified as early as the 1960s, legislation restricting its use did not pass until the psychological and medical community established problems with the accuracy of the polygraph and labor unions raised questions about its effects on employment opportunities.

Several new privacy issues were emerging in the early 1990s. Probably the most important concerned the issue of genetic privacy. The mapping of the human genome brings with it significant advances for medical research and treatment but also raises the possibility that data bases will be constructed containing genetic information on all Americans or on some subset of the population. Data bases of genetic information are of potential interest to many organizations, but especially to employers, doctors, and insurance companies. At the same time, such data bases raise fundamental questions of individual privacy as genetic information provides a complete picture of one's biological destiny. Another unresolved issue involved the private sector's use of personal information. In effect, personal information—especially about buying patterns and life-style—has become a commodity that is exchanged. Some advocate that individuals be given property rights with respect to such information so they can exert some economic control over its uses. Others argue that individuals should be able to opt in or out of schemes that exchange information for marketing purposes. Similar proposals are raised with respect to new communications services, such as a telephone service that allows a call's recipient to see the caller's number. The harmonization of privacy, or data protection, legislation among the European nations is also reigniting debates in the United States about the need for a governmentwide agency to monitor and advise on privacy issues; such organizations exist in most European countries, Canada, and Australia.

[*See also* Civil Liberties.]

BIBLIOGRAPHY

Burnham, David. *The Rise of the Computer State.* 1983.
Flaherty, David H. *Protecting Privacy in Surveillance Societies.* 1989.
Regan, Priscilla M. "Privacy, Government Information, and Technology." *Public Administration Review* 46 (1986): 629–634.
Rule, James B., et al. *The Politics of Privacy: Planning for Personal Data Systems as Powerful Technologies.* 1980.
Westin, Alan F. *Privacy and Freedom.* 1967.

PRISCILLA M. REGAN

PRIVATE BILL. A bill that applies only to a named individual (which may be a public body or a corporation), usually granting some benefit from government not otherwise authorized, is a private bill; when enacted, it becomes a private law. Most bear titles declaring them "for the relief of" the individual, but no authority explicitly defines them.

Early private laws often provided pensions, settled monetary and land claims, and, especially after the Civil War, corrected records of military service and restored political rights to former rebels. They also permit citizens to accept foreign honors. Even the First Congress enacted a few; the 14th (1815–1817) enacted over one hundred, the 49th (1885–1887), one thousand; and the 59th (1905–1907), six thousand. With enactment of a general pension statute, the figure then dropped below two hundred.

The Legislative Reorganization Act of 1946 forbade private bills concerning pensions, military records, bridge-building projects, and tort claims; it substituted administrative remedies, including the Tort Claims Act. After the Immigration Act of 1924 and with the disruptions connected with World War II, however, the number of private bills on immigration rose, accounting for the majority of private bills after 1937. Most Congresses from the 69th (1925–1927) on enacted more than five hundred private laws; the 81st–83d (1949–1955) enacted one thousand each. Numbers declined thereafter, as Congress increasingly delegated administrative discretion over both immigration and claims; each Congress from the 97th (1981–1983) to the 102d (1991–1993) enacted fewer than sixty.

By 1810 the House had established special procedures for private bills; from 1839, private bills were listed on a separate calendar; and from 1900, practices were instituted that allowed one objection to block passage. Since 1935, the Private Calendar may be called on first and third Tuesdays, and any bill to which two members object is recommitted. Each party appoints official objectors for this purpose; bills they find problematic are often simply passed over, or difficulties are worked out before the calendar call; recently, some objectors have also been members of a subcommittee handling such measures. Committees may, but seldom do, rereport recommitted measures under procedures that allow passage by majority vote in the House as in Committee of the Whole.

The Senate usually considers private bills by unanimous consent; party policy committee staff review them as reported. The president sometimes vetoes private measures, often because he considers them inequitable or advocates reexamination of general law instead. Most are pocket vetoes, and few are overridden.

Most private bills begin in the House, usually at the request of individuals or their attorneys. The comptroller general rarely, but often effectively, exercises authority to recommend a private bill. Both chambers refer most private bills to their Judiciary committees, although bills dealing with foreign claims, veterans' benefits, and public lands go elsewhere. A few also address patents or copyrights, but most concern immigration or claims, and their processing is routine. House subcommittees handle these categories; Senate staff prepare recommendations for the full committee. Each panel has rules specifying required documentation and criteria for favorable consideration; they normally act only if the sponsor requests, then request a report from the appropriate agency.

Claims bills forgive government overpayments, waive statutes of limitations for claims on the government, and redress torts not covered by the Tort Claims Act. The House Subcommittee on Administrative Law considers no bills on federal pay or social security. After creating the Court of Claims in 1855, Congress incrementally expanded its own power to refer a measure there; today such reports are occasionally requested and usually followed. After a 1966 ruling suggesting that such recommendations might unconstitutionally amount to advisory judicial opinions, Congress provided that not judges but trial commissioners report.

Immigration bills permit entry, residence, or citizenship to individuals otherwise ineligible. The panels usually decline cases for which administrative remedy is authorized. From the 1960s, many such bills were introduced solely because the Immigration and Naturalization Service would stay deportation when a report was requested; evidence suggested that some introductions were corruptly procured (later, the 1980 Abscam operation used purported requests for similar action). In response, the House Immigration subcommittee in 1969 broadened and the Senate Judiciary Committee in 1979 adopted a practice of requesting reports only when they intended action. Congress formerly used the one-house legislative veto, invalidated in *Immigration and Naturalization Service v. Chadha* (1983), to reverse court orders suspending deportation.

Private bills rest on practices of the British Parliament that have roots in Roman law. In enacting them, Congress is sometimes viewed as a last resort, but might better be understood as acting to establish equity in cases where no alternative resort exists. Some fear that private laws violate equal protection or constitute bills of attainder, but those private laws acting to the benefit rather than the detriment of individuals, at least, seem to meet constitutional requirements. Some also fear that such laws violate separation of powers, but courts seem to regard them to be at least as legitimate as administrative determinations.

[*See also* Public Law.]

BIBLIOGRAPHY

Congressional Quarterly Inc. *Congressional Quarterly's Guide to Congress.* 4th ed. Edited by Mary Cohn. 1991.
U.S. House of Representatives. *Cannon's Precedents of the House of Representatives of the United States,* by Clarence Cannon. 74th Cong., 1st sess., 1935. Vol. 7, secs. 850–871.
U.S. House of Representatives. *Deschler's Precedents of the United States House of Representatives,* by Lewis Deschler. 94th Cong., 2d sess., 1977. H. Doc. 94-661. Vol. 7, chap. 22, part C; chap. 24, sec. 3.
U.S. House of Representatives. *Hinds' Precedents of the House of Representatives of the United States,* by Asher C. Hinds. 59th Cong., 2d sess., 1907. Vol. 4, secs. 3266–3303.

RICHARD S. BETH

PRIVILEGE. Privilege is a parliamentary status granting priority of consideration. Permanent privilege is conferred on an item by the standing rules of the chamber, its precedents, the Constitution, or by statute. Temporary privilege can be conferred in the House by the adoption of a special rule from the House Rules Committee, and in the Senate by a unanimous consent agreement.

"Privileged business" is matter entitled by definition to priority, and in some cases, immediate floor consideration. Examples include conference reports, amendments in disagreement from the other body, or messages from the president. "Privileged motions" are granted a higher precedence than other motions, and if offered on the floor may intervene and suspend or supersede the pending business. Examples include the motions to adjourn, recess, or table.

A "question of the privileges of the House" asserts that the collective integrity, dignity, or safety of the House has in some way been impaired. It takes the form of a resolution that must be disposed of by the chamber. There is no counterpart in the Senate.

A "question of personal privilege" entitles a member to address the chamber for up to one hour in the House (unlimited in the Senate), to express personal umbrage taken at an event or statement, or to assert a violation of constitutional rights, an affront to reputation, or an impediment to conduct as a member. It may be expressed in the form of a resolution that requires floor disposition, or it may be limited to a discussion of the offense.

BIBLIOGRAPHY

Kravitz, Walter. *American Congressional Dictionary.* 1993. Pp. 206–209.

U.S. House of Representatives. *Constitution, Jefferson's Manual, and Rules of the House of Representatives, 102d Congress.* Compiled by William Holmes Brown. 101st Cong., 2d sess., 1990. H. Doc. 101-256. See Rules IX; XI, clause 4; XVI, clause 4; and XXIV, clause 1.

ILONA B. NICKELS

PRIZES. *See* Awards and Prizes.

PROCTOR, REDFIELD (1831–1908), Republican senator from Vermont. Proctor was appointed to the Senate in 1891 and was elected in 1892 and reelected in 1898 and 1904, serving until his death in March 1908. While chairman of the Agriculture and Forestry Committee, he played a key role in securing an increase in funds for the Department of Agriculture, from $3 million in 1897 to $11.5 million in 1907. He supported the conservation efforts of Chief Forester Gifford Pinchot and urged President Theodore Roosevelt in 1905 to promote a pure food law. As a member of the Committee on Military Affairs, Proctor supported the following policies: structural reform of the army (including the creation of a general staff), pay increases for and professionalization of the officer corps, reformation of the National Guard, and the enlistment of Indian soldiers.

On 17 March 1898, Proctor spoke to the Senate on his recent fact-finding trip to Cuba. His moving yet restrained account of the suffering and devastation inflicted on the Cuban people infuriated the public and fueled the demand for American intervention to end Spanish rule. Highly regarded as a responsible and conservative senator who was not prone to emotionalism, Proctor had a special effect on the American business community. Until Proctor's address this segment of the public had tended to dismiss reports of human suffering in Cuba as yellow journalism. Proctor's close relationship to the McKinley administration and the unfounded supposition that his speech reflected official policy added further credibility to his remarks. His address played an enormous role in propelling America into war with Spain.

BIBLIOGRAPHY

Bowie, Chester W. "Redfield Proctor: A Biography." Ph.D. diss., University of Wisconsin, 1980.

Linderman, Gerald F. *The Mirror of War: American Society and the Spanish-American War.* 1974. Chap. 2.

Partridge, Frank. "Redfield Proctor." *Vermont Historical Society Proceedings* (1915): 59–123.

ROBERT S. SALISBURY

PROGRESSIVE MOVEMENT. The Progressive movement of the twentieth century is as remarkable in retrospect as it was to its participants. Its major features constituted the first American response to egregious social ills stemming from rapid industrialization, urbanization, and immigration. A social justice campaign launched by social workers, social science professionals, and progressive politicians set a new agenda for government, an agenda demanding legislative solutions. The catalyzing voice of a remarkable group of journalists, the muckrakers, galvanized middle class indignation by exposing in graphic detail the travesty and corruption characterizing much of American industrial society. The effect was to expand the Progressive movement from a state-level to a national-level locus. A regulatory state was legislated at the state and national levels; precedents were established for social insurance and other welfare policies; direct democracy and the professionalization of governance were fostered; and an inexorable shift in political authority from the state to the national level began, thereby ushering in a permanent alteration in the balance of power accorded each in the U.S. federal system.

Congress played a central role in the rise and fall of the Progressive movement. The operating rules of the House of Representatives were democratized in 1910 when a coalition of insurgent Republicans and Democrats removed the entrenched Speaker of the House, Joseph G. Cannon, and with him the dictatorial tactics he used to control committee assignments and the flow of legislation. In place of "one-man rule," political power shifted to the two parties' House leadership, a more democratic form of internal governance and one that remained the

Landmark Progressive Era Legislation

TITLE	YEAR ENACTED	REFERENCE NUMBER	DESCRIPTION
Newlands Reclamation Act	1902	32 Stat. 388–390	Financed Western irrigation projects from public land sales.
Elkins Act	1903	32 Stat. 847–849	Prohibited railroad rebates.
Hepburn Act	1906	34 Stat. 584–595	Extended rate setting and other Interstate Commerce Commission powers.
Meat Inspection Act	1906	34 Stat. 674–679	Regulated meat-packing industry.
Pure Food and Drugs Act	1906	34 Stat. 768–772	Strengthened regulation of quality of food and drugs.
Payne-Aldrich Tariff Act	1909	36 Stat. 11–118	Lowered tariff rates, but not enough to satisfy critics of protection.
Mann-Elkins Act	1910	36 Stat. 539–557	Strengthened Interstate Commerce Commission, created short-lived Federal Court of Commerce.
White Slave–Trade Act (Mann Act)	1910	36 Stat. 825–827	Prohibited interstate transportation of women for immoral purposes.
Federal Reserve Bank Act (Owen-Glass Act)	1913	38 Stat. 251–275	Established Federal Reserve Bank system to regulate national currency.
Sixteenth Amendment	1913[1]	36 Stat. 184	Made a federal income tax constitutional.
Seventeenth Amendment	1913[1]	37 Stat. 646	Provided for direct election of U.S. senators.
Underwood-Simmons Tariff Act	1913	38 Stat. 114–202	Democratic measure lowering tariff rates.
Clayton Antitrust Act	1914	38 Stat. 730–740	Extended federal antitrust power established by Sherman Act.
Smith-Lever Act	1914	38 Stat. 372–375	Provided federal aid for agricultural extension programs.
Federal Trade Commission Act	1914	38 Stat. 717–724	Established regulatory commission to oversee business trade practices.
La Follette Seaman's Act	1915	38 Stat. 1164	Regulated employment and working conditions of seamen.
Adamson Act	1916	39 Stat. 721–722	Set eight-hour work day on interstate railroads.
Federal Farm Loan Bank Act	1916	39 Stat. 360–384	Created system for long-term agricultural credit administered by Federal Farm Loan Board.
Keating-Owen Child Labor Act	1916	39 Stat. 675–676	Regulated child labor on basis of interstate commerce power; held unconstitutional in 1918.
Smith-Hughes Act	1917	39 Stat. 929–936	Provided federal grants-in-aid for vocational education.
Eighteenth Amendment	1919[1]	40 Stat. 1050	Prohibited manufacture and sale of liquors.
Second Child Labor Act	1919	40 Stat. 1057	Regulated child labor through taxation; found unconstitutional in 1922.
Transportation Act (Esch-Cummins Act)	1920	41 Stat. 456–459	Encouraged railroad consolidation; included "recapture clause" to help weaker railroads.
Nineteenth Amendment	1920[1]	41 Stat. 362	Extended suffrage to women.

[1]Date ratified

norm thereafter. While party rule contributed to the rise of congressional seniority as a criterion for committee membership, it was an improvement over what it replaced.

Splits in the Republican party led to the presidential candidacy of Theodore Roosevelt under the banner of the Progressive party in 1912, which fostered the election of Democratic president Woodrow Wilson as well as a bumper crop of Democratic candidates to the Congress in the congressional elections of 1912 and 1914. Wilson's "New Freedom" legislative agenda, passed by Congress between 1913 and 1916, was the product of new political conditions that included exceptional cohesion of the Democratic party enforced by the Democratic cau-

MISS DEMOCRACY "LAN' SAKES, WHAT'LL I DO WITH 'EM?
NOVEMBER 1912

DEMOCRATIC MAJORITIES OF 1912. Cartoon showing Miss Democracy, with the White House tucked under her arm, carrying figures representing the House and Senate. In the 1912 November elections, Woodrow Wilson was elected president, and the Democratic party gained a commanding majority in the House and a slim but workable majority in the Senate. The Democratic victories were the result of a split in Republican party ranks produced by Theodore Roosevelt's independent Progressive (Bull Moose) party candidacy. Clifford K. Berryman, *Washington Evening Star*, 7 November 1912.

U.S. SENATE COLLECTION, CENTER FOR LEGISLATIVE ARCHIVES

cus in the 63d Congress (1913–1915), coalitions between insurgent Republicans and Democrats, and the representation of a wide range of splinter parties in Congress (51 members of the House elected in 1914 represented minor parties, such as Progressives and Socialists, solely or in combination with a major party affiliation).

Leading congressional figures in the rise and development of progressivism in Congress include Robert M. La Follette, Jr. (R-Wis.), Albert B. Cummins (R-Iowa), Miles Poindexter (R-Wash.), Albert J. Beveridge (R-Ind.), Moses E. Clapp (R-Minn.), George W. Norris (R-Nebr.), William E. Borah (R-Idaho), Joseph L. Bristow (R-Kans.), Henry D. Clayton (D-Ala.), Atlee Pomerene (D-Ohio), William Hughes (D-N.J.), James Beauchamp (Champ) Clark (D-Mo.), James K. Vardaman (D-Miss.), Morris Sheppard (D-Tex.), Oscar W. Underwood (D-Ala.), and Luke Lea (D-Tenn.). While southerners were not absent from the cadre of progressive reformers in Congress, support for policy innovation characterizing this period more often came from westerners and midwesterners of both parties. Organized opposition was typically a product of big business interests in the East, represented in Congress by the conservative wing of the Republican party.

Congress furthered the Progressive movement by passing landmark regulatory and social legislation. Congress also passed major amendments to the Constitution, which were subsequently ratified by the states, attesting to a progressive legislative commitment to improving democratic governance and advancing social and economic reforms. The Sixteenth Amendment (1913) provided for a national income tax; the Seventeenth Amendment (1913) established the direct election of senators; the Nineteenth Amendment (1920) guaranteed the right to vote to women; and the Eighteenth Amendment (1919) misguidedly instituted prohibition, which was eventually repealed by the Twenty-first Amendment (1933). Congress's progressive legislation enlarged the scope of the public sector and of federal authority as well, thereby establishing precedents and features of governance that would have long-term importance for the subsequent development of the modern American state.

[*See also* Eighteenth Amendment; New Freedom; Nineteenth Amendment; Seventeenth Amendment; Sixteenth Amendment.]

BIBLIOGRAPHY

Burnham, Walter Dean. *The Current Crisis in American Politics.* 1982.

Jones, Charles O. *The Minority Party in Congress.* 1970.

Keller, Morton. *Regulating a New Economy: Public Policy and Economic Change in America, 1900–1933.* 1990.

Link, Arthur, and William B. Catton. *American Epoch: A History of the United States since 1900.* Vol. 1. 1980.

McDonagh, Eileen Lorenzi. "Representative Democracy and State Building in the Progressive Era." *American Political Science Review* 86 (1992): 938–950.

Skocpol, Theda. *Protecting Soldiers and Mothers: The Politics of Social Provision in the United States, 1870s–1920s.* 1992.

Skowronek, Stephen. *Building a New American State: The Expansion of National Administrative Capacities, 1877–1920.* 1982.

EILEEN L. MCDONAGH

PROGRESSIVISM. *See* History of Congress, *article on* Progressivism and Normalcy.

PROHIBITION. Prohibition refers to outlawing the manufacture, transportation, and sale of alcoholic beverages. National prohibition, legitimized by the Eighteenth Amendment and the Volstead Act of 1919, was in force from 16 January 1920 to 6 December 1933. During the nineteenth and twentieth centuries state and local governments passed prohibition laws as well, some of which also forbade the personal possession of alcoholic beverages.

Prohibition advocates, often motivated by religious convictions as to the desirability of removing barriers to personal salvation and improved communities, directed their attention primarily at businesses that supplied liquor. Prohibitionists believed that liquor businesses, with the law's sanction, enticed customers to drink and consume ever larger quantities of alcohol. The reformers believed that outlawing the liquor businesses would allow Christians especially to persuade all persons to abstain from alcoholic beverages and would eventually result in a national culture of sobriety. Prohibitionists were convinced that eliminating liquor consumption would improve the well-being of the American people. They thus fostered the political theory of modern liberalism: the power of the state should be enlarged to ensure the conditions that allow individual freedom—in this case, freedom from the dangerous drug of alcohol, which condemned so many to lives of poverty and ill-health.

Prohibition remained a matter largely of local and state reform in the nineteenth century. The issue seriously intruded on the affairs of Congress only after 1910. Powerful congressional leadership and partisanship had prevented the full membership from considering prohibitory legislation. The prohibitionists cooperated with other reformers to enlarge the House Committee on Rules and reduce the power of the Speaker and longtime committee chairmen. The change allowed various reformers, including prohibitionists, to bring popular legislation to the floor of the House. The drys first secured congressional legislation—the Webb-Kenyon Act of 1913, passed over President William Howard Taft's veto—to reduce the power of the liquor trades to ship liquor into dry areas and to enact prohibition in the District of Columbia. In 1913 the Anti-Saloon League and a coalition of other reform organizations announced a campaign to achieve national prohibition through a constitutional amendment. The Eighteenth Amendment was submitted to the states for ratification on 18 December 1917.

REP. JOHN PHILIP HILL (R-MD.). Determined to make America "wet," 1926. LIBRARY OF CONGRESS

REP. WILLIAM D. UPSHAW (D-GA.). Determined to keep America "dry," 1926.   LIBRARY OF CONGRESS

A number of issues remained, however. Once the states ratified the amendment in 1919, legislation for enforcement was necessary. The resulting Volstead Act proved controversial because it relied primarily on the Treasury Department, whose agents had been responsible for collecting alcohol taxes, instead of the Justice Department. Presidents Warren G. Harding and Calvin Coolidge appointed unsympathetic enforcement officials, and prohibitionists remained disappointed with the results. Although President Herbert Hoover supported prohibition and enforcement responsibilities were shifted to the Justice Department in 1930, the reform quickly lost favor during the depression that began in 1929. Opponents argued that reviving the liquor businesses would create employment and wealth in the face of economic calamity. President Franklin D. Roosevelt supported repeal. In 1933 Congress initiated, and the states quickly ratified, the Twenty-first Amendment, repealing prohibition.

The per capita consumption of alcoholic beverages by the drinking-age population dropped substantially under national prohibition. Drinking rates returned to their preprohibition levels by the 1970s, forcing Congress to attend to the problems of alcohol abuse. In 1970 Congress established the National Institute of Alcohol Abuse and Alcoholism to channel funds for research and treatment of drinkers. In 1991, faced with continuing high rates of alcohol-related traffic accidents and other abuses, Congress mandated colleges and universities to launch programs aimed at curbing widespread alcohol abuse among students. Although prohibition was never again seriously considered, the liquor interests opposing regulation labeled the new attention "neo-prohibition."

[See also Alcoholic Beverages in Congress; Alcohol Policy; Eighteenth Amendment; National Prohibition Act; Twenty-first Amendment.]

BIBLIOGRAPHY

Blocker, Jack S. American Temperance Movements: Cycles of Reform. 1989.
Clark, Norman H. Deliver Us from Evil: An Interpretation of American Prohibition. 1976.

K. AUSTIN KERR

PROHIBITION ACT. See National Prohibition Act.

PROTECTIONISM. See Tariffs and Trade.

PUBLIC LANDS. The making of public land policy may not rank among the most glamorous subjects in the history of Congress. Who but the most specialized scholar knows that the famous 1830 Webster-Hayne debate in the Senate had to do with a proposal for the elimination of the General Land Office's post of surveyor general? Yet the history of congressional policy toward the public lands touches on important themes ranging over the past two centuries of American life, including national attitudes toward the West, the environment, and Native Americans.

The public domain consists of federally owned land and as of 1994 makes up more than a quarter of the land area of the fifty states. It once comprised the entirety of all the states except for the original thirteen and Vermont, Kentucky, Tennessee, Texas, and Hawaii. In all, nearly two billion acres were at one time owned by the United States. The job of Congress in setting public land policy has been to decide what to do with this magnificent patrimony.

Public lands and public land policy make up one of the longest index entries to the *Congressional Record* and its predecessor the *Congressional Globe*. Early on, both houses found it necessary to have standing committees on the public lands, the House in 1805 and the Senate in 1816. These committees necessarily worked closely with the executive department charged with administering the public lands, starting with the Treasury Department and, after 1812, the more specialized General Land Office. In 1849 Congress removed the General Land Office from Treasury and placed it in the newly created Interior Department.

Congress itself has helped write the history of its own public land policies by authorizing periodic Public Lands Review commissions, the first in 1879 and the most recent in 1968. The commissions were created at times of national debate about land policy and the future of the public lands. Each commission has included among its documents a historical perspective on policy-making. The first such effort, Thomas Donaldson's massive *The Public Domain* (1881), contained every imaginable summary statistic about the survey and disposition of the public domain.

Paul W. Gates, the leading modern historian of U.S. public land policy, writing for the 1968 Review Commission, suggested a basic periodization for U.S. public land history, one that is generally accepted by modern historians. Policy was driven from the 1790s to the Great Depression of the 1930s by the desire to promote settlement and growth in the American West. This was best accomplished, Congress reasoned, by transferring the public lands to millions of private farmers. At times this central goal was modified by other congressional needs. For example, during the first fifty years of congressional policy-making, according to Gates, there was a strong countertendency to use the public lands to generate revenue to help pay the public debt. From the 1840s through the Civil War, Congress made frequent use of the public domain to promote the interests of certain parties, ranging from veterans of past wars to newly organized railroad companies. Gates found that the postbellum era was characterized by an "incongruous" land policy. Congress passed a homestead measure during the Civil War, but at the same time maintained a cash sales policy and promoted corporate ownership of land. Congress took important conservation measures in the Progressive era, but the basic imperative toward western growth and development did not come to a close until the Great Depression. Writing from the vantage point of 1968, Gates cautiously characterized the decades since the New Deal as a period of multiple-purpose use of the public domain.

The Public Lands and the Public Debt. One of the lasting achievements of the federal government under the Articles of Confederation was the establishment of the public domain, first by general agreement of the states to give up their western land claims and then by the passage of the two Northwest Ordinances. The first ordinance, enacted in 1785, provided the basis for future public land administration. It specified the rectangular survey system of townships and ranges, and defined the section of 640 acres (one square mile) as the basic unit of public land. Public land surveying followed this principle from the Ohio River lands bordering Pennsylvania all the way to the Pacific Ocean, heedless of the vagaries of terrain. In today's age of air travel people look down from the sky on the fruits of the rectangular survey when they see the distinctive checkerboard pattern of the land.

The Confederation Congress faced two basic problems of land policy that would engage future congresses over the next century: what should be the price, if any, for public land, and what should be the amount sold or donated? Congress decided against a policy of free land in 1785, despite the precedent of "headrights" from some of the old southern colonies. Instead, it decided to sell the public domain to individuals for a minimum of one dollar an acre. In practice, this amounted to just a penny or two an acre in coin, because Congress allowed purchasers to pay with the severely depreciated Continental paper currency. Other noteworthy features of the Northwest Ordinance of 1785 included a provision that land should first be surveyed and then offered for sale at a public auction, and that one section from each township should be reserved for the benefit of local public education. The minimum tract for purchase was set at 640 acres.

The legislature established under the federal Constitution initially reaffirmed the land policy of the Confederation Congress. Not until 1796 did the new Congress change its land policy in any significant way. In that year Albert Gallatin led a move to change the minimum price to two dollars an acre, with a provision allowing buyers up to a year's credit to complete their purchases. This meant a significant rise in land prices, given the fact that the value of federal currency had risen dramatically during the Washington administration. The Land Act of 1796 may be seen in retrospect as the high point for a policy that sought to maximize revenue from public land sales. Both the Treasury faction of Federalists around Alexander Hamilton and the opposition party led by Jefferson and Madison agreed that the public lands must be safeguarded as collateral for the national debt.

The Promotion of Individual Western Settlement and Growth. Public land legislation in the century and a quarter after the Land Act of 1796 may best be characterized as a series of measures designed to promote the changing needs of individual and family farms and ranches. Thomas Jefferson is often identified with the ideal of using the public domain to maintain Americans as individual farmers, but this policy was widely approved by Congress throughout the nineteenth century. Settlers were pouring into the Northwest Territory, especially Ohio, after 1800 and soon began a clamor to amend some of the provisions of the 1796 Land Act. Some complained that the price of land was too high, while others petitioned Congress to reduce the minimum tract for purchase from 640 acres to a lesser figure. Still others noted that the federal credit term of one year did not leave sufficient time for a settler to pay his debt. Congress acted on all these complaints over the next few years. Much of the legislative history of public land law in the early republic was a matter of tinkering with the Land Act of 1796.

In 1800, for example, the tract size was reduced to 320 acres and credit was extended over a five-year period. The Land Act of 1800 also provided for the establishment of land offices in Ohio staffed by federal officials, where purchasers could scrutinize the records of the official surveys without having to go to Philadelphia to conduct their land business. Here was the origin of the American phrase "doing a land-office business," signifying a booming market. In 1804 the minimum acreage for purchase was again halved to a quarter-section, 160 acres. The price, credit, and quantity limits remained constant until 1820, when in an effort to reduce land speculation, the minimum tract size was again halved to eighty acres, credit sales were abolished, and the price was reduced to $1.25 an acre. Congress now insisted that prospective buyers pay cash at the land office.

The figure of $1.25 an acre stood as what Congress called the "cash-entry" price until cash sales were halted in 1890. Yet cash sales at $1.25 an acre

were declining in relative importance in the alienation of the public lands as early as the 1840s. Congressional land grants for various purposes, as discussed below, accounted for part of the shift. Another reason for the move away from cash-entry sales at $1.25 an acre was a policy implemented in 1854 called "graduation." This was an attempt by Congress to set prices by matching supply and demand. Congress and the General Land Office set the supply by determining when new tracts of land should be surveyed and declared open to public entry.

Slowing or speeding the process of offering new lands had an indirect effect on the demand for public land already offered; as several recent studies have shown, the demand for public land was driven mainly by the level of commodity prices and not just by the supply of public land offered by the General Land Office. Congress and several Democratic administrations had encouraged the rapid opening of new land districts, so that by the advent of the Pierce administration in 1853, some 25 million acres of offered public land remained unsold. To encourage more rapid sales, the General Land Office was instructed by Congress to reduce the price on unsold land by a fifth for every five years that a tract remained on the market. The effect of graduated land prices was most evident in the South, where millions of acres in Alabama, Mississippi, Louisiana, and Arkansas had their prices reduced to as low as twelve and a half cents an acre.

During the 1820s and 1830s the House and Senate committees on public lands received numerous petitions from western settlers requesting congressional permission to occupy without charge parcels on the public domain for short periods of time, in effect, postponing the time when they had to pay for their claims. This practice, known as preemption or more derisively as "squatting," was illegal and took up a great deal of congressional time. Only the U.S. Army could enforce the law against illegal occupation of the public domain and prevent preemptors from occupying their parcels without payment. The army had no desire to make war on settlers, but from time to time troops were dispatched to remove squatters.

Congress periodically passed special bills forgiving trespassing in various land districts and finally in 1830 enacted a statute forgiving all prior preemptions, provided that the preemptors paid what they owed. After several extensions of this law, Congress passed a more general bill in 1841 legalizing future preemptions but only on land surveyed by the

General Land Office. The law allowed settlers to pre-empt their parcels for up to fifteen months before they had to make payment, provided they could show or "prove up" evidence that they had made rudimentary improvements to the tract. The Pre-emption Act of 1841 left out another class of pre-emptors seeking congressional forgiveness, those who "squatted" on unsurveyed land, particularly Indian land where title had not yet passed to the United States. The strength of sentiment behind preemptors was sufficient for Congress to grant even this right in 1853, so that preemptors could legally become pioneers, staking a claim to 160 acres before the surveyor had even arrived. The basic proof statement specified by the Preemption Act of 1841 required a description of the house built by the preemptor as well as an account of the land cleared and brought into production.

The same approach to settlers and public land administration informed the congressional crafting of the greatest of all land laws, the Homestead Act of 1862. The act had a long gestation period in Congress before becoming law. Earlier versions had been proposed in the 1840s and were seriously debated and voted on during the Pierce administration. A homestead bill actually passed Congress in the Buchanan administration but was vetoed by the president. Homestead might be regarded as the ultimate reform of the old 1796 Land Act in that the minimum purchase price was eliminated entirely. But as in the Preemption Act of 1841, Congress very much wanted the General Land Office to keep an eye on the activities of the settlers before letting title pass from the federal government to private owners. Over seventy years after the passage of the Homestead Act, settlers filed more than one million homestead claims to public land parcels totaling over 200 million acres. The peak years for homestead entries were just before World War I, when for several years over 10 million acres were claimed.

Although the Homestead Act became the central feature of land policy through the end of the nineteenth century, Congress adopted several supplementary policies as well. In 1873 it passed the Timber Culture Act to encourage homesteaders to enter an additional quarter section with the provision that the entrant had to plant forty acres in trees. The Desert Land Act of 1877 granted tracts of 640 acres to those who pledged to construct irrigation works that brought water to previously dry land. Both acts were less than successful in execution, and in the 1890–1891 winter session Congress halted entries under the Timber Culture Act and also ended cash sales and preemptions.

At the same time Congress formulated a policy of using the public domain to increase mining output. The Mining Act of 1872 set prices of $2.50 an acre for placer-mined lands and $5.00 an acre for lode mining. Fraud and evasion flourished under the Mining Act, as they did under the Timber Act, and Congress moved in 1909 and 1910 to separate the surface use of public land from subsoil mining use.

Congress continued to make homesteading more attractive in the first decade of the twentieth century by increasing the maximum acreage that a settler could claim. Nebraskans were first allowed to claim up to 640 acres in 1904 under the Kincaid Act, and in 1909 a similar privilege was extended to nine other western states under the Enlarged Homestead Act.

In the western Great Plains and intermountain states, much of the public domain was used by ranchers who grazed their livestock for free on the public lands. Congress sought to turn much of this remaining land into private property when it passed the Stock Raising Homestead Act of 1916, granting 640-acre homesteads to Great Plains ranchers. This was the last of the great legislative acts designed to grant public lands to individuals who wished to become self-supporting farmers or ranchers. The agricultural downturn of the 1920s, and especially the Great Depression, permanently changed the old Jeffersonian notion. In 1934 and 1935 most of the public domain was withdrawn from further entries under the various land laws. The era in which the public domain was used primarily to promote new farms and ranches came to an end.

Congress as Landed Proprietor. The goal of turning public land into private property was shared by most in Congress throughout the nineteenth century, but there was much room for disagreement over how to bring about this end. Congress continually faced conflicts over how best to manage the public domain. Should the public lands be administered largely for the benefit of prospective western settlers and landowners? Or should the older, nonpublic land states receive some benefit, too? These questions dominated much of the public land debate between Andrew Jackson's Democrats and Henry Clay's Whigs. The latter group fought long and hard, but ultimately without much success, to have a portion of the revenue from land sales "distributed" back to the states. Clay engineered a distribution bill through both houses in the 1832–1833 session, but President Jackson vetoed it. When the Whigs finally came to power in 1841, the newly sworn-in president, John Tyler, signed a distribution bill into law, but it was repealed the next year when the public debt rose sufficiently to convince the Whigs that federal revenues could not stand such an outflow to the states.

Within the larger context of using the public lands to promote western settlement, Congress did come to see the public lands as a substitute for making actual expenditures. Proponents of "proprietorship" argued that Congress could make grants of the public lands to achieve desired goals of national policy. Congress used this power sparingly in the early decades of the nineteenth century, primarily to increase enlistments in the army during times of national emergency. It resorted to such a policy before and during the War of 1812: some 29,000 men took advantage of the bounty and at the war's end claimed over 4 million acres of public land, mainly in western Illinois.

When war with Mexico broke out in 1846, Congress repeated the procedure in the Ten Regiments Act of February 1847. In all, about 90,000 men received 13 million acres of public land. The terms of their land grants were more generous than those given to the army and militia veterans of the War of 1812. As many as 475,000 men had seen some federal service against the British and their Indian allies, and many among the great majority who did not receive land bounties were jealous of the treatment accorded the Mexican War soldiers. Therefore in 1850, 1852, and 1855 Congress passed acts that redressed the inequity and granted more than 47 million new acres in land bounties, most of which went to the now elderly veterans of the War of 1812 and to their widows and minor children. One study estimates that 95 percent chose to sell their land warrants in a secondary market. Warrant brokers in turn sold discounted warrants to frontier bankers and settlers for use in the West.

The unprecedented size of the grants to veterans unleashed a flood of new requests for Congress to act in its proprietor role. Why not make grants of land directly with the express purpose of resale? In 1854 the House and Senate passed the so-called Dix bill, named after the Massachusetts reformer Dorothea Dix and designed to grant 10 million acres of public land for the benefit of the indigent insane. President Pierce vetoed the bill, but after the Republicans came to power in 1861, Congress passed similar legislation granting land for purposes other than the direct promotion of western settlement. The Morrill Land-Grant College Act of 1862 used public lands for the benefit of all the states. Here was an updated version of Henry Clay's old distribution idea: allot acreage, not the proceeds of land sales, on the basis of a state's population, and let the states do with public land grants what they wanted, so long as the proceeds were used to create agricultural colleges. The result was that New York, the state with the largest population, got the most public land. New York in turn entrusted its land grants to the upstate financier Ezra Cornell, who located millions of acres in the pine forests of northern Wisconsin, holding many valuable tracts until they rose in market value to ten and twenty times the land office price of $1.25 an acre. The profits from this sale led to a sizable endowment for New York State's agricultural college, named in Cornell's honor by a grateful legislature.

The most extensive and enduring application of congressional proprietorship of the public domain was the land grants in the 1850s and 1860s for the promotion of internal improvements, most notably railroads. Illinois Democrat Stephen A. Douglas put together the legislation authorizing land grants to aid the construction of a railroad from Chicago to Mobile in 1850. Hard on the heels of his triumphant legislative maneuvering of the Compromise of 1850, Douglas sought to bind up the nation with railroads built with federal land assistance. The Chicago-Mobile line, later known as the Illinois Central, set the pattern for later railroad land grants: alternating sections within a strip of land several miles wide on each side of the projected line. The lands reserved by the General Land Office were doubled in price to $2.50 an acre, which in effect insured the government against any loss of revenue. Congress intended the land to be resold to raise money for construction costs, and railroads like the Illinois Central opened offices to encourage emigration to railroad-owned lands.

The Illinois Central land grant was soon followed by other land grants for internal improvements in the 1850s, including one for constructing a canal and locks around the St. Mary's River, running from Lake Superior to Lake Huron at Sault Sainte Marie, Michigan. More than 25 million acres of public land were donated to various internal improvement projects in the 1850s, when Democrats controlled both House and Senate. Yet the biggest grants came after the outbreak of the Civil War, when the Republicans controlled Congress. Congress gave over 90 million acres to aid in the construction of transcontinental railroads between

1861 and 1871. The largest beneficiary by far was the Northern Pacific Railway, intended to run from Duluth to Tacoma, which received a land grant of 38 million acres in its 1864 enabling act.

Congress, the Public Lands, and Indian Affairs. Textbook maps of the expansion of the United States usually show acquisitions from negotiations with European nations or by conquest, starting with the Peace of Paris in 1783, continuing through the purchase of the Louisiana Territory, Florida, and the Mexican Cession of 1848, ending with the purchase of Alaska and the acquisition of Hawaii. The general claim of sovereignty, however, did not give clear title; that remained to be negotiated with the hundreds of American Indian nations that occupied the land. The numerous treaties signed between the United States and assorted American Indian nations between 1790 and 1871 provided the essential basis for legal title to the public lands, and the subsequent basis of private ownership of the land.

The general sequence of events in the history of the American West for a century after the 1790s was as follows: peace treaties with Native American landholders; land cession treaties granting title to the United States; Indian removal or reservation agreements; General Land Office surveys; land district auctions and sales; in-migration of new settlers; and finally, territorial governments leading to statehood. Sometimes, particularly in Kansas, this idealized sequence of events became jumbled, with the settlers preceding the army and the treaty makers. But the essential point remains that new additions to the supply of the public domain came primarily from a host of treaties and agreements between the United States and American Indians.

The pace of treaty making and Indian land cessions expanded considerably after the War of 1812, led in large part by the actions of Gen. Andrew Jackson in negotiating agreements with the Five Civilized Nations of the South. Jackson's postwar actions became general congressional policy in 1830 with the passage of the Indian Removal Act. The rash of treaties entered into under that act often included assorted grants of public lands to interested parties. Sometimes the treaty interpreters received land grants for their troubles, and in some cases, as with the Mississippi Choctaws and the Lake Superior Chippewas, mixed-blood tribal members were granted quarter sections of public land if they chose to remain in the ceded territory.

The intended land grants reflected long-standing notions of reformers that if American Indians were granted land in fee simple ownership, then old tribal loyalties would be cast aside and a new Indian man would emerge, similar to the American yeoman farmer. For much of the nineteenth century this was an article of faith for "friends of the Indian," and in 1887 the idea was made official federal Indian policy in the General Allotment Act, also known as the Dawes Severalty Act. This legislation granted 160 acres to every head of household (in itself, an inexact representation of the complexity of American Indian family structure), with lesser acreage awarded to minors and dependents. The Dawes Act also had the foreseen consequence of separating over 120 million acres of what was once Indian reservation land and bringing it into the public domain, where it was entered by homesteaders and ranchers under other land laws. What had started as an idealistic, if misguided, attempt to reform the personality of Indian people degenerated into little more than a grab of the tribal land base throughout the West.

Congress and Conservation: The Reserving of the Public Lands. In the twentieth century, Congress has used the public lands once again as a proprietor, not only to promote the aggressive immediate development of natural resources, but also for their long-term conservation and use. Economic development has remained the primary congressional goal, but in a more planned and less unregulated manner. By the close of the nineteenth century, most of the public domain suitable for family farming had been alienated into private ownership. What remained was arid lands on the western Great Plains and in the intermountain region, as well as considerable timberland that had not yet been logged. Starting in 1891, Congress gave the president the right to withdraw land from the public domain and reserve it for future forest use. More than 40 million acres were withdrawn in the 1890s, and after Theodore Roosevelt's accession to the presidency in 1901, another 150 million acres were taken from the public domain and transformed into national forests under the administration of the Department of Agriculture.

In addition to reserving timberland for future production, Congress passed a series of measures in the first two decades of the twentieth century designed to use the public domain for irrigation and hydroelectric power generation. The Reclamation Act of 1902, sponsored by the aptly named Francis G. Newlands (D-Nev.), aimed to promote the construction of irrigation works by the Bureau of Reclamation, to be funded by the fees and commissions received by the General Land Office. It was expected that the irrigation projects would be remunerative to the federal government, because the arid lands brought into production would generate new land-office fees and water-use payments. The Reclamation Act even had a Jeffersonian clause limiting the beneficiaries under the act to landowners holding no more than 160 acres. In practice the act was soon evaded by large corporate landowners, and the Bureau of Reclamation grew into an empire unto itself, with its single-minded goal of transforming the West into an agricultural domain.

The best-known public lands are the national parks, administered by the Department of the Interior. Starting with Yellowstone National Park in 1872, the National Park Service has grown in the size and scope of its mission. Most, although not all, national parks and national monuments consist of lands withdrawn from the public domain. Yellowstone, with more than 8 million acres, is still the largest of the forty-eight national parks, but the National Park Service also maintains sites such as the comparatively tiny one at Hot Springs, Arkansas. A separate category of public lands is the acreage classified as wilderness areas under the Wilderness Act of 1964 and the Alaska Wilderness Act of 1980.

Congressional public land policy of the later twentieth century has been characterized by a vigorous debate between those who want a more rapid development of the natural resources on the public lands and those who wish to see more land designated as wilderness areas. The Public Land Law Review Commission that operated in the late 1960s acknowledged that the public domain would never be opened up to widespread private alienation, as in the nineteenth and early twentieth centuries, but not until 1976 did Congress finally repeal most of the old nineteenth-century land laws. The Federal Land Policy and Management Act of that year directed the Bureau of Land Management (the reorganized General Land Office) to determine by 1991 the extent of acreage that should be withdrawn from grazing use and declared wilderness areas. Some of the bitterest political disputes of the 1980s over land policy arose because of conflict between the Interior Department and Congress over implementing the 1976 statute. Congress had asked the Bureau of Land Management to study 25 million acres of public land for inclusion in the National Wilderness Preservation System. Interior secretaries James Watt and William Clarke wanted none of the land taken from ranchers and only grudging-

ly allowed the transfer of 300,000 acres from grazing land to wilderness.

A review of congressional policy toward the public lands reveals the alternating and sometimes conflicting goals of promoting both individual land ownership and other social policies. Landmark legislation such as the Homestead Act of 1862 and the Reclamation Act of 1902 came after decades of debate over the terms and intent of public land disposal to private ownership. This does not mean that congressional policy has been constant or unchanging in such broad areas as western regionalism, environmentalism, and Indian affairs. Rather, looking at congressional public land policy within this framework helps the modern policymaker and student better understand the mix of idealism and expediency that has characterized the past.

[See also Crédit Mobilier; Environment and Conservation; Homestead Act; Indian Treaties; Internal Improvements; Morrill Land-Grant College Act; National Parks and Forests; Railroads; Territories and Possessions.]

BIBLIOGRAPHY

Donaldson, Thomas C. The Public Domain: Its History with Statistics. 1881.

Feller, Daniel. The Public Lands in Jacksonian Politics. 1984.

Gates, Paul Wallace. History of Public Land Law Development. 1968.

Hibbard, Benjamin Horace. History of the Public Land Policies. 1924.

Oberly, James W. Sixty Million Acres: American Veterans and the Public Lands before the Civil War. 1990.

Opie, John. The Law of the Land. 1987.

Robbins, Roy. Our Landed Heritage. 1942.

Rohrbough, Malcom. The Land Office Business. 1968.

Worster, Donald. Rivers of Empire. 1986.

Zaslowsky, Dyan. These American Lands: Parks, Wilderness, and the Public Lands. 1986.

JAMES W. OBERLY

PUBLIC LAW. Every measure that completes the lawmaking process prescribed by the Constitution is thereby enacted into law. Except for private measures, every enacted bill or joint resolution becomes a *public law.* By contrast, concurrent and simple resolutions, if adopted, do not make law. Also, joint resolutions proposing constitutional amendments do not become law but go to the states for ratification.

The format of acts of Congress, which include bills and joint resolutions passed by Congress, is prescribed by law. The enacting clause of a bill reads, "Be it enacted by the Senate and House of Representatives of the United States of America in Congress Assembled"; the resolving clause of a joint resolution replaces the first three words by "Resolved." Statute also prescribes that this clause appear only once, at the beginning, and that the measure be divided into numbered sections, each containing "as nearly as may be, a single proposition or enactment." Appropriations, especially in general appropriations bills, are usually set forth in captioned paragraphs rather than numbered sections. In long measures, sections are often grouped into titles, and sometimes into parts, chapters, or other divisions.

The lawmaking process is completed on the date when (1) the president signs, (2) the period expires during which he may veto, or (3) Congress completes action to override a veto. On that date the law is enacted and, unless otherwise specified in law, takes effect. It is sent to the Archivist of the United States for publication, initially in pamphlet form as a "slip law"; an annual volume, *United States Statutes at Large*, compiles all public laws enacted during a session of Congress (and, under separate headings, private laws, concurrent resolutions adopted, treaties, presidential proclamations, and certain presidential recommendations on which Congress may act). Between 1950 and 1984, these functions were carried out by the General Services Administration, and before that by the State Department.

The *Statutes* identify public laws by date of enactment and number them by Congress and order of enactment within the Congress (e.g., P.L. 91-510). Before the 85th Congress (i.e., before 1957), laws were numbered only within a Congress and commonly cited by date of enactment and *Statutes* chapter number. Public laws are also cited by *Statutes* volume and page number (e.g., 84 Stat. 1410).

New law often amends or repeals provisions of previous public law. Under the direction of the House Law Revision Counsel, most new public laws are codified as revisions or additions to the *United States Code*, organized topically under fifty titles, some of which have been reenacted as statutes in their codified form. Codified provisions of law may be cited to the *Code* (e.g., 2 U.S.C. § 166). The first edition of the *Code* was released in 1926. Federal law had been comprehensively revised and reenacted in the *Revised Statutes* of 1875 and 1878, and some current law still traces to these revisions.

BIBLIOGRAPHY

1 U.S. Code, chap. 2.

RICHARD S. BETH

PUBLIC UTILITY HOLDING COMPANY ACT. *See* Wheeler-Rayburn Public Utility Holding Company Act.

PUBLIC WORKS. The development of legislative procedures and of relations between Congress and the executive branch for authorizing public works and for appropriating funds to carry them out may be examined through three distinct categories of public works programs. In the first, the basic authorizing or appropriating legislation designates individual projects—that is, the choice of projects is made in the legislative process. Typically, the authorizing statutes are omnibus: each includes a significant number of projects, and the projects are built by direct federal spending. The water resources program of the U.S. Army Corps of Engineers is an important example in this category (see table 1).

Statutes in the second category authorize lump-sum appropriations for programs of public works, including formulas for allocating the money among beneficiaries, typically in the form of grants to state and local governments. The statutes define the characteristics of state and local projects that are eligible for federal funding, but choice of the projects themselves is not made in the legislative process, as in the first category; the projects are selected and built by state and local governments. The federal aid highway program, established in 1916, is the principal public works program in this category (see table 1).

Statutes in the third category authorize lump-sum appropriations for programs and define the characteristics of projects that are eligible for federal funding. The choice of projects is not made in the legislative process; instead the statute delegates this authority to a department or agency in the executive branch. The federal program of grants-in-aid for airports is an example.

The categories have led to different forms of relations between Congress and the executive, to different procedures for legislative choice, and to different trade-offs between the local or geographically specific benefits and the general or national benefits of governmental programs.

TABLE 1. *Federal and Federally Financed Nondefense Public Works, 1940–1990 (in billions of constant 1987 dollars)*

| | DIRECT FEDERAL CAPITAL | | | | | CAPITAL FINANCED BY FEDERAL GRANTS | | | | | | |
| | OUTLAY | | | COMPOSITION OF OUTLAY | | OUTLAY | | | COMPOSITION OF OUTLAY | | | |
FISCAL YEAR	EXPEN-DITURE	AS % OF TOTAL FEDERAL OUTLAYS	AS % OF GDP	WATER AND POWER PROJECTS[1]	OTHER	EXPEN-DITURE	AS % OF TOTAL FEDERAL OUTLAYS	AS % OF GDP	TRANS-PORTA-TION[2]	COMMU-NITY DEVEL-OPMENT	NATURAL RESOURCES AND ENVI-RONMENT[3]	OTHER
1940	19.0	21.2	2.1	NA	NA	4.2	4.7	0.5	1.6	2.6	—	—
1945	1.6	0.2	0.1	1.1	0.5	1.1	0.2	0.1	0.2	0.9	—	—
1950	7.2	3.1	0.5	4.9	2.2	2.6	1.1	0.2	2.5	—	—	0.1
1955	5.0	1.6	0.3	3.6	1.4	3.9	1.2	0.2	2.8	0.2	0.1	0.7
1960	7.3	2.1	0.4	3.8	3.5	13.8	3.6	0.7	12.4	0.4	0.4	0.6
1965	10.5	2.6	0.5	4.9	5.6	19.5	4.2	0.7	16.0	2.3	0.6	0.6
1970	7.3	1.3	0.3	4.3	3.0	27.9	3.6	0.7	14.0	5.0	1.1	1.7
1975	9.3	1.5	0.3	5.8	3.5	20.6	3.3	0.7	10.6	4.7	4.3	1.0
1980	10.0	1.4	0.3	5.8	4.2	27.7	3.8	0.9	14.3	7.1	6.0	0.2
1985	12.1	1.2	0.3	4.7	7.3	25.8	2.6	0.6	16.5	5.2	3.7	0.3
1990	14.1	1.2	0.3	4.8	9.3	24.9	2.2	0.5	16.8	3.4	3.0	1.5

[1]In addition to projects of the Army Corps of Engineers, includes projects of the Tennessee Valley Authority and the Bureau of Reclamation, of the Bonneville Power Administration and other power marketing agencies, and of nuclear power plants of several agencies.
[2]Mostly highways
[3]Since 1975, mostly pollution control facilities
SOURCE: Budget of the U.S. Government for fiscal year 1994. Historical tables 9.1, 9.2, 9.6.

Public Works, 1789–1865. From its earliest years, the federal government supported the construction and maintenance of forts, arsenals, and armories; the improvement and protection of coastal harbors that were related to national defense or foreign commerce, including the erection of numerous lighthouses; and the construction of public buildings required for federal activities that are explicitly authorized in the Constitution, such as customhouses, post offices, and court houses. But the government's constitutional power to construct roads, canals, and river and inland harbor works—so-called internal improvements—was strongly contested. It was generally conceded that the government had authority to build internal improvements in the territories, but there was intense disagreement in Congress, among pre–Civil War presidents, and among political parties and factions on whether the United States had similar powers within the sovereign states. It was not until after the Civil War that the constitutional dispute over internal improvements was largely ended.

While the debate over constitutionality continued, Congress, under ever-increasing pressures from western settlers, passed bills authorizing internal improvements in the territories, many of them roads, and military and post roads in both states and territories. In 1806, a majority in Congress voted to lay out and then build a national pike from Cumberland, Maryland, to the Ohio River. (The Cumberland Road was subsequently continued from the Ohio River to the Mississippi River, through the states or territories of Ohio, Indiana, Illinois, and Missouri.) Congress sought to avoid the question of the constitutionality of this nonmilitary internal improvement by providing that the states of Pennsylvania, Maryland, and Virginia were to give their assent to construction by the federal government within their limits. The strategy continued until 1822 when, for the first time, an appropriation was made for a river improvement within a state without previously obtaining that state's approval.

Another strategy was for the federal government to subsidize construction of works to be built by the states. The government owned huge areas of land in all states emerging from territorial status that it continued to sell or otherwise dispose of. Beginning with Ohio, when it was admitted to the Union in 1802, and adopted for all states admitted thereafter, 5 percent (in some cases, 3 percent) of the government's proceeds from sale of the public lands was paid to the states to aid them in building roads, canals, and other projects. Approximately one-third of the money appropriated by Congress for roads between 1802 and 1882 consisted of payments to the states from these funds. In addition, the national government made large grants of land to the new states for internal improvements. The states either sold the land to raise money for building roads, canals, river improvements, railroads, and projects for draining farm lands and protecting them from floods, or used the land as rights of way for the improvements. More than 80 million acres of federal land were donated between 1822 and 1889—3.3 million for wagon roads, 4.6 million for canals, 2.2 million for river improvements, 7.8 million for "internal improvements," which could be any combination of these purposes, and 64 million acres of federal swamplands in fifteen states. Money derived from the sale of swamplands was to be used to reclaim them, although some states used part of the income for other purposes such as grants in aid of railroad construction. The value of the land grants is difficult to calculate because state records are incomplete and money from the sale was used for a variety of purposes.

Between 1802 and the end of the Civil War, the federal government appropriated approximately $18 million for rivers, harbors, and canals and $16 million for roads (which includes the 5-percent funds but not the value of land grants).

In the postwar period federal appropriations for rivers and harbors increased significantly. Those for road construction virtually stopped and were not renewed for fifty years, when an entirely new program of federal aid to the states was initiated. Road work was turned over to the states, and they in turn left it to counties or other local authorities. The collapse of the federal program can be attributed principally to the rapid spread of railroads, which were often aided by federal land grants.

Congress Dominates Rivers and Harbors Policy. From the end of the Civil War until the mid 1930s Congress controlled policy and legislation relating to the improvement of rivers and harbors. The presidents, viewed as a group, did not have a profound influence. In order to initiate and perfect policy in this area of technical engineering, Congress coopted the U.S. Army Corps of Engineers to serve as its agent. West Point was the only engineering school in the United States until 1825, so the army had within its ranks a high percentage of the nation's trained engineers. The engineers and Congress considered the corps in its civil (not military) activities to be outside the executive branch. Rather, they were, "engineer consultants to and contractors for the Congress of the United States." As the corps saw it, Congress had designated the corps members as its agents in finding the facts upon which the legislature might act. Thus, the corps operated "in pursuance of law as an agency of the legislative branch."

In their reports to Congress, the engineers tried to focus on the engineering aspects of improvements, leaving Congress to determine commercial value and, above all, policy. Indeed, an influential chief of engineers said in a 1912 public address, "It has been the established policy of the engineering department to avoid as far as possible any action that might be misconstrued into an effort on our part to decide for Congress what it should do in rivers and harbors work." Yet Congress, confronted with overenthusiastic endorsements by individual legislators and local interests, sought from the corps information that the corps was reluctant to consider, forcing Congress to repeatedly direct its agent by law to collect and report the data.

This unusual pattern of legislative-executive relations developed and prospered because the principal activity of the legislative process was the selection of projects. The Rivers and Harbors Act of 1826 included twenty-two items distributed over ten states. Subsequent omnibus acts, enacted each year or biennially, authorized and appropriated funds for conducting surveys, initiating the construction of new projects, continuing construction of projects underway, and for repairing and maintaining completed projects. In each category the projects were specified. The House committee of jurisdiction (Commerce, 1844–1882; Rivers and Harbors, 1883–1946; Public Works, 1946–) composed these bills based on data provided by the corps.

The first step in considering the improvement of a river or harbor was for the proponents to petition Congress to direct the corps to make an engineering survey to determine the most suitable plan for improvement and whether the plan was justifiable economically. The rivers and harbors acts authorized the surveys and directed the corps to submit its survey reports directly to Congress, without intervention by other agencies or the president. The surveys provided the basis for congressional deliberation on new projects.

The Annual Report of the Chief of Engineers was the basis for decisions on funding continuing construction of unfinished projects and repair and maintenance of completed ones. The annual reports, which Congress in 1866 required the corps to prepare, included for each authorized project an estimate of cost for its completion, the amount that could be "profitably expended" in the next fiscal year, and, as far as practicable, the tonnage of commerce that would be benefited by its completion.

Finally, there were the estimates of appropriations for the next fiscal year. Prepared by each department and bureau, these were submitted to the secretary of the Treasury who combined them into a Book of Estimates, which was forwarded to Congress. It was the predecessor of today's Budget except that neither the Treasury secretary nor the president had authority, except in certain limited cases, to alter an agency's estimates. For rivers and harbors appropriations, the total of the amounts that could be profitably expended in the next fiscal year on each project, as reported by the chief of engineers in the annual report, was many times greater than the lump-sum amounts proposed by the corps and the secretary of War in the Book of Estimates. For this reason, the Estimates included the advice "to be expended upon such works as may be directed by Congress." These data, in addition to petitions and memorials from project supporters and the testimony of members of Congress, accompanied by their constituents, were the menu presented to the House committee.

It was expedient for the legislative committee to distribute money widely in order to prevent strong congressional opposition or damaging amendments. At the same time, it was necessary to keep the total reasonable in terms of the condition of the national treasury—to compose bills that would avoid presidential veto. The committee attempted to solve the problem in part by providing partial or piecemeal funding. It typically approved a large number of small appropriations. As a result, numerous projects were under construction at any given time but with allotments so small that completion and the realization of their benefits were delayed for many years beyond the targets planned in the survey reports.

Having composed the bills after a great deal of tedious work, the committee sought to protect them in the House against amendments that would add projects and expenditures. The committee used procedures that limited drastically time for debate and the freedom of members to offer amendments, principally suspension of the rules. To consider a bill under suspension in the House requires a two-thirds majority vote. If this is obtained, debate is limited to forty minutes and no floor amendments are permitted except those proposed by the committee. Twelve of the sixteen annual rivers and harbors bills that passed the House between 1866 and 1883 were considered under suspension of the rules, indicating broad and bipartisan House satisfaction with its procedures and the committee's work. Also, the House and Senate committees agreed jointly that projects would not be included in omnibus bills if the corps had not conducted a survey or if a completed survey was unfavorable. Although this rule was violated on numerous occasions, it was a powerful tool used by the committees against those who sought to offer amendments on the floor that would authorize such projects.

Despite broad contentment among the people's elected representatives with the results of corps-Congress relations, rivers and harbors bills have been relentlessly attacked since the Civil War. By 1832, the disparaging epithet *logrolling* (the trading of votes by legislators to secure favorable action on projects of interest to each one) had been firmly attached to this legislation. President Andrew Jackson, an opponent of internal improvements, said in a letter to his political associate Amos Kendall that he was determined "to stop this corrupt, log-rolling system of legislation." Rivers and harbors bills were later called *pork barrel* legislation: a derisive term referring to the practice whereby legislators dip into the federal treasury for "pork" or funds for local projects. (The expression is believed to derive from the pre–Civil War practice of distributing salt pork to slaves from large barrels.)

The condemnations of logrolling and pork barrel were related to the more basic criticism that the rivers and harbors bills resulted in waste, funding projects with local but few national benefits, and in a simple accumulation of individual projects without a framework of national policies to justify them. Although the pattern of corps-congressional relations, as it had developed since the great debates on the constitutionality of internal improvements, tended to discourage debate on national policies to justify the projects being authorized, critics exaggerated the absence of national benefits. An analysis by the office of the chief of engineers of the much-criticized 1890 Rivers and Harbors Act, based on commercial tonnage, found that 59 percent of the appropriations were for works of purely national benefit, 22 percent for works of large national benefit, 18 percent for works of comparatively small national benefit, and as little as 0.003 percent for works of only local benefit.

To curtail logrolling, President Chester A. Arthur proposed that each project be considered as a separate bill or, alternatively, that the Constitution be amended to give the president a line-item veto. But Congress did not give serious consideration to these reforms.

The paramount criticism was that logrolling was immoral. In a scathing 1888 study of rivers and harbors legislation, Harvard professor Albert Bushnell Hart asserted that "the number of members who believe in a river and harbor bill, as in itself meritorious, is not sufficient to pass it," and that members of Congress therefore resorted to logrolling. Emory Richard Johnson, professor of transportation and commerce and later dean of the Wharton School at the University of Pennsylvania, took issue with most of Hart's contentions (*Annals of the American Academy of Political and Social Science*, vol. 2, 1892). But he, too, found logrolling to be immoral: "'Log-rolling' is opposed to wise and honorable legislation, and is to be condemned. . . . I condemn it; but do so mindful that no practice so much in vogue can exist without a reason, and do so mindful of the difficulty of suggesting a cure."

Today, journalists continue to use pork barrel and logrolling as terms of scathing disparagement, as did Brian Kelly, a *Washington Post* editor, in a 1992 book, *Adventures in Porkland: How Washington Wastes Your Money and Why They Won't Stop*. But many political scientists who study decision making in Congress, and who frequently use rivers and harbors legislation as an empirical source for their theories, are no longer bothered by the question of morality of logrolling. Interested primarily in the rational foundations of legislative behavior, these scholars begin with legislators' preferences, which they typically assume to be related to reelection, and proceed to construct models that connect elec-

TENNESSEE VALLEY AUTHORITY PROJECT. Senators on an inspection tour, 27 June 1959.   TENNESSEE VALLEY AUTHORITY

torally induced preferences to legislative organization, legislative behavior, and legislative policy. In this context, logrolling is simply one of several methods of coalition building; it has no moral component.

Bringing the Civil Works Functions of the Corps into the Executive Branch. The Budget and Accounting Act of 1921 had a profound effect on Congress-corps relations. The Book of Estimates, compiled by the secretary of the Treasury and over which the president had little control, became the President's Budget, prepared by the Budget Bureau, over which he had considerable control. On the congressional side, the budget estimates were handled by newly invigorated Appropriations committees in each house rather than by the Rivers and Harbors Committee in the House and the Commerce Committee in the Senate, as had been the case. Furthermore, whereas the rivers and harbors bills until 1921 included both authorizations of new projects and appropriations for new and ongoing projects, appropriations were now separated from authorizations, which remained under the jurisdiction of the legislative committees.

Because the appropriations for rivers and harbors under the new budget system were typically consolidated into several lump sums and individual projects were not designated in the statute, some observers concluded that Congress had forfeited to the executive control over the allocation of funds to individual projects and that the problem of partial or piecemeal appropriations had been largely solved. But this was not necessarily the case. Although not designated in the appropriations acts, individual projects to which Congress intended the lump sums to be allocated were named in the Appropriations Committee reports that accompanied the bills or in the committee hearings. Although nonstatutory, the procedures retained considerable control for Congress.

With appropriations stripped from them, the authorization bills were more difficult to compose and enact. With fewer items to review, the Rivers and Harbors Committee gave more careful scrutiny to each project and enforced more rigorously its rule that every new project have the corps's approval. The restrictions diminished opportunities for logrolling or coalition building. At the same time, the direct mode of corps-congressional relations remained in place for authorization legislation although it had been attenuated for water project appropriations.

As part of its New Deal, the Roosevelt administration made a sustained effort to bring the civil functions of the Corps of Engineers fully into the executive orbit. The campaign had four related parts. First, Roosevelt wanted the executive to develop national water resource policies that would be presented to Congress for adoption and would provide the framework for consideration of individual projects. The policies were to be formulated by a National Resources Board (subsequently called the National Resources Committee and later the National Resources Planning Board [NRPB]), with the participation of the corps and other agencies. Both the corps and Congress opposed the concept. The engineers continued to regard the development of policy as the sole duty of Congress, and Congress supported the corps in its claim.

Second, the president wanted to make the NRPB a permanent statutory agency in the Executive Office of the President, to "serve as a general staff in the husbanding of our natural resources." Roosevelt had established and funded the board in 1934 as a temporary agency without legislative approval. The proposal to give the agency permanent status, along with other proposals for administrative reorganization, became the subject of one of the most bitter controversies between Congress and the president during the tenure of Franklin D. Roosevelt. The watered-down reorganization bill finally adopted in 1939 contained no provision for a planning board. Supporters of the Corps of Engineers were the chief source of opposition to planning board legislation.

The board continued to operate on a temporary basis. However, the long fight to obtain permanent status ended in June 1943 when the Congress abolished the agency. The board's conflicts with the corps contributed significantly to its demise.

The president also sought to alter the practice that excluded the executive office and other agencies from reviewing and evaluating the corps's survey reports before they were submitted to Congress. For some years, the executive departments and agencies had been required to submit to the Budget Bureau their proposed reports and testimonies on pending legislation to determine whether they were in accord with the president's program. If they were not, the agencies were expected to withhold or revise the reports, but could nonetheless submit them, providing that they informed Congress that their recommendations were not in accord with the president's program. In 1940, Roosevelt issued an executive order that required the corps to follow a similar procedure for its survey reports. The corps was to submit its reports to the Budget Bureau, which would ask the NRPB to review them in light of national policies and potential conflicts with other existing or proposed developments. On the basis of the NRPB evaluations and additional budgetary considerations, the Budget Bureau, then, would inform the corps of the relationship of each survey report to the program of the president.

How effective was the order? From January 1941 to August 1948, the Executive Office of the President (EOP) cleared 914 Corps of Engineers reports; 478 recommended no federal improvements and were cleared by the EOP with no objection. Of the remaining 436 reports supporting construction, 360 were cleared with no objection to authorization. Forty-four reports were held to be wholly or partially not in accord with the president's program. The Corps of Engineers transmitted reports on all contested projects to Congress with its own favorable recommendations, and Congress authorized 36 projects. Clearly, the Executive Office of the President had not been effective in convincing either the Corps of Engineers or Congress to consider its views on the projects.

Sen. John H. Overton (D-La.), who for many years chaired the subcommittee that handled corps projects, said that his committee and Congress paid little or no attention to the recommendation and evaluations of the NRPB, although these were the views of the president. Congress based its decisions directly on the recommendations of the chief of engineers.

The final part of the Roosevelt administration's campaign to bring the corps to heel relates to the Administrative Reorganization Act of 1939. The central provision of the legislation gave the president authority to submit to Congress plans to reorganize and consolidate government agencies and functions. The plans took effect unless they were vetoed by both houses of Congress within sixty days. It was generally known that secretary of the Interior Harold L. Ickes intended to ask the president to submit a plan that would transfer the engineers' civil functions to his department and that Roosevelt was sympathetic. Congress, therefore, added a provision to the bill that exempted the engineers and their rivers and harbors functions from all of its provisions, thus ensuring that the president, under his reorganization authority, could not transfer corps functions to any other agency. Thus, the Roosevelt effort failed on all four fronts. The corps remained the engineering consultant to the Congress.

The long-standing pattern of legislative-executive relations began to change, however, in the mid 1950s. The corps began to act as if it were in fact part of the executive branch of government, reporting to the president directly and to Congress only through the president. The engineers began to cooperate as well as any public works agency officials in clearing their project reports with the Budget Bureau, and they became leaders among federal agencies in developing presidential policies for water resources. Remarkably, when the corps changed its posture, so did the congressional committees. They no longer expected the corps to perform as part of the legislative branch.

The old nexus dating back to the early nineteenth century had finally been broken by several developments. The corps could not ignore the increasingly effective controls exercised by the Budget Bureau during the Eisenhower administration over the budgets and legislative programs of all executive agencies. The leadership of the corps changed with the retirement of Gen. Lewis A. Pick as chief of engineers. The corps's efforts to respond to the growing environmental movement were not entirely successful. The engineers, among other measures, began to include environmental quality as an objective in the design of their projects and added environmental experts to their planning staffs in Washington and all district offices. Still environmental leaders opposed almost all dams and other structures, which significantly dampened Congress's enthusiasm for them. Finally, in the 1970s decision theory, with its focus on program objectives, evaluation of alternative means for achieving objectives, and evaluation of program results in terms of objectives, came to dominate policy planning as taught in the schools of public policy and practiced in the bureaucracy. By contrast, the corps's civil works program, and above all the process by which it was authorized, remained fixed on individual projects, and for this reason, it was associated in the minds of many public officials and opinion leaders with pork barrel.

Although bills authorizing the construction of new water projects were usually enacted at least every two years, none was proposed by the corps or enacted by Congress between 1970 and 1986. In reporting the Water Resources Development Act of 1986, the committees spoke of it as a major step in creating "a nationally coordinated water resources use policy," but it was more nearly another omnibus project authorization bill, albeit a small one. The basic form of the legislation had not changed very much.

Roads, 1916–1991. When the federal government once again took up the issue of roads in 1916, after a hiatus of more than half a century, it decided to aid the states in building them. The choice of projects was not to be made in the legislative process. As a consequence, legislative procedures and legislative-executive relations regarding the construction of roads developed very differently than for road projects before the Civil War and for water projects.

Preparing for a deeper involvement in road building, the House in 1913 established a Committee on Roads. The rule authorizing the committee stipulated that "it shall not be in order for any bill providing general legislation in relation to roads to contain any provisions for any specific road, nor for any bill in relation to a specific road to embrace a provision in relation to any other specific road." The debate on adoption of the rule makes clear the House's intention that roads be a "category two" public works program. As the member who became the first chairman of the new committee explained it, "We all know the vice of omnibus-bill legislation, and the purpose of these two exceptions . . . is to make it impossible to have any logrolling or an omnibus bill."

The first federal-aid highway act of 1916 and the acts of 1921, 1956, and 1991 spelled out the principles and procedures that govern the road program. The federal-aid highway program is a federally assisted state program. States are responsible for planning, construction, and maintenance of highways and for determining which projects will be federally financed, subject to approval of the secretary of Transportation (initially the secretary of Agriculture). Although state highway departments design all federally aided projects, the federal government sets uniform design standards—maximum cost per mile, for example, and that all Interstate highway segments have at least four lanes and be built to accommodate the traffic anticipated for a twenty-year period.

The program consists of several designated systems of interconnected roads. The 1916 act was silent on the location of roads entitled to receive federal aid, but Congress in 1921 required that each state, through its state highway department, designate a system of highways, not exceeding 7 percent of the total mileage in the state, upon which all federal funds should be spent. The system was to be divided into two categories: primary or interstate highways, to receive no more than 60 percent of federal aid, and secondary or intercoun-

ty roads. The 1944 act added a third category, urban extensions of the primary system, and together they became known as the ABC systems.

The highway act of 1956 designated a fourth category, the Interstate system of approximately 42,000 miles to be completed at an accelerated rate. By 1990, twenty years beyond the initial target date of 1970, the system was more than 99 percent complete (in miles of road). The highway act of 1991, therefore, inaugurated a new system, the National Highway System of about 155,000 miles, to include highways in the Interstate program, a major portion of those in the primary program, and a system of connecting principal arterials. The specific segments of highway to be included in the new national system are to be selected by the states, approved by the secretary of Transportation and designated by Congress in law.

Both the federal and state governments participate directly in program funding. The 1916 act adopted a matching ratio of 50 percent federal and 50 percent state funds, which remained in effect for almost forty years. In 1956, the federal contribution to the then new Interstate system was set at 90 percent of costs, which was increased to 100 percent in 1991. The federal share for the ABC programs was raised from 50 percent to 70 percent in 1970, to 75 percent in 1978, and to 80 percent in 1991.

Users pay a significant part of the costs of highway programs. The 1916 requirement that states pay 50 percent stimulated the imposition of state gasoline taxes to generate the matching funds. Over the years, the federal government has adopted a number of so-called excise taxes on highway users, including taxes on gasoline and other motor fuels, tires, new automobiles, trucks, and other vehicles, and annual use taxes on heavy vehicles based on their gross weight.

Income from the excise taxes was deposited in the treasury's general fund. The 1956 act, however, authorized the Highway Trust Fund into which most of the taxes were deposited and from which the expenditures for most highway programs were appropriated.

Federal highway funds are apportioned among the states by formulas. The traditional formula for the ABC systems, prescribed initially in the 1916 act, included area, population, and road mileage, each having a weight of one-third. Authorization in 1956 of the Interstate system was accompanied by sharp disagreement between the House and Senate on the apportionment formula to be used, and the act contained a two-stage compromise. The Senate version, which retained the area-population-road mileage formula that favored large, less populated states was adopted for the first three years; after that, the House version, which contained a new cost-to-complete formula favoring urban eastern states, would govern.

Congress fashioned a major overhaul of apportionments in 1991, when long-standing formulas were abandoned for most systems. The new method combines an average of the money received by a state in each of the previous five years with a number of additional factors related principally to fuel consumption and traffic volume. Also, each state was guaranteed a minimum apportionment equal to 90 percent of the federal gasoline tax dollars paid by its motorists. Finally, the act provides for several lump-sum payments to states in addition to the formulas.

The two public works programs—water resources and roads—have developed under widely different modes of executive-legislative relations. There is no parallel in the case of roads to the role of the Corps of Engineers before the 1950s, when it acted as if it were part of the legislative branch, not responsible to the president, while eschewing recommendations to Congress on policy, holding that policy should be the exclusive concern of elected representatives.

The biennial authorization bills for water resources are devoted almost exclusively to projects, while those for roads are devoted almost exclusively to programs. The executive has played a minor role as initiator of rivers and harbors bills and a major role in highway bills. Floor debate on rivers and harbors bills has been discouraged lest it result simply in pressure to add projects; floor debate on the highway bills has been vigorous.

Also, compare the conduct of the office of a member of Congress in seeking approval for a water project and for a road that will serve the district. For a water project, the member becomes involved in the legislative process, sponsoring a provision in a rivers and harbors act that directs that corps to make a survey of the project and later, if the survey is favorable, another provision in a subsequent act that authorizes the project. Then, the member must persuade the corps to assign the now-authorized project a high priority so that it will be included in the list of projects to be funded in the current Budget. The member must also ensure that the Appropriations committees state their intention that the project is to be included among those to be funded from a lump-sum appropriation.

By contrast, surveying and designing a road project and assigning it a priority is the responsibility of the state highway department, which submits its plans to the Federal Highway Administration for approval. If the federal agency for any reason delays or rejects the plans, the state agency may seek the assistance of a member of Congress to press its case. In doing this, however, the member does not become involved in the legislative process but rather in providing constituency service, which is largely independent of legislative work.

Recent Trends in Highway Legislation. Three recent developments in the procedures by which Congress composes and considers highway bills threaten to compromise the pattern of executive-legislative relations on highways established in 1916.

The first is a proliferation of categorical programs. Beginning with the 1970 highway act, Congress has added a large number of specific purpose programs to the four designated systems. Because each program has its own design standards and matching ratio, federal influence over spending and federal red tape have increased as have opportunities for logrolling or coalition building in the legislative process.

Periodic efforts to consolidate programs were unsuccessful until 1991. The Surface Transportation Act of that year created a new, well-financed program, the Surface Transportation Program, that states may use for a variety of roads providing that they are not classified as local or rural minor collector roads. The act authorized the transfer to this flexible program of many of the categorical programs, thus alleviating somewhat the threat to long-standing procedures.

The second development is the proliferation of highway demonstration projects. These are presumably projects that demonstrate novel road-building techniques, and as such they are individually named in the highway acts, along with the techniques that they are to demonstrate and how they are to be financed. The program began modestly in 1974 and has grown steadily. The Surface Transportation Act of 1987 included 120 projects to cost approximately $1 billion, and the 1991 act included 450 projects at an estimated cost of $4.5 billion.

In the first few years, such projects were restricted to those that demonstrated novel road-building techniques, but by 1980 few projects could legitimately support such a claim. The justifications presented for them were so embarrassingly weak that the committees decided to delete from the bills all language justifying the projects as demonstrations. As one informed observer has said, most of the projects demonstrate nothing more than the ability of members of Congress to get money for their districts. President Ronald Reagan vetoed the 1987 highway bill in large part because of the demonstration projects, but Congress overrode his veto.

While Congress designates highway demonstration projects as in "category one" public works programs, there are no generally accepted procedures for selecting or financing them, as there are for water projects. In all likelihood the Public Works Committee has no survey reports to study. Survey reports would have to come from the state highway agencies, and they have opposed the proliferation of demonstration projects, which are often low on the state's priority list and may require the state to allocate resources to roads that, although important to the member of Congress and his or her constituents, have little significance in terms of the state's transportation needs. Also, the mix of federal and state funding for such projects has become a contentious issue. Realizing that demonstration projects have become a reality, some states have sought to channel them toward their priorities instead of those of their state's congressional members. The Nevada Department of Transportation, for example, opened a Washington office, hired a lobbyist in 1989, and began pushing its own list of demonstration projects on Capitol Hill.

How did all this happen when the 1913 rule which prohibits the inclusion of specific roads in general roads legislation is still in effect and had been followed conscientiously for sixty years? The usual way to enforce a House rule of this type, when a committee proposes to violate it, is for a member to raise a point of order against the offending section of the bill. The Public Works Committee circumvented the enforcement procedure by asking the Rules Committee in each case to include in the rule governing debate on the bill a provision waiving points of order. Once the House approves the rule for the bill, there is no way to enforce the general rule of the House. It is interesting to note that in 1913, when the House was debating the legislative procedures for roads, which were to be very different than those for rivers and harbors, Rep. John J. Fitzgerald (D-N.Y.) proposed to strengthen the prohibition against specifying roads in bills by adding the following language: "nor shall the Committee on Rules report a rule . . . providing for the consideration of such a bill." He said that unless this provision is contained in the rule, "the experience of the House is that it will not be possible, though perhaps it may be in the immediate future, to prevent omnibus bills." Although his language was not enacted, Fitzgerald was prescient.

The third recent development relates to the overhaul of apportionment formulas in the 1991 act. Negotiations in the conference committee turned into what *Congressional Quarterly* has called a "formula free-for-all." Alternate formulas were not debated in terms of their impact on national highway policy; "instead they provided congressional aides a starting point to punch numbers into computers in a high-tech search for the best deal for a particular state." (*Congressional Quarterly Weekly Report*, 23 November 1991, p. 3448). In the end, in addition to revising formulas for the several highway programs, the act authorized approximately $1 billion per year to pay to states with apportionments under the new formulas that would be less than 90 percent of the federal gasoline taxes paid by their motorists.

Reflecting on the legislative outcome in 1991, especially the demonstration projects and the apportionment formulas, the secretary of Transportation said, "What we have is controlled pork." On the other hand, referring to the special projects, the chairman of the House Transportation Appropriations Subcommittee complained, "Demonstration projects get 2 percent of the funding and 98 percent of the attention."

[*For discussion of related public policy issues, see* Housing Policy; Interstate Highway System; Internal Improvements; Transportation. *See also* Commerce, Science, and Transportation Committee, Senate; Environment and Public Works Committee, Senate; Public Works and Transportation Committee, House; Rural Post Roads Act.]

BIBLIOGRAPHY

Arnold, R. Douglas. *Congress and the Bureaucracy.* 1979.

Arnold, R. Douglas. *The Logic of Congressional Action.* 1990.

Krehbiel, Keith. *Information and Legislative Organization.* 1992.

Maass, Arthur. *Congress and the Common Good.* 1983.

Maass, Arthur. *Muddy Waters: The Army Engineers and the Nation's Rivers.* 1951.

Maass, Arthur. "Public Investment Planning in the United States: Analysis and Critique." *Public Policy* 18 (1970): 211–243.

Pross, Edward L. "A History of Rivers and Harbors Appropriations Bills, 1866–1933." Ph.D. diss., Ohio State University, 1938.

Wheeler, Porter K. *Highway Assistance Programs: A Historical Perspective.* 1978.

ARTHUR MAASS

PUBLIC WORKS AND TRANSPORTATION COMMITTEE, HOUSE.

The major predecessor of the Committee on Public Works and Transportation was the Committee on Public Buildings and Grounds, established in 1837. The Legislative Reorganization Act of 1946 combined that committee with those on Flood Control, Rivers and Harbors, and Roads into a new Public Works Committee. In 1974 further legislative reforms added transportation to the committee's jurisdiction, giving it its present name. The committee's Senate counterpart is the Environment and Public Works Committee.

The committee's jurisdiction now covers all legislation relating to flood control and improvement of rivers and harbors; highway safety and construction or maintenance of roads and post roads; pollution of navigable waters; public buildings and grounds of the federal government; public works benefiting navigation, including bridges and dams; water power; water transportation; civil aviation; most transportation covered by the Interstate Commerce Commission; and nonrailroad transportation regulatory agencies. It oversees the Capitol and congressional office buildings; the buildings and grounds of the Botanic Garden, the Library of Congress, and the Smithsonian Institution; and the purchase of sites for and construction of post offices, customhouses, federal courthouses, and federal government buildings in the District of Columbia. In 1993, Superfund environmental cleanup legislation (the Comprehensive Environmental Response, Compensation and Liability Act of 1980) was added to the committee's oversight jurisdiction.

As a result of the 1974 reforms, the committee surrendered jurisdiction over District of Columbia parks and its authority to report "privileged bills" authorizing rivers and harbors improvements. Newly added jurisdiction concerned revolving funds for the Southeastern and Southwestern Power Administrations, provision of school facilities for U.S. Army Corps of Engineers construction works, acquisition of corps flood-control project lands, construction of the John F. Kennedy Center for the Performing Arts and the East Wing annex to the National Gallery of Art, land transfers from the Corps of Engineers to Indian tribes, and truck transportation regulation.

The committee deals with a range of federal agencies, including the Defense, Transportation, Interior, and Commerce departments as well as the Environmental Protection Agency, the Tennessee Valley Authority, and the Federal Aviation Administration. It also involves state and local governments and state, municipal, and regional special authorities as it considers legislation and performs oversight functions in intergovernmental matters such as interstate highways, airports, and dam construction.

From the 1870s to the present, the committee (and its chief predecessor, Buildings and Grounds) has generally ranked in the middle in terms of its attractiveness to members. The 103d Congress (1993–1995) represented a major exception, with the committee becoming the most sought-after assignment among House freshmen, in part because of campaign promises by President Bill Clinton to emphasize transportation, environment, and other infrastructure ventures in his administration. Consequently, the House leadership expanded the committee from fifty-seven to sixty-three members, making it the House's largest panel.

The Public Works and Transportation Committee attracts members seeking prestige and federal largess for their districts as well as those interested in the subject matter. George Goodwin, Jr. (1970), classified it as a "clientele" committee, and Stephen S. Smith and Christopher J. Deering (1984) categorized it as a "constituency" committee. James T. Murphy (1990) found that during the 90th Congress (1967–1969), members gave "image building" in their districts as their primary reason for choosing this committee: 60 percent of the members joined because of district benefits, 19 percent were interested in helping their state congressional delegations, and 21 percent could not get slots on other committees. Smith and Deering later surveyed junior members for their committee preferences and reported that almost all Public Works respondents had selected it for constituency-related motivations, including reelection.

Public Works members can benefit constituents by promoting projects in their states and districts. Gerald S. Strom (1975) found strong support for the hypothesis that states represented on Public Works received more average policy benefits than did states not represented on the committee.

Of the many groups attempting to influence Public Works and Transportation Committee legislation, perhaps those associated with transportation (particularly highways) and environmental interests

House Public Works Committee Chairmen since 1947

George A. Dondero (R-Mich.)	1947–1949
William M. Whittington (D-Miss.)	1949–1951
Charles A. Buckley (D-N.Y.)	1951–1953
George A. Dondero (R-Mich.)	1953–1955
Charles A. Buckley (D-N.Y.)	1955–1965
George H. Fallon (D-Md.)	1965–1971
John A. Blatnik (D-Minn.)	1971–1975
Robert E. Jones, Jr. (D-Ala.)	1975–1977
Harold T. Johnson (D-Calif.)	1977–1981
James J. Howard (D-N.J.)	1981–1988
Glenn M. Anderson (D-Calif.)	1988–1991
Robert A. Roe (D-N.J.)	1991–1993
Norman Y. Mineta (D-Calif.)	1993–

are the most vocal. State and local governments also try to affect committee decisions. Demands made by various groups, however, do not necessarily promote conflict on the committee.

This committee has sometimes met opposition from the president (regardless of party) as the administration has tried to exert budgetary control over the expenditure of funds for public works projects. Committee authorizations often increase budgetary pressures because members want projects for their districts. Occasionally, the president has had to retreat to save the programs he has favored.

Patterns of partisanship have varied. Julius Turner (1951) characterized the Public Works Committee in the 1940s as "moderately partisan." By the 1960s, James T. Murphy found the committee substantially more partisan, exhibiting patterns both of party conflict and of cooperation. The two parties rarely agreed on either regional allocation issues—those that benefited a minority in each party—or traditional party issues. For example, differences arose over aid to economically depressed areas, the authority of the federal government, and the federal government's position in the economy.

During the 1960s and 1970s, party differences emerged in disagreements over issues such as support for public versus private power; whether federal, state, or local governments should assume responsibility for water pollution; how to distribute the financial burden of the interstate highways; and economic development. The parties also disagreed over the extent to which the federal government could approve state water-quality standards, promulgate federal standards, and penalize states for noncompliance (Murphy, 1974; Parker and Parker, 1985).

In the 1980s and early 1990s, bipartisanship supplanted partisanship as the norm, particularly on infrastructure issues. Although many committee issues inspire disagreements, most do not break down along party lines. Regional and individual philosophical differences are more likely to engender conflict, particularly on transportation and environmental issues. For example, depending on the region they represent, members may diverge on which types of transportation to emphasize (e.g., coal slurry pipelines versus railroads to transport coal; roads versus mass transit to move people) or on the definition of federally protected wetlands. Nevertheless, by the early 1990s the committee showed a bipartisan consensus on the need to rebuild the nation's infrastructure. And in 1993 the committee's new chairman, Norman Y. Mineta (D-Calif.), with a reputation as a consensus-builder, was working closely with the ranking minority member to try to tailor public works programs to benefit as many states as possible.

Many differences are worked out at the staff level, with cooperation among the full and subcommittee staffs, majority and minority. Often disagreements are pragmatic, not philosophical. For example, there is widespread agreement on relevant concepts, such as the desirability of clean drinking water, the transferability of transportation funds from one pot to another, and the need for "intermodality"—that is, using various modes of transport to move goods and people at the cheapest cost. Disagreements arise regarding the practical application of these concepts—for example, over the portion of the cost the federal government should shoulder versus that taken on by the states. Disagreements most often stem from constituencies, not parties, although partisan philosophical differences may arise over the question of how to pay for public works programs.

Although Public Works has a tradition of strong central direction, reforms in the 1970s fragmented it and other committees, diminishing the chair's control. Subcommittees assumed more independence in setting the legislative agenda, and their chairs gained influence on the House floor, often replacing committee chairs as legislative floor managers.

Subcommittees handle most of the committee's legislation, although the full committee does sometimes deal with major bills. In addition, the committee's more senior members have served on almost all its subcommittees and therefore have experience and an interest in all facets of the committee's legislation. The Intermodal Surface Transportation Efficiency Act of 1991, for example, was a joint effort involving every subcommittee, but much of the work was done at the full committee level.

The full committee seldom challenges subcommittee recommendations because members' preferences are taken into account when the subcommittees write legislation. Members begin their negotiations with the idea of being fair to as many states as possible. In 1993, the committee maintained six subcommittees, structured to accommodate both constituency- and policy-oriented members: Aviation, Surface Transportation, Economic Development, Investigations and Oversight, Water Resources and Environment, and Public Buildings and Grounds.

The Public Works and Transportation Committee deals with nuts-and-bolts legislation understandable to everyone and generally does not concern itself with esoteric issues. Since most disagreements are worked out in the committee, legislation often is reported unanimously and has relatively high success rates on the House floor. Bills that make it to the floor usually pass, often by large margins.

The leadership of the committee turned over twelve times between 1947 and 1993. In 1990, Democratic committee members successfully persuaded the House Democratic caucus to oust chairman Glenn M. Anderson (D-Calif.), whose leadership they found weak.

[*See also* Commerce, Science, and Transportation Committee, Senate; Environment and Public Works Committee, Senate.]

BIBLIOGRAPHY

Cooper, Kenneth J. "The House Freshmen's First Choice." *Washington Post*, 5 January 1993, p. A13.
Ferejohn, John A. *Pork Barrel Politics: Rivers and Harbors Legislation, 1947–1968*. 1974.
Goodwin, George, Jr. *The Little Legislatures: Committees of Congress*. 1970.
Murphy, James T. "Political Parties and the Porkbarrel: Party Conflict and Cooperation in House Public Works Committee Decision Making." *American Political Science Review* 68 (March 1974): 169–185.
Parker, Glenn R., and Suzanne L. Parker. *Factions in House Committees*. 1985.
Smith, Steven S., and Christopher J. Deering. *Committees in Congress*. 2d ed. 1990.
Stewart, Charles III. "Committee Hierarchies in the Modernizing House." *American Journal of Political Science* 36 (1992): 835–856.
Strom, Gerald S. "Congressional Policy Making: A Test of a Theory." *Journal of Politics* 37 (1975): 711–735.
Turner, Julius. *Party and Constituency*. 1951.

ANDRÉE E. REEVES

PUERTO RICO. On 17 April 1898, Congress issued the declaration of the Spanish American War. With it began America's experiment in managing an overseas territorial empire. Three months later, U.S. troops landed in Puerto Rico and took possession of the Spanish colony with very few casualties. Thus, the island and its people were "ceded" as property by Spain to the United States, by virtue of the Treaty of Paris of 1898.

In May 1900, Congress enacted the Foraker Act establishing a civil government and formally making the island an unincorporated territory of the United States. This statute set up a government under a governor appointed by the U.S. president, an elected lower House of Delegates, a local judiciary, and a federal district court for the island.

Through the Jones Act of 1917, Congress approved a second organic statute that gave Puerto Rico a bill of rights and granted U.S. citizenship to all persons born on the island. The act created a two-house legislative body elected by the citizens, although the executive officers were still presidentially appointed.

The territory's development toward self-government continued after World War II. In 1947, Congress, through the Elective Governor Act, provided for the election of the governor. In 1948, in the first general election held on the island, Luis Muñoz-Marín became its first elected governor. Two years later, at the insistence of Muñoz, Congress approved the Federal Relations Act, which provided for the organization of a constitutional government in Puerto Rico and reenacted parts of the Jones Act of 1917 as a "new" organic statute that would regulate federal-territorial relations under the constitutional government, now designated a commonwealth. In 1952, an overwhelming 73 percent majority of Puerto Ricans approved the constitution and the Federal Relations Act, two instruments that have defined the self-government of the island to the present time.

Today, Puerto Rico remains a commonwealth under the sovereignty of Congress, through Article IV, section 3 of the U.S. Constitution. Puerto Ricans are full U.S. citizens, although on the island they are not protected by all provisions of the U.S. Constitution and they are not allowed to vote in presidential or congressional elections.

By virtue of the Federal Relations Act, the residents of Puerto Rico do not pay federal personal income tax, and they are represented in Congress by one resident commissioner, whose right to vote in the House is limited. In spite of significant economic progress achieved since 1950, 59 percent of Puerto Rico's citizens still live below the poverty level. Most U.S. industrial corporations located on the island are tax exempt by virtue of Section 936 of the Internal Revenue Code. Puerto Rico is the eighth largest market for U.S. goods.

Since the early part of the twentieth century, more than 210,000 Puerto Ricans have served in the U.S. armed forces during major wars. Puerto Rican soldiers suffered extremely high casualty rates during the Korean, Vietnam, and Persian Gulf wars.

The century-long territorial relationship has not been devoid of controversy. Although 94 percent of the electorate wants to keep close ties to the United States, either through commonwealth or statehood status, during the last thirty years there has been growing support for making the island a state of the Union. Puerto Rico also has an independence movement, which despite its activism has not garnered more than 6 percent of the vote in recent general elections.

The debate over the island's status became a nationwide issue during the 101st Congress (1989–1991), when House and Senate committees considered bills to enact a plebiscite to choose from among the three options. This would have allowed the citizens of Puerto Rico to express a mandate for constitutional change. The bills died in committee after intense debate, but the issue remains alive. Those advocating statehood have demanded admission into the Union as a civil rights issue and to end five centuries of "colonial" rule and economic deprivation and injustices. Opponents of statehood claim that Congress will deny admission because of racial and cultural biases. Furthermore, they prefer the other two options of continued commonwealth status or independence, arguing that admission into the Union would endanger the identity, represented by the island's rich Hispanic culture and its use of the Spanish language, and would cause economic disruptions, particularly to tax exempt industries.

BIBLIOGRAPHY

Dávila-Colón, Luis R. "The Blood Tax: The Puerto Rican Contribution to the United States War Effort." *Revista del Colegio de Abogados de Puerto Rico* 40 (1979): 603–638.
Dávila-Colón, Luis R. "Equal Citizenship, Self-Determination, and the U.S. Statehood Process: A Constitutional and Historical Analysis." *Journal of International Law* 13 (Spring 1981): 315.
Documents of the Constitutional History of Puerto Rico. Edited by the Office of the Commonwealth of Puerto Rico in Washington, D.C. 2d ed. 1964.
García-Passalacqua, Juan M. *Puerto Rico: Equality and Freedom at Issue.* 1984.
Perusse, Roland I. *The United States and Puerto Rico: Decolonization Options and Prospects.* 1987.

LUIS R. DÁVILA-COLÓN

PUJO INVESTIGATION.

On 12 April 1912, when public concern over the power of America's large financial institutions ran high, the Banking and Currency Committee of the newly Democrat-controlled House created a subcommittee to look into "the concentration of money and credit." Arsène P. Pujo of Louisiana was its titular head. But the subcommittee's work was primarily in the hands of its counsel, Samuel J. Untermyer, a New York lawyer outspokenly critical of large concentrations of capital.

The New York legislature's Armstrong committee investigation of large life insurance companies in 1905 was Untermyer's model. Even before beginning his work, he was convinced "that there is a close and well-defined 'community of interest' and understanding among the men who dominate the financial destinies of our country."

The committee held hearings in the spring of 1912 and in the winter of 1912–1913 after the presidential election. It focused on the major investment banking firms, most notably, J. P. Morgan and Company. Untermyer demonstrated the existence of interlocking networks of investments and directorates linking the leading investment banks, trust and insurance companies, and large industrial and railroad corporations. The climax of the hearings came when the seventy-six-year-old J. P. Morgan took the stand in early 1913. Morgan staunchly insisted that his influence stemmed more from trust and character than from financial power.

The committee recommended the adoption of legislation to prevent further concentration of wealth, to restore competition in capital markets, and to subject Wall Street to some government regulation. The Federal Reserve Bank Act of 1913 and the Clayton Antitrust and Federal Trade Commission acts, both of 1914, were in part responses to these recommendations. But the investment and capital markets did not come under serious government supervision until the New Deal.

[*See also* Clayton Antitrust Act; Federal Reserve Bank Act; Federal Trade Commission Act.]

BIBLIOGRAPHY

Carosso, Vincent P. *Investment Banking in America.* 1970. Chapter 6.

MORTON KELLER

PURE FOOD AND DRUGS ACT (1906; 34 Stat. 768–772).

Local laws protecting consumers from spoiled meat and adulterated bread and wine became inadequate as commercial food processing and the use of organic chemistry to modify natural products developed during the nineteenth century. New creations, such as oleomargarine as an unacknowledged substitute for butter and corn syrup added to honey and maple syrup, also threatened established interests. Pioneer consumer advocates like George T. Angell emphasized threats to health, but early efforts to secure broad federal legislation owed more to food processors whose competitors cheapened their products with adulterants. The first such bill, influenced by British legislation, was introduced in 1879. Every Congress thereafter debated one or more comprehensive food and drug bill until the Pure Food and Drugs Act was approved in 1906. Single-issue bills, such as those to bar imports of adulterated drugs (1848) and to tax oleomargarine (1886), fared better.

Harvey W. Wiley, chief chemist of the Department of Agriculture, became a focal figure in the drive to secure a federal law. He directed a government study revealing the composition—and the adulteration—of a range of foods. He conceived the "Poison Squad" experiments, testing chemical preservatives in the controlled diets of young men and concluding that the results were harmful. Wiley served as adviser for the first major congressional hearing on food problems, conducted in 1898 by Sen. William E. Mason of Illinois. Thereafter, Wiley kept in touch with members of both houses concerned with the developing bill. At private meetings, he sought to reconcile differences among advocates of legislation.

Wiley worked persistently to increase public interest in the bill and to sustain allegiance of groups pressing for its passage: state chemists, women's clubs, the American Medical Association, many pharmacists, and segments of the food processing industries. In the final years of this effort, congressional leaders of the cause were Senators Henry C. Hansbrough and Porter J. McCumber of North Dakota and Weldon B. Heyburn of Idaho and Representatives William P. Hepburn of Iowa and James R. Mann of Illinois. In late 1905 President Theodore Roosevelt announced his support for a pure food bill.

Muckraking played an indispensable part in arousing public interest. The major documents were Samuel Hopkins Adams's sharp critique in *Collier's* of patent medicine abuses and Upton Sinclair's depiction in his novel *The Jungle* of unhygienic packinghouse conditions. The latter led also to a meat inspection law signed by Roosevelt on the same day, 30 June 1906, he signed the Pure Food and Drugs Act.

The food and drug law, concerned with products entering interstate commerce, was basically an honest labeling law, grounded in the concept that an adequately informed consumer could avoid deception and danger. Misbranding was illegal: no statement or design in labeling could be "false or misleading in any particular." One type of information was required: the names and amounts of certain dangerous drugs, especially alcohol and narcotics. The *United States Pharmacopoeia* and *National Formulary* provided the legal standard; drugs not included in these volumes, especially patent medicines, had to match in content what their label declared. The law proscribed adulterated food, including adulteration by added poisonous ingredients that might endanger health and any "filthy, decomposed, or putrid substance." However, penalties for violations were slight.

This law much improved the marketplace, but efforts at enforcement revealed inadequacies and led to major controversies. The 1906 law was replaced in 1938 by a more rigorous measure, the Food, Drug, and Cosmetic Act. Much amended, this remains the basic governing statute.

BIBLIOGRAPHY

Anderson, Oscar E., Jr. *The Health of a Nation: Harvey W. Wiley and the Fight for Pure Food.* 1958.
Bailey, Thomas A. "Congressional Opposition to Pure Food Legislation." *American Journal of Sociology* 36 (1930): 52–64.
Young, James Harvey. *Pure Food: Securing the Federal Food and Drugs Act of 1906.* 1989.

JAMES HARVEY YOUNG

Q

QUALIFICATIONS OF MEMBERS. *See* Members, *article on* Qualifications.

QUAY, MATTHEW S. (1833–1904), senator from Pennsylvania (1887–1904) and, during that period, the state's most visible Republican boss. A recipient of the Medal of Honor for his exploits at Fredericksburg during the Civil War, Quay relied heavily on the support of veterans. Generally indifferent to national legislation, he refused to accept the chairmanship of a significant Senate committee. Although he served on such prestigious committees as Commerce, Territories, Indian Affairs, and Manufactures, his career-long duty was with the Committee on Public Buildings and Grounds, of which he did become chairman. Never in the limelight, this committee offered its own peculiar rewards because from time to time every senator needed the chairman's support in pushing projects, most often new post office buildings. Frequently, a senator's prestige at home—sometimes reelection—hinged on passage of such a measure. Aware of the subtle power of this chairmanship, Quay exercised a quiet influence over all senators and demanded quid pro quo when necessary.

By this technique he added new dimensions to senatorial power, discipline, and compromise. Focused more on his state's needs than on national legislative programs, he championed no principle, not even the doctrine of protection. Although he did speak on the tariff, he merely demanded specific schedules for the iron and steel producers of his state.

MATTHEW S. QUAY. Widely believed to be part Native American, Quay donned American Indian attire for a publicity photograph to express solidarity with Indians.

LIBRARY OF CONGRESS

1655

His voice was seldom heard on the Senate floor, partly because he was not a gifted speaker and partly because of his habitual absenteeism. He listened attentively when he was in the chamber, not to contribute subsequently to the discussion but to understand the beliefs and attitudes of his colleagues so that he might bargain more successfully with them in the committee rooms and dining halls where he conducted his most effective work.

BIBLIOGRAPHY

Crist, Robert G, ed. *Pennsylvania Kingmakers*. 1985.
Kehl, James A. *Boss Rule in the Gilded Age: Matt Quay of Pennsylvania*. 1981.

JAMES A. KEHL

QUORUM. The Constitution specifies in Article I that "a majority of each House shall constitute a quorum to do business." (When in Committee of the Whole, the House is not bound by this requirement, and the quorum is set at one hundred in Rule XXIII.) The question of what constitutes a "house" in this context—all of the members provided for by statute or some lesser number determined by circumstance—remained open for some time.

During the Civil War, the seceding states did not choose representatives, and in 1861 House Speaker Galusha A. Grow ruled that a quorum consisted of "a majority of those chosen" rather than simply a majority of the total seats provided for by statute. In 1890 this was clarified by Speaker Thomas B. Reed to mean all members "chosen and living." The current interpretation was established in 1903, when Speaker Joseph G. Cannon ruled that "a quorum consists of a majority of those Members chosen, sworn, and living, whose membership has not been terminated by resignation or by the action of the House."

In the Senate, the path to the current interpretation was quicker. Although originally reluctant to embrace the House's view, in 1864 the Senate formally adopted a rule stating that a quorum consisted of "a majority of the Senators duly chosen." A revision of the Senate rules in 1868 amended this to read "a majority of the Senators duly chosen and sworn."

Both the House and Senate operate under the general assumption that a quorum is present unless demonstrated otherwise. In the House, whether operating as the House or in Committee of the Whole, the rules discourage raising points of order questioning the presence of a quorum. Another factor in House practice is the provision in Rule XV that allows the Speaker to direct the clerk to record the names of members who do not vote in determining the presence of a quorum. This change was Speaker Reed's response to "disappearing quorums," caused when members refused to respond to quorum calls to delay or prevent the House from conducting business. House rules also greatly restrict the applicability of such points of order in the House and in Committee of the Whole. Quorum calls are rarely permitted except in conjunction with a recorded vote.

In the Senate, however, quorum calls are quite common, and that body's rules and practices allow senators to suggest the absence of a quorum at virtually any time; furthermore, the chair has no power to count for a quorum (except under cloture). This has led to the distinction between a "live" quorum call—designed to ascertain the presence of an actual quorum, in response to a point of order—and "constructive delay"—when a quorum call is designed as a means of suspending proceedings to accomplish some other action.

When the absence of a quorum is determined, no business can be transacted except a call of the House or Senate, a motion to secure a quorum, or a motion to adjourn (although a motion to recess is also in order in the Senate if pursuant to a prior order or unanimous consent agreement).

Committees are given great flexibility in establishing the size of a quorum. A majority of the panel's membership is necessary to make a quorum to report a measure, but for other action it can be set by committee rules as low as one-third the membership. A quorum in committees needs to be established by the physical presence of the members. Proxies or other means of polling the members do not count in determining a quorum. Both Senate and House committees, however, sometimes use what is called a "rolling quorum" by which the members may record their presence on a ledger, so that a quorum may not necessarily be physically present at all times. For a hearing, Senate rules allow for a quorum of less than one-third, and the House specifically allows for quorums as small as only two.

[*See also* Quorum Call.]

BIBLIOGRAPHY

U.S. House of Representatives. *Constitution, Jefferson's Manual, and Rules of the House of Representatives, 103d Congress*. Compiled by William Holmes Brown. 102d Cong., 2d sess., 1993. H. Doc. 102-405. Rules XI, XV, XXIII.
U.S. House of Representatives. *Hinds' Precedents of the*

House of Representatives of the United States, by Asher C. Hinds. 59th Cong., 2d sess., 1907. Vol. 4, chap. 86.

U.S. Senate. *Senate Procedure, Precedents, and Practices,* by Floyd M. Riddick. 97th Cong., 1st sess., 1981. S. Doc. 97-2.

JAMES V. SATURNO

QUORUM CALL. [*This entry includes separate discussions of the quorum call in each house of Congress. See also* Quorum; House of Representatives, *article on* Daily Sessions of the House; Senate, *article on* Daily Sessions of the Senate.]

In the House

There are two calls of the House that can be used to ascertain the presence of a quorum (usually 218 members): (1) the call ordered on motion and (2) the automatic call. A point of no quorum may not be entertained unless the pending question has been put to a vote, but the Speaker may, at his discretion, recognize a member for a motion for a quorum call of the House at any time. If the motion is agreed to, the roll is called until a quorum answers or until the House adjourns.

The automatic call ensues when a quorum fails to vote on any question that requires a quorum, a quorum is not present, and objection is made for that reason. Following the announcement of a voice or division vote, if the Speaker sustains a point of no quorum from the floor, the yeas and nays are considered as ordered on the pending question. Members vote and thereby indicate their presence as part of the same action.

In the Committee of the Whole, the first time the Committee finds itself without a quorum (one hundred members) on any day, the chairman invokes a quorum call. The chairman may refuse to entertain a point of order that a quorum is not present during general debate only. After a quorum has been established once on that measure during a day, the chairman has put the pending question to a vote. At that point, the chair may use either a regular quorum call or a "notice" quorum call, whereby the call is "vacated" as soon as one hundred members are present.

BIBLIOGRAPHY

U.S. House of Representatives. *Deschler's Precedents of the United States House of Representatives,* by Lewis Deschler. 94th Cong., 2d sess., 1977. H. Doc. 94-661. Vol. 5.

U.S. House of Representatives. *Constitution, Jefferson's Manual, and Rules of the House of Representatives, 103d Congress.* Compiled by William Holmes Brown. 102d Cong., 2d sess., 1992. H. Doc. 102-405.

THOMAS G. DUNCAN

In the Senate

The practice of the quorum call is based on the constitutional requirement that a majority of the Senate must be present for the Senate to transact business. While quorum calls were originally used to require senators' presence on the Senate floor, they have assumed a different character in the modern legislative process. In practice, quorum calls are used to fill the time between transactions of business and are primarily a delaying mechanism.

Quorum calls are a typical feature of any extended debate in the Senate. They allow Senators to negotiate and discuss pending items away from the Senate floor. There is no limit on the length of a quorum call, and during contentious debates quorum calls have been known to last several hours.

A quorum call begins when any senator who has the floor states to the presiding officer, "I suggest the absence of a quorum." A quorum call can be brought to an end by unanimous consent to "dispense with the calling of the roll." However, such consent must come before the chair announces that a quorum is not present. When a quorum call goes to completion and the chair announces that a quorum is not present, a majority of the Senate must appear or the Senate must adjourn. Because unanimous consent is required to suspend a quorum call, a single senator can force the attendance of a majority of senators on the Senate floor.

BIBLIOGRAPHY

U.S. Senate. *Senate Procedure, Precedents, and Practices,* by Floyd M. Riddick. 97th Cong., 1st sess., 1981. S. Doc. 97-2.

ROBERT B. DOVE

R

RACKETEER INFLUENCED AND COR-RUPT ORGANIZATIONS ACT (RICO)
(1970; 18 U.S.C. secs. 1961–1968). In 1970, Congress enacted the Organized Crime Control Act (84 Stat. 922–962), Title IX of which is known as the Racketeer Influenced and Corrupt Organizations Act (RICO). RICO grew out of study by congressional committees and presidential commissions of organized and white-collar crime.

RICO introduced into the law the concepts of "enterprise"—defined as various licit organizations (corporations, partnerships, unions, etc.) in the legitimate sphere as well as various illicit organizations in the underworld—and "pattern"—defined as related conduct extending over a substantial period. RICO then prohibited patterns of violence, selling illegal goods, political corruption, or commercial fraud by, through, or against licit or illicit enterprises.

Criminally, RICO is enforced by imprisonment, fines, and forfeitures of illicit proceeds and interests in enterprises. As such, RICO's aim is to take the profit out of crime. Civilly, the statute is enforced by government injunctions and private enforcement suits for treble damages and counsel fees. Here, too, RICO's goal is to make crime unprofitable; civil sanctions under RICO also encourage victims to help themselves to overcome the effects of crimes done against them.

Approximately 125 criminal RICO indictments are returned each year: 48 percent against white-collar crime; 39 percent against organized crime; and 13 percent against violent groups. About a thousand RICO suits are filed each year, principally against fraud. RICO has been widely criticized by defense attorneys and business groups. Nevertheless, RICO has had a devastating impact on political corruption, on organized crime families, and on violent-crime groups, including neo-Nazi hate groups and terrorist organizations.

BIBLIOGRAPHY

Blakey, G. Robert, and Thomas Perry. "An Analysis of the Myths that Bolster Effort to Rewrite RICO." *Vanderbilt Law Review* 43 (1990): 851–1101.
U.S. Senate. *The Federal Government's Use of the RICO Statute and Other Efforts against Organized Crime.* 101st Cong., 2d sess., 1990. S. Rept. 101-407.

G. ROBERT BLAKEY

RADICAL REPUBLICANS.
From its beginnings in the mid 1850s, the Republican party attracted a small but influential group of political abolitionists, soon known as Radicals, who took an uncompromising stand against slavery and its extension into the western territories and helped shape the party's free-labor ideology. Among the key early congressional Radicals were Senators Charles Sumner and Henry Wilson of Massachusetts, Salmon P. Chase and Benjamin F. Wade of Ohio, Zachariah Chandler of Michigan, and Representatives Thaddeus Stevens of Pennsylvania and James M. Ashley of Ohio. Joined during the war by influential representatives such as George S. Boutwell of Massachusetts, William D. Kelley of Pennsylvania, Samuel Shellabarger of Ohio, and Henry Winter Davis of Maryland, the Radicals pushed for aggressive prosecution of the war and constantly pressured President Abraham Lincoln

and their moderate congressional colleagues to add emancipation to the Union's war aims.

Advocating rigorous requirements for restoring the South to the Union, they clamored for suffrage and civil rights for the freedpeople in the early reconstruction period. Viewing President Andrew Johnson's reconstruction policy as far too lenient to ex-Confederates and offering little protection for the freedpeople, the Radicals led the congressional break with Johnson in 1866 and later spearheaded the move to impeach him. Although they were often forced to compromise with the larger moderate wing of the party, the Radicals still played a significant role in shaping reconstruction legislation, including the Thirteenth, Fourteenth, and Fifteenth Amendments. Their influence declined as northern support for further reconstruction measures and protecting the freedmen waned after 1868, and most had passed from the political scene by the early 1870s.

BIBLIOGRAPHY

Benedict, Michael Les. *A Compromise of Principle: Congressional Republicans and Reconstruction, 1863–1869.* 1974.

Trefousse, Hans L. *The Radical Republicans: Lincoln's Vanguard for Social Justice.* 1968.

TERRY L. SEIP

RADIO. *See* Press.

RAILROADS. Congress has faced some of its most persistent and perplexing problems in dealing with the railroads. For nearly a century, "the railroad question," more consistently than any other subject, epitomized major issues of economic policy and the functioning and constitutional role of Congress.

The history of Congress's handling of railroads divides into four periods: 1825 to 1850, 1850 to 1887, 1887 to 1920, and 1920 to the present. Several interrelated themes persist: the evolution of railroads from an experimental to the dominant to a declining mode of transportation, the transformation of government's role from one that was marginal and passive to that of an active and powerful force, and the development of an ever more centralized and elaborate system of regulation. Congress was both a mirror and a director of change, shaped by an ambivalent political ideology that preferred private initiative and suspected the worst of government

yet lost no opportunity to seek a helping hand from that government. As a complicated and often confused but dominant theme, railroad policy has few peers in the history of Congress and the nation.

From the outset, questions of congressional action concerning railroads have focused on assistance or regulation; notions that the federal government should manage or own railroads have been rare. In both the first and second periods, when railroads seemed harbingers of utopia and controls were anathema to enterprise, Congress dealt mostly with appeals for help. Until 1850, most of these were as small as the industry itself.

Early Years, 1825–1850. By 1850, the railroad system was well into its adolescence, but until 1850 railroad officials had had only marginal contacts with the nation's government. The meager role of Congress in this formative period reflected the pervasiveness of capitalism; the predominance of small, local enterprises without interstate commerce; fear of centralized power; and wariness of any business with monopolistic potential. The Jacksonian era was no time for a national economic policy.

In 1825, with the railroads still but a freakish toy, a House committee recommended building an experimental line in the District of Columbia; the matter went no further. Requests began trickling in, and in 1831 Congress gave the Baltimore & Ohio permission to extend a branch into Washington, granting right-of-way and setting maximum rates. The acorn of congressional aid was planted.

To midcentury, Congress sidled into this major growth industry of the century, largely through its dispatch of other business. Army engineers who had been surveying for roads and canals for military and postal use were allowed to do so for railroads as well. In 1838 the proliferating rail lines were made eligible for mail contracts, and in 1845 Congress enacted a comprehensive law on the subject. The burning issue of the tariff came to include debates over special rates for iron used in railroads, incidentally giving rise to a coherent railroad lobby in the capital.

Despite earlier funding for the Cumberland Road, direct financial aid for transportation was politically impossible after 1830. A less troublesome form of subsidy lay in the vast stretches of government land, chunks of which had been routinely set aside to support approved activities. Railroad companies found two uses for such land: rights-of-way and as an endowment to be sold or used as collateral. A number of canal companies had received land for

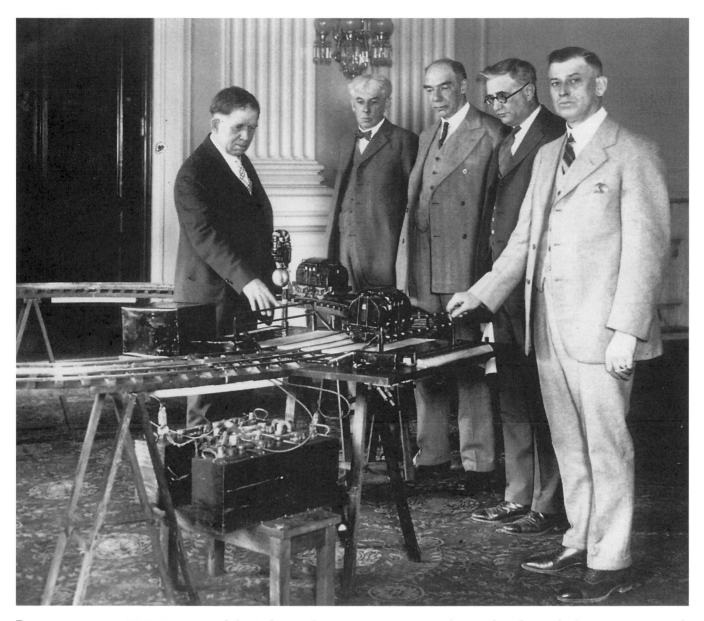

RAILROAD SAFETY. W. T. Ferguson of the Safety Railway Crossing Co., *standing within the track*, demonstrates a railroad crossing gate to members of Congress at the Capitol. *Left to right*, Representatives J. Alfred Taylor (D-W.Va.), James V. McClintic (D-Okla.), Henry R. Rathbone (R-Ill.), James French Strothers (R-W.Va.), c. 1925.

both purposes, and in 1833 Congress began to authorize the transfer of canal lands for railroad use. The railroad land grant era thus entered through a side door. Before 1850, however, this seemingly painless form of subsidy, although much requested, remained politically unacceptable for railroads in direct form. Grants of rights-of-way, more limited but very valuable, fared better, beginning with a Florida grant in 1835 and culminating in a general

right-of-way grant statute in 1852. Almost surreptitiously, the principle of encouraging railroad construction through subsidy was established.

A few people raised the idea of having the national government build and operate railroads, but in the U.S. constitutional and political milieu, the notion was doomed. The idea of a "national" project appeared seriously only in Asa Whitney's first proposal for a Pacific railroad in 1845. His plan for federal ownership and operation stirred such opposition that he soon abandoned it. By 1850, it was clear that Congress preferred to be involved with railroads only on a piecemeal basis and that its preferred mode was subsidy.

Large-scale Federal Aid, 1850–1887. With the Land Grant Act of 1850, railroads emerged as a central concern of Congress, and federal aid in their construction became the core of congressional practice. Requests for land grants had become numerous, reflecting a growing fancy for the wondrous machine and the expanding scale of new projects. As the population sprawled and sectional tensions mounted, using railroads to unify the country became ever more attractive.

The act of 1850 granted about 3.75 million acres to aid construction of a railroad from Chicago to the Gulf of Mexico. The Illinois Central and the Mobile & Ohio were to receive alternating sections of land for six miles on both sides of the track. Government and the public would benefit from the enhanced value of remaining lands and from provisions for the free transport of government traffic and the carrying of mail at rates fixed by Congress. To preserve constitutional propriety, the lands were granted to the states for transmission to the companies.

In its scale and as a precedent, the 1850 act was a landmark. The government had used its land to spur economic development and as a source of largesse for private activity. Yet the presumed general benefit to the nation seemed vague, and provisions for governmental control were perfunctory. Deference to state sovereignty was only formal, and the lobbying of private groups made Congress appear to be making policy by default rather than by initiative. Unsurprisingly, the grant to the Illinois Central invited others to seek similar favors. During

LAND GRANTS, 1878. For railroads and wagon roads, marked as shaded areas on the map of the United States.

the next seven years, Congress was persuaded to provide grants for forty additional railroad projects in ten states along the Mississippi River and the Gulf of Mexico. More than 24 million acres were offered, always through state governments.

The era of federal subsidy reached full flower in the Pacific Railway acts of 1862 and 1864. Congress had debated projects and routes for a transcontinental railroad since 1845, but regional rivalries were too strong and private pressures too weak. Although arguments over the role of government varied, nearly all assumed government would have a substantial part in so costly and risky an enterprise. Under expert pressure from burgeoning railroad interests in California, Iowa, and Kansas, the first Pacific Railway Act was adopted in 1862, after Southern contenders for the route had seceded.

The 1862 act was a definitive event in the history of railroads and congressional economic policy. As amended in 1864, it afforded legitimacy and massive government help to private economic endeavor, with perfunctory supervision of the results. The laws created the Union Pacific, the first corporation chartered by Congress since the Bank of the United States, and promised to it and to California's Central Pacific twenty sections of land and as much as $48,000 in government bonds for each mile of track. The loan was secured by a second mortgage, repayable in thirty years. Public controls were minimal: inspection of newly built track and minority membership on the Union Pacific's board of directors, devices easily manipulated by the companies. Departures from the precedents of the 1850s were striking: the Union Pacific was a federal corporation; lands were given directly to the companies; and, most notable, the government lent its credit in addition to the usual grant of land. The measure blended well with the general concept of government as a helpful auxiliary in a private-enterprise economy.

During the next few years, Congress applied most principles of the Pacific Railway acts to other comparable western projects. The land grants for the Northern Pacific (1864), Atlantic & Pacific (1866), and Texas & Pacific (1871) doubled the acreage granted per mile, but the loan of bonds was not repeated. Altogether, Congress offered more than 116 million acres for transcontinental railroads before disillusionment set in. Meanwhile, grants through the states continued until 1872.

Although the granting of subsidies stopped, its consequences lingered in political debate and congressional interest. The public became disillusioned when utopia failed to follow the track, and the size, vicissitudes, and sometimes dubious behavior of the subsidized railroads brought them under constant attack. Slipshod legislation and a government ill equipped for oversight compounded the problem. Had land-grant railroads met the conditions for receiving their lands? Would the bond-aided railroads repay their debts to the government? Members of Congress wrestled with such questions for two decades. An act of 1890 required the forfeiture of "unearned" lands. The Thurman Act in 1878 sought to force the first Pacific railroads to create a sinking fund for repaying their debt. In 1887 Congress created the Pacific Railway Commission, which produced a voluminous report that reinforced the suspicion that the government's venture in subsidizing railroads had become a burden to

"THE SENATORIAL ROUND-HOUSE." Political cartoon commenting on the influence of railroad companies in the U.S. Senate. The plaque in front of the presiding officer reads: "The Rail-Road States of America." The paper beneath the central figure's foot reads: "Beck's Bill, to prevent members of Congress from accepting fees from subsidized railroads." Wood engraving after Thomas Nast, *Harper's Weekly*, 10 July 1886.

LIBRARY OF CONGRESS

all. Meanwhile, suspicions of a government corrupted by railroads, and by its own officers, shadowed public figures and produced the century's most lurid scandal in the Crédit Mobilier affair in 1873. By 1887 the nation's railroad system was nearly complete, and Congress had played a significant, though haphazard and controversial, part. But the era of subsidy was yielding to an era of federal regulation.

Federal Regulation, 1887–1920. The Interstate Commerce Act of 1887 initiated federal regulation of railroads and the modern era of governmental economic regulation more generally. The pervasive effects of railroads generated complaints from a variety of interests, including many railroad companies, and the growing reach of the companies limited the value of state regulatory efforts. Also, the controls in the land-grant acts had been incidental and largely futile. The act of 1887 was wholly regulatory, although hesitantly so. The complexity of the subject called for a new response: an independent regulatory commission. By creating the Interstate Commerce Commission (ICC), Congress took its first step toward the formation of the modern bureaucratic state.

Mounting agitation for federal regulation since the early 1870s had yielded a host of proposals and copious information, notably the report of the Senate's Select Committee to Investigate Interstate Commerce (known as the Cullom committee) in 1886. Clashing interests combined with timidity and inexperience in federal controls to produce a law that had great importance as symbol and precedent but that was modest in its immediate effect. The law launched a generation of preoccupation with "fair" rates by requiring that all rates be "reasonable and just." It prohibited rebates to favored shippers, the pooling of traffic among railroads, and per-mile rates higher for short than for long hauls. The idea was to deter companies from devious practices by compelling them to publicize rates and report to the government. The ICC would gather information, hear complaints, and order changes in rates. It could not initiate changes or prescribe rates, and its orders depended upon the courts for enforcement. It was hardly a recipe for active control or systematic policy-making, but it led in those directions.

A hardened public suspicion of railroads, the depression of the 1890s, and the modest impact of the ICC kept the railroad question high on the political agenda and even built support for nationalizing the railroads. Further regulation was, however, incremental. In a series of laws, most notably the Hepburn Act of 1906, Congress expanded the commission's rate-making authority and created a special Commerce Court to hear appeals. Both Congress and the commission focused on rates, neglecting evidence of changes in railroading and the economy that called for greater efficiency and carrying capacity and rates sufficient to encourage investment and reward enterprise. By 1916, rate-setting had become a tangle of intricate rules and clashing interests complicated by state regulations; railroad leaders complained that their industry was being gradually suffocated.

World War I added a new calculation to the public's concern with railroads. Even before America's entry into the war, the volume of traffic and the urgency of handling it portended a breakdown. In 1916 Congress passed the Adamson Act, authorizing an eight-hour day on railroads, in order to forestall a crippling strike. With war a reality in 1917, and on authority of the Army Appropriation Act of 1916, President Woodrow Wilson proclaimed government control of the railroads late in the year. Three months later, on 21 March 1918, Congress passed the Railroad Control Act, implementing the president's action. The law provided for compensation to railroad owners, proper maintenance of the property, and its return to the owners within twenty-one months after ratification of a peace treaty. The experience that followed was instructive for the companies, the railroads, and Congress alike.

The Transportation Act of 1920 returned the railroads to "normalcy" and recast the meaning of normalcy. In the process, it illustrated a central fact of congressional life, "the ability of . . . organized business groups to utilize the political power of the federal government to solve essentially private economic problems" (K. Austin Kerr, *American Railroad Politics, 1914–1920*, 1968, p. 229). While returning the railroads to private control, the act mixed the Progressive approach to railroad regulation with ideas quite alien to prewar reformers. The principle of regulation was reaffirmed and its scope widened, with the ICC more powerful than ever. But new approaches were behind some of the added powers, such as the authority to set minimum rates and the duty to assure companies of a fair rate of return. The commission would also supervise new securities issues and review proposed mergers. With an eye to strengthening the railroad system, the act required that half of all "excess" profits be returned to the government (the so-called recapture clause) for assistance to weak companies. Most strikingly, Congress reversed its traditional

Landmark Railroad Legislation

Title	Year Enacted	Reference Number	Description
Land Grant Act of 1850	1850	9 Stat. 466	Launched policy of federal subsidy for railroad construction through grant of public lands to aid in construction of Illinois Central and Mobile and Ohio railroads.
Pacific Railway Act	1862	2 Stat. 489	Began federal encouragement of transcontinental railroad building with grant of land and credit; chartered Union Pacific.
Interstate Commerce Act	1887	24 Stat. 379	Opened era of federal regulation of railroads and independent regulatory commissions with creation of Interstate Commerce Commission.
Adamson Act	1916	39 Stat. 721	Landmark in railroad and labor legislation; authorized eight-hour day for railroad labor.
Railroad Control Act	1918	40 Stat. 451	Provided for federal management of all railroads.
Transportation Act of 1920	1920	41 Stat. 456	Postwar act returned railroads to private control and considerably expanded federal regulatory role.
Regional Rail Reorganization Act of 1973	1974	87 Stat. 986	Attempted to reverse deterioration of railroad system by merging many northeastern railroads into Conrail.
Staggers Rail Act of 1980	1980	94 Stat. 1895	Endorsed competition as the preferred policy for railroads; substantially eased restrictions on rates, mergers, and abandonment of lines.

fondness for competition by directing the commission to plan for consolidation of railroads into a few systems. Wartime experience and the chaotic results of earlier regulation had created a new regulatory order.

Decline and Deregulation after 1920. In the years after 1920, the railroad question steadily drifted away from center stage. This does not mean that regulatory questions had been satisfactorily resolved. Indeed, the micromanagement that Congress prescribed in 1920 appears to have played a significant part in the gradual decline of the railroads. It proved too inflexible, inhibiting of entrepreneurial energy, and vulnerable to political pressure to accommodate the changes necessary. The rise of less-regulated competition from trucks, buses, automobiles, airplanes, and water-borne traffic required the railroads to adapt, but they were hampered by the regulatory system. The government-by-experts that Congress prescribed in 1887 and elaborated through 1920 proved inadequate to its task.

Congress adjusted its policies but did so hesitantly, still haunted by the old image of railroads as predatory monopolies. New laws in 1935 and 1940 brought highway and water carriers under federal control in principle, but regulation was applied selectively and failed to offset the advantages of nearly free thoroughfares supplied by government. World War II brought no repetition of government operation, but by midcentury the railroads, alone among modes of commercial transport, remained tightly regulated.

Since then, regulatory policy has been substantially modified. The Transportation Act of 1958 moved cautiously toward deregulation, and during the decade starting in 1971 Congress moved dramatically to dismantle the regulatory system. The creation of Amtrak in 1971 and Conrail in 1973 sought to salvage passenger service and a segment of freight traffic through subsidized, publicly owned corporations. A 1976 law offered greater flexibility in setting rates, effecting mergers, and abandoning burdensome routes. The Staggers Rail Act of 1980 made the most striking changes. It embraced competition as the preferred policy, lifted most restrictions on rates, and greatly liberalized rules for mergers and abandonment. Regulatory policy was returning to its hands-off origins.

Relations between Congress and the railroads have in many respects mirrored American politics and congressional behavior. Largely reactive to private activity, Congress successively moved through indifference, generosity, near-punitive control, and reluctant permissiveness. It has played a significant role both in fostering and in complicating the development of railroads as a central feature of the economic life of the United States.

[*See also* Hepburn Act; Interstate Commerce Act; Pacific Railroad Acts; Transportation.]

BIBLIOGRAPHY

Keeler, Theodore E. *Railroads, Freight, and Public Policy.* 1983.

Martin, Albro. *Railroads Triumphant: Railroads and the Transformation of American Society.* 1991.

Mercer, Lloyd J. *Railroads and Land Grant Policy: A Study in Government Intervention.* 1982.

Skowronek, Stephen. *Building a New American State: The Expansion of National Administrative Capacities, 1877–1920.* 1982.

WALLACE D. FARNHAM

RANDALL, SAMUEL J. (1828–1890), Democratic representative from Pennsylvania, Speaker of the House (1876–1881). A native Philadelphian, he was first elected to Congress in 1863 after a decade in state politics; he retained his House seat until his death. During the Civil War and Reconstruction eras, Randall, a committed unionist, gained national prominence for his opposition to Radical Republicanism. By 1875 he had captured control of the Democratic party in Pennsylvania and expected his

SAMUEL J. RANDALL.   *PERLEY'S REMINISCENCES,* VOL. 2

national and state reputations to propel him to the speakership that year, but an urban-agrarian split in the party's ranks caused the position to go to Michael C. Kerr of Indiana. When Kerr died in 1876, Randall was the party's overwhelming choice to replace him for the second session of the 44th Congress, and he continued as Speaker for the next two Congresses, serving a total of five years in that role.

Because of his parliamentary skills Randall brought increased power to the speakership. Although James G. Blaine (R-Maine) had earlier extended the prestige of the office, Randall undertook a systematic revision of the rules of the House. In reducing the overlapping 166 rules to 45 he provided the Speaker with additional powers that were a springboard to the Reed Rules of 1890.

Randall's revision converted the Rules Committee to a standing committee with the stipulation that all changes had to be referred to it in advance of enactment, and by interpretation he established the Speaker's right of recognition. He was challenged when he introduced the practice of recognizing committee chairmen in preference to all others, but he maintained that a Speaker's ruling was as absolute in House procedures as the judgment of the Supreme Court in interpreting a law.

Given his service on committees such as Rules, Appropriations (as chairman), and Banking and Currency and his five years as Speaker, Randall seemed destined for national leadership in the Democratic party, but he was sidetracked by the tariff issue. He was a leading candidate for the presidential nomination in 1884 but was bypassed in favor of Grover Cleveland. When Cleveland carried the general election, Randall cooperated with the administration until the president's 1887 message calling for "a tariff for revenue only."

Although they had tilted toward such a policy since the Civil War, the Democrats had avoided a clear-cut statement on the tariff. They feared that it would become disruptive because the party included pockets of protectionism, of which Pennsylvania was one. Since his arrival in Congress, Randall had always endorsed at least moderate protection. When it became necessary to line up on one side of the issue or the other, he declared his unwavering commitment to protectionism. His views on the tariff go far in explaining his success as a Democrat in a Republican state and city; during his entire congressional tenure he was the only Democrat elected to Congress from Philadelphia.

After a two-year hiatus the Democrats regained

control of the House in 1883. Randall was again considered for the speakership but was passed over in favor of John G. Carlisle of Kentucky, largely because of Randall's protectionist stand. Randall preferred not to sacrifice the policy of his state for personal acclaim at the national level. His subsequent refusal to acquiesce in Cleveland's tariff dictum was further proof of this determination. Thereafter, the administration directed state patronage away from Randall, and his prestige within the party was in decline at the time of his death.

BIBLIOGRAPHY

House, Albert V. "The Contributions of Samuel J. Randall to the Rules of the National House of Representatives." *American Political Science Quarterly* 29 (1935): 837–841.

House, Albert V. "The Political Career of Samuel Jackson Randall." Ph.D. diss., University of Wisconsin, 1934.

House, Albert V. "The Speakership Contest of 1875: Democratic Response to Power." *Journal of American History* 52 (1965): 252–274.

JAMES A. KEHL

JOHN RANDOLPH. Randolph's contemporary Ben Perley Poore wrote that the senator "used to enter the Senate Chamber wearing a pair of silver spurs, carrying a heavy riding-whip, and followed by a favorite hound, which crouched beneath his desk."

PERLEY'S REMINISCENCES, VOL. 1

RANDOLPH, JOHN (1773–1833), representative and senator from Virginia, early defender of southern nationalism. John Randolph of Roanoke was born into a great Virginia planter family, which was at once a burden and a source of pride to him. His political career stretched from the administration of Thomas Jefferson to that of Andrew Jackson. His political principles, an old-fashioned variant of English country Whiggery, remained nearly intact throughout. His was a voice of opposition temperamentally unsuited to party government. Randolph became his generation's most committed (and at times shrill) voice of the slaveholding South, a voice deeply mistrustful of the nationalist and expansionist imperatives of the mainstream. He insisted on calling himself "of Roanoke," an attachment to estates evoking the English country gentry and classical detachment of the public and private.

Randolph first stood for Congress in 1799, making a name for himself by publicly debating the formidable Patrick Henry. He won the sixth congressional district, a seat he would hold until 1813. Republicans around him expected Randolph to enter the ranks of the Jeffersonian majority. In 1800, at the age of twenty-eight, he was made chair of the Committee on Ways and Means, a pivotal committee for the new administration.

Randolph soon broke with Jefferson and his secretary of State James Madison. Randolph's distrustful nature was not suited to the compromises necessary for day-to-day legislation. He stood for the defense of ordered liberty and opposed power accruing to government; he shared none of the Jefferson administration's new emphasis on democracy. A fiery, witty, and often caustic speaker, Randolph held a deep mistrust of accrued power and looked with suspicion, bordering on paranoia, at those who opposed him politically. In Congress he soon drew attention for his attacks on a standing army and his criticisms of Jefferson's negotiations with Spain over Florida as an undue exercise of executive power. Although he supported the Louisiana Purchase, Randolph opposed a $2 million appropriation for Spain, which he called a bribe. Relations with Jefferson and Madison worsened after Randolph's disastrous handling of Federalist justice Samuel Chase's prosecution in 1805. In 1806 Randolph began to publish his "Decius" letters in a Richmond paper, openly attacking what he considered to be the dangerously democratic tendencies of the Jeffersonian coalition. Randolph called himself a tertium quid and gathered around him a small circle of southerners ("the quids") disaffected from Jefferson.

Randolph opposed Jefferson's embargo and the War of 1812 and mistrusted western expansion as dangerous to the South's interests. His antiwar stance cost him his congressional seat in 1813, but he was returned in 1815. He sat in the House from 1815 to 1817 and from 1819 to 1825 and then in the Senate from 1825 to 1827. He followed a consistent path of opposition to economic nationalism and the expansion of the national government, opposing the second Bank of the United States, the tariff, and internal improvements.

Randolph's political career took a second turn in the 1820s. During the Missouri controversy he emerged as a leading spokesman for southern sectionalism. Angered at Henry Clay's defection to the hated John Quincy Adams in 1824, Randolph fought a duel against the southern nationalist in April 1826. In his state's constitutional convention of 1828 to 1830 Randolph led the conservatives of eastern Virginia against western forces seeking a more democratic constitution. Initially a supporter of Andrew Jackson, he soon broke with the president over a perceived aggrandizement of executive power. He disagreed with Jackson's proclamation of force against South Carolina, although he did not support John C. Calhoun's doctrine of nullification either.

In his last two years, Randolph was in all probability insane. A tormented slaveholder, during his dementia he abused his slaves, to whom he ordinarily was kind. Randolph died in Philadelphia on 24 May 1833.

BIBLIOGRAPHY

Adams, Henry. *John Randolph.* 1896.
Dawidoff, Robert. *The Education of John Randolph.* 1979.
Kirk, Russell J. *John Randolph of Roanoke.* 1978.

JOHN F. WALSH

JEANNETTE RANKIN. First woman member of Congress.
LIBRARY OF CONGRESS

RANKIN, JEANNETTE (1880–1973), the first woman elected to the U.S. Congress and the only member to vote against entering both World War I and World War II. Rankin (R-Mont.) was first elected in 1916, four years before the Nineteenth Amendment gave women the right to vote. At that time, Montana was one of several western states that had already enfranchised women.

An activist in the movement for women's suffrage, Rankin also worked for international peace, an eight-hour workday for women, tax-law reform, stronger national defense, legislation for children's rights, and the prohibition of alcoholic beverages. Rankin lost her seat in 1919, a victim of redistricting and of her own highly unconventional views. Her career in Congress then suffered a twenty-five-year hiatus between the world wars. Before her reelection in 1940, she pursued her political interests as an advocate and lobbyist for peace and consumer groups.

Rankin acquired notoriety as the only member of Congress to oppose both world wars. When she cast the only vote against World War II, the Capitol police had to protect her from the patriotic fervor of bystanders so she could return to her offices unharmed. "America should be ready to defend its own shores, but foreign wars are no part of the American way of life," she asserted. The pressures on Rankin were so intense after this dissenting vote that her second term was said to have ended, for all practical purposes, the day the Japanese bombed Pearl Harbor.

In 1968, Rankin led several thousand women in a demonstration on the steps of the Capitol to protest the Vietnam War. In her honor, the group was called the Jeannette Rankin brigade.

BIBLIOGRAPHY

Tolchin, Susan J. *Women in Congress.* 1976.

SUSAN J. TOLCHIN

RAYBURN, SAM (1882–1961), representative from Texas, chairman of the Committee on Interstate and Foreign Commerce (1931–1937), Democratic floor leader (1937–1940, 1947–1949, and 1953–1955), and Speaker of the House (1940–1947, 1949–1953, and 1955–1961). Samuel Taliaferro Rayburn demonstrated exceptional skill as a lawmaker and leader almost from the day he entered the House on 4 March 1913. He rose through hard work and the seniority system to become one of the most powerful and respected of all House Speakers. His forty-eight years, eight months, and twelve days of continuous House service exceeded that of any predecessor.

The eighth of William and Martha Rayburn's eleven children, he was born in Roane County, Tennessee, on 6 January 1882. He was five years old when his parents joined the great migration to Texas. Settling in rural Fannin County, north of Dallas, the Rayburns established a forty-acre cotton farm, on which all the children worked. Rayburn's interest in politics was kindled early and, in part, grew out of his esteem for his own congressman, the brilliant and imperious Joseph W. Bailey. After attending East Texas Normal College for two years and teaching locally for three years, he was elected at age twenty-four to the Texas House of Representatives. He served three two-year terms, the last term as Speaker. In 1912, he was elected U.S. representative in Texas's 4th Congressional District.

Committee Years. One of 270 House Democrats elected in the Wilson landslide, Rayburn was named to the active and prestigious House Committee on Interstate and Foreign Commerce. His years on the Texas legislature's Common Carriers Committee, which dealt with railroad regulation, helped him grasp quickly the broad range of federal regulatory issues upon which his House committee was beginning to focus in 1913.

The freshman earnestly attended committee sessions, did his homework, and soon caught the eye

SAM RAYBURN.   SAM RAYBURN LIBRARY

of Chairman William C. Adamson. Despite his junior status, he was invited in 1913 to author one of President Woodrow Wilson's priority bills, a measure to regulate the sale of railroad stocks and bonds. Wilson, having second thoughts about the bill, later asked Rayburn to put it aside. The young lawmaker refused. Defiantly, he continued to seek the bill's enactment, winning respect for his tenacity but angering Wilson and prompting the president to support Rayburn's electoral opponent in 1916.

In 1917, Rayburn sponsored the War Risk Insurance Act, which reformed a chaotic veterans' pension system. His skillful handling of debate on the measure won the approval of House leaders, who declared him a rising star and began inviting him to after-hours gatherings in their Capitol hideaways. Rayburn later attributed much of his success to the informal tutoring of senior colleagues, such as Chairman William C. Adamson and fellow Texan John Nance Garner, whose trust and loyalty he cultivated. When he became a House leader, Rayburn also encouraged promising young members, often inviting them to his own after-hours "Board of Education." They in turn gave him devoted and valuable service as his lieutenants.

Although he had no major role in legislative battles during the period of Republican control of the House from 1919 through 1931, Rayburn continued to win reelection and to advance in seniority. In December 1931, with the return of a Democratic majority in the House, he was elevated to chairman of the Interstate and Foreign Commerce Committee.

From 1933 to 1937, Rayburn's committee handled many of President Franklin D. Roosevelt's most urgent and controversial New Deal proposals. He personally managed a succession of bills to regulate the securities industry, a targeted villain of the Depression. The ensuing legislative battles, among the fiercest ever seen in Congress, pitted the farm-reared, meagerly educated Texan against some of the ablest lawyers, accountants, publicists, and lobbyists that Wall Street could enlist.

Unwilling to accept the White House's hastily drafted bills, Rayburn scrutinized and rewrote each measure sent to his committee. He insisted that all such legislation meet his high standards for precision, fairness, and enforceability, and he so instructed the team of young New Deal lawyers, headed by brilliant Benjamin V. Cohen and Thomas G. Corcoran, who helped him draft the bills' final language.

Between 1933 and 1937 Rayburn coauthored six major New Deal laws: the Emergency Railroad Transportation Act of 1933; the Truth-in-Securities Act of 1933; the Stock Exchange Act of 1934 (which created the Securities and Exchange Commission); the Federal Communications Act of 1934 (which created the Federal Communications Commission); the Public Utility Holding Company Act of 1935; and the Rural Electrification Act of 1936.

Majority Leader. The death of Speaker Henry T. Rainey in 1934 provided Rayburn an opportunity to seek the office that since childhood had been his life's goal. Letting ambition overwhelm his characteristic patience, he challenged the heir-apparent, Democratic majority leader Joseph W. Byrns, for the vacant speakership and was soundly beaten. He did not repeat the mistake when Speaker Byrns died in 1936. Rather than contest Majority Leader William B. Bankhead's claim on the higher office, he ran to succeed Bankhead as majority leader and in January 1937 was elected over the odds-on favorite, Rules Committee chairman John J. O'Connor.

Rayburn proved ill suited for the role of floor leader. Although a forceful speaker, he lacked the verbal agility and zest for partisan combat that the job requires. His own loyalty to Roosevelt never wavered, but he could not control other party members who were increasingly rebellious of the president's dominance. During his four years as Democratic leader, commanding in 1937 and 1938 the most lopsided party majority since 1867 (331 Democrats to 89 Republicans), the House was noted for its unruliness and sparse accomplishment. He tried but could not sell Roosevelt's plan to enlarge the Supreme Court. His inability in 1937 to produce votes for a wage-and-hour bill resulted in the president's worst House defeat.

Speaker. Where Rayburn excelled was in presiding over the House, which, because of Speaker Bankhead's frequent illnesses, he was often required to do. His innate fairness, coupled with his broad and growing knowledge of the House rules and precedents, made him a popular and effective presiding officer. In 1939 he was named Speaker pro tempore. He also continued to serve as majority leader. The double duty was arduous and exhausting, but it uniquely prepared him to succeed Bankhead, who died on 15 September 1940. The next day, the House unanimously elected Rayburn as its forty-second Speaker.

His first interval as Speaker lasted until 3 January 1947. He presided for much of that time over a quarrelsome and divided House. Prior to World War II, Rayburn led House efforts to enact President Roosevelt's war-preparedness agenda. In January 1941 his strict interpretation of the House's germaneness rule thwarted isolationists seeking to cripple FDR's lend-lease bill authorizing the first of a series of transfers of U.S. weapons to beseiged European nations. The following August, in a masterful display of parliamentary skill and raw power, Rayburn battled for enactment of Joint Resolution 290, a politically unpopular measure to extend the draft. After one of the House's most dramatic roll calls, the resolution was passed, 203 to 202. Its defeat would have forced much of the army to disband barely four months before the Japanese attack on Pearl Harbor.

Rayburn's leadership was repeatedly tested during World War II as a brief period of House unity at the war's onset yielded to a new era of contention in 1943. Republicans, strengthened in the 1942 elections, joined with southern Democrats to form an effective majority that dealt Rayburn and Roosevelt one defeat after another. Significantly, a conservative coalition controlled the Rules Committee, where two southern Democrats often voted with four Republicans to prevent administration bills from reaching the House floor.

Still, under Rayburn's prodding, the House gave

Roosevelt most of the wartime laws he sought. *Time* magazine, in a 27 September 1943 cover article on Rayburn, praised him as "the great compromiser"—the best since Henry Clay. Rayburn, however, expressed disappointment at his failure to speed war appropriations and to curb conservative attacks on unpopular wartime agencies. Following the election of a Republican majority in 1946, he surrendered the speakership to Joseph W. Martin, Jr., of Massachusetts and stepped into an unaccustomed new role as leader of the minority party. His performance as minority leader from 1947 to 1949 won him the *Collier's* Award for distinguished service to the nation.

The Democratic sweep of Congress and the presidency in 1948 brought Rayburn his second tenure as Speaker, lasting from 3 January 1949 to 3 January 1953. He continued to serve as the Truman administration's chief House advocate, often hammering out compromises to salvage Fair Deal bills. To thwart his old nemesis, the Rules Committee, he supported the so-called twenty-one-day rule, a procedural change that allowed committee chairmen, under certain conditions, to bypass the Rules Committee and bring bills directly to the House floor. After two years, Rayburn decided that the new rule created more problems than it solved and joined in rescinding it.

After another two-year interval as minority leader in 1953 and 1954, Rayburn began his final period as Speaker on 5 January 1955. For the first time leading a Democratic-controlled House in a Republican administration—and with the Senate also under Democratic control—he sought to avoid the political stalemate often associated with divided government. He was joined by Senate Democratic leader Lyndon B. Johnson, a fellow Texan and a Rayburn protégé, in declaring a suspension of partisan criticism of Republican foreign policy. His views on the limits of partisanship were deep-seated. While reserving the right to oppose the administration's domestic programs, he said the nation must speak internationally with only one voice—the president's.

His quest for a bipartisan foreign policy occasionally took extreme forms, as when he publicly rebuked Democrat Henry S. Reuss in 1958 for a speech faulting President Dwight D. Eisenhower's decision to land troops in Lebanon. Until the Lebanon crisis subsided, Rayburn declared, he no longer would recognize House members "to talk about foreign affairs." Despite objections from Democratic National Chairman Paul Butler and others, who argued that no presidential decisions should be off limits to examination by the opposing party, Rayburn and Johnson kept Democratic criticism of Eisenhower's foreign policy to a minimum through the 1950s.

In 1961, pressure from restless liberals, heightened by the election of a new Democratic president, finally forced Sam Rayburn to challenge the conservative-dominated Rules Committee, long notorious as a graveyard for progressive initiatives. The resulting clash of two determined septuagenarians—Rayburn and Rules chairman Howard W. Smith of Virginia—was epic and conclusive. In the end, by a five-vote margin, the House accepted Rayburn's proposal to enlarge the committee and thereby destroy the conservatives' slender majority.

It was to be his final battle. On 12 June 1961, he completed sixteen years and 273 days as Speaker, doubling Henry Clay's record. A few weeks later, his health began to fail. He declined rapidly and died of cancer on 16 November 1961.

Place in History. "Mr. Sam," as he was widely known, stood 5 feet 6 inches, and was, for many years, totally bald. He had an expressive face with hot brown eyes that flashed when he was angry. Basically shy, with simple tastes, he seldom sought credit or publicity. The House was his life and, as he often said, his love. He was little known outside of Washington and his district until television coverage of the Democratic National Convention, over which he presided in 1948, 1952, and 1956, made him a national celebrity. As a result, he has never received adequate recognition for his contributions, particularly as an architect of the New Deal.

He refused to be labeled a liberal or a conservative. "Call me a progressive conservative, or a conservative progressive—just be sure the word 'progressive' is in there," he would say. Reversing the usual pattern, he grew more progressive as he advanced in years. After a lifetime of countenancing racial segregation, he provided the essential support that helped bring about the Civil Rights Act of 1957, the first civil rights law in eighty years.

In his later years, Rayburn was a legend unto himself, viewed by many Americans as the embodiment of the House and principal guardian of its traditions and prerogatives. The orientation of each new House member in the 1950s and early 1960s included Rayburn's gentle discourse on their responsibilities to their constituents and the House. His philosophy, which over the years he had distilled into an assortment of pithy truisms, stressed honesty, discretion, cooperation, and diligence. Savored by old and new members alike, these Rayburnisms, as they were known, contained a wealth of practical political advice:

Any new member who wants to stay here a long time must keep in mind that he has two constituencies: the people who sent him here and the colleagues with whom he must serve.

A man doesn't have to be brilliant to make a success here. All you need is a reasonable amount of intelligence and the willpower to tend to your own business.

The fellow who jabbers all the time gets no attention. If he gives the House some meat when he speaks, the members will quiet down and listen.

I found out early in life that I never have to explain anything I haven't said.

Legislation should never be designed to punish anyone.

In this House, the people who get along the best, go along the most.

One of the wisest things ever said was, "Wait a minute."

A politician has got to have publicity to live, but he can damn well get too much of it.

There are no degrees of honesty; a man is either honest or he isn't.

When pressed, as in 1941 and 1961, Rayburn did not flinch from using the full powers of his office. But he was never a tyrant in the mold of Thomas B. Reed or Joseph G. Cannon. His leadership style, by and large, was one of quiet persuasion, combined with patience and a willingness to compromise. He relied on friends in both major parties and on his own persuasive powers, enhanced by an unblemished reputation for fairness, loyalty, and integrity. As a powerful, innovative Speaker, he ranked with Clay, Reed, and Cannon. As a master legislator, leader, and all-around House member, he arguably has had no equal.

BIBLIOGRAPHY

Champagne, Anthony. *Congressman Sam Rayburn.* 1984.
Dorough, C. Dwight. *Mr. Sam.* 1962.
Dulaney, H. G., and Edward Hake Phillips. *Speak, Mr. Speaker.* 1978.
Hardeman, D. B., and Donald C. Bacon. *Rayburn: A Biography.* 1987.
Mooney, Booth. *Roosevelt and Rayburn.* 1971.
Steinberg, Alfred. *Sam Rayburn: A Biography.* 1975.

DONALD C. BACON

RAYBURN-WHEELER ACT. *See* Wheeler-Rayburn Public Utility Holding Company Act.

REAGAN, JOHN H. (1818–1905), Democratic representative and senator from Texas, postmaster general of the Confederacy, first chairman of the Texas Railroad Commission, and coauthor of the Interstate Commerce Act. Born in Tennessee, John Henninger Reagan migrated to Texas in 1839. He served briefly as a judge and in the state legislature before being elected to the 35th and 36th Congresses (1857–1861). He advocated a stronger defense of the frontier, asking for five additional regiments to protect Texas. Like many southern Democrats, Reagan supported the Buchanan administration's stand in behalf of the Lecompton constitution. He supported Texas's secession from the Union, and resigned from Congress on 15 January 1861.

From 1861 to 1865, Reagan served as postmaster general of the Confederacy. Together with Jefferson Davis, he was captured by Union troops near Abbeville, Georgia, in May 1865, and was imprisoned at Fort Warren in Boston Harbor for five months. After receiving amnesty in 1874, Reagan ran for Congress and was easily elected. He supported government economy by advocating civil service reform as well as opposing exorbitant mail-carrying fees by railroads. He favored low tariffs, the remonetization of silver, and river and harbor improvements. As chairman of the House Committee on Commerce from 1877 to 1887 (except in the 47th Congress), Reagan played a major role in the drafting and passage of the Interstate Commerce Act, although the final bill was less rigorous than his initial proposal.

On 31 January 1887 Reagan was elected to the U.S. Senate. In the 51st Congress (1889–1891) he introduced bills providing for unlimited coinage of silver, regulation of trusts, and irrigation and settlement of arid lands in New Mexico and Texas, and he vigorously opposed the McKinley Tariff Act. He resigned from the Senate on 23 April 1891 upon accepting appointment to the newly formed Texas Railroad Commission.

BIBLIOGRAPHY

Procter, Ben H. *Not Without Honor: The Life of John H. Reagan.* 1962.

BEN PROCTER

REAGAN, RONALD W. (1911–), 40th president of the United States and conservative political leader, noted for his anticommunist views but also for signing the first treaty that reduced U.S.-Soviet nuclear arsenals. Ronald Wilson Reagan followed a unique path from Hollywood to the White House. He redefined the nation's political agenda in his eight years as president (1981–1989), during which he displayed considerable skill at mobilizing public opinion to persuade Congress to pass his budget and tax reduction proposals. But Reagan failed to persuade the American people or Congress that providing military aid to anticommunist rebels in Nicaragua, known as the Contras, was in the national interest. His success with Congress declined in the final years of his second term after his influence was weakened by revelations that he had approved secret U.S. arms sales to Iran in an effort to free American hostages in Lebanon.

He was born in Tampico, Illinois, the son of an itinerant shoe salesman and a devout mother who encouraged his early interest in dramatics. The significant political influence on Reagan's early life was President Franklin D. Roosevelt, whose administration rescued his family from poverty by providing work for his father and brother during the Depression. Reagan became an ardent Democrat and patterned his later radio speeches after Roosevelt's "fireside chats." After working as a sports announcer in Des Moines, Reagan in 1937 moved to Hollywood, where he launched a successful film career that included a critically acclaimed role in *Kings Row* (1942). Reagan made training films for the army during World War II, then plunged into union activity for the Screen Actors Guild, which he served as president for six years. Hollywood was then a target of investigations by the House Committee on Un-American Activities. Reagan, who had briefly belonged to two organizations that were communist-influenced, cooperated with the Federal Bureau of Investigation. While initially critical of the House committee's disregard for civil liberties, he helped the Screen Actors Guild implement a blacklist of actors who refused to cooperate.

As late as 1950, Reagan was a prospective Democratic candidate for an open House seat, but was rejected by the Los Angeles County Democratic Central Committee on the grounds that he was too liberal. But his politics were changing. Reagan's film income had made him wealthy, and he increasingly resented federal income taxes, then at historically high peacetime levels. His conservatism deepened after he became the spokesman for General Electric and host of its weekly television program, "General Electric Theater" (1954–1962). In an unusual political apprenticeship, Reagan toured GE plants throughout the country, developing a speech with an antigovernment theme. Eventually, Reagan became too controversial for GE, which fired him.

By now, he was an avowed conservative. In 1960, Reagan supported a Republican presidential candidate for the first time, backing Richard M. Nixon against John F. Kennedy. In 1962, he changed his voter registration to Republican. On 27 October 1964, he made his political debut on national television, on behalf of Republican presidential candidate Barry Goldwater, with a rousing partisan version of his GE speech. Goldwater lost in a landslide, but Reagan became a national hero to conservatives. Largely discounted by Democrats, Reagan ran in 1966 for governor of California and defeated two-term incumbent Governor Edmund G. (Pat) Brown by nearly one million votes.

The eight years Reagan spent in Sacramento, where Democrats controlled both houses of the legislature for all but two years, shaped the strategy and style he would later use in dealing with Congress. Legislators tended to dismiss Reagan as a celebrity who gave rousing speeches but knew little about governance. Reagan, in turn, was suspicious of the professional politicians in the legislature. Relatively little was accomplished during his first term. But after Reagan was reelected in 1970, he showed a pragmatic willingness to negotiate that he credited to his experience with the Screen Actors Guild. He also displayed considerable skill in using his popularity to pressure legislators. "I made them see the light by making them feel the heat," he often said. In his second term, Reagan and Democratic legislative leaders negotiated significant welfare reform and tax legislation.

Reagan ran abortively for president in 1968, before Nixon was nominated and elected. After Nixon was forced to resign over the Watergate scandal, Reagan opposed President Gerald R. Ford for the Republican nomination in 1976. While Reagan's challenge fell short, he made such a strong showing that he easily won the nomination in 1980. He defeated President Jimmy Carter in an election that also gave Republicans control of the Senate.

Reagan had pledged during the campaign to cut income tax rates, increase military spending, and balance the federal budget—promises that independent candidate John B. Anderson said could be accomplished only "with mirrors." Democrats were even more skeptical. When Reagan arrived in Washington, House Speaker Thomas P. (Tip) O'Neill, Jr., warned him that he had reached "the big leagues," where bills would move less swiftly than in Sacramento. But Reagan rallied public support for his policies and was so popular in the districts of southern Democratic House members known as "boll weevils" that it was difficult for them to oppose him. With considerable help from the "two Bakers"—White House chief of staff James A. Baker and Senate majority leader Howard H. Baker—Reagan won congressional approval of his

RONALD REAGAN. As president, addressing Republican senators in the White House, October 1981. Photograph by Michael Evans, the White House.   COURTESY OF THE RONALD REAGAN LIBRARY

major proposals: a huge reduction in income tax rates and a budget bill that vastly boosted military spending.

Reagan's talents as a performer and communicator were his strong suit in politics. Following the pattern he had established in Sacramento, he dealt with Congress by staking out a strong public position and making television and radio speeches designed to pressure vulnerable members. Typically, he then compromised and presented the result as a victory. But Reagan also used his charm and storytelling proclivities to establish personal relations with Democratic leaders of Congress, including O'Neill and Rep. Dan Rostenkowski (D-Ill.), chairman of the House Ways and Means Committee. He worked with these Democrats and a Republican-controlled Senate that usually backed Reagan on big-ticket items to produce the Tax Reform Act of 1986, which matched the budget bills as the most important domestic legislation of the Reagan years.

Paradoxically, Reagan's success with Congress may have undermined his presidency by producing an economic legacy that is widely viewed as his greatest failing in the White House. The tax cuts and military spending increases were not offset by comparable reductions in domestic spending, and the budget deficit soared out of control. Though he made some highly publicized spending cuts, Reagan was unwilling to take the political risk of trying to brake the growth of Social Security or other popular entitlement programs with built-in and escalating costs. He never once submitted a budget plan that could raise the money to pay for the programs he thought necessary, and the budgets passed by Congress made additional cuts that compounded the problem. Reagan's faith that the tax cuts would spur economic activity to such an extent that the government would receive added revenues from lower rates proved unfounded. As a result, the national debt nearly tripled during the Reagan presidency, the trade deficit quadrupled, and the United States became a debtor nation. This legacy of debt and deficits overshadowed the economic accomplishments of the Reagan years, which included a substantially lower inflation rate and the longest peacetime recovery in history.

In the midst of this recovery Reagan proclaimed that it was "morning again in America," and he was reelected in 1984 over Democratic candidate Walter F. Mondale in a forty-nine–state landslide. But Reagan proposed few new programs in his second term except for the 1986 tax reform bill. He did, however, succeed in winning congressional approval over protectionist opposition of a free trade agreement with Canada that he saw as the first step toward a hemispheric trading block that included Mexico. Reagan's ability to influence Congress on domestic issues dwindled after 1986, when Democrats regained control of the Senate, and Reagan's popularity declined during investigations into the Iran-contra scandal. Democrats, including some who had gone along with Reagan during the first term, accused the administration of systematic deception in its effort to circumvent the congressional ban on military aid to the Contras.

Nonetheless, the final years of the Reagan presidency were fruitful ones for U.S.-Soviet relations, which were badly frayed during the first term. Reagan, who in 1983 had denounced the Soviet Union as "the focus of evil," formed a constructive relationship with Mikhail Gorbachev after Gorbachev became Soviet leader in 1985. They held five summits and in 1987 signed the Intermediate Nuclear Forces (INF) treaty, the first U.S.-Soviet pact to reduce nuclear arsenals. Reagan's reputation as an anticommunist was so unassailable that he was able to prevail easily over conservative opposition to the treaty, which was overwhelmingly ratified by the Senate. The INF treaty marked what Reagan called a "new era" in U.S.–Soviet relations and contributed significantly to the end of the Cold War.

BIBLIOGRAPHY

Anderson, Martin. *Revolution: The Reagan Legacy.* 1990.
Cannon, Lou. *President Reagan: The Role of a Lifetime.* 1991.
Stockman, David A. *The Triumph of Politics: How the Reagan Revolution Failed.* 1986.

LOU CANNON

REALIGNMENTS. *See* Alignments and Realignments.

RECESS. *For discussion of adjournment and recess in the House and Senate, see* Adjournment and Recess.

RECESS APPOINTMENTS. Under Article II, section 2 of the Constitution, the president has the power to "fill up Vacancies that may happen during the Recess of the Senate, by granting Commissions which shall expire at the End of their next Session." The Framers empowered the president to make recess appointments, without Senate confirmation, because they anticipated long periods each year when Congress would be in adjournment.

In recent decades congressional sessions have expanded to fill most of the year. As a consequence, presidents make far fewer recess appointments now than in the early days of the Republic. In fact, the principal purpose of recess appointments now is to circumvent the confirmation process. Between 1981 and 1984, for example, Ronald Reagan made more than ten recess appointments to the board of directors of the Legal Services Corporation. Generally, these were individuals whose conservative views would have generated substantial Senate opposition to their nominations.

The ambiguous phrase "Vacancies that may happen during the Recess of the Senate" was long a subject of controversy. Did it mean simply vacancies that may occur during a recess, or all vacancies that happen to exist during a recess even though they may have occurred while the Senate was in session? Since James Madison's time, despite Senate opposition, presidents have given the constitutional language a broad construction and used recess appointments to fill any existing vacancies. A U.S. Court of Appeals supported the broader interpretation in an important 1962 decision, *United States v. Alloco.*

BIBLIOGRAPHY

Congressional Quarterly Inc. *Congress and the Nation.* Vol. 6: 1981–1984. 1985.
Corwin, Edward S. *The Constitution and What It Means Today.* 1978.

G. CALVIN MACKENZIE

RECOGNITION. The Speaker of the House's power of recognition derives from clause 2 of House Rule XIV, which states, "When two or more Members rise at once, the Speaker shall name the Member who is first to speak. . . ." This rule was adopted in 1789, the first year of Congress; and its origins may be traced to Section XVII of Thomas Jefferson's *Manual of Parliamentary Practice.*

In the early days of the House, following adoption of clause 2 of Rule XIV, business proceeded upon recognition by the Speaker of individual members. During this time, the Speaker simply recognized the first member to rise to his feet. In the early nineteenth century, as the membership and work load of the House increased, it became necessary to establish and adhere to a fixed order of business. Rule XXIV, adopted in 1811, was an early attempt by the House to establish a schedule for House business. Rule XXIV necessarily affects recognition practice, requiring that the Speaker recognize certain types of business before others. Nevertheless, in practice, Rule XXIV does not bind the House to a daily routine and, in fact, allows the House considerable freedom to schedule matters it deems most important.

As legislation in the nineteenth and twentieth centuries continued to grow in volume and complexity, the House Committee on Rules evolved as the primary tool of the House democratic leadership to schedule legislation. The Rules Committee makes certain legislation in order and establishes procedures governing its consideration by reporting to the House a special order of business. The Speaker has a close relationship to the Rules Committee, recommending Rules Committee nominees directly to the Democratic caucus and suggesting to the Rules Committee which measures to make in order. Furthermore, the Speaker retains authority to schedule a measure because clause 1 of Rule XXIII gives the Speaker discretion to determine when to proceed to the consideration of a measure recommended to be made in order by the Rules Committee (after the recommendation is adopted by the House). Thus, the Speaker's power of scheduling is derived not only from his Rule XIV power of recognition but also from his close relationship to the Rules Committee and his ability to schedule measures made in order by the House.

While the Senate has a rule similar to Rule XIV of the House governing recognition (Paragraph 1 [a] of Rule XIX), the presiding officer of the Senate does not have the Speaker's comparable power to schedule legislation. In the Senate, whose Rules Committee has no comparable scheduling role, the schedule and procedures governing consideration of legislation are normally established by unanimous consent agreement negotiated by the party leaders.

While recognition rests with the Speaker's discretion and is not subject to appeal, the Speaker's authority ordinarily is constrained by the House rules and long-standing practices of the House. For example, the Speaker is obliged to recognize a member who represents a committee reporting a bill for allowable motions to expedite the bill and must recognize a member proposing to offer a motion of higher privilege. Similarly, during the amendment process under the five-minute rule, the chairman of the Committee of the Whole is constrained to alternate recognition between majority and minority party members, giving priority to members of the reporting committee.

In some situations, however, the Speaker's discretion on recognition is not constrained. Absolute discretion extends, for example, to motions to suspend the rules, which are in order on Monday and Tuesday of each week. The Speaker may also decline to recognize a member not proceeding under the Consent Calendar (a calendar reserved for noncontroversial bills under clause 4 of House Rule XIII) who desires to ask unanimous consent to set aside the rules in order to consider a bill not otherwise in order. Similarly, recognition for one-minute speeches by unanimous consent and the order of such recognition are entirely within the discretion of the Speaker; and when the House has a heavy legislative schedule, the Speaker may refuse to recognize members for such speeches until the completion of legislative business.

So that members are on notice, the Speaker has announced several policies by which he confers recognition in those situations where his discretion is absolute. For example, the Speaker has declared a policy (first enunciated on 15 December 1981) of conferring recognition upon members to call up unreported bills and resolutions by unanimous consent only when the measures are cleared by the majority and minority floor and committee leadership. Similarly, the Speaker has declared a policy (first enunciated on 8 August 1984) for recognition of one-minute and special-order speeches: recognition alternates between majority and minority members, and speeches of five minutes or less are recognized first before longer special-order speeches.

On the other hand, the Speaker in some situations has declined to curtail or limit his discretion and does not announce in advance whom he will recognize if a certain parliamentary situation develops. For example, pending a vote on ordering the previous question, the Speaker has declined to indicate who might be recognized if the motion ordering the previous question was defeated.

Finally, the Speaker only recognizes a member with respect to a particular matter and such recognition does not extend to a motion relating to another matter. For that reason, the Speaker will first inquire, "for what purpose does the Gentleman [or Gentlewoman] rise?" Such an inquiry does not confer recognition; rather ultimate recognition will be granted to the member seeking recognition only for a stated purpose. Similarly, if the recognized member yields to another member for presentation of other business, the member loses the floor, as, for example, when the member in charge of a pending resolution in the House yields to another member to offer an amendment.

BIBLIOGRAPHY

U.S. House of Representatives. *Constitution, Jefferson's Manual, and Rules of the House of Representatives, 103d Congress.* Compiled by William Holmes Brown. 102d Cong., 2d sess., 1992. H. Doc. 102-405.

U.S. Senate. *Riddick's Senate Procedure, Precedents, and Practices,* by Floyd M. Riddick and Alan S. Frumin. 101st Cong., 2d sess., 1992. S. Doc. 101-28.

MUFTIAH McCARTIN

RECOMMITTAL. The motion to recommit, one of several variations of the parliamentary motion to refer, has a significant place in House procedure. The motion often provides the final political confrontation on a measure before the vote is taken on passage. House Rule XVI, clause 4 specifies that after the previous question is ordered on passage, one motion to recommit is in order, and priority in recognition goes to a member opposed to the bill. The motion may be with or without instructions. A "straight" motion (which, if adopted, sends the bill back to the reporting committee) is not debatable. If instructions are included, ten minutes of debate are permitted, divided equally between the proponent and a member opposed, usually the floor manager of the bill. The instructions can be to amend the measure ("The committee is instructed to report the bill forthwith with the following amendment: . . . "). The amendments proposed by the motion must be germane to the bill, but if one motion is ruled out as improper, another may be entertained. If the House recommits, the bill manager immediately responds ("Pursuant to the instructions of the House, I report the bill with the following amendment: . . . "). The question is then put on the amendment; if adopted, it becomes part of the bill to be engrossed (put in its perfected form, with all adopted amendments added to the intro-

duced text). After the third reading the question recurs on passage.

The importance of the motion is demonstrated by the fact that the Committee on Rules is precluded from reporting a special order that prevents its being offered (Rule XI, clause 4). Given the modern tendency to expedite the amendment process by adopting closed or modified closed rules for the consideration of many pieces of legislation, the motion has gained renewed significance as one of the options available to the minority to establish its legislative record. The minority in the House has by various parliamentary maneuvers resisted attempts to limit the free and full use of the motion.

The special recommittal motion in Rule XVI applies only to bills and joint resolutions, but Rule XVII extends the motion to commit (or recommit) to any measure, including resolutions and conference reports. This rule, however, provides no guarantee of the right of the minority to recognition. Precedents dictate that such recognition is appropriate when a measure reported from a committee is regularly before the House, but when an unreported matter is called up as privileged, recognition does not depend on party affiliation. When a conference report is before the House, a minority member who qualifies as being opposed is entitled to recognition to move to recommit. Recommittal of a conference report is only in order in the house first acting on the report, since adoption of the report in either body dissolves the conference committee.

In the Senate the motion to recommit is not a "minority" motion, but it is sometimes used by supporters to salvage a bill after it has become weighed down with amendments. It is also applied to conference reports when the Senate wishes to dispose of the report adversely.

BIBLIOGRAPHY

U.S. House of Representatives. *Constitution, Jefferson's Manual, and Rules of the House of Representatives, 103d Congress.* Compiled by William Holmes Brown. 102d Cong., 2d sess., 1992. H. Doc. 102–405.

U.S. House of Representatives. *Deschler's Precedents of the United States House of Representatives,* by Lewis Deschler. 94th Cong., 2d sess., 1977. H. Doc. 94–661.

WILLIAM HOLMES BROWN

RECONCILIATION. Established in section 310 of the Congressional Budget Act of 1974, reconciliation is a procedure in which House and Senate committees are instructed in a budget resolution to recommend changes in spending and revenue laws within their jurisdiction. It has been used under current practices since 1980, exclusively for the purpose of deficit reduction.

Reconciliation begins with instructions in the concurrent resolution on the budget. House and Senate committees with jurisdiction over mandatory spending (principally entitlements) or revenue laws are instructed in the budget resolution to recommend changes in those laws to bring spending and revenue levels in line with the totals set forth in the resolution. The committees' recommendations are forwarded to the House and Senate Budget committees, which normally combine the proposals into an omnibus measure for House and Senate action. The Congressional Budget Act establishes expedited procedures in the House and Senate for consideration of reconciliation legislation, and in the Senate prohibits the inclusion of so-called "extraneous matter" (provisions unrelated to deficit reduction) in reconciliation measures.

Reconciliation is not used to change discretionary spending (spending controlled by the Appropriations committees). Other enforcement procedures, based on points of order (objections raised under House or Senate rules to the consideration of legislation), are used to make annual appropriations measures conform to the budget resolution.

Reconciliation legislation has been the principal legislative vehicle for congressional action to reduce the deficit since 1980. In particular it has been used to implement broad deficit reduction agreements between the president and congressional leaders.

[See also Congressional Budget and Impoundment Control Act of 1974.]

BIBLIOGRAPHY

U.S. House of Representatives. Committee on the Budget. *A Review of the Reconciliation Process.* 98th Cong., 2d sess., 1984. Committee Print 9.

U.S. House of Representatives. Committee on the Budget. *The Whole and the Parts: Piecemeal and Integrated Approaches to Congressional Budgeting.* Report prepared by Allen Schick. 100th Cong., 1st sess., 1987. Committee Print 3.

EDWARD DAVIS

RECONSIDER, MOTION TO. [*This entry includes separate discussions of motions to reconsider:* In the House *and* In the Senate.]

In the House

The motion to reconsider a question may be offered by a member of the majority in voting thereon. It may be offered on the same day the question is decided or on the succeeding day for the consideration of that type of business, but the motion may not be repeated. It has been used in the House of Representatives since 1789 and was first stated in the standing rules in 1802.

The motion to reconsider is not admitted in the Committee of the Whole. The "majority" means the prevailing side in a vote. On a tie vote, all those voting "no" qualify to offer a motion to reconsider. On an unrecorded vote, all those voting qualify. In standing committees, all those voting in person qualify. Any member may object to the chair's customary statement that by unanimous consent a motion to reconsider is laid on the table, in which case a qualifying member may offer a formal motion to reconsider.

The motion to reconsider is subject to the motion to lay on the table. It may not be applied to negative votes on adjournment, recess, resolving into the Committee of the Whole, the question of consideration, suspension of the rules, or overriding a veto. It may not be applied to a partially executed order of the previous question. In modern practice, adoption of a motion to reconsider a question on which the previous question has been ordered does not render the question debatable or amendable unless the vote on the previous question is separately reconsidered.

BIBLIOGRAPHY

U.S. House of Representatives. *Constitution, Jefferson's Manual, and Rules of the House of Representatives, 103d Congress.* Compiled by William Holmes Brown. 102d Cong., 2d sess., 1992. H. Doc. 102–405.

JOHN V. SULLIVAN

In the Senate

A single motion to reconsider is in order following almost any vote of the Senate. The purpose of the motion is to provide senators with an opportunity to change their minds about their vote. It can be made or entered only by a senator who voted with the prevailing side or who did not vote, and only on the day of the vote or one of the next two days of session. In practice, motions to reconsider are routinely tabled, that is, killed immediately following any vote. The typical scenario following a vote involves an immediate motion to reconsider that is then followed immediately by a motion to table the motion to reconsider. The motion to table is routinely adopted by unanimous consent.

It is extremely rare for senators to use the motion to reconsider for the purpose for which it was created. On those rare occasions when it is allowed to follow its course, however, it can be extremely important. For example, in 1987, President Ronald Reagan's veto of the Highway bill was sustained in the Senate by one vote. The following day a motion to reconsider was entered and the Senate voted again. One senator changed his vote and the veto was overridden.

BIBLIOGRAPHY

U.S. Senate. *Senate Procedure, Precedents, and Practices,* by Floyd M. Riddick. 97th Cong., 1st sess., 1981. S. Doc. 97-2.

ROBERT B. DOVE

RECONSTRUCTION.

The process of restoring the seceded southern states to the Union began during the Civil War and lasted until the last Republican governments were overthrown in the South in 1877. From the beginning, Congress and the president engaged in an acrimonious dispute over which branch had primary responsibility for determining the terms of readmission. Arguing that the Union was indissoluble and secession illegal, Abraham Lincoln and then Andrew Johnson maintained that the southern states were merely out of their normal relationship with the Union and that the pardoning power gave the president the constitutional right to set conditions for readmission.

Congress, on the other hand, had the right to determine its membership and assumed that it had the power to guarantee each state a republican form of government. In addition, some Radical Republicans, such as Sen. Charles Sumner of Massachusetts, developed theories of territorialization, arguing that the seceded states had committed suicide and reverted to the status of territories over which Congress had constitutional control. Thaddeus Stevens of Pennsylvania, leader of the House Radicals, went a step further and asserted that the seceded states had forfeited all constitutional rights and should be treated as "conquered provinces."

While questions regarding readmission requirements for white southerners were important, much of the rancor involved in the process of reconstruction stemmed from disagreements over the future of the nearly four million slaves freed by the war.

Most southern whites, reluctant enough to give up slavery, could not envision—let alone tolerate—racial equality; racism was nearly as sharp in the North, particularly among Democrats and conservative Republicans. From the opposite end of the political spectrum, Radical Republicans argued that the federal government had both the power and responsibility to work the freedmen into a truly equitable position in American society. Between these extremes and holding the balance of power were the moderate Republicans. Far more circumspect than the Radicals on the race question, the moderates were also more wary of extending the government's enhanced wartime activism into reconstruction. The intransigence of Johnson and southern conservatives, the Radicals' constant pushing, and the immediate postwar climate of enlarged federal power would ultimately force the moderates closer to the Radical position. Still, they were the critical force in shaping the final plan for readmission.

Wartime Reconstruction Efforts. As the Union army occupied portions of the Confederacy, Lincoln and Congress faced the intertwined problems of what to do about slaves who came within Union lines and how to provide a loyal government for the occupied territory. The Confiscation Act of July 1862 confirmed the practice of some military leaders, who declared slaves to be contraband of war and specified that those coming within Union lines could not be returned to their owners. Pushed by Radical Republicans, Lincoln moved cautiously in 1862 toward using emancipation as a war measure, issuing in September the preliminary Emancipation Proclamation, which declared all slaves in Confederate-held territory free as of 1 January 1863.

As portions of Arkansas, Louisiana, Tennessee, and Virginia came under Union army control, Lincoln appointed military governors to establish federal administrative authority. And in a Proclamation of Amnesty and Reconstruction in December 1863, he offered a pardon to all who would take an oath of future loyalty to the Union and agree to emancipation, excluding only high-ranking Confederate officials. Once 10 percent of those who voted in 1860 had taken the oath, loyalists could hold elections for a new state government, which Lincoln promised to recognize. Lincoln's plan was clearly designed to undermine the Confederate war effort while carefully avoiding volatile questions about the future status of the ex-slaves. With Lincoln's encouragement, the Union-held areas of Louisiana, Tennessee, and Arkansas implemented his plan—with frankly narrow bases of support and considerable opposition to emancipation in the broader population.

Concerned with the leniency of Lincoln's plan, in July 1864 Congress adopted a stricter approach. Sponsored by Sen. Benjamin F. Wade of Ohio and Rep. Henry Winter Davis of Maryland, the plan stipulated that when at least 50 percent of the 1860 electorate had sworn future loyalty, those who could swear to an additional "ironclad oath" that they had never aided or abetted the Confederacy could select delegates to a constitutional convention to prohibit slavery, repudiate Confederate war debts, and establish a new government. A Radical-supported provision to extend suffrage to the freedmen failed, but the Wade-Davis bill did take some steps toward recognizing the legal rights of blacks. Not wanting to be locked into any particular plan, Lincoln pocket vetoed the bill and was promptly denounced by its sponsors in a manifesto advising him to "confine himself to his Executive duties . . . and leave political reorganization to Congress." Meanwhile, congressional Republicans refused to recognize the state governments organized under Lincoln's plan, but Lincoln and Congress cooperated to send the Thirteenth Amendment, abolishing slavery, to the states in January 1865.

Johnsonian Reconstruction. Thrust into the presidency by the assassination of Lincoln at the war's end in April 1865, Andrew Johnson was a Jacksonian Democrat who believed in strict construction and states' rights but whose Unionism led him to remain in the Senate when his home state of Tennessee seceded. After Lincoln appointed him military governor of Tennessee in 1862, Johnson reluctantly supported emancipation but believed blacks to be innately inferior and incapable of fitting into American society in anything more than a subservient position. Initially, however, even the Radicals took hope from his frequent wartime assertions that "treason must be made odious, and traitors must be punished and impoverished."

But it soon became apparent that Johnson saw reconstruction as his responsibility and that he sought a quick and lenient restoration of the South. With Congress out of session, Johnson recognized the existing Unionist governments in Arkansas, Louisiana, Tennessee, and Virginia and implemented his own plan of reconstruction for the other states in proclamations of amnesty and reconstruction beginning in late May. Although he required high-ranking Confederate leaders and wealthy southerners to appeal to him personally for pardon, all others needed only to swear future loyalty to be able to vote and hold office. He appointed provisional governors to conduct voter registration and the election of delegates to constitutional conventions, which were to nullify the ordinances of secession, repudiate Confederate war debts, and abolish slavery. Other than requiring legislative approval of the Thirteenth Amendment, Johnson was content to leave the freedpeople's future to southern whites. By December 1865, most states had satisfied Johnson's requirements. To his thinking, Congress needed only to seat the southern delegations to complete the process.

The Evolution of Congressional Reconstruction. Initially hopeful that the Thirteenth Amendment, ratified in December 1865, would prompt the southern states to guarantee basic civil rights for the freedpeople, congressional Republicans were sorely disappointed with the actions of southern whites under presidential reconstruction. Johnson's generous pardoning policy freed former Confederate leaders to hold office, and seemingly unrepentant southern legislatures enacted black codes severely restricting the liberties of the former slaves. When Congress reconvened in December 1865, the Republican majority refused to seat representatives from the Johnsonian governments and charged a new joint committee with consideration of additional reconstruction legislation. Although committee membership included several prominent Radicals such as Stevens, the moderate majority, led by Sen. William Pitt Fessenden of Maine, clearly hoped to work with Johnson to modify his plan.

While the Joint Committee on Reconstruction compiled testimony on the conditions in the South, moderate Illinois senator Lyman Trumbull, chairman of the Judiciary Committee, reported two measures designed to supplement Johnsonian reconstruction by offering greater protection for the ex-slaves. The first strengthened and extended the life of the Freedmen's Bureau, a federal agency established in March 1865 to assist the ex-slaves in their transition to freedom, and easily passed both houses with conservative as well as moderate Republican support. Republicans assumed that Johnson would go along with the modification, but the chief executive stubbornly took strict constructionist grounds in a sharply worded veto on 19 February and days later rashly denounced Radical Republicans Stevens and Sumner as traitors. After failing to override the veto, in late March Congress passed the second of Trumbull's bills, the Civil Rights Act, offering the first definition of national citizenship and making civil rights a federal as well

"AWKWARD COLLISION ON THE GRAND TRUNK COLUMBIA R.R." Political cartoon commenting on the conflict between President Andrew Johnson and Congress over control of reconstruction of the South and the severity of its terms. Johnson and Rep. Thaddeus Stevens (R-Pa.) are portrayed as the drivers of railroad engines that stand nose to nose on the same track. In the caption Johnson says, "Look here! One of us has got to go back." Stevens replies, "Well, it ain't me that's going to do it—you bet!" Wood engraving, *Frank Leslie's Budget of Fun*, November 1866.   LIBRARY OF CONGRESS

as a state concern by enumerating specific guarantees of equality before the law. Johnson disagreed with Trumbull's use of the Thirteenth Amendment as constitutional justification for the bill and vetoed it as an unconstitutional extension of federal powers. His reaction further antagonized the moderate Republicans, who led the override of his veto in early April. As the breach with Johnson widened, Congress also overrode his veto of a new Freedmen's Bureau bill in July. Further hurting Johnson's cause in the North was continuing southern obstreperousness, underscored by antiblack race riots in Memphis in early May and in New Orleans at the end of July.

In the interim, the joint committee reported the proposed Fourteenth Amendment, and after more than a month of floor debate and modification, Republicans mustered the requisite two-thirds majority to send the amendment to the states in mid June. Borrowing language from the Civil Rights Act, the amendment established the first constitutional definition of national citizenship and imposed limitations on state action with the privileges and immunities, due process, and equal protection clauses. In an effort to encourage black suffrage, it also reduced congressional representation in proportion to the number of adult males disenfranchised, prohibited officeholding for those who had violated a prewar oath to support the United States by endorsing the rebellion (until Congress removed that disability), and validated the U.S. debt and invalidated the Confederate debt. Although Congress failed before the end of the session to provide any explicit procedure for southern states to follow, the implication was that if they approved the Fourteenth Amendment, Congress would consider their readmission. When Republican-controlled Tennessee ratified, Congress readmitted the state in late July. But the other ten former Confederate states, acting in part on Johnson's advice, rejected the Fourteenth Amendment.

Johnson's late-summer effort to put together a coalition of conservative Republicans and Democrats to combat Congress and take his case to the northern public turned into a disaster. In the November congressional elections, the North returned an even stronger anti-Johnson majority to both houses. The breach with Johnson now insurmountable, Congress took full control of the reconstruction process when it reconvened in December 1866. The more extreme Radicals such as Stevens pushed for harsh proscription of the rebels, including long-term disfranchisement and confiscation and redistribution of their land to the former slaves. But moderate Republicans, such as Senators Trumbull, Fessenden, and John Sherman of Ohio, and Representatives John A. Bingham of Ohio and James G. Blaine of Maine, turned back most Radical proposals, and Congress passed the Reconstruction Act over Johnson's veto on 2 March 1867.

Supplemented by subsequent legislation, the act became the final congressional plan for restoring the ten remaining former Confederate states to the Union. Declaring the Johnsonian governments to be provisional only, it divided the ten states into five districts, each under the command of a Union general. Each state was to register all adult males "of whatever race, color, or previous condition," who in turn would elect delegates to a constitutional convention; excluded from participation were those prohibited from officeholding under the proposed Fourteenth Amendment. The delegates were to draft a new state constitution and explicitly provide for impartial male suffrage. After a majority of registered voters ratified the constitution, the state could hold elections and the new state legislature was to ratify the Fourteenth Amendment. Upon congressional approval of the process, the states would be readmitted.

When southern whites failed to take the initiative to launch the process, Congress in the Second Reconstruction Act on 23 March authorized the military commanders to register voters and initiate the elections for the conventions. In July, a third measure clarified the classes of southerners excluded by the Fourteenth Amendment from participating in the electoral process and authorized military commanders to remove obstructionist state and local officials from office. Finally, in March 1868, after conservative voters boycotted the election ratifying Alabama's new constitution, Congress provided that a simple majority of those voting would be sufficient for ratification.

Throughout the process, Congress had to pass every piece of reconstruction legislation over Johnson's vetoes. And when Johnson worked to curb the authority of the military district commanders, Congress limited his influence with an amendment to an army appropriation bill in March 1867. It also passed a Tenure of Office Act requiring Senate approval for Johnson's removal of cabinet and other appointed officials—designed in particular to protect Radical secretary of War Edwin M. Stanton, whose support was crucial to congressional reconstruction. With Congress out of session in August, Johnson requested Stanton's resignation and, upon his refusal, suspended him, making Gen. Ulysses S. Grant the interim replacement.

Radicals had pushed for impeachment of Johnson as an impediment to reconstruction throughout 1867, but failed to attract moderate Republican support until early 1868 when the Senate refused to concur in Stanton's suspension and Johnson countered by replacing Stanton with Gen. Lorenzo Thomas in an apparent violation of the Tenure of Office Act. The House immediately voted to impeach Johnson (126 to 47) and formulated eleven articles of impeachment, most centering on the president's violation of the Tenure of Office Act. Johnson's trial before the Senate began in mid March, but House prosecutors, going up against Johnson's able defense lawyers, had problems making their case stick, and some senators worried about the institutional ramifications of conviction. On 16 May the Senate acquitted Johnson by one vote (35 to 19) on Article 11, a summary of all the

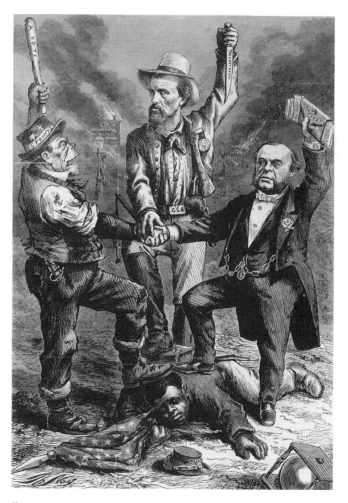

"THIS IS A WHITE MAN'S GOVERNMENT." Political cartoon portraying southern defiance over reconstruction. A thug with a bottle in his pocket and a club in his hand, a Confederate soldier holding a dagger of "the lost cause," and a wealthy man with a wallet full of "capital for votes" stand on the back of a black Union soldier. In the background, a school and an orphanage for black children burn. The cartoon's caption reads, "'We regard the Reconstruction Acts (so called) of Congress as usurpations, and unconstitutional, revolutionary, and void.'—*Democratic Platform.*" Woodcut after Thomas Nast, *Harper's Weekly*, 5 September 1868.   LIBRARY OF CONGRESS

charges. After his acquittal on two other articles ten days later, the Senate abandoned the effort to convict Johnson, and he remained obstinate until the end of his term in March 1869. Overall, Johnson's acrimonious relationship with Congress sharply undercut the need for a unified northern response to the task of reconstruction.

Implementation and Retreat. Congress readmitted six states in July 1868, and while the process continued to unfold in the remainder of the former

Confederacy, Congress moved to enfranchise blacks nationally with the Fifteenth Amendment. The decision reduced the hypocrisy of requiring black suffrage in the South while many northern states denied it. Well aware of significant northern opposition, Congress, over the protests of its remaining Radicals and newly admitted southern Republicans, framed the amendment negatively, stating only that suffrage could not be denied or abridged on the basis of "race, color, or previous condition of servitude." Still, the nationalization of suffrage, finally ratified on 30 March 1870, was seen as a capstone to congressional reconstruction. When the last four ex-Confederate states were readmitted in 1869 and 1870 with the additional requirement of ratifying the Fifteenth Amendment, the process of readmission was complete.

In the South, the newly enfranchised blacks provided the primary electorate for Republican governments that replaced those created under Johnson. While a majority of officeholders were carpetbaggers (northern natives who had migrated south after the war) and scalawags (southern whites who joined the Republicans), blacks served at all levels of state government except the gubernatorial; during the course of reconstruction, fourteen southern blacks served in the House and two in the Senate. Throughout the period, African Americans made significant progress in establishing their own educational, religious, and other community institutions as well as avidly participating in Republican politics.

From their beginnings, however, the southern Republican regimes faced intimidation from terrorist organizations such as the Ku Klux Klan as well as constant harassment from conservative Democrats. Responding to appeals from southern Republicans for protection, Congress passed three enforcement acts in 1870 and 1871. The first two prohibited state officials and others from using fraud and intimidation to limit voting, designated authorities to institute proceedings against violators in federal courts, and established federal supervisors for registration and congressional elections. The third, known as the Ku Klux Klan Act, empowered the president to suspend the writ of habeas corpus in rebellious areas and to use military force to suppress terrorist groups conspiring to deprive citizens of political rights.

While the legislation helped curb terrorist activity, the use of federal authority in the South was intermittent and often timid. Aided by congressional passage of a general amnesty in 1872 and a quickly waning northern commitment to further reconstruction measures, conservatives regained control in state after state through the use of economic and physical intimidation and election fraud. Southern Republican pleas for help fell on increasingly deaf ears as Congress and the Grant administration, retreating from the wartime legacy of an activist central government, took less and less action to protect them from conservatives dedicated to restoring "home rule." Additional enforcement legislation failed to pass Congress in 1875, but the few remaining Radicals and southern Republicans did secure a final civil rights bill prohibiting racial discrimination in places of public accommodation, transportation systems, and juries. The measure had little effect, however, and in 1883 the Supreme Court invalidated most of its provisions.

The disputed election of 1876 between Republican Rutherford B. Hayes and Democrat Samuel J. Tilden provided the finale to reconstruction. Bitter clashes between Democrats and the lingering Republican regimes in Florida, Louisiana, and South Carolina produced sets of dual electoral returns, one favoring Tilden, the other Hayes. Tilden needed but one of the disputed electoral votes to win; Hayes needed them all. Lacking precedent to handle the disputed returns, the Republican-controlled Senate and the Democrat-controlled House finally agreed to an electoral commission to be composed of five representatives, five senators, and five members of the Supreme Court to hear legal arguments from each side. Only the concurrence of both houses of Congress could reverse the tribunal's final decision in the disputed cases, so when the commission awarded the electoral votes of the three southern states to Hayes and the Republican Senate approved, his election was ensured. As the commission rendered its decisions, House Democrats threatened a filibuster to delay the electoral count, but ultimately northern Democrats feared the consequences of an interregnum, and southern Democrats extracted pledges from Hayes's supporters that he would agree to "home rule" for the South. Democrats allowed the completion of the count on the eve of Hayes's inauguration, and his withdrawal of military support for Republican regimes in Louisiana and South Carolina brought closure to Reconstruction.

Reconstruction on Balance: The Unfinished Revolution. Given the limitations posed by society in both North and South, the congressional attempt to work the freedpeople into an equitable position in American society proved to be an impossible task. Even within the dominant Republican party, the Radicals, imbued with faith that an activist government could foster racial egalitarianism, were frequently forced to compromise with moderates and conservatives who worried about expanding federal influence, altering federal-state relationships, and maintaining political power. Dearly held beliefs in the sanctity of private property and opposition to special privilege prompted the overwhelming northern rejection of Radical proposals for confiscation and redistribution to give the freedpeople an economic start. Persistent racism in both North and South prohibited acceptance of equality in social rights; even universal, as opposed to impartial, suffrage was unattainable. Congress thus opted for a patchwork political solution that did little to permanently touch the economic and social core of the problem. Charged with implementing the final plan, southern Republicans were sharply limited in what they could accomplish, and their conservative rivals, who saw the final plan as promoting revolutionary and totally unacceptable change, never accorded them political legitimacy. Plagued by their own destructive factionalism, southern Republicans were soon abandoned by their northern creators and overwhelmed by the violent tactics of their opponents.

Still, in attempting to cope with the problems of reconstruction and race, Congress made contributions of long-range significance. The three constitutional amendments, the promise of which remained unfulfilled for so long, provided a legal basis for the civil rights revolution of the 1950s and 1960s, and the Civil Rights acts of 1866 and 1875 and surviving remnants of the enforcement acts are still evoked in racial discrimination cases. To hold mid-nineteenth-century Americans strictly accountable for failing to establish the full equality of blacks is to overlook the advances that were made and to deny the enormous complexity of the problems of race that remain evident in late twentieth-century America. As historian Eric Foner has noted, despite the advances made in civil rights in recent times, reconstruction remains an unfinished revolution.

[See also Fifteenth Amendment; Fourteenth Amendment; Radical Republicans; Reconstruction Committee, Joint.]

BIBLIOGRAPHY

Belz, Herman. Reconstructing the Union: Theory and Policy during the Civil War. 1969.

Benedict, Michael Les. A Compromise of Principle: Congressional Republicans and Reconstruction, 1863–1869. 1974.

Brock, W. R. An American Crisis: Congress and Reconstruction, 1865–1867. 1963.

Foner, Eric. Reconstruction: America's Unfinished Revolution, 1863–1877. 1988.

Gillette, William. Retreat from Reconstruction, 1869–1879. 1979.

Hyman, Harold M. A More Perfect Union: The Impact of the Civil War and Reconstruction on the Constitution. 1973.

Keller, Morton. Affairs of State: Public Life in Late Nineteenth Century America. 1977.

TERRY L. SEIP

RECONSTRUCTION COMMITTEE, JOINT.

Distressed with the leniency of President Andrew Johnson's plan of reconstruction and the South's imposition of restrictions such as the black codes on the freed slaves, Congress, by concurrent resolution in December 1865, created the Joint Committee of Fifteen on Reconstruction. The Republican majority charged the committee to consider all questions and proposals relating to the restoration of the southern states to the Union, to conduct hearings, and to create appropriate reconstruction legislation. Senator William Pitt Fessenden of Maine chaired the committee of nine representatives and six senators; other influential members included Thaddeus Stevens of Pennsylvania, the senior House member and leading Radical on the committee; Representatives John A. Bingham of Ohio, Roscoe Conkling of New York, Elihu B. Washburne of Illinois, and George S. Boutwell of Massachusetts; and Senator Reverdy Johnson of Maryland, one of three Democratic members. Rounding out the committee were Democratic representatives Henry Grider of Kentucky and Andrew J. Rogers of New Jersey, Republican representatives Justin S. Morrill of Vermont and Henry T. Blow of Missouri, and Republican senators James W. Grimes of Iowa, Jacob M. Howard of Michigan, George H. Williams of Oregon, and Ira Harris of New York.

With Republican moderates in control, the joint committee served as a vital deliberative body and clearinghouse for reconstruction legislation through the second and lame-duck sessions of the 39th Congress. In addition to considering all reconstruction proposals except the Freedmen's Bureau and Civil Rights bills, which originated in the Senate Judiciary Committee, the committee compiled an influential report from the often damaging testimony of witnesses on conditions in the South under Johnsonian reconstruction. Amid the building tension between Johnson and Congress, the committee clustered various congressional proposals into a proposed Fourteenth Amendment and reported it on 30 April 1866. By mid June Republicans were able to muster the requisite two-thirds majority to send the modified amendment to the states for consideration. Designed to protect the freedpeople, the amendment defined national citizenship and then imposed limitations on state action against citizens with the privileges and immunities, due process, and equal protection clauses in the important first section. In an indirect effort to encourage black suffrage, the amendment also reduced congressional representation in proportion to the number of adult male citizens disenfranchised, prohibited from holding office those who had violated an oath to support the United States by supporting the Confederacy (until that disability was removed by a two-thirds vote of Congress), validated the U.S. debt and invalidated the Confederate debt, and authorized Congress to enforce the amendment's provisions with appropriate legislation. Although Congress failed to pass procedural legislation at this point, the implication was that if the ex-Confederate states approved the amendment, Congress would consider their readmission. Only Tennessee, already safely under Republican control, did so; the other ex-Confederate states, acting in part on Johnson's advice, rejected the amendment and, for the moment, it failed to be ratified.

The South's action necessitated additional reconstruction legislation, and therefore during the lame-duck session of the 39th Congress the joint committee worked on a military government bill for the South and reported it to the House in early February 1867. After much debate and modification, Congress passed the Reconstruction bill (including the requirement of black male suffrage and approval of the Fourteenth Amendment), which, supplemented by subsequent legislation, became the final congressional plan for restoring the remaining ten ex-Confederate states to the Union.

[See also Fourteenth Amendment.]

BIBLIOGRAPHY

Benedict, Michael Les. *A Compromise of Principle: Congressional Republicans and Reconstruction, 1863–1869.* 1974.
James, Joseph P. *The Framing of the Fourteenth Amendment.* 1956.

TERRY L. SEIP

RECORDS OF DEBATE. During its first century, Congress gradually came to endorse and then direct the compilation of a systematic and comprehensive record of debate. The constitutional requirement that the House of Representatives and Senate keep journals of their proceedings included no provision for a record of debate in the legislative chambers; earlier legislatures in Great Britain and America provided few precedents. The British Parliament and colonial assemblies generally discouraged the printing of any debates. Although the British Parliament ceased to prosecute printers after the 1770s, that body failed to provide an official record of debate until 1909. The Continental Congress and the Constitutional Convention met in secret sessions, and the former published only a journal of official proceedings. When early state governments and ratification conventions opened their sessions, however, printers were quick to meet the public demand for summaries of debates.

Early in the First Congress, the House voted to open sessions to the public, thereby making debates accessible to reporters. Several newspapers printed accounts of House debates, and one short-lived publication, Thomas Lloyd's *Congressional Register,* was devoted exclusively to summaries of proceedings in the House. Without officially commissioning any publication of records, the House, in the interest of greater accuracy, soon provided reporters with seats on the floor of the chamber. The Senate met in secret session until December 1795, after which reporters also printed summaries of debates in that body. Following the relocation of the government to Washington, D.C., the Senate chamber could not accommodate reporters, and no record of debate survives for 1800 to 1802. Thereafter, the District's *National Intelligencer,* a thrice-weekly newspaper, printed accounts of debates in both bodies of Congress. Other newspapers periodically printed their own summaries of debates.

Beginning with the session of 6 December 1824, Joseph Gales, Jr., and William Seaton, congressional printers and the editors of the *National Intelligencer,* initiated the *Register of Debates,* a forerunner of the *Congressional Record.* The *Register,* issued after the close of each session, presented regular summaries of debates in a dedicated publication. In an effort to recover the record of debate from the First Congress through the conclusion of the first session of the 18th Congress on 27 May 1824, Gales and Seaton also published the *Annals of Congress,* which reconstructed debates from various published sources, the stenographers' notes from the *National Intelligencer,* and the House and Senate journals. Gales and Seaton published two volumes of the *Annals* in 1834 but suspended work until 1849, when a congressional subscription allowed them to prepare forty more volumes; they completed publication in 1856.

The record of debate in the *Annals of Congress* and the *Register of Debates,* like the newspaper reports that preceded them, were summaries of speeches and floor action rather than a verbatim record of debates in the House and Senate. Deficiencies in recording methods, omission of entire speeches, political biases, and the editors' limited access to sources compromised the accuracy and reliability of the debate summaries. Some members of Congress presented printers with texts of their remarks that may or may not have reflected their spoken words, while others revised speeches after delivering them on the floor. Any researcher seeking a complete record of debates from these years must consult the various sources used by Gales and Seaton.

Beginning with the opening session of the 23d Congress in 1833, Francis Blair and John C. Rives, who replaced Gales and Seaton as official printers of Congress, began publication of the *Congressional Globe* in direct competition with the *Register of Debates.* The two publications coexisted until 16 October 1837, when Gales and Seaton discontinued the *Register of Debates.* The *Congressional Globe* continued to publish summaries of debates that were recorded by reporters of the *Globe* newspaper owned by Blair and Rives; the record suffers from the same omissions, political bias, and deficiencies of earlier publications. After the *Globe* newspaper failed in 1845, however, the *Congressional Globe* achieved greater accuracy in its reporting.

In the first official endorsements of a printed record of debate, the Senate in 1848 and the House in 1850 contracted with local newspapers and the *Congressional Globe* to publish a record of debate in the respective bodies. The contracts were also the beginning of efforts to compile a verbatim record of debate. Aided by the development of Pitman shorthand, reporters were able to transcribe more accurate records and avoid the frequent charges of political motivation in the inclusion or exclusion of speeches. In 1855, Congress moved a step closer to official sponsorship of compiling the record when it agreed to pay *Congressional Globe* reporters; in 1863, it appropriated money for reporting debates. In 1865, it required the *Congressional Globe* to begin daily printing of debates.

The government funding of reporters of debate, the desire for a more accurate record, and the establishment of the Government Printing Office in 1860 convinced Congress to oversee directly the printing of its debates after the *Congressional Globe*'s contract expired in 1873. Under the title of *Congressional Record,* Congress initiated its own reporting with the proceedings for 4 March 1873, at the opening of the 43d Congress. The format remained the same as the *Congressional Globe*'s for nearly seventy years, and both House and Senate retained the *Globe* reporters for compilation of the *Congressional Record.*

The inception of the *Congressional Record* did not end the prolonged debate over the compilation of a verbatim record. According to a statute of 12 January 1895, the *Congressional Record* is supposed to publish a "substantially verbatim report of the proceedings." Government direction of the publication and improved methods of recording debate solved many of the problems of earlier publications, but members still may revise and extend their remarks and submit for publication remarks not spoken in the chambers.

[*See also* Congressional Record; Debate, Reporters of.]

BIBLIOGRAPHY

Amer, Mildred. *The Congressional Record: Content, History, and Issues.* Congressional Research Service, Library of Congress. CRS Rept. 93-60. 1993.

McPherson, Elizabeth Gregory. "The History of Reporting the Debates and Proceedings of Congress." Ph.D. diss., University of North Carolina, 1940.

Springer, Michelle M. "The *Congressional Record:* Substantially a Verbatim Report?" *Government Publications Review* 13 (May–June 1986): 371–378.

BRUCE A. RAGSDALE

REED, DANIEL A. (1875–1959), representative from New York, ardent fiscal conservative, senior Republican member of the House Ways and Means Committee (1949–1959) and its chairman (1953–1955). Reed was elected to the House of Representatives from New York in 1918 and rose to a position of influence as a member of the Committee on Ways and Means, which exercises jurisdiction over tax, trade, and social security legislation. He was a strong proponent of limited government, low taxes, and tariff protection for U.S. industry and liked to boast that during the 1930s he had cast more votes against President Franklin D. Roosevelt's New Deal programs than any other member of Congress. Reed became the senior Republican on the Ways and Means Committee in 1949 and continued to oppose new federal programs and tax increases proposed by the Truman administration.

After the 1952 election, in which both a Republican president, Dwight D. Eisenhower, and Republican majorities in the House and Senate were elected, Reed became chairman of the Ways and Means Committee. As chairman, Reed was determined to enact tax cuts that had been promised by his party during the election campaign, and he repeatedly clashed with Eisenhower over tax issues in 1953. Eisenhower preferred to defer tax cuts in favor of balancing the federal budget and worked successfully with Republican Speaker Joseph W. Martin, Jr., to thwart Reed's efforts to pass immediate reductions.

Reed worked more closely with the Eisenhower administration during 1954, helping to pass a number of important administration initiatives, including revisions in the social security program, excise tax reductions, and a major revision of the tax code. After Democrats regained control of the House in 1955, Reed again became the ranking minority member on the Ways and Means Committee, a position he held until his death in 1959.

BIBLIOGRAPHY

Morris, John D. "The Ways and Means of Dan Reed." *New York Times Magazine*, 5 July 1953.
U.S. House of Representatives. Committee on Ways and Means. *The Committee on Ways and Means: A Bicentennial History*, by Donald R. Kennon and Rebecca M. Rogers. 100th Cong., 2d sess., 1989. H. Doc. 100-244.

RANDALL STRAHAN

REED, DAVID A. (1880–1953), conservative Republican senator from Pennsylvania (1922–1935), a proponent of protective tariff legislation, and strident critic of the New Deal. Born into a wealthy, upper-class family in Pittsburgh, Reed attended Princeton University and the University of Pittsburgh Law School. Through his family, Reed was associated with the Andrew Carnegie financial empire and as a young lawyer defended the corporation's interests.

After the death of Sen. William E. Crow, Reed was appointed to Crow's unfinished term and was elected shortly thereafter in 1922. Immediately regarded as the representative of Secretary of the Treasury Andrew W. Mellon, Reed became the servant of numerous Pennsylvania industrial and commercial interests, as his predecessors traditionally had been.

From his position on the Senate Finance Committee, Reed espoused the high protective tariff favored by the state's manufacturing interests. Reflecting the state's nativist elements, Reed co-offered the Reed-Johnson Immigration Act of 1924, which established national origins quotas favorable to the entry of northern European immigrants and restrictive to other nationalities. Seeking to bolster his political base in a divided state party, in 1927 Reed advocated the contested senatorial seating of Philadelphia machine boss William S. Vare despite charges that Vare had spent more than $800,000 and manipulated the vote to procure the seat. In fact, Reed detested the plebeian Vare, claiming later that the electorate that gave Vare a majority were "dunderheads."

Snobbish and in his speeches frank to the point of tactlessness, Reed nonetheless was regarded as one of the most able and intelligent of the conservative Republican Old Guard and became an outspoken opponent of the New Deal policies of Franklin D. Roosevelt. Challenged for reelection in 1934 by liberal governor Gifford Pinchot in the primary, Reed was eventually defeated by Democrat Joseph F. Guffey.

BIBLIOGRAPHY

Tucker, Ray T. "Leader of the Status Quo: A Portrait of Senator David Aiken Reed." *Outlook and Independent*, 25 December 1929.

RICHARD C. BURNWEIT

REED, THOMAS B. (1839–1902), Republican representative from Maine, Speaker of the House, author of the Reed Rules designed to streamline House procedure. Thomas Brackett Reed was born in Portland, the son of a fisherman. A graduate of Bowdoin College, he studied law and was admitted to the bar in California before serving in the Union navy in 1864 and 1865. After the Civil War he returned to Portland and practiced law.

In the late 1860s Reed served three terms in the Maine legislature, where he exhibited skills as a debater and legislative technician that later blossomed in Washington. He so impressed his colleagues that the legislature elected him in 1870 to a three-year term as state attorney general.

Reed first ran for Congress in 1876. He narrowly defeated a two-term Republican incumbent for the party's nomination and went on to beat his Democratic opponent by one thousand votes out of thirty thousand. He was reelected eleven times, usually by comfortable margins. His district, comprising the state's two southernmost counties, boasted a diversified economy with manufactures exceeding $25 million annually, substantial shipping and commerce, and agricultural interests based in corn and livestock. From this secure political base, Reed charted an independent course in Congress.

Although he arrived in Congress just as the Republican party's support for Reconstruction was drawing to a close, he continued to champion black suffrage rights. But he also recognized the party's need to transcend sectionalism and to espouse an activist government agenda to foster economic growth through a protective tariff, a stable currency, and subsidies for business.

Reed rose rapidly in the ranks of the House, less by cultivating friendships with colleagues than by dint of high intelligence, hard work, and great skill at parliamentary maneuver. Standing six feet three inches and weighing 275 pounds, he was a commanding physical presence, but he spoke, in an unappealing, high-pitched drawl, and his relatively few set speeches moved his colleagues more by the force of their logic and argument than by their style. He was most impressive in spontaneous give-and-take in the House, where he used pungent wit to maximum effect. Among Reed's gems: he once defined "statesman" as "a politician who is dead"; when his constituents petitioned him to secure a disused army cannon for a Civil War monument, he replied, "I am not in the junk business." Reed's insulting barbs evoked laughter from his friends and raised the hackles of his enemies. He was a respected and feared antagonist in debate.

Reed took his seat in the 45th Congress in 1877. Initially, he received relatively minor committee assignments but later was appointed a minority member of a special committee created by the House Democratic majority to investigate the disputed 1876 presidential election. The Democrats' aim was to discredit Rutherford B. Hayes's claim to the presidency and damage Republican chances in 1880. Thanks largely to Reed, however, the plan backfired. Through skillful cross-examination of Democratic witnesses, he unearthed evidence showing their party to have been at least as guilty of chicanery as the Republicans.

Also during his first term Reed voted against the Bland-Allison Act of 1878, which reinstituted the coinage of silver on a limited basis. Later that year,

THOMAS B. REED.   LIBRARY OF CONGRESS

fervently embracing the sound money doctrines that were becoming a Republican party hallmark, he beat back a Greenback challenge to his reelection.

Reforming House Rules. Since Republicans were in the minority during his first two Congresses, Reed, an eager student of parliamentary maneuver, learned much about legislative obstructionism. As minority party representatives had done for decades, he and other Republicans sometimes resorted to the "disappearing quorum" by being present but refusing to vote in order to prevent a quorum. A proposed rule change in January 1880 that would have allowed the Speaker to count nonvoting members as present won little support from either party and met strong denunciation from Reed. Arguing that minorities generally had not abused the disappearing quorum, he defended it as a necessary means to prevent harmful or partisan legislation by the majority. His words returned to haunt him.

Republicans won control of the House in 1880, and when the 47th Congress convened, Reed received eleven votes for Speaker in the Republican caucus. Though only in his third term, he became chairman of the Judiciary Committee. He also joined the Rules Committee and scored his first notable success in reforming House procedures. Typically, each new House began with the consideration of contested elections, and the minority resorted to dilatory motions and other tactics to postpone the seating of majority party members. Through skillful maneuvering, Reed persuaded the House to amend its rules to permit the Speaker to limit such obstructionist tactics. Afterward, election disputes were settled more expeditiously, clearing the way for substantive business.

The Democrats regained a majority in the House in 1883 and controlled the 48th through the 50th Congresses. Even so, Reed's prominence continued to grow. In the 48th Congress he retained membership on the Judiciary and Rules committees and joined Ways and Means. In the 49th and 50th Congresses he was the Republican nominee for Speaker.

Although again a member of the minority, Reed still bridled at cumbersome House procedures. In 1884 he offered rules amendments to overhaul the calendar system. Traditionally, bills were acted on in the order in which they were reported from committees; as a result, many important measures requiring lengthy committee consideration never reached the floor. Reed proposed a "morning hour" during which committees in succession could report bills to be voted on. But the Democrats rejected Reed's reform. His proposals lost again at the beginning of the 49th Congress. This time, though, Reed joined the majority on the Rules Committee in obtaining a watered-down amendment that forced the Appropriations Committee to share with several others the right to report spending measures directly to the House.

Reed fought for rules reform not merely for its own sake but to expedite consideration of substantive measures. Democrats' obstructionism, he believed, reflected their lingering adherence to outdated Jeffersonian notions of small government. In Reed's view, Democrats embodied a crippling negativism while Republicans embraced activist government measures to benefit the nation and the economy. On the stump and in the House, he championed the Republican program of a protective tariff (particularly as a means to maintain wages), a stable and noninflationary currency, pensions for Union veterans, business subsidies (especially transportation enterprises), and a strengthened national defense. Less enthusiastic about

government regulation of business or direct aid to farmers or labor, Reed favored a trickle-down approach to government intervention in the economy that, he argued, would benefit all. He recognized, however, that no one would gain from government largess if archaic House rules continued to block needed legislation.

With the election of Benjamin Harrison in 1888, Republicans won control of the presidency and both houses of Congress for the first time in fifteen years. The moment seemed propitious for the enactment of their program, but their razor-thin majority in the new House caused lingering anxiety. The 51st Congress would not convene until December 1889; in the interim Reed published magazine articles advocating reform in the way the House did business. "Rules should not be barriers," he wrote in the October 1889 issue of the *North American Review*, "they should be guides."

The Speakership. When the House convened, Reed won the speakership and referred the question of the rules to the Rules Committee, which he chaired. Little of importance transpired before the Christmas recess, but speculation abounded as to how Reed would deal with the quorum question. The answer came on 29 January 1890. A quorum required 165 votes, but when a roll call in a pending election contest resulted in 161 yeas and 2 nays, Reed ordered the clerk to list Democrats in the hall as present and refusing to vote and declared that a quorum was met. The ruling sparked a storm of protest from Democrats. When Rep. James B. McCreary (D-Ky.) denied the Speaker's right to count him as present, Reed replied, "The Chair is making a statement of fact that the gentleman from Kentucky is present. Does he deny it?" Three days of wrangling ensued, but, sustained by his Republican colleagues, Reed made his interpretation of the quorum stick.

In early February the Rules Committee reported a new set of rules largely drafted by Reed and embodying many reforms he had advocated since the 47th Congress. Their principal aim was to expedite business. First, the proposed rules permitted the Speaker to count nonvoting members as present for purposes of a quorum. Second, the Speaker could refuse to entertain dilatory motions. Third, the Committee of the Whole, used by the House to facilitate consideration of measures, would require a quorum of only one hundred members; furthermore, the committee could end debate on any part of a bill it was considering. Finally, Reed's Rules revamped provisions dealing with the order of business by creating a "morning hour" for action on committee bills, as Reed had earlier advocated. Reed defended the proposed rules as vital to break the obstructionist grip of the minority and to ensure majority rule in the House. On 14 February the House adopted them.

Thus empowered, House Republicans joined the Republican Senate to make the 51st Congress one of the most productive of the nineteenth century. Its landmark legislation included the Sherman Antitrust Act, the McKinley Tariff Act, the Sherman Silver Purchase Act, the Meat Inspection Act, the Dependent Pension and Disability Act, a ban on using the mails for lotteries, and the Forestry Reserves Act for forest preservation. The House also passed the Lodge federal elections bill, which called for federal court supervision of congressional elections with the primary aim of restoring the right to vote to blacks in the South. The bill failed in the Senate, but it stood as another symbol of Republican activism.

Ironically, in their hour of greatest legislative success, the Republicans suffered their worst electoral defeat. In the 1890 congressional elections Democrats denounced "Czar" Reed for his aggressive dominance of the House. They blamed high prices on the McKinley tariff, portrayed the Lodge bill as threatening a revived reconstruction complete with black rule, and otherwise assailed the activism of the Republican "Billion-Dollar Congress." Although Reed easily won reelection, House Republicans were reduced to a mere 88 seats compared to the Democrats' 235.

In the minority for the next two Congresses, House Republicans in each nominated Reed for Speaker. In the 52d Congress, over Reed's spirited protest, the Democrats threw out his rules and returned to the rules of the 50th Congress. In 1892 the Democrats won both houses of Congress and elected Grover Cleveland to the presidency, giving them control of both the executive and legislative branches for the first time since before the Civil War. But Republicans had gained enough House seats that, under Reed's leadership, they presented Democratic Speaker Charles F. Crisp (D-Ga.) with a revived "disappearing quorum." Their aim was to force Crisp to adopt Reed's method of counting a quorum, and in April 1894 Crisp caved in. Ever since, nonvoting members have been counted toward a quorum.

The depression following the panic of 1893 and the Democrats' apparent incapacity to deal with it led to a Republican landslide in the 1894 House elections. At the opening of the 54th Congress, Republicans triumphantly returned Reed to the Speaker's chair and reinstated the rules of the 51st Congress.

This was the high-water mark of Reed's political career. He never wanted a Senate seat. Reed did, however, aspire to the presidency in 1896, though with little reason to hope for success. As Republicans surveyed the field of candidates for their nominating convention, Reed assessed his chances by declaring, "They might do worse, and they probably will." Although he had become the undisputed leader of the House, in the wider field of presidential politics, Reed's prickly personality stood little chance against the good-natured geniality of William McKinley, who was nominated and elected.

McKinley carried with him strong Republican majorities in the 55th Congress, and the House elected Reed to his third and last term as Speaker. In a special session immediately after McKinley's inauguration, Reed and his Maine friend, Ways and Means chairman Nelson Dingley, Jr., easily secured House passage of the highly protectionist Dingley Tariff Act. In the field of foreign affairs, however, Reed disagreed with most of his Republican colleagues. He regarded war with Spain over Cuba as ill-advised and opposed the annexation of Hawaii. He deplored the acquisition of the Philippines and Puerto Rico as a risk-filled violation of the foreign policy traditions of the Republic. Acquiring overseas possessions, he believed, would overextend U.S. responsibility and jeopardize national unity.

Disenchanted with the McKinley administration but unwilling to make an open break with his party, Reed chose to retire from public life, resigning his House seat in September 1899. He moved to New York, where he launched a lucrative legal practice. Although mentioned as a possible antiimperialist candidate for president in 1900, he had no taste for such a race. In December 1902, he collapsed while visiting the Capitol and died soon thereafter.

BIBLIOGRAPHY

McCall, Samuel W. *Thomas B. Reed.* 1914.
Mooney, Booth. *Mr. Speaker: Four Men Who Shaped the United States House of Representatives.* 1964.
Offenberg, Richard Stanley. "The Political Career of Thomas Brackett Reed." Ph.D. diss., New York University, 1963.
Robinson, William A. *Thomas B. Reed: Parliamentarian.* 1930.

CHARLES W. CALHOUN

REED'S RULES. A major revision of House rules was enacted in 1890 after a period during which legislative business in the House of Representatives had become increasingly subject to delay and obstruction by minorities. Because Speaker Thomas B. Reed of Maine played a critical role in winning approval of these procedural reforms, the new rules became known as Reed's Rules.

By the late 1880s legislative business in the House had slowed to a trickle as minority factions readily availed themselves of opportunities to block action on pending legislation. Two delaying tactics were most common: the disappearing quorum and the use of dilatory motions. Minorities could bring the business of the chamber to a halt by refusing to vote, thereby depriving the House of the quorum needed to conduct official business. In addition, members opposing legislative action frequently demanded votes on motions such as those to recess or adjourn, simply for purposes of delay. Criticism of obstructionism arose primarily from House Republicans who sought a more active legislative agenda; leading House Democrats defended existing House procedures as necessary for the protection of minority views and interests.

The most vocal of the Republican critics of rules allowing minority obstructionism was Reed. First elected to the House in 1876, he rose steadily through Republican ranks. In 1889, when Republicans controlled the House for the first time in six years, Reed was elected Speaker. In an essay published just before the 51st Congress (1889–1891) convened, Reed made clear his intention to "establish rules which will facilitate the public business—rules unlike those of the present House, which only delay and frustrate action."

In what remains one of the most dramatic (and at times humorous) episodes in the history of the House, in January 1890 Reed asserted the Speaker's authority to count as present for purposes of establishing a quorum those members who were in the chamber but were refusing to vote. When Kentucky Democrat James B. McCreary objected to being counted as present, Reed replied: "The Chair is making a statement of fact that the gentleman from Kentucky is present. Does he deny it?" When two days later a member of the Democratic minority made a motion to adjourn in order to delay proceedings, Reed ruled that the Speaker would no longer allow motions made only for purposes of delay.

In February 1890 Reed introduced and won enactment of new rules that formalized the Speaker's authority to refuse dilatory motions and count non-voting members as present. Also included were rules changes to increase the efficiency of deliberations in the Committee of the Whole. The new rules allowed the majority party greater control over legislative procedures, primarily by enhancing the prerogatives of the Speaker. Together with previously existing authority to appoint members of standing committees and direct legislative business as chairman of the Rules Committee, Reed's Rules provided the institutional framework for a period of strong Speakers and centralized party leadership in the House that continued until the revolt against Speaker Joseph G. Cannon in 1910.

BIBLIOGRAPHY

Galloway, George B. *History of the House of Representatives.* 1976.
Peters, Ronald M., Jr. *The American Speakership.* 1990.
Robinson, William A. *Thomas B. Reed: Parliamentarian.* 1930.

RANDALL STRAHAN

REFERRAL. With rare exceptions, measures introduced in either house of Congress are transmitted to the committee or committees of appropriate jurisdiction in that chamber. This transmission is called referral. The responsibility for determining referral lies with the Speaker of the House and the presiding officer of the Senate. Because of the thousands of bills referred during each Congress and the complex jurisdictional arrangements that exist, the parliamentarian in each chamber advises the presiding officer regarding appropriate referrals. The parliamentarians are also available to advise individual members about possible referrals prior to a bill's introduction.

In the House, referral decisions are generally based on Rule X, which delineates committee jurisdiction, and on a review of prior bill referrals, which together are presumed to create precedent for future referrals. Bills can be referred to a single committee or, since 1974, to more than one. If several committees can justify jurisdiction based on the Rules and precedent, the Speaker can refer a bill jointly, or concurrently, to all the panels that have jurisdiction. In a joint referral the entire measure is referred simultaneously to the appropriate committees. A split referral allows the Speaker to divide the measure into its component parts, by title or section, and to refer only designated portions to the relevant committees. A sequential referral enables the Speaker to refer a bill to a single committee, or jointly to several committees, after the committee or committees of original referral report out the measure. Most sequential referrals have time limits imposed for consideration—for example, thirty or sixty days—and usually the committee(s) that receives the measure may review only those matters within its jurisdiction rather than the entire bill. Several thousand bills are multiply referred during each Congress. Multiple referral generally implies a complex measure, and such a bill is less likely to survive than a simpler measure because of the multiple committee involvement and because all panels receiving a referral must act before the measure can go to the full House. In the case of a sequential referral, however, a panel usually must act before the deadline, or the bill will be taken from it automatically.

In the Senate, the process of referral is based on Rule XXV and, as in the House, on precedent. However, the Senate refers bills according to "predominant" jurisdiction, preferring to allow only a single committee with responsibility over the "subject matter which predominates" in the measure to consider the bill. Since Rule XXV was revised in 1977, the topical jurisdiction language is presumed to be more modern and therefore able to accommodate consideration of bills by single committees.

Multiple referrals are possible in the Senate, and can be invoked using one of three methods: a unanimous consent request propounded on the floor for a specific bill referral; a unanimous consent standing agreement that is negotiated among the relevant committees and is considered binding; or, since 1977, by motion of the joint party leadership. The first option is rare, the second is used sparingly, and the third has never been invoked.

[See also Committees, article on Committee Jurisdictions.]

BIBLIOGRAPHY

Tiefer, Charles. Congressional Practice and Procedure. 1989.
U.S. House of Representatives. Constitution, Jefferson's Manual, and Rules of the House of Representatives, 103d Congress. Compiled by William Holmes Brown. 102d Cong., 2d sess., 1992. H. Doc. 102-405.
U.S. Senate. Committee on Rules and Administration. Rules and Manual of the United States Senate. 102d Cong., 1st sess., 1992. S. Doc. 102-1.

JUDY SCHNEIDER

REFORM. See Reorganization of Congress.

REGULATION AND DEREGULATION. Federal regulation may be broadly or narrowly defined. Broadly defined, such regulation includes any effort by the national government to control the behavior of smaller governmental entities, business firms, or individuals. In a sense, therefore, nearly everything that government does may be deemed regulatory. Most discussion of federal regulation, however, focuses specifically on attempts by government to control business activity.

Four main concerns of such narrowly defined regulation may be distinguished. First, regulation may constrain the ability of firms to enter and exit markets. Second, it may directly govern the prices that firms can charge customers. Third, it may limit the competitive practices available to firms, especially as regards price setting, market structure, and disclosure of a product's ingredients, relative quality, or contingent impacts. Fourth, it may aim to improve the quality of specific work practices or products, often in the interest of enhanced human health and safety. Congress has established a wide variety of agencies charged with enforcing regulatory laws through administrative action. And, as discussed in detail below, Congress attempts to influence these agencies through diverse means and toward many perceived ends.

Although regulation is today both pervasive and controversial, Congress had enacted relatively little regulatory legislation before the twentieth century. The earlier federal government was quite modest in size and scope. As James Q. Wilson put it, "Washington was content to operate the post office, issue the currency, devise a tariff, distribute the public lands, and fight the Indians" (1980, p. viii). This state of affairs prevailed for decades despite the availability of constitutional provisions (especially the commerce clause and the necessary and proper clause) that would later serve as the foundation for a vastly more powerful and diversified national bureaucracy. Increased regulation of business constituted a significant portion of government's greater reach.

Economic Regulation. In 1887 Congress passed the Interstate Commerce Act, which created the Interstate Commerce Commission (ICC), the first major federal regulatory agency. Like later economic regulatory agencies, the ICC emerged from the lobbying of various stakeholders (in this case, chiefly railroads and farm interests) that combined to generate a congressional perception of regulatory confusion between the states, unfairness to various shippers, and excessive competition among railroads. The railroads and the shippers with whom they contracted had partially overlapping concerns. Anxious to achieve a predictable competitive environment, railroads wanted an end to rate wars, secret concessions, and rebates. Efforts to achieve such results by forming voluntary cartels were neither wholly successful nor enduring; the incentive of individual members to violate cartel agreements proved difficult to combat through purely private action. Shippers, on the other hand, were similarly concerned about both rate stability and frequently discriminatory rate setting; short hauls in some instances were more costly than longer ones. Beginning with Illinois in 1871, several states moved to regulate railroads, attempting to fill the void created by federal inaction. The resulting inconsistent state regulation added impetus to the call for a unified regime of national regulation.

With the advent of trucking and interstate bus service, these modes of surface transportation were also brought under ICC jurisdiction with the Motor Carrier Act of 1935. The railroads wanted to constrain rival transport modes, and trucking interests saw considerable economic benefit in a system of controlled entry. While private interest benefits surely constituted the major political force behind regulation of all three modes of surface transport, both the original regulatory regime and subsequent enlargements of it were routinely defended as in the public interest. This has been a theme common in the politics of economic regulation. The nation as a whole, it has been claimed, benefits from the stability and managed growth that regulation yields.

Congress extended regulation to other modes of transport for many of the same reasons as lay behind the creation of the ICC. In creating the Civil Aeronautics Board (CAB) in 1938, Congress acted to protect the young industry of civil aviation from unfettered competition. The Federal Maritime Commission (FMC), successor to the U.S. Shipping Board created under the Shipping Act of 1916, reflected the lobbying of ocean shippers (i.e., firms that send goods by sea) who had turned to Congress for relief from what they held to be the predations of ocean carriers. As a result the authorizing legislation reflected predominately the views of shippers rather than carriers. Indeed, the Shipping Act was approved over the opposition of the carriers, an outcome that might not have been possible but for the outbreak of World War I. With carrier capacity vastly diminished, resulting in high freight rates, the act seemed a way to lower rates by increasing the number of available ships and reducing collusion among carriers.

The creation of the Shipping Board exemplifies the role a crisis can play both in reshaping the overall political agenda and in galvanizing, at least temporarily, a political coalition sufficient to overcome entrenched resistance. A broadly similar dynamic has operated repeatedly in the congressional politics of regulation, resulting in either the creation of a new agency or the enhancement of an existing regulatory mandate. Crises may emanate from broad economic or political forces (such as depression or war) or from more narrow ones.

The banking and securities industries were brought under stringent regulation for the first time as a direct result of the special political atmosphere generated by a widespread economic crisis, the Great Depression of the 1930s. As Robert E. Litan recounts in *What Should Banks Do?* (1987), some six thousand banks failed in the 1920s, but these were overwhelmingly "small, mostly rural institutions with capital less than $100,000." But between 1930 and 1933 "nearly 9,000 of the nation's 25,000 commercial banks failed. The casualty list included many larger urban institutions" (p. 25). Congress responded by creating systems of insurance for both savings bank and commercial bank deposits, by bringing state-chartered institutions under federal supervision, and by strictly separating commercial and investment banking functions (the last achieved under the Glass-Steagall Act of 1933). To regulate and restore public faith in the stock and bond markets, Congress enacted strong disclosure requirements in the Securities Act of 1933 and created the Securities and Exchange Commission (SEC) with the Securities Exchange Act of 1934.

More recently, in response to the crisis in the savings and loan industry that began in the mid 1980s, Congress enacted the Financial Institutions Reform, Recovery, and Enforcement Act of 1989, massively reorganizing regulation of savings and loan institutions. The act also abolished the Federal Home Loan Bank Board, whose authority was transferred to a new Office of Thrift Supervision in the Treasury Department.

Of course, most crises spawning new economic regulation are less pervasive. The Communications Act of 1934 created the Federal Communications Commission (FCC). Like its predecessor, the Radio Act of 1927, this act was intended to regulate what had been disorganized and destructive access to the electromagnetic spectrum. Like the CAB, the FCC was the product of a Congress that wanted to nurture an infant industry (and an industry generally eager to be nurtured), while responding to public criticism.

While much of the economic regulatory legislation that Congress has enacted is industry-specific, antitrust law is an important exception. Federal lawmaking in the field began in 1890 with congressional passage of the Sherman Antitrust Act, which broadly (and, some critics would say, too vaguely) declared illegal the pursuit of monopoly and other activities found to be "in restraint of trade or commerce." As Robert Bork notes, the act's framers intended it to strike generally at "cartels, horizontal mergers of monopolistic proportions, and predatory business tactics," such as "the . . . extraction of railroad rebates by the Standard Oil [Company]" (1978, p. 20). Congress thereafter extended the scope of antitrust law with the Clayton Antitrust Act of 1914, the Federal Trade Commission Act of the same year, and the Federal Anti–Price Discrimination (Robinson-Patman) Act of 1936. Though consumer protection was ostensibly the primary motivation behind these statutes, later critics of antitrust would argue that they resulted in considerable harm to consumers. Indeed, Bork suggests that, whether they knew it or not, the members of Congress who supported the Robinson-Patman Act were actually "sacrificing consumers for the benefit of small merchants" (p. 63).

Health and Safety Regulation. While the years 1880 to 1940 (and particularly the Progressive and New Deal periods) saw the rise of economic regulation, in the 1960s and 1970s there emerged a second and more compressed surge in regulation of a quite different sort. This later era emphasized initiatives intended neither to coddle infant industries nor to constrain competition for the sake of market stability and economic fairness. Instead, Congress enacted a large number of statutes aimed at safeguarding health, safety, and the environment.

Businesses sometimes support (or at least do not strongly oppose) such regulation. They may embrace it as a way to retain consumer confidence, to avoid the inconsistencies of state regulation, to fend off even harsher government controls, or because they calculate a regulated environment to be more profitable. (Examples of the last would be a firm offering a product or service mandated by regulation, or a firm with a market position relative to competitors that improves due to the distribution of regulatory benefits and costs.) In large measure, however, health and safety regulation has sprung from political victories by labor, environmental, and consumer activists over business opposition. Perhaps the most dramatic example of such a victory came in 1966, when Congress passed the National Traffic and Motor Vehicle Safety Act, enforced since 1970 by the National Highway Traffic Safety Administration (NHTSA), thus vindicating the automotive safety crusade of a young attorney named Ralph Nader.

Though alarmist, moralistic appeals through the media would become part of the stock-in-trade of the advocates of strong health and safety regulation, the basic dynamic did not originate with Nader nor did such regulation commence only in the 1960s. The Food and Drug Administration (FDA) traces its origins to the Pure Food Act of 1906 (also known as the Pure Food and Drugs Act), enacted partly due to journalist Upton Sinclair's stomach-churning descriptions of abuses in the meat-packing industry in his novel *The Jungle*.

Health and safety regulation, like economic regulation, has often been enacted in the wake of a crisis that succeeds at least for a time in capturing the attention and votes of members of Congress. Successive enhancements in FDA's regulatory mandate exemplify, perhaps more than any other agency, an inclination toward crisis-driven legislation, for the agency's responsibilities have grown largely in lockstep with highly publicized episodes of identifiable harm to specific victims. After more than one hundred people died from Elixir of Sulfanilimide, Congress boosted the agency's power with the Food, Drug, and Cosmetics Act of 1938. A wave of severe birth defects triggered by the thalidomide catastrophe in Europe prompted the passage of the Drug Amendments of 1962, requiring both manufacturers and FDA to evaluate drug effectiveness as well as safety. The Dalkon Shield episode, in which thousands of users of a defective intrauterine device developed painful infections and serious injuries, helped to generate the climate that led to the passage of the Medical Device Amendments of 1976. In 1979 two soy-based infant formulas, inadvertently rendered chloride deficient, were found to cause serious metabolic disturbances, thus prompting a recall, a wave of publicity, and a congressional investigation that resulted in the Infant Formula Act of 1980. A year after the deaths of seven people who had taken cyanide-laced Tylenol capsules, Congress passed the Federal Anti-Tampering Act of 1983.

The decade extending roughly from the mid 1960s to the mid 1970s spawned a dizzying array of important federal regulatory statutes aimed at protecting workers, consumers, and the environment. A few of the more prominent examples suggest the breadth and significance of congressional innovation. The National Environmental Policy Act of 1969 (NEPA) created the now-familiar requirement of the environmental impact statement. The Clean Air Act of 1970 and the Federal Water Pollution Control Act Amendments of 1972 established stringent standards and emission reduction targets. The Federal Environmental Pesticide Control Act of 1972 enhanced the existing regime of pesticide regulation. The Occupational Safety and Health Act of 1970 created a new agency, the Occupational Safety and Health Administration (OSHA), with a strong mandate to reduce workplace hazards. The Consumer Product Safety Act of 1972 likewise established a new agency, the Consumer Product Safety Commission (CPSC) with a similarly broad responsibility: protecting consumers against otherwise unregulated products posing "unreasonable risk" of injury. Existing agencies such as the FDA and the FTC also received additional regulatory responsibility.

Overall, the congressional politics of health and safety and of economic regulation differ dramatically. Programs that control the price of goods or services or entry into an economic activity usually incite attention and sustained interest mainly from those rather narrow elites with perceptible stakes in the costs and benefits of regulation. The average citizen (or voter) will typically perceive little if any difference in disposable income or personal welfare due to the creation or routine operation of these economic regulatory programs. The resulting indifference has huge political implications, often allowing the dominance of policy-making by a one-sided alliance of regulated firms, agency officials, and congressional committees—the sort of symbiotic arrangement traditionally identified as an "iron triangle." (The politics of such distributive benefits as farm subsidies and veterans' benefits have most commonly been described this way.) Students of regulation have differed regarding the precise dynamic by which business interests come to dominate economic regulatory policy-making. Some have argued that business has an intended dominance at birth and others believe that it is due to a more evolutionary process resulting from the inevitable waning over time of more disinterested attention. By either mechanism, a strong, and likely commanding, position for regulated firms is the result.

The politics of health and safety regulation diverge sharply from this pattern. The environmental and consumer regulatory legislation of the 1960s and 1970s resulted from broad social movements that exhibited great resourcefulness and institutional staying power. In their struggles with business interests, advocacy organizations committed to stringent regulation successfully cultivated external financial support (from grassroots dues and foundations, among other sources) and contacts or alliances with both well-positioned members of Congress and the national media. Organized labor perceived in legislation concerning workplace hazards not only powerful symbolism but also a means through which to win management concessions unavailable through collective bargaining. While the arcana of rate schedules and other competitive arrangements elicit little citizen interest, health and safety regulatory issues have proved persistently salient to a mass public. Indeed, so popular has been the concept of environmental protection that every major-party presidential candidate (or would-be candidate) since the early 1970s has felt compelled to proclaim firm commitment to the cause, and most legislation that emerges from Congress enjoys considerable bipartisan support. The public's strong interest in health and safety has offered advocates of regulatory stringency important leverage not only in creating new programs but also in transforming the political environments of existing ones. For example, the policy network that characterized regulation of civilian nuclear power during the 1950s and 1960s was far more cohesively business oriented and promotional than it is today. The increasing prominence of safety concerns both inside Congress and beyond substantially altered the balance of power.

Agency Structure. Regulatory agencies vary importantly not only in their respective mandates but also in the means through which they exercise them. Along with substantive authority and funding, Congress's structural choices are crucial for defining how and how well an agency of any kind will operate. The range of organizational options varies across two key dimensions: administrative location and leadership cohesiveness. The first dimension varies according to whether an agency resides inside or outside an executive department. The second dimension involves a choice between a collective, "commission-type" leadership or a single agency head. The resulting four structural types are described below.

Landmark Regulatory Laws

Title	Year Enacted	Reference Number	Description
Interstate Commerce Act	1887	49th Cong., 2d sess., chap. 104	Created the first major federal regulatory agency, the Interstate Commerce Commission, to regulate railroad pricing and market entry.
Sherman Antitrust Act	1890	51st Cong., 1st sess., chap. 647	First major federal antitrust statute; declared illegal any "contract, combination in the form of trust or otherwise, or conspiracy, in restraint of trade among the several States, or with foreign nations. . . ."
Pure Food and Drugs Act	1906	P.L. 59-384	First major federal food and drug law. Prohibited mislabeling; gave regulatory power to the Bureau of Chemistry in the Department of Agriculture, which later became the Food and Drug Administration.
Federal Reserve Act	1913	P.L. 63-46	Created the Federal Reserve Board, with broad powers to control the money supply and bank operations.
Federal Trade Commission Act	1914	P.L. 63-203	Created the Federal Trade Commission, empowered to prevent "unfair and deceptive" competitive practices by businesses.
Clayton Antitrust Act	1914	P.L. 63-212	Supplemented existing antitrust law to enhance regulation of price discrimination, exclusive dealing, acquisitions, and interlocking directorates.
Shipping Act	1916	P.L. 64-260	Created the U.S. Shipping Board, precursor to the Federal Maritime Commission, to regulate prices for merchant shipping.
Securities Act of 1933	1933	P.L. 73-22	Created securities registration and disclosure requirements as conditions of market participation.
Banking Act of 1933 (Glass-Steagall Act)	1933	P.L. 73-66	Provisions of the act mandated the stringent separation of commercial and investment banking activities.
Securities Exchange Act of 1934	1934	P.L. 73-291	Created the Securities and Exchange Commission to regulate the securities market.
Communications Act	1934	P.L. 73-416	Created the Federal Communications Commission, empowered to regulate access to the electromagnetic spectrum in accordance with "the public interest, convenience and necessity."
National Labor Relations Act	1935	P.L. 74-198	Created the National Labor Relations Board to oversee labor-management relations; recognized the right to organize and to bargain collectively.
Civil Aeronautics Act	1938	P.L. 75-706	Created the Civil Aeronautics Authority (later renamed the Civil Aeronautics Board) to oversee pricing and market entry in commercial aviation.
Food, Drug, and Cosmetic Act	1938	P.L. 75-717	Empowered the Food and Drug Administration (FDA) to require that products be proved safe before marketing.
Federal Aviation Act	1958	P.L. 85-726	Created the Federal Aviation Agency (later, Administration) to regulate air safety.
Drug Amendments of 1962	1962	P.L. 87-781	Empowered the FDA to require that products be proved effective.
National Traffic and Motor Vehicle Safety Act	1966	P.L. 89-563	First major automotive safety law; created regulatory power for what became the National Highway Traffic Safety Administration in 1970.
National Environmental Policy Act	1969	P.L. 91-190	Created the Council on Environmental Quality and required that federal activities be formally evaluated for their environmental impact.

Landmark Regulatory Laws (Continued)

Title	Year Enacted	Reference Number	Description
Occupational Safety and Health Act	1970	P.L. 91-596	Created the Occupational Safety and Health Administration to promulgate regulations and conduct inspections regarding workplace health and safety.
Clean Air Amendments (Clean Air Act) of 1970	1970	P.L. 91-604	Authorized the Environmental Protection Agency (EPA) to establish national ambient air quality standards, to approve state plans implementing emission controls, and to set emission levels for both stationary and mobile pollution sources.
Federal Water Pollution Control Act Amendments 1972 (Clean Water Act)	1972	P.L. 92-500	Authorized the EPA to use effluent guidelines and the issuance of permits to regulate industrial and other of discharges into the nation's water supply.
Federal Environmental Pesticide Control Act	1972	P.L. 92-516	Revised the existing Federal Insecticide, Fungicide, and Rodenticide Act (FIFRA) to empower the EPA to register and evaluate pesticides, to certify them for specific uses, and to suspend, restrict, or cancel those that pose unreasonable risk to humans or the environment.
Consumer Product Safety Act	1972	P.L. 92-573	Created the Consumer Product Safety Commission, charged with regulating nearly all consumer products not otherwise regulated to prevent "unreasonable risk" of injury.
Medical Device Amendments of 1976	1976	P.L. 94-295	Amended the Food, Drug, and Cosmetic Act to authorize FDA regulation of medical devices according to a three-class scheme of stringency; most stringently regulated class III devices require premarket approval by the FDA.
Toxic Substances Control Act	1976	P.L. 94-469	Authorized the EPA to screen new chemical entities for their safety, to require safety testing by manufacturers, to gather information on existing chemicals, and to control chemicals proved to pose a risk.
Resource Conservation and Recovery Act	1976	P.L. 94-580	Updated the Solid Waste Disposal Act to provide "cradle to grave" management of various products posing waste disposal concerns and to encourage recycling and conservation.
Airline Deregulation Act	1978	P.L. 95-504	Deregulated commercial aviation and abolished the Civil Aeronautics Board (CAB).
Motor Carrier Act	1980	P.L. 96-296	Significantly deregulated the trucking industry but retained a role for the Interstate Commerce Commission (ICC).
Staggers Rail Act	1980	P.L. 96-448	Significantly deregulated the railroad industry, retaining a diminished role for the ICC.
Comprehensive Environmental Response, Compensation, and Liability Act (Superfund)	1980	P.L. 96-510	Established a fund to finance hazardous waste cleanup; gave the EPA authority to seek compensation from responsible parties.
Financial Institutions Reform, Recovery, and Enforcement Act	1989	P.L. 101-73	Massively restructured supervision of the savings and loan industry following widespread failures and management abuses; terminated the Federal Home Loan Bank Board.
Clean Air Act Amendments	1990	P.L. 101-549	Ended a thirteen-year impasse that prevented revision of of 1990 the Clean Air Act; imposed new controls on sulfur dioxide emissions (associated with acid rain), toxic chemicals, ozone depleting substances, and mobile source emissions.

Independent regulatory commissions. In some instances Congress has created multimember commissions formally separate from any executive department. Independent regulatory commissions usually include five to seven members appointed by the president for staggered terms, with some requirement of partisan balance among appointees. Each appointee is subject to Senate confirmation but can be dismissed only for reasons of "inefficiency, neglect of duty, or malfeasance in office." This organizational format is politically attractive when Congress and the president want to use the regulatory structure to assuage intensely competitive interests. Imposing a collective leadership of this sort lessens the likelihood of overwhelming influence by any single firm, sector, or political party and so makes it easier for contending players to unite behind passage of enabling legislation.

This format has also appealed to Congress as a way of restricting presidential influence. (Such motivations apparently explain why the ICC, originally located in the Department of the Interior, was placed outside any department in 1889.) A system of multiple commissioners means that the president may appoint the chairman but not (at least, generally speaking, not all at once) the entire leadership of the agency. And in the event that the president is displeased with one or more commissioners that Congress happens to like, the legislature retains the upper hand; the president cannot dismiss on purely political or policy grounds. (Franklin D. Roosevelt's attempt to do just that resulted in the Supreme Court's rebuff in *Humphrey's Executor v. United States* [1934].)

However, if, as was the case for many years after the 1980 presidential election, one party with a well-defined regulatory policy agenda consistently controls the White House, the president's hand is dramatically strengthened. Unscheduled vacancies, combined with the budget process and the power to appoint a strong chairman, shift the balance even more. Nevertheless, even today Congress remains strongly inclined to view independent regulatory commissions as extensions of the legislative branch. From this perspective, commission independence should apply only to executive branch authority.

Regulatory agencies constructed roughly according to this format include the Interstate Commerce Commission (ICC), the now-defunct Civil Aeronautics Board (CAB), the Federal Trade Commission (FTC), the Federal Communications Commission (FCC), the Federal Maritime Commission (FMC), the Securities and Exchange Commission (SEC), the Consumer Product Safety Commission (CPSC), the National Labor Relations Board (NLRB), the Commodity Futures Trading Commission (CFTC), and the Nuclear Regulatory Commission (NRC).

Single-administrator departmental agencies. In many other instances Congress has lodged regulatory responsibilities within executive branch departments, with agencies headed by a single administrator. Prominent examples include the National Highway Traffic Safety Administration (NHTSA) in the Department of Transportation, the Occupational Safety and Health Administration (OSHA) in the Department of Labor, and the Food and Drug Administration (FDA) in the Department of Health and Human Services.

According to a classic argument, adjudicatory or quasijudicial functions are best carried out by independent commissions, while rule making (thought to depend more on effective coordination) ought to be the province of executive departments. Historically, however, self-interest has been a more telling factor in the creation of an agency of one type or the other. As Terry M. Moe points out, once they could no longer resist the passage of what was to become the Occupational Safety and Health Act, business interests attempted to cut the best deal they could by endorsing an independent commission to implement the law. Organized labor, on the other hand, sought and won supervision by the Labor Department under an assistant secretary, an arrangement far more favorable to the unions than an independent commission. By the same token, there is no inherent logic for withholding meat and poultry inspection programs from FDA jurisdiction. Yet these reside in the Department of Agriculture, primarily because that is where farm interests and their congressional allies have wanted them (Moe, 1989, pp. 297–306).

Single-administrator independent agencies. Among major regulatory bureaucracies, the Environmental Protection Agency (EPA) has been the primary example of this organizational arrangement (though the Senate did briefly approve a similar architecture for what became the CPSC). Significantly, the EPA's structure mirrors that of an executive department; an administrator sits at the organizational apex, with a deputy administrator and assistant administrators below. Given the agency's birth in a 1970 presidential reorganization plan consolidating a diverse array of existing bureaucracies, the commission format would have been unlikely for political, if not practical, reasons. The EPA's unique status was the result of three concerns. First, the White House under Richard M. Nixon was bent on enhanced presidential management. A second factor was environmentalists' anxiety about placing a new environmental agency in an executive department, such as Commerce or Interior, heavily influenced by competing interests. Finally, as is often the case in regulatory politics, business interests could see an important advantage in having to comply with a single national agency rather than fifty separate state programs. Had Congress enacted a statute creating the agency, a commission would have been the far more likely result. It is telling that a serious proposal to change the EPA to a multimember commission structure emerged only once—from angry congressional Democrats in the wake of a major scandal in 1982 and 1983 that embarrassed the Reagan administration into overhauling the agency's leadership. By 1993, in the wake of Bill Clinton's election to the presidency, Congress appeared to be on the verge of elevating the EPA to departmental status.

Departmental regulatory commissions. Placing a multimember commission within an executive department might seem a peculiar structural choice. (The National Transportation Safety Board, which investigates accidents and makes safety recommendations, takes this form—it resides in the Department of Transportation—though it has no regulatory authority.) However, when there exists a desire to recognize and placate intensely competitive interests while also connecting the outcomes of such contests to broader policy ends, the departmental regulatory commission is an appealing option. Congress chose this hybrid when it created the Federal Energy Regulatory Commission (FERC) within the new Department of Energy. The secretary of Energy and FERC share power in complex ways, the outline of which is beyond the scope of this essay.

Congressional Oversight. In creating an agency Congress also generates for itself a set of ongoing opportunities and responsibilities. Individual members of Congress, driven by their particular constituents' preferences, will over time have myriad opportunities to push the agency in particular directions (perhaps challenging the executive branch in the process). Congressional responsibilities include decisions to reauthorize agencies, appropriate funds for them, confirm appointees, and correct errant performance. Working largely through the institution's committee and subcommittee structure, members have both continuing and episodic incentives to monitor and influence agency behav-

ior and do so through a variable set of tasks and tools best encompassed by the term *congressional oversight*.

For many years, the most common criticism of congressional oversight was its scarcity. Scholars, journalists, policy advocates, and members of Congress long bemoaned a lack of attention by Congress to the details of administration. The principal reason for this inattention, it was said, was the lack of political incentive; members were rewarded by their constituents, their peers, and the press for creating programs but not for overseeing them once they had been created. This lack of incentive was thought to apply particularly to oversight of economic regulatory bureaucracies. In 1957 House Speaker Sam Rayburn (D-Tex.) engineered the creation of a new oversight and investigations subcommittee of the House Committee on Interstate and Foreign Commerce specifically because of concern about the lack of scrutiny of such agencies as the SEC and the FCC. And as recently as 1980, scholar Robert A. Katzmann regarded congressional oversight of the FTC as at best episodic and somewhat casual (Katzmann, 1980).

Today the estimation of close observers both inside and outside academia is rather more complex. Recent theoretical and empirical work by scholars tends to portray oversight (and the more general notion of legislative influence) as both more subtle and more substantive than in the traditional critique. There is also widespread recognition that under certain circumstances the incentives of members to engage in oversight can be quite powerful. Congressional "micromanagement" is now a more common criticism than insufficient oversight. This reflects Congress's bolstered institutional capacity to monitor and influence executive branch behavior and the political incentives generated by constituency interests and an extended period of divided government. Particularly in the realm of health and safety regulation, congressional Democrats during Republican administrations have proved both aggressive and skilled at using the various tools of oversight to criticize policies believed dangerous to the public. In using oversight hearings and other devices to challenge Republican management of regulation, congressional Democrats built on the foundation of the public's fondness for the general idea of health and safety. During the 1980s House Energy and Commerce Committee chairman John D. Dingell (D-Mich.) used his control over the committee staff, combined with his chairmanship of the oversight and investigations subcommittee, to build an unprecedented reputation as a zealous and fearsomely effective oversight entrepreneur, particularly (though by no means exclusively) in the area of health and safety regulation.

Deregulation and Regulatory Reform. In health and safety regulation Dingell and other Democrats were particularly exercised by Reagan (and later Bush) administration efforts to promote a vision of regulatory implementation both less adversarial and less stringent than many thought either legal or prudent. Despite the low esteem in which the public held government as a whole, efforts to promote such goals as a cleaner environment, healthier workplace, and safer drugs and medical devices remained popular. Combined with the control of crucial committees and subcommittees by defenders of regulatory stringency, this meant that the path to major statutory deregulation in the health and safety realm was often effectively blocked. For example, for more than two decades from the time of its enactment in 1970, the Occupational Safety and Health Act remained completely impervious to amendment. For most of that period, both the Senate Labor Committee and the House Education and Labor Committee remained firmly controlled by political allies of organized labor. What is more, OSHA (like the FDA) enjoyed a permanent authorization, thus denying its critics a natural opportunity to force its reconsideration. (Opponents had a somewhat easier time in the more exposed appropriations process, where they could amend annual funding bills on the floor to constrain OSHA's authority.)

These political realities effectively forced on the Reagan and Bush presidencies a strategy of administrative deregulation. Its basic elements included constraining proposed agency budgets, appointing strong-willed agency leaders committed to the administration's perspective, and controlling the content and pace of day-to-day regulatory implementation. In pursuit of this last objective, only weeks after it assumed office the Reagan administration issued Executive Order 12291 (supplemented later by Executive Order 12498), granting the Office of Management and Budget (OMB) unprecedented power to review proposed regulations for their cost effectiveness. Dingell and other congressional Democrats harshly criticized the administration's strategy in general and its approach to regulatory review in particular. They even attempted to cut off funding for the Office of Information and Regulatory Affairs (OIRA), the OMB unit responsible for policing regulatory proposals before both public discussion and final promulgation. Unfortunately for critical congressional Democrats, OMB review remained by nature largely abstract in the public eye and by design largely invisible to congressional scrutiny. Therefore Democrats seized every opportunity in oversight hearings to link whatever concrete victimization or scandal was under examination to the larger pattern of administrative deregulation in general and to OMB review in particular.

On the other hand, at least since the mid 1970s Congress has viewed price and market-entry deregulation far more favorably. This might seem somewhat peculiar. After all, organized stakeholders can be expected both to pay close attention to regulatory programs directly beneficial to them and to resist unfavorable change. Given public indifference, how would the political impetus for deregulation arise? And how might the impulse to deregulate gather majority support in Congress, where vested interests ordinarily are expected to be both active and influential?

Martha Derthick and Paul J. Quirk (1985) answer these questions by emphasizing the power both of ideas and of effective legislative leadership. They note that by the late 1970s, price and entry regulation had long been a target of economists, who had mounted a sustained, coherent, and virtually unanimous attack on its underlying justifications. This procompetition critique gained added political impetus from the increasing visibility of economists in national policy debates, from the infiltration of economists into leadership of the regulatory apparatus, and from the transformation of deregulation into both an anti-inflation and a consumerist cause that liberals and conservatives alike could support.

The most dramatic (even drastic) legislative results of these developments were the Airline Deregulation Act of 1978 (which, among other things, abolished the CAB) and the Motor Carrier Act of 1980, which retained the ICC but significantly deregulated trucking. Well before congressional action, the chairmen of both the CAB and the ICC had taken positions strongly in favor of deregulation, both in public remarks and through administrative discretion. In fact Alfred E. Kahn, President Jimmy Carter's appointee to head the CAB, was a distinguished academic economist whose commitment to deregulation was not only well known but also a major reason for his selection.

Strong presidential and congressional leadership

was crucial to promoting deregulatory legislation. Eager to find an issue on which to make a mark, Sen. Edward M. Kennedy (D-Mass.) settled on airline price and entry reform, which he effectively championed as a potential boon to consumers. It could be vividly demonstrated that regulated interstate air fares cost passengers more than unregulated intrastate flights of comparable distance. Though Kennedy chaired the Subcommittee on Administrative Practice and Procedure of the Judiciary Committee (rather than of Commerce, where Nevada senator Howard W. Cannon chaired the subcommittee with formal jurisdiction), the Judiciary subcommittee offered him suitably broad jurisdiction to initiate high-profile investigations such as his extensive probe of pharmaceutical regulation. Kennedy's persistent aggressiveness in holding hearings and attracting attention to the airline deregulation issue proved vital to generating and sustaining legislative momentum. Presidents Gerald R. Ford and Jimmy Carter also strongly endorsed deregulation.

The forces arrayed on behalf of the status quo were not nearly so aggressive or effective. As Derthick and Quirk (1985) write:

> In contrast with the abundant and committed leadership supporting reform, congressional leadership for the opposition was scarce and hesitant. In each case, the industries had difficulty recruiting well-placed congressional spokesmen and maintaining their allegiance. The main representatives of the opposition were, with few exceptions, more junior members of the legislative committees or senior members who did not hold positions of leadership or were not members of the relevant committees. Instead of forcefully defending regulatory limits on competition, they preferred to obscure their positions in debate and sought to avoid confrontation. (P. 113)

This weakness in creating effective legislative allies, combined with administrative initiatives and the political appeal of deregulation as an idea, fatally undermined the proregulation position of both the airline and trucking industries.

The political victories of the advocates of deregulation in such issues as aviation, trucking, telecommunications, and railroads have not been replicated in all areas of price and entry control. Where academic analysis is less unified or persuasive, where a predicted near-term result of deregulation is not lower prices but higher ones, and where the opponents of deregulation are well positioned or tenacious, the prospects for congressional enactment of deregulatory policy dim considerably. That is why the politics and provisions of the Natural Gas Policy Act of 1978 differed so fundamentally from the airline pricing reforms enacted at almost the same time. Although many economists perceive natural gas regulation as undesirable and can doubtless find a receptive audience among the gas-producing states of the sunbelt, their arguments are cold comfort to legislators and voters from northern states accustomed to purchasing energy at regulated prices.

Nor has Congress moved to dismantle the system of agricultural marketing orders under which prices and market entry are carefully controlled for a wide variety of farm commodities. Indeed, in one of its few collective challenges to the system of OMB regulatory review created by Executive Order 12291, Congress voted in 1983 to forbid the agency from spending any funds to examine agricultural marketing orders. In their repeated struggles to protect a cherished system of price supports, farm interests have both won and lost, but they remain a long way from being completely vanquished.

The same holds true for the maritime industry, which continues effectively to defend the FMC (as well as outright subsidies from the Maritime Administration in the Department of Transportation) as necessary for protecting an endangered industry whose survival bears significantly on larger issues of trade and national security. The congressional committees that oversee these programs remain unpersuaded of the need for drastic change.

During the period that price and market-entry deregulation reached the national political agenda, some of the same forces that propelled the issue forward also fostered an intense interest in reform of regulatory procedure. But while the advocates of price and entry deregulation managed to focus on a few narrow targets and unite behind a relatively well-defined theme, the more general notion of regulatory reform spawned a dizzying array of proposals grounded in differing visions of effective regulation in particular and proper bureaucratic governance in general.

Some criticisms focused on regulatory delay and administrative inefficiency, others on a perceived imbalance among the interests participating in regulatory decision making. (It is worth noting that the tensions inherent in these diagnoses alone would have constituted a significant challenge to congressional reformers; a reformer could hardly enhance public participation and scrutiny without risking additional delay and inefficiency.) Another criticism, heavily promoted by economists, was that agencies were insufficiently sensitive to the broad social costs imposed by their decisions. This concern prompted calls for regulatory (i.e., cost-benefit and cost-effectiveness) analysis as a component of agency decision making and for direct congressional management of social costs through a "regulatory budget" analogous to a traditional expenditure budget.

An alleged historical failure (despite successful deregulation) to consider whether regulatory programs (or indeed *any* program) might outlive their usefulness gave rise to proposals for "sunset" and "zero-based" budgeting provisions. Under the first, programs would expire after a set period unless explicitly reauthorized, while the second would require reconsideration of complete program budgets (not just incremental increases or cuts) with every budget cycle. Such proposals arose from a general sense that government bureaucracy had departed too far from genuine control by either the citizenry or its elected representatives.

Perhaps the most popular proposal in this vein was for broader application of the legislative veto. Congress had either employed or considered several different versions of the device since the 1930s, all boiling down to a statutory requirement for congressional approval of a proposed administrative action before it becomes effective. Although the Supreme Court ultimately held the legislative veto to be an invalid legislative infringement on executive authority (in *Immigration and Naturalization Service v. Chadha* [1983]), the years immediately before that landmark decision witnessed considerable debate over whether and how to expand use of the device. Among health and safety regulatory programs, Congress wrote legislative veto provisions into the authorizing statutes of both the FTC and the CPSC.

In the end the extensive debate over procedural reform bore only modest legislative fruit. In 1982 the Senate unanimously passed an omnibus package of reforms (S. 1080), including legislative veto and regulatory analysis requirements, only to see it die in the House Rules Committee at the end of the 97th Congress, a victim of opposition by Democratic committee chairmen fearing the loss of power that such a vehicle might entail. The last major change enacted before the Reagan presidency was the Paperwork Reduction Act of 1980, a law that, like the 1982 Senate bill, attempted to satisfy the congressional quest for symbolic reform while leaving essentially undisturbed the powerful alliances and constituencies behind particular regulatory programs. (Ironically, the law also created the Office of Information and Regulatory Affairs, later the target of so much congressional wrath.)

The power of such constituencies to block change has been apparent in the reluctance of Congress to embrace a pure market-incentive approach to pollution control. Such an approach emphasizes emissions taxes or tradable emissions allocations in lieu of detailed regulatory directives. While Congress embraced trading of sulfur dioxide emissions allowances in section 403(b) of the Clean Air Act Amendments of 1990, it has shunned tax schemes. Both environmental and business communities have mistrusted the potential implementation of emissions taxes. The former fear too low a tax, while the latter anticipate higher taxes than either necessary or affordable. On the other hand, environmentalists have welcomed a different sort of regulatory reform for clean air and clean water laws: deadlines for achieving clearly defined regulatory goals. In that respect, if not in others, environmental legislation avoided the vague standards for which earlier economic regulation had often been criticized. Predictably, strict deadlines have sometimes caused problems, threatening unacceptable costs or inconvenience.

The 1992 election set the stage for significant change, with Bill Clinton's presidency promising an immediate and sharp departure from the Reagan-Bush era theme of regulatory relief. For example, the day of Clinton's inauguration marked the end of the Council on Competitiveness, a secretive White House "back door" through which businesses could appeal to escape stringent regulation, chaired by Vice President Dan Quayle since its March 1989 creation. Congressional Democrats, labor unions, environmentalists, and consumer advocates had stridently criticized the council. On the other hand, the Reagan Executive Order 12291 and Executive Order 12498 were initially retained pending review, indicating that even a Democratic administration would be cautious about relinquishing tools that might bolster presidential interests. Perhaps most significant was the consolidation of congressional and executive branch leadership under one party for the first time since 1980, a development widely believed to enhance the prospects for statutory innovation on many fronts, regulation among them.

[*For discussion of related public policy issues, see* Commerce Power; Economic Policy; Oversight. *See also* Bankruptcy; Copyright, Trademarks, and

Patents; Small Business Legislation; *and numerous other entries on particular areas of public policy and particular legislation mentioned herein.*]

BIBLIOGRAPHY

Aberbach, Joel D. *Keeping a Watchful Eye: The Politics of Congressional Oversight.* 1990.

Alexis, Marcus. "The Political Economy of Federal Regulation of Surface Transportation." In *The Political Economy of Deregulation: Interest Groups in the Regulatory Process.* By Roger G. Noll and Bruce M. Owen. 1983.

American Enterprise Institute. *Government Regulation: Proposals for Procedural Reform.* 1979.

Behrman, Bradley. "Civil Aeronautics Board." In *The Politics of Regulation.* Edited by James Q. Wilson. 1980.

Bork, Robert. *The Antitrust Paradox: A Policy at War with Itself.* 1978.

Derthick, Martha, and Paul J. Quirk. *The Politics of Deregulation.* 1985.

Fesler, James W., and Donald F. Kettl. *The Politics of the Administrative Process.* 1991.

Foreman, Christopher H., Jr. "Legislators, Regulators, and the OMB: The Congressional Challenge to Presidential Regulatory Relief." In *Divided Democracy: Cooperation and Conflict between the President and Congress.* Edited by James A. Thurber. 1991.

Foreman, Christopher H., Jr. *Signals from the Hill: Congressional Oversight and the Challenge of Social Regulation.* 1988.

Friendly, Henry J. *The Federal Administrative Agencies: The Need for Better Definition of Standards.* 1962.

Katzmann, Robert A. *Regulatory Bureaucracy: The Federal Trade Commission and Antitrust Policy.* 1980.

McCubbins, Mathew D., and Thomas Schwartz. "Congressional Oversight Overlooked: Police Patrols versus Fire Alarms." *American Journal of Political Science* 28 (1984): 165–179.

Mansfield, Edward. "Federal Maritime Commission." In *The Politics of Regulation.* Edited by James Q. Wilson. 1980.

Moe, Terry M. "The Politics of Regulatory Structure." In *Can the Government Govern?* Edited by John E. Chubb and Paul E. Peterson. 1989.

Nadel, Mark V. *The Politics of Consumer Protection.* 1971.

U.S. Senate. Committee on Governmental Affairs. *Study on Federal Regulation: Regulatory Organization.* 95th Cong., 1st sess., December 1977. Vol. 5.

Wilson, James Q. *The Politics of Regulation.* 1980.

CHRISTOPHER H. FOREMAN, JR.

RELIGION. A primary influence in U.S. history, religion has left its imprint on partisan battles and congressional enactments over the past two centuries. The intensity of religious disputes impinging on Congress has, of course, waxed and waned as circumstances have changed. But, appropriately enough, the rules for most subsequent religious engagement with the political sphere were charted by actions of the First Congress as it struggled to delineate founding principles by which a religiously pluralistic nation might operate.

The Debate over the First Amendment. The First Congress began its work in spring 1789 by considering proposed constitutional language on religious freedom. Born out of agitation for a bill of rights and offered as a congressional campaign promise by James Madison, the religion clause of the First Amendment was, in fact, one of the first pieces of legislation considered by the new Congress. It represented a historic break with European tradition in its prohibition of an established church for the new nation and its guarantee that the national government would not infringe on the free exercise of religious faith. But those first sixteen words of the Bill of Rights—"Congress shall make no law respecting an establishment of religion or prohibiting the free exercise thereof"—have been the subject of heated commentary, voluminous litigation, and varying interpretations by the Supreme Court. What exactly was the legislative intent of the First Congress, and what did the amendment mean in practical terms?

While scholars dispute the broad historical context, records of the congressional debate indicate that bargaining and compromise contributed to the legislative consensus. Introduced by Madison in June 1789, the legislation went through several versions in both chambers before a conference committee bill was passed by the necessary two-thirds of the House on 24 September and the Senate on 25 September. Madison's sweeping approach was amended to accommodate critics. For example, many Anti-Federalists feared that the new Constitution was inhospitable to religion. Thus Madison's attempt to include what he called "rights of conscience" in the language of the amendment—which, it was feared, would require government neutrality concerning religion versus atheism—was dropped from the final version. A second concern was that the national government might interfere with state practices and constitutions, including established churches in several of the former colonies. Madison, in fact, wanted to prohibit both the national and state governments from infringing religious liberty, but the final version, acknowledging states' rights, applied only to the federal govern-

FIRST PRAYER IN CONGRESS. A print commemorating the event celebrated as the first prayer in Congress, Carpenters Hall, Philadelphia, 7 September 1777. The image includes an account of the event during the Continental Congress, its visual depiction, and the invocation offered by Episcopalian clergyman Jacob Duché.

ment (Malbin, 1978). Moreover, the amendment's shrewd language—"respecting *an* establishment"—both prohibited Congress from establishing a national church and simultaneously protected established state churches from congressional interference.

Interpretation of the First Amendment religion clause has varied tremendously. Not until the 1940s, for example, did the Supreme Court apply it to the states. And though many state constitutions contained provisions for religious liberty, a number of states had legally established churches that continued into the nineteenth century. Moreover, early Congresses sometimes operated as if the amendment prohibited nonsectarian support for religion but at other times acted as if such aid was allowed. The same year it passed the First Amendment, for example, Congress reenacted the Northwest Ordinance, introducing section 3 of the law in this manner: "Religion, morality, and knowledge being necessary to good government and the happiness of mankind, schools and the means of learning shall forever be encouraged" (1 Stat. 50, 52 [1789]).

Nineteenth-Century Reform and the Abolitionists. Even though religious organizations in the early nineteenth century agitated for a broad range of social reforms, from the prohibition of dueling to prison reform, Congress was able to avoid many of these issues because they were deemed state matters. Occasional issues, however, aroused national religious concern. From 1810 until 1830, for example, Congress was petitioned by Christians protesting Sunday mail delivery as a violation of the Sabbath. Church leaders up and down the eastern seaboard remonstrated against government policy, especially in the wake of comprehensive postal legislation in 1825. Though opponents of Sunday delivery ultimately failed, the tactics they used would be copied on such momentous issues as Indian policy and slavery (Stokes, 1950, vol. 2, pp. 12–14.)

Religious people's consciences were piqued by the plight of the Cherokee people, who struggled for a decade and a half to resist Georgia's expropriation of their ancestral land. From the early 1820s until their forcible relocation in 1838, the Cherokee appealed to Congress for justice. Many church leaders, in turn, took up the cause of the Cherokee, most of whom belonged to Christian denominations and lived in well-established communities. Two prominent Christian laymen championed the Cherokee cause—U.S. senator Theodore Frelinghuysen, of New Jersey, president of the American

RABBI ABRAHAM DE SOLA. Delivering the opening prayer in the House of Representatives, 9 January 1873.

LIBRARY OF CONGRESS

Bible Society, and Jeremiah Evarts, editor of the nation's premier Protestant journal. Evarts presented the definitive legal petition of the Cherokee Nation to government representatives in Washington, and, when the Georgia legislature annexed Cherokee lands late in 1829, Senator Frelinghuysen attempted unsuccessfully to nullify its effect with provisos attached to the 1930 enabling federal legislation. Six years later, at President Andrew Jackson's urging, the Senate narrowly approved a new "treaty" with the Cherokee that led to their forced removal in the Trail of Tears to Oklahoma (Stokes, 1950, vol. 1, pp. 708–714).

By the mid-nineteenth century the growing sectional split over slavery had brought that religiously infused dispute to the national stage. Morally energized by waves of revivals, churches in the North were drawn increasingly into the abolitionist movement. In 1854 Congress was presented with a petition signed by more than three thousand New England ministers opposing the Kansas-Nebraska bill, which allowed the extension of slavery into new territories. While some members of congress viewed

SENATE CHAPLAIN ZEBARNEY THORNE PHILLIPS. Offering an invocation in the Senate on 21 February 1939, the day the Senate began the practice of opening each daily session with a prayer.

OFFICE OF THE HISTORIAN OF THE U.S. SENATE

such political action by clergy as inappropriate, religious agitation played the key role in solidifying northern opposition to slavery (Reichley, 1985).

Parochial Aid and Grant's Indian Policy. While state governments eventually followed the national example in disestablishing state churches, Protestant hegemony produced a form of cultural "establishment" in the nineteenth century, complete with use of the King James version of the Bible in public schools. In self-defense, Roman Catholics developed their own parochial school system. This deep Protestant-Catholic cleavage shaped partisan alignments for more than a century. But Congress did not become involved until the Catholic constituency became strong enough to influence state school-aid policy, raising the ire of the Protestant majority.

In the wake of the Civil War, Catholics intensified their efforts for state funding of church-run schools, aided by Democratic party machines that had assimilated waves of Catholic immigrants. Protestant fealty to the Republican party in the North produced the Blaine amendment, an attempt by the Republican administration of Ulysses S. Grant to amend the U.S. Constitution to prohibit any state

governmental aid to parochial schools. Introduced in the House by Rep. James G. Blaine of Maine in 1875, the amendment became a symbol of anti-Catholic prejudice because of Blaine's association with the charge that the Democrats were the party of "rum, Romanism, and rebellion." The proposed constitutional amendment was notable, however, because it explicitly sought to extend the religion clause of the First Amendment to the states. Passing the House, the bill fell short of the two-thirds needed in the Senate. Strong Catholic opposition, coupled with a desire by some to leave the issue to the states, convinced enough senators to vote against the amendment or to abstain. While Republican platforms from 1876 to 1892 called for an end to government aid to sectarian schools, the issue was not brought before Congress again.

President Grant took a more accommodating church-state posture in crafting his so-called Indian peace policy. Endeavoring to promote peace through the assimilation of Native Americans, Grant turned to churches for Indian education. This approach was not entirely new. Since the federal government did not operate schools, Congress found it convenient to grant churches the privilege of providing schools on reservations. After the Civil War, church leaders (notably Quakers) demanded reform of corrupt Indian agencies. Grant responded by agreeing to appoint Indian agents from lists the churchmen provided, a practice that expanded from 1869 onward, to the point that different denominations were formally assigned to particular tribes and given responsibility for education and relief of specific Indian groups. Ironically, the same House of Representatives that passed the Blaine amendment appropriated enormous sums to sectarian religious schools on reservations. Indeed, in the last quarter of the nineteenth century Roman Catholics alone received $4.5 million from the federal government for their Indian schools in the West. While the policy thrived from the 1870s to the end of the century, some Protestant groups became skittish about receiving government support and withdrew from the program. Catholics, in contrast, expanded their federally funded efforts with private money, sparking renewed anti-Catholic agitation. In 1894 Congress began debating the wisdom of the policy, and thereafter appropriations were cut, until in 1899 legislation declared an end to the remarkable experiment in federal support for sectarian schools (Stokes, 1950, vol. 2, pp. 285–292).

The Mormon Controversy. The struggle between Mormons and the U.S. government was the most serious church-state clash of the nineteenth century. The Mormon church, organized as the Church of Jesus Christ of Latter-day Saints, had sprung from the visions of New York farmer Joseph Smith in 1830. The fervent, disciplined religious sect he fashioned aroused the enmity of neighbors, and Smith's followers were successively chased out of New York, Missouri, and Illinois. Smith's militaristic posture provoked a near war in Missouri, with the governor issuing an extermination order against the Mormons. Retreating to Illinois, Smith was eventually seized and hanged by a lynch mob in 1844. Smith's successor, Brigham Young, led the faithful to the Salt Lake Valley to found what amounted to a theocratic nation (Ahlstrom, 1972).

The federal government stayed aloof from the Mormons until the Territory of Utah came under United States control in 1848, after the Mexican War. The taming of Mormon theocracy by congressional action ensued. The Mormon practice of polygamy, so repugnant to orthodox Christian culture, especially aroused congressional ire. In 1862 the First Antipolygamy Act outlawed polygamy in the territories, and the Supreme Court upheld the statute in 1879. Congress then followed with a more draconian law, the Edmunds Act of 1882, which punished polygamy by imprisonment and disfranchisement and which resulted in confiscation of much church property. Finally, in 1890, the leader of the Mormon church issued a declaration against plural marriages and pledged loyalty to the law of the United States. This barrier removed, Utah was admitted as a state in 1896 (Stokes, 1950, vol. 2, pp. 275–285).

From Prohibition to Pacifism. Animated by America's enormous per capita consumption of hard liquor in the nineteenth century, Christian prohibitionists formed what became the most successful pressure group in U.S. history, the Anti-Saloon League (Clark, 1976). Founded in Oberlin, Ohio, in 1879, the clergy-led movement pursued shrewd tactics through a vast network of ministers, affiliated churches, and publications. The league initially fought for the local option to regulate or close down saloons, a strategy that isolated "wet" areas. State after state was captured, and the movement ultimately became strong enough to gain congressional support for the Eighteenth Amendment, which banned the production and sale of alcoholic beverages. Even unsympathetic members voted for prohibition for fear of electoral defeat. After passing both houses of Congress on 22 December 1917, the amendment sailed through state legislatures, gaining the three-quarters necessary for ratification on 19 January 1919. Congress then passed the Volstead Act, the enabling legislation for the amendment, in September 1919 and quickly overrode President Woodrow Wilson's veto. The law went into effect in January 1920 and lasted until prohibition was repealed by the Twenty-first Amendment in 1933. The prohibition era marked the high-water mark of Protestant domination of American culture, and Congress would never again be so swayed by a single religiously based movement.

At about the same time as prohibition was introduced, the increasing international responsibilities of the United States intensified clashes between the government and those claiming religious objection to war. For much of the nation's history Congress had included provisos in draft laws exempting members of historically pacifist churches (principally Quakers, Mennonites, and Brethren). During the Civil War, for example, Congress first exempted Quakers from the draft in the 1863 Conscription Act and then others in 1864 (Stokes, 1950, vol. 3, pp. 264–266). In World War I, Congress only went so far as to offer noncombatant service to conscientious objectors, a policy which led to imprisonment of those who would not agree even indirectly to aid the war. On the eve of World War II, Congress again took up the draft and again exempted persons belonging to well-established pacifist churches. Church leaders, however, lobbied for broader interpretation of the religious exemption, and the Selective Training and Service Act of 1940 was amended to include more generous language encompassing religious training and belief, not just membership in pacifist denominations (Stokes, 1950, vol. 3, pp. 293–296). During the Vietnam era, religious organizations again pushed to liberalize conscientious objector provisions in Selective Service legislation and administration.

Religious Exemption from Taxation. Deeply rooted in common law and centuries of tradition, the practice of exempting religious entities from taxation has been affirmed by Congress on a number of occasions. The most compelling argument for such an exemption is that it promotes freedom of religion by limiting government interference with church life. One of the few challenges to the religious exemption occurred in 1875, when President Grant proposed a constitutional amendment to allow the taxation of state and local church property. Though aimed at the Roman Catholic Church, the proposal was so unpopular that it failed to gain congressional sponsorship. Since then, Congress has consistently reaffirmed its support for religious exemptions. In the first modern income-tax statutes, the Revenue Act of 1894 and the Revenue Act of 1913, Congress authorized taxation only on "net income," thus excluding nonprofit organizations. In 1942 Congress overruled an attempt by District of Columbia commissioners to tax church property not specifically devoted to religious purposes. Finally, as tax law has grown increasingly complex from the 1930s on, Congress has codified the religious exemption in numerous sections of the Internal Revenue Code. Though a few limitations have been written into law, these provisions generally have been in favor of broad religious exemption from taxation (Kelley, 1977).

The Growing Religious Presence on Capitol Hill. Up to World War II, Congress dealt with religious constituencies only periodically, as particular issues arose. The mid-twentieth century, however, marked the growth of a permanently organized religious presence in Washington. Precursors included the United Methodist Church, which established a Washington office in 1916 to promote prohibition; the National Catholic Welfare Council, which

set up shop in 1919; and the Society of Friends (Quakers), which opened the first full-time registered religious lobby in Washington in 1943, principally to protect conscientious-objector status (Reichley, 1985). The real growth of religious lobbies, however, came in the post–World War II era, when the prominence and reach of the federal government acted as a magnet for church lobbies. By the 1990s the full spectrum of religious pluralism in the United States was engaged in congressional lobbying—liberal Protestants, conservative evangelicals, African American denominations, Catholics, Jews, and Muslims (Hertzke, 1988).

Initial activity was modest. From the end of World War II through the administration of Dwight D. Eisenhower pacifist churches pushed for demilitarization while officials of mainline denominations offered polite testimony favoring labor, welfare, civil rights, and foreign aid legislation. Federal aid to education produced the greatest contentiousness, with Protestants and Roman Catholics squaring off on whether parochial schools would receive government assistance.

The pace quickened in the 1960s. Inspired by Martin Luther King, Jr., clergy and laypeople flocked to the capital in 1964 in a lobbying campaign to persuade members of Congress to vote for the historic Civil Rights Bill. The liberal National Council of Churches played a pivotal role in planning civil rights strategy and in organizing an effective grassroots campaign in the Midwest among wavering Republican senators who were members of mainline denominations (Findlay, 1990).

The success of this effort sparked religious advocacy on a broad front. By the mid 1970s, for example, a religious antihunger lobby emerged to promote domestic and international food programs. Led by international church relief agencies, domestic church missions, and Bread for the World (formed by Arthur Simon, brother of Sen. Paul Simon of Illinois), the antihunger lobby claimed success in enhancing international food aid and response to famines. Domestically, it contributed to increases in funding for the Women, Infants, and Children program and food stamps.

Galvanized by the movement to end the Vietnam War, liberal Christians also created a permanent lobby against facets of U.S. foreign policy that they deemed militaristic or supportive of right-wing dictators. This effort intensified during the administration of Ronald Reagan as churches became the prime focus for opposition to national security policy. The nuclear freeze movement in the early

Landmark Legislation

Title	Date Enacted	Reference Number	Description
Selective Training and Service Act	1940	54 Stat. 885	Military draft legislation that provided expanded religious conscientious objector status during World War II.
Civil Rights Act	1964	P.L. 88-352	One of the truly landmark pieces of congressional legislation, it began the era of the second reconstruction in the South. Religious lobbying was especially critical in building support among moderate Republican senators in the Midwest.
Hyde amendments	Late 1970s–	—	Numerous riders attached to different pieces of congressional legislation, routinely proscribing any use of federal funds for abortion. Backed aggressively by pro-life evangelical groups and Catholic lobbyists. Reenacted in 1993 after an extensive legislative battle.
Civil Rights Restoration Act	1988	P.L. 100-259	Object of intense religious lobbying, passed only after "abortion neutral" language was included. Its aim was to restore civil rights remedies in light of Supreme Court rulings that narrowed the effect of the law. Viewed as intrusive by some conservative evangelical groups but supported by liberal church leaders.
Equal Access Act	1984	P.L. 98-377	Designed to prohibit school districts from discriminating against high school religious clubs. Passed in wake of the defeat of the school prayer amendment, it accommodated the concerns of diverse Christian groups about the status of student religion in the public schools. Vigorously opposed by Jewish groups.
Child-Care Programs	1990	P.L. 101-508	Contained parental choice provisions in response to religious concerns about impact of federal law on religiously run day-care centers.
Religious Freedom Restoration Act	1993	P.L. 103-141	Broadly supported by diverse religious groups, it was a response to the 1990 Supreme Court case, *Oregon v. Smith*, in which Justice Antonin Scalia, writing for the majority, denied that the government had to demonstrate a "compelling state interest" to justify a restriction on religious practice. The law restored this stringent standard in church-state jurisprudence.

1980s, for example, was infused with church support and gained an enormous boost when the nation's Roman Catholic bishops drafted a pastoral letter, *God's Promise and Our Response*, that was widely interpreted as supporting the freeze. Congressional support for a freeze resolution grew to such an extent that in 1983 the administration offered its own version to forestall an embarrassing snub in the House. Funding for the MX nuclear missile was also opposed by liberal Protestant groups and the Catholic bishops. Finally, churches mounted the principal grassroots pressure against the Reagan administration's program of military aid to the Contras fighting the Marxist Sandinista government in Nicaragua. This pressure contributed to the passage of the Boland Amendment, which restricted U.S. military support for the Contras (Hertzke, 1988).

The Jewish lobby also intensified its national focus in the era. Groups such as the American Jewish Committee, B'nai B'rith, and the American Israel Public Affairs Committee (AIPAC) earned the reputation as the most effective lobbies in Washington. In the 1970s these groups lobbied successfully for provisions that tied favored trade status for the Soviet Union to its liberalization of Jewish emigration. In the 1980s Jewish groups fought to check what they saw as violations of church-state separation advocated by the so-called religious right. And throughout this era the unified and vigorous Jewish lobby fought successfully to maintain close ties between the United States and Israel, protecting generous U.S. aid and opposing arms sales to Arab countries.

Infused with deep religious undercurrents, the debate over abortion emerged in the 1970s as one of the most contentious national issues. Notable congressional battles involved federal funding for abortion and the use of fetal tissue in medical research. The U.S. Catholic Conference, allied with conservative evangelical groups, successfully battled against abortion funding for more than a decade. Leading the fight was Rep. Henry J. Hyde (R-Ill.), a devout Catholic who succeeded in attaching his antiabortion amendment to numerous pieces of legislation. The Hyde Amendments virtually eliminated public funding for abortion from the 1980s into the 1990s. During the administration of George Bush the use of fetal tissue in medical research and treatment became the focus of opposing pro-life and pro-choice camps. Despite efforts by Catholic and religious right lobbies, the Democrat-controlled Congress passed legislation in 1992 to remove the ban on use of fetal tissue. The ban remained in effect, however, when Congress failed to override President Bush's veto. Another battle loomed over the Freedom of Choice bill, an effort by pro-choice forces to protect abortion rights by national statute. Through the early 1990s, the abortion issue continued to cleave Congress.

In the 1980s the conservative fundamentalist Christian movement mounted a major offensive on Capitol Hill (Moen, 1989). The religious right had gained steam in the late 1970s by blocking the Equal Rights Amendment, which passed Congress in 1972 but fell three states short of ratification by its 1982 deadline. Conservative evangelicals and fundamentalists also successfully pushed for heavier federal restrictions on pornography and for guidelines for the National Endowment for the Arts restricting the use of tax dollars for art deemed blasphemous or obscene. On abortion they backed restrictions and supported conservative Supreme Court nominees likely to be sympathetic toward reversing *Roe v. Wade* (1973). By far the most intense lobbying was over school prayer, banned from public schools by the Supreme Court in the 1960s. Backed by President Reagan, fundamentalists in 1984 mobilized millions of members to flood Congress with letters and calls of support for the proposed school prayer amendment. Fierce opposition by liberal Protestant and Jewish organizations and civil liberties groups kept proponents from gaining the necessary two-thirds support needed for passage. In the wake of the school prayer defeat, however, Congress passed the 1984 Equal Access Act, which sanctioned religious clubs in high schools. Religious-right lobbyists viewed this as a partial victory in their war against secularism in public education (Hertzke, 1988).

The growing number and diversity of religious lobbies clearly challenged Congress in the 1980s and 1990s. Such seemingly secular concerns as day care and civil rights became battlegrounds in the war over religious values. The Civil Rights Restoration Act of 1988, for example, was held hostage until "abortion neutral" language, backed by the Catholic Conference, was added to it. A similar dynamic delayed passage until 1993 of the broadly supported Religious Freedom Restoration Act, which sought to strengthen religious grounds for exemptions from secular law. Federal day-care legislation, in turn, sparked a long and complex church-state debate because a good share of U.S. child-care facilities were run by churches. Congress, in its landmark 1990 day-care legislation, ultimately included a certificate option designed to allow parents to use religiously oriented centers. Critics charged that this represented a foot in the door for educational vouchers. Educational choice, in fact, became the rallying cry of an unusual alliance of Catholics and conservative Protestants, the latter formerly opposed to government aid to parochial schools. Expressing discontent with secular public schools, evangelical Protestants joined Catholics in petitioning Congress for tax credits and vouchers that would enable parents to send their children to schools that taught their own religious values.

In the 1990s Congress found itself routinely petitioned by churches and religious groups on issues ranging from the Persian Gulf War to tax policy. Yet the diversity of religious voices increasingly conformed to Madison's vision of "sect checking sect." While each religious viewpoint enjoyed periodic, if modest, success with Congress, none dominated the system, and none is likely to do so in the foreseeable future.

[See also Bill of Rights; Chaplains.]

BIBLIOGRAPHY

Adams, James L. *The Growing Church Lobby in Washington.* 1970.

Ahlstrom, Sydney. *A Religious History of the American People.* 1972.

Benson, Peter C., and Dorothy L. Williams. *Religion on Capitol Hill: Myths and Realities.* 1986.

Clark, Norman H. *Deliver Us From Evil: An Interpretation of American Prohibition.* 1976.

Ebersole, Luke Eugene. *Church Lobbying in the Nation's Capital.* 1951.

Findlay, James F. "Religion and Politics in the Sixties: The Churches and the Civil Rights Act of 1964." *Journal of American History* 77 (1990): 66–92.

Hertzke, Allen D. *Representing God in Washington: The Role of Religious Lobbies in the American Polity.* 1988.

Kelley, Dean M. *Why Churches Should Not Pay Taxes.* 1977.

Malbin, Michael. *Religion and Politics: The Intentions of the Authors of the First Amendment.* 1978.

Moen, Matthew C. *The Christian Right and Congress.* 1989.

Reichley, A. James. *Religion in American Public Life.* 1985.

Stokes, Anson Phelps. *Church and State in the United States.* 3 vols. 1950.

ALLEN D. HERTZKE

REMOVAL POWER.

The power of the president to remove executive officials received close attention from the members of the First Congress. Some members thought that the Senate's role in appointments meant that it should also participate in removals. A few thought that impeachment constituted the only method of removing officials. A third school believed that the power of Congress to create an office implied the right to attach to that office the procedure for removal. After lengthy debate, the First Congress decided that the power to remove the heads of executive departments (at that time Foreign Affairs, Treasury, and War) belonged exclusively to the president as part of the executive power. Congress offered independence from presidential removal, however, to officers, such as the comptroller in the Treasury Department, who carried out adjudicative functions.

By passing the Tenure of Office Act of 1867, Congress attempted to restrict the president's ability to fire cabinet officers by requiring the Senate's approval for all suspensions and removals. President Andrew Johnson vetoed the bill, claiming it violated the intent of the First Congress, but Congress overrode the veto. Johnson fired Secretary of War Edwin M. Stanton in August 1867, setting the stage for the president's impeachment by the House of Representatives. The effort to convict fell one vote short in the Senate. After a confrontation between Congress and President Grover Cleveland, Congress repealed the Tenure of Office Act in 1887.

The Supreme Court decided a number of removal cases from 1839 to 1922, but *Myers v. United States* (1926) represents the first major judicial decision on the removal power. Chief Justice William Howard Taft argued that the president's removal power was largely unrestricted, but his opinion was too broad and required adjustments by future Courts. In *Humphrey's Executor v. United States* (1935), the Court upheld the right of Congress to specify grounds of removal for members of independent regulatory commissions. The particular statute at issue, governing the Federal Trade Commission, permitted the president to remove a commissioner only for inefficiency, neglect of duty, or malfeasance in office. A similar decision was handed down in *Wiener v. United States* (1958). A significant later case concerned the independent counsel, who may be removed by the president only for "good cause." The Reagan administration attacked the statute on numerous grounds, including the removal clause, but in *Morrison v. Olson* (1988) the Court upheld this restriction on the president's removal power by a vote of 7 to 1.

The original intent of the removal power was to protect the unity and responsibility of the presidency. Only with the power to fire subordinates could the president be made accountable. Congress, however, has always taken an interest in removals, sometimes applying pressure to drive executive officials out of government. Scholars have estimated that members of Congress are responsible for more firings and reassignments of executive branch personnel than are caused by presidential initiatives. At other times Congress intervenes to protect officials, such as agency whistle-blowers, who are threatened with removal. Because of its interest in implementing executive programs and having access to agency information, Congress will always take a keen interest in the suspension and removal of federal employees.

[*See also* Morrison v. Olson; Myers v. United States.]

BIBLIOGRAPHY

Corwin, Edward S. *The President's Removal Power under the Constitution.* 1927.

Fisher, Louis. *Constitutional Conflicts between Congress and the President.* 1991.

Hart, James. *The American Presidency in Action.* 1948.

LOUIS FISHER

REORGANIZATION OF CONGRESS.

Conventional wisdom to the contrary, Congress renews itself regularly; at the start of each session, it inevitably adopts some institutional changes, most often minor and perhaps merely cosmetic, but occasionally fundamental. The accretion of change—any shift, intended or inadvertent, gradual or abrupt, in Congress's method of procedure—dramatically alters the contours of the legislative institution but does so in a more-or-less random or unobtrusive fashion over extended periods.

Reform—more conscious efforts to reshape institutional structures and processes—occurs less frequently, most often in response to members' perceptions that their assembly is an ineffective policy-maker or that it is at risk of losing the public approbation necessary to sustain its legitimacy. The years 1910 to 1911 and 1970 to 1977 saw notable manifestations of the reform impulse. More rarely still, reform is embodied in a major statute, a legislative reorganization act, such as those enacted in 1946 and 1970.

Whatever form it takes, change continually alters Congress. The committee-centered institution of the 1980s was a far cry from the party-dominated legislature of the early twentieth century, and the 1990s promise significant change as Congress reels under the burden of both ineffective policy-making and a series of scandals that have undermined its popular standing.

Perspectives on Change and Reform. Self-conscious change—reform and reorganization—most often reflects events in Congress's environment, in the form of international or domestic crises that raise new issues to the top of the legislative agenda and demand efficient organizational forms for effective resolution. In addition, membership turnover may bring new people with different backgrounds, experiences, and perspectives to Congress; newcomers may require new modes of action to achieve their legislative goals. Alternatively, events and new issues may induce incumbent members to reassess their views, leading, among other things, to reorganization of Congress.

The problem confronting would-be reformers is to construct a set of institutional forms that implement their vision of an improved legislature. Several images of the ideal Congress exist, but none has generated consensus or broadly energized lawmakers. At one extreme is an executive-force theory that envisions a Congress subordinate to the president, the only person capable of providing the nation with the leadership it needs. An alternative answer to an immobilized and obstructionist Congress is a responsible political party system. Disciplined, cohesive congressional parties could pass programs with dispatch, either supporting the executive or imposing legislative priorities. Adherents of the "literary" theory revere the tradition of checks and balances and separation of powers they see embedded in the text of the Constitution; they look to Congress to check the power-seeking president and to deter radical policy initiatives. Finally, congressional supremacists (reflecting the Whig tradition of the mid-nineteenth century) envision a dominant first branch of government as the prime mover in national politics, able to set policy and to oversee its implementation.

These broad visions of an altered Congress have inspired little interest beyond academic circles; rather, reform and reorganization have proceeded more pragmatically, more incrementally, in response to contemporary political pressures. One strand of change has sought to make Congress more responsible, more capable of enacting effective policy with dispatch. A responsible legislature resolves policy problems successfully and efficiently. A second set of changes has emphasized responsiveness, the capacity of Congress to consider carefully and act in accordance with the expressed preferences of those—citizens, organized groups, local and state governments, and presidents and federal bureaucrats—whom its actions will affect. There is a tension between responsibility and responsiveness: a responsible Congress will act rapidly and decisively; a responsive assembly will move slowly, waiting for those with opinions to voice them and for some basic agreement to emerge. A third focus of change has been accountability, the ability of citizens to discover what Congress and its members have done and to hold them to account what they have, or have not, accomplished. Responsibility, responsiveness, and accountability—concepts narrower than the broad philosophic visions—offer benchmarks against which to assess Congress's performance.

Reorganization and Reform, 1946–1992. Recent reformers have sought to improve congressional performance in each of these three areas. A major effort has been made to enhance the legislature's decision-making prowess, that is, to make Congress more responsible. Earlier reforms, beginning with the 1910–1911 revolt against the domineering Speaker of the House, Joseph G. Cannon (R-Ill.), brought down a centralized party apparatus and led to the emergence of a fragmented, atomized institution where individual members enjoyed considerable freedom to pursue their own career interests from positions of strength within independent committees and subcommittees. The lessons of the Depression and World War II suggested that a more efficient Congress was in order.

Thus, the Legislative Reorganization Act of 1946 sought to streamline a chaotic committee system, paring the number of House committees to nineteen (from forty-eight) and of Senate panels to fifteen (from thirty-three) and rationalizing their jurisdictions. Recognizing that Congress (following

TABLE 1. *Landmarks of Legislative Reorganization*

1910–1911	"Revolt" against Speaker of the House Joseph G. Cannon (R-Ill.). Stripped the Speaker of the ability to manage House affairs through control of powerful political parties; marked the advent of the modern committee-centered Congress.
1921	Budget and Accounting Act (42 Stat. 20–27). Assigned the president the task of submitting a unified executive budget to Congress; initiated contemporary budget practices.
1946	Legislative Reorganization Act of 1946 (60 Stat. 812–852). Sought to restructure the committee system, create a comprehensive budget process, and provide Congress with improved information resources.
1961	House Rules Committee enlarged.
1970–1977	Major postwar reform era, beginning formally with passage of the Legislative Reorganization Act of 1970 (84 Stat. 1140–1204). Simultaneously decentralized the congressional process, strengthened the political parties, and opened congressional deliberations to public scrutiny.
1985	Balanced Budget and Emergency Deficit Control (Gramm-Rudman-Hollings) Act (99 Stat. 1038). Revised the budget process significantly.
1990	Budget Enforcement Act (P.L. 101-508). Major revision of the budget process.
1992–	Revival of interest in broad congressional reform. Creation of a Joint Committee on the Organization of Congress.

the procedures of the 1921 Budget and Accounting Act) had not handled its fiscal responsibilities competently, the act called for a legislative budget, an omnibus bill that would treat revenues and expenditures in unified fashion. Finally, the act provided Congress with vastly enlarged information resources and analytic capacity in the form of professional personal and committee staff and a bigger and better Legislative Reference Service in the Library of Congress. The reformers, following the recommendations of a Joint Committee on the Organization of Congress, hoped to make Congress better able to address effectively the nation's pressing policy problems.

The 1946 legislation was less than a total success. Changes in the legislative agenda and members' career interests led to the creation of new committees (four in the House, one in the Senate) and, more significantly in the long term, to the proliferation of subcommittees. The new budget process did not work; here, too, the goals of individualistic, election-oriented members prevailed over the need for efficiency, and budgeting almost immediately reverted to its previous form, with fiscal decisions parceled out among thirteen virtually autonomous Appropriations subcommittees. Only the increase in information resources endured; Congress continues to call on its own expertise to buttress its policy-making efforts.

In the 1960s, reformers focused on the House Rules Committee, the "traffic cop" that, among other things, manages the flow of legislation to the House floor. In the previous decade, two conservative southern Democrats, including the chairman, voted frequently with the four Rules Republicans,

all conservatives, to deadlock the twelve-member committee at 6 to 6, thus preventing the majority Democrats' policy initiatives from reaching the floor. Following the 1960 election, the liberal bloc in the House narrowly (217 to 212) won a difficult fight to enlarge the committee to fifteen members, ostensibly giving the majority an 8 to 7 working margin. In the 1970s, the Democrats empowered the Speaker, subject to caucus approval, to nominate Rules members; they set the ratio of members from the majority and minority parties at "2 to 1 plus 1" (currently nine Democrats and four Republicans). In the 89th Congress (1965–1967), the Democrats adopted a "twenty-one-day rule" that in effect prevented the committee from holding up bills for more than three weeks. (The ensuing Congress, however, repealed the rule.) Overall, the reformers succeeded in harnessing the sometimes defiant Rules Committee to the party leadership, smoothing the flow of legislation to the House floor.

In the mid 1960s and after, learning from its inability to exert its collective influence with respect to the war in Vietnam and the Watergate scandals, Congress launched a new effort to enhance institutional responsibility. As a consequence of agitation for change from the Democratic Study Group (an informal caucus of liberal Democrats) and the recommendations of a new Joint Committee on the Organization of Congress, the Legislative Reorganization Act of 1970 inaugurated an unprecedented period of reform. In the ensuing years, the House Democratic Caucus adopted a wide variety of other changes; reform in the Senate was considerably more restrained. Efforts to make Congress more responsible followed two tracks: reclaiming traditional authority ceded unwisely to the president and instituting a more efficient decision-making process.

To resist executive domination, Congress enacted the War Powers Resolution in 1973. Passed over Richard M. Nixon's veto, the act circumscribed the commander in chief's ability to commit the armed forces to combat by empowering Congress to compel the president to withdraw troops sent into the field at any time, or within sixty days of deployment if Congress did not declare war or extend the sixty-day period by law. Also, to regain control over federal expenditures, the legislature enacted the Congressional Budget and Impoundment Control Act of 1974. The law was designed to allow Congress to produce a coherent, comprehensive budget that compared revenues and expenditures, thus offering a clear picture of the deficit. The act also created new procedures that permitted Congress to curb the president's capacity to impound—refuse to spend—duly authorized and appropriated funds. The act did not stem the flow of red ink—members found creative ways to evade its strictures—and Congress modified it with the Gramm-Rudman-Hollings Balanced Budget Act (1985) and the Budget Enforcement Act (1990). The former exacted automatic spending cuts if the deficit exceeded prescribed levels; the latter abandoned a focus on the deficit and sought instead to impose spending limits (caps) on domestic, military, and international outlays. Third, building on the precedent of the 1946 Reorganization Act, Congress gave itself new staff and support agency information resources to enable it to countervail the executive with its own expertise.

A second dimension of the attempt to enhance responsibility was to make the policy-making process less fragmented. To that end, the House Democratic Caucus (in a Democratic-controlled Congress) sought to limit the independence of individual committee chairs. It decreed that seniority (length of committee service) would no longer automatically determine who would preside in the committee room; it empowered its Steering and Policy Committee to recommend chairs using other criteria and retained the right to vote to reject that panel's nominations. The Speaker of the House won new authority to control the Steering and Policy Committee; to nominate, subject to caucus approval, members of the Rules Committee and thus to exercise some influence over the conditions under which bills were considered on the House floor; to regulate the flow of legislation to and from committee (through the prerogative to refer bills to several panels); and to create ad hoc committees and task forces to facilitate systematic treatment of complex policy issues. These changes, reformers hoped, would give the majority party improved capacity to centralize congressional operations and enact policy more efficiently.

In the Senate, the major effort to advance responsibility was a limitation of the minority's capacity to filibuster—to use unlimited debate to tie up the chamber and defeat or substantially weaken controversial legislation (such as civil rights bills). Until 1975, a two-thirds majority of those present and voting (sixty-seven votes if all senators were in attendance) was required to invoke cloture (end debate). After that year, a constitutional three-fifths majority (sixty votes) could force Senate action.

In the 1970s, Congress also put in place significant reforms for responsiveness, reflecting the desire of dissatisfied lawmakers for greater participation and influence on policy. Substantial pieces of committee power were reallocated to the rank and file. The consolidation of full committees under the 1946 Legislative Reorganization Act led to the proliferation of subcommittees—to facilitate Congress's division of labor and to provide senior members with positions of influence. At the time of the act, there were approximately 97 House subcommittees; by the 94th (1975–1977) Congress there were 151; by the 103d (1993–1995), the number declined to 120. In the Senate, there were roughly 34 subcommittees in 1946; the number peaked at 140 in the 94th Congress, but fell back to 86 in the 103d.

New rules reined in the full committee chairs, limited the committee and subcommittee chairmanships that any individual could hold, and established procedures that enabled more members to attain desirable subcommittee assignments. A "subcommittee bill of rights" required that subcommittees have fixed jurisdictions and that legislation within their jurisdictions be referred automatically to them; it also authorized subcommittees to meet at the pleasure of their members, to write their own rules, and to manage their own budgets and staffs. In 1975, the Democratic Caucus mandated that all House committees with more than twenty members create a minimum of four subcommittees. These reforms democratized the House; more members, responding to more diverse constituency and group interests, occupied positions from which they could exercise some influence over some parts of the legislative agenda. But the reforms also made responsible decision making more problematic: the increased number of players with greater ability to influence policy made forging coalitions to enact meaningful legislation more difficult.

Another route to reorganization and reform led toward increased accountability. To restore its popular standing, damaged by policy failure and a series of highly publicized scandals, the legislature enacted a set of reforms designed to expose its operations to citizens' scrutiny. Members were to conduct the public's business in public: committees were to meet in open session; votes in committee and on the floor were to be recorded; and proceedings were made available for live television coverage on the C-SPAN network. Both the House and Senate adopted codes of ethics, including financial disclosure provisions, intended to deter or expose conflicts of interest. The Federal Election Campaign Act (1971), as interpreted by the Supreme Court in *Buckley v. Valeo* (1976) and amended subsequently by Congress, set up an election finance system that limited contributors' donations but not candidates' expenditures. Moreover, it stipulated that candidates report in detail the sources—individuals and political action committees (PACs)—of their funds and the uses to which they put the money; the Federal Election Commission, which administers the campaign act, publishes this data. Both the ethics codes and the campaign statute aim to permit concerned citizens to discover to whom, if anyone, senators and representatives are financially beholden and to assess whether members' personal or political interests impinge on matters about which they must vote or otherwise act. Dissatisfied voters can exact retribution at the ballot box.

These reforms of the 1970s failed to revive Congress's flagging reputation. A series of new revelations further undercut public support for the legislature: charges of ethical improprieties led to the resignations in 1989 of House Speaker James C. Wright, Jr. (D-Tex.) and Majority Leader Tony Coelho (D-Calif.); more than three hundred members wrote overdrafts on the House bank; a group of senators, the so-called Keating five, were chastised for ethically dubious relations with a savings and loan executive; and the public became aware of members' perquisites (e.g., subsidized meals and beauty services and free [franked] mail) that made the lawmakers appear to be a pampered elite.

Further reforms ensued in 1991 and 1992. As a quid pro quo for a sizable salary increase, the House and Senate gave up honoraria paid to members by various interests for speeches and articles. The House Bank was shut down, the franking privilege limited, and other perquisites eliminated or reduced; professional administrators, particularly a director of Non-Legislative and Financial Services, assumed responsibility for day-to-day House operations. Again, the intent of these changes was to demonstrate that Congress acts openly and aboveboard and thus to rekindle public confidence in the legislature.

The Impact of Reorganization and Reform. In the short term, reform favored responsiveness (fragmentation) over responsibility (centralization) while simultaneously enlarging the potential for (if not the reality of) accountability. On balance, Congress has neither often reclaimed authority from, nor regularly imposed its programmatic judgments on, the executive. The War Powers Act has not enabled the legislature to impose its will systematically on the president. Reshaping the budget process— in the 1974 act and with the Gramm-Rudman-Hollings experiment with automatic spending cuts or the efforts of 1990 and after to cap spending—has not reduced outlays or the growth of the deficit. Even enlarged legislative expertise has produced mixed results. Congress does have greater access to more and better data with which to propose legislative alternatives to executive initiatives, but politically motivated lawmakers often have little incentive to use policy analysis or, if they do, may find themselves overwhelmed with a surfeit of data.

Nor has the House majority party's new authority—control over committee chairs, the Speaker's enhanced influence over committee assignments and the Rules Committee, and the multiple referral power—consistently produced cohesive partisan majorities. To be sure, a curious concatenation of events at the end of the 1980s—increased party polarization stemming from divided government and greater ideological homogeneity among the Democrats, coupled with Speaker Jim Wright's aggressive use of the full panoply of leadership powers—led to somewhat greater party cohesion among members, who came to recognize the need to pull together to enact party programs. Whether such centralization and its attendant party discipline will continue under Speaker Thomas S. Foley (D-Wash.) and his successors remains questionable.

More significantly, recent legislative change has made Congress more responsive. The breach of the seniority tradition, the allocation of leadership positions among a wider array of more junior members, the devolution of authority to independent subcommittees at the expense of full committee chairs, and the provision of greater staff and analytic resources have, especially in the House, afforded more members, responding to more interests, a piece of the policy-making action. Enhanced responsiveness, however, has not been without cost. Responsibility, or policy-making efficiency, has suffered. Specialization and expertise have declined; fewer members have the capacity to formulate coherent and effective policies on any given subject. With more participants possessing influence, assembling coalitions at the multiple stages of the lawmaking process becomes more difficult, requiring more negotiation and compromise among more interests and reducing the possibilities for truly innovative programs.

The contemporary Congress is more accountable, but this also is not necessarily an unmixed blessing. In principle, the campaign and financial disclosure rules make the public better able to ferret out members' potential ethical and economic conflicts of interest; in reality, there is little evidence that citizens are inclined to do so. There has been no diminution in charges of ethical and campaign malfeasance, as the House bank and post office scandals and the Keating five affair amply illustrate. Moreover, the necessity of acting openly, in public, forces members to protect their political flanks; with lobbyists, journalists, and administrative officials monitoring their behavior, they may be reluctant to take the political risks that responsible policy-making entails.

Yet incumbents have continued to win reelection in overwhelming numbers. In 1992, 88 percent of incumbents seeking reelection retained their seats, down only slightly from the rates of over 90 percent that characterized the 1980–1990 decade. Electoral margins, however, decreased significantly in both 1990 and 1992, and 67 retirements in the latter year coupled with the defeat of 43 incumbents brought 110 new members to the House. Eighty-two percent of incumbent senators seeking new terms (twenty-two out of twenty-seven seeking reelection) won in 1992; newcomers to the 103d Senate totaled fourteen. Although more vulnerable, incumbents continue to win in impressive numbers.

Reorganization and Reform in the 1990s. Reorganization and reform have thus changed the nature of congressional responsibility, responsiveness, and accountability incrementally, but sometimes with unexpected results. In consequence, a number of items remain on the reform agenda, and Congress has established another Joint Committee on the Reorganization of Congress to explore them. Some attention will go to improving legislative responsibility. Recognizing that a decentralized decision-making process contributes substantially to congres-

sional policy-making immobilism, senior members proposed another joint committee to tackle such issues as simplification of the tangled and overlapping committee jurisdictions, reducing the excessive use of subcommittees, streamlining the complicated budget process, and strengthening the position of party leaders in relation to the committees and their chairs. Such changes would move Congress toward party-based centralization, reducing responsiveness to parochial constituency interests and enabling the legislature to move policy initiatives forward more efficiently. Term limitations—barring members from serving more than twelve years in Congress or more than six or eight years as committee chairs—would, proponents argue, concentrate member attention on policy and the national interest rather than on reelection concerns.

Greater attention will likely be given to accountability. Campaign finance and congressional ethics seem certain to be subjects of intensive and extensive debate. High reelection rates for incumbents, achieved with the help of campaign contributions from political action committees, are inviting targets. Career-oriented legislators, critics allege, place electoral above other concerns and make concessions to special interests to gain financial support for excessively and increasingly expensive media-driven campaigns; they vote themselves abundant perquisites to the same end, it is said. Spending limits, restrictions on PAC contributions, and public funding of campaigns emerge as possible remedies, but consensus has proved elusive. Minority Republicans reject spending caps and public finance as inimical to their efforts to unseat Democratic incumbents. Sitting Democrats are disinclined to limit PACs, a significant source of their contributions.

Continuing controversy over legislative ethics—highlighted by the House bank and Keating five scandals, among others—has spawned a host of reform issues. Most significant is the need to define "proper" constituency service. When does a legitimate effort to serve residents of the members' states or districts become a self-serving exercise of policy-making power or unwarranted interference in administrative matters? Limitation of member perquisites is likely to proceed apace, salary increases and use of franked mail will be difficult to sustain, and staff resources will not grow and may even be reduced. Pressure to ensure coverage of Congress under worker safety and antidiscrimination laws, from which it has exempted itself, will not diminish. The legislature will face increasing demands to organize and display its activities in ways that promote the public's ability to evaluate the propriety of congressional performance.

Congress, in short, has changed and continues to change. Reorganization and reform proceed, sometimes dramatically in response to singular events, more often quietly and in evolutionary rather than revolutionary fashion. The institution tries, haltingly and incrementally in most instances, to balance its needs to be responsible, responsive, and accountable. On the whole, these efforts produce a mixed record of success and failure, guaranteeing that reorganization and reform will continue to animate at least some members of Congress as well as attentive observers of the national legislature.

[*See also* Balanced Budget and Emergency Deficit Control Act; Buckley v. Valeo; Budget and Accounting Act; Budget Enforcement Act of 1990; Cannon Revolt; House Bank; Legislative Reorganization Acts; Organization of Congress Committee, Joint.]

BIBLIOGRAPHY

Center for Responsive Politics. *"Not for the Short Winded": Congressional Reform, 1961–1986*. 1986.

Davidson, Roger H. "The Advent of the Modern Congress: The Legislative Reorganization Act of 1946." *Legislative Studies Quarterly* 15 (1990): 357–373.

Davidson, Roger H., David M. Kovenock, and Michael K. O'Leary. *Congress in Crisis: Politics and Congressional Reform*. 1966.

Davidson, Roger H., and Walter J. Oleszek. *Congress against Itself*. 1977.

Kravitz, Walter. "The Advent of the Modern Congress: The Legislative Reorganization Act of 1970." *Legislative Studies Quarterly* 15 (1990): 375–399.

Magleby, David B., and Candice J. Nelson. *The Money Chase: Congressional Campaign Finance Reform*. 1990.

Ornstein, Norman J., ed. *Congress in Change: Evolution and Reform*. 1975.

Rieselbach, Leroy N. *Congressional Reform*. 1986.

Rohde, David W. *Parties and Leaders in the Postreform House*. 1991.

Sheppard, Burton D. *Rethinking Congressional Reform: The Reform Roots of the Special Interest Congress*. 1985.

LEROY N. RIESELBACH

REPORTERS OF DEBATE. *See* Debate, Reporters of.

REPRESENTATION. Literally, *representation* means to make present again, so that constituents' opinions are faithfully translated into public policy by their elected representatives. Public officials, especially members of Congress, are also expected to have their own positions on questions of public policy. Thus, there is a tension between whether legislators should follow their own views of what the best policies are or whether they should simply reflect the opinions of their constituents. Should they follow Edmund Burke, the eighteenth-century British political philosopher and member of Parliament, and be "trustees" of the public interest? Or should they behave as instructed "delegates"?

Burke told voters in his Bristol constituency that local interests ought not dictate policy decisions in Parliament. Legislators must look out for the national interest and use their best judgment to determine what that is, for ultimately Bristol's interest is the same as that of all England. Adherents of the "delegate" role follow the dictum of former Speaker of the House Thomas P. (Tip) O'Neill (D-Mass.): "All politics is local." The principal duty of a public official is to represent constituency interests faithfully in a legislative body. Legislators who do this are more faithfully making their constituents present in the legislature—and this, after all, is what democracy is all about.

Delegates please their constituents by speaking forcefully for their policy views in a national forum. The voters will in turn signal their pleasure by reelecting such legislators. Delegates must engage in a continuing struggle to determine public opinion and to reconcile the conflicting views of many different constituencies in a single national policy. Trustees face no such problem. They must only have a clear vision of what good policy should be. If voters reject the legislator's vision, they may, and often do, cast ballots against the incumbent, as Burke himself learned. Trustees agree to a trade-off. In return for autonomy in actions in the legislature, trustees risk defeat when their votes stray too far from public opinion. Delegates protect themselves from defeat on the issues, but they have virtually no autonomy. Elections are essential to accountability for trustees; they are less central to keeping delegates in line.

More legislators claim to be trustees than delegates or "politicos," who sometimes follow public opinion and at other times use their own judgment. Yet legislators are always cognizant of public opinion and often appear to be slaves to it. How do they know what their constituents want—and how often do they get it right? Until the 1940s there were no scientific public opinion polls; even now, polls are too expensive for members of Congress to use routinely. The mail is an unreliable source of constituency opinion, because extremists of both the left and the right are far more likely than centrists to take the trouble to communicate their views in writing. Much correspondence results from organized efforts that mobilize only a small part of a constituency. Legislators have to rely on their own instincts, which have sharpened as they have grown up and made careers in their constituencies.

Good politicians know the pulses of their constituencies. In the aggregate, agreement between legislators and constituents is quite strong. Yet representatives often misperceive their own constituents' views on key questions of public policy. On a few highly controversial issues, legislators are likely to have a clear view of public opinion, but these situations are atypical of legislator-constituency relations. Legislators' own views are far better predictors of their voting behavior in Congress and other chambers than are constituents' attitudes. Delegates do not perceive constituency opinion any better than trustees.

For the representational nexus to work, constituents must know legislators' positions and roll-call behavior. Few do, and even fewer cast their ballots for legislators primarily on policy grounds. Senate elections are more strongly affected by issues than are contests for the House. It is harder for senators to please diverse constituencies on policy grounds than it is for members of the House, whose districts are usually much more homogenous. House members often try to secure leeway in voting on issues by stressing other aspects of representation. They emphasize their local roots, their common culture with their constituents. Legislators underscore the symbolic nature of representation when they tell constituents, "I am one of you." On the one hand, they seek to reassure voters that they are faithfully re-presenting constituency views in the legislature. They also emphasize the uniqueness of the district by implicitly claiming, "We are not them. We have our own interests." On the other hand, legislators make the voters' task more difficult. They downplay the role of issues when they stress the role of personal trust between the legislator and the district. In turn, legislators buy more freedom of action from their constituents, whom they urge to judge them on other grounds.

Whom should representatives represent? The implicit assumption in most studies of representation is that elected officials should respond to the entire geographic constituency. Yet this may be difficult in heterogenous districts and entire states. Senators and many representatives may instead choose to pay closer attention to their electoral coalitions in the primary and general elections. Legislators may perceive the views of their supporters more accurately than the positions of the entire district. A large segment of the electorate may go unrepresented.

Both students of Congress and members themselves have increasingly expanded the concept of representation. In the past, debates revolved around whether members should be delegates or trustees. The focus was on public policy. There were also questions of symbolic representation. Could whites represent blacks? Could men represent women? These questions were mostly subsidiary to the delegate-trustee issue. Now, virtually everything a representative does falls under the rubric of representation. Providing constituency benefits such as a new post office, informing constituents through regular mailings, running errands for constituents, and even creating media images are now important aspects of representation.

[See also Accountability; Constituency Outreach; Constituency Service.]

BIBLIOGRAPHY

Davidson, Roger H. *The Role of the Congressman.* 1969.

Miller, Warren E., and Donald E. Stokes. "Constituency Influence in Congress." *American Political Science Review* 57 (1963): 45–57.

Uslaner, Eric M. "Legislative Behavior: The Study of Representation." In *Annual Review of Political Science.* Vol. 1. Edited by Samuel Long. 1986.

Wahlke, John C., Heinz Eulau, William Buchanan, and Leroy C. Ferguson. *The Legislative System.* 1962.

ERIC M. USLANER

REPRESENTATIVE. A person selected, most commonly through an election, to act on behalf of a larger number of people in a decision-making body is called a representative. Representatives are expected to be typical of their constituents, and a representative chamber is expected to be a condensation of the nation.

The House of Representatives, with its 435 members and two-year terms, was designed to be the legislative chamber with closer ties to popular opinion. As such, its members are called "representatives." This was not the initial expectation for senators, who were originally appointed for six-year terms to shield them from the public's shifting ideas.

Usually the links between representatives and their constituents depend on policy agreement.

Some people also demand symbolic representation, in which politically important groups are represented by one of their own. In this view, blacks can best represent blacks, women can best represent women. Some political systems even reserve seats for designated groups in decision-making bodies. The Democratic party initiated quotas in order to ensure inclusion of blacks, women, and young people in its convention in 1972. Symbolic representation does not inevitably result in better policy congruence between leaders and their constituents.

Both policy-based and symbolic representation must confront the issue of whom representatives should represent. Must legislators pay attention to their entire constituencies or only to those who voted for them? Is representation simply a matter of following constituency preferences on all issues, or should representatives exercise independent judgment? These are all controversial issues in the study of representation that have no ready answers.

[See also Senator.]

BIBLIOGRAPHY

Dexter, Lewis Anthony. "The Representative and His District." In *New Perspectives on the House of Representatives*. 2d ed. Edited by Robert L. Peabody and Nelson W. Polsby. 1969.
Pitkin, Hanna Fenichel. *The Concept of Representation*. 1967.

ERIC M. USLANER

REPUBLICAN PARTY. The Republican party has been one of the two major parties in the United States almost from the moment of its founding in the mid 1850s. During most of its first seventy-five years it was the accepted majority party in national politics. While it generally has been the minority party in Congress since the early 1930s, since the 1952 election of Dwight D. Eisenhower as president the Republican party usually has been competitive and often dominant in presidential politics.

The Republican party has largely been the more conservative of the two major national parties in the sense of promoting probusiness policies, opposing high taxes, favoring strong national defense, advocating stringent law enforcement measures, and espousing the moral views of culturally dominant (until the 1960s) middle-class Protestants. The party has carried on the broad ideological tradition launched by Alexander Hamilton and then promulgated by the earlier Federalist and Whig parties. Like all major U.S. political parties, however, the Republican party has been a coalition of economic and regional as well as ideological groups, and it has included a large element of pragmatism in its approach to politics.

The impetus behind the formation of the Republican party was the 1854 passage of the Kansas-Nebraska Act, opening western territories to slavery. The Whigs, who had championed the conservative tradition with considerable success during the 1840s, were divided and destroyed by differences over slavery between their northern and southern wings. The other major party, the Democrats, was also racked by disputes over slavery. Simultaneously, the national political scene was torn by the meteoric rise of the American (or Know-Nothing) party, fed by nativist reaction against immigrants and Catholics.

During the winter of 1854 hundreds of meetings to protest the Kansas-Nebraska Act were held throughout the North. Some of these meetings called for formation of a new national party. The gathering most often credited with founding the Republican party was held in the small town of Ripon, Wisconsin, on the night of 20 March 1854. The new party took the name *Republican*, according to one of its founders, to attract Democrats who traced their political lineage to the Republican party of Thomas Jefferson and to appeal to the sizable block of German voters in the Midwest who associated the term with the failed German revolution of 1848.

Unlike earlier antislavery parties, the Republicans embraced a broad program of economic and social proposals, including a high protective tariff, government support for industry, extension of public education, and construction of a railroad to the Pacific. In its first election, in the fall of 1854, the Republican party won a plurality in the U.S. House of Representatives and captured fifteen of sixty Senate seats. Two years later the party's first presidential candidate, Gen. John C. Fremont, explorer of the West, lost narrowly to his Democratic opponent, James Buchanan. The Democrats regained control of the House, but in the midterm elections of 1858, Republicans again won a plurality in the House and made further headway in the Senate.

By 1860 the conflict over slavery had become so acute that the Democrats' northern and southern wings divided, nominating separate candidates for president. Rejecting the presidential candidacy of their best known congressional leader, William H. Seward of New York, the Republicans nominated Abraham Lincoln of Illinois, whose elective experience was limited to one term as a Whig member of the House in the 1840s. (A fourth party, the Constitutional Union, dedicated to preserving the Union at any cost, fielded its own candidate.) Against divided opposition Lincoln carried every northern state and was elected president with a plurality of only 40 percent of the popular vote. Afterward, southern states seceded from the Union, and most of their representatives in Congress withdrew, causing a sharp drop in Democratic strength. The Republicans achieved clear majorities in both houses.

Congressional Republicans not only supported Lincoln's call for military action against the South but also pushed the most extensive legislative program that had ever been enacted, including the Homestead Act of 1862, distributing public lands to small farmers; the Agricultural College Act of 1862, giving land to states for "agricultural and mechanical colleges" (the basis of most state universities); an increased protective tariff; the National Banking Act of 1863, providing capital for industrial growth; creation of the first national paper currency; and chartering of the Union Pacific and Central Pacific railroads. In 1865, the Republican Congress, with Lincoln's support, passed the Thirteenth Amendment, abolishing slavery.

Although some leaders of the so-called Radical Republicans in Congress, such as Sen. Charles Sumner of Massachusetts and Rep. Thaddeus Stevens of Pennsylvania, were at times critical of Lincoln's conduct of the war and his delay in moving against slavery, the bond of party generally preserved a close working relationship between the president and the congressional majority. Lincoln was effective with Congress in part because he built in the executive branch a vast patronage machine that aided Republican candidates in congressional elections.

The Gilded Age. After war's end and Lincoln's assassination in 1865, congressional Republicans quarreled with his successor, Andrew Johnson, a former Democratic senator from Tennessee, over his administration's lenience toward the former slaveholding class in the South. When Johnson set out to purge Radical Republicans from Congress in the midterm elections of 1866, House Republicans established their own campaign committee—the ancestor of the current National Republican Congressional Committee. (The parallel Senate Republican campaign committee was not founded until passage in 1913 of the Seventeenth Amendment requiring the direct election of senators.)

Radical Republicans triumphed over Johnson's candidates in the congressional elections of 1866 and two years later nominated and elected as president Ulysses S. Grant, who had led Union armies to victory in the Civil War. Under Grant, the federal patronage machine was placed at the disposal of four Radical Republican senators: Roscoe Conkling of New York, Simon Cameron of Pennsylvania, Zachariah Chandler of Michigan, and Oliver H. P. T. Morton of Indiana. John A. Logan of Illinois joined them after his election to the Senate in 1871.

The Radical Republican bosses in the Senate, who soon became known as "stalwarts," devoted much of their attention to maintaining the state machines that assured their reelections. They also enacted measures promoting industry and supported civil rights for newly enfranchised blacks in the South. In the House, Speaker James G. Blaine of Maine pursued a somewhat independent course but was, if anything, even more closely allied with business.

The financial panic of 1873, coupled with the gradual return to power of white supremacists in the South, restored Democratic fortunes. The 1874 midterm elections reduced the Republicans to a minority in the House for the first time since 1858. The Republican candidate, Gov. Rutherford B. Hayes of Ohio, narrowly won the 1876 presidential election on the basis of disputed returns from three southern states still occupied by federal troops. As part of the deal through which congressional Democrats accepted Hayes's election, Republican leaders agreed to withdraw federal backing from problack southern state administrations. The South became a Democratic—and white supremacist—preserve for more than eighty years.

From 1874 to 1894 the two major parties were closely competitive at the national level. The Republicans won three presidential elections and the Democrats two. The Republicans controlled the Senate in all except two Congresses (those elected in 1878 and 1892), but the Democrats held majorities in the House in all except two (those elected in 1880 and 1888). Democratic national strength, however, was largely dependent on almost solid support from the South. In much of the North, including such major cities as Philadelphia, Boston, Pittsburgh, Cleveland, and Cincinnati, the Republicans were generally dominant. In twenty-one northern states casting a total of 715 electoral votes in the four presidential elections from 1880 to 1892, the Republicans won all but forty-five votes.

Republican unity on roll-call votes in Congress during the period, though varying somewhat from year to year, was generally high, sustained in part

REPUBLICAN HEADQUARTERS IN CHICAGO. Built for the meeting of the Republican convention of 1860.

HARPER'S PICTORIAL HISTORY OF THE GREAT REBELLION

by shared probusiness ideology and in part by the influence of Republican state machines, which controlled nominations and used patronage to enforce discipline. Moderate conservatives such as Sen. John Sherman of Ohio occasionally persuaded congressional Republicans to support measures such as the Sherman Antitrust Act of 1890, aimed at restraining the power of business trusts. But a second generation of Senate bosses, along with House conservatives such as Speaker Thomas B. Reed of Maine and Rep. William McKinley of Ohio, generally sustained party cooperation with business. Under Reed's leadership in the closely divided House elected in 1888, Republicans enhanced the power of the Speaker to facilitate passage of legislation favored by the majority.

Responding in 1896 to the challenge of populist Democrat William Jennings Bryan, the Republicans nominated McKinley, who in 1893 had become governor of Ohio, for president. Riding on the coattails of McKinley's decisive victory, Republicans achieved large majorities in both houses of Congress, which they maintained for more than a decade.

The Progressive Era. Having defeated Bryan and the populists, the victorious Republicans soon fell to quarreling among themselves. Republicans who called themselves progressives attacked the business trusts, which were closely allied with party conservatives, like Senators Marcus A. Hanna of Ohio and Thomas C. Platt of New York, and with the patronage-based state machines. One group of progressives, exemplified by Gov. Robert M. La Follette of Wisconsin, concentrated on broadening public participation in government and breaking up business monopolies. Another group, exemplified by Gov. Theodore Roosevelt of New York, emphasized rationalization of government. In 1900 McKinley, to the horror of most conservatives, chose Roosevelt as his running mate for vice president. Soon after his landslide reelection, McKinley was assassinated and Roosevelt was president.

As president, Roosevelt often made common cause with such progressive congressional Republicans as George W. Norris of Nebraska, elected to the House in 1902, and La Follette, elected to the Senate in 1905. But he also maintained cordial ties with congressional conservatives, led by House Speaker Joseph G. Cannon of Illinois and Sen. Nelson W. Aldrich of Rhode Island. His reward was enactment of a series of moderate economic and governmental reforms.

Roosevelt's chosen successor, William Howard Taft of Ohio, elected president in 1908, favored many of the progressives' governmental goals but cast his political lot with Cannon and Aldrich. The result was revolt by progressive Republicans in Congress and a growing split within the party. In 1910 House progressives led by Norris formed an alliance with Democrats to reduce drastically the Speaker's authority, thereby curbing Cannon's power.

In 1912 both Roosevelt, who had broken with Taft, and La Follette raised the progressive banner to launch separate campaigns for the Republican presidential nomination. When Taft was renominated, by a narrow margin, Roosevelt entered the general election on a Progressive party ticket. With the normal Republican vote divided, Woodrow Wilson, the Democratic candidate, was elected president with 42 percent of the popular vote. The Progressive party also ran candidates for the Senate and House, enabling the Democrats to win many congressional elections with pluralities. The Democrats gained a huge majority in the House and organized the Senate for the first time since 1894.

Progressive Republicans like La Follette and Norris, elected to the Senate in 1912, supported much of Wilson's liberal domestic program, but when World War I began in Europe in 1914, most western progressives were bitterly critical of the administration's tilt toward the Allied powers. Foreign involvement, the progressives argued, would undermine domestic reform. Most congressional progressive Republicans were among the small minority who voted against Wilson's call for war against Germany in 1917, but Roosevelt, who had returned to the Republican party, faulted Wilson for not being sufficiently aggressive in favoring the Allies.

As the war ended in 1918, voters rejected Wilson's plea for continued Democratic control of Congress and installed Republican majorities in both houses. Senate progressives, led by La Follette, Norris, and Hiram W. Johnson, elected from California in 1916, opposed Wilson's proposal that the United States enter the newly conceived League of Nations. Conservative Republicans in the Senate, led by Henry Cabot Lodge of Massachusetts, were prepared to accept the League with stipulated reservations. Wilson ordered Senate Democrats to reject Lodge's conditions, and the result was a three-way division and defeat of the League.

The 1920s were Republican years, with party victories in three straight presidential elections and substantial majorities in Congress. Conflict between conservative and progressive Republicans continued, particularly over the proposed McNary-Haugen bill, providing federal support for farm prices. Western progressives warmly supported the bill, while conservatives in Congress and the White House opposed it.

Minority Status. Onset of the Great Depression at the beginning of the 1930s brought an end to the Republican era that had lasted with few interruptions since the Civil War. Voters blamed economic hard times on incumbent Republicans and their laissez-faire economic philosophy. In 1932 Franklin D. Roosevelt swept into the presidency and the Democrats won large majorities in both houses of Congress. After Roosevelt's election to a second term in 1936, the Republican minority in the Senate had shrunk to sixteen, and in the House to eighty-nine (one-fifth of the total).

Progressive Republicans, including Johnson and Wisconsin's Robert M. La Follette, Jr., elected to succeed his father in 1925, supported most of Roosevelt's New Deal domestic program. Progressives, however, joined conservative Republicans and southern Democrats in 1937 to oppose Roosevelt's attempt to pack the Supreme Court, which had been declaring much New Deal legislation unconstitutional.

Republican conservatives, led by Senators Arthur H. Vandenberg of Michigan and Robert A. Taft of Ohio and House minority leader Joseph W. Martin, Jr., of Massachusetts, doggedly resisted the administration's moves toward construction of a national welfare state. After Republicans gained seventy-five seats in the House and seven in the Senate in the 1938 midterm elections, conservative Republicans joined southern Democrats in the so-called conservative coalition, which for the next twenty years blocked most liberal legislation.

When World War II began in Europe in 1939, isolationist progressives like Johnson, La Follette, and Sen. William E. Borah of Idaho joined conservatives like Vandenberg and Taft in demanding strict nonintervention by the United States. Internationalist Republicans, mainly from the Northeast, backed Roosevelt's efforts to support the powers allied against Nazi Germany. After Japan bombed Pearl Harbor in December 1941, intraparty conflict between isolationists and internationalists virtually ceased for the duration of the war.

After Roosevelt's death and the end of the war in 1945, the national mood swung toward conservatism. In 1946 the Republicans won majorities in both houses of Congress. Under Taft's leadership, Congress in 1947 enacted the Taft-Hartley Act, restraining some of the powers organized labor had acquired under the New Deal. Struggles between internationalists and isolationists resumed. Vandenberg, who had converted to internationalism during the war, helped Harry S. Truman, Roosevelt's successor, win approval for U.S. aid to rebuild western Europe as a bulwark against communism and the Soviet Union. Democrats regained control of Congress in 1948, riding on the coattails of Truman's upset victory in the presidential election over the Republican candidate, Gov. Thomas E. Dewey of New York.

In 1952 internationalists, led by Dewey and backing Gen. Dwight D. Eisenhower for the Republican presidential nomination, waged a showdown fight with isolationists, who supported Taft. Eisenhower was nominated and elected, bringing with him small Republican majorities in both congressional houses. For a time after Taft's death in 1953 isolationism nearly vanished in the Republican party. Most conservatives swung to a militant form of foreign interventionism, assuming that the United States was locked in life-or-death combat with international communism.

In the 1954 midterm elections Democrats regained control of both the Senate and the House. A long period began in which Republicans more often than not held the White House, but Democrats maintained majorities in the House and usually in the Senate. Democratic landslide victories in congressional elections in 1958, 1964, and 1974 weakened the conservative coalition against liberal legislation. House minority leader Charles A. Halleck of Indiana nevertheless continued to work closely with conservative southern Democrats as a means of gaining Republican leverage against the Democratic majority. At the beginning of 1965, Rep. Gerald R. Ford of Michigan supplanted Halleck as minority leader, in part on a promise to break the alliance with the southern Democrats and work more aggressively for a Republican majority in the House.

The South's shift to the Republican side in most presidential elections after 1964 helped increase Republican representation from that region in the House, but simultaneous decline of Republican representation from the Northeast and Midwest resulted in little change overall.

Republican Resurgence. While Republican strength in the House in the 1980s generally paralleled that of the late 1950s, the geographic composition of the Republican minority was substantially different. During Eisenhower's second term, 36 percent of House Republicans were from the Northeast and 35 percent from the Midwest, while only 3 percent were from the South. In the 1980s, the portion of House Republicans from the Northeast had fallen to 22 percent and from the Midwest to 26 percent, while the share from the South had grown to 22 percent.

While authority within the House Democratic majority was decentralized during the 1970s, many Republicans, particularly senior members, were able to wield considerable influence by establishing close relationships with their Democratic counterparts on House committees. With return to the more centralized direction of the majority in the 1980s, however, Republicans found their role in the House power structure greatly reduced.

Rep. Robert H. Michel of Illinois, who became minority leader when Ford became vice president in 1974, generally took a bargaining approach to the Democratic leadership. In the more partisan atmosphere of the House in the 1980s, many Republicans, regardless of ideology, began to demand a more confrontational strategy. One result was election of Rep. Newt Gingrich of Georgia, a conservative firebrand, as minority whip in 1991.

In the Senate during this period, Republicans were generally more competitive in numbers than they were in the House. For six years after Ronald Reagan's election as president in 1980 Republicans formed the Senate majority. Republican influence in the Senate was also enhanced by a series of forceful and highly visible party leaders: Everett M. Dirksen of Illinois, Hugh Scott of Pennsylvania, Howard H. Baker, Jr., of Tennessee, and Bob Dole of Kansas.

Republican unity on roll-call votes in both the Senate and the House, which had fallen during the 1960s and 1970s, rose sharply during the 1980s, particularly in 1981, the first year of Reagan's presidency, when united Republicans joined with some conservative Democrats to enact much of the administration's conservative program. Increased Republican unity reflected in part the ideological line Reagan drew in national politics, producing greater congressional unity in both parties, and in part the decreasing number of progressive Republicans elected to Congress from the Northeast and Far West.

Stepped-up campaign activity by the National Republican Senatorial Committee (NRSC) and the National Republican Congressional Committee (NRCC) may also have contributed to increased Republican unity on roll-call votes. From 1978 to 1982 staff and spending by both campaign committees more than quadrupled. After 1982 NRCC spending fell somewhat, as did NRSC's after 1986, but at the end of the decade, spending by both committees remained far higher than it had been earlier.

At the beginning of the 1990s the Republican minorities in the Senate and House were more unified, more ideological, and more combative than they had been at almost any previous time in history. Congressional Republicans, deeply frustrated with their long confinement to minority status, eagerly sought a strategy that would produce a long-awaited national party realignment—or at least an occasional change in party control of Congress.

[*See also* Radical Republicans.]

BIBLIOGRAPHY

Goldman, Ralph M. *The National Party Chairmen and Committees: Factionalism at the Top.* 1990.
Jones, Charles O. *The Minority Party in Congress.* 1970.
Kehl, James A. *Boss Rule in the Gilded Age.* 1981.
Mayer, George H. *The Republican Party, 1854–1964.* 1964.
Moos, Malcolm. *The Republicans.* 1956.
Rae, Nicol C. *The Decline and Fall of the Liberal Republicans from 1952 to the Present.* 1989.

A. JAMES REICHLEY

RESCISSION. The permanent cancellation of spending provided by law is called a rescission. It is one of two types of impoundments (executive actions to withhold spending) defined in the Impoundment Control Act of 1974. The other type is deferral (an action to delay spending temporarily).

The Impoundment Control Act of 1974 establishes procedures for congressional consideration of impoundments and sets forth the conditions under which the president may rescind or defer spending. It was enacted after the unprecedented impoundments of the late 1960s and early 1970s by President Richard M. Nixon.

Under the act, whenever the president decides to propose a rescission, he must submit a special message to Congress specifying the amounts to be rescinded and giving the reasons for his belief that the spending should be canceled. Unless the rescission is approved by Congress in law, funds proposed to be rescinded must be released within forty-five calendar days of congressional session. (The forty-five-day time period is broken only by the sine die adjournment of a Congress or adjournments of either house for more than three days.) Typically, Congress includes rescissions, both those proposed by the president and those generated within Congress, in annual appropriations measures. Separate rescission bills are less common.

Pressure to reduce the deficit prompted efforts to strengthen the president's rescission authority. Presidents Ronald Reagan and George Bush called for the enactment of so-called enhanced rescission authority, which would permit proposed rescissions to remain in effect unless overturned by Congress. President Bill Clinton has endorsed proposals to grant the president expedited rescission authority. Such proposals generally would establish expedited procedures for Congress to consider the president's rescission recommendations, but would still require congressional approval for the rescissions to become effective.

[*See also* Congressional Budget and Impoundment Control Act of 1974; Impoundment.]

BIBLIOGRAPHY

Middlekauff, William Bradford. "Twisting the President's Arm: The Impoundment Control Act as a Tool for Enforcing the Principle of Appropriation Expenditure." *Yale Law Journal* 100 (1990): 209–228.
Thurber, James A., and Samantha L. Durst. "Delay, Deadlock, and Deficits: Evaluating Proposals for Congressional Budget Reform." In *Federal Budget and Financial Management Reform.* Edited by Thomas D. Lynch. 1991.

EDWARD DAVIS

RESOLUTIONS. Resolutions are one of the two general types of measures on which the House of Representatives and Senate act. There are three forms of resolutions: simple, concurrent, and joint. Each may originate in either house. Simple resolutions are designated as "H. Res." or "S. Res.," concurrent resolutions as "H. Con. Res." or "S. Con. Res.," and joint resolutions as "H.J. Res." or "S.J. Res."—all followed by an identifying number.

In contrast to bills, simple and concurrent resolu-

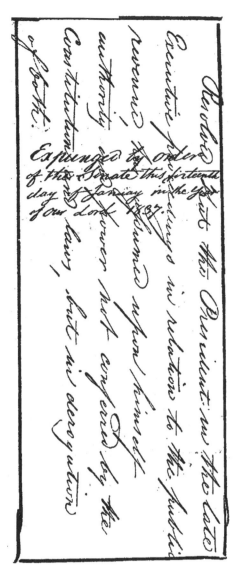

EXPUNGED RESOLUTION. Dated 1834, censuring President Andrew Jackson for removing deposits from the Bank of the United States. The resolution declared that Jackson had thereby "assumed upon himself authority and power not conferred by the Constitution and laws, but in derogation of both." The resolution was expunged from the Senate Journal on 16 January 1837, "by order of the Senate."   *PERLEY'S REMINISCENCES,* VOL. 1

tions do not become law, even after being approved by one or both houses of Congress. These resolutions usually address questions concerning the internal operations of Congress or express a non-statutory opinion of one or both houses. Like bills, joint resolutions do become law once signed by the president or enacted without his signature or over his veto. Traditionally, constitutional amendments

also take the form of joint resolutions but are not submitted for presidential approval.

Simple resolutions of the House or Senate relate only to the house of Congress in which they are proposed and require no action by the other house. Many simple resolutions address "housekeeping" questions and other matters of internal organization and procedure. The House establishes its rules at the beginning of each Congress by adopting a simple House resolution, and either house may change its rules at any time by adopting simple resolutions. By simple resolutions, the House and Senate assign members to their committees and determine committee budgets. Questions concerning the conduct of members also are decided by votes on simple resolutions of the House or Senate.

The most common and important simple resolutions are House resolutions affecting its order of business on the floor. These resolutions, also known as special orders or special rules, are reported by the House Rules Committee and recommend procedures for debating and amending individual measures on the floor. Each house also adopts simple resolutions to express "the sense of the House" or "the sense of the Senate." These are expressions of opinion or preference that may be intended to influence actions by the president or executive branch officials, but they have no binding force.

The Senate also acts on executive resolutions, especially resolutions of ratification by which it gives its advice and consent to the ratification of treaties the president has submitted. The House occasionally considers resolutions of inquiry asking the president or an executive branch official to provide it with certain facts or documents that the House determines it needs in order to fulfill its constitutional responsibilities.

When the House or Senate adopts a simple resolution, the other house is not even officially informed because it may take no action on the resolution. By contrast, concurrent resolutions require adoption by both houses. The House and Senate must pass the same concurrent resolution and reach complete agreement on its text before they have successfully completed legislative action on it.

Concurrent resolutions are used to express "the sense of Congress," instead of the opinion of only one house. These resolutions also can be used for organizational questions affecting both houses: for example, joint committees may be created and abolished by concurrent resolutions. Similarly, concurrent resolutions are used to fix the date and time at which both houses will adjourn for more than three days and at the end of each session of Congress. In addition, budget resolutions take the form of concurrent resolutions because they are not intended to become law. They only prescribe a budget plan that is supposed to guide both houses during their subsequent consideration of revenue, appropriations, and other spending bills.

In their potential effect, joint resolutions are indistinguishable from bills. Like a bill, a joint resolution requires passage by both houses, which must reach complete agreement on its text. Also like a bill, almost every joint resolution that Congress passes is presented to the president for his approval or disapproval.

Joint resolutions often are considered more appropriate than bills when the statutory purpose to be achieved is limited or temporary. For example, joint resolutions are used to continue the availability of appropriations temporarily until annual appropriations bills are enacted. These are called continuing resolutions. On the other hand, some major, permanent laws have taken the form of joint resolutions, such as the War Powers Resolution of 1973, which attempted to establish conditions and procedures relating to presidential decisions to use U.S. armed forces without first securing a declaration of war from Congress. The fact that this law was enacted by Congress as a joint resolution instead of a bill did not enhance or diminish its statutory force once both houses approved it over President Richard M. Nixon's veto. Unlike bills, joint resolutions (and other resolutions) may include preambles, stating the facts or reasons prompting Congress to approve them.

Congress also acts on constitutional amendments in the form of joint resolutions. Once approved by both houses, a joint resolution for this purpose is not presented to the president. Instead, it is submitted directly to the states for them to consider for ratification.

BIBLIOGRAPHY

U.S. House of Representatives. *Deschler's Precedents of the United States House of Representatives*, by Lewis Deschler. 94th Cong., 2d sess., 1977. H. Doc. 94-661. Vol. 7, pp. 323–425.

U.S. Senate. *Senate Procedure, Precedents, and Practices*, by Floyd M. Riddick. 97th Cong., 1st sess., 1981. S. Doc. 97-2. Pp. 367–373, 975–985.

STANLEY BACH

REVENUE SHARING. The State and Local Fiscal Assistance Act of 1972 established the General Revenue Sharing (GRS) program. GRS allowed fifty states and thirty-nine thousand local governments (counties, cities, townships, and Indian tribal governments) to receive revenues from the national government. One-third of GRS funds went to states for state use and two-thirds went to localities. Over the fourteen-year course of the program, $85 billion was dispersed to states and localities. GRS was terminated for states in 1980 and for localities in 1986. Annually, localities received a constant $4.6 billion between 1981 and 1986.

Sharing of funds under GRS required no application on the part of the receiving government, and funds could be used for practically any recognized state and local function. GRS was used, for example, to fund one-time capital projects such as the construction of public buildings, roads, and parks; to augment operating expenditures; and to lower local tax rates.

A philosophy of more closely linking various levels of government—federal, state, and municipal—underlay the GRS program. GRS welded together the federal government's greater capacity to raise revenues with state and local governments' greater ability to set spending priorities sensibly. A number of the program's significant features represented departures from other federal programs or were otherwise controversial. First, GRS revenues had very few strings attached, making the program extremely flexible. Second, GRS made maximum use of state and local governmental structures, thus making it economical to administer. Third, GRS was based on a formula (population, tax effort by state and local government, and per capita income) that targeted funds to governments with greatest fiscal need. Finally, GRS expanded political participation by requiring public hearings to obtain citizens' comments on the proposed uses of GRS allocations.

GRS was terminated in 1986 for reasons related to its philosophy and funding. The program provided funds to all states and localities whether they needed them or not. Some critics contended that GRS did not sufficiently aid the most needy local governmental units. More important, the growing federal budget deficit during the 1980s made it politically difficult to continue maintaining congressional support for the GRS program. As the federal deficit grew it became difficult to justify sharing revenues with many localities that had budget surpluses. The Reagan administration and congressional leaders contended that the states, rather than the federal government, (through GRS), were better positioned fiscally to aid localities.

The termination of GRS significantly reduced or entirely eliminated federal aid to local governments. Fiscally distressed localities were particularly badly affected by GRS's termination. In many localities, particularly those facing fiscal stress, GRS had constituted as much as 23 percent of total revenues. The loss of GRS funds forced many local governments to seek alternative state and local revenues. Localities began relying more heavily on increased taxes, user fees, and service charges to raise revenues. Many local governments reduced or eliminated some services. Another effect was an increasing fiscal disparity among local jurisdictions.

GRS termination contributed to an overall shrinking of federal aid to states and localities. GRS's termination left many states with a greater obligation to aid localities, and the states generally did increase such aid. In many states, GRS losses to localities were compensated with state revenue sharing and other aid programs. Termination further contributed to shaping an intergovernmental system in which states and localities increasingly formulate their own mixes of raising revenues and allocating expenditures without federal participation.

[*See also* Grant-in-Aid.]

BIBLIOGRAPHY

Marando, Vincent. "General Revenue Sharing: Termination in City Response." *State and Local Government Review* 22, no. 3 (1990): 98–107.

U.S. House of Representatives. Committee on Government Operations. *The Impact of the Proposed Elimination of the General Revenue Sharing Programs on Governments.* Hearings before the Committee. 99th Cong., 1st sess., 1985. No. 49-3530.

VINCENT L. MARANDO

RHODE ISLAND. The last of the original thirteen states to ratify the Constitution, Rhode Island did not in fact send delegates to the Constitutional Convention in 1787. Rhode Islanders also refused to follow the recommended ratification process and rejected ratification attempts eleven times before finally accepting the Constitution in May 1790 by two votes. Accompanying Rhode Island's ratification were twenty-one suggested amendments, most of which would have weakened the new federal government.

Two basic reasons lay behind this obstreperous behavior. First, Rhode Islanders did not want to trade subjection to Parliament for subordination to Congress. Rhode Island had been the freest and most independent of all of Britain's colonies, and its people feared and resisted strong central government. Quick to rebel against Parliament in 1775, the Rhode Island General Assembly unanimously ratified the Articles of Confederation in 1778 because the Articles created just the sort of central government it wanted: one with little or no power over the states.

The second reason was the state war debt. In the election of 1786 the Country party gained power and pledged to pay off the state debt by the issuance of paper money—something that Rhode Island's neighbors and the British government had hated during the colonial era, when Rhode Island had frequently resorted to issuing paper money. The new Constitution prohibited this practice. It is no coincidence that the Country party remained in power until the state debt was liquidated in 1790 and that Rhode Island joined the Union that same year.

Rhode Island's House delegation has always been small. The state started in 1790 with a single representative; a second seat was gained late that year as a result of the 1790 census. A third representative was added in 1912, but the state reverted to two representatives in 1932.

Rhode Island's most influential congressional figure was Republican senator Nelson W. Aldrich (1881–1911), who was sometimes called the "General Manager of the United States." While no other member of the Rhode Island delegation has matched Aldrich in power, others have risen to positions of respect and influence. Sen. Theodore F. Green (1937–1961), a staunch New Deal and Fair Deal supporter, was chairman of the Foreign Relations Committee from 1951 to 1959. The first U.S. senator of Italian extraction, John O. Pastore (1950–1976) was chairman of the Joint Committee on Atomic Energy. Sen. Claiborne Pell (1961–), chairman of the Foreign Relations Committee and famous for the "Pell grants" to college students, in 1992 became the longest-serving senator from Rhode Island. An outstanding congressman was John E. Fogarty (1941–1967), frequently called "Mr. Public Health" because he supported the massive expansion of federal expenditures for public health, medical research, and aid to the mentally retarded.

During most of the period from 1865 to 1930, Republicans dominated the Rhode Island delegation to Congress—a stability that allowed Aldrich to serve for so long in an era of tumultuous political change elsewhere. His power in Congress resulted in part from his having survived when most Republican senators were defeated in the 1890s. The Great Depression ushered in a political revolution in Rhode Island and produced forty years of Democratic domination of the state. But Democratic infighting fractured the state party in the early 1970s, and in 1976 John H. Chafee became the first Republican elected to the Senate from Rhode Island since 1930. In 1980 Claudine Schneider (1981–1991) became the first Republican the state had elected to the House of Representatives since 1938. Rhode Island is lopsidedly Democratic on the state level, but since 1980 half the members of its congressional delegation have been Republicans.

BIBLIOGRAPHY

Kellner, George H., and J. Stanley Lemons. *Rhode Island: The Independent State.* 1982.
McLoughlin, William. *Rhode Island: A History.* 1978.
Polishook, Irwin H. *Rhode Island and the Union, 1774–1795.* 1969.

J. STANLEY LEMONS

RICO. *See* Racketeer Influenced and Corrupt Organizations Act (RICO).

RIDDICK, FLOYD M. (1908–), parliamentarian emeritus, U.S. Senate. Riddick is a foremost expert on parliamentary procedure in general and Senate procedures in particular. He compiled the first comprehensive volume of Senate procedures and precedents since that prepared by Henry H. Gilfry in 1919. In 1947, as a legislative staff analyst for the U.S. Chamber of Commerce, Riddick created, and was the first editor of, the Daily Digest. The Digest provided for the first time a daily index and summary of the *Congressional Record,* making the *Record* accessible not only to congressional staff and members but also to the researcher and the general reader. He became assistant parliamentarian of the Senate in 1951 and was named parliamentarian in 1964, serving until 1974.

Riddick is the author of *Congressional Procedure* (1941); *Congress in Action* (coauther, 1948); *U.S. Congress: Organization and Procedure* (1949); *Senate Procedure,* the compilation of all Senate precedents since 1884 (4 eds., 1958, 1964, 1974, 1981); and *Riddick's Rules of Procedure* (1985).

Riddick, who graduated from Duke University in 1931 and received a master of arts from Vanderbilt University in 1932 and a Ph.D. from Duke University in 1935, has also received honorary degrees from Duke University and Goucher College. He has conducted mock Senates on a number of college campuses across the country. Riddick has served as consultant to the Senate Rules Committee since his retirement in 1974.

BIBLIOGRAPHY

Brownson, Charles B. *Congressional Staff Directory.* 1971.

ROBERT B. DOVE

RIDERS. Riders are amendments, or sometimes provisions of bills, that are unrelated to the bills' principal subjects and purposes. *Rider* is an unofficial term, not recognized in the rules or precedents of either house of Congress, that sometimes is used imprecisely to refer to legislative proposals that can be presented to one house or the other in several different ways.

Congressional committees may write bills containing provisions on any subjects within their respective jurisdictions. If a committee includes a provision on one subject in a bill that primarily addresses another subject, some members and observers might call that provision a rider. Most often, however, *rider* refers to House or Senate floor amendments that either are not germane to the bill being considered or are so-called legislative or limitation amendments proposed during consideration of an appropriations bill.

Germaneness. The House rules generally require that each amendment be germane to the text it would amend. Germaneness is related to relevance and pertinence, but it is a more technical requirement that the House interprets and applies by reference to a large and complex body of published precedents. No nongermane amendment may be considered if a point of order is made and sustained against it. However, the Rules Committee may report a resolution, or special rule, for considering a particular measure that also waives clause 7 of Rule XVI, the germaneness rule, so that one or more nongermane amendments can be offered to it.

The Senate has no such general germaneness requirement. Senate floor amendments must be germane only if offered to a general appropriations or budget measure, if offered under cloture, or if offered under a unanimous consent agreement or a statutory provision that permits only germane amendments to a particular measure or class of measures. At all other times, senators are free to offer nongermane amendments to the bills the Senate considers on the floor. In this way, a senator can compel the Senate to consider, debate, and cast a vote concerning any policy proposal that he or she considers sufficiently important and timely to propose as a nongermane amendment. This right also makes the Senate floor schedule rather unpredictable because of the possibility that senators will offer unexpected nongermane amendments on subjects unrelated to the pending measure.

Members and observers sometimes have nongermane amendments, especially those originating in the Senate, in mind when they speak of riders. Such an amendment is thought to be riding, or perhaps even enjoying a free ride, on the bill to which it is attached. At other times, however, the rider at issue is what is more formally known as a legislative or limitation amendment to a general appropriations bill.

Appropriations Amendments. The general purpose and effect of House and Senate rules is to separate decisions about the funding levels for federal programs from decisions about what federal programs should be established and funded and how those programs should operate. To this end, House rules preclude bills that create programs or change their operating authority from also including the appropriations to pay for them. The same rule also protects appropriations bills from "legislative" provisions and amendments—those that are intended to change the existing law that the bill's appropriations will implement. Like the germaneness requirement, however, this proscription may be waived as part of the Rules Committee's "order of business resolution," or special rule, which the House may adopt before considering an appropriations bill.

In addition, House procedures can permit members to propose amendments to appropriations bills that limit the purposes for which the appropriated funds may be used without making permanent changes in federal programs and authorities. Examples of limitation amendments were those offered to appropriations bills, especially for the Department of Health, Education, and Welfare (later Health and Human Services), to prohibit the funds appropriated in such bills from being used to pay for or encourage abortions. Senators also can propose limitation amendments, and they can effectively decide by a simple majority vote to circumvent the prohibition in their rules against considering a legislative amendment to an appropriations bill.

The effect of riders, whether as nongermane amendments or as legislative or limitation amendments to appropriations bills, can be to delay the legislative process and to distract members from concentrating on the purposes of the bill to which the riders are attached. On the other hand, offering riders sometimes has been the only way in which members have been able to present critical policy issues for votes on the House or Senate floor.

[*See also* Germaneness.]

BIBLIOGRAPHY

Bach, Stanley. "Germaneness Rules and Bicameral Relations in the U.S. Congress." *Legislative Studies Quarterly* 7 (1982): 341–357.

U.S. House of Representatives. *Deschler's Precedents of the United States House of Representatives*, by Lewis Deschler. 94th Cong., 2d sess. 1977. H. Doc. 94-661. Vol. 8.

U.S. Senate. *Senate Procedure: Precedents and Practices*, by Floyd M. Riddick. 97th Cong., 1st sess., 1981. S. Doc. 97-2. Pp. 119–170.

STANLEY BACH

RIVES, WILLIAM CABELL (1793–1868), representative and senator from Virginia, opponent of Jacksonian fiscal policy. Rives was born 4 May 1793 in Amherst County, Virginia. He attended the College of William and Mary, studied law under Thomas Jefferson, and served in the Virginia House of Delegates (1817–1820, 1822–1823) before his election to the 18th Congress as a member of the House. He served from 1823 until 1829, resigning to accept an appointment as minister to France.

Rives served three partial terms in the Senate. First elected in 1832, he resigned in 1834 when the Virginia legislature instructed him to oppose Andrew Jackson's withdrawal of government deposits from the Bank of the United States. Elected to the seat left vacant by John Tyler's resignation, he served until the term expired in 1839. Party divisions prevented the legislature from electing a successor until 1841, when a Whig majority reelected Rives to the term expiring in 1845. He chaired the Naval Affairs Committee (24th and 25th Congresses, 1836–1839) and the Foreign Relations Committee (27th Congress, 1841–1842).

Rives's positions on the tariff and internal improvements and moderate states' rights philosophy initially aligned him with the Jacksonians. Disappointed by Jackson's refusal to endorse him for the vice presidency in 1836 and convinced that the hard money policy of the 1836 Specie Circular

WILLIAM CABELL RIVES. Lithograph by Charles Fenderich, 1839.   LIBRARY OF CONGRESS

would wreak havoc on Virginia's economy, he emerged as a leader of the conservative Democrats during his second Senate term (1836–1839). An advocate of state banks, he joined the Whigs' unsuccessful effort to defeat President Martin Van Buren's Independent Treasury bill, and joined the party by 1843.

Rives was minister to France during Zachary Taylor's administration (1849–1853) and a delegate to the Second Confederate Congress before ill health forced his retirement in 1861. He died on 25 April 1868. His defection from Jacksonian ranks was prompted by many of the same concerns that energized the Whig opposition in the late 1830s and, as Jean E. Friedman suggests in *The Revolt of the Conservative Democrats: An Essay on American Political Culture and Political Development, 1837–1844* (1979), reflects the conservative Democrats' rejection of the emerging political party system.

BIBLIOGRAPHY

Liston, Ann Elizabeth. "W. C. Rives: Diplomat and Politician, 1829–1853." Ph.D. diss., Ohio State University, 1972.
McCoy, Drew R. *The Last of the Fathers: James Madison and the Republican Legacy.* 1989. Chap. 8, "Legacy: The Strange Career of William Cabell Rives."

JO ANNE MCCORMICK QUATANNENS

ROBINSON, JOSEPH T. (1872–1937), representative and senator from Arkansas, Senate Democratic leader (1923–1937), New Deal advocate. Known for his fiery temper, devotion to duty, and loyalty to a succession of presidents, Joseph Taylor Robinson was the first formally elected Senate floor leader to consolidate and employ the full powers of that office. His determination and his skill in pushing President Franklin D. Roosevelt's initiatives through the Senate won him wide recognition—and criticism.

He was a complex, driven man, admired and at the same time feared by many of his colleagues. As majority leader, he pushed the Senate to rare efficiency. He threatened cloture and discharge motions, long sessions, and canceled holidays to prod senators into completing their work. He used his intricate knowledge of the body's rules and procedures to thwart filibusters and other dilatory tactics. His commanding presence and unblemished record of integrity allowed him to conduct vast amounts of minor business by unanimous consent.

Robinson was noted for his well-crafted speeches, fierce loyalty to friends and party, passion for detail, and ruthlessness in debate. When fully aroused, he could terrify an opponent, conveying, as one journalist put it, "the impression of brute animal strength and the willingness to use it." His voice roaring, his face crimson, he would pound his desk, gesture wildly, and stomp his feet to drive home a point.

Before entering the Senate in 1913, Robinson served for ten years as the representative of Arkansas's 6th Congressional District. In the House, as in the Senate, he served on a succession of committees, seldom staying long on any. He remained a lifelong conservative on fiscal and states' rights matters but a progressive on antitrust, child labor, free trade, and other issues. His spirited condemnation of religious intolerance won him national acclaim and a spot on the Democratic ticket as Alfred E. Smith's vice presidential running mate in 1928. His most significant legislative initiative was the Federal Anti–Price Discrimination (Robinson-Patman) Act of 1936, protecting small merchants against predatory pricing by chain stores.

One of the young progressives on whom President Woodrow Wilson depended, he was a staunch defender of Wilson's handling of the war with Germany and a firm ally in Wilson's fight for ratification of the Treaty of Versailles. Wilson praised him as the "moral and intellectual leader of the Senate." As Senate minority leader in the 1920s, Robinson

JOSEPH T. ROBINSON. *Left,* with Sen. Charles Curtis (R-Kans.), 1920s. LIBRARY OF CONGRESS

also maintained cordial relations with Republican presidents Calvin Coolidge and Herbert Hoover and occasionally supported their programs.

Robinson is most remembered—and sometimes faulted—for his subservient loyalty to Democratic presidents. Commanding a huge Senate majority during the first administration of Franklin D. Roosevelt, he worked intimately with the White House to enact the president's program. Starting in 1933 with the Emergency Banking Relief Act, he forced the usually independent Senate to accept administration proposals with minimal debate. When it adjourned on 15 June 1933, Roosevelt's so-called Hundred Days Congress had enacted a vast array of far-reaching measures to counteract the Depression and improve social conditions. Although some of the new laws were poorly drafted and based on dubious theory, Robinson was unabashedly proud of his role in their enactment.

The Senate leader, ignoring his own failing health, drove himself relentlessly as Roosevelt's chief Senate advocate. "One must fill his place to the end by rendering the best service of which he is capable," he once wrote. Although by 1936 his enthusiasm for the New Deal had waned, he remained loyal to the president and rarely criticized White House policies.

In 1937, despite misgivings, he accepted his hardest and last chore for the president: winning Senate passage of the Judiciary Reorganization Act, Roosevelt's audacious scheme to expand, and thereby liberalize, the Supreme Court. A motivating factor for Robinson was the near certainty that Roosevelt intended to name him to one of the proposed new seats. Whether Robinson could have salvaged the widely criticized Court-packing plan remains debatable. He believed that he had garnered sufficient support for a modified bill. But on 14 July, at the peak of Senate debate on the issue, he suffered a fatal heart attack. All hope for the plan died with him. Freed from their commitment to Robinson, the senators voted to send the bill back to the Judiciary Committee for permanent burial.

BIBLIOGRAPHY

Bacon, Donald C. "Joseph Taylor Robinson: The Good Soldier." In *First among Equals.* Edited by Richard A. Baker and Roger H. Davidson. 1991.

MacLeish, Archibald. "The Senator from Arkansas." *Fortune,* January 1937, pp. 88–108.

Vervack, Jerry J. "Joseph Taylor Robinson, Twenty-third Governor." In *The Governors of Arkansas: Essays in Political Biography.* Edited by Timothy P. Donovan and Willard B. Gatewood, Jr. 1981.

DONALD C. BACON

ROBINSON-PATMAN ACT. *See* Federal Anti–Price Discrimination Act.

RODINO, PETER W., JR. (1909–), Democratic representative from New Jersey (1949–1989) and chairman of House Judiciary Committee hearings in the Impeachment Inquiry of President Richard M. Nixon. Rodino's steady, careful handling of the complex political and legal issues underlying the 1974 impeachment inquiry earned him national respect. In the wake of the Watergate burglary and cover-up and Nixon's firing of the special prosecutor, Rodino as House Judiciary Committee chairman (1973–1989) established a special nonpartisan staff to investigate. He asserted the constitutional "sole power" of the House to impeach and steered a balanced course between congressional advocates and opponents of impeachment. His committee defined the law of presidential impeachment and firmly established the duty of Congress to hold the executive accountable for breach of duty and abuses of power, as intended by the Constitution.

Rodino, a Democrat, received bipartisan support from a majority of committee members on three proposed articles of impeachment: criminally related charges concerning the Watergate break-in, noncriminal charges related to Nixon's alleged abuse of presidential power; and presidential refusal to comply with congressional subpoena. Although Nixon resigned before the House could vote to impeach, Rodino would have acted as manager (or chief prosecutor) for the House in the Senate trial that would have followed.

Rodino, an Italian-American Catholic and World War II veteran from Newark, New Jersey, represented the urban, ethnically diverse 10th District for forty years. His consistently strong record of support for civil rights legislation in the 1960s, including fair employment and open housing, enabled him to continue in office even as his original constituency shifted to become more than 50 percent African American. He maintained good relations with labor, fought in the 1980s to save the Legal Services Corporation, and supported the 1981 extension of the Voting Rights Act. He was involved with immigration and naturalization issues, and was a leader in securing passage of the 1965 Immigration Reform Act, which eliminated the national origins quotas then existing. He was also concerned with narcotics abuse, an increasingly serious problem in his heavily urbanized district.

BIBLIOGRAPHY

Lukas, J. Anthony. *Nightmare: The Underside of the Nixon Years.* 1975.

White, Theodore H. *Breach of Faith: The Fall of Richard M. Nixon.* 1975.

DAGMAR S. HAMILTON

ROGERS, EDITH NOURSE (1881–1960), Democratic representative from Massachusetts (1925–1960), veterans' advocate, and author of legislation creating the Women's Army Corps and the GI Bill of Rights. First elected to the House in 1925 to fill the unexpired term of her late husband, John Jacob Rogers, Edith Nourse Rogers was reelected to the House for the next thirty-five years, until her own death in 1960.

Rogers spent her entire adult life working in some way to assist veterans. During World War I she served as a volunteer caring for disabled soldiers in France and in the United States. By 1922 her skill in assessing veterans' needs was well known, and she was appointed President Warren G. Harding's personal representative to inspect veterans' hospitals. Presidents Calvin Coolidge and Herbert Hoover reappointed her to that position. During her service in the House, Rogers was sometimes called the "veterans' voice in Congress." She served on the Committee on Veterans' Affairs and became that panel's most senior member; she chaired the committee in the 80th and 83d Congresses and was the committee's ranking Republican member when the Democrats were the majority party in the House. Rogers also served on the Committee on Foreign Affairs from 1933 to 1947;

EDITH NOURSE ROGERS.   LIBRARY OF CONGRESS

1955 by Sidney Yudain, an aide to a Connecticut representative, and, although privately owned, it was operated in the early years from an office in the Capitol.

For its first thirty-one years, the tabloid-size newspaper came out weekly, was eight pages long, had a circulation of no more than four thousand, and had a staff of four. In 1986, the paper was purchased by Arthur Levitt, Jr., then chairman of the American Stock Exchange. Levitt hired James K. Glassman, former publisher of the *New Republic* and the *Atlantic Monthly*, as editor and Mary Glassman as publisher. The newspaper expanded to twice-weekly publication in 1989 and by early 1994 was averaging thirty-six pages, with a staff of thirty and a circulation of 15,000. Some 11,000 copies are distributed free to congressional offices, and another 4,000 copies go to subscribers—mostly lawyers, lobbyists, journalists, and scholars—who pay $210 per year.

The newspaper, headquartered at 900 Second Street, N.E., is financed primarily through the sale of advertising to corporations, trade unions, and associations that encourage Congress to support or oppose particular pieces of legislation or generally promote their own images. In 1992, the *Economist* magazine, based in London, purchased the Glassmans' share of *Roll Call* and in 1993 bought the remainder of the stock from Levitt. The Glassmans

she resigned that committee to devote her full attention to issues concerning disabled veterans.

Reportedly, some of Rogers's colleagues were surprised when she won her early reelections, but came to respect her skill as a legislator. She was adept at representing both management and labor interests of the Massachusetts textile industry and received strong support from both constituency groups. She was also strongly supported by veterans' groups, not only in her congressional district, but nationally as well.

BIBLIOGRAPHY

Obituary. *New York Times*, 11 September 1960.
U.S. Congress. *Congressional Record.* 83d Cong., 1st sess., 30 June 1953. See Hon. Edith Nourse Rogers, pp. 7821–7824.

MARY ETTA BOESL

ROLL CALL. *Roll Call* is a twice-weekly publication that can best be described as a small-town newspaper that covers Congress. It was founded in

ROLL CALL. House Administration Committee chairman Charlie Rose (D-N.C.) reading a copy prior to a committee meeting, July 1994.   MAUREEN KEATING

left *Roll Call* in 1993, and Stacy Mason then became editor.

A nonpartisan newspaper, *Roll Call* focuses on House and Senate electoral politics and on the internal workings of Congress, rather than on legislation and public policy. Its concerns include Capitol Hill security, rules, ethics, leadership and committee appointments and internal elections, campaign finance, and redistricting, as well as personal information about members, including health and families.

The newspaper's outspoken editorials are widely read, and columnist George Will in 1992 termed *Roll Call* "the feisty newspaper that covers Congress and can be called . . . the conscience of Capitol Hill." On 19 September 1991, *Roll Call* was first to report that hundreds of members of the House had overdrawn their accounts at the House bank; the ensuing scandal resulted in the retirement or electoral defeat of about fifty members.

BIBLIOGRAPHY

Roll Call. 1955–.

JAMES K. GLASSMAN

ROOSEVELT, FRANKLIN D. (1882–1945),

New York Democratic state senator and governor, assistant secretary of the Navy, thirty-second president of the United States. Franklin Delano Roosevelt's extraordinary leadership during two profound national crises—the Great Depression and World War II—did much to shape the "modern" presidency so that the chief executive rather than Congress served as "the steward of the public welfare," to use Theodore Roosevelt's phrase. It fell to Franklin D. Roosevelt to expand and institutionalize the changes in the executive office that had begun under Theodore Roosevelt and Woodrow Wilson during the Progressive era and that had been reversed in the 1920s. After Franklin Roosevelt's long tenure, a new understanding of presidential responsibilities would endure, a vision followed by conservative Republicans as well as by progressive Democrats.

As Roosevelt took the oath of office on 4 March 1933, some fifteen million were unemployed, about one-third of the work force. He quickly gave notice of his intention to act boldly to deal with the crisis at hand. In his inaugural address, he warned that if

Congress shall fail to take [action] and in the event that the national emergency is still critical, I shall ask the Congress for one remaining instrument to meet the crisis—broad executive power to wage a war against the emergency, as great as the power that would be given to me if we were in fact invaded by a foreign foe.

The First Hundred Days. Roosevelt lost no time in translating his intentions into action. On 5 March 1933, he issued the "Bank Holiday Proclamation" suspending "the heavy and unwarranted withdrawal of gold and currency from our banking institutions." It was an unprecedented peacetime exercise of executive power. On the same day, Roosevelt issued another executive order to call Congress into special session. Four days later, he introduced the Emergency Banking Relief bill, which marshaled the full resources of the Federal Reserve Board to support the faltering banks. The bill was enacted in fewer than eight hours, with many legislators who had not even read the legislation endorsing it; forty-five minutes later, with photographers recording the scene, Roosevelt signed it into law. More far-reaching legislation such as the National Industrial Recovery Act and the Agricultural Adjustment Act took longer to pass, but by mid June Congress had ratified an array of measures to provide relief, bring about recovery, or achieve reform. The volume and significance of the legislation was so great that the period of time in which it was passed became known as the First Hundred Days.

Thus did the Roosevelt administration bring the presidency into its own as the primary source of popular and legislative leadership. In becoming the nation's legislative leader, Roosevelt relied on popular fear in an emergency, but he also displayed remarkable skill in influencing Congress and the public. He made good use of political patronage, dangling jobs before Democratic members of Congress but postponing all appointments until he had the legislation he wanted.

Just as important, Roosevelt used the mass media to go over the heads of members of Congress. He was the first president to take full advantage of the press conference, dazzling reporters twice a week with his charm and knowledge of government. Roosevelt's "fireside chats," broadcast on radio, were also a revolutionary advance in the presidential use of the mass media. Their purpose was to educate the American people, to shape public opinion in support of a specific piece of legislation, or, as in the first of the chats, to enlist popular support for a particular course of action. With Roosevelt's masterful use of the media, legislators were made only too aware of the temper of their constituents.

old age pensions for those who are now too old to build up their own insurance; it is, of course, clear that for perhaps thirty years to come funds will have to be provided by the states and the Federal government to meet these pensions. Second, compulsory contributory annuities which in time will establish a self-supporting system for those now young and for future generations. Third, voluntary contributory annuities by which individual initiative can increase the annual amounts received in old age. It is proposed that the Federal government assume one half of the cost of the old age pension plan, which ought ultimately to be supplanted by self-supporting annuity plans.

The amount necessary at this time for the initiation of unemployment compensation, old age security, children's aid and the promotion of public health, as outlined in the report of the Committee on Economic Security, is approximately one hundred million dollars.

The establishment of sound means toward a greater future economic security of the American people is dictated by a prudent consideration of the hazards involved in our national life. No one can guarantee this country against the dangers of future depressions but we can reduce these dangers. We can eliminate many of the factors that cause economic depressions and we can provide the means of mitigating their results. This plan for economic security is at once a measure of prevention and a method of alleviation.

We pay now for the dreadful consequence of economic insecurity - and dearly. This plan presents a more equitable and infinitely less expensive means of meeting these costs. We cannot afford to neglect the plain duty before us. I strongly recommend action to attain the objectives sought in this report.

THE WHITE HOUSE,
January 17, 1935.

SOCIAL SECURITY. The final page of Franklin D. Roosevelt's original presidential message proposing social security legislation, 17 January 1935.   NATIONAL ARCHIVES

The Second New Deal. Roosevelt's political gifts were sorely tested during the 74th Congress (1935–1937). Although the 1934 congressional elections added to the Democratic majorities in both houses—only the second time since the early nineteenth century that a president gained supporters in each chamber in the middle of a term—journalists and public officials predicted that the new Congress would prove unmanageable. The party leadership and many strategic committee posts in the House and Senate were now held by conservative Democrats, a sign that Congress was less willing to follow the president's lead. By 1935, the paralyzing financial panic had eased; moreover, the reforms Roosevelt sought during the latter part of his first term would bring enduring changes in the political economy. It was one thing for legislators to accept temporary emergency measures to ameliorate the severe hardships of the Depression, but it was another thing entirely for them to approve programs that implied a new philosophy of government, one that guaranteed individual men and women protection from the uncertainties of the marketplace. These factors combined to strengthen the anti-Roosevelt forces within the Democratic party, particularly southern Democrats in Congress, who had little sympathy for the New Deal. Collaborating with the Republicans, they formed a conservative coalition against Roosevelt's policies. This opposition was abetted by an unreconstructed segment of the business community, whose concerns were embodied in organizations such as the Liberty League, which denied that the federal government had any right to regulate commercial activity.

The New Deal's critics also included a majority of the Supreme Court. In 1935 and 1936, the Court struck down a greater number of important national laws than in any other comparable period in history. Among its adverse decisions was *Schechter Poultry Corporation v. United States* (1935), which declared that the discretionary authority that Congress had granted, at Roosevelt's request, to the National Recovery Administration (the leading economic agency of the early New Deal) was an unconstitutional delegation of legislative power to the executive.

Defying the growing opposition to his policies, FDR steered a new reform package through Congress—the Second New Deal, as it was called—that entrusted an enlarged set of federal agencies and boards with new regulatory and social tasks. The First New Deal, enacted during the heady early days of the administration, involved programs administered by agencies and personnel ostensibly empowered for emergency purposes. The second brought laws such as the Social Security Act and the Wagner-Connery National Labor Relations Act (also called the Wagner Act), both passed in 1935, that converted emergency programs into ongoing obligations of the national government.

Furthermore, Roosevelt's first term led Americans to expect that the president would take the lead within what he called the new "economic constitutional order." Traditionally, legislation had been for-

ANTI-ROOSEVELT CAMPAIGN BUTTON. From the 1944 presidential election. "Sidney" refers to Sidney Hillman, chairman of the Political Action Committee of the Congress of Industrial Organizations (CIO), which played a vital role in mobilizing the increasingly politically apathetic public to vote for Franklin D. Roosevelt. A confidant of the president, a Jew, an immigrant, and a former socialist radical, Hillman was the target of campaign propaganda. During the Democratic convention, Roosevelt allegedly had told party officials regarding their choice of his running mate, "Clear it with Sidney."

COLLECTION OF DAVID J. AND JANICE L. FRENT

mulated in consultation with, if not in deference to, congressional party leaders and drafted by legislative staff. But now Congress frequently received legislation fully drawn up by the White House staff and often passed it without significant change. Moreover, Roosevelt used press conferences to announce important legislative proposals to reporters and the public before communicating them to Congress.

Not every major public policy innovation during the 1930s originated in the White House, however. Some New Deal programs, such as the Tennessee Valley Authority, had long been on the public agenda but needed the impetus of a national crisis to be enacted. Other measures, such as the Wagner Act, redounded to the president's political benefit even though he had supported them only haltingly. That Roosevelt was hailed for the initiatives of New York senator Robert F. Wagner and others signified the public's growing tendency to think of the president as the government.

The 1936 election ensured that the important political changes that had occurred since 1932 would endure. Sweeping support of Roosevelt's leadership and his New Deal programs came in 1936, when Roosevelt won 60 percent of the popular vote—the largest plurality ever by a presidential candidate—and carried all but two states. This election, which also again strengthened the Democratic hold on both houses of Congress, marked the Democrats' emergence as the nation's new majority party.

Constitutional Crisis. Roosevelt's triumphant reelection deflected the nation's attention from a gathering storm that soon erupted into a full-blown constitutional crisis. Roosevelt argued that the modern presidency conformed to sound constitutional principles. "The only thing that has been happening," he told the nation in a fireside chat on 7 May 1933, "has been to designate the President as the agency to carry out certain of the purposes of Congress. This was constitutional and in keeping with past American traditions." Such was not the view, however, of Roosevelt's opponents in Congress. Indeed, by the end of Roosevelt's first term, Congress was chafing at its subordinate position and looking for an opportunity to rebuke this popular president who threatened to turn Congress into a rubber stamp. That opportunity came in early 1937, with Roosevelt's proposal of two controversial reorganization bills.

The first was an executive reorganization bill sent to Congress in January 1937. It sought to expand significantly the staff support of the executive office and presidential authority over the personnel and structure of the executive branch, including federal offices and regulatory commissions hitherto subject to considerable congressional influence.

The second reorganization bill was the so-called Court-packing plan, sent up to Capitol Hill some three weeks after the executive reform measure. The bill provided that for every Supreme Court justice who failed to retire within six months of reaching the age of seventy, the president could appoint a new justice. Six of the nine justices already were seventy or older, which meant that Roosevelt would be able to enlarge the court to fifteen members. Presumably, these new justices would overcome the Court's resistance to the New Deal.

Congress rejected these proposals. But changes in the judiciary's personnel and rulings during Roosevelt's presidency eliminated what had been seen as the constitutional barriers to national consolidation and to the delegation of authority to the executive branch. Moreover, the Executive Reorganization Act of 1939, though considerably weaker than Roosevelt's original proposal, not only provided authority for the creation of the Executive Office of the President, which included the White House Office and the Bureau of the Budget, but also enhanced the chief executive's control over federal agencies.

Still, the bitter fights over Court packing and executive reorganization entailed a considerable political cost. The Court issue, especially, brought Roosevelt's mastery over Congress and his party to an end. It served as a lightning rod for the New Deal's opponents, sparking a resurgence of congressional independence and the strengthening of the bipartisan conservative coalition, which would continue to block presidential reform initiatives until the mid 1960s.

Roosevelt's first response to the new ideological fissure was to try to unseat entrenched conservative Democrats in the 1938 elections. He intervened in one gubernatorial and several congressional primary campaigns in a bold effort to replace recalcitrant

PRESIDENT FRANKLIN D. ROOSEVELT. Signing the Tennessee Valley Authority Act, 18 May 1933.

TENNESSEE VALLEY AUTHORITY

Democrats with candidates who were "100-percent New Dealers." This attempted purge marked an unprecedented effort by a president to stamp his policies on his party.

The purge campaign failed; all but two of the incumbent Democrats whom Roosevelt opposed were renominated. Moreover, the campaign, which was widely condemned as an assault on the constitutional system of checks and balances, galvanized political opposition to Roosevelt, apparently contributing to the heavy Democratic losses in the 1938 elections. Since Roosevelt's unhappy experience in 1938, presidents generally have shied away from open intervention in House and Senate primaries.

Foreign Policy. The economic crisis that dominated Roosevelt's first two terms as president was displaced in the late 1930s by the approach of World War II. The war both reinforced and recast the flow of power to the executive. For one thing, it gave Roosevelt the opportunity to break settled tradition by running for unprecedented third and fourth terms in 1940 and 1944. Furthermore, under conditions of total war, Roosevelt was empowered not only to direct military operations abroad but to manage economic and social affairs at home. In 1942, Roosevelt demanded that Congress create an effective program of wage and price controls. If Congress did not act by 1 October, Roosevelt warned in his Labor Day message, "I shall accept the responsibility and I will act." Congress's acquiescence, however reluctant, indicated, as historian Ellis Hawley has noted, that "as depression gave way to war, another expansion of presidential authority was under way, linked chiefly now to the creation of a national security and warfare state rather than a welfare one."

Congress, the courts, and the states remained central to the structure and activities of the political order spawned by the Roosevelt "revolution." But Roosevelt's legacy included a more powerful and prominent executive office. That and his long tenure created serious concern about the danger of concentrating too much power in the White House. The president's death in April 1945 caused most Americans to weep, openly and unashamedly, for the passing of a mighty leader. "Even so," historian Barry Karl has written, "they hoped they would never need such heroic presidential leadership again." Two years later, Congress, with popular approval, passed the Twenty-second Amendment, which imposed a two-term limit on the president. Thus, although Roosevelt had recast the presidency in his own image, establishing it as the central actor in U.S. constitutional government, the place of this modern executive in the political system was an uneasy and unsettled one.

BIBLIOGRAPHY

Burns, James MacGregor. *Roosevelt: The Lion and the Fox.* 1956.
Freidel, Frank. *Franklin D. Roosevelt: A Rendezvous with Destiny.* 1990.
Greenstein, Fred I. "Nine Presidents in Search of the Modern Presidency." In *Leadership in the Modern Presidency.* Edited by Fred I. Greenstein. 1988. Pp. 296–352.
Leuchtenburg, William E. "Franklin Roosevelt: The First Modern President." In *Leadership in the Modern Presidency.* Edited by Fred I. Greenstein. 1988. Pp. 7–40.

SIDNEY M. MILKIS

ROOSEVELT, THEODORE (1858–1919), twenty-sixth president of the United States. Roosevelt strengthened the power of the executive office, pursued regulation of the economy, and expanded the world role of the United States. Roosevelt's relations with Congress were good at the outset of his presidency, and he had significant success in achieving his domestic legislative goals from 1901 to 1906. Resistance to his policies stiffened during the last two years of his administration, and he left office with his standing on Capitol Hill at a low ebb.

Roosevelt became president on 14 September 1901 following the death of William McKinley from an assassin's bullet. Only forty-two years old when he assumed his duties, Roosevelt had been a state legislator in New York and a cattle rancher in the Dakotas during the 1880s. He had served on the Civil Service Commission from 1889 to 1895, in which role he learned firsthand about congressional patronage practices. After a term on the New York City Board of Police Commissioners, Roosevelt was assistant secretary of the Navy under McKinley until the war with Spain erupted in 1898. Following military service in Cuba, Roosevelt was elected governor of New York, and then the Republican party nominated him as McKinley's running mate in 1900.

McKinley had broadened the power of the executive relative to Congress during his presidency, and Roosevelt built on that precedent. The result was growing friction between the executive and the legislature during the eight years of Roosevelt's administrations. During the early years relations between Roosevelt and Capitol Hill were relatively

COTTON CAMPAIGN BANNER. For Theodore Roosevelt's 1900 campaign as William McKinley's vice presidential running mate. The banner shows Roosevelt in his 1st Volunteer Cavalry (Rough Rider) uniform.

COLLECTION OF DAVID J. AND JANICE L. FRENT

amicable. The new president wanted to be nominated for a full term in 1904, and he worked hard to avoid confrontations with the lawmakers. He cooperated with Republican leaders in Congress—Sen. Nelson W. Aldrich and, after 1902, Speaker of the House Joseph G. Cannon. Early in his term, Roosevelt decided not to continue McKinley's campaign for tariff reciprocity, a gesture that pleased Republican protectionists in Congress.

As a result, the first three years of Roosevelt's presidency produced constructive legislation. The Newlands Act (1902) set up a system of irrigation projects for the West. A congressional act in 1902 cleared the way for negotiations with Colombia about a canal across Central America. During the short congressional session from 1902 to 1903, Roosevelt secured enactment of the Elkins Act to outlaw railroad rebates and of legislation to facilitate the work of the Justice Department in filing an-

titrust suits. Faced with the opposition of Standard Oil and other corporations to a measure to create a Bureau of Corporations in the new Commerce Department, Roosevelt effectively publicized the lobbying tactics of these big businesses to win congressional passage. After a revolution in Panama, the Senate approved the Hay-Bunau-Varilla treaty (1904) granting the United States the right to build the Panama Canal. His achievements with Congress formed one element in Roosevelt's 1904 campaign for the presidency, which culminated in a landslide victory.

His second term was stormier. Roosevelt's opinion of the Senate and the House had diminished during his first years in office, and he began to be more assertive in his private criticisms of lawmakers who disagreed with him. Some of them, he said, were "scoundrels and crooks," while others were "fools" (Gould, p. 11). He chafed under the power of the Senate to approve treaties that the executive had negotiated with foreign governments. "I do not much admire the Senate," he said in 1905, "because it is such a helpless body when efficient work for good is to be done" (Gould, p. 149). To advance his programs, Roosevelt sent Congress numerous special messages. In time the legislators came to resent the hectoring tone of these documents and the personal attacks that they often contained.

Following his election in 1904, Roosevelt proposed legislation to increase the regulatory power of the Interstate Commerce Commission (ICC) over the nation's railroads. To win approval of the law, Roosevelt made public speeches, wooed individual legislators, and leaked information to friendly reporters. After a protracted struggle with Nelson Aldrich and his conservative Republican allies, the Hepburn Act, which significantly enhanced the authority of the ICC, was passed in 1906. Roosevelt also induced Congress to act favorably on the Pure Food and Drugs Act and on an amendment to the Agricultural Appropriation Act giving the federal government the power to inspect the meat-packing industry. By 1906, however, Roosevelt confronted a congressional Republican party that was divided over the issue of government regulation. Many of these laws required support from the Democrats to achieve enactment.

Tensions with Capitol Hill surfaced first in foreign affairs. Early evidence of friction came in 1905, when the Senate took up ten arbitration treaties that the Roosevelt administration had signed with foreign powers. Senators complained that the pacts gave the executive too much power in foreign affairs. Amendments were inserted to assert senatorial prerogatives, and Roosevelt withdrew the treaties.

In 1905 the Roosevelt administration also submitted a protocol to allow the U.S. government to collect the debts of the Dominican Republic. Democrats in the Senate said that the president had exceeded his constitutional authority. Roosevelt then accomplished the same ends with a modus vivendi that irritated his critics in the Senate. When the president sent in the treaty to carry out the provisions of the Algeciras Conference of 1906 that involved France and Germany, the Senate again insisted on substantive reservations that forbade American participation in issues that were "entirely European in their scope" (Gould, p. 194).

On the domestic scene, the president's policy toward the conservation of natural resources also aroused congressional opposition. Roosevelt and his chief forester, Gifford Pinchot, wished to make decisions about conservation without having constantly to consult Congress. A reaction occurred in 1907 when western lawmakers introduced language in an agricultural bill to limit the power of the president to create forest reserves in the West. Roosevelt signed the bill, but before he did so he set up twenty-one new forest reserves.

The president also created the Keep Commission to streamline the workings of the federal government. This innovation found few friends on Capitol Hill, and Congress tried to limit by law the power of such commissions in the future.

On election night, 1904, Roosevelt had announced that he would not be a candidate for president in 1908. The approaching end of his administration made Congress more ready to oppose him. The president endorsed the reelection of Republican lawmakers during the election of 1906, but relations with Congress did not improve. Roosevelt wished "that the same men who get elected on the issue of standing by me would not at once turn and try to thwart me" (Gould, p. 244). Congress increasingly resented the constant flow of presidential messages. When he sent five in one week in December 1906 there were complaints about "such unwonted activity."

Roosevelt kept pressing Congress to pass more regulatory laws, but his audience was less and less receptive to his pleas. During the 1906 to 1907 session, the president obtained little of his proposed program. The economic downturn following the panic of 1907 worsened prospects for presidential-congressional cooperation as 1908 began. "The

feeling at the Capitol against anything and everything the President wants is very bitter," said a friend of Roosevelt in early 1908. Speaker Cannon complained, "That fellow at the other end of the Avenue wants everything from the birth of Christ to the death of the devil" (Gould, p. 281).

During the congressional session of 1907–1908, Roosevelt and the Congress battled over banking legislation, naval appropriations, and corporate regulation. Some legislation did emerge, however, including the Aldrich-Vreeland Act, which concerned banking. Angry members of the House endeavored to limit the right of the executive to use Secret Service agents to investigate government departments and Congress. Senators conducted hearings about Roosevelt's ouster of African American soldiers from the army after a shooting incident at Brownsville, Texas, in 1906. Despite these wrangles, the public sided with Roosevelt. "In a marked degree," said one newspaper, "the President, rather than Congress, possesses the confidence of the people" (Gould, p. 292).

After William Howard Taft won the presidential election of 1908, Roosevelt's last congressional session produced a series of squabbles that endured to the end of his term. Efforts continued to reduce the president's use of the Secret Service as an investigative agency. When Roosevelt suggested that "only criminals need fear our detectives" (Gould, p. 292), the House responded with a resolution to table the special message and that section of the president's annual message that dealt with the Secret Service. The resolution passed by a vote of 212 to 36. The House felt vindicated, but again the public cheered the president. "When Roosevelt attacks Congress," said the San Francisco *Bulletin*, "the people feel that he is making their fight" (Gould, p. 294).

Because of Roosevelt's assertion of presidential power, clashes with Congress were almost inevitable. In the public mind, Roosevelt usually had the better of the struggles. Whether a more conciliatory approach would have produced better relations between Congress and president is impossible to say. Had the president been more discreet in private and less critical in public, it is likely that Congress might have been more disposed to accept some of his programs. For Roosevelt, harmony with Congress was not the point. As he said in 1909, "I have been full President right up to the end—which hardly any other President ever has been" (Gould, p. 293). His handling of Congress from 1901 to 1909 reflected the working out of that basic principle.

Roosevelt had started some innovations that had important implications for the modern presidency in its relations with Congress. His expanded use of messages to push his programs on Capitol Hill became a favored technique of his successors. The president also played a greater role in the shaping of actual legislation. In his campaign for the Hepburn Act, Roosevelt also showed how a forceful chief executive could mobilize public opinion behind a reform program.

BIBLIOGRAPHY

Blum, John Morton. *The Republican Roosevelt.* 1954.
Gould, Lewis L. *The Presidency of Theodore Roosevelt.* 1991.

LEWIS L. GOULD

ROSS, EDMUND G. (1826–1907), senator from Kansas, most vilified of the Republican "seven martyrs" who voted for acquittal in the 1868 impeachment trial of President Andrew Johnson. Edmund Gibson Ross was born in Ashland, Ohio, on 7 December 1826. In 1856 he came to Kansas, where he published newspapers in Topeka and Lawrence.

EDMUND G. ROSS. LIBRARY OF CONGRESS

After Kansas senator James H. Lane committed suicide in 1866, Gov. Samuel J. Crawford appointed Ross, a fellow veteran of the Civil War, to the interim position in an attempt to avoid a factional fight among more prominent Republicans. In January 1867 the Kansas legislature elected Ross to fill out the term in a contest whose outcome was apparently influenced by bribery.

The Senate's vote of 35 to 19 on whether to impeach Andrew Johnson fell one vote short of the required two-thirds margin. After the impeachment trial Ross successfully solicited patronage appointments for his supporters from the president, citing his critical vote. He and the other party dissenters were not reelected in 1870, when the turnover of incumbents was large, regardless of how they had voted on impeachment. Ross joined the Liberal Republican party in 1872 and ran unsuccessfully for governor of Kansas as a Democrat in 1880. He moved to the Territory of New Mexico and was appointed governor (1885–1889) by President Grover Cleveland. In the 1890s Ross found a sympathetic audience for magazine accounts of his heroic version of his vote. His view of what had happened was generally adopted in John F. Kennedy's Pulitzer Prize–winning *Profiles in Courage* (1956).

BIBLIOGRAPHY

Bumgardner, Edward. *The Life of Edmund G. Ross, the Man Whose Vote Saved a President.* 1949.
Plummer, Mark A. "'Profile in Courage?' Edmund G. Ross and the Impeachment Trial." *Midwest Quarterly* 27 (1985): 30–48.

MARK A. PLUMMER

ROTUNDA. *See* Capitol, *article on* Dome and Great Rotunda.

RULE, SPECIAL. Also known as a special order, order of business resolution, or rule, a special rule is a simple resolution of the House of Representatives, usually reported by the Committee on Rules, to permit the immediate consideration of a legislative measure, notwithstanding the usual order of business, and to prescribe conditions for its debate and amendment. The authority of the Rules Committee to report special rules can be traced to 1883. Prior to that time, bills could not be considered out of their order on the calendars of the House except by unanimous consent or under a suspension of the rules, which required a two-thirds vote. Since special rules reported from the Rules Committee required only a majority vote in the House, the new practice greatly facilitated the ability of the majority leadership to depart from the regular order of business and schedule major legislation according to the majority's priorities.

In addition to giving a bill privileged status for consideration at any time after the rule's adoption, a special rule establishes the amount of time for general debate on the bill and how that time is to be allocated. Usually the time is equally divided between the chairman and ranking minority member of the committee or committees reporting the bill.

Special rules also provide for the type of amendment process to be followed once general debate has been concluded. Under an open rule, any member may offer germane amendments. Under a closed rule, no amendments are permitted. Between open and closed rules are modified open and modified closed rules, which limit the amendment process to only those amendments referred to in the rule. The text of such amendments, who may offer them, and how long they may be debated are often contained in the Rules Committee's report on the resolution.

Studies have documented a significant increase, beginning in the 1980s, in the frequency of special rules that restrict the amendment process. This trend has been variously attributed to increasing legislative complexity, member independence, member partisanship, and leaders' desire for predictable results.

Special rules are also used to waive points of order against bills or amendments and thereby permit their consideration notwithstanding their violation of House rules. In this regard, special rules are often necessary to waive points of order for matters that would otherwise be privileged for floor consideration without a rule, such as appropriations bills and conference reports.

Special rule resolutions are subject to one hour of debate in the House, controlled by the majority party manager for the Rules Committee. Half this time is traditionally yielded to the minority. The resolutions may not be considered by the House on the same day they are reported from the Rules Committee except by a two-thirds vote of the House. They may not be amended unless the majority manager offers an amendment or yields to another member for that purpose, or unless the previous question (the motion to end debate and proceed to a final vote) is defeated. If the previous question is defeated, its leading opponent is recog-

nized for one hour of debate and the right to amend the rule in a similar fashion.

[*See also* Previous Question.]

BIBLIOGRAPHY

Bach, Stanley, and Steven S. Smith. *Managing Uncertainty in the House of Representatives: Adaptation and Innovation in Special Rules.* 1988.

U.S. House of Representatives. *Deschler's Precedents of the United States House of Representatives,* by Lewis Deschler. 94th Cong., 2d sess., 1976. H. Doc. 94-661. Vol. 6.

DONALD R. WOLFENSBERGER

RULES AND ADMINISTRATION COMMITTEE, SENATE.

The Senate Committee on Rules and Administration is responsible for the internal management of the Senate. Many issues handled by Rules and Administration are of little interest to the general public, but are of intense interest to senators. The panel administers a number of housekeeping tasks such as room assignments, committee budgets, parking, computer systems, expense vouchers, and the Senate restaurant. Senate rules and proposals for the reorganization of the Senate are considered by the committee.

The Rules and Administration Committee also is responsible for legislation establishing federal election laws. Issues such as voter registration, election reform, regulation of campaign contributions, and campaign spending limits fall under its purview. Rules and Administration is one of seventeen standing committees in the U.S. Senate in the 103d Congress (1993–1995).

History and Jurisdiction. Rules and Administration is the oldest committee in the Senate. One of its predecessors, the Joint Committee on Enrolled Bills, was established by the First Congress in 1789. In addition, on the second day that the Senate had a quorum (7 April 1789) it established the first of a series of special committees to prepare a system of rules for conducting business. From 1789 until 1874, the Senate established nine temporary committees to review and revise its rules.

A standing Committee on Rules was established in December 1874. From the time it was made permanent in 1874, until the Legislative Reorganization Act of 1946, the Rules Committee had a narrow and specific focus, the rules of the Senate. The committee completed two general and comprehensive revisions to the rules of the Senate in 1877 and

SEN. WENDELL H. FORD (D-KY.). *Left*, chairman of the Senate Committee on Rules and Administration (1987–), and Sen. Dianne Feinstein (D-Calif.) before a committee markup, 18 March 1993.

R. MICHAEL JENKINS, CONGRESSIONAL QUARTERLY INC.

in 1884, and also considered individual legislative proposals that related to changing Senate rules.

When the committee system was modernized by the Legislative Reorganization Act of 1946, the jurisdiction of the committee was significantly expanded and it was renamed the Committee on Rules and Administration. The functions and duties of the following committees were merged under Rules and Administration: Enrolled Bills; Library; Audit and Control of the Contingent Expenses of the Senate; Printing; Privileges and Elections; and Rules. In 1947, the Senate transferred responsibilities for the enrollment of bills to the secretary of the Senate, but the remaining tasks have been retained, and jurisdiction has been expanded into additional areas.

In the 1990s the Senate Committee on Rules and Administration was responsible for (1) administration of the Senate office buildings and the Senate wing of the Capitol, including the assignment of office space; (2) congressional organization relative to rules and procedures, and Senate rules and regulations, including floor and gallery rules; (3) investigation of corrupt practices; (4) credentials and qualifications of members of the Senate, contested elections, and acceptance of incompatible offices; (5) federal elections generally, including the election of the president, vice president, and members of Congress; (6) the Government Printing Office, and the printing and correction of the *Congressional Record;* (7) meetings of the Congress and attendance of members; (8) payment of money out of the contingent fund of the Senate; (9) presidential succession; (10) purchase of books and manuscripts and erection of monuments in memory of individuals; (11) the Senate library and statuary, art, and pictures in the Capitol and Senate office buildings; (12) services to the Senate, including the Senate restaurant; and (13) the United States Capitol and congressional office buildings, the Library of Congress, the Smithsonian Institution, and the Botanic Gardens.

The Rules and Administration Committee also has the responsibility to make a continuing study of the organization and operation of the Congress of the United States and recommend improvements with a view toward strengthening the Congress, simplifying its operations, improving its relationships with other branches of the U.S. government, and enabling it better to meet its responsibilities under the Constitution of the United States; and it should identify any court proceeding or action that is of vital interest to the Congress and call such proceeding or action to the attention of the Senate.

Characteristics. Most issues considered by the committee are of scant interest to the general public, and of little value to senators in terms of impressing constituencies and earning votes toward reelection. The Senate Committee on Rules and Administration can be characterized as internally focused. The bulk of its work is looking after administrative tasks that keep the Senate functioning as smoothly as possible. Occasionally the committee will become involved in a comprehensive congressional reorganization study such as hearings in the 102d Congress (1991–1993) to establish a Joint Committee on the Organization of Congress. The committee may also become involved in a contested election, such as the 1974 dispute over who won the Senate election in New Hampshire.

Some issues under the committee's jurisdiction, such as voter registration and campaign practices, are of interest to selected constituency groups. For example, in the 102d Congress, the committee held a series of hearings on proposals for campaign finance and campaign ethics reforms.

Another characteristic of the committee is the likelihood that members of the Senate leadership will be appointed to serve on the committee. Since 1969, the Senate Republican leader has served concurrently on Rules and Administration: Hugh Scott (R-Penn.), minority floor leader from 1969 to 1976; Howard H. Baker (R-Tenn.), minority and majority floor leader from 1977 to 1984; and Bob Dole (R-Kans.), majority and minority floor leader from 1985 to 1992. Robert C. Byrd (D-W.Va.) was a member of the Rules and Administration Committee as well as majority and minority floor leader from 1977 to 1988. Wendell H. Ford (D-Ky.) served as chairman of the Rules and Administration Committee, and as the Senate majority whip during 1991 and 1992.

The Senate Rules and Administration Committee can also be characterized as relatively small and simply structured. In the 103d Congress, the committee has sixteen senators; only two standing committees had fewer members. Rules and Administration is one of only four standing committees in the Senate that do not have subcommittees.

[*See also* Rules Committee, House.]

BIBLIOGRAPHY

Pincus, Walter. "Senate Official Told to Clear Vouchers." *Washington Post,* 14 March 1989, p. 5.

U.S. Senate. *History of the Committee on Rules and Administration.* 96th Cong., 1st sess., 1980. S. Doc. 96-27.

"Who's Who in Federal Elections." *FEC Journal of Election Administration* (Summer 1989): 12–34.

MARY ETTA BOESL

RULES AND PROCEDURES. *For discussion of rules and procedures in the House and Senate, see under* House *and under* Senate.

RULES COMMITTEE, HOUSE. A procedural committee known as the Committee on Rules has jurisdiction over "the rules and joint rules . . . and order of business of the House," and authority "to report at any time" on such matters (House Rules X, clause 1[q], and XI, clauses 4[a] and [b]).

In Congresses of the late twentieth century, the Rules Committee consisted of thirteen members, nine from the majority party and four from the minority party. This heavy majority party ratio of 2 to 1 plus 1 reflected the committee's status since the mid 1970s as an "arm of the leadership" and "legislative gatekeeper." The committee of the 1990s served principally to assist the majority leadership in scheduling bills for floor action. Bills were scheduled by means of special rules that gave them priority status for consideration in the House and established procedures for their debate and amendment.

During its first century, however, the Rules Committee exercised a quite different and more limited role—that of recommending changes in the standing rules for the House. At other times it has acted independently of House leadership. The evolution and changing roles of the Rules Committee in many respects mirror the historical development of the House itself and the changing relationships among its leaders, members, committees, and parties.

Evolution of the Committee's Role. On 2 April 1789, the second day of the First Congress, the House voted to establish a select committee of eleven members "to prepare and report such standing rules and orders of proceedings as may be proper to be observed in the House." On 7 April the select committee reported back to the House a set of four rules that the House adopted without amendment. These rules dealt with the duties of the Speaker, decorum and debate, bill procedure, and procedure for the Committee of the Whole.

On 13 April, the select committee reported eight additional rules, which the House adopted over the next two days, relating to committee service, leaves of absence, creation of a standing committee on elections, an oath of office for the clerk, and the appointment and duties of the sergeant at arms. With its final report the first Rules Committee was dissolved—but not to fade into history. In less than two weeks, it had established a set of rules that would endure at the heart of House parliamentary practice for the next two centuries.

Early role. For ninety years, the Rules Committee remained a temporary, select committee, appointed at the beginning of each Congress for the purpose of recommending changes in the rules of the previous Congress and then going out of existence. Its role was so minor that in five Congresses it was not even established and in others it made no reports.

There were hints during this period, though, of the larger role the Rules Committee would eventually assume of reordering the House's legislative business. On 16 June 1841, the House adopted a resolution extending the rules of the previous Congress for the balance of the first session but also giving the Rules Committee "leave to report at all times," rather than once, in the usual single report.

Less than a month later, on 6 July, the Rules Committee took advantage of this authority by reporting an amendment to House rules that would permit the House by majority vote, rather than the two-thirds vote otherwise required, to terminate all debate in the Committee of the Whole and thereby bring a bill to a final vote back in the House. The Speaker overruled a point of order against this amendment on grounds that the 16 June resolution had given the Rules Committee authority to make "reports in part at different times, and by 'piece meal.'" The Speaker's ruling was upheld on appeal and the rule was subsequently adopted. A motion was immediately made under the authority of this rule to terminate all debate at 7:00 P.M. that day on a pending public lands bill that for several days had

been subject to minority delaying tactics in the Committee of the Whole. The motion was agreed to by majority vote and all debate on amendments was terminated at 7:00 that evening (though the minority continued to offer scores of nondebatable amendments for several more hours before the measure was finally reported back to the House). The Rules Committee had for the first time exercised its authority to intervene in the consideration of a specific bill.

Other foretokens of the modern Rules Committee came in the 31st and 32d Congresses (1849–1853), when the House briefly elevated it to standing committee status, and in 1858, when the House created a special rules revision committee that included the Speaker as one of its members. A year later, the Speaker was made the chairman of the select committee on rules.

In 1880, when the House again undertook a comprehensive overhaul of House rules, it reduced the number from 166 to 44, and designated as one of the forty-two House standing committees a Committee on Rules with jurisdiction over "all proposed action touching on the rules and joint rules." Moreover, the Speaker retained the authority to chair the newly permanent Rules Committee and to appoint the chairmen and members of other standing and select committees.

The Reed Rules. Between 1880 and 1910, the modern Rules Committee emerged as the Speaker's committee and the legislative scheduling agent for the House. Its first chairman (1880), Speaker Samuel J. Randall (D-Pa.), used his authority to bolster the influence of the speakership, establishing that all future rules changes should be referred to the Rules Committee and that its reports could be brought to the floor at any time.

The powers of the Committee and the speakership continued to grow when Republicans took control of the House in 1881. One of the first to recognize the potential of the Rules Committee was Thomas B. Reed (R-Maine). Appointed to the Rules Committee in January 1882, Reed, then in his third term, assumed a leadership position by engineering rules changes and Speaker's rulings designed to eliminate dilatory tactics used by the minority.

The most significant early example of this, and also the first recorded instance of a modern-day special rule reported by the Rules Committee, occurred on 26 February 1883. Reed called up a resolution reported by the Rules Committee that would allow the House by majority vote, rather than by the two-thirds vote required under the suspension rule, to suspend the rules and request a conference with the Senate on a controversial tariff bill.

A point of order was made by Rep. Joseph C. S. Blackburn (D-Ky.) against the resolution on grounds that the Rules Committee did not have authority to report the resolution since it was neither a rule nor an amendment to House rules. Speaker J. Warren Keifer (R-Ohio), chairman of the Rules Committee, overruled the point of order on grounds that the resolution was "reported as a rule from the Committee on Rules." The Speaker went on to explain that, just as the Rules Committee could report a rule to suspend or repeal every rule of the House, subject to approval by the House, so too could it do so "though [the rule] may apply to a single great and important measure now pending before Congress."

When Republicans again took over the House in the 51st Congress (1889–1891) after a six-year hiatus, Reed was elected Speaker and thus became chairman of the Rules Committee as well. He moved immediately to rely on the Rules Committee to control legislative business on the floor through the use of special orders. Reed would later describe the role of the Rules Committee as a steering committee "to arrange the order of business and decide how and in what way certain measures shall be considered."

Reed also moved swiftly as Speaker to eliminate minority obstruction of floor business by issuing rulings from the chair that outlawed dilatory motions and "disappearing quorums." He then directed the codification of his rulings from his position as Rules Committee chairman. Known as the Reed Rules, the rules changes of 1890 helped to consolidate the power of the Speaker and the Rules Committee and to enable the majority party in the House to establish and expedite its legislative agenda without undue minority obstruction.

The Cannon Revolt. The power of the speakership and the Rules Committee continued to grow under Speaker Joseph G. Cannon (R-Ill.), who held that position from 1903 to 1910. From his two pinnacles of power, Cannon ruled the House with such an iron fist that his nickname soon changed from "Uncle Joe" to "Czar Cannon." Cannon was a strong believer in party discipline and did not hesitate to use his power in appointing committee members and chairmen and in removing those who did not toe the line.

His tactics and conservative philosophy eventually fomented a revolt by a group of progressive Republican insurgents, led by Rep. George W. Norris

(R-Nebr.) and joined by the minority Democrats. On 17 March 1910, Norris offered a resolution as a matter of constitutional privilege to change House rules by removing the Speaker as chairman and a member of the Rules Committee and by expanding its membership from five to fifteen, to be chosen by state groupings.

A point of order was made against the resolution on grounds that it was not privileged under the Constitution. Cannon allowed debate on the point of order and resolution to continue until 19 March, when he sustained the point of order by citing an 1878 precedent involving a ruling by Democratic Speaker Randall. Cannon's decision was appealed to the House and was overturned, 182 to 162. The Norris resolution was subsequently adopted, 191 to 156, after he amended it to provide for a ten-member committee elected by the House. Although the Norris resolution did not strip the Speaker of his power to appoint committees, the same effect was achieved in 1911. When the Democrats took control of the House that year, they adopted rules requiring the election of committees by the House.

Rules in a decentralized era. Although the Cannon revolt dealt a blow to the speakership, the Rules Committee's powers remained undiminished, and for the next twenty-seven years it continued to function as an arm of the majority leadership in scheduling legislation for the floor. The revolt did, however, lead to a period of decentralization in the House in which committees came to act as independent power centers, bolstered by the institutionalization of the seniority system. This trend gradually caught up with the Rules Committee as well.

The committee had played a key role in expediting much of President Franklin D. Roosevelt's New Deal legislation during his first term by reporting closed rules on major legislation, particularly during Roosevelt's famous First Hundred Days. A total of ten closed rules were reported in the 73d Congress (1933–1935). But a reaction against Roosevelt's increasingly liberal policies began to set in during the 74th Congress (1935–1937)—a reaction echoed on the Rules Committee, which John J. O'Connor (D-N.Y.), a New Deal skeptic, had just taken over as chairman.

By Roosevelt's second term, beginning in 1937, the Rules Committee had ceased to function as an arm of the majority leadership and instead came under the control of a coalition of conservative Democrats and Republicans, which held sway until 1961. Only during the brief periods of Republican control of the House in the 80th and 83d Congresses (1947–1949 and 1953–1955) did the committee revert to its majority-supporting role.

Rearming the leadership. The first major chink in the conservative coalition's armor was lodged in 1961, when Speaker Sam Rayburn (D-Tex.), acting in concert with the new administration of President John F. Kennedy, moved to enlarge the committee from twelve to fifteen members, including two additional Democrats and one Republican.

The resolution to enlarge the Rules Committee (H. Res. 127) was reported by the Rules Committee by a vote of 6 to 2 on 14 January 1961, with only committee Democrats in attendance. Chairman Howard W. Smith (D-Va.) and William M. Colmer (D-Miss.) cast the dissenting votes. Following an hour of debate on the resolution on 31 January, which included impassioned pleas from Rayburn and Smith on opposing sides, the House adopted the resolution by a vote of 217 to 212. Only two Republicans voted for the resolution, and sixty-four Democrats voted against it.

Despite some slight improvement in the enlarged Rules Committee's record of cooperation with the leadership, it continued to obstruct floor consideration of certain education, labor, and civil rights bills for the duration of the Kennedy administration. By the 90th Congress (1967–1969), the committee had become much more cooperative with the majority leadership, mainly because of the elevation of Colmer to the chairmanship following Smith's primary defeat in 1966. Although of similar ideological bent to Smith, Colmer viewed the role of the committee in a different way, in part reflecting his own threatened ouster from the committee and the adoption of committee rules in 1967 permitting a committee majority to circumvent a recalcitrant chairman.

By the mid 1970s, in tandem with a liberal reform revolution sweeping the House, the Rules Committee was fully restored as an arm of the leadership. With the departure of Colmer in 1972, the succeeding Democratic chairmen (Ray J. Madden [Ind.], 1973–1976; James J. Delaney [N.Y.], 1977–1978; Richard W. Bolling [Mo.], 1979–1982; Claude Pepper [Fla.], 1983–1989; and John Joseph Moakley [Mass.], 1989–) reflected this more liberal orientation of the House.

The Democratic Caucus was instrumental to the House reform movement. At the beginning of the 93d Congress (1973–1975), the Caucus adopted a rule placing restrictions on the Rules Committee's ability to grant closed rules. At the beginning of the 94th Congress (1975–1977), it gave the Speaker au-thority to nominate all Democratic Rules Committee members to the caucus.

The reform movement also precipitated enormous decentralization of power in the House, partially because of the growth and institutionalization of semiautonomous subcommittees and the new practice of referring bills to more than one committee. This decentralization in turn posed a challenge to the leadership and the Rules Committee to draw things back together for unified legislative action.

The Rules Committee's centralizing role under the leadership was most apparent in the growth during the 1980s of "complex" and "restrictive" special rules that both limited and structured the amendment process on major legislation. Whereas restrictive rules constituted only 15 percent of all rules in the mid 1970s, by the end of the 1980s they made up 55 percent, according to a Rules Committee minority staff study.

Many restrictive rules were worked out in cooperation with the minority and were adopted by wide margins. Others continued to run into strong opposition on grounds that they unfairly limited

REP. RICHARD W. BOLLING (D-MO.). Chairman of the House Committee on Rules (1979–1983), seated in the committee hearing room in the Capitol, conferring with Rep. Delbert L. Latta (R-Ohio), a senior Republican on the committee, *far left,* c. 1980.

CONGRESSIONAL QUARTERLY INC.

amendments in order to produce predictable results.

Original Jurisdiction and Reform. The authority of the Rules Committee to amend the standing rules of the House is often referred to as its original jurisdiction. Indeed, this was the sole function of the committee for most of its first century. But even when it was a select committee between 1789 and 1880, its members were reluctant to propose sweeping House reforms through rules changes. The major rules reforms of 1860 and 1880 were generated by specially appointed panels.

Even after the Rules Committee became a standing committee, its members' reluctance to make it an agent of reform in the House continued. With the rise of "King Caucus" following the 1910 revolt against Speaker Cannon came the practice of reporting House rules changes at the beginning of a Congress from the majority party caucus instead of waiting for the Rules Committee to act. This practice continued in the late twentieth century.

Moreover, further rules reforms of any magnitude are often initiated by special entities outside the Rules Committee. This is done in part to ensure broader institutional representation and support, but also because so much of the Rules Committee's time is consumed with granting special rules for bills from other committees. For example, the 1946 and 1970 Legislative Reorganization acts originated in joint House-Senate committees; the 1974 Budget Act in a joint study committee on the budget; and the House Committee Reform Amendments of 1974 in a bipartisan select committee (followed by a major rewrite in a Democratic caucus committee). But in most such reform efforts, not only were Rules Committee members represented on the special panels, but the committee itself retained final review authority and the right to recommend substantive changes. This was especially true with the 1970 Legislative Reorganization Act and the 1974 Budget Act.

After the mid 1970s, the Rules Committee increased its staff resources considerably and created two subcommittees for original jurisdiction matters, giving it still greater potential to play a major role in House reform efforts.

In sum, the great paradox of the Rules Committee is that while it was originally created to develop a set of standing rules and uniform order of business for the House, its principal role in the 1990s is to devise special rules that depart from the standing rules and the regular order. This development, over a two-century period, reflects the growing complexity of the Congress and the issues it confronts, the changing relationships among its internal components, and the ultimate need for a mechanism to assist the leadership in coordinating and processing the business of the Congress in an orderly and expeditious fashion.

As an arm of the leadership of both parties, the committee is at the center of both political and legislative battles, performing precarious balancing acts between majority will and minority rights, leadership needs and membership demands, and a wide range of public policy options. The flexibility of the committee over the years to adapt to changing circumstances and help bring order out of uncertainty is the best measure of its continuing utility and necessity.

[*See also* Cannon Revolt; House of Representatives, *article on* House Rules and Procedures; Reed's Rules; Rule, Special; Speaker of the House.]

BIBLIOGRAPHY

Bolling, Richard. *Power in the House.* 1968.

Galloway, George B. *History of the United States House of Representatives.* 1961.

Oppenheimer, Bruce I. "The Rules Committee: New Arm of Leadership in a Decentralized House." In *Congress Reconsidered.* Edited by Lawrence C. Dodd and Bruce I. Oppenheimer. 1st ed. 1977.

U.S. House of Representatives. *Deschler's Precedents of the United States House of Representatives,* by Lewis Deschler. 94th Cong., 2d sess., 1977. H. Doc. 94-661. Vol. 4.

U.S. House of Representatives. Committee on Rules. *A History of the Committee on Rules.* 97th Cong., 2d sess., 1983. Committee Print.

DONALD R. WOLFENSBERGER

RURAL ELECTRIFICATION ACT OF 1936

(49 Stat. 1363–1367). The administration of Franklin D. Roosevelt created the Rural Electrification Administration (REA) in 1935 by executive order, and it was given congressional statute authority when Sen. George W. Norris (R-Nebr.) and Rep. Sam Rayburn (D-Tex.) sponsored the Rural Electrification Act in 1936. The REA provided funding for electric cooperatives whose members were the recipients of electrical service. It also gave technical and administrative guidance to the cooperatives. Farmers took advantage of the opportunity and quickly formed electrical co-ops. By the end of 1941 the percentage of farms with electricity had jumped to approximately 35 percent, up from 10 percent in 1930.

World War II and the need for military matériel brought a delay in constructing rural power lines, and it was disappointing for the still unserved families to wait. Toward the end of the war, however, Congress began to reappropriate funds for the REA, and the construction of rural lines resumed at a fast pace. Particularly due to the prodding of Rep. John E. Rankin (D-Miss.), the REA received more funding than it requested for several years after the war. Generously financed, the REA program moved ahead at full speed, and by 1955 the United States had achieved 90 percent rural electrification.

The impact of electrification was staggering. The REA reported that families used their new service primarily for lighting, radio, and ironing. Indoor bathrooms, running water, and other such electricity-dependent conveniences were installed as quickly as financially possible by the families. Public health improved, particularly in those areas where communicable diseases were transmitted through the use of outhouses prior to the availability of electrical service. With refrigeration, family diet also improved. The REA, still active, is regarded as one of the great achievements of the New Deal. Today Congress continues to fund the REA program, and the cooperatives receive technical and administrative assistance as they have in the past. Funding is not as generous now only because the great need for rural electrification has been met. But the REA still enjoys strong congressional support.

BIBLIOGRAPHY

Brown, D. Clayton. *Electricity for Rural America: The Fight for the REA.* 1980.
Childs, Marquis. *The Farmer Takes a Hand.* 1953.

D. CLAYTON BROWN

RURAL POST ROADS ACT (1916; 39 Stat. 355–359). Key elements of modern national highway policy were established by the Rural Post Roads Act of 1916 (also known as the Federal Aid Road Act), which for the first time since the mid-nineteenth century authorized funds for U.S. road construction. The bill appeared at a time of growing popular support for better roads, a movement that had been gaining momentum since the 1890s. From 1911 to 1916, numerous highway bills were proposed. One approach was a "rental" plan calling for annual federal payments, typically $25 per mile, to counties building post roads. The main alternative, favored by automotive interests, was a national highway commission charged with building a fifty-one-thousand-mile national road network. The legislation passed in 1916, however, was molded by Logan W. Page, chief of the Department of Agriculture's Office of Public Roads and a reforming engineer, whose influence has been compared by some to that of conservationist Gifford Pinchot. Page worked closely with a Senate committee—he even furnished the committee's statistician—and with outside groups to promote a federal aid plan.

Federal aid meant that the federal and state governments shared responsibility and expenses. The federal government paid 50 percent of the cost (up to $10,000 per mile) of building post roads outside towns with populations above 2,500. The states (not the counties) planned, constructed, and maintained the roads; federal engineers inspected plans and the finished highways. The states, however, were required to establish highway departments under the control of engineers and to adopt suitable construction standards; Page's Office of Public Roads had to approve both. To fund construction, Congress appropriated $75 million over five years—$5 million in 1917, rising to $25 million in 1921. To forestall political bickering, funds were allocated according to a formula based on population, area, and road mileage. Indeed, the basic premise of the bill was typically progressive: that roads should be removed from politics and their control given to engineers. This technical orientation remained at the heart of American highway programs well into the 1960s.

BIBLIOGRAPHY

Dearing, Charles L. *American Highway Policy.* 1942.
Holt, W. Stull. *The Bureau of Public Roads: Its History, Activities, and Organization.* 1923.
Seely, Bruce E. *Building the American Highway System: Engineers as Policy Makers.* 1987.
U.S. House of Representatives. *Report of the Joint Congressional Committee on Federal-Aid in the Construction of Post Roads.* 63d Cong., 3d sess., 1915. H. Doc. 1510.

BRUCE E. SEELY

RUSSELL, RICHARD B. (1897–1971), Democratic senator from Georgia, chairman of the committees on Appropriations and Armed Services, and anti–civil rights leader. Richard Breward Russell, Jr., was born in Winder, Georgia; his parents were Judge Richard Brevard Russell and Ina Dillard Russell. Russell attended the University of Georgia and received a law degree in 1918. He was elected

RICHARD B. RUSSELL. In his office, January 1967.

as a Democrat to the state general assembly in 1920, and for the next fifty years devoted most of his time to politics and public service. He never married.

After ten years as a state legislator, Russell was voted Georgia's governor in 1930 and elected to the U.S. Senate in 1932. His affable personality, intelligence, excellent speaking ability, fairness, and honesty combined to make him an unbeatable political candidate. He never lost an election.

Russell was sworn in to the Senate on 10 January 1933. Working mainly behind the scenes, he gradually became a strong force in that body. He was appointed to the Appropriations Committee in 1933 and served in that position until his death, chairing the committee from 1969 to 1971. His other committee assignments included Naval Affairs and, later, the committees on Armed Services, Immigration, and Manufactures. He was chairman of the Armed Services Committee from 1951 to 1953 and from 1955 to 1969. As a member of the Immigration Committee in the 1930s and 1940s, he strongly opposed any relaxation of the immigration laws. Russell was a strong supporter of agricultural interests. He devised the school lunch program.

By the 1940s Russell had become one of the most influential Democratic senators. Because of his stature, integrity, and impartiality, he was selected in 1951 to head the committee that investigated the firing of Gen. Douglas MacArthur. In 1964 he served on the Warren Commission to investigate the assassination of President John F. Kennedy.

Russell fought the civil rights movement vigorously. Raised in a segregated environment and believing that the races should be kept apart, he fought antilynching laws, fair employment practices, school desegregation, integration of the armed forces, and similar measures. By the 1940s Russell had assumed leadership of the Southern Caucus, a group of southern senators who organized to block civil rights legislation. He was the principal author of the 1956 Southern Manifesto opposing the Supreme Court's *Brown v. Board of Education* decision. Opponents of civil rights prevailed on him to seek the Democratic presidential nomination in 1952; though he failed to win the nomination, he and his allies blocked effective civil rights legislation for more than two decades.

A strong advocate of U.S. military power as a means of maintaining world peace, Russell worked hard as chairman of the Armed Services Committee to keep the nation militarily powerful. He opposed U.S. involvement in Vietnam, but once America was committed, he favored a military victory. He did not, however, believe that the United States should police the world, and he consistently voted against foreign aid after 1952.

Russell made numerous positive contributions to American political life. He was heavily involved in most of the leading issues considered by Congress during his thirty-eight-year senatorial career. Moreover, he was a jealous guardian of the U.S. Senate as an institution. But he failed to achieve true national greatness because of his unchanging views on race relations. The permanence of his contributions and his stature among his colleagues are symbolized on Capitol Hill by the Russell Senate Office Building.

BIBLIOGRAPHY

Fite, Gilbert C. *Richard B. Russell, Jr.: Senator from Georgia.* 1991.

Potensiani, David D. "Look to the Past: Richard B. Russell and the Defense of Southern White Supremacy." Ph.D. diss., University of Georgia, 1981.

GILBERT C. FITE